THE ENCYCLOPEDIA
OF THE
KOREAN WAR

SECOND EDITION

THE ENCYCLOPEDIA
OF THE
KOREAN WAR

A Political, Social, and Military History

SECOND EDITION

VOLUME II: M–Z

Dr. Spencer C. Tucker
Volume Editor

Dr. Paul G. Pierpaoli Jr.

Associate Editor and
Editor, Documents Volume

Professor Jinwung Kim
Dr. Xiaobing Li
Dr. James I. Matray

Assistant Editors

 ABC-CLIO

Santa Barbara, California • Denver, Colorado • Oxford, England

Copyright © 2010 by ABC-CLIO, LLC

Library of Congress Cataloging-in-Publication Data

The encyclopedia of the Korean War : a political, social, and military history / Spencer C. Tucker, volume editor ; Paul G. Pierpaoli, Jr., associate editor and editor, documents volume ; Jinwung Kim, Xiaobing Li, James I. Matray, assistant editors — 2nd ed.
    p. cm.
  Includes bibliographical references and index.
  ISBN 978-1-85109-849-1 (hard copy : acid-free paper) — ISBN 978-1-85109-850-7 (ebook)
 1. Korean War, 1950-1953—Encyclopedias.   I. Tucker, Spencer, 1937–   II. Pierpaoli, Paul G., 1962–   III. Kim, Jinwung.
IV. Li, Xiaobing, 1954–   V. Matray, James Irving, 1948–
  DS918.E53 2010
  951.904'203—dc22

                                        2010000681

14 13 12 11 10   1 2 3 4 5

This book is also available on the World Wide Web as an ebook.
Visit abc-clio.com for details.

ABC-CLIO, LLC
130 Cremona Drive, P.O. Box 1911
Santa Barbara, California 93116–1911

This book is printed on acid-free paper
Manufactured in the United States of America

To Dr. Paul G. Pierpaoli Jr.,
Korean War scholar, colleague, friend.

About the Editors

Spencer C. Tucker, PhD, graduated from the Virginia Military Institute and was a Fulbright scholar in France. He was a U.S. Army captain and intelligence analyst in the Pentagon during the Vietnam War, then taught for 30 years at Texas Christian University before returning to his alma mater for 6 years as the holder of the John Biggs Chair of Military History. He retired from teaching in 2003. He is now Senior Fellow of Military History at ABC-CLIO. Dr. Tucker has written or edited more than 25 books, including ABC-CLIO's award-winning *The Encyclopedia of the Cold War* and *The Encyclopedia of the Arab-Israeli Conflict*, as well as the comprehensive *A Global Chronology of Conflict*.

Paul G. Pierpaoli Jr., PhD, is the author of *Truman and Korea: the Political Culture of the Early Cold War* (1999). He has published widely in a variety of venues, including book chapters and *The Journal of Military History*. He served as the assistant editor of *Diplomatic History* from 1992 to 1994 and has been the assistant editor on many ABC-CLIO projects, including *The Encyclopedia of the Arab-Israeli Conflict* and *The Encyclopedia of the Spanish-American and Philippine-American Wars*. Dr. Pierpaoli received his MA and PhD from The Ohio State University and has served on the faculties of numerous schools, including Hampden-Sydney College and the University of Arizona.

Contents

Volume I: A–L

List of Entries, xi
List of Maps, xix
Foreword, xxi
Preface, xxv
General Maps, xxvii
Introduction, xxxvii
Entries, 1
Index, I-1

Volume II: M–Z

List of Entries, xi
List of Maps, xix
General Maps, xxi
Entries, 527
Appendix A, 1005
Appendix B, 1021
Appendix C, 1027
Chronology, 1031
Glossary, 1051
Selected Bibliography, 1055
List of Editors and Contributors, 1069
Categorical Index, 1073
Index, I-1

Volume III: Documents

List of Documents, xi
Documents, 1079
Index, I-1

List of Entries

Abductees, South Korean
Aces
Acheson, Dean Gooderham
Acheson's National Press Club Speech
Active Defense Strategy
Adams, Edward
ADCOM
Aerial Combat
Aeromedical Evacuation
African Americans and the Korean War
Agenda Controversy
Airborne Operations
Aircraft
Aircraft Carriers
Airfields
Airpower in the Korean War
Alexander-Lloyd Mission
Allison, John Moore
Almond, Edward Mallory
Amphibious Force Far East
An Chang Ho
An Ho Sang
Antiwar Sentiment in the United States
ANZUS Treaty
Armistice Agreement
Armor, Tanks
Armored Vests
Artillery
Artillery, Antiaircraft
Atomic Bomb
Atomic Bomb, Threat to Use

Atomic Energy Commission, U.S.
Atrocities
Attlee, Clement Richard
Austin, Warren
Australia

Baillie, Hugh
Bajpai, Girja Shankar
Baldwin, Hanson Weightman
Barkley, Alben William
Barr, David Goodwin
Baruch, Bernard
Battle Fatigue
Bazooka
Bebler, Ales
"Bed-Check Charlies"
Belgium
Bendetsen, Karl Robin
Berendsen, Sir Carl August
Bevan, Aneurin
Bevin, Ernest
Biological Warfare
Blacklists
Blair House Meetings
Bloody Ridge, Battle of
BLUEHEARTS, Operation
Boatner, Haydon Lemaire
Bohlen, Charles Eustis
Bolté, Charles Lawrence
Bond, Niles W.
Bonnet, Henri

xi

Border Clashes
Bowles, Chester Bliss
Bowling Alley
Bradley, Omar Nelson
Bradley-Bohlen Mission to Korea
Brainwashing
Bricker, John William
Bridgeford, Sir William
Bridges, Henry Styles
Briggs, Ellis Ormsbee
Briscoe, Robert Pierce
"Bug-out Fever"
Bunker Hill, Battle of
Burke, Arleigh Albert

Cairo Declaration
Cambridge Five
Campbell, Archibald
Canada
Cassels, Sir James
Casualties
Cates, Clifton Bledsoe
Cease-fire Negotiations
Censorship and the Korean War
Central Intelligence Agency
Chae Pyong Dok
Chai Chengwen
Chang Myon
Chang Taek Sang
Changjin Reservoir Campaign
Chaplains, U.S. Army and Republic of Korea Army
Chauvel, Jean Michel Henri
Cheju-do Prisoner of War Uprising
Cheju-do Rebellion
Chemical Warfare
Chen Yi
China, People's Republic of
China, People's Republic of, Army
China, People's Republic of, Navy
China, People's Republic of, People's Liberation Army Air Force
China, People's Republic of, United Nations Representation
   Question
China, Republic of
China Hands
China Lobby
Chinese Civil War
Chinese Economic and Military Aid to North Korea
Chinese Offensive, First
Chinese Military Disengagement
Chinese Offensive, Second
Chinese Offensive, Third
Chinese Offensive, Fourth
Chinese Offensive, Fifth

Chinese Offensive, Sixth
Chinese Offensives, Summer
Chinese People's Volunteer Army
Chipyong-ni, Battle of
Cho Man Sik
Cho Pyong Ok
Choe Tok Sin
Choe Yong Gon
Chondogyo Movement
Chong Il Gwon
Chongchon River
Chongchon River, Battle of
Choson Democratic Party
Chunchon, Battle of
Church, John Huston
Church Survey Mission to Korea
Churches and the War, Korean
Churches and the War, U.S.
Churchill, Sir Winston
Civil Defense, U.S.
Civil Liberties in the United States
Civilian Internee Issue
CLAM-UP, Operation
Clark, Joseph James
Clark, Mark Wayne
CLEANUP I and CLEANUP II, Operations
Close Air Support
Clubb, Oliver Edmund
Cold War, Origins to 1950
Collins, Joseph Lawton
Collins Visit to Tokyo
Collins-Sherman Visit to Tokyo
Collins-Vandenberg Discussions in Tokyo
Collins-Vandenberg Visit to Tokyo
Colombia
COMMANDO, Operation
Committee on the Present Danger
Connally, Thomas Terry
Containment
Controlled Materials Plan
Cordier, Andrew Wellington
Cory, Thomas J.
Coulter, John Breitling
COURAGEOUS, Operation
Cutler, Robert

Dam Raids of 1953
DAUNTLESS, Operation
Davidson, Garrison Holt
Davidson Line
Davies, John Paton
Dean, Arthur Hobson
Dean, William Frishe

Defectors
Defense Production Act
Demilitarized Zone
Democratic National Party
Democratic Party, United States
Demographics, Korean
Deng Hua
Detachment 2
Dodd-Colson Prisoner of War Incident
Doyle, James Henry
Draft
Drumright, Everett Francis
Du Ping
Dulles, John Foster
Dulles's Trip to Korea

Economic Stabilization Agency
Eden, Robert Anthony
Eighth Army, U.S.
Eisenhower, Dwight David
Eisenhower's Trip to Korea
Election, U.S. Presidential
Elections, U.S. Midterm
Elsey, George McKee
Emmons, Arthur B., III
Entezam, Nasrollah
Ethiopia
European Defense Community
EVERREADY, Operation
Executive Order 9981

Fallout Shelters
Far East Air Force
Far East Command
Fechteler, William Morrow
Film and the Korean War
Finletter, Thomas Knight
Forward Air Controllers
Foster, William Zebulon
France
Franks, Oliver
Freeman, Paul LaMarch, Jr.

Gao Gang
Gay, Hobart Raymond
Geneva Conference
Geneva Convention
Germany, Federal Republic of
Gloucester Hill, Battle of
Graham, William Franklin
Graves Registration
Great Debate
Greece

Grenades
Gromyko, Andrei
Gross, Ernest Arnold
Guo Moruo

Haman Breakthrough
Hammarskjöld, Dag
Han Kyong Jik
Han Pyo Uk
Han River Operations
Harriman, William Averell
Harrison, William Kelly, Jr.
Hausman, James Harry
Heartbreak Ridge, Battle of
Helicopters, Employment of
Helicopters, Types and Nomenclature
Henderson, Loy Wesley
Hershey, Lewis Blaine
Hess, Dean Elmer
Hickerson, John Dewey
Hickey, Doyle Overton
Higgins, Marguerite
Hiss, Alger
Historiography of the Korean War
Ho Ka I
Hodes, Henry Irving
Hodge, John Reed
Hoengsong, Battle of
Hoge, William Morris
Hollywood Ten
Home-by-Christmas Offensive
Hong Kong, British Crown Colony of
Hong Xuezhi
Hook, Battles of the
Hope, Leslie Townes
Hospital Ships
Hot Pursuit
House Un-American Activities Committee
Housewives United
HUDSON HARBOR, Exercise
Hull, John Edwin
Human Wave Attacks
Hungnam, North Korea
Hungnam Evacuation
Hydrogen Bomb

Imjin River
Imjin River, Battle of
Inchon Landing
India
Indochina War, Impact on Korea
Industrial Base, U.S.
Industrial Dispersion

Infiltration
Internal Security Act
Iron Triangle
Isolationist Sentiment in the United States

Jackson, Charles Douglas
Jamieson, Arthur B.
Japan
Japan, Economic Impact of the Korean War on
Japan, Post–World War II U.S. Occupation of
Japan Logistical Command
Japanese Peace Treaty
Jebb, Sir Gladwyn
Jessup, Philip Caryl
Jet Aircraft, First Manned Clash in History
Jiang Jieshi
Jiang Jieshi's Offer of Nationalist Troops to Fight in Korea
Johnson, Louis Arthur
Johnson, Ural Alexis
Joint Chiefs of Staff
Jooste, Gerhardus Petrus
Joy, Charles Turner
Juche Ideology

Kaesong
Kaesong Bombing Proposal
Kaesong Neutral Zone Controversy
Kaesong Truce Talks
Kang Kon
Kansas-Wyoming Line
Kapyong, Battle of
Katzin, Alfred G.
Kean, William Benjamin
Keiser, Laurence Bolton
Kelly Hill, Battle of
Kennan, George Frost
Kennan-Malik Conversations
KILLER, Operation
Kim Chaek
Kim Chong Won
Kim Il Sung
Kim Jong Il
Kim Ku
Kim Kyu Sik
Kim Paek Il
Kim Sae Sun
Kim Sok Won
Kim Song Su
Kim Tu Bong
Kim Ung
Kimpo Airfield
Kingsley, John Donald

Kinsler, Francis
Kirk, Alan Goodrich
Knowland, William Fife
Kochang Incident
Koje-do
Koje-do Prisoner of War Uprising
Kojo Amphibious Feint
K1C2
Korea, Climate and Geography of
Korea, Democratic People's Republic of, 1945–1953
Korea, Democratic People's Republic of, 1953–Present
Korea, Democratic People's Republic of, Air Force
Korea, Democratic People's Republic of, Army
Korea, Democratic People's Republic of, Economy
Korea, Democratic People's Republic of, Invasion of the Republic of Korea
Korea, Democratic People's Republic of, Navy
Korea, Democratic People's Republic of, United Nations Command Occupation of
Korea, History of, to 1945
Korea, History of, 1945–1947
Korea, Japanese Occupation of
Korea, Republic of, 1947–1953
Korea, Republic of, 1953–Present
Korea, Republic of, Air Force
Korea, Republic of, Army
Korea, Republic of, Demonstrations for Unification
Korea, Republic of, Economy
Korea, Republic of, Korean Service Corps
Korea, Republic of, Marine Corps
Korea, Republic of, National Defense Forces
Korea, Republic of, National Defense Forces Scandal
Korea, Republic of, Navy
Korea, Republic of, Occupation of by Democratic People's Republic of Korea
Korea, Republic of, Political Crisis
Korea, Topography of
Korea Aid Bill of 1947
Korea Aid Bill of 1950
Korea Military Advisory Group
Korean Augmentation to the United States Army
Korean Communications Zone
Korean Democratic Party
Korean Independence Party
Korean Provisional Government
Korean War Veterans Memorial, U.S.
Kum River, Battle of
Kunu-ri, Battle of

Lampe, James S.
Latin America
Lattimore, Owen

Lay, James S.
Lee Myung Bak
Lemnitzer, Lyman Louis
Leviero, Anthony Harry
Li Kenong
Liberal Party
Lie, Trygve Halvden
Lightner, Edwin Allan, Jr.
Limb, Ben C.
Lin Biao
Lippmann, Walter
Literature of the Korean War, Korean
Literature of the Korean War, U.S.
LITTLE SWITCH and BIG SWITCH, Operations
Lloyd, John Selwyn
Lodge, Henry Cabot, Jr.
Logistics in the Korean War
Lovett, Robert Abercrombie
Lowe, Frank E.
Luxembourg, Grand Duchy of

MacArthur, Douglas
MacArthur Hearings
Machine Guns
Makin, Norman
Makins, Sir Roger
Malenkov, Georgii
Malik, Jacob
Manchuria
Manchurian Sanctuary
Mao Zedong
March First Movement
Marshall, George Catlett
Marshall, Samuel Lyman Atwood
Marshall Plan
Martin, Joseph William
Massive Retaliation
Matthews, Francis Patrick
Matthews, Harrison Freeman
McCarran, Patrick Anthony
McCarthy, Joseph Raymond
McCarthyism
McClure, Robert Alexis
McGarr, Lionel Charles
"Meat Grinder" Strategy
Media and the Korean War
Medicine, Military
Medics, Combat
Menon, Kumara Padmanabha Sivasankara
Menon, Vengalil Krishnan Krishna
Menzies, Robert Gordon
Merchant, Livingston Tallmadge

Mexico
Meyer, Clarence Earle
Meyer Mission
Michaelis, John Hersey
MIG, Operation
MiG Alley
Milburn, Frank William
Military Air Transport Service
Military Armistice Commission
Military-Industrial Complex
Military Intelligence
Military Sea Transport Service
Mine Warfare, Sea
Mines, Land
Mines, Sea
Missing in Action
Mobile Army Surgical Hospital
Mobilization
Moffett, Howard Fergus
Molotov, Viacheslav Mikhailovich
Monclar, Ralph
MOOLAH, Operation
Morrison, Herbert Stanley
Mortars
Mu Chong
Muccio, John Joseph
Munich Analogy
Munsan-ni Airborne Operation
Murphy, Charles Springs
Murphy, Robert Daniel
Music of the Korean War, Korean
Music of the Korean War, U.S.
Muste, Abraham Johannes

Najin, Bombing of
Naktong Bulge, First Battle of
Naktong Bulge, Second Battle of
Nam Il
Namsi, Battle of
Napalm
National Emergency Declaration
National Security Act
National Security Council
National Security Council Report 68
National Security Resources Board
Naval Battles
Naval Forces Far East
Naval Gunfire Support
Needham, Joseph
Nehru, Jawaharlal
Netherlands
Neutral Nations Repatriation Commission

Neutral Nations Supervisory Commission
New Look Defense Policy
New Zealand
Nie Rongzhen
Nitze, Paul Henry
Nixon, Richard Milhous
No Name Line, Battle of
Noble, Harold
Nogun-ni Railroad Bridge Incident
Norstad, Lauris
North Atlantic Treaty Organization
North Korean Offensive, Delaying of
Northern Limitation Line
Nuclear Warfare

O'Donnell, Emmett
Office of Defense Mobilization
Office of Price Stabilization
Old Baldy, Battle of
Oliver, Robert Tarbell
Oppenheimer, Robert
Organized Labor
Osan, Battle of
Outpost Harry, Battle for

Pace, Frank, Jr.
Pacific Pact
Padilla Nervo, Luis
Paek In Yop
Paek Son Yop
Paek Song Uk
Paek Tu Jin
Pak Hon Yong
Pak Sun Chon
Pandit, Vijaya Lakshmi Nehru
Pang Ho San
Panikkar, Sardar K. M.
Panmunjom Security Agreement
Park Chung Hee
Partridge, Earle Everard
Pearson, Lester Bowles
Peng Dehuai
Peruvian Prisoner of War Settlement Proposal
Philippines
Pierce, Robert Willard
PILEDRIVER, Operation
Pistols
Pleven Plan
Plimsoll, James
Pohang, Battle of
Point Four Program
Police Action

Pongam-do Prisoner of War Uprising
Pork Chop Hill, Battle of
Potsdam Conference
Price Gouging
Price and Wage Freeze Order
Prisoner of War Administration, Communist
Prisoner of War Administration, United Nations Command
Prisoner of War Code of Conduct
Prisoners of War, Rescreening of
Psychological Warfare
Pueblo Incident
Puller, Lewis Burwell
PUNCH, Operation
Punchbowl
Pusan
Pusan Perimeter and Breakout
Pyon Yong Tae
Pyongyang
Pyongyang, March to and Capture of

Qin Jiwei
Quesada, Elwood Richard

Radford, Arthur William
Radhakrishnan, Sarvepalli
Railroads, Korean National
RATKILLER, Operation
Rau, Sir Benegal Narsing
Recoilless Rifles
Reconnaissance
Red Ball Express
Red Cross
Refugees
Relief Efforts, Missionary
Repatriation, Voluntary
Republican Party, United States
Rest and Recuperation
Return-to-Seoul Movement
Revolt of the Admirals
Rhee, Syngman
Rhee, Syngman, Assassination Attempt on
Rhee's Release of North Korean Prisoners of War
Ridgway, Matthew Bunker
Rifles
RIPPER, Operation
Roberts, William Lynn
Robertson, Sir Horace
Robertson, Walter Spencer
Robertson Mission
Rocket Artillery
"Rolling with the Punch"
Rosenberg, Julius

Rotation of Troops System
ROUNDUP, Operation
Ruffner, Clark Louis
RUGGED, Operation
Rusk, David Dean
Ryan, Cornelius Edward

Sanctuaries
Sasebo, Japan
SATURATE, Operation
SCATTER, Operation
Schuman Plan
Scorched Earth Policy
Searchlights
Sebald, William Joseph
2nd Logistical Command
Seoul
Seoul, Fall of
Seoul, Recapture of
Seoul City Sue
Service, John Stewart
Shaw, William Hamilton
Shepherd, Lemuel Cornick, Jr.
Sherman, Forrest Percival
Short, Joseph H., Jr.
SHOWDOWN, Operation
Shtykov, Terentii Fomich
Sin Ik Hui
Sin Song Mo
Sin Tae Yong
Sino-Soviet Treaty of Friendship and Alliance
SMACK, Operation
Smith, Oliver Prince
Smith, Walter Bedell
Son Won Il
Son Yang Won
Song Chin U
Song Shilun
South Africa, Union of
Southeast Asia Treaty Organization
Soviet Air War in Korea
Soviet Airfield Incident
Soviet Security Council Boycott
Soviet Union
Special Operations
Spellman, Francis Joseph
Spender, Sir Percy Claude
St. Laurent, Louis Stephen
Stalin, Joseph
Steel Plants, Truman's Seizure of
Stevenson, Adlai Ewing
Stockholm Peace Appeal

STRANGLE, Operation
Strategic and Tactical Airlift in the Korean War
Stratemeyer, George Edward
Struble, Arthur Dewey
Student Volunteer Troops, Republic of Korea
Submachine Guns and Light Machine Guns
Sukchon and Sunchon Airborne Operation
Supung and the Korean Electric Power Plant Campaign
Symington, William Stuart, III

Taegu, Defense of
Taejon, Defense of
Taejon Agreement
Taft, Robert Alphonso
Taft-Hartley Act
TAILBOARD, Operation
Taiwan, Neutralization of
Tasca, Henry Joseph
Task Force Kean
Task Force Smith
Taylor, Maxwell Davenport
X Corps
Thailand
Thimayya, Kadenera Subayya
3rd Logistical Command
38th Parallel, Decision to Cross
38th Parallel, Division of Korea at
Thomas, Norman Mattoon
THUNDERBOLT, Operation
Tomlinson, Frank Stanley
Triangle Hill, Battle of
Tripartite Meetings
Troopships
Truce Talks
Truman, Harry S.
Truman Doctrine
Truman-Eisenhower Transition Meeting
Truman Loyalty Program
Truman's Cease-fire Initiative
Truman's Domestic Agenda and the Korean War
Truman's Recall of MacArthur
Tsarapkin, Semion Konstantinovich
Tsiang Ting Fu Fuller
Turkey
Twining, Nathan Farragut
Tydings Committee

Underwood, Horace Grant
Underwood, Horace Grant, II
Underwood, Horace Horton
United Kingdom
United Nations and the Korean War

United Nations Additional Measures Committee
United Nations Cease-Fire Group
United Nations Civil Assistance Command in Korea
United Nations Collective Measures Committee
United Nations Command
United Nations Command Air Assets
United Nations Command Ground Forces, Contributions to
United Nations Commission for the Unification and
    Rehabilitation of Korea
United Nations General Assembly Resolution 376 (V)
United Nations General Assembly Resolution 377 (V)
United Nations General Assembly Resolution 498 (V)
United Nations Good Offices Committee
United Nations Korean Reconstruction Agency
United Nations Peace Observation Commission
United Nations Sanctions on China
United Nations Security Council Resolution 82
United Nations Security Council Resolution 83
United Nations Security Council Resolution 84
United Nations Security Council Resolution 85
United States, Home Front
United States Air Force
United States Army
United States Army Engineers
United States Army Military Police
United States Army Rangers
United States Army Signal Corps
United States Coast Guard
United States Marine Corps
United States National Guard
United States Naval Construction Battalions
United States Navy
United States Navy Air Operations
United States Reserve Forces
United States–Republic of Korea Mutual Defense Treaty
Universal Military Training and Service Act
Unsan, Battle of
U.S. Policy toward Korea, Pre-1950
U.S. Policy toward Korea, 1950–1953
U.S. Policy toward Korea, 1953–Present

Van Fleet, James Alward
"Van Fleet Load"
Vandenberg, Hoyt Sanford
Voorhees, Tracy Stebbins
Vyshinskii, Andrei Ianuarovich

Wage Stabilization Board
Wake Island Conference
Walker, Walton Harris

War Crimes Trials
Washington Conference
Webb, James Edwin
West, Sir Michael M. A. R.
Weyland, Otto Paul
White Horse Hill, Battle of
Whitney, Courtney
Williams, George Z.
Willoughby, Charles Andrew
Wilson, Charles Edward
WOLFHOUND, Operation
Women in Defense Production Administration Committees
Women on the Home Front, United States and Korea
Women in the Military during the Korean War
Won Yong Dok
Wonju, Battle of
Wonsan, North Korea
Wonsan Landing and Evacuation
World Vision
Wrong, Humphrey Hume
Wu Xiuquan

Xie Fang

Yalu Bridges Controversy
Yalu River
Yang Dezhi
Yang Yu Chan
Yi Chong Chan
Yi Hak Ku
Yi Hyong Gun
Yi Kwon Mu
Yi Pom Sok
Yi Sang Jo
Yi Sung Yop
Yi Tong Hwi
Yim, Louise
Yo Un Hyong
Yongchon, Battle of
Yosu-Sunchon Rebellion
Younger, Kenneth
Yu Chae Hung
Yun Chi Yong

Zhang Hanfu
Zhang Tingfa
Zhou Enlai
Zinchenko, Konstantin E.
Zorin, Valerian

List of Maps

General Maps

Map Key   xxiii

Korean Peninsula   xxx

Korean War, 1950–1953   xxxi

Korean Peninsula Railroads   xxxii

North Korean Invasion of South Korea, June 25–28, 1950   xxxiii

Chinese Intervention in the War, October 25–November 1, 1950   xxxiv

Demarcation Line, 1953   xxxv

Entry Maps

Armistice Conference Area, October 1951   45

Battle of the Changjin Reservoir, November 1950   123

Chinese Second Offensive, November–December 1950   158

Battle of the Chongchon River, November 28–December 1, 1950   175

UNC on the Defensive, April 21–May 19, 1951   224

Inchon Invasion, September 15, 1950   353

UNC Offensive, May 20–June 24, 1951   398

UNC Counteroffensive, January 25–April 22, 1951   408

Areas of MiG-15 Operations   577

Pusan Perimeter, August 1950   710

Inchon-Seoul Campaign, September 1950   773

Redeployment of X Corps, October–November 1950   838

UNC Pursuit, September 23–30, 1950   888

Changjin Reservoir Withdrawal, December 1–11, 1950   917

UNC on the Defensive, December 31, 1950–January 24, 1951   963

Advance toward the Yalu River, October 20–24, 1950   983

General Maps

Map Key

Generic Troops		Brigade
Cavalry		Regiment
Forces/Troops/Infantry		Battalion
Armored		Company
Armored Cavalry		Fortification/Redoubts
Mechanized		Fort/Station/Military Base
Air Assault		Battery/Artillery
International Boundary		Palisade
Major Roads		City
Minefields/Landmines		State Capital
Battle Site		Capital (of country)
Railroad		Bridge/Pass
Army Group		Hills
Army		Military Camp
Corps		Swamp
Division		Surrender

Korean Peninsula

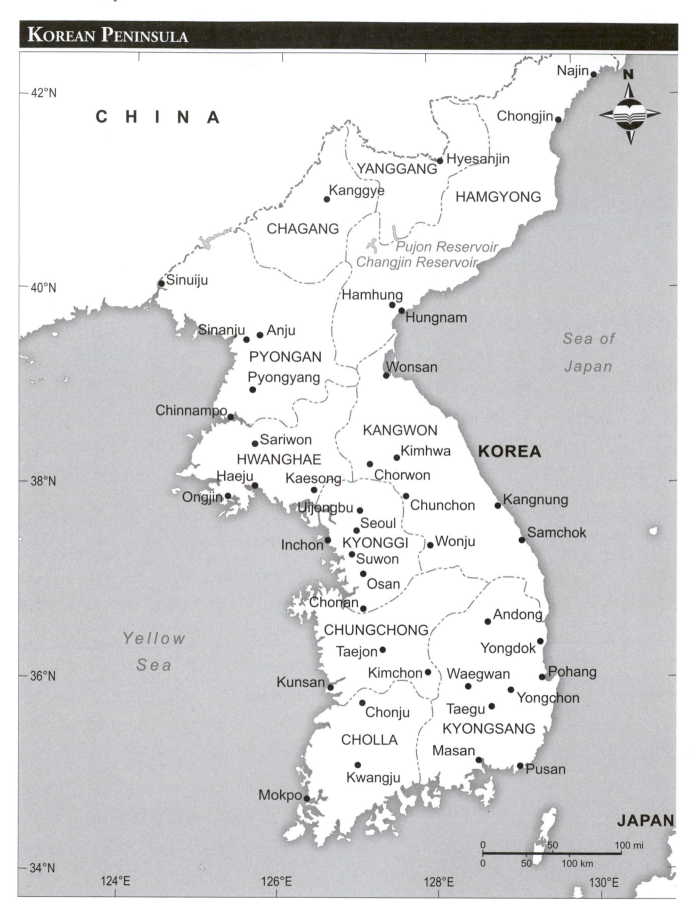

CHINA

Najin

Chongjin

YANGGANG   Hyesanjin

Kanggye   HAMGYONG

CHAGANG

Pujon Reservoir
Changjin Reservoir

Sinuiju

Hamhung

Sinanju   Anju   Hungnam

PYONGAN   Sea of
Japan

Pyongyang   Wonsan

Chinnampo

KANGWON

Sariwon   KOREA

HWANGHAE   Kimhwa

Haeju   Kaesong   Chorwon

Ongjin   Chunchon   Kangnung

Uijongbu
Seoul   Samchok

Inchon   KYONGGI   Wonju

Suwon

Osan

Chonan   Andong

CHUNGCHONG   Yongdok

Taejon   Pohang

Kimchon   Waegwan   Yongchon

Kunsan   Taegu   KYONGSANG

Chonju   Masan   Pusan

CHOLLA

Kwangju

Mokpo   JAPAN

Yellow
Sea

Sea of
Japan

42°N

40°N

38°N

36°N

34°N

124°E   126°E   128°E   130°E

N

0   50   100 mi
0   50   100 km

KOREAN WAR, 1950–1953

SOVIET
UNION

N

125°E

130°E

MANCHURIA

Vladivostok

CHINA

Tunghwa

Chongjin

Yalu R.

Kanggye

Changjin
(Chosin)
Reservoir

Chosan

Chongchon R.

Changjin
(Chosin)

Iwon

Sinuiju

Hagard

40°N

NORTH
KOREA

Hungnam

Sea of
Japan

Yongdok

Wonsan

Imjin R.

Pyongyang

Iron
Triangle

Ongjin
Peninsula

Pork
Chop
Hill

Pyonggang

38th Parallel

Kumhwa

Chorwon

Yangyang

Kaesong

Panmunjom

Chunchon

Inchon

Seoul

Samchok

Osan

Han R.

TAEBAEK MTS.

SOUTH
KOREA

SOBAEK MTS.

Kum R.

Yondok

Yellow

Sea

Taejon

Kumchon

Pohang

Naktong R.

Kunsan

Taegu

CHIRI
MTS.

35°N

Masan

Pusan

JAPAN

Mokpo

Koje-do
Island

Korea Strait

Tsushima
(Japan)

Tsushima Strait

Limit of North Korean advance,
Jun-Sep 1950

Limit of United Nations advance,
Nov 1950

Limit of Chinese advance,
Jan 1951

Armistice Line, Jul 27, 1953

Battle site

Principal railroads

Principal Chinese railroad
supply lines

Principal roads

0   50   100 mi

0   50   100 km

Korean Peninsula Railroads

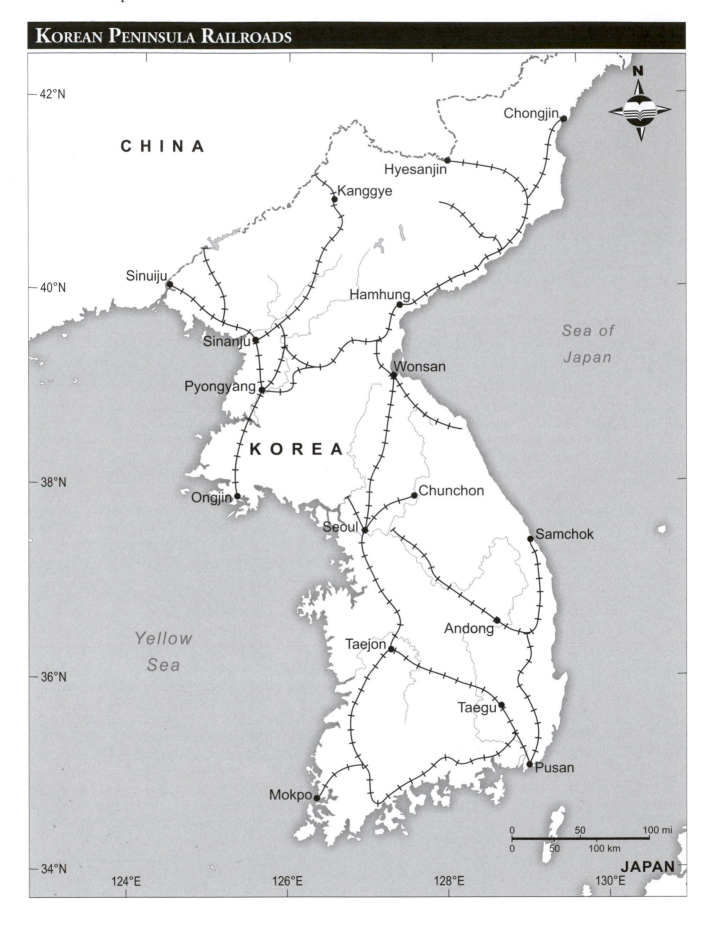

NORTH KOREAN INVASION OF SOUTH KOREA, JUNE 25–28, 1950

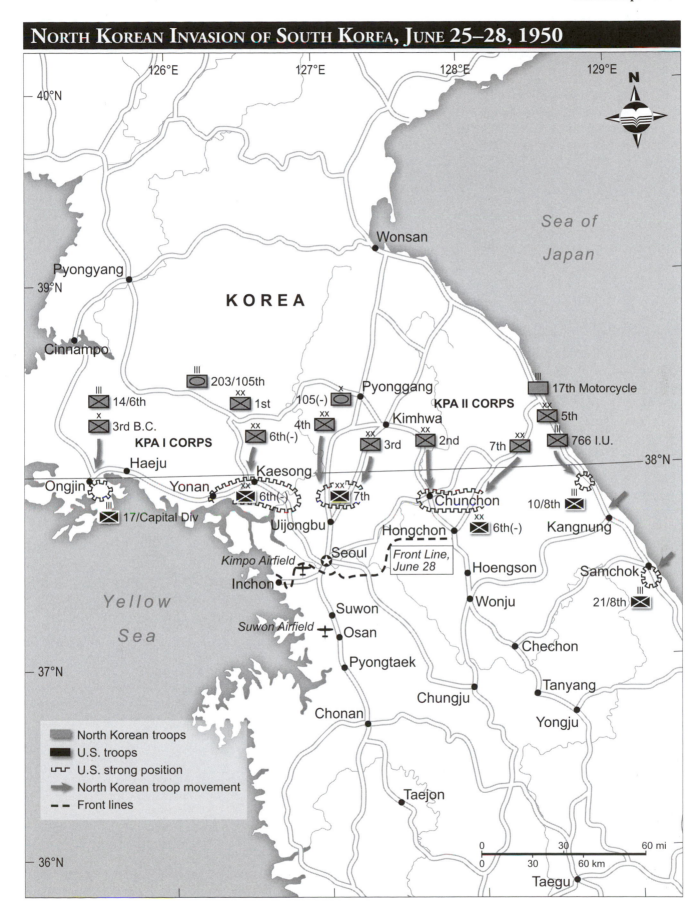

CHINESE INTERVENTION IN THE WAR, OCTOBER 25–NOVEMBER 1, 1950

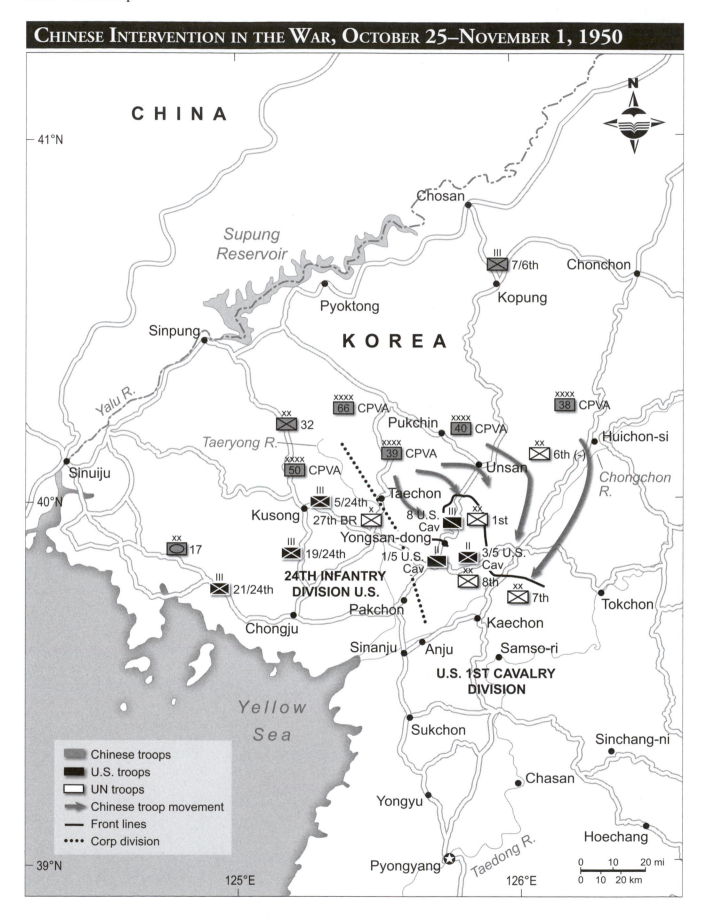

DEMARCATION LINE, 1953

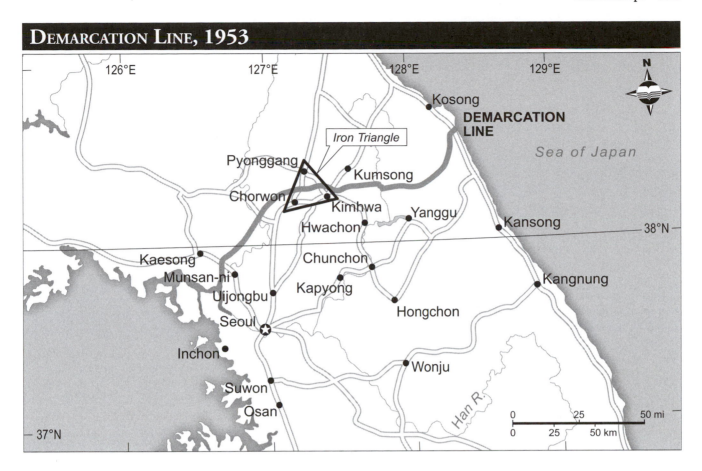

M

MacArthur, Douglas

Birth Date: January 26, 1880
Death Date: April 5, 1964

U.S. Army general and supreme commander of United Nations Command (UNC) forces during the Korean War. Douglas MacArthur, son of Civil War hero and career U.S. Army officer General Arthur MacArthur, was born on January 26, 1880, at Arsenal Barracks, Little Rock, Arkansas, and spent much of his youth on frontier army posts. He attended the U.S. Military Academy at West Point, graduating at the head of his class and as first captain in 1903. Following service in the Philippines and Japan, he became an aide to President Theodore Roosevelt from 1906 to 1907. MacArthur took part in the 1914 occupation of Veracruz, Mexico, and he served on the U.S. Army general staff from 1913 to 1917.

After the United States entered World War I in April 1917, MacArthur went to France as chief of staff of the 42nd Division. Promoted to temporary brigadier general, he took part in the Second Battle of the Marne. MacArthur then led the 8th Infantry Brigade in the St. Mihiel and Meuse-Argonne Offensives and, at the end of the war, commanded the 42nd Division.

Following occupation duty in Germany, MacArthur returned to the United States as superintendent of West Point from 1919 to 1922, carrying out much-needed reforms. He again served in the Philippines during 1922–1930 (in 1928–1930 he commanded the Philippine Department). MacArthur next served as chief of staff of the army from 1930 to 1935. His reputation suffered from the 1932 Bonus Army Incident, when he employed force to oust a protest by World War I veterans in Washington, DC In 1935, MacArthur returned to the Philippines as advisor to the Philippine government in establishing an army capable of resisting a Japanese invasion.

In August 1936, he accepted the post of field marshal of Philippine forces, and in December 1937, he retired from the U.S. Army.

Recalled to active service with the U.S. Army as a major general in July 1941, MacArthur received command of all U.S. forces in the Philippines. He was quickly elevated to lieutenant general and then general. Believing his forces could defend the islands, MacArthur scrapped the original, sound plan to withdraw into the Bataan Peninsula. As a result of his refusal to allow Major General Lewis Brereton to launch an immediate retaliatory air strike against the Japanese on Taiwan (then known as Formosa) in response to the attack on Pearl Harbor, half of the American bombers and one-third of the fighters in the Philippines were caught and destroyed on the ground by the Japanese on December 8.

Although the Japanese force invading the Philippines was only 57,000 men, half the number of his own troops, many of MacArthur's men were poorly trained (a number were recent inductees) and they were thinly spread. The Japanese had little difficulty taking Manila and much of the island of Luzon. MacArthur then ordered his forces to implement the original plan of withdrawing into the Bataan Peninsula. The bases there were not ready and the retreating troops had to abandon stocks of supplies and ammunition in the process. Over the next months, MacArthur spent most of his time on Corregidor. Rather than see MacArthur become a prisoner of the Japanese, President Franklin D. Roosevelt ordered him to Australia on February 22, 1942, where he became supreme commander of Allied forces in the Southwest Pacific. MacArthur also was awarded the Medal of Honor, which many defenders of Bataan and Corregidor believed was undeserved. Officials in Washington were also chagrined by MacArthur's acceptance of a $500,000 payment from his friend Philippine president Manuel Quezon.

General Douglas MacArthur shown addressing a joint session of Congress on April 19, 1951, following his relief from command. (National Archives)

In Australia, MacArthur developed a deliberate strategy to return to the Philippines. The slow pace of the Allied advance led Washington to insist on a leap-frogging approach that would bypass strongly held Japanese islands and positions such as Rabaul on New Britain Island and Truk. In the spring of 1944, MacArthur's troops invaded New Guinea and isolated Rabaul. By September, they had taken Morotai and the rest of New Guinea.

In a meeting with Roosevelt in Hawaii in July 1944, Admiral Chester Nimitz, who commanded forces in the Central Pacific, proposed moving against Taiwan, while MacArthur lobbied to retake the Philippines. Both moves sought to deny Japanese forces access to key resources in southeast Asia. Roosevelt agreed to allow MacArthur to retake the Philippines, and Nimitz shifted his resources against Okinawa. In October, U.S. forces under MacArthur's command invaded Leyte. They then secured Luzon during January–March 1945, then next, the southern Philippines.

The invasion of Japan proved unnecessary, and MacArthur, promoted to general of the army in December 1944, presided over the formal Japanese surrender ceremony on the battleship *Missouri* in Tokyo Bay on September 2, 1945. President Harry S. Truman named MacArthur commander of Allied occupation forces in

Japan. In this position he, in effect, governed Japan as a benevolent despot, presiding over the institution of a new democratic constitution and domestic reforms. When MacArthur took command in Tokyo, he also gained responsibility for the U.S. occupation of southern Korea (Korea having been a colony of Japan). Officials in Washington, meanwhile, ordered Lieutenant General John Hodge and his XXIV Corps from nearby Okinawa to occupy Korea south of the 38th Parallel in accordance with agreements reached in mid-August with the Soviets, who occupied Korea north of the parallel. Unfortunately, Hodge lacked diplomatic skills and had little understanding of Korea or its people. South Korea was plagued with internal turmoil throughout the U.S. occupation, but MacArthur was too busy with Japanese affairs to pay much attention to it, despite repeated pleas from Hodge.

MacArthur's sole trip to Korea during the occupation was on August 15, 1948, to witness the inauguration of the Republic of Korea (ROK, South Korea) and its first president, Syngman Rhee. After the ceremony, MacArthur assured an anxious Rhee that, in the case of communist aggression, he would defend Korea "as I would California." This pledge conflicted with later statements made by Truman administration officials, which excluded Korea from the U.S. defensive perimeter. These later public declarations may have given communist leaders in Pyongyang, Beijing, and Moscow the impression that the United States lacked interest in Korea and would not intervene there in the event of an invasion by the Democratic People's Republic of Korea (DPRK, North Korea) into South Korea.

Soviet troops were withdrawn from Korea in December 1948, followed by U.S. occupation troops in June 1949, in accordance with a United Nations (UN) agreement. The Soviets supplied their North Korean client state with an abundance of tanks, heavy artillery, and military aircraft. President Rhee repeatedly pleaded with the United States for airplanes, ships, and heavier weapons, but the Truman administration, fearful that the Nationalist Rhee might use them in a military effort to reunite the peninsula, denied the requests. Weapons provided to the Republic of Korea Army (ROKA, South Korean Army) were limited to small arms and light artillery.

By 1950, MacArthur's Far East Command (FEC) was in no shape to fight a war. Drastic cutbacks in the U.S. defense budget had severely reduced its troops and equipment. The four divisions making up the U.S. Eighth Army deployed in Japan were all severely under strength, each consisting of about 12,800 troops instead of the authorized strength of 18,900 each. MacArthur must bear some responsibility for allowing readiness and training in his command to deteriorate until, after five years of soft occupation duty, it was unfit to engage a determined foe in combat. A U.S. Army study described the FEC on the eve of war as "flabby and soft, still hampered by an infectious lassitude, unready to respond swiftly and decisively to a full-scale emergency."

That emergency occurred on June 25, 1950, when North Korea launched a full-scale invasion of South Korea. That same day, MacArthur dispatched a cargo ship bearing ammunition, with an air and naval escort, to the beleaguered South Koreans, thus establishing U.S. intervention. Two days later President Truman approved the use of U.S. air and naval forces south of the 38th Parallel, but he gave no authorization for the use of ground troops.

On June 29, MacArthur flew to Korea to view the situation for himself. What he saw there dismayed him. The South Korean capital, Seoul, had already fallen, and roads were jammed with refugees and troops of the defeated ROKA heading south. MacArthur realized that U.S. troops would have to be thrown "into the breach" if South Korea was to be saved. He also already envisaged a later amphibious landing, far behind enemy lines, which could offset the enemy's superior numbers and "wrest victory from defeat."

The next day, MacArthur, now back in Tokyo, received authorization from Washington to utilize limited ground forces to protect the southern port of Pusan, toward which ROKA forces were retreating. MacArthur was also permitted to use air assets against targets north of the 38th Parallel. MacArthur informed Washington that this was not sufficient; U.S. troops would have to be committed in force to avert total defeat. President Truman then decided to give MacArthur "full authority to use the ground forces

under his command." The United States was now fully committed to a war in Asia.

On July 8, Truman formally selected MacArthur to command UNC forces in Korea. MacArthur was the obvious candidate for the position, but at least one prescient observer (correspondent James Reston) noted that "diplomacy and a vast concern for the opinions and sensitivities of others are the political qualities essential to his new assignment, and these are precisely the qualities General MacArthur has been accused of lacking in the past."

MacArthur threw Lieutenant General Walton Walker's Eighth Army into battle against the North Koreans immediately after receiving consent from Washington. Task Force Smith, an ad hoc group of 430 men from the U.S. 24th Infantry Division, was rushed to the peninsula ahead of the main U.S. forces in an attempt to slow the North Korean advance. However, this small, ill-equipped force was badly mauled in its first action at Osan against the Korean People's Army (KPA, North Korean Army) and was forced to retreat along with its ROKA allies. The Eighth Army was gradually forced back until the only Korean soil under UN control was a perimeter around the vital port of Pusan. Walker was contemplating further withdrawals when, on July 27, a "grim faced" MacArthur arrived at Eighth Army headquarters and informed Walker and his staff that further retreat would be "unacceptable." Shortly thereafter, Walker issued his famous "stand or die" order to the Eighth Army.

With United Nations Command (UNC) lines stabilized along the Pusan Perimeter, the Joint Chiefs of Staff (JCS) suggested that MacArthur send a senior officer to meet in Taiwan with Chinese Nationalist leader Jiang Jieshi (Chiang Kai-shek) to assess defenses on Taiwan and inform Jiang that U.S. Navy ships would intercept any Nationalist raids against the People's Republic of China (PRC) on the mainland. Truman was already concerned about the possibility of Chinese intervention in Korea and was determined not to provoke Beijing over the sensitive issue of Taiwan.

MacArthur decided to make the trip to Taiwan himself. A strong advocate of Taiwan and convinced of its importance to U.S. defense, MacArthur issued statements following the meeting that seemed to imply Taiwan-American military cooperation. Reaction in Washington was swift, as numerous officials made clear to MacArthur the president's intention to keep Taiwan neutral.

The matter seemed resolved until, on August 20, MacArthur sent a letter to the Veterans of Foreign Wars (VFW) convention in Chicago in which he stridently pleaded the case for U.S. defense of Taiwan. Truman, outraged by what he considered to be public defiance of his foreign policy, ordered MacArthur to retract his message. But the damage had already been done. The U.S. press had published the text of the letter amid speculation of a rift between Truman and MacArthur. It was at this time, Truman later recalled, that he first considered relieving the general.

The situation in Korea, meanwhile, remained grave for UNC forces, still confined to their defensive positions around Pusan. MacArthur, eschewing a frontal assault to break the stalemate, gave full attention to his scheme for landing U.S. troops deep in the enemy's rear. The plan, christened Operation CHROMITE, called for a two-division (X Corps) amphibious assault on the port of Inchon, on North Korea's west coast, 20 miles from Seoul. The invaders would seize the capital, cutting the lines of communication of the KPA, while the Eighth Army broke out of the Pusan Perimeter. The KPA would be caught and destroyed in a massive pincer movement. But the general had to convince skeptical members of the JCS that the risky plan would work with a minimum of casualties. The plan was bold. Inchon was less than ideal for an amphibious operation. It had very high tides and swift currents and lacked landing beaches (the troops would have to assault the heart of the city over sea walls).

MacArthur acknowledged the difficulties involved and assured his superiors that surprise was guaranteed because the North Koreans would never suspect such a daring operation. "We shall land at Inchon" he said, "and I shall crush them!" The JCS and President Truman finally gave their reluctant approval.

Operation CHROMITE occurred on September 15, while MacArthur watched the U.S. 1st Marine Division landings from the bridge of the command ship USS *Mount McKinley*. North Korean resistance was light as the marines seized Inchon. MacArthur had been correct; the North Koreans were taken by surprise. U.S. and ROKA troops then moved to capture Seoul while the bulk of communist forces, far to the south, disintegrated and fled northward following the breakout of the Eighth Army from the Pusan Perimeter. The Inchon Landing had worked brilliantly, just as MacArthur had predicted. It was the high point of his career, and a dangerous aura of invincibility now surrounded the general.

On September 26, UNC forces recaptured Seoul, and three days later, MacArthur presided over the ceremony reinstating President Rhee's government in the capital. MacArthur's forces were now on the 38th Parallel. He favored pursuing KPA troops into North Korea, but the popular myth that he ordered troops across the parallel on his own authority is not true.

President Truman decided, and the UN resolved, that UNC forces should enter North Korea, destroy remaining KPA forces, and reunite the peninsula under a democratic government. MacArthur received the directive from the JCS on September 27. He was warned, however, not to allow non-ROKA forces to enter any of the northern provinces bordering China. On October 1, ROKA troops crossed the parallel. Two days later, the Chinese issued a warning, largely ignored in Washington, that U.S. troops entering North Korea would "encounter Chinese resistance." Chinese troops began entering North Korea on October 14.

Supremely confident of impending victory, MacArthur unwisely split his forces, sending X Corps by sea to land on the east coast at Wonsan and Iwon and the Eighth Army north toward Pyongyang, which fell on October 19. The two forces were dangerously divided by the rugged Taebaek mountains and could not be mutually supporting.

On October 15, 1950, MacArthur met with President Truman (their first and only meeting) on Wake Island. They met with members of the JCS and discussed a wide array of topics over a span of only two hours. MacArthur was asked if he thought Chinese intervention likely. He responded negatively and assured everyone present that even if the Chinese did enter the conflict there would be "the greatest slaughter" of Chinese troops. MacArthur and Truman then departed, seemingly in agreement about the progress of the war. Flying back to his headquarters in Tokyo that same day, MacArthur grumbled that the meeting had been a mere political junket in which the president was trying to bask in the reflected glow of the successful general. He feared that the Wake meeting had been a political ambush in which his comments would be used against him if things turned sour in Korea. For his part, Truman found MacArthur imperious.

On October 24, MacArthur, ignoring the JCS directive forbidding non-ROKA troops to enter the provinces along the Yalu River, ordered all his forces north. The JCS remonstrated briefly, then relented. On October 25, Chinese troops initiated their first engagements of the war with UNC forces. Believing this was no minor action, General Walker wisely withdrew the bulk of his Eighth Army back behind the Chongchon River. MacArthur wanted an immediate resumption of the offensive, but Walker demanded time to resupply, and MacArthur reluctantly agreed. Not until November 20 were supply elements able to deliver the 4,000 tons daily required for offensive operations, and Walker agreed to resume the offensive on November 24. MacArthur confidently predicted it would "get the boys home by Christmas."

On the night of November 25–26, the Chinese attacked on a massive scale. The next day, some 180,000 Chinese troops struck the Eighth Army. On November 27, X Corps was attacked by another 120,000 Chinese. UNC forces, divided by the Taebaek mountains, were forced into full retreat. Troops of X Corps were surrounded near the Changjin (Chosin) Reservoir and were compelled to break out southward toward the port of Wonsan, suffering heavy casualties in the process. With his forces in full retreat, MacArthur informed Washington that "we face an entirely new war."

This brought another test of wills with Washington. MacArthur demanded that restrictions on the bombing of Yalu bridges be lifted. Washington gave way, but the attacks, restricted to the North Korean ends of the bridges, were largely ineffective in stopping the Chinese. MacArthur, stung by press criticism, lashed out at Washington, blaming restrictions placed on his forces as the reason for the UNC disaster. On December 6, Truman issued directives obviously aimed at MacArthur that ordered government officials to use "extreme caution" when making public statements and to have all public statements cleared by Washington before release to the press.

On December 29, MacArthur received a new directive informing him that the original goal of Korean unification was being scrapped. "Korea," the general was told, "is not the place to fight a major war." MacArthur railed at what he regarded as the loss of fighting spirit in Washington. He responded with his own demands for a naval blockade of China, air and naval bombardment of the

Chinese mainland, and utilization of Nationalist troops from Taiwan. He informed the JCS that if these demands were turned down, then defeat and evacuation were the only alternatives for UNC forces. But MacArthur was proven wrong by the new ground commander of the Eighth Army, Lieutenant General Matthew Ridgway, who had taken command following General Walker's death in a jeep accident. Ridgway stabilized UNC lines south of the 38th Parallel and even launched counterattacks against the Chinese. No evacuation would be necessary.

Increasingly disturbed by the stalemate in Korea and Washington's restrictions, MacArthur issued a statement that violated Truman's directive, predicting a "savage slaughter" and further stalemate if his methods for waging war were not adopted. The press dubbed it the "Die for Tie" statement. No rebuke came from Washington. On March 24, 1951, MacArthur effectively torpedoed a planned peace initiative when he insulted the communists' ability to wage war and called on the Chinese to admit defeat. This open defiance convinced Truman, the president later claimed, that the general had to go.

Another factor also motivated Truman's decision to relieve MacArthur. U.S. military leaders were worried about a Chinese and Soviet military buildup in Asia and thought the UNC commander should have standing authority to retaliate against any communist escalation. Having recommended deployment of atomic weapons to forward Pacific bases for this purpose, they were fearful that MacArthur might provoke an incident to widen the war. Moreover, U.S. allies never would consent to providing discretion to the UNC commander to order an atomic retaliation so long as MacArthur held this position.

Meanwhile, MacArthur provided Truman with a reason that the president could rely on publicly to justify the recall when the general sent an inflammatory letter to House Minority Leader Joseph Martin in which he again savaged U.S. foreign policy. After Martin read this letter on the floor of Congress, the policy rift between MacArthur and Truman made headlines. Truman received the support of his military and civilian advisors in the decision that his press secretary announced before dawn on April 11. In Tokyo one of the general's aides, Colonel Sidney L. Huff, heard the news on the radio and informed Jean MacArthur, who interrupted an embassy luncheon to whisper the news to her husband. After a moment of silence, MacArthur remarked, "Jeannie, we're going home at last" (he had not been to the United States in 14 years).

MacArthur returned to a tumultuous welcome, enjoying ticker-tape parades through cities across America. He addressed a joint session of Congress, giving an epic speech worthy of a Shakespearean actor, and he refused to simply fade away. He testified at the congressional investigation of his dismissal and there again attacked Truman administration policies in Asia. He toured the country in full uniform, giving shrill, often extremist speeches at every stop. But gradually he lost his following among the public and the chance for a run for the presidency, which he seemed to covet.

In 1952, MacArthur met with President-Elect Dwight D. Eisenhower and presented a plan for victory in Korea. It called for, among other things, the creation of a radioactive wasteland across the peninsula near the Yalu River to stem the Chinese flow of men and supplies. Eisenhower tucked the plan in his pocket, thanked MacArthur politely, and ignored the proposal.

MacArthur spent his remaining years quietly, living with his wife in New York City's Waldorf Hotel and writing his memoirs. He visited briefly with presidents John Kennedy and Lyndon Johnson, urging both to avoid war in Asia at all costs. MacArthur died on April 5, 1964, in Washington, DC He is buried in Norfolk, Virginia.

DUANE L. WESOLICK AND SPENCER C. TUCKER

See also

China, Republic of; Eighth Army, U.S.; Far East Command; Hodge, John Reed; Inchon Landing; Jiang Jieshi; Joint Chiefs of Staff; MacArthur Hearings; Martin, Joseph William; Pusan Perimeter and Breakout; Rhee, Syngman; Ridgway, Matthew Bunker; Task Force Smith; X Corps; 38th Parallel, Decision to Cross; Truman, Harry S.; Truman's Cease-fire Initiative; Truman's Recall of MacArthur; United Nations Command; Wake Island Conference; Walker, Walton Harris; Yalu Bridges Controversy

References

Blair, Clay. *The Forgotten War: America in Korea, 1950–1953.* New York: Times Books, 1987.

———. *MacArthur.* New York: Times Books, 1977.

Hastings, Max. *The Korean War.* New York: Simon and Schuster, 1987.

James, D. Clayton. *The Years of MacArthur,* Vol. 3, *Triumph and Disaster, 1945–1964.* Boston: Houghton Mifflin, 1985.

MacArthur, Douglas. *Reminiscences.* New York: McGraw-Hill, 1964.

Manchester, William. *American Caesar: Douglas MacArthur, 1880–1964.* Boston: Little, Brown, 1978.

Rovere, Richard, and Arthur Schlesinger. *The General and the President, and the Future of American Foreign Policy.* New York: Farrar, Straus and Young, 1951.

Schaller, Michael. *Douglas MacArthur: Far Eastern General.* New York: Oxford University Press, 1989.

MacArthur Hearings
Start Date: May 3, 1951
End Date: June 25, 1951

Hearings conducted by the U.S. Senate Foreign Relations and Armed Services Committees to inquire into General Douglas MacArthur's removal from command of U.S. Forces in the Far East and United Nations Command (UNC) in Korea and President Harry S. Truman's Far East policy.

MacArthur's removal in April 1951 caused widespread public outrage in the United States, leading several state legislatures to condemn the action. Longtime critics of President Truman's China policy and old-guard Republicans demanded a congressional investigation. The Democrats, who controlled the Senate, established a joint committee and named Senator Richard B. Russell of Georgia chairman. Republican senators wanted the hearings broadcast over radio and television, but the Democrats secured closed hearings and the daily issuance of censored transcripts to protect classified information. The 26 senators on the two committees were permitted to ask questions in order of their seniority, resulting in the duplication of questions, which produced a hodgepodge of testimony in no particular order.

The first witness on May 3 was General MacArthur himself. He testified for three days. The Democrats treated him with great deference but asked questions to show his variance with administration policy. MacArthur's testimony was an amplification of his April 19 speech to a joint session of Congress arguing for a complete military victory over the People's Republic of China (PRC).

MacArthur stated that his forces could have stopped the Chinese at the end of 1950 had he been allowed to bomb Manchurian bases. He also stated that his proposals would have resulted in the defeat of the Chinese had he been allowed to execute the plans. These proposals were a naval blockade of China, naval attacks on Chinese coastal industrial sites, dispatch of Chinese Nationalist troops to Korea, and the insertion of Nationalist guerrillas along the coast of mainland China. MacArthur denied that the Soviet Union would have entered an expanded war, and he wanted the United States to defeat China, despite allied opposition to such a course.

Senator Brien McMahon of Connecticut told MacArthur that he had been wrong about Chinese intervention in Korea and asked if he could also be wrong about Soviet intervention. If the Soviets intervened, Senator McMahon asked, how could the United States defend itself? MacArthur replied that it was not his responsibility to determine defense needs, as he was only a theater commander. McMahon replied that MacArthur had made the point that he wanted to make: that the president and his advisers had to look at the Korean War from a global viewpoint. McMahon pointed out that MacArthur, as a theater commander, lacked knowledge of worldwide defense needs and was not in a position to know the ramifications of expanding the war into China.

MacArthur professed not to understand why he was relieved of command or why his March 24 ultimatum to the Chinese, threatening an attack on China proper, would cause problems for Truman while the president was trying to secure a negotiated settlement. He blamed politicians for causing the stalemate by exercising control over strategic decisions, such as bombing Manchuria, that should have best been left to military professionals. MacArthur stated that he and the Joint Chiefs of Staff (JCS) were in full agreement on policy and that it was President Truman and his secretary of state who had made it impossible to win the war.

After MacArthur finished testifying, six administration witnesses refuted his testimony. These included Secretary of Defense George C. Marshall, chairman of the JCS General Omar N. Bradley, army chief of staff General J. Lawton Collins, air force chief of staff General Hoyt C. Vandenberg, chief of naval operations Admiral Forrest P. Sherman, Secretary of State Dean G. Acheson, and State Department legal counsel Adrian S. Fisher. Marshall testified that MacArthur's policy risked a world war and the loss

of allied support, while Sherman believed that a naval blockade would be difficult to maintain with the British and Soviets controlling three Chinese ports. Vandenberg said the United States would have to double the size of its strategic bombing force to be able to bomb China effectively. But Bradley was the most powerful critic of MacArthur's desire to attack China. He asserted that war with China would be the "wrong war, at the wrong place, at the wrong time, and with the wrong enemy."

On the issue of MacArthur and the JCS agreeing on military policy, all the witnesses contradicted MacArthur's statement that their message of January 12, 1951, supported his desire for total victory. The JCS proposed a naval blockade and aerial reconnaissance of China and removal of restrictions on the Nationalists, contingent on the near-defeat of UNC forces. This JCS proposal had never been approved as policy.

With regard to MacArthur's insubordination, Marshall cited six occasions when the general had failed to secure approval for public statements as directed by the president. Collins related how MacArthur had disregarded a directive that he send only ROKA troops near the Chinese border along the Yalu River.

Acheson was quizzed mainly on the administration's China policy. Afraid that the senators' questions would not make administration policy clear, Acheson presented a prepared statement. His argument was that the United States did not "lose" China to communism; the corruption of the administration of Jiang Jieshi (Chiang Kai-shek) and his failure to broaden the base of the government caused internal collapse. Acheson argued that there was no connection between the Yalta Agreements and the communist victory in China.

Last to testify were supporters of Republican critics of Far East policy, but even they opposed MacArthur's desire to expand the war. General Albert C. Wedemeyer remarked that it was better to withdraw from Korea than to broaden the war.

On August 17, 1951, the committee decided to send the transcript of the hearings to the Senate without a majority or minority report but allowed committee members to append their concluding statements if they so desired. Eight old-guard Republican senators stated that MacArthur's removal was not justified and that Truman's foreign policy was disastrous. By this time, however, the political passions aroused by MacArthur's dismissal had subsided.

JOHN L. BELL

See also

Acheson, Dean Gooderham; Bradley, Omar Nelson; Collins, Joseph Lawton; Jiang Jieshi; Joint Chiefs of Staff; MacArthur, Douglas; Marshall, George Catlett; Sherman, Forrest Percival; Truman, Harry S.; Vandenberg, Hoyt Sanford

References

Acheson, Dean. *Present at the Creation: My Years at the State Department.* New York: Norton, 1969.
Bradley, Omar N., and Clay Blair. *A General's Life: An Autobiography.* New York: Simon and Schuster, 1983.

James, D. Clayton. *The Years of MacArthur,* Vol. 3, *Triumph and Disaster, 1945–1964.* Boston: Houghton Mifflin, 1985.

Kaufman, Burton I. *The Korean War: Challenges in Crisis, Credibility and Command.* 2nd ed. New York: McGraw-Hill, 1997.

U.S. Senate Committee on Armed Services and the Committee on Foreign Relations. *Inquiry into the Military Situation in the Far East and the Facts Surrounding the Relief of General of the Army Douglas MacArthur from His Assignments in That Area.* 82nd Cong., 1st sess. Washington, DC: U.S. Government Printing Office, 1951.

Wilz, John E. "The MacArthur Hearings of 1951: The Secret Testimony." *Military Affairs* 39(4) (December 1975): 167–173.

Machine Guns

Automatic weapons generally classified as light (one-man weapons issued in standard rifle calibers), medium (often requiring a crew), and heavy (fitted to heavier mounts and ranging from rifle calibers to .50 caliber or higher). Both United Nations Command (UNC) and communist forces issued large numbers of machine guns deployed in a variety of roles: ground, armored, aircraft, and antiaircraft.

No entirely new machine gun designs saw service in Korea. Most were of World War II vintage, and a significant number of weapons bore World War I–era dates of manufacture. However, nations that participated in the Korean War renewed machine gun development in the early 1950s. Their efforts led to such innovations as the more versatile, general-purpose machine guns that appeared soon after the war ended.

Although the various UNC contingents (notably the United Kingdom) issued their own weapons, most relied on the United States for the majority of their machine gun issues. The People's Republic of China (PRC) and the Democratic People's Republic of Korea (DPRK, North Korea) found it expedient to field examples of virtually any machine guns used prior to 1950. These included Japanese weapons captured by the Soviets in Manchuria and U.S. and Chinese weapons abandoned by the Chinese Nationalists during China's civil war. Communist ordnance stores thus included a bewildering variety of captured U.S. .30- and .50-caliber machine

Machine guns in action defending against communist forces in the central part of the Korean front, February 22, 1951. (National Archives)

During fighting north of the Chongchon River, a weapons squad leader in the U.S. 2nd Infantry Division points out a North Korean position to his machine gun crew, November 20, 1950. (National Archives)

guns, World War II Japanese 6.5-mm, 7.7-mm, 12.7-mm, and 13.2-mm weapons, as well as German 7.92-mm MG34s and MG42s. Later in the conflict, the communists also issued thousands of machine guns that were either of Soviet manufacture or Chinese copies of Soviet designs.

U.S. forces and most of their UNC allies fielded light and medium company- and battalion-level machine guns that used the standard .30-06 U.S. rifle cartridge. The U.S. Browning water-cooled Model 1917A1 and air-cooled Models 1919A4 and A6 machine guns saw extensive service in Korea. They were not only the standard U.S. infantry machine guns but also were so ubiquitous that they can be considered at least substitute standard for their allies and, when the guns were captured, by the communists as well. Designed by prolific weapons innovator John Browning, all three weapons had won fame in World War II; the M1917A1 also claimed World War I service.

Other than their cooling systems, the Brownings were virtually identical in their method of operation. They were recoil-operated, belt-fed weapons, the 1917A1 achieving 450–600 rounds per minute; the 1919A4, 400–550 rounds per minute; and the 1919A6, 400–500 rounds per minute. The M1917A1 weighed 41 pounds with water and was typically mounted on the 53.15-pound M1917A1 tripod. The 31-pound 1919A4 served as an antiaircraft

weapon and, in fixed mode, aboard tanks and other armored vehicles. Fitted to the 16.22-pound M2 tripod, the M1919A4 joined the M1919A6 as the most widely used allied infantry machine guns in Korea. The 32.5-pound 1919A6 was fitted with a shoulder stock, carrying handle, and bipod for ground use. Belgium's Fabrique Nationale d'Armes de Guerre also manufactured large numbers of the .30-caliber Browning, supplying them to the Belgian government as well as other nations.

Few weapons approach the reputation and versatility of the Browning .50-caliber M2 machine gun series. The basic M2 evolved from a World War I John Browning prototype mated with a Winchester-designed cartridge. Early models were water cooled, but soon after their introduction, an air-cooled version appeared for aircraft use. These models were soon joined by a heavier-barreled M2 that was capable of longer sustained fire. The air-cooled M2 weighed 65 pounds, 2 ounces and was capable of 800 rounds per minute, whereas the M2HB (heavy barrel) weighed 84 pounds and fired at 500 rounds per minute.

Very similar in appearance to the .30-caliber Browning, the M2 heavy machine gun proved itself in both aircraft and antiaircraft roles during World War II. The M2 was a recoil-operated, belt-fed weapon that saw service in Korea aboard tanks and other armored vehicles and aircraft—most notably the North American F-86

Sabre. It could also be tripod mounted in an infantry role. The antiaircraft M2HB saw considerable success as a heavy ground-support weapon when fired from the M45 quad mount. Its massive firepower proved a devastating counter to Chinese "human-wave" attacks.

The British Vickers Machine Gun Mark I closely rivaled the Browning designs in longevity of service and popularity among the troops who manned it. The Mark I was adopted in 1912 and manufactured in both England and Australia. It served the British Commonwealth until being declared obsolete in 1968. The Mark I, when mounted on the Mark IVB tripod, served as the standard heavy infantry machine gun for Commonwealth troops. It also proved its versatility in naval, aircraft, antiaircraft, tank, and other armored vehicle roles.

The belt-fed, water-cooled Vickers was capable of automatic fire only, achieving a cyclic rate of 450–550 rounds per minute. A modified Maxim design using a gas-assisted recoil system of operation, the Mark I was issued with either smooth or corrugated water jackets. It was chambered for the standard British .303-caliber rimmed rifle cartridge.

Although relatively heavy at 90 pounds (unloaded with tripod), slow firing (450 rounds per minute), and prone to misfeeds owing to its rimmed cartridge, the Vickers nevertheless commanded the loyalty of its crews. Other than its cartridge problems, the weapon itself was well designed and constructed. Most important, it was reliable under the harshest conditions.

Commonwealth tank and other armored vehicle machine guns included the U.S. .30-caliber Browning machine gun and the 7.92-mm Besa machine gun. The Besa was based on a pre–World War II Czech design and chambers the German 7.92-mm rimless service cartridge. The Besas, in Marks 1, 2, 2*, 3, and 3*, are gas-operated, belt-fed weapons featuring adjustable cyclic rates. The Besa was particularly highly regarded by its crews for its high rate of fire (low: 450–550 rounds per minute; high: 750–850 rounds per minute) and long-range accuracy.

Still recovering from World War II, France issued a hodge-podge of domestic and foreign machine guns, primarily U.S. .30-caliber Brownings, but also British Brens and Vickers, as well as World War II German 7.92-mm MG34s and MG42s. The 27.48-pound French 7.5-mm Model 1931A tank and fortress machine gun was developed before World War II. Its design was based on the famous Browning automatic rifle; it was gas operated and capable of automatic fire only. The M1931A achieved an impressive rate of sustained fire at 750 rounds per minute, owing to its heavy barrel. After World War II, the M1931A was adapted to either the 32.15-pound French M1945 tripod or the 16.22-pound U.S. M2 tripod for infantry use. It also saw use as a fixed tank and armored vehicle machine gun. The Model 1931A accepted either a box or side-mounted 150-round drum magazine.

Communist forces tended to rely heavily on captured U.S. and Japanese ordnance early in the war, later replacing those weapons lost to attrition with Soviet, Soviet-captured, and Chinese copies of Soviet machine guns. In short, as with many armies of guerrilla origin, the communists used whatever was available, regardless of condition or quality.

Owing to their ready availability, many types of Japanese machine guns saw communist service in Korea. These most probably included the 6.5-mm Taisho 3, Taisho 11, Type 91, and Type 96, as well as the 7.7-mm Type 92, Type 97, and Type 99. Other weapons included the 7.92-mm Type 98, a copy of the German MG15, and the .303 Type 89, a copy of the British Vickers. The 13.2-mm Type 93 was the standard Japanese heavy-caliber machine gun—a dramatic contrast to the diminutive reduced-power training machine guns that were also pressed into emergency service.

These Japanese weapons presented a host of logistical liabilities. Although the weapons were relatively plentiful, ammunition proved scarce. Both the Chinese and the North Koreans found it necessary to manufacture new cartridges for them—a daunting task, considering the wide variety of Japanese service calibers. To compound the ammunition problem, most World War II Japanese machine guns can best be characterized as somewhat eccentric in design.

The Type 92 is representative of most Japanese machine guns. It was a modified French Hotchkiss design and saw wide use in World War II as well as in Korea. The Type 92's advantages—it was well made and was capable of accepting both the 7.7-mm semirimless Type 92 round and the Type 99 rimless round—were more than offset by its flaws. The Type 92 weighed a hefty 122 pounds unloaded with tripod, and it fired at a slow 450-rounds per minute cyclic rate. Furthermore, its strip-fed ammunition required oiling before loading to facilitate extraction—a cause of frequent jamming under dusty or other adverse conditions. Still, expediency dictated the Type 92's continued use throughout the war.

As existing stocks of weapons were depleted, the Soviet Union stepped in to replace them with machine guns from its own considerable stocks of domestic and captured weapons. Early Soviet machine guns were based on Maxim designs. These included the water-cooled Model 1910 Maxim (SPM), the air-cooled Maxim Tokarev, and the Maxim Koleshnikov. All were belt-fed, recoil-operated weapons chambered for the rimmed Russian 7.62-mm rifle cartridge. The Model 1910 was mounted on the Sokolov two-wheeled carriage, and the Tokarev and Koleshnikov were fitted with bipods for infantry use. Their cyclic rate was 500–600 rounds per minute. The 7.62-mm Goryunov SG43 replaced the Maxim M1910 as the Soviet battalion-level and armored vehicle machine gun. It was gas operated and fed by either a 250-round drum or belt. It had a cyclic rate of 600–700 rounds per minute.

JEFF KINARD

See also

Pistols; Rifles; Submachine Guns and Light Machine Guns

References

Hobart, F. W. A. *Pictorial History of the Machine Gun.* London: Ian Allan, 1971.

Hogg, Ian, and John Weeks. *Military Small Arms of the Twentieth Century.* Chicago: Follett, 1973.

Smith, W. H. B. *Small Arms of the World,* 9th ed. Harrisburg, PA: Stackpole, 1969.

Willbanks, James H. *Machine Guns: An Illustrated History of Their Impact.* Santa Barbara, CA: ABC-CLIO, 2004.

Magrin-Vernerey, Raoul Charles

See Monclar, Ralph

Makin, Norman
Birth Date: March 31, 1889
Death Date: July 20, 1982

Australian politician, government official, and ambassador to the United States (1946–1951). Born on March 31, 1889, in Petersham, Sydney, Norman John Oswald Makin was educated at Broken Hill Public School. In 1919, he entered public life as a member of the federal parliament representing the Australian Labour Party and remained there until 1946. In 1929, he was Speaker of the House of Representatives, and from 1941 to 1946 he served in the Australian war cabinet and the advisory war council as minister for the navy and minister of munitions.

In 1946, when Australia's Washington, DC, legation was upgraded to an embassy level, Makin became his country's first ambassador to the United States. He also led the Australian delegation at the United Nations (UN), was elected to the first UN Security Council in 1946, and served as the latter's first president. Although Australia's Labour government was defeated in the general election of December 1949, the successor Conservative administration of Robert Menzies did not replace Makin until May 1951.

Makin's major contribution during the Korean War was to push for the conclusion of a regional security pact between the United States and Australia, which came to fruition in 1951 with the ANZUS (Australia–New Zealand–U.S.) Treaty. In late June 1950, he reported to his superiors in Canberra that, because U.S. officials were grateful for Australia's speedy support over Korea, this was an appropriate time to press the United States to conclude such an arrangement.

As with other Australian officials, Makin expressed his country's reservations over aspects of U.S. policy on the war. In late 1950, he communicated to U.S. leaders Australian concerns that, in retaliation for the People's Republic of China (PRC) intervention in Korea, the United States might respond in such a way as to broaden and escalate the conflict. During and after British prime minister Clement Attlee's December 1950 visit to the United States, Makin laid out his own country's reservations on any potential U.S. use of atomic weapons in the war, views that essentially echoed those of Attlee.

In late 1950, Makin discussed with U.S. officials suggestions by Australian minister for external affairs Percy C. Spender that the United States might withdraw its recognition of Jiang Jieshi's (Chiang Kai-shek) Guomindang (GMD, Nationalist) government of Taiwan (then known as Formosa) to obtain a peace settlement with the PRC. In February 1951, Makin also warned the U.S. State Department of Australia's fears that, as the tide of war turned again in Korea, UN forces might repeat their earlier mistake of crossing the 38th Parallel and pushing far north into the Democratic People's Republic of Korea (DPRK, North Korea). Although U.S. officials tended to resent and sometimes ignored such warnings and suggestions from their allies, such caveats did exercise a restraining influence on the more extreme U.S. policy makers.

Makin left Washington in May 1951 and returned to politics, sitting in the House of Representatives from 1954 until he retired in 1964. He died in Glenelg on July 20, 1982.

PRISCILLA ROBERTS

See also

ANZUS Treaty; Attlee, Clement Richard; Australia; Jiang Jieshi; Menzies, Robert Gordon; Spender, Sir Percy Claude

References

Barclay, John St. J. *Friends in High Places: Australian-American Diplomatic Relations.* Melbourne: Oxford University Press, 1985.

Bridge, Carl, ed. *Munich to Vietnam: Australia's Relations with Britain and the United States since the 1930s.* Melbourne: Melbourne University Press, 1991.

Harper, Norman. *A Great and Powerful Friend: A Study of Australian American Relations between 1900 and 1975.* St. Lucia: Queensland University Press, 1987.

McIntyre, W. David. *Background to the Anzus Pact: Policy-Making, Strategy, and Diplomacy, 1945–55.* New York: St. Martin's, 1995.

O'Neill, Robert J. *Australia in the Korea War, 1950–1953.* 2 vols. Canberra: Australian War Memorial/Australian Government Publishing Service, 1981, 1985.

Makins, Sir Roger
Birth Date: February 3, 1904
Death Date: November 9, 1996

British career diplomat and deputy undersecretary of state for Foreign Affairs (1948–1952) and British ambassador to the United States (1953–1956). Born in London on February 3, 1904, Roger Mellor Makins was educated at Christ Church College, Oxford, where he won first-class honors in history. He was called to the bar in 1927 and joined the Foreign Office the following year. His first overseas posting was to Washington, DC, where he married the daughter of U.S. senator Dwight F. Davis and began the earliest of what would be many close ties with numerous influential and prominent Americans.

For the rest of his career, Makins remained one of the strongest British advocates of a close Anglo-American relationship, which he considered should be the essential keystone of British foreign policy. This outlook, which he saw as a means of ensuring Britain's status as the "third world power," informed all his subsequent professional activities. During the 1930s Makins also served in Norway and the League of Nations, and in the Second World War he spent 1943 to 1945 in northwest Africa in various staff capacities for the resident minister, Harold Macmillan, who described Makins as "never satisfied with second best." Makins's tireless work, enormous competence, intellectual brilliance, and economic ability all won great respect.

Makins spent 1945 through 1947 as minister at the British embassy in Washington, focusing particularly on economic issues and atomic energy; he also undertook much public relations work explaining British policies publicly and privately to Americans, an enterprise in which his U.S. connections and knowledge were especially valuable. In 1948, Makins returned to the Foreign Office as deputy undersecretary of state, where he concentrated once more on economic issues, especially the implementation of the European Recovery Plan.

As a career official, Makins remained in place when in autumn of 1951 the Conservatives ousted Clement Attlee's Labour government. He gave politicians of both parties advice that consistently reflected his well-matured view—shared by a number of influential senior civil servants—that Britain should remain an important international force, active in Commonwealth, European, and world affairs, and that to do so it needed U.S. support.

Makins's political superiors, whether Labour or Conservative, generally concurred in his arguments that they must persuade inexperienced U.S. officials not to overreact in Korea while neglecting the European interests that he considered a higher priority. Makins accompanied Prime Minister Clement Attlee on his December 1950 visit to the United States, when the prime minister demurred at the use of atomic weapons, suggested U.S. conciliation of China, and urged the speedy opening of armistice talks, points the British continued to put forward for the remainder of the war.

In 1953, Makins replaced Oliver Franks as British ambassador in Washington, when the Korean armistice negotiations were in their final months, and as the settlement's multifarious details were determined, he worked closely with the Eisenhower administration. Throughout his four-year ambassadorship he attempted to alleviate those difficulties in the Anglo-American relationship that were created or at least enhanced by often tactless U.S. secretary of state John Foster Dulles.

On returning to Britain in 1956, Makins became joint permanent secretary of the treasury and, on his retirement in 1959, spent five years as chairman of Britain's Atomic Energy Authority. In 1964, Makins was ennobled as Lord Sherfield. From 1966 to 1970, he chaired the Hill Samuel Group, and from 1974 to 1979, he was Warden of Winchester College, Oxford. Makins held numerous directorships and served in various capacities on many public bodies. He died on November 9, 1996, in Basingstoke, England.

PRISCILLA ROBERTS

See also

Attlee, Clement Richard; Bevin, Ernest; Churchill, Sir Winston; Eden, Robert Anthony; United Kingdom

References

Butler, Rohan, and M. E. Pelly, eds. *Documents on British Foreign Policy Overseas*, Series 2, Vol. 4, *Korea, 1950–1951*. London: HMSO, 1995.

Edwards, Jill. "Roger Makins: 'Mr. Atom.'" In *British Officials and British Foreign Policy, 1945–50*, edited by John Zametica, 8–38. Leicester, UK: Leicester University Press, 1990.

Kelly, Saul. "Roger Makins, 1953–56." In *The Washington Embassy: British Ambassadors to the United States, 1939–77*, edited by Michael F. Hopkins, Saul Kelly, and John W. Young, 91–109. New York: Palgrave Macmillan, 2009.

Lowe, Peter. *Containing the Cold War in East Asia: British Policies toward Japan, China and Korea, 1948–1953*. Manchester, UK: Manchester University Press, 1997.

MacDonald, Callum A. *Britain and the Korean War*. Oxford, UK: Blackwell, 1990.

Stueck, William W., Jr. *The Korean War: An International History*. Princeton, NJ: Princeton University Press, 1995.

Malenkov, Georgii
Birth Date: January 8, 1902
Death Date: January 14, 1988

Soviet political leader who initiated diplomatic moves to end the Korean War (1952–1953) and premier of the Soviet Union (1953–1955). Born on January 8, 1902, in Orenberg, Russia, Georgii Maximilianovich Malenkov joined the Bolshevik Party in 1920. After working in the Organizational Bureau (Orgburo) of the Central Committee between 1925 and 1930, Malenkov became secretary of the Moscow Orgburo. Using his control over personnel dossiers, Malenkov established a power base within the Moscow Party organization, and in 1939, he became a member of the Central Committee.

Despite close ties to Soviet security ministers Nikolai Yezhov and Lavrentii Beria and deep involvement in the 1930s "Great Terror," Malenkov was perhaps the most pacifistic of Joseph Stalin's inner circle with regard to foreign policy. After the Soviet dictator died on March 5, 1953, Malenkov emerged at the head of the new "collective leadership" and quickly moved to resume peace talks in Korea. On March 15, 1953, the Soviet government offered to obtain the release of British and French citizens seized by the Democratic People's Republic of Korea (DPRK, North Korea) at the outset of the Korean War. On March 28, presumably under Soviet prompting, the North Korean regime rendered a favorable response to the United Nations (UN) proposal for an agreement permitting supervised voluntary repatriation of all prisoners of war. Two days later, Chinese Foreign Minister Zhou Enlai returned

Georgii M. Malenkov was a Soviet political leader. Perhaps the most pacifistic of Soviet leader Joseph Stalin's inner circle, he initiated diplomatic moves during 1952–1953 to end the Korean War. (Library of Congress)

to Beijing after attending Stalin's funeral and proposed that truce negotiations resume.

It is unlikely that this policy of accord was of Malenkov's devising; the Soviet "peace offensive" began in the autumn of 1952. Malenkov presented a commanding front as a politician, yet he followed policy more often than he created it. Ruthless in internal affairs, he was charitable in foreign affairs and is often credited with helping end the Greek Civil War in 1948–1949. It was Malenkov who delivered the keynote address at the 19th Communist Party of the Soviet Union (CPSU) Congress in October 1952 that announced the Soviet Union's peaceful diplomatic intentions in Korea.

Ironically, Malenkov probably played a key role in persuading the Chinese to intervene in Korea as well. He met Mao Zedong, leader of the People's Republic of China (PRC) during Mao's 1949–1950 visit to Moscow, and scholars believe that Malenkov visited Beijing in the autumn of 1950 regarding the Chinese intervention across the Yalu River.

In his speech at the 19th CPSU Congress, Malenkov spoke of the U.S. "attack on the Korean People's Republic." In 1951, he participated in Stalin's "war cabinet" along with Beria, Andrei Zhdanov, and Viacheslav Molotov—all hard-line Stalinists. Yet as

premier of the Soviet Union from 1953 to 1955, he reduced the defense budget in favor of consumer goods and incentives for collective farmers.

By 1955, Malenkov had lost in the struggle to succeed Stalin. His involvement in the purges of the 1930s and the Leningrad Affair of 1948–1949, his ties to Yezhov and Beria, and his refusal to retreat from Stalinist tactics had isolated him in the Soviet Politburo. In June 1957, Malenkov was ousted, along with Molotov and other hard-liners, for plotting to replace Nikita Khrushchev as premier. He became the director of a hydroelectric station in Kazakhstan and retired in 1964. His membership in the CPSU was revoked that same year. Malenkov died in Moscow, unrepentant, on January 14, 1988.

TIMOTHY C. DOWLING

See also

Mao Zedong; Molotov, Viacheslav Mikhailovich; Soviet Union; Stalin, Joseph; Zhou Enlai

References

Ebon, Martin. *Malenkov: Stalin's Successor.* New York: McGraw-Hill, 1953.

MacDonald, Callum. *Korea: The War before Vietnam.* New York: Free Press, 1987.

Medvedev, Roy. *All Stalin's Men.* Garden City, NY: Anchor Press/ Doubleday, 1984.

Malik, Jacob
Birth Date: 1906
Death Date: February 12, 1980

Soviet diplomat and representative to the United Nations (UN) during the first years of the Korean War. Born in 1906 in Kharkov, Russia, Jacob (Iakov) Alexandrovich Malik was in 1925 accepted to the Kharkov Institute of Economics. He graduated in 1930 and then continued his studies at the Institute for Diplomatic and Consular Officials. In 1937, he began his diplomatic career as a member of the Press Department of the People's Commissariat for Foreign Affairs. In 1939, he was appointed to the Soviet Embassy in Japan, and in 1942, he became Soviet ambassador to Japan. In August 1946, Malik became deputy minister for foreign affairs, and in 1948, he became the representative of the Soviet Union to the UN.

Like other Soviet diplomats, Malik did not have much room to express personal initiative while at the UN. He was expected to closely follow the orders of Soviet leader Joseph Stalin. Thus, on January 13, 1950, on Moscow's orders, Malik walked out of the Security Council to protest the UN refusal to seat the People's Republic of China (PRC) in place of Nationalist China on Taiwan (then known as Formosa). This action indicated that Soviet officials perceived a demonstrative stand in support of China as being more important than their participation in the council's work.

Jacob A. Malik, Soviet representative to the United Nations Security Council, raises his hand to cast the only dissenting vote on the resolution calling on the People's Republic of China to withdraw its troops from Korea in December 1950. (Department of Defense)

The absence of a Soviet representative on the Security Council definitely played into the hands of Western powers, as it allowed them to control its sessions and made UN intervention in Korea possible. There is little doubt that, had he been present at the council proceedings, Malik would have exercised his right of veto. U.S. secretary of state Dean G. Acheson later characterized Malik's absence as a "long helpful Russian boycott."

Moscow finally thought it appropriate to return to the Security Council in August when it was Malik's turn to preside. Earlier that summer, the other 10 members of the council decided at an informal meeting that if the Soviet boycott continued, they would pass the presidency of the council to the United Kingdom, the next member in alphabetical order. On July 27, 1950, however, Malik indicated that he would return to the council on August 1 and preside over its meetings.

Malik's presidency that month made the sessions frustrating and unfruitful. Some of the issues he brought to the Security Council included recognition of the representative of China and "peaceful settlement of the Korean question."

Procedural issues dominated the 13 Security Council meetings under Malik's presidency. The outspokenly anti-American Malik also condemned the United States for "aggression" in Korea and for making the UN an instrument of U.S. foreign policy.

At the end of May 1951, at the Truman administration's initiative, U.S. diplomat George F. Kennan met with Malik to discuss the possibility of a resolution of the Korean conflict. During their second meeting in early June, Malik spoke of Soviet interest in a cease-fire in Korea, noting that the U.S. should work directly with the Democratic People's Republic of Korea (DPRK, North Korea) and China, as the Soviet Union was not a belligerent. Then, in a UN address on June 23, 1951, Malik suggested that the two warring sides discuss an armistice based on the 38th Parallel, but he made no reference to the withdrawal of foreign troops from Korea. In 1952, at a meeting of the UN Disarmament Commission, Malik accused the United States of distributing germ-infested foodstuffs in Korea.

In September 1952, Valerian Zorin replaced Malik as Soviet UN representative. In 1953, Malik became ambassador to Great Britain, and from 1960 to 1968, he was deputy foreign minister. In 1968, Malik again returned to the UN as Soviet representative, where he served until 1976. He died in Moscow on February 12, 1980.

NATALIA PETROUCHKEVITCH

See also

Acheson, Dean Gooderham; Biological Warfare; China, People's Republic of, United Nations Representation Question; Kennan, George Frost; Kennan-Malik Conversations; Soviet Security Council Boycott; Soviet Union; Stalin, Joseph; Zorin, Valerian

References

Bailey, Sydney D. *The Korean Armistice.* New York: St. Martin's, 1992.
Hastings, Max. *The Korean War.* New York: Simon and Schuster, 1987.
Lowe, Peter. *The Origins of the Korean War.* New York: Longman, 1997.
Paige, Glenn D. *The Korean Decision, June 24–30, 1950.* New York: Free Press, 1968.

Stairs, Denis. *The Diplomacy of Constraint: Canada, the Korean War, and the United States.* Toronto: University of Toronto Press, 1974.

Stueck, William W., Jr. *The Korean War: An International History.* Princeton, NJ: Princeton University Press, 1995.

Whiting, Allen S. *China Crosses the Yalu.* Stanford, CA: Stanford University Press, 1960.

Manchuria

Chinese province that played a crucial role in the Korean War. Manchuria is the closest Chinese province to Korea and shares the majority of the border with the Democratic People's Republic of Korea (DPRK, North Korea). Manchuria's border with North Korea mostly follows the Yalu and Tumen rivers. Manchuria is an important raw materials base for China, and leaders of the People's Republic of China (PRC) were concerned about having U.S. forces in close proximity to it. Indeed, Chinese concerns over U.S. forces invading North Korea helped bring about the Chinese decision to intervene militarily in the war.

In the late 19th and early 20th centuries, both Russia and Japan had endeavored to control Manchuria. The Japanese had secured important economic concessions in the province thanks to their defeat of Russia in the Russo-Japanese War of 1904–1905. Then in 1931, the Japanese Guandong (Kwantung) Army took over the entirety of the province, and Japan set up the puppet state of Manchukuo. The province reverted back to China following the Second World War, but the precipitous efforts of Nationalist leader Jiang Jieshi (Chiang Kai-shek) to control it brought about an early military defeat at the hands of Mao Zedong's communists. Manchuria provided the avenue for China to become involved in the Korean War. It also was the pipeline for much of the Chinese/Soviet logistical effort.

As forces of the Korean People's Army (KPA, North Korean Army) were pushed toward their border with China, Chinese troops massed north of it. Following the Chinese military intervention, United Nations Command (UNC) commander General Douglas MacArthur requested approval from Washington, DC, to bomb the bridges across the Yalu River over which supplies passed from Manchuria into North Korea. Although Truman authorized strikes on the Korean side only, many Chinese troops and supplies had already moved into North Korea, and the Yalu was soon frozen, allowing the movement of supplies across it without the benefit of the bridges.

During the remainder of the Korean War, Manchuria continued to serve as the resource base and conduit for Chinese military and armaments to enter Korea.

David R. Buck

See also

China, People's Republic of; Chinese Offensive, First; Chinese Offensive, Second; Chinese Offensive, Third; Chinese Offensive, Fourth; Chinese Offensive, Fifth; Chinese Offensive, Sixth; Chinese Offensives, Summer; Jiang Jieshi; Logistics in the Korean War; MacArthur, Douglas; Manchurian Sanctuary; Mao Zedong; Yalu Bridges Controversy

References

Appleman, Roy E. *Disaster in Korea: The Chinese Confront MacArthur.* College Station: Texas A&M University Press, 1989.

Manchurian Sanctuary

The term sanctuary denotes an area or region enjoying specially favored treatment in view of the belligerent status of its occupiers. After intervention by the People's Republic of China (PRC) in the Korean War, Manchuria, a Chinese province that shares a long common border with the Democratic People's Republic of Korea (DPRK, North Korea), served as a supply center and air base for communist forces, including Soviet air forces.

To prevent the conflict from escalating into another world war, United Nations Command (UNC) forces were not permitted to attack or bomb Manchuria. The concept of Manchurian sanctuary was developed to explain the special status of the region during the Korean War. Yet UNC commander General Douglas MacArthur argued that this was not justified from a military point of view.

On November 6, 1950, MacArthur stated that the flow of Chinese troops and supplies over the Yalu River bridges jeopardized UNC forces in Korea. The only way to stop this movement was destruction of the bridges by air attack. MacArthur indicated that he planned to employ 90 Boeing B-29 Superfortress aircraft to strike the international bridge at Sinuiju spanning the Yalu. Authorities in Washington, DC, suspended the operation, over MacArthur's strong protests, in the belief that the communist side might consider it a prelude to an attack on Manchuria itself. MacArthur replied that the operation was within the scope of the rules of warfare and of resolutions and directives he had received. Washington did authorize MacArthur to proceed with bombing in North Korea near the frontier, including targets at Sinuiju and the Korean side of the Yalu River bridges, but the effort had little effect.

MacArthur also complained that Washington was refusing to allow aerial reconnaissance beyond the Manchurian border despite the need to gather normal field intelligence on communist intentions and capabilities. In his speech to Congress on April 19, 1951, after he was relieved of his command, MacArthur argued that simple military necessity mandated the removal of restrictions on air reconnaissance of Manchuria.

Nonetheless, Washington's directive to MacArthur on August 5, 1950, authorized aerial reconnaissance of all Korean territory, including coastal waters up to the Yalu River on the west and up to but short of the Korean-Soviet international boundary on the east; these authorizations were subject to the understanding that such operations would be conducted from as far south of the frontiers of Manchuria or the Soviet Union as practical and that in no cases would those frontiers be overflown.

Following the massive Chinese military intervention in late November 1950, MacArthur announced the beginning of "an entirely new war." Bombing the Yalu bridges was soon a moot point, as the Yalu froze over, making it impossible for UNC air power to interdict the flow of troops and supplies from Manchuria. As a result, MacArthur advocated doing away with the Manchurian sanctuary altogether. His insistence on removing the sanctuary privilege was tantamount to spreading the area of hostilities into Chinese territory.

Chairman of the Joint Chiefs of Staff (JCS) General Omar N. Bradley dismissed MacArthur's argument that only the Chinese enjoyed the sanctuary privilege. Large-scale communist air attacks from Manchurian bases could deal a severe blow to crowded airfields in South Korea and Japan. A communist air attack on Pusan, the well-illuminated UNC supply center, could cripple UNC logistic capabilities. Thus, the sanctuary privilege was not a unilateral practice. During the war, the Soviet Union provided only air cover for Chinese forces in Manchuria. Its air force never struck behind the UNC front line or endeavored to destroy supply ports such as Pusan and Inchon. This self-imposed Soviet restraint cannot be construed as resulting from Soviet premier Joseph Stalin's goodwill or a desire to minimize bloodshed; it was based strictly on strategic calculations.

As Chinese forces captured Seoul and advanced south, their lines of communications became long enough for UNC air forces to cause them serious logistic troubles. The increase in the effectiveness of UNC air attacks on Chinese forces within Korea undermined MacArthur's argument that it was necessary to strike Chinese territories directly to halt communist advances. The United States then seized the opportunity to hold and stabilize a line in Korea without doing away with the Manchurian sanctuary.

YOUNGHO KIM

See also

Bradley, Omar Nelson; Joint Chiefs of Staff; Logistics in the Korean War; MacArthur, Douglas; Stalin, Joseph

References

Shu Guang Zhang. *Mao's Military Romanticism: China and the Korean War, 1950–1953.* Lawrence: University Press of Kansas, 1995.

Spanier, John W. *The Truman-MacArthur Controversy and the Korean War.* Cambridge, MA: Harvard University Press, 1959.

Stueck, William W., Jr. *Rethinking the Korean War: A New Diplomatic and Strategic History.* Princeton, NJ: Princeton University Press, 2004.

U.S. Department of State, Bureau of Public Affairs. *Foreign Relations of the United States, 1950,* Vol. 7, *Korea.* Washington, DC: U.S. Government Printing Office, 1976.

Mao Zedong
Birth Date: December 26, 1893
Death Date: September 9, 1976

Communist revolutionary and leader of the People's Republic of China (PRC) (1949–1976). A great visionary, Mao Zedong was also one of history's deadliest tyrants. Mao was born on December

Communist revolutionary and leader of the People's Republic of China Mao Zedong. Mao played a key role in the creation of a unified Chinese state, but he was also one of history's greatest tyrants. Tens of millions of Chinese died as a result of his policies. (Hulton Archive/Getty Images)

26, 1893, in a peasant home in Hunan Province. A rebel even in his youth, he was educated at his village primary school and subsequently entered high school in Changsha, the provincial capital. Mao was in Changsha when, on October 10, 1911, revolution broke out against the last of the Qing dynasty emperors. Mao joined the revolutionary army but saw no fighting and returned to his studies after six months as a soldier.

After graduating from the provincial teacher training college, Mao went to Beijing (then known as Peking), where he worked as an assistant librarian at Beijing University and began to learn about Marxism. In July 1921, he attended the founding congress of the Chinese Communist Party (CCP) in Shanghai. Seeing Marxist theories through a Chinese prism, Mao believed, unlike many of his more orthodox comrades, that revolution in China had to begin among peasants rather than in an embryonic industrial working class. During the 1920s, he spent much of his time organizing peasant unions in his native Hunan Province.

At the end of the decade, when the communists were fighting a guerrilla war for survival against the Guomindang (GMD, Nationalist) government led by Jiang Jieshi (Chiang Kai-shek), Mao retreated farther into the countryside instead of joining other communist leaders in suicidal urban uprisings. By 1934, Mao's base in Jiangxi Province was under heavy pressure from Nationalist troops. That October, some 86,000 communists slipped through the Nationalist blockade and began a 6,000-mile retreat that became known as the Long March. Mao, in political eclipse when the march began, became the party's supreme leader during the trek, a role he never relinquished. At the end of the Long March, with only about 4,000 left from the original force, Mao and his comrades established a new base in Yenan (Yan'an) in northwestern China.

Between 1937 and 1945, Mao and his army fought a new enemy—the Japanese. In that conflict, Mao and his commanders refined the art of "people's war." Mao summed up the strategy of warfare in only 16 Chinese characters: "The enemy advances, we retreat; the enemy camps, we harass; the enemy tires, we attack; the enemy retreats, we pursue." Mao's communists also forged an uneasy and tenuous alliance with the Nationalists in order to defeat the Japanese.

The Red Army became a political as well as a military weapon. Instead of victimizing the peasantry, as Chinese soldiers had done from time immemorial, Mao's troops sought to win over the rural population to their cause. Instead of looting, raping, and destroying, communist soldiers were ordered to pay for food, respect women, and help repair war damage. The ideal, and to an extent the reality, was an army that commanded public support and could, in Mao's most famous simile, swim among the people as fish swim in the sea. By the fall of 1945, Mao's army had grown to some 1.27 million men, supported by militia numbering another 2.68 million.

Following Japan's defeat in 1945, the struggle between communists and Nationalists resumed, but by now the tide was running strongly in Mao's favor. By the fall of 1949, the Nationalist government and what remained of its army had fled to the island of Taiwan (then known as Formosa). On October 1, 1949, Mao stood under China's new flag, red with five gold stars, and officially proclaimed the People's Republic of China (PRC). Mao's army, the People's Liberation Army (PLA, Chinese Communist Army), numbered 4 million men.

The communists were not gentle in establishing their regime, however. "A revolution is not the same thing as inviting people to dinner or writing an essay or painting a picture or embroidering a flower," Mao once wrote. "It cannot be anything so refined, so calm and gentle." In the first years of the People's Republic of China, hundreds of thousands, perhaps millions, were executed as landlords or capitalist exploiters. Millions more were imprisoned or tortured for real or imaginary crimes against the revolution, or simply for having a privileged background. Rigid ideological controls were imposed on educators, artists, and the press.

In late 1949, when pressed to support Korean reunification under the auspices of the Democratic People's Republic of Korea (DPRK, North Korea), Mao demurred, not wishing to involve his fledgling regime in a potential war with the West. By the spring of 1950, however, North Korean leader Kim Il Sung renewed his lobbying efforts in Moscow to attain Soviet leader Joseph Stalin's approval for an attack against the Republic of Korea (ROK, South Korea) to attain Korean unity under communist rule. Stalin now agreed to the plan, but only if North Korea could convince the Chinese to go along. In May 1950, Kim Il Sung and Pak Hong Yong traveled to Beijing to meet personally with Mao. During two days of meetings, Mao expressed his skepticism with the North Korean plan but finally told Kim Il Sung that China "could" provide troops should the Americans intervene. The North Koreans interpreted this as a green light for an invasion of the south, which was scheduled as early as June.

Less than a year after Mao came to power, the outbreak of war in Korea presented him with difficult choices. His priority was on consolidating his new government and rebuilding China. But a North Korean defeat would bring hostile foreign forces to China's northeastern border and, Mao feared, might encourage Jiang to send his forces back across the Taiwan Strait to reopen the civil war on the mainland. A defeat would also send the wrong message to the world about the communist commitment to worldwide revolution. The key issue for China was whether the counterattacking U.S. forces would halt at the 38th Parallel in the fall of 1950 or continue their advance into North Korea. If the latter, Mao decided, China had no choice but to enter the war. As a result, as early as July 1950, Mao began mobilizing troops in the border region; by the end of the month, 255,000 Chinese troops were massed along the Chinese–North Korean border.

On October 8, the day after the first U.S. troops moved onto North Korean territory, Mao issued the official directive: "It has been ordered that the Northeast Border Defense Army be turned into the Chinese People's Volunteers [CPVA, Chinese Army; the name was a fig leaf, a transparent device for China to go to war with the United States without formally avowing it] and that the Chinese People's Volunteers move immediately into the territory of Korea to assist the Korean comrades in their struggle."

Mao's decision to intervene in Korea was costly indeed, and it cost the life of his oldest son. Mao Anying, age 28, was killed in a U.S. air strike on a CPVA command post in November 1950, just weeks after the intervention began. In less than three years of fighting in Korea, China suffered almost 1 million military casualties. The war drained away precious resources that could have been used to rebuild the Chinese economy, but Mao did use the conflict to consolidate his power by engaging in a massive propaganda campaign that portrayed the United States as the great enemy of the revolution.

For many ordinary Chinese, life gradually improved in the years following 1949. But Mao was impatient for faster progress. Uninformed about economics and technology, and convinced that the sheer muscle power of China's huge population could accomplish any goal if it were just mobilized properly, he began in 1958 dreaming of a "Great Leap Forward" that would hurl China out of poverty and backwardness and create a modern, prosperous state virtually overnight.

The Great Leap Forward produced numerous follies, but the worst calamity occurred in agriculture. Intoxicated by his own visions and seduced by crackpot theorists, Mao decreed an overnight transition from family or small cooperative farms to vast People's Communes, while calling for absurdly high increases in grain production. The results were devastating. From 1959 to 1961, as many as 30 million Chinese died as a direct or indirect result of Great Leap Forward policies. Many simply starved to death.

In the wake of the disaster, Mao withdrew from day-to-day administrative details. But he nursed a deep grievance against those whom he imagined had sabotaged his plan. In 1966, Mao struck back with the Great Proletarian Cultural Revolution, an event so irrational and bizarre that recorded history shows nothing else quite like it. Proclaiming "rebellion is justified," Mao urged China's youth to rise up against the party bureaucracy and against the "four olds": old habits, old customs, old culture, and old thinking.

At Mao's call, brigades of youthful Red Guards waving the little red book of Mao's thoughts spread out to "make revolution" in schools, factories, and offices throughout China. Within months, the country was in chaos. Red Guard groups splintered into rival mobs, each determined to outdo the other in rooting out enemies and tearing down everything that symbolized incorrect thoughts or China's past. Teachers, managers, intellectuals, and anyone suspected of insufficient revolutionary purity were paraded before howling mobs and forced to confess their misdeeds. Savage beatings were common. Many victims died under torture; constant physical and mental harassment drove others to commit suicide.

Among those persecuted were almost all of the old cadres—party workers and Red Army soldiers whose struggle and sacrifice had brought the communists to power. Meanwhile, the glorification of Mao reached extraordinary heights. His face on giant placards gazed out from virtually every wall in China. Badges with his image became part of the national dress. Schoolchildren and office workers began every day with bows before Mao's picture. Not even the frenzy of leader worship could stem a growing sense that something was wrong, however. In the torrent of slogans and accusations, the movement's goals grew steadily more inexplicable.

China paid a heavy price for Mao's mad fantasies: the educational system was shattered for years; economic losses were ruinous; much of China's rich artistic legacy was destroyed; society was fractured; and ideals crumbled. After two years of chaos, order was gradually restored, often at gunpoint by PLA units, but a mood of fear and uncertainty persisted through the remaining years of Mao's rule.

The Red Guards were disbanded, and millions of young people were sent from towns and cities to work as farm laborers. Out loud, nearly all of them obediently vowed willingness to "serve the people" wherever they were sent. But inwardly, many were confused, disillusioned, and hurt.

On July 28, 1976, a disastrous earthquake struck northern China. Nearly 250,000 people were killed, and physical destruction was immense, even in Beijing, 100 miles from the epicenter.

In Chinese tradition, such disasters were thought to signal the end of a dynasty. The communist regime officially scorned such superstitions, but to many Chinese the old beliefs were vindicated when, at 10 minutes past midnight on September 9, 1976, Mao died.

Believing that sheer willpower and human muscles could overcome any obstacle, Mao had turned China into a gigantic laboratory for his experiments in transforming human society. But when his grandiose dreams failed, instead of recognizing that his policies were flawed, Mao tore China apart in mad witch-hunts for the "demons and monsters" who had frustrated his efforts.

Mao's career was rich in contradictions. He proclaimed Marxism his lifelong faith, but his revolutionary ideas owed little to Marx and much more to ancient Chinese sagas of bandits and peasant rebellions. He preached simplicity and egalitarianism but had himself glorified as a virtual god-king. He declared war against China's feudal past and its oppressive traditions, but his reign, rife with arbitrary cruelties and constant intrigues, mirrored many of the worst aspects of imperial despotism. After Mao's death, Deng Xiaoping, whom Mao had twice expelled from the leadership, regained power, and within a few years Deng reversed nearly all of Mao's policies. In the end, it was the pragmatic Deng rather than the visionary Mao who laid the groundwork for economic reforms that transformed China in the 1980s and 1990s.

ARNOLD R. ISAACS

See also
China, People's Republic of; Chinese Civil War; Chinese People's Volunteer Army; Jiang Jieshi; Zhou Enlai

References
Chang, Jung. *Wild Swans: Three Daughters of China.* New York: Simon and Schuster, 1991.

Chang, Jung, and Jon Halliday. *Mao: The Unknown Story.* New York: Knopf, 2005.

Chen Jian. *Mao's China and the Cold War.* Chapel Hill: University of North Carolina Press, 2000.

Goncharov, Sergei N., John W. Lewis, and Xue Litai. *Uncertain Partners: Stalin, Mao, and the Korean War.* Stanford, CA: Stanford University Press, 1993.

Li, Zhisui. *The Private Life of Chairman Mao.* Translated by Tai Hung Chao. New York: Random House, 1994.

Salisbury, Harrison E. *The New Emperors: China in the Era of Mao and Deng.* Boston: Little, Brown, 1992.

Spence, Jonathan. *The Search for Modern China.* New York: Norton, 1990.

March First Movement
Start Date: March 1, 1919
End Date: April 30, 1919

Independence movement precipitated by Koreans against Japanese colonial rule and perhaps the most significant nationalist event in modern Korean history. After Japan annexed Korea in 1910, Koreans began organizing into a variety of groups whose sole objective was to win Korea's independence. Some members of these nationalist groups were studying in the United States, and they tried to persuade the U.S. government to assist in their fight for independence. Others worked from headquarters in China or at home in Korea.

Inspired by U.S. president Woodrow Wilson's Fourteen Points and concept of "self-determination of peoples" enunciated during World War I, the leaders of several Korean nationalist groups planned to demonstrate against their Japanese colonial rulers. This was spurred by the death of former Choson dynasty ruler King Kojong in January 1919 and rumors that he had been poisoned by a Japanese doctor. After much discussion, the nationalists decided to draft a declaration of independence, which they planned to read at Pagoda Park in Seoul, at 2:00 p.m. on March 1, 1919, two days before the former ruler's funeral. Thirty-three representatives of the nationalist groups signed the declaration of independence and a petition, both of which were sent to the governments of the United States and Japan and to the Paris Peace Conference then underway. Additionally, organizers had thousands of copies made and distributed to various localities.

Evidence suggests that initially the organizers did not plan to provoke a national uprising. They simply assumed this would be a nonviolent action by a small group of nationalist representatives expressing the desires of the Korean people. As the day drew near, the planners changed the location of the demonstration from Pagoda Park to a restaurant near the park. They feared that the park would give the more radical nationalists the opportunity to transform a dignified occasion into a volatile uprising.

On March 1, 1919, residents of Seoul and citizens from local areas began arriving at Pagoda Park to hear the declaration of independence. When none of the nationalist representatives arrived, at 2:00 p.m., a schoolteacher stood up and read the declaration to the crowd. When he finished, the crowd joined him in chanting "Long live Korea, long live Korean independence!" The crowd then moved into the streets and began marching down Chongno, one of Seoul's principal thoroughfares. More and more people joined the march, and by day's end tens of thousands of Korean citizens had participated in the demonstration. Similar events occurred elsewhere in the country; between 500,000 and 2 million Koreans participated in these demonstrations from March 1 until the end of April.

The demonstration was so well coordinated and planned in such secrecy that it caught the Japanese government in Korea completely by surprise. Although the demonstrators conducted themselves peacefully, the Japanese reaction was severe. The Japanese government immediately imposed restrictions on traffic, outlawed assemblies and street demonstrations, and closed several markets. The Japanese searched and destroyed houses, schools, and churches, looking for documents and those individuals responsible. According to one government report, between March 1 and April 30, more than 7,500 people were killed and some 16,000 were injured. More than 46,000 Koreans were arrested.

The March First Movement was truly a nationwide demonstration, involving every segment of Korean society. Students, teachers, and graduates from the mission schools led the demonstrations in the countryside. Most noteworthy, for the first time in Korean history, several thousand Korean women participated in these demonstrations, establishing their place as partners with men in the struggle for independence.

The events also brought new nationalist leaders to the fore. Many of those involved in the movement fled abroad, and in the Chinese city of Shanghai several of them organized what became the best-known Korean nationalist organization, the self-styled Korean Provisional Government. It elected Syngman Rhee as its first president.

The March First Movement did not bring Korea's liberation from Japanese rule, but with the help of U.S. and other foreign missionaries, the events of March 1, 1919, and Korea's struggle against a brutal Japanese colonial government became known to the world. Missionaries serving in Korea did not join the movement, but they were sympathetic to Korea's plight and approved of the nonviolent nature of the demonstrations. More important, they witnessed the events and reported in detail what they saw to their respective governments. In doing so, they succeeded in building international outrage against the Japanese for the cruel nature of their rule. This eventually forced the Japanese government to modify and somewhat reform its policy toward Korea after 1919.

MARK R. FRANKLIN

See also

Korea, Climate and Geography of; Korea, History of, to 1945; Rhee, Syngman; U.S. Policy toward Korea, Pre-1950

References

Bark, Dong Suh. "The American-Educated Elite in Korean Society." In *Korea and the United States: A Century of Cooperation,* edited by Young Nok Koo and Dae Sook Suh, 263–280. Honolulu: University of Hawaii Press, 1984.

Cumings, Bruce. *Korea's Place in the Sun: A Modern History.* New York: Norton, 1997.

Ku, Dae Yeol. *Korea under Colonialism: The March First Movement and Anglo-Japanese Relations.* Seoul: Seoul Computer Press, 1985.

Lee Chong Sik. *The Politics of Korean Nationalism.* Berkeley: University of California Press, 1963.

Nahm, Andrew C. *Korea, Tradition and Transformation: A History of the Korean People.* Elizabeth, NJ: Hollym International, 1988.

Shin, Young Il. "American Protestant Missions to Korea and the Awakening of Political and Social Consciousness in the Koreans between 1884 and 1941." In *U.S.-Korean Relations,* edited by Tae Hwan Kwak et al., 196–222. Seoul: Seoul Computer Press, 1982.

Marshall, George Catlett
Birth Date: December 31, 1880
Death Date: October 16, 1959

One of the foremost soldier-statesmen of the 20th century; chief of staff of the U.S. Army (1939–1945), special envoy to China (1945–1946), secretary of state (1947–1949), and secretary of defense

(1950–1951). Born in Uniontown, Pennsylvania, on December 31, 1880, George Catlett Marshall graduated from the Virginia Military Institute in 1901. Commissioned in the infantry in 1902, he then served in a variety of assignments, including in the Philippines. He attended the Infantry and Cavalry School, Fort Leavenworth, in 1906 and was an instructor in the Army Service Schools from 1907 to 1908.

After the United States entered World War I, Marshall went to France with the American Expeditionary Forces as operations and training officer of the 1st Division in June 1917. Promoted to lieutenant colonel in 1918, he became deputy chief of staff for operations of the U.S. First Army in August and was the principal planner of the Saint-Mihiel Offensive of September 12–16. He earned admiration for his logistical skills in directing the repositioning of hundreds of thousands of men quickly across the battlefront after his success in the Meuse-Argonne Offensive of September 26–November 11. After working on occupation plans for Germany, Marshall reverted to his permanent rank of captain and, from 1919 to 1924, worked as aide to General John J. Pershing, who served as chief of staff of the army from 1921 to 1924. Marshall was promoted to major in 1920 and lieutenant colonel in 1923.

Marshall served in Tianjin (Tientsin), China, with the 15th Infantry Regiment from 1924 to 1927. He was assistant commandant in charge of instruction at the Infantry School, Fort Benning, Georgia, from 1927 to 1932, where he helped to train many officers who would serve as generals during World War II. Promoted to colonel in 1932, he served in various assignments in the continental United States, including instructor with the Illinois National Guard from 1933 to 1936. He advanced to brigadier general in 1936 and assumed command of the 5th Infantry Brigade.

Marshall became head of the War Plans Division in Washington, DC, with promotion to temporary major general in July 1938, then deputy chief of staff in October. President Franklin D. Roosevelt advanced him over many more senior officers to appoint him chief of staff of the U.S. Army on September 1, 1939, the day that German armies invaded Poland. He was promoted to permanent major general and simultaneously to temporary general the same day that he became chief of staff.

As war began in Europe, Marshall worked to revitalize the American defense establishment. Supported by pro-Allied civilian senior leaders, such as Secretary of War Henry L. Stimson, Marshall instituted and lobbied for programs to recruit and train new troops; expedite munitions production; assist Great Britain, China, and the Soviet Union in resisting the Axis powers; and coordinate British and American strategy. After the United States entered the war on December 7, 1941, Marshall presided over an increase in U.S. armed forces from a mere 200,000 troops to a wartime maximum of 8.1 million men and women. Marshall stressed the tactical basics of firepower and maneuver and he supported mechanization and the most modern military technology. For all this he became known as the Organizer of Victory.

General George C. Marshall was chief of staff of the U.S. Army during World War II. Known as the "Organizer of Victory," Marshall oversaw the creation and successful employment of the largest military force in U.S. history. After the war, as secretary of state, he helped develop what became known as the Marshall Plan for the reconstruction of Europe. During 1950–1951, he served as secretary of defense, in which post he helped to reconstitute the U.S. military to fight the Korean War. (Library of Congress)

Marshall was a strong supporter of opening a second front in Europe as early as possible, a campaign that was deferred by strategic necessity until June 1944. Between 1941 and 1945, he attended all the major Allied wartime strategic conferences, including those at Placentia Bay, Washington, Quebec, Cairo, Tehran, Malta, Yalta, and Potsdam. Marshall was the first to be promoted to the newly authorized five-star rank of general of the army in December 1944. Perhaps Marshall's greatest personal disappointment was that he did not hold field command, especially that of the European invasion forces. Roosevelt and the other wartime chiefs wanted him to remain in Washington, and Marshall bowed to their wishes. Marshall was a major supporter of the army air forces and he advocated employment of the atomic bomb against Japan in August 1945.

Marshall retired in November 1945 but, on the urging of President Harry S. Truman, he returned to public service as special envoy to China (1945–1946) in a fruitless effort to bridge the gap between Guomindang (GMD, Nationalist) leader Jiang Jieshi

(Chiang Kai-shek) and communist leader Mao Zedong. He again answered Truman's call to serve as secretary of state (1947–1949) and next was president of the American Red Cross (1949–1950). One of his greatest achievements as secretary of state was his inauguration of a massive economic aid program to Western Europe, which bore his name—the Marshall Plan.

In August 1950, Truman again persuaded Marshall to come out of retirement and replace Defense Secretary Louis Johnson, who was forced to resign on September 12, 1950. Truman had been upset by Johnson's feuding with other cabinet members, especially Secretary of State Dean Acheson, and Johnson had taken considerable blame for the poor state of readiness of U.S. armed forces at the start of the Korean War. Truman decided by late June to remove Johnson but waited to sound out Marshall and see if his views were in accord with his own and those of Acheson regarding Korea. A fierce congressional fight over Marshall's confirmation occurred as a result of hysteria over the communist victory in China. Marshall met these personal attacks, as with all others, with calm logic and dignity.

Marshall's top priority as secretary of defense was to secure additional personnel for the armed forces to meet the demands of both Korea and Europe, while at the same time maintaining an adequate reserve. He secured the appointment of Anna M. Rosenberg as assistant secretary of defense for manpower and brought Robert A. Lovett back into government service. Marshall also restored harmony between the defense and state departments. Early on he established a good working relationship with the military chiefs. Chairman of the Joint Chiefs of Staff (JCS) General Omar N. Bradley had served under Marshall in the Second World War and the two men worked well together, as was the case with Bradley's successor, General J. Lawton Collins. Marshall respected and worked well with the heads of the air force and navy, General Hoyt S. Vandenberg and Admiral Forrest P. Sherman.

The Inchon Landing and the Pusan Perimeter breakout preceded Marshall's confirmation as secretary of defense, but he participated in the decisions providing United Nations Command (UNC) commander General Douglas MacArthur with instructions on conducting operations north of the 38th Parallel. A secret signal from Marshall to MacArthur on September 29 reaffirmed the Truman administration's commitment to an advance into the Democratic People's Republic of Korea (DPRK, North Korea). Marshall put it in these words, "We want you to feel unhampered strategically and tactically to proceed north of the 38th Parallel." In part, this was intended to avoid complications related to securing United Nations (UN) approval for a decision that the Truman administration previously had made to seek forcible reunification. Accordingly, he advised MacArthur against advance announcements that might precipitate a new vote in the UN.

For some time, the top figures in the Truman administration had worried about a clash with the People's Republic of China (PRC). PRC leader Mao Zedong (Mao Tse-tung) had already decided in early October to send Chinese forces to the aid of North

Korea, so MacArthur was mistaken when at the Wake Island meeting on October 15 he informed Truman with unbridled confidence that the Chinese would not act. After the initial Chinese military actions with units from the Republic of Korea (ROK, South Korea) and the United States at the end of October, neither Marshall nor the JCS made any effort to halt MacArthur's advance.

Marshall opposed granting MacArthur permission to bomb the Yalu River bridges unless the security of all his forces was directly threatened; but after MacArthur predicted dire results if nothing was done, Truman authorized the strikes against the Korean side of the bridges. Marshall supported the recommendation from the JCS authorizing "hot pursuit" of communist aircraft into Manchurian airspace, but allied reaction caused the proposal to be dropped. Marshall and the JCS were generally supportive of MacArthur because of traditional Pentagon reluctance to supervise field commanders too closely and the fact that MacArthur was no ordinary commander.

Following the second, and massive, Chinese military intervention, rather than criticize MacArthur, Marshall and the JCS sought ways to help him. At the meeting of the National Security Council on November 28, Marshall agreed with the president and the JCS that all-out war with China must be avoided. The United States should continue to work through the UN and maintain allied support for the war. When the JCS instructed MacArthur to withdraw X Corps from its exposed position, Marshall inserted a statement that the region northeast of the waist of Korea (running from approximately Anju in the west to Hungnam in the east) was to be avoided except for military operations essential to command security.

In the debate over what to do about the changed military situation in Korea, Marshall opposed a cease-fire with the Chinese. He believed that would represent a "great weakness on our part" and admitted that the United States could not in "all good conscience" abandon the South Koreans. When British prime minister Clement Attlee suggested negotiations with the Chinese, Marshall expressed opposition. He pointed out that it was almost impossible to negotiate with the Chinese Communists, and he also expressed fear of the effects on Japan and the Philippines of concessions to the Chinese. At the same time, Marshall sought ways to avoid a wider war with China. When many in Congress favored an expanded war with China, Marshall was among administration leaders who in February 1951 stressed the paramount importance to the United States of Western Europe.

In the April 6, 1951, meeting between President Truman and his closest advisers to discuss the firing of General MacArthur, Marshall urged caution, pointing out that if MacArthur were recalled Congress might obstruct military appropriations. Later that morning, Truman asked Marshall to review all messages between Washington and Tokyo over the past two years. When the five men met again the next morning, Marshall declared that he shared Averell Harriman's view that MacArthur should have been dismissed two years earlier for flouting administration directives over occupation policies in Japan. Given the political risks involved, Marshall and the other men involved in the decision to remove MacArthur exhibited a considerable degree of courage.

In the Senate hearings that followed the general's dismissal, Marshall defended the decision. Longtime rivals, in many ways, Marshall and MacArthur represented the different viewpoints of Europe first versus concentration on Asia, and limited war versus total war.

Marshall defended the concept of limited war in Korea; he hoped it would "remain limited." He said that there was no easy solution to the Cold War short of another world war, the cost of which would be "beyond calculation." As a result, the Truman administration's policy was to contain communist aggression by different methods in different areas without resorting to total war. Such a policy was not "easy or popular." Marshall believed that the Western alliance had to be kept intact, the United States must rearm as quickly as possible, the status quo should be maintained, and Taiwan (then known as Formosa) should "never be allowed" to come under communist control.

By now the Truman administration was under heavy attack. In June 1951, when Senator Joseph McCarthy demanded the resignations of Acheson and Marshall and threatened Truman with impeachment, he all but called Marshall a communist. The unjust attacks against him may well have confirmed Marshall's decision to step down from a position he had agreed to hold only for six months to a year. In any case, McCarthy's attack ended Marshall's usefulness as a nonpartisan member of the administration. At Truman's request he stayed on until September 1, 1951, when he officially resigned. He was replaced by his deputy, Robert A. Lovett. For Marshall it was the end of 50 years of dedicated government service.

Apart from all his other services, as secretary of defense, Marshall had restored morale in the armed forces, rebuilt a cordial relationship between the Defense and State departments, increased the size and readiness of the armed forces, and assisted Truman in the crisis over the MacArthur firing. These were not inconsiderable achievements. Awarded the Nobel Prize for Peace for the Marshall Plan in 1953, he was the first soldier so honored. Marshall died in Washington, DC, on October 16, 1959.

SPENCER C. TUCKER

See also

Acheson, Dean Gooderham; Attlee, Clement Richard; Bradley, Omar Nelson; Collins, Joseph Lawton; Harriman, William Averell; Johnson, Louis Arthur; Joint Chiefs of Staff; Lovett, Robert Abercrombie; MacArthur, Douglas; McCarthy, Joseph Raymond; Sherman, Forrest Percival; Truman, Harry S.; Truman's Recall of MacArthur; Vandenberg, Hoyt Sanford

References

Acheson, Dean. *Present at the Creation: My Years in the State Department*. New York: Norton, 1969.

Pogue, Forrest C. *George C. Marshall*, Vol. 4, *Statesman, 1945–1959*. New York: Viking, 1987.

Stoler, Mark A. *George C. Marshall: Soldier-Statesman of the American Century*. New York: Twayne, 1989.

Marshall, Samuel Lyman Atwood
Birth Date: July 18, 1900
Death Date: December 17, 1977

One of the most influential, albeit controversial, military historians of the 20th century. Born on July 18, 1900, in Catskill, New York, Samuel Lyman Atwood Marshall, widely known as Slam after his initials, gained all of his direct military experience as a reservist, first receiving his commission from the ranks during World War I at age 17. For the next 60 years, he pursued parallel careers as a reserve officer and as a journalist and writer. As a reporter and a military columnist for the *Detroit News*, he covered many of the world's major conflicts.

During World War II, Marshall was the chief historian of the U.S. European Theater of Operations. He recruited many of the historians and initiated the work that led to the widely respected *U.S. Army in World War II* series. Marshall's own books about World War II include *Night Drop* (1962) and *Bastogne: The First Eight Days* (1946).

Marshall pioneered the technique of conducting direct interviews with participants of combat actions as soon as possible after the events. As a result of these interviews, Marshall in 1947 wrote *Men against Fire,* a penetrating analysis of the U.S. infantryman and small-unit cohesion and effectiveness. Marshall pointed out many problems with U.S. combat performance and offered recommendations to correct them. The U.S. Army adopted many of his recommendations.

As a reserve colonel, Marshall served in Korea as a military analyst and historian with the army's Operations Research Office. Despite other negative press stories at the time, Marshall wrote a report praising the combat performance of African American soldiers in the 2nd Infantry Division's partially integrated 9th Infantry Regiment. This was at a time when the army was still having great difficulty coming to terms with and implementing President Harry S. Truman's 1948 executive order to integrate the armed forces.

During his several trips to Korea, Marshall continued to file stories with his newspaper, write articles for the *Combat Forces Journal* (later titled *ARMY* magazine), and gather material, which he used for his books. His Korean War volumes include *The River and the Gauntlet* (1953) and *Pork Chop Hill* (1956), which later became a movie starring Gregory Peck. Marshall also wrote the Medal of Honor recommendation for Captain Lewis Millett, who led his Company E, 27th Infantry in a bayonet charge near Soamni in February 1951.

During the Vietnam War, as a retired reserve brigadier general, Marshall made several trips to the war zone under U.S. Army sponsorship. With Colonel David H. Hackworth he wrote *Vietnam*

Primer, which the army published as *DA Pamphlet 525-2.* Over 2 million copies of the lessons-learned manual were printed. Marshall wrote five other books on Vietnam battles.

During his lifetime, Marshall was widely regarded as an outstanding military historian and an astute analyst of combat operations. His close friend acclaimed writer Carl Sandburg called him "the greatest of writers on modern war." Marshall himself worked hard to cultivate this image. The army could always count on him to present the organization in its most positive light, and that in turn opened many doors. Marshall delighted in his close associations with the great and the near-great high-ranking commanders of the day.

In the years since his death, a far more mixed opinion of Marshall has emerged. A disillusioned Hackworth once called him "the Howard Cosell of combat" and "the Army's top apologist." Yet in his 1987 book, *The Korean War,* historian Max Hastings still referred to Marshall as "perhaps America's finest combat historian of the twentieth century."

Some historians have criticized Marshall's work by indicating flaws and inconsistencies in both his data and his much-vaunted interview techniques. Marshall, nonetheless, did have a profound impact on the post–World War II U.S. Army and its training doctrine. Many veterans of infantry combat continue to agree that regardless of the flaws in Marshall's data or data collection methods, his conclusions in *Men against Fire* were correct. Marshall died in El Paso, Texas, on December 17, 1977.

DAVID T. ZABECKI

See also

African Americans and the Korean War; Executive Order 9981; Truman, Harry S.

References

Marshall, S. L. A. *Bringing up the Rear: A Memoir.* San Rafael, CA: Presidio, 1979.

———. *Men against Fire.* New York: William Morrow, 1947.

———. *Pork Chop Hill: The American Fighting Man in Action, Korea, Spring, 1953.* New York: William Morrow, 1952.

———. *The River and the Gauntlet: Defeat of the Eighth Army by the Chinese Communist Forces, November 1950, in the Battle of the Chongchon River, Korea.* New York: William Morrow, 1953.

Spiller, Roger J. "S. L. A. Marshall and the Ratio of Fire." *Journal of the Royal United Services Institution* 133(4) (Winter 1988): 67–71.

Williams, Frederick D. *SLAM: The Influence of S. L. A. Marshall on the United States Army.* Fort Monroe, VA: U.S. Army Training and Doctrine Command, 1990.

Marshall Plan

Massive U.S. economic aid program for Western Europe proposed in 1947, designed chiefly to rebuild war-torn economies and serve as a bulwark against communist encroachment, named for Secretary of State George C. Marshall. In the wake of World War II, Europe experienced a severe economic crisis because of the crippling effects of nearly six years of war. The United States had attempted to promote European recovery through limited reconstruction loans, relief assistance, German war reparation transfers, and new multilateral currency and trade arrangements. By the winter of 1946–1947, however, it was apparent that these piecemeal stabilization efforts were not working. Millions of West Europeans were unemployed, inflation and shortages were rampant, and malnutrition had become a widespread concern.

The central problem facing Europe was low industrial productivity. Industrial and agricultural production lagged far behind prewar levels, as the wartime destruction or disruption of factories and equipment had led to dramatically decreased industrial output. Adequate funds were not available for reconstruction and replacement, and none of the nations involved had the wherewithal to raise large amounts of capital on their own. To make matters worse, basic building-block industrial materials such as steel and coal were scarce.

The growing economic troubles fed frustration, hopelessness, and despair. And many Europeans had begun to seek extreme political solutions to their troubles. Alienated from capitalism, some began turning to communism as an alternative. In France, Italy, and Germany, the crisis had eroded government support and lent credence to communist promises of economic stability. In Great Britain, serious financial woes forced policy makers to reduce international agreements that had helped restrict the spread of communism. Only by eliminating the economic conditions that encouraged political extremism could European governments withstand the influence of communism, and nobody seemed to understand that better than the United States.

U.S. policy makers believed that rejuvenated West European economies would provide a strong demand for American goods and help maintain the United States as the world's leading economic power. They also envisioned Western Europe as an integral part of a multilateral economic system of free world trade crucial to the liberal-capitalist world order that Washington, DC, had in mind for itself and its allies. Clearly, unity and prosperity in Western Europe would create an economy able to generate high productivity, decent living standards, and political stability that would resist communist advances.

The European Recovery Program, which came to be known as the Marshall Plan, would serve to strengthen shaky pro-American governments and ward off the inroads being made by domestic communist parties and other left-wing organizations sympathetic to the Soviet Union. U.S. undersecretary of state Dean G. Acheson, who helped formulate the plan, argued that U.S. foreign policy had to harness U.S. economic and financial resources to preserve democratic institutions and to expand capitalism abroad. He also saw the Marshall Plan as necessary for long-term national security. Thus, the plan emerged as an all-embracing effort to revive the economies of Western Europe. The plan was unprecedented in terms of the massive commitment of U.S. dollars, resources, and international involvement.

First formally proposed by Secretary of State Marshall on June 5, 1947, in a speech at Harvard University, the plan originally applied to all of Europe. Aid was not directed publicly against communism specifically but toward the elimination of dangerous economic conditions across all of Europe. Accordingly, the United States controversially planned to reconstruct Germany as an industrial power. Marshall had concluded that German resources, manpower, expertise, and production were absolutely essential to European recovery. For success, the plan had to allow full German participation but at the same time prevent German industrial power from becoming linked to militarism and a future threat to peace.

Additionally complicating matters was Marshall's belief that the objective of the Soviet Union was to delay European economic recovery and therefore exploit the consequent misery and political instability. Yet Marshall did not want his nation to assume the responsibility for permanently dividing Europe. Thus, to avoid having the plan viewed as anti-Soviet, he invited the Soviet Union and its East European satellite states to participate in implementation of the plan. Nations eligible to receive economic assistance would be defined by those countries that were willing to cooperate fully with the U.S. proposal. All the while, U.S. policy makers fully counted on Moscow's rejection of the plan.

President Harry S. Truman believed that the United States should not unilaterally devise a plan for recovery and force it on the Europeans. Instead, the particular aid initiatives came from the Europeans and represented not a series of individual requests but rather a joint and integrated undertaking by all European countries in need of U.S. assistance. In other words, the United States wanted a lasting cure for Europe's problem and not a mere quick fix. The U.S. role would be to assist in the drafting of a program and to support that program with its resources.

The Soviet Union together with Poland, Czechoslovakia, France, Great Britain, and 12 other European nations gathered at the first planning conference, convened in Paris on June 27, 1947. Soviet Foreign Minister Vyacheslav Molotov demanded that each country be allowed to fashion its own plan and present it to the United States. Georges Bidault and Ernest Bevin, the foreign ministers of France and Britain, respectively, opposed Molotov. Bidault and Bevin, in line with U.S. wishes, stressed that the Marshall Plan had to be a continent-wide program to take advantage of the economies of the continent as a whole, or, seen in another light, to take advantage of the economies of scale rendered only through a jointly administered effort. As the United States had predicted, the Soviets quickly withdrew, denouncing the plan as an imperialist, anti-Soviet tool. Molotov warned that if Germany were to be revived, then the continent would be divided. Poland, Czechoslovakia, Hungary, and Romania still expressed interest in the Marshall Plan, but the Soviet Union pressured them into withdrawing.

The Soviets left Paris chiefly because participation in the plan would have required the disclosure of extensive statistical information about the Soviet Union's financial condition and also would have given the United States some control over the Kremlin's internal budget. Additionally, George F. Kennan, father of the U.S. containment policy and director of the State Department's Policy Planning Staff, had earlier made it clear that aid would not be advanced to nations that refused to open their economies to U.S. exports. These requirements were unacceptable to the Soviets, as Kennan realized. The Soviets were not willing to abandon the exclusive orientation of their economy.

The Soviets kept their finances a well-guarded secret and set about weakening the Marshall Plan. In response, they formed the Cominform on July 6, 1947, to help coordinate international propaganda aimed at torpedoing the plan. On July 12, 1947, the Soviet Union negotiated trade agreements with its communist satellites that diverted to Eastern Europe a substantial amount of trade that had previously gone to Western Europe. Finally, later that year, the Soviets proposed the Molotov Plan for East European recovery as an alternative to the Marshall Plan. Lengthy negotiations thus ensued without the Soviets or their client states. Participating nations laid the groundwork for the recovery plans and requested $28 billion to be spent over the course of four years.

On March 15, 1948, the U.S. Senate endorsed the plan by a 69–17 vote after the House had approved it by a 329–74 margin but only allocated $17 billion in aid. The Marshall Plan passed despite growing conservative objections to international agreements. The communist-led overthrow of the Czechoslovakian government and the Soviet Union's badgering of Finland for military bases had apparently convinced U.S. legislators of the seriousness of the Soviet threat.

When the plans were finalized, the United States created the Economic Cooperation Administration (ECA) and named Paul Hoffman as its head. The ECA made the ultimate determination of specific aid and projects to be undertaken. The fundamental way in which the Marshall Plan contributed to increased European productivity was by furnishing capital, food, raw materials, and machinery that would have been unavailable without U.S. help. The ECA made U.S. funds available to foreign governments to buy goods that were primarily obtained from their own private agricultural and industrial producers. The ECA also authorized purchases in other countries, especially Canada and Latin America. These policies also helped to reduce excessive demand on raw materials in the United States, thereby protecting the U.S. economy from inflationary pressures. The plan additionally benefited non-European countries and contributed to the development of multilateral trade. Recipients of the largest amounts of aid were Britain, France, Italy, the Federal Republic of Germany (FRG, West Germany), and the Netherlands.

Participating European governments sold U.S.-financed goods to their own people. The payments received were placed in special funds that were employed where they could best serve economic recovery and ensure financial stability. Italy used its funds for public works projects, such as replacing bombed-out bridges. The British reduced government debt to check inflation.

From 1948 to 1952, approximately $13.5 billion in Marshall Plan aid went to the revitalization of Western Europe and guided it onto the path of long-term economic growth and integration. By 1950, industrial production in Marshall Plan countries was 25 percent higher than 1938 levels, while agricultural output had risen 14 percent from the prewar level. The volume of intra-European trade among Marshall Plan beneficiaries increased dramatically, while the balance-of-payments gap dropped significantly. Britain had sufficiently recovered by January 1951 so that Marshall Plan aid was suspended at that time, a full year and a half before the scheduled termination of the program. It should be noted, however, that the onset of the Korean War in June 1950 and the autumn 1950 decision to deploy U.S. troops to Western Europe to bolster North Atlantic Treaty Organization (NATO) defenses also contributed to increased European productivity.

The Marshall Plan also advanced European unification and integration. The United States sought a single large market in which quantitative restrictions on the movement of goods, monetary barriers, and trade tariffs had been largely eliminated. The creation of an integrated free market modeled after the United States would encourage the growth of consumer demand and large-scale industry. It would also permit more efficient use of materials and labor while stimulating competition. The West Europeans removed a number of economic barriers and established subregional agreements, such as the European Coal and Steel Community (ECSC). The success of the Marshall Plan ultimately paved the way for the establishment of the Common Market in 1958.

The Marshall Plan did not cure all of Europe's problems. Productivity advanced considerably but leveled off by 1952, the last year of the plan. Europe's dollar gap had also begun to widen. The Korean War and concomitant rearmament program diverted resources and manpower to defense production, thereby creating scarcities of certain commodities. As a result, inflation became problematic beginning in 1951.

The intensification of the Cold War and especially the onset of the Korean War hastened the end of the Marshall Plan. The Mutual Security Act of 1951, signed during the Korean War, provided a new strategy for European recovery that largely superseded the Marshall Plan. The act made military security rather than economic self-reliance the major objective of U.S. policy in Western Europe. Aid recipients had to sign new agreements assuring the fulfillment of military obligations and promising to maintain European defensive strength. The ECA was abolished in favor of a Mutual Security Agency that was responsible for supervising and coordinating all foreign aid programs—military, technical, and economic.

CARYN E. NEUMANN

See also

Acheson, Dean Gooderham; Bevin, Ernest; Containment; Kennan, George Frost; Marshall, George Catlett; Molotov, Viacheslav Mikhailovich; Stalin, Joseph; Truman, Harry S.

References

Gimbel, John. *The Origins of the Marshall Plan.* Stanford, CA: Stanford University Press, 1976.

Hoffmann, Stanley, and Charles Maier, eds. *The Marshall Plan: A Retrospective.* Boulder, CO: Westview, 1984.

Hogan, Michael J. *The Marshall Plan: America, Britain, and the Reconstruction of Western Europe, 1948–1952.* New York: Cambridge University Press, 1987.

Mayne, Richard. *The Recovery of Europe: From Devastation to Unity.* London: Weidenfeld and Nicolson, 1970.

Milward, Alan S. *The Reconstruction of Western Europe, 1945–51.* Berkeley: University of California Press, 1984.

Martin, Joseph William
Birth Date: November 3, 1884
Death Date: March 7, 1968

Journalist, publisher, Republican congressman from Massachusetts, Speaker of the House of Representatives (1947–1949, 1953–1955), and outspoken critic of Korean War policies. Born on November 3, 1884, in North Attleboro, Massachusetts, Joseph William Martin was a newspaper reporter from 1902 to 1908 and then became publisher of his hometown newspaper. He served in the state legislature (1912–1917) and then in 1924 he won election to the U.S. House of Representatives, where he served for over four decades. Martin was assistant floor leader to the Republican minority, chairperson of the GOP Congressional Campaign Committee, and, in 1939, House Republican leader. He received consideration as a possible presidential nominee in the election of 1940. When Republicans won a House majority in 1946, he became Speaker in January 1947. When President Harry S. Truman won an unexpected victory in 1948 and the Democrats gained control of Congress, the isolationist and fiscally conservative Martin reverted to his former role as minority leader in 1949.

Representative Martin sharply criticized Truman's Korean War policies as too Eurocentric and unaggressive. In a February 12, 1951, speech, he expressed anxiety about an administration preoccupation with Europe that was debilitating America's strength in Asia. He suggested that the Nationalist Chinese army on Taiwan (then known as Formosa) should be used to establish a secondary Asian front to ease the strain on the United Nations (UN) in Korea. Martin added, "There is good reason to believe that General [Douglas] MacArthur favors such an operation [and] there should be no limitation on force once war was declared." The congressman forwarded a transcript of his address to MacArthur, accompanied by a cover letter requesting the United Nations Command (UNC) commander's "views on this point, either on a confidential basis or otherwise."

Responding in a letter on March 19, MacArthur agreed with Martin. The general concurred with his views on Taiwan, assailed the idea of limited war, and declared, "There is no substitute for victory." On April 5, Martin read the text of the correspondence during a session of the House of Representatives. Despite

During his 42 years in the U.S. House of Representatives from 1925 to 1967, Joseph W. Martin became one of the most influential legislators of his generation. (Library of Congress)

MacArthur's claim that his letter was "merely [a] routine communication as I turn out by the hundred," he had indeed confided to a partisan critic of the Truman administration who employed his comments for political advantage. The general's response to Martin neglected a request of nondisclosure.

MacArthur's letter to Martin was a direct violation of a directive that the Joint Chiefs of Staff (JCS) had sent to all military personnel on December 6, 1950. "Officials overseas, including military commanders and diplomatic representatives," it declared, "should . . . exercise extreme caution in public statements, to clear all but routine statements with their departments, and to refrain from direct communication on military or foreign policy with newspapers, magazines or other publicity media." This gag order clearly targeted MacArthur in response to his recent public criticism of the Truman administration's refusal to escalate the war following intervention by the People's Republic of China (PRC).

MacArthur's prior assertions had angered President Truman, but the general's letter to Martin violated a direct order and was an unambiguous act of insubordination. This final act of open defiance provided the president with clear justification for no longer disregarding MacArthur's challenge to his constitutional powers as commander in chief and architect of foreign policy. According to Truman, the general's letter to Martin was "the last straw" leading to MacArthur's dismissal on April 11. However, there was a more compelling factor motivating the recall. U.S. military leaders were worried about a Chinese and Soviet military buildup in Asia and thought the UNC commander should have standing authority to retaliate against any communist escalation. Having recommended deployment of atomic weapons to forward Pacific bases for this purpose, they were fearful that MacArthur might provoke an incident to widen the war. Moreover, U.S. allies never would consent to providing discretion to the UNC commander to order an atomic retaliation so long as MacArthur held this position.

After receiving news of MacArthur's recall, Republican leaders, among them senators Robert A. Taft and Kenneth S. Wherry, assembled in Martin's office. When they emerged, the minority leader informed the press that a congressional probe of Truman administration military and foreign affairs was in order, and they wanted MacArthur to present his opinions to Congress. Furthermore, Martin said the subject of impeachment came up, suggesting indictments of other administration figures as well as the president.

Martin sought to turn the Korean War issue into an electoral triumph in 1952. When MacArthur returned to the United States, he tendered Martin support for a presidential bid. Martin chaired the 1952 Republican National Convention, where the general gave the keynote address. Support for MacArthur to be the Republican nominee soon evaporated, however. At the convention Martin charged that the Democrats, success at hand, "decided the best way to win was to lose." Later, the joint report on the Democratic Eighty-second Congress, published by Martin and Senate Minority Leader Styles Bridges, alleged that the majority party had no answer for the endless Korean conflict.

As a result of Dwight D. Eisenhower's overwhelming electoral victory in 1952, in which the Republicans regained control of both houses of Congress, Martin again became Speaker in January 1953. He lost the position in 1955 once the Democrats regained control of the House and Senate, and, four years later, he was removed as Republican floor leader. In 1966, he was thwarted in a renomination bid in the Republican primary for a House seat. Martin died in Hollywood, Florida, on March 7, 1968.

RODNEY J. ROSS

See also

MacArthur, Douglas; MacArthur Hearings; Taft, Robert Alphonso; Truman, Harry S.; Truman's Recall of MacArthur

References

Caridi, Ronald J. *The Korean War and American Politics: The Republican Party as a Case Study*. Philadelphia: University of Pennsylvania Press, 1968.

James, D. Clayton. *The Years of MacArthur*, Vol. 3, *Triumph and Disaster, 1945–1964*. Boston: Houghton Mifflin, 1985.

Martin, Joseph. *My First Fifty Years in Politics*. New York: McGraw-Hill, 1960.

Schaller, Michael. *Douglas MacArthur: The Far Eastern General*. New York: Oxford, 1989.

MASH

See Mobile Army Surgical Hospital

Massive Retaliation

A U.S. defense doctrine first conceived in 1953 and publicly enunciated by Secretary of State John Foster Dulles in January 1954. Massive Retaliation was predicated on the predominance of U.S. nuclear forces in the 1950s. Under Massive Retaliation, the Dwight D. Eisenhower administration put U.S. adversaries—principally the Soviet Union—on notice that any offensive provocation—be it conventional or nuclear—would be met with swift, overwhelming nuclear retaliation. The magnitude of the nuclear response would be sufficient to cripple or destroy an aggressor's military and civilian infrastructure and would involve the deaths of millions of people.

Massive Retaliation was meant as a form of ultimate deterrence, meaning that it was designed to prevent an aggressor from launching any sort of military offensive, nuclear or conventional. In the 1960s, as Soviet nuclear capabilities reached parity with those of the United States, Massive Retaliation was replaced—at least in part—by Mutual Assured Destruction (MAD). It promised a crushing retaliatory nuclear blow to any nation that launched a preemptive nuclear strike against the United States.

The genesis of the Massive Retaliation plan came in the 1953 Solarium Project, so named because many of its meetings were convened in the White House solarium. In the spring of 1953, while the Korean War still raged, President Eisenhower decided to gather a group of senior military and civilian strategists charged with advising him on the best course of action in prosecuting the Cold War. Eisenhower was chagrined with the stalemate in Korea and worried that the nation's massive military spending would have a deleterious effect on the American political economy. Divided into three teams, the advisors were given six weeks to analyze and defend a specific Cold War strategy. One team was to study a strategy that would have the United States maintaining just enough military might to defend against aggression while simultaneously helping its allies to rearm and avoiding a general war. Another team was to analyze and defend a position in which the United States would draw a line in Europe, which, if crossed by the Soviets in any way, would trigger a military attack on the Soviet Union. The third team held the position that the United States should aggressively roll back the Soviet Union and attempt to liberate its satellites. In the end, when Eisenhower met with the teams, he stated his preference for the first option, noting that the second two were too bellicose and expensive. Massive Retaliation would thus be a cost-effective way to defend the United States and its allies.

Project Solarium and Massive Retaliation helped to inform the Eisenhower administration's New Look defense posture, which eschewed the buildup of large conventional forces in favor of more cost-effective nuclear forces. In a speech on January 12, 1954, Secretary of State Dulles first enunciated the concept of Massive Retaliation, stating that "local defense must be reinforced by the further deterrent of massive retaliatory power." Herein lay the coining of the term "Massive Retaliation." Eisenhower was not only concerned about the size of the defense budget; he was also worried about the great disparity between the number of Soviet troops in Eastern Europe and the number of allied troops in Western Europe. This disparity gave the Soviet Union a considerable advantage should it decide to launch a military offensive into West Germany and Western Europe. Massive Retaliation, it was hoped, would prevent such a scenario without the need for a large number of conventional (and more costly) forces.

In fact, what Eisenhower did was merely to codify, in a more systematic fashion, what the Harry S. Truman administration had already begun to emphasize: air power and nuclear weapons. Indeed, for Fiscal Year 1953, the last year of the Truman defense budgets, the U.S. Air Force was allotted nearly one-half of the total $46.6 billion. Of the $21.1 billion allocated to the U.S. Air Force, 60 percent was dedicated to the development and procurement of more aircraft, including guided missiles capable of delivering nuclear payloads. In a significant sense, there was in reality nothing new to Eisenhower's New Look defense doctrine, including Massive Retaliation.

Critics of Eisenhower and Dulles—both military and civilian—decried what they saw as an overreliance on nuclear weapons, which left the United States two choices in case of a Soviet military adventure—capitulation or all-out war. In the end, the alleged cost-effectiveness of Massive Retaliation was illusory. In 1958, the U.S. Army was still 50 percent larger than it was at the start of the Korean War, and the inexorable march toward technical supremacy ensured that new aircraft and missiles would be ever more costly. When the John F. Kennedy administration was inaugurated in 1961, it made a conscious decision to deemphasize Massive Retaliation, adopting Flexible Response as a better way to respond to regional threats and small-scale military offensives.

PAUL G. PIERPAOLI JR.

See also

Dulles, John Foster; Eisenhower, Dwight David; Mobilization; New Look Defense Policy

References
Dockrill, Saki. *Eisenhower's New Look: National Security Policy, 1953–1961.* New York: St. Martin's, 1996.
Pierpaoli, Paul G., Jr. *Truman and Korea: The Political Culture of the Early Cold War.* Columbia: University of Missouri Press, 1999.
Sherry, Michael S. *The Rise of American Airpower: The Creation of Armageddon.* New Haven, CT: Yale University Press, 1995.

Matthews, Francis Patrick
Birth Date: March 15, 1887
Death Date: October 19, 1952

Attorney, banker, corporate executive, and U.S. secretary of the navy (1949–1951). Born on March 15, 1887, in Albion, Nebraska, Francis Patrick Matthews graduated from Creighton University in 1913. A prominent Catholic layman, Matthews became president

Francis P. Matthews, secretary of the navy from May 1949 to July 1951. Matthews had no knowledge of the navy when he became secretary and became very unpopular with many senior naval officers. (Naval Historical Center)

of the National Thrift Assurance Company, the Securities Investment Corporation, and an Omaha bank. He also served as general counsel for the Reconstruction Finance Corporation. A supporter of President Harry S. Truman in the 1948 campaign, Matthews helped influence the Nebraska delegation in Truman's favor. He was nonetheless surprised when Truman appointed him successor to John L. Sullivan as secretary of the navy in 1949.

Taking office on May 25, 1949, during the tumultuous Revolt of the Admirals, Matthews admitted incautiously to the press that his only qualification for the post was ownership of a small boat on a Minnesota lake. Dubbed Rowboat Matthews, the new secretary immediately earned the enmity of many sailors by playing a key role in forcing out chief of naval operations Admiral Louis Denfeld during the controversy over the B-36 bomber and the canceled supercarrier *United States*. In the course of the congressional hearings, Matthews painted such a rosy picture of navy morale that he was literally jeered by officers in the audience.

Matthews deepened this chasm of distrust by enthusiastically supporting Secretary of Defense Louis Johnson in the latter's severe pruning of the navy's budget and by striking at Denfeld's supporters. One of the prominent victims of this purge was Captain Arleigh Burke, who Matthews illegally removed from the promotion list to flag rank. Matthews also attempted to quash

criticism within the navy of its sister services. On the positive side, Matthews appointed as Denfeld's successor Admiral Forrest Sherman, who got Burke reinstated and convinced Congress to fund a nuclear submarine and to pay more attention to naval aviation.

Despite the outbreak of the Korean War, Matthews was slow to reverse course from shrinking the navy. He failed, for instance, to push forward the supercarrier project, leaving the task to Congressman Carl Vinson. Worse, in an August 1950 public speech commemorating the sesquicentennial of the Boston Naval Shipyard, Matthews issued a call for preventive war against the communist bloc, arguing that Americans should become "the first aggressors for peace." Both the State Department and the Oval Office repudiated his remarks. After being dressed down by President Truman for "talking out of turn about foreign policy," Matthews was, in the president's words, "very contrite." Nonetheless, his days as secretary of the navy were numbered.

Following a Far Eastern inspection tour, on June 28, 1951, Matthews was named ambassador to Ireland. He formally left the secretary's post on July 31. Dan A. Kimball succeeded him. Matthews cannot be ranked among the effective civilian leaders of the navy. Malcolm Cagle and Frank Manson, in *The Sea War in Korea*, mention him only once in the entire volume. Paolo Coletta's biographical sketch of Matthews concludes, "Completely unversed in the ways of the Navy and of Washington, he broke the chain of competent men James V. Forrestal had trained." His principal accomplishment was to install Forrest Sherman as chief of naval operations. Matthews died of a heart attack on October 19, 1952, in Omaha, Nebraska.

MALCOLM MUIR JR.

See also
Burke, Arleigh Albert; Johnson, Louis Arthur; Revolt of the Admirals; Sherman, Forrest Percival; Truman, Harry S.

References
Barlow, Jeffrey G. *Revolt of the Admirals: The Fight for Naval Aviation, 1945–1950*. Washington, DC: Naval Historical Center, 1994.

Cagle, Malcolm W., and Frank A. Manson. *Sea War in Korea*. Annapolis, MD: Naval Institute Press, 1957.

Coletta, Paolo E. "Francis P. Matthews, 25 May 1949–31 July 1951." In *American Secretaries of the Navy*, Vol. 2, *1913–1972*, edited by Paolo E. Coletta, 783–827. Annapolis, MD: Naval Institute Press, 1980.

Matthews, Harrison Freeman
Birth Date: May 26, 1899
Death Date: October 19, 1986

U.S. diplomat. Born in Baltimore, Maryland, on May 26, 1899, Harrison Freeman Matthews (known as H. Freeman Matthews) graduated from Princeton University in 1921, finishing a master's degree the following year. Matthews completed postgraduate courses at the École Libre de Sciences Politiques in Paris in 1922 and 1923. His first career post with the U.S. Foreign Service was in Budapest in 1923, and he also held posts in Madrid, Havana, and Bogotá.

Matthews was the first U.S. representative to the Francisco Franco government of Spain after the Spanish Civil War. During World War II, he worked at the U.S. embassy in Paris, then at Vichy when the Germans occupied France. Relocating to London, Matthews was General Dwight D. Eisenhower's political adviser and assisted with strategic plans for the 1942 invasion of North Africa.

In the following year, Matthews began work as director of European affairs at the State Department. He became influential in U.S. foreign policy and advised presidents Franklin D. Roosevelt and Harry S. Truman. Matthews attended wartime conferences at Potsdam, Yalta, and Cairo, as well as postwar foreign ministers' meetings in Moscow and Paris.

Appointed ambassador to Sweden in 1947, Matthews served in that post until 1950, when he became the deputy undersecretary of state to Secretary of State Dean G. Acheson. In this position Matthews participated in discussions about policy making and diplomatic efforts during the Korean War. He acted as a liaison between the State and Defense departments, an especially difficult job while the temperamental Louis A. Johnson was secretary of defense. Matthews offered advice regarding the conduct of the Korean War and related diplomatic efforts, and he has been credited for providing the initiative that helped efforts in seeking a cease-fire and armistice in May 1951. Throughout his career, Matthews was involved in complex diplomatic situations, calmly deliberating answers to difficult questions.

Aware that during the post–World War II Berlin Crisis communication with the Soviet Union's United Nations (UN) representative had helped resolve issues, Matthews suggested that the spring 1951 military stalemate in Korea might be ended through informal contact with the Soviet ambassador at the UN. Matthews suggested to Acheson that George F. Kennan should attempt to talk secretly to Jacob A. Malik, the Soviet Union's UN representative, to assess Soviet attitudes toward a cease-fire. Acheson agreed, and Kennan reported that Malik told him on June 5, 1951, that the Soviets wanted peace but that the United States needed to contact the Chinese and North Koreans. During a June 23, 1951, radio address, Malik suggested both sides should withdraw to the 38th Parallel and begin cease-fire and armistice talks. Although the armistice did not occur in 1951, Matthews's efforts to begin negotiations were helpful in encouraging future deliberations at the Kaesong truce talks.

Working closely with Undersecretary of State James E. Webb during the Korean War, Matthews remained in office until 1953. He began work as ambassador to the Netherlands in 1953 and became ambassador to Austria four years later. While in that post he supervised meetings with U.S. president John F. Kennedy and Soviet Union leader Nikita Khrushchev. Matthews retired from the Foreign Service in May 1962 and was chairman of the U.S. section of the Permanent Joint Board on Defense for the United States and Canada for six years. He died on October 19, 1986, in Washington, DC

Elizabeth D. Schafer

See also

Acheson, Dean Gooderham; Cease-fire Negotiations; Johnson, Louis Arthur; Kaesong Truce Talks; Kennan, George Frost; Kennan-Malik Conversations; Malik, Jacob; Potsdam Conference; Truce Talks; Truman, Harry S.; Webb, James Edwin

References

Acheson, Dean G. *Present at the Creation: My Years in the State Department.* New York: Norton, 1969.
Current Biography, 1945. New York: H. W. Wilson, 1946.
Who Was Who in America, 1951–1960. Chicago: Marquis, 1963.

McCarran, Patrick Anthony
Birth Date: August 8, 1876
Death Date: September 28, 1954

U.S. Democratic senator from Nevada, zealous anticommunist, and sponsor of the 1950 Internal Security Act (McCarran Act). Patrick Anthony McCarran was born in Reno, Nevada, on August 8, 1876, and graduated from the University of Nevada in 1901. The son of Irish immigrants, he was raised on a sheep farm and returned to farming and ranching after he received his university degree.

In 1902, local Democrats urged McCarran to run for office, and he was elected to the state legislature in 1903. He read law on his own and in 1905 passed the state bar exam. McCarran then served as a county prosecutor, chief justice of Nevada, and chair of the Nevada State Board of Bar Examiners. After two previously unsuccessful runs for the U.S. Senate, he won a Senate seat in 1932, the same year that swept the Democrats and Franklin D. Roosevelt to power.

Although a Democrat, McCarran was a conservative in the mold of many such politicians from the Southwest. He was often critical of President Roosevelt's New Deal programs and helped defeat the president's 1937 court-packing scheme. McCarran was an able and effective legislator, having sponsored important bills such as the 1938 Civil Aeronautics Act and the 1945 Federal Airport Act. But the rather reclusive senator would become best known for his virulent anticommunism, which he stoked with a vengeance after the end of World War II.

McCarran was certainly one of the most important figures in the Red Scare and McCarthyism that emerged in the late 1940s. He headed the Senate Internal Security Subcommittee, which had investigated both the Roosevelt and Harry S. Truman administrations. In 1950, just as Senator Joseph McCarthy was launching his anticommunist witch-hunt, McCarran sponsored the Internal Security Act (also known as the McCarran Act), which was passed in September 1950 over President Truman's veto. This legislation required that all communist or communist-inspired organizations in the United States register with the U.S. attorney general. The bill also made it illegal to conceal membership in a communist organization when applying for government employment or using a passport. As well, the act stipulated that communists or other people deemed subversive or a danger to the public welfare could be detained or deported. Naturalized citizens who fell into the last category could face denaturalization and, ultimately, deportation. Finally, the legislation established the Subversive Activities Control Board, which was empowered to investigate any person suspected of engaging in un-American activities.

In June 1952, McCarran and fellow Senator Francis Walter introduced the McCarran-Walter Act, which imposed stricter regulations on immigration and tightened laws relating to the admission and deportation of "dangerous aliens" as defined by the Internal Security Act. McCarran died in Hawthorne, Nevada, on September 28, 1954, but his legacy as a significant contributor to Cold War anticommunist hysteria would live on for decades.

PAUL G. PIERPAOLI JR.

See also

Internal Security Act; McCarthy, Joseph Raymond; McCarthyism

References

Pittman, Von Vernon, Jr. "Senator Patrick A. McCarran and the Politics of Containment." Unpublished PhD dissertation, University of Georgia, 1979.

Ybarra, Mike. *Washington Gone Crazy: Senator Pat McCarran and the Great American Communist Hunt.* Hanover, NH: Steerforth, 2004.

McCarran Act

See Internal Security Act

McCarthy, Joseph Raymond
Birth Date: November 14, 1908
Death Date: May 2, 1957

Divisive U.S. Republican senator and the best-known exponent of the sweeping charges of domestic communism that helped to create a political climate of hysteria and suspicion in the United States during the Korean War. His efforts ultimately bore his name: "McCarthyism." Born in Grand Chute, Wisconsin, on November 14, 1908, to a farming family of modest circumstances, Joseph Raymond McCarthy was educated at Little Wolf High School, Manawa, and Marquette University, where he earned an LL.B. in 1935. He then practiced law in Wisconsin.

An early interest in politics led to McCarthy's 1939 election as judge of the 10th Judicial Circuit in Wisconsin, a position he left in 1942 to join the military. Although McCarthy's war record was rather undistinguished, he inflated it greatly and ran for the U.S. Senate as a Republican. After losing in 1944, he succeeded two

years later in defeating the veteran senator Robert M. La Follette Jr. During the campaign, McCarthy characterized his opponent as "communistically inclined." McCarthy's early years in the Senate were legislatively vacuous and distinguished principally by his persistent disregard for, and violation of, that body's traditions, privileges, and etiquette, as well as his ability to alienate powerful colleagues in both parties.

On February 9, 1950, seeking an issue on which to focus a successful reelection campaign, McCarthy used the occasion of a speech at Wheeling, West Virginia, to state that he possessed a list of acknowledged communists employed by the U.S. State Department. Various Republicans had made similar charges since the mid-1930s against officials in the administrations of Franklin D. Roosevelt and Harry S. Truman. The distinctive features of McCarthy's countless allegations were their seeming veracity and his willingness not only to deliberately make numerous untruthful statements, but also to repeat them even when they were shown to be lies.

The timing of his speech was opportune in that he delivered it three weeks after Alger Hiss, a former State Department official and suspected Soviet agent, was convicted for perjury in misstating the extent of his procommunist sympathies and contacts during the 1930s and early 1940s. McCarthy was also fortunate in that senior Republican politicians, however distasteful they might have found his tactics, were prepared to tolerate them as a means to reclaiming the presidency in 1952 for the Republican Party, after 20 years of Democratic dominance. Although a congressional investigation chaired by Democratic senator Millard Tydings of Maryland found no evidence to substantiate McCarthy's charges, McCarthy continued to reiterate these and similar allegations against other Democratic officials with undiminished vigor.

The communist takeover of mainland China in October 1949 and indications that the United States might abandon the rump Guomindang (GMD, Nationalist) regime of Jiang Jieshi (Chiang Kai-shek) on Taiwan (then known as Formosa) won McCarthy favor with the China Lobby, those American partisans of Jiang who were determined to ensure continuing U.S. support for him. The unexpected outbreak of the Korean War in June 1950, following suggestions made six months earlier in a speech by Secretary of State Dean Acheson that Korea lay outside the U.S. defensive perimeter, gave new credibility to McCarthy's accusations of traitorous incompetence in the State Department. Thus, it is entirely fair to state that the Korean War fully unleashed McCarthyism.

During the Truman administration's remaining years, McCarthy and McCarthyism flourished unchecked, subjecting numerous State Department officials, particularly such Asian experts as John Paton Davies, John Stewart Service, and John Carter Vincent, as well as such higher officials as Acheson, President Truman, and even General George C. Marshall, to generally unsubstantiated but persistent charges that they were either subversive communist agents, or at least naive and unreliable fellow-travelers. Numerous Americans, including government officials, civil servants

Republican senator Joseph McCarthy from Wisconsin speaks in front of a television camera in 1953. McCarthy's anticommunist "witch-hunts" led to the term "McCarthyism." (Library of Congress)

at all levels, academics, entertainment figures, and writers, like-wise became the targets of similar allegations, which were often unfounded and undocumented, rarely substantiated, sometimes malicious, but often extremely difficult to disprove. Such allegations were capable of ruining careers and denying numerous opportunities to otherwise well-qualified individuals.

McCarthy's charges certainly hampered the Truman administration's freedom of action in dealing with the Korean War, particularly with respect to the nonrecognition of China and its policies toward Taiwan, and subjected it to intense criticism over such matters as the replacement of General Douglas MacArthur as commander in chief of the United Nations Command (UNC) forces in April 1951. China specialists who attracted McCarthy's opprobrium, if they were not dismissed, tended to be shifted from Asian positions to presumably less sensitive assignments in Europe or elsewhere, and within the State Department vast amounts of time and energy were devoted to refuting his charges.

During the 1952 election campaign McCarthy flourished; although Republican candidate Dwight D. Eisenhower disliked the

senator's tactics, political expediency led him to acquiesce in them and implicitly endorse McCarthy's allegations. It was thought particularly disgraceful that Eisenhower failed to publicly defend his World War II commander, General Marshall, from groundless accusations by McCarthy. The Republican capture of both houses of Congress that year and his own reelection initially seemed to give McCarthy further power; in 1953 he became chairman of both the Senate Committee on Government Operations and its Permanent Subcommittee on Investigations. Ironically, however, the Republican victory contained the seeds of McCarthy's own defeat, as the party leaders, no longer shackled by their eagerness to defeat the Democrats, found McCarthy's penchant for bullying, lying, and seeking publicity increasingly embarrassing and sought to dissociate themselves from his excesses.

In 1954 McCarthy extended his investigations to the military, a move the armed forces resisted, and he also launched increasingly harsh attacks on the Eisenhower administration, which eroded his support within his own party. In early 1954 televised hearings on alleged subversive activities in the U.S. Army exposed all the unattractive and outlandish aspects of McCarthy's methods to the U.S. public, features deliberately emphasized by respected broadcaster Edward R. Murrow. On July 11, 1954, a fellow Republican, Senator Ralph E. Flanders of Vermont, introduced a resolution calling for McCarthy's censure, and on December 2, after lengthy hearings, the Senate voted 67–22 to condemn him for behavior described as "contemptuous, contumacious, and denunciatory" and obstructive of justice.

Although still a senator, McCarthy spent his final years in relative obscurity, largely ignored by his colleagues, the president, and the press. On May 2, 1957, he died of complications due to alcoholism at the naval hospital in Bethesda, Maryland.

Priscilla Roberts

See also

Acheson, Dean Gooderham; China Lobby; Davies, John Paton; Jessup, Philip Caryl; Jiang Jieshi; MacArthur, Douglas; Marshall, George Catlett; McCarthyism; Nixon, Richard Milhous; Service, John Stewart; Truman, Harry S.; Truman's Recall of MacArthur

References

Kepley, David R. *The Collapse of the Middle Way: Senate Republicans and the Bipartisan Foreign Policy, 1948–1952.* New York: Greenwood, 1982.

Landis, Mark. *Joseph McCarthy: The Politics of Chaos.* Selingrove, PA: Susquehanna University Press, 1987.

Oshinsky, Daniel M. *A Conspiracy So Immense: The World of Joe McCarthy.* New York: Free Press, 1983.

Reeves, Thomas C. *The Life and Times of Joe McCarthy.* Lanham, MD: Madison Books, 1997.

Rovere, Richard H. *Senator Joe McCarthy.* New York: HarperCollins, 1986.

McCarthyism

Militantly anticommunist American movement of the late 1940s and 1950s, named after its best-known exponent (Republican senator Joseph R. McCarthy of Wisconsin), which created a climate of often hysterical and paranoid antiradicalism in the United States, giving rise to generally outrageous and far-fetched allegations that many prominent U.S. officials were either Soviet agents or fellow-travelers with dangerously procommunist sympathies.

The roots of McCarthyism lay in the long-standing antiforeign tradition of the United States, dating back at least to the mid-19th century, one early manifestation of which was the "Know-Nothing" party, followed later by the Red Scare of 1919 just after the end of World War I. Conservative opposition to the New Deal during the 1930s and 1940s gave new intensity to this antiforeign outlook, leading to the establishment during the 1930s of no fewer than three congressional committees to investigate communist penetration of government, the best known of these being the House Un-American Activities Committee (HUAC).

Set up in 1938 and chaired by Congressman Martin Dies, HUAC investigated charges that President Franklin Roosevelt's and, later, Harry S. Truman's administration officials had radical or pro-Soviet sympathies or connections. Such fears gained new credibility with the development of the Cold War and concomitant growing anxiety in the later 1940s over the Soviet Union and its influence. In 1947 HUAC regained public attention when it probed the communist ties of several leading Hollywood figures.

Historians such as Ronald J. Caridi and Richard M. Freeland have held the Truman administration partially responsible for the increasing plausibility of McCarthyism in the later 1940s. They cite the president's deliberate invocation of the Soviet threat in such foreign policy messages as the Truman Doctrine speech of February 1947; the establishment, by Executive Order 9385 on March 3, 1947, of the Federal Loyalty Program, which monitored U.S. government servants; and accusations by Truman supporters during the 1948 election that rival Democratic politician Henry A. Wallace and his Progressive Citizens of America Party were naive in dealing with the Soviets and penetrated by communist influences.

After 1948, when Republican candidate Thomas E. Dewey unexpectedly lost the presidential election to Truman, such leading Republicans as Robert A. Taft undoubtedly tolerated and encouraged charges that the Truman administration was effectively honeycombed with communists, regarding such tactics, distasteful though they might be, as a potential means of ending the 20-year Democratic monopoly of the presidency.

McCarthyism reached a peak, and also found a name for itself, when Senator McCarthy, apparently seeking an issue on which to win reelection to the Senate, charged in a February 9, 1950, speech at Wheeling, West Virginia, that he possessed a list of known communists currently serving in the State Department. Three weeks earlier, former State Department official and alleged Soviet agent Alger Hiss had been convicted of perjury for having testified to his lack of previous communist connections; Secretary of State Dean Acheson's public refusal to ostracize his old friend Hiss would make him, in turn, the target of similar allegations.

McCarthy's apparently well-documented, although in fact ill-founded and exaggerated, charges led to the establishment of a congressional investigating committee under Senator Millard Tydings. Although the committee found no evidence to substantiate the charges, McCarthy continued to repeat these and many other accusations of the same nature against a wide variety of targets. The growing China Lobby, eager to ensure continued U.S. support for the unpopular nationalist regime of Jiang Jieshi (Chiang Kai-shek), which in 1949 had been ejected from the Chinese mainland to its island redoubt of Taiwan (then known as Formosa) by communist forces, was also quick to argue that any U.S. official who was less than uncritically committed to Jiang's cause was ipso facto a communist agent.

The unexpected eruption of the Korean War in June 1950, together with several well-publicized contemporaneous espionage cases involving well-placed American, Canadian, and British spies, gave yet more plausibility to claims that the United States was riddled with secret communist sympathizers. Indeed, the Korean War fully unleashed McCarthyism. To many, particularly Republicans, Truman's decision in April 1951 to replace the insubordinate but vehemently—and publicly—anticommunist General Douglas MacArthur, the commander in chief of United Nations Command (UNC) forces, seemed to confirm suspicions that communist influence extended to the highest levels of the U.S. government. Prominent U.S. leaders, among them Truman, Acheson, and Secretary of Defense George C. Marshall, together with numerous junior State Department and other officials, particularly those responsible for Asian policy, were subjected to charges that they were covertly acting in the interests of the Soviet Union and international communism. Rebutting such allegations was time-consuming and hampered the charged individuals' effectiveness; in some cases promising diplomatic careers, such as those of John Paton Davies, John Stewart Service, and John Carter Vincent, were ended by persistent claims of procommunist sympathies, and even those less affected, such as Charles E. Bohlen or Philip C. Jessup, sometimes found confirmation in subsequent appointments difficult.

Although in 1953 McCarthy became chairman of both the Senate Committee on Government Operations and its Permanent Subcommittee on Investigations, his influence declined rapidly after Republican president Dwight D. Eisenhower's electoral victory in November 1952, in part because of the increasing discomfort and embarrassment that his excesses provoked among leading Republicans. In 1954, when McCarthy attempted to investigate alleged subversion in the armed forces, he met determined opposition from the military, and later that year, after televised hearings in which his aggressive bullying and unabashedly untruthful tactics alienated many Americans as well as his colleagues, he was censured by the Senate and lost virtually all his political influence.

In the long run, McCarthyism contributed to the U.S. recognition of Jiang's nationalist regime on Taiwan as China's only legitimate government and the consequent nonrecognition for more than 20 years of the communist People's Republic of China (PRC). The persistent attacks on the State Department's Asian specialists, which in most cases led to their resignations, also created a serious long-term deficit of U.S. diplomatic expertise in that area. The legacy of McCarthyism was also apparent in the reluctance of U.S. officials in the 1950s and 1960s to abandon Asian regimes to communism for fear of the political consequences, an outlook that undoubtedly contributed to the subsequent U.S. involvement in Vietnam.

PRISCILLA ROBERTS

See also

Acheson, Dean Gooderham; Bohlen, Charles Eustis; China Lobby; Davies, John Paton; Eisenhower, Dwight David; Hiss, Alger; Jessup, Philip Caryl; Jiang Jieshi; MacArthur, Douglas; Marshall, George Catlett; McCarthy, Joseph Raymond; Nixon, Richard Milhous; Service, John Stewart; Taft, Robert Alphonso; Truman, Harry S.; Truman Loyalty Program; Truman's Recall of MacArthur

References

Caridi, Ronald J. *The Korean War and American Politics: The Republican Party as a Case Study.* Philadelphia: University of Pennsylvania Press, 1968.

Caute, David. *The Great Fear: The Anti-Communist Purge under Truman and Eisenhower.* New York: Simon and Schuster, 1978.

Freeland, Richard M. *The Truman Doctrine and the Origins of McCarthyism: Foreign Policy, Domestic Politics, and Internal Security, 1946–1948.* New York: New York University Press, 1985.

Fried, Richard M. *Nightmare in Red: McCarthyism in Perspective.* New York: Oxford University Press, 1991.

Griffith, Robert. *The Politics of Fear: Joseph R. McCarthy and the Senate.* 2nd ed. Amherst: University of Massachusetts Press, 1987.

Kepley, David R. *The Collapse of the Middle Way: Senate Republicans and the Bipartisan Foreign Policy, 1948–1952.* New York: Greenwood, 1982.

Schrecker, Ellen. *Many Are the Crimes: McCarthyism in America.* Boston: Little, Brown, 1998.

McClure, Robert Alexis

Birth Date: March 4, 1897
Death Date: January 1, 1957

U.S. Army major general, chief of the Psychological Warfare Division during the Korean War, and originator of the idea of voluntary repatriation of prisoners of war (POWs). Born in Matoon, Illinois, on March 4, 1897, Robert Alexis McClure attended the Kentucky Military Institute (1912–1915). He was commissioned in the U.S. Army in 1916 and served in the Philippine Islands and in China. During the interwar years McClure attended the Infantry and Cavalry Schools, the Command and General Staff School, and the Army War College. He later taught at the Infantry School and Army War College before becoming the military attaché in London.

In October 1942, during World War II, McClure was appointed chief of the Psychological Warfare Service attached to the Operation TORCH task force in the invasion of North Africa. Task force commander General Dwight Eisenhower charged him with conducting psychological warfare against Axis forces. Following a reorganization of the Anglo-American Allied Force Headquarters, McClure, promoted to brigadier general, became chief of the Information, News, and Censorship Division, which included a new Psychological Warfare Branch. He continued in that position through 1943 as Allied forces liberated North Africa and invaded Sicily and Italy.

As one of the highest-ranking officers with any experience in psychological warfare, McClure was asked by Eisenhower to join Supreme Headquarters, Allied Expeditionary Force, as chief of the new Psychological Warfare Division in January 1944. Here McClure coordinated Anglo-American civilian and military strategic and tactical propaganda campaigns against Germany.

In July 1945 McClure became director of the Information Control Division of the U.S. military government in Germany; he remained in that post until 1947. Between 1947 and 1950 he was chief of the U.S. Army Civil Affairs Division and commandant of Fort Ord, California.

When the Korean War began in June 1950, McClure became head of the Department of the Army's Psychological Warfare

Major General Robert A. McClure was chief of the U.S. Army's Psychological Warfare Division during the Korean War and is credited with originating the idea of voluntary repatriation of prisoners of war. (Bettmann/Corbis)

Division and played a leading role in promoting the use of psychological warfare in Korea. McClure was a founder of what would become the U.S. Army Special Warfare Center and School at Fort Bragg, North Carolina, and he served as its first director, from April 1952 until March 1953.

McClure was instrumental in persuading army officials and U.S. president Harry S. Truman's administration to adopt a position opposing the forcible repatriation of communist POWs. On the eve of the truce talks in July 1951, McClure approached U.S. Army chief of staff General J. Lawton Collins regarding the possible fate of prisoners who had fought under the nationalists in the Chinese Civil War. These individuals, McClure had learned, were forced to join the communist cause, and he feared that harsh punishments, even execution, awaited them upon their return.

To forestall this possibility, McClure recommended that instead of sending the POWs back to the People's Republic of China (PRC) against their will, the United States should undertake to send them to the nationalist-led Republic of China (ROC) on Taiwan (then known as Formosa), a territory still officially considered part of China. McClure believed that by doing so the United States could avoid repeating its World War II experience of forcibly repatriating prisoners to the Soviet Union, where many were subsequently executed or sent to labor camps. Such a policy would also enhance United Nations (UN) psychological warfare by giving new assurance to communist soldiers considering surrender that they would not be repatriated against their will. Finally, McClure concluded that the

publicity surrounding the announcement that thousands of POWs had chosen not to return home would seriously weaken communism and be a major propaganda triumph for the United States.

Collins submitted McClure's idea to the Joint Chiefs of Staff on July 6, 1951. Shortly thereafter, Washington informed the commander in chief of United Nations Command (UNC) General Matthew B. Ridgway that he could develop a position based on the principle of voluntary repatriation. The communist delegations at the truce talks refused to accept this policy and for the next 18 months rejected out of hand all attempts at compromise concerning this issue. This position created an impasse that stalled progress toward a peace settlement or armistice.

In February 1952 McClure proposed a new idea that avoided the term of "voluntary repatriation" altogether. Under this plan, the UN would agree to a prisoner exchange, but would exclude those claiming that they were impressed into communist service, those who did not reside in an area controlled by the communists, or those who claimed political asylum. Men in these categories would be referred to the governments concerned under item 5 of the proposed armistice agreement. In this manner the issue of repatriation would become a postwar issue, separated from the talks seeking an end to the fighting. The POW issue was settled on April 26, 1953, when both sides accepted the idea of voluntary repatriation that included an extensive screening process.

In 1953 McClure became chief of the U.S. military mission to Iran, remaining in that position until his retirement in 1956. He died in Shalimar, Florida, on January 1, 1957.

Clayton D. Laurie

See also
Collins, Joseph Lawton; Eisenhower, Dwight David; Joint Chiefs of Staff; Ridgway, Matthew Bunker

References
Hermes, Walter G. *U.S. Army in the Korean War: Truce Tent and Fighting Front.* Washington, DC: Office of the Chief of Military History, 1966.

Laurie, Clayton D. *The Propaganda Warriors: The American Crusade against Nazi Germany.* Lawrence: University Press of Kansas, 1996.

———. "The U.S. Army and Psychological Warfare Organization and Operations, 1918–1945." Washington, DC: U.S. Army Center of Military History. Unpublished manuscript.

Who Was Who in America, 1951–1960. Chicago: Marquis, 1963.

McGarr, Lionel Charles
Birth Date: March 5, 1904
Death Date: November 3, 1988

U.S. Army officer. Born in Yuma, Arizona, on March 5, 1904, Lionel Charles McGarr graduated in 1928 from the U.S. Military Academy at West Point. Commissioned in the infantry, McGarr's early postings were with the 25th Infantry Regiment and the 21st Infantry Regiment in Hawaii. He graduated from the Infantry School at Fort Benning, Georgia, then returned to Hawaii, serving as an instructor with the National Guard until it was activated in 1940. He was reassigned to headquarters in Hawaii but returned to the mainland in mid-1941 to join the 3rd Infantry Division at Fort Lewis, Washington.

After the United States entered World War II, McGarr saw action in North Africa, Sicily, Italy, and southern France. By the end of the war, McGarr had participated in four major amphibious assaults and had been wounded on five occasions. Promoted to colonel in 1945, McGarr became chief of staff of the 3rd Infantry Division, a post he held until returning to the United States in 1946.

McGarr was then assigned to Fort Myer, Virginia, and he graduated from the National War College in June 1947. He was next assigned to the Intelligence Division of the Army General Staff. McGarr held several commands over the next few years in the United States and abroad, but the beginning of the Korean War led to his assignment in Korea.

Advanced to brigadier general, McGarr served as assistant division commander of the 2nd Infantry Division. He then took command of the United Nations Command (UNC) prison camp system in Korea, presiding over 13 island and mainland camps that housed some 120,000 North Korean and Chinese prisoners of war.

Following the war McGarr held a variety of commands and was promoted to major general. He served as the commanding general in the Panama Canal Zone in 1954 before returning to the United States to command the U.S. Army Command and General Staff College at Fort Leavenworth, Kansas. Promoted to lieutenant general in 1960, McGarr served as chief of the United States Military Assistance Advisory Group (MAAG), Vietnam. In this position he was responsible for the U.S. effort to advise and train the Army of the Republic of Vietnam (ARVN) to deal with the communist insurgency.

McGarr retired in 1962. He settled in Lafayette, California, where he died on November 3, 1988.

JEFFREY B. COOK

See also

Prisoner of War Administration, United Nations Command

References

"Lionel Charles McGarr." *Assembly: Association of Graduates, United States Military Academy,* May 1990, 131–132.

Spector, Ronald H. *Advice and Support: The Early Years of the U.S. Army in Vietnam, 1941–1960.* New York: Free Press, 1985.

"Meat Grinder" Strategy

Start Date: January 1951
End Date: June 1951

An offensive strategy used by the U.S. Eighth Army in Korea (EUSAK) during the first half of 1951 that emphasized deliberate advances supported by firepower. This helped the United Nations Command (UNC) regain the initiative in the Korean War. Although it did not produce operations that achieved decisive results, it was an ideal complement to the strategy of attrition that focused on inflicting maximum punishment on communist forces rather than securing terrain objectives pursued by the UNC during the second half of the war's first year. The strengths of this strategy included simplicity, control, reduced UNC casualties, and maximum use of firepower; its drawbacks included a deliberate sacrifice of maneuver, little chance for individual initiative, predictability, and a decidedly negative impression on the public.

Eighth Army commander Lieutenant General Matthew B. Ridgway developed this approach in early 1951. Eighth Army continued to employ it under Lieutenant General James A. Van Fleet's leadership until the battlefield situation stabilized in June 1951. Although the U.S. press criticized the strategy as excessively brutal and the U.S. State Department viewed the term "meat grinder" as reducing the intent of Eighth Army operations to little more than wanton killing, the strategy was one of the main components of the Eighth Army's rebirth in early 1951, and it was largely responsible for the UNC's ability to recapture Seoul and reposition itself along and above the 38th Parallel in its final locations.

The intervention by the People's Republic of China (PRC) into the Korean War in the fall and winter of 1950 had forced the Eighth Army to withdraw well below the 38th Parallel by the beginning of January 1951. This and the arrival of General Ridgway to command the Eighth Army in late December 1950 were important precursors to the development of the "meat grinder" strategy. The Eighth Army was a beaten unit in the wake of the Chinese intervention, and its leaders had to do something to restore its sagging spirit or risk being driven off the Korean Peninsula entirely. Upon his arrival and after assessing the Eighth Army's senior leadership, Ridgway relieved 1 of 3 corps commanders and 5 of 6 division commanders, and he supported the relief of 19 of 47 regimental commanders during the first six weeks of 1951. The combination of these two events made it imperative for the Eighth Army to take the offensive quickly and to develop plans for offensive actions that would be relatively simple to execute.

After conducting his own reconnaissance of the Eighth Army's front and the success of Operations WOLFHOUND, THUNDERBOLT, and ROUNDUP, as well as Task Force Johnson, Ridgway initiated Operation KILLER using the "meat grinder" strategy. Beginning by drawing the I, IX, and X Corps together to eliminate any gaps between units, Ridgway launched his offensive with a number of predetermined phase lines to control the movement of the units involved. Moving methodically from phase line to phase line, Ridgway directed that the attacking units completely destroy all communist units in their paths, prevent any gaps from developing between units, and adhere precisely to his movement instructions. During the conduct of the operation, Ridgway coordinated massive artillery and close air support with the units' employment of their organic firepower, particularly tanks, machine guns, and mortars. This produced a plodding but unstoppable advancing juggernaut. While preventing units from exploiting local successes and denying individual commanders any initiative, Operation KILLER was a

The destruction caused by the "meat grinder" strategy was undeniable, but such harsh tactics were essential to the recapture of Seoul. Here, a Marine Corps tank and infantry move along a war-torn street, March 1951. (National Archives)

successful endeavor, and it signaled a dramatic battlefield reversal in favor of the UNC, during which the Eighth Army seized the initiative from communist forces.

Building on the triumph of the method and the operation, Ridgway launched additional operations of similar design to capitalize on his success. Operations RIPPER, COURAGEOUS, RUGGED, and DAUNTLESS followed the basic outline of KILLER: closing gaps between units and then attacking methodically by moving under Ridgway's direction between a series of predetermined phase lines that made maximum use of all available firepower.

Using this strategy, Eighth Army was attacking in corps strength by the end of January 1951 and in army strength by the middle of February 1951. By March 1951 the UNC had recaptured Seoul and recrossed the 38th Parallel. Once north of the Han River, the Eighth Army used the "meat grinder" technique to "elbow forward" and improve its overall defensive position. After absorbing the Chinese Fifth Offensive, Van Fleet used the "meat grinder" method again in June 1951 during Operation PILEDRIVER to recapture lost territory and move farther north.

Despite the limitations inherent in the "meat grinder" strategy, its greatest strength was that the Eighth Army's new leadership could successfully execute it while undertaking offensive operations that were essential in transforming the Eighth Army

from a beaten unit to a competent and confident fighting organization. In addition, the methodical advance dictated by the "meat grinder" approach maximized the Eighth Army's firepower advantage, minimized U.S. casualties, and allowed the soldiers to experience some much-needed battlefield success during the first half of 1951. Although this strategy did limit individual initiative and opportunities for exploitation, it helped Ridgway, Van Fleet, and lower-level commanders to control combat operations and ensure that they continued to support the limited political objectives of the United Nations (UN). While the term itself was very unpopular and the strategy employed was not perhaps the most elegant or sophisticated method of waging war, the "meat grinder" strategy was particularly well suited for the situation faced by Eighth Army in the first half of 1951.

KELLY C. JORDAN

See also

Chinese Offensive, Fifth; Close Air Support; COURAGEOUS, Operation; DAUNTLESS, Operation; Eighth Army, U.S.; KILLER, Operation; PILEDRIVER, Operation; Ridgway, Matthew Bunker; RIPPER, Operation; RUGGED, Operation; Van Fleet, James Alward

References

Appleman, Roy E. *Ridgway Duels for Korea.* College Station: Texas A&M University Press, 1990.

Blair, Clay. *The Forgotten War: America in Korea, 1950–1953*. New York: Times Books, 1987.

Hoyt, Edwin P. *The Day the Chinese Attacked, Korea, 1950: The Story of the Failure of America's China Policy*. New York: McGraw-Hill, 1990.

Matray, James I., ed. *Historical Dictionary of the Korean War*. New York: Greenwood, 1991.

Mossman, Billy C. *United States Army in the Korean War: Ebb and Flow, November 1950–July 1951*. Washington, DC: U.S. Army Center of Military History, 1990.

Ridgway, Matthew B. *The Korean War*. Garden City, NY: Doubleday, 1967.

Media and the Korean War

The Korean War was the last major U.S. conflict covered primarily by print journalism. Stories on the war by the Associated Press (AP), United Press (UP), and the International News Service (INS) wire services ran in newspapers and magazines. Improvements in communications technology enabled stories to reach publication just hours after a battle occurred.

Radio was also a key component of Korean War journalism. The number of radio stations in the United States increased significantly after World War II, and in 1945 there were 960 AM radio stations and 50 FM stations in the United States. By 1950 there were 2,300 AM radio stations and 760 FM stations. Included were four national radio networks, of which NBC and CBS were the most popular. Americans listened nightly to reports about the war on these stations and their affiliates.

Television was still a novelty, and few American households had a TV set, especially in the first year of the war. Satellites, of course, were more than a decade away. But visual images of the war appeared in regular newsreel footage of the war, which was shown before feature films in movie theaters. Going to movies was very popular at the time, and so these newsreels reached tens of millions of Americans each week. Such newsreel footage took several days to reach the United States, however.

Many of the war correspondents who reported live from Korea were seasoned veterans of war reporting, most having served in a similar capacity during World War II. When the war began, there were only 5 journalists in the Republic of Korea (ROK, South Korea), but by September 1950 there were 238 there, and this number would later increase to 270. The number of journalists in Korea was far fewer than the 419 journalists who covered the Vietnam War 20 years later.

There were two groups of journalists in the Korean War: those who reported from the front lines, where the action was most intense, and those who reported from the general safety of allied headquarters. Journalism was not without risks, especially for those who sought to be close to the action. Over the course of the war, 15 journalists were killed in action. Jim Becker of the AP cynically remarked that it was a contest between the U.S. Air Force (USAF) and the communists as to who could kill the most

journalists. Death on the battlefield was not the fate of others, however. One, Frank Noel, an AP photographer, was captured by the Chinese People's Volunteer Army (CPVA, Chinese Army) in 1951 and held prisoner for the remainder of the war.

From the beginning of the war there was a conflict of interest between the military and the press. Correspondents often encountered problems with military protocols regarding journalists. Ironically, it was the journalists themselves who called for full military censorship at the beginning of the war in order to limit competition among themselves and to reduce the risk of security breaches, as well as to improve the quality of reporting. For example, news of the Inchon Landing on September 15, 1950, appeared in newspapers while the troops were still at sea.

Commander of the United Nations Command (UNC) General Douglas MacArthur at first refused to implement censorship of the press. He called on journalists to act responsibly, but at the same time he warned them not to reveal troop movements and the locations of UNC forces. Press censorship was finally imposed on December 21, 1950. Reportedly, this was favored by almost 90 percent of the journalists. Censorship remained in effect until the end of the war.

From the beginning of the war, journalists wrote about the many problems facing the UNC. They questioned the involvement of the United Nations (UN) and whether South Korea was worth saving. Journalists showed the human side of the conflict by picturing soldiers suffering from malaise, disillusionment, homesickness, wounds, the cold, and other problems. Two reporters flew to Japan, where they investigated the lack of preparedness, including equipment shortages, of allied troops at the beginning of the war. Military authorities refused to permit these journalists to return to Korea because they feared their stories would affect morale. Journalists also covered corruption in South Korean president Syngman Rhee's government by showing how South Korean police profited from selling army supplies and how brothels and alcohol were made available to troops.

After censorship went into effect, journalists were severely limited in what they were allowed to write. They were always told to report their stories from "Somewhere in Korea" and were forbidden to mention a specific unit by name until that information had been released by official sources; they also had to obtain permission from the authorities to write about any military action. They could not disclose the nationality of troops and were not allowed to report the number of casualties after a battle.

In January 1951 all journalists covering the UNC were placed under military jurisdiction and given a list of possible punishments if they disobeyed military policies regarding censorship. MacArthur later expelled 17 journalists who had questioned his policies and been openly critical of the UNC war effort. The editor of *Stars and Stripes* was fired after he published a photograph of General William Dean in captivity. A few journalists later chose to return to the United States in order to freely express their views on the war without censorship or fear of reprisal.

Correspondents with the United Nations Command (UNC) at the armistice building in Panmunjom, South Korea, on July 23, 1953. (Department of Defense)

Official news sources were often slanted. The Public Information Office of the Far East Command (FEC) released news stories on the war, but these were biased to the point of being little more than propaganda. Some topics that appealed to journalists but were not given full attention included the possible employment of the atomic bomb, disunity among the different UNC nations, the behavior of allied troops as prisoners of war (POWs), and the Panmunjom peace talks.

At the peace talks, the correspondents were not allowed to speak with the UNC delegates, and they were denied access to maps and documents used by the military. This angered many reporters, and some turned to communist reporters for information. The latter were happy to provide information and disinformation to Western reporters, much to the embarrassment of the UNC. UNC commander Lieutenant General Matthew B. Ridgway henceforth prohibited contact between allied reporters and their communist counterparts to reduce the possibility of compromising military security.

Two of the best-known communist reporters were Alan Winnington of the *London Daily Worker,* and Australian Wilfred Burchett. In earlier wars it would have been considered treason if a member of an allied nation had reported from the enemy's camp,

and this situation was perhaps a first in war journalism. Burchett unleashed a propaganda attack, accusing the UNC of employing germ warfare in Korea. He claimed that the UNC had toxic gases in bullets and artillery shells and had released bacterial warfare agents such as lice, ticks, and beetles against the communist side to spread typhus and bubonic plague. The United States was slow to respond to these charges, helping to lend credence to the reports. The charges were later revealed to have been a deliberate communist propaganda hoax.

Another first in war journalism was Marguerite Higgins, female correspondent for the *New York Herald Tribune.* Told several times to leave the battlefield because it was no place for a woman, she helped pioneer the way for female reporters in later wars.

Journalists played an important role in the Korean War. They provided firsthand coverage from the battlefield and took considerable risks to inform the American public about the war. Several, including Higgins and Keyes Beech, won the Pulitzer Prize for their efforts in covering the war.

JAMES R. MAHALA

See also
Biological Warfare; Dean, William Frishe; Film and the Korean War; Higgins, Marguerite; Literature of the Korean War, Korean;

Literature of the Korean War, U.S.; MacArthur, Douglas; Rhee, Syngman; Ridgway, Matthew Bunker

References

Beech, Keyes. *Tokyo and Points East*. Garden City, NY: Doubleday, 1964.

Braestrup, Peter. *Battle Lines: Report of the Twentieth Century Fund Task Force on the Military and the Media*. New York: Priority Press, 1985.

Higgins, Marguerite. *War in Korea: Report of a Woman Combat Correspondent*. Garden City, NY: Doubleday, 1951.

Kahn, E. J., Jr. *The Peculiar War: Impressions of a Reporter in Korea*. New York: Random House, 1952.

Mercer, Derrik. *The Fog of War: The Media on the Battlefield*. London: Heinemann, 1987.

Medicine, Military

Although it began only a half decade after the end of World War II, the Korean conflict engendered signal advances in military medicine, including the refinement of the Mobile Army Surgical Hospital (MASH), helicopter transport of the sick and wounded, and improvements in the treatment of vascular injuries, head injuries, and shock. Many of these techniques ultimately were translated to civilian medicine and have since become standards of care.

Military medicine was in a tenuous state when Korean People's Army (KPA, North Korean Army) forces invaded the Republic of Korea (ROK, South Korea) on June 25, 1950; it was, if anything, in a worse situation than the combat arm of the military.

After World War II, in response to those still in uniform and to civilians at home, military doctors were rapidly demobilized. Between June 1945 and June 1950, the Army Medical Corps lost 86 percent of its officers and 91 percent of its enlisted personnel. In an attempt to replenish the supply, residencies were opened at a number of army hospitals with the intent that, in return for being paid during postgraduate training, the new specialist physicians would serve for a time in the military. Unfortunately the program was new, the potential help was still in the process of being trained, and the predicted nadir of physician supply was June 1950.

In addition, civilian physicians were in relatively short supply, and those in domestic practice were busy, prosperous, and unenthusiastic about service in Korea. A specific draft for physicians was not instituted until August 1950, and it produced no direct help in Korea until January 1951. Nevertheless, by 1952 90 percent of physicians serving in Korea were draftees.

The first military medical contingent in Korea was the Advance Command and Liaison Group of 15 officers and 2 enlisted men dispatched by the Far East Command (FEC) on June 27, 1950. Its mission was to care for American refugees fleeing the KPA and to begin replenishing supplies lost in the fall of Seoul.

The medical aspect of the war can be divided into three parts: offensive operations, defensive operations against invading forces and during withdrawal, and static defensive operations. These distinctions are important because the rate and type of injury differ among the three.

For the first time in the history of military medicine, data on battle and nonbattle (further subdivided into disease and injury) casualties were collected on punch cards and returned to Washington for computer analysis by the Medical Department and the Surgeon General. The Adjutant General collected an entirely separate set of data, and the two sets do not uniformly agree. Surgeon General records report 18,769 killed in action, 77,788 wounded in action and admitted to treatment facilities, and 14,575 with wounds not requiring admission. The Adjutant General's records report 19,658 killed in action and 79,526 wounded in action. Only the Surgeon General collected data on disease and nonbattle injury. A total of 443,163 patients were admitted to treatment facilities during the war; this included 365,375 nonbattle admissions (82.4 percent). Of these, 290,210 were for disease, and 75,165 were for nonbattle injury. Over the course of the war, 30 of each 1,000 active-duty personnel were killed in action, 121 of each 1,000 were admitted for battle injury, and 570 of each 1,000 were admitted for disease or nonbattle injury. In general all of these incidences declined as the war progressed.

The most common battle injuries were penetrating wounds (57 percent) and fractures (23 percent), although the specific mechanism of injury varied with the type of combat. Average casualties per division per day were 119 in withdrawal, 77 in defense against a main force, and 67 in offense against a main force. In addition, the death rate among casualties was 25.2 percent in defense and only 14.6 percent in offense. Death rates also varied according to the weapon with which the casualty was inflicted: 28.4 percent for small arms, 23.8 percent for mines and booby traps, 18.4 percent for artillery, and 10.8 percent for hand grenades.

Army hospitals in Korea performed 89,974 surgical procedures throughout the duration of the conflict. Fifty-nine percent of those admitted with battle wounds required some sort of surgery, and the case-fatality rate was 2.5 percent (compared to 4.5 percent during World War II). Many patients required more than one operation, with the average being 1.2 procedures per wounded patient admitted. Surgery in Korea tended to be quick and of the salvage variety, with definitive treatment left to rear-area hospitals.

One of the most important technical advances during the war was the increased use of whole-blood transfusions to resuscitate patients in shock. A wounded soldier received an average of 3.3 pints of whole blood, although transfusions of 15 to 30 units were not unusual. This practice placed a predictable strain on the donation system, with 21,188 pints collected in the United States and 22,099 pints collected in Japan in 1950 alone. Caucasian and native Japanese blood supplies were segregated, although it is not known whether this was done for medical or racial reasons.

Neurosurgery posed a particularly difficult problem, both because of the complexity of the injuries and the extreme shortage of trained personnel. By 1952 a special evacuation path through the 8209th (and later the 8063rd) MASH units, commanded by Lieutenant Colonel Arnold Meirowsky, was established to care for wounds of the head and spinal cord.

Wounded soldiers of K Company, 38th Regiment, 2nd Infantry Division, being treated at a forward aid station near Old Baldy, September 19, 1952. (National Archives)

Vascular injuries posed another technical challenge. Use of vein grafts to repair arterial injuries was a significant advance, and by 1951 these repairs resulted in salvaging 85 percent of limbs with major vascular disruptions. Cold injuries were an especially common cause of nonbattle traumatic admissions. During 1950 there were 1,791 cases of cold injury, for an incidence of 34 per 1,000. Medics were particularly hampered in the actions around the Changjin and Pujon reservoirs when the cold caused medicine, intravenous fluids, and plasma to freeze and become unusable.

Infectious disease was a persistent problem. Of those treated for nonbattle-related causes and not requiring admission, 90 percent had infectious or parasitic disease. The most common problems were respiratory disease (20 percent), ill-defined febrile illnesses, and diarrheal disease. The latter was especially severe early in the war when hygienic facilities were lacking. Gastrointestinal disease (especially shigellosis) occurred at a rate of 120 per 1,000 per year in August 1950. Other common infectious problems were encephalitis, polio, hemorrhagic fever, hepatitis, and venereal disease.

Malaria and plague were locally endemic but never became a serious problem for United Nations (UN) troops.

The third most common disease problem was neuropsychiatric (NP) illness. The frequency of disability from psychiatric illness varied greatly with the stage of the war. Early in the war, young psychiatrists were stationed at the rear. Inexperienced and far removed from the battlefields, these doctors tended to be liberal in sending home soldiers with psychiatric complaints. As the war progressed, physicians were moved closer to the front and became less sympathetic, and the rate of psychiatric disability dropped. A second factor was the kind of fighting going on at the time. The rate of NPs dropped from 249 per 1,000 before the Pusan breakout, to 18.4 per 1,000 during the advance, although it rose again when the winter weather set in.

Deployment of medical facilities proceeded rapidly in the fall of 1950. By November, four MASH units, with bed capacities increased from a planned 60 to 150, had been established in Korea, along with three 400-bed semimobile evacuation hospitals, four 400-bed field

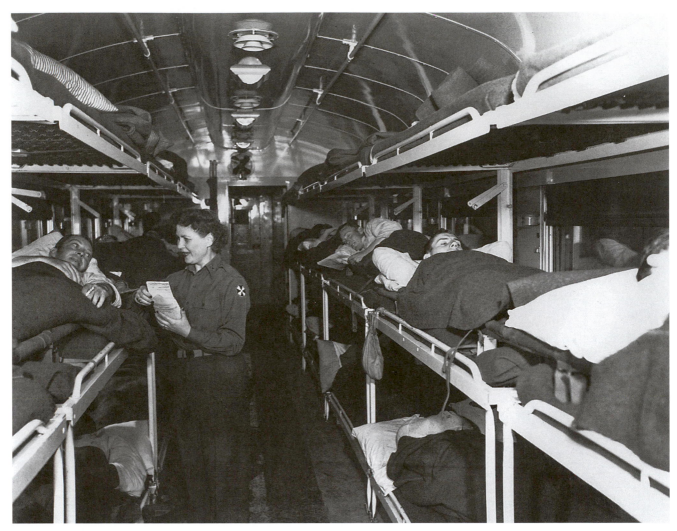

Casualties aboard a U.S. Army hospital evacuation train in Korea. (National Archives)

hospitals, one station hospital, and three hospital ships. Two additional MASH units were deployed in 1951, and one of the evacuation hospitals was moved to Japan in December 1950. After the Chinese entered the war, three additional evacuation hospitals were committed, but they functioned as immobile station hospitals. The field hospitals were converted to treat prisoners of war (POWs).

The evacuation sequence from facility to facility was from battalion aid station, to regimental collecting station, to division clearing station, to evacuation hospital at Pusan, to Korean airfields, to the 118th Station Hospital at Fukuoka (Kyushu, Japan), to other army hospitals in Japan (Osaka and Tokyo), to Tripler Army Hospital (Hawaii), to either Travis Air Force Base (California) or Lackland Air Force Base (Texas), to zone-of-the-interior hospitals. Patients requiring emergency stabilization or surgery could be sent from either the regimental collecting stations or the division clearing stations to the MASH units. From there, the stabilized patients were sent on either to the evacuation hospital at Pusan or directly to Fukuoka. Of admissions for battle injury, 10 percent received final disposition at a forward unit (aid, clearing, or collecting station), 57 percent at army hospitals in the FEC,

6 percent at nonarmy hospitals (navy or air force), and 26 percent at hospitals in the United States. These figures include both discharge and death, although 96 percent of all deaths occurred in one of the FEC hospitals. Eighty percent of division wounded eventually returned to duty.

Transport changed as the war progressed. Because the terrain in Korea was difficult, the initial stages of transport were by hand-carried litter, especially when combat units were moving either in advance or retreat. From the aid and clearing stations, transport was primarily by rail. Early in the war, gasoline-powered rail cars ("Doodlebugs") carried patients from the front at Chochiwon to Taejon. They held 17 litters or 50 ambulatory patients and traversed the 30 miles in about 45 minutes. As the front stabilized later in the war, formal rail transport was more frequent. Rail facilities were brought to within 8,000 yards of the front line, and evacuation trains typically comprised eight ward cars, two orderly cars, a kitchen car, a dining car, a pharmacy car, an officer personnel car, and a utility car.

Because of both improved transport (both rail and air) and treatment facilities located relatively close to the front line, a remarkable 58 percent of soldiers wounded in battle received medical care within two hours of injury, and 85 percent were treated within six hours. The median time from wound to first care was 90 minutes, and 55 percent of casualties were hospitalized the same day they were wounded—a number that rose to nearly 100 percent by 1953.

Early in the war, evacuation from Pusan to Fukuoka was principally by ship, with hospital ships, troop transports, and even ferries pressed into service. This relatively slow and expensive method of transport was quickly replaced by air evacuation. In the first year of the war, Douglas C-47 Skytrains (Dakotas) were utilized, although as the war progressed, Douglas C-54 Skymasters became available. The longer range of the C-54s allowed direct transfer to Honshu, and transports were divided 40–40–20 percent between Itazuki Air Base (Fukuoka), Itami Air Base (Osaka), and Tachikawa Air Base (Tokyo).

Because there was an initial shortage of all physicians and a persistent lack of some specialists, a tactical decision was made to substitute triage and transport for personnel. The army realized that the best use could be made of scarce personnel by concentrating them in hospitals in rear areas. Patients who were predicted to recover in fewer than 30 days were kept at Pusan; those expected to recover in 30 to 120 days were kept in Japan; and those anticipated to have prolonged recovery were returned to the United States. A complex of evacuation units grew around the 8054th Evacuation Hospital at Pusan. The 8054th was initially in the Pusan Middle School but grew to several buildings with 1,200 beds that handled up to 12,000 admissions a month. It was assisted by the Swedish Red Cross Hospital, the First Prisoner-of-War Hospital, and several hospital ships and specialized units.

The overall record of army medicine in Korea compares favorably to that of World War II. The case-fatality rate for those wounded in battle in the earlier war was 4.5 percent, dropping to 2.5 percent in the latter. In addition, these rates dropped as the war progressed—the rate for 1950 is not known, but for 1951 it was 2.1 percent, and by 1952 it was down to 1.8 percent. Of those wounded but not killed in Korea, 87.9 percent returned to duty, 8.5 percent were separated as disabled, and 1.4 percent were separated for administrative reasons. Overall, medical care in Korea was characterized by rapid transport, effective early resuscitation and surgery, and some advances in surgical technique and decline in mortality rates from battle injury.

JACK McCALLUM

See also

Aeromedical Evacuation; Hospital Ships; Mobile Army Surgical Hospital

References

Apel, Otto F., Jr. *MASH*. Lexington: University Press of Kentucky, 1998.
Cleaver, Frederick. *U.S. Army Battle Casualties in Korea*. Chevy Chase, MD: Operations Research Office, 1956.
Cowdrey, Albert E. *United States Army in the Korean War: The Medic's War*. Washington, DC: U.S. Army Center of Military History, 1987.
Smith, Allen D. "Air Evacuation—Medical Obligation and Military Necessity." *Air University Quarterly* 6 (1953): 98–111.

Medics, Combat

In any armed conflict, medical services are extremely important. Korea was no exception. In the combat zone, medical treatment started on the battlefield. Enlisted men of a regimental medical company were called "medics" in the army and "corpsmen" by U.S. Marine Corps units. Marine corpsmen were actually navy hospital corpsmen assigned to Marine units as combat medics. In army units one medic was attached to each rifle platoon, with a total of seven medics in a rifle company. Marine units were similarly manned. Most combat patrols included a medic.

These medical personnel had to deal with all manner of wounds and injuries, including those caused by small arms, heavy weapons, mortars, and artillery fire. Depending on the time of year, they also dealt with frostbite and heat prostration, as well as various illnesses and communicable diseases.

Medics, usually unarmed, carried out their duties in the heat of battle. With only small first-aid kits, they often accomplished medical near-miracles. Battlefield casualties, once treated, were evacuated to the battalion aid station by litter bearers. Many of these bearers were men of the Korean Service Corps. Some wounded had to find their own way to the rear if they were judged to be "walking wounded."

Depending on the seriousness of their injuries, the wounded men were then evacuated by jeep, ambulance, or helicopter to the regimental collecting station, the division clearing station, or a Mobile Army Surgical Hospital (MASH). Early in the war some fixed-wing liaison aircraft were also used for medical evacuation. Combat soldiers had a high regard for the medics and always felt better when medics were present during an operation.

The number of medics who received medals for valor attests to their bravery. Medics received 8 of the 131 Medals of Honor awarded in the Korean War. Of these, four (three posthumous) were awarded to army medics and four (all posthumous) went to navy hospital corpsmen serving with marine units.

NORMAN R. ZEHR

See also

Aeromedical Evacuation; Hospital Ships; Medicine, Military; Mobile Army Surgical Hospital

References

Apel, Otto F., Jr. *MASH*. Lexington: University Press of Kentucky, 1998.
Cowdrey, Albert E. *United States Army in the Korean War: The Medic's War*. Washington, DC: U.S. Army Center of Military History, 1987.
Jordan, Kenneth N., Sr. *Forgotten Heroes*. Atglen, PA: Schiffer Military/Aviation History, 1995.
Meid, Pat, James M. Yingling, Nicholas Canzona, et al. *U.S. Marine Operations in Korea, 1950–1953*. 5 vols. Washington, DC: U.S. Marine Corps Historical Branch, 1962–1972.

Menon, Kumara Padmanabha Sivasankara
Birth Date: October 18, 1898
Death Date: November 21, 1982

India's ambassador to the People's Republic of China (PRC), 1947–1948, and then to the Union of Soviet Socialist Republics, 1952–1961; chairman of the United Nations Temporary Commission on Korea (UNTCOK), 1948. Born in Kottayam, Kerala State, India, on October 18, 1898, Kumara Padmanabha Sivasankara Menon graduated from Madras Christian College in 1918 and attended Christ Church, Oxford University, in Great Britain, earning a master's degree with honors.

Menon returned to India and there became a career civil servant, working first in Madras between 1922 and 1925. From 1925 to 1943 he worked in the Foreign and Political Department in New Delhi. During World War II Menon was appointed agent-general to China to promote Sino-Indian cooperation in the war effort. After India's independence in 1947, Menon became that nation's first ambassador to China.

In late 1947 the nine-nation UNTCOK came into being, and in January 1948 Menon became its chairman. The choice of Menon was no accident, as his reputation and success in forming a solid relationship with China was well known. Commission members were also aware that Koreans would identify with the representative of an Asian nation that had recently won independence from a Western colonial power.

In a January 21, 1948, speech Menon called for free elections throughout the entire Korean Peninsula. To ensure these elections, he set up three committees: one to study the means for securing a free atmosphere for the forthcoming elections; another to study Korean public opinion; and the third to develop an electoral system for Korea. This last committee was to study existing Korean electoral laws, in both northern and southern Korea, and recommend a mechanism compatible with these and United Nations (UN) General Assembly requirements.

Commission goals were to hold free and unfettered elections; to ensure maximum voter turnout; and to create an atmosphere promoting voter enthusiasm. Not only must electors be free to vote, but candidates of all parties, including those of the extreme left and right, must also have freedom. Menon believed that both Eastern and Western ideologies could coexist. He hoped that Korea might be able to take concepts from both camps and evolve its own system.

North Korea and the Soviet Union balked at allowing UN-supervised elections. The Soviet Union refused to cooperate and denied commission members entry into northern Korea. As a result, elections were held only south of the 38th Parallel on May 10, 1948. Menon feared that electing a national government in southern Korea would "set off a vaster cataclysm in Asia and the world." He wanted any partial-peninsula election to be held for the selection of representatives to consult with UNTCOK only and not for the establishment of a divided Korea. However, as a result of U.S. pressure on the commission, the Interim Committee agreed to hold elections in as much of Korea as was accessible—namely the portion of the peninsula south of the 38th Parallel.

After completing his assignment as chairman of UNTCOK, Menon returned to India as foreign secretary. In 1950 he helped establish full diplomatic relations with China. This recognition irritated Washington and dampened relations between India and the United States. Menon preferred to steer India's foreign policy along the same lines as Yugoslavia's by aligning neither with the East nor the West. From 1952 to 1961 he was Indian ambassador to the Soviet Union, Poland, and Hungary. There he established an Indo-Soviet bond that would last for decades after his retirement.

Following his tour as ambassador, Menon retired from foreign service and became president of the India-Soviet Cultural Society and chairman of the Indian Institute of Russian Studies. He wrote several books, including his autobiography *Many Worlds, The Flying Troika* (extracts from his diary), and *Delhi-Chungking*, which describes a four-month journey he made on foot and on horseback to China during World War II. Menon died of undetermined causes on November 21, 1982, in Ottapalam, India.

WILLIAM H. VAN HUSEN

See also
China, People's Republic of; India

References
Candee, Marjorie Dent, ed. *Current Biography, 1957*. New York: H. W. Wilson, 1958.
Stueck, William W., Jr. *Rethinking the Korean War: A New Diplomatic and Strategic History*. Princeton, NJ: Princeton University Press, 2004.

Menon, Vengalil Krishnan Krishna
Birth Date: May 3, 1896
Death Date: October 5, 1974

Indian politician, diplomat, and representative to the United Nations (UN) in 1952 who played a crucial part in the negotiations leading to the Korean Armistice Agreement. Born on May 3, 1896, in Calicut (Kozhikode) in the state of Kerala, the son of an Indian lawyer of the Malabar aristocracy, Vengalil Krishnan Krishna Menon (known simply as V. K. Krishna Menon) graduated from the Madras Presidency College in 1918. He was then attracted to Annie Besant's Theosophical Society and also became active in the movement for Indian home rule. Moving to England, he earned a first-class bachelor of science degree and a master's degree. in political science from the London School of Economics, and he also worked ardently for the Indian nationalist cause.

Menon became a well-connected member of the British Labour Party, forming close relationships to such leading lights as Harold Laski, Sir Stafford Cripps, and Aneurin Bevan; and for 14 years, beginning in 1934, he served on the St. Pancras Borough Council. It

Strong anticolonialist V. K. Krishna Menon, head of the Indian delegation to the United Nations (UN), is shown addressing the UN General Assembly on June 24, 1955. (Bettmann/Corbis)

was partly from his influence that in 1944 the Labour Party passed a resolution demanding independence for India. Menon was also a close friend of Indian president Jawaharlal Nehru, whom he met in 1927 and with whom he worked for Indian independence. At Nehru's request, Menon represented the Indian Congress Party in various international venues, publicizing and furthering the Indian nationalist cause. Both Menon and Nehru, whose political views had received a sympathetic hearing from many British intellectuals, made a distinction between the British government and its policies and the country's people. From 1947 to 1952 Menon served as Indian high commissioner in London, where he was instrumental in keeping India within the British Commonwealth; he then became India's representative to the UN, a position he held until 1962.

Sharp-tongued, obsessive, and vain, Menon alienated many U.S. officials, who both resented his bitter anticolonial outbursts and his commitment to Indian nonalignment, and they wrongly considered him pro-Soviet in outlook. As a leading nonaligned Asian nation with a recent anticolonial history and socialist leanings, India did, however, possess useful contacts with the Soviets and even more with the Chinese.

When he took up his UN position in 1952, Menon followed a policy consonant with the broad objectives of India's nonaligned stance of preventing further escalation of the war while facilitating negotiations among the major belligerents and their allies and patrons. By late 1952 the Panmunjom truce talks had reached an impasse over the issue of the repatriation of prisoners of war (POWs), and the war was at a stalemate. Menon immediately tried to suggest a compromise, and in November 1952 he formally introduced a settlement proposal in the UN. After significant modifications, this proposal laid the foundation for an eventual agreement on POWs, which was concluded on June 8, 1953. In early 1954, when an anticipated postarmistice Korean political conference intended to deal with this and other matters did not take place, Menon again moved to further the peace process, suggesting that any as-yet unrepatriated POWs should be returned to their original captors or custodians, who would be left responsible for their release, thereby circumventing a contentious issue.

As India's representative to the UN, Menon later made substantial contributions to resolving crises in Indochina and Cyprus. He was immensely popular with the Indian general public, who appreciated his strong defense of India's position on Kashmir and Goa in the UN. His anticolonial attacks on Western nations on these issues and over Suez, his strong support for the 1955 Bandung Conference of Afro-Asian nations and a somewhat brief Sino-Indian entente, and his failure to condemn the 1956 Soviet intervention in Hungary all won him the bitter antagonism of U.S. secretary of state John Foster Dulles and other U.S. officials, as well as conservative Indians. Despite this opposition, Nehru appointed Menon minister without portfolio in 1956 and minister of defense from 1957 to 1962. In the latter capacity Menon was generally held responsible for the debacle suffered by India in the 1962 Sino-Indian War, a disaster from which his career never recovered. Menon died in New Delhi on October 5, 1974.

PRISCILLA ROBERTS

See also

Bevan, Aneurin; Dulles, John Foster; India; Nehru, Jawaharlal

References

Brecher, Michael. *India and World Politics: Krishna Menon's View of the World.* London: Oxford University Press, 1968.

Gopal, Sarvepalli. *Jawaharlal Nehru: A Biography.* 3 vols. Cambridge, MA: Harvard University Press, 1976.

Iyer, V. R. Krishna. *Nehru and Krishna Menon.* Delhi: Konark, 1993.

Prior, Katherine. "Menon, (Vengalil Krishnan) Krishna (1896–1974)." In *Oxford Dictionary of National Biography: From the Earliest Times to 2000,* 60 vols., edited by H. C. G. Matthew and Brian Harrison, 37:815–817. Oxford: Oxford University Press, 2004.

Raychaudhuri, T. "Menon, Vengalil Krishnan Kunji-Krishna." In *Dictionary of National Biography, 1971–1980,* edited by Lord Blake and C. S. Nicholls, 560–561. Oxford: Oxford University Press, 1986.

Stueck, William W., Jr. *The Korean War: An International History.* Princeton, NJ: Princeton University Press, 1995.

Robert G. Menzies was prime minister of Australia throughout the Korean War and a strong supporter of United Nations action there. (Corbis)

Menzies, Robert Gordon

Birth Date: December 20, 1894
Death Date: May 15, 1978

Attorney, politician, and prime minister of Australia throughout the Korean War. Born at Jeparit, Australia, on December 20, 1894, to a storekeeper who later became a member of the Legislative Province of Victoria State, Robert Gordon Menzies was educated at private schools and at Melbourne University, where he read law and won first-class honors. Menzies proceeded to practice law, specializing in constitutional law. By the late 1920s he had not only won an outstanding professional reputation but was also making a handsome income. Within 11 years of his entry into politics in 1928, Menzies had become leader of the United Australia Party (UAP), and from 1939 to 1941 he served as prime minister. After several years in opposition, during which the politically astute Menzies skillfully reconstituted the elements supporting the UAP

as the right-of-center Liberal Party, he was reelected prime minister in 1949.

Prime Minister Menzies consulted with both the British and U.S. governments over Korea, but his own inclination was to follow the British line whenever possible. His government viewed the outbreak of the Korean War as part of a global struggle between communism and democracy, and on June 27, 1950, it responded by sending a squadron of heavy bombers to assist British Commonwealth forces combating the communist insurgency in Malaya. U.S. president Harry S. Truman's administration put considerable pressure on its international allies and supporters, including Australia, to contribute military assistance to United Nations Command (UNC) forces fighting in Korea. On June 29, after the British sent naval vessels to Korea, Menzies followed suit, committing an Australian destroyer and a frigate, and the following day, under some pressure from U.S. Far East commander General Douglas MacArthur, Menzies added a fighter squadron of F-51 Mustangs from the Royal Australian Air Force, which was already based in Japan.

Menzies and the British were both initially reluctant to commit ground troops, and discussions Menzies held in London with the British cabinet in July 1950 initially reinforced his predilections on this question. The British changed their minds after Menzies's departure by sea for the United States, and during his absence the Australian cabinet, led by Minister of External Affairs Percy C. Spender, decided to commit the 3rd Battalion of the Royal Australian Regiment. Upon his arrival Menzies learned of this about-face and immediately capitalized on it to enhance Australia's prestige in the United States. In Washington he addressed both houses of Congress and secured a World Bank loan of $250 million. Although Menzies personally doubted whether a security pact with the United States was necessary and thought its American political prospects were poor, the ANZUS (Australia-New Zealand-U.S.) Treaty, which was negotiated in 1951, was greatly facilitated by the Australian contribution to Korea.

Despite Menzies's firm support for the U.S. position on Korea, he, along with the British, was not totally uncritical of the U.S. stance. Less than anxious to tarnish Australia's advantageous image as a loyal U.S. ally or damage the new Australian-American alliance, he generally expressed Australian misgivings within a Commonwealth framework and left the British, Canadians, or Indians to take the lead in questioning U.S. policies. Menzies shared British concerns that the United States might escalate the war by attacking mainland Chinese territory or that it might employ atomic weapons. He fully endorsed British prime minister Clement Attlee's attempt, on his December 1950 visit to the United States, to dissuade Americans from use of their nuclear capabilities. In February 1951, as UN forces regained ground after the first shock of Chinese intervention, Australia expressed its concern that the UN forces might once more push too far into the Democratic People's Republic of Korea (DPRK, North Korea).

Menzies remained prime minister until his retirement in 1966, and throughout that time he remained a loyal ally to both Britain and the United States, joining the Southeast Asia Treaty Organization (SEATO) in 1954, sending Australian troops to assist the United States in Vietnam, and always regarding communism as the greatest international and Asian menace, to be combated at all costs. In retirement he wrote two volumes of memoirs. He died in Melbourne on May 15, 1978.

PRISCILLA ROBERTS

See also

ANZUS Treaty; Attlee, Clement Richard; Australia; MacArthur, Douglas

References

Cain, Frank, ed. *Menzies in War and Peace.* St. Leonards, New South Wales, Australia: Allen and Unwin, 1997.

Martin, A. W. *Robert Menzies: A Life.* Carlton: Melbourne University Press, 1993.

Menzies, Robert. *Afternoon Light: Some Memories of Men and Events.* London: Cassell, 1967.

———. *The Measure of the Years.* London: Cassell, 1970.

O'Neill, Robert J. *Australia in the Korea War, 1950–1953.* 2 vols. Canberra: Australian War Memorial/Australian Government Publishing Service, 1981, 1985.

Prasser, Scott, J. R. Nethercote, and John Warthurst, eds. *The Menzies Era: A Reappraisal of Government, Politics and Policy.* Sydney: Hale and Iremonger, 1995.

Merchant, Livingston Tallmadge
Birth Date: November 23, 1903
Death Date: May 15, 1976

U.S. deputy assistant secretary of state for Far Eastern affairs from 1949 to 1951 and special assistant to the secretary of state on mutual security affairs from 1951 to 1952. Born in Boston, Massachusetts, on November 23, 1903, into a long-established prominent New England family, Livingston Tallmadge Merchant was descended from one of the men who signed the Declaration of Independence in 1776. After study at Princeton University, he joined the New York and Boston firm of Scudder, Stevens, and Clark as an investment counselor.

In 1942, soon after the United States entered World War II, Merchant joined the Department of State, serving as assistant chief of the Division of Defense Materials until 1945, when he became chief of the War Areas Division. Both positions called upon Merchant's special expertise in economic matters, as did his subsequent assignment as counselor for economic affairs in the U.S. embassy in Paris. He formally joined the Foreign Service in 1947, when he was serving as chief of the State Department's Aviation Division. Throughout his long diplomatic career, Merchant was a skilled and able bureaucrat and administrator rather than an innovative thinker or broad strategist.

Merchant's first Asian posting was as counselor of the U.S. embassy in Nanjing from 1948 to 1949. He witnessed firsthand the collapse of Jiang Jieshi's (Chiang Kai-shek's) Guomindang (GMD, Nationalist) government to the Communists. Disillusioned by the former's corruption and inefficiency, Merchant and other State Department Asian experts favored some form of rapprochement between the United States and Mao Zedong's new People's Republic of China (PRC) as both desirable and inevitable. Serving from 1949 to 1951 as deputy to Dean Rusk, the assistant secretary of state for Far Eastern Affairs, Merchant shared his superior's unassuming personal style and adopted the posture of a loyal team player, a professional approach that Foreign Service personnel generally tended to favor. While both men contributed to sometimes heated debates on U.S. Asia policy, including relations with China, Japan, Korea, and Indochina, neither was strongly identified with one particular viewpoint or outlook, and both men escaped the worst of the often bitter ensuing recriminations.

As Rusk's deputy, Merchant attended many of the most crucial policy meetings on the Korean War and was privy to the highest policy debates and decisions, although he initially tended to function as an observer rather than a key participant. He handled much of the war's routine diplomacy and, as his experience grew, over time he became more involved in policy formulation and more inclined to express his personal views. As special assistant to the secretary of state on mutual security affairs (1951–1952), deputy for political affairs to the U.S. special representative in Europe (1952–1953), and assistant secretary of state for European affairs (1953–1956), Merchant dealt with the war's broader implications for U.S. defense policy. During the administration of U.S. president Dwight D. Eisenhower, Merchant's European responsibilities also imposed on him the task of representing to his superiors in the State Department, including Secretary John Foster Dulles, the strong conviction of America's European allies that the war should be brought to an early conclusion. Merchant fulfilled this charge conscientiously.

In the later 1950s Merchant rose to become undersecretary of state for political affairs, the third-highest position in the State Department. He also served two separate terms as ambassador to Canada, during 1956–1958 and 1961–1962. After his retirement in 1962, Merchant was executive director of the World Bank from 1965 to 1968. He died on May 15, 1976, in Washington, DC

PRISCILLA ROBERTS

See also

Dulles, John Foster; Jiang Jieshi; Mao Zedong; Rusk, David Dean

References

McMahon, Robert J. "Livingston T. Merchant." In *Dictionary of American Biography, Supplement Ten, 1976–1980,* edited by Kenneth T. Jackson, 528–529. New York: Scribner, 1995.

U.S. Department of State, Bureau of Public Affairs. *Foreign Relations of the United States, 1950,* Vol. 7, *Korea.* Washington, DC: U.S. Government Printing Office, 1976.

———. *Foreign Relations of the United States, 1951,* Vol. 7, *Korea and China.* Washington, DC: U.S. Government Printing Office, 1983.

———. *Foreign Relations of the United States, 1952–1954,* Vol. 15, *Korea.* Washington, DC: U.S. Government Printing Office, 1984.

Mexico

Latin American nation covering 769,000 square miles. Mexico, with a 1950 population of 28.485 million people, is bordered by the United States to the north and Guatemala and Belize to the south. Its east coast is on the Gulf of Mexico; its west coast is on the Pacific Ocean. Mexico is a federated, representative democratic republic, divided into numerous states, not unlike the United States. It has three branches of government: executive, legislative, and judicial. The president of Mexico is both head of state and government and is commander in chief of Mexican armed forces. By the mid-20th century, Mexican politics were dominated by the Institutional Revolutionary Party (PRI), although the National Action Party (PAN) had by then begun to make inroads at the federal level. Miguel Alemán Valdés of the PRI was president during most of the Korean War (until November 30, 1952); he was succeeded by

Adolfo Ruiz Cortines, who led Mexico until 1958. Cortines, too, was associated with the PRI.

From the American point of view, Mexico was the most important Latin American nation, and Washington was hoping for the same type of support during the Korean War that Mexico had provided during World War II. During that conflict, Mexico had worked closely with the United States to provide strategic materials and even labor needed for the U.S. war effort. Mexico was one of only two Latin American nations to furnish combat troops, a fighter squadron that saw action in the Pacific, during World War II. Once the war ended, Mexico wanted to maintain the close wartime economic ties to promote its own rapid industrialization but was more reluctant to maintain the close military ties. Mexico supported the Inter-American Treaty of Reciprocal Assistance signed in Rio in 1947 but was unenthusiastic—if not downright suspicious—of U.S. efforts to create closer military links in the name of hemispheric defense. Like other Latin American nations, Mexico was disenchanted with the U.S. emphasis on strategic concerns and doubted the seriousness of the communist threat to the hemisphere in general or to Mexico in particular.

After the Democratic People's Republic of Korea (DPRK, North Korea) invaded the Republic of Korea (ROK, South Korea) in June 1950, Mexico supported the U.S. position on the major resolutions relating to the war in the United Nations (UN) General Assembly and offered to provide foodstuffs and medical supplies for the conflict. The United States, however, wanted a Mexican troop commitment, hoping that this might encourage contributions from other Latin American countries. In April 1951 U.S. officials made a formal request to a Mexican delegation in Washington headed by Foreign Minister Manuel Tello that Mexico contribute a division to the fighting in Korea. Tello replied that public opinion in Mexico would not support sending Mexican troops outside of Mexican territory and reminded U.S. officials that the U.S. government had earlier agreed with Mexico's view that support for military action in Korea did not obligate Mexico to send troops there. Tello also indicated that Mexico would not be able to bear the cost of supporting a division in the field, since the United States had a policy of requiring reimbursement for any expenses incurred by the U.S. government in equipping, training, transporting, or maintaining troops of other nations in connection with Korean service. Tello particularly emphasized the problem of sending Mexican troops to Korea with presidential elections scheduled in Mexico for July 1952; the Mexican Senate would have to approve any commitment of Mexican forces outside the country, a process that would almost certainly spark a major debate over the constitutionality of such a move, in addition to raising the volatile question of national sovereignty.

Washington continued to work for a promise of Mexican troops, hoping that the growing economic ties between the two countries might produce a change in Mexico's position. The United States had granted Mexico "most-favored nation" status in trade, even though no trade agreement was in force. The United

States also backed loans to Mexico from the U.S. Export-Import Bank and the World Bank, as well as a growing program of technical assistance under the Point IV Program. Washington made a final effort to enlist Mexican military support at a meeting in Mexico City in early 1952. The United States wanted to reach an agreement with Mexico under the U.S. Mutual Security Act of 1951, which provided U.S. military assistance in exchange for a promise from the recipient country to participate in "missions important to the defense of the Western Hemisphere." Mexican officials were so nervous about the appearance of making a military commitment that the joint press release announcing the meeting put the emphasis on improving Mexico's defensive capabilities rather than on hemispheric defense.

When negotiations began in February 1952, the Mexican delegation again cited domestic political and constitutional problems that prevented the signing of a standard military assistance agreement. Negotiations quickly reached an impasse, although U.S. negotiators strung out the proceedings, fearing that an abrupt termination of the negotiations might discourage other Latin American nations from signing similar agreements. The end came when the U.S. delegation announced that it would have to return to Washington for consultation and further instructions. Mexico never signed a military assistance pact and never provided troops for UN operations in Korea.

While the United States unsuccessfully attempted to gain Mexico's military support, Mexico continued to provide diplomatic support for U.S. efforts. One of the most important developments in this area was Mexico's proposal in the UN aimed at breaking the deadlock over the repatriation of prisoners of war (POWs), which had become the single biggest obstacle to an armistice. On September 2, 1952, Mexico's permanent representative to the UN, Luis Padilla Nervo, presented a letter to UN Secretary-General Trygve Lie containing a proposal from Mexican president Miguel Alemán.

Alemán's plan was later offered as a draft resolution in the General Assembly on November 1, 1952. The plan recognized the principle of voluntary repatriation, which had been supported by the United States. The difficult question of what to do with those refusing repatriation would be handled by granting them temporary asylum with any UN member agreeing to the proposal. Those refusing repatriation would be given immigrant status and allowed to seek employment. Those who originally refused repatriation but later changed their minds would be returned to their home countries under UN auspices. The United States originally welcomed the proposal but later backed a proposal by the Indian delegation and suggested to Padilla Nervo that any action be deferred. Alemán's proposal was never voted on by the General Assembly, but its submission did help promote an eventual resolution of the POW controversy.

Although Mexico never provided the kind of military support that the United States thought appropriate, it did provide important economic and diplomatic support for the goals being pursued by the United States and the UN in Korea. It was perhaps unrealistic for U.S. officials to expect that Mexico would make a larger military contribution (a division) to the Korean War, a conflict that Mexico considered both distant and nonthreatening, than it had in World War II, when a much more obvious and immediate military threat was present. Mexico had also undergone a lengthy process of reducing military influence in politics; Mexican politicians feared that military involvement in Korea ran the risk of returning the military to politics with a larger portion of the national budget.

Don M. Coerver

See also

Colombia; Latin America; Padilla Nervo, Luis; Peruvian Prisoner of War Settlement Proposal; Repatriation, Voluntary

References

Langley, Lester. *Mexico and the United States: The Fragile Relationship.* Boston: Twayne, 1991.

Parkinson, F. *Latin America, the Cold War, and the World Powers, 1945–1973.* Beverly Hills, CA: Sage, 1974.

U.S. Department of State, Bureau of Public Affairs. *Foreign Relations of the United States, 1950,* Vol. 7, *Korea.* Washington, DC: U.S. Government Printing Office, 1976.

———. *Foreign Relations of the United States, 1951,* Vol. 2. Washington, DC: U.S. Government Printing Office, 1979.

———. *Foreign Relations of the United States, 1952–1954,* Vol. 4. Washington, DC: U.S. Government Printing Office, 1984.

———. *Foreign Relations of the United States, 1952–1954,* Vol. 15, *Korea.* Washington, DC: U.S. Government Printing Office, 1984.

Meyer, Clarence Earle
Birth Date: August 14, 1891
Death Date: March 15, 1965

U.S. oil company executive and economic mediator in Korea. Born on August 14, 1891, in East Ashford, New York, Clarence Earle Meyer graduated from Syracuse University in 1913. He began his career with the Standard Oil Company, marketing petroleum products in China. He then worked in the company's Hong Kong office when Standard Oil Company merged with its competitor, the Vacuum Oil Company, to create first the Socony-Vacuum Oil Corporation and then, in 1933, the Standard Vacuum Oil Company. The next year Meyer was named general manager of the Standard-Vacuum Oil Company in Japan. He was imprisoned there for seven months in solitary confinement after the United States declared war on Japan following the Japanese attack on Pearl Harbor in December 1941.

After his repatriation in 1942, Meyer was the petroleum attaché at the U.S. embassy in London. Three years later he returned to the United States to serve as director of the Standard-Vacuum Oil Company. He was vice president in charge of the company's business in China and Japan from 1946 to 1950. Meyer was also director of the Far East–American Council of Commerce and Industry from 1945 to 1950. He retired from business in 1950 and began a

U.S. businessman Clarence E. Meyer during April–May 1952 led a mission to South Korea to help resolve exchange rate issues between the United States and the Republic of Korea. (Bettmann/Corbis)

seven-year U.S. government career, especially assisting the State Department with financial matters. Meyer was chief of missions for the U.S. Economic Cooperation Administration in Vienna, Austria, and for the Mutual Security Agency in the Far East.

During the Korean War President Harry S. Truman appointed Meyer director of a presidential mission in April and May 1952 to resolve exchange rate issues between the United Nations Command (UNC) and the Republic of Korea (ROK, South Korea). The South Korean government had advanced Korea's currency, the won, to the UNC to finance military operations during the war. By February 1952 a dispute about the currency exchange rate had escalated into what was called the Suspense Account Controversy.

South Korea suffered extremely high wartime inflation, with prices in early 1952 reaching almost 40 times the 1947 level. The South Korean government balanced its budget and tightened credit, believing that advancing currency to the United Nations (UN) forces was the primary cause of inflation. The Koreans wanted to settle won advances, amounting to $70 million, to prevent hyperinflation. The ROK government hoped to keep the conversion rate at 6,000 won to $1 and expressed disfavor with the UNC's joint control of Korea's foreign reserves. The United States argued that it needed the $70 million of advances to use after the war for the rehabilitation of Korea and that the conversion rate should be 10,000 to 1. South Korea did not want to permit the UNC

to control Korea's foreign exchange. It also demanded that all won advances be settled quickly so that Korea would have funds to buy imports to sell to Koreans. The resulting profits would be taken out of circulation in an effort to stop inflation.

UNC commander Lieutenant General Matthew B. Ridgway was determined to stop UNC spending of won and suggested that President Truman send a special mission to help improve economic relations between Korea and the United States. Meyer led what became known as the Meyer Mission in the spring of 1952 to negotiate with South Korea. Its primary goal was to work with the ROK to stabilize the South Korean economy through improved use of U.S. economic aid and application of anti-inflationary measures. The mission also sought decisive debate about how to reimburse the Korean government and establish the rate of exchange regarding advances of won to UNC forces.

On May 24, 1952, Meyer secured the Agreement on Economic Coordination, which promised to settle won advances made since January 1952. Claims made during the first 18 months of the war were delayed for settlement until after March 31, 1953. The UNC promised to repay South Korea all won that had been sold to UN troops from January 1952 to May 1952 at the rate of 6,000 to 1. Outstanding won balances drawn after June 1, 1952, were to be settled at an agreeable conversion rate. The UNC would also pay $4 million monthly to South Korea to apply against the settlement.

These payments helped to slow inflation. Meyer and the Korean government representatives also created the Combined Economic Board. Consisting of ROK and UNC representatives, this board strove to coordinate South Korean foreign exchange to stabilize finances and reconstruct the postwar Korean economy.

Meyer's expertise in Asian business matters helped ensure the successful conclusion of the agreement. By June 1953 Prime Minister Paek Tu Jin, formerly the ROK finance minister, visited the United States seeking future economic aid. During the course of his stay, he noted that the Meyer Mission had satisfactorily resolved the currency exchange issue and that it was no longer a problem.

Following the Korean War assignment, Meyer was a member of missions to the Far East for the U.S. International Cooperation Administration. He was director of economic aid and chief of economic affairs at the U.S. embassy in Tokyo through 1957. Meyer also performed economic evaluations for the U.S. Department of State in Taiwan, the Philippines, and Honduras and worked for the Standard Oil Company in Australia. He won awards for public service and was president of the Japan-American Society in 1960. Meyer died on March 15, 1965, in Washington, DC

ELIZABETH D. SCHAFER

See also

Korea, Republic of, 1947–1953; Meyer Mission; Paek Tu Jin; Truman, Harry S.; U.S. Policy toward Korea, 1950–1953

References

National Cyclopedia of American Biography, Vol. 51. New York: James T. White, 1969.

U.S. Department of State, Bureau of Public Affairs. *Foreign Relations of the United States, 1950,* Vol. 7, *Korea.* Washington, DC: U.S. Government Printing Office, 1976.

———. *Foreign Relations of the United States, 1952–1954,* Vol. 15, *Korea.* Washington, DC: U.S. Government Printing Office, 1984.

Who Was Who in America, 1951–1960. Chicago: Marquis, 1963.

Meyer Mission

Start Date: April 10, 1952
End Date: May 24, 1952

U.S. mission to the Republic of Korea (ROK, South Korea) to deal with financial and currency exchange concerns. On April 10, 1952, President Harry S. Truman appointed Economic Cooperation Administration official Clarence E. Meyer as the head of a special mission to South Korea. The objective of the mission was to reach an agreement with Seoul "on measures which would promote the stability of the Korean economy and facilitate the military operations of the United Nations Command in Korea." Meyer was also to work out appropriate arrangements for control and coordination of the foreign exchange resources in South Korea.

In the spring of 1951 South Korea was experiencing massive inflation. The Seoul government saw the advances of its currency, the won, for use by United Nations (UN) forces as the basic cause of inflation. The government recommended immediate and full settlement of outstanding won advances ($70 million) to pay for imports, which could then be sold to Koreans. South Korea was also determined to keep the artificial current conversion rate of won to dollars (6,000 to 1) for future transactions.

U.S. officials believed that the $70 million advance would be inefficient because of the instability of the Korean economy. Instead of "premature reconstruction and development," they suggested using the amount after the war for basic rehabilitation. In his report to Washington, Meyer emphasized that South Korea should make every effort to utilize its earnings of foreign exchange to achieve the maximum counterinflationary effect.

The agreement concluding the Meyer Mission provided for the establishment of a combined economic board composed of one representative each from South Korea and the United Nations Command (UNC). The board's recommendations were directed toward the development of a program designed to provide maximum support to the UNC military effort in Korea, to relieve the hardships of the Korean people, and to develop a stable Korean economy. The board also was to coordinate all foreign currency exchange in South Korea.

The agreement provided for a schedule of monetary adjustments in South Korea. Government experts in Washington concurred that the current won-to-dollar rate of 6,000 to 1 was unrealistic and should be at least 10,000 to 1. Under the terms of the agreement, the UNC agreed to repay to South Korea all won sold to UN troops at the 6,000-to-1 rate for the period January–May 1952.

Thereafter the UNC agreed to pay $4 million per month on account to be applied in settlement for Korean currency used by its forces. In addition, as soon as practicable after March 31, 1953, the UNC was to make full and final settlement at realistic conversion rates for any won used by UNC forces between June 1, 1952, and March 31, 1953.

The South Korean government used these foreign exchange payments with some success to curb inflation. However, while the agreement provided for certain responsibilities of the board in economic coordination and reconstruction, in practice the organization concentrated its efforts primarily on the financial relations between the UNC and South Korea.

ZSOLT VARGA

See also

Meyer, Clarence Earle; Truman, Harry S.; United Nations Korean Reconstruction Agency

References

U.S. Department of State, Bureau of Public Affairs. *Foreign Relations of the United States, 1950,* Vol. 7, *Korea.* Washington, DC: U.S. Government Printing Office, 1976.

———. *Foreign Relations of the United States, 1952–1954,* Vol. 15, *Korea.* Washington, DC: U.S. Government Printing Office, 1984.

Michaelis, John Hersey

Birth Date: August 21, 1912
Death Date: October 31, 1985

U.S. Army officer, commander of the 27th Infantry Regiment during the Korean War. His superb leadership made the 27th the best-known U.S. command of the Korean War and earned Michaelis two battlefield promotions. Born at the Presidio of San Francisco, California, on August 21, 1912, John Hersey ("Mike") Michaelis attended grammar and high school in Lancaster, Pennsylvania. He then served in the army for a year before being appointed to the U.S. Military Academy at West Point.

Graduating in 1936, Michaelis was commissioned in the infantry and assigned to Fort Thomas, Kentucky. Tours of duty in the Philippines and Fort Benning, Georgia, followed. During World War II Michaelis served with the 502nd Parachute Infantry Regiment, 101st Airborne Division. When the regimental commander broke his leg and became incapacitated, division commander Major General Maxwell D. Taylor appointed the 32-year-old Michaelis to the command. Michaelis was severely wounded in Holland; after he returned from the hospital, during the Battle of the Bulge, Taylor secured his promotion to full colonel and made him division chief of staff.

After the war Michaelis, along with a number of other young temporary colonels, was reduced in rank to lieutenant colonel. Michaelis served in the Pentagon from 1945 to 1948, the last two years as senior aide to Chief of Staff and General of the Army

Dwight D. Eisenhower. Eisenhower rated him as one of four lieutenant colonels "of extraordinary ability."

Michaelis was then assigned to Eighth Army headquarters in Japan. At the beginning of the Korean War he received command of the 27th Infantry Regiment as it arrived in Korea. His leadership of that regiment earned Michaelis and the 27th an enviable combat reputation. Known to many in the regiment as "Iron Mike," Michaelis was soon promoted to colonel and, in February 1951, to brigadier general and assistant commander of the 25th Infantry Division. At age 38, he was the youngest general in the U.S. Army.

In early May 1951 Michaelis left Korea. The next year he became commandant of cadets at West Point. Subsequent assignments included commanding general, U.S. Army Alaska; V Corps; Allied Land Forces, Southeast Europe; and U.S. Fifth Army. From 1969 until his retirement as a full (four-star) general in 1972, Michealis served as commander in chief, United Nations Command (UNC), U.S. Forces, Korea and U.S. Eighth Army.

Michaelis retired to St. Petersburg, Florida. He died on October 31, 1985, of a heart attack at his summer home in Dillard, Georgia.

UZAL W. ENT

See also

Eisenhower, Dwight David; Taylor, Maxwell Davenport

References

Assembly: Association of Graduates, United States Military Academy. July 1989.

Blair, Clay. *The Forgotten War: America in Korea, 1950–1953.* New York: Times Books, 1987.

MIG, **Operation**
Event Date: July 1951

United Nations Command (UNC) effort to secure a Mikoyan-Gurevich MiG-15 aircraft. The swept-wing MiG-15, which made its combat debut in Korea in November 1950, quickly demonstrated its superiority over the straight-winged U.S. fighters in action at that time. It was also a match for the North American F-86 Sabre brought in specifically to counter it.

The MiG not only posed a threat to UNC bombing operations in North Korea, but also to U.S. bombers in the event of a war with the Soviet Union. Because so little was known in the West about the MiG, efforts were made to try and capture one to study its characteristics. The U.S. Far East Air Force (FEAF) formed a special guerrilla unit specifically to secure MiG parts, which it obtained in crashes. In April 1951 a technical team landed by helicopter to inspect a wreck. They blew the MiG-15 apart with grenades to secure some of the pieces but were soon driven off. The same month U.S. Navy units searched unsuccessfully for a MiG that had crashed at sea near the mouth of the Yalu River.

On July 9, 1951, a communist pilot ejected from a MiG northwest of Pyongyang. His aircraft continued out to sea and crashed on a sandbar off Sinmi-do in the Yalu Gulf. Operation MIG was the effort to capture that downed aircraft. It included the British aircraft carrier *Eagle* and cruiser *Birmingham,* Republic of Korea Navy (ROKN, South Korean Navy) small craft, and a lifting barge procured in Japan. On July 20–21, under cover of bombardment, the MiG was lifted off and taken to Pusan. It was then transported for evaluation to Wright-Patterson Air Force Base in Ohio, where it provided information on both engine performance and airframe.

The air force remained anxious to secure an undamaged MiG for combat evaluation, and in Operation MOOLAH, it offered cash incentives toward that end. No MiG was obtained until after the armistice, however, when Korean People's Army (KPA, North Korean Army) pilot No Kum Sok defected with his aircraft to Kimpo Airfield in the Republic of Korea (ROK, South Korea). He said he had not been aware of the financial incentive.

Although the MiG-15 and F-86 aircraft may have been well matched in characteristics, ultimately UNC command pilots made the difference over their communist counterparts, and F-86 Sabres eventually compiled an impressive 7:1 victory ratio over their MiG-15 opponents.

SPENCER C. TUCKER

See also

Aircraft; MiG Alley; MOOLAH, Operation

References

Bruning, John R. *Crimson Sky: The Air Battle for Korea.* Dulles, VA: Brassey's, 1999.

Futrell, Robert F. *The United States Air Force in Korea, 1950–1953.* Rev. ed. Washington, DC: Office of the Chief of Air Force History, 1983.

MacDonald, Callum. *Korea: The War before Vietnam.* New York: Free Press, 1987.

Matray, James I., ed. *Historical Dictionary of the Korean War.* Westport, CT: Greenwood, 1991.

No, Kum Sok, with J. Roger Osterholm. *A MiG-15 to Freedom: Memoir of the Wartime North Korean Defector Who First Delivered the Secret Fighter Jet to the Americans in 1953.* Jefferson, NC: McFarland, 1996.

Schuetta, Laurence V. *Guerrilla Warfare and Airpower in Korea, 1950–1953.* Montgomery, AL: Aerospace Studies Institute, Air University, 1964.

MiG Alley

A 6,500-square-mile airspace in northwest Korea, site of the most intense jet aircraft combat throughout the Korean War. In early 1950 the communists established a MiG-15 base at the Manchurian border city of Dandong (Antung) to guard vital railroad bridges over the adjacent Yalu River. On November 8, 1950, the first jet-versus-jet combat resulted in the downing of a Soviet-built Mikoyan-Gurevich MiG-15 by a U.S. Lockheed F-80 Shooting Star. MiG Alley quickly evolved as a testing ground for new jet tactics as U.S., Soviet, and Chinese pilots pitted their skills and aircraft against one another. Russian and Chinese MiG-15 pilots enjoyed a number of advantages over their United Nations Command

AREAS OF MiG-15 OPERATIONS

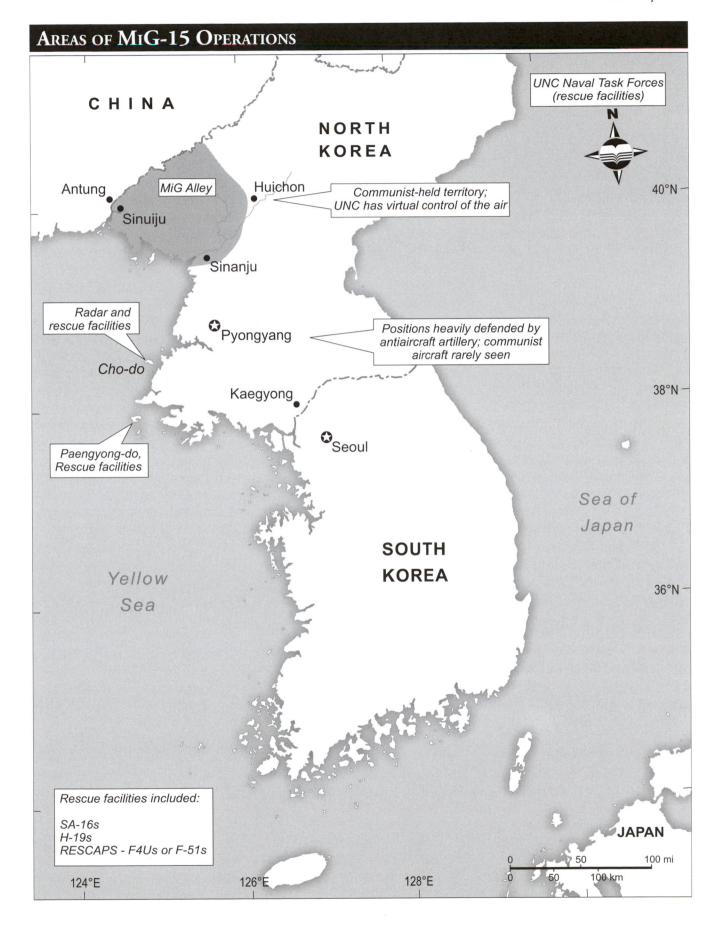

CHINA

NORTH KOREA

UNC Naval Task Forces (rescue facilities)

N

Antung   *MiG Alley*   Huichon   Communist-held territory; UNC has virtual control of the air

Sinuiju

40°N

Sinanju

Radar and rescue facilities

Pyongyang   Positions heavily defended by antiaircraft artillery; communist aircraft rarely seen

Cho-do

Kaegyong   38°N

Paengyong-do, Rescue facilities

Seoul

Sea of Japan

Yellow Sea

SOUTH KOREA

36°N

Rescue facilities included:

SA-16s
H-19s
RESCAPS - F4Us or F-51s

JAPAN

0   50   100 mi
0   50   100 km

124°E   126°E   128°E

(UNC) counterparts. The MiG-15 was superior in some respects to the North American F-86 Sabre, the most advanced U.S. fighter. Moreover, United Nations (UN) pilots, based below the 38th Parallel, were fighting over hostile territory and were severely limited in operational time over the Alley.

Typically, U.S. pilots were more aggressive and better trained and had often honed their combat skills in World War II. In contrast, communist pilots exhibited a wide diversity of combat effectiveness. Skilled MiG pilots, or "honchos" in U.S. pilot parlance, won grudging respect as dangerous opponents, whereas novice communist pilots, exhibiting little training, earned the derisive label of "nimwit."

As the war progressed, U.S. MiG Combat Air Patrols (MIGCAPS) effectively countered such communist tactics as southbound "trains" of up to 80 MiGs each. On July 22, 1953, the last jet combat in MiG Alley ended when Sabre pilot Lieutenant Sam P. Young scored his first kill, a MiG-15.

JEFF KINARD

See also

Aircraft; Jet Aircraft, First Manned Clash in History

References

Bruning, John R. *Crimson Sky: The Air Battle for Korea.* Dulles, VA: Brassey's, 1999.

Crane, Conrad C. *American Air Power Strategy in Korea, 1950–1953.* Lawrence: University Press of Kansas, 1999.

Futrell, Robert F. *The United States Air Force in Korea, 1950–1953.* Rev. ed. Washington, DC: Office of the Chief of Air Force History, 1983.

Sherwood, John Darrell. *Officers in Flight Suits: The Story of American Air Force Fighter Pilots in the Korean War.* New York: New York University Press, 1996.

Werrell, Kenneth P. *Sabres over MiG Alley: The F-86 and the Battle for Air Superiority in Korea.* Annapolis, MD: Naval Institute Press, 2005.

U.S. Army lieutenant general Frank William Milburn commanded I Corps during its breakout from the Pusan Perimeter in September 1950. (Bettmann/Corbis)

Milburn, Frank William
Birth Date: January 11, 1892
Death Date: October 25, 1962

U.S. Army general and commander of the U.S. I Corps during the Korean War. Born on January 11, 1892, in Jasper, Indiana, Frank William Milburn graduated from the U.S. Military Academy at West Point and was commissioned a second lieutenant of infantry in June 1914. Between 1914 and 1918 he served with the 5th, 33rd, and 15th Infantry regiments in the Panama Canal Zone. He then returned to the United States for duty at Camp Beauregard, Louisiana.

In the immediate post–World War I period, Milburn served with the 5th Infantry at Camp Zachary Taylor, Kentucky, and with the 28th Infantry at Camp Dix, New Jersey; attended the Infantry School at Fort Benning, Georgia; and was assigned to the student officer training camp at Plattsburg Barracks, New York. He also served as an instructor at the Infantry School at Fort Benning,

Georgia, from 1922 to 1926, after which he was the professor of military science and tactics of the Reserve Officer Training Corps at the University of Montana, where he was also football coach. He then attended the two-year course at the Army Command and General Staff School at Fort Leavenworth, Kansas, graduating in 1933. He was assigned briefly to Fort Sheridan, Illinois, as post adjutant and executive officer of the 12th Brigade.

Milburn subsequently returned to Fort Leavenworth, where he was an instructor at the Command and General Staff School from 1934 to 1938. After service with the 29th Infantry at Fort Benning, Milburn became plans and operations officer of the 8th Infantry Division at Fort Jackson, South Carolina, in July 1940. In May 1941 he was reassigned to duty as a regimental commander with the 6th Infantry Division at Fort Leonard Wood, Missouri.

Having been promoted to brigadier general in February 1942, Milburn assumed command of the 83rd Infantry Division at Camp Breckinridge, Kentucky, in August 1942. He was promoted to major general the next month, and in December 1943 he assumed command of XXI Corps at Camp Polk, Louisiana. In October 1944 Milburn took XXI Corps to Europe and commanded it in operations there until July 1945, when he became the acting commander of the U.S. Seventh Army. In September 1945 he briefly commanded the XXIII Corps in Europe, and that November he returned to the United States to command V Corps at Fort Jackson. Milburn returned to Europe in May 1946 as commanding general of the 1st Infantry Division. Following his promotion to lieutenant general, Milburn became acting commander of the U.S. Army Europe (USAREUR) in June 1949, and two months later he was officially assigned as deputy commander of USAREUR, a position in which he served until 1950.

On August 10, 1950, IX Corps was activated at Fort Sheridan, Illinois, and Milburn was assigned to command it. With a small group of staff officers, he left Fort Sheridan for Korea by air on September 5, 1950. On September 11 commander of the U.S. Eighth Army in Korea (EUSAK) General Lieutenant Walton H. Walker reassigned Milburn to command I Corps at Taegu for the breakout from the Pusan Perimeter. When Walker was killed in an automobile accident near Uijongbu on December 23, 1950, Milburn assumed command of the Eighth Army until the arrival of Lieutenant General Matthew B. Ridgway on December 25.

Milburn subsequently commanded I Corps, consisting of the 3rd and 24th U.S. Infantry divisions, the 1st Republic of Korea Army (ROKA) Infantry Division, the Turkish Brigade, and the British 29th Infantry Brigade. He commanded forces in the drive north toward the Yalu River, the capture of Pyongyang, and the Battle of Chongchon River, as well as during the subsequent withdrawal of United Nations (UN) forces from North Korea in November–December 1950. He then led the I Corps in the defense against the communist 1951 spring offensive and the subsequent UN counteroffensive.

Milburn retired from active duty in April 1952. He was then athletics director at Montana State University in Missoula, Montana, until 1954. He died in Missoula on October 25, 1962.

CHARLES R. SHRADER

See also

Ridgway, Matthew Bunker; Walker, Walton Harris

References

Ancell, R. Manning, and Christine M. Miller. *The Biographical Dictionary of World War II: Generals and Flag Officers—The U.S. Armed Forces.* Westport, CT: Greenwood, 1996.

Appleman, Roy E. *United States Army in Korea: South to the Naktong, North to the Yalu.* Washington, DC: Office of the Chief of Military History, 1961.

Matray, James I., ed. *Historical Dictionary of the Korean War.* Westport, CT: Greenwood, 1991.

Schnabel, James F. *United States Army in the Korean War: Policy and Direction, the First Year.* Washington, DC: Office of the Chief of Military History, Department of the Army, 1972.

Military Air Transport Service

Primary organization furnishing air transportation for the U.S. armed forces. The Military Air Transport Service (MATS) was created on June 1, 1948, by a merger of the Air Transport Command (ATC) and the Naval Air Transport Service (NATS). MATS

A U.S. Air Force C-119 Flying Boxcar provided by the Military Air Transport Service (MATS) prepares to transport paratroopers to Korea from southern Japan on July 2, 1953. MATS was the primary organization furnishing air transportation for the U.S. armed forces during the Korean War. (National Archives)

was placed under the command and direction of the chief of staff of the U.S. Air Force (USAF), with the consent of the secretary of defense. The commander was either an air force or navy officer. MATS's primary responsibility was to provide air transportation for all departments and agencies of the Department of Defense and for other government agencies as authorized.

General Henry H. Arnold, then commander of the U.S. Army Air Corps (renamed U.S. Army Air Forces [USAAF] on June 22, 1941), created the first U.S. military air transport unit, the Air Corps Ferrying Command (ACFC), in May 1941, primarily to dispatch Lend-Lease aircraft to Great Britain. By 1942 it had flown almost 1,350 aircraft to Britain. Following the December 1941 Japanese attack on Pearl Harbor, ACFC missions were expanded, and air routes to the various theaters of war were developed to systematize the U.S. transport system. At the same time, new models of transport aircraft, which had more payload and range, were purchased. These included the Curtiss-Wright C-46 Commando, the Douglas C-47 Skytrain (Dakota), and later the Douglas C-54 Skymaster.

In July 1942 USAAF officials changed ACFC's designation to ATC. Commanded by Major General William H. Tunner, ATC had one of its greatest successes with the resupply of China from India beginning in December 1942. This operation was called "Flying the Hump" by its pilots because the routes crossed the perilous Himalayan Mountains. ATC aircraft delivered 650,000 tons of supplies to beleaguered Guomindang (GMD, Nationalist) Chinese forces holed up in Chongqing (Chungking).

U.S. Air Force Transport Aircraft Specifications

Aircraft	Span	Length	Height	Gross Weight (pounds)	Top Speed (mph)	Range (miles)	Ceiling (feet)
Curtiss C-46	108' 1"	76' 4"	21' 9"	56,000	269	1,200	27,600
Douglas C-47	95' 6"	63' 9"	17' 0"	26,000	230	1,600	24,000
Douglas C-54	117' 6"	93' 10"	27' 6"	62,000	265	2,000	22,000
Douglas C-124	173' 3"	127' 2"	48' 3"	175,000	298	6,280	22,050
Fairchild C-119	109' 3"	86' 6"	26' 6"	72,700	281	1,630	21,580

In June 1948, when the Department of Defense formed MATS, it charged the new organization to manage all strategic airlifts. To accomplish this, four squadrons were created under MATS: Naval Air Transport Service; Air Weather Service; Air Rescue Service; and Airways and Air Communications Service.

The first big challenge for MATS after World War II was the Soviet blockade of Berlin, which began less than a month after MATS was formed. By September 1949 the blockade had been broken by General Tunner and his crews, who flew nearly 1.8 million (of the total 2.35 million) tons of supplies to West Berlin during Operation VITTLES.

Just nine months later, the Korean War began. This time MATS operated a strategic logistics and supply pipeline of nearly 11,000 air miles from the United States to Japan to Korea. In nearly three years, MATS delivered 80,000 tons of cargo and 214,000 combat troops and support personnel to the Korean Theater of Operations. Air Rescue Service personnel saved hundreds of pilots and crews who were able to ditch or parachute off the Korean coast and many who bailed out over land, some in enemy territory. Last but not least, the subsequent aeromedical evacuation airlift returned more than 65,000 wounded personnel to the United States.

Major General Tunner commanded in-theater airlift, cargo, and transport assets from August 26, 1950, to February 8, 1951. Officially, he commanded the Far East Air Forces (FEAF) Combat Cargo Command (Provisional) and 315th Air Division (Combat Cargo). He had actually arrived in July 1950 to take charge of airlifting United Nations (UN) and U.S. troops and supply assets to Korea with about 250 mostly Fairchild C-119 Flying Boxcars (some C-46s, C-47s, and C-54s as well) scraped together by air force chief of staff General Hoyt Vandenberg in an effort to stem the Korean People's Army (KPA, North Korean Army) advance. Among the first units airlifted to Korea were the 187th Airborne Regiment of the 101st Airborne Division and portions of the 1st Marine Division.

One of the biggest early airlift assignments for MATS and FEAF Combat Cargo Command was the evacuation of U.S. citizens (including many civilian dependents) out of the Republic of Korea (ROK, South Korea) to Japan. The success of ferrying civilians out and troops in helped solidify the Pusan Perimeter and allowed General Douglas MacArthur to execute his daring Inchon Landing in September 1950. The ability of MATS and other airlift personnel to rapidly deploy vital men and materials to Korea throughout the war proved decisive in stemming the North Korean advance in 1950 and ultimately preserved the ROK.

Following the Korean War, Tunner and others pushed for larger and more technologically advanced cargo/transport aircraft. In the 1950s this push led to the development and deployment of propeller-driven cargo aircraft such as the Douglas C-124 Globemaster II, Lockheed C-130 Hercules (mostly for tactical airlift), and Douglas C-133 Cargomaster. Clearly, the workhorse of this era was the C-124, known to pilots in Korea who flew it as the "Crowd Killer."

The 1960s saw the development of the first strategic jet airlift aircraft, the C-141 Starlifter. Entering the inventory in 1965, the Lockheed C-141 (modified to be the "B" model in the 1970s and 1980s) and its much larger sister jet "trash hauler," the Lockheed C-5 Galaxy (in service in 1969), proved particularly effective in providing strategic airlift support to such theaters of operation as Southeast Asia and the Persian Gulf.

In 1966 Congress recognized how important strategic airlift had become. As a result, it redesignated MATS as the Military Airlift Command, headquartered at Scott Air Force Base, Illinois. Military Airlift Command was placed on the same level as other air force combat elements such as the Tactical Air Command and Strategic Air Command. In 1992, after the Persian Gulf War, in the air force's general reorganization, the command's designation was changed to Air Mobility Command.

WILLIAM HEAD

See also

Aircraft; MacArthur, Douglas; Military Sea Transport Service; Vandenberg, Hoyt Sanford

References

Futrell, Robert F. *The United States Air Force in Korea, 1950–1953*. Rev. ed. Washington, DC: Office of the Chief of Air Force History, 1983.

Thompson, Wayne. "The Air War over Korea." In *Winged Shield, Wing Sword: A History of the United States Air Force*, edited by Bernard C. Nalty, 3–52. Washington, DC: U.S. Air Force History and Museum Program, 1997.

Tunner, William H. *Over the Hump*. Reprint. Washington, DC: Office of Air Force History, 1985.

Military Armistice Commission

Commission to supervise the implementation of the July 17, 1953, Korean Armistice Agreement, to monitor activity and investigate armistice violations inside the Demilitarized Zone (DMZ) and the Han River Estuary, to negotiate the settlement of armistice violations, and to act as a channel of communication between the two sides. In the months immediately after the signing of the Armistice Agreement, the Military Armistice Commission (MAC) also supervised the activities of the Neutral Nations Repatriation Commission, the Committee for Repatriation of Prisoners of War, and the Committee for Assisting the Return of Displaced Civilians.

During the truce talks, both sides quickly agreed on the need for a military armistice commission with equal representation from both sides, but they differed as to the nature and scope of its activities. The United Nations Command (UNC) sought to establish a supervisory mechanism with the power of inspection throughout Korea in order to verify and enforce armistice compliance and to prevent a military buildup. The Korean People's Army (KPA, North Korean Army)–Chinese People's Volunteer Army (CPVA, Chinese Army) side accepted the idea of armistice supervision inside the DMZ, but rejected the notion of MAC inspections in the Democratic People's Republic of Korea (DPRK, North Korea) outside the DMZ. When, after months of negotiations, the UNC accepted a KPA-CPVA proposal for inspections outside the DMZ by teams of neutral nations, the way was clear for agreement on the composition and functions of the MAC. The commanders of the opposing sides would be solely responsible for enforcement of and compliance with the armistice. The MAC would supervise the armistice inside the DMZ, while the Neutral Nations Supervisory Commission would carry out inspections and conduct investigations outside the DMZ and report its findings to the MAC.

The MAC consisted of five members from each side, at least three of whom had to be general or flag officers. It was a joint organization with no chairman and would meet at the call of either side to discuss charges of armistice violations and other armistice-related matters. Each side's component of the MAC was authorized to have "staff assistants" and a secretariat to perform administrative functions. In addition, the armistice provided for 10 Joint Observer Teams (JOTs), reduced to 5 teams in 1955, each composed of two to three field-grade officers from each side plus additional support personnel. The MAC could dispatch these JOTs to the DMZ or the Han River Estuary to investigate alleged armistice violations.

The commission held its first meeting on July 28, 1953, the day after the Armistice Agreement was signed. Its early work consisted of supervising the withdrawal of military forces from the DMZ, overseeing the repatriation of prisoners of war (POWs) and the remains of war dead, delineating the MAC Headquarters Area, and establishing procedural rules for the operation of the MAC and its subordinate organizations. These matters were easily settled, but the commission proved entirely unable to adjudicate armistice violations. Nor were the JOTs able to reach agreement on the circumstances of the alleged violations they investigated. After 1967 the KPA-CPVA rejected all further UNC proposals for JOT investigations. The last official JOT action, conducted in 1976, surveyed and delineated the boundary between the two sides in

the Panmunjom conference area following a clash between the guard forces in which two UNC officers were killed by KPA guards.

Although most MAC activity consisted of unproductive allegations and denials, the commission did some useful work. Serious incidents could be defused at MAC meetings; noncontroversial administrative actions, such as the return of remains, were often carried out in a businesslike and nonconfrontational manner; and the commission was a useful channel of communication. Beginning in 1971, the governments of North Korea and the Republic of Korea (ROK, South Korea) also found it convenient to use the MAC conference facilities to carry out dialogue.

From 1953 to 1991 the UNC senior member was a U.S. officer. When the UNC appointed a South Korean major general from the Republic of Korea (ROK, South Korea) as senior member in 1991, the KPA rejected his credentials and refused to attend further MAC meetings. In 1994 the KPA unilaterally withdrew from the MAC, but it continued to maintain a negotiating organization at Panmunjom under the title "Korean People's Army Panmunjom Mission." Later that year, the Chinese government recalled the CPVA MAC delegation.

Despite these changes, much of the administrative and communications work of the MAC continues, and talks below the plenary level still take place from time to time. In this manner the last vestiges of the MAC continue to operate.

Donald W. Boose Jr.

See also

Agenda Controversy; Armistice Agreement; Demilitarized Zone; Kaesong Truce Talks; Neutral Nations Repatriation Commission; Neutral Nations Supervisory Commission; Truce Talks

References

Hermes, Walter G. *U.S. Army in the Korean War: Truce Tent and Fighting Front*. Washington, DC: Office of the Chief of Military History, 1966.

U.S. Department of State, Bureau of Public Affairs. *Foreign Relations of the United States, 1951*, Vol. 7, *China and Korea*. Washington, DC: U.S. Government Printing Office, 1983.

Wilhelm, Alfred D., Jr. *The Chinese at the Negotiating Table*. Washington, DC: National Defense University Press, 1996.

Military-Industrial Complex

An interlocking alliance among the U.S. military establishment, defense industries, and research-oriented universities that during the Cold War created a separate, stand-alone economy dedicated to national security imperatives. President Dwight D. Eisenhower, in his farewell address of January 1961, was perhaps the first public official to warn the public about the dangers of the burgeoning military-industrial complex, thereby raising awareness of a process that had begun in earnest a decade before, during the Korean War. Indeed, Eisenhower helped popularize the term "military-industrial complex."

Eisenhower, like others who worried about this phenomenon, feared that the military-industrial complex had the potential to wield great power by absorbing vast amounts of the nation's resources, granting undue influence to nonelected government bureaucrats and corporate executives, and perhaps subverting the democratic process as a result. Eisenhower's warning was in fact somewhat ironic, considering that his administration had been instrumental in the growth of the complex.

The military-industrial complex arose in the early 1950s in response to the needs of both the Cold War and the Korean War. In America's fight against communism, resources had to be harnessed to develop new military and defense technologies. Much of the research for these endeavors was conducted at large research-intensive universities. The Massachusetts Institute of Technology (MIT) and Stanford University were among the top research schools in these areas. Defense-oriented industries often provided much of the capital and additional resources to fund research and development. In turn, these companies were usually rewarded with sizable government contracts to produce military hardware and weapons systems, many of which had originated in university laboratories. In almost every case, both university and industrial research and development (R&D) was initiated by the U.S. Department of Defense. Thus, a tightly connected military-industrial-academic reciprocal relationship was created.

The Cold War military-industrial complex was born out of the decision by President Harry S. Truman's administration to engage the United States in a massive military rearmament program after the outbreak of the Korean War in June 1950. Between 1950 and 1953, the U.S. defense budget increased almost fourfold, from $13.5 billion in 1950 to more than $52 billion in 1953. The vast majority of those funds, however, did not go to the war in Korea, but instead were earmarked for long-term rearmament programs designed to keep the United States one step ahead of its Cold War rival, the Soviet Union.

Even after Eisenhower tried to rein in defense spending in the mid-1950s, the defense budget fell only slightly and certainly remained at least three times as high as the pre–Korean War level. The Korean rearmament program essentially gave teeth to the National Security Council's seminal NSC-68 report of early 1950, which envisioned a huge military buildup.

Pivotal in fueling the military-industrial complex was the late-1950 decision to create a permanent U.S. industrial base that would provide the United States with excess industrial capacity that could swing into high gear at the first sign of war. Such a decision resulted in the government-sponsored construction of a military-oriented industrial sector that was of little use for civilian applications.

It is important to note that Eisenhower was not against the military, big industry, or academia. In fact, he was a proponent of all. As a five-star army general, he appointed mostly businessmen and industrialists to his cabinet, and he briefly served as president of Columbia University. He was also supportive of the scientific community, establishing the new post of special assistant to the president for science and technology in 1957. It was also his administration that embarked on the deployment of intercontinental ballistic missiles (ICBMs), U-2 reconnaissance planes, and orbiting satellites, all of which utilized the military-industrial complex.

But if Eisenhower encouraged the development of these relationships, why did he alert the nation to the dangers inherent in a scientific-technological-industrial elite? The answer may be that Eisenhower's address was directed at what science adviser Herbert York called the "hard-sell technologists and their sycophants," who invented the missile gap and tried to exploit the 1957 launch of the Soviet satellite *Sputnik 1* and the Gaither Report to instill fear that Americans were losing ground to the Soviets. Clearly, what Eisenhower was warning against was not so much the work of his own science advisers, but rather that of the scientific-technological elite, comprising special interest groups that had sprung from the emphasis on military research and development in industry and academia.

The military-industrial complex, which still exists today, has provided many benefits to society. Superior weapons technology, satellites, nuclear reactors, silicon chips, chemotherapies, molecular genetics, and particle physics have all benefited from the military-industrial-academic alliance. In many ways, the military-industrial complex is simply a continuation of the evolving big science of the prewar years. Most Americans viewed this growth as a positive development for national security and economic health.

On the downside, however, the military-industrial complex has resulted in the creation of a separate economy whose products, such as nuclear weaponry, are not likely to be used commercially and add little or nothing to long-term economic productivity. It also has made some industries too reliant on defense contracts, the results of which were glaringly apparent in the early 1990s when the end of the Cold War brought about sharp cuts in defense spending, which in turn fueled unemployment and a deep industrial downturn. Finally, many of the jobs in the defense-oriented sector require advanced education and training, meaning that America's working class has largely been left out of the military-industrial complex's largesse. The military-industrial complex also bypassed many northern and midwestern cities, which severely debilitated their economies. All in all, the phenomenon first brought to light in the early 1960s has been a mixed blessing.

VALERIE ADAMS

See also

Eisenhower, Dwight David; Industrial Base, U.S.; National Security Council Report 68

References

Brands, H. W. "The Age of Vulnerability: Eisenhower and the National Insecurity State." *American Historical Review* 94 (October 1989): 963–989.

Hogan, Michael J. *A Cross of Iron: Harry S. Truman and the Origins of the National Security State, 1945–1954.* New York: Cambridge University Press, 1998.

Leslie, Stuart. *The Cold War and American Science: The Military-Industrial-Academic Complex at MIT and Stanford.* New York: Columbia University Press, 1993.

Pierpaoli, Paul G., Jr. *Truman and Korea: The Political Culture of the Early Cold War.* Columbia: University of Missouri Press, 1999.

Military Intelligence

U.S. military intelligence during the Korean War proved to be a roller coaster of triumphs and failures, innovations, and botched opportunities. Most high-ranking U.S. military officers disdained anything resembling unconventional intelligence-gathering techniques, which resulted in failures to counter communist tactics and strategies. United Nations Command (UNC) commander General Douglas MacArthur relied on the conventional intelligence estimates of his Far East Command (FEC) G-2, chief of intelligence General Charles Willoughby, rather than trust those of the newly organized Central Intelligence Agency (CIA).

In the late 1940s the fledgling CIA infiltrated agents into the People's Republic of China (PRC) and the Democratic People's Republic of Korea (DPRK, North Korea), who reported preparations for Kim Il Sung's June 1950 invasion of the Republic of Korea (ROK, South Korea). U.S. intelligence failed to discover the preparations because the Korean People's Army (KPA, North Korean Army) delivered orders by courier rather than sending them by radio. When KPA troops moved near the 38th Parallel, MacArthur's staff concluded that the increased activity was some type of agricultural project.

Five days before the KPA attacked South Korea, CIA chief Roscoe Hillenkoetter sent intelligence estimates to President Harry S. Truman and his cabinet indicating that the KPA could mount a coordinated attack at any time. Both Washington and MacArthur's FEC ignored the warnings, and as a result U.S. and Republic of Korea Army (ROKA, South Korean Army) troops were totally unprepared for the onslaught that drove them to the brink of disaster.

Preparations for MacArthur's September 15, 1950, amphibious operation at Inchon necessitated substantial intelligence on the landing beaches. On September 1 a reconnaissance team clandestinely slipped ashore to check the high tides, mudflats, and beach defenses near Inchon. Critical information from this team allowed the FEC to correct its erroneous tide charts and adjust the landing plan, assisting in a successful operation. On the night before the invasion, the team infiltrated Palmi-do, an island that had an abandoned lighthouse atop a 219-foot peak. The team lit the light to guide the invasion force and then evacuated to waiting ships.

By the end of September UNC forces had recaptured Seoul and stood along the 38th Parallel. MacArthur sought to free all of Korea from communist domination, and with United Nations (UN) concurrence he launched a coordinated attack across the parallel, intending to advance north to the Yalu River, the border between North Korea and Chinese Manchuria.

Through radio broadcasts, Chinese officials in Beijing warned the UNC not to invade North Korea, but U.S. and UN officials ignored these warnings. On October 1, 1950, ROKA troops crossed the 38 Parallel. Chinese foreign minister Zhou Enlai then summoned Sardar K. M. Panikkar, the Indian ambassador to China, to a meeting in which Zhou sent a message to the UN that the PRC would intervene militarily if UNC forces followed. MacArthur ignored the warning and assured President Truman and the Joint Chiefs of Staff that China would not enter the conflict because its People's Liberation Army (PLA, Chinese Communist Army) was not prepared for any large assault. Truman regarded the Chinese threat as a "bald attempt to blackmail the UN." MacArthur on his part promised a "great slaughter" if Chinese troops attacked UNC forces.

Again FEC analysis proved faulty because officers ignored agent reports and because they lacked methods of decrypting PLA radio messages. The PRC used the Mandarin dialect, and MacArthur's staff lacked trained linguists. Nationalist Chinese analysts easily read Beijing's messages, but U.S. officers distrusted the nationalists' self-serving transcripts.

The FEC nevertheless had other sources that indicated large numbers of Chinese forces gathering across the Yalu. Despite a shortage of trained photo reconnaissance interpreters, the 91st Strategic Reconnaissance Squadron, which flew from Japan, provided some indication of unusual Chinese troop movements in Manchuria. CIA agents confirmed reports of PLA movements, but analysts believed that the Chinese were capable of "intervening effectively but not necessarily decisively."

Between October 14 and 19, three Chinese armies crossed the Yalu into North Korea. UN intelligence failed to understand Chinese march discipline and combat capabilities. These Chinese armies marched 286 miles in 16–19 days from Manchuria to combat-assembly areas. Marches began after dark and ended before daylight, when all troops were hidden from UN air reconnaissance. PLA officers had the authority to shoot anyone who disobeyed orders to remain concealed. By late October 1950 more than 210,000 Chinese troops had infiltrated into North Korea, literally under the noses of the UNC.

On October 25 these Chinese forces, known as the Chinese People's Volunteer Army (CPVA, Chinese Army), struck the UNC in its drive toward the Yalu. Numerous CPVA prisoners indicated that six Chinese armies in two army groups opposed the U.S. Eighth Army in Korea (EUSAK) and X Corps. Both photo reconnaissance in Manchuria and Korean civilians confirmed movements of large formations of CPVA, but MacArthur ignored all indications of intervention and ordered UNC forces to resume the offensive.

On November 25 Chinese troops attacked en masse and, in a sustained drive, forced UNC divisions to retreat south of Seoul. Historian David Rees claims that "Inchon was imagination and intuition over sound military logic. The intelligence failure two months later was that too."

When Lieutenant General Matthew B. Ridgway arrived in Korea, his initial intelligence briefing concerning the CPVA was a big "goose egg" on a map with 175,000 scrawled inside it. By early 1951 the UNC actually faced about 400,000 Chinese troops with a few reorganized KPA divisions numbering just fewer than 100,000 men. Ridgway immediately reorganized his intelligence structure and began relying on his own subordinates rather than FEC staff in Japan. Ridgway also initiated the Li Mi Project to screen Korean refugees for KPA spies. UNC counterintelligence teams discovered hundreds of spies, guerrillas, and saboteurs among the refugees scattered across South Korea.

Poor organization and interservice rivalry inhibited most U.S. intelligence efforts in Korea. Combined Command for Reconnaissance Activities Korea and its supposed subordinate Joint Advisory Commission, Korea (JACK), constantly bickered for funding and scarce assets. The CIA, presumably under JACK, ran numerous, still classified, successful covert operations into North Korea, infiltrating Korean agents by parachute, small boats, and "line crossers." North Koreans, trained by the United States, jumped behind the front lines from high altitude Boeing B-26s in a precursor to U.S. Army's High Altitude Low Opening operations. Military intelligence officers ignored much valuable information brought back by these clandestine operatives.

The army, air force, navy, and Marines all ran separate intelligence-gathering systems, including patrols, prisoner snatches, photo reconnaissance, radio interception, and a series of covert operations. Each service shared its information with only its higher headquarters. Agents employed by one service sold information to other services; sometimes one report might be sold four or five times. Because individual services refused to coordinate covert missions, agents sometimes called in air strikes on one another.

On January 25, 1953, the United States dropped a "Green Dragon Team" of 97 men 40 miles from Pyongyang in an effort to form a popular guerrilla resistance in North Korea, but the mission was compromised. When Fairchild C-119 Flying Boxcars attempted to resupply the team, they met intense antiaircraft fire, and an air strike was called on the area. This was the last attempt to use paramilitary intelligence measures before the armistice in July 1953.

STANLEY S. McGOWEN

See also

Central Intelligence Agency; Joint Chiefs of Staff; Kim Il Sung; MacArthur, Douglas; Panikkar, Sardar K. M.; Ridgway, Matthew Bunker; Truman, Harry S.; Willoughby, Charles Andrew; Zhou Enlai

References

Appleman, Roy E. *Disaster in Korea: The Chinese Confront MacArthur.* College Station: Texas A&M University Press, 1989.

Blair, Clay. *The Forgotten War: America in Korea, 1950–1953.* New York: Times Books, 1987.

Breuer, William B. *Shadow Warriors: The Covert War in Korea.* New York: Wiley, 1996.

Evanhoe, Ed. *Dark Moon: Eighth Army Special Operations in the Korean War.* Annapolis, MD: Naval Institute Press, 1995.

Heinl, Robert D. *Victory at High Tide: The Inchon-Seoul Campaign.* Philadelphia: Lippincott, 1968.

Malcom, Ben S. *White Tigers: My Secret War in North Korea.* Washington, DC: Brassey's, 1996.

Mossman, Billy C. *United States Army in the Korean War: Ebb and Flow, November 1950–July 1951.* Washington, DC: U.S. Army Center of Military History, 1990.

Rees, David. *Korea: The Limited War.* New York: St. Martin's, 1990.

Stueck, William W., Jr. *Rethinking the Korean War: A New Diplomatic and Strategic History.* Princeton, NJ: Princeton University Press, 2004.

Military Sea Transport Service

U.S. unified logistics organization established by the 1947 National Security Act to handle ocean transportation of all the military services. The Military Sea Transport Service (MSTS) actually came into being in October 1949, when it absorbed the Naval Transportation Service and the shops and seagoing functions of the Army Transportation Corps. The Korean War broke out as this transfer of army troopships to MSTS was in progress; the transfer was completed as scheduled on July 1, 1950. Established in the Navy Department, MSTS was essential to the U.S. war effort. The Military Air Transport Service (MATS) of the U.S. Air Force moved supplies, but most troops and supplies went from the continental United States to Korea by sea.

When the Korean War began, MSTS had 50 transports, 48 tankers, 25 cargo ships, and 51 miscellaneous smaller craft. This was only slightly more than 1.5 million deadweight tons and could not begin to meet the requirements of U.S. forces in Korea. Chief reliance fell on civilian ships under MSTS charter. MSTS chartered 87 civilian ships, and it also brought out of the reserve mothball fleet a number of World War II ships. Soon after the start of hostilities MSTS returned to service 15 of these older ships, and over the next months it reconditioned and returned to service groups of 20, 30, 40, and 25 ships. Until the latter could be made ready, MSTS chartered 13 foreign ships. Early in 1951 the Maritime Administration let contracts for a $350 million program to build 50 new, fast cargo ships.

MSTS included chartered vessels, navy-manned (USS) and civil service–manned (USNS) transport and cargo vessels, and oil tankers from the Armed Services Petroleum Purchasing Agency. It also controlled the fleet of 12 freighters and 39 tank landing ships (LSTs) owned by the Shipping Control Administration Japan (SCAJAP). As a consequence of the war, military cargo handled by Japanese ports jumped from 125,000 tons in May 1950 to 1.4 million tons in September. The average thereafter was 1.2 million tons.

Two-thirds of the traffic by sea to and from Japan went through the port of Yokohama. Pusan was the only deep-water port in Korea capable of handling a high volume of traffic; an excellent harbor, it could berth up to 29 oceangoing ships at a time. The LSTs proved invaluable, as 12–15 of these could unload at the same time over the beach. Pusan's total discharge potential was

Landing ships, tank (LSTs) of the Military Sea Transport Service (MSTS) land the U.S. Army's 31st Infantry Regiment at the port of Inchon in South Korea on September 18, 1950. (National Archives)

40,000–45,000 tons per day. By late 1952 Pusan and its outports were handling about 1 million tons of cargo per month; all other ports in the Republic of Korea (ROK, South Korea), of which Inchon was the most important, were handling about a third of that total.

By the autumn of 1950, MSTS had under its control 404 vessels of different kinds, of which 350 were in ocean service, although not all of these were in the Pacific. From June 1950 to June 1953 MSTS moved to, from, and within the Far East some 52,111,299 tons of cargo; 21,828,879 tons of petroleum; and 44,918,919 passengers.

SPENCER C. TUCKER

See also

Japan Logistical Command; Logistics in the Korean War; Military Air Transport Service; 2nd Logistical Command; United States Navy

References

Cagle, Malcolm W., and Frank A. Manson. *Sea War in Korea.* Annapolis, MD: Naval Institute Press, 1957.

Field, James A., Jr. *History of United States Naval Operations, Korea.* Washington, DC: U.S. Government Printing Office, 1962.

Huston, James A. *Guns and Butter, Powder and Rice: U.S. Army Logistics in the Korean War.* Selinsgrove, PA: Susquehanna University Press, 1989.

Marolda, Edward J. *The U.S. Navy in the Korean War.* Annapolis, MD: Naval Institute Press, 2007.

Mine Warfare, Sea

The naval mine has, since its introduction in the mid-19th century, become a mainstay of modern warfare. The North Sea Mine Barrage, a large minefield laid by the British and U.S. navies in the North Sea during World War I, inhibited the movement of German U-boats. Mines released by U.S. Navy submarines and dropped by U.S. Army Air Forces (USAAF) B-29 bombers sank hundreds of Japanese warships, merchant ships, and smaller coasting vessels during World War II. Enemy-laid mines also exacted a heavy toll on Allied shipping in both world wars.

Thus, when President Harry S. Truman ordered U.S. armed forces into action in Korea at the end of June 1950, U.S. naval leaders took steps to deal with the mine threat. In early July Vice Admiral C. Turner Joy, the commander of Naval Forces, Far East (NAVFE), ordered Mine Squadron 3 to clear mines laid by the Korean People's Army (KPA, North Korean Army) from the approaches to Pohang on Korea's eastern coast. The United Nations Command (UNC) was desperate to stop the southward advance of the KPA and sought to deploy troops ashore at Pohang.

Accordingly, Lieutenant Commander D'arcy V. Shouldice, in command of fleet minesweeper *Pledge* and motor minesweepers *Kite, Chatterer, Redhead, Partridge, Osprey,* and *Mockingbird,* carried out a sweep of the approaches to the port and was able to

Lieutenant Dan F. Chandler briefs Underwater Demolition Team members on a beach at Wonsan on the east coast of North Korea, October 26, 1950. The "Frogmen" helped destroy a North Korean minefield offshore. (Naval Historical Center)

confirm that the communists had not mined those waters. As a result, on July 18, 1950, the U.S. Army's 1st Cavalry Division disembarked there and soon added its combat power to that of the units on the Pusan Perimeter. Minesweepers also ensured that there were no mines around the port of Pusan, which was Korea's largest port and essential to the UNC logistical effort.

The UNC was fortunate that it did not have to deal with North Korean minefields in the first critical months of the war because the allied navies did not then have available adequate mine-countermeasure resources. Owing to postwar demobilization and defense budget cuts, the World War II force of 500 mine-warfare vessels, manned primarily by naval reserve sailors, had been reduced to a worldwide contingent of 2 destroyer minesweeper divisions, 2 fleet minesweeper divisions, and 21 smaller craft. During the postwar years the navy devoted much more of its attention and resources to the development of new aircraft carriers, jet aircrafts, and shipboard surface-to-air missile systems than to mine warfare ships and equipment.

Freedom from North Korean sea mines did not last long. As allied forces carried out operations in preparation for the large-scale amphibious assault at Inchon, they discovered mine-laying activity. On September 4, 1950, crewmen on the U.S. destroyer

McKean spotted mines in the water near Chinnampo, and several days later two British warships destroyed a number of floating mines in the same area. Then, on September 10 the crew of Republic of Korea Navy (ROKN, South Korean Navy) *PC 703*, a former U.S. Navy submarine chaser, encountered a North Korean ship laying mines in the approaches to Inchon. Commander Yi Hung So's ship dispatched the communist mine-laying vessel with one shot from its deck gun. Allied warships en route to the landing sites at Inchon on September 13–14 saw mines piled on the shore for laying or already in the water. As they continued their passage up Flying Fish Channel, the destroyers *Mansfield, DeHaven, Lyman K. Swenson,* and *Henderson* used their guns to eliminate the mines. The North Koreans had begun their mine-laying operation too late to stop General Douglas MacArthur's landing at Inchon on September 15.

No sooner were UNC ground troops safely ashore at Inchon, however, than Soviet-made mines began to take a toll on UNC ships along the periphery of the Korean Peninsula. On September 26, off the Democratic People's Republic of Korea (DPRK, North Korea), the U.S. destroyer *Brush* struck a mine that killed 13 sailors, wounded 34 more, and put the ship out of action. Two days later, the *YMS 509* of the ROKN sustained damage from a "floater" on the south coast. The next day the *Mansfield,* spared at Inchon, hit a mine in North Korean waters that sent it to a shipyard in Japan. Then, in one day, October 1, communist mines destroyed the wooden-hulled U.S. minesweeper *Magpie,* killing or injuring its entire crew of 33 men, and badly damaged the ROKN *YMS 504.* Although sailors were killed and ships damaged in these separate incidents, UNC operations were not seriously disrupted.

The same could not be said of the planned allied landing at Wonsan, when an armada of 250 warships and transports, the latter carrying 50,000 marines and soldiers of the U.S. X Corps, waited idly offshore as minesweepers worked to clear an approach route through waters containing more than 3,000 mines laid by the North Koreans with the direct assistance of Soviet advisers.

On October 10, 1950, Captain Richard C. Spofford's Mine Squadron 3, warned by the helicopter crew from U.S. cruiser *Worcester* that mines were present in the waters off Wonsan, began its dangerous clearance mission. During that day and the next two, Spofford's nine vessels, assisted by helicopter and Martin PBM-5 Mariner seaplane spotters, cleared a 12-mile-long lane toward the landing site. The ships neutralized more than 30 mines, while the men of Underwater Demolition Team 3 marked another 50 mines for later destruction. In midmorning of October 12, however, the minesweeper *Pirate* hit a mine and quickly sank, losing six of its crewmen, and an hour later the minesweeper *Pledge* and six of its sailors met the same fate. Shore batteries added to the danger and difficulty of the operation. By October 18, two days before the planned landing, the minesweeping force had almost cleared all moored contact mines from the approach lane to the beach. That day, however, magnetic influence mines destroyed the ROKN *YMS 516;* half of its crew was lost. Discovery of these new weapons stalled the operation. Finally, on October 25 the way was clear for X Corps to deploy ashore at Wonsan. The operation, however, would be an "administrative landing," since Republic of Korea Army (ROKA, South Korean Army) ground units had already liberated Wonsan on October 11.

At one point Rear Admiral Allan Smith, in charge of the advance force at Wonsan, cabled the navy's Washington headquarters that "we have lost control of the seas to a nation without a navy, using pre–World War I weapons, laid by vessels that were utilized at the time of the birth of Christ." His words and the experience at Wonsan energized the navy's mine warfare community.

Allied fortunes improved in the operation to clear mines from the approaches to Chinnampo on Korea's west coast. This port served Pyongyang, which was occupied by the fast-advancing U.S. Eighth Army in Korea (EUSAK) on October 19. The closer UNC ground troops got to North Korea's border with the People's Republic of China (PRC) in the late autumn of 1950, the longer was the supply line from Inchon. The ground units needed a port opened farther north.

Consequently, even before the Wonsan operation was over, Admiral Joy ordered establishment of a new mine-clearance force for Chinnampo. This ad hoc group included the destroyer *Forrest*

Royal; the destroyer minesweepers *Thompson* and *Carmick;* the small minesweepers *Pelican, Swallow,* and *Gull* (newly arrived from the United States); the ROKN *YMS 502, YMS 306, YMS 513,* and *YMS 503; LST Q-007;* the high-speed transport *Horace A. Bass,* with Underwater Demolition Team 1 embarked; and the dock landing ship *Catamount,* carrying 14 minesweeping boats, 13 Japanese-manned minesweepers, and the salvage ship *Bolster.* U.S. Navy PBM seaplanes and helicopters and Royal Navy Sunderland aircraft were used not only to spot mines but also to destroy them with their machine guns. Helicopters were also found useful in minesweeping operations.

The group began its work on October 28, when aircraft began searching for the more than 300 mines that North Koreans who had been involved in the mine-laying operation claimed were in the water. On November 6 a Korean-manned tug, with U.S. Navy commander Donald N. Clay on board, steamed from Chinnampo to the Yellow Sea to prove that the channel was free of mines. Then ROKN *YMS 503* made the passage from the sea to the port. The docking of hospital ship *Repose* in Chinnampo on October 20 signaled the opening of the port to seagoing support vessels. Not a man or a ship was lost while carrying out the successful mine-clearance operation at Chinnampo.

The stabilization of the fighting front around the 38th Parallel from 1951 to 1953 ushered in a new era in mine warfare. Because the UNC navies had driven communist combatants from the sea early in the war, communist forces did what they could to deny the UNC use of the waters off North Korea. They made liberal use of sea mines along both coasts and covered their minefields with shore batteries. They deployed the mines from junks and sampans and released them in rivers that carried them to the sea. On occasion, nature aided the communists, such as when fierce Asian typhoons tore mines loose from their moorings and spread them far and wide.

Between 1951 and 1953 the UNC mine-clearance force often went in harm's way to threaten amphibious assaults, land guerrillas behind the lines, and open waters close offshore from which warships could bombard targets ashore. Nighttime sweep operations also became more frequent, as did the seizure of communist mine-laying junks and sampans. These operations compelled the communists to spread their forces and distracted them from concentrating on the ground war, but not without cost. From 1951 to 1953 mines sank the U.S. minesweeper *Partridge* and tug *Sarsi* and the ROKN ships *JMS 306* and *PC 704.* Many other UNC mine-clearance ships were damaged by mines or shore fire.

During the Korean War enemy mines caused 70 percent of all U.S. Navy casualties and sank the only four U.S. naval vessels lost in combat. The Korean War showed clearly that in the future the sea mine would be the weapon of choice for many of the U.S. Navy's adversaries and a fixture of late-20th-century naval warfare.

EDWARD J. MAROLDA

See also
Joy, Charles Turner; Korea, Republic of, Navy; Truman, Harry S.; United States Navy

References

Cagle, Malcolm W., and Frank A. Manson. *Sea War in Korea*. Annapolis, MD: Naval Institute Press, 1957.

Field, James A., Jr. *History of United States Naval Operations, Korea*. Washington, DC: U.S. Government Printing Office, 1962.

Lott, Arnold S. *Most Dangerous Sea: A History of Mine Warfare and an Account of U.S. Navy Mine Warfare Operations in World War II and Korea*. Annapolis, MD: U.S. Naval Institute, 1959.

Marolda, Edward J. *The U.S. Navy in the Korean War*. Annapolis, MD: Naval Institute Press, 2007.

Melia, Tamara Moser. *"Damn the Torpedoes": A Short History of U.S. Naval Mine Countermeasures, 1777–1991*. Washington, DC: Naval Historical Center, 1991.

Mines, Land

Land mines are explosive devices designed to kill or maim enemy troops and/or destroy or cripple tanks and other vehicles. Land mines were used with great—and deadly—effect in the Korean War. Land mines first appeared in modern form during the American Civil War (1861–1865). During World War I (1914–1918), German innovators buried artillery shells or boxes full of explosives connected to a triggering device as a counter to British tank attacks. As tanks increased in battlefield importance, mines became a vital defensive weapon. Mines underwent major technological changes during World War II (1939–1945), with particular emphasis on the development of antitank mines capable of destroying or damaging armored vehicles. These mines proved slow to emplace and easy to remove, however, with the result that they were often redeployed by an enemy. To prevent tampering, German engineers designed a series of antipersonnel mines that could be emplaced around antitank mines. German and Italian mine researchers also investigated the creation of nonmetallic mines, making their detection much more difficult. By the end of the war, mines had accounted for more than one-fifth of Allied tanks lost in combat.

The massive emphasis placed on the development of mines in World War II allowed their use on an unprecedented scale

U.S. Army engineers pull antitank mines into position in Yongdong, South Korea, in July 1950. (AP/Wide World Photos)

during the Korean War. Furthermore, the Korean War demonstrated a need for new methods of delivery and deployment of mines, stimulating another round of technological advances in land mine design during the 1950s. The human-wave attacks launched by units of the Chinese People's Volunteer Army (CPVA, Chinese Army) during the war showed the need for antipersonnel and anti-infiltration defenses that could be emplaced and left unmanned, leading to a series of new and increasingly lethal mines. Mines are a cheap, efficient weapon. They can replace manpower in guarding vital areas, especially key pieces of terrain such as road junctions or airstrips that must be used by an adversary.

When the Korean War devolved into a stalemate near the 38th Parallel in the spring of 1951, both sides constructed defenses-in-depth guarded by massive mine fields. The United Nations Command (UNC) forces emplaced hundreds of thousands of antipersonnel and antitank mines on or near the 38th Parallel, many of which remain in place today.

Land mines were often improvised to fulfill a particular battlefield need. One of the most expensive and destructive of such mines was the American X-200. This mine, based on earlier German models from World War II, contained five gallons of napalm (a highly volatile gelatinous mixture of gasoline, polystyrene, and benzene) that could be command detonated or triggered by a tripwire. By the end of 1952 more than 10,000 X-200 mines were emplaced along the front lines.

Mine research during and after the Korean War resulted in a series of new mine designs. One of the most effective antipersonnel mines was first demonstrated in 1952. The M18 Claymore mine, created by Norman MacLeod, initially consisted of a simple box with a layer of explosives covered by metal squares. When detonated, the manufactured shrapnel was expelled conically in a predetermined direction. By 1957 the M18A1 appeared; it had a shaped charge of plastic explosives and a load of 700 steel balls. The mine is designed to decimate attacking units. Upon detonation it fires the projectiles in a 60-degree arc that is deadly to a range of 150 feet or more.

Other major innovations in mine warfare during the Korean War included antipersonnel mines that could be deployed via aircraft. This involved scattering mines over a wide area to deny an avenue of approach to enemy infantry. This method proved both quick and efficient and was soon expanded to include small mines delivered via artillery that could be called in to halt an attack as it developed.

Despite efforts to ban the use of land mines in modern warfare, including the Ottawa Treaty of 1997, the Korean demilitarized zone along the 38th Parallel remains one of the most heavily mined areas in the world. Some estimates place the number of still-active land mines in Korea at more than 1 million.

PAUL J. SPRINGER

See also

Armor, Tanks; Demilitarized Zone; Human Wave Attacks

References

Matthew, Richard A., Bryan McDonald, and Ken Rutherford, eds. *Landmines and Human Security: International Politics and War's Hidden Legacy.* Albany: State University of New York Press, 2004.
Prokosh, Eric. *The Technology of Killing: A Military and Political History of Antipersonnel Weapons.* London: Zed Books, 1995.
Sloan, C. E. E. *Mine Warfare on Land.* London: Brassey's, 1986.

Mines, Sea

Sea mines are underwater explosive devices that are designed to sink or damage marine vessels or discourage an enemy's use of a particular area. Mines are frequently used by smaller powers as an inexpensive alternative to controlling an area of operations. The Democratic People's Republic of Korea (DPRK, North Korea) employed mine warfare to some effect against United Nations Command (UNC) forces between 1950 and 1952. Indeed, 14 U.S. Navy ships were damaged or sunk by North Korean mines. The most costly incident for the UNC came on June 12, 1951, when the U.S. destroyer *Walke* struck a mine, killing 26 and wounding 35. The final loss came on August 30, 1952, when a South Korean tug struck a mine near Hungnam, killing 4 of its crew and wounding 4 others.

Several types of mines were used in the war. These included magnetic mines, or those with a magnetic trigger that explodes the mine when a metal-hulled ship enters the magnetic field surrounding the mine. Another type was the contact mine, which explodes when a ship directly strikes it. Acoustic mines were also employed in a limited number. These detonated when the sound of a ship's engines came within a preset range of the mine. The acoustic mines tended to lose their effectiveness quickly because of saltwater or marine animals invading the listening devices.

The predominant mine employed by the North Koreans was the Soviet KB (North Atlantic Treaty Organization designation MKB). "KB" stands for "Korabel'naya Mina," or shipboard mine, which was introduced in 1940; it was a large five-horned contact mine with a 506-pound (230-kilogram) explosive charge of TNT and moorable to a depth of 853 feet (260 meters). The North Koreans laid these mines at night using civilian sampans and junks in order to hide their mine-laying activities. It is estimated that the Soviet Union provided some 1,500 of these mines to the North Koreans. The majority of them were laid around Wonsan to protect against a UNC landing at that point.

The United States never engaged in any mine-laying projects of its own. This was largely because of the offensive nature of UNC naval operations in Korea. The UNC did have to engage in extensive minesweeping operations to remove North Korean–laid mines, however. These operations forced the U.S. Navy to expand its minesweeping program.

JEFFERY SEYMOUR

See also

Helicopters, Employment of; United States Navy; Wonsan, North Korea; Wonsan Landing and Evacuation

References

Cagle, Malcolm W., and Frank A. Manson. *Sea War in Korea.* Annapolis, MD: Naval Institute Press, 1957.

Hartmann, Gregory K. *Weapons That Wait.* Annapolis, MD: U.S. Naval Institute Press, 1979.

Levie, Howard S. *Mine Warfare at Sea.* Boston: Kluwer Academic, 1992.

Melia, Tamara Moser. *"Damn the Torpedoes": A Short History of U.S. Naval Mine Countermeasures, 1777–1991.* Washington, DC: Naval Historical Center, 1991.

Morison, Samuel L. *Guide to Naval Mine Warfare.* Arlington, VA: Pasha Publications, 1995.

Missing in Action

A tragic and enduring legacy of the Korean War remains the thousands of servicemen categorized as missing in action (MIA). Although statistics vary from nation to nation and from source to source, the most reliable figures of U.S. soldiers missing in action are found in a 1994 report sponsored by the U.S. Department of Defense. This extensive RAND report establishes the total number of U.S. body-not-returned (BNR) cases of the Korean War at 8,140. Of this number, 5,945 BNR cases have been positively verified as dead, either by repatriated U.S. soldiers or extensive documentation provided by U.S. forces in Korea. Death cannot be firmly established for the remaining 2,195 cases, mostly soldiers, whose whereabouts remain unknown.

Military officials and historians have offered various explanations for the MIAs in the Korean War. In a conflict characterized by the unfettered use of heavy ordnance, bodies of soldiers were often obliterated beyond recognition or recoverability. In the confusion of battle, soldiers were lost in the rugged terrain of densely wooded areas or swampy marshes. Aircraft incidents in which planes went down at sea or in remote mountainous areas also account for some missing servicemen. Defections to the other side help explain the high number of MIAs among North Korean and South Korean forces.

Contributing to the high figures of missing U.S. soldiers was an antiquated U.S. recovery policy that had been practiced during World War II. The United Nations Command (UNC) established temporary cemeteries throughout the Korean Peninsula from Pusan to the Yalu River. Bodies were temporarily interred in various sites until the United States adopted a new repatriation policy in December 1950. Consequently, armed service personnel often recovered, buried, exhumed, and reburied the bodies of soldiers several times before repatriation took place. Needless to say, many were simply lost in the process.

MIA cases remain intricately tied to the prisoner of war (POW) issue. During the conflict, Chinese People's Volunteer Army (CPVA, Chinese Army) forces and the Korean People's Army (KPA, North Korean Army) forced thousands of POWs to march on foot to the rear. Many UNC servicemen perished during these long death marches. Survivors suffered through the horrible conditions of makeshift POW camps, collection points, and detainment centers. Most U.S. captives were released during the POW exchange following the July 1953 armistice, but 389 Americans who were positively known to be alive in communist POW camps were never repatriated.

The UNC's Military Armistice Commission repeatedly raised this issue, but KPA and CPVA representatives denied any knowledge of the whereabouts of these missing Americans. To add insult to injury, between 1990 and 1992 the Democratic People's Republic of Korea (DPRK, North Korea) turned over 46 sets of remains to U.S. authorities, but forensic experts could not authenticate a single set as American.

From October 1991 to April 1993 the U.S. Department of Defense funded two research projects to determine whether any American servicemen and civilians were transported to the Soviet Union or its satellites during World War II, the early Cold War, and the Korean War, but evidence remains inconclusive. Despite this, the U.S. government and its citizens continue efforts to recover and repatriate the remains of persons missing in action during the Korean War.

MATTHEW D. ESPOSITO

See also

Armistice Agreement; Casualties; LITTLE SWITCH and BIG SWITCH, Operations; Prisoner of War Administration, Communist; Truce Talks; United Nations Command

References

Cole, Paul M. *POW/MIA Issues,* Vol. 1, *The Korean War.* Santa Monica, CA: RAND Corporation for the National Defense Research Institute, 1994.

Mossman, Billy C. *United States Army in the Korean War: Ebb and Flow, November 1950–July 1951.* Washington, DC: U.S. Army Center of Military History, 1990.

Mobile Army Surgical Hospital

The idea of mobile hospitals with their tentage, supplies, and personnel able to accompany military units dated to the American Expeditionary Forces (AEF) in World War I. General Douglas MacArthur deployed mobile surgical units in the Pacific during World War II but with limited success. Between 1948 and 1949 five Mobile Army Surgical Hospitals (MASH units) were created, but none were based in the Pacific.

When the Korean War began in 1950, the necessity for such units was evident, and three MASH units were activated: the 8055th on July 1, the 8063rd on July 17, and the 8076th on July 19. The 8055th left Sasebo for Pusan on July 6 and proceeded by train directly to Taejon. The 8063rd left July 18 for Pohang to support the 1st Cavalry Division. The 8076th arrived in Pusan on July 25

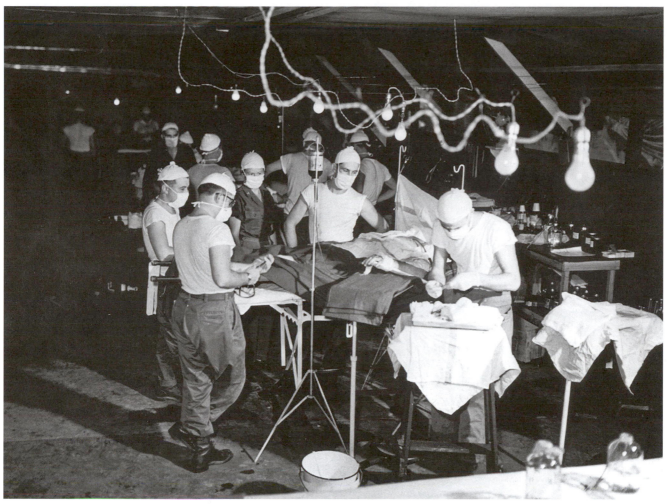

An operation being performed on a wounded soldier at the 8209th Mobile Army Surgical Hospital (MASH), located only 20 miles behind the front line, August 4, 1952. (National Archives)

and moved up the Taejon-Taegu corridor to support the Eighth Army. All three would follow their combat units after the United Nations Command (UNC) breakout from the Pusan Perimeter and the subsequent UNC invasion of the Democratic People's Republic of Korea (DPRK, North Korea).

In 1951 the 8225th MASH unit was deployed, and an additional unit was organized by the Norwegians and sent to Uijongbu the same year. Two additional MASH units, one of which (the 8209th) specialized in caring for neurosurgical cases, were deployed in 1952.

The MASH was initially intended to be a 60-bed unit to provide early treatment and triage. Each was to have a headquarters detachment, a preoperative and shock treatment area, an operating section, a postoperative area, a pharmacy, an X-ray section, and a holding ward. It was to be staffed by 14 medical officers, 12 nurses, 2 Medical Service Corps officers, 1 warrant officer, and 97 enlisted men. One of the medical officers was assigned as commander, and there were 2 anesthesiologists, 1 internist, 4 general medical officers, and 5 surgeons. The number of beds, mission, and staffing never exactly fit the plan. Because of the excess of

wounded over treaters, especially in the early part of the war, the MASH units grew into small evacuation hospitals. At one point, just the holding area alone of the 8076th had 200 beds.

MASH units received patients (usually by rail or helicopter) from aid or collecting stations. After the patients were stabilized they were transferred either to the evacuation hospitals at Pusan or directly to one of the Far East Command's facilities in Japan.

Early in the war there was a severe shortage of personnel to staff MASH units. Residency programs in the army hospital system were tapped to provide partially trained specialists on temporary duty (TDY). These young physicians and dentists were often asked to perform jobs for which they had little or no training; it was not uncommon for dentists to give anesthesia, psychiatric residents to operate on abdomens, and radiologists to repair fractures.

Both lack of training and high volume led to less than fastidious surgical techniques. Open wounds were cleaned but not closed, leaving the definitive surgery to hospitals farther down the chain. A typical abdominal operation involved making a large incision, after which any visible bleeding was controlled. Then the gut was examined for visible perforations, which were clamped and repaired. The abdominal cavity was then rinsed to clean out loose food and parasites (some of which were worms up to a foot long). The viscera were then replaced and the patient closed.

The doctor shortage was eased by the draft of 1950, but a new set of problems arose. Fully 90 percent of military physicians in Korea were drafted, and many had served in World War II as enlisted men. They had only recently completed their medical training and begun busy civilian practices, and they had little enthusiasm for their new predicament and little inclination to cooperate with military rules and discipline. As the war progressed and the lines stabilized, MASH units became fixed hospitals, relatively remote from the front lines, staffed with female nurses and with access to a variety of recreational facilities and temptations. Major Kryder van Buskirk ran the 8076th MASH in a way both typical and readily recognized by those familiar with Richard Hooker's (Dr. Richard Hornberger) 1968 novel *M*A*S*H*. These men were capable of working or playing for long hours with singular dedication.

Although quirky and often confused, the pattern of care begun in Korea's MASH units joined the helicopter transport model in forming the template for the shock-trauma services now present in virtually every large city in the United States.

JACK MCCALLUM

See also

Aeromedical Evacuation; MacArthur, Douglas; Medicine, Military

References

Apel, Otto F., Jr., and Pat Apel. *MASH: An Army Surgeon in Korea.* Lexington: University Press of Kentucky, 1998.

Cleaver, Frederick. *U.S. Army Battle Casualties in Korea.* Chevy Chase, MD: Operations Research Office, 1956.

Cowdrey, Albert E. *United States Army in the Korean War: The Medic's War.* Washington, DC: U.S. Army Center of Military History, 1987.

Horwitz, Dorothy, ed. *We Will Not Be Strangers: Korean War Letters between a M.A.S.H. Surgeon and His Wife.* Urbana: University of Illinois Press, 1997.

Reister, Frank. *Battle Casualties and Medical Statistics: U.S. Army Experience in the Korean War.* Washington, DC: Office of the Surgeon General, 1973.

Mobilization

The rapid calling up of U.S. armed forces was a key factor in staving off defeat in the Korean War. In June 1950 the United States was unprepared for war. All branches of the armed services were suffering under defense cutbacks mandated by Congress and President Harry S. Truman's administration. The cuts had enjoyed wide public support following World War II.

As a consequence, the three U.S. Army divisions in Japan in General Douglas MacArthur's Far East Command committed to the initial fighting had only two rather than the allotted three battalions each per regiment. Within these there were only two artillery batteries, one antiaircraft artillery battery, and one light tank company rather than the standard three medium tank companies.

On June 30, 1950, Congress passed the Selective Service Extension Act. This gave the president the authority to call up the National Guard and organized reserves to active service for a period of 21 months. The next month the Selective Service issued a call for 50,000 draftees for September who would be ready to be sent to Korea by the end of the year.

The army had to call up the National Guard and the active reserve. The figures were substantial, involving a total of 591,487 regular troops, 324,761 National Guard troops, and 184,015 active reservists. Also called up were 324,602 inactive volunteer reservists and 91,800 inactive reservists. By August 14, 1950, 1,457 National Guard units had been called for service. During the course of the war, the army reserve contributed 244,300 officers and men. Most were from the untrained and unpaid inactive and volunteer reserves rather than from active units.

In June 1950 the U.S. Marine Corps had 74,279 officers and men on active duty worldwide. The 1st Marine Division was so short of manpower that other units had to be stripped to bring it up to strength before it could be deployed to Korea. On July 19, 1950, the Organized Marine Corps Reserve was called to active duty, and it was followed by the Volunteer Marine Corps Reserve on August 15. Of all these personnel, 99 percent of the reserve officers, and 77.5 percent of the enlisted personnel were World War II veterans. By October 1951 all U.S. Marine Corps units had been activated.

The U.S. Navy had to call up reserves as well. It also recalled some of its mothball reserve fleet of older seagoing vessels. The navy also called up fighter squadrons; 22 reserve fighter squadrons were added to the Seventh Fleet Strike Force.

The U.S. Air Force had also suffered from defense cutbacks. Drawn from the Air National Guard, 145 North American F-51 Mustang aircraft were placed into active service. Soon afterward, troop carrier wings and fighter-bomber wings were called to service. A total of 22 wings of the Air National Guard and 10 wings of the Air Force Reserve were called up, numbering altogether some 100,000 personnel.

This military mobilization was vital in enabling the United States to stave off defeat in Korea. Fortunately, despite the defense cutbacks, the reservists were available, and with or without training, many were soon in battle and playing a vital role in the war.

SEAN WILLIAMS

See also

Far East Command; United States National Guard; United States Reserve Forces

References

Field, James A., Jr. *History of United States Naval Operations, Korea.* Washington, DC: U.S. Government Printing Office, 1962.

Futrell, Robert F. *The United States Air Force in Korea, 1950–1953.* Rev. ed. Washington, DC: Office of the Chief of Air Force History, 1983.

Giusti, Ernest H. *The Mobilization of the Marine Corps Reserve in the Korean Conflict.* Washington, DC: Historical Branch, G-3 Division Headquarters, U.S. Marine Corps, 1967.

Moffett, Howard Fergus
Birth Date: August 16, 1917

Physician, U.S. Navy officer, and missionary in Korea. Born on August 16, 1917, in Pyongyang, Korea, Howard Fergus Moffett was the fourth son of Drs. Samuel A. Moffett and Mary Fish Moffett, well-known American physicians and Presbyterian missionaries to Korea. The younger Moffett spent a large part of his early life in the northern part of Korea. He went to the United States for his higher education, graduating from Wheaton College in Wheaton, Illinois, in 1939. He pursued a medical degree at Northwestern University Medical School, graduating from there in 1943. After interning at Charity Hospital, New Orleans, he served for three years in the U.S. Navy as a medical officer during World War II. He held a commission as a lieutenant in the Naval Medical Corps Reserve.

As soon as the war ended Moffett tried to return to Korea as a Presbyterian missionary, but he had to spend a year in China before he received permission to enter Korea in late 1948. He then began working at the Presbyterian Hospital in Taegu. When the Korean War broke out in June 1950, Moffett and his wife evacuated to Tokyo with other U.S. nationals. Moffett applied for active military service and was returned to active duty on July 27, 1950.

Because the U.S. Navy had no direct action within the Pusan Perimeter and because his medical and language skills were badly needed inside Korea, Lieutenant Moffett was sent back to Taegu in a U.S. Air Force uniform instead. His position with the Fifth Air Force was to manage the Presbyterian Hospital in Taegu. While the city was under heavy shelling, Moffett remained there from July to September 1950, keeping the hospital operational.

Following the northward advance after the breakout from the Pusan Perimeter in the autumn of 1950, Moffett was the first missionary to arrive in Pyongyang City, his birthplace. Because he knew the area so well, he was sent by the commander of the Fifth Air Force, Lieutenant General Earle E. Partridge, to locate a suitable base for a headquarters. To assist the U.S. military occupation of the city, Moffett contacted members of the local Christian community for support. U.S. soldiers who saw him working with Korean civilians and interpreting for U.S. chaplains, military personnel, and foreign visitors mistook him for a chaplain.

When United Nations Command (UNC) forces evacuated Pyongyang following the massive Chinese military intervention, Moffett chose to stay a little longer to assist the refugees instead of flying south directly with Ambassador John J. Muccio. Moffett's military uniform secured him access to the military pontoon bridge across the Taedong River, and he used this means to evacuate many carloads of Korean refugees.

Back in Taegu, Moffett continued to run the Presbyterian Hospital until 1953. He then returned to the United States and took a three-year residency in internal medicine at Hines V. A. Hospital in Chicago before returning to Korea in 1956. He continued to serve in Korea until 1993. He now lives in California in retirement.

KAI YIN ALLISON HAGA

See also
Muccio, John Joseph; Partridge, Earle Everard; Relief Efforts, Missionary

References
Clark, Donald N. *Living Dangerously in Korea: The Western Experience 1900–1950.* Norwalk, CT: East Bridge, 2003.

Haga, Kai Yin Allison. "An Overlooked Dimension of the Korean War: The Role of Christianity and American Missionaries in the Rise of Korean Nationalism, Anti-Colonialism, and Eventual Civil War, 1884–1953." Unpublished PhD dissertation, College of William and Mary, 2007.

Park, Chung-Shin. *Protestantism and Politics in Korea.* Seattle: University of Washington Press, 2003.

Rhodes, Harry A., and Archibald Campbell, eds. *History of the Korean Mission Presbyterian Church in the USA,* Vol. 2, *1935–1959.* New York: United Presbyterian Church in the U.S.A., 1964.

Molotov, Viacheslav Mikhailovich
Birth Date: March 9, 1890
Death Date: November 8, 1986

Soviet foreign commissar and minister during 1939–1949 and 1953–1956. Born Viacheslav Mikhailovich Skriabin on March 9, 1980, in Kukarka, Viatka Province (now Omsk Oblast), Molotov had been a Bolshevik since 1906 and a staunch supporter of Joseph Stalin as early as 1922. This dogged loyalty was rewarded in 1939 when Molotov replaced Maxim Litvinov as commissar for foreign affairs. The title was changed to the more traditional "foreign minister" during World War II, when he gained great prominence as Stalin's right-hand man in complex wartime diplomacy.

In the immediate postwar years, Molotov was renowned in Washington, DC, for his dour demeanor and hard line on Cold War issues. This prominence may have cost him his job in March 1949, however, when the notoriously jealous and suspicious Stalin replaced him with Andrei Vyshinskii. Although Stalin sent Molotov's wife into exile in Siberia and may have planned to execute him, Molotov continued to serve after 1949 as first deputy chairman of the Soviet Union Council of Ministers, but he did not regain the foreign minister's portfolio until 1953.

One turning point in the Korean War came in August 1950 when Chinese and Soviet officials met to discuss possible responses in the event that United Nations Command (UNC) forces crossed the 38th Parallel. The Soviet delegation, headed by Molotov, wanted to avoid direct conflict with the United States but recognized the unacceptability of a Western overthrow of the Soviet Union's client state of the Democratic People's Republic of Korea (DPRK,

Soviet hardliner Viacheslav Molotov was a loyal supporter of Joseph Stalin. Molotov was Soviet foreign minister during 1939–1949. This photograph is from ca. 1955. (Library of Congress)

North Korea). Both parties apparently agreed that Chinese forces, with indirect Soviet assistance, would be used to support Kim Il Sung's regime, triggered by a crossing of the 38th Parallel by UNC troops.

After Stalin's death on March 5, 1953, Molotov's rhetoric softened abruptly when he took back the position of foreign minister. Part of a new ruling troika with Georgi Malenkov and Lavrenti Beria, Molotov worked to revive the Korean armistice negotiations. He did not play a direct role in the Panmunjom discussions, but he did try to pressure the participants when progress stalled on the issue of prisoner of war repatriation.

When Nikita Khrushchev used his position as first secretary of the Communist Party of the Soviet Union to fight his way to the top of the Soviet hierarchy, Molotov was one of the losers. Removed as foreign minister in May 1956, Molotov joined an ultimately unsuccessful attempt to depose Khrushchev in 1957. Stripped of his remaining posts, Molotov was given the relatively mild punishment of exile as Soviet ambassador to the Mongolian People's Republic during 1957–1960. He never regained prominence in Soviet public life. Molotov spent the last two decades of his life in a modest dacha in Zhukovka, where he died on November 8, 1986.

EDWARD SHARP

See also

China, People's Republic of; Cold War, Origins to 1950; Malenkov, Georgii; Mao Zedong; Soviet Union; Stalin, Joseph; Truce Talks; Vyshinskii, Andrei Ianuarovich

References

Beloff, Max. *Soviet Policy in the Far East, 1944–1951.* London: Oxford University Press, 1953.

Chuev, Felix. *Molotov Remembers.* Chicago: Ivan R. Dee, 1993.

MacKenzie, David. *From Messianism to Collapse: Soviet Foreign Policy, 1917–1991.* New York: Harcourt Brace College Publishers, 1994.

Zubok, Vladislav, and Constantine Pleshakov. *Inside the Kremlin's Cold War: From Stalin to Khrushchev.* Cambridge: Harvard University Press, 1996.

Monclar, Ralph
Birth Date: February 7, 1892
Death Date: June 3, 1964

French Army general and commander of French forces in the Korean War. Raoul Charles Magrin-Vernerey was born in Budapest, Hungary, on February 7, 1892. He is best known by his pseudonym of Ralph Monclar. Educated at the Lycée Victory Hugo of Besançon and at the Petit Séminaire of Ornans, he attempted to join the Foreign Legion when he was 15 years old but was rejected because of his age. Entering the French military academy of Saint-Cyr in 1912, he graduated in 1914 and was promoted to second lieutenant that August when he rejoined the 60th Infantry Regiment. Monclar distinguished himself in World War I, during which he received 11 citations for bravery. Wounded seven times, he was awarded 90 percent disability. He ended the war as a captain.

Posted to the Levant after the war, Monclar commanded various posts in Syria, Morocco, Algeria, and Indochina, earning two additional citations for bravery and becoming known for his bravado and great courage under fire. In 1924 he transferred to the Foreign Legion and took part in the Rif War in Morocco in 1927. Sent to the Middle East in 1928, he commanded a battalion. He again served in the Foreign Legion during 1931–October 1941, being posted both to Morocco and Tonkin in Indochina. He was promoted to lieutenant colonel in June 1938.

In February 1940 Monclar took command of two battalions of the Foreign Legion in Norway and distinguished himself in the initial Allied victory at Narvik. Evacuated from Norway with the Allied departure from that country, he joined Free French forces in Britain in late June 1940. It was at this point that he adopted the name of Ralph Monclar (for the village of Monclar-de-Quenncy in Tarn-et-Garonne), perhaps to protect his family in France. Monclar then fought against Axis forces in Eritrea. In June 1941 he refused to fight in Syria against other Frenchmen who were loyal to the Vichy regime. Subsequently promoted to general, he held various commands in the Levant and took part in the pacification of northern Syria. After the end of World War II, in 1946 Monclar took command of troops in Algeria, and during 1948–1950 he was inspector general of the French Foreign Legion.

In 1950 on the eve of retirement, Monclar gave up his rank as lieutenant general to serve as a lieutenant colonel and command the highly effective French Battalion in Korea, which he proclaimed as "my finest hour." One of the more colorful officers of the war, Monclar sported a monocle, a beret, and a bright red scarf and employed a cane to compensate for his limp. Reaching mandatory retirement age, he returned to France in 1951, and in 1962 he became governor of the Invalides in Paris. Monclar died in Val-de-Grace, Paris, on June 3, 1964.

SPENCER C. TUCKER

See also
France

References
Blair, Clay. *The Forgotten War: America in Korea, 1960–1953.* New York: Random House, 1987.

des Vollerons, Edme. *Le Général Monclar, un condottière du Xxe siècle.* Paris: Economica, Hautes études militaires, ISC, 2000.

Thiébaud, Jean-Marie. *La Présence française en Corée de la fin du XVIIIe siècle à nos jours.* Paris: L'Harmattan, 2005.

MOOLAH, **Operation**
Event Date: April 1953

Launched in April 1953 during the final stages of the Panmunjom armistice talks, Operation MOOLAH offered $100,000 and political asylum to the first communist pilot of an undamaged Mikoyan-Gurevich MiG-15 who defected with his airplane to the United Nations Command (UNC) and $50,000 to any subsequent imitators.

Operation MOOLAH's objectives were, first, to acquire a Soviet-built MiG for assessment and evaluation, something that the U.S. Air Force had long hoped to accomplish, and, second, to subject communist forces to psychological pressure as truce negotiations reached a critical stage. Lieutenant General Mark W. Clark, commander in chief of UNC forces in Korea, was an enthusiastic supporter of the scheme, which according to him was devised over a bottle of brandy in Seoul by United Press correspondent Dick Applegate. Other accounts credit Harvard University's Russian Research Center. On learning of the potential scheme in November 1952, Clark embraced it enthusiastically, although he waited until April 1953 to announce the offer, quite possibly to deprive the outgoing Harry S. Truman administration of any possible kudos. The air force budgeted $250,000 for the operation.

UNC shortwave radio broadcasts in Korean, Chinese, and Russian—since it was believed correctly that despite Soviet claims of neutrality a number of Russian pilots were flying MiGs over the Democratic People's Republic of Korea (DPRK, North Korea)—publicized the operation's details, as did almost 2 million leaflets in those languages dropped along the Yalu River and over North Korean airfields.

Operation MOOLAH's effects remain problematic. Clark, an enthusiastic supporter, claimed that it forced the communists to ground all planes until their pilots had undergone loyalty checks. The Far East Air Force more cautiously suggested that the break in flights probably owed more to bad weather, although the official U.S. Air Force history speculated that since aircraft bearing Soviet markings scarcely appeared in the skies after the offer, the Soviets in particular might have removed their pilots from combat missions. UNC radio propaganda on the operation in Russian was jammed, whereas broadcasts in Korean and Chinese experienced no such interference. Even before Operation MOOLAH, however, MiG pilots had become reluctant to venture into battle against the U.S.-made North American F-86F Sabres, which had just come into service.

The first communist pilot to defect did not do so until September 21, 1953, several months after the armistice was concluded. Lieutenant No Kum Sok of the Korean People's Air Force (KPAF, North Korean Air Force), who landed his MiG-15 at Kimpo Airfield, claimed that he was unaware of any reward and was motivated solely by personal considerations. Although President Dwight D. Eisenhower had approved the original offer, he now found it somewhat embarrassing. The war had ended, and although he believed that the Central Intelligence Agency (CIA) was morally obliged to fulfill its promise, he thought that $100,000 was a great deal to pay for an airplane that he considered "no longer of any great interest to us." Eisenhower also disliked the idea of bribing individuals to defect, believing it preferable that they do so from ideological conviction. Lieutenant No was therefore persuaded to reject the reward as such, and instead the Committee for Free Asia, a CIA-funded organization, provided him with an equivalent sum in technical education and financial assistance.

At this time, the United States also withdrew the offer of $50,000 to any subsequent communist pilot who defected and even offered to return the Soviet-made aircraft to its "rightful owner." Clark later speculated that the reason the Soviets never took up the latter suggestion was because this would have flagrantly disproved their contemporaneous claim that as a "neutral" power in the Korean conflict, the Soviet Union was entitled to voting representation in this capacity at a forthcoming international conference scheduled to discuss Korean political problems.

Although some observers questioned the actual value of this particular aircraft, given that it was a relatively old model, Clark had no such reservations, claiming that it "was the first combat MiG we ever laid hands on long enough to test." This, he argued, later enabled U.S. pilots to shoot down at least a dozen similar airplanes. Lieutenant No also provided valuable intelligence information on communist violations of the armistice, particularly on the transfer of MiGs from Manchuria to supposedly nonmilitary bases within North Korea.

PRISCILLA ROBERTS

The Mikoyan Gurevich MiG-15 fighter flown to Kimpo Airfield on September 21, 1953, by defecting Democratic People's Republic of Korea Air Force (North Korean Air Force) lieutenant No Kum Sok. (National Archives)

See also

Clark, Mark Wayne; Eisenhower, Dwight David; MIG, Operation

References

Ambrose, Stephen E. *Eisenhower.* 2 vols. New York: Simon and Schuster, 1983–1984.

Bailey, Sydney D. *The Korean Armistice.* New York: St. Martin's, 1992.

Clark, Mark W. *From the Danube to the Yalu.* New York: Harper and Row, 1954.

Foot, Rosemary J. *A Substitute for Victory: The Politics of Peacemaking at the Korean Armistice Talks.* Ithaca, NY: Cornell University Press, 1990.

Futrell, Robert F. *The United States Air Force in Korea, 1950–1953.* Rev. ed. Washington, DC: Office of the Chief of Air Force History, 1983.

No, Kum Sok, with J. Roger Osterholm. *A MiG-15 to Freedom: Memoir of the Wartime North Korean Defector Who First Delivered the Secret Fighter Jet to the Americans in 1953.* Jefferson, NC: McFarland, 1996.

Morrison, Herbert Stanley

Birth Date: January 3, 1888
Death Date: March 6, 1965

British Labour Party politician and foreign secretary from March to October 1951. Born on January 3, 1888, to a London police constable and his wife, a former domestic servant, Herbert Stanley Morrison was educated at state schools. He completed his formal schooling at age 14 and quickly moved into journalism and, from April 1915 onward, into Labour Party politics. In 1922 Morrison became the mayor of Hackney Borough in London, and in 1921 he won a seat on the London County Council, which he soon came to dominate and would continue to do so until 1940. Among his major achievements in London were the creation of the London Passenger Transport Board, slum clearance, the building of Waterloo Bridge, and reform of welfare provisions.

Elected to Parliament in 1923 and 1929, between 1929 and 1931 Morrison served as minister of transport in Ramsay MacDonald's Labour government, losing his seat in the general election of 1931. Returned to Parliament in 1935, in the national wartime coalition government of 1940 Morrison was first minister of supply and then home secretary and minister of home security. In the latter capacity he used his knowledge of London and its inhabitants to assist its people in enduring the wartime blitz with their sanity and sense of humor intact. In the 1945 Labour government Morrison served successively as lord president of the council, chancellor of the exchequer, and again lord president, positions in which he continued to concern himself almost exclusively with domestic affairs.

In 1951 when Ernest Bevin's illness left the post of foreign secretary vacant, Prime Minister Clement Attlee hesitated over whether to appoint Morrison, who it seems gave the appearance, deliberately or not, of coveting the job and so obtained it by default, a prize that he may later have regretted. Attlee soon regarded the appointment as an error, and he and U.S. secretary of state Dean Acheson both remarked acidly on Morrison's ignorance of world affairs. Even so, during Morrison's tenure Anglo-American friction over East Asia diminished, partly because of the recall of General Douglas MacArthur, which alleviated fears that Britain might be drawn into a broader war against the People's Republic of China (PRC).

Morrison's personal preoccupation with the concurrent Iranian crisis also reduced tensions, inasmuch as the British muted their criticisms of U.S. policies in Asia in the hope of winning U.S. support in the Middle East. In addition, PRC intransigence in the spring of 1951 in rejecting all moves toward a negotiated settlement and attempting instead to keep fighting until it had driven United Nations Command (UNC) forces from Korean territory radically improved America's image in British eyes.

In May 1951 Britain voted for a selective United Nations (UN) embargo on China and accepted Acheson's suggestion of a moratorium on the perennially difficult question of PRC representation in the UN. Morrison also endorsed the principle that the UN commander in Korea be authorized to attack Manchurian military bases should North Korean or Chinese forces launch an unexpected air assault on his troops, although he did insist on prior American consultation with the British. In addition, in May Morrison made a speech supporting the position of the World War II Cairo Declaration of 1943 that Taiwan (then known as Formosa) was part of China but opposing its return to the PRC until the Korean crisis had ended.

Morrison did not merely echo U.S. policy but instead continued to reveal the same fears of imprudent provocation of China that Attlee demonstrated in 1950. Although Morrison shared Acheson's view that it was unlikely that an armistice would ultimately lead to a settlement of all outstanding political questions in Asia, Morrison refused to preclude the possibility of such a comprehensive scheme. Emphasizing Hong Kong's vulnerability to PRC pressure or takeover and the need to avoid driving China entirely into the Soviet camp, he was reluctant to broaden the war should armistice negotiations fail. He was also somewhat fearful that domestic political pressures might lead Washington to recklessly expand the war beyond the bounds of prudence. He was therefore only ready to endorse somewhat limited moves, such as bombing Yalu power stations. In December 1950 an irritated Acheson, who already thought that Beijing was part of the communist conspiracy, complained of "familiar exegesis" on the part of Morrison and, by extension, on the part of Britain.

Morrison's tenure as foreign secretary ended when the Labour Party lost the October 1951 election. Conservative Anthony Eden replaced him. In opposition, Morrison remained a highly effective parliamentarian and party spokesman, contributing frequently to debates, but he lost the Labour leadership contest of 1955 to Hugh Gaitskell. Morrison died on March 6, 1965, at Sidcup.

PRISCILLA ROBERTS

See also

Acheson, Dean Gooderham; Attlee, Clement Richard; Bevin, Ernest; Eden, Robert Anthony; MacArthur, Douglas; Truman's Recall of MacArthur

References

Butler, Rohan, and M. E. Pelly, eds. *Documents on British Foreign Policy Overseas,* Series 2, Vol. 4, *Korea, 1950–1951.* London: HMSO, 1995.

Donoughue, Bernard, and G. W. Jones. *Herbert Morrison: Portrait of a Politician.* London: Weidenfeld and Nicolson, 1973.

MacDonald, Callum A. *Britain and the Korean War.* Oxford, UK: Blackwell, 1990.

Morgan, Kenneth O. *Labour in Power, 1945–1951.* Oxford, UK: Clarendon, 1985.

Morrison, Lord of Lambeth. *Herbert Morrison: An Autobiography.* London: Odhams, 1960.

Stueck, William W., Jr. *The Korean War: An International History.* Princeton, NJ: Princeton University Press, 1995.

———. *Rethinking the Korean War: A New Diplomatic and Strategic History.* Princeton, NJ: Princeton University Press, 2004.

Mortars

The need for indirect methods of fire to assist infantry other than air strikes has traditionally been filled by artillery, but the hilly, mountainous terrain of the Korean Peninsula often rendered artillery fire impractical. This void was filled by mortars, high-angle–firing weapons designed to fire over heights and enemy fortifications. In the Korean War the U.S. Army employed three types of mortars: the 60-millimeter (mm) (three per rifle company), the 81-mm (three per infantry battalion), and the 107-mm, more commonly known as the 4.2-inch (six per infantry regiment). British Commonwealth forces used a 3-inch mortar. On the communist side the Korean People's Army (KPA, North Korean Army) and the Chinese People's Volunteer Army (CPVA, Chinese Army) utilized a 61-mm mortar at company level, an 82-mm mortar at battalion level, and a 120-mm mortar at the regimental level. The slightly larger diameters of the 61-mm and the 120-mm enabled the KPA and the CPVA to take advantage of captured U.S. mortar ammunition for the American 60-mm and the 107-mm in their own mortars; however, the U.S. troops could not use any captured communist ammunition because the rounds were too big to fit in the U.S. mortar bores.

Conventional rounds were not the only types of projectiles employed by the United Nations Command (UNC). The 2nd Chemical Mortar Battalion, with three 4.2-inch heavy mortar companies, provided direct support of infantry units. It saw heavy action in November and December 1950. During the Chinese Spring Offensive of April 1951, elements of the Republic of Korea Army (ROKA, South Korean Army) collapsed, leaving the 2nd Chemical Mortar Battalion trapped, but most of its elements managed to reach UNC lines. In October 1952, most probably to dispel communist propaganda that the United States was employing

Members of a U.S. Army heavy mortar company fire at communist positions west of Chorwon, South Korea, on February 7, 1953. Mortars are muzzle-loading, short-range, high-trajectory weapons designed to fire over obstacles. (National Archives)

chemical weapons against noncombatants, the army dissolved the 2nd Chemical Mortar Battalion.

Of U.S. mortars used in Korea, the 107-mm (4.2-inch) may have seen the most action. It saw extensive use with the U.S. 8th Cavalry Regiment at Unsan and the U.S. 9th Infantry Regiment at Kunu-ri, which came under heavy Chinese pressure at the end of November 1950.

Mortar fire was also very important in fighting over Heartbreak Ridge between September 1951 and November 1952. Artillery and mortar support fire for the battle during September 13–15, 1951, alone created an army-wide ammunition shortage after the expenditure of nearly 120,000 60-mm, 81-mm, and 107-mm (4.2-inch) mortar rounds.

Mortars were effective in both offensive and defensive operations. On November 30, 1950, U.S. Army troops of Task Force Faith, named for their commander Lieutenant Colonel Don Faith, were assaulted by the CPVA 80th Division. U.S. commanders believed that the Chinese had orders to take the position at any

cost, so the soldiers were ordered to retreat, but in the process they used mortar and artillery fire to inflict heavy casualties on the attackers. U.S. and UNC forces also used mortar fire with great effect in March 1951 in Operation RIPPER, when they drove Chinese forces back across the 38th Parallel.

Mortars played an important role in the Korean War by providing mobile infantry support fire in all types of terrain and in conditions and locations where standard artillery was impractical. In the so-called Forgotten War, mortars may be the forgotten weapon, but their supporting fire was responsible for saving entire UNC units.

WILLIAM B. HARRINGTON

See also
Chemical Warfare; RIPPER, Operation

Reference
Blair, Clay. *The Forgotten War: America in Korea, 1950–1953.* New York: Times Books, 1987.

Mu Chong
Birth Date: 1905
Death Date: October 1952

Korean People's Army (KPA, North Korean Army) general and commander of its II Corps at the start of the Korean War. Mu Chong (his family name of Kim has usually been omitted) was born in Kyongsong, North Hamgyong Province, in present-day North Korea, in 1905. After joining the March First Movement of 1919, he went to China in 1923 and graduated from Henan Military Academy.

Mu Chong began his military career with the warlord Yen Hsishan and developed an expertise in artillery. An artillery lieutenant during the Northern Expedition, Mu Chong joined the Chinese Communist Party in 1925. In 1927 he was sentenced to death by the Guomindang (GMD, Nationalist) court at Wuchiang but fled to Shanghai. In 1929 he was arrested again but escaped to Hong Kong. Thereafter, he reportedly became chief of artillery in the People's Liberation Army (PLA, Chinese Communist Army). He was the only Korean to survive the Long March, cultivating a friendship with Peng Dehuai.

In 1939 and 1940 Mu Chong established a Korean unit within the PLA. Early the following year, this unit was developed into the North China Korean Youth Federation. Six months later, in combination with new arrivals from the Korean Volunteer Corps, which was receiving Nationalist backing in Nanjing, the federation was reorganized into the North China Korean Independence League, with Kim Tu Bong as its chairman. Under the league the Korean Volunteer Army was established, with Mu Chong as its commander.

Following the 1945 liberation of Korea, Mu Chong was elected in absentia a member of the Central People's Committee at the Committee for the Preparation of Korean Independence organized in Seoul, but in December 1945 he returned to northern Korea. In the initial period of liberation, he was highly regarded as the vice commander of the Eighth Route Army, or the Chinese communist choice to assume leadership in Korea, much to the great displeasure of Kim Il Sung. However, Mu Chong would hold no official position in the northern leadership until the autumn of 1946, when he became deputy chief for artillery in the Peace Preservation Corps, from which the KPA developed. Evidently, Kim Tu Bong served as the principal spokesman for the Yenan (Yan'an) Chinese exile faction in northern Korea. In March 1948 Mu Chong was elected a member of the Central Committee of the North Korean Workers' Party.

Mu Chong was ineffective during the Korean War and was demoted to the less important post of commander of the KPA VII Corps. At the third regular meeting of the Central Committee of the Korean Workers' Party held on December 4, 1950, he was removed from the body on charges that he was responsible for the loss of Pyongyang that fall. It is believed that Kim Il Sung purged him because Mu Chong's Chinese connection might have heightened his politico-military position following Chinese military intervention in the Korean War. The Chinese leadership helped Mu Chong to return to China; however, he was dying of gastroenteritis and returned to Pyongyang, where he died in October 1952.

HAKJOON KIM

See also
Korea, Democratic People's Republic of, 1945–1953; Korea, Democratic People's Republic of, 1953–Present; March First Movement

References
Chungang Ilbo, ed. Pirok: Choson Minjujuui Inmin Konghwaguk [The Secret Records of the Democratic People's Republic of Korea]. Seoul: Chungang Ilbo, 1992.
Cumings, Bruce. The Origins of the Korean War. 2 vols. Princeton, NJ: Princeton University Press, 1981, 1990.
Millett, Allan R. The War for Korea, 1945–1950: A House Burning. Lawrence: University Press of Kansas, 2005.
Suh, Dae Sook. Kim Il Sung: The North Korean Leader. New York: Columbia University Press, 1988.

Muccio, John Joseph
Birth Date: March 19, 1900
Death Date: May 19, 1989

First U.S. ambassador to the Republic of Korea (ROK, South Korea) (1949–1952). Born on March 19, 1900, in Valle Agricola, Italy, John Joseph Muccio saw service in the U.S. Army during World War I. He then acquired U.S. citizenship and in 1921 graduated from Brown University. Appointed to the U.S. Foreign Service two years later, Muccio held posts in Europe, Asia, and Latin America. In August 1948 he became President Harry S. Truman's special representative to South Korea and then, on March 21, 1949, the first U.S. ambassador to South Korea.

Muccio presided over the U.S. embassy, the Korea Military Advisory Group (KMAG), an Economic Cooperation Administration branch, and the Joint Administrative Services, the mission's supply office. Despite disagreements with South Korean president Syngman Rhee, Muccio established a working relationship with him as well as developed an admiration for Rhee's intelligence and historical insights. Nevertheless, Muccio recognized Rhee's reverence for General Douglas MacArthur, commander of the U.S. Far East Command, and feared his suspicious nature. Characterizing the South Korean leader as an "egomaniac," Muccio feared that Rhee might launch an attack against the Democratic People's Republic of Korea (DPRK, North Korea) with the goal of reuniting Korea under his leadership.

Muccio endorsed Rhee's wish for a permanent U.S. military role in Korea and his government's request for $10 million in additional aid for 1950. A few weeks before North Korea invaded South Korea, Muccio informed the U.S. Congress of South Korea's military inferiority, an assessment that many in the Truman administration did not agree with. Muccio worried that North Korea's

John J. Muccio was the first U.S. ambassador to the Republic of Korea. He held that post during 1949–1952. (Time & Life Pictures/Getty Images)

military advantage would give it the winning edge in case of an all-out assault of South Korea. He cited North Korean advantages in artillery, armor, and aircraft supplied by the Soviet Union.

Ambassador Muccio officially notified Washington of the outbreak of the Korean War on June 25, 1950. In a dispatch sent almost six and a half hours after the beginning of the invasion, he announced that North Korea had mounted a full-scale unprovoked attack. At a meeting of the United Nations (UN) Commission on Korea, Muccio expressed confidence in the capability of Republic of Korea Army (ROKA, South Korean Army) troops, but he also pressed the Department of State to back a KMAG plea to General MacArthur for more ammunition for the ROKA. When Rhee considered a sudden departure from Seoul, Muccio warned that this could demoralize ROKA troops. Muccio's own decision to stay braced Rhee, at least temporarily.

Under the pressure of advancing Korean People's Army (KPA, North Korean Army) forces, Muccio elected to evacuate U.S. civilians from Seoul via Inchon and Kimpo Airfield but delayed this step for a time, despite the misgivings of some military personnel, in hopes of preserving South Korean morale. Once Rhee departed Seoul, the State Department ordered Muccio to follow, and the ambassador joined Rhee in Taejon.

Muccio conferred with MacArthur on several occasions after the war's outbreak and traveled with the general to meet President Truman at Wake Island in October 1950. Muccio and MacArthur were the only participants in the general's party to take prominent roles in the discussions. Muccio later described MacArthur as irritated and uncomfortable and stated that the general complained of being "summoned for political reasons" and suggested that the president was "not aware that I am still fighting a war." In his own remarks, Muccio spoke about Korean political and economic conditions. Both he and MacArthur endorsed a reconstruction aid package and expressed fear of President Rhee's weakened political status. Before their departure, Truman awarded Muccio the Medal of Merit.

In 1952 Muccio pressed Rhee to comply with the pending ceasefire and found the South Korean president uncooperative. Despite his reputation of being Rhee's "best and most patient friend in the American community," Muccio urged the State Department to ponder UN intervention through the ROKA. On June 25, 1952, the State Department directed Muccio and new United Nations Command (UNC) commander Lieutenant General Mark W. Clark to begin contingency planning in case action was required to stop Rhee's meddling. In November 1952 Muccio was succeeded by Ellis O. Briggs and returned to the United States.

Muccio retired from the Foreign Service in 1961. He died in Washington, DC, on May 19, 1989.

RODNEY J. ROSS

See also

Briggs, Ellis Ormsbee; Church, John Huston; Clark, Mark Wayne; Korea Military Advisory Group; MacArthur, Douglas; Rhee, Syngman; Seoul; Truman, Harry S.; Wake Island Conference

References

Goulden, Joseph C. *Korea: The Untold Story of the War.* New York: Times Books, 1982.

James, D. Clayton. *The Years of MacArthur,* Vol. 3, *Triumph and Disaster, 1945–1964.* Boston: Houghton Mifflin, 1985.

Paige, Glenn D. *The Korean Decision, June 24–30, 1950.* New York: Free Press, 1968.

Stueck, William W., Jr. *Rethinking the Korean War: A New Diplomatic and Strategic History.* Princeton, NJ: Princeton University Press, 2004.

Munich Analogy

Historical analogy positing that appeasement only invites further aggression. In the belief that they were preventing a war with Nazi Germany, British prime minister Neville Chamberlain and French premier Édouard Daladier, during a September 1938 conference in Munich, Germany, agreed to cede German-speaking areas of Czechoslovakia to German dictator Adolf Hitler.

Seemingly emboldened by the British and French concession at Munich, six months later Hitler sent German troops to occupy the remainder of Czechoslovakia. The acquisition of Czechoslovak military hardware, especially artillery but also tanks and aircraft, in addition to war industries immensely benefited the German war machine. On September 1, 1939, German forces invaded Poland, starting World War II.

Cold War–era politicians often used the Munich example as a reason to stand firm in the face of foreign hostile behavior. They applied the Munich Analogy especially in the face of perceived Soviet aggression. The Munich reference illustrates both the power and limitations of analogical reasoning. The 1947 Truman Doctrine and the U.S. intervention in the Korean War in June 1950 assumed that communist aggression had to be countered to forestall a third world war. Indeed, President Harry S. Truman specifically compared the North Korean attack upon South Korea to Nazi aggression in the late 1930s. This analogy helped him make a quick and decisive decision to intervene in the war. President John F. Kennedy, whose Harvard undergraduate thesis "Why England Slept" (1940) dissected the causes of laggard British rearmament before World War II, also invoked the lessons of the 1930s during the 1962 Cuban Missile Crisis.

But the Munich Analogy can be carried too far. British prime minister Anthony Eden conflated Egyptian nationalism with fascism, which set the stage for Britain's disastrous participation in the 1956 Suez Crisis. President Lyndon Johnson's misapplication of the analogy to Vietnam rationalized a strategically dubious conflict and ignored the profound dissimilarities between Nazi Germany and the Democratic Republic of Vietnam (DRV, North Vietnam) and the goals of their governments. The Vietnam War did not fully discredit this analogy, however, as President George H. W. Bush carelessly likened Iraqi president Saddam Hussein to Hitler prior to the 1991 Persian Gulf War.

JOSEPH ROBERT WHITE

See also

Containment; Truman, Harry S.; Truman Doctrine

References

Khong, Yuen Foong. *Analogies at War: Korea, Munich, Dien Bien Phu, and the Vietnam Decisions of 1965.* Princeton, NJ: Princeton University Press, 1992.

May, Ernest R. *"Lessons" of the Past: The Use and Misuse of History in American Foreign Policy.* New York: Oxford University Press, 1973.

Record, Jeffrey. *Making War, Thinking History: Munich, Vietnam, and Presidential Uses of Force from Korea to Kosovo.* Annapolis, MD: Naval Institute Press, 2002.

Weinberg, Gerhard L. "Reflections on Munich after 60 Years." *Diplomacy & Statecraft* 10(2/3) (July/November 1999): 1–12.

Munsan-ni Airborne Operation
Start Date: March 23, 1951
End Date: March 27, 1951

The second of two United Nations Command (UNC) Korean War airborne operations, the first being the operation at Sukchon and Sunchon during October 20–23, 1950. Both operations were carried out by the 4,000-man U.S. Army 187th Airborne Regimental Combat Team (ARCT) commanded by Brigadier General Frank S. Bowen Jr. The Munsan-ni operation of March 23–27, 1951, also included the 2nd and 4th Ranger companies.

UNC commander Lieutenant General Matthew B. Ridgway planned the Munsan-ni operation, code-named TOMAHAWK, to trap elements of the Chinese People's Volunteer Army (CPVA, Chinese Army) and the Korean People's Army (KPA, North Korean Army) that were withdrawing north above the Han River to the Imjin River before advancing UNC forces in Operation COURAGEOUS (March 22–31, 1951). The airborne forces were to drop into the Munsan-ni Valley some 20 miles northwest of Seoul and there set up a blocking position on the Seoul-Kaesong road, where they would be joined by an armored task force from I Corps that was to link up with the paratroops within 24 hours of the airborne drop and provide the hammer to the anvil provided by the airborne forces. The Ranger companies were to secure the village of Munsan-ni itself.

Planning was begun on March 21, and fighter-bombers of the 452nd Bombardment Group, Light, strafed, rocketed, and bombed communist forces in the drop area. Protected by Fifth Air Force fighters, on the morning of March 23 the 314th Troop Carrier Group and 437th Troop Carrier Wing transports—a collection of Curtiss C-46 Gooney Birds, Douglas C-47 Sky Trains, Fairchild C-82 Packets, and Fairchild C-119 Flying Boxcars—departed the K-2 airstrip at Kimpo for the short flight to Munsan-ni. The drop occurred at 500–600 feet and included more than 3,400 men and 220 tons of equipment and supplies. It was the first airborne operation in which heavy equipment, to include trucks and artillery, was parachuted into enemy-held territory. On March 24 and 26–27, C-119s and C-46s dropped an additional 264 tons of supplies.

Bowen had designated two drop zones (DZs), one a mile northeast of Munsan-ni and the other three miles to the southeast, but the air force mistakenly dropped almost the entire airborne force into the northern DZ. Overcoming several minor complications, the 187th ARCT consolidated at the northern DZ. The airborne troopers and Rangers soon controlled Munsan-ni and overcame scattered resistance from communist infantry, supported by mortar fire. Combat casualties totaled 19, while 84 casualties were incurred in the drop itself. Communist casualties totaled 136 dead and 149 captured.

TOMAHAWK came too late. The bulk of the communist units had already withdrawn north of the Imjin River. After being delayed by numerous communist mines, the UNC armored task force, known as Task Force Growden for its commander Lieutenant Colonel John S. Growden Jr., linked up with the 187th ARCT beginning on the evening of March 23. With little that either could accomplish at Munsan-ni, these units were then assigned the task of coming up behind a Chinese division that was blocking the route north of Uijongbu and holding up the advance of the U.S. 3rd Infantry Division. This mission was accomplished by March 27, and a linkup was secured the next day with elements of the U.S. 3rd Infantry Division. Unfortunately for the UNC, the Chinese had held open the road from Uijongbu long enough to withdraw their main units. On March 29 the 3rd Division took over the 187th ARCT positions, and on March 30 General Bowen moved his men by train back to Taegu.

SPENCER C. TUCKER

See also

Airborne Operations; Ridgway, Matthew Bunker; Sukchon and Sunchon Airborne Operation

References

Appleman, Roy E. *Ridgway Duels for Korea.* College Station: Texas A&M University Press, 1980.

Mossman, Billy C. *United States Army in the Korean War: Ebb and Flow, November 1950–July 1951.* Washington, DC: U.S. Army Center of Military History, 1990.

Ridgway, Matthew B. *The Korean War.* Garden City, NY: Doubleday, 1967.

Murphy, Charles Springs
Birth Date: August 20, 1909
Death Date: July 28, 1983

Special counsel to the president (1950–1953), speechwriter from 1947 onward, and a close personal friend to President Harry S. Truman. Born on August 20, 1909, in Wallace, North Carolina, Charles Springs Murphy joined the civil service in 1928 as a postal clerk in Wilmington, Delaware; he earned a bachelor's degree and a law degree from Duke University by attending night school. Murphy then moved to Washington to work as assistant counsel in the Office of the Legislative Counsel of the U.S. Senate, scrutinizing the language of draft bills to ensure that there were no inaccuracies or errors. In this capacity Murphy, a Democrat, became acquainted with and won the respect of the novice senator Harry S. Truman of Missouri, who often called upon his expertise and for whom he wrote the bill establishing the wartime committee to investigate the World War II–era defense industry that Truman chaired.

In 1947 President Truman chose Murphy as a presidential administrative assistant responsible for steering bills through the numerous congressional pitfalls and hazards that they faced. In 1950 Truman selected Murphy to succeed Clark Clifford as special counsel to the president, his principal responsibility being to ensure the legislative success of programs initiated by the White House. Murphy was known for his meticulous attention to detail and his deep knowledge both of Congress and of legislation in progress. Many viewed the unassuming lawyer as the most able member of Truman's staff.

The plain-spoken Truman also valued Murphy's talent for expressing the president's thoughts in simple and comprehensible words and phrases compatible with his own personality, and the president used him as a major speechwriter. The two men found

Charles S. Murphy was a close friend and special counsel to U.S. president Harry S. Truman during 1950–1953. (AP/Wide World Photos)

each other highly congenial, and Murphy regularly attended sessions of Truman's so-called Little Cabinet, late-night meetings of a circle of the president's friends and advisers who discussed and decided political and legislative strategies over poker and bourbon. Murphy played an important part in developing the campaign strategy for the presidential election of 1948 in which the supposedly unelectable incumbent won a dramatic upset victory.

Murphy's role in U.S. policy toward the Korean War was relatively limited and essentially supportive. He was present at the November 28, 1950, meeting when Truman told his staff that Chinese intervention in the war had destroyed all hope of a quick and easy victory. Murphy helped to draft several of the president's speeches on the war, including his statement of June 27, 1950, and his December 16 declaration of a national emergency that demanded much higher defense spending, partial mobilization, price and wage controls, and restoration of the draft.

Truman discussed with Murphy his April 1952 seizure of the steel plants, a move that the Supreme Court ultimately declared unconstitutional. He was one of the entourage at Truman's October 1950 Wake Island meeting with General Douglas MacArthur. The following April, when the president finally fired the general, Murphy advised him on public relations tactics.

Overall, Murphy's role was to support and assist the president rather than to initiate policy. This pattern continued into later years, when Murphy assisted his financially straitened former boss in approaching top political figures to win congressional legislation granting all presidents a pension. Even later, Murphy was one of the comparatively few guests invited to attend Truman's 1972 funeral and memorial ceremonies.

After Truman left office, Murphy went into private law practice in Washington. He returned to government in 1961 when President John F. Kennedy appointed him undersecretary of agriculture. From 1965 to 1968 Murphy was chairman of the Civil Aeronautics Board, and in 1968 he also became counselor to the embattled President Lyndon B. Johnson. Murphy returned to private law practice when Richard Nixon became president in 1969, but behind the scenes the Democratic Party valued Murphy's advice and regarded him as a respected elder statesman. Murphy died in Anne Arundel County, Maryland, on July 28, 1983.

PRISCILLA ROBERTS

See also

MacArthur, Douglas; Truman, Harry S.; Wake Island Conference

References

Hamby, Alonzo L. *Man of the People: A Life of Harry S. Truman.* New York: Oxford University Press, 1995.
McCullough, David. *Truman.* New York: Simon and Schuster, 1992.

Murphy, Robert Daniel
Birth Date: October 28, 1894
Death Date: January 9, 1978

U.S. diplomat and ambassador to Japan during 1952–1953. Born in Milwaukee, Wisconsin, on October 28, 1894, to an Irish laborer's family, Robert Daniel Murphy worked his way through Marquette University and George Washington University Law School, after which he joined the Foreign Service in 1920. Early assignments were followed by 10 years in Paris (1930–1940).

During World War II, Murphy undertook various confidential assignments for President Franklin D. Roosevelt, helping to prepare the ground for the invasion of North Africa, among other missions. From September 1944 until 1949 Murphy was the political adviser in occupied Germany, working closely with deputy military governor Lieutenant General Lucius D. Clay. Both men became early supporters of the economic rehabilitation of the western occupation sectors of Germany, and both generally urged a hard line against Soviet demands. This was particularly the case during the 1948–1949 Berlin Blockade, when Murphy believed that administration policy was overly conciliatory.

After 18 generally uneventful months as U.S. ambassador to Belgium, in 1952 Murphy was appointed ambassador to Japan, the first U.S. diplomat since the war to hold that position. At this time, President Harry S. Truman's administration regarded Murphy's lack of previous Asian experience as a positive asset, since

many of its Far East experts had come under McCarthyite attack for views allegedly overly sympathetic to Asian communism, a charge from which Murphy's well-known hawkish reputation protected him. In this post Murphy worked closely with General Lieutenant Mark W. Clark, commander of United Nations Command (UNC) forces in Korea, to bring about an armistice in Korea. Here again, Murphy's uncompromising outlook was much in evidence. Murphy believed that the Soviet Union and the People's Republic of China (PRC) were using the Democratic People's Republic of Korea (DPRK, North Korea) for their own ends but that both powers feared extension of the war to China. Murphy maintained that the United States should drive the Chinese People's Volunteer Army (CPVA, Chinese Army) back into Manchuria, as he believed that UNC forces were capable of doing, rather than restricting its troops to a limited war. The UNC could then force a peace settlement on the Chinese and North Koreans. Murphy also found himself frustrated by what he believed to be intransigent and unreliable maneuvering by South Korean president Syngman Rhee, who stubbornly refused to improve his country's relations with Japan.

When Dwight D. Eisenhower, Murphy's old friend and military associate from World War II, assumed the presidency in 1953, he appointed Murphy assistant secretary of state for United Nations (UN) affairs but delayed his transfer until after the armistice had been concluded. Murphy found his role as political adviser during the concluding stages of the armistice negotiations personally difficult, and the contrast with his experiences in Europe at the end of World War II, when the United States was dealing from a victorious position, was especially galling. He continued to believe that the United States should have fought the Korean War to a similar victorious end.

In August 1953 after the Korean Armistice Agreement had been signed, Murphy unenthusiastically took up his UN duties, blaming that organization for having exercised a major "restraining influence" on U.S. prosecution of the war in Korea. Later that year Eisenhower promoted Murphy to deputy undersecretary of state, placing him third in the department. Until Murphy's retirement in 1959, he was a troubleshooter undertaking particularly sensitive missions, with Eisenhower dispatching him to deal with the French during the Suez Crisis of 1956 and to Lebanon in 1958 to prepare that nation for the arrival of U.S. troops. Although retired, in 1969 Murphy advised President Richard Nixon on top diplomatic appointments, and under Gerald Ford, Murphy served on the Foreign Intelligence Advisory Committee. Murphy died in New York City on January 9, 1978.

PRISCILLA ROBERTS

See also

Clark, Mark Wayne; Eisenhower, Dwight David; Rhee, Syngman

References

Foot, Rosemary J. *A Substitute for Victory: The Politics of Peacemaking at the Korean Armistice Talks.* Ithaca, NY: Cornell University Press, 1990.

Funk, Arthur L. "Murphy, Robert Daniel." In *American National Biography*, 24 vols., edited by John A. Garraty and Mark C. Carnes, 16:143–144. New York: Oxford University Press, 1999.

McMahon, Robert J. "Robert D. Murphy." In *Dictionary of American Biography: Supplement Ten, 1976–1980*, edited by Kenneth T. Jackson, 571–573. New York: Scribner, 1995.

Murphy, Robert D. *Diplomat among Warriors*. Garden City, NY: Doubleday, 1964.

Music of the Korean War, Korean

South Korean music relating to the Korean War comprises both popular contemporary songs and songs in the classical style. Nevertheless, an overwhelming majority of Korean War music consists of popular songs composed in the 1950s. The songwriter Yu Ho and the composer Pak Si Chun were two prominent figures who jointly produced a number of popular songs relating to the war. About the time that South Korean and United Nations Command (UNC) forces marched north across the 38th Parallel in the autumn of 1950, the two men turned out a famous field song titled "Chonu ya Chal Chara" (Rest in Peace, Fellow Soldiers), which was sung by the singer Hyon In. Containing such lyrics as "jumping over the dead bodies of fellow soldiers," the "Naktong River," "Water of the Han River," and the "38th Parallel," this song was a favorite among South Korean soldiers at the time. Even now, Korean War veterans are still stirred when they sing or hear it.

In 1952 these two musicians produced another well-known song, "Chonson Yagok" (Night Song of the Front), which was a tune about the fall of Seoul on January 4, 1951. Pak Si Chun also composed "Ibyol ui Pusan Chongojang" (Farewell at Pusan Station). This song, which came out in 1953, dealt with the return of the South Korean government to Seoul on August 15, 1953. The words of the song were written by Ho Tong A. In 1951, Pak Si Chun composed "Kutseora Kumsun a" (Be Stout-Hearted, Kumsun), the words of which were written by Kang Sa Rang. This song expressed a man's reluctance to leave his girlfriend. Yu Ho wrote the words to the song "Chincha Sanai" (A Confirmed Man), which has been called the most popular martial song of South Korean forces. The music was composed by Yi Hung Ryol in 1973.

Among other songs relating to the Korean War, "Tanjang ui Mia-ri Kogae" (The Heartbreaking Mia-ri Pass) was released in 1959. It expressed a wife's pining for her husband who had been kidnapped by retreating North Korean forces and had passed through the Mia-ri Pass just north of Seoul to be taken to the Democratic People's Republic of Korea (DPRK, North Korea). Songs such as "Kum e Pon Nae Kohyang" (My Hometown Seen in a Dream) (1951), "Panmunjom ui Talbam" (Moonlight at Panmunjom) (1956), "Sampalson ui Pom" (Spring at the 38th Parallel) (1959), and "Kum e Pon Taedonggang" (The Taedong River Seen in a Dream) (1956) described the homesickness of North Korean refugees who had fled to the Republic of Korea (ROK, South Korea).

Singer and actress Rosemary Clooney rose to stardom in the 1950s. With five gold records to her credit, she was well known for her jazz and popular song interpretations. (AP/Wide World Photos)

Songs such as "Hae do Hana Tal do Hana" (The Sun and the Moon Are One and the Same) (1949), "Nambuk Tongil" (North-South Korean Unification) (no date), "Kagora Sampalson" (The 38th Parallel Should Be Gone) (1947) manifested the pain that Koreans suffered after the division of their country. The distinctive feature of these Korean songs dealing with division and war was that they almost all expressed feelings of sorrow and deplorability. A typical lamentation in the classical style, "Pimok" (Tomb Wood) (1967) also had the same character.

When North Korea launched its surprise military attack across the 38th Parallel against South Korea on June 25, 1950, the United States took the lead in forming the United Nations (UN) coalition to repel the invasion. South Koreans therefore considered the United States as their savior. Korean gratitude toward the United States led to a great outpouring of affection for the country, which produced several American-aspiration songs such as "San Francisco" (1954), "America Chinatown" (1953), and "Arizona Cowboy" (1953). Unlike most Korean War–era songs, the tunes dealing with the United States were as a whole characterized by their cheerful and bright overtones. This phenomenon was closely related to rising pro-Americanism that reached its climax in the 1950s and the 1960s.

This pro-American sentiment also gave rise to interest in American popular songs among Koreans. In the 1950s the favorite American pop singer was Patti Page. Her songs, including "Tennessee Waltz," "Changing Partners," and "I Went to Your

Dizzy Gillespie was a trumpet virtuoso who, with Charlie Parker, instigated the bop revolution. (Library of Congress)

Wedding" sung in an elegant rhythm of triple time, commanded great popularity among South Koreans.

Finally, unlike lyrical songs of South Korea, the Korean War–era songs of North Korea, which consist of tunes that celebrate the defense of the fatherland and death-defying resistance, have a strongly ideological bent to them. This phenomenon appears in North Korean literature as well as in music.

Jinwung Kim

See also

Literature of the Korean War, Korean; Music of the Korean War, U.S.

References

Hanguk Chonjaeng kwa Taejung Kayo [The Korean War and Popular Songs]. A Music Exhibition. Pusan, South Korea, June 22–August 31, 2007.

Howard, Keith. *Korean Music.* Burlington, VT: Ashgate, 2006.

———. *Korean Pop Music: Riding the Wave.* Folkstone, Kent, UK: Global Oriental Publishing, 2006.

Music of the Korean War, U.S.

The Korean War unfolded during what many would argue was the greatest sea change in American music history. The war saw a continuation of the big-band style of music of the 1940s, which was by then already on its way out; the emergence of popularized rhythm and blues (R&B) by artists such as Memphis Slim, T-Bone Walker, and John Lee Hooker; and the moanin' blues, a particular style of country-western music that featured the nasal-voiced Hank Williams singing to the accompaniment of blues chord progressions.

Looming just over the horizon, however, was the advent of rock and roll, a term first coined in 1951 by Cleveland disc jockey Alan Freed but not truly popularized until 1955, when rock-and-roller Bill Haley released his smash hit "Rock around the Clock." The year before, a young and still unknown singer named Elvis Presley released "That's Alright Mama," a bluesy number that borrowed heavily from African American soul and country-western music. Presley would be credited largely for the transformation to rock and roll, but Haley and others helped put it on the map and ushered in a new style of music that persists to the present day.

During the early 1950s, however, American music was still largely dominated by the light melodies and sweet sentimental lyricism of popular music, which is what most American soldiers listened to while serving in Korea. The music was performed by the last vestiges of the big bands of the 1940s and was often sung by vocalists such as Pat Boone, Rosemary Clooney, Nat King Cole, Frank Sinatra, Perry Como, Tony Bennett, Doris Day, and many others. This music was not considered controversial in either its style or lyricism, and it reflected the fragile political and social consensus of the post–World War II United States.

Unlike World War I and World War II, the Korean War did not produce many wartime or propaganda-style songs. Perhaps this was because the war was an unpopular one and because many Americans had a difficult time understanding the cause, course, and goals of the conflict.

In 1951 Arthur "Big Boy" Crudup lamented the war from a personal African American perspective in his song "I'm Gonna Dig Myself a Hole." Capturing the frustration of the conflict, he sang: "Well, I ain't got no one to love me, all I got is gone . . . I might dig myself a hole . . . You know when I come up, there won't be no wars around." The hole metaphor also alludes to nuclear warfare, during which the only place presumably safe would be a bunker in the ground.

In 1951 the Louvin Brothers produced a song meant to keep those on the home front connected to the war. Titled "Weapon of Prayer," the song implored Americans to pray for their compatriots serving in the Korean War, suggesting that prayer and God's love were the ultimate weapons with which to wage the conflict. Meanwhile, some servicemen sang songs from World War II, as many Korean War GIs had also served in that conflict.

Rock and roll emerged concomitant to the Korean War, and although it would not become widely popular until after the conflict ended, it was about to set the American musical and cultural scene on its head. Unlike the predictable and noncontroversial music of the first few years of the 1950s, rock and roll was seen as scandalous by many adults because of its up-tempo beat, reliance on guitars and drums instead of large bands and orchestras, and provocative lyrics. Its earliest adherents, such as Elvis Presley, made it seem even more over the top with his suggestive hip gyrations and sexual innuendoes. In its early years, rock and roll was especially frowned upon in the American South, and many radio stations there refused to play it because of its clear connections with African American–inspired blues, soul, and jazz genres.

Meanwhile, during the early 1950s jazz musicians were helping to radically transform that genre as well. Whereas jazz of the big-band era had emphasized large bands and orchestras and flowing melodies, the new jazz featured smaller groups, such as quintets, quartets, and trios, that emphasized edgier melodies, improvisational riffs, and long solos. While some big-band–era songs were simply rearranged and given faster tempos, the jazz impresarios also wrote much new music, which better fit the new jazz style that had now come to be called be-bop. Be-bop was popularized by Dizzy Gillespie, Miles Davis, Charlie Parker, Thelonious Monk, and others. Clearly, while the popular American music was somewhat predictable during the Korean War, just underneath the surface of this seeming conformity lurked revolutionary changes.

PAUL G. PIERPAOLI JR.

See also

Music of the Korean War, Korean

References

Cook, Richard, and Brian Morton. *The Penguin Guide to Jazz.* 7th ed. New York: Penguin, 2004.

Davis, Ronald L. *A History of Music in American Life*, Vol. 3, *1920–Present.* Huntington, NY: Krieger Publishing, 1981.

Starr, Larry, and Christopher Waterman. *American Popular Music: From Minstrelsy to Mp3.* New York: Oxford University Press, 2006.

Muste, Abraham Johannes
Birth Date: January 8, 1885
Death Date: February 11, 1967

Quaker minister, union organizer, radical, pacifist, and antiwar activist. Abraham Johannes Muste was born in Zierikzee, Netherlands, on January 8, 1885. At the age of six, he moved with his family to Grand Rapids, Michigan, where he spent much of his youth. From 1909 to 1914 he was a minister in the Dutch Reformed Church. In 1914 he joined the Congregational Church, and from 1918 to 1926 was a member of the Society of Friends (Quakers). He was a dedicated pacifist during World War I. As a Quaker minister, he also became involved in union organizing.

During the 1920s and 1930s, Muste largely eschewed religion and became more radicalized as he continued to agitate for the labor agenda. He actually conferred with Leon Trotsky in Norway in 1936 but had a sudden change of heart upon his return to the United States that same year. Muste now rejected radical Marxism and dedicated his efforts to nonviolent pacifism, mainly through the peace organization Fellowship for Reconciliation (FOR). In 1940 he became executive secretary of FOR, a position that he would hold for the remainder of his life.

During World War II, Muste was outspoken in his criticism of the war, arguing that waging war against the Axis powers only encouraged them to resort to even more brutality. He also actively promoted conscientious objection and draft evasion as a way to register personal contempt for warfare. Muste and FOR pioneered the concept of peaceful passive resistance, which would soon be taken up by Mohandas Gandhi in India and later by the the U.S. Civil Rights Movement that began in the mid-1950s.

As the Cold War settled in during the late 1940s, Muste became even more dedicated to peace, arguing that the horror of modern warfare and atomic weapons necessitated a step back from the precipice and demanded the implementation of worldwide disarmament. Muste soon became involved in the War Resisters' League and had made opposition to the nuclear arms race one of his signature causes.

Muste vociferously opposed the Korean War, once again imploring Americans not to support the war effort and to resist the draft, much as he had during World War II. As a show of his distaste for what he termed U.S. militarism, he refused to pay federal income taxes from 1948 to 1952 because he believed that the taxes would be used for military purposes. In 1960 he was compelled to pay his back taxes, with interest and penalties, under threat of imprisonment. He paid the taxes unwillingly. By the 1950s Muste had come to be admired by many for his dedication to pacifism and his intellectual prowess that linked nonviolent civil disobedience with modern religion and theology.

During the 1960s Muste became one of the first individuals to speak out against the U.S. war effort in Vietnam. He attended numerous antiwar demonstrations and was a major presence in New York's antiwar organization Fifth Avenue Peace Parade Committee. Despite his advanced age, in 1966 Muste was chosen to head up the Spring Mobilization to End the War in Vietnam, a nationwide movement that planned mass antiwar demonstrations in 1967. Muste's unique background as a one-time political radical, labor organizer, minister, and peace activist allowed him to act as a highly effective mediator among the competing antiwar factions. In April 1966 he traveled to Saigon to advance the peace agenda, and he went to Hanoi in January 1967. The following month, on February 11, 1967, Muste died of a heart attack in New York City.

PAUL G. PIERPAOLI JR.

See also

Antiwar Sentiment in the United States

References

Hentoff, Nat. *Peace Agitator: The Story of A. J. Muste.* New York: Macmillan, 1963.

Robinson, Jo Ann. *Abraham Went Out: A Biography of A. J. Muste.* Philadelphia: Temple University Press, 1981.

Myong Nyon

See Pak Sun Chon

N

Najin, Bombing of
Start Date: August 1950
End Date: August 1951

Port and industrial center in northeastern Korea only 60 miles from Vladivostok and less than 20 miles from the Soviet border, which became a controversial bombing target because of its installations and location. Najin (also called Rashin or Racin) in 1950 contained key oil storage tanks and railway yards as well as docks frequented by Soviet ships. It was included in the early target lists of major industrial concentrations prepared both by the Strategic Air Command (SAC) and the Joint Chiefs of Staff (JCS), but the Far East Air Force (FEAF) Bomber Command could not divert adequate resources to strategic bombing until the ground situation had stabilized and additional SAC reinforcements arrived.

Boeing B-29 Superfortresses attacked the city on August 12, 1950, but cloud cover forced them to deliver their bomb loads by radar, and the results were poor. The inaccurate bombing and news reports that the mission was designed to hinder Soviet submarine operations from the ice-free port heightened U.S. State Department fears that the action might widen the war, and protests were lodged with both President Harry S. Truman and Secretary of Defense Louis Johnson.

Although Johnson defended the raids, U.S. Air Force chief of staff General Hoyt Vandenberg instructed Lieutenant General George Stratemeyer of the FEAF to delay further attacks until targets could be reevaluated. Johnson and JCS chairman General Omar Bradley requested permission from the National Security Council to resume the attacks in October, but by then United Nations Command (UNC) F-51 Mustangs had strafed a Chinese airfield, and the U.S. Navy had shot down a Soviet aircraft. A worried Truman ordered the State Department and the Defense Department to study the matter, and the JCS decided on its own to order no further attacks against Najin because of the increased tensions.

Najin again became an issue after Chinese intervention in the war. On February 15, 1951, General Douglas MacArthur complained that the communist side was taking advantage of the port's immunity from air attack to build up reinforcements and supplies. He asked to be permitted to take advantage of good weather to destroy docks, marshaling yards, and storage facilities by visual bombing. Major General Maxwell Taylor, U.S. Army assistant chief of staff for operations, recommended at a February 16 meeting that U.S. Army chief of staff General J. Lawton Collins ask the JCS to lift restrictions, but the JCS expressed concern about the bombers being intercepted or hitting Soviet ships in the harbor. MacArthur replied that there were no indications that Soviet ships were using the port, while the only source for possible fighters to defend the city were Soviet airfields near Vladivostok, "and such an overt act of war is not considered likely." Taylor again recommended that Collins get approval for the air attacks at the next JCS meeting on February 19, but Secretary of Defense George Marshall, Secretary of State Dean Acheson, and President Truman all agreed that the limitations should not be removed at that time. The JCS informed MacArthur of its decision on February 21. The prohibition against bombing Najin generated much debate in May 1951 during the congressional hearings concerning the relief of MacArthur and the overall situation in the Far East.

MacArthur's successor, Lieutenant General Matthew B. Ridgway, tried to get the restrictions lifted later that summer. He cabled the JCS that aerial reconnaissance had revealed "extensive stockpiling of materiel and supplies" at the port, and with its highway

U.S. Air Force Bomber Specifications

Aircraft	Span	Length	Height	Gross Weight (pounds)	Top Speed (mph)	Range (miles)	Ceiling (feet)
Boeing B-29	141' 3"	99' 0"	29' 7"	137,500	364	4,200	32,000
Douglas B-26	70' 0"	50' 0"	18' 6"	35,000	355	1,400	22,100
N.A. RB-45	96' 0"	75' 11"	25' 2"	110,721	570	2,530	40,250

and rail complex funneling supplies to all areas in the south, it was "a principal focal point for intensifying the enemy supply build-up in the battle area." In reply to queries about his specific plans, Ridgway assured the JCS that because of uncertain weather conditions, he would mount only one or two normal visual strikes against the marshaling yard, and he guaranteed that the border would not be violated.

The Air Staff supported Ridgway's request for many reasons. An attack would hamper the communist supply buildup and might pressure their negotiators out of "dilatory tactics" at the armistice talks. It was in keeping with current JCS directives to conduct no military operations within 12 miles of Soviet Union territory, and it would show the communists that "all of their sanctuaries are not privileged." Najin was also considered "the last major profitable

strategic target in Korea." The Air Staff discounted diplomatic concerns about a secret treaty between the Democratic People's Republic of Korea (DPRK, North Korea) and the Soviet Union giving the Soviets a long-term lease on the port, noting that another port covered in the same agreement had been bombed repeatedly with no Soviet reaction.

The JCS agreed with the Air Staff arguments and, after getting presidential approval, authorized Ridgway to attack Najin. Since the port lay beyond the range of Fifth Air Force fighters, carrier jets provided cover for 35 B-29s, which carried out the mission in good weather on August 25, 1951. Bomber Command hit the target area with a reported 97 percent of the more than 300 tons of bombs dropped, and no follow-up raids were necessary.

CONRAD C. CRANE

The North Korean port city of Najin (Rashin) was an important target during the Korean War because of its oil storage facilities and railroad yards, but it was difficult to strike because of its proximity to the Soviet Union. (Corbis)

See also

Acheson, Dean Gooderham; Aircraft; Bradley, Omar Nelson; Collins, Joseph Lawton; Johnson, Louis Arthur; Joint Chiefs of Staff; MacArthur, Douglas; Marshall, George Catlett; Ridgway, Matthew Bunker; Stratemeyer, George Edward; Taylor, Maxwell Davenport; Truman, Harry S.; Vandenberg, Hoyt Sanford

References

Crane, Conrad C. *American Air Power Strategy in Korea, 1950–1953.* Lawrence: University Press of Kansas, 1999.

Futrell, Robert F. *The United States Air Force in Korea, 1950–1953.* Rev. ed. Washington, DC: Office of the Chief of Air Force History, 1983.

Schnabel, James F. *United States Army in the Korean War: Policy and Direction, the First Year.* Washington, DC: Office of the Chief of Military History, Department of the Army, 1972.

Schnabel, James F., and Robert J. Watson. *The History of the Joint Chiefs of Staff: The Joint Chiefs of Staff and National Policy,* Vol. 3, *The Korean War.* Wilmington, DE: Michael Glazier, 1979.

U.S. Senate. *Military Situation in the Far East: Hearings before the Committee on Armed Services and the Committee on Foreign Relations.* 82nd Cong., 1st sess. Washington, DC: U.S. Government Printing Office, 1951.

Naktong Bulge, First Battle of

Start Date: August 5, 1950
End Date: August 19, 1950

Key battle in August 1950 involving U.S. and Republic of Korea Army (ROKA, South Korean Army) forces against Korean People's Army (KPA, North Korean Army) troops along the Naktong River. In early August, Major General John H. Church's 24th Infantry Division numbered 9,882 men (half its authorized strength). An attachment of 486 soldiers and operational control of the 2,000-man ROKA 17th Infantry Regiment brought its aggregate strength to 12,368 men. Rated combat efficiency was 53 percent.

The division manned a 34-mile front; army doctrine, however, called for division fronts (at full strength) to be only 9 miles. The northern 30,000-yard sector was held by the ROKA 17th Infantry, while the next 12,000-yard sector was held by the U.S. 21st Infantry with the 14th Engineer Combat Battalion. The Heavy Mortar Company was on line south of the 21st. Next, in the bulge of the Naktong, was the 34th Infantry on a 16,000-yard front. Everywhere the division front was held by isolated squad and platoon enclaves, with huge gaps between them. The 3rd Battalion, 34th Infantry, manned the regimental front with I, L, and K companies, from north to south. The 1st Battalion, 34th Infantry, formed the regimental reserve, while the 19th Infantry was the division reserve.

At one minute after midnight on August 6, 1950, 800 members of the KPA 4th Division quietly crossed the Naktong and drove deep into the gap between I and L companies of the 34th Infantry. A counterattack by the 1st Battalion of the 34th Infantry saw its Company A reach the front line, but in effect the counterattack failed. A subsequent attack by the 19th Infantry and the

24th Recon Company relieved some pressure but failed to stay the KPA's advance.

The ROKA 17th Infantry thwarted a KPA river-crossing attempt on the night of August 6–7. The next morning the Eighth Army withdrew the 17th Infantry. Its place was taken by Task Force Hyzer, named for Lieutenant Colonel Peter C. Hyzer, commanding officer of the 3rd Engineer Combat Battalion. It consisted of Hyzer's battalion, a light tank company (less its tanks), and the 24th Recon Company. At the same time Eighth Army commander Lieutenant General Walton H. Walker reduced the 24th Infantry Division's front by 20,000 yards, assigning this to the 1st Cavalry Division on the 24th Infantry's right flank.

Counterattacks and fighting during August 7–10 proved fruitless, although the newly arrived 9th Infantry Regiment of the U.S. 2nd Division was thrown into the battle. KPA troops now approached the town of Yongsan in the 24th Division rear area, and the 2nd Battalion, 27th Infantry Regiment, of the 25th Division was committed to the southern flank of the 24th Division, attacking successfully northeast toward the town.

On August 10 Church formed Task Force Hill, named for Colonel John G. Hill, commander of the 9th Infantry. It included the 9th Infantry (less its 3rd Battalion), the 19th and 34th Infantry regiments, and the 1st Battalion, 21st Infantry. But the force was inadequate.

KPA forces now cut the main supply route east of Yongsan. A series of ad hoc defensive positions were formed along this route by headquarters, military police, reconnaissance, and engineer troops, but most soon fell to enemy attack. On August 12 elements of the KPA 10th Division crossed the Naktong and seized a large terrain mass on the division's northern flank (Hill 409) but never moved beyond that point.

On August 13 the 2nd Battalion of the 27th Infantry, joined by the 3rd Battalion, attacked again, driving closer to Yongsan and making contact with 1st Battalion of the 21st Infantry and the freshly arrived 1st Battalion of the 23rd Infantry of the U.S. 2nd Division. This meeting opened the supply route.

Task Force Hill was not sufficiently strong to continue attacking on August 14 and 15. The KPA struck the 1st Battalion of the 21st Infantry shortly after midnight on August 15 and then attacked all across the front, penetrating the lines of the 2nd Battalion of the 9th Regiment, 2nd Division. Continuing on August 16, the KPA pushed the 2nd Battalion of the 19th Regiment back some 600 yards and forced the 1st Battalion of the 34th Infantry to give ground.

On August 17 Task Force Hill was disbanded, its components reverting to division control. That day the 1st Marine Provisional Brigade (5th Marine Regiment, artillery battalion, and tank company) was committed to the fray, attached to the 24th Division.

The Marine 2nd Battalion attacked the KPA on Obong-ni Ridge. The army's 9th Infantry, on the marines' right, was to attack at the same time. The commanders of the 5th Marines and 9th Infantry decided to have the marines attack first and then support the army attack. This proved to be a mistake, for KPA troops in the army's zone poured deadly fire into the flanks and rear of the attackers. This coupled with very stubborn resistance limited the marines to the seizure of a single knob on the ridge. Then the 9th attacked and eliminated the threat to the marines from that quarter.

The Marine 1st Battalion continued the assault on Obong-ni, taking two-thirds of the ridge. The marines defeated a KPA counterattack that night and then the next morning seized the remainder of Obong-ni and a promontory across the valley from it. Army units also continued attacking north of the marines on August 18, some them taking heavy casualties. But KPA troops were dislodged and began fleeing toward and across the Naktong, hastened by heavy and accurate air, artillery, and mortar fire.

By August 19 the United Nations Command (UNC) had restored the river line but at the high cost of more than 1,800 casualties. The KPA 4th Division, which had numbered about 8,000 men, was reduced to some 3,500 men and lost all of its artillery and heavy equipment.

Uzal W. Ent

See also

Church, John Huston; Naktong Bulge, Second Battle of; Walker, Walton Harris

References

Appleman, Roy E. *United States Army in Korea: South to the Naktong, North to the Yalu.* Washington, DC: Office of the Chief of Military History, 1961.

Blair, Clay. *The Forgotten War: America in Korea, 1950–1953.* New York: Times Books, 1987.

Ent, Uzal W. *Fighting on the Brink: Defense of the Pusan Perimeter.* Paducah, KY: Turner, 1996.

Geer, Andrew. *The New Breed: The Story of the U.S. Marines in Korea.* Nashville, TN: Battery Press, 1989.

Montross, Lynn, et al. *U.S. Marine Operations in Korea, 1950–1953.* 5 vols. Washington, DC: U.S. Marine Corps Historical Branch, 1954–1972.

Naktong Bulge, Second Battle of
Start Date: August 31, 1950
End Date: September 9, 1950

Second key battle in August–September 1950 involving U.S. and Republic of Korea Army (ROKA, South Korean Army) forces against the Korean People's Army (KPA, North Korean Army) along the Naktong River. On August 24, 1950, the U.S. 2nd Infantry Division relieved the 24th Infantry Division on the Naktong. An adjustment of the 2nd Infantry Division and 1st Cavalry Division sectors gave the 2nd Division a front of more than 32 miles. Eighth Army commander Lieutenant General Walton H. Walker believed that with the defeat of the KPA 4th Division earlier in the month, the U.S. 2nd Division would be on a relatively quiet front where it could gain experience but without serious fighting.

The division had but seven infantry battalions available. The 3rd Battalion, 9th Infantry Regiment, was defending the airfield at Yonil, and the 3rd Battalion, 23rd Infantry, was attached to the 1st Cavalry Division. 2nd Division commander Major General Laurence B. "Dutch" Keiser placed his 38th Infantry in the north on a front of almost 12 miles, with the 23rd Infantry (minus the 3rd Battalion) in the center defending somewhat less than 10 miles and with the 9th Infantry (minus the 3rd Battalion) in the south, including the bulge, defending about 11.5 miles.

The 1st Battalion, 9th Infantry, held the southern half of the regimental sector with three companies on line; the 2nd Battalion, 19th Infantry, held the north with two companies. One company was in reserve.

The 23rd Infantry placed all three companies of the 1st Battalion on line. The 2nd Battalion (minus Company E) was in reserve. Company E was sent to the 9th Infantry as an additional reserve unit. The 38th Infantry outposted the Naktong with two companies, while two others were on the regimental flank. Its 3rd Battalion was in reserve.

Supported by artillery and mortar fire, elements of the KPA 9th Division crossed the Naktong between 9:30 p.m. and midnight on August 1, striking the 9th Infantry Regiment. The KPA 2nd Division attacked the 23rd Infantry at the same time, overrunning Company C. The attack was so swift and surprising that it also overran the reinforced company-sized Task Force Manchu, which had been assembled in Company B's position in preparation for a raid across the river. Although one or two river-front units still held out, by dawn on September 1 the KPA had already taken Obong-ni Ridge and most of the neighboring Cloverleaf Hill. In one memorable episode, Sergeant Ernest R. Kouma's tank battled the KPA all night and then fought its way through eight miles of KPA-held territory. Kouma was later awarded the Medal of Honor.

The story was the same in the 23rd Infantry's sector; some troops of the KPA 2nd Division attacked frontally, while others exploited gaps to attack command posts (CPs), supply points, and mortar and artillery positions and to ambush reinforcements. Companies B and C were all but destroyed.

Part of the KPA 10th Division also attacked the 38th Infantry, overrunning Companies E and F. Elements of three KPA divisions (the 2nd, 9th, and 10th) attacked the 2nd Division. By daylight on September 1 the KPA had split the 2nd Division in two, and KPA units had reached Yongsan, deep in the division's rear. South of the 2nd Division, elements of the KPA 6th and 7th divisions had penetrated 25th Division's lines, but the division's 27th Infantry was successfully counterattacking.

Remnants of the 9th Infantry, the division engineers, reconnaissance company, part of the division's tank battalion, and some automatic antiaircraft carriers then formed a scratch force to defend Yongsan.

General Keiser appointed division artillery commander Brigadier General Loyal Haynes to lead the defense of the division's northern sector and assistant division commander Brigadier

A Korean People's Army (North Korean Army) soldier who had been captured by U.S. marines on September 4, 1950, during the Second Battle of the Naktong Bulge. (National Archives)

General Sladen Bradley to do the same in the south. Meanwhile, General Walker attached the Marine Brigade to the 2nd Division at 1:30 p.m. on September 2 and alerted the 19th Infantry (24th Division) for possible commitment.

The army-marine counterattack on September 3 was marked by considerable confusion. The local army commander told the marines that the line of departure was secured; it was not. The marines had to seize it before launching the planned attack.

The Marine 2nd Battalion attacked from south of Yongsan along the main supply route. Shortly thereafter, it was stopped by stubborn KPA defenders, but the Marine 1st Battalion, attacking on the 2nd Battalion's left, dislodged this force. The marines ended the day with the two battalions somewhat scattered but having driven back the KPA. On September 4 the 1st and 3rd battalions continued the attack, forcing KPA units to retreat farther. The marines experienced heavy KPA artillery fire and infantry probes that night.

Early on September 5 a strong KPA counterattack against the 9th Infantry north of the marines was thwarted by artillery and the marines' machine-gun fire. Then the marines began their attack, headed for Obong-ni Ridge. Simultaneously, elements of the 9th, 23rd, and 38th regiments of the 2nd Division also attacked.

Throughout this period the 23rd Regiment, aided by the 3rd Battalion, 38th Infantry, took on the KPA 2nd Division and thoroughly defeated it. Fighting in the 23rd Regiment's sector

continued until September 16, when most of the KPA forces were eliminated. In the far north of the division sector, the KPA 10th Division, after making its initial attacks, retreated onto massive Hill 409.

In this Second Battle of the Naktong River the KPA 2nd and 9th divisions lost between them more than 10,000 men. There is evidence that elements of the KPA 4th Division also took part in the battle, but to what extent and with what loss is unknown. KPA forces of varying sizes remained in the 2nd Division sector, engaging in some bloody battles, until the 2nd broke out of the perimeter later in September.

UZAL W. ENT

See also

Keiser, Laurence Bolton; Naktong Bulge, First Battle of; Walker, Walton Harris

References

Appleman, Roy E. *United States Army in Korea: South to the Naktong, North to the Yalu.* Washington, DC: Office of the Chief of Military History, 1961.

Blair, Clay. *The Forgotten War: America in Korea, 1950–1953.* New York: Times Books, 1987.

Ent, Uzal W. *Fighting on the Brink: Defense of the Pusan Perimeter.* Paducah, KY: Turner, 1996.

Geer, Andrew. *The New Breed: The Story of the U.S. Marines in Korea.* Nashville, TN: Battery Press, 1989.

Montross, Lynn, et al. *U.S. Marine Operations in Korea, 1950–1953.* 5 vols. Washington, DC: U.S. Marine Corps Historical Branch, 1954–1972.

Nam Il
Birth Date: June 5, 1913
Death Date: March 7, 1976

General and political figure in the Democratic People's Republic of Korea (DPRK, North Korea) and chief North Korean delegate at the Korean armistice negotiations. Born on June 5, 1913, at Kyongwon County, North Hamgyong Province, in present-day North Korea, the son of a farmer who later fled to Soviet Russia to escape the Japanese, Nam Il graduated from a teacher's college in Tashkent. Forsaking a teaching career, he attended the Smolensk Military School in the Soviet Union. As a Soviet Army captain, he fought in the Battle of Stalingrad. Later, as chief of staff of a division, he helped the Soviet Army take Warsaw.

Nam arrived in Pyongyang in August 1946, one year after Soviet forces had liberated North Korea from Japanese control. He then became vice minister of education of the North Korean People's Committee under Soviet auspices. In September 1948, on the establishment of the DPRK, Nam was named to the same post. The Ministry of Education was soon a propaganda vehicle for the new regime.

Nam helped the Defense Ministry plan the North Korean attack on the Republic of Korea (ROK, South Korea) on June 25, 1950.

General Nam Il, senior Democratic People's Republic of Korea delegate to the truce talks, shown leaving the negotiations after they had adjourned for the day, November 30, 1951. (National Archives)

With the beginning of the Korean War, he became vice chief of staff of the Korean People's Army (KPA, North Korean Army). In December 1950 he became its chief of staff with the rank of lieutenant general, replacing Kang Kon who had been killed in battle.

Nam was regularly elected to the Central Committee of the Korean Workers' Party. When armistice negotiations began in July 1951, he became head of the North Korean delegation, a position that he held for the remainder of the talks. The chain-smoking Nam had considerable nervous energy, although he seldom displayed emotion. He was also known for rudeness, lack of courtesy, and tasteless remarks. U.S. officials soon realized that Nam, despite his title, was subordinate to Chinese representative Xie Fang.

Nam met United Nations (UN) proposals with a filibuster, obviously unable to proceed without specific authorization from superiors. After a day or two, he would speak firmly on the matter under discussion. Shortly before the signing of the truce agreement, Nam was promoted to full general so that he would outrank Lieutenant General William K. Harrison Jr., who signed for the United Nations Command (UNC).

In August 1953, a month after the agreement, Nam became foreign minister, a post he held until 1959. Entirely subservient to North Korean leader Kim Il Sung, Nam was one of the few Korean officials of Soviet background to survive Kim's purge of Soviet Koreans after the Korean War. In 1954 Nam led the North Korean delegation at the Geneva Conference and proposed the reunification of Korea on the basis of North-South parity while excluding the UN and all external forces. South Korea opposed this plan, and no agreement could be reached.

In 1957 Nam was promoted to North Korean vice president, a post he held until his death on March 7, 1976, at Pyongyang, reportedly in an automobile accident. Nam received a state funeral.

HAKJOON KIM

See also
Armistice Agreement; Geneva Conference; Harrison, William Kelly, Jr.; Kang Kon; Xie Fang

References
Bailey, Sydney D. *The Korean Armistice.* New York: St. Martin's, 1992.

Foot, Rosemary J. *A Substitute for Victory: The Politics of Peacemaking at the Korean Armistice Talks.* Ithaca, NY: Cornell University Press, 1990.

Goulden, Joseph C. *Korea: The Untold Story of the War.* New York: Times Books, 1982.

Joy, C. Turner. *How Communists Negotiate.* New York: Macmillan, 1955.

Matray, James I., ed. *Historical Dictionary of the Korean War.* Westport, CT: Greenwood, 1991.

Namsi, Battle of
Event Date: October 1951

Air battle in and around Namsi, a town in northwestern North Korea not far from what was commonly known as MiG Alley. With the Korean War in stalemate in mid-October 1951, U.S. intelligence discovered three 7,000-foot hard-surfaced airstrips in a 20-mile radius in northwestern Korea near Saamchon, Taechon, and Namsi. Each had antiaircraft guns, major revetments, and some 1,000 workers for rapid runway repair.

Brigadier General Joe W. Kelly, commander of Bomber Command of the Far East Air Force (FEAF), was assigned to destroy the fields. Up to that time, most Boeing B-29 Superfortress raids had occurred during daylight, with no real MiG opposition. On average the B-29s flew 16 sorties a day, with three flights of three bombers each attacking rail and road targets or two flights of four bombers attacking bridges.

To destroy the airfields, Kelly planned to send three flights of three B-29s using short-range navigation (SHORAN) guidance beacons and receiving direct escort from Republic F-84 Thunderjets and indirect escort from North American F-86 Sabre patrols tying down enemy MiGs. The raids were planned along four SHORAN arcs. Flak and the lower altitude limits at which SHORAN beams could be received dictated bombing altitudes.

On October 18, 1951, nine B-29s of the 19th Bomb Group (19BG) attacked Saamchon, and nine from the 98th Bomb Wing (98BW) attacked Taechon. The 19BG successfully dropped 306 100-pound bombs on target, but the 98BW failed to rendezvous with its fighter escort and went on to secondary targets. The same thing happened three days later. Thus far, no MiGs had defended the airfields.

On October 22, 9 B-29s of the 19BG, escorted by 24 F-84s, bombed Taechon and were attacked by 40 MiG-15s. One B-29 crashed in the sea, but its crew was rescued. The next day, 9 more B-29s of the 307th Bomb Wing, supported by 55 F-84s, bombed Namsi. One B-29 aborted at the start. The rest were attacked by 50 MiGs diving through the formations. At the same time 100 other MiGs struck 34 nearby patrolling F-86s, effectively diverting them from the main fight. In the 20-minute battle, each of the three B-29 flights lost at least 1 bomber. The communists lost 4 MiGs (3 to the B-29 gunners), while 1 U.S. F-84 was lost. Only 1 of the bombers that survived the attacks did not have major damage as well as dead and wounded men on board.

One air force official called it "one of the most savage and bloody air battles of the Korean War." Still, the campaign continued the next day when 8 98BW B-29s bombed bypass railway bridges at Sunchon. Supported by 16 Royal Australian Air Force Gloster Meteors and 10 F-84s, they were attacked by 70 MiGs with similar results. Another B-29 went down, while 7 sustained heavy damage. For two days, FEAF commander General Otto P. Weyland halted operations. On October 27, 8 B-29s of the 19BG, 16 Meteors, and 32 F-84s were ravaged by 95 MiGs.

In many ways, the October raids proved to be the high tide for the communist air forces in the war. It was also, as historian Robert Futrell noted, the "swan song of Superfortress daytime operations over Korea."

The *U.S. Air Force Statistical Digest* for fiscal year 1953 officially reported that in one week United Nations Command (UNC) aircraft had engaged 2,166 MiG sorties and shot down 32 of them (24 by F-86s). The FEAF lost 15 aircraft: 7 F-86s, 5 B-29s, 2 F-84s, and 1 Lockheed RF-80 Shooting Star. The B-29 losses were particularly staggering, because before October 1951 only 6 had been lost in 17 months; now 5 had gone down in only one week. In addition, 8 B-29s were severely damaged, with 55 crewmen dead and 12 wounded.

The results of the October 1951 campaign were mixed. Kelly decided to fly all future B-29 raids at night. The communists, for the time being, continued to build up their Korean bases and increase the number of their MiG jets. In December they flew 3,997 sorties. At the same time, U.S. leaders could no longer ignore the need to upgrade FEAF aircraft. In early November, U.S. Air Force chief of staff General Hoyt Vandenberg began replacing Lockheed F-80 Shooting Stars with an initial deployment of 75 new F-86s. In addition, B-29 operations began to use the SHORAN radar system with ever-improving results. By the end of 1951, air force reports determined that the "medium bombers [had] . . . scored damages" at Namsi, Taechon, and Saamchon "faster than Red laborers could effect repairs."

Between January 1952 and April 1953, the communists made little effort to repair their Korean airfields, opting instead to fly out of Manchurian fields that were immune from UNC attack. As truce talks languished between April and June, laborers rebuilt the airstrips to regain the initiative. Once again, UNC aircraft destroyed them. The day that the final armistice was signed on July 27, 1953, reconnaissance reports stated that all airfields in North Korea were unserviceable for jet aircraft landings. In short, the air battles over Namsi, Taechon, and Saamchon in October 1951, although costly and tactically confining, taught the FEAF important lessons that eventually assured UNC air superiority during the Korean War.

WILLIAM HEAD

See also

Aircraft; United States Air Force; Vandenberg, Hoyt Sanford; Weyland, Otto Paul

References

Futrell, Robert F. *The United States Air Force in Korea, 1950–1953.* Rev. ed. Washington, DC: Office of the Chief of Air Force History, 1983.

Jackson, Robert. *Air War Korea, 1950–1953.* Osceola, WA: Motorbooks International, 1998.

Mark, Eduard. *Aerial Interdiction: Air Power and the Land Battle in Three Wars.* Washington, DC: Center for Air Force History, 1994.

Nalty, Bernard C., and Wayne Thompson. *Within Limits: The U.S. Air Force and the Korean War.* Honolulu: University Press of the Pacific, 2005.

Thompson, Wayne. "The Air War over Korea." In *Winged Shield, Wing Sword: A History of the United States Air Force,* edited by Bernard C.

Nalty, 3–52. Washington, DC: U.S. Air Force History and Museum Program, 1997.

Napalm

Incendiary weapon employed by United Nations Command (UNC) forces in the Korean War. The term napalm is derived from the first few letters of two of the fatty acids contained in coconut oil, naphthenate and palmitate, which were added to gasoline to produce an incendiary gel first used in bombing raids over Japan in World War II. In time, the term came to designate the gel itself. This early form of napalm was employed in the Korean War as opposed to Napalm-B, composed of gasoline, benzene, and polystyrene, which is a more free-flowing gel developed for use in the Vietnam War. Napalm resembles syrup or jelly; can be translucent, pale, or brownish in color; and burns at between 800 and 1,200 degrees Celsius in air.

UNC forces used napalm-based weaponry and munitions extensively in Korea. On the ground, napalm was projected by flamethrowing tanks, portable flamethrowers worn on the back, specially charged land mines, and 55-gallon drums wired with explosives. One method, known as napalm "golden rain," worked much like a primitive fuel-air explosive. It was created by spraying a napalm mixture into the air above the Korean People's Army (KPA, North Korean Army) troop positions, literally showering them with fire.

U.S. Far East Air Force (FEAF) and U.S. Navy and Marine Corps aircraft employed napalm in close air support missions, for interdiction, and in strategic bombing. In a close air support role, 500-pound bombs filled with thermite and napalm were highly successful against communist armor. When dropped against the Soviet-built T-34 tank, even a near-miss would result in this incendiary mixture igniting the rubber parts of the treads, which would then catch the rest of the tank on fire. Special bunker-busting napalm bombs were also employed against fixed-point targets.

Against troop concentrations, napalm achieved mixed results. In the case of a direct hit, napalm proved to be very effective because of its adhesiveness and high burning temperatures. In such instances it usually produced two forms of casualties: severe burn cases and carbon monoxide poisoning cases. In a near-miss scenario, however, communist troops were usually able to outrun

U.S. Air Force napalm attack on suspected communist military positions in a Korean village, 1950. (National Archives)

A Korean village attacked by napalm. Prisoner interrogation determined that napalm bombs were the most feared of all weapons used by the U.S. Far East Air Forces in Korea. (National Archives)

the napalm blast. Still, this exposed them to UNC machine-gun and artillery fire while they sought new cover.

Napalm was also employed, along with other aerial munitions, against railroads and roadways. The intent was to slow and disrupt lines of communication so that communist military forces would not be adequately supplied and reinforced with matériel and soldiers. Napalm was very effective against trains, truck convoys, and the wooden bridges over which they traveled. By December 1951, however, communist forces had effectively countered these attacks. Men and supplies were moved at night, antiaircraft artillery increasingly protected key bridges and rail lines, and even damages resulting from "maximum-effort" operations were repaired within four to seven days.

Napalm was also used along with other incendiary munitions for strategic bombing purposes—confusingly referred to as close air support or interdiction from about January 1951 onward for policy reasons. During the course of the war, the FEAF Bomber Command devastated the major North Korean cities of Pyongyang, capital of the Democratic People's Republic of Korea (DPRK, North Korea), along with Chinnampo, Najin (Rashin), Chongjin,

and Wonsan. One attack upon Pyongyang on July 11, 1952, saw 1,400 tons of bombs and 23,000 gallons of napalm delivered by 1,254 aircraft. Such incendiary raids were on a scale with those that took place over Germany and Japan in World War II.

The FEAF dropped 32,557 tons of napalm ordnance during the course of the Korean War. This was more than twice the total napalm tonnage dropped by the U.S. Army Air Forces (USAAF) during World War II. This was in addition to the 10,000–12,000 tons of napalm dropped by navy and marine aircraft. Napalm represented 6.8 percent of the total tonnage of ordnance delivered by the FEAF. At its height, U.S. monthly production of napalm bombs was estimated to be at about 2,000, compared with 20,500 high-explosive bombs.

ROBERT J. BUNKER

See also

Close Air Support

References

Bjornerstedt, Rolf. *Napalm and Other Incendiary Weapons and All Aspects of Their Possible Use.* Report of the Secretary-General. New York: United Nations, 1973.

Futrell, Robert F. *The United States Air Force in Korea, 1950–1953.* Rev. ed. Washington, DC: Office of the Chief of Air Force History, 1983.

Lumsden, Malvern. *Incendiary Weapons.* Stockholm International Peace Research Institute. Cambridge, MA: MIT Press, 1975.

Stockholm International Peace Research Institute. *Incendiary Weapons.* Cambridge, MA: MIT Press, 1975.

National Emergency Declaration

Declaration issued by U.S. president Harry S. Truman on December 16, 1950. This presidential declaration was in response to the intervention in the Korean War by forces of the People's Republic of China (PRC). The first major Chinese offensive had actually begun nearly three weeks earlier, on November 25, 1950. However, it took the Truman administration a number of days to decide on a course of action in response to what became a stunning military setback for United Nations Command (UNC) forces. Not surprisingly, the administration came under intense pressure by both political parties to move quickly and decisively to stem what by then had become one of the longest withdrawals in U.S. military history.

The reasons for an emergency declaration were numerous. First, Truman wanted to rally the American public around what had clearly become an entirely new war. This was vitally important, as recent polls had indicated a 25 percentage-point drop in U.S. support for the war since October 1950. Second, by publicly placing the United States on emergency war footing, he sent a powerful signal to U.S. adversaries, especially the Union of Soviet Socialist Republics (USSR, Soviet Union), that the country was readying itself to fight a far wider conflict. Third, Secretary of Defense George C. Marshall, whom Truman admired and trusted implicitly, had urged Truman to make such a declaration. Marshall's advice carried enormous weight with the president. Finally, Truman used the declaration to begin a dramatic increase in industrial and economic mobilization, an effort that had begun months earlier but had been spotty and haphazard at best.

Truman readied the nation for the emergency declaration in a nationally broadcast speech on the evening of December 15. The speech, which was broadcast over both radio and television, informed the nation about the new threat it now faced in Korea and the steps that would be taken to meet the demands of the crisis.

Formally signing the emergency declaration the following day, Truman also announced the creation of a new and powerful mobilization agency, the Office of Defense Mobilization (ODM). Selected to head the new agency was Charles E. Wilson, president of General Electric. Vested with sweeping powers to mobilize the nation and its resources for war, Wilson was entrusted with a massive military buildup. His agency would also oversee the imposition of price and wage controls, which would be in place by the end of January 1951.

PAUL G. PIERPAOLI JR.

See also

Antiwar Sentiment in the United States; Isolationist Sentiment in the United States; Marshall, George Catlett; Mobilization; Office of Defense Mobilization; Truman, Harry S.; Wilson, Charles Edward

References

McCullough, David. *Truman.* New York: Simon and Schuster, 1992.

Pierpaoli, Paul G., Jr. *Truman and Korea: The Political Culture of the Early Cold War.* Columbia: University of Missouri Press, 1999.

National Security Act
Event Date: July 26, 1947

Act signed by U.S. president Harry S. Truman on July 26, 1947, that consolidated the U.S. armed forces and reorganized the military establishment, established the Central Intelligence Agency (CIA), and created the National Security Council (NSC) and the National Security Resources Board (NSRB). Although major reorganizations of the U.S. military services had been suggested for decades, it was not until December 19, 1945, that Truman finally set into motion a major revamping of the nation's defense establishment. On that date, the president followed up the many studies undertaken by the military services during World War II and sent a message to Congress indicating his support for a consolidation of the armed forces. Numerous congressional hearings followed throughout 1946, and legislation reflecting Truman's ideas, modified to obtain the support of the military, was put forward in 1947.

The National Security Act ultimately secured passage, and Truman signed it on July 26, 1947. It went into effect on September 18, 1947. The legislation received bipartisan support and was a logical progression in the Truman administration's evolving Cold War policies, which sought to gird the United States for a protracted struggle with the Union of Soviet Socialist Republics (USSR, Soviet Union) and worldwide communism. Indeed, the Truman Doctrine and the Marshall Plan, also launched in 1947, and the formation of the North Atlantic Treaty Organization (NATO) in 1949 all fit into this larger Cold War dynamic.

The act established the U.S. Army, U.S. Navy, and U.S. Air Force as separate and equal entities headed by civilian administrators, called secretaries. The three service secretaries in turn fell under a single civilian secretary of defense who had cabinet-level status. The old Navy and War Departments were abolished and replaced by a new organization known as the National Military Establishment. The secretary of defense had authority over all parts of the National Military Establishment and was directed by the president to eliminate duplication of effort between the services in defense procurement, supply, transport, health care, research, and storage. He was also to coordinate the national defense budget and its preparation in all parts of the National Military Establishment. The Joint Chiefs of Staff (JCS) held a prominent place in the new organization and continued to formulate strategy, issue military directives, and recommend defense policy to the secretary of defense, the National Security Council, and the president.

The National Security Act of 1947, in addition to dealing with the military services, for the first time brought some rationalization to the nation's intelligence community. The act officially established the CIA from parts of the World War II–era Office of Strategic Services (OSS) and charged the new agency with coordinating the intelligence-gathering activities of all government departments.

The NSC was another creation of the 1947 law. It was to coordinate the foreign and military policies of the nation and to advise the president on national security matters. Finally, the act created the NSRB to coordinate all military, civilian, and industrial capacities that might be needed for emergency mobilization or future war.

The National Military Establishment underwent reorganization on August 10, 1949, with greater authority being granted to the secretary of defense to allow him to enforce cooperation between the services. Thus, in 1949 the National Military Establishment was renamed the Department of Defense and was thereafter to consist of the Departments of the Army, Navy, and Air Force, each directed by a civilian secretary, the JCS, the War Council, the Munitions Board, and the Research and Development Board.

By the beginning of the Korean War in June 1950, the military services of the United States had largely overcome the organizational difficulties caused by conformity with the 1947 act and were able to meet the mobilization and deployment needs presented by the war in a relatively more efficient and timely manner than was possible during earlier 20th-century military conflicts.

CLAYTON D. LAURIE

See also

Central Intelligence Agency; Joint Chiefs of Staff; National Security Council; National Security Resources Board; Truman, Harry S.

References

Brune, Lester H. *Chronological History of United States Foreign Relations, 1776 to January 20, 1981*, Vol. 2. New York: Garland, 1985.

Hogan, Michael J. *A Cross of Iron: Harry S. Truman and the Origins of the National Security State, 1945–1954*. New York: Cambridge University Press, 1998.

Leffler, Melvyn P. *A Preponderance of Power: National Security, the Truman Administration, and the Cold War*. Stanford, CA: Stanford University Press, 1992.

Rearden, Steve L. *History of the Office of the Secretary of Defense*, Vol. 1, *The Formative Years, 1947–1950*. Washington, DC: Historical Office, Office of the Secretary of Defense, 1984.

National Security Council

U.S. agency within the Executive Office of the President, established by the 1947 National Security Act. The close relationship with Great Britain in World War II, especially the experience with the Combined Chiefs of Staff, helped U.S. planners recognize the need for a similar U.S. organization. This experience was applied during World War II to the development of the organizational structure of the U.S. Joint Chiefs of Staff (JCS), as well as to the development of the staff and subcommittee structure of the State-War-Navy Coordinating Committee (SWNCC), established in December 1944 to provide a more regular channel of communication between the State Department and the U.S. military on politico-military matters. The "Committee of Three," established during the war and subsequently abolished, was, in a sense, one of the predecessors of the National Security Council (NSC).

In the immediate postwar period, numerous individuals and groups advocated some kind of high-level coordinating mechanism for national security. President Harry S. Truman was also a strong proponent of a unified military establishment and the creation of centralized national security apparatus. One of the more comprehensive of these studies, and the first to suggest the name "National Security Council," was the report prepared by Ferdinand Eberstadt for Secretary of the Navy James Forrestal in September 1945 as a result of the controversy over unification of the armed services. The NSC, established by the enactment of the National Security Act of 1947, flowed from this.

The act, passed by a Republican Congress and approved by a Democratic president, is best known as the legislation that provided for unification of the armed services. However, it was the intent of Congress in passing the act to provide a comprehensive program for the future security of the United States. Title I of the act provides coordinating mechanisms in three other areas of national security activity: national security policy; intelligence; and military, industrial, and civilian mobilization. The NSC, the Central Intelligence Agency (CIA), and the National Security Resources Board (NSRB) were created to coordinate the various activities of the existing executive departments and agencies in these three fields, respectively.

The act provided that the function of the NSC should be to "advise the president with respect to the integration of domestic, foreign, and military policies relating to the national security so as to enable the military services and other departments and agencies of the government to cooperate more effectively in matters involving the national security." The CIA was placed under the NSC. The NSC was composed of the president; the secretaries of state, defense, army, navy, and air force (service secretaries were excluded in the 1949 amendment to the act); and the chairman of the NSRB. There was no single national security adviser until the advent of President Dwight D. Eisenhower's administration in 1953. That same year, Eisenhower dissolved the NSRB by folding its responsibilities into a slightly reorganized Office of Defense Mobilization (ODM).

YOUNGHO KIM

See also

Central Intelligence Agency; National Security Act; National Security Resources Board; Office of Defense Mobilization

President Harry S. Truman with members of the National Security Council on August 19, 1948. From left to right, clockwise around the table: Assistant Secretary of the Air Force Cornelius Vanderbilt Whitney, Secretary of the Army Kenneth Royall, Executive Secretary of the National Security Council Sidney Souers, National Security Resources Board Chairman Arthur M. Hill, Director of Central Intelligence Roscoe Hillenkoetter, Secretary of Defense James Forrestal, Secretary of State George C. Marshall, President Truman, and Undersecretary of the Navy W. John Kenney. (Harry S. Truman Presidential Library)

References

Central Intelligence Agency. *Organizational History of the National Security Council during the Truman and Eisenhower Administrations.* Washington, DC: U.S. Government Printing Office, 1988.

Hogan, Michael J. *A Cross of Iron: Harry S. Truman and the Origins of the National Security State, 1945–1954.* New York: Cambridge University Press, 1998.

Leffler, Melvyn P. *A Preponderance of Power: National Security, the Truman Administration, and the Cold War.* Stanford, CA: Stanford University Press, 1992.

National Security Council Report 68
Event Date: April 14, 1950

A response by U.S. president Harry S. Truman's administration to the first atomic explosion, in late August 1949, detonated by the Union of Soviet Socialist Republics (USSR, Soviet Union) as well as the October 1949 communist victory in the Chinese Civil War (1945–1949). The top secret report, labeled National Security Council Report 68 (NSC-68), was released to the president on April 14, 1950. Its principal author was Paul H. Nitze, director of the State Department's Policy Planning Staff.

The basic premise of NSC-68 was that because the Soviets had developed a workable atomic bomb, a hydrogen (thermonuclear) bomb would not be far behind. The drafters of NSC-68 estimated that by 1954, "the year of maximum danger," the Soviets would be capable of launching a crippling preemptive strike against the United States. According to NSC-68, the United States could not prevent such a blow without a massive increase in its military and economic capacities. Should the report not be heeded, in case of Soviet aggression the United States would be forced into appeasement or nuclear war. Nitze and other policy makers believed that the key to avoiding this dilemma and preserving free-world security lay in a vast conventional and nuclear rearmament. NSC-68 also called for greater foreign aid, along with expanded military assistance to the Western allies, additional funding for information and propaganda campaigns, better intelligence gathering, and an expansion of nuclear weapons programs.

Alarmed by the report's recommendations and likely costs, Truman initially shelved the plan. Only after the sudden outbreak of the Korean War in June 1950 did he agree to begin enacting the NSC-68 rearmament program. Full implementation came in response to the massive military intervention by the People's Republic of China (PRC) in the conflict. Thanks in part, at least, to the Korean War, U.S. defense expenditures quadrupled, going from $13.5 billion before the war to more than $54 billion by the time Truman left office in January 1953. The lion's share of this massive rearmament program in fact was not directed to the Korean War but instead went toward fulfilling a long-term U.S. mobilization base as envisioned in NSC-68. Indeed, NSC-68 put muscle into Truman's containment policy.

Although subsequent administrations would tinker with the recommendations in NSC-68, the report nonetheless guided U.S. national security and military mobilization planning for almost a generation after its drafting. Fundamentally, NSC-68 was underpinned by the traditional Cold War mentality. Many of its critics have argued that the report overstated the nature and extent of the Soviet threat. Others have maintained that NSC-68 was a wise and prudent response to a real and present Soviet danger. Still others have pointed out that although NSC-68 may paint a somewhat distorted picture of the Soviet Union, this distortion results more from what is now known from newly opened Eastern bloc archives as opposed to what was known to officials at the time. Whatever the case, it is a truism that NSC-68 was a seminal and paradigmatic document that resulted in militarization of U.S. strategy in the Cold War.

JOSH USHAY

See also

Atomic Bomb; Containment; Hydrogen Bomb; Industrial Base, U.S.; National Security Council; Nitze, Paul Henry; Truman, Harry S.

References

Gaddis, John Lewis. *Strategies of Containment: A Critical Appraisal of Postwar American National Security.* New York: Oxford University Press, 1982.
———. *We Now Know: Rethinking Cold War History.* New York: Oxford University Press, 1998.
Leffler, Melvyn P. *A Preponderance of Power: National Security, the Truman Administration, and the Cold War.* Stanford, CA: Stanford University Press, 1992.
May, Ernest R. *American Cold War Strategy: Interpreting NSC 68.* Boston: Bedford Books, 1993.
Pierpaoli, Paul G., Jr. *Truman and Korea: The Political Culture of the Early Cold War.* Columbia: University of Missouri Press, 1999.

National Security Resources Board

Independent advisory board created by the National Security Act of 1947 and responsible chiefly for long-term mobilization planning and civilian war planning. The National Security Resources Board (NSRB) reported directly to the president (who was a permanent board member) and was designed to be the domestic counterpart of the National Security Council (NSC), also created by the National Security Act. During the Korean War the NSRB operated as the principal mobilization agency from September 9, 1950, to December 16, 1950, at which time, in response to the massive military intervention of the People's Republic of China (PRC), President Harry S. Truman established the Office of Defense Mobilization (ODM). The ODM superseded the NSRB and assumed many of its responsibilities.

From 1947 to 1949 the NSRB had as its permanent members the president of the United States, the chairman of the NSRB (appointed by the president), as well as the secretaries of state, defense, army, navy, and air force, and additional members serving at the discretion of the president. From 1947 to 1950 the NSRB was chiefly a contingency-planning board. It mapped out strategies for civilian and industrial mobilization, manpower allocation, raw materials distribution, and conversion to a wartime economy; coordinated the efforts of federal agencies; supervised the stockpiling of critical war matériel; and advised on the relocation of strategic industries, government agencies, and economic activities in time of war. In short, the NSRB was responsible for ensuring that the United States was ready and able to undertake industrial and economic mobilization for war.

In its first years the NSRB was a highly ineffective organization, partly because its responsibilities fell upon numerous individuals rather than one leader. Indeed, until 1949 the chairman did not exercise sole control over the board. The job of the NSRB was also made more difficult because the board was unable to retrieve from defense planners in the Pentagon firm figures upon which to base its mobilization plans.

Arthur Hill was the first NSRB chairman. His tenure lasted only until 1948. From 1948 to early 1950 the agency was headed by John R. Steelman, a Truman confidante and assistant to the president. He maintained the title "acting" chairman. The fact that the NSRB did not have a full-time chairman for nearly two years demonstrates Truman's ambivalence toward the NSRB and the NSC. He simply distrusted them and believed that relying on them too much invited military interference in civilian affairs. In 1950 Truman named W. Stuart Symington, first secretary of the air force, to take the helm of the NSRB. On the eve of the Korean War, the White House took renewed interest in the NSRB by placing it in the hands of an experienced bureaucrat with experience in military matters.

When the Korean War broke out in June 1950, Symington was among the first presidential advisers to recommend the imposition of economic controls. Symington was particularly concerned about the soaring prices and dwindling supply of key industrial materials. After Congress passed the Defense Production Act in September 1950, which empowered the president to place the nation on a war footing, Symington, who had been lobbying the

White House to place him in control of mobilization matters, was given that opportunity on September 9. Now the NSRB was charged with coordinating current and future mobilization agencies as well as overseeing the possible imposition of economic controls.

Between September and December 1950, the NSRB proved incapable of meeting the exigencies of the crisis. Some of the problems stemmed from internal bureaucratic issues, including the Pentagon's unwillingness to share information with the NSRB. Other problems were a consequence of the changing war goals between September and December and, of course, the Chinese intervention in Korea in late November. When Truman decided to declare a national emergency on December 16, 1950, he created the ODM, realizing that he needed a new and more powerful mobilization agency to handle the crisis. The ODM effectively usurped all of the NSRB's enhanced powers. By early 1951 the NSRB had been all but emasculated and was once again restricted to long-term planning. In October it came under the aegis of the ODM.

In April 1951 Symington left the NSRB to become head of the Reconstruction Finance Corporation; he was replaced by Jack Gorrie, who was the last chairman of the agency. Before it was organized out of existence by President Dwight D. Eisenhower's administration in 1953, the NSRB was heavily involved in industrial dispersion programs. These were ways by which the federal government tried to locate new factories and industry away from city centers to render them less vulnerable to a nuclear attack.

PAUL G. PIERPAOLI JR.

See also

Defense Production Act; Mobilization; National Emergency Declaration; National Security Council; Office of Defense Mobilization; Symington, William Stuart, III

References

Dorwart, Jeffery. *Eberstadt and Forrestal: A National Security Partnership.* College Station: Texas A&M University Press, 1991.
Pierpaoli, Paul G., Jr. *Truman and Korea: The Political Culture of the Early Cold War.* Columbia: University of Missouri Press, 1999.

Naval Battles

As in modern conflicts involving the U.S. Navy, during the Korean War the U.S. Navy and allied navies had to eliminate their enemy's presence at sea before concentrating on the conflict ashore. Soon after the Democratic People's Republic of Korea (DPRK, North Korea) invaded the Republic of Korea (ROK, South Korea) on June 25, 1950, the Republic of Korea Navy (ROKN, South Korean Navy)—composed of submarine chaser *Paektusan* (PC 701), a tank landing ship (LST), 15 minesweepers and minelayers, and 7,000 men—sortied from port in search of the Korean People's Navy (KPN, North Korean Navy). It did not take long for *Paektusan*, the crew of which had only recently brought its ship (formerly *USS Whitehead*) to South Korea from the United States, to locate

prey. *Paektusan* discovered a KPN 1,000-ton steamer off the east coast in the vicinity of the South Korean port of Pusan. The ROKN combatant sank the KPN ship, perhaps preventing seizure of the one port that would become vital to the United Nations Command (UNC) forces fighting ashore.

In the meantime, UNC help was on the way. With the outbreak of war, U.S. Naval Forces Far East (NAVFE) commander Vice Admiral C. Turner Joy dispatched 1 light cruiser, 4 destroyers, 4 amphibious ships, 1 submarine, 10 minesweepers, and an attached frigate of the Royal Australian Navy to Korean waters. Almost simultaneously, U.S. Pacific Fleet commander in chief Admiral Arthur W. Radford transferred his subordinate Seventh Fleet to Admiral Joy's operational control. That fighting fleet, under Vice Admiral Arthur D. Struble, steamed from its home port of Subic Bay, Philippines, on June 27, 1950, made a show of force off the coast of the People's Republic of China (PRC), and then headed for Korean waters. Struble's aircraft carrier *Valley Forge,* heavy cruiser *Rochester,* 8 destroyers, 3 submarines, and a number of logistic support ships would be most welcome in the combat theater. The British Commonwealth soon complemented these U.S. naval forces with the aircraft carrier *Triumph,* 2 light cruisers, 3 destroyers, and 3 frigates. In July the United States strengthened the ROKN with 3 decommissioned U.S. submarine chasers, additional LSTs, and logistic ships and craft.

In the early hours of July 2, 1950, as the allied fleets converged on Korea, the U.S. cruiser *Juneau,* British cruiser *Jamaica,* and British frigate *Black Swan* discovered 4 torpedo boats and 2 motor gunboats of the KPN that had just finished escorting 10 craft loaded with ammunition south along the coast in the East Sea (Sea of Japan). The outgunned KPN torpedo boats turned and sought to press home a torpedo attack but, before they could launch their weapons, the Anglo-American flotilla ended the threat; only 1 torpedo boat survived U.S.-British naval gunfire to flee the scene. After this one-sided battle and for the remainder of the war, North Korean naval leaders decided against contesting control of the sea with the UN navies. Surviving KPN units eventually took refuge in Chinese and Soviet ports.

Freed early from the threat of attack by KPN combatants, major UN warships could concentrate on the ground campaign. At this critical time for UN ground troops—then fighting to hold a precarious lodgment in South Korea—the fleet's carrier-based aircraft, battleships, cruisers, and destroyers poured bombs and shells on North Korean troops, tanks, and vehicles pushing down both coasts of South Korea.

The UNC navies still had much to do to deny the KPN use of the sea, however. During July, August, and early September, UNC combatants, especially ROKN ships, were needed to disrupt KPN seaborne attempts to resupply the fast-advancing North Korean ground forces. Early in July, ROKN minesweeper *YMS 513* sank three communist supply craft at Chulpo on the southwestern coast; on the other side of the peninsula, *Juneau* located and destroyed the ammunition ships that figured in the July 2 sea battle. On July

22 *YMS 513* sank another 3 supply vessels near Chulpo. Five days later submarine chasers *PC 702* and *PC 703,* newly provided by the United States, steamed up the west coast of Korea and, west of Inchon, sank 12 North Korean sampans loaded with ammunition. During the first week of August *YMS 302* and other ROKN units destroyed another 13 communist supply craft off the west coast. Between August 13 and 20, the ROKN engaged North Korean supply vessels five times. In one instance, *YMS 503* sank 15 such vessels and captured another 30.

Combat action was especially heavy on the south coast during the last week of August 1950, when the North Korean command was desperate to reinforce and resupply its troops trying to penetrate the Pusan Perimeter. Motor minesweepers *YMS 503, YMS 504, YMS 512,* and *YMS 514,* and *PC 702* sank numerous North Korean craft; a number of the embarked troops drowned, while many others were captured.

At the end of the month, the ROKN frustrated a North Korean attempt to seize the port of Pohang on the Pusan Perimeter with troop-laden small boats. Finally, as the UN navies converged on Inchon for the amphibious assault that would turn the tide in the fall of 1950, *PC 703* sank a KPN mine-laying craft and three other vessels in waters off the Yellow Sea port.

Having secured control of the sea off Korea, the UNC could proceed with exploitation of that strategic advantage. With little fear from North Korean counteraction at sea, UN naval forces under Joy deployed U.S. marine and army troops and South Korean soldiers ashore at Inchon on September 15, landed other ground forces at Wonsan in northeastern Korea during October, and safely withdrew those forces from Hungnam in December 1950 when China's entry into the war once again altered the strategic balance. While the fortunes of war on the ground changed a number of times before the July 27, 1953, armistice, UNC forces never lost control of the sea.

EDWARD J. MAROLDA

See also

Joy, Charles Turner; Korea, Democratic People's Republic of, Navy; Korea, Republic of, Navy; Radford, Arthur William; Struble, Arthur Dewey; United States Navy

References

Cagle, Malcolm W., and Frank A. Manson. *Sea War in Korea.* Annapolis, MD: Naval Institute Press, 1957.

Field, James A., Jr. *History of United States Naval Operations, Korea.* Washington, DC: U.S. Government Printing Office, 1962.

Jane's Fighting Ships. London: S. Low, Marston, 1949–1950, 1951–1952.

Marolda, Edward J. *The U.S. Navy in the Korean War.* Annapolis, MD: Naval Institute Press, 2007.

Naval Forces Far East

At the beginning of the Korean War, U.S. Naval Forces Far East (NAVFE), a command existing since 1947, was the principal naval organization directly subordinate to General of the Army Douglas MacArthur's Far East Command (FEC), with its general headquarters in Tokyo, Japan. Vice Admiral C. Turner Joy, commander of NAVFE from August 26, 1949, directed an organization divided into four principal components: Amphibious Force Far East (Task Force 90); Naval Forces, Philippines (Task Force 93); Naval Forces, Marianas (Task Force 94); and Naval Forces, Japan (Task Force 96).

In June 1950 these organizations lacked resources. For warships, Joy could count only one light cruiser (*Juneau*) and four destroyers at his immediate disposal in Task Force 96, a unit especially weak in mine warfare vessels. His amphibious force (Task Force 90) totaled five ships, including only one landing craft (*LST-611*). Moreover, joint training had been woefully inadequate. In June 1949 MacArthur had directed that the three services conduct amphibious exercises, but the first major landing was not scheduled until the fall of 1950.

After the shooting started in Korea on June 25, 1950, authorities in Washington, DC, acted quickly to bolster Joy's forces. On June 27 the Seventh Fleet, based in the Philippines and under the direct control of the commander in chief of the Pacific Fleet, was assigned to NAVFE. Its first warships—the aircraft carrier *Valley Forge,* heavy cruiser *Rochester,* and eight destroyers—reached Japanese waters by June 28 and were soon in action. Designated as Task Force 77, this striking force was soon bolstered by other United Nations Command (UNC) warships and supported by a replenishment unit dubbed Task Group 77.7 (soon redesignated Task Force 79). Henceforth the principal combatant component of the Seventh Fleet—and thus of NAVFE—was Task Force 77, built around its fast carrier forces.

During the next three years 4 vice admirals commanded the Seventh Fleet: Arthur D. Struble (May 6, 1950, to March 28, 1951), Harold M. Martin (March 28, 1951, to March 3, 1952), Robert P. Briscoe (March 3 to May 20, 1952), and J. J. Clark (May 20, 1952, through the end of the war). During the war 13 rear admirals rotated command of Task Force 77.

In a major reorganization on September 12, 1950, the naval operating commands were recast. Added to the Seventh Fleet organization was Task Force 72, which included the ships involved in the Formosa Patrol. For work closer to the Korean Peninsula, the United Nations Blockading and Escort Force (Task Force 95) was established. Its principal elements included Task Group 95.1 (west coast group), Task Group 95.2 (east coast group), Task Group 95.6 (minesweeping group), and Task Group 95.7 (Republic of Korea Navy [ROKN, South Korean Navy]). During the conflict NAVFE activated additional commands, including two large aviation units: Fleet Air Wing 6 (commissioned August 4, 1950) and Fleet Air Wing 14 (operational on October 16, 1952). Also created was the Logistic Support Force (Task Force 92) on April 3, 1951.

As units rushed to the theater, NAVFE ballooned. In aircraft carriers, the force went from 1 in June to 8 U.S. and British by October 1950. The numbers of battleships, cruisers, and destroyers climbed from 18 to 64. During the same period, the total of warships at the disposal of NAVFE rose from 86 to 274. Such increases in matériel were reflected in personnel. In June 1950, 10,990 U.S. sailors were in the western Pacific; by the end of July 1951 comparable figures totaled 74,335.

In contrast to many of its components, NAVFE enjoyed remarkable command continuity. When Joy stepped down on June 4, 1952, he was replaced by Briscoe, who held his post until the end of the war.

MALCOLM MUIR JR.

See also

Briscoe, Robert Pierce; Joy, Charles Turner; MacArthur, Douglas; Struble, Arthur Dewey; United States Navy

References

Cagle, Malcolm W., and Frank A. Manson. *Sea War in Korea.* Annapolis, MD: Naval Institute Press, 1957.

Field, James A., Jr. *History of United States Naval Operations, Korea.* Washington, DC: U.S. Government Printing Office, 1962.

Marolda, Edward J. *The U.S. Navy in the Korean War.* Annapolis, MD: Naval Institute Press, 2007.

Naval Gunfire Support

If, in the thinking of many defense analysts in the late 1940s, the aircraft carrier was obsolete in the nuclear age, the gunship seemed positively antediluvian. Yet during the Korean War, the battleship, cruiser, and destroyer once again proved their utility, especially in the support of friendly troops ashore and in the interdiction of communist forces' communications.

With the great drawdown of the fleet in the five years following World War II, the number of battleships on active duty in the U.S. Navy dropped from 23 to 1, while cruisers went from 90 to 23. Similar drastic cuts took place in destroyer strength. After all, the Soviet surface fleet was negligible, and the most sensitive targets in the communist bloc were far removed from coastal areas.

When Korean People's Army (KPA, North Korean Army) forces crossed the 38th Parallel and invaded the Republic of Korea (ROK, South Korea), the U.S. Navy had only 1 cruiser and 4 destroyers on duty in Japanese waters. But these were in action at Mukho within four days and, rapidly reinforced by gunships from the Seventh Fleet, they provided support to hard-pressed United Nations Command (UNC) troops retreating toward Pusan. From distant waters came the navy's only active battleship, the *Missouri,* and additional cruisers and destroyers. These U.S. ships were bolstered by gunships from Australia, Canada, Great Britain, New Zealand, and the Netherlands. Over the next three years, the U.S. Navy reactivated the remaining Iowa-class battleships (*Iowa, New Jersey,* and *Wisconsin*), 5 heavy cruisers, and 104 destroyers.

During the conflict, naval gunfire provided strong support to important United Nations (UN) operations. For instance, two U.S. and two British cruisers plus six U.S. destroyers assisted the U.S. Marine landing at Inchon on September 15, 1950. At Hungnam

that December, after the massive Chinese intervention, surface warships, including the *Missouri,* covered the withdrawal of ground troops with a large portion of their supplies; in the effort, two heavy cruisers, the *St. Paul* and *Rochester,* expended 3,000 8-inch shells. By the spring of 1951, Secretary of the Navy Francis P. Matthews cited naval gunfire support as one of the key assets of the UN in the conflict.

In fact, shore bombardment had become the primary task of surface warships. Missions included firing in support of fixed positions at the front (in contrast to fluid targets encountered in an amphibious assault); securing both flanks of the UNC battle line; and interdicting rail and road lines running along the northeast coast of Korea. In January 1952 this last effort was formally code-named DERAIL; its greatest success came the next month, when shore bombardment halted railroad traffic into Wonsan for weeks. But the navy simply did not have enough gunships to maintain this tempo of operations indefinitely.

The overall record is impressive. U.S. warships in one 11-month period undertook 24,000 fire support missions, during which they expended 414,000 projectiles. Many ships did a great deal of shooting. For instance, the destroyer *Swenson* fired 5,709 rounds of 5-inch ammunition in 4 months.

The big guns of the battleships turned in the most effective performance. Their 2,700-pound armor-piercing shells proved particularly devastating against such hard targets as railroad tunnels. One Marine Corps report concluded that the 16-inch guns were "pound for pound . . . the most efficient rifles in the Korean War." Analysts calculated that a battleship could destroy a bridge in less than half an hour with 60 rounds of 16-inch ammunition. In comparison, at least 12 aircraft sorties were required to achieve a similar result with the attendant risk to aircraft and their crews. During the war the four battleships fired more than 20,000 16-inch projectiles—a much larger number than they had shot in World War II.

Between June 25, 1950, and May 31, 1953, navy gunships fired 4,069,626 rounds. In the first two years of the war, the warships claimed the destruction of 3,334 buildings, 824 vessels and small craft, 14 locomotives, 214 trucks, 15 tanks, 108 bridges, 93 supply dumps, and 28,566 troops.

These intensive operations revealed certain problems: early in the war, the army and navy possessed neither effective liaison nor a standard doctrine for fire control. Both omissions reflected the prewar sentiment that naval gunfire support was obsolete. Also missing in 1950 were dedicated spotting aircraft: the navy had removed its last float planes from battleships and cruisers two years earlier. Given the exigencies of combat, gunships began experimenting with their helicopters for this work.

With the high pace of operations came a variety of problems, including bore erosion, accidents, and blast damage to ship structures. The cruiser *Helena* did so much shooting that its entire main battery had to be replaced. Its sister ship, the *St. Paul,* suffered a serious turret fire in April 1952 that killed 30 men.

The battleship *New Jersey* firing its 16-inch guns in support of United Nations Command (UNC) forces near the 38th Parallel. (National Archives)

Communist forces also hit back. Surface warships were struck on 85 separate occasions, with the damage usually being superficial. On May 7, 1952, however, the destroyer *James C. Owens* took 6 hits that resulted in 10 crew casualties. Even the battleships were not immune; both the *New Jersey* and *Wisconsin* were slightly damaged by land-based gunfire. Mines presented a more severe threat to vessels operating close inshore: five destroyers were damaged by these underwater weapons.

Despite such drawbacks, UN soldiers attested to the effectiveness of naval gunfire support. Both army and marine troops gave it high praise, often comparing it favorably with divisional artillery. Top commanders agreed with these favorable assessments. In December 1950 General Douglas MacArthur noted that communist forces frequently conducted their offensives well inland to avoid the effects of warship bombardment. After the trench stalemate developed in the spring of 1951, Lieutenant General Matthew B. Ridgway declared that naval gunfire relieved him of any concern for his flanks. Some analysts noted tellingly that UN front lines near the coast were invariably forward of the battle line inland.

Despite this excellent performance, naval gunfire support suffered cuts during the post–Korean War defense realignment, as adherents of President Dwight D. Eisenhower's "New Look" defense policy concluded that Korean conditions had been "artificial." Thus, all four battleships, most of the cruisers, and many of the destroyers were consigned to mothballs or the scrap heap. Ironically, the Vietnam War would once again prove the utility of the gunship to hard-pressed troops ashore.

MALCOLM MUIR JR.

See also

Helicopters, Employment of; Helicopters, Types and Nomenclature; Hungnam Evacuation; Inchon Landing; MacArthur, Douglas; Naval Forces Far East; New Look Defense Policy; Ridgway, Matthew Bunker; United States Navy

References

Cagle, Malcolm W., and Frank A. Manson. *Sea War in Korea*. Annapolis, MD: Naval Institute Press, 1957.

Field, James A., Jr. *History of United States Naval Operations, Korea*. Washington, DC: U.S. Government Printing Office, 1962.

Marolda, Edward J. *The U.S. Navy in the Korean War*. Annapolis, MD: Naval Institute Press, 2007.

Muir, Malcolm, Jr. *Black Shoes and Blue Water: Surface Warfare in the United States Navy, 1945–1975*. Washington, DC: Naval Historical Center, 1996.

———. *The Iowa-Class Battleships: Iowa, New Jersey, Missouri, and Wisconsin*. Poole, Dorset, UK: Blandford, 1987.

Reilly, John C., ed. *Operational Experience of Fast Battleships: World War II, Korea, Vietnam*. Washington, DC: Naval Historical Center, 1989.

Needham, Joseph

Birth Date: December 9, 1900
Death Date: March 24, 1995

British-born biochemist and Sinophile who pioneered the study of Chinese scientific and technological achievements and who corroborated the bogus claims that the United States had employed biological weapons during the Korean War. Born Noel Joseph Terence Montgomery Needham (although he was known professionally only as Joseph Needham) in London on December 9, 1900, Needham attended Cambridge University, where he received an undergraduate degree in 1921, a master's degree in January 1925, and a doctorate in October 1925. Specializing in developmental biology, he worked for a number of years as a researcher at Gonville and Caius College, Cambridge University.

Needham's first significant links to China came in 1936, when three Chinese scientists began to work with Needham in his laboratory. One of them taught Needham classical Chinese, and thereafter he demonstrated an abiding curiosity regarding China's scientific and technological heritage.

Needham began to conduct intensive research into Chinese scientific history and soon began numerous collaborative efforts with Chinese and British historians who were doing work on the subject. Traveling to China, Needham was director of the Sino-British Science Cooperation Office in Chongqing from 1942 to 1946. In 1945 he published the first of what would be many books on Chinese science and technology. Thereafter, he traveled extensively throughout China gathering material that would eventually inform his subsequent works, including *Science and Civilization in China*, a multivolume study that is considered one of the most significant English-language works on the subject.

In 1948 Needham returned to Great Britain, where he taught biochemistry until 1966 and continued to work on his research. In the meantime, he traveled regularly to China, even after the October 1949 triumph of Mao Zedong's Communist revolution, where he was hailed a minor hero for his work about and passion for Chinese history and civilization. Needham was apparently quite taken by Chinese communism, and admired Mao and his determination to remake Chinese society.

From 1952 to 1953, during the Korean War, the Chinese government asked Needham to serve as an observer in the Democratic People's Republic of Korea (DPRK, North Korea). This was an effort to bolster its propaganda campaign that alleged U.S. use of biological warfare. Needham joined several scientists from the People's Republic of China (PRC) and North Korea, and agreed that there was evidence that biological weapons had been employed in North Korea. The British and U.S. governments vehemently denied that any such weapons were deployed or used in the conflict. Not surprisingly, Needham's reputation was somewhat tarnished after the affair, and his biographer later argued that he had been "pitilessly duped" by the Chinese communists. No evidence since then has pointed to the use of biological weapons during the Korean War, at least not by United Nations Command (UNC) forces. Moreover, Soviet documents reveal that Moscow knew Beijing's charges were fraudulent shortly after they were made public. Experts have since argued that naturally occurring epidemics linked to poor health and sanitation conditions had precipitated the large number of civilian deaths in North Korea and China in 1950 and 1951.

Needham continued to conduct research on Chinese scientific history, receiving many rewards and honors for his contributions to the field. He authored more than 20 books, many on Chinese scientific history, but also on chemical embryology, biochemistry, and the history of embryology. Throughout his work on Chinese science and technology, he emphasized that four significant, world-altering inventions had originated in China: the compass, gunpowder, paper, and printing. These innovations had placed China on the cutting edge of technological and scientific achievement. Yet, China was eventually eclipsed by the technological prowess of the West. Needham attributed this development in part to the interaction of Confucianism and Taoism on Chinese society and the Chinese scientific community. Arguing that Chinese scientific thought had grown more diffuse over time, limiting its ability to produce cutting-edge technologies, Needham asserted that in the end the more independent-minded inquisitiveness of Western scientific thought eventually won out.

In the early 1980s Needham was diagnosed with Parkinson's disease, which slowed him considerably. Nevertheless, in 1985 he was on hand for the opening of the Needham Research Institute at Cambridge University. The institute fosters the study of Chinese and East Asian medicine, science, and technology, with an emphasis on the history of science and technology. On March 24, 1995, Needham died of natural causes at his home in Cambridge, England.

Paul G. Pierpaoli Jr.

See also
Biological Warfare

References
Needham, Joseph. *A Selection of the Writings of Joseph Needham*. Jefferson, NC: McFarland, 1994.

Winchester, Simon. *The Man Who Loved China: The Fantastic Story of the Eccentric Scientist Who Unlocked the Mysteries of the Middle Kingdom*. New York: Harper, 2008.

Nehru, Jawaharlal
Birth Date: November 14, 1889
Death Date: May 27, 1964

Indian nationalist politician and prime minister of India from 1947 to 1964. Born on November 14, 1889, at Allahabad in Uttar Pradesh, a northern state of India, Jawaharlal Nehru was born into a prominent upper-caste family. His father was a lawyer and nationalist leader in the Indian Congress Party. Nehru attended school at Harrow and then graduated from Trinity College at Cambridge University in England. Afterward, he returned to India, where he became involved in the independence movement against British colonial rule. In the mid-1930s Nehru served as Mahatma Gandhi's chief lieutenant. When independence was secured in 1947, Nehru was selected as the first prime minister of independent India, serving until his death in 1964. An ardent nationalist, he perceived foreign policy, especially toward Asia, regionally rather than globally.

During the Korean War Nehru diplomatically endorsed a policy of nonalignment. A scholar-statesman, Nehru was known for his pacifist philosophy. Uncomfortable with militarism, Nehru strove to minimize potential superpower conflicts; he also was concerned because India shared a border with the People's Republic of China (PRC). Nehru wanted to resolve the Korean issue peacefully through compromise, appeasement, and accommodation, instead of resorting to warfare. Nehru's diplomacy was compared to a tightrope act in which he criticized aggression but refused to align with the East or West. Neither the United States nor the Union of Soviet Socialist Republics (USSR, Soviet Union) liked Nehru's nonalignment policy and wanted India to declare allegiance to one side or the other.

After June 25, 1950, when the Democratic People's Republic of Korea (DPRK, North Korea) invaded the Republic of Korea (ROK, South Korea), India's chief delegate to the United Nations (UN), Sir Benegal N. Rau, voted for the UN Security Council resolution condemning North Korean aggression. Nehru and other Indian leaders instructed Rau not to commit India to any further actions without deliberations, however. Nehru discussed the situation with U.S. ambassador Loy W. Henderson, and the Indian government issued a statement in support of the second UN Security Council resolution on June 27, which called on member states to offer assistance to South Korea in order to force the North Koreans to withdraw to the 38th Parallel.

Nehru accepted the passing of these resolutions but did not endorse the U.S. idea that the North Korean invasion had been directed by the Soviet Union. He thought that President Harry S. Truman was overreacting to a war of local origins that should be resolved by Koreans. Nehru also resented U.S. interference with his efforts to convince the Soviet Union and China not to intervene in Korea. During the second week of July 1950, he issued the first Indian peace initiative to the United States, Soviet Union, and China, in which he asked for China to be seated in the UN, for the

Jawaharlal Nehru was the first prime minister of independent India during 1947–1964, during which time he followed a strict policy of nonalignment. (Library of Congress)

Soviet Union's UN Security Council boycott to end, for a cease-fire in Korea, and for hope of future reunification. The Soviets and Chinese politely acknowledged Nehru's requests but did not commit to fulfilling them. The United States responded angrily about the suggestion of diplomatic recognition of China and said that that demand should not be a condition for ending the war. Despite this discouragement, Nehru continued his efforts to achieve Chinese diplomatic recognition and a cease-fire.

Nehru was frustrated by the attitudes of political and military leaders toward him and India. For the most part, the Western powers in Korea did not listen to his ideas, and China told the UN secretary-general that India's views were unimportant because India had not sent soldiers to the conflict. World leaders did not support a 13-member Asian-Arab bloc in the General Assembly that Nehru helped to establish, with the purpose of promoting a cease-fire and addressing East Asian concerns. As a result, Nehru sank into a depression during 1950. Nevertheless, he continued to speak against war, demand tolerance, and promote international goodwill.

Throughout the Korean War Nehru attempted to keep open lines of communication with Washington, DC, Moscow, and Beijing in hopes of negotiating a settlement. His initiatives, however, were never fully supported by the communist powers and often made Truman angry. In the fall of 1950 Nehru tried to prevent the war's expansion by sending warnings to Washington and London via Indian ambassador to China, Sardar K. M. Panikkar. Chinese foreign minister Zhou Enlai had told Panikkar that Chinese troops would enter the war if United Nations Command (UNC) troops moved north of the 38th Parallel. The Western powers ignored the warnings.

In January 1951 the Commonwealth prime ministers met in London, where Nehru sought to convince the United States not to condemn China and to accept its claim to Taiwan (then known as Formosa) and membership in the UN. The other Commonwealth leaders refused to support Nehru, and he suggested staging a conference between the United States, China, Great Britain, and the Soviet Union. Nehru believed that the United States had too much influence on policy in Korea, such as approving the bombing of North Korean power plants along the Yalu River. He wrote that he feared that the future of the UN and of world peace "might be decided without proper consultations, and might ultimately depend on the discretion of military commanders who would naturally think more of local military objectives than of large questions affecting the world."

When Truman dismissed General Douglas MacArthur in April 1951, Nehru urged China to seek a diplomatic resolution to the war. China decided to enter negotiations, however, by submitting demands and concerns through the Soviet Union instead of India. Nehru was isolated from Korean War negotiations until Ambassador Chester B. Bowles and Eleanor Roosevelt visited India and urged him to convince the Chinese to file its complaints of bacteriological warfare independently of truce talks. China withdrew these allegations and urged India to lobby for the repatriation of prisoners of war (POWs) through Great Britain. China had demanded that all POWs be returned.

In late 1952, when the Panmunjom truce talks were stalled, Nehru asked Indian ambassador to the UN V. K. Krishna Menon to initiate a compromise regarding Item 4 on POW repatriation. The Indian proposal called for a cease-fire, the repatriation of prisoners wanting to return, and the establishment of a repatriation commission of four neutral powers to monitor the exchange of remaining prisoners, but China and the Soviet Union rejected the idea. However, the Indian peace initiatives and Menon's POW settlement proposal ultimately established the foundation for the July 1953 Armistice Agreement. The United States and China mutually accepted the repatriation commission's final POW agreement, ending the stalemated war. Nehru praised the agreement as an "outbreak of peace."

After the Korean War, Nehru tried to boost India's industrial and economic development. He also focused on encouraging peace within India by creating new states to appease indigenous tribes and such religious factions as the Sikhs. Despite his efforts, violent riots erupted over such issues as Kashmir and government control of private schools.

Seeking to perpetuate his policy of peaceful coexistence and nonalignment during the Cold War, Nehru refused to join the Soviet or Anglo-American blocs. Active in international diplomacy, he participated in the 1954 Geneva Conference, and he supported disarmament and a ban on nuclear weapons. In 1956 he joined Yugoslavian president Josip Tito and Egyptian president Gamal Abdel Nasser to denounce colonialism and promote a global system of collective security.

In 1961 Nehru ordered Indian troops into Portuguese-controlled areas of the subcontinent. The next year India and China fought along their common border as an unprepared Indian military failed to prevent Chinese troops from gaining Indian territory. Nehru dismissed Menon, his defense minister. In January 1964 Nehru became ill during a session of the Indian Congress. He died in New Delhi on May 27, 1964.

ELIZABETH D. SCHAFER

See also

Armistice Agreement; Bowles, Chester Bliss; Cease-fire Negotiations; China, People's Republic of, United Nations Representation Question; Henderson, Loy Wesley; India; Menon, Vengalil Krishnan Krishna; Panikkar, Sardar K. M.; Rau, Sir Benegal Narsing; Repatriation, Voluntary; Soviet Security Council Boycott; Soviet Union; Truce Talks; Truman, Harry S.; Truman's Recall of MacArthur; Zhou Enlai

References

Brown, Judith M. *Nehru: A Political Life.* New Haven, CT: Yale University Press, 2003.

Doody, Agnes G. "Words and Deeds: An Analysis of Jawaharlal Nehru's Non-Alignment Policy in the Cold War, 1947–1953." Unpublished PhD dissertation, Pennsylvania State University, 1961.

Gopal, Sarvepalli. *Jawaharlal Nehru: A Biography.* 3 vols. Cambridge, MA: Harvard University Press, 1976.

Nanda, Bal Ram. *Jawaharlal Nehru: Rebel and Statesman.* New York: Oxford University Press, 1995.

Nehru, Jawaharlal. *Jawaharlal Nehru: An Autobiography.* New Delhi: Oxford University Press, 1980.

———. *Letters to Chief Ministers, 1947–1964.* 5 vols. Edited by G. Parthasarathi. New Delhi: Oxford University Press, 1985–1989.

Netherlands

Small Western European nation encompassing 16,033 square miles, about twice the size of the U.S. state of New Jersey. The Netherlands is one of the most densely populated areas of Europe; its population in 1950 was 10.14 million. The nation is bordered to the north by the North Sea, to the southwest by Belgium, and to the east by Germany (then West Germany). The Netherlands is a parliamentary, constitutional monarchy. The monarch at the time of the Korean War was Queen Juliana, who was constitutionally head of state but not of government, although her executive powers were fairly broad. In practice, however, monarchs have not exercised these powers in the last 75 years or so, and their role has been mainly ceremonial. Politics in the early 1950s were dominated chiefly by the Catholic People's Party (later part of the Christian Democrats) and the Labor Party. Willem Drees of the Labor Party presided as the Dutch prime minister during the Korean War; he governed from 1948 to 1958.

As a signatory power of the North Atlantic Treaty Organization (NATO) and the Western European Union defensive alliance of 1948, the Netherlands agreed to provide a battalion of troops to the United Nations (UN) efforts in Korea following the outbreak of war on the divided peninsula. The advance party of the Netherlands force arrived in Korea on October 24, 1950. The entire battalion arrived in Pusan a month later, on November 23, immediately before the opening of the Chinese offensive.

Following processing at the United Nations Command (UNC) Reception Center at Taegu, the battalion was attached to the U.S. Eighth Army. As such it represented part of the only reserve available to U.S. commander Lieutenant General Walton H. Walker. By the next month, the Netherlands force was assigned, along with the French Battalion, to the U.S. 2nd Division as divisional reserve.

The battalion took part in the fierce defensive battles of the first two weeks of January 1951, helping the 2nd Division fend off strong Korean People's Army (KPA, North Korean Army) V Corps attacks southwest of the town of Wonju. In these actions the Dutch held Hill 247 and assisted in the killing or capturing of some 1,100 KPA troops. The fighting ranged north of Wonju to Hoengsong and back again by mid-February. On February 13 the battalion fought a gallant rear-guard action in which Dutch commander Lieutenant Colonel M. P. A. den Ouden personally confronted elements of a Chinese breakthrough that had reached the edge of the battalion's command post. Den Ouden and a number of his staff were killed; other members of the battalion staff were wounded. The excellent covering fire provided by the Dutch troops nevertheless allowed a number of U.S. units to withdraw safely.

In March and April, indications arose that the Chinese were about to resume their offensive in the higher ranges of the Taebaek Mountains southeastward from the Soyang River. Launched on May 16, that offensive again pushed U.S. and Republic of Korea Army (ROKA, South Korean Army) forces back. Included again were the U.S. 2nd Division and its attached Dutch Battalion. The Dutch drew the assignment to counterattack any Chinese or North Korean breakthrough. This occurred at the juncture of the lines of the U.S. 38th and 23rd Infantry regiments, where an ROKA covering force was collapsed back into the U.S. line by advancing communist forces. The Dutch only partially fulfilled their mission, confronted as they were by successive waves of thousands of Chinese troops, who literally walked upright through a hail of artillery and small-arms fire directed at the breach. At one point on May 17, the battalion broke under the pressure, though its commander, Lieutenant Colonel W. D. H. Eekhout, quickly regained control of his troops. U.S. commanders subsequently pulled the battalion out of the line and sent it two miles to the rear to rest and reorganize at the village of Hangye. By May 28, however, communist forces had been pushed back to about the 38th Parallel.

In the ensuing fighting around Hwachon Reservoir, Dutch troops and the rest of the 2nd Division helped cut off and destroy communist units attempting to escape the UN counteroffensive. In the words of Lieutenant General Matthew B. Ridgway, the Dutch Battalion and the 2nd Division performed brilliantly and displayed extraordinary heroism in the face of numerically vastly superior communist forces.

In the spring of 1952 the Dutch Battalion was assigned to the guard units on Koje-do off the southern coast of South Korea. There, it assisted in physically suppressing anti-UN demonstrations among Chinese and North Korean prisoners of war (POWs).

In general, the Dutch Battalion fit in well among UN forces and conducted itself admirably in a largely defensive, and occasionally offensive, role between 1950 and 1953. No significant cultural or linguistic difficulties arose between troops from the Netherlands and other contingents as, for example, plagued the Turkish Brigade. Dutch preferences for greater amounts of bread and potatoes in their rations than provided U.S. forces caused some initial logistical problems. These, however, were fairly quickly overcome and generated no serious frictions in any case. For its service in Korea, the battalion earned a U.S. Presidential Unit Citation.

D. R. DORONDO

See also

Ridgway, Matthew Bunker; Walker, Walton Harris

References

Hermes, Walter G. *U.S. Army in the Korean War: Truce Tent and Fighting Front.* Washington, DC: Office of the Chief of Military History, 1966.

Mossman, Billy C. *United States Army in the Korean War: Ebb and Flow, November 1950–July 1951.* Washington, DC: U.S. Army Center of Military History, 1990.

Neutral Nations Repatriation Commission

Commission created by the 1953 Korean Armistice Agreement to oversee the final screening of prisoners of war (POWs) from both sides in the Korean War who refused repatriation to their countries of origin. Indian representative to the United Nations (UN) V. K. Krishna Menon had proposed the establishment of a Neutral Nations Repatriation Commission (NNRC) to guarantee each POW freedom of choice. The UN resolution of December 3, 1952, provided the format for the June 8, 1953, POW agreement that set up the NNRC. It consisted of five representatives: two from neutral states friendly to the United States—Sweden and Switzerland—and two from communist states—Poland and Czechoslovakia. Neutral India was the fifth member, and the Indian representative, Major General Kadenera Subayya Thimayya, served as chairman and executive agent of the NNRC. India also agreed to provide a brigade of about 6,000 troops to guard the prisoners while they were being held in compounds within the demilitarized zone (DMZ) near Panmunjom. Major General S. P. P. Thorat had actual command of the troops of the Indian Custodian Force (CFI) supporting the NNRC.

The South Korean government of President Syngman Rhee opposed the Armistice Agreement and insisted that POWs held by the United Nations Command (UNC) refusing repatriation be

Recently repatriated United Nations Command (UNC) prisoners of war (POWs) arrive in ambulances in Panmunjom on April 21, 1953. The Neutral Nations Repatriation Commission oversaw the agreed-upon armistice decision that no prisoner would be forced to return home against his will after the war. (National Archives)

released in South Korea rather than being transferred to NNRC jurisdiction. Rhee also strongly objected to the selection of India as arbitrator of the POW issue. He regarded India as procommunist and therefore not neutral. Because the South Korean government refused to permit the Indian custodial troops on South Korean soil, the UNC transported all of them to the DMZ by helicopter. Although Rhee ordered the release of some 27,000 anticommunist POWs on June 18, 1953, the armistice was concluded with the agreement that all remaining nonrepatriated POWs be handed over to NNRC custody. The United States had insisted on a provision that this be completed within 60 days of the conclusion of the armistice. POWs from both sides were then to remain under NNRC jurisdiction for an additional 90 days while representatives of the countries involved endeavored to persuade them to return home. After this, the postwar Korean political conference would hold them for an additional 30 days. At the conclusion of this time, the NNRC would disband and the remaining POWs would become civilians.

On September 22, 1953, the CFI received from the communist side 359 UNC nonrepatriated POWs: 23 Americans, 1 British, and 335 South Koreans. Two days later, the NNRC took control from the UNC of 7,890 North Korean and 14,702 Chinese POWs. The countries of origin all sent representatives to try to convince the POWs to return home, but the NNRC had difficulty in getting the POWs to attend these sessions, which anticommunist leaders among the POWs opposed. The communist side constantly insisted that the NNRC force the POWs to attend, but the NNRC was unable to break the control of the anticommunist POW organizations over the prisoners and to guarantee conditions for the explanations. If the prisoners would not attend, the explanations could not take place. On several occasions POWs assaulted their guards and attempted to break out of the camps.

UNC representatives were able to meet with only 60 UN POWs. POWs of both sides were under strong and resolute leadership, and only about 3 percent of those who received the briefings decided to accept repatriation. Both sides sought to exploit the repatriation issue for their own propaganda advantage.

The persuasion process was to end on December 24, 1953. The communists demanded that it continue until all POWs had been briefed, but the UNC refused any extension in the time limit beyond that specified in the armistice terms. India sided with the UNC on this and, in a majority ruling, the commission advised both sides that the briefings had ended.

During the subsequent 30 days, until January 22, 1954, there was to be a political conference of representatives of the two sides and the NNRC to decide the fate of prisoners not yet briefed. The NNRC was to retain the custody of the POWs within that period. That conference did not convene because of antagonisms between the UNC and the communist side.

On January 20, 1954, the CFI began the transfer of POWs back to UNC custody. The delivery of 21,805 men to the UNC was completed by January 21. During this time, 104 additional prisoners sought CFI protection and asked for repatriation or asylum. No doubt other prisoners would have chosen repatriation if the opportunity to do so had been available. Only 137 of the communist nonrepatriates and 10 of the UNC nonrepatriates opted to return home.

Rejecting the position of the NNRC's Polish and Czechoslovakian representatives, on February 18, 1954, the Indian, Swedish, and Swiss members adopted a resolution to dissolve the NNRC three days later. Although the NNRC effort was disappointing to both sides, its activities nevertheless created precedents and established patterns that were followed in subsequent conflicts.

SUNGHUN CHO

See also

Menon, Vengalil Krishnan Krishna; Prisoners of War, Rescreening of; Rhee, Syngman; Thimayya, Kadenera Subayya

References

Bailey, Sydney D. *The Korean Armistice.* New York: St. Martin's, 1992.
Neutral Nations Repatriation Commission. *The Final Report of the Neutral Nations Repatriation Commission.* 1954.
Thimayya, Kadenera Subayya. *Experiment in Neutrality.* New Delhi: Vision Books, 1981.

Neutral Nations Supervisory Commission

Commission established to supervise the provisions of the 1953 Korean Armistice Agreement dealing with the introduction of military personnel, weapons, and equipment and to investigate armistice violations outside the demilitarized zone (DMZ). The truce negotiations that led to the formation of the Neutral Nations Supervisory Commission (NNSC) dealt with the "concrete arrangements" for the cease-fire and armistice.

When negotiations on these arrangements began on November 27, 1951, the two sides had already agreed in principle to the establishment of a Military Armistice Commission (MAC) to supervise the armistice. The United Nations Command (UNC) side now proposed that the MAC include Joint Observer Teams with freedom of movement throughout Korea. It was also proposed that, while both sides should be permitted to rotate their personnel and replace equipment, there should be no "reinforcement" (no increase in the numbers of military personnel and other war equipment) while the armistice was in effect. On December 3, 1951, North Korean and Chinese negotiators proposed a complete ban on the introduction of any new troops and equipment and introduced the idea of supervision of this ban by nations "neutral in the Korean War."

The UNC eventually accepted the idea of neutral nations supervision, so long as both sides were permitted to rotate (but not reinforce) their troops and equipment; that the "neutral" countries be mutually acceptable; and that the NNSC be subordinate to the MAC. Negotiations on this issue stalled for several months when the North Korean and Chinese negotiators proposed including the Union of Soviet Socialist Republics (USSR, Soviet Union); however, the two sides eventually agreed on Czechoslovakia and Poland (nominated by the North Koreans and Chinese) and Sweden and Switzerland (nominated by the UNC). They also agreed on a rotation figure of 35,000 military personnel per month through five ports of entry for each side. These were Inchon, Kangnung, Kunsan, Pusan, and Taegu in the Republic of Korea (ROK, South Korea); and Chongjin, Hungnam, Manpo, Sinanju, and Sinuiju in the Democratic People's Republic of Korea (DPRK, North Korea).

With the signing of the Armistice Agreement on July 27, 1953, the NNSC went into operation, moving into camps close to the Panmunjom conference site and establishing its operating procedures. It organized 20 Neutral Nations Inspection Teams (NNITs). Ten would operate at the ports of entry and 10 mobile teams would be available to investigate violations in other areas outside the DMZ if requested to do so by the MAC or by the senior MAC member of either side.

From the beginning, the inspections were controversial. North Korea restricted NNIT access at their official ports of entry and was accused by the UNC of bringing equipment in through other locations. The South Korean government accused the Czech and Polish members of spying, and periodically threatened to expel them. Tension also developed within the NNSC between the Poles and Czechs on one side and the Swiss and Swedes on the other. With a four-member, two-faction commission, deadlocks occurred frequently.

In 1956 the UNC unilaterally suspended NNIT operations in South Korea, citing communist violations and the obstructive attitude of the Czechs and Poles. The NNSC withdrew its inspection teams but continued to meet weekly at Panmunjom to review reports submitted by the two sides on the rotation of troops and replacement of equipment. As the years went by, both sides found the restrictions against introducing new equipment to be unrealistic and burdensome. In 1957 the UNC, arguing that North Korea persistently violated the armistice prohibitions on introducing new equipment, unilaterally suspended its adherence to that provision.

The NNSC supervisory system was now essentially defunct, but the commission served for many years as an informal channel of communication between the two sides and a moderating influence in the potentially volatile Panmunjom conference area. With the end of the Cold War, however, North Korea became disenchanted with Poland and Czechoslovakia. When Czechoslovakia broke up, North Korea refused to either recognize the Czech Republic as its NNSC successor or to nominate a replacement, and so in April 1993 the Czech delegation withdrew from the NNSC. In 1995 North Korea evicted the Polish delegation and severed all contact with the NNSC. The Swiss and Swedish NNSC delegations nonetheless continue to meet weekly, and Poland sends a representative several times a year to sign and validate NNSC documents. Representatives of the three nations also meet periodically in Europe to discuss NNSC business. Thus, a small and tenuous NNSC mechanism survives more than a half a century after its establishment.

DONALD W. BOOSE JR.

See also

Armistice Agreement; Demilitarized Zone; Kaesong Truce Talks; Military Armistice Commission; Neutral Nations Repatriation Commission; Truce Talks

References

Bailey, Sydney D. *The Korean Armistice.* New York: St. Martin's, 1992.

Hermes, Walter G. *U.S. Army in the Korean War: Truce Tent and Fighting Front.* Washington, DC: Office of the Chief of Military History, 1966.

U.S. Department of State, Bureau of Public Affairs. *Foreign Relations of the United States, 1951,* Vol. 7, *China and Korea.* Washington, DC: U.S. Government Printing Office, 1983.

———. *Foreign Relations of the United States, 1952–1954,* Vol. 15, *Korea.* Washington, DC: U.S. Government Printing Office, 1984.

New Look Defense Policy

Embraced by President Dwight D. Eisenhower's administration on October 30, 1953, through National Security Council (NSC) policy document NSC-162/2, the New Look defense policy was designed to implement U.S. military policy in a more cost-effective way without losing any ground in the Cold War. During the 1952 presidential election, Eisenhower had criticized President Harry S. Truman's administration both for being soft on communism and for risking the economic health of the nation because of high defense expenditures and budget deficits. Once in office, the Eisenhower administration sought a new policy that would fulfill its election pledges and address the events that unfolded during 1953. These included a swift end to the Korean War and reduced defense expenditures.

Following the start of the Korean War in June 1950, the defense budget had nearly quadrupled by 1953, a fact that greatly troubled Eisenhower. In fact, the majority of these added expenditures did not go to the war in Korea, but rather toward the global military buildup envisioned in NSC-68, which had been drafted in early 1950. Nevertheless, Korean War spending and implementation of the Cold War rearmament program had placed significant strains on the U.S. economy and federal budget. Working with his treasury secretary, George Humphrey, and his director of the Bureau of the Budget, Joseph Dodge, the new president proposed a policy of fiscal conservatism that would help balance the budget and allow the nation to wage the Cold War without risking its economic well-being.

The need for a new defense posture was highlighted further when the policy-making apparatus of the Eisenhower administration ground to a halt as its leading protagonists were racked by indecision in the wake of Soviet leader Joseph Stalin's death in March 1953 and the East German uprising in June of the same year. Leading members of the NSC argued over how best to exploit these situations and whether or not the United States should seize the initiative and attempt to roll back communism.

In May 1953 Eisenhower launched Operation SOLARIUM, which established three task forces to study and debate the future of U.S. military policy. Task Force A was headed by U.S. State Department veteran George F. Kennan and advocated a scenario loosely based on the containment policy already in place; Task Force B, led by Major General James McCormack, proposed a more muscular type of containment that would emphasize nuclear deterrence; and Task Force C, headed by Admiral Richard L. Conolly, examined the potential of a policy that would liberate Eastern Europe by rolling back communism. By July 1953 all three task forces had reported their findings to the NSC, although they were unable to reach consensus on the preferred course of action. Ultimately, the approach chosen would borrow from all three recommendations.

Discounting the 1950 NSC-68 policy document that presumed 1954 would be the "year of maximum danger," NSC 162/2 instead outlined a plan that would see the United States prepare for a long-haul struggle, with no set end date. The document called for greater use of covert operations and psychological warfare, an increase in aid to European and Asian allies, and a readiness to use nuclear weapons as a first response to any Soviet aggressive action, be it conventional or nuclear. At the same time, the New Look would decrease reliance on conventional forces, which, it was hoped, would bring down defense expenditures. Eisenhower eventually initialed the document on October 30, 1953. The policy was soon put into place, although U.S. defense budgets fell only marginally during 1954–1958 before rising once more. The rearmament effort during the Korean War–era had clearly driven the 1953 decisions, and implicit in the New Look strategy was an acknowledgment that the United States would heretofore eschew wars like the one in Korea.

BEVAN SEWELL

See also

Containment; Eisenhower, Dwight David; Kennan, George Frost; National Security Council; National Security Council Report 68

References

Bowie, Robert, and Richard Immerman. *Waging Peace: How Eisenhower Shaped an Enduring Cold War Strategy.* New York: Oxford University Press, 1998.

Dockrill, Saki. *Eisenhower's New Look: National Security Policy, 1953–1961.* New York: St. Martin's, 1996.

Gaddis, John Lewis. *Strategies of Containment: A Critical Appraisal of Postwar American National Security Policy.* New York: Oxford University Press, 1982.

New Zealand

English-speaking South Pacific island nation situated approximately 1,000 miles to the southeast of Australia, with a population of 1.9 million in 1950. New Zealand's land area covers 104,454 square miles. New Zealand is a parliamentary democracy, and during the Korean War was dominated by the New Zealand National Party, which came to power in 1949; it would retain power for much of the next 45 years. New Zealand also maintains direct ties to the British monarch. Sir Sidney George Holland was prime minister during the Korean War, governing from 1949 to 1957. Holland's government was strongly anticommunist and allied itself on most issues with the United States and other Western powers. In September 1951 Holland's government signed the Australia-New Zealand-United States (ANZUS) Treaty, which bound New Zealand closely to the United States and which gave it a modicum of security in case of attack.

New Zealand was one of the first countries to answer the United Nations (UN) call for assistance in Korea. When the war began, U.S. leaders asked that New Zealand deploy a force as a part of the United Nations Command (UNC). Prime Minister Holland and Chief of the General Staff Major General Sir Keith Lindsay Stewart initially contemplated joining forces with Australia, but the British Commonwealth powers were unable to reach quick agreement on either the type or size of their military commitment. Thus, on July 26, 1950, the New Zealand government unilaterally decided to send naval and ground forces to Korea.

On December 31, 1950, 1,231 New Zealand officers and troops arrived in Korea as part of the 16th Field Regiment, Royal New Zealand Artillery. Commanded by Lieutenant Colonel J. W. Moodie, this unit was the nation's principal military commitment, and in January 1951 it was attached to the 27th British Commonwealth Brigade. In April 1951 the artillery unit was followed by part of a divisional signals regiment, a transport platoon, and a light aid detachment.

New Zealand ground forces coordinated well with Australian troops and, because many members of the New Zealand contingent had not been adequately trained in technical matters, Australian artillery officers were attached to supervise their performance. New Zealand soldiers were also incorporated into other Australian units.

In the first week of February 1951, the New Zealanders provided fire support to the U.S. 24th Division, helping its advance to Chuam-ni. In April 1951 the New Zealanders also supported the 6th Division of the Republic of Korea Army (ROKA, South Korean Army) above Seoul at the beginning of the Chinese People's Volunteer Army's (CPVA, Chinese Army) spring offensive. Hindered by rugged terrain, the New Zealanders experienced difficulty transporting their equipment and were unable to provide effective support. The ROKA defense collapsed and the New Zealand troops disengaged, moving south to Kapyong, where the Commonwealth Brigade was in reserve. U.S. IX Corps commander Lieutenant General William M. Hoge ordered the New Zealanders again to move forward, protected by the British Middlesex Battalion. Again the South Koreans retreated, and the New Zealand artillery regiment withdrew to Kapyong, where the U.S. 213th Field Artillery Battalion reinforced the New Zealanders with 155-millimeter self-propelled howitzers. The unit played a vital role by shelling directly in front of Canadian troops and foiling a Chinese advance.

CPVA assaults continued until May 1, when the New Zealanders helped the U.S. 24th Division decisively defeat the CPVA offensive in their sector and advance to Line Kansas. For their role in the fighting, South Korean president Syngman Rhee awarded the 16th New Zealand Field Artillery Regiment a presidential unit citation. The New Zealanders later provided artillery support at the Battle of Maryong-san Mountain, where they fired more than 50,000 rounds in support of UNC forces.

In 1951 the United States urged New Zealand to send additional troops. By this time, however, New Zealanders already constituted about 5 percent of the Commonwealth Division forces, and the request was refused. Later, the New Zealanders did increase their transportation force from a platoon-size unit to a company.

In July 1951 the United States suggested the formation of a joint Australian–New Zealand force, but New Zealand officials stated their preference to remain with other Commonwealth forces. Thus, the New Zealand contingent was merged into the 1st Commonwealth Division when that force was formed that same month. In late 1952 the UNC again requested additional New Zealanders for Korean service, but the appeal was denied. The New Zealand force reached its maximum strength of 1,389 men in 1953, consisting of volunteers who rotated annually on an individual basis.

New Zealand also contributed 1,350 men of its naval forces. Their first naval contingent, the frigates HMNZ *Pukaki* and *Tutira*, departed for Korea on July 3, 1950. It was the start of a deployment that lasted for the duration of the war. Within a month these ships had joined the Blockading and Escort Force of the U.S. Naval Command Far East in the Yellow Sea. Other New Zealand naval units patrolled near Wonsan, while still others participated in the screening force at Inchon. The frigates *Taupo, Rotoiti, Kaniere,* and *Hawea* patrolled the coast. In 1951 and 1952, in a combined endeavor with South Korean Marines and the U.S. Navy, these ships shelled communist guerrillas and insurgents on the islands in the Han River estuary.

A total of 3,794 New Zealanders served in the Korean War, with casualties of 22 killed and 79 wounded in action, 16 dead from other causes, and 1 missing. One New Zealander was repatriated in Operation BIG SWITCH. While New Zealand's manpower contribution to the war was dwarfed by U.S. and ROKA forces, on a per capita basis it was second only to that of the United States.

CLAYTON D. LAURIE

See also

Australia; Hoge, William Morris; Kapyong, Battle of; LITTLE SWITCH and BIG SWITCH, Operations; Rhee, Syngman

References

Barclay, C. N. *The First Commonwealth Division: The Story of British Commonwealth Land Forces in Korea, 1950–1953.* Aldershot, UK: Gale and Polden, 1954.

Carew, Tim. *Korea: The Commonwealth at War.* London: Cassell, 1967.

McGibbon, Ian C. *New Zealand and the Korean War.* 2 vols. Auckland: Oxford University Press, 1996.

Mossman, Billy C. *United States Army in the Korean War: Ebb and Flow, November 1950–July 1951.* Washington, DC: U.S. Army Center of Military History, 1990.

Republic of Korea, Ministry of National Defense. *The History of the United Nations Forces in the Korean War.* 6 vols. Seoul: War History Compilation Commission, 1967–1975.

Nie Rongzhen
Birth Date: December 9, 1899
Death Date: May 14, 1992

People's Republic of China (PRC) marshal, acting chief of staff of the People's Liberation Army (PLA, Chinese Communist Army), and vice chairman of the Central Military Commission of the Chinese Communist Party (CCP) during the Korean War. Born in Jiangjin County, Sichuan Province, on December 9, 1899, Nie Rongzhen (Nieh Jung-ch'en) joined the CCP in 1922 and was sent to the Union of Soviet Socialist Republics (USSR, Soviet Union) to study the military and defense industry in 1924–1925. He became a deputy director of the Red Army's Political Department in the late 1920s and political commissar of its First Army Group during the Long March of 1934–1935.

During the war against Japan (1937–1945), Nie served as commander and political commissar of the North China Military Region. He worked with Mao Zedong closely on a daily basis after the CCP leadership moved from Yenan (Yan'an) to North China during the Chinese Civil War (1945–1949). Nie protected the CCP headquarters by defeating the Nationalist attacks and personally saved Mao's life once in an air raid. He became one of Mao's closest working colleagues and trusted generals. When Mao founded the PRC in October 1949, Nie was appointed mayor of Beijing and deputy chief of the PLA General Staff. He ran the General Staff because Zhou Enlai, as its chief, was preoccupied as Chinese premier and foreign minister. In 1950 Nie became acting chief of the General Staff and vice chairman of the Central Military Commission.

As Mao's senior aide in Beijing, Nie shared the responsibility of war preparation, intelligence, training, and mobilization. In January 1950 Nie met the North Korean military delegation, headed by Kim Kwang Hyop, who requested a transfer of two PLA divisions whose soldiers were of Korean origin. Nie agreed that all the Korean national soldiers in the Chinese army would be transferred to the Korean People's Army (KPA, North Korean Army). At the meetings, Kim also asked Nie to fully equip the two divisions before their leaving for the Democratic People's Republic of Korea (DPRK, North Korea). Nie viewed the request favorably and reported it to Mao on January 21. Mao approved the next day.

After the Korean War began in June 1950, Nie paid special attention to intelligence work. In July the General Staff sent more than 100 Chinese intelligence officers to North Korea under Colonel Chai Chengwei. Nie sought every possible means to obtain timely information on all aspects of the front. In August, based on his sources, he reported to Mao about a possible major U.S. counteroffensive against the KPA, which had penetrated deep into the Republic of Korea (ROK, South Korea), making its rear areas vulnerable. In the meantime he cabled Deng Hua and the commanders of the Northeast Border Defense Army (NBDA) along the Chinese–North Korean border to be combat-ready by the end of August. Later, Nie ordered these five armies to finish all the preparation before September 30.

After the CCP leadership made the decision in early October to send the Chinese People's Volunteer Army (CPVA, Chinese Army) into the Korean War, Nie's General Staff issued orders for the CPVA to cross the Yalu River into North Korea. Thereafter, Mao asked Nie and the General Staff to focus on CPVA operations. Meeting with Mao on daily basis, Nie took part in high command decision making, planned major operations, and shared the responsibility of mobilization, transportation, rotation, and logistics for the troops involved. On October 27 Nie proposed to Mao sending the 9th Army Group, including three armies, from east China to Korea as reinforcement. After Mao's approval on the same day, Nie began to work with Song Shilun, army group commander, on their preparation. On November 7 the 150,000 men of the 9th Army Group began to cross the Yalu River. They participated in the CPVA's second offensive later that month. On November 26 Nie reported to Mao of his plan to mobilize security and police forces. Mao approved his plan the next day. After one month of reorganization, Nie mobilized 120,000 men for the service. In January, after training, they were sent to the Korean front. In February Nie made a detailed arrangement for the 19th Army Group of three armies to enter Korea. In March he and the General Staff arranged for the 3rd Army Group to enter Korea. Later, the General Staff began to rotate the PLA units. By the end of the war about 73 percent of the Chinese infantry troops had been rotated into Korea (25 of 34 armies, or 79 of 109 infantry divisions). More than 55 percent of the tank units, 67 percent of the artillery divisions, and 100 percent of the combat engineering divisions had also been sent to Korea.

Mao did not always agree with Nie. After the Chinese Second Offensive, General Peng Dehuai planned another offensive south of the 38th Parallel and presented the plan to the General Staff on December 15, 1950. Nie believed that, after days of constant movement and fighting, the CPVA troops were exhausted and still poorly provisioned. He urged a postponement of the new offensive until February 1951. Mao disagreed and approved Peng's plan to launch the third offensive before the end of December. During the third offensive the CPVA faced mounting problems beyond shortages of food and ammunition. The CPVA and KPA lost more than 10,000 men during the eight-day campaign.

Nie faced great problems in logistics of the CPVA, which consumed an unprecedented amount of war matériel. During the first two offensives, the CPVA met only 25 percent of the food needs of its frontline troops. Nearly half of the CPVA troops did not have weapons and ammunition. In January 1951 Nie went to Manchuria, visited the logistics depots, and met with commanders to resolve some of the problems. In May the CPVA established its Logistics Department in Korea. That month, Nie and the General Staff put together an order to purchase weapons and equipment from the Soviet Union in order to arm 60 Chinese infantry divisions to meet wartime demand. The Soviet Union delivered the arms and equipment for 10 divisions in 1951, 16 divisions in 1952, and 40 divisions in 1953. The Soviets also shared technology for the production of rifles, machine guns, and artillery pieces.

Both CPVA equipment and logistics improved in the war. More than 6 million tons of supplies were shipped into Korea during the war. For the years 1950–1953, China's military spending represented 41 percent, 43 percent, 33 percent, and 34 percent of its total government annual budget.

After 1954 Nie was one of the party's 11 top national leaders as a member of the Standing Committee of the CCP Politburo. In 1955 he became one of 10 generals promoted to marshals in China. In 1958 when the Chinese leadership decided to develop atomic bombs, Nie headed China's nuclear and missile programs as director of the National Science and Technology Commission from 1958 to 1967. He also served as chairman of the National Defense Science and Technology Committee and director of the CCP Central Committee's Science Commission. He served as vice premier from 1959 to 1966. Nie died in Beijing on May 14, 1992.

XIAOBING LI

See also

Chai Chengwen; Chinese Offensive, Third; Chinese People's Volunteer Army; Deng Hua; Mao Zedong; Peng Dehuai; Song Shilun; Zhou Enlai

References

Chen Jian. *China's Road to the Korean War: The Making of the Sino-American Confrontation.* New York: Columbia University Press, 1994.

Han Huaizhi et al. *Dandai Zhongguo Jundui de Junshi Gongzuo* [Contemporary Chinese Military Affairs]. Beijing: Zhongguo Shehui Kexue Chubanshe [China's Social Science Press], 1989.

Li Xiaobing, Bin Yu, and Allan R. Millett, eds. and trans. *Mao's Generals Remember Korea.* Lawrence: University Press of Kansas, 2001.

Nie Rongzhen. *Nie Rongzhen Huiyilu* [Memoir of Nie Rongzhen]. Beijing: Jiefangjun Chubanshe [PLA Press], 1984.

———. *Nie Rongzhen Junshi Wenxuan* [Selected Military Papers of Nie Rongzhen]. Beijing: Jiefangjun Chubanshe [PLA Press], 1992.

Roe, Patrick C. *The Dragon Strikes: China and the Korean War, June–December 1950.* Novato, CA: Presidio, 2000.

Zhang Shu Guang. *Mao's Military Romanticism: China and the Korean War, 1950–1953.* Lawrence: University Press of Kansas, 1995.

Nitze, Paul Henry

Birth Date: January 16, 1907
Death Date: October 19, 2004

National security and arms control expert, academic, and director of the U.S. State Department's Policy Planning Staff (PPS) from 1950 to 1953. Born in Amherst, Massachusetts, on January 16, 1907, to an academic family, Paul Henry Nitze graduated from Harvard University with a bachelor's degree in economics in 1928, whereupon he entered the New York investment bank of Dillon, Read & Company. Among his colleagues was James V. Forrestal, who became undersecretary of the navy in 1940 and took Nitze with him as his assistant. During World War II Nitze held high office in the Board of Economic Warfare and the Foreign Economic Administration, and from 1944 to 1946 he was vice chairman of the U.S. Strategic Bombing Survey. As deputy director of the Office of International Trade Policy in the State Department, 1946–1948, and deputy to the assistant secretary of state for economic affairs, 1948–1949, Nitze helped to formulate and implement the Marshall Plan.

In 1949 Nitze became assistant to George F. Kennan, Soviet expert and formulator of the highly influential containment policy, who then headed the State Department's PPS. By the end of the year Kennan had resigned his position, and Nitze succeeded him. As with fellow Soviet expert Charles E. Bohlen, Kennan depreciated the creation of the North Atlantic Treaty Organization (NATO). He argued forcefully but unsuccessfully that the Soviets did not pose a major military threat to European security and that the ratification of a Western European military alliance with the United States would antagonize the Union of Soviet Socialist Republics (USSR, Soviet Union) and destroy any prospects for long-term European peace and German unification, yet provide little real protection against potential nuclear attack. Secretary of State Dean G. Acheson, by contrast, was a strong supporter of the new alliance, as was the temperamentally hawkish Nitze, who had for several years advocated a hard-line position toward the Soviet Union. In his new post he helped to formulate NATO's fundamental structure and to convince Congress to ratify the treaty.

In January 1950, responding to the autumn 1949 Soviet detonation of an atomic bomb and the communist victory in China, Acheson asked Nitze to chair an interdepartmental study group that would conduct a full review of U.S. foreign and defense

An expert on arms control, Paul H. Nitze was director of the State Department's Policy Planning Staff during 1950–1953. This photo was taken in 1952. (Hulton Archive/Getty Images)

policy, the first comprehensive survey of its kind. Its report, National Security Council Report 68 (NSC-68), which was handed to President Harry S. Truman in April 1950, was largely written by Nitze, and the document argued his (and Acheson's) view that the Soviets were determined on world domination and that by 1954 they would possess nuclear strength sufficient to destroy the United States. To meet this challenge, Nitze recommended that the United States should make itself the leader of the noncommunist world and should rebuild the West until it far surpassed the Soviet Union economically. More significantly, NSC-68 envisaged that the United States would take primary responsibility for the entire noncommunist world's defense and security against outside attack and should possess the ability both to repel a full-scale invasion and to handle limited peripheral wars. To carry out this mission, NSC-68 recommended a massive enhancement of the Free World's military capabilities, and in particular a massive increase in U.S. defense spending, the strengthening of NATO's nuclear forces, and the development of more advanced nuclear weapons. NSC-68 estimated that the United States could devote up to 20 percent of its gross national product to defense expenditures without major economic disruptions. Truman, eager to cut government spending and balance the budget, initially rejected these recommendations, preferring a more modest and limited military and foreign policy.

The outbreak of the Korean War greatly enhanced the credibility of NSC-68's analysis and prescriptions, and within a few weeks Truman began to implement a permanent massive increase of United States defense spending and commitments, including the commitment of substantial U.S. land forces to NATO and the acquisition of additional military bases and allies throughout the world. The U.S. defense budget rose from $13 billion to $52 billion in less than 2 years. The broad framework of defense capabilities, commitments, and objectives laid out in NSC-68 would in many respects characterize U.S. Cold War strategy for the subsequent 40 years.

Nitze agreed enthusiastically with the original U.S. decision to intervene in the Korean conflict. Initially he argued against crossing the 38th Parallel, because he feared this might bring Soviet or Communist Chinese forces into the war, but when presentations by John M. Allison, director of the Office of Northeast Asian Affairs, and John Paton Davies, PPS China expert, discounted this possibility, the PPS submitted a memorandum endorsing an attempt to unify all Korea under one Western-oriented noncommunist government. Truman was cautious in accepting these recommendations, authorizing General Douglas MacArthur to pursue North Korean forces as far as the Yalu River but to neither occupy nor unify the country. After the November 1950 Chinese military intervention, Nitze once again embraced caution, believing that Soviet forces would enter the war only if the overthrow of the Chinese government seemed likely or United Nations (UN) forces came too close to the Soviet border.

After Dwight D. Eisenhower became president in 1953, Nitze, who was politically unacceptable to the Republican right, retired from the government to head the Foreign Service Educational Foundation. He remained active in Democratic politics, generally advocating the hawkish foreign policies also favored by his friend and patron Acheson. He subsequently held numerous second-rank positions within the national security apparatus, though he never attained the highest-level positions of secretary of state, secretary of defense, or national security adviser, which was his ultimate ambition.

Nitze served under President John F. Kennedy as assistant secretary of defense for international security affairs, participating in the deliberations during crises over Berlin and Cuba. From 1963 to 1967 he was secretary of the navy, where he became a proponent of a negotiated Vietnam peace settlement and de-escalation of the ground war. He was one of the "Wise Men," the members of President Lyndon B. Johnson's ad hoc Task Force on Vietnam, which in March 1968 recommended U.S. withdrawal from the Vietnam conflict. Nitze was deputy secretary of defense, 1967–1969; a member of the U.S. delegation to the Strategic Arms Limitations Talks (SALT) held at Helsinki, Finland, 1969–1974; head of the U.S. delegation at the Geneva Arms Control Talks, 1981–1984; and a presidential adviser on arms control, 1984–1989.

In the 1970s Nitze was one of the founders of the second Committee on the Present Danger, which argued that U.S. defenses were dangerously inadequate and attacked SALT II as ineffective. His relatively hard-line views on security won him both respect and office from Ronald Reagan's Republican Party. Interested for decades in the training and education of foreign policy experts, Nitze also founded and endowed the Washington, DC-based Paul H. Nitze School of Advanced International Studies of Johns Hopkins University, where in his official retirement he kept an office, held a senior research appointment, and remained actively engaged with the intellectual interests that had preoccupied him for almost 60 years. Nitze died in Washington on October 19, 2004.

PRISCILLA ROBERTS

See also

Acheson, Dean Gooderham; Allison, John Moore; Bohlen, Charles Eustis; Davies, John Paton; Kennan, George Frost; National Security Council; National Security Council Report 68; North Atlantic Treaty Organization; Truman, Harry S.

References

Callahan, David. *Dangerous Capabilities: Paul Nitze and the Cold War.* New York: HarperCollins, 1990.

May, Ernest R. *American Cold War Strategy: Interpreting NSC 68.* Boston: Bedford Books, 1993.

Nitze, Paul H., with Ann M. Smith and Steven L. Rearden. *From Hiroshima to Glasnost at the Center of Decision: A Memoir.* New York: Grove Weidenfeld, 1989.

Rearden, Steven L. *The Evolution of American Strategic Doctrine: Paul H. Nitze and the Soviet Challenge.* Boulder, CO: Westview, 1984.

———. "Paul H. Nitze: The Last of the Cold Warriors." *Diplomatic History* 17(1) (Winter 1993): 143–146.

Talbott, Strobe. *The Master of the Game: Paul Nitze and the Nuclear Peace.* New York: Knopf, 1988.

Nixon, Richard Milhous

Birth Date: January 9, 1913
Death Date: April 22, 1994

U.S. congressman and senator who served as vice president of the United States from 1953 to 1961 and president of the United States from 1969 to 1974. Born into a grocer's family in Yorba Linda, California, on January 9, 1913, Richard Milhous Nixon graduated from Whittier College in 1934 and Duke University Law School in 1937. He then began the practice of law in Whittier, California. After stints during World War II with the Office of Price Administration in Washington, DC, and as an aviation ground officer in the Pacific theater, Nixon served two terms (1947–1950) in Congress before winning election to the Senate in the 1950 campaign.

Nixon, a Republican, quickly became notorious for red-baiting, a reputation he won through service on the House Un-American Activities Committee (HUAC), where he aggressively participated in the Alger Hiss espionage investigation. In his 1950 senate campaign, he likewise characterized his opponent, Congresswoman Helen Gahagan Douglas of California, as the "Red Lady," tactics that made him a bête noire of the Democratic Party.

Using the tailgate of his car as his podium, Rep. Richard Nixon (R-Calif.) addresses a crowd during his campaign for the U.S. Senate nomination on April 22, 1950. (AP/Wide World Photos)

Nixon supported President Harry S. Truman's decision to intervene in Korea but, like other Republicans, he frequently attacked the specifics of the administration's war policies. He ascribed much responsibility for the outbreak of war to what he characterized as the administration's weak, ineffective, and insufficiently anticommunist policies, particularly its failure to intervene on Jiang Jieshi's behalf in the Chinese Civil War, which he blamed for the subsequent communist takeover of China. Predictably, he developed close ties to the China Lobby, although political opportunism seems to have underpinned his anticommunism. Nixon's rhetoric grew increasingly harsh when United Nations Command (UNC) forces failed to hold North Korean territory after Chinese intervention in late 1950, a tendency further exacerbated by Truman's recall of UNC commander General of the Army Douglas MacArthur the following spring. Nixon went so far as to introduce an unsuccessful Republican Senate resolution demanding MacArthur's reinstatement.

Nixon's selection in 1952 as Dwight D. Eisenhower's running mate in the presidential election was largely due to his anticommunist credentials and the party's desire to appease the Republican right wing after its favored candidate, Senator Robert A. Taft, failed to win the nomination. Whereas Eisenhower presented a relatively moderate image, Nixon took the low road, launching ferocious assaults on the Truman administration, in which the

Korean situation featured prominently, often as a symbol of the failure of Truman's containment policy.

Nixon initially claimed to believe that total victory in Korea was attainable, a position that Eisenhower, who hoped that the Panmunjom armistice talks would deliver a settlement, forced him to modify. In late 1953, well after he became vice president, Nixon privately claimed that he shared the view of the columnist Joseph W. Alsop, who argued that the July 1953 Korean truce settlement deprived the United Nations (UN) of victory. National Security Council (NSC) records, however, reveal that he was less than persistent in urging this viewpoint within the Eisenhower administration, behavior that probably reflected his uneasy relationship with the president.

In November 1953 Nixon visited the Republic of Korea (ROK, South Korea) on Eisenhower's instructions to extract from President Syngman Rhee a pledge to take no action against the Democratic People's Republic of Korea (DPRK, North Korea) without informing Eisenhower. Nixon, in whose later foreign policies pragmatism and stated ideology were likewise often at odds, pressed Rhee to exercise even greater circumspection when dealing with North Korea. According to his own memoirs, Nixon succeeded in winning the South Korean president's verbal admission that he recognized that South Korea "could not possibly act alone." Rhee's letter to Eisenhower on the subject, however, merely provided the requested assurance that Rhee would take no unilateral action against North Korea without notifying the U.S. government. Rhee and Nixon also agreed that Rhee might continue his belligerent public statements, though it remains unclear whether Eisenhower had authorized his deputy to endorse this stance.

After narrowly losing the 1960 presidential election to John F. Kennedy and a subsequent trouncing in the 1962 California gubernatorial race, Nixon announced he would leave politics. In 1968, however, he narrowly defeated Democratic candidate Hubert H. Humphrey to become the 37th president of the United States. His victory inaugurated several decades of Republican dominance in the White House, an achievement for which Nixon deserved much of the credit. Foreign policy dominated his presidency. After his efforts to secure victory in Vietnam failed, he withdrew U.S. forces. He opened relations with the People's Republic of China (PRC), inaugurated détente with the Union of Soviet Socialist Republics (USSR, Soviet Union), and undertook a major reconceptualization of the role of the United States in the world in light of its diminished international weight. One aspect of the latter was the U.S. insistence that such allies as South Korea bear more of the burden of their own defense. The Watergate scandal, which drove Nixon to resign in August 1974, undercut his foreign and domestic policy successes.

Nixon spent his final two decades in a dogged crusade for rehabilitation, publishing extensively on international affairs and recasting himself as a respected elder statesman and foreign policy expert. He died in New York City on April 22, 1994.

PRISCILLA ROBERTS

See also

China Lobby; Eisenhower, Dwight David; Jiang Jieshi; MacArthur, Douglas; National Security Council; Rhee, Syngman; Taft, Robert Alphonso; Truman's Recall of MacArthur; U.S. Policy toward Korea, 1953–Present

References

Ambrose, Stephen E. *Nixon.* 3 vols. New York: Simon and Schuster, 1987–1991.

Caridi, Ronald J. *The Korean War and American Politics: The Republican Party as a Case Study.* Philadelphia: University of Pennsylvania Press, 1968.

Kepley, David R. *The Collapse of the Middle Way: Senate Republicans and the Bipartisan Foreign Policy, 1948–1952.* New York: Greenwood, 1982.

Morris, Roger. *Richard Milhous Nixon: The Rise of an American Politician.* New York: Henry Holt, 1990.

Nixon, Richard. *RN: The Memoirs of Richard Nixon.* New York: Grosset and Dunlap, 1978.

Wicker, Tom. *One of Us: Richard Nixon and the American Dream.* New York: Random House, 1991.

No Name Line, Battle of
Start Date: May 16, 1951
End Date: May 18, 1951

Battle for one of several battle tactical lines established mainly in the spring of 1951 during the several Chinese offensives. Other lines included Lincoln, Utah, Kansas, Missouri, Quantico, and Wyoming. These lines generally constituted both desired defensive and offensive positions. The No Name Line was an eastward extension of Line Lincoln that had its westward terminus in the Seoul area. The No Name ran in a northeastward direction from a point about midway between the towns of Chunchon and Hongchon for a distance of about 18 miles, ending a mile or so southeast of the village of Ogumal on the Inje-Hangye/Hongchon road (now Korean National Highway 44).

Generally, in the spring and early summer of 1951, the front lines in Korea were below or above the No Name Line, except in May, when the line was manned by four divisions of the X Corps—the U.S. 1st Marine and 2nd Army divisions, and the Republic of Korea Army (ROKA, South Korean Army) 5th and 7th divisions. These four divisions occupied a northeast diagonally twisting line south of the Soyang River and parallel to the Kansong-Hongchon road.

By May 14 the X Corps G-2 assistant chief of staff for intelligence determined that large numbers of communist troops—the Chinese People's Volunteer Army (CPVA, Chinese Army) and Korean People's Army (KPA, North Korean Army)—were in the central sector and that a major attack there was imminent. U.S. Eighth Army headquarters expressed doubt about this intelligence and continued to believe that communist forces would aim for Seoul in the west. On May 16, contrary to the Eighth Army's assessment, the communists launched their Sixth Offensive and burst upon X Corps with 15 CPVA and 5 KPA divisions, altogether some 175,000 men. The CPVA directed their attack primarily on the ROKA units on the right, where resistance promptly collapsed.

The ROKA troops abandoned most artillery and crew-served weapons and even rifles as they fled to the rear. Two dozen U.S. advisers with the ROKA troops were either killed or captured. Historian Clay Blair wrote, "The ROK bugout, involving about 40,000 men, was the largest and most disgraceful of the Korean War." It left a great gap on the X Corps' right flank and exposed the entire rear of the eastern United Nations Command (UNC) position, directly imperiling the 2nd Division, which now faced CPVA troops on three sides. With the departure of the ROKA troops on the right, the CPVA concentrated on the U.S. 2nd Division.

During the next three days the 2nd Division carried out a ferocious defense of its positions and inflicted heavy casualties on the attackers. The 2nd fired awesome amounts of artillery: 17,000 rounds on May 16 and 38,000 rounds on May 18. The division's position, so far forward of the main line of resistance, was perilously untenable. On May 18 it was ordered to withdraw to Hangye to the rear of the No Name Line. The 2nd Division commander assessed communist casualties in the fighting at more than 20,000 men.

On May 20 the UNC launched a counteroffensive that pushed the communists back to the No Name Line and beyond. This offensive continued throughout the summer, and by August and September it had reached well beyond the 38th Parallel to the areas that would become known as Bloody Ridge, Heartbreak Ridge, and the Punchbowl. The No Name Line did not thereafter become a location for frontline combat.

SHERMAN W. PRATT

See also
Chinese Offensive, Sixth

References

Blair, Clay. *The Forgotten War: America in Korea, 1950–1953.* New York: Times Books, 1987.

Hastings, Max. *The Korean War.* New York: Simon and Schuster, 1987.

Munroe, Clark C. *The Second United States Infantry Division in Korea, 1950–1951.* Tokyo: Toppan Printing, n.d. [1952].

Pratt, Sherman W. *Decisive Battles of the Korean War: An Infantry Company Commander's View of the War's Most Critical Engagements.* New York: Vantage Press, 1992.

Noble, Harold

Birth Date: January 19, 1903
Death Date: December 22, 1953

U.S. diplomat. Born in Pyongyang on January 19, 1903, to U.S. missionaries living in Korea, Harold Noble graduated from Ohio Wesleyan University in 1924, and the next year he completed a master's degree at Ohio State University. He was an instructor at Ewha College in Seoul between 1926 and 1928. In 1929 he obtained a teaching fellowship from the University of California at Berkeley and completed a doctorate in history there in 1931. That same year he became a professor of history at the University of Oregon. During 1939–1940 he taught at Third College in Kyoto, Japan. He was also awarded a Rockefeller fellowship in Chinese and Japanese studies. During World War II Noble served in the U.S. Marine Corps and saw service in New Zealand, New Caledonia, and the Solomon Islands as a combat intelligence officer, company commander, and a Japanese language officer.

After the war Noble was a foreign correspondent for the *Saturday Evening Post* in Japan, Korea, China, and Australia. In 1947 he became chief of the publications branch of the Civilian Intelligence Section of the Far East Command. Noble foresaw the forthcoming war in Korea and even predicted its outbreak in an article he wrote.

His many diplomatic positions included that with general headquarters of the Far East Command in Tokyo during 1947–1948; chief of the Political Liaison Office Headquarters in Seoul, Korea, 1948; member of the U.S. delegation to the United Nations (UN) General Assembly, 1949–1951; and political attaché and first secretary at the U.S. embassy to the Republic of Korea (ROK, South Korea).

Noble was an important figure in the Korean War, as he was perhaps the most important U.S. influence on South Korean president Syngman Rhee. Rhee had learned to speak English from Noble's father, and Noble was a longtime associate of Rhee's. Noble wrote several of Rhee's speeches, acted as a conduit during negotiations between Rhee and U.S. ambassador John Joseph Muccio, and was the U.S. diplomat assigned to stay with Rhee when the latter was in Taejon after the June 1950 North Korean invasion.

Just before the start of the Korean War, Noble was working to ensure that Rhee would permit free elections in South Korea. He was not in Korea at the time of the North Korean invasion but was immediately recalled by Muccio to serve as chief liaison officer to Rhee.

Noble was a staunch opponent of the Democratic People's Republic of Korea (DPRK, North Korea) and a fervent supporter of South Korea. He publicly expressed his desire for forcible reunification of the two Koreas and was subsequently reprimanded for this.

Dissatisfaction with U.S. policies led Noble to resign from the Foreign Service, and in July 1951 he left Korea. He became an executive with the Committee for Free Asia in San Francisco. He was a member of the board of editors of the *Pacific Historical Review;* he was a contributing editor for the *Far Eastern Quarterly;* and he wrote articles and coauthored a book, *What It Takes to Rule Japan* (1946). Noble was in the process of writing another book on Asian affairs when he died of a heart attack on December 22, 1953, on an airplane flight from Honolulu to the continental United States.

MONICA SPICER

See also
Muccio, John Joseph; Rhee, Syngman

References
Findling, John. *Dictionary of American Diplomatic History.* Westport, CT: Greenwood, 1980.
Matray, James I., ed. *Historical Dictionary of the Korean War.* Westport, CT: Greenwood, 1991.

Nogun-ni Railroad Bridge Incident
Event Date: July 1950

Site of alleged massacre of South Korean civilians by U.S. soldiers of H Company of the 2nd Battalion, 7th Cavalry Regiment of the 1st Cavalry Division in July 1950. The railroad bridge at Nogun-ni is located near that town a few miles southwest of Hwanggan, North Chungchong Province, central Republic of Korea (ROK, South Korea). A few days after their deployment to Korea, soldiers of the U.S. 1st Cavalry Division allegedly fired on civilians at the Nogun-ni railroad bridge, killing up to 300 people.

In 1997 some 30 Korean survivors of the Nogun-ni incident filed for compensation with the South Korean government. A low-level South Korean commission found that civilians had been killed at Nogun-ni but that there was no proof of U.S. involvement. In 1998 a national panel rejected the claim on the basis that the statute of limitations had expired. The incident surfaced again when it received major press coverage in the United States in September 1999, and U.S. Secretary of Defense William S. Cohen ordered a new review of the historical evidence with a report to be issued upon its conclusion.

Allegedly, on July 26, 1950, U.S. troops instructed some 500 residents of Nogun-ni and nearby villages to gather near railroad tracks at Nogun-ni. U.S. veterans recall the subsequent events differently, although they are in agreement on a preponderance of women and children among the refugees at the bridge. Reports had circulated among U.S. troops that Korean People's Army (KPA, North Korean Army) infiltrators might attempt to use refugees to penetrate the battalion's defenses.

On July 26 the civilian refugees were resting near the railroad tracks when they suddenly came under a strafing attack by U.S. aircraft; reportedly upwards of 100 refugees were killed and those who remained sought cover under the railroad bridge. Over the next several days U.S. soldiers kept the refugees pinned down under the bridge and fired on them. Some veterans recall receiving fire from the civilians at the bridge and say that they found disguised KPA soldiers among the dead. Others do not recall being fired upon and say they saw only civilians there. The Korean claimants recall only three days of carnage. On July 29 the 7th Cavalry pulled back and the KPA moved into the area. A North Korean newspaper reported several weeks later that KPA troops had found about 400 bodies in the area.

A 2001 report by the U.S. Army inspector general concluded that the Nogun-ni incident was not a deliberate or premeditated massacre of civilians but rather a tragic result of a savage war and ill-trained U.S. and South Korean troops. The Pentagon insisted that no soldiers were ordered to shoot civilians in the vicinity of the bridge. The U.S. government thus admitted that civilians had been fired upon, but the precise number of those killed varies widely; the U.S. military has estimated 50–100; the South Koreans claim as many as 250. The Democratic People's Republic of Korea (DPRK, North Korea) continues to claim 400 or more. Before leaving office, President Bill Clinton issued a formal statement of deep regret over the incident. There are still many people, both in the United States and South Korea, however, who believe that what happened at the railroad bridge was more nefarious than an unfortunate accident of war.

The events at Nogun-ni must be seen against the background of the initial deployment of U.S. troops from Japan, the vast majority of whom were poorly trained and without combat experience, and their injection into the desperate fighting that marked the retreat of United Nations (UN) forces to the Pusan Perimeter. UN troops had regularly come under fire from North Korean infiltrators utilizing civilian refugees as human shields. As a consequence, U.S. commanders had indeed issued orders authorizing troops to fire on civilians as a defense against disguised KPA soldiers.

SPENCER C. TUCKER

See also
Atrocities

References
Bateman, Robert L., III. *No Gun Ri: A Military History of the Korean War Incident.* Mechanicsburg, PA: Stackpole Books, 2002.
Hanley, Charles J., Sang-hun Chol, and Martha Mendoza. *The Bridge at No Gun Ri: A Hidden Nightmare from the Korean War.* New York: Henry Holt, 2001.

Norstad, Lauris
Birth Date: March 24, 1907
Death Date: September 12, 1988

U.S. Air Force general, supreme allied commander of the North Atlantic Treaty Organization (NATO), and early advocate of deploying tactical nuclear missiles to defend Western Europe against communist attack. Born the son of a minister in Minneapolis, Minnesota, on March 24, 1907, Lauris Norstad graduated from the U.S. Military Academy at West Point in 1930. Commissioned in the cavalry, he soon transferred to the Army Air Corps and received fighter pilot training.

Following a series of operational assignments, Norstad graduated from the Air Corps Tactical School in 1939. Promoted to captain in 1940, in November of the same year he became the assistant chief of staff for intelligence at General Headquarters, Air Force.

General Lauris Norstad was U.S. Air Force deputy chief of staff for operations and acting vice chief of staff when the Korean War began. From 1956 until his retirement in 1963 he was Supreme Allied Commander Europe (SCAEUR) for the North Atlantic Treaty Organization. (NATO Photos)

He was promoted to major in June 1941 and to lieutenant colonel in January 1942. In February 1942 Norstad was a member of the personal advisory council of Lieutenant General Henry Arnold, commander of Army Air Forces, and carried out studies of air strategy issues. He was promoted to colonel in July 1942.

In 1943 Norstad began overseas service, first with the Twelfth Army Air Force and later with the Northwest African Air Force. In these positions he helped plan and implement air support for the Allied landings in North Africa, Sicily, and Italy. After his promotion to brigadier general in 1944, Norstad helped plan Boeing B-29 (Superfortress) raids against Japan, climaxing in the atomic bombings of Hiroshima and Nagasaki in August 1945. In June 1945 he was promoted to major general. During the immediate postwar period Norstad served as assistant chief of air staff and played a leading role in the shaping of an independent U.S. Air Force.

When the Korean War began in June 1950, Norstad was the air force deputy chief of staff for operations and acting vice chief of staff. He accompanied W. Averell Harriman on a fact-finding mission to Tokyo in August 1950 and returned with a recommendation that Lieutenant General Matthew B. Ridgway replace Lieutenant General Walton H. Walker as Eighth Army commander

if Walker should become a casualty in the fighting in Korea. In October 1950 Norstad was named to command the U.S. Air Force in Europe and assumed additional duty as commander of allied air forces in Central Europe under Supreme Headquarters Allied Powers Europe (SHAPE) in April 1951.

In 1952 Norstad became the youngest American ever to become a full (four-star) general. Between 1953 and 1956 he was air deputy of SHAPE; from November 1956 until his retirement in 1963 he served as SHAPE commander. During his time with NATO he worked for increased conventional military preparedness as well as an independent NATO nuclear capability. He favored the expansion of the West German military and stockpiling of nuclear weapons on German soil. During his tenure in Brussels, Belgium, Norstad was also a strong advocate for a NATO nuclear force command and was instrumental in increasing from 30 to 100 the number of short-range tactical nuclear missiles in Europe.

During the 1961 Berlin crisis, Norstad advised President John F. Kennedy to publicize the fact that the United States would use nuclear weapons to protect the city, and he was disappointed when the president refused to do so. Norstad also differed with Kennedy on whether land-based or submarine-based nuclear weapons should be deployed to defend Western Europe and whether Britain and France should have veto power concerning their use. These differences led to his resignation in January 1963.

After his retirement Norstad became president of the international division of the Owens-Corning Fiberglass Corporation, a position he held until 1972. He continued to speak out on defense issues, focusing on the creation of a separate NATO nuclear force and on the need to maintain U.S. troop levels in Europe. Norstad died in Tucson, Arizona, on September 12, 1988.

CLAYTON D. LAURIE

See also

Harriman, William Averell; North Atlantic Treaty Organization; Ridgway, Matthew Bunker; Walker, Walton Harris

Reference

Jordan, Robert S. *Norstad: Cold War NATO Supreme Commander, Airman, Strategist, Diplomat.* London: Palgrave Macmillan, 2000.

North Atlantic Treaty Organization

Mutual defense alliance initially comprising the United States and 11 Western European nations. The North Atlantic Treaty Organization (NATO) came into being on April 4, 1949, and originally was a collective security alliance in response to the growing concerns over aggression by the Union of Soviet Socialist Republics (USSR, Soviet Union) and the spread of communism into Western Europe. The member states mutually declared that an attack against any one of its members would be considered an assault against all.

The European member states hailed NATO as a new U.S. commitment to the defense of Western Europe. The Korean War, however, shifted U.S. foreign policy to East Asia, and the Western

The first meeting of the North Atlantic Treaty Organization convenes in Washington, D.C., on September 17, 1949. (NATO Photos)

Europeans believed that increased U.S. military involvement in Korea might damage the flow of military aid to them. These fears soon vanished once President Harry S. Truman's position on the war became clear. Indeed, Washington, DC, believed that a communist triumph in Asia would pave the way for an attempt to repeat the process in Europe, as did U.S. Far East commander General Douglas MacArthur.

Nevertheless, NATO members had to address hard realities laid bare by the Korean War. The military and organizational weakness of NATO in 1950 demanded quick remedies in the face of the crisis. Rearmament in Europe was scarcely under way at the outbreak of war in June 1950. Also, NATO had only 12 divisions. Efforts to rearm, spurred forward by U.S. secretary of state Dean G. Acheson, resulted in a substantial increase in defense spending by Britain and France. In the autumn of 1950 the United States also pledged to send four additional U.S. divisions to Europe, despite the opposition of some in Congress over diverting resources to Europe in time of war in Asia.

These steps proved to be inadequate and raised the explosive issue of allowing military participation by the Federal Republic of Germany (FRG, West Germany) in the alliance. Europeans, especially the French, lodged strong protests. The desperate need for manpower, however, produced a proposal by French economic planner Jean Monnet. In October 1950 he introduced the Pleven Plan, named for French premier René Pleven, which called for a European defense force at the command of NATO that would include West German units. Monnet's plan led to the creation of the European Defense Community (EDC) in May 1952. Although the plan ultimately failed (ironically, rejected by the French government), it laid the foundation for West Germany's eventual inclusion in NATO in 1955.

Organizational changes in the command structure of NATO resulted from rearmament and particularly the German question. Command of the military forces of the alliance rested with the Supreme Headquarters Allied Powers Europe (SHAPE), created in January 1951. At that time, General Dwight D. Eisenhower became NATO's first supreme commander. Political restructuring took the form of a council of deputies under the leadership of a secretary-general to carry out the policies of the alliance. These changes, with the exception of continued expansion of the alliance, remain largely unchanged to the present.

ERIC W. OSBORNE

See also

Acheson, Dean Gooderham; European Defense Community; France; Truman, Harry S.; United Kingdom

References

Kaplan, Lawrence S. *NATO and the United States.* New York: Twayne, 1994.

Kaufman, Burton I. *The Korean War: Challenges in Crisis, Credibility and Command.* 2nd ed. New York: McGraw-Hill, 1997.

MacDonald, Callum. *Korea: The War before Vietnam.* New York: Free Press, 1987.

North Korea

See Korea, Democratic People's Republic of, 1945–1953; Korea, Democratic People's Republic of, 1953–Present

---

North Korean Offensive, Delaying of
Start Date: July 5, 1950
End Date: August 4, 1950

As soon as President Harry S. Truman made the decision to send ground combat troops to Korea, U.S. commander in the Far East General Douglas MacArthur dispatched U.S. forces there from Japan. Major General William F. Dean's 24th Infantry Division was the first division to enter Korea, and Dean assumed command of all U.S. Army forces there. His mission was to delay the advance of the Korean People's Army (KPA, North Korean Army) as long as possible until substantial U.S. reinforcements could be sent to Korea. Dean immediately formed a task force headed by Lieutenant Colonel Charles B. Smith, which would fly to the Republic of Korea (ROK, South Korea) and move into blocking positions north of Osan. Task Force Smith, as it came to be known, consisted of two reinforced rifle companies and a field artillery battery. In the meantime the rest of the division was assembled to move to Pusan by ship and thence to the front.

Task Force Smith took up position south of Suwon, where the main highway to Seoul passed through a low saddle in a small ridge. Its first contact with the KPA came on the morning of July 5, 1950, when a tank column approached. When the KPA tanks got within 700 yards of the dug-in U.S. infantry, they were taken under fire by recoilless rifles and 2.36-inch bazookas. These weapons were not effective in stopping the tanks. U.S. 105-millimeter howitzer fire did, however, knock out 2 lead tanks, but 30 tanks behind them kept moving around and through the U.S. troops. Later, KPA infantry arrived and outflanked the U.S. position. By early afternoon the U.S. defensive position became untenable. Colonel Smith, fearful of being cut off, then withdrew his men.

The success of this first KPA contact with the U.S. Army made time even more important for United Nations (UN) forces. Other U.S. units would now have to make sacrifices to delay the KPA

until sufficient resources could be put together to stop the North Korean drive. Geography acquired importance, and rivers became excellent obstacles to slow KPA tanks. General Dean and his planners selected important terrain features where U.S. forces would fight. Such places as Chonan, Pyongtaek, Taejon, and the Kum River were points where U.S. forces would try to block the KPA advance.

The next U.S. unit positioned to block the KPA advance was the 34th Infantry Regiment of the 24th Division. At Ansong and Chonan, however, battalions of the regiment were outflanked and became disorganized. Again the 2.36-inch rockets proved incapable of knocking out the North Korean tanks, and regimental commander Colonel Robert Martin died trying to stop a tank with one. Infiltrating KPA infantry produced both casualties and confusion among U.S. troops.

Dean decided on the Kum River as his next line of defense, with the 34th and 21st regiments to defend this line. By July 12, the 34th Regiment had blown the Kum River bridges and withdrawn behind the river. Here the first real defense in the war occurred. The dogged defense of the Kum River line by two battalions of the 21st delayed two of the best North Korean divisions for three days. In spite of this determined defense, the 16th KPA Regiment made a night crossing through gaps in the division position, surprising and overrunning the 63rd Field Artillery Battalion, and by July 16 the KPA was poised to attack Taejon from the west.

During the early days of the war, bad weather had limited the use of U.S. air power. Not only did heavy rain delay air strikes but early morning fog provided cover for attacking North Koreans. On July 9 and 10 the skies cleared, and the Fifth Air Force carried out heavy strikes on KPA columns. Massive U.S. air strikes proved highly effective in destroying KPA tanks, artillery, and trucks.

On July 13 Lieutenant General Walton H. Walker arrived in Korea to take over command of the defense and build up U.S. forces, now known as the Eighth Army. At the same time, two new divisions, the 25th and 1st Cavalry, arrived from Japan. Walker needed two additional days to deploy these divisions in defensive positions. To secure this time, Walker ordered Dean's 24th Division to make a stand at Taejon. It was important that Dean be there to keep up the morale of his troops as well as to set an example for leaders of the Republic of Korea Army (ROKA, South Korean Army).

On July 20 the North Koreans assaulted Taejon by crashing into the defenders and then flanking them in the rear. In the midst of this activity, Dean suddenly found himself fighting as part of an antitank team. New 3.5-inch bazookas had just been airlifted from the United States, and with this new weapon Dean was able to knock out several KPA tanks. In spite of this brief success, by late afternoon on July 20 the overall situation for the 24th Division in Taejon was hopeless. Despite mass confusion, most U.S. units were able to withdraw from the city, and more than 75 percent of the troops involved survived. Dean was cut off and later taken prisoner.

The last 10 days in July and the first week in August were crucial to U.S. efforts to delay the KPA long enough for the Eighth Army to establish a foothold. Both sides were racing against the clock as the North Koreans made an all-out effort to complete their conquest of South Korea before the U.S. forces could complete their buildup. At the same time the United States rushed in every available man in an effort to stem the North Korean tide.

On July 22 the 24th Division turned over its frontline positions at Yongdong to the newly arrived 1st Cavalry Division. To the right of this division at Sangju was the recently arrived 25th Division. Both divisions engaged in fierce struggles with KPA units west of the Naktong River. Over the next week the U.S. divisions slowly withdrew to the east side of the river. General Walker had decided that the Eighth Army would make a final defensive stand behind the Naktong. Despite taking heavy casualties, KPA units were able to infiltrate between the two U.S. divisions. With their defensive positions untenable, both U.S. divisions made preparations to withdraw. Walker, an aggressive combat leader in Europe under General George S. Patton during World War II, was furious with the situation, and on July 29 he issued his famous "stand or die" order.

Some have criticized Walker's order because KPA success was more a result of the paucity of numbers of defenders rather than of weaknesses in their fighting ability. In any case, Walker needed to build up the morale of the Eighth Army. Certainly one of Walker's greatest contributions in the Korean War was his tenacious and brilliant military defense in the early days of fighting.

While most of the Eighth Army concentrated on blocking KPA forces north and northeast of Taegu, the KPA 6th Division carried out a rapid and wide envelopment south to the Strait of Korea and then east to outflank the U.S. troops and drive toward the port of Pusan, the major access point for U.S. forces into Korea. KPA leaders understood the terrain well and knew that a dash along the coast from the west would avoid the obstacle posed by the Naktong River until just outside Pusan. By July 25 the KPA 6th Division was at Sunchon, poised to take Chinju, only 55 miles from Pusan.

When Walker realized the KPA 6th Division goal, he quickly moved the understrength, exhausted 24th Division to block the envelopment. By July 26 the 24th Division, minus its 21st Regiment, held a 30-mile defensive front from Kochang to Chinju.

The situation was critical. Newly arriving units were immediately sent to help cover this broad front. Among the units were the 1st and 3rd Infantry battalions of the 29th Regiment from Okinawa, Japan, with 400 brand-new recruits who had never trained with the regiment. Both battalions were immediately sent to the front to face two attacking KPA divisions. The 3rd Battalion, attached to the 35th Infantry Regiment of the 25th Infantry Division, ran head first into the North Korean 6th Division; most of the 3rd Battalion's officers were killed in the ensuing fighting and the unit as a whole suffered 50 percent casualties. At the same time, the 1st Battalion was attached to the 27th Infantry Regiment of the 25th Infantry Division. It encountered the KPA 4th Division

and suffered many casualties. In two days of fighting during July 26–27, the two battalions sustained a combined 618 casualties. In September 1950 these two battalions were absorbed into the regiments to which they were attached and ceased to function as units of the 29th Regiment.

The Eighth Army had at last reached a point where it could no longer continue to withdraw and still retain a foothold on the Korean Peninsula. Walker shifted other units south to meet the onslaught, such as the 27th Regiment ("Wolfhounds"). Bitter fighting in which U.S. units incurred heavy casualties finally slowed down the attacking KPA 4th and 6th divisions. As new units arrived, Walker rushed them into the line. These units included the 5th Marine Brigade from California and the 5th Regimental Combat Team from Hawaii. At this point Walker was willing to concede to the KPA all of Korea except the area east of the Naktong River, known as the Pusan Perimeter. The Eighth Army would spend the next 45 days in costly fighting to defend this area of some 5,000 square miles.

DANIEL R. BEIRNE

See also

Dean, William Frishe; MacArthur, Douglas; Task Force Smith; Truman, Harry S.; Walker, Walton Harris

References

Appleman, Roy E. *United States Army in Korea: South to the Naktong, North to the Yalu.* Washington, DC: Office of the Chief of Military History, 1961.

Blair, Clay. *The Forgotten War: America in Korea, 1950–1953.* New York: Times Books, 1987.

Fehrenbach, T. R. *This Kind of War: A Study in Unpreparedness.* New York: Macmillan, 1962.

Leckie, Robert. *Conflict: The History of the Korean War, 1950–1953.* New York: Putnam, 1962.

Toland, John. *In Mortal Combat: Korea, 1950–1953.* New York: William Morrow, 1991.

Northern Limitation Line

Disputed maritime demarcation line between the Democratic People's Republic of Korea (DPRK, North Korea) and the Republic of Korea (ROK, South Korea) in the Yellow Sea. The Northern Limitation Line (NLL) was set by U.S. General Mark W. Clark, head of United Nations Command (UNC) forces, on August 30, 1953. The NLL was created because UNC and communist forces had failed to reach an agreement on the maritime border during the armistice talks. The UNC claimed a 3-nautical-miles boundary while North Korea insisted on a 12-nautical mile boundary. The NLL was based on a 3-nautical-mile limit, recognized in the 1950s, extending from the Han River estuary and running between North Korea's mainland and five offshore islands, which now remain under the administrative control of South Korea. The NLL was not included in the Korean Armistice Agreement that ended the Korean War in July 1953.

The NLL is not a de jure border, because the UNC unilaterally drew it and presented it to North Korea as a fait accompli. But it has nevertheless served as a de facto maritime border between the two Koreas. In fact, although North Korea officially ignored the NLL, declaring 12-nautical mile territorial waters in March 1955 and then establishing a 50-nautical mile military zone, it tacitly recognized the line. The communist nation even acknowledged the boundary as a virtual maritime border at a meeting of the Military Armistice Commission in 1963.

In many cases, since the 1970s, when it began provoking South Korea by crossing the NLL, North Korea recognized the border as the sea boundary with its southern neighbor. In the 1992 Inter-Korean Basic Agreement, the two Koreas agreed that they would abide by the waters over which they had exercised jurisdiction so far, thereby recognizing the NLL as a de facto sea border, while also committing to future negotiations that might draw a new borderline. In short, the NLL has functioned as the essential maritime demarcation line (DML) and the zone along the line has served as the maritime demilitarized zone (DMZ) between the two Koreas.

When North Korea felt it necessary to heighten tensions with South Korea, however, its forces violated the NLL deliberately. After declaring its disapproval of the DMZ on land in April 1996, North Korea began to intrude past the NLL more frequently. In 1999, North Korea claimed a more southerly maritime DML, which would make the five islands under South Korean control a part of its territory as well. Disputes between North and South Korean vessels have often occurred in this area and the issue of the NLL has periodically arisen during inter-Korean talks. Deadly skirmishes took place there in 1999 and 2002.

North Korea caused a naval confrontation by crossing the NLL with its forces on June 13, 1999. The North Koreans did not want to start a war, but they purposefully caused a confrontation. They intended to make the NLL a disputed issue through continuous military confrontation in the zone south of the maritime line. The confrontation escalated into a mini naval war. Threatened by the persistent ramming operations of the Republic of Korea Navy (ROKN, South Korean Navy), the North Korean patrol boats fired first, but they were answered by a hail of fire from more modern and better-armed vessels, initiating a 14-minute battle. North Korea lost the skirmish and failed to carry out its original plan.

Amid improving relations between North and South Korea, another naval clash occurred in the zone south of the NLL. On June 29, 2002, one of the two North Korean patrol boats that had crossed the NLL opened fire on a South Korean patrol boat. Two South Korean warships returned fire. The battle continued for about 20 minutes until the North Korean ships returned to their territorial waters. One of the ROKN speedboats suffered a direct hit and was sunk. Six South Korean sailors were killed and 19 others were wounded. North Korea's provocation was clearly intentional. After the two naval engagements, North Korea has continued to infringe on the NLL.

As the progressive Roh Moo Hyun administration actively pursued its engagement policy with North Korea, the NLL became a hot issue in South Korea, and conservatives expressed concern over the possibility of scrapping the NLL. On October 13, 2007, Roh stated that the NLL was originally a boundary line for South Korea's naval operations rather than an official border. Roh's remark on the status of the NLL sparked a hot debate in South Korea. On August 10, 2007, the South Korean unification minister had maintained that the NLL was not a border or territorial concept but a security concept. The unification minister was severely criticized by conservatives for expressing his "readiness" to give up the NLL to North Korea and his willingness to redraw the maritime DML between North and South Korea.

When the South Korean Ministry of Defense sounded out the UNC on changing the NLL during the Roh administration, the UNC answered that the NLL would not be up for negotiation and that changing or redrawing it would not be a matter to be decided solely by the two Koreas. The NLL will likely remain a bone of contention between the two Koreas for some time to come.

JINWUNG KIM

See also

Armistice Agreement; Clark, Mark Wayne; Demilitarized Zone

References

Cumings, Bruce. *Korea's Place in the Sun: A Modern History*. New York: Norton, 1997.

Oberdorfer, Don. *The Two Koreas: A Contemporary History*. Rev. and updated ed. New York: Basic Books, 2001.

NSC-68

See National Security Council Report 68

Nuclear Warfare

The June 25, 1950, invasion by the Democratic People's Republic of Korea (DPRK, North Korea) of the Republic of Korea (ROK, South Korea) was viewed by many influential policy makers in the Harry S. Truman administration as the opening Soviet salvo in World War III. While the Soviets were not a direct military threat in the Korean theater of operations, they had endorsed the attack and made it possible by training and equipping the Korean People's Army (KPA, North Korean Army) that launched it. The view that the invasion was part of a general Soviet offensive was reinforced by the Soviets' detonating their own atomic bomb in 1949, which broke the U.S. monopoly on nuclear weapons; fielding of vast conventional military forces on the eastern border of the still-recovering Western European democracies; and signing of the Sino-Soviet Pact of February 1950, which provided for mutual assistance in case of attack.

The advent of nuclear weapons prompted the U.S. Navy to procure long-range aircraft capable of delivering these from aircraft carriers. The North American AJ-1 Savage, pictured here in 1951, was the first navy aircraft specifically built for this purpose. (National Museum of Naval Aviation)

U.S. nuclear warfare strategy in regard to the communist threat dealt with both strategic and operational-level concerns. With regard to strategic policy, the general concept of preventive war had formed in the late 1940s and continued into the early 1950s. It was based on lessons learned from World War II—namely, that the Allies should have moved more quickly against German and Japanese aggression because such action may have forestalled a war or ended it sooner and because this was the moral thing to have done. This perception was strengthened by the view that bombing an adversary with nuclear weapons, derived from the experience with Japan, could achieve a quick and decisive U.S. victory.

As early as the Berlin crisis of 1948, the possibility of such a preemptive nuclear strike had been considered. President Harry S. Truman had agreed to put into effect plan BROILER, which would have authorized U.S. forces to drop up to 100 atomic bombs on the Soviet Union if the Soviets attempted to obstruct the airlift of supplies into Berlin. With the start of the Korean War, high-ranking policy makers in the Truman administration considered the use of nuclear weapons against the Soviet Union. As a result of the North Korean invasion of South Korea, nonnuclear components of

atomic bombs were allowed to leave the continental United States in July 1950 and were stockpiled in the United Kingdom.

There was popular support in the United States for the use of atomic weapons against the Soviet Union. In August 1950, Secretary of the Navy Francis Matthews gave a speech advocating such a position to 100,000 cheering supporters at the Boston Naval Yard.

The November 1950 entrance of the People's Republic of China (PRC) into the war once again raised the specter of the use of nuclear weapons. Indeed, by then, a good number of U.S. citizens believed that World War III was at hand. While answering a reporter's question in a press conference late that month, President Truman did not rule out the nuclear option and even stated that it might be up to field commanders to make such a decision. This statement was clarified later that day by the White House, which made it clear that only the president, and not a general such as Douglas MacArthur, could authorize the use of nuclear weapons. During this period the Joint Chiefs of Staff (JCS) never recommended using atomic bombs in the conflict. Its rationale was that these weapons should be used only in case of forced evacuation from the peninsula or to stave off an impending military disaster. Still, after Chinese forces crossed the Yalu River in late 1950, the JCS requested that nonnuclear atomic bomb components be placed aboard the aircraft carrier *Franklin Roosevelt,* which was then stationed in the Mediterranean. Truman endorsed the request.

As the Korean War entered its static phase of opposing trench lines and as armistice talks dragged on, in January 1952, President Truman again considered the use of nuclear weapons. These thoughts were discussed with his aides and written down in his journal but were not made known to the public. His idea, which was never carried out, was to issue an ultimatum to the communist side either to end the war or risk nuclear annihilation.

Shortly after he took office in 1953, President Dwight D. Eisenhower had his senior policy makers examine the possibility of using nuclear weapons against China and North Korea. In May 1953, the JCS urged the National Security Council to consider their use to resolve the war if armistice negotiations broke down. Administration officials concurred with the JCS recommendation in NSC-147. Because of the 1950 Sino-Soviet Pact, the Soviet Union would be directly drawn into the war. This might lead to implementing war plan SHAKEDOWN, which called for Convair B-36 Peacemaker bombers to drop hundreds of atomic bombs on the Soviet Union. Fortunately for all involved, the signing of the armistice in July 1953 precluded further discussion of this option.

Nuclear operational planning focused on the Korean theater and was based on the needs of U.S. military commanders. It was little more than a sidebar compared to strategic-level issues. With the Chinese entry into the war, General MacArthur requested the right to use nuclear weapons if necessary, and, in late December 1950, he generated a list of targets for atomic destruction. In all, 34 atomic bombs would be required. After MacArthur was relieved of his command, his successor, Lieutenant General Matthew B. Ridgway, in May 1951, renewed the earlier request, this time for 38 atomic bombs. Nothing came of these requests, as President Truman retained control of the nuclear arsenal. MacArthur also supported the idea of "a radioactive by-product cordon," essentially rendering the Manchurian–North Korean border an uninhabitable waste land, as did others.

In the fall of 1951, the U.S. Air Force simulated the use of atomic bombs on the battlefield in Exercise HUDSON HARBOR. Individual Boeing B-29 Superfortress bombers flew from Okinawa to North Korea in simulated runs. However, with identifiable concentrations of communist forces being rare, the exercise was considered operationally unsound. Although U.S. nuclear weapons influenced the strategic conduct of the war and possibly forced the communists to make concessions leading to the eventual settlement of the war, they had no impact on theater operations.

ROBERT J. BUNKER

See also

Eisenhower, Dwight David; Joint Chiefs of Staff; MacArthur, Douglas; Ridgway, Matthew Bunker; Truman, Harry S.

References

Buhite, Russell D., and William Christopher Hamel. "War for Peace: The Question of an American Preventive War against the Soviet Union, 1945–1955." *Diplomatic History* 14 (Summer 1990): 367–384.

Herken, Gregg. *The Winning Weapon: The Atomic Bomb in the Cold War, 1945–1950.* Princeton, NJ: Princeton University Press, 1981.

Hewlett, Richard G., and Francis Duncan. *Atomic Shield, 1947/1952: A History of the United States Atomic Energy Commission,* Vol. 2. Berkeley: University of California Press, 1990.

James, D. Clayton. *The Years of MacArthur,* Vol. 3, *Triumph and Disaster, 1945–1964.* Boston: Houghton Mifflin, 1985.

Snyder, Jack. *Atomic Diplomacy in the Korean War.* Washington, DC: Pew Charitable Trusts, 1993.

Wheeler, Michael O. *Nuclear Weapons and the Korean War.* McLean, VA: Center for National Security Negotiations, 1994.

O'Donnell, Emmett

Birth Date: September 15, 1906
Death Date: December 26, 1971

U.S. Air Force general who commanded the Far East Air Force (FEAF) during July 1950 to January 1951. Born on September 15, 1906, in Brooklyn, New York, Emmett "Rosie" O'Donnell Jr. graduated from the U.S. Military Academy, West Point, in 1928 and was commissioned a second lieutenant in the infantry. He soon switched to the U.S. Army Air Corps and graduated from flying school in 1929. Promoted to captain in 1935, he was assigned to the 18th Reconnaissance Group at Mitchell Field, New York. He then graduated from the Air Corps Tactical School at Maxwell Field, Alabama. In 1940, he commanded a squadron of the 11th Bombardment Group in Hawaii. He was promoted to major in January 1941.

Assigned to the Philippines as part of the U.S. buildup there in the fall of 1941, O'Donnell commanded a squadron of Boeing B-17 Flying fortresses of the 14th Bombardment Group. After the Japanese air attack on Clark Field, he led a retaliatory U.S. raid against Japanese shipping. He was then assigned to Java. Later he was assistant chief of staff of the new Tenth Air Force in India, which ferried supplies to Allied forces over the "Hump." He was advanced to lieutenant colonel in January 1942 and to full colonel in March.

In 1943, O'Donnell returned to the United States to serve on the Army Air Forces Advisory Council. In 1944, he took command of the 73rd Bomb Wing in Kansas. Promoted to brigadier general in February 1944, he trained the 73rd in the new Boeing B-29 Superfortress for bombing operations against Japan and then relocated with it to Saipan in the Marianas. On November 24, 1944, O'Donnell led 111 B-29s against industrial targets in Tokyo, the first attack on the Japanese capital since the Doolittle Raid of April 1944.

After the end of the war, O'Donnell was assigned as head of the Engineering Division of the Air Technical Service Command (later the Air Matériel Command). He then served as deputy director of information for the air force during 1946–1947. Promoted to major general in February 1947, he was then deputy director of public relations. In 1948, he served on the Canada–United States Joint Board on Defense. That October, he took command of the Fifteenth Air Force at Colorado Springs, Colorado, within the Strategic Air Command.

On July 13, 1950, several weeks after the Korean War began, O'Donnell was ordered to move both the 22nd and the 92nd Bombardment Groups to Japan and organize them as the Far East Bombing Command. Within 36 hours of arrival, O'Donnell's aircraft were striking targets in the Democratic People's Republic of Korea (DPRK, North Korea).

O'Donnell was highly critical of employing his big bombers in a close air support role; he instead wanted them used against communist industrial and command centers. O'Donnell also proposed that his bombers strike communist staging areas and supply lines in Manchuria. He continued to believe that had bombing attacks been carried out early across the border into the People's Republic of China (PRC) before China had been able to build up its air defenses and a large number of Mikoyan-Gurevich MiGs, China could have been prevented from sending significant material aid and then large numbers of men to aid the Korean People's Army (KPA, North Korean Army).

O'Donnell left Korea in January 1951. At the MacArthur hearings that spring, he testified that U.S. bombers should have struck Manchuria in November 1950. With all strategic targets destroyed in North Korea, U.S. bombers were left to "blow up haystacks." Nonetheless, he opposed MacArthur's victory plan in Korea, believing it would severely undermine U.S. air capability against the Soviet Union.

In 1953, O'Donnell was assigned as deputy chief of air force personnel and advanced to lieutenant general. In August 1959, he was promoted to full (four-star) general and given command of the U.S. Pacific Air Forces. He retired on July 31, 1963. After employment as a business consultant, O'Donnell died in McLean, Virginia, on December 26, 1971.

CLINT MUNDINGER AND SPENCER C. TUCKER

See also
Close Air Support; MacArthur Hearings; United States Air Force

References
Appleman, Roy E. *United States Army in Korea: South to the Naktong, North to the Yalu.* Washington, DC: Office of the Chief of Military History, 1961.
Bruning, John R. *Crimson Sky: The Air Battle for Korea.* Dulles, VA: Brassey's, 1999.
Futrell, Robert F. *The United States Air Force in Korea, 1950–1953.* Rev. ed. Washington, DC: Office of the Chief of Air Force History, 1983.
Who Was Who in America, 1951–1960. Chicago: Marquis, 1963.
Wolk, Herman S. *The Struggle for Air Force Independence.* Washington, DC: Air Force History and Museums Program, 1997.

Office of Defense Mobilization

U.S. government agency created by executive order on December 16, 1950, in response to President Harry S. Truman's declaration of a national emergency. After the massive intervention by the People's Republic of China (PRC) in the Korean War, the Truman administration drastically accelerated the mobilization program. To implement this stepped-up process, Truman created the Office of Defense Mobilization (ODM) and appointed Charles E. Wilson, president of the General Electric Company, to direct its activities. The ODM replaced the older National Security Resources Board, which had been charged with directing mobilization at the beginning of the war.

In creating the ODM, Truman gave it unprecedented powers to mobilize the whole of America's civilian, industrial, and military resources. The major responsibilities of the ODM were to execute the mandates of the Defense Production Act, to ensure an adequate supply of war matériel to the soldiers in Korea, and to begin the long-term buildup of all of the nation's military forces, specifically those forces prescribed in NSC-68.

Falling under the aegis of the ODM were its various constituent agencies, the most important of which were the National Production Authority (NPA), the Defense Production Administration (DPA), and the Economic Stabilization Agency (ESA). Managerially organized by Charles Wilson, the ODM was designed to function as a policy-making and coordinating agency only. Thus, the NPA, DPA, ESA, and other already existing cabinet-level agencies carried out operational and other day-to-day mobilization activities. Organizationally, the ODM and its constituent parts

resembled the typical large, vertically integrated, multidivisional corporation of the day, nearly mirroring the management structure of the General Electric Company. In this sense, the ODM was patterned after the War Production Board of World War II.

The ODM made extensive use of industry advisory committees throughout its life span. These advisory committees, composed of nearly all sectors of the industrial economy, worked together with the ODM and other mobilization officials to establish and implement industrial and military production schedules. The use of such committees helped to keep operational functions out of the ODM and also served to ensure that key elements of the private sector worked together on matters of prices, wages, industrial output, and materials allocations.

In general the ODM functioned well. During the Korean War, the U.S. industrial base, military and civilian production, and weapons development grew at a rapid pace. As examples, by the end of the war, aircraft plants churned out nearly 1,000 piston-driven planes per month, four times the number produced in mid-1950, while five times as many jet aircraft were being produced than in mid-1950.

After Charles Wilson resigned as ODM director in April 1952, the agency was headed successively by John R. Steelman and Henry H. Fowler. The ODM continued in existence after the war was over. In 1958, however, President Dwight D. Eisenhower consolidated the ODM and the Federal Civil Defense Agency into one agency under the new banner of the Office of Civil Defense and Mobilization (OCDM). In 1978, that agency was consolidated with several others to form the Federal Emergency Management Agency (FEMA), which remains today as the lineal descendent of the ODM.

PAUL G. PIERPAOLI JR.

See also
Defense Production Act; Economic Stabilization Agency; Eisenhower, Dwight David; National Security Council Report 68; Truman, Harry S.; United States, Home Front; Wilson, Charles Edward

References
Hogan, Michael J. *A Cross of Iron: Harry S. Truman and the Origins of the National Security State, 1945–1954.* New York: Cambridge University Press, 1998.
Pierpaoli, Paul G., Jr. *Truman and Korea: The Political Culture of the Early Cold War.* Columbia: University of Missouri Press, 1999.
Vawter, Roderick W. *Industrial Mobilization: The Relevant History.* Washington, DC: National Defense University Press, 1983.

Office of Price Stabilization

U.S. government agency that, under the direction of the Economic Stabilization Agency (ESA), administered price controls during the Korean War. Created by executive order on September 9, 1950, the Office of Price Stabilization (OPS) did not become fully operational until January 1951, at which time the Truman administration had decided to freeze prices because of rising inflation. The OPS was responsible for administering the general price freeze of

January 1951, as well as setting subsequent price control policies that gradually superseded the general freeze.

The OPS administered price guidelines through 13 regional and 84 district offices maintained by the Department of Commerce throughout the United States. It also acted as an enforcement agency of its price regulations and worked with the Department of Justice to prosecute merchants and individuals suspected of breaking or circumventing pricing regulations. Also, the OPS used myriad industry advisory committees and consumer advisory committees to keep key groups in society working collaboratively on mobilization and price stabilization issues. In addition to these unpaid advisors, at its peak of operations, the OPS employed 12,300 workers, the most by far of any Korean-era mobilization agency.

OPS regulations provided set price ceilings for virtually all services and commodities sold in the United States, with the notable exception of food products selling below the Department of Agriculture's price parity program for farmers. The OPS considered requests for price increases above the ceilings or for exemptions from the regulations on a case-by-case basis.

By the spring of 1952, with inflation in retreat, the OPS began lifting or suspending controls on a large number of commodities. OPS guidelines were modestly successful in keeping inflation in check during the early months of the war. However, they did pose problems for some manufacturers, especially smaller producers who could not easily adjust output by emphasizing products that had an inherently higher profit margin. President Dwight D. Eisenhower completely liquidated the OPS in the spring of 1953.

PAUL G. PIERPAOLI JR.

See also

Defense Production Act; Economic Stabilization Agency; Mobilization; Price Gouging; United States, Home Front

References

Hogan, Michael J. *A Cross of Iron: Harry S. Truman and the Origins of the National Security State, 1945–1954.* New York: Cambridge University Press, 1998.

Pierpaoli, Paul G., Jr. *Truman and Korea: The Political Culture of the Early Cold War.* Columbia: University of Missouri Press, 1999.

Rockoff, Hugh. *Drastic Measures: A History of Wage and Price Controls in the United States.* New York: Cambridge University Press, 1984.

Old Baldy, Battle of
Start Date: June 26, 1952
End Date: March 26, 1953

This battle saw near continuous fighting from June 26, 1952, to March 26, 1953, on and near Hill 275, also known as Old Baldy because of the absence of trees at its summit. In mid-1952 the

United Nations Command (UNC) troops erecting barbed wire as part of their defensive position on Old Baldy. (National Archives)

A member of the U.S. 5th Marine Regiment scans communist lines with his binoculars, April 7, 1952. (National Archives)

front line of the U.S. 45th Division occupied a position south of the Yokkok-chon River valley. The need for forward defensive positions became apparent because the proximity of forces of the Chinese People's Volunteer Army (CPVA, Chinese Army) allowed them easy view of the division's troop movements.

In early June 1952, 45th Division commander Major General David Ruffen established a network of forward outposts to shield troop movements. The operation, which took place on June 6, was a success and encountered little resistance except at two hills, one of which was Hill 275 (Old Baldy). Sporadic fighting over Old Baldy escalated on June 26 as CPVA forces attempted to retake the outposts in a series of failed counterattacks that lasted until June 29. Another CPVA attempt to retake the hill on July 3–4 met with similar results.

This Chinese failure did not deter them from further attacks. The CPVA launched a new offensive that overran Old Baldy on the night of July 17–18. Retaking the hill proved difficult because of lashing rain that turned the terrain into a quagmire, but the U.S. 23rd Infantry Division accomplished the feat on August 1. Another Chinese

assault in September had brief success, but United Nations Command (UNC) forces regained control on September 21.

Fighting during the ensuing months was not as heavy, but by March 20, 1953, intelligence reports confirmed that a large-scale communist assault in the area of Old Baldy was imminent. At the time, the commander of the U.S. 31st Infantry Regiment and an accompanying Colombian battalion, Colonel William B. Kern, had charge of the area encompassing Old Baldy. Kern entrusted its defense to the Colombian battalion, commanded by Lieutenant Colonel Alberto Ruiz-Novoa.

On March 23, the Chinese launched a coordinated assault on Old Baldy and neighboring Pork Chop Hill. A massive artillery and mortar barrage on Old Baldy destroyed most of the UNC bunkers before a Chinese infantry regiment of about 3,500 men seized the hill. Repeated UNC counterattacks on March 24–25 were unsuccessful and produced heavy casualties. Kern finally decided to abandon the effort and withdrew his forces during the night of March 25–26. The remnants of Ruiz-Novoa's battalion also managed to escape. Eighth Army commander Lieutenant General

Maxwell D. Taylor canceled further plans to retake the hill because he did not consider it essential terrain.

The Battle of Old Baldy typified the seesaw hill battles in the static phase of the Korean War. Its loss led to renewed assaults on neighboring Pork Chop Hill. The Chinese occupation of Old Baldy outflanked UNC troops on Pork Chop Hill, which eventually led to its capture as well.

ERIC W. OSBORNE

See also

Pork Chop Hill, Battle of; Taylor, Maxwell Davenport

References

Hermes, Walter G. *U.S. Army in the Korean War: Truce Tent and Fighting Front.* Washington, DC: Office of the Chief of Military History, 1966.

Kaufman, Burton I. *The Korean War: Challenges in Crisis, Credibility and Command.* 2nd ed. New York: McGraw-Hill, 1997.

Rees, David. *Korea: The Limited War.* New York: St. Martin's, 1990.

Oliver, Robert Tarbell
Birth Date: 1909

U.S. academic, close friend of President Syngman Rhee of the Republic of Korea (ROK, South Korea), and prominent writer on Korean affairs. Born in Sweet Home, Oregon, in 1909, Robert Tarbell Oliver graduated from Pacific College in Oregon and received his Ph.D. from the University of Wisconsin in speech and communication. He was on the faculty at Bucknell University, at Syracuse University, and later at Pennsylvania State University.

In September 1942, Oliver was invited to meet Korean nationalist Syngman Rhee in Washington, DC, by Reverend Edward Junkin, pastor of the Presbyterian Church in Lewisburg, Pennsylvania, where Oliver was on leave during the war from the faculty of Bucknell University. Oliver became a close friend and associate of Rhee until the latter's death in 1965. Oliver served as an advisor to President Rhee and to the Korean Commission and the Korean delegation to the United Nations (UN). He first began to write and lecture on Korea in 1943 to promote Korean independence.

From 1947, Oliver managed the Washington Bureau of the Korean Pacific Press and was editor of the monthly magazine *Korean Survey.* He registered with the Department of Justice as an agent of South Korea.

Oliver wrote many newspaper articles on Korea and a number of Rhee's speeches. He also frequently exchanged letters with Rhee. When Seoul was captured by forces of the Democratic People's Republic of Korea (DPRK, North Korea) at the end of June 1950, Rhee's files were seized and were soon quoted by North Korea and the Soviet Union in the course of a propaganda campaign. Portions of these letters were made public in incomplete quotations taken out of context by the communist countries in an attempt to blame South Korea and Rhee for the outbreak of the Korean War. In reality, Oliver had objected to any belligerent actions by South

Korea. He wrote to Rhee on September 30, 1949, "On the question of attacking northward . . . it is very evident to us here that any such attack now, or even talk of such an attack, is to lose American official and public support and will weaken our position among other nations."

From 1944 through 1978, Oliver wrote a half dozen books on Korea. He also wrote several books on public speaking and communications and served as the president of the American Speech Association. Oliver retired to Chestertown, Maryland.

YOUNGHO KIM

See also

Rhee, Syngman

References

Oliver, Robert T. *The Case for Korea: A Paradox of United States Diplomacy.* Washington, DC: Korean American Council, 1945.

———. *Korea: Forgotten Nation.* Washington, DC: Public Affairs Press, 1944.

———. *Syngman Rhee: The Man behind the Myth.* New York: Dodd, Mead, 1955.

———. *Syngman Rhee and American Involvement in Korea, 1942–1960: A Personal Narrative.* Seoul: Panmun Books, 1978.

———. *Why War Came in Korea.* New York: Fordham University Press, 1950.

Oppenheimer, Robert
Birth Date: April 22, 1904
Death Date: February 18, 1967

U.S. physicist and nuclear scientist. Born in New York City on April 22, 1904, Julius Robert Oppenheimer attended the Ethical Culture School of New York and Harvard University, graduating from the latter after three years in 1925 with honors and a degree in chemistry. Turning to physics, he spent a year pursuing graduate work at the Cavendish Laboratory and then switched to the University of Göttingen, Germany, and the new field of theoretical quantum physics, receiving his doctorate in March 1927. He pursued postdoctoral studies for two years in the United States, Holland, and Switzerland before accepting a joint appointment at the California Institute of Technology (Caltech) and the University of California, Berkeley. An inspiring teacher, he quickly attracted a generation of enthusiastic graduate students to Caltech and Berkeley, which became leading international centers of quantum physics. Although Oppenheimer published extensively on spectra, particles, neutron stars, and black holes, his personal scientific contribution was less outstanding, and he was never a serious contender for a Nobel Prize.

In October 1941, Oppenheimer began fast-neutron research for the U.S. government in connection with atomic bomb development. One year later, he became director of the central laboratory for bomb design and development at Los Alamos, New Mexico, supervising the Manhattan Project. In this enormously

Known for his involvement in the development of the atomic bomb, J. Robert Oppenheimer was also a major influence on the quantum physics of his day. Allegations regarding his patriotism and Oppenheimer's opposition to the development of a hydrogen bomb led the U.S. government to withdraw his security clearance, although he remained a professor at Princeton University. (Library of Congress)

demanding position, his skillful leadership, capacity to absorb and process information, concern for the team of 1,500 people working under him, and ability to negotiate the often difficult relationship between individualistic scientists and governmental demands for conformity became legendary. After the 1945 atomic explosions over Hiroshima and Nagasaki, the exhausted Oppenheimer, who told President Harry S. Truman that "I feel we have blood on our hands," hoped that the bomb's destructiveness might eventually force nations to abandon war.

Leaving Los Alamos in late 1945, Oppenheimer became director of the Institute for Advanced Study at Princeton two years later and quickly transformed it into the world's leading center for theoretical physics while simultaneously enhancing its existing reputation in humanist studies. As the most prestigious American advisor to the 1945–1946 Acheson-Lilienthal Committee on Nuclear Power and the U.S. Atomic Energy Commission (AEC), he advocated international control of atomic energy and lectured extensively, seeking to enhance popular scientific understanding. Initially, Oppenheimer opposed the development of the hydrogen (thermonuclear) bomb, which led many to question his motives.

In 1953, growing McCarthyism, anticommunist sentiment, and resentment by some colleagues—notably Edward Teller—of Oppenheimer's earlier reluctance to develop a hydrogen bomb led the American government to withdraw his security clearance. This was done on the grounds that his wartime evasiveness over potential security problems and prewar left-wing and communist associates, including his brother, a former fiancée, and his wife, had permanently compromised his status. A full-scale inquiry held in 1954 at Oppenheimer's insistence confirmed this verdict. Later evidence revealed that the Federal Bureau of Investigation (FBI) had blatantly infringed Oppenheimer's civil rights by tapping his telephone and providing transcripts of his legal consultations to the inquiry's members.

In 1994, retired Soviet spy General Pavel A. Sudoplatov claimed in his memoirs that Oppenheimer had passed atomic secrets to Soviet agents, but major errors in his account led most in the scientific community to doubt this. Although excluded from governmental counsels, Oppenheimer retained his academic position at Princeton until June 1966, where he published several books on science for the educated general reader. He died in Princeton, New Jersey, on February 18, 1967.

PRISCILLA ROBERTS

See also

Atomic Bomb; Atomic Energy Commission, U.S.; Hydrogen Bomb; McCarthyism

References

Goodchild, Peter. *J. Robert Oppenheimer: Shatterer of Worlds.* Boston: Houghton Mifflin, 1981.

Herken, Gregg. *Brotherhood of the Bomb: The Tangled Lives and Loyalties of Robert Oppenheimer, Ernest Lawrence, and Edward Teller.* New York: Henry Holt, 2002.

Kunetka, James W. *Oppenheimer: The Years of Risk.* Englewood Cliffs, NJ: Prentice Hall, 1982.

Rhodes, Richard. *Dark Sun: The Making of the Hydrogen Bomb.* New York: Simon and Schuster, 1995.

———. *The Making of the Atomic Bomb.* New York: Simon and Schuster, 1995.

Schweber, S. S. *In the Shadow of the Bomb: Bethe, Oppenheimer, and the Moral Responsibility of a Scientist.* Princeton, NJ: Princeton University Press, 2000.

York, Herbert F. *The Advisors: Oppenheimer, Teller, and the Superbomb.* New York: Freeman, 1975.

Organized Labor

The American Federation of Labor (AFL) and the Congress of Industrial Organizations (CIO) were for many years the principal labor coalitions in the United States, including during the period of the Korean War. For many years they remained two separate entities despite strong interest in a merger, which was finally achieved in 1955. Both organizations had within their ranks dozens of smaller labor union groups, representing a multitude of chiefly industrial workers. As such, both the AFL and CIO were major players in the Korean War–era industrial mobilization program.

Philip Murray headed the CIO until 1952; he was succeeded by Walter Reuther, who led the organization until its 1955 merger with the AFL. William Green presided over the AFL until 1952, at which time George Meany became president. Meany then led the newly formed AFL-CIO from 1955 to 1979. These men were intimately involved in industrial mobilization during the war and were particularly active in the wage and price control setup created in January 1951.

Because the Korean War was a limited conflict, and not a total war like World War II, there was much initial uncertainty concerning the degree to which the federal government could directly control the activities of labor and management in the private sector. During World War II, for example, U.S. president Franklin D. Roosevelt's administration had been able to exact a no-strike pledge on the part of organized labor. Yet no such pledge was forthcoming during the Korean War. Generally, President Harry S. Truman was sympathetic to labor's cause, but this did not stop him from asserting his authority when it became necessary. In the first trying months of the conflict, labor leaders conferred with Truman administration officials and pledged full cooperation in regard to the Korean War and major emergencies that might confront the nation.

On September 9, 1950, the day after he signed the Defense Production Act into law, the president announced a plan for economic and industrial mobilization for the war, which would be part of a broader, bigger buildup to wage the ongoing Cold War. That same day, Truman named W. Stuart Symington, chairman of the National Security Resources Board (NSRB), to head the mobilization and economic stabilization program. At this stage, however, neither price controls nor wage controls were in the immediate offing.

American labor leaders, including the CIO's Philip Murray and the AFL's William Green, met with Symington in Washington, DC, on July 11, 1950. Although they reiterated their earlier pledge to cooperate with the government, they stopped short of a no-strike pledge. Union leaders also insisted that organized labor be fully represented in the planning and implementation of national economic stabilization and manpower policies. To accomplish this, a labor committee was appointed to confer with Symington and others at the federal level on mobilization for the war. The committee, called the Wage Stabilization Board (WSB), included three labor leaders (including one each from the AFL and CIO), three leaders from industry, and three at-large "public" members.

Even before creation of the WSB, organized labor's actions threatened the war effort. On August 25, 1950, faced with an imminent national railroad strike, Truman ordered the U.S. Army to seize and operate the lines if rail workers went on strike. A confrontation was averted when the Brotherhood of Railroad Trainmen and the Order of Railway Conductors, the two unions directly involved, ordered their members to cooperate with the

government. The strike was postponed indefinitely, but army management of the nation's railroads began on August 27 under Major General Frank A. Heileman, the U.S. Army's chief of transportation. The railroads' corporate executives remained in place, however. This was Truman's third seizure of the railroads since 1945, and the fifth such seizure by a U.S. president since 1918. In May 1952 the army returned operation of the railroads to civilian management and unions, following the settlement of a labor dispute that had endured for three years.

Also in August 1950, President John L. Lewis of the United Mine Workers Union informed AFL president William Green that miners would not be bound by any general no-strike pledge. Later, the CIO's United Steel Workers canceled a scheduled strike and referred the matter to a special meeting in Atlantic City. This was in reaction to pressure from the White House, which had referred the matter to the WSB. President Truman publicly urged the workers and management to keep working and producing. These events clearly reflected the priority given by Green and other AFL leaders to aid the Korean War effort by avoiding strike actions.

Labor was not always pliable to the government's wishes, however. Indeed, in February 1951 all three labor union leaders resigned their positions with the WSB over the board's refusal to grant a 12-percent wage increase that would replace the general wage freeze of January 25. The United Labor Policy Committee (UPLC), representing 15 million workers, publicly excoriated the Truman administration's economic stabilization policies. Also at issue was labor's general annoyance with mobilization chief Charles E. Wilson, whom the UPLC accused of ignoring the needs and involvement of labor. Labor thus boycotted the mobilization program until April 17, 1951, when a compromise was reached that brought labor leaders back to the table. Among other changes, the WSB was increased to 18 members, with equal representation among labor, industry, and the public. Thereafter, labor continued to be involved in mobilization and stabilization policies, but strikes were not infrequent, especially during 1952–1953. By late 1952, the AFL, CIO, and other labor groups had begun to question the efficacy of wage and price controls and to publicly question the need for their continuation.

In 1952 the Truman administration confronted one of the most serious conflicts in U.S. labor-management relations history. In November 1951 the United Steel Workers, representing some 600,000 members, announced plans to secure improvements in working conditions and a significant wage increase when their contracts expired early the following year. The steel companies refused to grant a wage increase without the ability to raise the price of steel, which the government tightly controlled.

Truman refused to invoke the 1947 Taft-Hartley Act, including an 80-day injunction against a strike, or "cooling-off period," legislation that he had deplored and unsuccessfully vetoed. Instead, he turned to the WSB to mediate a compromise. In the end, the WSB's best solution alienated both parties, and steel-plant owners refused to grant the WSB's recommended pay increase without a concomitant hike in the price of steel. After the steel workers voted to strike beginning April 9, 1952, a move that was supported by both the AFL and CIO, Truman moved to seize the nation's steel mills on April 8 to avert a strike and a potentially devastating blow to the rearmament program. The move was immediately challenged in the courts, and on June 2 the U.S. Supreme Court decided against Truman's action, deeming it unconstitutional. Meanwhile, a White House effort to secure enabling legislation from Congress also failed.

Later that day, all 600,000 steel workers went on strike. Not until July 24, when Truman granted the wanted wage increases and steel-price hikes, would the strike end. As 1952 progressed, wage and price controls were diluted, and many Americans chafed under such government meddling. Strikes were on the increase, and a donnybrook between the United Mine Workers and their employers precipitated another crisis in the late fall of 1952. In December Truman overruled his own WSB by granting the miners the full wage increase they sought. This compelled the chairman of the WSB, Archibald Cox, to resign on December 4, 1952. Two days later all of the industry representatives resigned, and the WSB essentially ceased to function.

ARTHUR I. CYR AND PAUL G. PIERPAOLI JR.

See also

Defense Production Act; Economic Stabilization Agency; National Security Resources Board; Steel Plants, Truman's Seizure of; Wage Stabilization Board; Wilson, Charles Edward

References

Goldberg, Arthur J. *AFL-CIO: Labor United*. New York: McGraw Hill, 1955.
McCullough, David. *Truman*. New York: Simon and Schuster, 1992.
Pierpaoli, Paul G., Jr. *Truman and Korea: The Political Culture of the Early Cold War*. Columbia: University of Missouri Press, 1999.
Truman, Harry S. *Memoirs*. 2 vols. Garden City, NY: Doubleday, 1956.

Osan, Battle of
Event Date: July 5, 1950

First battle of the Korean War involving U.S. troops, specifically Task Force Smith. Named for its commander, Lieutenant Colonel Charles B. "Brad" Smith, Task Force Smith comprised 406 officers and enlisted men from the 1st Battalion of the 21st Infantry Regiment and 134 officers and men from the 52nd Field Artillery Battery (Battery A plus small contingents from the Headquarters and Service Batteries). It was the first U.S. Army combat unit to enter Korea after the invasion of the Republic of Korea (ROK, South Korea) by the Democratic People's Republic of Korea (DPRK, North Korea).

Task Force Smith arrived in South Korea by air near Pusan and moved north to Taejon by train, arriving there on the morning of July 2, 1950. The men of the task force were confident, believing that as soon as the North Koreans saw their American uniforms they would run away. Smith ordered his men to rest while he and his staff officers drove north to reconnoiter. Some three miles north of Osan, Smith found an ideal blocking position, a line of low rolling hills about 300 feet above the level ground. This position commanded the main railroad line to the east and afforded a clear view to Suwon, about eight miles north.

On July 4, the task force was joined at Pyongtaek by part of the 52nd Field Artillery Battalion: some of the Headquarters and Service Batteries and all of A Battery with 5 105-mm howitzers (1 howitzer was left behind at Pyongtaek), 73 vehicles, and 134 men under the command of Lieutenant Colonel Miller O. Perry. In the late afternoon of July 4, Smith, Perry, and others made a reconnaissance of the position Smith had selected. The combined infantry and artillery then moved out of Pyongtaek by truck, arriving at the position around 3:00 a.m. The U.S. line was about one mile in length and was bisected by the Suwon-Osan road.

In cold, rainy weather, the men dug foxholes and laid telephone lines to 4 of the howitzers, placed in a concealed position some 2,000 yards to the south. One 105-mm howitzer was positioned halfway between the battery and the infantry to enfilade the road and serve as an antitank gun. Artillery volunteers formed 4 .50-caliber machine gun and 4 2.36-inch bazooka teams and joined the infantry position to the north. The infantry vehicles were located just to the south of their position, and the artillerymen concealed their trucks just north of Osan. The U.S. forces were vulnerable to flanking attacks, lacked the means to stop tanks, and had no reserves.

At dawn on July 5, Smith ordered his artillery, mortars, and machine guns to conduct registration fire. Steady rain precluded air support. Shortly after 7:00 a.m., the U.S. forces detected movement to the north. Within half an hour, a column of eight T-34 tanks of the Korean People's Army (KPA, North Korean Army), part of the 107th Tank Regiment of the 105th Armored Division, approached across the open plain from Suwon.

At 8:00 a.m., the U.S. artillery received a request for a fire mission, and at 8:16 it opened fire against the tanks about 2,000 yards in front of the infantry position. The high-explosive (HE) rounds had no effect on the tanks, which had their hatches closed, but they did kill a number of KPA infantrymen riding on them. The battery had only six armor-piercing high-explosive antitank (HEAT) rounds available (one-third of the total on hand when the 52nd was loading at Sasebo, Japan), all of which were given to the single howitzer forward. Antitank mines would have stopped the enemy advance but there were none in Korea. Smith ordered 75-mm recoilless rifle fire withheld until the column of tanks reached 700 yards range. The recoilless rifle crews then scored direct hits, again without apparent effect. The tanks stopped and opened fire with their 85-mm main guns and 7.62-mm machine guns.

Second Lieutenant Ollie Connor engaged the tanks as they entered the infantry position, firing 22 2.36-inch bazooka rounds at the enemy armor as it passed through and out of the position. All rounds were fired from close range, and a number were fired at the more vulnerable rear ends of the T-34s. The 2.36-inch rounds

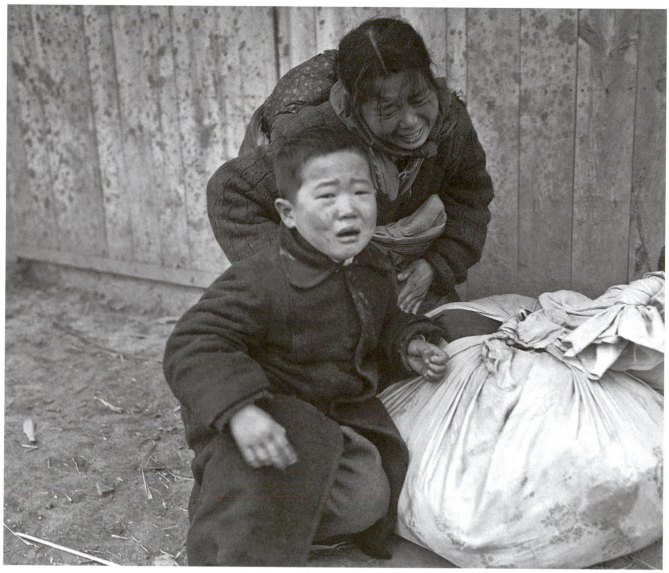

A Korean mother, bent over in pain, sobs as she halts with her child, unable to continue her flight from the fighting around Osan, south of Seoul, January 14, 1951. (AP/Wide World Photos)

could not penetrate the T-34 armor, but Connor is credited with disabling two of the tanks. The 3.5-inch bazooka round would have been effective, but there were none in country.

As they approached the lone 105-mm gun forward, the two lead tanks were hit and damaged, probably by HEAT rounds. One caught fire and two of its crew members came out of the turret with their hands up; a third came out with a burp gun and fired it against a U.S. machine gun position beside the road, killing an assistant gunner, possibly the first U.S. ground soldier fatality of the Korean War. The third tank through the pass, however, knocked out the forward 105-mm howitzer with cannon fire. The other tanks then swept on south past the U.S. artillery battery, which fired HE rounds against them. One tank was disabled and ultimately abandoned.

Additional KPA tanks soon swept past the U.S. position, causing some of the battery crewmen to run from their guns.

Officers and noncommissioned officers continued to service the guns, and the men returned. One other tank was disabled by a hit in the track. By 10:15 a.m., the last of 33 North Korean tanks had driven through the U.S. position, killing or wounding some 20 Americans by machine gun and artillery fire. Most of the vehicles parked immediately behind the infantry position were destroyed. The tanks also severed the wire communications link with Battery A.

Fortunately for the U.S. forces, there was no accompanying infantry; the tankers were unable to locate the artillery battery firing on them, and the T-34s rumbled on toward Osan. A lull of about an hour followed. The steady rain continued and the defenders used the time to improve their position. At about 11:00 a.m., three more tanks were sighted advancing from the north. Behind them was a column of trucks, followed by long columns of infantry on foot, the 16th and 18th regiments of the North Korean

4th Division. The column was apparently not in communication with the tanks that had preceded it.

It took about an hour for the head of the column to reach a point about 1,000 yards from the U.S. position, when Smith ordered fire opened. U.S. mortars and machine guns swept the KPA column but did not stop the three tanks. They advanced to within 300 yards and raked the ridge with shell and machine gun fire. Smith had no communication with the artillery battery, which he believed had been destroyed.

Smith held his position as long as he dared, but casualties among his men rapidly mounted. The Americans were down to fewer than 20 rounds of ammunition apiece and the North Koreans threatened to cut off their position. With KPA tanks to the rear of the American position, Smith consolidated his force in a circular perimeter on the highest ground east of the road. The North Koreans were by now employing mortar and artillery fire. Around 4:30 p.m., Smith ordered a withdrawal, remarking, "This is a decision I'll probably regret the rest of my days." He planned an orderly leapfrogging withdrawal, with one platoon covering another, but under heavy KPA fire many weapons and much equipment were simply abandoned. Many men had not received word of the withdrawal, including three of the eight platoon leaders present. It was at this point that the Americans suffered most of their casualties.

The infantry withdrawal was disorganized from the start. The men came out for the most part in small groups. Some went south toward Osan, but west of the road; others headed west for a short distance, then south to the road leading east from Osan. Most of the infantry passed through or near the battery position.

Shortly after ordering the infantry to withdraw, Smith set out to find Perry. He discovered the artillery still in position east of the road. Smith was surprised to find the battery position intact with only Perry and one other man wounded. The artillerymen disabled their howitzers by removing sights and breechblocks. The men then withdrew into Osan, when they discovered KPA tanks near the southern edge of the town. They then turned back and drove east out of Osan. Fortunately for them, there was no KPA pursuit.

At Chonan, only 185 men of the task force could be accounted for. Subsequently, C Company commander Captain Richard Dashner came in with 65 more, bringing the total near 250. More men trickled back to U.S. positions during the following week. One survivor even made it from the west coast by sampan (boat) to Pusan. In the battle, approximately 150 U.S. infantrymen were killed, wounded, or missing. All 5 officers and 10 enlisted men of the forward observer liaison, machine gun, and bazooka group were lost. KPA casualties in the battle before Osan were approximately 42 dead and 85 wounded. The KPA also had four tanks destroyed and two or three damaged but repairable. In the Battle of Osan, Task Force Smith had held up the KPA advance for perhaps seven hours.

The North Koreans continued their offensive south against more and more units of the 24th Division. On July 6, they forced a U.S. withdrawal from the next blocking position at Pyongtaek,

held by the 34th Regiment. The 21st Regiment imposed another slight delay on the KPA in front of Chochiwon, but both regiments suffered heavily in these actions. These and other battles taking place until July 21 did purchase time for the 1st Cavalry and 25th Infantry divisions to arrive from Japan.

SPENCER C. TUCKER

See also

Dean, William Frishe; MacArthur, Douglas; Task Force Smith; Truman, Harry S.; Walker, Walton Harris

References

Appleman, Roy E. *United States Army in Korea: South to the Naktong, North to the Yalu.* Washington, DC: Office of the Chief of Military History, 1961.

Collins, J. Lawton. *War in Peacetime: The History and Lessons of Korea.* Boston: Houghton Mifflin, 1969.

Gugeler, Russell A. *Combat Actions in Korea.* Rev. ed. Washington, DC: U.S. Army, Center of Military History, 1987.

Rees, David. *Korea: The Limited War.* New York: St. Martin's, 1990.

Outpost Harry, Battle for
Start Date: June 10, 1953
End Date: June 18, 1953

One of the bloodiest of the so-called hill battles that marked the final days of the Korean War. This series of clashes along the stalemated front line erupted as forces of the Chinese People's Volunteer Army (CPVA, Chinese Army) and of the Korean People's Army (KPA, North Korean Army) sought to strengthen their bargaining position at the Panmunjom Truce Talks.

The site of the fighting was a hill with a 1,270-foot elevation located about 60 miles north of Seoul in an area known as the Iron Triangle. It sat some 425 yards in front of the United Nations Command (UNC) main line of resistance (MLR) and only 320 yards from the CPVA lines. The name for the hill came from Greek forces calling it Outpost Haros, Greek for "death." The hill's exposed position made it a tempting target for the Chinese. In addition, Outpost Harry was strategically important because it blocked Chinese observation of UNC forces in the area and shielded the MLR from direct Chinese artillery fire. The loss of Outpost Harry would render that sector of the MLR indefensible and force the U.S. Eighth Army to withdraw some six miles to the next viable and defensible position.

In June 1953, the UNC understood Outpost Harry's importance and fully anticipated a major communist offensive against the position. Chinese shelling and probing actions in the area had intensified over the previous weeks. Furthermore, during the first week of June, UNC aerial reconnaissance revealed substantial CPVA troop reinforcements opposite Outpost Harry as well as increasing trench construction forward of the Chinese lines.

Outpost Harry was held by a company of the U.S. 15th Regiment, 3rd Infantry Division—a unit with considerable combat

The bodies of Chinese soldiers killed during a communist attack on Outpost Harry, held by the U.S. 3rd Infantry Division, on June 12, 1953. (AP/Wide World Photos)

experience in Korea. The Americans shared responsibility for the outpost with the Greek Brigade. The Americans and their Greek allies had been actively deepening their own trench line and reinforcing the outpost's bunkers. U.S. engineers brought in 55-gallon drums of napalm to strengthen the perimeter's defenses, which they wired for firing. The UNC issued orders that Outpost Harry was to be held at all costs.

The Chinese attack opened at 6:00 p.m. on June 10 with an intense artillery barrage, followed by an attack of 3,600 CPVA troops. They faced two platoons of American soldiers from K Company, 15th Regiment, a ratio of 30 to 1. Charging through their own artillery fire that they hoped would keep the Americans pinned down, the Chinese seemed certain to overrun the hill. The defenders, however, called in massive artillery in front of their defenses, killing large numbers of Chinese. Although the CPVA infantry penetrated the American trench line, they were unable to overrun the American bunkers. A counterattack led by Sergeant Ola L. Mize drove the Chinese back. By the time American reinforcements arrived at 8:00 a.m. the next morning, only 12 Americans from the original 2 platoons had not been killed or wounded but U.S. forces still held the hill.

The pattern established during that first night persisted over the next eight days. Most of the fighting occurred at night. The Chinese would withdraw at dawn, not wanting to expose themselves to U.S. firepower in daylight. American and UNC forces would spend the day evacuating the dead and wounded, repairing damaged defenses, and moving up fresh units to relieve the survivors of the previous night's fighting. These relief and reinforcing operations were carried out in the face of intense Chinese shelling and also sniper fire from nearby hilltops.

During the night of June 11–12, the CPVA again attacked, repeating the same tactics—a massive artillery barrage with infantry moving through their own barrage to try to overrun the defenders pinned in their bunkers. The Americans again held, thanks to heavy artillery and armored support.

The most ambitious Chinese assault occurred on the night of June 12–13. After an initial attack failed, the Chinese regrouped and mounted a three-pronged effort from the north, northeast, and northwest. A reinforced company from the 15th Regiment held on, with help from a diversionary attack by a U.S. tank battalion on the east flank. Two more attacks—one on June 14–15 against four companies from the 15th Regiment, and one on June 18 against a combined U.S./Greek force—both failed. After June 18, the CPVA made no further attempts to take Outpost Harry.

Over the course of the eight-day battle, the Chinese suffered an estimated 4,200 casualties. Reportedly the communists fired 88,000 artillery rounds at Outpost Harry. In its successful effort to hold the hill, the UNC rotated seven companies from the U.S. 5th and 15th Infantry Regiments to and from the hill along with armored units and a company from the Greek Brigade. U.S. casualties totaled 183 killed and 606 wounded.

The siege and battle for Outpost Harry was typical of the fighting that occurred during the period of stalemate in Korea, which lasted from mid-1951 until the July 27, 1953, armistice. Both sides used these engagements for tactical and/or political advantage. As with these other battles, the outcome of the struggle for Outpost Harry proved that both sides were too well entrenched for significant military gains to be possible.

WALTER F. BELL

See also

Chinese Offensives, Summer; Iron Triangle; Truce Talks

References

Dyhouse, Tim. "The Siege of Outpost Harry." *VFW Magazine* 90(9) (May 2003): 34–35.

Hermes, Walter G. *U.S. Army in the Korean War: Truce Tent and Fighting Front.* Washington, DC: Office of the Chief of Military History, 1966.

Peters, Richard, and Xiaobing Li. *Voices from the Korean War: Personal Stories of American, Korean, and Chinese Soldiers.* Lexington: University Press of Kentucky, 2004.

P

Pace, Frank, Jr.
Birth Date: July 5, 1912
Death Date: January 8, 1988

Attorney, director of the U.S. Bureau of the Budget (1949–1950), and U.S. secretary of the army (1950–1953). Born on July 5, 1912, in Little Rock Arkansas, Frank Pace Jr. was educated at Princeton and Harvard universities and became a lawyer specializing in tax law. Service during World War II as a stateside administrator in the Air Transport Command whetted his appetite for public service. After working in the Justice and Post Office departments in Washington, he became assistant director, then director, of the Bureau of the Budget (BOB) in 1949. His efficient service as BOB director helped him secure the position of secretary of the army in April 1950.

As army secretary, Pace was responsible for the training, operations, preparedness, and effectiveness of the U.S. Army. When the Korean War erupted on June 25, 1950, Pace and other presidential advisers recommended to President Harry S. Truman that the U.S. government do all in its power short of war to assist the Republic of Korea (ROK, South Korea). When U.S. Far Eastern Command commander General Douglas MacArthur asked to use U.S. troops in combat on June 30, 1950, because of South Korea's near military collapse, Pace concurred and obtained presidential approval. This action marked U.S. entry into the ground war. When MacArthur's forces were approaching the Yalu River in November 1950, Pace contributed to the directive that they should stop at the heights south of the Yalu. On November 28, 1950, Pace advised President Truman that, because of massive Chinese intervention in the war, the United States should fully implement NSC-68 as soon as possible, which would put the United States on a constant war footing during the Cold War.

When President Truman decided to relieve MacArthur in April 1951, he wanted Pace, who was in Asia at the time, to deliver the message; but Pace was in Korea and out of contact with Washington. With the press about to break the story, the Truman administration released the news first, and MacArthur learned of his dismissal from his wife. She had been informed by one of MacArthur's aides, who heard it over the radio. Pace did inform Lieutenant General Matthew B. Ridgway that he was MacArthur's replacement.

Under Pace's tenure and during the Korean War, the army increased in size from 600,000 to 1.5 million men. New training camps were opened, and National Guard divisions and reservists were called to active duty. Nearly 3 million soldiers served during the war. To share risk among combat troops, Pace instituted a point system whereby troops with sufficient points could rotate out of the combat zone. Racial enlistment quotas and segregated units were abolished, and African American replacements filled vacancies in white combat units. By the end of Pace's tour in January 1953, the army was almost fully integrated.

The army was also reorganized: chiefs of infantry, cavalry, and artillery were abolished, and the new branches of armor, transportation, and military police were established. Pace supported the development of army tactical nuclear weapons, especially the 280-mm atomic cannon.

One of Pace's actions had a long-reaching impact on the army. The Key West Agreement of 1948 had restricted the army to small airplanes and helicopters in roles that would not duplicate air force missions of close air support, transport, or reconnaissance. To meet battlefield needs in Korea in 1951 and 1952, Pace secured two agreements from Secretary of the Air Force Thomas K. Finletter that expanded the functions of army aviation and the size of

Frank Pace Jr. served as U.S. secretary of the army during the Korean War. (Hulton Archive/Getty Images)

the battle zone in which aircraft could operate. These agreements enabled the army to rapidly expand its aviation in the 1950s.

After he left office, Pace served as executive vice president, president, and chairman of the General Dynamics Corporation from 1953 to 1963. He also sat on numerous presidential commissions, task forces, and panels under both Republican and Democratic presidents. From 1968 to 1972, Pace was the first chairman of the Corporation for Public Broadcasting. Pace also served on the boards of numerous philanthropic and civic organizations and founded two not-for-profit service associations: the International Executive Service Corps and the National Executive Service Corps. Pace died in Greenwich, Connecticut, on January 8, 1988.

JOHN L. BELL

See also
Finletter, Thomas Knight; National Security Council Report 68; Ridgway, Matthew Bunker; Truman, Harry S.; Truman's Recall of MacArthur; United States Air Force; United States Army

References
Bradley, Omar N., and Clay Blair. *A General's Life: An Autobiography.* New York: Simon and Schuster, 1983.
Collins, J. Lawton. *Lightning Joe: An Autobiography.* Baton Rouge: Louisiana State University Press, 1979.

"Frank Pace, Jr., Former Secretary of the Army and Executive, Dies." *New York Times,* January 10, 1988.
Roosevelt, Kermit. "The Army's Bright Young Boss." *Saturday Evening Post,* October 28, 1950.
Weigley, Russell F. *History of the United States Army.* Bloomington: Indiana University Press, 1984.

Pacific Pact

Abortive attempt in 1950 to establish an anticommunist Asian mutual security organization. The Pacific pact scheme, spearheaded by the Philippines, Taiwan (then known as Formosa), and the Republic of Korea (ROK, South Korea), prefigured the Southeast Asia Treaty Organization (SEATO) and the bilateral Asian-U.S. security pacts concluded later in the 1950s.

The communist victory in China in October 1949 altered the course of U.S. foreign policy in Asia. Guomindang (GMD, Nationalist) forces led by Jiang Jieshi (Chiang Kai-shek) were driven off the mainland and onto Taiwan. U.S. policy makers believed that the "loss" of China to communism rendered defense of South Korea impractical. Previously, the United States had referred to South Korea as a testing ground of U.S. resolve and a battleground between democracy and communism. President Harry S. Truman had gone so far as to suggest that aid to South Korea should be considered equivalent to that for Western Europe.

Even so, from at least 1947, U.S. policy toward Korea was somewhat ambiguous. In June 1947, Congress shelved the Korean Aid Bill, and the State, War, and Navy departments announced their intention of minimizing U.S. financial and military commitments and withdrawing all U.S. troops within two years. In 1949, the official U.S. attitude became still more cautious and ambivalent. The U.S. Congress refused to approve the first year of a three-year $500 million aid bill until February 1950 (after initially rejecting it), although it soon approved a second year. On January 12, 1950, moreover, Secretary of State Dean Acheson excluded South Korea when he detailed the U.S. defense perimeter in the course of a major speech.

South Korean president Syngman Rhee responded to the new U.S. policy by requesting an official commitment from the United States comparable to the North Atlantic Treaty Organization (NATO) in Europe. On May 16, 1949, Rhee issued a public statement calling for "a solution to the grave threat against Korea and all Asia by aggressive forces of communism." At the least, Rhee wanted a public declaration of U.S. intent to defend a reunited, independent Korea. Earlier, Rhee had made similar requests. On one occasion, he stated that he wanted a "statement by President Truman that the United States would consider an attack against South Korea as an attack against itself."

In requesting a Pacific pact, Rhee found an immediate ally in nationalist Chinese leader Jiang, who had been trying since 1948 to persuade the United States to expand its commitment to noncommunist forces in Asia. He too wanted a pledge equivalent to the one the United States had extended to western Europe. Thus, on May 11, 1949, Nationalist Chinese ambassador to the United States V. K. Wellington Koo suggested to Acheson the creation of a Pacific pact. The next day, the Australian prime minister echoed the request, and two days later Rhee followed suit.

Washington turned down this request for a formal alliance. On May 18, 1949, Acheson stated publicly that a Pacific pact was premature. He also suggested that any such pact would indefinitely commit U.S. troops to the Nationalist Chinese in their fight against the communists on mainland China. Acheson concluded by saying that the United States favored Indian prime minister Jawaharlal Nehru's policy that called on Asian nations to work to end their conflicts before the creation of formal alliances.

Rebuffed by the United States, Jiang and Rhee sought allies in the Pacific. In July 1949, Jiang traveled to the Philippines, where he met with Prime Minister Elpidio Quirino, who endorsed the idea of an anticommunist Pacific pact. Quirino claimed that such an arrangement did not seek or require U.S. sanction, despite the intent of the members to "do our bit in the American-led crusade against Communism." Jiang next traveled to South Korea, where he and Rhee issued a joint statement proposing an organizational conference of anticommunist Pacific countries.

This did not alter the U.S. stance. In August 1949, President Truman told Quirino that the United States would "watch sympathetically" as noncommunist Asia worked to bring about mutual security. Quirino also found a less-than-enthusiastic U.S. Congress. A further setback occurred in September, when the North Atlantic Council of Foreign Ministers, meeting in Washington, concurred with the U.S. position that a communist victory in China was inevitable and further efforts to assist the Nationalists' military would therefore be pointless. Thus, the foreign ministers rejected participation in a Pacific pact. In addition, Nehru again characterized the creation of such an alliance as premature.

Nevertheless, Quirino organized a conference. During May 26–30, 1950, representatives from India, Indonesia, the Philippines, Ceylon, Pakistan, and Thailand met in Baguio in the Philippines. Noticeably absent were Rhee and Jiang. Neither attended nor sent representatives because India and Indonesia refused to deviate from their neutral stance even before the conference began.

In the end, the Baguio Conference produced little of a concrete nature. No formal Pacific pact emerged, and there was no mutual security declaration. In fact, the official proclamation implied that the representatives opposed Great Power intervention in Asia altogether.

Less than one month later, forces of the Democratic People's Republic of Korea (DPRK, North Korea) crossed the 38th Parallel and invaded South Korea, beginning the Korean War. Although early moves for a Pacific pact proved fruitless, the outbreak of the Korean War greatly alarmed many Asian nations and subsequently was a major contributory factor in persuading the United

States to establish the 1954 SEATO pact and to negotiate bilateral security treaties with both Taiwan and South Korea.

Mark A. T. Esposito

See also

Acheson, Dean Gooderham; Jiang Jieshi; Korea Aid Bill of 1947; Mao Zedong; Nehru, Jawaharlal; North Atlantic Treaty Organization; Rhee, Syngman; Southeast Asia Treaty Organization; Truman, Harry S.

References

Colbert, Evelyn S. *Southeast Asia in International Politics, 1941–1956.* Ithaca, NY: Cornell University Press, 1977.

Hess, Gary R. *The United States' Emergence as a Southeast Asian Power, 1940–1950.* New York: Columbia University Press, 1987.

Mabon, David W. "Elusive Agreement: The Pacific Pact Proposals of 1949–1951." *Pacific Historical Review* 57(2) (May 1988): 147–177.

Oliver, Robert T. *Syngman Rhee: The Man Behind the Myth.* New York: Dodd, Mead, 1955.

Stueck, William W., Jr. *The Korean War: An International History.* Princeton, NJ: Princeton University Press, 1995.

———. *Rethinking the Korean War: A New Diplomatic and Strategic History.* Princeton, NJ: Princeton University Press, 2004.

Padilla Nervo, Luis
Birth Date: August 19, 1898
Death Date: September 9, 1985

Mexican diplomat, head of the Mexican Delegation to the United Nations (UN) (1945–1952), and president of the Sixth Session of the UN General Assembly (1951–1952). Although Mexico drew closer to the United States economically in the 1940s and 1950s, it always tried to maintain an independent foreign policy both in international affairs in general and at the UN in particular. Luis Padilla Nervo was one of the principal architects of that policy. Born on August 19, 1898, in Zamora, Michoacan, Mexico, Luis Padilla Nervo received a law degree from the National Autonomous University of Mexico and also attended the University of Buenos Aires, George Washington University, and the University of London. He entered the Mexican diplomatic corps in 1918 and served variously between 1933 and 1945 as Mexico's minister to El Salvador, Panama, Uruguay, Denmark, Cuba, and the United States. Padilla was part of the Mexican delegation to the San Francisco Conference of 1945 that established the UN, and he subsequently served as head of the Mexican delegation to the UN from 1945 to 1952.

As head of the Mexican delegation, Padilla exercised considerable influence among the Latin American nations, which initially composed approximately 40 percent of the membership of the General Assembly. Padilla worked unsuccessfully at the San Francisco meeting of the UN in 1945 to get a permanent "Latin American" seat on the Security Council. Mexico, however, did become the first Latin American nation to be elected to one of the nonpermanent seats on the Security Council in 1946, making Padilla the first Latin American to serve on that powerful body.

Mexican diplomat Luis Padilla Nervo headed his country's delegation to the United Nations during 1945–1952. He is shown here during the Pan-American Conference of March 1954. (Time & Life Pictures/Getty Images)

After the attack on the Republic of Korea (ROK, South Korea) by the Democratic People's Republic of Korea (DPRK, North Korea) in June 1950, Padilla supported UN military involvement in Korea as well as UN resolutions calling for a greater role for the General Assembly in cases of international aggression and branding the People's Republic of China (PRC) as an aggressor after its intervention in Korea. Although supporting a military response, Padilla continued to work for a diplomatic solution to the conflict. He was one of three veteran diplomats assigned to the UN's Good Offices Committee, which had the responsibility of bringing China into negotiations to end the war.

Mexico also had a representative on the UN's Additional Measures Committee (AMC), exploring economic sanctions against China; Mexico was part of the committee trying to delay sanctions for fear that they might provoke a widening of the war. Under growing U.S. pressure, Mexico and the AMC approved a resolution calling for a selective embargo, which was later approved by the General Assembly on May 18, 1951, without a negative vote, although several nations abstained or were absent. While Padilla supported a peaceful resolution in Korea, he opposed an appeal being considered by a bloc of Asian and African countries to halt the fighting along the 38th Parallel because it would have bypassed the Good Offices Committee.

As president of the Sixth Session of the General Assembly (1951–1952), Padilla continued his efforts to bring about a negotiated end to the war. He was at the center of an ultimately unused Mexican effort to resolve the problem of dealing with the repatriation of prisoners of war (POWs), an issue that had deadlocked the armistice talks. Although he supported the U.S. position on key resolutions relating to the conduct of the war, in other areas, such as UN membership, disarmament, UN trusteeships, and economic development, Padilla staked out an independent position for Mexico. In his parting remarks as outgoing president of the assembly in October 1952, Padilla commented on the need for reconciliation between the United States and the Soviet Union and called for renewed efforts to bring the war to a negotiated conclusion.

After leaving the UN at the end of his term as president of the General Assembly, Padilla continued his distinguished diplomatic career as Mexico's minister of foreign relations, a post he held from 1952 to 1958. He then returned to head the Mexican delegation at the UN from 1958 until 1963, when he was appointed to the International Court of Justice, where he served until 1973. By the end of his career he had received decorations from 24 African, Asian, European, and Latin American countries.

Padilla effectively used his position at the UN during the Korean conflict to help maintain Latin American support for UN policy in Asia without blindly adhering to the positions adopted by the United States on other issues. Padilla died in Mexico City on September 9, 1985.

Don M. Coerver

See also
Latin America; Mexico

References
Faust, John R., and Charles L. Stansifer. "Mexican Foreign Policy in the United Nations: The Advocacy of Moderation in an Era of Revolution." *Southwestern Social Science Quarterly* 44 (September 1963): 121–129.

Houston, John A. *Latin America in the United Nations.* New York: Carnegie Endowment for International Peace, 1956.

Stueck, William W., Jr., ed. *Korean War in World History.* Lexington: University Press of Kentucky, 2004.

———. *The Korean War: An International History.* Princeton, NJ: Princeton University Press, 1995.

Paek In Yop
Birth Date: 1922

General of the Republic of Korea Army (ROKA, South Korean Army) and educator. Born in Kangso, North Pyongan Province, in the Democratic People's Republic of Korea (DPRK, North Korea) in 1922, Paek In Yop is the younger brother of well-known ROKA general Paek Son Yop. Paek In Yop graduated from the Japanese Military Academy in 1945 and became a second lieutenant in the Japanese army.

Following the Second World War, Paek became a colonel in the National Constabulary of the Republic of Korea (ROK, South Korea) and was appointed commander of the 17th Regiment in the Ongjin peninsula. He was a key figure in border fighting with North Korean forces during the period 1948–1949. Paek's regiment was long identified with the "Haeju attack" theory of the beginning of the Korean War—namely, that the war was initiated by ROKA forces. This has, however, been proved false. Soon after the outbreak of the war, the 17th Regiment was compelled to withdraw because of resupply problems.

On August 7, 1950, Paek became commander of the Capital Division. He distinguished himself in the later fighting, and in 1953 he studied at the U.S. Army War College. He then became commander of the ROKA VI Corps as a lieutenant general. Paek graduated from the ROK National Defense College in 1953 and retired from the military in 1962.

In 1964, Paek and his elder brother, Paek Son Yop, founded the Sonin School in Inchon City.

CHOO SUK SUH

See also
Border Clashes; Paek Son Yop

References
Millett, Allan R. *The War for Korea, 1945–1950: A House Burning.* Lawrence: University Press of Kansas, 2005.

Paik Sun Yup. *Kun kwa Na* [The Army and I]. Seoul: Taeryuk Yongu-so, 1989.

Paek Son Yop
Birth Date: November 23, 1920

Officer of the Republic of Korea Army (ROKA, South Korean Army) who rose from division commander with the rank of colonel at the beginning of the Korean War, to corps commander, and then to full general and chief of staff of the army. Born in Kangso, South Pyongan Province, near Pyongyang, on November 23, 1920, Paek Son Yop graduated from the Japanese Manchurian Military Academy in 1941. During World War II, he was a Japanese army lieutenant. After his return to Korea following its liberation in 1945, Paek graduated from the U.S. military government's Military English-Language School and joined the Korean constabulary as a company commander.

When the Korean People's Army (KPA, North Korean Army) began its invasion of the Republic of Korea (ROK, South Korea) on June 25, 1950, Paek commanded the ROKA 1st Division at Kaesong, two miles below the 38th Parallel on the Seoul-Pyongyang highway. On the day of the invasion, his division conducted a surprisingly effective defense and held its positions south of the Imjin River for nearly three days. But his own division was threatened with being cut off by the main KPA attack from the Uijongbu area when the ROKA 7th Division was forced to give way. Paek then removed his division to the Han River, where he took up positions on June 28.

Paek established a reputation as an excellent combat leader. In August 1950, he played an important role in the valiant and bloody defense of Taegu, a key point on the axis of the KPA main attack, which was vital in enabling United Nations Command (UNC) forces to hold the Pusan Perimeter. Although Paek received proper credit for the defense of Taegu, his success was in part the result of fire support from the neighboring U.S. 1st Cavalry Division, which helped compensate for the lack of his own artillery.

During the Pusan Perimeter breakout and subsequent counterattack, Paek and his division came under U.S. I Corps command, the first time ROKA formations were with U.S. Army units at the division level. During the October 1950 UNC/ROKA race to Pyongyang, Paek's division, despite being on foot, beat UNC motorized units to the capital of the Democratic People's Republic of Korea (DPRK, North Korea) and took the city on October 19. During the subsequent advance north of the Chongchon River, on October 25, Paek first encountered Chinese units above Unsan. When he immediately reported this fact to commanding general of I Corps Frank W. Milburn, it was the first U.S. knowledge of direct military intervention by the People's Republic of China (PRC) in the war. Many U.S. generals, including Milburn, 1st Cavalry Division commander Hobart R. Gay, and Eighth Army commander Walton H. Walker, regarded Paek as one of very best ROKA generals.

Promoted to major general in April 1951, Paek commanded the ROKA I Corps then positioned on the east coast of Korea north of the 38th Parallel. In July, when truce talks began, Paek represented the South Korean government as one of five UNC delegates. From

November 1951 to April 1952, he commanded Task Force Paek, consisting of the ROKA Capital and 8th divisions. With this force, he conducted Operation RATKILLER, which successfully wiped out communist guerrillas operating in the Chiri-san area in the southern part of Korea. This force killed or captured more than 10,000 guerrillas.

In January 1952, Paek was promoted to lieutenant general and given command of the new ROKA II Corps. Unlike I Corps, the new corps had, in addition to its infantry divisions, an organic artillery battalion and quartermaster and engineer assets.

U.S. Eighth Army commander General James A. Van Fleet was so impressed by Paek's ability that in July 1952 he recommended him to President Syngman Rhee as ROKA chief of staff. Paek served twice in that position: from 1952 to 1954 and from 1957 to 1959. On January 31, 1953, Paek was, at age 32, promoted to full (four-star) general, the first individual in the ROKA to hold that rank.

In May 1953, the U.S. government prepared a contingency plan to remove Rhee from office, as the president was then attempting to sabotage the truce talks. In drawing up their plan, the Americans assumed Paek would side with the United States even though they had not consulted him. The plan was never implemented, as Rhee finally agreed to the U.S. position regarding the truce.

In 1959, Paek became chairman of the South Korean Joint Chiefs of Staff, and the next year he retired from the army. Thereafter he served successively as ambassador to Taiwan, France, Canada, and 13 other nations. From 1969 to 1971 he was minister of transportation.

To Woong Chung and Mark R. Franklin

See also

Gay, Hobart Raymond; Kaesong Truce Talks; Milburn, Frank William; Pusan Perimeter and Breakout; RATKILLER, Operation; Rhee, Syngman; Taegu, Defense of; Van Fleet, James Alward; Walker, Walton Harris

References

Appleman, Roy E. *United States Army in Korea: South to the Naktong, North to the Yalu.* Washington, DC: Office of the Chief of Military History, 1961.

Hermes, Walter G. *U.S. Army in the Korean War: Truce Tent and Fighting Front.* Washington, DC: Office of the Chief of Military History, 1966.

Millett, Allan R. *The War for Korea, 1945–1950: A House Burning.* Lawrence: University Press of Kansas, 2005.

Paik Sun Yup. *From Pusan to Panmunjom.* Washington, DC: Brassey's, 1992.

———. *Kun kwa Na* [The Army and I]. Seoul: Taeryuk Yongu-so, 1989.

Paek Song Uk

Birth Date: 1897
Death Date: 1981

Buddhist scholar, minister of the interior of the Republic of Korea (ROK, South Korea), and educator. Born in Seoul in 1897, Paek Song Uk was educated at the Buddhist Central School, which later became Tongguk University. A supporter of Korean independence, he was exiled to Shanghai, China, after he joined the March First Movement of 1919. It was at this time that he met Syngman Rhee, a generation older and already one of the foremost leaders of the Korean Nationalist movement. Paek left Korea and lived in France and Germany for several years. In 1925, the University of Wurzburg awarded him a doctorate in Buddhism.

Returning to Korea, Paek spent many years pursuing Buddhist scholarship at a temple on Kumgang-san Mountain. When Rhee returned to Korea in 1945 after the country's liberation from the Japanese, Paek resumed contact with him and became one of his strongest supporters. During Rhee's subsequent bitter disputes and conflicts with Lieutenant General John R. Hodge, commander of U.S. occupation forces, Paek remained his staunch ally, publicly stating that Rhee was the only Korean leader capable of uniting the country and heading a future South Korean government.

Paek's one period of high political office was short and ill fated. In February 1950, Rhee, who became the first president of South Korea in 1948, asked Paek's opinion as to the desirability of establishing a parliamentary system, as the opposition in the National Assembly had suggested. Paek expressed strong disapproval of the idea, whereupon Rhee promptly named him interior minister, a post in which he exercised direct authority over the local and central bureaucracies and, even more important, the police, who were responsible for maintaining internal security, a mandate that South Korean leaders tended to define very broadly.

Paek used his position to orchestrate and direct a nationwide propaganda and terror campaign against the creation of a parliamentary system, which was probably partly responsible for the National Assembly's failure to pass a constitutional amendment supporting the switch to such a political system. Simultaneously, Rhee also pressured the National Assembly by threatening to postpone the imminent elections scheduled for the coming May. His tactics, however, proved counterproductive when U.S. officials warned that, if the elections did not take place on time, anticipated U.S. economic and military aid would not be forthcoming, a threat that forced Rhee to accept a compromise and end this particular crisis.

After the invasion by the Democratic People's Republic of Korea (DPRK, North Korea) on June 25, 1950, Paek (whom Harold J. Noble, at that time first secretary at the U.S. embassy in Seoul, described as a superstitious "fatalist and military pessimist"), was Rhee's only cabinet member to refuse to desert Seoul until the government as a whole left the capital. His courage, however, coexisted with a "gloomy" outlook that so depressed Rhee that on the day the war began, Paek's "defeatism" led the president to demand his resignation.

Paek clung to office for only another month. By mid-July, Noble, Lieutenant General Walton H. Walker, commander of the U.S. Eighth Army in Korea, and U.S. ambassador John J. Muccio had all come to regard him as "a serious menace to the successful prosecution of the war so pessimistic that he even infected high police officers with his defeatism." They were determined to replace Paek with the more positive and dynamic Cho Pyong Ok, a course of action that they daily recommended to the reluctant Rhee. Although the president preferred the loyal and malleable Paek to Cho or any other contender, ultimately he followed their advice, dismissed Paek, and appointed Cho.

In 1952, Paek ran unsuccessfully for vice president, his last major excursion into politics. From 1953 to 1961, he served as president of Tongguk University, his alma mater, and after he retired he continued to lecture privately on Buddhism. Paek died in 1981.

PRISCILLA ROBERTS

See also

Hodge, John Reed; Korea, Republic of, 1947–1953; Muccio, John Joseph; Noble, Harold; Rhee, Syngman; Walker, Walton Harris

References

Cumings, Bruce. *The Origins of the Korean War.* 2 vols. Princeton, NJ: Princeton University Press, 1981, 1990.

Dobbs, Charles M. *The Unwanted Symbol: American Foreign Policy, the Cold War, and Korea, 1945–1950.* Kent, OH: Kent State University Press, 1981.

Noble, Harold J. *Embassy at War.* Seattle: University of Washington Press, 1975.

"Paek Song Uk." In *Historical Dictionary of the Korean War,* edited by James I. Matray, 506–507. Westport, CT: Greenwood, 1991.

Paek Tu Jin
Birth Date: October 7, 1908
Death Date: September 5, 1992

Banker, finance minister, and prime minister of the Republic of Korea (ROK, South Korea). Born in Sinchon, Hwanghae Province, in present-day North Korea on October 7, 1908, Paek Tu Jin grew up in Seoul. He graduated from the College of Commerce of Tokyo Imperial University in 1934. He joined Choson Central Bank in 1934 and served as a trustee there from 1945 to 1950.

A staunch supporter of South Korean president Syngman Rhee, Paek was appointed chief of the foreign aid management agency in 1949. After the outbreak of the Korean War in June 1950, he became president of the Korea Industrial Bank. The next year, Rhee appointed him both finance minister and the chief of the Planning Agency, thus making him his chief financial advisor.

As chief financial officer of Korea, Paek faced enormous problems, perhaps the most pressing of which was controlling chronic inflation. Paek employed the common-sense approach of cutting nonmilitary expenditures as much as possible and collecting taxes, by force if necessary. Paek played a major role in South Korea–U.S. economic relations. Both he and Rhee believed that the serious inflation resulted from the advance payments in won, the South Korean currency, to the United Nations Command

(UNC) for maintenance costs in Korea. In May 1952, Paek finally secured an economic cooperation agreement with Clarence Meyer, representing the U.S. government. In February 1953, Paek implemented a currency reform that replaced the old won with a new won at the rate of 100 to 1. When Henry Tasca visited South Korea, Paek worked out a program with him for a long-range reconstruction program.

In 1952, Rhee designated Paek acting prime minister, succeeding Chang Taek Sang. Paek became prime minister in April 1953 and served until 1954. In 1960, Paek was elected to the South Korean National Assembly, but he could not serve out his term because of the May 1961 military coup d'état that removed Rhee from power. Paek became presidential adviser to the ruling Democratic Republican Party in 1967. From 1967 to 1980, he served as an assemblyman. He was again prime minister during 1970–1971, and he was elected Speaker (chairman) of the National Assembly in 1971. In 1973, he also chaired the Yujong Hoe club, consisting of assemblymen selected by President Park Chung Hee.

Paek was again elected Speaker of the National Assembly in 1979, but in the 1980s, he held no official position. Paek died in Seoul on September 5, 1992.

CHOO SUK SUH

See also

Meyer, Clarence Earle; Rhee, Syngman; Tasca, Henry Joseph

References

Lyons, Gene M. *Military Policy and Economic Aid: The Korean Case, 1950–1953.* Columbus: Ohio State University Press, 1961.

Matray, James I., ed. *Historical Dictionary of the Korean War.* Westport, CT: Greenwood, 1991.

Paek Tu Jin. *Paek Tu Jin Hoegorok* [Memoirs of Paek Tu Jin]. Seoul: Taehan Kongnon-sa, 1975.

Pak Hon Yong
Birth Date: May 1, 1900
Death Date: December 1955

Minister of foreign affairs and a vice premier of the Democratic People's Republic of Korea (DPRK, North Korea) during the Korean War; one of the key leaders of the Korean communist movement. Pak Hon Yong was born on May 1, 1900, in Yesan, South Chungchong Province, in southern Korea. He joined anti-Japanese activities in the Koryo Communist Youth League in Shanghai as early as 1919 and was one of the original members of the Koryo Communist Party formed in Shanghai in 1921. In 1925, in Seoul, he formed both the Korean Communist Party (KCP) and the Korean Communist Youth League.

The Japanese arrested him three times—in 1921, in 1924, and in 1933—in connection with his communist activities. In 1933, he was imprisoned for six years when he reentered Korea from Shanghai in an effort to reconstruct the KCP. Upon his release in

1939, he achieved some success in uniting existing Korean communist factions in the Kom Kurup (Communist Group). In 1941, he went underground for the duration of the Pacific War, working as a laborer in a South Cholla Province brick factory. On August 15, 1945, when the Japanese surrendered, he left for Seoul, saying, "I go to begin my future."

After the liberation of Korea, Pak was the key leader in the short-lived, stormy period of communist ascendancy in southern Korea. Called in 1945 "the greatest leader of Korean communism," he took the lead in the February 1946 formation of Minjon (Democratic National Front), a leftist coalition in southern Korea, and the autumn 1946 creation of the Namrodang (South Korean Workers' Party), a merger of the political Left in southern Korea. As the leader of the "domestic" faction, Pak was the logical choice to be national leader of post-1945 Korean communism because of his indigenous support, long party experience, and strong intellectual qualifications.

In August 1945, the Americans intervened in Korea, occupying the peninsula south of the 38th Parallel in accordance with World War II agreements with the Soviets. Since their fundamental objectives and the means they used in reaching them differed so radically, U.S. occupation authorities and the communists in southern Korea were destined to come into conflict. After the 1946 Autumn Harvest Uprisings (or October People's Resistance), the southern Left saw its strength dissipate and the center of gravity move to Pyongyang. Pak and other southern communist leaders were forced to move north, to be ensconced in secondary positions there.

On the September 1948 establishment of the Democratic People's Republic of Korea, Pak became a vice premier with Kim Chaek and Hong Myong Hui under Premier Kim Il Sung. Pak also held the important cabinet position of minister of foreign affairs, and he was made vice chairman of the Korean Workers' Party—a fusion of the northern and southern parties—as well as a member of the all-important seven-member military committee of the party. According to some writers, Pak urged the North Korean invasion of the Republic of Korea (ROK, South Korea) in an effort to advance his political fortunes against his rival Kim Il Sung. But both men wanted a war against South Korea to reunify their country under communism. A secret conference was held in March 1950 in Pyongyang that was attended by North Korea's top leaders. Kim Il Sung opened for discussion the possibility of military action against South Korea. Pak spoke strongly in favor of such a course, asserting that if the Korean People's Army (KPA, North Korean Army) invaded South Korea, 200,000 underground South Korean communists would emerge to fight with the northern forces. But in the summer of 1950, the southern population was generally apathetic regarding the North Korean occupation. Few rose up voluntarily to greet the KPA, which was one of the reasons for the North Korean failure.

After North Korea's military defeats in the fall of 1950, the rivalry between Kim Il Sung and Pak intensified. Kim complained to the Chinese that Pak "has no determination to start a guerrilla struggle in the mountainous area." Pak's fate was sealed by the North Korean failure to conquer South Korea.

After the conclusion of the Armistice Agreement, Pak and the southern communists were made scapegoats for the debacle of the war. Kim Il Sung and his allies blamed Pak for failing to produce an uprising in South Korea that would lead to a communist victory. Pak, the loser in the power struggle with Kim, was purged. In December 1955, Kim, who emerged as the "maximum leader," had Pak executed on a charge of spying for the "U.S. imperialists."

JINWUNG KIM

See also
Kim Il Sung

References

Cumings, Bruce. *Korea's Place in the Sun: A Modern History*. New York: Norton, 1997.

Matray, James I., ed. *Historical Dictionary of the Korean War*. Westport, CT: Greenwood, 1991.

Millett, Allan R. *The War for Korea, 1945–1950: A House Burning*. Lawrence: University Press of Kansas, 2005.

Scalapino, Robert A., and Lee Chong Sik. *Communism in Korea*. 2 vols. Berkeley: University of California Press, 1973.

Pak Sun Chon
Birth Date: September 19, 1898
Death Date: January 9, 1983

Female politician in the Republic of Korea (ROK, South Korea) and a member of the National Assembly during the Korean War. Pak Sun Chon was born Myong Nyon at Tongnae, now part of the city of Pusan, on September 19, 1898. She converted to Christianity in 1908 and graduated from Ilsin Girls' School at Tongnae in 1917. Pak took part in the March First Movement in 1919 while she was teaching at Uisin Girls' School in Masan, South Kyongsang province. Because of her involvement in the March uprising and other anti-Japanese activities, Pak was sought by the Japanese police. She subsequently married a man in Sunchon, South Cholla Province, and changed her name to Sunchon to conceal her identity. She pretended that her husband had deserted her.

In 1926, Pak traveled to Tokyo to study at Nippon Women's College. While attending college, where she majored in sociology, she married Pyon Hui Yong, a Korean student studying in Japan. After graduating that same year, Pak returned to Korea and lived at her husband's home at Koryong, North Kyongsang Province. There she and her family farmed for 13 years. She also operated day nurseries in the busy farming season and night schools in the off season, actively advocating the teaching of *hangul* (the Korean written language) and mathematics to children and women. After giving birth to seven children, in 1939 she moved to Seoul and engaged in educational work, running a private school out of her home.

Following Korea's liberation on August 15, 1945, Pak decided to participate in Korea's nation building, and three days later, on August 18, with Yim Yong Sin and others, organized the Women's Union for National Foundation. On November 5, 1946, she established the Association of the Patriotic Women for Rapid Realization of Independence, becoming its first president. The organization was later renamed the Korean Women's Association, and Pak served as its president for six years.

In the National Assembly election held on May 30, 1950, just before the outbreak of the Korean War, Pak was elected to the body on a Korean Women's Association ticket from Seoul. She stood as an independent candidate for the next National Assembly election held on May 20, 1954, but failed to win reelection. She was, however, reelected in the following elections: May 2, 1958; July 29, 1960; and November 26, 1963 on a Democratic Party ticket, and again on June 8, 1967, as a member of the New Democratic Party. Serving as an opposition lawmaker, she engaged in the struggle against the dictatorships of presidents Syngman Rhee and Park Chung Hee. She also fought for the extension of women's rights. On July 18, 1963, Pak was elected president of the Democratic Party, an opposition party to Park Chung Hee's military regime.

In the National Assembly election of November 1963, the ruling Democratic Republican Party won almost two-thirds of the assembly seats while receiving only one-third of the popular vote. The main reason for the discrepancy was that opposition parties each ran their own candidates in many districts. In other words, the failure of the opposition to unite against the government party led to its crushing defeat. The opposition, therefore, had to form a united front. Finally, on May 3, 1965, two opposition parties, the Democratic Politics Party of former president Yun Po Son and the Democratic Party of Pak Sun Chon were merged into the Democratic People's Party, a united opposition party against the Park Chung Hee regime. On June 14, 1965, Pak defeated Yun Po Son to become the elected president of the new party and thus was the leader of the first main opposition party in the Park's Third Republic (1963–1972). The Democratic People's Party was renamed the New Democratic Party on February 11, 1967.

Pak Sun Chon retired from political life in 1971. During 1980–1983, she was a member of the Advisory Council on National Affairs and was also the chairperson of the Promotion Committee for the Construction of the Independence Hall, located at Chonan, South Chongchong Province. She died in Seoul on January 9, 1983.

JINWUNG KIM

See also

Korea, Republic of, 1947–1953; Korea, Republic of, 1953–Present; Park Chung Hee; Rhee, Syngman

References

CTN. *Minjujuui ui Jeanne d'Arc Pak Sun Chon* [Jeanne d'Arc of Democracy: Pak Sun Chon]. Seoul: CTN, 1999.

Kim, Min-ha. *Han'guk Chongdang Chongchi Ron* [On the Korean Party Politics]. Seoul: Kyomunsa, 1976.

Soh, Chung'hee Sarah. *Women in Korean Politics*. Boulder, CO: Westview, 1993.

Pandit, Vijaya Lakshmi Nehru
Birth Date: August 8, 1900
Death Date: December 1, 1990

Indian politician, diplomat, and ambassador to the United States and chief delegate to the United Nations (UN) during the Korean War. Born on August 8, 1900, in Allahabad, India, Vijaya Lakshmi Nehru Pandit was, like her brother, future Indian prime minister Jawaharlal Nehru, active in the Indian movement to secure independence from Britain. She was arrested several times. After India became independent in 1947, Pandit served the new government in a variety of key diplomatic posts, including those of ambassador to the Soviet Union and then to the United States and Great Britain.

As Indian ambassador to the United States during the Korean War, Pandit closely followed her country's nonaligned stance, worked to keep the conflict from spreading, and sought to bring the war to a peaceful conclusion. She was certainly friendlier toward, and less skeptical of, the West than her brother, and

Vijaya Lakshmi Pandit was the Indian ambassador to the United States and chief delegate to the United Nations during the Korean War. Pandit closely followed her country's policy of nonalignment and worked to bring about a peaceful end to the conflict. (Library of Congress)

on occasion she sought to soften his criticisms of the policies of the Harry S. Truman administration. This was a difficult period in U.S.-Indian relations for, although Pandit was well respected by Truman administration officials—Secretary of State Dean G. Acheson found her "a most charming lady"—they also viewed Indian policies as, at best, naive.

Pandit played little role in V. K. Krishna Menon's prisoner of war (POW) proposals that helped to end the war, in part because of personal animosity and in part because she did not think that Menon would be able to secure a compromise on the matter.

In 1953, Pandit was elected president of the General Assembly, the first woman to hold that post. In India, she was governor of Maharashtra from 1962 to 1964. In 1970, she moved to Dehra Dun, in the Himalayan foothills of north India. Outraged by the proclaimed state of emergency, she campaigned against her niece Prime Minister Indira Gandhi and was a factor in the latter's fall from power. Ailing for some years, Pandit died on December 1, 1990.

SPENCER C. TUCKER

See also

Acheson, Dean Gooderham; India; Menon, Vengalil Krishnan Krishna; Nehru, Jawaharlal

References

Pandit, Vijaya Lakshmi. *The Scope of Happiness: A Personal Memoir.* New York: Crown, 1979.

Reid, Escott. *Envoy to Nehru.* New York: Oxford University Press, 1981.

Stueck, William W., Jr. *The Road to Confrontation: American Policy toward China and Korea, 1947–1950.* Chapel Hill: University of North Carolina Press, 1981.

Pang Ho San
Birth Date: 1916
Death Date: 1959

General of the Korean People's Army (KPA, North Korean Army) and one of its ablest commanders during the Korean War. Pang Ho San was born sometime in 1916 in the north Hamgyong Province, present-day North Korea. He helped form the liberation movement against Japanese occupation as a young man and went to the Soviet Union to study from 1937 to 1939. In 1940, Pang entered the People's Liberation Army (PLA, Chinese Communist Army). From 1945 to 1948, during the Chinese Civil War, he fought against Guomindang (GMD, Nationalist) forces led by Jiang Jieshi (Chiang Kai-shek) and was a political commissar of Lee Hung Gwang's detached troops.

In 1949, Pang entered the Democratic People's Republic of Korea (DPRK, North Korea) as commander of 166th Division, made up entirely of Korean soldiers, part of the Chinese forces released by Mao Zedong, leader of the People's Republic of China (PRC). The 166th Division was soon reorganized and expanded and became the 6th Division of the KPA. Pang continued in command.

During the Korean War, especially its early stages, Pang and his division fought with great effectiveness against the Republic of Korea Army (ROKA, South Korean Army). Taking the offensive, his division occupied much of southwestern Korea and made a quick advance toward Jinju and Masan.

During the crisis precipitated by the successful United Nations Command (UNC) amphibious operation at Inchon in September 1950, Pang withdrew his division from South Korea with minimal casualties. At war's end, North Korean leader Kim Il Sung praised Pang highly. In June 1956, he received the Gold Star Medal with the title of Hero of the Korean Democratic Republic.

In August 1958, Pang was named commander of KPA V Corps and president of the Army War College. In 1959, however, he was purged after being suspected of having had connections to the so-called 1956 August Anti-Party Incident, in which the pro-Chinese faction was charged with having engaged in antiparty and antigovernment activities. The place and exact date of his death are unknown, but undoubtedly Pang Ho San was executed on Kim's orders sometime in 1959.

LEE JUCHEON

See also

Kim Il Sung; Korea, Democratic People's Republic of, Army

References

Scalapino, Robert A., and Lee Chong Sik. *Communism in Korea.* 2 vols. Berkeley: University of California Press, 1973.

Suh, Dae Sook. *Korean Communism, 1945–1980: A Reference Guide to the Political System.* Honolulu: University Press of Hawaii, 1981.

———. *The Korean Communist Movement, 1918–1948.* Princeton, NJ: Princeton University Press, 1967.

Panikkar, Sardar K. M.
Birth Date: June 3, 1895
Death Date: December 10, 1963

Indian politician, ambassador to China from 1947 to 1952, and diplomatic conduit for communications between the People's Republic of China (PRC) and the Western powers during the Korean War. Born on June 3, 1895, at Travancore, India, Sardar K. M. Panikkar was educated at Madras Christian College and Christ Church College, Oxford, where he gained first class honors in modern history. After reading for the bar, Panikkar returned to India and spent short spells as a university professor and editor of the *Hindustan Times*. He then became a public servant, serving in the administrations of several of the Indian princely states. His most senior positions were as foreign minister of Potiala and prime minister of Bikaner State from 1944 to 1947.

Before Indian independence in 1947, Panikkar was also a member of the Indian delegations at numerous international gatherings and conferences. Throughout his life he wrote extensively on India's history and politics and on international relations, and he became known as a brilliant although far from objective scholar and diplomat, dedicated to the cause of Afro-Asian nationalism. In 1947, he became India's ambassador to China. Panikkar withdrew briefly from China after the Communist Party's final victory in the Chinese Civil War and its proclamation of the People's Republic of China on October 1, 1949, but in December of that year Indian Prime Minister Jawaharlal Nehru of India recognized the new regime and, somewhat unconventionally, reassigned Panikkar to Beijing. Panikkar's outspoken support for Asian nationalism, the Chinese revolution, India's nonaligned Cold War policies, and Panikkar's scholarly accomplishments were assets that helped him to develop warm and friendly relations with China's new leaders.

During the Korean War, Panikkar routinely informed secretary-general of the Ministry of External Affairs Sir Girja Bajpai of his conversations regarding Korea with Chinese foreign minister Zhou Enlai and other Chinese leaders. Bajpai, in turn, relayed these messages to the British and U.S. governments, with whose personnel he enjoyed good relations. The British Foreign Office tended to give considerable credence to his reports, whereas U.S. officials were more skeptical, deploring what they considered Panikkar's procommunist sympathies and therefore characterizing his observations as unreliable.

Panikkar initially reported that China's leadership seemed relatively uninterested in Korea and that a Chinese military intervention appeared unlikely. In late September 1950, after the success of General Douglas MacArthur's Inchon counteroffensive raised the possibility that United Nations (UN) forces would cross the 38th Parallel dividing the two Korean states, Chinese leaders began to express serious concern over Korea. The most dramatic incidents of Panikkar's involvement with Korea then ensued. On September 25, 1950, acting chief of staff of the Chinese People's Liberation Army (PLA, Chinese Communist Army) General Nieh Yen Jung warned Panikkar that China would intervene militarily should UN forces cross the parallel. In a speech of September 30, Zhou publicly made the same threat.

Disregarding these warnings, on October 1, units of the Republic of Korea Army (ROKA, South Korean Army) crossed the 38th Parallel. On October 3, earlier Chinese warnings were reinforced when Zhou summoned Panikkar to a midnight meeting, at which Zhou emphasized that China was prepared to tolerate the presence of South Korean forces in North Korea, but "American intrusion into North Korea would encounter Chinese resistance." Panikkar immediately cabled this information to Delhi, and it was communicated to both British and U.S. diplomatic representatives. The British were relatively receptive, and although some U.S. State Department officials, notably O. Edmund Chubb and U. Alexis Johnson, argued that the threat of Chinese intervention should not be ignored, top U.S. leaders, including President Harry S. Truman, Secretary of State Dean Acheson, and MacArthur, argued that to hold back at the parallel would be interpreted as evidence of U.S. weakness and irresolution.

On October 8, the UN, at U.S. insistence, passed a resolution authorizing its forces to cross into North Korean territory, and on October 25, Chinese troops joined the fighting. Panikkar feared that the war would escalate further and that the United States would extend bombing raids to Manchuria, possibly provoking Soviet intervention. He remained in Beijing until 1952, encouraging all moves to bring about a negotiated peace settlement, efforts in which Indian diplomats at the UN were also deeply involved.

After leaving China, Panikkar was successively Indian ambassador to Egypt and to France. In 1961, he returned to the academic world as vice-chancellor of Jammu and Kashmir University in Srinagar. He died at Mysore, India, on December 10, 1963.

PRISCILLA ROBERTS

See also

Acheson, Dean Gooderham; Bajpai, Girja Shankar; Clubb, Oliver Edmund; Inchon Landing; India; Johnson, Ural Alexis; MacArthur, Douglas; Nehru, Jawaharlal; Truman, Harry S.; Zhou Enlai

References

Gopal, Sarvepalli. *Jawaharlal Nehru: A Biography.* 3 vols. Cambridge, MA: Harvard University Press, 1976.
Kux, Dennis. *Estranged Democracies: India and the United States, 1941–1991.* New Delhi: Sage, 1993.
Panikkar, K. M. *In Two Chinas: Memoirs of a Diplomat.* London: Allen and Unwin, 1955.
Stueck, William W., Jr. *The Korean War: An International History.* Princeton, NJ: Princeton University Press, 1995.
Wolpert, Stanley. *Nehru: A Tryst with Destiny.* New York: Oxford University Press, 1996.

Panmunjom Security Agreement
Event Date: October 22, 1951

The October 22, 1951, Panmunjom Security Agreement relocated the truce talks from Kaesong to Panmunjom and designated the conference site, the base camps of the two sides, and corridors along the roads leading from the base camps to Panmunjom as neutral areas.

Security and access in the conference area had been an issue from the beginning of the truce talks. Kaesong was not under the control of either side when the United Nations Command (UNC) agreed on July 3, 1951, to hold the talks there. By the time the negotiations began on July 10, however, troops of the Korean People's Army (KPA, North Korean Army) and the Chinese People's Volunteer Army (CPVA, Chinese Army) had occupied the town, giving them possession of the negotiation site and control of the conference setting. During the initial negotiations, the KPA-CPVA refused to allow journalists to accompany the UNC delegation, citing security considerations. The UNC then proposed a five-mile radius Kaesong neutral zone and threatened to change the conference site if the Chinese and North Koreans continued to insist that restrictions on the movements of UNC personnel at Kaesong were necessary for their safety. On July 15, the KPA-CPVA agreed to establish the neutral zone.

Despite this agreement, however, security and access in the conference site continued to be an issue. On August 4, a company of Chinese combat troops marched through the conference area. When the UNC protested, the KPA-CPVA apologized for the incident. They in turn made a series of accusations against the UNC, alleging air attacks and other violations of the neutral zone. On August 22, the KPA-CPVA charged the UNC with bombing and strafing the conference site itself and unilaterally recessed the talks. Apparently, the Chinese wanted a pause in the talks while they reassessed their battlefield position and their negotiating strategy.

Although the UNC expressed willingness to resume the talks, it had concluded that the Kaesong conference site was disadvantageous. It was also concerned that the Chinese and North Koreans were taking advantage of the large neutral zone to reconstitute their forces in that area, which lay along the main avenue of approach into South Korea.

When the Chinese completed their strategic reassessment in mid-September and decided not to conduct a new major military offensive, the KPA-CPVA side offered to resume negotiations. The UNC, however, declined to resume the negotiations at Kaesong. After several weeks of bargaining, the KPA-CPVA side agreed on October 24 to a new conference site at Panmunjom, midway between the two sides, and ratified an agreement reached by the liaison officers on October 22.

The Panmunjom Security Agreement established a circular area 1,000 yards in radius as the conference site. Armed personnel were excluded from that area except for each side's security detachment of 2 officers and 15 men equipped with small arms. The two sides would share in equipping and maintaining the conference facilities. Each side could determine the composition of its own delegation, which would have freedom of movement within the conference site. Three-mile radius areas centered on the two sides' base camps at Kaesong and Munsan and a corridor extending 200 meters (218 yards) on either side of the Kaesong-Panmunjom-Munsan road were also designated as neutral zones. No hostile acts were to be permitted within or against these areas, nor could aircraft fly over them, except under uncontrollable weather or technical conditions.

When the talks resumed on October 25, 1951, the UNC accepted a KPA-CPVA proposal to establish a joint office of the liaison officers to deal with the administration of the security agreement and to investigate and settle violations. Under a subsequent liaison officer agreement of November 24, 1951, the UNC agreed to allow safe passage between Pyongyang and Kaesong of two daily KPA-CPVA convoys of up to six trucks and three jeeps each.

The Panmunjom Security Agreement largely removed the issue of equity and security from the truce talks agenda and set the stage for substantive negotiations. However, the long recess, the charges and countercharges, and the difficulty of reaching the agreement did nothing to alleviate an atmosphere of hostility and mistrust that continued to permeate the talks.

DONALD W. BOOSE JR.

See also

Kaesong Neutral Zone Controversy; Kaesong Truce Talks; Truce Talks

References

Chen Jian. *Mao's China and the Cold War.* Chapel Hill: University of North Carolina Press, 2000.

Goodman, Allan E., ed. *Negotiating While Fighting: The Diary of Admiral C. Turner Joy at the Korean Armistice Conference.* Stanford, CA: Hoover Institute Press, 1978.

Hermes, Walter G. *U.S. Army in the Korean War: Truce Tent and Fighting Front.* Washington, DC: Office of the Chief of Military History, 1966.

Stueck, William W., Jr. *Rethinking the Korean War: A New Diplomatic and Strategic History.* Princeton, NJ: Princeton University Press, 2004.

U.S. Department of State, Bureau of Public Affairs. *Foreign Relations of the United States, 1951,* Vol. 7, *China and Korea.* Washington, DC: U.S. Government Printing Office, 1983.

Park Chung Hee
Birth Date: November 14, 1917
Death Date: October 26, 1979

Army officer in the Republic of Korea Army (ROKA, South Korean Army) during the Korean War and later president of the Republic of Korea (ROK, South Korea) from 1963 to 1979. Park Chung Hee was born at Kumi, in present-day South Korea's North Kyongsang Province, on November 14, 1917. He graduated from the Taegu Teachers' College and entered the Military Officer Training Academy of the Manchurian Imperial Army in Changchun, China, in April 1940. He attended the Japanese Military Academy from 1942 to 1944, was commissioned a lieutenant, and then served in Japan's Guandong (Kwantung) Army in Manchuria until the end of World War II.

Park returned to southern Korea in May 1946 and became an officer in the Constabulary Army during the U.S. occupation of the southern half of Korea. In early October 1946, while suppressing a riot at Taegu, South Korean police under the direction of the U.S. military government killed Park's closest brother, a regional leader of the Left. This event led Park to join the South Korean Workers' Party (SKWP), which was established in late November of that year. Immediately after the Yosu-Sunchon Rebellion collapsed in late October 1948, South Korean President Syngman Rhee moved quickly to suppress dissent and to strengthen his control over his security forces. The first target was the constabulary. The South Korean government arrested Park, then a major, in November 1948 on charges that he had led a communist cell in the Constabulary Army. In February 1949, Park was sentenced to life imprisonment by a military court. Subsequently, however, Rhee commuted his sentence to 10 years in prison on the urging of several high-ranking Korean military officers and after his active

Park Chung Hee, Republic of Korea Army, general during the Korean War (South Korean Army) was the president of his country during 1963–1979. He ruled South Korea with an iron fist but ushered in a period of impressive economic growth. (UPI/Bettmann/Corbis)

their attempts to initiate needed reforms, their efforts largely failed and antigovernment violence increased. Taking advantage of the situation, a group of young military officers helped Park seize power in a military-led coup on May 16, 1961.

Park was promoted to lieutenant general in August 1961 and to general in November 1961. Following the coup, he was consecutively elected president in 1963, 1967, 1971, 1972, and 1978. Initially, he embarked on a generally successful economic modernization program that brought stability and increased prosperity to his country. From 1965 to 1973, he dispatched more than 47,000 South Korean troops to Vietnam at the request of the U.S. government. Beginning in the early 1970s, however, public resistance against his authoritarian regime escalated, and by the mid-1970s the once-flourishing South Korean economy was on the skids. Park's iron-fisted rule ended abruptly when his director of the Korean Central Intelligence Agency, Kim Chae Gyu, assassinated him in Seoul on October 26, 1979.

Today, Park is remembered less as the ruthless dictator who retarded South Korea's political development than as the father of the country's remarkable economic renaissance. He has been cited as the country's greatest president, thanks to the impressive economic progress and development that began under his regime.

JINWUNG KIM

See also

Chang Myon; Korea, Republic of, Economy; Korea, Republic of, 1953–Present; Rhee, Syngman; Yosu-Sunchon Rebellion

References

Cho, Kap Che. *Nae Mudom e Chim ul Paetora: Kundaehwa Hyongmyongga Park Chung Hee ui Pijanghan Saengae* [Spit on My Tomb: The Heroic Life of Park Chung Hee, a Revolutionist for Modernization]. 8 vols. Seoul: Choson Ilbo-sa, 1998.

Cumings, Bruce. *Korea's Place in the Sun: A Modern History*. New York: Norton, 1997.

Oberdorfer, Don. *The Two Koreas: A Contemporary History*. Rev. and updated ed. New York: Basic Books, 2001.

assistance in the arrest of other SKWP members in the army. Park ultimately served almost no time in jail.

On June 30, 1950, immediately after the Korean War began, Park returned to active service as a major and served as an intelligence officer. He was promoted to lieutenant colonel that September and to colonel in April 1951. As a colonel, he became the artillery commander of II Corps in February 1953 and of III Corps in May 1953. Advanced to brigadier general in November 1953, he became commander of the 5th Division in July 1955 and of the 7th Division in September 1957.

Appointed major general in March 1958, Park became chief of staff of the First Army. In July 1959, he headed the 6th District Command, which had responsibility for the defense of Seoul. He then commanded, in succession, the Quartermaster Base and the 1st District Command. In September 1960, Park became chief of the operations staff of the ROKA and, that September, deputy commander of the Second Army.

In April 1960, mass antigovernment demonstrations forced the aging Rhee from power. That July, national elections brought a coalition government to power, with Yun Po Son as figurehead president and Chang Myon (John M. Chang) as premier. Despite

Partridge, Earle Everard
Birth Date: July 7, 1900
Death Date: September 7, 1990

U.S. Air Force (USAF) general and commander of the U.S. Fifth Air Force in Japan and Korea, 1948–1951. Born in Winchendon, Massachusetts, on July 7, 1900, Earl Everard Partridge served in the U.S. Army in World War I. He then studied one year at Norwich University before attending the U.S. Military Academy at West Point. Graduating in 1924, he was commissioned in the Army Air Service. Subsequent assignments included flying instructor and service in observation and pursuit squadrons. Partridge also advanced his professional education in the late 1930s with study at the Air Corps Tactical School and the Command and General Staff School. During World War II he

Painting of U.S. Air Force general Earle E. Partridge, commander of the Far East Air Forces during March 1954–June 1955. Partridge commanded the Fifth Air Force in Japan and Korea during 1948–1951. (Department of Defense)

was chief of staff of the 12th Bomber Command in North Africa and then of the Fifteenth Air Force in Italy. He was advanced to brigadier general in December 1942 and to major general in May 1944. In June 1944 Partridge commanded the 3rd Bombardment Division in Britain and later was deputy commander of the Eighth Air Force there.

In 1948 Partridge became commander of the Fifth Air Force in Japan. After the Korean People's Army (KPA, North Korean Army) invaded the Republic of Korea (ROK, South Korea) on June 25, 1950, U.S. commander in the Far East General Douglas MacArthur ordered Partridge, acting commander of the Far East Air Forces (FEAF), to evacuate Americans from Korea, attack KPA invasion forces, and resupply the Republic of Korea Army (ROKA, South Korean Army). Major General Partridge thus led the air force into the Korean War.

Initially, the USAF operated under very difficult conditions. Nonetheless, it contributed greatly to the September rout of KPA forces. Fifth Air Force executed missions of close air support

(CAS), interdiction, air superiority, and reconnaissance. Partridge located his headquarters next to that of the U.S. Eighth Army in Korea (EUSAK), and he and Lieutenant General Walton H. Walker established a close working relationship. Partridge frequently piloted Walker in a North American T-6 Texan.

Partridge soon discovered that his Lockheed F-80 Shooting Star jets based in Japan did not have the range to remain long over targets in Korea, despite the addition of wing drop tanks. The F-80s could not operate from the primitive fields in Korea, so he converted six squadrons to old propeller-driven North American F-51 Mustangs operating from dirt strips. Flying both from Japan and Korea, his squadrons devastated KPA forces and helped prevent the destruction of the Eighth Army. In July his aircraft destroyed many communist planes and established U.S. air superiority over all Korea. His planes also destroyed railroad and highway bridges in July and August to interdict resupply to KPA forces along the Pusan Perimeter and to isolate the Inchon invasion site. Lacking sufficient numbers of forward air controllers (FACs) for CAS, Partridge developed "Mosquito" flights of T-6s to direct air strikes.

In July and August 1950, Partridge tried to coordinate navy and Marine CAS in support of EUSAK. The marines coordinated their CAS attacks with the air force, and the navy tried to do the same, but launchings at sea were dependent on the weather, and when the carriers did launch, the air force often lacked the controllers to put them on targets when they arrived over the battlefield. The navy thereupon moved its carriers farther north along the west coast of Korea to launch interdiction strikes. Later, naval aviation acted independently on the east coast.

After the Inchon Landing on September 15, when EUSAK invaded the Democratic People's Republic of Korea (DPRK, North Korea), Partridge's planes blasted a path for it. His provision of CAS was made easier in October when EUSAK received sufficient numbers of radios to open a strike-request network. Partridge also supplied FACs to every army unit down to regiment. North Korean resistance had almost ceased when on November 1, 1950, Partridge received a shock: fast Chinese People's Volunteer Army (CPVA, Chinese Army) MiG-15 jets operating from Manchuria attacked his F-51s, and his F-51s and F-80s could not match them in speed. But in December, Partridge received higher performance Republic F-84 Thunderjets and North American F-86 Sabre jets that prevented the MiGs from attacking EUSAK troops.

As the Eighth Army and X Corps withdrew before the Chinese onslaught, Partridge exerted every effort to provide air support. His most important mission was CAS. One new technique utilizing flares enabled Martin B-26 Marauders to attack at night. As a result, CPVA troops, who tended to remain concealed during the day and move at night, were often caught in the open and mauled. As United Nations Command (UNC) forces fell back before superior Chinese numbers, Partridge evacuated airfields at Pyongyang and elsewhere in the north, relying on Suwon, Taegu, Pusan, and even Japan.

In early 1951 Partridge's airmen discovered that the Chinese were improving airfields in northwest North Korea, in the area known as MiG Alley. Fearful that the Chinese would move fighter-bombers to these fields to support a spring ground offensive, Partridge ordered the fields to be repeatedly bombed to prevent their use. This campaign was successful, and the Chinese gave up their effort in July 1951. The CPVA Spring Offensive of 1951 thus had no air support, and the attackers on the ground paid a high price from artillery fire and Fifth Air Force bombs.

When Partridge departed Japan in the summer of 1951, his command had made substantial contributions to the UNC war effort. In his new assignment as head of the Air Research and Development Command during 1951–1953, Partridge focused on improving weapons used by airmen in Korea. One of his achievements was increasing the speed of the F-86 to make it more competitive with Chinese MiG-15s. During 1954–1955, Partridge returned to Japan as commander of Far East Air Forces (FEAF). After serving as chief of Continental Air Defense Command during 1955–1959, he retired from the air force in July 1959. In 1960 he became a trustee of the Aerospace Corporation. Partridge died on September 7, 1990, in Jupiter, Florida.

JOHN L. BELL

See also

MacArthur, Douglas; United States Air Force; Walker, Walton Harris

References

Appleman, Roy E. *United States Army in Korea: South to the Naktong, North to the Yalu.* Washington, DC: Office of the Chief of Military History, 1961.

Candee, Marjorie Dent, ed. *Current Biography, 1954.* New York: H. W. Wilson, 1955.

Futrell, Robert F. *The United States Air Force in Korea, 1950–1953.* Rev. ed. Washington, DC: Office of the Chief of Air Force History, 1983.

Partridge, Earle E. *Air Interdiction in World War II, Korea, and Vietnam: An Interview with Earle E. Partridge, Jacob E. Smart, and John W. Vogt.* Washington, DC: Office of Air Force History, U.S. Air Force, 1986.

Pearson, Lester Bowles
Birth Date: April 23, 1897
Death Date: December 27, 1972

Canadian politician, diplomat, and secretary of state for external affairs during the Korean War. Born in Newtonbrook, Ontario, on April 23, 1897, Lester Bowles Pearson began his professional career as a history professor but soon moved into the Canadian diplomatic service. He was first appointed secretary to the Canadian High Commission in London in 1935, and then held the same position in Canada's legation in Washington, DC, in 1942. Pearson became Canadian ambassador to the United States in 1945 and, the following year, deputy minister for external affairs in Ottawa. In 1948 Pearson ran for, and won, a seat in the Canadian House of Commons and a place in Prime Minister Louis St. Laurent's cabinet as secretary of state for external affairs. He was in this position when the Korean War broke out in June 1950.

The invasion of the Republic of Korea (ROK, South Korea) by the Democratic People's Republic of Korea (DPRK, North Korea) surprised Pearson, as did the decision by U.S. president Harry S. Truman's administration to become militarily involved in the war. Nonetheless, Pearson soon realized the need for Canadian participation in the United Nations (UN) force to be sent to Korea. Not only was he an ardent believer in collective security, but he also knew that Canada must participate if it was to have any influence in the operation. As the war evolved, Pearson became one of its most active diplomatic figures, especially in the UN, where he often headed the Canadian delegation. He was particularly important as president of the General Assembly during the crucial last phase of the war in 1952–1953, and he was heavily involved in attempting to influence the United States, which provided the lion's share of the troops in the United Nations Command (UNC).

Pearson and the Canadian government doubted the wisdom of having any involvement in Asia, believing that the focus of the Cold War lay in Europe and involved the North Atlantic Treaty Organization (NATO). However, if the battle against communism were to be fought in a limited way in Korea, then it would have to be under the UN umbrella. In addition, the Canadians saw the UN as a forum to influence U.S. policies, a view shared by the British and some other nations. Pearson used the UN to present a Canadian perspective of the Korean War, one that was limited and moderate in geographical extent, in strategy, and in ultimate goals.

Because of Pearson's activities in brokering UN policies on Korea, Washington sometimes saw him as either a nuisance or a counterproductive agent who seemed to work against the interests of the United States. Yet Pearson repeatedly emphasized his government's basic agreement with U.S. policy and its commitment to contain communist expansion. More than once he warned the Soviet Union not to assume that there was any breach in fundamental beliefs between the United States and Canada, and he insisted that Canada was still America's closest friend and staunchest ally.

Pearson tried to perform his balancing act of molding and restraining U.S. positions informally and discreetly. This was the quiet diplomacy of cajoling and prodding the United States into what Pearson and the Canadian leadership believed were more moderate policies toward the war. If this type of diplomacy failed, then the Canadians had to determine how important a specific issue was and whether it was worth publicly criticizing the Americans for it. On occasion, in a number of speeches to various groups, Pearson did "go public." This was a tactic guaranteed to infuriate the U.S. State Department.

Some of the issues that concerned Pearson during the war dealt with specific military strategy. For instance, the Canadian government did not want a widened war. Of primary concern was the possibility of doing anything that could bring the People's Republic of China (PRC) into the conflict. Because of that, General Douglas MacArthur's rhetoric and actions were often viewed with suspicion or even outright alarm. Canada agreed, but only with great reluctance, with the decision to have UNC forces move across the 38th Parallel into North Korea. Pearson believed that this act was done more to fulfill U.S. foreign policy goals than to enforce UN resolutions that called only for a restoration of the prewar status quo. The Canadian government opposed plans to bomb Chinese bases in Manchuria or pursue communist aircraft into Chinese airspace. Pearson was one of a number of Western leaders who was vocal in questioning MacArthur's role and who applauded his eventual dismissal.

Pearson was part of the UN Cease-fire Group that in late December 1950 tried to explore ways to end the fighting. On this issue he tended to agree more with the U.S. position of wanting a cease-fire on the battlefield before any substantive issues could be discussed. He and St. Laurent worked diligently with the Indian government to broker a compromise over the prisoner of war (POW) repatriation dispute, in this case breaking with the U.S. State Department and causing a good deal of hard feelings in Washington.

Pearson was also associated with the unsuccessful attempt to block a U.S.-sponsored UN condemnation of the Chinese as aggressors. He eventually voted with the U.S. on this resolution but still believed it to be an unwise step in the process of ending the war. In the spring of 1952, Pearson was openly upset over the use of Canadian troops, without prior consultation, to help guard rebellious prisoners on Koje-do, an island POW camp where the U.S. administration had failed badly at keeping order.

Pearson continued on at External Affairs after the war and in 1956 helped arrange a solution to the Suez Crisis, for which he received the Nobel Peace Prize in 1957. In 1958 he succeeded St. Laurent as leader of the Liberal Party, and in 1963 and 1965 became prime minister in minority governments. In that office he once more was critical of U.S. Asian policy, this time in Vietnam. Pearson retired from public life in 1967 and died in Ottawa on December 27, 1972.

ERIC JARVIS

See also

Canada; Cease-fire Negotiations; Koje-do Prisoner of War Uprising; MacArthur, Douglas; North Atlantic Treaty Organization; Repatriation, Voluntary; St. Laurent, Louis Stephen; 38th Parallel, Decision to Cross; United Nations Cease-Fire Group; Wrong, Humphrey Hume

References

Granatstein, J. L., and Norman Hillmer. *For Better or for Worse, Canada and the United States to the 1990s.* Toronto: Copp Clark Pitman, 1991.

Melady, John. *Korea: Canada's Forgotten War.* Toronto: Macmillan, 1983.

Stairs, Denis. *The Diplomacy of Constraint: Canada, the Korean War, and the United States.* Toronto: University of Toronto Press, 1974.

Stueck, William W., Jr. *The Korean War: An International History.* Princeton, NJ: Princeton University Press, 1995.

Peng Dehuai
Birth Date: October 24, 1898
Death Date: November 29, 1974

Marshal of the People's Republic of China (PRC); commander and political commissar of the Chinese People's Volunteer Army (CPVA, Chinese Army) during the Korean War. Born in Wushi Village, Xiangtan County, Hunan Province, on October 24, 1898, Peng Dehuai (Peng Te Huai) ran away from home as a child and supported himself by means of manual labor. In 1919 he joined the army and in 1920 became a lieutenant. He was then involved in an assassination attempt against Fu Liangzao, governor of Hunan Province, and was arrested. Nothing is known of the terms of his imprisonment.

In 1926 Peng joined the Guomindang (GMD, Nationalist) army with the rank of major and took part in the Northern Expedition. He secretly joined the Chinese Communist Party (CCP), and he left the GMD army in early 1928. That year he joined the CCP's Red Army, becoming the commander of its Fifth Army in 1936. During the Long March (1934–1935), he became one of Mao Zedong's closest lieutenants, second only to Lin Biao. Peng was vice commander of the Eighth Route Army under Zhu De during 1937–1945.

Peng's record as a military commander during the Chinese Civil War (1945–1949) was at best spotty. Of 29 battles he personally directed until 1949, he had 15 victories and 14 defeats. He fought best when fighting defensively for survival. He was less successful when fighting offensively, but he was an effective tactician and campaigner. He did not build a group of loyal supporters.

At the time of the outbreak of the Korean War, Peng was in northwest China (Xinjiang Province) consolidating CCP control. During the war he retained his posts as the deputy commander in chief of the People's Liberation Army (PLA, Chinese Communist Army) and commander of the First Field Army.

Peng commanded Chinese forces intervening in Korea from October 1950 to September 5, 1954. Peng arrived in northeast China in October to lead the intervention forces. He was officially named commander on October 8, the same day that the CPVA was ordered "to march speedily to Korea."

On October 10, 1950, Peng cabled Mao Zedong informing him that, contrary to Peng's original plan to send only two armies and two artillery divisions across the Yalu River, he now intended "to mass all forces south of the Yalu in case bridges are blown." Mao agreed with this plan, and on October 13, 1950, the Central Military Commission formally sanctioned sending Chinese troops into Korea.

Peng's forces began crossing the Yalu River on October 14, and on October 25 the CPVA had its first clashes with United Nations Command (UNC) forces. From October 1950 to June 1951 the Chinese fought five major "counterattacks" under Peng's direction, albeit with detailed guidance from the General Staff (Nie Rongzhen), Zhou Enlai, and Mao in Beijing. Zhou provided detailed guidance of all logistics operations and daily operations.

General Peng Dehuai commanded the Chinese People's Volunteer Army during the Korean War. In 1955 he was named 1 of 10 Chinese marshals. (Xinhua News Agency)

Peng initially attacked along the whole front in a series of three campaigns: October 25–November 1, 1950; mid-November 1950–December 12, 1950; and December 30, 1950–January 11, 1951. During late November or early December 1950, Mao Zedong's only son, Mao Anying, who served as Peng's Russian-language interpreter, died during a U.S. air attack on Peng's headquarters. Peng, who had been entrusted to protect Anying, blamed himself for the death.

During the Fourth Campaign, January 25–March 1951, the Chinese offensive broke down south and southeast of Seoul, and Li Tianyu was forced to evacuate Seoul on March 14. On April 22 Peng launched the Fifth Campaign with the aim of retaking Seoul, but UNC forces under Lieutenant General James A. Van Fleet broke the Chinese offensive north of Seoul. By May 21, 1951, the front line was at a standstill.

In July 1951 armistice negotiations began at Kaesong. Between May and July 1953 Peng launched a series of offensives against Old Baldy and Pork Chop Hill. On July 11, 1953, Chinese and Korean People's Army (KPA, North Korean Army) forces launched a massive five-army offensive against the Republic of Korea Army (ROKA, South Korean Army). The U.S. 3rd Division counterattacked, ending major communist forces' hostilities for the remainder of the war. Peng then concentrated on building elaborate defensive positions for what he later styled an "active defense in positional warfare."

On July 27, 1953, Peng signed the Armistice Agreement worked out at Panmunjom. Kim Il Sung awarded him the National Flag Order of Merit, First Class, and conferred on him the title "Hero of the Korean Democratic People's Republic" on July 31, 1953. Peng left the Democratic People's Republic of Korea (DPRK, North Korea) on August 11, 1953, returning to a hero's welcome in Tiananmen Square in Beijing. He resigned as the CPVA commander on September 5, 1954. Yang Dezhi of the North China (Fifth) Field Army succeeded him.

Peng viewed the Korean War more as a strategic than an operational success. In his memoirs he wrote, "signing the armistice, I thought that the war had set a precedent for many years to come—something the people could rejoice in." But Peng continued, "tactically the war revealed to the PLA's leaders just how weak their forces were and just how thin the line that separated success from failure. The victory had been nearly pyrrhic in nature."

The Korean War experience convinced Peng that the PLA needed to modernize its forces for conventional warfare. He placed priority on military training over politics and stressed the importance of modern equipment, professionalism, and new technology to support modern warfare. Following his time in Korea, Peng turned to the Soviet Union to provide a model for modernization and professionalism.

Appointed minister of defense at the First National People's Congress on September 28, 1954, Peng initiated a program for modernization of the PLA on October 1 when he issued Order No. 1, which required the PLA to study the Soviet models, grasp modern warfare, obey orders, and honor discipline. He initiated further reforms (the Four Great Systems) in 1955. On September 27, 1955, Peng was named one of 10 marshals of the PLA.

Mao Zedong dismissed Peng from all posts on September 17, 1959, accusing him of leading an "anti-Party clique." At the beginning of the Cultural Revolution (1966–1976), Peng was arrested and brought to Beijing, where he was publicly criticized between January and February 1967. He was imprisoned in April 1967 and later tortured. In 1974, when he fell seriously ill, Mao ordered that Peng receive no medical care. He died on November 29, 1974. Peng was posthumously rehabilitated as "a great revolutionary fighter and loyal member of the Party" at the Third Plenum of the 11th CCP in 1978.

SUSAN M. PUSKA

See also

China, People's Republic of, Army; Chinese People's Volunteer Army; Deng Hua; Gao Gang; Mao Zedong; Van Fleet, James Alward; Xie Fang; Zhou Enlai

References

Domes, Jurgen. *Peng Te Huai, The Man and the Image.* Stanford, CA: Stanford University Press, 1985.

Li Xiaobing, Bin Yu, and Allan R. Millett, eds. and trans. *Mao's Generals Remember Korea.* Lawrence: University Press of Kansas, 2001.

Peng Dehuai. *Memoirs of a Chinese Marshal: The Autobiographical Notes of Peng Dehuai (1989–1974).* Beijing: Foreign Language Press, 1984.

Whitson, William W., with Chen-Hsia Huang. *The Chinese High Command: A History of Communist Military Politics, 1927–71.* Westport, CT: Praeger, 1973.

Wilhelm, Alfred D., Jr. *The Chinese at the Negotiating Table.* Washington, DC: National Defense University Press, 1996.

Wilkinson, Mark F. *The Korean War at Fifty: International Perspectives.* Lexington, VA: John A. Adams Center for Military History and Strategic Analysis, 2004.

Zhang Shu Guang. *Mao's Military Romanticism: China and the Korean War, 1950–1953.* Lawrence: University Press of Kansas, 1995.

Peruvian Prisoner of War Settlement Proposal
Event Date: November 1952

Unimplemented United Nations (UN) resolution aimed at resolving the issue of repatriating prisoners of war (POWs). As armistice negotiations stalled, the main issue increasingly revolved around the question of repatriating POWs. The United States was pressing for voluntary repatriation of prisoners, while the People's Republic of China (PRC) and the Democratic People's Republic of Korea (DPRK, North Korea) insisted on a forced repatriation of all prisoners. The U.S. view had been shaped by the unfortunate results of forced repatriation after World War II, as well as by the composition and numbers of prisoners held by the United Nations Command (UNC). The PRC and DPRK were alarmed by the propaganda implications of the large numbers of their soldiers that the UNC claimed did not want to be repatriated.

The continuing impasse over repatriation produced a suspension in armistice talks in October 1952 and led to a number of offers of mediation by different countries, as well as proposals in the UN General Assembly—meeting that same month—to deal with the problem. One of the proposals for settling the POW controversy came from Peru, which submitted its proposition to the UN General Assembly on November 3, 1952. The centerpiece of the Peruvian plan was voluntary repatriation. The proposal called for the creation of a commission composed of representatives from the principal combatant nations as well as two representatives selected by the General Assembly. One neutral country that was not a member of the UN would also be invited to send a representative, who would serve as chair of the commission. The commission would preside over the immediate return of all prisoners who "freely expressed" a wish to be repatriated. Prisoners who declined repatriation would be located in a "neutralized zone"—neutral nations or UN Trust Territories—until a final agreement could be reached concerning their disposition. The UN never acted on the proposal, which was publicly rejected by the Soviet Union at the UN on November 10, 1952.

Although the Peruvian proposal was never implemented and had a brief diplomatic life span, it did help push forward a resolution of the repatriation issue. The United States was uneasy over the proposal's vagueness regarding treatment of those who refused repatriation, but U.S. diplomats frequently referred to the proposal in their discussions concerning an acceptable solution to the problem. U.S. Secretary of State Dean Acheson asked the Peruvian delegation to the UN to defer action on their proposal until the General Assembly considered a proposal from India dealing with repatriation. The Assembly approved the Indian proposal, and the Peruvian proposal, no longer needed, was never submitted to a vote. The Indian delegation admitted that their plan had been influenced by the Peruvian proposal and by another proposal put forward by the Mexican delegation.

The Peruvian POW proposal represented a long-standing interest of Latin American nations in mediating between the superpowers. In the context of the Korean War, it also demonstrated the general diplomatic support on most issues that the United States enjoyed among Latin American nations. On the specific issue of POWs, the proposal incorporated the most important point sought by the United States—no forced repatriation of prisoners.

DON M. COERVER

See also

Acheson, Dean Gooderham; Armistice Agreement; India; Latin America; Mexico; Padilla Nervo, Luis; Repatriation, Voluntary; Truce Talks

References

Houston, John A. *Latin America in the United Nations.* New York: Carnegie Endowment for International Peace, 1956.

Stueck, William W., Jr. *The Korean War: An International History.* Princeton, NJ: Princeton University Press, 1995.

———. *Rethinking the Korean War: A New Diplomatic and Strategic History.* Princeton, NJ: Princeton University Press, 2004.

U.S. Department of State, Bureau of Public Affairs. *Foreign Relations of the United States, 1950,* Vol. 7, *Korea.* Washington, DC: U.S. Government Printing Office, 1976.

———. *Foreign Relations of the United States, 1952–1954,* Vol. 15, Part I. Washington, DC: U.S. Government Printing Office, 1984.

Philippines

Southeast Asian nation encompassing 186,000 square miles with a 1950 population of 21.131 million people. An archipelago of 7,108 islands, the Philippines is located between the Philippine Sea and the South China Sea. The nation is south of Taiwan, north of Indonesia and eastern Malaya, and about 750 miles east of Vietnam. After receiving its independence from the United States in 1946, the Philippines, a constitutional republic with a president that is both head of state and government, was ruled by the Liberal Party, a center-left party. Elpidio Quirino, who succeeded Liberal Party president Manuel Roxas, served as president from 1948 to 1953.

Philippine interest in Korea was marked by various diplomatic initiatives before 1950. Its United Nations (UN) delegation endorsed a resolution passed on November 14, 1947, creating the UN Temporary Commission on Korea (UNTCOK), a body designed to oversee Korean elections. The UN General Assembly agreed with the U.S. recommendation that Manila should participate in UNTCOK. Filipino president Manuel Roxas assigned Senator Melecio Arranz, and then replaced him with Rufino Luna, as envoy to the commission. Luna supported an Interim Committee resolution of February 26, 1948, for elections in sections of Korea accessible to UNTCOK. According to Luna, an independent and unified Korea was the aim of the pending election. Roxas favored noninvolvement in Korea's domestic matters and a negotiated unity by Koreans themselves. The Philippines participated in additional UN agencies regarding the Korean Peninsula, such as the Commission on Korea (a follow-up to UNTCOK), the Additional Measures Committee, and the Commission on Unification and Rehabilitation of Korea.

Within UNTCOK the Philippine government encouraged U.S. efforts to recognize the Republic of Korea (ROK, South Korea). Manila tendered diplomatic acknowledgment on August 22, 1948, seven days after South Korean president Syngman Rhee's inauguration, but waited until February 1953 to institute official ties. The next year, Rhee considered a Pacific security pact, an idea promoted by Elpidio Quirino. Despite the fact that the idea originated from Thomas H. Lockett (an officer in the U.S. embassy in Manila) and Philippine interest, as reflected in a meeting between Quirino and Jiang Jieshi (Chiang Kai-shek) of the Republic of China (ROC, Taiwan), the United States objected and the proposition languished.

Once war began in June 1950, the Philippines, after briefly considering neutrality, endorsed the U.S. decision to stand behind South Korea. Now the recipient of increased U.S. military aid, the Quirino administration weighed the extent of Philippine entanglement. Since the General Military Council and opposition nationalist party resisted the employment of Filipinos beyond the homeland, Quirino pondered the use of volunteers or American-outfitted units.

At first Quirino limited Manila's contribution to the sending of material goods. But Philippine Foreign Minister Carlos Romulo and Filipino ambassador to the United States Joaquin Elizalde favored a troop commitment and labored to surmount the military and political obstacles. Before committees of the Philippine senate, Romulo argued that a troubled Korea's proximity meant repercussions for the archipelago and reasoned that the national constitution's repudiation of war still permitted military intervention. On August 10 the Philippine house approved a proposal to give "every possible assistance," and President Quirino initially committed a 5,000-man regimental combat team (RCT) to the United Nations Command (UNC). Senator Claro Recto, an advocate of an independent policy that shunned loyalty to the United States, scorned the decision.

The leading Philippine contingent reached Korea by September 19, 1950, with four battalions of combat units alternating in and out during the war. Early arrivals were provisioned from mutual security moneys allotted to Manila, with later equipment provided on a repay arrangement through the U.S. Eighth Army. Notwithstanding morale difficulties owing to cold weather and operational conditions, Filipino soldiers performed with merit. Some took part in Operation KILLER, begun on February 21, 1951, in which UNC and Republic of Korea Army (ROKA, South Korean Army) forces regained lost ground and advanced toward the Han River. A general retreat of UNC forces saw many Filipino troops taken prisoner. Despite two years of confinement and alleged indoctrination, none of the Filipino prisoners of war (POWs) became communists.

Although Philippine authorities supported the U.S. Korean policy, the Manila press defended General Douglas MacArthur after his dismissal. President Quirino asked him to make a stopover in the islands, but Ambassador Elizalde warned about partiality in the controversy. Meanwhile, the Philippines endorsed UN resolutions concerning the means of Korean unification; the establishment of a cease-fire; condemnation of, and sanctions against, the People's Republic of China (PRC); and an accounting of enemy atrocities against war prisoners. Manila supported the 1953 Armistice Agreement.

RODNEY J. ROSS

See also

Jiang Jieshi; KILLER, Operation; Rhee, Syngman; United Nations Additional Measures Committee; United Nations Commission for the Unification and Rehabilitation of Korea

References

Dobbs, Charles M. *The Unwanted Symbol: American Foreign Policy, the Cold War, and Korea, 1945–1950.* Kent, OH: Kent State University Press, 1981.

Meyer, Milton Walter. *A Diplomatic History of the Philippine Republic.* Honolulu: University of Hawaii Press, 1965.

Stueck, William W., Jr. *The Korean War: An International History.* Princeton, NJ: Princeton University Press, 1995.

Pierce, Robert Willard
Birth Date: October 8, 1914
Death Date: September 6, 1978

Christian evangelist and relief organizer. Robert (Bob) Willard Pierce was born on October 8, 1914, in Fort Dodge, Iowa. He studied for the ministry at Pasadena Nazarene College in California but did not graduate. In 1936 he began working as a traveling evangelist. Later, he briefly served as a youth pastor in the Los Angeles Evangelistic Center. In August 1944 Pierce joined the Youth for Christ (YFC) movement and became YFC vice president at large.

Pierce visited China as a YFC representative in July 1947 and returned a changed man, for he had found his mission—to aid the helpless and support missionary works in Asia. He produced his first Christian documentary film, *China Challenge,* which led to a Litt.D. degree from Northwestern College in Minneapolis. His focus now set on Asia, Pierce began planning visits to Japan and Korea.

In April 1950 Pierce visited the Republic of Korea (ROK, South Korea) and participated in the "Saving the Nation Evangelistic Crusade," preaching in Taegu, Pusan, Seoul, Taejon, and Inchon. About 25,000 new converts made public confessions during his nine-week tour. He also visited at least 40 high schools, speaking to as many as 100,000 students. He also met with South Korean president Syngman Rhee and preached to South Korean troops before he left in June.

Once the Korean War began, Pierce flew back to Korea as a war correspondent for the American Christian Press. He spent two weeks in Korea. When he saw the scope of the suffering caused by the war, he decided to make an appeal to the American people. Thus, on September 22, 1950, in Portland, Oregon, he formed World Vision, Inc., a missionary aid organization originally designed for Korean relief work.

Within a month Pierce was back in Korea, now as a United Nations (UN) war correspondent. He captured on film the plight of the many hundreds of thousands of refugees as they fled before advancing Korean People's Army (KPA, North Korean Army) and later Chinese People's Volunteer Army (CPVA, Chinese Army) troops. He also preached to U.S. troops and visited prisoner of war (POW) camps. In early 1951 he published *The Untold Story of Korea* and released a film, *The 38th Parallel,* which documents conditions in Korea prior to the Korean War. A year later he produced another emotion-packed documentary, *The Flame.* His graphic depiction of suffering women and children shocked many Americans and brought an outpouring of funds to purchase relief supplies. This period also marked the beginning of the World Vision Child Sponsorship Program.

Throughout the war, Pierce's radio broadcasts, films, and reports fueled the tremendous humanitarian response of American churches. His service was so deeply appreciated by the South Korean government that it awarded him three times the Medal for Public Welfare Service, Korea's highest award given to a foreigner.

In the ensuing decades, Pierce's interests in Asia continued. Indeed, his works expanded from Korea to India, Taiwan, Hong Kong, Japan, and Vietnam. After he resigned from World Vision in 1968, he began another relief organization, Samaritan's Purse. Pierce died on September 6, 1978, in Los Angeles, California.

KAI YIN ALLISON HAGA

See also

Churches and the War, U.S.; Relief Efforts, Missionary

References

Dunker, Marilee Pierce. *Man of Vision: The Candid, Compelling Story of Bob and Lorraine Pierce, Founders of World Vision and Samaritan Purse.* Waynesboro, GA: Authentic Media, 2005.

Haga, Kai Yin Allison. "An Overlooked Dimension of the Korean War: The Role of Christianity and American Missionaries in the Rise of Korean Nationalism, Anti-Colonialism, and Eventual Civil War,

1884–1953." Unpublished PhD dissertation, College of William and Mary, 2007.

Pierce, Bob. *The Korean Orphan Choir: They Sing Their Thanks.* Grand Rapids, MI: Zondervan Publishing House, 1965.

———. *The Untold Korean Story.* Grand Rapids, MI: Zondervan Publishing House, 1951.

PILEDRIVER, **Operation**
Start Date: June 1, 1951
End Date: June 13, 1951

Last United Nations Command (UNC) offensive of the Korean War, before the establishment of lines just north of the 38th Parallel. On May 27, 1951, U.S. Eighth Army in Korea (EUSAK) commander Lieutenant General James A. Van Fleet issued Operational Order PILEDRIVER, directing the Eighth Army to attack into the "Iron Triangle" (an area described by Pyonggang in the north, Chorwon in the west, and Kimhwa in the east), just north of the 38th Parallel, roughly in the center of the Korean Peninsula, which witnessed some of the fiercest fighting of the entire conflict. The purpose of the offensive was to solidify the UNC position along the Kansas-Wyoming Line.

The operation called for I Corps to drive to the areas bounded by Chorwon and Kimhwa; IX Corps to seize the area from Hwachon north to Samyang-ni; and X Corps to attack north from the east side of the reservoir and, with the Republic of Korea Army (ROKA, South Korean Army) I Corps, to seize the area to Kojin-ni on the east coast and clean out the Punchbowl north of Sohwa, another fortified zone that communist forces had previously used as a springboard for their offensives.

Van Fleet, who believed that communist forces were severely weakened and that a continuation of the UNC attack north could destroy them, expected rapid progress. When the operation commenced on June 3, however, UNC forces immediately encountered unexpectedly stiff resistance, particularly in the I Corps sector. In moving forward, the 1st Cavalry Division ran into three communist defensive lines in the Yonchon area. At the same time, the 3rd Division, attacking north toward Chorwon, met heavy resistance and was hit by a vicious Chinese People's Volunteer Army (CPVA, Chinese Army) counterattack; one of the division's battalions was driven back across the Hantan River. The 25th Division was also held up by tenacious Chinese troops defending the high ground on its objective.

The next day Lieutenant General Edward M. Almond's X Corps on the right flank resumed its attack toward the Punchbowl. For five days the battle raged. So little progress was made that the 7th Marines, on reserve after their rugged battle on the ridge, were sent to the front with the 1st Marines on their right and the ROKA Marines on their left. At 2:00 a.m. on June 11, the ROKA Marines took their Korean People's Army (KPA, North Korean Army) foes by surprise in a night attack, resulting in the wholesale slaughter

Private First Class Roman Prauty, a gunner with the 31st Regimental Combat Team, fires his 75-mm recoilless rifle in support of infantry units during Operation PILEDRIVER, on June 9, 1951. (Department of Defense)

of the North Koreans and allowing UNC forces to advance to the Punchbowl.

By June 10, aided by round-the-clock close air support (CAS), the 3rd Division, the ROKA 9th Division, and the 10th Philippine Battalion had gained the high ground south of Chorwon at the western foot of the triangle base, while the 25th Division and the Turkish Brigade fought to within three miles of Kimhwa. The next day the communists abandoned Chorwon and Kimhwa, and on June 13 two tank-infantry task forces, one from Chorwon and the other from Kimhwa, entered the ruins of Pyonggang, the apex of the triangle, and found it deserted as well. However, UNC forces discovered that the communists were positioned in strength on the high ground north of Pyonggang, and I Corps forces subsequently withdrew.

Units of IX Corps also pushed northeast from Kimhwa toward Kumsong and likewise found the line heavily defended by communist troops, who were in the process of establishing a strong defensive line. These UNC units also pulled back to Kimhwa.

Because the Iron Triangle was dominated by surrounding heights, neither side attempted thereafter to hold the low ground in strength, though Chinese troops struck back on June 17 and recaptured Pyonggang.

Operation PILEDRIVER had a twofold significance. First, it was the last offensive of the Korean conflict before the establishment of lines just north of the 38th Parallel. Second, the Iron Triangle would be from that point forward a no-man's-land, belonging to neither side.

JAMES H. WILLBANKS

See also

Almond, Edward Mallory; Iron Triangle; Kansas-Wyoming Line; Milburn, Frank William; Punchbowl; X Corps; Van Fleet, James Alward

References

Appleman, Roy E. *Ridgway Duels for Korea*. College Station: Texas A&M University Press, 1990.

Blair, Clay. *The Forgotten War: America in Korea, 1950–1953*. New York: Times Books, 1987.

Middleton, Harry J. *The Compact History of the Korean War.* New York: Hawthorn Books, 1965.

Rees, David. *Korea: The Limited War.* New York: St. Martin's, 1990.

Pistols

Pistols are short-range, personal sidearms generally carried by officers and specialized personnel.

Designed by John Browning, the U.S. .45-caliber Model 1911A1 pistol was the standard sidearm of U.S. forces in Korea. Adopted in 1911, the Model 1911 was a recoil-operated semiautomatic pistol that was fed by a seven-round magazine. The U.S. government also purchased commercially available sidearms, including the Colt .32 and .380-caliber automatic pistols, the Colt Detective Special Revolver, Colt Police Positive Revolver, Colt Special Official Police Revolver, and the Smith and Wesson Military and Police Revolver. All were chambered for the .38-caliber Special cartridge.

Other United Nations (UN) contingents, notably Belgium, France, and the United Kingdom, issued their own small arms. A John Browning design, the highly successful 9-millimeter (mm) FN Browning High Power Pistol served as the standard military sidearm of Belgium as well as of Denmark, the Netherlands, the Republic of China (ROC, Taiwan), the United Kingdom, and Canada. Originally manufactured by Fabrique Nationale d'Armes de Guerre (FN) of Herstal lez Liège, the High Power resembled Browning's earlier design, the Colt Model 1911A1, in appearance and mechanism. Significant changes included the 9-mm caliber and its 13-round magazine capacity.

There was also little standardization in French sidearm issues. Post–World War II armorers faced a logistical nightmare of captured German 9-mm P08 Lugers and P-38s, U.S. .45-caliber 1911s and 1911A1s, prewar French 7.65-mm M1935s, and the new French 9-mm M1950. The M1950 was a nine-round hybrid of the M1935 series and Colt 1911 series designs chambered for the 9-mm cartridge. It resembled its forbearers in both appearance and function.

The .38-caliber Enfield "Pistol" No. 2 Mark I was the standard sidearm of British Commonwealth troops. The Enfield was a six-chambered, top-break, double-action revolver. Its cousin, the No. 2 Mark I*, was introduced during World War II and was a double action–only weapon. Commonwealth troops also carried the Canadian Inglis-manufactured 9-mm Browning High Power, as well as numbers of U.S. Colt 1911s and 1911A1s, and obsolescent British .455-caliber Webley revolvers.

The most common sidearms in communist service were the German Mauser Models 1896 and 1912 "Broomhandles," and the Russian Tokarev Models 1895 and 1933. The Tokarev Model 1933 was a modified Browning design. The People's Republic of China (PRC) also manufactured the Model 1933, designating it as Type 51. The Model 1933 was a recoil-operated semiautomatic pistol that was fed by an eight-round magazine. The Soviets also furnished numbers of their obsolescent 7.62-mm Model 1895

double-action revolvers. The Mauser Model 1912 "Broomhandle" semiautomatic pistol was a particular favorite among Chinese troops. It was chambered for either the 7.63-mm Mauser cartridge or the 9-mm parabellum cartridge. China also produced a number of copies in U.S. caliber .45. The Mauser accepted a wooden shoulder stock/holster and was fed by a 10-round integral magazine.

JEFF KINARD

See also

Machine Guns; Rifles; Submachine Guns and Light Machine Guns

References

Hogg, Ian, and John Weeks. *Military Small Arms of the Twentieth Century.* Chicago: Follett, 1973.

Smith, W. H. B. *Small Arms of the World,* 9th ed. Harrisburg, PA: Stackpole, 1969.

Pleven Plan
Event Date: October 24, 1950

Plan proposed by French prime minister René Pleven in October 1950 to build an integrated, supranational West European defense force to repel potential Soviet threats. The plan was a natural successor to the Schuman Plan, which had sought to integrate the economy of the Federal Republic of Germany (FRG, West Germany) into the larger European economy, ultimately resulting in the European Coal and Steel Community (ECSC). The Pleven Plan was also a response to the deteriorating international situation, exacerbated by the September 1949 Soviet atomic bomb testing, the October 1949 victory of communist forces in the Chinese Civil War, and most critically, the outbreak of the Korean War in June 1950 and the large-scale commitment of U.S. forces to that theater. The French plan sought to integrate West Germany into a European defense structure without allowing Bonn to rearm unilaterally. French leaders also did not relish the idea of West German admittance to the North Atlantic Treaty Organization (NATO). Thus, the Pleven Plan would have effectively bypassed such a scenario.

In 1949 the United States, Great Britain, and France agreed that to defend Germany properly required the restoration of its autonomy. Most American and European policy makers were convinced that only a fully integrated Germany could stanch the threat of internal communist subversion or, worse still, a military invasion from the East. They did not agree, however, on the means by which to achieve this integration.

The defense of Germany and the restoration of its role as an equal partner caused the Western governments to realize that rearming Germany would require a German military contribution, but not one in which Germany acted unilaterally. The Americans, British, and French thought that the best way to achieve such a goal would be in establishing an integrated European force.

In September 1950, at the New York conference of foreign ministers, the Americans proposed an integrated European army under the aegis of NATO, in which German military units would have no capacity for independent action. This army would be led by a NATO commander—the Supreme Allied Commander Europe (SACEUR)—with a sizable American military contribution. French concerns about a rehabilitated Germany caused Paris initially to balk at this plan.

On October 24, 1950, Pleven announced a plan of his own for a European army. Worked out by Jean Monnet, the French architect of West European integration, this project aimed at avoiding any autonomous German control over German troops. According to the Pleven Plan, German troops were to be recruited and trained not by the German government but rather by a supranational European army integrated within the existing NATO military structures, alongside NATO troops. The plan would include a European defense minister responsible to the control and supervision of a European assembly. German armed forces would thus exist only within an integrated European military arrangement.

Both the British and the Germans opposed the Pleven Plan. The British believed that instead of leading to the creation of an Atlantic Community, such an arrangement would dilute Atlanticism by excluding direct American involvement. It would also, they pointed out, complicate—or even duplicate—the existing organizational structures of NATO. Bonn rejected the plan because German troops would clearly be in a subservient role. Moreover, it was a project that would have required member nations to relinquish a certain degree of national sovereignty, which did not sit well.

Soon the plan evolved into the abortive European Defense Community (EDC), debated at length by the Western alliance and finally defeated, rather ironically, by the French themselves in 1954. By then, with American reassurances of protection, the presence of British troops in Germany, and the end of the Korean War, many of France's fears concerning a resurgent, belligerent Germany were allayed, and the Pleven Plan and the EDC were subsumed by the admission of West Germany into NATO.

SIMONE SELVA AND PAUL G. PIERPAOLI JR.

See also

European Defense Community; France; Germany, Federal Republic of; North Atlantic Treaty Organization

References

Ruane, Kevin. The *Rise and Fall of the European Defense Community: Anglo-American Relations and the Crisis of European Defense, 1950–55.* New York: St. Martin's, 2000.

Trachtenberg, Marc. *A Constructed Peace: The Making of the European Settlement, 1945–1963.* Princeton, NJ: Princeton University Press, 1999.

Plimsoll, James

Birth Date: April 25, 1917
Death Date: May 8, 1987

Australian diplomat and representative on the United Nations Commission for the Unification and Rehabilitation of Korea

James Plimsoll (right), chairman of the United Nations Interim Korean Commission, is greeted by T. W. Eckersley, acting head of the diplomatic mission in Tokyo, on Plimsoll's arrival at Haneda Airport, Tokyo, on November 15, 1950. (AP/Wide World Photos)

(UNCURK), 1950–1952. Born in Sydney, Australia, on April 25, 1917, James Plimsoll was educated at Sydney High School and the University of Sydney. He spent four years working in the Economics Department of the Bank of New South Wales before joining the Australian army in 1942. In 1945, while still in the military, he became a member of the Australian delegation to the Far Eastern Commission, a post he held for several years. This experience impelled him to change his career and become a professional diplomat. While on the Far Eastern Commission, he indicated to John M. Allison, then chief of the U.S. State Department's Division of Northeast Asian Affairs, that Australians would find a moderate Japanese peace settlement enabling that country to regain its international position far more tolerable if it were coupled with a security pact between Australia and the United States. This was also the position taken by Sir Percy Spender, who became Australia's minister of external affairs shortly afterward.

On October 8, 1950, the United Nations (UN) established UNCURK. This came at a time when UN officials optimistically anticipated victory in Korea in the near future but were by no means delighted by the prospect that Syngman Rhee, the autocratic leader of the Republic of Korea (ROK, South Korea), would simply extend his authority over the entire country. UNCURK was a seven-nation body, the representatives of which were expected to arrive in Korea in mid-November. Meanwhile, they were to form an Interim Committee to "assume provisionally all responsibilities" for governing the Democratic People's Republic of Korea (DPRK, North Korea) until arrangements for unifying the country could be finalized. Plimsoll was appointed Australia's representative on UNCURK, and he immediately set to work attempting to draft an acceptable scheme for nationwide elections that would not necessarily result in a government controlled by Rhee, and for interim arrangements that would ensure that the United Nations Command (UNC), not Rhee, governed UN-occupied North Korean territory.

Plimsoll arrived in Korea in late November, by which time Chinese People's Volunteer Army (CPVA, Chinese Army) intervention had eradicated prospects of any imminent UNC victory. Even so, UNCURK's personnel remained in Korea, despite the dilution of their authority when the UN subsequently established both the UN Cease-fire Group and the UN Korean Reconstruction Agency. One major reason for this continued presence in Korea was the fact that the fairly youthful and inexperienced Plimsoll swiftly found himself on a personal footing with the elderly and intractable Rhee. This enabled him to exert a certain moderating influence on that authoritarian leader's policies. Plimsoll was heavily involved in UNCURK's efforts to restrain the South Korean police and prison authorities.

Plimsoll cooperated closely with U.S. ambassador John J. Muccio in these efforts, a relationship that helped to reinforce the developing Australian-American alliance. U.S. officials, appreciative of Plimsoll's role, strongly resisted his government's attempts to assign him to other duties and insisted that he remain in Korea. They argued that only by staffing UNCURK with representatives of Plimsoll's high caliber could the commission win respect and acceptance.

The climax of Plimsoll's service on UNCURK came in the South Korean political crisis of mid-1952, after Rhee declared martial law and arrested opposition members of the National Assembly so as to force the passage of a constitutional amendment likely to win him a third term as president. In a personal interview with Rhee, Plimsoll warned him that his behavior had shocked other countries throughout the world and that it would jeopardize continuing UN support for South Korea. Plimsoll subsequently served as an important intermediary in Western negotiations with Rhee, although the stubborn president effectively came through this crisis victoriously, obtaining the constitutional amendment he sought and winning a landslide election in August.

In late 1952, when an armistice in Korea seemed imminent and the victory of Dwight D. Eisenhower in the U.S. presidential elections was about to remove many of Plimsoll's most fervent American admirers, the Australian government finally recalled him to Canberra to be assistant secretary of the Department of External Affairs. In his later career, he served with distinction as secretary of the department; as ambassador to Washington, Moscow, and

Tokyo; and as high commissioner in London. In 1982 Plimsoll was appointed governor of Tasmania. He died at Government House, Hobart, on May 8, 1987.

Priscilla Roberts

See also

Eisenhower, Dwight David; Muccio, John Joseph; Rhee, Syngman; United Nations Commission for the Unification and Rehabilitation of Korea

References

Luard, Evan. *A History of the United Nations*, Vol. 1, *The Years of Western Domination, 1945–1955*. London: Macmillan, 1982.

O'Neill, Robert J. *Australia in the Korea War, 1950–1953*. 2 vols. Canberra: Australian War Memorial/Australian Government Publishing Service, 1981, 1985.

Stueck, William W., Jr. *The Korean War: An International History*. Princeton, NJ: Princeton University Press, 1995.

Yoo, Tae Ho. *The Korean War and the United Nations*. Louvain, Belgium: Librairie Desbarax, 1964.

Pohang, Battle of
Start Date: July 1950
End Date: September 1950

Battle that was part of the communist plan to take the Pusan Perimeter at the beginning of the Korean War. By the end of the summer in 1950 the initial Korean People's Army (KPA, North Korean Army) thrust to crush the Pusan Perimeter had failed. Only in the east had the lines of the perimeter defense changed markedly. There Republic of Korea Army (ROKA, South Korean Army) defenses had collapsed against a renewed KPA attack on Yongdok, and the 3rd ROKA Division had to be evacuated by sea. The ROKA then went back into action against the KPA, which by this time had moved into the east coast port of Pohang. ROKA troops retook the town, but with the KPA so close, the U.S. Air Force (USAF) evacuated its nearby base at Yonil (USAF Field K-3). The KPA command ordered its 12th Division to attack through the ROKA 8th Division behind the Yongdok front and capture Pohang by July 26, 1950. However, ROKA forces fought tenaciously, and it was the end of July before the KPA reached the outskirts of Andong.

In early August there was an uneasy lull in the fighting across the entire front as both sides girded for the next round of bitter fighting. By August 15 the only KPA hope for victory was to launch a massive coordinated offensive around the perimeter before the United Nations Command (UNC) forces got any stronger. Two new KPA divisions were brought up for this offensive, making an assault force of 13 infantry divisions, 1 armored division, and 2 armored brigades. The KPA renewed their attacks all along the Pusan Perimeter.

U.S. Eighth Army in Korea (EUSAK) commander Lieutenant General Walton Walker called this new KPA offensive the "last gasp" of an "over-extended enemy." Nevertheless, it was a

The U.S. Navy heavy cruiser *Helena* fires 10 8-inch shells to drop two spans of a bridge at Kanggu Hang, 23 miles north of Pohang, during heavy fighting in the summer of 1950. (Naval Historical Center)

forceful move, and the Pusan Perimeter almost cracked in several places. In the east, KPA forces from the 5th and 12th divisions retook Pohang on September 3, despite an intense U.S. sea and land bombardment. The battle for the town consumed five days and resulted in heavy casualties in the KPA divisions as well as in the defending ROKA 3rd and Capital divisions, both of which had given way and then suddenly collapsed in the face of the KPA assault.

The KPA continued to push to the south to the outskirts of Kyongju, and at Yongchon they cut the lateral road running east from Taegu, threatening this key city from the "back door."

Walker moved up everything he could spare to stop the KPA advance: the 21st Infantry Regiment, units of the 19th Regiment, and finally the 24th Division, whose place along the Naktong River had been taken by the 2nd Infantry Division. With this assistance and highly effective support from warships firing from offshore, ROKA forces finally rallied sufficiently to retake some of the lost ground. In the end, however, the KPA offensive in the east collapsed as much from its logistical difficulties as from anything else.

JAMES H. WILLBANKS

See also
Pusan Perimeter and Breakout; Walker, Walton Harris

References

Alexander, Bevin. *Korea: The First War We Lost.* New York: Hippocrene Books, 1986.

Appleman, Roy E. *United States Army in Korea: South to the Naktong, North to the Yalu.* Washington, DC: Office of the Chief of Military History, 1961.

Blair, Clay. *The Forgotten War: America in Korea, 1950–1953.* New York: Times Books, 1987.

Point Four Program

Foreign-aid program of President Harry S. Truman, announced in January 1949 and first funded beginning in 1950. As the Cold War deepened in 1947–1948, the Truman administration sought ways to keep communist influences out of the developing world. A major part of this effort took the form of direct and indirect assistance to nations of the developing world in technical assistance, loans, investments, and the like. The Point Four Program marked an attempt to fulfill those goals and acted as a sort of Marshall Plan to poorer nations. Point Four, however, was on a scale far less grand than that of the Marshall Plan. The program received its name because it was the fourth point of Truman's foreign policy

A nurse visits a family in La Paz, Bolivia, through the Servicio Cooperativo Interamericano de Salud Publica, a cooperative Point Four Program, on February 13, 1951. (National Archives)

initiatives enunciated in his inaugural address on January 20, 1949.

The Point Four Program began in earnest in early 1950. As policy makers weighed their options as to what types of aid should be emphasized, a consensus soon emerged that technical assistance to the developing world was the single best way to effect change there. The focal point of such aid would be in the areas of education, agriculture, public health, and medical care. The U.S. government relied principally on the private sector to plan and build the necessary infrastructure, which it reimbursed in cash, tax credits, or other types of incentives. All but a small amount of the aid that went to the Point Four Program was administered bilaterally between the United States and recipient nations through the U.S. Department of State's Technical Cooperation Administration.

The Point Four Program was, in the end, rather limited in scope. It had no sooner gotten off the ground when the Korean War began in June 1950. The war shifted the U.S. focus from international aid programs such as Point Four to rearmament and military readiness. Furthermore, after the Korean War, a good

deal of Point Four assistance tended to be funneled into military and military support programs in recipient nations, rather than to educational, health care, or agricultural endeavors.

The advent of Dwight D. Eisenhower's presidency in January 1953 marked the practical end of the Point Four Program as a stand-alone entity. Eisenhower, who eschewed handing out large amounts of foreign aid (at least in his first term), ordered the Point Four Program absorbed into general foreign assistance programs. Although Point Four's immediate legacy was quite modest, it did set the stage for such future programs as the International Finance Corporation (1956), the Inter-American Development Bank (1961), and the Alliance for Progress (1961).

PAUL G. PIERPAOLI JR.

See also
Marshall Plan

References
Kaufman, Burton I. *Trade and Aid: Eisenhower's Foreign Economic Policy, 1953–1961.* Baltimore, MD: John Hopkins University Press, 1982.

Mack, Robert T., Jr. *Raising the World's Standard of Living: The Coordination and Effectiveness of Point Four, United Nations Technical Assistance, and Related Programs.* New York: Citadel Press, 1953.

Police Action

Term used by President Harry S. Truman to describe the U.S. military response in the Korean War. Article I, Section 8, of the U.S. Constitution reserves for Congress the right to declare war. In this, the framers of the constitution sought to place the power to wage war with the people through their elected representatives, as opposed to placing this authority with the executive branch or with the cabinet, as in the British system.

Truman's action was not unique. Earlier U.S. presidents had temporarily committed U.S. military forces without a formal declaration of war; the Barbary Wars and Quasi-War with France are but two examples. In the case of Korea, however, there was not the excuse of a direct attack on U.S. citizens or their property, and none of the other deployments solely on the basis of presidential authority had been as long term or as costly.

On June 27, 1950, citing the threat posed by international communism and in what he called the most difficult decision of his presidency, Truman committed U.S. forces to the Korean fighting without a congressional vote. Only after the fact did he communicate this decision to his cabinet and to congressional leaders of both parties.

Truman's message to the American people amounted to a declaration of war in which he not only committed U.S. fighting forces to Korea but also announced an acceleration of military assistance to France for its war in Indochina. Truman, while he did not originate the phrase himself, agreed with a newsman's characterization of the fighting in Korea as a "police action." This connoted what Truman sought: a short and limited action. He also said U.S. forces had merely to defeat "a bandit raid." When pressed on the matter, he cited as justification the United Nations (UN) Security Council resolution calling on member states to provide military support to the Republic of Korea (ROK, South Korea), although its passage came after Truman had committed U.S. forces to active participation in the war.

In effect, Truman brought the United States into a war by executive decision through the guise of UN resolutions. The president believed that he had to act quickly, but his decision to proceed on his own vastly increased presidential power set a precedent that surfaced again during the Vietnam War, when President Lyndon B. Johnson used the August 1964 Tonkin Gulf Resolution as justification for waging an undeclared war in Indochina. Of course, Congress can halt any U.S. military venture simply by cutting off funding, but such action is quite difficult once troops have been committed and American blood has been shed.

SPENCER C. TUCKER

See also
Truman, Harry S.

References
Javits, Jacob K. *Who Makes War: The President versus the Congress.* New York: William Morrow, 1973.
LaFeber, Walter. *The American Age: United States Foreign Policy at Home and Abroad, 1750 to the Present.* New York: Norton, 1994.
Truman, Harry S. *Memoirs.* 2 vols. Garden City, NY: Doubleday, 1956.

Pongam-do Prisoner of War Uprising
Event Date: December 14, 1952

Communist prisoner of war (POW) uprising that occurred at United Nations Command (UNC) Camp No. 1C on Pongam-do, a small island west of Koje-do and near Pusan, in the Republic of Korea (ROK, South Korea). The UNC garrison on Pongam-do consisted of about 100 U.S. administrative personnel and a Republic of Korea Army (ROKA, South Korean Army) security battalion. The camp had two separate areas that housed civilian internees (CIs). These CIs had been held in the infamous Compound 62 on Koje-do, which had erupted with violence on February 18, 1952. They had been transferred to Pongam-do in July, when the large Koje-do compounds were broken up.

Between December 7 and 13, POW camp authorities on Pongam-do intercepted several messages indicating imminent coordinated riots. Concerned that the CIs might break out of their enclosures, the commanding general of the Korean Communications Zone, Major General Thomas W. Herren, alerted the UNC to his possible need for reinforcements from the mainland. On December 12, however, he informed the commander in chief of the UNC that he believed no immediate danger of a mass breakout existed and that prisoner plans were not of a nature to warrant additional reinforcements. Meanwhile, the camp commander took the precaution of doubling his alert forces to provide for any contingency.

At noon on Sunday, December 14, 1952, CIs in Enclosure 2 began mass demonstrations in their respective compounds. An estimated 3,600 of some 9,200 prisoners in six of the eight compounds of Enclosure 2 were involved in the riot, but Enclosure 1 was quiet. The probable prisoner objective was to break out of the compounds and capture UNC personnel to bargain with camp authorities and embarrass the UNC. The instigators also sought to influence negotiations at the truce talks then in progress and to provoke world opinion.

The camp on Pongam-do was situated on steep, terraced, and windswept terrain. The approach to the buildings housing the POWs was from below, an aid to prisoners throwing stones and other objects down on the guards. It also inhibited the effective use of such mass-control weapons as concussion and tear-gas grenades. In any case, at the time of the uprising, the wind was blowing across the steep hill, and tear gas could not be used effectively.

Prominent POW Uprisings during the Korean War

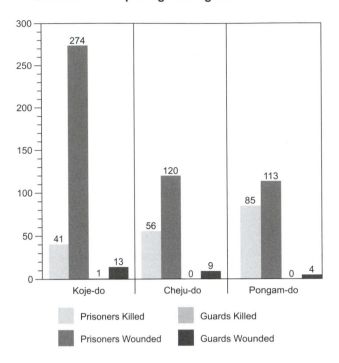

of special riot-type weapons. Other incidents at Pongam-do later in December, while on a smaller scale, resulted in the deaths of 14 CIs and injuries to an additional 86.

SUNGHUN CHO

See also

Koje-do Prisoner of War Uprising; Prisoner of War Administration, United Nations Command

References

Cho, Sunghun. "Hanguk Chonjaeng Chung UN Kun ui Poro Chongchaek e Kwanhan Yongu" [A Study of UN Forces POW policies during the Korean War]. PhD dissertation, Academy of Korean Studies, Seoul, 1999.

Headquarters U.S. Army Pacific. "The Handling of Prisoners of War during the Korean War." 1960. Unpublished document.

Millett, Allan R. *Their War in Korea: American, Asian, and European Combatants and Civilians, 1945–1953*. Princeton, NJ: Princeton University Press, 2002.

If the use of tear gas had been possible, the riot quite probably would have been quelled with fewer fatalities.

Orders, warning shots, and riot guns had no effect on the demonstrating POWs. The limited number of security personnel available also inhibited camp authorities. This situation prevented the simultaneous dispatch of significant numbers to each of the six compounds involved. As a result, almost from the start of the rioting, camp authorities resorted to machine gun and rifle fire to prevent a mass outbreak. Clearly, the threat of another Koje-do situation conditioned events.

Camp authorities soon quelled the riot, and throughout the disturbances they maintained uncontested control. In the course of suppressing the demonstrations, however, 85 prisoners were killed and another 113 were wounded. The injured were later moved to the field hospital at nearby Koje-do. Two U.S. soldiers and two ROKA soldiers were injured by thrown rocks.

At Panmunjom, communist truce negotiators condemned the actions by the UNC in suppressing the demonstration, questioning why it was necessary to shoot prisoners who were shouting slogans and demonstrating. They demanded that the UNC take immediate steps to end such "brutalities." The Soviet Union even submitted to the UN General Assembly on December 21, 1952, a protest over the "mass murder of Korean and Chinese POWs" by U.S. armed forces on Pongam-do.

Although the Soviet UN resolution failed to pass, killings of POWs, no matter how justified, caused the UNC considerable embarrassment. The Pongam-do uprising revealed the need for intensive training for security personnel in riot control and the use

Pork Chop Hill, Battle of
Start Date: March 23, 1953
End Date: July 11, 1953

Name given to a number of small, violent battles fought during the Korean War on and around the western side of the Korean Peninsula near the 38th Parallel. Hill 234 became known as Pork Chop Hill because of its shape. The hill was originally taken from the Chinese People's Volunteer Army (CPVA, Chinese Army) by United Nations Command (UNC) forces on June 6, 1952, and was made into a defensive outpost, one of many such positions making up the UNC line.

The UNC outposts were located on hills or ridges and were built for all-around defense. It was a system, created by the stalemated nature of the war in 1952–1953, that emphasized small-group combat fought on a seemingly endless number of hills crossing the center of the peninsula. Victories in these engagements were used, particularly by the Chinese who usually initiated the combat, as propaganda in the long-running peace talks being held at Panmunjom.

In November 1952 CPVA troops attacked Pork Chop Hill, which was successfully defended by a battalion from Thailand. The most serious attempts to capture the hill, however, came in the spring and summer of 1953. On March 23 the CPVA launched simultaneous assaults against Pork Chop Hill and the nearby hill known as Old Baldy. Old Baldy was lost by UNC forces, but a U.S. battalion managed to hang on to a portion of Pork Chop Hill; a counterattack retook all of the hill on March 24. U.S. Eighth Army in Korea (EUSAK) headquarters then decided to give up Old Baldy, but Pork Chop Hill, which now stuck out into the communist lines, was maintained as a fortified outpost.

Perhaps the best known of the struggles for the hill began after 10:00 p.m. on April 16, 1953. By moving swiftly and silently, CPVA

Medical personnel assist a U.S. soldier from Pork Chop Hill. He had been wounded during the heavy fighting there during March–July 1953. (The Army Historical Foundation)

troops managed to arrive at Pork Chop Hill practically unobserved and penetrate the UNC defenses. They overwhelmed an under-strength U.S. force of only 76 men, including 20 who were strung out at listening posts in front of the hill, and 5 more who were on patrol at the time. This patrol was the only group that had seen the oncoming Chinese force, but it had been unable to relay a message back to the men on Pork Chop. In conjunction with a small number of survivors who had eluded the Chinese, attempts were then launched to try to retake the hill starting in the early hours of April 17 and lasting into the next day.

The UNC did not at first realize just how complete the CPVA's success had been, and as a result many of the units that moved up the rear of the hill were surprised when they came under communist fire almost immediately. They were routinely thrown back or cut off and surrounded. Confusion was common, and one U.S. unit even fired into one of its own companies by mistake. There were also shortages of water and ammunition and a lack of communication with headquarters. During the battle both sides pounded the hill with unusually heavy artillery barrages that had the effect of pinning everyone in their dugouts and battered trenches, thereby preventing either side from advancing successfully.

Throughout the battle, EUSAK command had to decide how many men it was prepared to lose in order to retake and hold Pork Chop Hill. This decision was dependent on the importance of preventing the Chinese from flaunting a victory at Panmunjom. In the end, it was determined that the hill must be kept, and a final

assault led to the recapture of the heights on April 18. Sporadic fighting for Pork Chop Hill continued into the summer of 1953.

What finally underlined the futility of the Battle of Pork Chop Hill was the decision later made by high command to give the hill back to the Chinese. The evacuation of the hill took place without difficulty on July 11, two weeks before the armistice. In a way, Pork Chop Hill symbolized the last two years of the Korean War. It was an example of the hopeless, bloody stalemate into which the war had devolved, and it pointed toward the type of limited warfare that both military personnel and civilians found to be so frustrating during the era of the Cold War. Pork Chop Hill ended up within the demilitarized zone (DMZ) created to separate the Republic of Korea (ROK, South Korea) and the Democratic People's Republic of Korea (DPRK, North Korea) at the war's conclusion.

ERIC JARVIS

See also

Chinese Offensives, Summer; Eighth Army, U.S.; Film and the Korean War; Literature of the Korean War, Korean; Literature of the Korean War, U.S.; Marshall, Samuel Lyman Atwood; Old Baldy, Battle of; Truce Talks

References

Hastings, Max. *The Korean War.* New York: Simon and Schuster, 1987.
Hermes, Walter G. *U.S. Army in the Korean War: Truce Tent and Fighting Front.* Washington, DC: Office of the Chief of Military History, 1966.
Marshall, S. L. A. *Pork Chop Hill: The American Fighting Man in Action, Korea, Spring, 1953.* New York: William Morrow, 1956.

Potsdam Conference
Start Date: July 17, 1945
End Date: August 2, 1945

Diplomatic conference at the end of World War II held in Potsdam, Germany, southwest of Berlin, from July 17 to August 2, 1945. The overall goals of the meeting, code-named "Terminal," included reaching agreement on how to manage postwar Germany, implement policies designed to bring about long-term peace in Europe, foster postwar rehabilitation in areas adversely affected by World War II, and deal with the Soviet entrance into the Pacific war. The conference participants also witnessed the Soviet Union accede to the principles of the December 1943 Cairo Declaration and discussed the future of Korea, albeit briefly.

The principals at Potsdam included President Harry S. Truman representing the United States, Joseph Stalin representing the Soviet Union, and Winston Churchill representing Great Britain. During the conference Churchill was ousted by British election results; Labour Party leader Clement Attlee replaced him.

Stalin demanded heavy reparations from Germany for the vast damage suffered by the Soviet Union in the war. He held out for a firm figure whereas Truman would agree only to the Soviet Union receiving a set percentage of a whole to be determined by the Germans' capacity to pay. The U.S. delegation also disagreed with the

U.S. president Harry Truman (center) shakes the hands of British prime minister Winston Churchill (left) and Soviet premier Joseph Stalin (right) during the first day of the Potsdam Conference in Germany, July 25, 1945. (Harry S. Truman Presidential Library)

Soviets over their very loose interpretation of "war booty," goods that could be confiscated without reference to reparations. Agreement was reached at Potsdam, however, that the Soviets would receive 25 percent of plants and industrial equipment removed from the Western zones. In return, the Soviets were to repay 15 of the total 25 percent in food and raw materials from their zone. The Soviets also received permission to seize German assets in Bulgaria, Hungary, Finland, Romania, and their zone of Austria. No agreement on reparations was ever reached, but it is estimated that the Soviets probably took about $20 billion (the total sum discussed at the Yalta Conference) from their zone of Germany alone.

The Allies also reached agreement on the "three D's" of democratization, denazification, and demilitarization. German leaders were also to be punished as war criminals, and that nation's resources were to be used to repair the damages that had been inflicted on its neighbors during the war. German industrial production was set at a level no higher than the average for Europe as a whole.

Korea was also a subject of discussion. Having agreed only on the need for a trusteeship as basic to the postwar status of Korea at the February 1945 Yalta Conference, U.S. diplomats at first hoped for further consideration of specifics about this formula at Potsdam. State Department officials regarded the Korean

Peninsula as a strategic area that could not be abandoned to the Soviet Union. During World War II, they developed a plan for a four-power trusteeship leading to the eventual independence of a unified Korean state. China, Great Britain, the Soviet Union, and the United States would share administrative responsibility for the territory until the Korean people were "ready" for independence according to the principles proclaimed in the Cairo Declaration. Truman's predecessor, President Franklin D. Roosevelt, believed that joint involvement in Korea would substitute cooperation for conflict in how Korea's neighbors dealt with this strategic country, as well as force the Soviets to assume equal responsibility for preserving peace and stability in the region. At the end of May 1945, during talks with presidential envoy Harry Hopkins, Stalin informally accepted the administrative scheme as the best solution for Korea. U.S. ambassador to the Soviet Union W. Averell Harriman confirmed in early July that the Soviets had embraced the proposal after talks with the Chinese and that they looked forward to a detailed examination of the arrangements at Potsdam.

The consultation never took place. This was because Truman, shortly after replacing Roosevelt as president, had begun to search for an alternative to trusteeship in Korea. Soviet imposition of control over Eastern Europe persuaded him that Stalin would seek the same outcome in East Asia. News of the successful testing of the atomic bomb on July 16 convinced the president that the United States could force Japan to surrender after an atomic attack and before the Soviets could declare war. This would allow the United States to occupy Korea unilaterally and avoid the possibility of "sovietization" in Korea. Truman did not raise the issue of Korea at Potsdam. When Stalin opened discussion of the trusteeship concept in general on July 22, with the suggestion that Korea be the first issue, British prime minister Churchill immediately turned the conversation to the subject of the Italian colonies in Africa. Churchill accused the Soviets of coveting these territories and using the trusteeship concept to get a foot in the door. The talks then slowly dissolved in acrimony.

Thereafter, Truman largely avoided the topic of Korea at the conference. Indeed, Truman seemed to take a tougher stance with the Soviets, buoyed as he was by the knowledge that the United States had developed an atomic weapon. Unlike American diplomats, U.S. military officials did not regard the Korean Peninsula as strategic. Their primary focus was securing an end to fighting in the Pacific Theater and invading the Japanese home islands. Accordingly, they reached agreement with their Soviet counterparts for shared responsibility divided at the 39th Parallel in Korea for military operations against Japan. But by early August, Operation BLACKLIST was developed, providing for prompt U.S. military occupation of Korea following Japan's surrender.

On July 26 the U.S. and British leaders issued a surrender ultimatum to Japan. Designed to weaken Japanese resistance to accepting defeat, the Potsdam Declaration held out some hope to the Japanese for the future. Although their country would be disarmed, occupied, and shorn of its conquests, Japan would be allowed access to raw materials after the war and have the opportunity for democratic development. If, however, Japanese leaders refused to surrender, the nation would be destroyed. The Soviet Union, several weeks away from a declaration of war against Japan, was not a party to this proclamation. After Japan's rejection of the Potsdam Declaration, the United States dropped an atomic bomb on Hiroshima on August 6. Two days later, the Soviet Union declared war on Japan, and four days after that the Red Army advanced into Korea.

On August 10 Japan requested surrender terms from the United States. In General Order Number One, the United States proposed that the dividing line for the acceptance of the surrender of Japanese forces in Korea be the 38th Parallel, which Stalin accepted without argument. The failure of Truman's gamble meant that, instead of unilateral U.S. occupation, no agreement was reached regarding the future of Korea until the December 1945 meeting in Moscow of the foreign ministers of China, Great Britain, the United States, and the Soviet Union. In the interim, the Soviet Union had become an indirect partner to the Cairo Declaration through both the Potsdam Declaration and its entry into the war against Japan. The Korean Peninsula had been liberated and occupied by Soviet and U.S. troops north and south of the 38th Parallel, respectively. Any diplomatic agreement, therefore, would be effective only if the occupiers could cooperate in arriving at an accord, which became increasingly more difficult with the emergence of the Cold War.

The Moscow Agreements of December 1945 essentially confirmed the Cairo Declaration and the original concept of trusteeship for Korea. Based on a Soviet draft in response to the initial U.S. proposal, the accord provided for four-power supervision of a provisional Korean government that would lead to a unified national government. The foreign ministers agreed that the trusteeship would last no more than five years. With American and Soviet troops on the spot, Chinese and British interests now clearly took a back seat to the competing world visions of the United States and the Soviet Union. The detailed arrangements for the joint administration of the Korean Peninsula contained in the Moscow Agreements thus came too late, and American actions in southern Korea undermined the accord almost immediately.

TIMOTHY C. DOWLING AND SPENCER C. TUCKER

See also

Attlee, Clement Richard; Cairo Declaration; Churchill, Sir Winston; Cold War, Origins to 1950; Harriman, William Averell; Stalin, Joseph; 38th Parallel, Division of Korea at; Truman, Harry S.

References

Cumings, Bruce. *The Origins of the Korean War.* 2 vols. Princeton, NJ: Princeton University Press, 1981, 1990.

Lowe, Peter. *The Origins of the Korean War.* New York: Longman, 1997.

Matray, James I. *The Reluctant Crusade: American Foreign Policy in Korea, 1941–1950.* Honolulu: University of Hawaii Press, 1985.

Stueck, William W., Jr. *Rethinking the Korean War: A New Diplomatic and Strategic History.* Princeton, NJ: Princeton University Press, 2004.

Price Gouging

Price gouging occurs when a store, dealer, or vendor charges more for an item than it is worth, or more than what the going price is for a similar or identical product. Price gouging occurred sporadically during the Korean War as a way to capitalize on the inflationary pressures created by the war or, more often, as a means by which to skirt government-imposed price controls.

When the Korean War began in June 1950, the U.S. economy was close to full employment, and industrial capacity was nearly maxed out. Only a small excess labor force and very little excess industrial capacity existed in the thriving economy. Thus, any new military spending and military production superimposed on the U.S. economy was likely to cause inflationary pressures, as consumers and factories competed for a static supply of raw materials, labor, and finished products. Continued high demand for finished goods and a briskly accelerating demand for industrial raw materials resulted in skyrocketing prices of materials like steel, aluminum, copper, manganese, rubber, cotton, and oil. This demand-pull inflation resulted in price increases at every level of the economy.

As soon as the war began in June 1950, U.S. consumers started buying—some might say hoarding—products at a record volume. Fearing that the war might grow bigger (57 percent of Americans believed by the end of June 1950 that World War III had begun), Americans purchased all manner of goods—food as well as more durable goods—as a hedge against future shortages or inflation. Of course, this activity served mainly to push prices even higher. In July 1950 alone, retail prices shot up by 8 percent. The price of rubber nearly quadrupled from $.34 to $.86 per pound, while tin shot up from $.76 per pound in June to $1.84 per pound in December 1950. With such galloping inflation and rising demand for raw materials, business and military planners alike fretted that materials shortages could stymie the rearmament drive and hamper industrial production.

These inflationary pressures notwithstanding, President Harry S. Truman's administration chose not to impose price controls on the economy, preferring instead to wait out the storm and hope that battlefield successes would mitigate the need for a fast and large military buildup. In the meantime, the administration exhorted Americans not to engage in hoarding and unnecessary purchases. It should come as no surprise that some less-than-scrupulous retailers took advantage of the war-induced panic by charging exorbitant prices for their products, essentially engaging in price gouging. Prior to the January 1951 imposition of mandatory price controls on virtually all products, the government took a dim view of price gouging but was unable, in most cases, to do anything about it. Furthermore, after the September 15, 1950, Inchon Landing moved U.S. forces in Korea from defense to offense, inflationary pressures eased, as Americans believed that the war would be short-lived.

When the People's Republic of China (PRC) intervened in the war in late November 1950, inflation once again soared, rising faster even than it had in the summer of 1950. The Truman administration's national emergency declaration in December 1950 and its decision to significantly increase both the size and pace of the rearmament effort had a deleterious effect on prices at both the wholesale and retail levels. Worse yet, prices for raw materials continued to rise even as supplies dwindled. The drastic reversal in the fortunes of war prompted the administration to freeze prices and wages on January 26, 1951. From then on, prices would be carefully set and maintained by the Office of Price Stabilization (OPS), operating under the aegis of the Economic Stabilization Agency (ESA) and the Office of Defense Mobilization (ODM).

The price freeze became an economic red herring for many retailers. Whenever a price freeze follows a period of high inflation, prices are invariably distorted. Because wholesale prices had risen faster than retail prices, myriad retailers were forced to replenish their inventories at higher prices while selling their products at a fixed price, making it virtually impossible to recover their costs in the short term. Also, those retailers who had attempted to hold down their prices before the freeze were at a disadvantage to those who had charged whatever the market would bear prior to January 26, 1951. In this case, price gouging hit the most conscientious retailers the worst.

Within weeks the OPS had begun to assemble an array of consumer and business advisory boards designed to help administer price controls and aid in their enforcement. Enforcement was carried out mainly at the local level, and when a violation was believed to have occurred, local and regional OPS officials were so notified. They in turn decided whether or not a violation had indeed occurred and then took the case to the U.S. Department of Justice for potential prosecution.

The first arrest involving an OPS pricing violation involved a Los Angeles Cadillac dealer, who had allegedly sold a 1950 Cadillac above the government-mandated price ceiling. The arrest garnered national attention, as the government tried to demonstrate that it was serious about price gouging. In the end, the dealer was sanctioned but not prosecuted. Had he been convicted, he could have received a minimum fine of $10,000 and a year in federal prison.

For the duration of the price-control period, which lasted until 1953, the government investigated hundreds of alleged violations. Price gouging was the most common complaint, although it is unclear just how many violators were actually prosecuted. As inflation began to ease during 1952, price gouging became less of a concern.

PAUL G. PIERPAOLI JR.

See also

Economic Stabilization Agency; Office of Price Stabilization

References

Pierpaoli, Paul G., Jr. *Truman and Korea: The Political Culture of the Early Cold War.* Columbia: University of Missouri Press, 1999.

Rockoff, Hugh. *Drastic Measures: A History of Wage and Price Controls in the United States.* New York: Cambridge University Press, 1984.

Price and Wage Freeze Order
Event Date: January 26, 1951

U.S. government order issued on January 26, 1951, that effectively froze prices and wages at the level they had attained on or before January 25, 1951. The freeze order was a response to accelerating inflation and materials shortages brought about by the Korean War. In truth, President Harry S. Truman's administration had been slow to respond to increasing inflationary pressures. First, it had lacked the administrative and organizational capacity to invoke controls before January 1951. Second, it had hoped that the war would be a short one and end by Christmas, as General Douglas MacArthur famously predicted. Finally, economic controls are never popular, and for political reasons the Truman White House chose not to invoke blanket price and wage controls, relying instead on voluntary controls, which simply did not work.

Further complicating the invocation of price and wage controls was considerable infighting within the Truman administration, as some believed that such controls were not yet needed; still others believed that the freeze order should wait until all of the organizational apparatuses were in place. Indeed, Truman's first director of the Economic Stabilization Agency (ESA), Alan Valentine, resigned in protest on January 19, 1951. The ESA was charged with overall coordination of wage and price controls. Valentine had sought to hold off on controls until his agency was administratively equipped to implement across-the-board controls. However, Charles E. Wilson, director of the Office of Defense Mobilization (ODM) and the nation's top mobilization official, wanted controls invoked immediately. Furthermore, Valentine disagreed with his chief price control officer, Michael V. DiSalle, head of the Office of Price Stabilization (OPS). DiSalle also believed that controls had to be applied quickly. On January 24 the ESA's second director was sworn into office, and he was prepared to invoke controls immediately. Eric Johnston, now in charge of the ESA, ordered controls into effect on January 26, 1951.

Realizing that a price and wage freeze would have to be followed as quickly as possible by a comprehensive, long-term anti-inflation strategy, Johnston ordered the freeze on January 26, which froze all applicable wages and prices as of January 25. What followed was a tortuous road of ad hoc price and wage adjustments to remedy inequities, and many weeks of strategy sessions that finally resulted in comprehensive wage and price guidelines, which were announced in mid-April 1951. These guidelines set the basic parameters of economic controls until they were abolished in the spring of 1953.

DiSalle and Cyrus Ching, chairman of the Wage Stabilization Board (WSB), announced the freeze order late in the afternoon of January 26 in Washington, DC Later in 1951 the WSB created a separate board to deal only with salaried workers, aptly named the Salary Stabilization Board.

The order froze applicable commodity prices at their highest attained level between December 19, 1950, and January 25, 1951.

This period marked the fastest acceleration in inflation. Exempt from the freeze were commodity trade-market margins and professional services. Farm products selling below government parity levels were also excluded from the freeze.

For wages, the freeze order applied to virtually all wages, salaries, and other types of compensation, effective January 25. Union representatives on the WSB were angry about the blanket freeze, however, and refused to sign the order in protest. They believed a freeze would hurt hourly, union workers and would undercut already negotiated labor contracts with employers.

Public reaction to the freeze was decidedly mixed. While some Americans believed that the freeze would dampen inflationary pressures, others groused that it represented too much government intrusion into economic affairs. The business community was not thrilled with controls either; while the more progressive industries and executives tepidly endorsed them, conservative groups, affiliated largely with the Chamber of Commerce and National Association of Manufacturers, assailed them as too intrusive and counterproductive. In the end, the consensus was that controls were needed to halt inflation and stymie materials shortages that might damage the war effort. But many at the time pointed out that had the Truman administration done more to curb inflation early in the war, blanket controls might not have been necessary.

PAUL G. PIERPAOLI JR.

See also

Economic Stabilization Agency; Office of Price Stabilization; Price Gouging; Wilson, Charles Edward

References

Pierpaoli, Paul G., Jr. *Truman and Korea: The Political Culture of the Early Cold War.* Columbia: University of Missouri Press, 1999.
Vawter, Roderick W. *Industrial Mobilization: The Relevant History.* Washington, DC: National Defense University Press, 1983.

Prisoner of War Administration, Communist

At the beginning of the Korean War, authorities in the Democratic People's Republic of Korea (DPRK, North Korea) and the People's Republic of China (PRC) did not anticipate the capture of large numbers of United Nations Command (UNC) prisoners. Ultimately these prisoners numbered some 90,000 people. The stated communist policy was humane treatment of prisoners of war (POWs). According to this policy the prisoners' lives would be protected, and medical care and treatment would be provided for the sick and wounded. But the lack of preparation stymied whatever good intentions the communist side might have had regarding POWs. There were no policies as to how POW camps should be operated, and there were no proper facilities for handling prisoners. Moreover, POWs came to be regarded as pawns in the ensuing ideological struggle.

Conditions in North Korean POW camps underwent three distinct phases: from June to November 1950, when Chinese People's Volunteer Army (CPVA, Chinese Army) forces entered the war; the winter of 1950–1951, when three temporary camps were established; and 1951–1953, when permanent camps were established.

During the first phase, the Korean People's Army (KPA, North Korean Army) had sole charge of UNC prisoners. Republic of Korea Army (ROKA, South Korean Army) POWs were taken first to Seoul and then to Pyongyang, where they remained until early September. Some of them were then moved to the vicinity of Manpo, where they were held until October 31, 1950. The KPA made use of whatever facilities were available in any given area in which they desired to establish a POW enclosure. Because in the first months of the war the KPA had no policy for handling POWs, there was no internal camp organization. Housing, food, and medical care were extremely primitive and limited. Despite facts to the contrary, the North Korean authorities claimed that they were treating their prisoners generously and well.

During the second period, in the winter of 1950–1951, the KPA and CPVA jointly administered the UNC POWs. However, the degree of contribution to be provided by each side was not clearly established, and the majority of POW deaths occurred during this time. The so-called "Death March" of early November 1950 transferred the POWs to camps in far northern Korea, again without any semblance of organization and under the control of security police. Upon their capture, unwounded and walking wounded prisoners were herded into groups for marching. Many marches were made in severely cold weather conditions and on foot, over rugged, even mountainous terrain. These marches resulted in the deaths of many POWs. During the marches there was little or no medical attention for the wounded. Malnutrition, lack of medical care, dysentery, pneumonia, and cold weather all took a heavy toll. And in many cases, sick and wounded prisoners were simply taken from the line of march by the guards; the most seriously wounded were either left behind or killed by small-arms fire or by bayonet.

Temporary camps along the route of march were known by different names, such as "Bean Camp," "Mining Camp," and "Death Valley." These temporary camps, first organized in November 1950, were all under KPA jurisdiction, but control passed to the Chinese in the middle of December. The prisoners were housed in huts, but food was inadequate and they died at an exceedingly high rate.

In the third period, beginning in the spring of 1951, the Chinese were in sole charge of the POW camps, with the exception of those housing South Korean POWs. Conditions began to improve that summer and continued to do so until the end of the war under the so-called lenient policy.

The headquarters for all communist POW camps was in Pyoktong, North Pyongan Province. Political officers worked in tandem at all levels with military officers in running the POW network. Decisions regarding POW policy came from the top, and individual camp commanders had little latitude to act on their own initiative.

Graves of American prisoners of war who had been killed by the Korean People's Army (North Korean Army), found beside an abandoned train where the bodies of other unburied American soldiers were also discovered. (National Archives)

Communist authorities announced the existence of camps numbered 1 to 17, but other camps have also been identified. Most camps were located in far northern Korea, near the Yalu River. Individual camps were divided into companies, which were the chief administrative unit. Companies averaged 200 men but ranged in size from 60 to 350 POWs. There were three to seven companies per camp. Each company was further broken down into four or five platoons of about 50 POWs each. Each platoon was further subdivided into five squads with approximately 10 POWs to a squad, which was the basic POW unit.

To facilitate camp control, the communists first allowed the prisoners to organize themselves along their own military lines, permitting the highest-ranking officer to serve as camp leader and to select his staff in accordance with normal military procedure. This system was abolished in early 1951 and replaced by one in which the communist authorities appointed the leaders.

Camp authorities appointed prisoners to the positions of platoon sergeant, squad leader, and assistant squad leader. Only those POWs who got along with the communists were selected for these positions. The platoon sergeant called roll and organized platoon details. The squad leader's primary duties consisted of checking the men on details, reporting squad roll call, and reading articles to the squad during indoctrination periods. There were many POW committees, such as mess, sanitation, recreation, and study.

To facilitate further handling of prisoners, the communists divided prisoners within each camp into companies and platoons along national and ethnic lines, by white Americans, African Americans, British, Turks, and other United Nations (UN) countries. Further segregation occurred among officers, noncommissioned officers, and enlisted men, as well as between "progressives" and "reactionaries." Progressives were either committed communists or potential converts. To protect them as a group and take proper retaliatory measures against reactionaries, the communists segregated the two groups. Progressives received much better treatment, while reactionaries were threatened, put on work details, and beaten.

A U.S. Army soldier, taken prisoner and then murdered by the Korean People's Army (North Korean Army), August 18, 1950. His boots have been taken and his hands are tied behind his back. (National Archives)

Prisoners were occasionally shifted between camps, companies, and platoons to prevent them from forming stable prison societies. The communists also kept firm control over the camps by means of an extensive informant system, augmented by close observation by instructors and guards. These techniques enabled the camp authorities to remain well informed of activities within the compounds.

The complete isolation of compounds from one another and from the outside world prevented the organization and planning of concerted resistance. Corporal punishment or solitary confinement in the "hole" were the most commonly used methods to deal with resistance. Indoctrination and utilization of POWs for propaganda purposes were important aspects of communist POW policy.

From July 1951 the communists had a developed plan to deal with POWs. Interrogation was conducted with a view of gaining tactical and strategic intelligence information. To this was added an effort to secure information of a personal nature to use in indoctrination sessions. In December 1950 the CPVA established an interrogation center 20 miles from "Death Valley" for detailed interrogation. The KPA used "Pak's Palace," established in April 1951, for POW interrogation.

The primary communist purpose in indoctrination was not to convert a prisoner to communism as much as to destroy his spirit or to place him under such mental pressure that he could be used for the captors' purposes. Persuasion and coercion were sometimes employed to force prisoners to accept communism. In Camp 5 the authorities transferred sergeants and officers to other camps to prevent their influencing the younger men who remained. Men who consistently made trouble were also moved to other camps, leaving behind groups of men between the ages of 18 and 24 who, although fairly intelligent, did not have much formal education and were from low-income groups.

The indoctrination program proceeded in stages and included lectures, discussions, and supplementary reading. Subjects included the Korean War, the contradictions between capitalism and socialism, and the advantages of communism. After completion of this formal indoctrination program, prisoners were encouraged to study on their own.

The communists also utilized prisoners to perform various tasks. These ranged from minimal maintenance duties to preserve some semblance of cleanliness in the camp to long, hard physical labor. ROKA POWs were not considered prisoners but were referred to as "liberated warriors." As such, they were organized into labor units known as "liberation units" and "liberation construction regiments" and were employed in direct support of the communist war effort. They worked in mines; dug air-raid shelters and underground bunkers; constructed airfields; planted, cultivated, and harvested crops; and built, repaired, and maintained roads, railway lines, and bridges.

UNC prisoners held by the communists during the Korean War had to endure horrific conditions. Although the exact number of those who died in captivity will never be known with certainty, it was undoubtedly quite high. One estimate puts the number of dead at about 15,000, including 8,334 Koreans and 6,137 Americans.

SUNGHUN CHO

See also

Casualties; Prisoner of War Administration, United Nations Command; Prisoner of War Code of Conduct

References

Biderman, Albert D. *Communist Techniques of Coercive Interrogation.* Lackland Air Force Base, TX: U.S. Air Force, 1956.

———. *March to Calumny: The Story of American POWs in the Korean War.* New York: Macmillan, 1963.

Carlson, Lewis. *Remembered Prisoners of a Forgotten War: An Oral History of Korean War POWs.* New York: St. Martin's, 2002.

Cho, Sunghun. "Hanguk Chonjaeng Chung Kongsanguk ui UN Kun Poro Chongchaek e Taehan Yongu" [Communist Policies Regarding UN POWs during the Korean War]. *Hanguk Kunhyondaesa Yongu* [Journal of Korean Modern and Contemporary History] 6 (1997): 217–266.

Kim, Haeng Bok. *Hanguk Chonjaeng ui Poro* [POWs in the Korean War]. Seoul: Korean Institute of Military History, 1996.

"U.S. Prisoners of War in the Korean Operation: A Study of Their Treatment and Handling by NK Army and the Chinese Communist Forces." Fort George G. Meade, MD: Army Security Center, 1954.

White, William L. *The Captives of Korea: An Unofficial White Paper on the Treatment of War Prisoners, Our Treatment of Theirs; Their Treatment of Ours.* New York: Scribner, 1955.

Prisoner of War Administration, United Nations Command

The United Nations Command (UNC) initially gave little thought to prisoner of war (POW) camps in the Republic of Korea (ROK, South Korea). The first camp, established at Pusan, held fewer than 1,000 prisoners. Numbers of POWs swelled, however, especially after the Inchon Landing of September 15, 1950, and the U.S. Eighth Army in Korea (EUSAK) breakout from the Pusan Perimeter. By November 1950 the UNC held more than 130,000 prisoners.

The Pusan camp was entirely inadequate to deal with so many POWs, and the sudden influx of prisoners into it revealed how inadequate planning had been. The camp was not only too small, but food and clothing were also in extremely short supply; there were insufficient guards for so many prisoners; and those who were on hand were unprepared for their duties. The quality

and numbers of guards did not improve and remained a major handicap in UNC camp administration. Prisoners who had been members of the Republic of Korea Army (ROKA, South Korean Army) but had been pressed into service in the Korean People's Army (KPA, North Korean Army) assumed positions of leadership among the prisoners. As they professed to be anticommunists, the ROKA guards gave them favorable treatment.

With Pusan incapable of handling so many prisoners, the UNC decided, for logistical as well as security reasons, to move the prisoners to new camps on Koje-do, an island 20 miles southwest of the port of Pusan. In January 1951 UNC authorities began the transfer of prisoners to Koje-do.

Colonel Hartley F. Dame, the first UNC commander on Koje-do, had several formidable obstacles to overcome in establishing the camp. Koje-do had no water resources, so the first order of business was to build dams and store rainwater to ensure a relatively adequate, independent supply of water sufficient for 118,000 indigenous inhabitants, 100,000 refugees, 150,000 prisoners, and the camp administration. Other major logistical problems included securing food, shelter, and other necessities. The South Korean government was responsible for providing the food and transporting it to the camp. Barracks for the prisoners, as well as other housing for the guards and camp administration personnel, had to be built. Construction began in January 1951, and by the end of the month 50,000 POWs had been transferred to the new camp from the mainland.

The camp, on the north coast of the island, was designed for four enclosures, each of which was divided into eight compounds. These compounds were to hold no more than 1,200 prisoners each, but they were soon crammed with up to five times the estimated number of prisoners, a major factor in the events that were to follow. Although Koje-do was considered an ideal place to hold POWs, it was also a small island, and there was no opportunity to enlarge the camps. Eventually the areas between the compounds were also used to hold prisoners.

The limited space, along with the limited number of guards and security personnel, who were inadequately trained and of a generally inferior quality, contributed to the inability of the administration to maintain adequate control. This situation was exacerbated by the belief that the war would not last long and that there was no need for a long-term solution. Thus, corrective actions were not taken.

Part of the problem—in fact a major part of it—was that ROKA troops were used as guards. Antagonism was common between the guards and the prisoners. Control weakened as tension and resentment grew from angry words and threats to physical attacks. The inadequacy of the guard situation was such that, to a considerable extent, the prisoners themselves ran the compounds, and staunch communists saw in this an opportunity to embarrass the UNC during cease-fire negotiations. Prisoner provocations reached a peak with the beginning of negotiations at Kaesong.

Communist prisoners of war in Compound 77, Koje-do, South Korea, May 27, 1952. (National Archives)

Many of the POWs who had professed strong anticommunist sentiments feared repatriation to the Democratic People's Republic of Korea (DPRK, North Korea). During attempts to screen the prisoners, they divided the POWs into two different groups—anticommunists and communists. North Korea and the People's Republic of China (PRC) sent agitator agents to be captured so that they could organize the prisoners and foment trouble in the camps. These agents formed the nucleus of prisoner resistance to screening.

Bloody clashes soon erupted in the compounds as POW kangaroo courts tried fellow prisoners, death penalties were carried out, and beatings and murders went unpunished. Camp administrators were not allowed to institute judicial actions against the troublemakers, resulting in a further erosion of authority within the camps.

The 2nd Logistical Command had charge of all prison camps. The chief of staff of the 2nd Logistical Command, Colonel Albert C. Morgan, requested more and better trained security personnel, but disturbances continued unabated in the camps when EUSAK commander General James A. Van Fleet inspected the camps. This resulted in a reorganization of the prison security forces.

Another problem was the rapid turnover in commanders on Koje-do. In September 1951 Colonel Maurice J. Fitzgerald assumed command. As a result of the disturbances and reorganization, the 8137th Military Police Group was activated that October. In addition to the three assigned battalions, four additional escort guard companies were attached to the group. By November a battalion of the 23rd Infantry Regiment was assigned to Koje-do, and by December there were more than 9,000 combined U.S. and ROKA forces on the island, although this was still far fewer than the 15,000 originally requested.

Despite an increase in security personnel, violence escalated. On December 18, 1951, a major disturbance between pro- and anticommunist forces led to more riots and demonstrations that left 14 dead and 24 injured. As commander of the 2nd Logistical Command Brigadier General Paul F. Yount pointed out, introduction of the screening process had led to the increased violence. Before that, U.S. military personnel had full access to compounds and administered them satisfactorily, although never to the degree desired. By December more than 37,000 prisoners had been reclassified as civilian internees (CIs). A second screening instituted by

A wounded North Korean prisoner, Taegu, South Korea. (Hulton-Deutsch Collection/Corbis)

the commander of the Koje-do camp, Colonel Fitzgerald, led to a major upheaval.

The second POW screening was an attempt to correct mistakes made in the first screening and to segregate nonrepatriates from those who wanted to be repatriated to North Korea or China. Communist POWs controlled Compound 62 and refused to admit screening teams. They stated that none of their numbers wanted to remain in South Korea. The South Korean screening teams were just as determined to fulfill their assigned duties.

On the morning of February 18, 1952, members of the 3rd Battalion of the 27th Infantry Regiment moved in, passing through the gates with bayonets fixed, and divided the camp into four segments. The prisoners grabbed makeshift weapons, including rocks and sticks, and attacked the troops. Completely unprepared for the violent resistance, the troops used concussion grenades in an attempt to stop the attack. When this tactic failed, they opened fire, killing 55 prisoners and wounding another 140. The 3rd Battalion suffered 1 killed and 38 wounded.

The UNC blamed the communist leaders among the POWs, and the Department of the Army directed UNC commander Lieutenant General Matthew B. Ridgway to point out that only 1,500 inmates took part and that only CIs, not POWs, were involved. Nonetheless, this event turned out to be a highly useful propaganda weapon for communist negotiators at the cease-fire talks.

On February 20, 1952, General Van Fleet appointed Brigadier General Francis T. Dodd as camp commandant and ordered him to tighten discipline and gain control of the situation. Unfortunately, the bloody confrontations were not over. Despite Dodd's

instructions, on March 13 another confrontation between ROKA troops and communist inmates resulted in the guards firing on inmates in retaliation for being attacked; 12 prisoners were killed and 26 wounded.

In April a new round of screening was undertaken. Again communist prisoners sought to obstruct the process; they refused to allow the screening teams into seven of the compounds. The screening went on, nevertheless. This led to the discovery that, of 170,000 prisoners, only 70,000 wished to return home. This brought negotiations at Panmunjom to a standstill as the communist negotiators renewed their attacks on the screening process.

General Van Fleet then informed General Ridgway that he intended to separate communist POWs from the anticommunists and remove the latter to the mainland. Despite the demands that this action would impose on personnel and equipment, Van Fleet believed that it would lessen the likelihood of violence. Unfortunately, the removal of the noncommunists resulted in a concentration of hard-liners among the communist prisoners who wished to return home. The POWs would no longer have to worry about fighting among themselves; they could now direct all their efforts against the UNC.

Unrest, tension, lack of moderating influences in the camps, and riots over food and other resources culminated in a riot on May 7, 1952, in which communist POWs seized General Dodd and announced that he would not be released until certain demands were met. They also warned that any attempts to secure his release by force would result in Dodd's death.

Van Fleet then appointed Brigadier General Charles F. Colson as the new camp commander and sent him to Koje-do to free Dodd by force, if necessary. Colson received an ultimatum from the prisoners stipulating a number of conditions for Dodd's safe release. Colson then signed a statement conceding that numerous POWs had been killed and wounded by UNC guards and guaranteeing "humane treatment" for UNC POWs in accordance with the principles of international law, as well as an end to "forcible" POW screening.

Dodd was released unharmed, but the communists exploited Colson's statement as proof of UNC atrocities, humiliating the United States and EUSAK and raising serious questions worldwide over the validity of the voluntary repatriation doctrine. Both Dodd's capture and Colson's statement were major international events and had a devastating impact on the UNC's international image.

Although a subsequent U.S. Army investigating board found both generals blameless, General Van Fleet and UNC commander Lieutenant General Mark W. Clark convened another board of inquiry that reversed the original decision, and both generals were reduced in rank to colonel and retired from the army.

General Clark assigned Brigadier General Haydon L. Boatner to command the camp with instructions to clean out the compounds and restore order. On June 10, 1952, Boatner sent in paratroopers backed by six M-47 Patton tanks, and after a battle of more than an hour, in which more than 150 prisoners were killed, he brought the situation under control. There was another public outcry, but this was the last major clash in the UNC prison camps.

The UNC also constructed new prison camps on Koje-do as well as on the mainland and on Cheju-do. In addition to a reduction in the numbers of POWs held in the new compounds, more UNC troops were added as guards—including those from the United Kingdom, Canada, and Greece. Boatner built new enclosures and moved 6,000 civilians away from the vicinity of the camps and to the mainland. On July 10, 1952, General Clark removed POW administration from EUSAK jurisdiction and placed it under the Korean Communications Zone of the Far East Command (FEC).

Another POW camp was established on Pongam-do, where one ROKA battalion and U.S. administrative personnel guarded and maintained 9,000 prisoners. On December 24, 1952, a riot broke out there. It was soon suppressed.

Less tumultuous times appeared to be in the offing, but the primary problem of POW repatriation remained. South Korean president Syngman Rhee, strongly opposed to an armistice that would leave Korea divided, saw the issue of forced repatriation as a means of breaking up the armistice talks. He ordered the release on the night of June 17–18, 1953, of noncommunist UNC prisoners from mainland camps. Some 27,000 militantly anticommunist POWs broke out of camps at Pusan, Masan, Nonsan, and Sangmudae and disappeared into the general South Korean population. Only 971 were recovered. U.S. troops subsequently replaced the South Korean security guards. After that, the UNC effectively maintained security and control of the camps.

PATRICIA WADLEY

See also

Boatner, Haydon Lemaire; Cheju-do Prisoner of War Uprising; Clark, Mark Wayne; Dodd-Colson Prisoner of War Incident; Koje-do Prisoner of War Uprising; Repatriation, Voluntary; Rhee's Release of North Korean Prisoners of War; Ridgway, Matthew Bunker; 2nd Logistical Command; Truce Talks; Van Fleet, James Alward

References

Blair, Clay. *The Forgotten War: America in Korea, 1950–1953*. New York: Times Books, 1987.

Hermes, Walter G. *U.S. Army in the Korean War: Truce Tent and Fighting Front*. Washington, DC: Office of the Chief of Military History, 1966.

Millett, Allan R. *Their War in Korea: American, Asian, and European Combatants and Civilians, 1945–1953*. Princeton, NJ: Princeton University Press, 2002.

Vetter, Hal. *Mutiny on Koje Island*. Rutland, VT: Charles E. Tuttle, 1965.

Prisoner of War Code of Conduct

The Military Code of Conduct for Prisoners of War, adopted in 1955, was a direct result of the ordeal of U.S. prisoners of war (POWs) held by both the Korean People's Army (KPA, North Korean Army) and the Chinese People's Volunteer Army (CPVA, Chinese Army). Before the establishment of the 1955 code, military personnel were merely expected to conduct themselves in a manner that would not bring dishonor upon their country, the military, or themselves. During preliminary and subsequent interrogations they were expected to give only their name, rank, and serial number. They were also expected to try to escape. They were still under military orders, but other than that there were no regulations to guide their conduct. The United States was a signatory of the Geneva Accords concerning the treatment of POWs. A subsequent protocol spelled out how POWs were to be maintained and what was expected of them.

The United States learned in World War II that prisoners were at the whim of their captors. The Germans generally followed the Geneva Accords, as did the Italians. The Japanese did not, and brutality was common. Prisoners were starved, medical care was virtually nonexistent, and there was no protecting power to guarantee proper treatment.

When the Korean War began, little thought was given to the POW issue, let alone to how prisoners would conduct themselves. Unfortunately for United Nations Command (UNC) personnel captured by the communists, the People's Republic of China (PRC) and the Democratic People's Republic of Korea (DPRK, North Korea) considered propaganda a tool of war and a potential weapon against a prisoner's own country. To that end, the communists carried out intense psychological and propaganda campaigns among prisoners. POWs were deprived of food, brutality was common, and medical care was sparse. The communists moreover refused to allow visits to their POW camps by the Red Cross or other international agencies.

The communists also instituted a regime to work on POW morale. Enlisted personnel were separated from noncommissioned officers, officers were isolated from their men, and any individual who showed leadership potential was removed. Prisoners were not allowed to consider themselves part of a military organization. The communists inflicted brutal punishment for the most trivial offenses, and deaths from mistreatment were not uncommon. POWs were also ordered to attend "schooling" and indoctrination classes. All this was done to try to break down the POWs' resistance to be able to use them for propaganda purposes.

Given these conditions and the length of time many of the men were prisoners, it is not surprising that some "cooperated" with the enemy. More shocking was the fact that 21 Americans refused repatriation. As a direct result of the Korean War experience, the U.S. military decided that both intensive ideological indoctrination and a policy of absolute noncompliance with any captor's demands were necessary. Furthermore, military officials decreed that a failure to follow this code should result in severe punishment. On August 17, 1955, President Dwight D. Eisenhower signed Executive Order 10631, which promulgated a code of conduct for members of the U.S. armed forces delineating exactly how members of the military were to conduct themselves as POWs.

PATRICIA WADLEY

See also
Brainwashing; Prisoner of War Administration, Communist

References
Biderman, Albert D. *March to Calumny: The Story of American POWs in the Korean War.* New York: Macmillan, 1963.
Carlson, Lewis. *Remembered Prisoners of a Forgotten War: An Oral History of Korean War POWs.* New York: St. Martin's, 2002.
Snyder, Don J. *A Soldier's Disgrace.* Dublin, NH: Yankee Books, 1987.

Prisoners of War, Rescreening of

June 1952 action by the United Nations Command (UNC) to determine the status of prisoners of war (POWs) it controlled, specifically those who wished to return home and those who would refuse repatriation. The UNC did not consider rescreening POWs to be desirable and believed that such a program might lengthen the odds of reaching an armistice agreement. It might also have strengthened communist allegations that the initial UNC screening was improper.

After the communist refusal to agree to an exchange of prisoners on the basis of an estimate of only 70,000 POWs desiring repatriation, the UNC cast about for any reasonable means to resolve the deadlock, while at the same time remaining firm on the issue of nonforcible repatriation. The UNC side then suggested verification and rescreening after the armistice, to be conducted under the most stringent criteria, to determine those who would actually resist repatriation. On April 23, 1952, the UNC proposed that joint Red Cross teams from the two sides, with or without military observers, be allowed to interview the prisoners to verify that those designated as nonrepatriates would forcibly resist being returned to the side from which they came. The UNC also proposed that all POWs of both sides be delivered in groups to the demilitarized zone (DMZ) and there be allowed to express their preferences on repatriation.

The communists rejected these proposals. Instead, they sought to establish the illegality of voluntary repatriation of POWs and halt the screenings. Communist agents also sought to instigate riots in the camps, leading to the capture of UNC Koje-do POW camp commander U.S. brigadier general Francis T. Dodd on May 7, 1952. The communist side said that the Dodd incident proved that voluntary repatriation and screening were only devices for the forceful retention of POWs. Certainly the incident undermined the previous confidence of allied governments, as well as public opinion, on the UNC's handling of POWs and the validity of the screening process.

The United Nations (UN) allies now pressed for some type of rescreening before an armistice that would allow communist observation and would contain a commitment by both sides to abide by the results. Worried about an indefinite suspension or even end to the negotiations, the UNC proposed a program for rescreening POWs before the armistice, in which independent observers would be drawn from countries not participating in the war. The UNC also invited the communists to participate in the rescreening process. But the communist side insisted that the very act of screening was illegal and unacceptable, and they continued to make a propaganda issue of the screening process.

As a consequence of the communist refusal to participate, rescreening was carried out unilaterally by the UNC without the participation of neutral or communist observers. The rescreening was conducted to determine whether a larger proportion of prisoners might want to be repatriated and to screen those prisoners not previously checked.

During the period June 23–30, 1952, previously unscreened POWs were interviewed. Each screening team consisted of 1–2 officers, 6–8 Korean interrogators from the Civil Information and Education Section, 4–6 fingerprint personnel, and 12 Korean interviewers. In general the procedure paralleled the one followed in April. Prisoners were first identified and fingerprinted, then taken to the interview tent. If a prisoner refused to answer the questions or indicated that he would not resist repatriation violently, he was placed on the list to be repatriated and assigned to a repatriate compound.

The rescreening occurred with less chance of violence because hard-core communist POWs and civilian internees (CIs) had already been transferred to other camps during Operation BREAKUP. The UNC stressed the objective nature of the screening, in which each POW was given the opportunity to make his own decision and was encouraged to return to communist control. The screening teams screened and identified some 50,000 POWs who had not been screened in April.

Of the 170,000 POWs, approximately 83,000 (76,600 North Korean and 6,400 Chinese) chose to be repatriated, while about 86,000 refused repatriation. The latter represented an increase of 16,000 over the April figure of those refusing repatriation. The UNC recommended to the U.S. Joint Chiefs of Staff that the UNC delegation at Panmunjom be authorized to submit a new final figure to the communists as soon as possible. But this suggestion led to a discussion over whether disclosing the revised figure would discredit the initial screening that had produced the figure of 70,000 refusing repatriation.

Finally, on July 13, 1952, the UNC informed communist negotiators of the revised figure. Korean People's Army (KPA, North Korean Army) Lieutenant General Nam Il, chief North Korean negotiator at the armistice negotiations, rejected the UNC contention that this was an impartial and valid count; he insisted that the final tally should be approximately 110,000 repatriates. The deadlock at Panmunjom over repatriation remained the major issue to be resolved before conclusion of an armistice.

The solution was for some independent and impartial body to reinterview all those POWs not wishing repatriation. The UNC presented new proposals on September 28, 1952, in which all POWs objecting to repatriation would be delivered to the DMZ, where they would be freed from the military control of both sides and interviewed by representatives of mutually agreed-upon countries or by an international committee. Such a plan was ultimately adopted, but the communist side initially remained firmly opposed to the principle of voluntary repatriation, fearing a propaganda defeat in the process.

SUNGHUN CHO

See also

Dodd-Colson Prisoner of War Incident; SCATTER, Operation; Truce Talks

References

Bailey, Sydney D. *The Korean Armistice.* New York: St. Martin's, 1992.

Cho, Sunghun. "Hanguk Chonjaeng Chung UN Kun ui Poro Chongchaek e Kwanhan Yongu" [A Study of UN Forces POW policies during the Korean War]. PhD dissertation, Academy of Korean Studies, Seoul, 1999.

Hermes, Walter G. *U.S. Army in the Korean War: Truce Tent and Fighting Front.* Washington, DC: Office of the Chief of Military History, 1966.

Vatcher, William H., Jr. *Panmunjom.* Westport, CT: Greenwood, 1973.

Psychological Warfare

Psychological warfare is the planned, systematized use of propaganda and other psychological tools to influence the attitudes, emotions, behavior, and actions of an enemy or adversary. Within a day of President Harry S. Truman's announcement that U.S. troops would assist the Republic of Korea (ROK, South Korea) in repelling the June 25, 1950, invasion by the Democratic People's Republic of Korea (DPRK, North Korea), propaganda leaflets were being dropped over the Korean Peninsula telling of the decision. Within another day, radio broadcasts from Tokyo carried the same message, making psychological warfare the first United Nations (UN) weapon used against North Korea. Following these early precedents, U.S. forces attached to the United Nations Command (UNC) used psychological warfare to an unprecedented degree relative to the size of the conflict. Although no definitive answer can be made as to its overall impact and effect, psychological warfare did serve as an "enhancer" to UNC conventional weapons.

The primary purpose of psychological warfare is to lower enemy morale and to influence populations to resist their leaders, abandon the war effort, surrender, or resist opposing forces less intently. Most practitioners recognize that propaganda rarely produces immediate results, but rather has a slow, cumulative effect. Tactically it works best against tired, hungry, cold, and demoralized troops, especially surrounded units, who feel abandoned or betrayed by their officers or leaders, or who feel overwhelmed by enemy numbers, firepower, or material might. During the Korean War most psychological warfare was used on the tactical level rather than at the strategic level.

By 1950 psychological warfare was a well-honed weapon in the U.S. arsenal, with an institutional history dating back to World War I. The Korean War experience also drew heavily on the same personnel, doctrine, methods, themes, weapons, and equipment used in both the European and Pacific theaters by U.S. and Allied civilian and military propagandists during World War II. Indeed, many propaganda leaflets and themes, such as the famous "surrender pass" leaflet first used in the earlier conflicts, were also used widely in Korea. The technology for delivering leaflets by aircraft and artillery dated back to World War II, and in some cases, such as the leaflet artillery shell, to World War I. Radio and loudspeaker broadcasts and equipment used during World War II again provided a significant component of the Korean War arsenal. Even psychological warfare tactical units and headquarters organizations, from the field to Washington, DC, could trace their origins to similar entities created during the earlier conflicts.

Unlike during World War I or World War II, however, the United States was quick to develop psychological warfare in 1950. Soon after the invasion, President Truman developed the Psychological Strategy Board (PSB) to formulate national policy and to coordinate campaigns with the military. The PSB was aided by social scientists of the Operations Research Office at Johns Hopkins University, who were later superseded by analysts and scholars belonging to the army's own Human Resources Research Office.

The U.S. Army, because of persistent pressure applied by Secretary of the Army Frank Pace Jr., created an unprecedented staff organization in the Pentagon on January 15, 1951: the Office of the Chief of Psychological Warfare, divided into Psychological Operations, Requirements, and Special Operations divisions. Brigadier General Robert A. McClure, who had commanded Allied psychological warfare efforts in Europe during World War II, was selected to lead the new office. McClure created a staff that drew heavily on the same talent he had used during the prior conflict. Capitalizing on this, he convinced the army to create a psychological warfare center at Fort Bragg, North Carolina, in April 1952 to provide training, equipment, and doctrinal support for all army psychological warfare units, including those in Korea.

U.S. psychological warfare in Korea had other strong supporters, in addition to Pace. They included General Douglas MacArthur, Lieutenant General Matthew B. Ridgway, and presidential adviser and assistant for Cold War planning C. D. Jackson, who, after his appointment in the spring of 1953, regularly advised a very interested President Dwight D. Eisenhower on the use of psychological warfare in Korea and in the larger struggle against world communism.

At the tactical level in Korea, the situation was initially not as far advanced as at Washington headquarters. Yet as early as 1947 Major General Charles A. Willoughby, MacArthur's assistant chief of staff for intelligence, recreated the World War II Psychological Warfare Section under Colonel J. Woodhall Greene to create contingency plans for the Far East. Although still a small group in June 1950, the Psychological Warfare Section, Far East Command (FEC), grew to 35 people by December and by 1952 had become the central planning and coordinating agency for all UNC psychological warfare activities in Korea.

Whatever the colour, race or creed,
All plain folks are brothers indeed.
Both you and we want life and peace,
If you go home, the war will cease.

Demand Peace!

Stop the War!

Greetings from The Chinese People's Volunteers

KOREA 1951

Chinese People's Volunteer Army propaganda Christmas card, dropped on United Nations Command lines in December 1951. (National Archives)

When North Korea invaded South Korea in June 1950, however, the only deployable U.S. Army psychological warfare unit was at Fort Riley, Kansas. This unit, the 25-member 1st Loudspeaker and Leaflet Company, was patterned after the five similar self-contained U.S. Army Mobile Radio Broadcast companies developed during World War II. The 1st Loudspeaker and Leaflet Company arrived in Korea on November 8, 1950, and served as the tactical propaganda unit of the U.S. Eighth Army in Korea (EUSAK) during the remainder of the war. In August 1951 this group was joined by the 1st Radio Broadcasting and Leaflet Group. It controlled all strategic psychological warfare operations in Korea, including the "Voice of the UN Command" broadcasts, which had begun the year before.

As during World War II, the propagandists in the U.S. Army units had backgrounds in journalism, art, advertising, radio, film, or the social sciences. The units employed South Koreans as radio announcers, leaflet writers, and linguists. Printing of leaflets took place in a specially created print shop in Yokohama. Propaganda leaflets drew heavily on themes and formats developed during World War II, which were adapted to new audiences in Korea. Colorful artwork was a perennial leaflet component, and themes included depictions of the horrors of combat, promises of food and medical treatment in captivity, descriptions of the incompetence

of communist officers and leaders, and exploitation of fears that the soldiers had for their own survival and safety. Other themes emphasized UNC firepower and material superiority; the mounting communist death toll on the battlefield; the backwardness of communist weapons, tactics, and matériel; the emptiness of communist ideology; and the injustice of the communist cause. Many communist prisoners of war (POWs) claimed that the signature of General MacArthur on a surrender pass convinced them that promises of good treatment in captivity would be honored, a similar response to that given by Axis soldiers viewing the same leaflet during World War II.

Once leaflet-production facilities were operational, psychological warfare officers (PWOs) attached to EUSAK headquarters would decide on suitable targets, either on their own initiative or after requests were received from division and corps commanders, many of whom had to first be indoctrinated as to the value of psychological warfare. After the target was determined, the PWO would contact Tokyo, giving the general content for leaflets and where the drop should occur. Tokyo then took the leaflets out of existing stocks or printed them specifically for a given situation or even a particular communist unit. From the printing plant, the leaflets were taken to air bases and loaded onto aircraft for drops directly over communist forces or for transport to the war zone for drops by Korea-based aircraft. Standard smoke artillery shells were also converted to leaflet use and allowed a broad distribution directly over communist positions during combat operations.

By the spring of 1951, plans were well under way to double the leaflet distribution effort of about 13 million propaganda leaflets per week. In response to these plans, General McClure continued to campaign to improve the air support he claimed he lacked during the first year in Korea.

As during both world wars, the vast majority of propaganda leaflets were delivered by aircraft, initially in loosely wrapped bundles that fell apart as they descended from low-flying planes. Later, air force personnel drew again on their World War II experiences and began using hollow aerial bombs, each with a capacity of 45,000 4-by-5-inch leaflets. Thirty-two bombs constituted an aircraft load. The bombs were released at 15,000 feet or higher, with fuses set to open at 1,000 feet.

By the end of the war, about 1 million individual leaflets could be distributed nightly by a single Boeing B-29 Superfortress. More than 2.5 billion leaflets were dropped over communist troops and civilians in North Korea by the end of the war, compared with 6 billion dropped during all of World War II.

In addition to leaflets, which were the primary medium of tactical psychological warfare, two Douglas C-47 Skytrain (Dakota) aircraft were made available to EUSAK to broadcast surrender messages over loudspeakers, a technology fully developed by the U.S. Navy in the Central Pacific and on Okinawa during World War II. These planes had loudspeakers mounted on their undersides so that they could point directly at the ground for better sound projection.

By the spring of 1951 plans were also under way to increase the 13 hours of daily radio broadcasts made in Korean by adding Chinese-language shortwave radio broadcasts audible to communist troops throughout Korea and into Manchuria. However, a shortage of receivers in communist hands and frequent disruptions of electrical power limited the effectiveness of strategic radio operations during the Korean War.

As in World War II, leaflet and radio propagandists often combined their efforts. In March 1953 the Fifth Air Force, in cooperation with EUSAK, began dropping a special leaflet that asked: "Where is the Communist Air Force?"—a direct throwback to the famous 1944 Office of War Information propaganda campaign asking "Where is the Luftwaffe?" These leaflets were dropped on communist troop concentrations, while Radio Seoul hammered the same theme, hoping to create demoralization, friction between the air forces and ground troops, and foolhardy sorties by communist pilots undertaken to disprove UNC allegations.

In a twist on the theme described above, on the night of April 26, 1953, two B-29s dropped more than 1 million leaflets along the Yalu River, offering $50,000 and political asylum to each Soviet, Chinese, or North Korean pilot who would deliver his jet to South Korea. The campaign was named Operation MOOLAH.

By 1953 psychological warfare in all its forms had become a standard UNC weapon. Leaflets, radio broadcasts, and loudspeakers were credited as major factors in the heavy increase of prisoners after July 1951, and interrogations of communist POWs showed that one in three were influenced to surrender by leaflets. Interrogations of civilians in North and South Korea further revealed that UNC radio broadcasts reached a considerable audience and stirred some civilian opposition to the communist regime. One authority found that Chinese enlisted men were the most amenable to UNC psychological warfare messages, while the hard-core North Korean officer corps was least inclined to believe or act on such appeals.

CLAYTON D. LAURIE

See also

Eisenhower, Dwight David; Jackson, Charles Douglas; MacArthur, Douglas; McClure, Robert Alexis; MOOLAH, Operation; Pace, Frank, Jr.; Ridgway, Matthew Bunker; Truman, Harry S.; Willoughby, Charles Andrew

References

Abner, Alan K. *Psywarriors: Psychological Warfare during the Korean War.* Shippensburg, PA: Burd Street Press, 2001.

Daugherty, William E., and Morris Janowitz, eds. *A Psychological Warfare Casebook.* Baltimore, MD: Johns Hopkins University Press, 1958.

Laurie, Clayton D. *The Propaganda Warriors: The American Crusade against Nazi Germany.* Lawrence: University Press of Kansas, 1996.

———. "The U.S. Army and Psychological Warfare Organization and Operations, 1918–1945." U.S. Army Center of Military History, Washington, DC. Unpublished manuscript.

Pease, Stephen E. *Psywar: Psychological Warfare in Korea, 1950–1953.* Harrisburg, PA: Stackpole, 1992.

Sandler, Stanley. "Cease Resistance: It's Good for You; A History of U.S. Army Combat Psychological Operations." Fort Bragg, NC: U.S. Army Special Operations Command, 1995.

Pueblo Incident
Event Date: January 23, 1968

Diplomatic and military confrontation between the Democratic People's Republic of Korea (DPRK, North Korea) and the United States. On January 23, 1968, four North Korean navy warships converged on and seized the USS *Pueblo*, touching off a major confrontation with the United States. Relations between the two nations had remained tense since the cessation of the Korean War in July 1953. The advent of major American involvement in the Vietnam War, beginning in the mid-1960s, had only further deteriorated relations between the two adversaries and emboldened the North Koreans to strike a more provocative stance.

Indeed, North Korea's hostility toward the Republic of Korea (ROK, South Korea) and the United States resulted in what can only be labeled as reckless behavior in 1968. On January 21, 1968, a unit of 31 North Korean commandos penetrated the demilitarized zone (DMZ) along the 38th Parallel and reached the northern edge of Seoul, with the acknowledged mission of assassinating South

The U.S. Navy intelligence-collection ship *Pueblo* in 1967, prior to its seizure off the coast of Wonsan by North Korea on January 23, 1968. (Naval Historical Center)

Korean president Park Chung Hee. When the commandos were within a mile of the Blue House (the South Korean presidential mansion), they were detected by South Korean police. A gun battle ensued, with all but three commandos killed. One was taken prisoner. Amid this tense atmosphere, the North Koreans seized the *Pueblo* on January 23, just two days later.

Captained by Commander Lloyd M. Bucher, the *Pueblo* (SGRT-21) was an American intelligence-gathering ship operating off the eastern coast of North Korea. Built by the U.S. Army in 1944 as a general-purpose supply vessel, it had been transferred to the U.S. Navy in 1966. Converted and commissioned in 1967 as an auxiliary general environmental research (AGER) ship, the *Pueblo* was actually designed for intelligence gathering. Essentially a small cargo vessel (850 tons and 177 feet in length), the ship was slow (12.5 knots) and only lightly armed, with .50-caliber machine guns. It was also equipped with the most sophisticated modern intelligence devices. Fully 27 members of its 82-man crew were cryptographic and intelligence personnel.

At the time of the attack, the *Pueblo* was in international waters, essentially unprotected with no U.S. warships within supporting range. Personnel onboard were supposedly conducting oceanographic research but were actually involved in gathering electronic intelligence on North Korea. When the ship was taken, Pyongyang claimed that it had entered North Korean territorial waters in Wonsan Bay. Washington insisted that the *Pueblo* had been at least 13 miles beyond the 12-mile limit imposed by North Korea.

During the actual seizure of the ship—the first U.S. warship to be surrendered to a foreign power since the War of 1812—one crewman was killed and several others, including Bucher, were wounded. The ship was then taken into Wonsan harbor under its own power. The North Koreans treated the ship's crew brutally, and on January 26 Japanese television aired a film made by the North Koreans in which Bucher and his crew signed a joint appeal to U.S. president Lyndon B. Johnson, asking him to apologize to the North Korean government for the intrusion of the *Pueblo*.

Crew members of USS *Pueblo* greet officers at the United Nations Advance Camp after almost a year in North Korean custody. (Naval Historical Center)

Meanwhile, North Korean radio stations broadcast Bucher's alleged confession, which stated that his ship had deliberately intruded into North Korea's territorial waters.

The seizure of the *Pueblo,* without a shot being fired in its defense, caused great controversy in the United States. Bucher was both condemned and praised, but certainly the responsibility for the ship's capture extended far up the chain of command. The ship was inadequately protected, and it received no support from any other source when attacked. Certainly the capture of the ship's sophisticated listening devices and cryptographic equipment was a great windfall for the communist intelligence services.

On January 24 U.S. secretary of state Dean Rusk described the seizure as "an act of war." The next day, President Johnson called up a number of U.S. Air Force Reserve, Air National Guard, and Navy Reserve units, a total of 14,787 personnel, and declared that American forces in and around South Korea would be strengthened. He also ordered the aircraft carrier *Enterprise* to take up a position off the North Korean coast. In the days and weeks to come, the task force included 3 cruisers, 5 carriers in addition to the *Enterprise,* 18 destroyers, and the *Pueblo*'s sister ship, the *Banner* (AGER-1). But the United States undertook no hostile action against North Korea, and Johnson announced that the U.S.

government would seek "a prompt and a peaceful solution to the problem."

Already heavily committed to the war in Vietnam, Washington did not wish to settle the *Pueblo* case by military force and risk war in Korea as well. Perhaps aware of this, Pyongyang defiantly declared that it was prepared to meet any eventuality and would deal any American attacks an "exterminating blow."

Taking a hint from a statement over Radio Pyongyang that the *Pueblo* case could be solved by direct negotiation, Washington initiated secret talks with the North Korean government at the truce village of Panmunjom in February 1968. By March 4 the United States and North Korea had met 10 times at Panmunjom. The North Koreans insisted that the United States must admit to and apologize for the supposed intrusion. Meanwhile, Radio Pyongyang reported on February 12 that Captain Bucher made a "second confession," and on March 4 Johnson received a letter purporting to be from *Pueblo* crewmen asking Washington to admit that the vessel had violated North Korean waters. From March 22 to April 2, the North Korean government circulated a series of letters allegedly written by the prisoners, and warned that a refusal to apologize could cost lives. Then, on September 13, Japanese newspapers reported a news conference in Pyongyang at which the *Pueblo* crewmen allegedly said that they had been ordered to intrude as close as three miles off the North Korean coast.

Ten months of negotiations finally led to a statement by the United States on December 21 acknowledging that the *Pueblo* "had illegally intruded into [North Korean] territorial waters." Washington also pledged that no U.S. ships would intrude into the territorial waters of North Korea in the future. Although U.S. chief negotiator Major General Gilbert H. Woodward read a statement inserted into the record disavowing the confession before signing the statement prepared by North Koreans, the North Korean government claimed a great moral as well as diplomatic victory. The next day, December 22, the North Korean government released Commander Bucher and the 81 *Pueblo* crew members. They did not return the *Pueblo*.

The *Pueblo* incident is part of what some historians have called a second Korean conflict. During 1966–1969, emboldened by the U.S. preoccupation with Vietnam, the North Korean government tested U.S. resolve to defend South Korea. During that period in Korea, U.S. casualties numbered 82 killed and 114 wounded. Also, 3 Americans were taken prisoner, not counting the 82 from the *Pueblo*. After 1969, when it became clear to the North Koreans that the United States was determined to remain firm in South Korea, the hostile actions diminished.

JINWUNG KIM

See also

Kim Il Sung; Korea, Democratic People's Republic of, 1953–Present; Korea, Republic of, 1953–Present; Rusk, David Dean

References

Armbrister, Trevor. *A Matter of Accountability: The True Story of the Pueblo Affair.* New York: Coward-McCann, 1970.

Bucher, Lloyd M. *Bucher: My Story.* Garden City, NY: Doubleday, 1970.

Hooper, Edwin B., et al. "The *Pueblo* Incident." *Naval History* 2(4) (Fall 1988): 53–59.

Lerner, Mitchell B. *The Pueblo Incident: A Spy Ship and the Failure of American Foreign Policy.* Lawrence: University Press of Kansas, 2002.

Puller, Lewis Burwell
Birth Date: June 26, 1898
Death Date: October 11, 1971

Iconic U.S. Marine Corps general. Born on June 26, 1898, in West Point, Virginia, Lewis Burwell "Chesty" Puller enrolled in the Virginia Military Institute in 1917 but, impatient to participate in World War I, dropped out to enlist in the Marine Corps in August 1918. Although his formal education was spotty, Puller read widely throughout his life and had a passion for the Civil War, especially the exploits of Confederate general Thomas J. "Stonewall" Jackson.

Disappointed not to see World War I service, Puller attended officer candidate school and was commissioned in the Marine reserves in June 1919. Caught in the reduction of the corps after the war, he was soon placed on the inactive list. Puller then promptly reenlisted in the Marines as a corporal. From 1919 to 1924 he served in the Haitian gendarmerie as acting first lieutenant. There he demonstrated the rapid marching, aggressive tactics, and leading from the front that became his hallmarks.

In 1924, on his return to the United States, Puller was commissioned a second lieutenant. During the next seven years he was stationed in Philadelphia; Quantico, Virginia; Pensacola, Florida (where he took aviation training but did not earn a pilot's wings); Hawaii; and Nicaragua. He served twice as commander of the Marine detachment on the cruiser *Augusta,* a second time in Nicaragua, and in Beijing (Peking), China, as commander of the Marine detachment at the U.S. legation. Between 1936 and 1939 he was an instructor at the Marine Basic School in Philadelphia, and during 1940–1941 he was with the 4th Marine Regiment in Shanghai, China, where he was promoted to major and battalion commander. Puller was next with the 7th Marines at Camp Lejeune, North Carolina, where he became a pioneer in jungle warfare training.

In September 1942 the 7th Marines landed on Guadalcanal, and Puller distinguished himself in the October 24–25 defense of Henderson Field. His half-strength battalion held off an entire Japanese regiment, killing more than 1,400 of the attackers. Promoted to lieutenant colonel, he commanded two battalions at Cape Gloucester, New Britain, when their regular commanders were wounded. In February 1944 he commanded the 1st Marine Regiment and landed with it on Peleliu in September. In November he returned to the United States for training duty at Camp Lejeune and was shortly thereafter promoted to colonel.

When the Korean War began, Puller actively sought a combat command. In August 1950 he returned to the 1st Marine Regiment at Camp Pendleton, California. Sent to Korea immediately thereafter, Puller led the 1st in the Inchon Landing of September 15 and in the subsequent recapture of Seoul. He then took part in the Changjin (Chosin) Reservoir campaign, for which he was awarded his fifth Navy Cross, the most awarded to an individual in Marine Corps history, for inspirational leadership during the Marine withdrawal. It was during this fighting that Puller remarked, "We've been looking for the enemy for some time now. We've finally found him. We're surrounded. That simplifies things." Promoted to brigadier general in January 1951, Puller was for a short time assistant divisional commander of the 1st Marine Division under Major General Oliver P. Smith.

In May 1951 Puller returned to the United States to command the 3rd Marine Brigade, later redesignated the 3rd Marine Division, at Camp Pendleton. Promoted to major general in September 1953, he returned to Camp Lejeune as commander of the 2nd Marine Division and was later deputy camp commander until his retirement for disability in November 1955, with the rank of lieutenant general.

Although he proved himself a competent staff officer, Puller was first and foremost a warrior. During his long career he won 53 decorations, probably the most in Marine Corps history. "Chesty" Puller was also perhaps the most colorful figure in Marine Corps history. Most comfortable when commanding troops in battle, he had only contempt for what he believed were bloated military staffs and their excess creature comforts. One "Pullerism" was "Paperwork will ruin any military force."

Puller died in Hampton, Virginia, on October 11, 1971. A chaplain who served with him in Korea said he was a man who "turned the air around him to heroism and romance and selflessness, who could make men act better than they really were."

SPENCER C. TUCKER

See also

Changjin Reservoir Campaign; Inchon Landing; Smith, Oliver Prince; United States Marine Corps

References

Dabney, William H. "The Next Stop Is Saigon." *Marine Corps Gazette* 82(6) (June 1998): 30–32.

Davis, Burke. *Marine! The Life of Lewis B. (Chesty) Puller, USMC (Ret.).* Boston: Little, Brown, 1962.

Hoffman, Jon T. "Lieutenant General Lewis Burwell Puller." *Marine Corps Gazette* 82(6) (June 1998): 27–30.

Jackson, Kenneth T., ed. *Dictionary of American Biography. Supplement Nine, 1971–1975.* New York: Scribner, 1994.

Montross, Lynn, et al. *U.S. Marine Operations in Korea, 1950–1953.* 5 vols. Washington, DC: U.S. Marine Corps Historical Branch, 1954–1972.

Schuon, Karl. *U.S. Marine Corps Biographical Dictionary.* New York: Franklin Watts, 1963.

Spiller, Roger J., ed. *Dictionary of American Biography*, Vol. 2. Westport, CT: Greenwood, 1984.

PUNCH, **Operation**
Start Date: February 5, 1951
End Date: February 9, 1951

Operation that cleared the way for the recapture of Seoul in 1951. Operation PUNCH began on February 5, 1951, the same day that X Corps implemented Operation ROUNDUP in the area of Hongchon, above the town of Hoengsong. PUNCH was actually an extension of the I and IX Corps push on the Seoul area in late January, code-named Operation THUNDERBOLT, and not part of the X Corps offensive. Operation PUNCH involved a task force built around the U.S. 25th Infantry Division, which was augmented by heavy artillery and armored units and by close air support. The mission of the

U.S. riflemen of the 25th Infantry Division keep a close watch on a burning house held by communist troops southwest of Seoul during Operation PUNCH, February 5–9, 1951. (AP/Wide World Photos)

task force was to destroy all communist troops in defensive positions in the Hill 440 complex just south of Seoul.

During February 5–9 Operation PUNCH forces pounded Hill 440. By February 9 the communist Chinese defenders had retreated across the Han River. More than 4,200 Chinese were killed (that number includes the battlefield count and not those carried from the field or wounded). United Nations Command (UNC) forces suffered only 70 casualties. Operation PUNCH cleared the way for I Corps' final assault on Seoul.

JAMES H. WILLBANKS

See also

Iron Triangle; ROUNDUP, Operation; Seoul; X Corps; THUNDERBOLT, Operation

References

Blair, Clay. *The Forgotten War: America in Korea, 1950–1953.* New York: Times Books, 1987.

Marshall, S. L. A. *Operation Punch and the Capture of Hill 404, Suwon, Korea, February 1951.* Baltimore, MD: Johns Hopkins University Press, 1952.

Middleton, Harry J. *The Compact History of the Korean War.* New York: Hawthorn Books, 1965.

Rees, David. *Korea: The Limited War.* New York: St. Martin's, 1990.

Punchbowl

Bowl-shaped valley about 4.4 miles in diameter surrounded by high hills and located about 5 miles north of Line Kansas, 19 miles north of the 38th Parallel, and 6 miles east of Heartbreak Ridge. The Punchbowl was first briefly held by United Nations Command (UNC) forces in April 1951, during the Operation PILEDRIVER offensive. After it was regained in early summer, it thereafter became mainly a no-man's-land vigorously patrolled by both UNC and communists units, which often set ambushes for each other. The high ground to the north of the Punchbowl was occupied by communists forces, while that to the south was controlled by UNC forces that from time to time included the U.S. 2nd, 3rd, 7th, and 40th Army divisions; the 1st Marine Division; and various Republic of Korea Army (ROKA, South Korean Army) divisions.

The high ground to the south and southwest of the Punchbowl was eventually, in the summer of 1951, mostly controlled by UNC forces. It provided jump-off points for some of the troops supporting or reinforcing 2nd Division regiments or others in attacks on the Heartbreak Ridge hills in August and September 1951.

At one point in the talks at Panmunjom, the communist delegates demanded that the Punchbowl, along with Heartbreak Ridge and some other key and hard-won high ground, be returned to them as a condition for agreeing to a cease-fire. The UNC rejected that demand, which was not again brought up by the other side. Today, the Punchbowl lies mostly just south of the 2.5-mile-wide (4-kilometer-wide) demilitarized zone (DMZ) with its northern rim at the southern DMZ boundary.

SHERMAN W. PRATT

See also

Bloody Ridge, Battle of; Heartbreak Ridge, Battle of; PILEDRIVER, Operation; Truce Talks

References

Blair, Clay. *The Forgotten War: America in Korea, 1950–1953.* New York: Times Books, 1987.

Command Reports, 2nd Infantry Division, August–September 1951. National Archives, Suitland, MD.

Millet, Allan R. *Drive North: U.S. Marines at the Punchbowl.* Washington, DC: U.S. Marine Corps, History and Museums Division, 2001.

Pratt, Sherman W. *Decisive Battles of the Korean War: An Infantry Company Commander's View of the War's Most Critical Engagements.* New York: Vantage Press, 1992.

Pusan

City in the southeastern corner of the Korean Peninsula, located on the Tsushima Strait. Pusan (also known as Busan) is the second-largest city and the largest trading port of the Republic of Korea (ROK, South Korea). When Korea was forced to sign the Kanghwa Treaty with Japan in February 1876, Pusan was opened to foreign trade along with Chemulpo (Inchon) and Wonsan. During the Korean War, Pusan was the temporary capital of South Korea after the capture of Taejon in the summer and early autumn of 1950.

By the beginning of August 1950 Lieutenant General Walton H. Walker's Eighth Army had been pushed below the Naktong River into the so-called Pusan Perimeter, where it struggled desperately to maintain a toehold on the peninsula. This perimeter was a line encompassing an area some 50 miles wide and 100 miles deep on the southeastern tip of the peninsula.

Control of the port of Pusan was absolutely vital to the United Nations Command (UNC) and survival of Walker's Eighth Army. Pusan possessed a large natural harbor and was Korea's chief seaport. Its docking facilities could handle up to 30 oceangoing ships at the same time and had a daily discharge capacity of up to 45,000 tons, but shortages of personnel and transportation assets held this to about 28,000 tons during the Pusan Perimeter campaign. Nonetheless, an excellent rail net connected the port with Miryang, Taegu, and Pohang.

Walker's forces daily became stronger as men and munitions poured into Pusan and the North Korean offensive stalled in the face of determined counterattacks. After the UNC's daring amphibious landing at Inchon on September 15, 1950, which entirely reversed the course of the war, Walker's force was able to break out of the Pusan Perimeter, trapping the Korean People's Army (KPA, North Korean Army) in a classic pincer movement.

At midnight on May 24, 1952, South Korean president Syngman Rhee declared martial law in Pusan and the surrounding region and jailed numerous members of the National Assembly. These actions became an embarrassment to the UN cause. Doubting his prospects to secure another term as president through the National Assembly, Rhee had sought to amend the constitution to provide for direct popular election of the president. This required action by the National Assembly, which resisted his appeal. In the end Rhee, under great pressure from the United States, resolved the issue but not before the National Assembly gave him his sought-after amendment. By the end of July the crisis was over, and nationwide presidential elections were held on August 5, 1952, during which Rhee handily won another term in office.

In early 1953 South Korea moved its government from Pusan back to Seoul, a move that the UNC vainly sought to postpone for security reasons. Today the city has a population of some 3.65 million people and is known for its beautiful beaches and port facilities.

JINWUNG KIM

See also

Inchon Landing; Pusan Perimeter and Breakout

References

Blair, Clay. *The Forgotten War: America in Korea, 1950–1953*. New York: Times Books, 1987.

MacDonald, Callum. *Korea: The War before Vietnam*. New York: Free Press, 1987.

Stueck, William W., Jr. *The Korean War: An International History*. Princeton, NJ: Princeton University Press, 1995.

Pusan Perimeter and Breakout
Start Date: August 1950
End Date: September 1950

The battle for the Pusan Perimeter was one of the most skillful mobile defense operations ever conducted by a U.S. commander. Beginning on July 5, 1950, when Task Force Smith was defeated by Korean People's Army (KPA, North Korean Army) forces near Osan, Lieutenant General Walton H. Walker's U.S. Eighth Army had suffered an unbroken string of defeats. From Chonan (July 6–8) to Chongju (July 10), Chochiwon (July 11–12), the Kum River (July 15–16), and finally Taejon (July 19–20), the KPA had continuously pushed Walker's understrength and poorly trained 24th Infantry Division southward down the Korean Peninsula. On July 25 meanwhile, the 1st Cavalry Division lost Yongdong.

Walker's mission became one of trading space for time, delaying and withdrawing until sufficient forces could be built up in Japan for General Douglas MacArthur's Far East Command to effect a deep turning movement by landing forces at Inchon, on the west coast. By the end of July, however, Walker had run out of space. If his forces withdrew any farther toward the key port of Pusan, he would have insufficient depth with which to maneuver the reserves necessary to counter KPA penetrations and eventually to mass for a counterattack and breakout.

Walker ordered his forces to withdraw behind the line of the Naktong River, and by August 1 the Pusan Perimeter (also known as the Naktong Perimeter) had been established. Three days earlier, on July 29, Walker issued his famous "Stand or Die" order. The Eighth Army at that point consisted of the still-understrength 24th and 25th Infantry divisions and the 1st Cavalry Division. Throughout the course of the campaign, the Eighth Army was reinforced by the 5th Regimental Combat Team (RCT), the 1st Marine Provisional Brigade, regiments of the 2nd Infantry Division, and the British 27th Infantry Brigade, all arriving through Pusan.

Walker also had operational control of the five surviving divisions of the Republic of Korea Army (ROKA, South Korean Army). The allied defensive perimeter consisted of a rectangle approximately 100 by 50 miles in the southeastern corner of Korea. On the western side, the line of defense ran along the Naktong River except for the southernmost 15 miles where the river turned east, away from the line. The northern boundary was a line through the mountains from Naktong-ni to Yongdok, on the east coast. The East Sea (Sea of Japan) formed the eastern boundary, and the Tsushima Strait formed the southern boundary.

General Kim Chaek was the KPA frontline commander in the battle for the Pusan Perimeter, with Lieutenant General Kang Kon as his chief of staff. Kang, however, was killed by a land mine on September 8 at Andong.

Walker had the advantage of operating on interior lines, and he had a robust logistics infrastructure within the perimeter. Pusan was in the southeastern corner. With its large natural harbor and its location on the Tsushima Strait, Pusan was Korea's chief seaport. Its docking facilities were capable of handling 30 oceangoing vessels simultaneously. The port had a daily discharge capacity of up to 45,000 tons, but shortages of personnel and transportation assets held the daily average to 28,000 tons during the campaign. Walker also had the advantage of an excellent rail loop that connected Pusan with Miryang, Taegu, and Pohang.

Walker positioned three of his still-understrength U.S. divisions along the Naktong. The 25th Infantry Division was in the south, the 24th Infantry Division in the center, and the 1st Cavalry Division in the north to just above Waegwan. Above the 1st Cavalry Division, the ROKA 1st Division held the north until the defensive line turned to the east. Across the northern flank of the line the ROKA 6th Division held the western portion, the 8th Division and Capital divisions held the center, and the 3rd Division held the eastern end, until the line reached the sea near Yongdok.

As U.S. forces continued to pour in through the port of Pusan, they were immediately rushed to the front lines. By mid-August the allies had more than 500 medium tanks in Korea, giving them a greater than 5-to-1 advantage in armor. On the sea flanks of the perimeter the U.S. Navy was able to provide effective naval gunfire support. The U.S. Fifth Air Force also held air supremacy, which meant that movement within the perimeter could be conducted without regard to cover and concealment. This, of course, enhanced Walker's mobility advantage.

Eleven KPA divisions initially faced the allies. From south to north along the Naktong were arrayed the 6th, 4th, 3rd, 2nd, 15th,

U.S. Eighth Army commander Lieutenant General Walton H. Walker crosses the Naktong River in his jeep fitted with a handrail. (National Archives)

and 1st divisions. From west to east along the northern flank of the perimeter the North Koreans had the 13th, 8th, 12th, and 5th divisions. The bulk of the 105th Armored Division was held in reserve. KPA forces also included the 766th Independent Infantry Regiment, in the northeast corner near Yongdok, and the 83rd Motorized Regiment, detached from the 105th Armored Division and in the southwestern corner near Kogang-ni. About the middle of August, elements of the newly formed 7th Division entered the southern end of the line north of the 6th Division. The 9th Division and elements of the 10th Division also entered the line south and north, respectively, of the 2nd Division.

Most of the KPA units, especially the 13th Division, had suffered heavy losses during the fight down the peninsula. The 105th Armored Division had only about 40 tanks left. Although intelligence estimates at the time painted a somewhat different picture, the allies actually held a slight numerical advantage, with some 92,000 troops to 70,000. Many of Walker's soldiers, however, were engaged in securing and operating his extensive logistics infrastructure within the perimeter.

The KPA's primary operational objective was to cut off and isolate the U.S. and South Korean forces on the Korean Peninsula,

thereby preventing them from reinforcing and building up to the point where they could go on the offensive. The North Korean geographic objective was the port of Pusan, the main point of entrance for allied reinforcements and logistics. From the KPA standpoint, the campaign's center of gravity was the forces of the Eighth Army and the ROKA. Once those forces were isolated and neutralized, Pusan would be wide open and vulnerable. Between August 5 and September 9 the KPA attacked the Pusan Perimeter along four widely separated concentric axes, all following natural approach corridors.

During August 5–14 the KPA tried to envelop the left (southern) flank of the United Nations Command (UNC) line, with one division and one armored regiment attacking along the Sunchon-Chinju-Masan-Pusan axis. Walker responded by reinforcing the 25th Infantry Division with the 5th RCT and the 1st Marine Brigade. Operating as Task Force Kean, the combined army-marine force launched the first allied counterattack of the war on August 7. Striking at the KPA 6th Division at Chinju, the poorly coordinated attack made only limited progress. After five days of back-and-forth fighting, Walker called off the counterattack and shifted his attentions to threats farther to the north.

During August 4–19 the KPA tried to penetrate the UNC line in the vicinity of Taegu with five infantry divisions echeloned in depth, supported by elements of the 105th Armored Division. This was a two-pronged attack originating around Sangju. One thrust approached Taegu from Kunwi in the north, and the other pointed south of Taegu. From Taegu the axis of attack led straight down the road and rail main lines of communication (LOCs) to Kyongsan, Miryang, Samnangjin, and Pusan.

General Walker considered the attack south of Taegu, an area known as the Naktong Bulge, to be the primary threat. Had KPA forces succeeded in this sector, they could have cut the Taegu-Pusan rail loop, threatening the very existence of the entire defensive perimeter. North of Taegu, Walker could still afford to trade some space for time. The North Koreans also helped the allies by poorly coordinating the two thrusts. This allowed Walker to continually shift his mobile and armored reserves behind the lines to the points of maximum danger.

Walker moved the 1st Marine Brigade and elements of the 27th Infantry Regiment up from the south and attached them to the 24th Infantry Division. On August 17 the 24th Infantry Division counterattacked the KPA 4th Division and cleared the bulge by the following night. On August 24 Walker moved the 2nd Infantry Division into the line and pulled the 24th Infantry Division back into reserve.

Meanwhile, north of Taegu the KPA 13th and 1st divisions forced their way across the Naktong and by August 9 had collapsed the northwestern corner of the perimeter, pushing the divisions of ROKA II Corps down on top of the 1st Cavalry Division. To protect his valuable mobile communications system, Walker was forced to evacuate his headquarters from Taegu to Pusan. He also shifted the 27th Infantry Regiment again farther north. The 27th Infantry and the ROKA 1st Division attacked on August 18 and established positions overlooking a long, flat, narrow valley that became known as the Bowling Alley. On August 19 Walker also shifted elements of the 23rd Infantry Regiment to reinforce the 27th Infantry Regiment. During the next six continuous nights, the KPA 13th Division unsuccessfully tried to drive the U.S. forces back.

Meanwhile, during August 9–19 the KPA 5th Division attempted to infiltrate and envelope the right (northern) side of the UNC line with three divisions and an independent regiment on the Yongdok-Pohang-Kyongju-Ulsan-Pusan axis. The North Korean objective was to drive all the way down the east coast to Pusan. The defensive battles along the northern flank were an operation primarily under the control of the ROKA I Corps. Walker did send a small task force of artillery and armor, and the South Koreans received massive U.S. air and naval support.

Both geography and hydrography provided perfect conditions for naval gunfire support of the ROKA 3rd Division. The straightness of the Korean east coast, the sea depth along the coast, and the high coastal terrain that forced the major roads right to the edge of the coast all meant that the KPA forces were almost constantly within range of the ships' guns. Naval gunfire and tactical

Private First Class Clarence Whitmore, a radio operator in the 24th Infantry Regiment, reads the news during a meal in a lull in the fighting near Sangju, South Korea, August 9, 1950. (National Archives)

air support from the Fifth Air Force helped the ROKA 3rd Division overcome its weakness in organic artillery.

Naval and air fires gave the ROKA units a further maneuver advantage by forcing the KPA forces to operate primarily at night and away from the main coastal roads. These fires also allowed the South Koreans to exploit both the advantage of falling back on interior lines and the advantage of UNC maritime superiority. The best example of this came during the August 16–17 evacuation of the ROKA 3rd Division from Toksong-ni by sea while the Fifth Air Force maintained a curtain of fire around the beach. By August 18 the 3rd Division was moving into battle positions near Pohang, some 25 miles to the south, and was still capable of continuing the fight. At that point, however, the Pusan Perimeter had been collapsed from the north to about half its original size.

Beginning on August 27 the North Koreans launched another round of attacks that fell on the same objectives as the earlier August drives. This time, the attacks were well coordinated and hit simultaneously. By September 3 Walker was forced to fight defensive battles in five different locations at the same time.

On the northern flank the ROKA 3rd Division was forced out of Pohang on September 6, and the KPA cut the east-west road to Taegu. In the center by September 10, the North Koreans had pushed the 1st Cavalry Division to within 15 miles of Taegu. Farther

PUSAN PERIMETER, AUGUST 1950

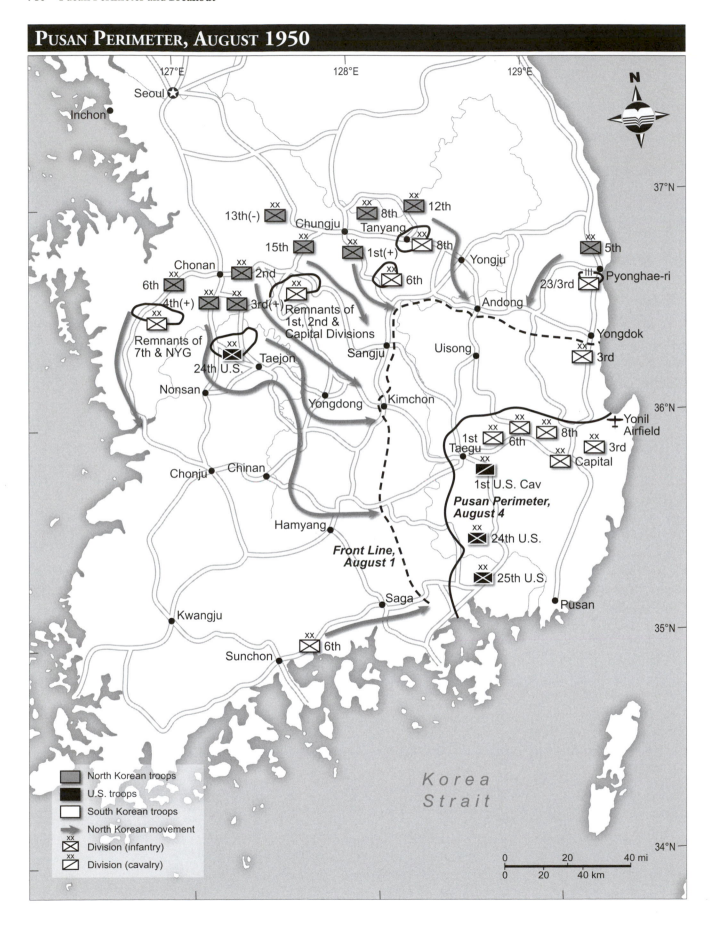

711 Pusan Perimeter and Breakout

south, the 2nd Infantry Division was driven back to just short of Yongsan in the Naktong Bulge. In the far south, the KPA broke through the 25th Infantry Division and again threatened Masan.

American casualties during the first two weeks of September 1950 were the heaviest of any comparable period in the war. Yet with the security of Pusan always in the forefront, Walker continued to shift his reserves from danger point to danger point inside his ever-shrinking perimeter. Attaching the 1st Marine Brigade to the 2nd Infantry Division, he ordered the clearing of the Naktong Bulge for the second time. He also centrally positioned one of the 24th Infantry Division's regiments where it could be used to reinforce either the 25th Infantry Division, the 2nd Infantry Division, or ROKA units in the north.

By September 12 the North Korean offensive reached its culminating point and stalled. The entire KPA was now overextended, dangerously out of position, and off balance. All of its effective combat power was arrayed around the Pusan Perimeter. Its land and sea LOCs were under constant attack by U.S. naval and air forces. The North Koreans were now a ripe target for a turning movement at operational depth. They still had close to 70,000 troops around the Pusan Perimeter. Inside, the Eighth Army now had 84,500 troops and the ROKA some 72,000.

The U.S. X Corps landed at Inchon on September 15. The Eighth Army began its breakout the next day. Walker wanted to wait one day after the Inchon Landing to let the reality of being cut off sink in for the North Koreans. On September 16, however, there was little sign that KPA forces were even aware of the situation to the north and west, despite a massive bombardment of psychological warfare leaflets and broadcasts.

The Eighth Army plan called for the breakout to be made by the newly activated U.S. I Corps just north of Taegu. I Corps at that point consisted of the 1st Cavalry Division, the 24th Infantry Division, the ROKA 1st Division, the 5th RCT, and the British 27th Infantry Brigade. The 5th RCT and the 1st Cavalry Division were supposed to seize a bridgehead over the Naktong near Waegwan. The 24th Infantry Division would then cross the river and drive along the Kimchon-Taejon-Suwon axis to effect a linkup with X Corps. Other units of the Eighth Army would conduct holding attacks along the perimeter to pin the North Koreans in place.

The Eighth Army experienced great difficulty in making the breakout. Walker's units were burned out after almost two months of heavy and continuous combat. They also lacked the proper river-crossing equipment, and ammunition was in short supply. Determined KPA troops held on grimly but finally showed signs of breaking on September 22. The next day, the North Koreans began a general withdrawal.

The allies pursued. The lead U.S. unit was Task Force Lynch, organized around the 1st Cavalry Division's 3rd Battalion, 7th Cavalry. At 8:26 a.m. on September 27 just north of Osan, Task Force Lynch linked up with elements of the U.S. 7th Infantry Division's 31st Infantry Regiment that had landed at Inchon. The battle for the Pusan Perimeter was over.

At the tactical level, the North Korean attacks had mostly been a series of poorly coordinated attempts to penetrate, infiltrate, and/or envelop the Pusan Perimeter. At the operational level, they added up to one big frontal attack, and a piecemeal one at that. The single biggest flaw in the KPA's operational concept was its inability to achieve the necessary mass at a decisive point. Its only hope had been to achieve overwhelming mass at one point, punch through the thinly held UNC lines, and drive straight for Pusan. The KPA failed to do this, although it came the closest at Taegu.

General Walker conducted an effective mobile defense. It was both active and flexible. The perimeter was thinly held, manned by a series of strong points on key terrain that commanded the principal river crossing sites, the major hills, and the road junctions. With his three U.S. divisions and all five South Korean divisions on line, Walker carefully husbanded and formed reserves with the units that were coming in through Pusan. The Eighth Army had two primary locations for holding reserves—Kyongsan and Samnangjin-Miryang—but the reserve forces were committed to wherever a trouble spot erupted. After a given situation was restored, the reserves were withdrawn for commitment elsewhere.

The Eighth Army's counterattacks in the south were conducted under the control of the division in the line, after being reinforced by commitment of Eighth Army reserves. For the counterattacks in the north, the counterattacking forces remained under Eighth Army control. At times, General Walker had to pull a regiment of a committed division out of the line and shift it elsewhere. For example, after the 25th Infantry Division had stopped the attack toward Masan (August 5–12), the 27th Infantry Regiment was pulled out of the line and sent north to assist the 24th Infantry Division at the Naktong Bulge (August 12–16) and then north again (August 18–25) to stop the KPA attack against Taegu on the Kunwi axis.

From the very start, General Walker had conducted his defense with the ultimate objective of shifting over to the offensive once the KPA attack had reached culmination. Critical to this was maintaining the viability of the internal LOCs, which would be essential to support and sustain any breakout. Walker therefore was able to give up far more ground in the north, where the original line of the perimeter was almost 40 miles from the apex of the LOC network at Yongchon. Along the western side of the perimeter the LOCs were much closer, giving the defenders far less flexibility.

By the time I Corps and X Corps linked up on September 27, the KPA had been all but annihilated. Only 20,000–30,000 of its troops besieging Pusan ever returned to North Korea. The defenders paid a high price as well. Between July 5 and September 16, Eighth Army casualties totaled 4,280 killed in action, 12,377 wounded, 2,107 missing, and 401 confirmed captured.

DAVID T. ZABECKI

See also

Bowling Alley; Inchon Landing; MacArthur, Douglas; Naktong Bulge, First Battle of; Naktong Bulge, Second Battle of; Naval Gunfire Support; Osan, Battle of; Taegu, Defense of; Task Force Kean; Task Force Smith; Walker, Walton Harris

References

Appleman, Roy E. *United States Army in Korea: South to the Naktong, North to the Yalu.* Washington, DC: Office of the Chief of Military History, 1961.

Blair, Clay. *The Forgotten War: America in Korea, 1950–1953.* New York: Times Books, 1987.

Ent, Uzal W. *Fighting on the Brink: Defense of the Pusan Perimeter.* Paducah, KY: Turner, 1996.

Hoyt, Edwin P. *The Pusan Perimeter.* New York: Stein and Day, 1984.

Robertson, William G. *Counterattack on the Naktong, 1950.* Fort Leavenworth, KS: Combat Studies Institute, 1985.

Pyon Yong Tae

Birth Date: December 15, 1892
Death Date: March 10, 1969

Educator, author, and diplomat for the Republic of Korea (ROK, South Korea). Born in Seoul on December 15, 1892, Pyon Yong Tae graduated from Posong High School in Seoul in 1909 and from Xinxing School in Manchuria in 1912. He studied at Xiehe University near Beijing (Peking), China, in 1915 and taught English at Chungang High School in Seoul from 1920 to 1943. To avoid any connection with Japanese colonial authorities during their national mobilization for World War II, in the spring of 1943 Pyon moved to a little farm at Pupyong, between Seoul and Inchon. From 1945 to 1949 he taught English at Korea University in Seoul. A prolific author, Pyon's literary works include *My Attitude toward Ancestor Worship* (1925), *Tales from Korea* (1943), and *Song from Korea* (1948).

In February 1949 South Korean president Syngman Rhee sent Pyon to the Philippines as his personal envoy, and he was successful in establishing official recognition of the South Korean government by the Philippines. During this trip Pyon had the opportunity to visit with General Douglas MacArthur in Tokyo. Pyon exposed Rhee's policy of unification through military means as being unrealistic and motivated by domestic politics. Pyon did, however, emphasize to MacArthur the need to strengthen South Korean military forces.

In February 1951 Pyon was a Korean delegate at the United Nations Economic Commission for Asia and the Far East (UNECAFE) held in Lahore, Pakistan. During this conference the Soviet delegate proposed that South Korea's associate membership in UNECAFE be ended because of its government's nondemocratic nature. Pyon made a strong impression in his shrewd responses to scathing attacks from the Soviet delegate; he was also able to disarm the Soviet attacks by dispassionately laying out the real situation in Korea. When the Soviet Union obstructed further activities of UNECAFE, its own membership was terminated.

Upon his return to Korea, Pyon became minister of foreign affairs. In the late spring of 1951 he went on a speaking tour in the United States in support of U.S. foreign aid around the world. He appealed to the American people to protect their own freedom and that of the rest of the free world by helping to rebuild South Korea, thereby forestalling the threat of communism.

Pyon led the South Korean delegation to the United Nations (UN) General Assembly Seventh Session, from October 1952 to March 1953. There he met with U.S. secretary of state Dean G. Acheson and stressed the necessity of a mutual defense treaty between South Korea and the United States. During the conference proceedings Pyon defended his government, which had been criticized in a report by the UN Commission for the Unification and Rehabilitation of Korea. He also refuted issues regarding prisoners of war raised by the Indian delegation.

Along with General Choe Tok Sin and Colonel Yi Su Yong, Pyon participated at the special UN General Assembly session held in August 1953 in preparation for carrying out Clause 60 of the Military Armistice Agreement on Korea. Pyon was successful in blocking Indian participation at the political conference that followed. He was also able to secure representation in its preparatory meeting, which included the ambassadors of the 16 nations that participated on the UN side in the Korean War. This strengthened the South Korean position at the ensuing political conference.

While Pyon was in the United States for the UN General Assembly Eightieth Session in September 1953, he helped dissuade U.S. politicians and journalists regarding possible neutralization of Korea and establishment of a buffer zone there. He also informed them about the reality of coercive persuasion tactics used by the communists on anticommunist prisoners of war.

The 1954 Geneva Conference provided another opportunity for Pyon to exhibit his diplomatic skills. He succeeded in frustrating both Nam Il's proposal to institute a Korean Commission with an equal number of members from the two Korean national assemblies and a Philippine proposal to establish a constitutional assembly with representatives from the two Korean states. At that time, President Dwight D. Eisenhower's administration was considering supporting a policy that would call for general elections in both the Democratic People's Republic of Korea (DPRK, North Korea) and South Korea, establishment of a buffer zone between the People's Republic of China (PRC) and North Korea, and the simultaneous withdrawal of Chinese and United Nations Command (UNC) military forces from Korea. Pyon dissuaded the U.S. delegates from supporting such a plan by reminding them of the previous negative experiences following negotiated arrangements with the communists. Subsequently, Pyon secured the support of 15 of the 16 nations participating in the Korean War on the UN side to endorse the South Korean proposal as outlined in a 16-nation communiqué, which included South Korea.

After serving as South Korean prime minister from June to November 1954, Pyon retired from government service. He received an honorary doctorate in literature from Korea University in May 1962 and became a professor at Seoul National University and Korea University in 1965. He died in Seoul on March 10, 1969.

Man-ho Heo

See also
Acheson, Dean Gooderham; Geneva Conference; MacArthur, Douglas; Nam Il; Rhee, Syngman

References
Chong In Hung, Kim Song Hui, et al., eds. *Chongchihak Sajon* [Dictionary of Political Science]. Seoul: Pakyong-sa, 1994.
Pyon Yong Tae. *Na ui Choguk* [Korea, My Country: Memoirs]. Seoul: Chayu Chulpan-sa, 1956.
———. *Oegyo Yorok* [The Other Story of Diplomacy]. Seoul: Hanguk Ilbo-sa, 1959.

Pyongyang

City located at the estuary of the Taedong River in the Democratic People's Republic of Korea (DPRK, North Korea). Pyongyang is currently the capital and largest city of North Korea. The city has direct access to the Yellow Sea via the Taedong River, which empties into Korea Bay at Nampo. It is about 100 miles north of the demilitarized zone (DMZ) near the 38th Parallel. Pyongyang, acclaimed the oldest city in Korea, is reportedly where Old Choson was founded in 2333 BCE by King Tangun, the mythic father of the Korean people. It served as the northern capital during the Koryo dynasty (918–1392).

During the Japanese occupation, Pyongyang was a major industrial and railroad center and, with almost half a million residents, the obvious choice to become the newly proclaimed North Korean regime's capital in 1948. Its current population is estimated to be between 2.5 million and 3.8 million people.

For reasons of both morale and strategy, after September 1950 Pyongyang's capture became one of the principal objectives for United Nations Command (UNC) forces, and it was taken by the advancing U.S. Eighth Army on October 19, 1950. U.S. and South Korean troops alike regarded it as a base for rest and recreation, and some incidents of looting occurred.

Following the late October 1950 Chinese intervention in the war, in mid-November the U.S. State Department proposed a halt to UNC offensive operations and a withdrawal to just north of Pyongyang and Wonsan. UNC commander General Douglas MacArthur rejected this and on November 24 commenced his final offensive.

The second (and massive) Chinese intervention of late November 1950 forced the UNC to evacuate Pyongyang on December 3, 1950, and two days later the city burned to the ground; whether accidentally or as a final vindictive act of retaliation on the part of UNC troops remains unclear. When communist forces retook Pyongyang, they circulated vivid pictures around the world of the devastated ruins in a major propaganda coup. From then until the 1953 armistice, the city was a major target for air raids by UNC air forces, often using delayed-action bombs that exploded as much as 72 hours after they were dropped. Bombing raids in the summer of 1952 also targeted five nearby dams that controlled the water supplies needed for the rice harvest, causing severe flooding

in much of North Korea. Pyongyang's population dwindled to 50,000 people. These residents, including Kim Il Sung's government, spent most of the daylight hours in a system of deep bunkers and trenches. One aim of the air raids was the psychological destabilization of Pyongyang's population, but as with similar bombing campaigns in other wars, civilian morale tended to survive relatively intact.

After the July 27, 1953, armistice, Pyongyang was rebuilt as a showplace for the North Korean government, although in the later 1990s the ravages of famine began to disturb its immaculate facade. It continues as the North Korean capital and as North Korea's special municipality.

PRISCILLA ROBERTS AND JINWUNG KIM

See also
Korea, Democratic People's Republic of, United Nations Command Occupation of; MacArthur, Douglas

References
Cumings, Bruce. *Korea's Place in the Sun: A Modern History*. New York: Norton, 1997.
Halliday, Jon, and Bruce Cumings. *Korea: The Unknown War*. New York: Pantheon, 1988.
Millett, Allan R. *Their War in Korea: American, Asian, and European Combatants and Civilians, 1945–1953*. Princeton, NJ: Princeton University Press, 2002.

Pyongyang, March to and Capture of
Start Date: October 7, 1950
End Date: October 20, 1950

The United Nations Command (UNC) invasion of North Korea officially began on October 7, 1950, after the failure of the government of the Democratic People's Republic of Korea (DPRK, North Korea) to respond to UNC commander General Douglas MacArthur's proclamation of the United Nations (UN) resolution demanding its surrender. The invading UNC force consisted of the U.S. I Corps of the Eighth Army in the west and the U.S. X Corps in the east.

The U.S. I Corps then driving on the North Korean capital of Pyongyang from the vicinity of Kaesong consisted of the 1st Cavalry Division followed by the 24th Infantry Division. In the east along the coast the Republic of Korea Army (ROKA, South Korean Army) I Corps had pushed ahead of U.S. X Corps and took the port city of Wonsan on October 11. Two weeks later, on October 25, X Corps forces landed at Wonsan by sea.

The 1st Cavalry Division ran into stubborn Korean People's Army (KPA, North Korean Army) resistance on its way to Kumchon. A strong KPA roadblock just north of Kaesong temporarily halted two battalions of the 5th Cavalry Regiment, and the 7th and 8th Cavalry regiments of the division quickly moved forward to aid in taking the town. The 7th Cavalry made a wide sweep to block the main highway north of Kumchon and create a pocket, into which the 5th and 8th Cavalry regiments slowly pushed the

Tanks and infantry of the 1st Cavalry Division in pursuit of Korean People's Army (North Korean Army) forces some 14 miles north of Kaesong on the way to Pyongyang. (National Archives)

KPA defenders. It took five days of fighting, however, before KPA resistance ceased and Kumchon fell. After this battle, the North Koreans limited their defense to slowing down advancing U.S. troops and ambushing lightly protected service units.

During this time, two other divisions moved on line with the 1st Cavalry. On the west the 24th Division moved toward the port of Chinnampo (Nampo). On the right the ROKA 1st Division moved toward Pyongyang. In addition, the 27th British Commonwealth Brigade, with its newly attached Australian 3rd Battalion, pushed through the 1st Cavalry Division in the center and took over the lead to Sariwon.

Attacking UNC units were moving so fast that they often over-ran many KPA units. Confusion over identity of uniforms affected both sides, and members of the 27th Brigade mistook stranded North Korean soldiers as South Korean troops. The North Koreans, on the other hand, thought that the Scot Argylls of the 27th Brigade were Soviet forces who had just entered the war to help them.

With the fall of Sariwon, the race for the capture of Pyongyang began. From the south, the U.S. I Corps continued to push rapidly north. From the southeast four ROKA divisions carried out a wide envelopment, racing one another to take the city. Capture of the North Korean capital now became a political objective. The North Koreans, however, were not prepared to give up their capital without a fight.

Two divisions led this race for Pyongyang: the U.S. 1st Cavalry and the ROKA 1st Division. On October 18 the 1st Cavalry Division was only 30 miles from the city, while the ROKA 1st Division was even closer but was being slowed by strong KPA resistance, the route in front of the ROKA division being heavily mined. As a consequence, on October 19 Company F of the 5th Cavalry Regiment became the first UNC unit to gain the North Korean capital; Company F entered southwestern Pyongyang at 11:00 a.m.

At almost the same time, the 2nd Battalion of the ROKA 12th Regiment arrived at the southern edge of the Taedong River. During the afternoon of October 19 the ROKA 11th Regiment secured Pyongyang Airfield. By nightfall most of the ROKA 1st Division was in the main part of the city north of the Taedong River. After dark the 8th Regiment of the ROKA 7th Division moved into Pyongyang from the east.

In spite of the quick capture of much of Pyongyang, the KPA continued to resist and planned a last-ditch defense at the administrative center of the city. However, the next morning, October 20, the ROKA 1st Division took the strongly fortified city administrative center with ease. North Korean defenders were too demoralized by the rapid approach of the Eighth Army to put up any fight and abandoned both guns and entrenchments. By midmorning the ROKA 1st Division reported the city secure. Shortly afterward, engineer boats were brought up, and the U.S. 5th Cavalry Regiment began crossing the Taedong River. By noon, both U.S. and ROKA forces had completely secured the city.

DANIEL R. BEIRNE

See also

MacArthur, Douglas; Pyongyang; X Corps

References

Alexander, Bevin. *Korea: The First War We Lost.* New York: Hippocrene Books, 1986.

Appleman, Roy E. *United States Army in Korea: South to the Naktong, North to the Yalu.* Washington, DC: Office of the Chief of Military History, 1961.

Blair, Clay. *The Forgotten War: America in Korea, 1950–1953.* New York: Times Books, 1987.

James, D. Clayton, with Anne Sharp Wells. *Refighting the Last War: Command and Crisis in Korea, 1950–1953.* New York: Free Press, 1993.

Whelan, Richard. *Drawing the Line: The Korean War, 1950–1953.* Boston: Little, Brown, 1990.

Q

Qin Jiwei

Birth Date: November 16, 1914
Death Date: February 2, 1997

Chinese general and commander of the Chinese People's Volunteer Army (CPVA, Chinese Army) Fifteenth Army during the Korean War. Born in Huangan, Hubei Province, China, on November 16, 1914, Qin Jiwei (Chin Chi Wei) in his long military career advanced steadily from soldier to People's Republic of China (PRC) minister of defense. Qin joined the Red Army in 1929 and the Chinese Communist Party (CCP) in 1930. He commanded a regiment in 1932 and a division of the Fourth Army during the Long March (1934–1935). Qin was a capable commander in the Second Field Army against the Japanese when they invaded China (1937–1945). He became commander of the Fifteenth Army in the Second Field Army during the Chinese Civil War (1945–1949).

Qin's Fifteenth Army entered the Democratic People's Republic of Korea (DPRK, North Korea) in March 1951 in the second wave of reinforcements. After participating in the CPVA's Fifth (Spring) Offensive, the Fifteenth Army was stationed in the Obong-san Mountain area. Some of its units were deployed on the hilltops of Sanggam-nyong, a strategically important position for the Chinese defense line that directly threatened Kimhwa on the 38th Parallel. Because the post was exposed to United Nations Command (UNC) attack, five companies from the 45th Division of the Fifteenth Army constructed tunnels to assist in its defense.

Qin directed the Chinese defense at Sanggam-nyong in a UNC attack during October 14–November 25, 1952, that saw some of the fiercest fighting of the Korean War. Qin's troops, deployed on two narrow hilltops of Sanggam-nyong at the front tip of the Obong-san ranges, absorbed numerous UNC assaults and bombardments. The Fifteenth Army defeated numerous assaults on the surface and used tunnels with great effectiveness, successfully defending the stronghold for more than one week before a large-scale Chinese counterattack ended the UNC offensive. The Chinese success there helped to strengthen the communist bargaining position in the armistice negotiations.

After the Korean War, Qin was promoted to deputy commander of the Yunnan Provincial Command and then deputy commander of the Kunming Regional Command. In 1955 he was promoted to lieutenant general. As a trusted officer under Deng Xiaoping, then political commissar of the Second Field Army, Qin was promoted to commander of the Chengdu Regional Command in 1974, commander of the Beijing Regional Command in 1978, and PRC minister of defense in 1988. That year he was promoted to general. He served in the latter post until 1993. Qin died on February 2, 1997.

RICHARD WEIXING HU

See also

China, People's Republic of, Army; Chinese Offensive, Fifth

References

National Defense University of China. *Zhongguo Jundui Shizhan Shilu* [War Cases of the Chinese Armed Forces], Vol. 4. Beijing: Guofang Daxue Chubanshe, 1993.

Peters, Richard, and Xiaobing Li. *Voices from the Korean War: Personal Stories of American, Korean, and Chinese Soldiers.* Lexington: University Press of Kentucky, 2004.

Qin Jiwei. *Qin Jiwei Huiyilu* [Qin Jiwei Memoirs]. Beijing: Jiefangjun Chubanshe, 1996.

Wu Rugao et al., eds. *Zhongguo Junshi Renwu Dacidian* [Dictionary of Chinese Military Figures]. Beijing: Xinhua Chubanshe, 1989.

Zhongguo Junshi Dabaike Quanshu [Chinese Military Encyclopedia]. Military History, Vols. 1–3. Beijing: Junshi Kexue Chubanshe, 1997.

Quesada, Elwood Richard
Birth Date: April 13, 1904
Death Date: February 9, 1993

U.S. Air Force general instrumental in developing the air-ground coordination techniques for close air support during World War II that were used by the U.S. Air Force in support of ground forces during the Korean War. Born in Washington, DC, on April 13, 1904, Elwood Richard Quesada attended the University of Maryland and Georgetown University. In 1924 he enlisted in the army as a private, becoming a flying cadet in the Army Air Service and receiving his commission upon graduation. In 1929 he won fame by joining fellow aviators and latter-day generals Carl Spaatz, Ira C. Baker, Frank Andrews, and Henry "Hap" Arnold in the record-setting flight of the *Question Mark*, a plane that the crew kept aloft for 151 hours through air-to-air refueling.

During the 1930s Quesada had several assignments as the personal pilot for a number of prominent government figures, including Secretary of War George H. Dern. Captain Quesada graduated from the Command and General Staff School at Fort Leavenworth, Kansas, in 1937. Other assignments included service as air attaché in Cuba and Argentina.

In late 1940 Quesada became the foreign liaison chief for Arnold, now commander of the Army Air Corps, and went with him to London in April 1941 to set up Lend-Lease operations with British air leaders. Three months later, in July 1941, Major Quesada assumed command of the 33rd Pursuit Group at Mitchell Field, New York. In December 1942 he was advanced to brigadier general and took command of the 1st Air Defense Wing, making preparations to go to North Africa. Once there, he took command of the XII Fighter Command. Quesada led his men in missions over Tunisia, Morocco, Sicily, Corsica, and southern Italy.

In the autumn of 1943 Quesada was summoned to England to command the IX Fighter Command (later renamed the IX Tactical Air Command). He led this group in preparations for the Allied invasion of France and was advanced to major general in April 1944. The day after D-Day (June 6, 1944) he established his headquarters on French soil. Quesada helped plan the breakout from the Normandy beaches, and he developed the air-ground coordination techniques for close air support that remain part of current U.S. military doctrine. Until the end of the war, he directed his command in operations in support of the Allied advance across France and Germany. During the Battle of the Bulge (Ardennes Offensive) he utilized radar to provide close air support in poor weather.

After the war, General Quesada went to Washington as assistant chief of staff for the U.S. Air Force. During 1946–1947 he commanded the Third Air Force, and in 1947–1948 he was the first commander of the Tactical Air Command. He then devoted his attention to several projects for the new Joint Chiefs of Staff (JCS) before assuming command of Joint Task Force Three at Enewetak (Eniwetok) during 1948–1951.

Quesada retired from the air force in 1951 as a lieutenant general. He then joined the aircraft manufacturer Lockheed as an executive. Four years later President Dwight Eisenhower appointed Quesada as his special assistant. During the next six years Quesada not only wrote the legislation establishing the Federal Aviation Agency (FAA) but also served as its first administrator, until January 1961. He then joined a successful real estate development company in the Washington, DC, area, for which he served as president from 1963 to 1977. He also sat on numerous corporate boards and was involved in civic projects in Washington, DC Quesada died on February 9, 1993, in Jupiter, Florida.

JAMES H. WILLBANKS

See also

Close Air Support; Eisenhower, Dwight David; Forward Air Controllers

References

Crane, Conrad C. *American Air Power Strategy in Korea, 1950–1953.* Lawrence: University Press of Kansas, 1999.

Frisbee, John L. *Makers of the United States Air Force.* Washington, DC: Air Force History and Museums Program, 1996.

Futrell, Robert F. *The United States Air Force in Korea, 1950–1953.* Rev. ed. Washington, DC: Office of the Chief of Air Force History, 1983.

Kohn, Richard H., and Joseph P. Harahan, eds. *Air Superiority in World War II and Korea: An Interview with General James Ferguson, General Robert M. Lee, General William W. Momyer, and Lieutenant General Elwood R. Quesada.* Washington, DC: Office of Air Force History, 1983.

Momyer, William W. *Air Power in Three Wars: WWII, Korea, Vietnam.* Washington, DC: Department of the Air Force, 1978.

Schlight, John. "Elwood R. Quesada: TAC Air Comes of Age." In John L. Frisbee, ed., *Makers of the United States Air Force,* 177–204. Washington, DC: Air Force History and Museums Program, 1996.

R

Radford, Arthur William
Birth Date: February 27, 1896
Death Date: August 17, 1973

U.S. admiral; commander in chief, Pacific, and commander in chief, U.S. Pacific Fleet, during April 1949–August 1953; and chairman of the Joint Chiefs of Staff (JSC) during 1953–1957. Born in Chicago, Illinois, on February 27, 1896, Arthur William Radford graduated from the U.S. Naval Academy, Annapolis, in 1916 and served aboard the battleship South Carolina during World War I. During the interwar period he became a naval aviator, spent three years with the Bureau of Aeronautics, and served with aviation units attached to the Colorado, Pennsylvania, and Wright. He eventually commanded a fighter squadron on the aircraft carrier Saratoga.

When World War II began in Europe, Radford was commander of the Naval Air Station in Seattle, Washington. He returned to sea duty in 1940 in the aircraft carrier Yorktown, then with the U.S. Pacific Fleet, and was aboard it at the time of the Japanese attack on Pearl Harbor, Hawaii, on December 7, 1941. Shortly thereafter, Radford became the director of the navy's aviation training program, which was then undergoing a major expansion. In April 1943 he was promoted to rear admiral and was again assigned to the Pacific Fleet, where he commanded a carrier division that participated in numerous amphibious operations, including the Gilbert Islands Campaign in November 1943. In May 1944 Radford became assistant deputy chief of naval operations for air in the Navy Department in Washington. He was promoted to vice admiral in 1945.

Following the war Radford held a number of posts, including vice chief of naval operations. He was a primary leader in the Revolt of the Admirals of 1949 over the Harry S. Truman administration's emphasis on a sizable U.S. Air Force strategic bomber capability at the expense of sea power.

Appointed commander in chief, Pacific, and commander in chief of the U.S. Pacific Fleet in April 1949, Radford was a strong anticommunist and a firm believer that the greatest threat to U.S. national security lay in Asia rather than in Europe. He did not, however, have any direct responsibility for U.S. forces in the Korean War because after its start one of Radford's subordinate commands, the newly formed U.S. Seventh Fleet, was placed under control of the commander in chief of the United Nations Command (UNC), General Douglas MacArthur. An advocate of an Asia First strategy and an admirer of General MacArthur, Radford supported the Inchon Landing and approved the long-range goal of a military reunification of the Korean Peninsula. He was present at the Wake Island Conference between President Harry S. Truman and MacArthur, later recalling that he had interpreted MacArthur's assurance that UNC forces could handle Chinese forces should they intervene to mean that the communists would not pose a problem so long as U.S. warplanes could strike their bases in Manchuria. As with MacArthur, Radford was frustrated by restrictions placed on the UNC after the intervention of the Chinese People's Volunteer Army (CPVA, Chinese Army). When in April 1951 Truman relieved MacArthur of his command, Radford gave the returning general a hero's welcome in Hawaii.

In late 1952 Radford joined president-elect Dwight D. Eisenhower on his trip to Korea. The admiral, then commander of the Philippine-Formosa area, made a favorable impression on Eisenhower, who the following summer nominated him as chairman of the JCS, a position that he accepted and held from 1953 until 1957.

Admiral Arthur W. Radford was commander in chief, Pacific, and commander in chief of the U.S. Pacific Fleet during April 1949–August 1953. During 1953–1957, Radford was chairman of the Joint Chiefs of Staff. (Corbis)

As Eisenhower considered alternatives for ending the stalemated Korean War, Radford reportedly recommended threatening the People's Republic of China (PRC) with attacks on their Manchurian bases and the use of atomic weapons. Radford suggested similarly aggressive measures to the president in the spring of 1954 following French pleas for U.S. military intervention in aid of the beleaguered garrison at Dien Bien Phu in Indochina.

Retiring from the navy in 1957 Radford entered the business world, yet he also served as a military adviser in the presidential campaigns of Republican vice president Richard M. Nixon in 1960 and Republican senator Barry Goldwater in 1964. Radford died in Washington, DC, on August 17, 1973.

CLAYTON D. LAURIE

See also

Eisenhower, Dwight David; Joint Chiefs of Staff; MacArthur, Douglas; Nixon, Richard Milhous; Revolt of the Admirals; Truman, Harry S.; Truman's Recall of MacArthur

References

Jurika, Stephen, Jr., ed. *From Pearl Harbor to Vietnam: The Memoirs of Admiral Arthur W. Radford.* Stanford, CA: Hoover Institution Press, 1980.
Who Was Who in America, 1951–1960. Chicago: Marquis, 1963.

Radhakrishnan, Sarvepalli

Birth Date: September 5, 1888
Death Date: April 16, 1975

Indian academic, scholar, ambassador to the Soviet Union (1949–1952), and president of India (1962–1967). Born on September 5, 1888, in Tiruttani in the state of Madras, Sarvepalli Radhakrishnan studied at Voorhees College, Vellore, and Madras Christian College. This led to an academic career as a distinguished philosopher and scholar. After holding a variety of university positions, Radhakrishnan was appointed to the King George V chair of moral philosophy at the University of Calcutta, where he remained for almost 20 years. As a visiting scholar, he also taught and lectured at numerous Western academic institutions, including All Souls College, Oxford; the University of London; and the University of Chicago.

Although not a member of the Congress Party, Radhakrishnan was friendly with both Mohandas K. Gandhi and Jawaharlal Nehru and made wide use of the Western contacts available to the Congress Party. Radhakrishnan won outstanding nationalist credentials in 1942 when, as vice-chancellor of Benares Hindu University, a center for Indian freedom fighters, he resisted the British viceroy's attempts to close down that institution. In 1947 Radhakrishnan was elected to the constituent assembly, and in 1949 Nehru appointed him Indian ambassador to the Soviet Union, a post in which Radhakrishnan convinced Joseph Stalin and other Soviet leaders that India was sincere in adopting a nonaligned posture. Radhakrishnan believed that India had the potential to serve as an ideological bridge between the antagonistic Cold War camps and thereby be an important force promoting world peace.

To Radhakrishnan, the Korean War initially seemed to offer an outstanding opportunity for India to play just such a conciliatory and mediating role. A few days after the war began in June 1950, India's Ministry of External Affairs instructed Radhakrishnan to explore with both Soviet officials and U.S. diplomats in Moscow the possibility of a negotiated peace settlement. Even before receiving this message, Radhakrishnan had begun to do just that, engaging in friendly conversations with Stalin and others. In early July Radhakrishnan suggested to Nehru that the United States be asked to support admission of the People's Republic of China (PRC) to the United Nations (UN) in exchange for Soviet support in the Security Council for an immediate cease-fire in Korea, the withdrawal of North Korean troops behind the 38th Parallel, and the creation of a united and independent Korean state.

These proposals became the foundation for Nehru's fruitless July peace initiative in which he sent messages calling for negotiations to Moscow, Washington, and Beijing. U.S. secretary of state Dean Acheson flatly turned him down while Stalin temporized, but with hindsight it seems unlikely that such proposals, an effective abdication of their position in the Democratic People's Republic of Korea (DPRK, North Korea), could ever have been acceptable to Soviet leaders. As the Korean War progressed, Radhakrishnan continued to support all peace initiatives but had little influence on policy.

In 1952 Radhakrishnan returned to India and successfully ran for election for the first of what would be two five-year terms as India's vice president. In 1962 he was elected president, and in that position he exercised a stabilizing influence during India's wars with China and Pakistan and in two prime ministerial transitions. Disillusioned with politics, after he left office in January 1967 he became a near recluse. Radhakrishnan died in Madras on April 16, 1975.

PRISCILLA ROBERTS

See also

Acheson, Dean Gooderham; India; Nehru, Jawaharlal; Stalin, Joseph

References

Copley, Antony R. H. "Radhakrishnan, Sir Sarvepalli." In *Dictionary of National Biography, 1971–1980*, edited by Lord Blake and C. S. Nicholls, 533–534. Oxford: Oxford University Press, 1986.

———. "Radhakrishnan, Sir Sarvepalli (1888–1975)." In *Oxford Dictionary of National Biography: From the Earliest Times to the Year 2000*, Vol. 45, edited by H. C. G. Matthew and Brian Harrison, 762–764. Oxford: Oxford University Press, 2004.

Gopal, Sarvepalli. *Jawaharlal Nehru: A Biography*. 3 vols. Cambridge, MA: Harvard University Press, 1976.

Kux, Dennis. *Estranged Democracies: India and the United States, 1941–1991*. New Delhi: Sage, 1993.

Reid, Escott. *Envoy to Nehru*. New York: Oxford University Press, 1981.

"Radhakrishnan, Sir Sarvepalli." In *Current Biography, 1952*, edited by Anna Rothe and Evelyn Lohr, 487–490. New York: H. W. Wilson, 1953.

Stueck, William W., Jr. *The Korean War: An International History*. Princeton, NJ: Princeton University Press, 1995.

Wolpert, Stanley. *Nehru: A Tryst with Destiny*. New York: Oxford University Press, 1996.

Railroads, Korean National

Both the United Nations Command (UNC) and communist forces in Korea relied on railroads as the principal means of meeting their requirements for surface transportation and movement of supplies over land. In June 1950 the Korean railway system, built by the Japanese in the early 20th century, was in relatively good condition despite some damage during World War II. However, the system was sparse, and the rugged Korean terrain limited railroad capacity and the flexibility of the rail network. Moreover, railway operations in Korea were hampered throughout the war by the destruction of facilities, the lack of indigenous operating and maintenance skills, and equipment deficiencies.

South Korean troops crowd aboard a train to escape advancing Chinese forces, end of 1950. (Time & Life Pictures/Getty Images)

In 1950 there were three principal rail lines in Korea. The main line (double-tracked, standard gauge, and well ballasted) extended some 250 miles north from the port of Pusan on the southeastern coast through rugged hills via Taegu, Taejon, and Yongdungpo to Seoul and then continued north up the western side of the peninsula via Pyongyang to Sinuiju on the Manchurian border. A second (single-tracked) line ran up the southeast coast from Pusan via Yongchon and Chechon to Wonju, where it turned eastward and terminated in the east-central mountains. The third principal line ran down the northeast coast from the Korean border with Manchuria and the Soviet Union via Hungnam and Wonsan to Yangyang just north of the 38th Parallel. There was no connection between the two east coast lines, and until the opening of the Seoul-Chunchon line in July 1951 there were no lateral lines across the peninsula south of the 38th Parallel, although in the north there were several single-track lateral lines. Feeder lines connected the port of Inchon and the other important ports and towns of southern and western Korea to the main line.

Capacity throughout the system was limited by steep grades and many curves, bridges, and tunnels, some of which made a 360-degree turn while climbing from one level to another. On the eastern single-track line, for example, there were 96 tunnels and 311 bridges in only 310 miles. On July 31, 1951, the capacity of the main line from Taejon to Yongdungpo was 18 trains (360 cars and 9,000 tons) per day. The southeast coast route could handle only about 9 trains and 3,000 tons per day.

Before World War II the Korean National Railways were run by Japanese management and technical personnel, and Koreans generally performed only menial tasks. In June 1950 the number of experienced Korean personnel was limited, and the levels of training and technical expertise were not high. Consequently, in August 1950 U.S. Army railway operating units were deployed to Korea and used to supervise Korean workers.

When the U.S. 3rd Transportation Military Railway Service began operations in August 1950, there were available to UNC forces only 270 miles of track, 280 locomotives, 4,300 freight cars, and 450 passenger cars, all in various states of disrepair. By January 1951 UNC forces had the use of 1,080 miles of railroads, 305 locomotives, and 5,225 usable cars, and that month they moved some 340,000 tons of freight. In June 1951, 3,397 trains were dispatched, 769,850 tons were hauled, and 211,486 passengers were transported. In the last year of the war (July 1952 to July 1953), monthly rail movements averaged 1.25 million tons and 300,000 passengers.

CHARLES R. SHRADER

See also

Logistics in the Korean War

References

Appleman, Roy E. *United States Army in Korea: South to the Naktong, North to the Yalu.* Washington, DC: Office of the Chief of Military History, 1961.

Huston, James A. *Guns and Butter, Powder and Rice: U.S. Army Logistics in the Korean War.* Selinsgrove, PA: Susquehanna University Press, 1989.

———. *The Sinews of War: Army Logistics, 1775–1953.* Washington, DC: Office of the Chief of Military History, 1966.

Logistical Problems and Their Solutions. APO 301: Headquarters, Eighth U.S. Army Korea, Historical Section and Eighth Army Historical Service Detachment (Provisional), 1952.

Rashin, Bombing of

See Najin, Bombing of

RATKILLER, **Operation**

Start Date: December 2, 1951
End Date: March 15, 1952

Four-phase Republic of Korea Army (ROKA, South Korean Army) campaign against Korean People's Army (KPA, North Korean Army) guerrilla units and independent bandit groups operating behind the main line of resistance within the Republic of Korea (ROK, South Korea) in late 1951 and early 1952. Because of the seesaw nature of the Korean War in 1950 and 1951 as well as the Inchon Landing (Operation CHROMITE) in September 1950, large numbers of KPA troops were cut off or purposely left behind in South Korea as guerrillas to hinder United Nations Command (UNC) operations and to harass South Korean military and civilian officials. Additional thousands infiltrated through the main line of resistance for the same purposes. During November 1951 there was a significant upsurge in raiding activities as North Korean guerrillas launched well-coordinated attacks on South Korean rail lines and installations. Although the raids were not in sufficient strength to inflict serious damage, Eighth Army commander General James Van Fleet decided to eliminate this irritation to the UNC.

In mid-November Van Fleet ordered the ROKA to set up a task force of the Capital and 8th divisions, minus artillery units. Van Fleet wanted the group organized and ready to stamp out guerrilla activity by the beginning of December 1951 in a four-phase operation. Because the region around Chiri-san contained the core of guerrilla resistance, Van Fleet directed that the first phase of the task force operations cover this mountainous stretch some 20 miles northwest of the city of Chinju.

On December 1, 1951, South Korean president Syngman Rhee took the first step in eliminating the guerrilla threat by declaring martial law in southwestern Korea. This restricted the movement of civilians, established a curfew, and severed telephone connections between villages. On the following day Task Force Paek, named after ROKA commander Lieutenant General Paek Son

Communist guerrillas, taken by the Republic of Korea Capital Division during Operation RATKILLER, being fed at a prisoner of war stockade. (National Archives)

Yop, initiated the antiguerrilla campaign code-named Operation RATKILLER.

Moving in from a 163-mile perimeter, Task Force Paek closed on Chiri-san. The ROKA 8th Division pushed southward toward the crest of the mountains, while the Capital Division moved northward to meet it. Blocking forces, composed of South Korean National Police, youth regiments, and area security forces, were stationed at strategic points to cut off possible escape routes. As the net was drawn tighter, groups of from 10 to 500 guerrillas each were flushed out, but only light opposition developed. After 12 days, on December 14, 1951, Task Force Paek ended the first phase of Operation RATKILLER with a total of 1,612 guerrillas reported killed and 1,842 captured.

Operations then shifted north to North Cholla Province for phase two of Operation RATKILLER, with the mountains around Chonju the chief objective. From December 19 to January 4, 1952, the ROKA 8th and Capital divisions ranged the hills to trap both guerrillas and independent bandits hiding in the rough terrain. By the end of December, it was estimated that more than 4,000 guerrillas or bandits had been killed and some 4,000 captured.

When phase three opened on January 6, 1952, Task Force Paek returned to the Chiri-san region to capture or liquidate guerrillas who had filtered back into the area after phase one. On January 19 the Capital Division carried out the most significant action of the campaign. While the ROKA 26th Regiment took up blocking positions north of the mountains, the ROKA 1st and Cavalry regiments attacked from the south in two consecutive rings. Although one small guerrilla group broke through the inner ring, it was caught by the outer circle of troops. What was believed to be the core of communist resistance forces in South Korea perished; some guerrillas were taken prisoner during this final drive. When phase three ended at the close of January 1952, a total of more than 19,000 guerrillas and bandits had been killed or captured in Operation RATKILLER.

The fourth and last phase was a mopping-up operation against light and scattered resistance. The ROKA 8th Division returned to the front in early February, while the Capital Division's mobile units sought to catch up with the remnants of the guerrillas. Operation RATKILLER officially terminated on March 15, 1952, when local authorities assumed the remaining tasks of securing the countryside. Operation RATKILLER must be rated a success. Although guerrilla activity continued after the close of the campaign, it was on a reduced scale.

CLAYTON D. LAURIE

See also

Paek Son Yop; Rhee, Syngman; Van Fleet, James Alward

References

Blair, Clay. *The Forgotten War: America in Korea, 1950–1953*. New York: Times Books, 1987.

Hermes, Walter G. *U.S. Army in the Korean War: Truce Tent and Fighting Front*. Washington, DC: Office of the Chief of Military History, 1966.

Rau, Sir Benegal Narsing
Birth Date: February 26, 1887
Death Date: November 29, 1953

Indian jurist, politician, diplomat, India's permanent representative at the United Nations (UN) during 1949–1951, and Indian representative on the Security Council during 1950–1951. Born in Mangalore in the South Kanara District of what was then British India on February 26, 1887, Benegal Narsing Rau was educated at Madras University, where he won first-class honors in three separate subjects, and at Trinity College, Cambridge, where he also earned a first-class honors degree in mathematics.

In 1910 Rau joined the Indian Civil Service and earned distinction as a legal specialist, particularly for his work in revising the Indian Statute Book in the mid-1930s. From 1934 to 1938 he served as India's deputy high commissioner in London. Appointed reforms commissioner in 1938, he served as a judge of the high court of Calcutta from 1939 to 1944; during 1944–1945 he served as prime minister of Jammu and Kashmir. Rau's legal expertise and his diplomatic skills alike were much in demand for difficult and potentially contentious assignments. During the 1940s he twice served as chairman of a committee in charge of codifying

Hindu law, and during 1946–1947 he was constitutional adviser to the governments of both India and Burma as they framed new constitutions in preparation for independence.

In 1948 Rau became a member of India's delegation to the UN, and in 1949 he was his country's permanent representative to that body. He was a staunch supporter of Prime Minister Jawaharlal Nehru's nonaligned and independent foreign policy. After India's recognition of the new People's Republic of China (PRC) in December 1949, Rau argued his country's case that the UN should also accept communist China's representatives on the grounds that only by such inclusion would China be forced to accept and respect international obligations and customs.

When forces of the Democratic People's Republic of Korea (DPRK, North Korea) invaded the Republic of Korea (ROK, South Korea) in late June 1950, Rau, India's nonpermanent representative on the UN Security Council, was serving as that body's president. He immediately convened the council in emergency session, and even though he felt some discomfort in doing so in the absence of instructions from his government, he voted for the June 25 Security Council resolution calling on North Korean troops to withdraw from South Korea. Still uncertain as to his government's position, on June 27 he abstained from the subsequent Security Council resolution requesting member states to contribute military forces to the United Nations Command (UNC) to accomplish this objective.

From the beginning of the Korean crisis, Rau tried to employ his charm and well-honed diplomatic skills to function as a voice of conciliation and moderation and also to carve out a distinctive role for India as a leading nonaligned nation. In August 1950 he was the leader in an abortive effort to set up a subcommittee of the Security Council's nonpermanent members to discuss UN objectives in Korea. As the fortunes of war began to favor UNC forces in September and early October 1950, Rau took the lead in efforts to deter their crossing of the 38th Parallel. From October 1950 when Chinese forces intervened, he was a dedicated supporter of a cease-fire. In December 1950 Rau attempted unsuccessfully to persuade PRC leaders to rein in their troops at the demarcating 38th Parallel.

Rau played a central role in drafting and steering through the General Assembly the UN resolution of December 14, 1950, that set up the three-person UN Cease-Fire Group, of which he was a member. In this capacity he initially succeeded in concentrating UN energies on the possibilities of a cease-fire, as opposed to the U.S. preference for pushing resolutions condemning the PRC. Soon, however, his efforts proved fruitless, as the Chinese followed in reverse the footsteps of the UNC forces and early in 1951 crossed the 38th Parallel. Even so, Rau's maneuvers contributed to delaying passage of such a resolution until February 1, 1951, when the military situation had once more begun to turn in favor of UNC forces. He also managed to moderate the resolution's language and recommendations sufficiently to reduce the possibility that the UNC would launch direct military attacks on the Chinese mainland, an abiding worry for Indian diplomats during the Korean War.

Although Rau would undoubtedly have welcomed serving on the UN Good Offices Committee established by the February 1 resolution, the Indian government's refusal to participate in its efforts denied him this chance. From then on, although he personally supported all efforts to bring about a cease-fire, his role in the Korean crisis diminished. His name was widely mentioned as a potential successor to the somewhat lackluster UN secretary-general Trygve Lie, who eventually stood down in 1953, but in late 1951 Rau left the UN to become a member of the International Court of Justice at The Hague. He died suddenly in Zurich, Switzerland, on November 29, 1953.

PRISCILLA ROBERTS

See also

Cease-fire Negotiations; India; Nehru, Jawaharlal

References

Barros, James. *Trygve Lie and the Cold War: The United Nations Secretary-General Pursues Peace, 1946–1953.* DeKalb: Northern Illinois University Press, 1989.

Gopal, Sarvepalli. "Rau, Sir Benegal Narsinga (1887–1953)." In *Oxford Dictionary of National Biography: From the Earliest Times to the Year 2000*, Vol. 46, edited by H. C. G. Matthew and Brian Harrison, 116–117. Oxford: Oxford University Press, 2004.

Kux, Dennis. *Estranged Democracies: India and the United States, 1941–1991.* New Delhi: Sage, 1993.

"Rau, Sir Benegal Narsing." In *Current Biography, 1951,* edited by Anna Rothe and Evelyn Lohr, 508–510. New York: H. W. Wilson, 1951.

Stueck, William W., Jr. *The Korean War: An International History.* Princeton, NJ: Princeton University Press, 1995.

Recoilless Rifles

Lightweight artillery developed for infantry use. Recoil, or the rearward action of a weapon as it is discharged, is an intrinsic problem of artillery. The laws of physics dictate that the forward-directed energy of an artillery projectile must be counterbalanced by an equal amount of energy directed to the rear. Conventional artillery has long compensated for this often considerable rearward action with various combinations of buffers and springs. Although they are generally effective, such systems invariably greatly increase the weight of the weapon, hindering mobility. As early as 1910, U.S. Navy experiments indicated that by redirecting a percentage of the blast rearward, the recoil and thus the weight of a weapon could be greatly reduced.

In the 1930s the German armaments firm Krupp renewed the recoilless weapon experiments in its search for a lightweight gun for airborne and mountain troops. Krupp's efforts resulted in the basic design still in use today. The Krupp technicians mounted a rocket nozzle to the breech of the gun to redirect half the energy of the ignited propellant rearward. They were thus able to virtually

A 75-mm recoilless rifle of the U.S. 7th Infantry Division in action in Korea. Recoilless rifles proved highly effective weapons in support of infantry during the war. (National Archives)

eliminate the weapon's recoil and, by eliminating its conventional recoil system, greatly reduce its weight as well.

The Krupp design, however, does incur some liabilities. Although the gun itself is relatively lightweight, the ammunition is considerably heavier than that of conventional artillery. To both propel its shell and counterbalance its recoil, a recoilless weapon charge requires twice the propellant of a normal gun. Moreover, the back-blast and flash generated by the weapon's discharge can both reveal its position and be hazardous to personnel behind the gun.

The best-known recoilless rifles were those introduced by the United States. First developed in 1943 by the Frankfort Arsenal, the weapon entered U.S. Army service in 1945 as the 57-millimeter (mm) M18 and 75-mm M20. These saw service in World War II. A projectile fired by an M18 could penetrate 1 inch of armor. The M20 weighed 114 pounds and was more than 7 feet in length, but its projectile was effective against 4 inches of armor. Both of these saw service in the Korean War as did a 105-mm, the M27. They quickly proved that their relative light weight, accuracy, destructive power, and general versatility far outweighed their liabilities.

The tendency of communist troops to establish bunkers high along Korea's innumerable hills frustrated the conventional artillery's efforts to neutralize them. These reinforced bunkers, dug beneath the ridge crests, were nearly impervious to indirect artillery fire and air attack. Infantry units, however, found their recoilless rifles mobile enough to handle within range of these positions; 75-mm recoilless rifle crews frequently exploited their guns' accuracy and flat trajectory to neutralize these bunkers with a single round at ranges up to 1,200 yards. Although lacking the range and destructive capabilities of the 75-mm gun, the 57-mm gun also had its merits. Many troops preferred it for its lighter weight and effectiveness.

Recoilless rifles also proved their versatility against armor and personnel. At close range the 75-mm guns were credited with the destruction of self-propelled guns as well as tanks. During one 1950 action south of Yudam-ni, a single recoilless rifle destroyed numerous Chinese pillboxes and machine-gun nests at ranges up to 1,300 yards. Switching to high-explosive ammunition, its crew then routed a company-size attack at a range of within 200 yards. Other recoilless rifle crews found 75-mm white phosphorous rounds particularly effective against enemy night attacks at long range.

Jeff Kinard

See also
Artillery; Machine Guns; Pistols; Rifles

References
Chant, Christopher, ed. *How Weapons Work.* London: Marshall Cavendish, 1976.

Marshall, S. L. A. *Commentary on Infantry Operations and Weapons Usage in Korea, Winter of 1950–51.* Chevy Chase, MD: Operations Research Office, 1951.

Reconnaissance

The seeking out and gathering of information about enemy forces, to include their location, positions, strength, firepower, types of equipment employed, potential movements, etc. Reconnaissance may be broken down into two categories: tactical and strategic. Tactical reconnaissance provides information regarding enemy forces that may be of immediate use to field commanders. Strategic reconnaissance yields information gathered for and distributed to war planners, who interpret it and apply it to operations development. All service branches conduct reconnaissance.

The U.S. Air Force conducted the bulk of United Nations Command (UNC) aerial reconnaissance missions during the Korean War, although it was handicapped at the start of the conflict by having only one specialized reconnaissance squadron in the Far East. Utilizing modified aircraft, given the prefix "R" (for "reconnaissance") to their designation, the Far East Air Force flew strategic-level reconnaissance with the Boeing RB-17 Flying Fortress and Boeing RB-29 Superfortress.

Only in January 1951 was the 67th Tactical Reconnaissance Wing assigned to the Fifth Air Force. The 67th Tactical Reconnaissance Wing flew the North American RF-51 Mustang, the Lockheed RF-80 Shooting Star, and the Glenn L. Martin RB-26 Invader. It also used the North American RF-86 Sabre jet to photograph the area of MiG Alley, the far north of Korea next to the Chinese Manchurian border. During the period April 1952 to March 1953, the 67th Reconnaissance Wing carried out an average of 1,792 reconnaissance sorties a month.

The 1st Marine Aircraft Wing's Marine Photographic Squadron (VMJ-1) was later assigned to the Fifth Air Force's command, which broke the tradition of U.S. Marine Corps command of its own air assets. The marines flew the McDonnell F2H-2P Banshee photo-jet aircraft.

Although overshadowed by the army and air force, UNC naval forces accounted for 30 percent of all U.S. reconnaissance operations during the Korean War. Ship patrols reported on North Korean mine-laying activities, and carrier-based missions provided both tactical and strategic intelligence. The UNC also used the Martin PMB-5S Mariner and the Royal Air Force's Sunderland, both flying boats (amphibious aircraft), for reconnaissance missions. Naval reconnaissance aircraft patrolled the skies along both the west and east coasts of Korea and along the coast of China.

U.S. Air Force sergeant James E. Kindseth analyzes an aerial photograph of communist gun positions in March 1952. Photo reconnaissance was an important tool in briefing pilots on how best to approach heavily defended targets. (National Archives)

Ground forces had the greatest need for tactical reconnaissance. In the air, the army employed VHF radio-equipped L-17s to direct air force tank-busting aircraft against communist positions. North American L-4 Navion and Stinson L-5 Sentinel small aircraft were also utilized to provide UNC forces information on communist positions to their front. In February 1951 the first Cessna L-19A Bird Dogs arrived in Korea. This magnificent aircraft soon replaced the L-4 and L-5 and became the backbone of U.S. Army aviation (reconnaissance, artillery spotting, occasional direction of air strikes, and general liaison) in Korea. The marines also used this aircraft, designated the OE-1. Observation helicopters were a new addition to the aviation units in Korea. The Hiller H-23A Raven was used for reconnaissance as well as other missions.

In the early stages of the war, the UNC neither appreciated the value of aerial photography nor made much use of it. Largely as a result of this, the UNC failed to detect the large numbers of Chinese People's Volunteer Army (CPVA, Chinese Army) troops moving into the Democratic People's Republic of Korea (DPRK, North Korea) in October and November 1950. Part of this had to do with the delay between the actual photography and the availability of the processed information. There were also few trained photo interpreters available. Aerial photography proved its effectiveness in the 2nd Infantry Division's success in crossing the Naktong River. Communist forces did their best to thwart aerial reconnaissance and photography by hiding during the day and moving only at night.

Although there were no military operations especially for intelligence or reconnaissance when the Korean War began, every

U.S. Air Force Reconnaissance, Observation, and Rescue Aircraft Specifications

Aircraft	Span	Length	Height	Gross Weight (pounds)	Top Speed (mph)	Range (miles)	Ceiling (feet)
Boeing RB-17	103' 9"	74' 4"	19' 1"	65,500	287	2,000	35,600
Boeing RB-50	141' 3"	99' 0"	32' 8"	168,400	385	4,650	37,000
Convair RB-36	230' 0"	162' 1"	46' 8"	328,000	381	8,000	42,500
Grumman SA-16	96' 8"	61' 3"	25' 10"	35,700	236	2,850	21,500
N.A. AT-6G	42' 0"	27' 9"	14' 0"	5,200	207	665	24,100

U.S. Army regiment had a special reconnaissance platoon, and each division had a reconnaissance company with a tank section (usually M-24 Chaffee light tanks). Frontline forces regularly sent out numerous foot patrols to collect information regarding communist forces. Corporal Gordon M. Craig, 16th Reconnaissance Company, 1st Cavalry Division, and Sergeant First Class Charles W. Turner, 2nd Reconnaissance Company, 2nd Infantry Division, were both awarded the Medal of Honor for actions behind communist lines in Korea.

Early in the conflict, specially trained soldiers known as line crossers would cross enemy lines mixed in with migrating civilians to collect intelligence. This process was short-lived and disappeared once the front lines became stable and civilians were forced to the rear.

Because the UNC dominated the skies over the Korean Peninsula during the war, communist forces were unable to utilize aerial photography, and their reconnaissance activities were limited largely to ground patrols.

JONATHAN D. ATKINS

See also

Aircraft

References

Bruning, John R. *Crimson Sky: The Air Battle for Korea.* Dulles, VA: Brassey's, 1999.

Field, James A., Jr. *History of United States Naval Operations, Korea.* Washington, DC: U.S. Government Printing Office, 1962.

Futrell, Robert F. *The United States Air Force in Korea, 1950–1953.* Rev. ed. Washington, DC: Office of the Chief of Air Force History, 1983.

Jackson, Robert. *Air War over Korea.* New York: Scribner, 1973.

Politella, Dario. *Operation Grasshopper.* Wichita, KS: Robert R. Longo, 1958.

Red Ball Express

Term used to describe a supply operation begun in September 1950 to meet the immediate emergency needs of United Nations Command (UNC) forces in Korea. The Red Ball Express was a highly organized and coordinated transportation operation supporting the UNC forces, which were then driving the Korean People's Army (KPA, North Korean Army) northward. Airlift was extremely limited at this time in the war, and the U.S. Navy was having to clear captured ports of mines before supplies could be moved through them. The term "Red Ball Express" was taken from a similar operation in the European theater during World War II that used truck convoys to move supplies from the Normandy beaches to the Allied front in eastern France.

The Red Ball Express cut some 12 hours off the normal 60 hours required to ship material from the U.S. supply depot in Yokohama, Japan, to the port of Pusan in the Republic of Korea (ROK, South Korea). It carried about 300 measurement tons a day, utilizing two express trains from the Yokohama depot to the port of Sasebo.

Once the supplies were in Korea, they moved north by rail and truck. Motor transport was especially critical as UNC forces advanced away from their supply depots at Pusan and Inchon. During the first months of the Red Ball Express, 76 percent of the Eighth Army's trucks operated around the clock. The U.S. 2nd Infantry Division was a primary contributor to the Red Ball Express, at one point providing 320 trucks to supply I Corps from the Han River.

As the war progressed South Korea's rail lines were rebuilt, and these took pressure off of supply by road. Throughout the war, similar rapid transportation of supplies played a vital role in supporting UNC forces. Once the Eighth Army's front stabilized, the supply situation became less critical. The supply lines were shortened, and additional aerial resupply became available. The Red Ball Express ended in the summer of 1952.

KEVIN J. FROMM

See also

Japan Logistical Command; Logistics in the Korean War; Railroads, Korean National; 2nd Logistical Command

References

Huston, James A. *Guns and Butter, Powder and Rice: U.S. Army Logistics in the Korean War.* Selinsgrove, PA: Susquehanna University Press, 1989.

Westover, John G. *Combat Support in Korea.* Washington, DC: Combat Forces Press, 1955.

Red Cross

International humanitarian relief organization dedicated to helping people in distress without regard to ethnicity, religion, national origin, or political affiliation. For more than 100 years the International Red Cross and its affiliates have provided aid in disaster and war. In the mid-19th century, Jean Henri Durant of Switzerland

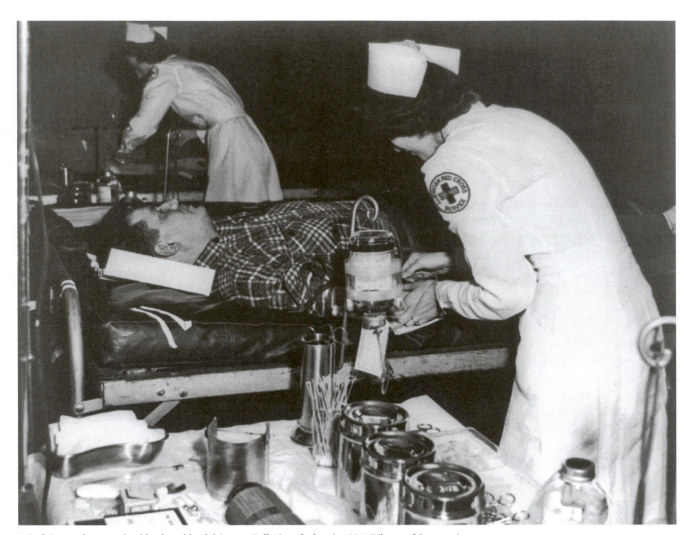

A Red Cross volunteer takes blood at a blood drive at a Bell Aircraft plant in 1951. (Library of Congress)

was the driving force lobbying for an organization to aid victims of man-made and natural catastrophes. The concept secured wide support. Clara Barton of the United States was only one of many influential figures supporting the concept. In 1863 representatives of 16 nations met in Geneva, Switzerland, to discuss the formation of such an organization. The envoys agreed on two necessities: a need for volunteers to aid victims in natural disasters and war and universally recognized neutrality for those administering the aid. Members named the organization the International Red Cross (IRC). By March 1882 the U.S. Congress had passed legislation that established the American Red Cross. In July of the same year President Chester Arthur signed the bill into law.

The IRC and the American Red Cross fulfilled many divergent roles during the Korean War. Soon after the 1950 incursion, the IRC offered to act as an intermediary between the belligerent forces. Also, medical experience during World War II had established the importance of extensive blood supplies. The U.S. surgeon general immediately launched a drive to collect whole blood, placing the American Red Cross in charge. Soon thereafter, the IRC expanded its processing capacity and eventually supplied 75

percent (961,000 units) of all the blood used during the conflict. In addition, organization personnel performed routine medical examinations to decide preliminary treatment. American women, serving as auxiliary personnel or Gray Ladies, supplied aid and comfort to the wounded during their recuperation in Tripler Hospital at Hickam Air Force Base, Hawaii.

From the outset of the conflict, the IRC stood ready to provide aid to those involved regardless of their political affiliation. But the Democratic People's Republic of Korea (DPRK, North Korea) and its allies frequently ignored the beneficent efforts of the IRC and typically sought to use them for political gain. The communist side repeatedly rejected humanitarian medical shipments and often shuffled United Nations Command (UNC) prisoners to various locations, successfully hampering attempts to confirm conditions and numbers. At one point, People's Republic of China (PRC) officials accused UNC forces of employing bacteriological warfare and using prisoners of war in atomic bomb experiments. An IRC investigation disproved the reports.

In the spring of 1952 riots erupted at the Koje-do prisoner of war camp in the Republic of Korea (ROK, South Korea). Political differences among the communist prisoners started the unrest, but the problems quickly involved South Korean and U.S. guards. In gaining control, sentries opened fire, killing several prisoners. The IRC subsequently evaluated camp conditions and offered suggestions to avoid future incidents. UNC officials adopted several proposals and thus eased tensions.

The American Red Cross arranged emergency leave for men who had serious family problems. This service was a valuable asset to the troops. The agency also maintained rest centers behind the lines.

Two IRC volunteers, both men, died of wounds sustained during the Korean War. The multiple agencies of the IRC continue to provide aid and assistance throughout the world in peace and war.

DEAN S. BRUMLEY

See also
Biological Warfare

References
Cowdrey, Albert E. *United States Army in the Korean War: The Medic's War.* Washington, DC: U.S. Army Center of Military History, 1987.
Hurd, Charles. *The Compact History of the American Red Cross.* New York: Hawthorne Books, 1959.
White, William L. *The Captives of Korea: An Unofficial White Paper on the Treatment of War Prisoners, Our Treatment of Theirs; Their Treatment of Ours.* New York: Scribner, 1955.

Refugees

Refugees during the Korean War were civilians who fled their homes in fear of imprisonment, reprisals, or execution. Most fled the communist forces rather than the United Nations Command (UNC). This dispersal scattered families and separated spouses, parents, children, and other relatives. As communist forces pushed south, refugees abandoned their homes and possessions and fled south.

Refugees stated that they fled to escape hardships such as forced labor and service in the Korean People's Army (KPA, North Korean Army). Others wanted to avoid retaliation for their own anticommunist activities or those by family members. Refugees were also afraid of Chinese soldiers after the People's Republic of China (PRC) entered the war. Many refugees decided to flee when encouraged by friends or neighbors or when ordered to leave by authorities. Alternatives to fleeing included going underground to fight the communists, hiding, or cooperating with the communist occupation forces.

Before the war, 3.5 million North Koreans had moved to the Republic of Korea (ROK, South Korea), while far fewer communist sympathizers had moved into the Democratic People's Republic of Korea (DPRK, North Korea). Numerous intellectuals, writers, and political figures were kidnapped from South Korea and taken to North Korea. Many who survived fled south after the invasion.

Some civilians used weapons to assist Republic of Korea Army (ROKA, South Korean Army) forces in the defense of cities, such as Taejon in July 1950. Most civilians, however, were refugees, carrying their belongings on A-frames and traveling on foot or sometimes by oxcart or railroad car. Following motorized military forces, the refugees were not protected from communist attacks. Thousands of refugees swarmed in masses on narrow roads and clustered waiting to cross bridges. Crowds of refugees risked death by climbing across the twisted metal of bombed bridges such as the Han River bridge at Seoul or the Taedong River bridge near Pyongyang. During winter, refugees suffered the hazards of crossing icy rivers with handmade rafts. Many left home without being able to tell their families where they were going or were separated from family members en route.

When Chinese forces entered the war in late October 1950 the flow of refugees expanded, and allied forces evacuated hundreds of thousands of civilians, many out of the port of Hungnam with the extraction of X Corps. Troops stockpiled food and straw at feeding stations, and refugees received inoculations and were dusted with DDT for lice. At Hungnam, UNC soldiers filled boats with many times their capacity but were unable to transfer all awaiting refugees, some of whom chose to drown themselves instead of risking their fate with the communists. Thousands of North Korean refugees were evacuated from other ports. Remaining refugees suffered from the scorched earth policy, which called for the destruction of all supplies from which the communist enemy could benefit. From December 1950 to January 1951 almost 1 million North Koreans, of a total population of 9.5 million, fled to South Korea.

Starvation and disease greatly affected refugees. Bitterly cold winter weather caused the loss of fingers and toes to frostbite, while other wounds festered without medical care. Smallpox also spread among refugees, who also felt constant fear and anxiety. Air raids and bombings threatened the columns of refugees moving south. As Eighth Army commander Lieutenant General Matthew B. Ridgway remarked on January 5, 1951, "The southward exodus of several million refugees before the oncoming communist flood presents perhaps the greatest tragedy to which Asia has ever been subjected."

The UNC offered refugees food, shelter, and medical care. The Civil Assistance Command, Korea, provided clothing, housing, sanitary water supplies, and an education program to rehabilitate refugees. Private relief efforts, such as the Red Cross, the International Refugee Organization, and CARE, attempted to assist refugees, but many people rejected charity. Chaplains and nuns who opened health clinics also offered humanitarian assistance. Servicemen arranged for shoes and clothing for homeless children and secured toys for orphans at Christmas. Operation CHRISTMAS KIDLIFT airlifted war orphans to Cheju-do. By the spring of 1951, with the stabilization of the fighting front, refugee relief work was more routine than emergency-based because the number of new refugees significantly decreased.

Efforts then centered on alleviating suffering, improving public health, and assisting in the recovery of the Korean economy.

Homeless, this brother and sister search empty cans for bits of food and try to keep warm beside a small fire in the railroad yards in Seoul, South Korea, November 17, 1950. (National Archives)

Moving refugees to safety was a priority, but attempts to place refugees in shelters in the Cholla provinces in southwestern Korea and other sites were not successful. Many refugees were determined to return to their homes.

Refugees presented dangers to the UNC war effort, as they hindered troop movement along crucial roads. Often KPA soldiers used refugees as shields, driving them ahead of themselves. KPA soldiers also disguised themselves as refugees, wearing traditional white robes over their uniforms, to infiltrate UNC lines. These fraudulent refugees served as a military weapon, harassing UNC forces, sabotaging equipment, and securing intelligence. Such agents endangered the safety of UNC troops, who experienced difficulty in determining who were refugees and who were not. Legitimate refugees were also at risk of being shot or captured if they were mistakenly considered to be spies. Military police set up checkpoints to screen columns and control refugee traffic from clogging supply routes or impeding military traffic.

After the war, some refugees were fortunate enough to be reunited with family members. However, many refugees never saw their loved ones again or their homes in North Korea. Not only was there physical separation, but communication was cut as well. Parents mourned missing children, and children searched for their parents and siblings. Many spouses never remarried, hoping to find their wife or husband. In the armistice talks, negotiators discussed the "ten million dispersed families" of North and South Korea. Such separation was devastating in a culture devoted to ancestor worship and rites such as the visiting of graves during the harvest festival (Chusok).

Efforts to reunite families were discussed during the armistice negotiations and in subsequent International Committee of the Red Cross meetings. Hoping to locate relatives, individuals published names and photographs of family members in newspapers. Although some contacts were established between families across North and South Korea, most refugees were not as fortunate.

In 1971 the IRC established a telephone line between North and South Korea at Panmunjom for the exchange of information about relatives. Even if families could not visit, they hoped to learn the fate and whereabouts of their relatives. Continued tensions between the two Koreas prevented reunions, and many former refugees have been frustrated in their efforts to locate family members. The theme of family separation has remained popular in Korean television and dramatic plots.

During the summer of 1983 the Korean Broadcasting System (KBS) televised a reunion telethon in which individuals held placards with names and photographs, which were then broadcast. On the first day alone 850 people gave their information, and 36 relatives were reunited. The telethon peaked with 238 reunions from 1,256 petitioners. Because of its popularity, the reunion telethon was rebroadcast every Friday for several months, reuniting more than 10,000 relatives. Although Koreans continued to employ posters, newspapers, and computers to search for lost family members, television has proved most useful for the illiterate.

Attempts to reunite families received a significant boost beginning in 2000 when South Korean president Kim Dae Jung's Sunshine Policy toward Pyongyang resulted in increased communications and exchanges between North and South Korea. The governments pursued closer ties, and family reunions were a part of the struggle to normalize relations between the two Koreas. But relations between Seoul and Pyongyang have since suffered setbacks, and there are still thousands of families whose loved ones remain unaccounted for.

ELIZABETH D. SCHAFER

See also

Civilian Internee Issue; Hungnam Evacuation; Infiltration; Nogun-ni Railroad Bridge Incident; RATKILLER, Operation; Red Cross; Ridgway, Matthew Bunker; Scorched Earth Policy; United States Army Military Police

References

Cummings, Bruce. *Korea's Place in the Sun: A Modern History.* New York: Norton, 1997.

Kim, Choong Soon. *Faithful Endurance: An Ethnography of Korean Family Dispersal.* Tucson: University of Arizona Press, 1988.

Millett, Allan R. *Their War in Korea: American, Asian, and European Combatants and Civilians, 1945–1953.* Princeton, NJ: Princeton University Press, 2002.

Red Cross Conference in Korea, from Aug. 12, 1971 to Nov. 22, 1972. Seoul: Office of the South-North Red Cross Conference, Republic of Korea National Red Cross, 1972.

Republic of Korea National Red Cross. *The Dispersed Families in Korea.* Seoul: Republic of Korea National Red Cross, 1977.

Riley, John W., Jr., Wilbur Schramm, and Frederick W. Williams. "Flight from Communism: A Report on Korean Refugees." *Public Opinion Quarterly* 15 (Summer 1951): 274–286.

Samuels, Gertrude. "Korea's Refugees—Misery on the March." *New York Times Magazine,* February 11, 1951, 10–11.

Worden, William L. "The Cruelest Weapon in Korea." *Saturday Evening Post* 223(33) (1951): 26–27, 134–136.

Relief Efforts, Missionary

On June 26, 1950, at the beginning of the Korean War, all U.S. civilians were directed to evacuate Korea. A few missionaries voluntarily stayed behind, however. From the U.S. Presbyterian Church, six men, led by Edward Adams, remained. A skeleton crew of Presbyterian men and single women also stayed, working at the two major mission stations in Chonju and Kwangju.

From June to October 1950 these missionaries were the major relief organizers inside the Pusan Perimeter. Those missionaries who had evacuated to Japan supported the effort with relief collections and by publishing an interdenominational newsletter on the Korean humanitarian crisis for American readers. Some evacuees traveled to the United States, giving lectures and seminars on Korea. They also wrote articles for church journals and the secular press on the Korean churches and the American military operations in Korea.

With the advance of the Korean People's Army (KPA, North Korean Army), approximately 1 million people left their homes and took to the road to Pusan. Taejon, located midway between Seoul and Taegu, became the largest refugee center in late June. When Taejon fell on July 18, refugees from there fled to Taegu, and it became the most overcrowded area. The roads to Pusan were choked with refugees as well. Feeding, clothing, and transporting these people proved an impossible task for the Republic of Korea (ROK, South Korea), as the army and all available resources were needed on the front. On July 22 Im Pyong Jik, South Korea's minister of foreign affairs, sent a letter to Colonel Alfred G. Katzin, the personal representative of the secretary-general of the United Nations (UN) in Korea, pleading for UN relief assistance. The UN agreed to help on July 31, but its organized relief effort did not actually begin until October. Until then, relief was up to private groups, and this largely meant missionaries.

Missionaries had several assets that would help in their work. They were the only civilians who still had their vehicles, they had an external means of support, they had connections with local churches to organize workers, and they had influence within the U.S. Army to obtain special permission for their activities. In Pusan, Edward Adams was able to secure a credit line for relief purposes with a New York bank and received permission to use materials owned by the Church World Service (CWS) that were stored in its Pusan warehouse. Missionaries in Tokyo arranged with the Economic Cooperation Administration (ECA) for transporting fresh supplies to Pusan in September 1950.

Although Christian relief supplies were distributed to all the refugees, missionaries usually left behind some materials for local churches. Churches thus became places for additional relief supplies. The effectiveness of the Christian relief effort lay in its collaboration with the authorities. The missionaries were in constant communication with South Korean and American officials to identify neglected areas and fill them.

This initial relief program operated by missionaries soon captured public interest in the United States and other Western countries. On October 19, 1950, American church leaders held a meeting at the office of the International Mission Committee (IMC) in New York City, with representatives from all major

Christian organizations and relief agencies. They decided to establish a formal Christian relief committee in Korea through the Korean National Christian Council (KNCC).

This meeting was timely because shortages were about to get worse, and the tide of war soon turned against United Nations Command (UNC) forces. Although Koreans in the Cholla regions were able to harvest their rice crop when the UNC pushed the North Koreans above the 38th Parallel in late September 1950, new shortages of clothing and fuel became the major concern because winter was fast approaching, and many refugees had only the clothes they wore.

Religious news in the United States highlighted Korean suffering. A joint effort through the CWS One Great Hour of Sharing was organized in December 1950. In the winter of 1950–1951 alone, the CWS shipped 223,000 pounds of clothing and 95,000 pounds of foodstuffs. Churches in England and Australia also sent funds and relief supplies to Pusan. These supplies were distributed to both Christians and non-Christians by the CWS.

Church relief organizers in the West discovered that whenever the label "Korea" was attached to a relief drive the public response was exceptional. Many Christian donors intended to send the relief supplies to Korean Christians only, especially women and children. These wishes could not be granted because supplies had to be sent through the UN; once in UN hands, individual charities lost control over how the materials were distributed.

Nevertheless, cooperation with the UN brought many benefits to all concerned. First, given the astronomical costs of shipping bulky goods to Asia, the charities could not have sent their materials without UN help. Second, the relief work established goodwill between Christian charities and the UN and the U.S. Army. The UN needed the experience, advice, and support of these Christian organizations. Third, Christians would, in turn, gain access to official information so that they could more effectively steer supplies to the neediest areas and reduce irregularities in distribution. Therefore, most religious groups participated in the UN effort and volunteered to collect and distribute relief supplies on behalf of the UN. By 1952 a total of 40 Christian organizations were carrying out relief programs in South Korea through the UN. From July 1950 to November 1952 they had offered more than $4.8 million in church donations for UN distribution, represented about 44 percent of the total donations by all U.S. voluntary agencies.

In 1953 when the UN eventually allowed private organizations to carry out their own distribution in Korea, Protestant churches in the United States sent a total of $271,341 in cash, almost $1.6 million in clothing, and almost 5.5 million pounds of relief supplies through the CWS. These figures did not include materials and funds sent through individual denominations for church reconstruction and the rehabilitation of Christian education and medical institutions. They also did not include contributions made through Catholic charities or materials sent directly through the UN relief agencies. Because of the Korean War, for the first time in U.S. church history Korea had replaced China

and Japan as the primary recipient of American relief materials in East Asia.

KAI YIN ALLISON HAGA

See also

Churches and the War, Korean; Churches and the War, U.S.

References

Clark, Donald N. *Living Dangerously in Korea: The Western Experience, 1900–1950.* Norwalk, CT: East Bridge, 2003.

Haga, Kai Yin Allison. "An Overlooked Dimension of the Korean War: The Role of Christianity and American Missionaries in the Rise of Korean Nationalism, Anti-Colonialism, and Eventual Civil War, 1884–1953." Unpublished PhD dissertation, College of William and Mary, 2007.

Rhodes, Harry A., and Archibald Campbell, eds. *History of the Korean Mission Presbyterian Church in the USA,* Vol. 2, *1935–1959.* New York: United Presbyterian Church in the U.S.A., 1964.

Repatriation, Voluntary

Policy developed by the United States for humanitarian and propaganda reasons stipulating that no communist prisoner of war (POW) would be forced to return home against his will after the war. President Harry S. Truman's administration debated the policy between July 1951 and late February 1952 after the issue was first raised by Brigadier General Robert A. McClure, chief of the U.S. Army's Psychological Warfare Division.

McClure had learned that many Chinese POWs had fought under Guomindang (GMD, Nationalist) leader Jiang Jieshi (Chiang Kai-shek) during the recent civil war in China and had then been impressed into communist service in Korea. McClure feared that many would face harsh punishments on their return, as had Soviet POWs in U.S. custody at the end of World War II. He further believed that a policy of voluntary repatriation would enhance the effectiveness of the United Nations (UN) psychological warfare campaigns.

Controversies surrounding voluntary repatriation stalled the truce talks for 16 months, and little consensus initially existed for the concept among U.S. and United Nations Command (UNC) military and political leaders; President Harry S. Truman was its main proponent. He was well aware of the fate of many Soviet citizens repatriated to the Soviet Union in accordance with wartime agreements at the end of the war in Europe.

The communists insisted on the return of all captured nationals, a demand that was strenuously opposed by the United States and the Republic of Korea (ROK, South Korea). Other UNC members argued that POW issues should not stand in the way of an armistice and that the voluntary repatriation concept seemed to contradict Article 118 of the 1949 Geneva Convention. In addition, it was very difficult to establish the true wishes of POWs while they were actually in custody.

When the concept was officially announced by UNC negotiators at the peace talks on January 2, 1952, the communists rejected it out of hand. But when UNC negotiators later indicated that as many as 116,000 out of 132,000 communist POWs and 38,500 civilian internees would probably elect to return home, giving the impression that voluntary repatriation would not discredit communist ideology, the Chinese agreed on April 2, 1952, to a POW screening to separate potential repatriates from nonrepatriates.

During the week-long Operation SCATTER, which began on April 8, 1952, the UNC produced figures contrary to original expectations, alleging that only 70,000 prisoners (7,200 civilians, 3,800 South Koreans, 52,900 North Koreans, and 5,100 Chinese) of the 170,000 total indicated any interest in returning to their homelands. The communists were livid when they were informed of the outcome of the screening on April 19, considering it a UNC plot to humiliate them. They walked out of the peace talks on April 28. As a result, UNC commander in chief Lieutenant General Matthew B. Ridgway, who personally opposed the policy, immediately sought permission from Washington to conduct a rescreening under the supervision of a neutral nation or the International Red Cross.

When the truce talks resumed on May 7, 1952, the communist delegation again refused to accept voluntary repatriation. The UNC was now less enthusiastic about rescreening because of the Koje-do POW uprising then under way, and the peace talks remained deadlocked over the issue for the remainder of the summer. Nonetheless, Lieutenant General Mark W. Clark, Ridgway's replacement as UNC commander in chief, did order rescreening after discovering that Operation SCATTER was marked by irregularities. The UNC then determined that at least an additional 10,000 POWs favored repatriation, bringing the final number to 83,000. The Chinese were assured that this new number of POWs would be returned as part of a new UNC POW offer made on September 28, 1952. When the communists rejected this approach, U.S. negotiators walked out of the peace talks on October 8, beginning another recess that lasted six months.

The deadlock over voluntary repatriation continued until three events changed the tone of the debate. The first was Dwight D. Eisenhower's assumption of the U.S. presidency in January 1953, the second was Soviet premier Joseph Stalin's death in March 1953, and the third was the successful Operation LITTLE SWITCH, which was carried out in April. Operation LITTLE SWITCH in particular set the stage for the final settlement of the voluntary repatriation issue and resulted in the communist plan to have all nonrepatriates sent to a neutral state until their fate could be finally determined. This idea was modified by the UNC on May 25, 1953, which proposed that a Neutral Nations Repatriations Commission (NNRC), consisting of representatives from four nations chaired by India, would be created to take responsibility for nonrepatriate prisoners within 60 days of the armistice.

During a 60- to 90-day period after that, the NNRC would maintain order and supervise both Chinese and North Korean prisoners in the POW camps. If nonrepatriates could not be convinced by their comrades to return home and if their fate could not be resolved by a postwar Korean political conference called for under Agenda Item 5 of the draft armistice agreement, the NNRC would be dissolved, and any remaining POWs would be released. Those prisoners willing to return home would be released in an operation designated BIG SWITCH. This proposal was accepted by the communists on June 8, 1953.

CLAYTON D. LAURIE

See also

Clark, Mark Wayne; Eisenhower, Dwight David; Jiang Jieshi; Koje-do Prisoner of War Uprising; LITTLE SWITCH and BIG SWITCH, Operations; McClure, Robert Alexis; Neutral Nations Repatriation Commission; Psychological Warfare; Ridgway, Matthew Bunker; Stalin, Joseph; Truman, Harry S.

References

Blair, Clay. *The Forgotten War: America in Korea, 1950–1953*. New York: Times Books, 1987.

Fehrenbach, T. R. *This Kind of War: A Study in Unpreparedness*. New York: Macmillan, 1962.

Hermes, Walter G. *U.S. Army in the Korean War: Truce Tent and Fighting Front*. Washington, DC: Office of the Chief of Military History, 1966.

MacDonald, Callum. *Korea: The War before Vietnam*. New York: Free Press, 1987.

Stueck, William W., Jr. *Rethinking the Korean War: A New Diplomatic and Strategic History*. Princeton, NJ: Princeton University Press, 2004.

Republican Party, United States

One of the two principal political parties in the United States at the time of the Korean War. Founded in 1854 as a reaction to the growing sectional crisis that culminated in the American Civil War (1861–1865), for many years the Republican Party was known as the "Party of [Abraham] Lincoln" and was indelibly linked to abolitionism. Until the advent of President Franklin D. Roosevelt's New Deal in 1932–1933, African Americans supported the Republican Party in large numbers, as did industrial and business interests in the Northeast and the Midwest. These latter groups found congenial the party's advocacy of federal government action to promote economic growth, which had its roots in the Republican absorption of the Whig Party program at the time of its creation. The party also enjoyed support from small merchants and farmers in the northern tier of the nation and garnered some support in the far West as well.

The Great Depression of the 1930s, however, and the promulgation of the Democratic Party's New Deal changed the dynamics of Republican support. African Americans, recently arrived immigrants, and many industrial laborers turned away from the Grand Old Party (GOP), as it is often called, in droves, which ensured a period of lengthy Democratic electoral dominance. As is the case today, the GOP of the 1950s generally stood for social and fiscal conservatism and limited government, although it still advocated policies and programs favoring the interests of business and industry.

By 1950 the Republican Party base continued to be found among the more conservative business interests in the Northeast and Midwest, with pockets of Republican dominance to be found in the intermountain West and far West. The GOP was quite weak in the South, from Virginia in the far North to the Gulf Coast and Texas in the far South. Indeed, the Southern states were heavily dominated by the Democratic Party, so much so that the region was called the Solid South.

The period of the Korean War marked an important ideological turning point for the party, as the more liberal wing, centered in the Northeast and typified by Thomas E. Dewey of New York and, later, Dwight D. Eisenhower, began to overshadow the older, more rightist wing of the party. Indeed, by 1952 when the Republicans won the White House and control of Congress, the first time that this had happened since 1928, the liberal wing of the GOP had come to accept the New Deal. Thus, it sought only to administer it more efficiently rather than trying to dismantle it altogether. Under Eisenhower, who took office in 1953, there were even some modest expansions to the New Deal, much to the consternation of the party's right wing. The Dewey-Eisenhower wing of the GOP also had an internationalist outlook and eschewed the isolationism of the right wing, whose chief spokesman was Republican senator Robert Taft of Ohio. The isolationists and internationalists had a brief contretemps after the Korean War broke out in 1950, but in the end the internationalist Republicans, whose standard-bearer was Eisenhower himself, prevailed.

Of course, no treatment of the Republican Party during the early 1950s would be complete without mention of the rabid politics of anticommunism, known as McCarthyism. Named for its chief instigator, Republican senator Joseph R. McCarthy of Wisconsin, McCarthyism remained a singular blight on U.S. politics for years after it had run its course in 1954. It also badly damaged the Republican Party, which had won control of Congress in 1952 only to lose it again in 1954 in large part because of the public backlash to McCarthy and his tactics. The GOP would not regain control of both houses of Congress for another 40 years.

McCarthy's anticommunist witch-hunt was more about his own personal and political demons than it was about party politics. However, the Republican Party's refusal to rein him in as he hurled baseless charges against thousands of Americans and violated civil liberties in the search of personal glory turned many Americans against the GOP. Even Eisenhower, perhaps the only politician who could have stopped McCarthy in his tracks, demurred from directly challenging the antic senator. While running for president in 1952, Eisenhower remained silent while McCarthy attacked the loyalty of many patriotic Americans including war hero and statesman General George C. Marshall, to whom Eisenhower owed much.

When the Korean War broke out in 1950, the idea of committing thousands of troops to a small nation thousands of miles from home—without a war declaration—raised the hackles of many Republicans, especially those in the isolationist wing of the party.

When President Harry S. Truman's administration began a massive rearmament program designed to fight the Korean War and wage the Cold War in perpetuity, these same Republicans joined the ranks of a number of southern Democrats, who also protested the effects that such an effort might have on the American system. Not only did the Korean-era mobilization program threaten fiscal responsibility, but it also greatly enlarged the size and scope of the federal government, which was anathema to conservative Republicans. Some conservative Democrats from the South joined these Republicans in their objections to a broadened—and indefinite—Cold War that threatened to strengthen the central government and erode individual initiative. At the core of this angst was concern that the Korean War and the attendant rearmament program would turn the United States into a regimented garrison state in which massive defense budgets and a skewed political economy would become day-to-day realities.

Initially, when President Truman decided to commit troops to Korea without a congressional war declaration or even a less-formal authorization to use force, he enjoyed broad bipartisan support. Viewed against the backdrop of the deepening Cold War and a series of sharp international crises that began with the 1948–1949 Berlin Blockade and Airlift, most politicians were ready to stand behind the president and supported his get-tough approach to the perceived Soviet challenge in Korea. However, by the late autumn of 1950, when the drive to defeat the Democratic People's Republic of Korea (DPRK, North Korea) suffered an agonizing reversal when the People's Republic of China (PRC) intervened, support for the president's war policies tumbled.

Republicans turned against Truman in large numbers. Worse still, from the conservative Republicans' perspective, was Truman's decision, on December 19, 1950, to send large troop deployments to Western Europe under the command of General Dwight D. Eisenhower. This precipitated what came to be known as the Great Debate, which pitted the conservative isolationist wing of the GOP against the internationalist wing. Led by former Republican president Herbert C. Hoover and Robert Taft, the isolationists argued against the stationing of any U.S. troops in Europe or Asia. The debate played itself out by the spring of 1951, and the internationalists prevailed. However, McCarthy and his supporters used the debate to deride Truman's war effort, which only emboldened them to continue their tirade against the Democrats.

The Great Debate also revealed the increasing unease of many Republicans with the Korean rearmament program, which they argued could be scaled back had the president not committed the nation to an open-ended military commitment around the globe. By late 1951, Truman's mobilization program faced serious challenges, not the least of which were Republican calls for an end to price, wage, and credit controls. Indeed, by 1952 the Republicans had managed to force sharp curtailments to the rearmament program and eviscerate many economic controls.

In 1952 the Republicans swept into power, taking the White House and both houses of Congress. McCarthyism was still on their side, but their biggest boost came from the backlash to the way in which the Korean War had been waged and the continuing economic controls. The Republicans' ascendance was fleeting, however. Indeed, the corrosive results of McCarthyism caught up with them, and voters turned against the party in the November 1954 congressional elections. Although Eisenhower would remain in the White House until 1961, after 1954 he never again enjoyed a Republican majority in Congress. It would not be until 1994 that the Republican Party would regain control of Congress. In the interim, the internationalist liberal wing would dominate the GOP, at least until the election of Ronald Reagan to the presidency in 1980.

PAUL G. PIERPAOLI JR.

See also

Antiwar Sentiment in the United States; Democratic Party, United States; Eisenhower, Dwight David; Great Debate; Isolationist Sentiment in the United States; McCarthy, Joseph Raymond; McCarthyism; Taft, Robert Alphonso; Truman, Harry S.

References

Caridi, Ronald J. *The Korean War and American Politics: The Republican Party as a Case Study*. Philadelphia: University of Pennsylvania Press, 1968.

Casey, Steven. *Selling the Korean War: Propaganda, Politics, and Public Opinion in the United States, 1950–1953*. New York: Oxford University Press, 2008.

Fried, Richard M. *Nightmare in Red: McCarthyism in Perspective*. New York: Oxford University Press, 1991.

Paterson, James T. *Mr. Republican: A Biography of Robert A. Taft*. Boston: Houghton Mifflin, 1972.

Pierpaoli, Paul G., Jr. *Truman and Korea: The Political Culture of the Early Cold War*. Columbia: University of Missouri Press, 1999.

Reichard, Gary W. *Politics as Usual: The Age of Truman and Eisenhower*. Arlington Heights, IL: Harlan Davidson, 1988.

Rest and Recuperation

Korean War policy initiated to restore troop morale. Early 20th-century warfare often had soldiers in combat, with no breaks, for the duration of a military conflict. The idea of limited wartime service and rotation of troops was introduced during World War II. In previous wars, soldiers occasionally visited rest areas behind the lines to restore their physical and emotional energy. Studies of World War II troops showed that casualty rates significantly increased when troops were in combat more than 180 days without relief. As a result of these findings and actual events in Korea, on December 30, 1950, the U.S. Eighth Army and the Japan Logistics Command formally established a rest and recuperation (R&R) program called Operation RELAX for servicemen. R&R was also known as Little R, while rotation home, which began in the spring of 1951, was called Big R.

Military leaders publicized R&R policies to troops in an effort to offer hope and enhance morale. Servicemen enthusiastically received the news that everyone would have a five-day R&R leave during their combat tour, usually in the sixth or seventh month of service. Priority was given to those who had been in Korea the longest, and this was not affected by rank or date of rank. Combat effectiveness of units would be retained by selecting individuals, not units, for R&R trips. R&R leaves were scheduled for specific dates so that soldiers could plan their R&R as if it were a holiday. Also, such itineraries ensured that transportation was available and that Special Service hotels and recreational facilities were not overwhelmed. A constant number of soldiers were transported to and from Japan on a daily basis.

The first Korean War soldiers to enjoy R&R were members of the 21st Regiment, 24th Division. They left Kimpo Airfield (Seoul) on a Douglas C-54 Skymaster transport. Unshaven, dirty, and exhausted, they wore their helmets and fatigues and carried weapons. Upon arrival in Japan, they were processed. At first, there were two reception centers: Camp Kokura near Ashiya Air Base on Kyushu and Camp McNeely near Haneda Air Base in the Tokyo-Yokohama area. A third processing center opened in February 1951 at Itami Air Base at Osaka. Railroads and buses were available to take soldiers to other destinations.

At the centers the soldiers were paid in Japanese currency, given clean uniforms, fed steak dinners, and told to rest and recuperate as they pleased. They left their uniforms, boots, and weapons at the center to be cleaned and repaired. Instructed as to the location of hotels where they could stay and possible activities, the men were ordered to report back to the center at midnight five days later. During R&R the men sampled entertainment around Japan. Some men arranged for their families and girlfriends to meet them in Japan. Others spent time talking to family in the United States by telephone.

Most soldiers spent R&R dining, dancing, sightseeing, and watching movies. Having saved their money while in service, they indulged in presents and souvenirs for themselves, their families, and members of their units in Korea. Some soldiers used the occasion for debauchery, and R&R was also known as I&I for "intercourse and intoxication," but many men were too tired from combat to do much more than sleep.

R&R helped restore soldiers by removing them from the hazards of combat and the desolation and stagnation of a war zone. Sleeping, eating, and bathing refreshed men and provided them with a sense of dignity. Momentarily escaping destruction, danger, and hardship, men savored comforts before returning to the daily risks of being in action. Returning to the reception centers, R&R soldiers received their weapons and equipment. Men were issued winter clothing as needed. A bus then transported them to Ashiya Air Base, where they departed for Seoul and the front.

The Fifth Air Force initially had a more informal R&R program for its forces. When airmen or officers could be spared for three days, they were allowed to go to Japan on available flights without being processed. There were no specific flights scheduled for air force personnel traveling on military orders for R&R, so plans were uncertain compared to army R&R. It was usually easier for

U.S. Navy sailors give their dinner orders to a Japanese waitress at the Maipei Hotel in Karuizawa, Japan, in April 1952. The sailors were on rest and recuperation (R&R) leave following extended sea duty aboard the carrier *Valley Forge*. (Naval Historical Center)

air force servicemen to get to Japan than to return; sometimes they waited several days for a flight to Korea. Airmen were allowed three-day leaves every month for awhile until the air force began scheduling R&R like the army did. In September 1951 the U.S. Far East Air Force (FEAF) standardized the R&R system by organizing packets of 46 people, with an officer or noncommissioned officer in charge, who were airlifted to and from Korea as a group.

Celebrations honored specific R&R passengers. For example, in April 1951 Combat Cargo and Japan Logistical Command hosted a welcome ceremony for Sergeant First Class George Quick, the 25,000th army R&R passenger. Governor Yasui Seiichiro gave Quick the keys to the city of Tokyo, and prominent officers attended a cocktail party in Quick's honor. A month later, the 75,000th army R&R passenger, First Lieutenant Napoleon L. Donato, was treated to similar events. By August 1951, 91,000 United Nations Command (UNC) officers and enlisted men had enjoyed R&R in Japan. Army corporal Ronald Allnut was the 100,000th passenger, and army master sergeant Richard J. Hartnett was the 200,000th R&R honoree. Similar events were staged for certain air force and Combat Cargo passengers to honor the total number of R&R recipients.

By the end of June 1953, the FEAF's 315th Air Division (Combat Cargo) had airlifted approximately 800,000 R&R passengers.

At first R&R soldiers were mostly American, but by the end of the war members of international forces affiliated with the UNC also enjoyed breaks from the front. Medical personnel and Red Cross workers also took R&R vacations from their duties. Because of the variety and number of R&R participants, the Japanese economy thrived from the money invested in luxury goods, meals, hotel rooms, and entertainment.

Soldiers needed this time away from combat duty and stress. Although rotation home was most desired, R&R enabled soldiers to continue their very hazardous yet often monotonous mission in Korea. R&R was indeed a pleasant interlude amid a savage war.

ELIZABETH D. SCHAFER

See also
Battle Fatigue; Japan Logistical Command; Kimpo Airfield; Rotation of Troops System; Strategic and Tactical Airlift in the Korean War; United States Air Force; United States Army

References
Fehrenbach, T. R. *This Kind of War: A Study in Unpreparedness.* New York: Macmillan, 1962.

Futrell, Robert F. *The United States Air Force in Korea, 1950–1953.* Rev. ed. Washington, DC: Office of the Chief of Air Force History, 1983.

Gray, Bob. "Seoul Liberty." *Leatherneck* 35 (1952): 43–45.

737 of the Admirals

Kellett, Anthony. *Combat Motivation: The Behavior of Soldiers in Battle.* Boston: Kluwer, 1982.

Thompson, Annis G. *The Greatest Airlift: The Story of Combat Cargo.* Tokyo: Dai-Nippon Printing, 1954.

Return-to-Seoul Movement

From late 1951 onward, South Korean president Syngman Rhee campaigned strongly to return his government from Pusan to Seoul, Korea's traditional capital ever since the Choson dynasty began in the late 14th century. Rhee accomplished his objective piecemeal in late 1952 and early 1953.

For Rhee, the relocation was filled with great symbolic, psychological, and political meaning. This step would signify that the Democratic People's Republic of Korea (DPRK, North Korea) had failed in its effort to conquer the Republic of Korea (ROK, South Korea), and it would confer additional legitimacy upon his domestically somewhat beleaguered government. Two successive United Nations (UN) commanders, lieutenant generals Matthew B. Ridgway and Mark W. Clark, opposed the transfer, fearing that should civilians return in large numbers to Seoul, it might prove militarily indefensible against a renewed communist offensive.

Seoul was uncomfortably close to the front, and in July 1952 the United Nations Command (UNC) deliberately created the Korean Communications Zone to handle rear-area issues, hoping to confine civilian activities to this sector while reserving the forward area, including the capital, for the military. Both U.S. commanders feared that returning the government to Seoul would once more entangle the UNC in civilian issues and confrontations with the Rhee government, detracting from their forces' fighting capabilities, which they considered their first priority.

Aid workers and foreign governments also opposed the move because they feared that the cost of rehabilitating Seoul, devastated after two successive "liberations" by communist and UN forces, would reduce the funds available for more immediate and essential relief work.

Such arguments carried no weight with Rhee, however, whose determination to return remained unwavering. After winning the South Korean presidential election of August 1952, he made Seoul his official residence, which forced all leading South Korean government officials, UN functionaries, and U.S. and other foreign representatives to travel there to transact business with him. By February 1953 civilians had begun to return to the city, and a piecemeal transfer of government offices was in progress.

For military reasons General Clark continued to oppose the move, although U.S. ambassador Ellis O. Briggs recommended that his country accept the shift of at least a few South Korean officials. On State Department instructions, in March 1953 the two men unsuccessfully attempted to persuade Rhee to return to Pusan. The notoriously stubborn president told them that he would remain there personally as would most key government officials, although he would for the time being leave their ministries in Pusan together with the legislature, with which his relations were poor.

As armistice talks progressed, the South Korean administration shifted inexorably to Seoul, and in May 1953 Briggs himself was obliged to relocate the U.S. embassy to Korea's traditional capital. Once the Armistice Agreement was signed, all remaining South Korean government agencies and officials, including the legislature, moved to Seoul.

PRISCILLA ROBERTS

See also

Briggs, Ellis Ormsbee; Clark, Mark Wayne; Rhee, Syngman; Ridgway, Matthew Bunker; Seoul; Seoul, Fall of; Seoul, Recapture of

References

Bailey, Sydney D. *The Korean Armistice.* New York: St. Martin's, 1992.

Clark, Mark W. *From the Danube to the Yalu.* New York: Harper and Row, 1954.

Foot, Rosemary J. *A Substitute for Victory: The Politics of Peacemaking at the Korean Armistice Talks.* Ithaca, NY: Cornell University Press, 1990.

Hermes, Walter G. *U.S. Army in the Korean War: Truce Tent and Fighting Front.* Washington, DC: Office of the Chief of Military History, 1966.

Oliver, Robert T. *Syngman Rhee and American Involvement in Korea, 1942–1960: A Personal Narrative.* Seoul: Panmun Books, 1978.

Stueck, William W., Jr. *The Korean War: An International History.* Princeton, NJ: Princeton University Press, 1995.

U.S. Department of State, Bureau of Public Affairs. *Foreign Relations of the United States, 1950,* Vol. 7, *Korea.* Washington, DC: U.S. Government Printing Office, 1976.

———. *Foreign Relations of the United States, 1952–1954,* Vol. 15, *Korea.* Washington, DC: U.S. Government Printing Office, 1984.

Revolt of the Admirals
Event Date: Late 1940s

Episode in the late 1940s involving an acrimonious debate over U.S. defense priorities in which navy leaders sharply disagreed with President Harry S. Truman's allocation of financial resources. The determination of U.S. Navy leaders to fight for their service came to be known as the Revolt of the Admirals. Its leaders were Secretary of the Navy John L. Sullivan and chief of naval operations Admiral Louis E. Denfield.

The revolt had been simmering for some time, as navy leaders believed that their service was being subordinated to both the U.S. Army and the fledgling U.S. Air Force, which was created in 1947. Part of the debate centered on President Truman's plan for unification of the armed forces that would place all the armed services under the new Department of Defense. It also concerned the continuing post–World War II defense drawdown and resulting shortage of funds for new weapons programs.

In the reorganization of the armed forces, army and air force leaders would have preferred to do away with the navy altogether.

At the least, the army sought to absorb the U.S. Marine Corps (USMC), while the air force wanted to take over naval aviation. The navy did keep its aviation, and the USMC's independence was preserved. However, navy suspicions were nevertheless heightened.

Of great concern to navy leaders was the priority assigned by the Truman administration to the army and air force in terms of funding. Truman questioned spending considerable sums on new ships that might easily be destroyed by atomic weapons. The air force insisted that priority go to strategic bombing and especially the Convair B-36 Peacemaker bomber. The B-36, the world's first intercontinental bomber and the U.S. Air Force's largest aircraft (popularly called the Aluminum Overcast), entered service in 1948.

Navy leaders sharply disagreed with the air force preoccupation with nuclear war. They believed that limited war was the most likely scenario in the nuclear age. The admirals also insisted that World War II in the Pacific had amply demonstrated the ability of carrier task forces to project force over great distances. The navy called for a new generation of supercarriers with supporting battle groups. These carriers were specifically designed to take the aircraft necessary to carry the multiton nuclear bombs of the period.

Secretary of Defense James V. Forrestal agreed with navy leaders and approved construction of the first supercarrier, the 65,000-ton flush-deck *United States* (CVA-58). Forrestal retired for health reasons at the end of March 1949, however. His replacement, Louis A. Johnson, wanted the air force to have a monopoly on strategic nuclear weapons and toward that end would order additional B-36 bombers. Johnson was also determined to cap defense expenditures, and he believed that the place to make large cuts was in naval programs.

On April 23, 1949, less than a month after taking office, Johnson canceled construction of the *United States,* the keel of which had already been laid. Sullivan resigned in protest. Another Johnson decision, that USMC air assets would be transferred to the air force, was rescinded but only following sharp congressional opposition.

Johnson promptly replaced Sullivan as secretary of the navy with a personal friend, Francis Matthews, known derisively in the navy as the "rowboat secretary" because of his complete lack of naval experience. Leading officers were outraged, and a research group, Op-23, headed by Captain Arleigh A. Burke began assembling data critical of the B-36. An anonymous document (later shown to have been written by a civilian assistant, later fired, in the Office of the Secretary of the Navy) then circulated, denigrating the B-36 and characterizing it as a "billion dollar blunder." The document also charged that Johnson had a personal financial interest in B-36 construction.

Subsequent hearings by the House Armed Services Committee found no evidence that Johnson had any financial interest in B-36 procurement. The committee also held that one service should not question the weapons of another and thus called into question testimony by the army and air force chiefs supporting Johnson's decision to cancel the *United States.* The committee also criticized the "summary manner" in which Johnson had made his decision, without proper consultation. In addition, the committee condemned the firing of Denfield, whom Johnson had sacked following his congressional testimony.

Gradually the matter died down, especially with the beginning of the Korean War. The onset of that conflict in June 1950 reinforced the important role played by aircraft carriers in the projection of U.S. military power. Under fire from all sides, especially given the lack of preparedness of the U.S. military to fight in Korea, Johnson resigned in September 1950. The Revolt of the Admirals did serve one positive function. It opened national debate on the role of nuclear weapons in the U.S. military establishment. Only after considerable wrangling was a consensus reached that multiple nuclear options would be the best response to the threat posed by the Soviet Union.

SPENCER C. TUCKER

See also

Burke, Arleigh Albert; Johnson, Louis Arthur; Matthews, Francis Patrick; United States Navy

References

Barlow, Jeffrey G. *Revolt of the Admirals: The Fight for Naval Aviation, 1945–1950.* Washington, DC: Naval Historical Center, 1994.

McFarland, Keith D., and David L. Roll. *Louis Johnson and the Arming of America: The Roosevelt and Truman Years.* Bloomington: Indiana University Press, 2005.

Palmer, Michael A. *Origins of the Maritime Strategy: American Naval Strategy in the First Postwar Decade.* Washington, DC: Naval Historical Center, 1988.

"Revolt of the Admirals." *Time* 54 (16) (October 17, 1949): 21–23.

Wouk, Herman S. "Revolt of the Admirals." *Air Force Magazine* 73 (5) (May 1988): 62–67.

Rhee, Syngman
Birth Date: April 26, 1875
Death Date: July 19, 1965

Korean nationalist leader and the first president of the Republic of Korea (ROK, South Korea), from 1948 to 1960. Born in Hwanghae Province, Korea, on April 26, 1875, to an aristocratic though impoverished Korean family, Syngman Rhee received an education that encompassed both Asian and Western traditions. After classical Confucian training, he studied at an American Methodist missionary school, where he learned English. By his late teens Rhee was a dedicated Korean nationalist, determined to prevent his country's domination by Japan. In 1896 he and like-minded associates formed the Independence Club, which the Korean government forcibly disbanded two years later. Rhee was arrested and tortured and remained in prison until 1904, during which time he converted to Christianity.

Upon his release, he went to study in the United States and, after some time at George Washington University and Harvard

Korean nationalist Syngman Rhee was the first president of the Republic of Korea (South Korea), beginning in 1948. Much criticized for his authoritarian methods, the conservative Rhee was driven from power in 1960. (Corbis)

young communist anti-Japanese guerrilla leader Kim Il Sung as their chosen protégé. From then until his fall from power in 1960, Rhee's often-stormy dealings with his U.S. sponsors would illustrate the numerous difficulties and pitfalls of the client-patron international relationships in which the United States engaged in Asia after World War II. The problems with Rhee were equally characteristic of U.S. relations with Chinese Guomindang (GMD, Nationalist) leader Jiang Jieshi (Chiang Kai-shek) and successive leaders of the Republic of Vietnam (RVN, South Vietnam) beginning in the mid-1950s.

By October 1945 two rival provisional governments had emerged: first the leftist Korean People's Republic (KPR), with a strong communist emphasis, and then the conservative Korean Democratic Party (KDP). Neither party was recognized by the occupying powers, which had committed themselves to setting up a four-power trusteeship to administer Korea for the indefinite future. Both political groupings nominated Rhee as one of their leaders and both united in opposing the trusteeship plan, but otherwise they had little in common.

Rhee himself quickly alienated his U.S. protectors by using fiercely anti-Soviet rhetoric and attacking the trusteeship scheme, tactics that dug a deep rift between him and Hodge. Initially, Rhee used his prestige as a patriotic scholar-statesman and longtime advocate of Korean independence to persuade leaders of both the KPR and KDP to join together and oppose Korean trusteeship in a Council for the Rapid Realization of Korean Independence, the one cause on which all could unite. Before long, hostility between elements of the Left and Right, together with Rhee's own undisguised antipathy for its communist members, led to its fragmentation. Rhee allied himself with officials of the KDP and with leaders from yet another exile group, the Chongqing-based Korean Provisional Government (KPG), closely tied to China's Guomindang, whose members also began to return that fall.

In December 1945 U.S. occupation authorities banned the KPG, using as a pretext its continuing claims to be the government of Korea. Although Hodge did not publicly endorse the more conservative KDP, he increasingly leaned in its favor. Even so, Rhee's obstinacy and outspokenness in dealing with the U.S. commander and other representatives quickly became and remained legendary.

By January 1946 each occupying power had established control in its own zone. During the next 20 months, successive attempts to reach agreement on the establishment of a four-power trusteeship overseeing a unified provisional government of all Korea—the strategy that the United States and the Union of Soviet Socialist Republics (USSR, Soviet Union) endorsed at the Moscow Conference of December 1945—ran aground because of the reluctance of both occupying powers to contemplate a settlement that their rival might be able to exploit to win a preponderant position on the Korean Peninsula. Talks finally collapsed in August 1947. Meanwhile, two separate and fundamentally different regimes began to emerge. In North Korea, the North Korean Workers' Party, under

University, in 1910 was awarded a Ph.D. from Princeton University, the first Korean to earn a doctorate there. His return to Korea that year coincided with the Japanese annexation of the country.

For the next 35 years Rhee remained in exile in the United States, advocating Korean independence and supported by donations from the Korean community and U.S. sympathizers. In 1919 he was elected president of the Korean Provisional Government, based in China, although some years later he lost this position because of charges of embezzlement of funds. During World War II Rhee became Korea's best-known political figure overseas, campaigning ardently for Korea's independence and, after the Japanese surrender in August 1945, its unification.

On October 16, 1945, a U.S. military aircraft returned the 70-year-old Rhee to Korea, which was then divided at the 38th Parallel into Soviet and U.S. zones of occupation. Each of the occupying powers swiftly moved to press its claims to political leadership and power of its preferred Korean candidate. On October 20 Rhee delivered an address at the welcoming ceremonies for the U.S. forces, attended by commander of U.S. forces in Korea Lieutenant General John R. Hodge, while the Soviets elevated

Kim Il Sung, strengthened its hold, and opposition to its rule was forcibly eliminated. In early 1947 elections in North Korea brought about the formation of the Supreme People's Assembly and North Korean People's Committee, headed by Kim Il Sung, as governing bodies. In South Korea, assassinations of politicians of every orientation became common, complicating the U.S. military government's unsuccessful attempts to organize a coalition of moderates that would exclude both rightist extremists such as Rhee and his counterparts on the Left.

Rhee campaigned vigorously throughout South Korea, his emotional demands for Korean independence reinforced his patriotic credentials and created solid bases of support inside the police and the bureaucracy. His followers established youth groups and unions opposed to those backed by the communists, and despite his poor relations with the Americans, by late 1947 Rhee's skill and acumen had positioned him to become the U.S. zone's indisputable leading political figure. In May 1948 elections in South Korea, held under United Nations (UN) authorization, conservative forces won a majority. Shortly thereafter, in a 180–16 vote, the new National Assembly elected Rhee as the first president of the newly established Republic of Korea (ROK, South Korea), which took over the responsibilities of the U.S. military government and quickly won U.S. diplomatic recognition.

Rhee almost immediately faced challenges from the National Assembly to his presidential authority over cabinet appointments and the establishment of a parliamentary system, which he beat back only by expending substantial political capital. By introducing land reform, however, he enhanced his standing with farmers, while compensating landowners with formerly Japanese industrial plants. He also instituted policies that successfully combated illiteracy.

Rhee's outlook was always that of a Confucian, authoritarian ruler governing for what he perceived as the good of the country, and he had little affinity for liberal democracy. He successfully and bloodily suppressed armed communist guerrilla uprisings in South Korea, backed by North Korea, and he purged suspected communists in the bureaucracy. Subsequently, Rhee and other politicians declared that the South Korean military forces should march north and unify the country on their terms, and in 1949 and 1950 there were frequent border clashes along the 38th Parallel, incidents in which neither side was guiltless.

These episodes along with Rhee's rhetoric alarmed U.S. officials, who decided in 1948 to withdraw their forces entirely from the peninsula, a process that was completed in June 1949. Although not unresponsive to Rhee's demands for weapons, the United States balked at his efforts to secure weapons with offensive capabilities, such as aircraft and tanks. U.S. representatives were also concerned by Rhee's reluctance to raise taxes to fight inflation and his readiness to postpone scheduled National Assembly elections. Even so, U.S. support assured South Korea substantial assistance from the UN as well as from the Economic Cooperation Administration, and the establishment of a training program for the South

Korean armed forces, to which the 500-strong U.S. Korea Military Advisory Group (KMAG) remained attached. Even so, by May 1950 Rhee's domestic political dominance was deteriorating; in a general election in which 85 percent of the population voted, his party won 56 seats in the Legislative Assembly, as opposed to 26 for the Democratic Nationalist Party (DNP) and other opposition groups and 128 independents.

The two Koreas bore responsibility for the sporadic border clashes. But on June 25, 1950, the Democratic People's Republic of Korea (DPRK, North Korea) launched a well-planned, full-scale invasion of South Korea. Recent findings from Soviet and East European archives have disproved earlier allegations by such historians and journalists as Bruce Cumings and I. F. Stone that Rhee, in collaboration with the United States, deliberately provoked the war.

Rhee initially ignored the U.S. ambassador's advice to leave Seoul and relocate his government at Pusan, stating that he preferred death at enemy hands to doing so, but the imminent prospect that this fate would materialize persuaded him to follow the counsel he had earlier rejected. Once United Nations Command (UNC) troops reversed the tide of war and achieved military success in the autumn of 1950, crossing the 38th Parallel, Rhee claimed the right to appoint provisional governors in liberated areas of North Korea. The UN refused; it claimed authority not only to govern such areas but also to institute Korea-wide elections once the war had ended.

Throughout the war Rhee demanded the unification of all Korea under his leadership and attempted to sabotage all measures that might undercut this goal. His aim of a united Korea was increasingly at odds with the U.S. and West European readiness to negotiate a settlement that would effectively restore the status quo ante bellum. In late 1950 Rhee told U.S. president Harry S. Truman that the Korean people demanded their country's unification and that he would refuse to recognize any settlement reached by the United States or other powers that did not accomplish this objective. This ultimatum further soured the always-poor relations between the two leaders, which remained frosty until Truman left office in 1953. Rhee was, however, sufficiently astute to realize that public or private criticism of UNC forces and tactics, even those with which he disagreed, such as the UNC policy of keeping South Korean troops under strict control and discipline, would be counterproductive. He enthusiastically endorsed General Douglas MacArthur's aim of expanding the war to Chinese territory and continuing it to complete victory, and he was shocked when in April 1951 Truman removed the outspoken general from the UNC command.

Other issues generated tension between the United States and Rhee. The war experience revealed the level of official corruption and maladministration in the National Defense Forces, whose survivors struggled back to Seoul in rags complaining of nonexistent supplies because of financial misappropriation. Atrocities by Republic of Korea Army (ROKA, South Korean Army) troops, most notably the February 1951 Kochang massacre, in which 719 villagers died (and the official investigation of which Rhee quickly ended), tarnished the image of the ROKA and led their U.S. allies to regard them with disgust. Increasingly, Western officials criticized Rhee's administration, but they did little to prevent his subverting of the constitution so as to remain president in the elections of 1952; even Truman merely expressed concern over the situation.

Rhee and newly appointed minister of the interior and political ally Yi Pom Sok organized a campaign of intimidation against his opponents and worked with the National Assembly, which was empowered to elect the president, to impose martial law on the temporary capital of Pusan in May 1952. Rhee threatened to disband the assembly if it failed to allow popular elections for the presidency.

In early July 1952, after an assassination attempt on Rhee that may well have been staged and that served as a pretext to arrest many of his opponents, the National Assembly bowed to Rhee's pressure, acceded to his demands, and amended the constitution to create an upper house and a popularly elected president. Predictably, in subsequent elections in August 1952, Rhee obtained 5 million votes and his closest opponent a mere 800,000. Rhee's repression of his political opponents and his intransigence led both the Truman and Dwight D. Eisenhower administrations to contemplate implementing Operation EVERREADY, a plan to remove him from power should he stand in the way of a truce.

For the remainder of the war, Rhee's greatest preoccupation was his ultimately unsuccessful effort to sabotage ongoing armistice negotiations and ensure that hostilities continued until all Korea was unified under his rule. By April 1953 both communist and UNC forces had wearied of war and were prepared to reach a compromise on the thorny issue of the repatriation of prisoners of war (POWs), which for 15 months had stalemated progress toward a settlement. Rhee promptly threatened to withdraw all ROKA troops from the UNC should the settlement permit any Chinese People's Volunteer Army (CPVA, Chinese Army) troops to remain on Korean soil, even in North Korea, and he rejected a U.S. offer of massive military assistance and economic aid for South Korean rehabilitation. On June 4, after the peace negotiators at Panmunjom had finally agreed on all aspects of the repatriation of prisoners of war, Rhee publicly stated the conditions on which he would endorse a settlement, mandating the simultaneous withdrawal of all UN and Chinese troops from Korean territory. He would accept this, he said, only on condition that South Korea should conclude a mutual security pact with the United States and receive massive economic aid and the commitment of substantial U.S. military and naval forces to South Korea.

Rhee made these demands secure in the knowledge that the communist side would find them unacceptable and continue to fight. After threatening to withdraw his troops—which by then constituted two-thirds of those manning the front line—from UNC command, Rhee hinted that even after an armistice they might refuse to lay down their arms. On June 18, 1953, he ordered

the release of some 27,000 POWs not scheduled for repatriation. Many were formed into labor battalions and enlisted in the ROKA; others vanished into the countryside. Rhee hoped this incident, which enraged communist delegates to the armistice talks, would generate recriminations so bitter as to sabotage the negotiations completely; but if anything, it made the exasperated participants on both sides even more determined to reach an agreement in which Rhee would be forced to acquiesce. UNC and communist representatives united in denouncing Rhee's unilateral action and agreed to resume their truce talks on July 12, 1953. The same day, the United States dispatched Assistant Secretary of State Walter S. Robertson to Seoul to persuade Rhee not to obstruct any settlement. After two weeks Robertson finally extracted Rhee's pledge to accept a cease-fire, which was then signed immediately, on July 27, 1953. In return, Rhee secured a U.S.–South Korean mutual defense treaty, which was concluded almost immediately, on August 8, 1953; $200 million in immediate economic aid, only the first installment of a long-term aid program; a pledge that the United States would walk out of the postwar reunification talks if the communists proved inflexible; and U.S. assistance in expanding the ROKA to 20 divisions.

While Rhee had driven a hard bargain, he found other consequences of the Korean War less attractive. Much as he hated the communists, he reserved his greatest antipathy for the Japanese, Korea's long-term enemies and oppressors, and often stated that, given the choice, he would join forces with the communists to fight Japan. From the late 1940s he greatly resented the U.S. Cold War–fueled policy of giving a higher priority to the revival of the Japanese economy than to that of Korea, and he was even more alarmed by the 1951 Japanese peace treaty with the United States, under which the two nations became de facto military allies.

When the Korean War ended, 78-year-old Rhee remained South Korean president until 1960, but he failed to meet popular expectations of modernization and political and economic development. His rule became increasingly personalized and authoritarian, and in April 1960 mass demonstrations against him, following charges of his having rigged the elections, led Rhee, under some U.S. pressure, to resign the presidency and return to private life. The following month he left Korea for exile in Hawaii, and five years later, on July 19, 1965, he died in Honolulu at age 90.

PRISCILLA ROBERTS

See also

Democratic National Party; EVERREADY, Operation; Hodge, John Reed; Jiang Jieshi; Kim Il Sung; Korea, Republic of, 1947–1953; Korea, Republic of, 1953–Present; Korean Provisional Government; MacArthur, Douglas; Rhee, Syngman, Assassination Attempt on; Rhee's Release of North Korean Prisoners of War; Robertson, Walter Spencer; Robertson Mission; Truman, Harry S.; Yi Pom Sok

References

Allen, Richard C. *Korea's Syngman Rhee: An Unauthorized Portrait.* Rutland, VT: Charles E. Tuttle, 1960.

Cumings, Bruce. *Child of Conflict: The Korean-American Relationship, 1943–1953.* Seattle: University of Washington Press, 1983.

———. *Korea's Place in the Sun: A Modern History.* New York: Norton, 1997.

Millett, Allan R. *The War for Korea, 1945–1950: A House Burning.* Lawrence: University Press of Kansas, 2005.

———. *Their War in Korea: American, Asian, and European Combatants and Civilians, 1945–1953.* Princeton, NJ: Princeton University Press, 2002.

Oliver, Robert T. *Syngman Rhee and American Involvement in Korea, 1942–1960: A Personal Narrative.* Seoul: Panmun Books, 1978.

Stueck, William W., Jr. *The Korean War: An International History.* Princeton, NJ: Princeton University Press, 1995.

———. *Rethinking the Korean War: A New Diplomatic and Strategic History.* Princeton, NJ: Princeton University Press, 2004.

Rhee, Syngman, Assassination Attempt on
Event Date: June 25, 1952

Purported attempt to assassinate South Korean president Syngman Rhee on June 25, 1952, during a ceremony in Pusan. This observance marked the second anniversary of the beginning of the Korean War and was attended by 50,000 people, including U.S. ambassador John J. Muccio. A lone gunman confronted Rhee and pulled the trigger of his pistol twice, but it misfired each time. The police then overpowered the suspect, 62-year-old Yu Si Tae. Under interrogation, he was said to have admitted his membership in the ultranationalist Blood and Justice Association.

The police claimed that this episode was only part of a larger plot involving the opposition Democratic National Party (DNP). Even today, it is still not altogether clear whether the attempt was a political ploy, stage-managed by Rhee, as the president's opponents alleged and as U.S. officials, including U.S. chairman of the Joint Chiefs of Staff General Omar N. Bradley and State Department official H. Freeman Matthews, were inclined to suspect.

In Rhee's defense, one might note that the assassination of political opponents was and would remain for some decades a reasonably common tactic in the violent and somewhat ungentlemanly political scene in both the Democratic People's Republic of Korea (DPRK, North Korea) and the Republic of Korea (ROK, South Korea), and no party was innocent of its use. Yet the timing and setting of this botched attempt proved so remarkably convenient for Rhee that it is difficult to believe it was purely coincidental.

Whatever its genesis, Rhee used the incident to his own political advantage. At the time, a political crisis had resulted from his attempts to change the constitution so as to win a third four-year term as president. To do so, Rhee and the newly appointed home minister and political ally Yi Pom Sok organized a campaign of intimidation against his opponents and the National Assembly, which was empowered to elect the president, by imposing martial law on the temporary capital of Pusan in May 1952 and threatening to disband the assembly if it failed to allow popular elections

for the presidency. The DNP was in the forefront of the opposition to these plans.

Rhee used the assassination attempt to justify the arrest of two DNP members and a campaign of political terror against his opponents, who ultimately acquiesced in his plans to change the constitution to allow the popular election of the president. Rhee promptly won this contest in August 1952 in a lopsided vote of 5 million to 800,000.

PRISCILLA ROBERTS

See also
Bradley, Omar Nelson; Democratic National Party; Matthews, Harrison Freeman; Muccio, John Joseph; Rhee, Syngman; Yi Pom Sok

References
Allen, Richard C. *Korea's Syngman Rhee: An Unauthorized Portrait.* Rutland, VT: Charles E. Tuttle, 1960.

Cumings, Bruce. *Child of Conflict: The Korean-American Relationship, 1943–1953.* Seattle: University of Washington Press, 1983.

Oliver, Robert T. *Syngman Rhee and American Involvement in Korea, 1942–1960: A Personal Narrative.* Seoul: Panmun Books, 1978.

Ra, Jong Il. "Political Crisis in Korea, 1952: The Administration, Legislature, Military and Foreign Powers." *Journal of Contemporary History* 27(2) (April 1992): 301–318.

Stueck, William W., Jr. *The Korean War: An International History.* Princeton, NJ: Princeton University Press, 1995.

———. *Rethinking the Korean War: A New Diplomatic and Strategic History.* Princeton, NJ: Princeton University Press, 2004.

Rhee's Release of North Korean Prisoners of War
Event Date: June 18, 1953

Release of prisoners of war (POWs) orchestrated by South Korean president Syngman Rhee that threatened to sabotage Korean War armistice talks. Although the talks had begun in July 1951, discord over repatriation of POWs became a major stumbling block, with a stalemate on the issue taking hold in May 1952. The communist side, however, returned to the peace table in April 1953 and showed signs of seeking a settlement.

Rhee remained adamant that the war should not end until Korea was unified under South Korean rule and the POW issue was settled. Throughout April and May 1953, he pressed the United States for permission to release Korean People's Army (KPA, North Korean Army) POWs because he feared that communist officials would take advantage of the Neutral Nations Repatriation Commission (NNRC) and coerce nonrepatriates to return home.

First dismissing Rhee's opposition to the peace settlement as bluff, President Dwight D. Eisenhower's administration soon began to take his threats of unilateral action more seriously. Yet Eisenhower's advisers convinced him that releasing North Korean POWs unilaterally or reopening negotiations on Item 4 might jeopardize the entire settlement. Eisenhower agreed, yet fears remained that Rhee would do something to sabotage the talks or would refuse to abide by any settlement.

By June 18, 1953, the Armistice Agreement was all but complete. At this time, however, Rhee unilaterally ordered the release of some 27,000 anticommunist North Korean POWs in protest of the proposed settlement. A United Nations Command (UNC) announcement of that date stated

> Between midnight and dawn today, approximately 25,000 (of 35,400) military anti-communist North Korean prisoners of war broke out of UNC POW camps at Pusan, Masan, Nonsan, and Sang Mu Dai, Korea. Statements attributed to high officials of the Republic of Korea now make it clear that the action had been secretly planned and carefully coordinated at top levels in the Korean Government and that outside assistance was furnished the POWs in their mass breakout. Republic of Korea (ROKA, South Korean Army) security units assigned as guards at the POW camps did little to prevent the breakouts and there is every evidence of actual collusion between the ROK guards and the prisoners. . . . U.S. personnel at these non-repatriate camps, limited in each case to the camp commander and a few administrative personnel, exerted every effort to prevent today's mass breakouts, but in the face of the collusion between the ROKA guards and the prisoners, their efforts were largely unsuccessful. The large quantities of non-toxic irritants employed proved ineffective because of the great numbers of prisoners involved in the nighttime breakouts. Nine prisoners were killed and sixteen injured by rifle fire. There were no casualties among U.S. personnel. As of 1 o'clock this afternoon 971 escaped POWs have been recovered. The ROKA security units which have left their posts at non-repatriate camps are being replaced by U.S. troops.

Although UNC officials denied any knowledge of or responsibility for Rhee's actions and issued a formal written apology at Panmunjom on June 20, the communist side denounced the release as a breach of faith.

The POW release prompted an immediate meeting of the National Security Council (NSC). Eisenhower was convinced that Rhee's move would cause the armistice to collapse, but Secretary of State John Foster Dulles and other administration officials believed that the communists would overlook the incident, as they too wanted an armistice. After further cabinet and congressional meetings, Eisenhower decided to send Assistant Secretary of State for Far Eastern Affairs Walter S. Robertson to meet with commander in chief of UNC General Mark W. Clark and Rhee in what became known as the "Little Truce Talks." These lasted 12 days.

Robertson, who arrived in Korea on June 25, 1953, had been instructed to offer Rhee long-term U.S. military and economic aid if he would cooperate, allaying any fears that the United States would abandon the Republic of Korea (ROK, South Korea). If Rhee did not cooperate, he was to be told that the United States would sign the armistice and withdraw its forces, leaving South Korea to

fight on alone. If this failed, Robertson and Clark had a plan to launch a coup d'état (Operation EVERREADY) to replace Rhee with Prime Minister Chang Taek Sang.

The talks, which occurred in the midst of a new communist offensive, were successful. On July 9 Rhee agreed, albeit reluctantly, to end his efforts to scuttle the settlement.

The unilateral POW release and the surprised reaction of the United States to it indicated to the communists that Rhee had acted on his own. Although this event did no more than delay the armistice, it forced the Eisenhower administration to deal with Rhee's fears. It also proved that the real POW issue all along had been the fate of Chinese, rather than North Korean, POWs.

CLAYTON D. LAURIE

See also

Armistice Agreement; Chang Taek Sang; Clark, Mark Wayne; Dulles, John Foster; Eisenhower, Dwight David; EVERREADY, Operation; National Security Council; Neutral Nations Supervisory Commission; Rhee, Syngman

References

Bailey, Sydney D. *The Korean Armistice.* New York: St. Martin's, 1992.

Blair, Clay. *The Forgotten War: America in Korea, 1950–1953.* New York: Times Books, 1987.

Clark, Mark W. *From the Danube to the Yalu.* New York: Harper and Row, 1954.

Hastings, Max. *The Korean War.* New York: Simon and Schuster, 1987.

Hermes, Walter G. *U.S. Army in the Korean War: Truce Tent and Fighting Front.* Washington, DC: Office of the Chief of Military History, 1966.

Millett, Allan R. *Their War in Korea: American, Asian, and European Combatants and Civilians, 1945–1953.* Princeton, NJ: Princeton University Press, 2002.

Ridgway, Matthew Bunker
Birth Date: March 3, 1895
Death Date: July 26, 1993

U.S. Army general, commander of the U.S. Eighth Army during the Korean War, and later commander in chief of United Nations (UN) forces in Korea. The son of an army officer, Matthew Bunker Ridgway was born at Fortress Monroe, Virginia, on March 3, 1895. He grew up on various military posts and graduated from the U.S. Military Academy at West Point in 1917, when he was commissioned in the infantry.

Unlike most of his classmates, Ridgway was not posted to France during World War I; instead, he served on the Mexican border. He returned to West Point to teach Romance languages and serve as head of athletics during 1918–1924. As one of only six officers in the regular army fluent in Spanish, he served with the 42nd Infantry in several high-level postings in Latin America during the 1920s. In the 1930s he attended the Army Infantry School, the Army Command and General Staff School, and the Army War College. Ridgway was then posted to the war plans division of the War Department General Staff from September 1939 to January

United Nations Command (UNC) commanding general Lieutenant General Matthew B. Ridgway slogs along a muddy path during his visit to a U.S. Marine Corps command post, May 1951. (National Archives)

1942. A protégé of chief of staff of the army General George C. Marshall, Ridgway was advanced to brigadier general in January 1942.

Ridgway was first assistant division commander, then commander of the 82nd Infantry Division, which became the 82nd Airborne Division, from March 1942 to August 1944. He was promoted to major general in August 1942. Ridgway parachuted with the division into France in the Normandy invasion of June 1944. From August 1944 to September 1945 he commanded the XVIII Airborne Corps. He was promoted to lieutenant general in June 1945.

Following the war Ridgway served as the U.S. Army representative on the UN military staff committee during 1946–1948. In August 1949 Ridgway became army deputy chief of staff for administration. When Eighth Army commander Lieutenant General Walton H. Walker was killed in a jeep accident on December 23, 1950, Ridgway was selected as his replacement.

Ridgway took over the Eighth Army during a very difficult period for the U.S. forces and the United Nations Command (UNC) in Korea. Chinese forces had pushed the UNC back below the 38th Parallel, and morale in the Eighth Army was low. In fact, the Joint Chiefs of Staff (JCS) had ordered a contingency plan for the possible evacuation of the UNC to Japan.

Ridgway employed his extraordinary motivational talents in Korea. He immediately removed incompetent or defeatist officers, and he improved reconnaissance and intelligence-gathering. He worked to improve conditions for the troops, ordering the supply services to provide better and more food, served hot. He secured warmer clothing for the bitter Korean winter, and he improved the Mobile Army Surgical Hospitals (MASHs), knowing that troops would fight better if they knew that they would receive proper medical care should they be wounded. Although Ridgway was forced to withdraw his troops to the south of the South Korean capital of Seoul in early January 1951, he restored their fighting spirit and, in February, launched a massive offensive, Operation KILLER. In that operation the Eighth Army retook Seoul and drove the Chinese back above the 38th Parallel, where the battle lines began to stabilize.

When President Harry S. Truman relieved General Douglas MacArthur of his command on April 11, 1951, Ridgway was appointed to MacArthur's former positions as UNC commanding general, commander in chief of U.S. armed forces in the Far East, and supreme commander of the allied occupation forces in Japan. Ridgway moved from the field to headquarters in Tokyo, where he oversaw the war for the next 13 months. Ridgway's accessibility, articulateness, and polish made him popular with the press, and he was elevated to national prominence and stature.

Having suffered devastating defeats in several failed offensives, the Chinese and North Koreans in July 1951 offered to begin negotiations at Kaesong, on the 38th Parallel. Official talks began on July 10, with the communists proposing an immediate cease-fire. Ridgway and the JCS rejected the suspension of military operations until a satisfactory peace was negotiated.

Lieutenant General James A. Van Fleet, new commander of the Eighth Army, proposed driving the communists far back into the Democratic People's Republic of Korea (DPRK, North Korea). Ridgway and the JCS believed that it would be a mistake to push deep into communist-held territory at this point. Instead, they wished to concentrate on punishing the communist forces along the parallel and employing air power to strike their long supply lines. Both sides strongly fortified their respective positions, and over the next two years some of the most bitter fighting of the war occurred. The war became one for yards rather than miles.

In late August 1951 the communists suspended negotiations and did not return to the table until October. Ridgway ordered a new series of attacks east of the Iron Triangle to pressure peace negotiations and to gain territory prior to an armistice agreement. The savage battles during the suspension of peace talks resulted in considerable UNC casualties, including 2,700 at Bloody Ridge and 3,700 at Heartbreak Ridge. The UNC gained important long-term defensive positions but at a cost of 60,000 casualties, 22,000 of whom were Americans. Ridgway emphasized that the UNC would not return to Kaesong, which was in communist territory, and on October 25 the talks resumed at Panmunjom, five miles east of Kaesong. Shortly thereafter, the communists offered to accept the existing battle lines as the permanent demarcation between North Korea and the Republic of Korea (ROK, South Korea) if a cease-fire were promulgated immediately. Ridgway rejected the proposal because he believed that military pressure was necessary to accomplish a favorable peace. Further, he was not willing to concede Kaesong, a former Korean capital, to the communists. The JCS did not consider Kaesong to be worth the cost, however, and instructed Ridgway to concede this issue.

While the peace talks stalled, Ridgway launched in November 1951 Operation RATKILLER, which eliminated 20,000 communist guerrillas and bandits in the mountains of South Korea. As 1952 began, repatriation of prisoners of war (POWs) became the divisive issue that would dominate the remainder of the war.

On May 12, 1952, Ridgway replaced General Dwight D. Eisenhower as supreme commander of allied powers in Europe and commander of the North Atlantic Treaty Organization (NATO). In October 1953 he became U.S. Army chief of staff. After disagreement with President Eisenhower's administration over its New Look defense policy (often dubbed "more bang for a buck"), which emphasized nuclear weapons at the expense of conventional forces, Ridgway retired from active duty in June 1955.

During the 1960s Ridgway urged limiting U.S. involvement in Vietnam, and in 1968, as one of the members appointed by President Lyndon B. Johnson to the senior advisory group known as the "Wise Men," he recommended U.S. extrication from Vietnam. Ridgway died on July 26, 1993, at Fox Chapel, Pennsylvania.

JOE P. DUNN

See also

Bloody Ridge, Battle of; Eisenhower, Dwight David; Heartbreak Ridge, Battle of; Joint Chiefs of Staff; Kaesong Truce Talks; KILLER, Operation; Marshall, George Catlett; Mobile Army Surgical Hospital; New Look Defense Policy; RATKILLER, Operation; Repatriation, Voluntary; Truce Talks; Truman, Harry S.; Truman's Recall of MacArthur; Van Fleet, James Alward; Walker, Walton Harris

References

Appleman, Roy. *Ridgway Duels for Korea*. College Station: Texas A&M University Press, 1990.

Blair, Clay. *The Forgotten War: America in Korea, 1950–1953*. New York: Times Books, 1987.

Ridgway, Matthew B. *The Korean War*. Garden City, NY: Doubleday, 1967.

Soffer, Jonathan M. *General Matthew B. Ridgway: From Progressivism to Reaganism, 1895–1993*. Westport, CT: Praeger, 1998.

Rifles

Rifles are medium- and long-range personal infantry weapons. The typical combatant during the Korean War, regardless of nationality, entered action armed with World War II or earlier weaponry. It fell to the nations with the largest stocks of existing small arms—the United States and the Union of Soviet Socialist Republics (USSR, Soviet Union)—to act as the primary sources of arms to the two sides in the war.

The United States provided the Republic of Korea Army (ROKA, South Korean Army) forces with U.S.-made weapons and supplemented the small arms issues of its United Nations Command (UNC) allied forces. Rifles and carbines were the standard infantry arms.

The U.S. .30-caliber M1 (Garand) rifle was the standard rifle for U.S. forces as well as many of their United Nations (UN) allies. The 9.5-pound gas-operated, semiautomatic Garand was chambered for the .30-06 cartridge. It was 43.6 inches in length overall and had a 24-inch barrel. The M1 was fed by 8-round stripper clips. Two telescopically equipped sniper versions, the M1C and the M1D, were also issued.

The U.S. .30-caliber M1 carbine was intended as a lightweight, semiautomatic weapon for company-grade officers and special troops. The M1 carbine weighed 5.5 pounds and measured a compact 35.6 inches in length with an 18-inch barrel. Chambered for the .30 caliber carbine cartridge, it had a 15- or 30-round detachable box magazine. Modifications included the M1A1, a folding-stock version intended for paratroops, and the selective-fire M2.

The Belgian army adopted the FN Self-Loading Rifle M1949 in U.S. caliber .30-06. Manufactured by Fabrique Nationale d'Armes de Guerre (FN) of Herstal, Belgium, it was a gas-operated semiautomatic weapon with a 10-round magazine capacity.

France issued domestic, U.S., British, and captured World War II German small arms. Many French soldiers carried the 7.5-millimeter (mm) MAS1936 rifle—a conventional bolt-action, pre–World War II design. Later models included the MAS1936 M51 (equipped with an integral grenade launcher) and the folding-stock 1936 CR39 rifle. The standard French service rifle—the semiautomatic 7.5-mm M1949 (MAS)—was simple to operate and maintain and was fed by a 10-round detachable magazine. Although it did not accept a bayonet, it was equipped with an integral grenade launcher and sights.

Great Britain and Canada issued the battle-proven yet relatively obsolete .303-caliber Enfield Rifle No. 4 Mark 1 (SMLE). Australia continued to use the earlier SMLE No. 1 Mark 3*. The Enfield was a robust bolt-action weapon fed by a detachable 10-round magazine. A sniper version, the Rifle No. 4 Mark I (T), was issued equipped with the No. 32 telescope.

The People's Republic of China (PRC) initially armed its own as well as the North Korean infantry with captured World War II Japanese, Chinese, and U.S. weapons abandoned by the Nationalists after the Chinese Civil War. As the war progressed, the Soviet Union replaced weapons lost to attrition with Soviet-made and captured World War II German armaments. The Chinese, in turn, eventually retooled their arsenals to copy the Soviet models.

A pre–World War I Russo-Belgian design, the bolt-action, 7.62-mm Mosin-Nagant series, was the most widely used communist rifle. The Model 1891 rifle, the Model 1891/30 rifle, and the Model 1944 carbine were all fed by five-round magazines and shared identical bolt actions. A sniper model of the M1891/30, equipped with either the PU or more powerful PE telescope, was also issued.

JEFF KINARD

See also
Machine Guns; Pistols; Submachine Guns and Light Machine Guns

References
Hogg, Ian, and John Weeks. *Military Small Arms of the Twentieth Century.* Chicago: Follett, 1973.
Smith, W. H. B. *Small Arms of the World,* 9th ed. Harrisburg, PA: Stackpole, 1969.

RIPPER, **Operation**
Start Date: March 6, 1951
End Date: March 31, 1951

March 1951 United Nations Command (UNC) military operation. In effect, Operation RIPPER was a continuation of Operation KILLER, but along the entire front. Its primary goal was to inflict maximum casualties and disrupt any new communist offensive. The secondary objective was to retake the South Korean capital of Seoul. Except for the Republic of Korea Army (ROKA, South Korean Army) 1st Division and the U.S. 3rd Division on the western front, the operation initially employed, from west to east: the U.S. 25th Infantry division (I Corps); 24th Infantry and 1st Cavalry divisions, British 27th Brigade, ROKA 6th and U.S. 1st Marine divisions (IX Corps); U.S. 2nd Infantry, ROKA 5th and U.S. 7th Infantry divisions (X Corps); ROKA 7th and 9th divisions (ROKA III Corps); and ROKA Capital Division (ROKA I Corps).

The offensive was to end on Phase Line Idaho, which ran northeast from the western boundary between the 3rd and 25th divisions to a point about 5 miles north of Kapyong, and then more or less east-northeast to 6 or 7 miles north of Chunchon. There it trended southeast across the eastern front of the IX Corps to a point about 15 miles north of the center of the X Corps front, then slightly north of east to the east coast. Phase Lines Albany, Buffalo, Buster, and Cairo were established to control the attack.

At 6:15 a.m. on March 7, the 25th Division conducted a model crossing of the Han River, preceded by an awesome 20-minute, 5,000-round bombardment from 148 artillery pieces. Four tanks added 900 main-gun rounds. Overcoming some initial resistance, the division gained Line Albany between March 11 and 13. The 24th, 1st Cavalry, ROKA 6th, and 1st Marine divisions met light to moderate resistance, gradually pinching out the ROKA 6th, and reaching Albany by dark on March 12th.

The marine advance took them through "Massacre Valley," where a 2nd Division force, Support Force 21st, had been ambushed and destroyed by communist forces in mid-February. There a 2nd Division team recovered five 155-millimeter howitzers, six M-5 tractors, four tanks, and a number of trucks. The 2nd and ROKA 5th and 7th divisions (X Corps) overcame skillful North Korean delaying actions and reached Albany by March 14. The ROKA III Corps also had little trouble advancing, and by March 13 the ROKA I Corps was beyond its portion of Line Idaho.

Thinking the communists might stoutly defend Hongchon, Eighth Army commander Lieutenant General Matthew B. Ridgway ordered that it be taken in a double envelopment. Accordingly, commanding general of IX Corps Major General William M. Hoge ordered the 1st Cavalry to attack on the 14th from the west while the 1st Marine Division approached from the east. Neither division met much resistance. The same was true of attacks by the 24th and ROKA 6th divisions, and the 25th Division in I Corps.

By nightfall on March 15, the 25th Division had completely outflanked Seoul, the 24th was on the banks of the Chongpyong Reservoir, the ROKA 6th was on high ground overlooking the Hongchon River, and the 1st Cavalry was on its banks. The marines, slowed by strong enemy positions, took the town of Hongchon and attained the riverbank later in the day.

A rifle platoon of the 24th Infantry Division fires on communist forces during Operation RIPPER (March 6–31), which retook the city of Seoul in 1951. (U.S. Army Military History Institute)

Of more value was the fact that the communists had abandoned Seoul without a fight. Third Division patrols crossed on March 12 to find communist shoreline positions vacant. More patrols crossed east and southeast of the city on March 14, while five from the ROKA 1st Division entered the city. Aerial reconnaissance revealed that the communist forces had withdrawn to strong positions about five miles north of the city.

Ridgway then ordered I Corps to take Seoul and occupy the first defensible terrain north of it. The ROKA 1st and U.S. 3rd divisions executed the order the next day, sending combat patrols farther north in search of communist forces.

In the meantime the 24th, ROKA 6th, 1st Cavalry, and 1st Marine divisions continued attacking. Only the 1st Cavalry met significant resistance. By nightfall on March 19, the bulk of IX Corps was on or near the Buster-Buffalo Line. The communists abandoned the area, allowing the IX Corps to attain Line Cairo and seize Chunchon unopposed on March 21, causing the cancellation of a projected drop just north of the city by the 187th Airborne and two U.S. Army Ranger companies.

In the east X Corps and the ROKA III Corps reached Line Idaho by March 17, and Ridgway ordered all three corps on the eastern front to patrol well beyond the 38th Parallel between the Hwachon Reservoir and Chunchon on the east coast.

Operation RIPPER secured Seoul without a fight. It also secured substantial territorial gains, but it fell short in inflicting significant casualties on communist forces. Between March 1 and 15 there were only 7,151 known communist dead.

UZAL W. ENT

See also

Hoge, William Morris; Ridgway, Matthew Bunker; Seoul

References

Appleman, Roy E. *Ridgway Duels for Korea*. College Station: Texas A&M University Press, 1990.

Blair, Clay. *The Forgotten War: America in Korea, 1950–1953*. New York: Times Books, 1987.

Mossman, Billy C. *United States Army in the Korean War: Ebb and Flow, November 1950–July 1951*. Washington, DC: U.S. Army Center of Military History, 1990.

Roberts, William Lynn
Birth Date: September 17, 1890
Death Date: November 27, 1968

U.S. Army brigadier general and commander of the Korea Military Advisory Group (KMAG) from its inception until just before the beginning of the Korean War. Born in Ohio on September 17, 1890, William Lynn Roberts attended the U.S. Military Academy at West Point, graduating in 1913. During World War I he served in France in the infantry and participated in the St. Mihiel and Meuse-Argonne offensives.

Roberts graduated from the Army Command and General Staff School in 1926 and then served as instructor there until 1930. He was an instructor at the Rank School during 1931–1932. Roberts was executive officer of the 21st Infantry Brigade in Hawaii during 1929–1940, before serving as professor of military science and tactics at the Citadel during 1940–1941. He was an instructor at the Army Command and General Staff College during 1942–1943. During 1943–1945 Roberts headed the Combat Command in the 10th Armored Division. He was promoted to brigadier general in May 1945.

During 1945–1946 Roberts was assistant divisional commander of the 4th Armored Division. Having been passed over for promotion to major general, he faced mandatory retirement in June 1950. In 1948 Roberts was assigned to Korea, where on May 20 he became adviser to the director of the Department of Internal Security in the U.S. military government. On the formal establishment of the Republic of Korea (ROK, South Korea), Roberts commanded the Provisional Military Advisory Group (PMAG) of some 100 men. On July 1, 1949, it expanded into KMAG, an organization of some 500 men. Roberts became chief of KMAG, with headquarters in Seoul.

As the closest military adviser to U.S. ambassador John J. Muccio, Roberts's mission was to train a South Korean army strong enough to deter any attacks from the Democratic People's Republic of Korea (DPRK, North Korea). Taking up the task with considerable zeal, Roberts was determined to be successful before he had to leave Korea, and he certainly did the best he could with the scant resources available. While he had direct communication with the Department of the Army on military matters, Roberts also regularly informed U.S. Far East Command commander General Douglas MacArthur on the status of the Republic of Korea Army (ROKA, South Korean Army).

Roberts directed the establishment of several technical schools, and in August 1949 he ordered that KMAG establish an infantry school to qualify Korean officers as platoon leaders, company commanders, and battalion staff officers. He also sought to prove to Congressmen and other U.S. visitors that military aid to South Korea was an excellent investment; he regularly stage-managed visits by VIPs and journalists to make the case for additional assistance. Publicly, Roberts had only praise for the ROKA; privately, he had doubts, most notably displayed in a long March

1949 letter to Lieutenant General Charles L. Bolté of the Joint Chiefs of Staff (JCS). In the letter Roberts warned about ROKA shortcomings, especially in confronting North Korean aircraft, tanks, and heavy artillery. In December, Roberts recommended through Ambassador Muccio that the United States sharply increase military aid to South Korea. His proposals included 10 North American T-6 Texan trainers, 40 North American F-51 (Mustang) fighter aircraft, 2 Douglas C-47 Skytrain (Dakota) cargo aircraft, signal equipment, 3-inch guns for the coast guard, 105-millimeter howitzers, and more machine guns and mortars (including 4.2-inch).

Roberts professed to be unconcerned about the Korean People's Army (KPA, North Korean Army) armor. Given his own long experience with tanks, Roberts should have known better when he stated that Korea was "not good tank country."

Overall, reports from Roberts and Muccio to Washington, DC, were optimistic in their assessment of ROKA capabilities and gave the false impression that it was the best in the Far East and lacked only aircraft and heavy artillery to be invincible. A week before the Korean War began, Roberts left Korea to retire from the army; Colonel W. H. Sterling succeeded him as the chief of KMAG. On his departure, Roberts again expressed confidence in ROKA capabilities. Stopping in Tokyo for a debriefing at MacArthur's headquarters, he told General Omar N. Bradley, the chairman of the JCS, that the ROKA could "meet any test the North Koreans imposed on it." This assessment led Bradley to write to the JCS after the KPA invasion, "After my talk with General Roberts, I am of the opinion that South Korea will not fall in the present attack unless the Russians actively participate in the action." Roberts retired from the army in September 1950. He died on November 27, 1968.

MONICA SPICER AND SPENCER C. TUCKER

See also
Bolté, Charles Lawrence; Bradley, Omar Nelson; Korea Military Advisory Group; MacArthur, Douglas; Muccio, John Joseph; Rhee, Syngman

References
Blair, Clay. *The Forgotten War: America in Korea, 1950–1953*. New York: Times Books, 1987.

Matray, James I., ed. *Historical Dictionary of the Korean War*. Westport, CT: Greenwood, 1991.

Sawyer, Robert K. *Military Advisors in Korea: KMAG in Peace and War*. Washington, DC: Office of the Chief of Military History, U.S. Army, 1962.

Robertson, Sir Horace
Birth Date: October 29, 1894
Death Date: April 28, 1960

Australian army officer and administrative commander in chief of the British Commonwealth Forces in Korea, 1950–1951. Born on October 29, 1894, in Melbourne, Australia, and educated at the Royal Military College at Duntroon, Horace Clement Hugh Robertson served with distinction at Gallipoli and in Palestine during World War I. He attended the Army Staff College at Camberley and proceeded to hold various staff and instructor positions in the interwar Australian army. During World War II he commanded the 19th Australian Army Brigade in the Libyan campaign, before returning to the Pacific theater to lead Australian troops in the southwest Pacific. In April 1946 he was named commander in chief of the British Commonwealth Occupation Forces in Japan, where he ranked second only to General Douglas MacArthur.

Although one of the ablest Australian military men of his generation, Robertson was frequently arrogant, tactless, and overbearing—characteristics that could and sometimes did bedevil his relations with peers and subordinates. Blunt and outspoken, he told the Japanese people on the third anniversary of the atomic bombing of Hiroshima in August 1948, "This disaster was your own fault. . . . The Japanese nation treacherously attacked us without warning."

Robertson remained on good terms with the often difficult and overbearing MacArthur, but his position as the first Dominion officer ever to command a British Commonwealth force that included British troops would in any case have been likely to cause some tensions, and Robertson's personality helped to exacerbate those strains. His time in Japan was marked by sharp disagreements with several of his subordinates and also with British military authorities in London and British officials in Tokyo.

When the Korean War began, Lieutenant General Robertson was appointed administrative commander in chief of British Commonwealth Forces in Korea, with overall responsibility for providing logistical and administrative support to the Commonwealth Division. The core of these forces was those Commonwealth troops still stationed in Japan, which, it had already been decided in May 1950, would shortly be withdrawn, and which were consequently understrength and poorly equipped. Robertson instituted a highly effective reinforcement, equipment, and training program for the one Australian infantry battalion still remaining in Japan, which was sent to Korea in September 1950.

During his time in Korea, serious tensions and disagreements continued to mar Robertson's dealings with British military officials in London and with British subordinates. At the same time, his good relations with the often prickly MacArthur allowed him to serve as an effective communications channel between the United Nations Command (UNC) commander in chief and his military and civilian superiors in Australia. Within a few days after the war began, he had won from them the decision to allow MacArthur to use the Royal Australian Air Force's 77th Squadron against North Korean troops. Contrary to MacArthur's original intentions, by Christmas 1950 Robertson had persuaded MacArthur to impose strict censorship on the reporting of the war, on the grounds that this was necessary to prevent the leakage of restricted information to the Chinese.

Robertson, who seems to have found the Americans more congenial than he did the British, was also on good terms with Lieutenant General Matthew B. Ridgway, MacArthur's successor. His efforts contributed to Australia's overall image as a loyal ally of the United States during the Korean War, which in turn played a major part in persuading U.S. officials to sign the 1951 ANZUS (Australia-New Zealand-United States) security pact. In December 1951 Robertson returned to Australia to become director general of recruiting. He retired in 1954 and died in Melbourne, Australia, on April 28, 1960.

PRISCILLA ROBERTS

See also

ANZUS Treaty; Australia; Far East Command; MacArthur, Douglas; Ridgway, Matthew Bunker

References

Farrar-Hockley, Sir Antony. *The British Part in the Korean War,* Vol. 1, *A Distant Obligation.* London: HMSO, 1990.

Grey, Jeffrey. *Australian Brass: The Career of Lieutenant General Sir Horace Robertson.* Cambridge, UK: Cambridge University Press, 1992.

———. *The Commonwealth Armies and the Korean War: An Alliance Study.* Manchester, UK: Manchester University Press, 1988.

O'Neill, Robert J. *Australia in the Korea War, 1950–1953.* 2 vols. Canberra: Australian War Memorial/Australian Government Publishing Service, 1981, 1985.

Wood, James. *The Forgotten Force: The Australian Military Contribution to the Occupation of Japan, 1945–1952.* St. Leonards, New South Wales, Australia: Allen and Unwin, 1998.

Robertson, Walter Spencer

Birth Date: December 7, 1893
Death Date: January 19, 1970

U.S. diplomat and assistant secretary of state for Far Eastern affairs, 1953–1959. Born on December 7, 1893, in Nottoway County, Virginia, Walter Spencer Robertson attended the Hoge Military Academy. He then studied at the College of William and Mary and Davidson College but left school in 1912 for a career in banking. During World War II he joined the U.S. Army Air Corps and served as a pursuit pilot. After the war he resumed his career with the Richmond, Virginia, banking and brokerage firm of Scott & Stringfellow, becoming a partner in 1925.

Robertson entered government service in 1943 during World War II as Lend-Lease administrator in Australia. The next year U.S. ambassador to China Patrick J. Hurley invited him to the embassy in Chongqing to be counselor for economic affairs; he later became chargé. He supervised U.S. economic activities in China until mid-1946, when he left government service to resume his business career.

Robertson was a great admirer and friend of Generalissimo Jiang Jieshi (Chiang Kai-shek). He was also one of the chief architects of U.S. pro-Nationalist China policy. Because of his conviction that U.S. policy before 1949 had helped Mao Zedong come to power, he urged that the United States not extend diplomatic recognition to the People's Republic of China (PRC). He believed that the Nationalists on Taiwan constituted the legitimate Chinese government.

Robertson joined Democrats for Eisenhower during the 1952 election campaign, and in January 1953 president-elect Dwight D. Eisenhower appointed him assistant secretary of state for Far Eastern affairs in the Department of State. In this post Robertson had a reputation for fervor and stubbornness in his beliefs. He was regarded as even more anticommunist than Secretary of State John Foster Dulles.

In late June 1953 President Eisenhower sent Robertson to the Republic of Korea (ROK, South Korea) in hopes of persuading President Syngman Rhee to accept the proposed armistice terms. Rhee had proclaimed these terms to be unsatisfactory, insisting that a U.S.–South Korean joint defense pact be followed by the reciprocal removal of United Nations Command (UNC) and communist military forces from Korea. He also opposed the employment of foreign troops on South Korean soil as guardians of prisoners of war (POWs) and protested any contact between communist officials and the captives. Rhee threatened a continuation of the war. Then, with communist military action intensifying, on June 17, 1953, Rhee breached the armistice terms by ordering South Korean guards to release communist POWs who were refusing repatriation.

Rhee turned down a request by Dulles to visit Washington, DC, for resolution of the impasse. Instead, he suggested that Dulles travel to Seoul. The secretary of state, considering such a journey ill-advised before a South Korean agreement to the armistice, elected to dispatch Robertson instead. Robertson lacked Korean expertise, but his staunch anticommunism led him to identify with Rhee.

Robertson arrived in South Korea amid popular demonstrations after a tirade by Rhee against the armistice accord. On June 26, 1953, Robertson began conversations with Rhee. While Robertson admired Rhee, he proved to be skillful in negotiating and was persuasive. He informed the South Korean president that the United States was not prepared to continue the war until Korea was reunified. Threatened with a withdrawal of the UNC and given concessions regarding U.S. military assistance for an expanded Republic of Korea Army (ROKA, South Korean Army) as well as the promise that the U.S. and South Korea would resume the war should the armistice fail, Rhee yielded. On July 9 Robertson received a pledge from Rhee that his government would not block the proposed armistice. Robertson departed Korea on July 11 with the crisis at an end.

Three years later, Eisenhower sent Robertson to Taiwan for talks with Jiang concerning the defense of the Quemoy and Matsu islands. After his resignation from the State Department in 1959, Robertson returned to Scott & Stringfellow. He died on January 19, 1970, in Richmond.

RODNEY J. ROSS

See also

Dulles, John Foster; Eisenhower, Dwight David; Jiang Jieshi; Marshall, George Catlett; Rhee, Syngman; Robertson Mission

References

Alexander, Bevin. *Korea: The First War We Lost.* New York: Hippocrene Books, 1986.

Goulden, Joseph C. *Korea: The Untold Story of the War.* New York: Times Books, 1982.

Stueck, William W., Jr. *The Korean War: An International History.* Princeton, NJ: Princeton University Press, 1995.

Robertson Mission
Start Date: June 22, 1953
End Date: July 12, 1953

U.S. diplomatic mission to Korea to convince Syngman Rhee, president of the Republic of Korea (ROK, South Korea), to agree to an armistice agreement with the communists. The mission had been planned months before its start on June 22, 1953, with the general objective to seek Rhee's support for the armistice negotiations. Following Rhee's release of 27,000 North Korean prisoners of war (POWs) on June 18, the mission, headed by Assistant Secretary of State for Far Eastern Affairs Walter S. Robertson, had a new emphasis. Now Robertson, United Nations Command (UNC) commander Lieutenant General Mark W. Clark, and Ambassador Ellis O. Briggs and Ambassador Robert D. Murphy recommended to Washington, DC, that the United States should go ahead "with full steam" and sign the armistice.

To achieve this goal the UNC had to convince the communists, who were outraged by Rhee's release of the POWs, that Seoul would abide by the provisions of a future armistice agreement. Legally, the UNC did not need the approval of the South Korean government to sign the armistice. It was a military agreement between military commanders, and South Korean forces had been placed under UNC control by President Rhee himself.

U.S. president Dwight D. Eisenhower sent Robertson to discuss a mutual defense treaty with Rhee to facilitate South Korean approval. Robertson was also allowed to outline U.S.–South Korean tactics for a postarmistice political conference with the communists, and he was also authorized to offer U.S. economic assistance to Seoul along the lines recommended by U.S. economist and special representative Henry Tasca's recent fact-finding mission to South Korea.

Robertson's first stop was in Tokyo, where Clark joined him, and they flew to Seoul together. Clark had his doubts about the wisdom of sending a special emissary to Rhee. He believed that "those who knew the problem intimately and had had personal contact with [Rhee] could make better use of a blank-check authority in dealing with him." Still, Clark gave his full support to the mission because he hoped Rhee might appreciate a special envoy straight from Washington. South Korean crowds, encouraged by Rhee's propaganda machine, "welcomed" the emissaries with such slogans as "Go North!" and "Don't Sell Out Korea!" to demonstrate that South Koreans wanted nothing less than the reunification of Korea.

At the beginning of the "Little Truce Talks," Rhee showed a willingness to accept Robertson's offers, but he soon threw in new conditions that seemed unacceptable to the United States. Rhee demanded the immediate withdrawal of Chinese forces from Korean soil, and he insisted that all POWs in South Korea would be guarded by South Korean armed forces and that no communist indoctrinators would be allowed to approach them. One of Robertson's tasks was to influence Rhee to agree to the transfer of POWs to the demilitarized zone (DMZ).

Washington instructed Robertson's team to convince Rhee that this was its last and best offer to him. Clark was allowed to put pressure on Rhee by indicating that the UNC was ready to resume negotiations with the communists. Clark was also permitted to let the South Korean president believe that Washington was even willing to withdraw its troops from the peninsula in order to end the war.

On July 8, 1953, the communists launched a massive offensive that devastated three South Korean divisions; only prompt U.S. military assistance halted the Chinese advance. The offensive was a signal to Seoul that a "march to the North" would not be so easy to accomplish. Rhee now dropped his demand for immediate Chinese withdrawal in return for a prompt start of negotiations over a U.S.–South Korean mutual defense pact.

During his visit to South Korea, Robertson met with Rhee every day. Although the two men never reached complete agreement, U.S. secretary of state John Foster Dulles believed that the current stage of negotiations was a good basis for an armistice and that the remaining differences could be solved at a postwar conference. The agreement concluding Robertson's visit pledged the United States to guarantee the creation of a mutual defense pact after an armistice. Washington also agreed to endorse long-term economic aid to South Korea, beginning with an initial $260 million. Political talks after the armistice were limited to 90 days, after which the United States and South Korea would withdraw and work out a different way to satisfy Seoul's demands. Robertson also promised that the United States would help expand South Korean armed forces to enable them to withstand any future aggression without foreign military aid. In return for all these, Rhee agreed to accept the armistice, yet without a promise to sign it.

As a result of the agreement, negotiations in Panmunjom resumed on July 10 and finally led to the Armistice Agreement of July 27, 1953. According to Clark, the significance of the Robertson mission was to prove that South Korea was not a puppet state under U.S. control, but a sovereign nation.

Zsolt Varga

See also

Armistice Agreement; Briggs, Ellis Ormsbee; Clark, Mark Wayne; Murphy, Robert Daniel; Prisoners of War, Rescreening of; Rhee, Syngman; Rhee's Release of North Korean Prisoners of War; Robertson, Walter Spencer; Tasca, Henry Joseph; Truce Talks

References

Berger, Carl. *The Korea Knot: A Military and Political History.* Philadelphia: University of Pennsylvania Press, 1957.

Clark, Mark W. *From the Danube to the Yalu.* New York: Harper and Row, 1954.

Paik Sun Yup. *From Pusan to Panmunjom.* Washington, DC: Brassey's, 1992.

Stueck, William W., Jr. *The Korean War: An International History.* Princeton, NJ: Princeton University Press, 1995.

———. *Rethinking the Korean War: A New Diplomatic and Strategic History.* Princeton, NJ: Princeton University Press, 2004.

Rocket Artillery

Artillery that employs rocket launchers instead of conventional guns or mortars. Both sides in the Korean War used artillery rockets and rocket launchers that had been developed and fielded during World War II. By modern standards these weapons were inaccurate and had very limited range. They were, however, capable of delivering short bursts of saturation fire on large areas, which generally produced a greater psychological than physical effect. The rocket artillery of the period fell into three basic categories: ship to shore, air to ground, and ground to ground.

The U.S. Navy used 5-inch, spin-stabilized shore bombardment rockets with a range of 5,000 yards. They were fired from World War II–era landing craft that had been refitted as rocket ships. These converted craft were designated as Landing Ship, Medium, Rocket (LSMR). At least six of these craft operated in Korean waters, supporting landing operations, such as the one at Inchon (September 1950), and evacuations, such as that of Hungnam (December 1950). One LSMR could fire a salvo of 1,020 rockets into an area 500 yards square, with 80 percent of the rockets expected to land in the target area. The first reloading took 45 minutes, and each subsequent reloading took 1.5 to 2 hours.

U.S. Air Force and Navy jet and propeller fighters carried 5-inch high-velocity aircraft rockets (HVARs) for use against ground targets. These fin-stabilized rockets weighed 140 pounds with a 20-pound high explosive or semi–armor-piercing warhead. They had a range of 1,000 yards. The Lockheed F-80 (Shooting Star) carried four HVARs.

The U.S. Army had a small number of multiple rocket launcher batteries in Korea. The standard field artillery rocket was the M-16, a 4.5-inch, spin-stabilized rocket first fielded in 1945. It was an improved version of the 4.5-inch, fin-stabilized M8 rocket introduced in 1943. The M-16 weighed 42.5 pounds and had a range of only 5,250 meters (5,700 yards), or less than half the range of the 105-millimeter (mm) light howitzer.

The M-16 rocket came with both smoke and high-explosive warheads. It was fired from a variety of towed or truck-mounted

A U.S. Army T-66 towed rocket launcher battery carrying out a fire-support mission in Korea, May 27, 1951. (National Archives)

launchers. The most commonly used was the T-66 towed rocket launcher. Weighing 1,240 pounds, the split-trail T-66 mounted 24 launching tubes. A single battery of 12 launchers was capable of delivering a volley of 288 rounds, the equivalent of 16 battalions of 105-mm howitzers.

Communist forces also had a limited number of Soviet-supplied rockets and rocket launchers. Used by the Korean People's Army (KPA, North Korean Army) for the first time during the Battle of Unsan on November 1–2, 1950, the 82-mm RS-82 rockets were fired primarily from a truck-mounted launcher. Introduced in 1941, the RS-82 weighed 17.6 pounds and had a range of 5,500 meters (6,000 yards).

After the Korean War the U.S. Army abandoned multiple rocket launchers in favor of larger, longer-range, single artillery rockets, such as the Little John and Honest John. In the late 1960s and early 1970s the unguided rockets were replaced with tactical guided missile systems, such as the Lance and Pershing. The Soviets also developed large free-flight rockets, such as the Frog, and tactical guided missiles, like the Scud, Scaleboard, and

SS-21. The Soviets, however, never abandoned multiple rocket launchers.

In the 1980s the U.S. Army and the North Atlantic Treaty Organization (NATO) resurrected multiple rocket launchers with the introduction of the Multiple Launch Rocket System (MLRS). The MLRS played a major role in the 1991 Persian Gulf War and the 2003 Anglo-American-led invasion of Iraq. With far greater accuracy, effective ranges now well beyond cannon artillery, and a sophisticated family of warheads, the MLRS only superficially resembles its Korean War ancestors.

DAVID T. ZABECKI

See also
Artillery; Unsan, Battle of

References
Bailey, Jonathan B. A. *Field Artillery and Fire Power.* Oxford, UK: Military Press, 1989.
Bellamy, Chris. *Red God of War.* London: Brassey's, 1986.
Hedekin, Thomas B. "Artillery Rockets." *Field Artillery Journal* (October 1946): 564–573.

U.S. marines fire a barrage of 4.5-inch rockets against Chinese forces in 1951. The M-16 4.5-inch was the standard U.S. Army field artillery rocket during the war. (National Archives)

"Rolling with the Punch"

United Nations Command (UNC) battlefield tactic employed in the Korean War from early January 1951, after the UNC withdrawal from north of the 38th Parallel, to about mid-February, after critical engagements at Chipyong-ni, Wonju, and elsewhere.

During this period the Chinese People's Volunteer Army (CPVA, Chinese Army) and Korean People's Army (KPA, North Korean Army) forces had been known to hesitate when meeting a U.S. unit with far superior firepower. Rather than continue a frontal assault, the communists would then halt in place, fan out to the flanks with their superior numbers, and attempt to surround, isolate, and annihilate the UNC units. UNC commanders also noted at this time that communist forces could not usually maintain the momentum of their assaults for much distance, because after advancing a short span, they had to wait for weak support and supply forces to catch up. Communist forces in that period had an ability to strike hard initially but could not maintain this over more than a short distance. Thus, if UNC forces resisted temporarily when attacked, then recoiled and maintained a short distance from communist forces, they could remain relatively safe from serious harm.

To counter the communist tactics, UNC battalions, especially those of the United States, would occupy blocking positions in mountain passes or elsewhere, with instructions to inflict as much damage on attacking forces as possible. Then, if it appeared they might be surrounded and cut off, they were to withdraw through and under covering fire from a companion unit in position to the rear and go into position behind that unit. The cycle would then be repeated. These actions became known as "rolling with (and just beyond) the punch." The tactic was largely abandoned after the Battle of Chipyong-ni, where it was established that there was little chance that U.S. units would be encircled.

SHERMAN W. PRATT

See also

Chipyong-ni, Battle of; Kapyong, Battle of; Wonju, Battle of

References

Appleman, Roy E. *Ridgway Duels for Korea.* College Station: Texas A&M University Press, 1990.

Boose, Donald. *U.S. Army Forces in the Korean War, 1950–1953.* Oxford, UK: Osprey, 2005.

Rosenberg, Julius

Birth Date: May 12, 1918
Death Date: June 19, 1953

U.S. engineer and Cold War spy who, along with his wife, Ethel, was executed in 1953 for treasonous activity. Born on May 12, 1918, in New York City, Julius Rosenberg was educated at Jewish schools and in his late teens became involved in radical politics. He studied electrical engineering at the College of the City of New York, and there he became a central figure in a close-knit group of engineering students who were members of the Young Communist League, some of whom he later recruited into Soviet espionage. He met fellow activist Ethel Greenglass at a union meeting, and the two were married in 1939.

During World War II Rosenberg worked as a civilian inspector for the U.S. Army Signal Corps but was dismissed in early 1945 when his past Communist Party membership surfaced. In 1943 he had the first of some 50 meetings with Alexander Feklisov, a Soviet intelligence officer, and began providing classified military information to him, reportedly including secrets related to the manufacture of the atomic bomb. Beginning in 1946, Rosenberg began a small and ultimately unsuccessful engineering enterprise with his brother-in-law, David Greenglass, who had previously worked as a machinist on the Manhattan Project.

On June 17, 1950, just eight days before the outbreak of the Korean War, the Federal Bureau of Investigation (FBI) arrested Rosenberg after a series of confessions from admitted spies Klaus Fuchs, Harry Gold, and David Greenglass, who turned witness for the prosecution. On August 11, 1950, Ethel Rosenberg was also arrested. The Rosenbergs' arrest electrified the nation, coming as it did at the beginning of McCarthyism and the Korean War.

The Rosenbergs' controversial trial began on March 6, 1951, deeply dividing a nation already polarized by McCarthyism and the Korean War. To some, the Rosenbergs personified the threat of atomic espionage and communist subversion; to others, they were unjust victims of McCarthyism and anti-Semitism. The Rosenbergs were convicted on March 29, 1951, of conspiracy to commit espionage in wartime and were sentenced to death six days later.

Although it now appears with considerable certainty that Julius—but not Ethel—was guilty of espionage, the verdict appeared shaky in 1951. The Rosenbergs remained on death row for 26 months while their lawyers filed appeals and as international outrage with the verdict intensified. Throughout the ordeal, both denied being communists and maintained their innocence.

Julius Rosenberg and his wife Ethel Rosenberg were convicted of espionage in 1951, including passing information to the Soviets relating to the atomic bomb. The two were sentenced to death and executed. (Library of Congress)

After President Dwight D. Eisenhower refused clemency, the Rosenbergs were put to death by electrocution on June 19, 1953, at Sing Sing Correctional Facility in Ossining, New York, the only two civilians executed for espionage during the Cold War. The Rosenbergs left behind two young sons, ages 6 and 10.

PHILLIP DEERY

See also

Hiss, Alger; McCarthyism

References

Carmichael, Virginia. *Framing History: The Rosenberg Story and the Cold War.* Minneapolis: University of Minnesota Press, 1993.

Feklisov, Alexander, and Sergei Kostin. *The Man behind the Rosenbergs.* New York: Enigma Books, 2001.

Radosh, Ronald, and Joyce Milton. *The Rosenberg File: A Search for the Truth.* New York: Holt, Rinehart and Winston, 1983.

Rotation of Troops System

U.S. military personnel policy during the Korean War. The rotation of troops was initially implemented during World War II. Previously, rest areas behind the lines provided soldiers a respite

U.S. Marine Corps staff sergeant Phillip Korei rejoins his wife and son, Phillip Jr., at Treasure Island, California, on September 26, 1951. He returned to the United States under the Korean War rotation plan. (Naval Historical Center)

from service, and units were placed in and out of combat together. Since the American Revolutionary War, soldiers had enlisted in a unit for a certain length of service time, ranging from a few months to until war's end. With the new rotation system, casualties were replaced by individuals, not by units. Soldiers did not remain in action for the duration of the military crisis. Instead, each serviceman was rotated home based on his time in combat.

When the Korean War began, military leaders considered the potential hazards of the harsh Korean climate on soldiers' morale and discussed limiting service time. Although some U.S. soldiers in Korea had fought in World War II, many of the reservists and national guardsmen called to service lacked active-duty experience and performed poorly in combat. These civilian soldiers wanted to go home, and most were unenthusiastic about their stay in Korea.

In the spring of 1951 U.S. political and military leaders realized that the war was not going to be resolved quickly; thus, they sought ways to equalize the burden of service. Troops soon heard rumors about a rotation-home policy. Since December 1950, the system of rest and recuperation, known as "R&R" and "Little R," allowed selected soldiers a five-day rest period in Japan away from combat dangers and stress. The "Big R," or rotation to the United States, enabled Korean War soldiers who had served for a certain time in the combat theater to be replaced. Replacements had to arrive before men could return home. On April 22, 1951, the first U.S. soldiers rotated out of Korea.

The rotation of troops system was based entirely on a point system. Each man received 4 points for every month spent in the combat zone. Three points were given for being located within the area between regimental headquarters and the front line, and 2 points were given for rear-echelon duties. Service in Japan counted for 1 point per month, except for soldiers wounded in combat, who received 4 points until they were reassigned. When a soldier accrued 36 points, he was rotated home and discharged, unless of course he preferred to reenlist. The average infantryman returned home within a year, assuming he survived combat and weather conditions.

The rotation of troops system was controversial in Korea and later in Vietnam. Military efficiency was hindered, as unqualified officers were often promoted because of personnel turnover. "Short-timers" became cautious in combat as the time neared for them to return home. Survival and beating the clock became more important than defeating the enemy, and returning home safely was the primary goal. Anthony B. Herbert, a decorated army soldier in Korea and later a lieutenant colonel, recalled, "There came a chance that I might make it home. I had given up on the idea long before, and the possibility was like a new lease on life. Like others, I began to fight a little more cautiously, to take fewer chances than before." Soldiers constantly talked about rotation home and sometimes protected high-point men on patrols and missions.

Individual rotation weakened unit cohesion and effectiveness. Experienced soldiers were replaced by reservists, national guardsmen, and draftees unfamiliar with the Korean terrain and mountain combat techniques. Military writer S. L. A. Marshall noted that the Chinese "sit there year after year. The longer they stay the smarter they get. Our youngsters keep moving in and out. They're smart and they've got guts, but they don't stay long enough to learn." Military leaders were acutely aware of the detrimental consequences of the rotation system by mid-1952, when 35,000 men were rotated monthly. Rotation created large demands for personnel and resulted in the drafting of 1.2 million more men, affecting such services as transportation.

ELIZABETH D. SCHAFER

See also

Battle Fatigue; Draft; Home-by-Christmas Offensive; MacArthur, Douglas; Marshall, Samuel Lyman Atwood; Rest and Recuperation; United States Army

References

Cohen, Eliot. *Citizens and Soldiers: The Dilemmas of Military Service.* Ithaca, NY: Cornell University Press, 1985.

Fehrenbach, T. R. *This Kind of War: A Study in Unpreparedness.* New York: Macmillan, 1962.

Kellett, Anthony. *Combat Motivation: The Behavior of Soldiers in Battle.* Boston: Kluwer, 1982.

Millett, Allan R., and Peter Maslowski. *For the Common Defense: A Military History of the United States of America.* New York: Free Press, 1984.

ROUNDUP, **Operation**

Start Date: February 5, 1951
End Date: February 11, 1951

Military operation mounted by the United Nations Command (UNC) in February 1951. In early 1951 Eighth Army commander Lieutenant General Matthew B. Ridgway decided to advance the center of the UNC line for an assault on Seoul, in the Republic of Korea (ROK, South Korea). He ordered Lieutenant General Edward M. Almond to launch his X Corps in an offensive to make contact with communist forces and ascertain their dispositions

and, if possible, their intentions. If the opportunity presented itself, Almond was to disrupt any assemblies for communist offensive operations. This attack was to be launched simultaneously with the I and IX Corps offensives THUNDERBOLT and EXPLOITATION. It was designed to be a limited offensive that would follow the successful implementation of Operation THUNDERBOLT, which had left the Eighth Army in control of the Han River on its left flank.

The primary objective of Operation ROUNDUP was to advance the central front northward in preparation for a coordinated assault on Seoul, compelling the communists to evacuate the capital of South Korea. Before launching the offensive, Ridgway moved troops from the western sector to reinforce X Corps and the Republic of Korea Army (ROKA, South Korean Army) III Corps in the center of the peninsula. He instructed X Corps and ROKA III Corps to coordinate an envelopment of Hongchon, which would bring them abreast and even a little above the two corps on the west.

Beginning on February 5, X Corps, consisting of the ROKA 5th and 8th divisions and supported by armored and artillery support teams from the 2nd and 7th divisions and the 187th Airborne Regimental Combat Team, advanced northward from Hoengsong toward Hongchon for several days; but resistance grew as UNC forces came closer to the main communist positions. Additionally, the terrain proved much rougher than anticipated. Narrow roads, sharp ridges, and broken ground slowed offensive operations.

Meanwhile, one Korean People's Army (KPA, North Korean Army) and two Chinese divisions had moved south from Seoul to halt the advance. Intelligence reports warned that a communist counterattack was possible, but X Corps commander Almond pressed forward. On the night of February 11, four armies of the Chinese People's Volunteer Army (CPVA, Chinese Army) counterattacked in force, striking ROKA forces spearheading the X Corps advance and breaking through to establish roadblocks behind UNC lines. X Corps was able to retreat to Wonju, but the ROKA 8th Infantry Division was nearly annihilated. It lost 7,500 men and all its equipment. U.S. support units, road-bound with their armor and artillery, were cut off and decimated, losing dozens of artillery pieces. The battle soon developed into a frantic defense of Hoengsong, but despite heroic efforts on the part of UNC forces, X Corps was forced to retreat south of Hoengsong at a cost of 11,800 casualties (1,900 of them American).

Ridgway ordered the establishment of defensive positions to halt the retreat, and X Corps was able to reestablish defensive lines north of Wonju. While the X Corps was trying to establish its defensive lines, the communists launched a new attack northwest of Wonju at the road junction of Chipyong-ni on X Corps' left flank. For three days, three Chinese divisions encircled and assaulted a defense perimeter manned by the 23rd Infantry Regiment and the French Battalion. The Chinese wanted Chipyong-ni because it was the key to the entire Eighth Army defense line, and they tried desperately to take it, despite sustaining severe punishment from air attacks as well as the embattled U.S. troops. The 23rd held its positions until relief arrived in the form of an armored task force from the 5th Cavalry Regiment.

In terms of its original objective, Operation ROUNDUP failed, but the hastily erected defenses and the valiant stand of the 23rd Infantry Regiment and the attached French Battalion halted the Chinese counterattack.

JAMES H. WILLBANKS

See also

Almond, Edward Mallory; Chipyong-ni, Battle of; Ridgway, Matthew Bunker; X Corps; THUNDERBOLT, Operation

References

Appleman, Roy E. *Ridgway Duels for Korea*. College Station: Texas A&M University Press, 1990.

Blair, Clay. *The Forgotten War: America in Korea, 1950–1953*. New York: Times Books, 1987.

Ruffner, Clark Louis
Birth Date: January 12, 1903
Death Date: July 26, 1982

U.S. army general, chief of staff, X Corps (1950–1951), and commander of the 2nd Infantry Division (1951). Clark Louis Ruffner was born in Buffalo, New York, on January 12, 1903. Graduating from the Virginia Military Institute in 1924, Ruffner was commissioned a second lieutenant in the cavalry that same year.

The first 10 years of Ruffner's career were spent in various cavalry units, and from 1937 to 1940 he was an assistant professor of military science and tactics at Norwich University. From 1940 to 1941 he attended the Army Command and General Staff School. Ruffner served first as assistant chief of staff and then deputy chief of staff for VII Corps during 1942–1943. Advanced to brigadier general in September 1943, he was chief of staff, U.S. Army Force Pacific Ocean Areas during 1944–1946. He was promoted to major general in March 1945.

Ruffner then held several posts at the Pentagon. In 1950 he became special projects officer to the chief of staff, Far Eastern Command. With the formation of X Corps, Ruffner became its chief of staff. During January to September 1951 Ruffner commanded the 2nd U.S. Infantry Division in Korea. During the Chinese Fifth Offensive Ruffner's division held the center of the United Nations Command (UNC) line. He was then transferred stateside, where he worked on national security matters in the office of the secretary of defense until the war ended in 1953.

From 1954 to 1956 Ruffner served as commanding general of the 2nd Armored Division. From 1956 to 1958 he was chief of the Military Assistance Group in the Federal Republic of Germany (FRG, West Germany). Promoted to lieutenant general in 1958, Ruffner became commanding general of the U.S. Third Army, which post he held until 1960. Advanced to four-star rank in 1960, Ruffner finished his career as the U.S. representative to the North Atlantic Treaty Organization (NATO) during 1960–1962. He retired from the army in October 1962. Ruffner died on July 26, 1982.

PAUL G. PIERPAOLI JR.

See also

Chinese Offensive, Fifth

References

Appleman, Roy E. *Escaping the Trap: The U.S. Army X Corps in Northeast Korea, 1950*. College Station: Texas A&M University Press, 1990.
———. *Ridgway Duels for Korea*. College Station: Texas A&M University Press, 1990.

RUGGED, Operation
Start Date: April 3, 1951
End Date: April 6, 1951

United Nations Command (UNC) military operation that unfolded in April 1951. By the end of March 1951, the U.S. Eighth Army was located generally just below the 38th Parallel, although Republic of Korea Army (ROKA, South Korean Army) troops on the east coast had moved a few miles above it. With the approval of General Douglas MacArthur, Eighth Army commander Lieutenant General Matthew B. Ridgway elected to continue the advance over the 38th Parallel in hopes of achieving maximum destruction of communist forces, which were assembling in a fortified area known as the Iron Triangle. Communist troops were already in this area in force and appeared to be preparing for the Chinese Fifth Offensive. By the first week in April allied intelligence reported the presence of Chinese People's Volunteer Army (CPVA, Chinese Army) troops (9 armies comprising 27 divisions) along with 18 Korean People's Army (KPA, North Korean Army) divisions.

Ridgway decided, under the circumstances, that it would be better for the Eighth Army to move forward than to stand in place. Accordingly, he ordered the commencement of Operation RUGGED, which called for a general advance to a new objective line, Line Kansas, which ran along commanding ground just north of the 38th Parallel, except along the Imjin River in the west, where UNC forces were to remain in position.

On April 5 United Nations (UN) forces moved forward in a general advance from positions across the peninsula. These included the U.S. 3rd, 24th, and 25th and the ROKA 1st divisions of the U.S. I Corps in the west; in central Korea it included the U.S. IX Corps, with the U.S. 1st Marine, 1st Cavalry, and ROKA 6th divisions; they were joined by the 4th Ranger Company of the 187th Airborne Regimental Combat Team, then in reserve. In the east, the U.S. X Corps, including the U.S. 2nd and 7th and the ROKA 5th divisions, also advanced; they were joined along the east coast of Korea by the ROKA I and III Corps, comprising four ROKA divisions.

These troops rapidly crossed the 38th Parallel and by April 9 reached defensive Line Kansas and began to dig in. With the success of this move, Ridgway decided to add another objective line in the west, which he named Utah. The purpose of this line, which was essentially a northern bulge of Line Kansas in the west, was to thrust UN troops to a point just south of Chorwon, the southwestern anchor of the Iron Triangle.

The result of this advance to Kansas-Utah was that UNC forces were in place just in time to defend against the Fifth Offensive, which began on April 22, 1951.

JAMES H. WILLBANKS

See also

Almond, Edward Mallory; Chinese Offensive, Fifth; Eighth Army, U.S.; Iron Triangle; Kansas-Wyoming Line; MacArthur, Douglas; Ridgway, Matthew Bunker; X Corps

References

Blair, Clay. *The Forgotten War: America in Korea, 1950–1953*. New York: Times Books, 1987.

Middleton, Harry J. *The Compact History of the Korean War*. New York: Hawthorn Books, 1965.

Rees, David. *Korea: The Limited War*. New York: St. Martin's, 1990.

Rusk, David Dean
Birth Date: February 9, 1909
Death Date: December 20, 1994

Long-time U.S. State Department official who played a key role in formulating Korean War policy and who was later U.S. secretary of state (1961–1969). Born into a family of modest means in Cherokee County, Georgia, on February 9, 1909, David Dean Rusk attended Davidson College in North Carolina and, after graduating in 1931, studied at St. John's College, Oxford University, as a Rhodes scholar. He studied and later taught government and international relations at Mills College between 1934 and 1940.

Rusk also briefly attended the University of Berlin in 1933. While there, he witnessed Adolf Hitler's rise to power as the chancellor of Germany, which had a profound impact on Rusk's life and worldview. Later, he equated communist aggression in Europe and Asia with Nazi expansion in Europe. The timid response to Hitler by the Western democracies at the 1938 Munich Conference appalled him, and during the Cold War he advocated meeting communist expansionism with strength in order to avoid another Munich.

A strong military heritage and experience in Asian affairs also affected Rusk's outlook. During the Civil War both his grandfathers had served in the Confederate Army, and Rusk followed his family's military tradition by joining the Reserve Officers' Training Corps (ROTC) in high school and in college, where he served as a cadet commander. During World War II Rusk was chief of war plans for General Joseph Stilwell in the China-Burma-India theater, and he held the rank of colonel when he left the U.S. Army.

In late 1944 Rusk accepted a position with the Pentagon, but he left that post in February 1945 for one in the State Department, where, working in the operations division, he and Charles H. Bonesteel III were largely responsible for the U.S. position promoting the 38th Parallel as the line dividing Korea between U.S. and Soviet occupation forces.

In 1947 Rusk became the State Department's director of special political affairs, working for Secretary of State George C. Marshall, whom he greatly admired. He then became deputy secretary of state in 1949. In 1949 and 1950, the State Department came under tremendous public scrutiny. The "loss" of China in October 1949 and the conviction of Alger Hiss for perjury in January 1950 led conservative critics, especially Republican senator Joseph R. McCarthy, to attack the department. Rusk had little role in developing Harry S. Truman's China policy, working instead on United Nations (UN) affairs. In 1950, however, Rusk became assistant secretary of state for Far Eastern affairs, volunteering for what was arguably the most difficult job at the State Department.

As early as May 1949, Rusk worried about U.S. policy in Korea. He believed that the United States had an "implied commitment" to the Republic of Korea (ROK, South Korea), and he fretted over Truman's decision to withdraw U.S. troops. Rusk also became an advocate of South Korea, saying in 1950 that although President Syngman Rhee's government was not democratic, it was progressing in that direction. Moreover, Rusk believed that South Korean military forces could repel an "unlikely" attack from the Democratic People's Republic of Korea (DPRK, North Korea).

When word first came that North Korea had invaded South Korea, Rusk and Secretary of State Dean G. Acheson closely monitored the situation for the rest of the night. At 3:00 a.m. on June 25, Rusk and Acheson formally requested a meeting of the UN Security Council. For the rest of the morning, Rusk worked with Acheson in forming policy options for Truman.

During two days of intense meetings at Blair House, Rusk was heavily involved in planning the response to the North Korean attack. Drawing on lessons he had seen in World War II, Rusk believed that the United States had to act to defend South Korea. He also insisted the matter be taken to the UN.

Even while United Nations Command (UNC) forces were battling the North Koreans along the Pusan Perimeter and before the successful Inchon Landing of September 15, 1950, State Department officials were debating whether UNC troops, once they took the offensive, should invade North Korea in an attempt to reunify the peninsula. Despite pronouncements from Beijing that the People's Republic of China (PRC) would fight if U.S. forces invaded North Korea, Rusk fully supported the decision to cross the 38th Parallel and advocated the reunification of the peninsula. Rusk did not seek a wider war, but he believed that Chinese military intervention was only a remote possibility.

UN commander General Douglas MacArthur also did not believe that China or the Union of Soviet Socialist Republics (USSR, Soviet Union) would intervene. During a meeting with Truman at Wake Island in October 1950, MacArthur told the president that there was "very little" chance that Soviet or Chinese forces would join the fray. In the midst of MacArthur's assessment, Rusk handed Truman a note in which he urged the president not to risk a wider war with either the Soviet Union or the PRC. Rusk subsequently fully supported Truman's decision to remove MacArthur from his commands.

Before leaving government service in 1952, Rusk held primary responsibility for shaping the peace treaty with Japan, working closely with future Secretary of State John Foster Dulles. In 1952 Rusk became president of the Rockefeller Foundation. He returned to government in 1961 as secretary of state in President John F. Kennedy's administration and remained in that capacity under President Lyndon B. Johnson. Many of Rusk's views as well as his defense of failed Vietnam War policies were based on his Korean War experience. Rusk was secretary of state until 1969. He then taught at the University of Georgia between 1970 and 1984 and was a frequent speaker in various venues. Rusk died in Athens, Georgia, on December 20, 1994.

MARK A. T. ESPOSITO

See also

Acheson, Dean Gooderham; Blair House Meetings; Dulles, John Foster; Japanese Peace Treaty; Korea, History of, 1945–1947; MacArthur, Douglas; Marshall, George Catlett; McCarthy, Joseph Raymond; McCarthyism; Munich Analogy; Rhee, Syngman; 38th Parallel, Decision to Cross; 38th Parallel, Division of Korea at; Truman, Harry S.; Wake Island Conference

References

Cohen, Warren I. *Dean Rusk*. Totowa, NJ: Cooper Square, 1980.

Rusk, Dean. *As I Saw It*. Edited by Daniel S. Papp. New York: Norton, 1990.

Schoenbaum, Thomas J. *Waging Peace and War: Dean Rusk in the Truman, Kennedy, and Johnson Years*. New York: Norton, 1988.

Zeiler, Thomas W. *Dean Rusk: Defending the American Mission Abroad*. Wilmington, DE: Scholarly Resources, 2000.

Ryan, Cornelius Edward

Birth Date: May 13, 1896
Death Date: June 6, 1972

U.S. Army general and chief of the Korea Military Advisory Group (KMAG) during 1951–1953. He is regarded, along with General James A. Van Fleet, as the "father" of the modern Republic of Korea Army (ROKA, South Korean Army). Born in Boston, Massachusetts, on May 13, 1896, Cornelius Edward "Mike" Ryan graduated from the University of Connecticut in 1917. The United States had entered World War I that April, and Ryan secured a commission in the infantry in 1918. He saw service with the 49th Infantry Regiment in France during July 1918–1919.

Ryan remained in the U.S. Army after the war. He attended the Tank School (1923–1924), the Massachusetts Institute of Technology (1924–1925), the French armor school (1927–1928), and the Army Command and General Staff College at Fort Leavenworth, Kansas (1938–1939). He served as a Reserve Officers' Training Corps (ROTC) instructor at the University of California (1930–1936) and the Army Infantry School at Fort Benning, Georgia (1939–1942). He also served with the 23rd Infantry (1936–1938).

During World War II Ryan served as an assistant operations officer, Third U.S. Army, in Europe during 1944–1945, followed by civil affairs and military government assignments in Germany during 1945–1947. He was promoted to brigadier general in 1945, and he commanded the U.S. sector of Berlin during May–September 1947.

When Van Fleet wanted a proven trainer to reform the ROKA, Lieutenant General Maxwell D. Taylor recommended Ryan, who had been serving as the commanding general, 101st Airborne Division (Training) since August 1950. Ryan had recently been cited for his effectiveness by a Congressional investigating committee. Van Fleet accepted Ryan, who arrived in Korea in May 1951 and assumed the challenge of improving the ROKA, a critical part of the U.S. plan to negotiate an end to the Korean War.

With Van Fleet's complete support, Ryan executed the Far East Command plan to enlarge the ROKA from 10 to 20 divisions by 1953 and to reorganize and retrain this army at the same time it doubled in size. Facing opposition and corruption in the Rhee government and in the ROKA itself, Ryan enlarged KMAG from 1,300 to 2,000 officers and men and divided it between a Field Training Command and a Replacement Training and Schools Command. The KMAG teams assigned to Korean corps and divisions advised their counterparts down to the regiment and separate battalion level and supervised a nine-week retraining program for all ROKA divisions. They reported ROKA positions through a separate communications net, controlled U.S. tactical air control parties and artillery support teams, and managed the flow of ammunition, gas, and vehicles to the ROKA. The most successful advisers with Ryan's approval sought ways to help ROKA officers with the chronic problems of paying, feeding, and providing health care for ROKA soldiers and their families, even if the aid was not strictly legal. One major success was forming 34 new artillery battalions for the ROKA. By late 1952 the army had 12 combat effective divisions with 6 more forming.

KMAG teams made the ROKA training system appropriate for a modern army. At Ryan's request, Van Fleet assigned proven commanders from the Eighth Army to ROKA divisions. Ryan placed accomplished advisers in training billets after frontline service. The ROKA schools stressed three priorities: (1) tactical leadership, (2) basic combat skills, and (3) individual technical qualification.

KMAG officers found training in a foreign culture through interpreters a challenge. They were discomfited by corporal punishment and abuse, which was common in the ROKA; Ryan urged them to convince their counterparts to use other forms of persuasion. Progressive Korean officers found his reform efforts inspiring, and Van Fleet reported that KMAG had exceeded his expectations in training the ROKA.

Promoted to major general and decorated for his Korean service, Ryan retired in June 1957. He died on June 6, 1972.

Allan R. Millett

See also

Korea Military Advisory Group; Taylor, Maxwell Davenport; Van Fleet, James Alward

References

Blount, John B. Lt. Gen. USA (Ret.), aide to Chief, KMAG, 1952–1953, "Thoughts on KMAG and General Ryan, Chief, KMAG." Oral memoir for Allan R. Millett, July 1995. In possession of author.

Gibby, Bryan R. "Fighting in a Korean War: The American Advisory Missions from 1946–1953." Unpublished PhD dissertation, Ohio State University, 2004.

Hausrath, Alfred. H. *The KMAG Advisor: Roles and Problems of the Military Advisor in Developing an Indigenous Army for Combat Operations in Korea.* Chevy Chase, MD: Operations Research Office, John Hopkins University, February 1957.

Meyers, Kenneth W. *KMAG's Wartime Experience 11 July 1951 to 27 July 1953,* Part 4, *Office of Military History Officer, Headquarters U.S. Army Japan, U.S. Military Advisory Group to the Republic of Korea.* Manuscript history, May 1958. U.S. Army Center of Military History, Fort Leslie J. McNair, Washington, DC.

"Ryan, Cornelius E., Maj. Gen. U.S. Army." Biographical files, U.S. Army Center of Military History, Fort Leslie J. McNair, Washington, DC.

Sawyer, Robert K. *Military Advisors in Korea: KMAG in Peace and War.* Washington, DC: Office of the Chief of Military History, U.S. Army, 1962.

S

Sanctuaries

Sheltered sites for troops. Sanctuaries were places of refuge, where forces were safe from attacks and from which they could stage operations against nearby opposing forces. In General Douglas MacArthur's September 27, 1950, military order for the United Nations Command (UNC) invasion of the Democratic People's Republic of Korea (DPRK, North Korea) after the Inchon Landing, he stressed that troops were not to cross the Chinese and Soviet borders, even if Chinese troops entered the war. Restrictions imposed on MacArthur by Washington, DC, also forbade air attacks on Chinese bases in Manchuria for fear of violating Soviet airspace.

In turn, although unstated, the communists did not attack U.S. bases and seaborne lines of communication between the Republic of Korea (ROK, South Korea) and Japan. Thus the port of Pusan, vital for supply operations, was able to operate fully lighted around the clock. President Harry S. Truman and his defense advisers accepted the idea of sanctuaries, preferring to contain any future fight with the Chinese in Korea rather than see an expansion of the war.

Manchuria was officially recognized as a sanctuary by the United Nations Command (UNC) and the United States in November 1950. Manchuria was a traditional invasion route against China proper. It was also a major resource base. In the 1930s Japan had used Korean bases to help conquer Manchuria and then invade China, and the presence of UNC forces near the Manchuria-Korea border in the fall of 1950 greatly alarmed the Chinese Communist leadership. Chinese People's Volunteer Army (CPVA, Chinese Army) forces used Manchuria to prepare for their entry into the Korean War in late October. Supply depots and airfields were built there to maintain communist forces in Korea and to mount air attacks against UNC air assets over North Korea. Siberia and the North Korean port town of Najin also were sanctuaries for communist forces, who built up industries, arsenals, and rail systems there safe from UNC attack.

The United States sought to keep Chinese forces out of the Korean War, fearing the Union of Soviet Socialist Republics (USSR, Soviet Union) might then enter the conflict because of the 1950 Sino-Soviet Treaty of Friendship and Alliance. Granting China a form of neutrality, which it was not legally entitled to because its forces were engaging UNC troops, was a sort of "gentlemen's agreement." Political restrictions would protect certain geographic regions from attack. Allied leaders recognized that Chinese army and air forces could consider as sanctuaries the area north of the Yalu River, serving as the North Korean and Chinese boundary, and the territory of Manchuria. Limiting military operations in the Korean War set a precedent for similar sanctuaries during the later Vietnam War.

U.S. military leaders agreed not to strike the Chinese bases in Manchuria. The Chinese, in turn, did not use these aircraft to interfere with UNC ground troops, or with bases outside Korea (primarily in Japan), and forces in transit to and from Korea. Chinese aircraft from Manchurian sanctuaries, however, routinely attacked allied aircraft in MiG Alley in northern Korea. Although some "hot pursuit" did in fact occur, there was a stricture against UNC fighters pursuing communist aircraft into Manchuria.

MacArthur criticized the Manchurian sanctuary as an "enormous handicap, without precedent in military history." Indeed, his frustration concerning prohibitions on bombing Manchuria, the Yalu River bridges, and power plants helped bring about his dismissal from command in April 1951. At the MacArthur hearings in May 1951 following his relief, he stressed that the Chinese

Two soldiers near Hyesanjin in North Korea gaze at the Yalu River and mountains of Manchuria in the distance. A temple and bridge, set on fire by U.S. Air Force bombers, still burn in the valley below. (Department of Defense)

could have been defeated if restrictions on bombing sanctuaries had been removed.

Although military strategists considered bombing airfields and supply lines in the sanctuaries after MacArthur's dismissal, including the possible use of atomic weapons to end the war, the sanctuaries remained safe from allied attacks despite continued launching of air strikes from Manchuria. The safety of the sanctuaries was ensured by the allies' fears of retaliation and an expanded war.

ELIZABETH D. SCHAFER

See also

China, People's Republic of, Army; China, People's Republic of, People's Liberation Army Air Force; MacArthur, Douglas; MacArthur Hearings; Manchuria; Manchurian Sanctuary; MiG Alley; Najin, Bombing of; Sino-Soviet Treaty of Friendship and Alliance; Soviet Air War in Korea; Truman, Harry S.; Truman's Recall of MacArthur; United States Air Force; Yalu Bridges Controversy

References

Futrell, Robert F. *The United States Air Force in Korea, 1950–1953.* Rev. ed. Washington, DC: Office of the Chief of Air Force History, 1983.

MacArthur, Douglas. *Reminiscences.* New York: McGraw-Hill, 1964.

Spurr, Russell. *Enter the Dragon: China's Undeclared War against the U.S. in Korea, 1950–1951.* New York: Henry Holt, 1988.

Wilz, J. E. "The MacArthur Hearings of 1951: The Secret Testimony." *Military Affairs* 39 (December 1975): 167–173.

Sasebo, Japan

Japanese port city on the western coast of the island of Kyushu. Sasebo became the major base for U.S. naval operations during the Korean War. Situated in Nagasaki Prefecture at the mouth of Omura Bay, Sasebo has a fine natural harbor. In the late 19th century it grew from a small village to a sizable naval base, which led to its partial destruction by Allied bombing during World War II. In June 1950 Sasebo, which was the headquarters of the U.S. Army's 34th Infantry Regiment, 24th Infantry Division, served as a secondary naval facility for U.S. Fleet Activities Yokuska.

During the Korean War Sasebo rapidly eclipsed Yokuska, which was located near Tokyo, 500 miles farther from the theater of war. Sasebo's convenient proximity to the Korean port of Pusan, a mere 156 nautical miles away across the Tsushima and Korean straits, gave it new importance as the chief wartime anchorage and center for the repair, refitting, and refueling of all U.S. naval forces in the Korean theater. The city also housed a large replacement depot for the U.S. Army. The majority of U.S. military personnel who served in Korea passed through Sasebo at least once during their tour of duty, either when embarking for Korea or when returning home.

PRISCILLA ROBERTS

See also

Japan; United States Navy

References

Cagle, Malcolm W., and Frank A. Manson. *Sea War in Korea.* Annapolis, MD: Naval Institute Press, 1957.

Karig, Walter. *Battle Report: The War in Korea.* New York: Rinehart, 1952.

Kim, Nam G. *From Enemies to Allies: The Impact of the Korean War on U.S.-Japan Relations.* San Francisco: International Scholars Publication, 1997.

Marolda, Edward J. *The U.S. Navy in the Korean War.* Annapolis, MD: Naval Institute Press, 2007.

Schonberger, Howard B. *Aftermath of War: Americans and the Remaking of Japan, 1945–1952.* Kent, OH: Kent State University Press, 1989.

SATURATE, **Operation**
Start Date: Winter 1952
End Date: Spring 1952

Aerial interdiction operation intended to disrupt communist rail lines and roads, thereby pressuring the North Koreans to accept the terms of armistice. On November 27, 1951, United Nations Command (UNC) commander Lieutenant General Matthew B. Ridgway halted a UNC offensive, resulting in a de facto cease-fire. To maintain the gains achieved by the recent offensive during ongoing armistice negotiations, he proposed to continue the Fifth Air Force's aerial interdiction campaign. Air force pilots were not happy at this prospect, especially if tactics used in Operation STRANGLE remained unchanged. Those missions had always been scheduled at the same morning or afternoon hours against predictable regular targets. Communist flak batteries were concentrated near the targets and took a heavy toll on UNC aircraft.

In January 1952 planners prepared for a new air campaign, Operation SATURATE, that would vary targets to avoid concentrated communist defenses. Even as analysts pondered how to improve aerial interdiction, the Far East Air Force (FEAF) commenced a bomber campaign against specific rail and road "choke points." The best known of these was the crossroads near Wadong.

Between January 26 and March 11, 1952, in this preliminary to Operation SATURATE, 77 Boeing B-29 Superfortress and 125 Martin B-26 Marauder sorties dropped 3,928 500-pound bombs on the target. It proved to be a disappointing effort, with only 18 rail and

Damage to a North Korean rail line in February 1952, during the United Nations Command (UNC) aerial bombing campaign known as Operation SATURATE. (National Archives)

15 road cuts. During the 45-day effort, rail traffic was blocked for only 7 days and road traffic for just 4.

Planning for Operation SATURATE called for more concentrated around-the-clock raids against shorter rail segments of the four main rail lines in the Democratic People's Republic of Korea (DPRK, North Korea). Fighter-bombers carried out daylight attacks, while B-26s struck the same targets at night. FEAF B-29s focused on bridges. The Fifth Air Force selected the targets. It also closely controlled the flights, varying the approaches, withdrawals, and altitudes. It shifted targets based on flak concentrations and weather, and it employed photo reconnaissance before, during, and after each raid.

Operation SATURATE officially commenced on February 25 and evolved into a race between U.S. airmen trying to destroy communist rail lines and repair personnel trying to fix them. One example of this general pattern occurred on March 25–26 in an attack against the Chongju-Sinanju line that crossed two small streams. Flak was minimal and weather good for the 307 fighter-bomber sorties that dropped 530 1,000-pound bombs and 84 500-pound bombs on the rail bed and bridges. That night, eight B-26s covered the target with 42 500-pound bombs.

The next day, 161 more fighter-bomber sorties dropped 322 1,000-pound bombs. In all, only one North American F-51 Mustang suffered minor flak damage. Aerial reconnaissance indicated that, aided by thawing mountain snows that caused flooding streams, the rail lines had become totally impassible.

Even so, by March 30 communist workers had repaired the roadbed, and by the next day they had replaced the track. The successful cut had lasted just five days, but to ensure continued success, the raids needed to be repeated—something dwindling FEAF resources would not allow. Raids through May had to be reduced in size.

Despite these problems, Fifth Air Force's focus on cutting shorter lengths of track and its ability to outguess communist flak placement generally validated the tactics of Operation SATURATE. One U.S. Air Force report noted that the Sinuiju-Sinanju line was "continually out of operation" throughout April and most of May.

By May, as fighter-bombers were in ever-increasing demand, 243 had been lost and 290 severely damaged since the beginning of aerial interdiction campaigns in June 1951. Concurrently, Fifth Air Force had received only 131 replacements. By late May the 49th and 136th Fighter-Bomber Wings, each of which was to have 75 aircraft, had only 41 and 39, respectively.

A fully-equipped Fifth Air Force could have maintained six major cuts, but the undermanned force simply found North Korea's 600 miles of track too extensive. In mid-May the operation ended. Nearly a year of rail and road interdiction had not had sufficient impact to cause communist forces to accept UNC armistice terms.

During these raids FEAF aircraft had flown 87,552 sorties and made 19,000 rail cuts, and had destroyed 34,211 vehicles, 276 locomotives, and 3,820 rail cars. Despite such numbers, communist forces were able to continue to supply their frontline troops and to build logistical dumps in forward areas. For example, in July 1951, at the height of Operation STRANGLE, the communists fired 8,000 artillery/mortar rounds. In May 1952, at the end of Operation SATURATE, they fired an estimated 102,000 rounds.

Ultimately, air force leaders were reminded that aerial interdiction is a very difficult and costly undertaking. They understood the significant impact of terrain, weather, climate, and communist defenses on such a campaign. They also grasped the need for continuous operations to counter the efforts of massed repair personnel.

The very nature of limited conflict deeply affected aerial operations in both Korea and Southeast Asia. Low-intensity conflict, by definition, seeks to limit the extent and expenditure of the engagement. It is full of political twists and turns, which also limit the full employment of military assets. In the case of Korea, and later Vietnam, political restraints on allied forces, especially air forces, and communist sanctuaries and resupply proved to be roadblocks that were nearly impossible to overcome. Chinese and Soviet resupply of arms and trucks in Korea was critical, and with Chinese supply areas off-limits to UNC attacks, these supplies were all but guaranteed.

The lessons of aerial interdiction during such operations as SATURATE came at a high price and should have been deeply ingrained in air power theory and doctrine and U.S. foreign policy when Vietnam unfolded less than a decade later. But to U.S. civilian and military leaders, Korea was the exception to the rule of international politics and military engagement. The strategic confrontation with the Union of Soviet Socialist Republics (USSR, Soviet Union) in Europe was the Cold War mainstream, not limited wars in Asia. Thus, in Vietnam most of the same problems arose again during the COMMANDO HUNT aerial interdiction operations of 1968–1972, with the same results.

WILLIAM HEAD

See also

Aircraft; Far East Air Force; Logistics in the Korean War; Ridgway, Matthew Bunker; STRANGLE, Operation

References

Bruning, John R. *Crimson Sky: The Air Battle for Korea*. Dulles, VA: Brassey's, 1999.

Futrell, Robert F. *The United States Air Force in Korea, 1950–1953*. Rev. ed. Washington, DC: Office of the Chief of Air Force History, 1983.

Mark, Eduard. *Aerial Interdiction: Air Power and the Land Battle in Three Wars*. Washington, DC: Center for Air Force History, 1994.

Thompson, Wayne. "The Air War over Korea." In *Winged Shield, Wing Sword: A History of the United States Air Force*, edited by Bernard C. Nalty, 3–52. Washington, DC: U.S. Air Force History and Museum Program, 1997.

SCATTER, **Operation**
Start Date: April 8, 1952
End Date: April 15, 1952

United Nations Command (UNC) code name for the screening of communist prisoners of war (POWs) to determine those who wished to be repatriated. During the armistice talks communist negotiators cited the Geneva Convention in demanding the unconditional repatriation of all POWs after the cessation of hostilities. The issue of POWs during the Korean War was not as simple as in some earlier wars, however. As increasing numbers of communist military personnel deserted or were otherwise captured by the UNC, it became evident that a substantial number of them believed that they would suffer death or injury if returned to communist control. Also, with the communists making a determined effort to organize their POWs, riots and disorders mounted, and murders and other atrocities became commonplace in the UNC-administered camps. Such conditions made camp reorganization imperative.

After armistice negotiations deadlocked over the issue of exchange of POWs, in early April 1952 the communist side requested an estimate of the number of POWs the UNC would repatriate. The UNC pointed out that this figure could be determined only by interviewing individual POWs. At that time, the UNC and the communist side assumed that only a relatively small percentage of prisoners would resist repatriation. Both sides supported screening to determine which POWs and civilian internees (CIs) desired repatriation and which did not.

At the suggestion of the UNC, the communist side issued an amnesty statement, and the UNC then began screening of the POWs in its custody. The plan to screen all internees, known as Operation SCATTER, was conducted by the 2nd Logistical Command and was carried out during April 8–15, 1952. Operation SCATTER was also designed to separate prisoners who selected repatriation from those who selected nonrepatriation, in order to minimize acts of violence between the opposing groups.

Before screening began, the UNC provided the communist side's official amnesty statement to all prisoners in UNC custody. POWs were told to carefully consider their individual decisions. They were warned of possible reprisals against their families if they refused to return; they were also told that no promises could be made as to their disposition if they refused to return and that they might remain in the camps for many months after repatriates had returned home.

On April 8 UNC teams began individual polling of the POWs. The interviews were conducted by unarmed UNC personnel, including Korean and Chinese linguists. Each prisoner, carrying his personal possessions, was called forward individually and interviewed in private. As soon as the prisoner reached a definite decision, either during or at the conclusion of the interview, he was removed to another camp if he refused repatriation; if not, he was kept in a Koje-do compound to await return to communist control. The program proceeded smoothly and with no incidents until UNC personnel attempted to enter the communist-controlled compounds. Camp authorities feared considerable loss of life if they attempted to do so. Therefore, authorities omitted screening of those compounds that had violently opposed the program and merely listed all of the POWs for return to communist control. Many individuals did seek, at risk of their lives, to express their desire not to return to communist control, and a number of them were murdered by fellow POWs as a result.

Pressed by the communist side in the armistice talks, the UNC in early April had released a figure of 116,000 likely repatriates. That seemed a reasonable estimate, but based on the screening of the POWs consenting to be interviewed, the UNC discovered to its surprise that only some 70,000 wanted repatriation, as follows: 7,200 CIs; 3,800 POWs of South Korean residence; 53,900 North Korean POWs; and 5,100 Chinese Communist POWs. The vast majority of Chinese POWs had refused repatriation and demanded to be sent to Taiwan (then known as Formosa). This was a very serious development, because it was clear that Beijing would never accept such an outcome.

The UNC defended the process, reporting that its estimate of 70,000 resulted from a carefully worked-out screening process in an atmosphere that guaranteed each POW freedom of choice. The UNC then affirmed the finality of the 70,000 estimate and indicated that this figure must be accepted in any further negotiations.

The screening necessitated moving those refusing repatriation to other camps to separate them from the communist prisoners. This effort, known as Operation SPREADOUT, took place from April 19 to May 1, 1952. It relocated some 80,000 nonrepatriate POWs and CIs from Koje-do UNC POW Camp One to new camps on the Korean mainland. Anticommunist Chinese POWs were sent to Cheju-do.

The screening results were not completely accurate, as many anticommunist enclosures had taken steps to ensure a majority for nonrepatriation. Some U.S. officials understood that the results would be unacceptable to the communist side and probably would lead them to charge the UNC with bad faith. Allied governments expressed concern that the number of nonrepatriates was too high in the anticommunist camps.

When on April 19 they were informed of the results of the first screening, communist negotiators were stunned. They insisted on the full repatriation of all POWs and at the same time sought to discredit the UNC screening. They protested that the 70,000 figure was the result of manipulation, and they claimed that the screening had not been impartial and was in violation of the Geneva Convention. The figure resulting from the Koje-do screening dealt a fatal blow to prospects of an early armistice.

SUNGHUN CHO

See also

Civilian Internee Issue; Prisoners of War, Rescreening of; Truce Talks

References

Bailey, Sydney D. *The Korean Armistice.* New York: St. Martin's, 1992.

Cho, Sunghun. "Hanguk Chonjaeng Chung UN Kun ui Poro Chongchaek e Kwanhan Yongu" [A Study of UN Forces POW policies during the Korean War]. PhD dissertation, Academy of Korean Studies, Seoul, 1999.

MacDonald, Callum. *Korea: The War before Vietnam.* New York: Free Press, 1987.

Stueck, William W., Jr. *The Korean War: An International History.* Princeton, NJ: Princeton University Press, 1995.

Schuman Plan
Event Date: May 9, 1950

Proposal announced on May 9, 1950, by French foreign minister Robert Schuman whereby France and the Federal Republic of Germany (FRG, West Germany) would pool their coal and steel industries. The plan was designed to eliminate 80 years of Franco-German rivalry, which had contributed to two world wars in less than a generation. It also marked the first significant step toward West European political and economic integration.

Schuman and Jean Monnet, France's leading proponent of European integration, argued that the Schuman Plan would transform intra-European relations in numerous ways. First, Franco-German production of heavy industry would necessitate joint control of the mineral-rich Ruhr and Saar regions, the geographical bone of contention between France and Germany. A basis of trust would thus be created between the French, who still feared another attack by Germany, and the Germans, who were concerned about permanent dismemberment by a vengeful former enemy.

Second, the successful implementation of the Schuman Plan would essentially solve the "German problem" by forcing West Germany to surrender some of its sovereignty in favor of integration into a larger European community. It was hoped that such an arrangement would stanch German militarism in the future. Yet Schuman and Monnet assured West Germany that should the plan go forward, it would serve as the first step toward a mutual defense pact that would assuage its fears of permanent disarmament. This would later be proposed as the European Defense Community (EDC).

Third, the plan symbolized European integrationists' vision of a supranational organization that would transcend the nationalism they believed had stoked two wars. Politically, therefore, Western Europe would become unified. Finally, the Schuman Plan could ultimately establish an economic bloc rivaling the United States and the Union of Soviet Socialist Republics (USSR, Soviet Union).

Informed of the proposal on May 8, 1950, West German chancellor Konrad Adenauer agreed that the Schuman Plan was based on equal rights for both nations and removed the Saar question from traditional Franco-German rivalry. He quickly wrote the French foreign minister and pledged that he would strongly urge West Germany's Bundestag (lower house of parliament) to approve the plan. Within days, the United States and Italy declared their approval, with the Benelux countries (Belgium, the Netherlands, and Luxembourg) not far behind. After nearly a month of negotiations, the British signed off on it, and on June 3, 1950, a joint communiqué was issued announcing mutual acceptance of the plan. On April 18, 1951, France, West Germany, Italy, and the Benelux countries signed the Schuman Treaty, thereby creating the European Coal and Steel Community (ECSC).

Signed only 22 days before the unexpected outbreak of war on the Korean Peninsula, the timing of the Schuman Plan could not have been more fortuitous. Indeed, it helped with European rearmament, which began in earnest in early 1951, solidified the North Atlantic Treaty Organization (NATO), shored-up Marshall Plan aid, ameliorated—to a degree—the economic dislocations and rising inflation caused by the Korean War, and assured that U.S. allies were working cooperatively to ensure a strong bulwark against potential Soviet expansionism in Europe. This in turn allowed U.S. policy makers to concentrate their immediate military efforts on the war in Korea.

CHRIS TUDDA

See also

European Defense Community; France; Germany, Federal Republic of; Marshall Plan; North Atlantic Treaty Organization

References

Duchêne, François. *Jean Monnet: The First Statesman of Interdependence.* New York: Norton, 1994.

Fransen, Fredric J. *The Supranational Politics of Jean Monnet: Ideas and Origins of the European Community.* Westport, CT: Greenwood, 1996.

Gillingham, John. *Coal, Steel and the Rebirth of Europe, 1945–1955: The Germans and the French from the Ruhr Conflict to Economic Community.* New York: Columbia University Press, 1991.

Hitchcock, William I. *France Restored: Cold War Diplomacy and the Quest for Leadership in Europe, 1944–1954.* Chapel Hill: University of North Carolina Press, 1998.

Monnet, Jean. *Memoirs.* Garden City, NY: Doubleday, 1978.

Scorched Earth Policy

Term implying the destruction of everything that might be useful to an advancing enemy force. With the massive Chinese military intervention in the war at the end of November 1950, the U.S. Eighth Army was forced to withdraw from the Democratic People's Republic of Korea (DPRK, North Korea). As United Nations Command (UNC) forces retreated, Eighth Army commander Lieutenant General Walton H. Walker ordered a scorched earth policy. He did so in the belief that the advancing Chinese People's Volunteer Army (CPVA, Chinese Army) forces, with their lengthening supply lines, would have to live off the land, which would be especially difficult in a harsh Korean winter.

Eighth Army engineers fired a large UNC supply dump in the North Korean capital of Pyongyang and destroyed bridges. Walker ordered that nothing of value be left behind. Eighth Army troops were to burn houses, kill livestock, and destroy food stocks as they retreated. The effect of these efforts on the CPVA forces is difficult to measure, but the policy certainly had catastrophic effects for the North Korean population. The scorched earth policy increased the number of North Koreans who fled south. Perhaps 1 million people left North Korea for the Republic of Korea (ROK, South Korea) in the winter of 1950–1951. As X Corps in eastern Korea withdrew, it too practiced a scorched earth policy, destroying everything that might be of use to communist forces, either by demolition or by naval gunfire.

Walker died in a jeep accident on December 23, 1950. Lieutenant General Matthew B. Ridgway succeeded him. On the morning of January 4, 1951, as the last UNC troops left Seoul, Ridgway ordered the four bridges over the Han River blown. At the same time, demolition charges destroyed the tidal basin at Inchon and supplies at Kimpo Airfield, including 1.6 million gallons of aviation gasoline, 9,300 tons of engineer material, and 12 railroad cars full of ammunition.

Ridgway then issued an order the same day to end the scorched earth policy. He declared that in the future demolitions would be limited to those that combined "maximum hurt to the enemy with minimum hurt to the civilian population." Water and power plants would be spared and bridges would be destroyed only if necessary to delay a communist advance. There was to be no more "destruction for destruction's sake."

SPENCER C. TUCKER

A U.S. soldier uses a flamethrower in March 1951 during the Korean War. As part of the United Nations Command (UNC) scorched earth policy, anything that might be useful to the enemy was destroyed. (Hulton Archive/Getty Images)

See also

Eighth Army, U.S.; Ridgway, Matthew Bunker; Walker, Walton Harris

Reference

Blair, Clay. *The Forgotten War: America in Korea, 1950–1953*. New York: Times Books, 1987.

Seabees

See United States Naval Construction Battalions

Searchlights

During the Korean War, both the United Nations Command (UNC) and communist forces employed searchlights in nighttime operations. These systems directed high-intensity light at military targets by manual-, radar-, or sound-controlled means and were usually mobile. Searchlights having intensity ranging up to tens of millions of candlepower existed, and some had beam ranges up to 30,000 feet. UNC ground searchlights were operated by engineer companies.

UNC use of searchlights centered primarily on battlefield illumination. For a short period in the late autumn of 1951, the U.S.

Air Force designated two bombers in each squadron of Douglas B-26 Intruders to be outfitted with 70 million–candlepower searchlights under their wings. Such searchlights had been used during World War II to locate German submarines. The searchlight had a range of some 2 miles, weighed 154 pounds, and operated on 72 volts DC. The searchlight beam was directed by the navigator sitting beside the pilot operating a joystick. It could not be used for longer than one minute at time, when it would have to be switched off to cool down for five minutes before it could be used again. After limited successes, the fragile searchlights were deemed unsuitable to hold up to the rigors of bombing operations. U.S. Army and Marine units holding defensive positions in October 1952 and March 1953 used searchlights in coordination with flares, both ground-launched and dropped from planes, to spot enemy movements. Searchlights were also employed by allied antiaircraft artillery searchlight batteries to illuminate communist aircraft and to light up ground forces by reflecting the beams off low-level clouds.

The communist side used searchlights principally in an air-defense role along the Yalu River, but after February 1952, they employed them farther south in support of flak units. Communist forces ultimately employed some 500 searchlights. They were positioned in clusters around key sites and in defensive belts but were constantly moved for defensive purposes.

ROBERT J. BUNKER

See also

Artillery, Antiaircraft

References

Futrell, Robert F. *The United States Air Force in Korea, 1950–1953*. Rev. ed. Washington, DC: Office of the Chief of Air Force History, 1983.

Hermes, Walter G. *U.S. Army in the Korean War: Truce Tent and Fighting Front*. Washington, DC: Office of the Chief of Military History, 1966.

Sebald, William Joseph

Birth Date: November 5, 1901
Death Date: August 10, 1980

U.S. State Department political adviser to U.S. Far Eastern commanders Generals Douglas MacArthur and Matthew B. Ridgway, 1946–1952. Born in Baltimore on November 5, 1901, William Joseph Sebald graduated from the U.S. Naval Academy at Annapolis in 1922. He served eight years in the navy, spending 1925 to 1928 as a language officer in Japan and then resigning in 1930 to earn a law degree. In 1933, Sebald returned to Japan to practice Japanese commercial law, returning to Washington, DC, in 1939, where he continued his legal practice until 1941. After wartime service as chief of the U.S. Navy's Pacific division of combat intelligence, Sebald turned to diplomacy, becoming an auxiliary U.S. Foreign Service officer in 1945 and a regular officer two years later.

In 1946, Sebald, one of few U.S. officials familiar with Japan's language and society, returned to Tokyo to join the U.S. occupation forces as legal assistant to MacArthur's acting political adviser, who died the following year. Sebald then took over three responsibilities: acting political adviser to MacArthur, representing State Department interests; chief of the diplomatic section of Far East commander General MacArthur's headquarters; and chairman and American member of the Allied Council for Japan, the largely ineffective international advisory body to the occupation forces. In 1950, he was named political adviser for Japan with the rank of ambassador. Sebald succeeded in developing an excellent relationship with the often difficult MacArthur and, therefore, served as a reliable conduit of information to the State Department, which the autocratic general otherwise tended to leave in the dark regarding his policies.

During the Korean War, Sebald continued to perform this function, exercising little influence on major decisions but participating in key meetings, observing, and reporting back to his superiors in Washington. On November 14, 1950, two weeks before forces from the People's Republic of China (PRC) intervened en masse, MacArthur described to Sebald his strategy for what he believed would be the war's final stages. This included intimidating China by bombing bridges crossing the Yalu River into China and, should the Chinese still prove intransigent, bombing key points in Manchuria, moves that State Department officials and many U.S. allies feared might well bring not only China but also the Soviet Union into the war. Sebald was normally present at MacArthur's meetings with the numerous Washington officials and other functionaries who for one reason or another paid visits to his combat headquarters.

Sebald remained in his post when Lieutenant General Matthew B. Ridgway replaced MacArthur, and he was heavily involved in the preparatory work for the conclusion of the Japanese peace treaty. In July 1951, the Joint Chiefs of Staff (JCS) declined to allow his participation in the impending Kaesong truce talks, fearing that as a nonmilitary figure his presence would draw attention to the negotiations' political nature and implications and perhaps suggest some connection existed between them and the impending Japanese treaty.

Sebald remained in Japan until early 1952, shortly before the U.S. occupation formally ended, and the State Department then replaced him with a regular ambassador. Sebald served as U.S. ambassador to Burma between 1952 and 1954 and as ambassador to Australia from 1957 until 1961, when he retired. For three years (1954–1957), he was assistant secretary of state for Far Eastern affairs. In retirement he wrote his memoirs. Sebald died in Naples, Florida, on August 10, 1980.

PRISCILLA ROBERTS

See also

Japan; Japanese Peace Treaty; MacArthur, Douglas; Ridgway, Matthew Bunker

References

James, D. Clayton. *The Years of MacArthur*, Vol. 3, *Triumph and Disaster, 1945–1964.* Boston: Houghton Mifflin, 1985.

Sebald, William J., with Russell Brines. *With MacArthur in Japan: A Personal History of the Occupation.* London: Cresset, 1967.

2nd Logistical Command

The principal logistical base for United Nations (UN) forces throughout the Korean War was the southeastern port of Pusan. A small U.S. Army detachment led by Lieutenant Colonel Lewis A. Hunt arrived in Korea on June 30, 1950, to organize logistical support of U.S. troops, and on July 4, Brigadier General Crump Garvin and his staff arrived in Pusan from Japan and established the Pusan Base Command, which immediately took over port operations and other logistical support for the U.S. Eighth Army in Korea (EUSAK). On July 13, 1950, the Pusan Base Command was reorganized and renamed the Pusan Logistical Command. During the desperate defense of the Pusan Perimeter from July to September 1950, personnel of the Pusan Logistical Command performed their critical logistical duties and also assisted in the fortification of the perimeter and prepared to take up defensive positions on the line if needed.

On September 19, 1950, the Pusan Logistical Command was redesignated as the 2nd Logistical Command, and Brigadier General Paul F. Yount subsequently assumed command from Brigadier General Garvin. The principal mission of the 2nd Logistical Command was to receive, store, and distribute supplies for the EUSAK and to forward EUSAK supply requisitions to the Japan Logistical Command. Headquarters of EUSAK, however, retained direct control of all requisitions for ammunition, petroleum products, and perishable foodstuffs. As of November 23, 1950, the 2nd Logistical Command controlled the port, depot, and transportation units at Pusan; the 3rd Logistical Command then operated UN logistical facilities on Korea's west coast, the UN Reception Center at Taegu, and a 400-bed Swedish Red Cross field hospital located in Pusan. The 2nd Logistical Command was also responsible for management of UN camps for prisoners of war (POWs) from the Democratic People's Republic of Korea (DPRK, North Korea) and the People's Republic of China (PRC). In November 1950, there were over 130,000 North Korean and Chinese POWs in camps operated by the 2nd Logistical Command at Pusan, Inchon, and Pyongyang.

As a result of the evacuation of Inchon in December 1950 and Chinese forces driving south, the 2nd Logistical Command absorbed most of the units of the 3rd Logistical Command, and it eventually controlled some 260 attached and assigned units and was responsible for the administration of all UN logistical and administrative facilities in Korea south of 36°30' north latitude. In September 1951, the 2nd Logistical Command had five subordinate area commands: the Pusan Area Command (operated by the 3rd Logistical Command); the Taegu Military Command; the Inchon-Seoul Area Command; the Kunsan Area Command; and the Sokcho-ri Area Command, all of which, except the Pusan Area Command, were operated by provisional units. U.S. military personnel assigned to the 2nd Logistical Command generally were used to supervise Korean laborers, who eventually numbered over 100,000 people. This made the 2nd Logistical Command a much larger organization than originally envisioned.

On October 16, 1952, the 2nd Logistical Command was transferred to the newly formed Korean Communications Zone (KCOMZ) and subsequently operated the Korean Base Section under KCOMZ. The outstanding performance of the 2nd Logistical Command during the Korean War proved the soundness of the logistical command doctrine.

Charles R. Shrader

See also

Eighth Army, U.S.; Japan Logistical Command; Korean Communications Zone; Logistics in the Korean War; 3rd Logistical Command

References

Appleman, Roy E. *United States Army in Korea: South to the Naktong, North to the Yalu.* Washington, DC: Office of the Chief of Military History, 1961.

Huston, James A. *Guns and Butter, Powder and Rice: U.S. Army Logistics in the Korean War.* Selinsgrove, PA: Susquehanna University Press, 1989.

———. *The Sinews of War: Army Logistics, 1775–1953.* Washington, DC: Office of the Chief of Military History, 1966.

Logistical Problems and Their Solutions. APO 301. Headquarters, Eighth U.S. Army Korea, Historical Section and Eighth Army Historical Service Detachment (Provisional), 1952.

Mossman, Billy C. *United States Army in the Korean War: Ebb and Flow, November 1950–July 1951.* Washington, DC: U.S. Army Center of Military History, 1990.

Senoe

See Brainwashing

Seoul

Capital and largest city in the Republic of Korea (ROK, South Korea) and the site of several major battles during the Korean War. Founded by General Yi Song Gye in 1394, Seoul, which means "capital," was originally called Hansong or Hanyang. Situated

Signs welcome sailors from the U.S. aircraft carrier *Boxer* (CV-21) and its escorts to the South Korean capital of Seoul on April 7, 1950. (Naval Historical Center)

in northwestern South Korea, about 32 miles to the southeast of Panmunjom and the 38th Parallel, the city offered an ideal location. The site was militarily defensible, a natural redoubt astride the navigable Han River, which bisects the city into northern and southern halves and flows into the Yellow Sea. The strategic port of Inchon, at the mouth of the Han, lies about 31 miles to the west of downtown Seoul and serves the capital city.

The Choson dynasty ruled the area until 1910, when the Japanese annexed Korea and renamed the city Kyongsŏng (Keijo). With the defeat of Japan at the end of World War II and the founding of the Republic of Korea in 1948, Seoul once again became the city's official name.

During the Korean War, Seoul changed hands four times. Troops of the Korean People's Army (KPA, North Korean Army) captured the city on June 28, 1950, only three days after they invaded South Korea. After the successful Inchon Landing (Operation CHROMITE) of September 15, 1950, United Nations Command (UNC) forces recaptured Seoul on September 28. UNC forces held the capital until January 3, 1951, when it again fell, this time to the Chinese People's Volunteer Army (CPVA, Chinese Army). UNC forces retook the city on March 14, 1951.

Although much of the city was left in ruins by the savage fighting, Seoul was rebuilt quickly and has developed into a major industrial area and one of the world's largest cities. Today, Seoul has a population of at least 10.5 million people, and the entire metropolitan area boasts a population of 24.47 million, meaning that almost half of all South Koreans live in Seoul or in the immediate areas surrounding it.

MARY L. KELLEY

See also

Inchon Landing; Seoul, Fall of; Seoul, Recapture of

References

Blair, Clay. *The Forgotten War: America in Korea, 1950–1953.* New York: Times Books, 1987.

Cumings, Bruce. *Korea's Place in the Sun: A Modern History.* New York: Norton, 1997.

Rees, David. *Korea: The Limited War.* New York: St. Martin's, 1990.

Riley, John W., Jr., and Wilbur Schramm. *The Reds Take a City: The Communist Occupation of Seoul.* New Brunswick, NJ: Rutgers University Press, 1951.

Seoul, Fall of

Start Date: June 25, 1950
End Date: June 29, 1950

Controlling the Republic of Korea (ROK, South Korea) capital of Seoul was important to both sides in the Korean War. Indeed, Seoul changed hands four times during the conflict. The city's location, with direct access to the port of Inchon via the Han River and less than 50 miles from the border between the Democratic

ROKA Organization and Strength as of June 26, 1950

Designation	Strength
ROKA headquarters	3,000
Replacement Training Command	9,016
Chonju Training Command	8,699
Kwangju Training Command	6,244
Pusan Training Command	5,256
3rd Division (1st Cavalry, 22nd, 23rd Regiments)	8,829
ROKA nondivisional troops	11,881
I Corps (activated July 5, 1950)	3,014
Capital Division (1st, 17th, 18th Regiments)	6,644
8th Division (10th, 16th, 21st Regiments)	8,864
II Corps (activated about July 15, 1950)	976
1st Division (11th, 12th, 15th Regiments)	7,601
6th Division (2nd, 7th, 19th Regiments)	5,727
Total assigned	94,570
Wounded and nonbattle casualties	8,699
Total effectives	85,871
Total in divisions	37,670

People's Republic of Korea (DPRK, North Korea) and South Korea, its industry, and the fact it was the South Korean capital and governmental center all contributed to its importance. North Korea made the capture of Seoul a priority for its June 1950 offensive.

The North Korean invasion of South Korea early on June 25, 1950, saw the Korean People's Army (KPA, North Korean Army) descend on an unprepared and unsuspecting South Korea. The prompt capture of Seoul was a primary goal. To cut off forces of the Republic of Korea Army (ROKA, South Korean Army) north of the Han River and secure the South Korean capital, the KPA deployed its 1st and 6th divisions along the Kaesong-Munsan-Seoul corridor, the 4th Division along the Tongduchon-Uijongbu-Seoul corridor, and the 3rd Division along the Pochon-Uijongbu-Seoul corridor. The ROKA 1st and 7th divisions and elements of the Capital Division were deployed north of Seoul and bore the brunt of the KPA shock troops at the beginning of the war. The ROKA 2nd, 3rd, and 5th divisions, deployed in the rear area as a reserve, then moved north of the Han River and on June 27 engaged KPA troops.

Seoul was under siege by the second day of the invasion, June 26. In the early hours of that day, Americans began to evacuate the city by ship along the Han River and out of the port at Inchon. The evacuation also occurred by air. It continued through the night and into the following day, until all 2,000 American dependents and other foreigners had been removed.

On June 27, four U.S. Air Force North American F-82 Twin Mustang propeller-driven night fighters and several Lockheed F-80 Shooting Star jet fighters of the Fifth Air Force covering the evacuation shot down three Korean People's Air Force (KPAF, North Korean Air Force) Yak-9 attack planes, which had attacked them. Four other Yak-9s were shot down later that same day.

As KPA forces advanced on Seoul, panic set in among the populace. Civilians as well as soldiers and government officials filled

U.S. tanks move through a roadblock and past men of the U.S. 1st Marine Division during the recapture of the South Korean capital of Seoul on September 25, 1950. (National Archives)

the streets, transporting such valuables as they could. Most fled the city south by one of the four bridges across the Han River, and from there many continued as far south as Pusan.

During the exodus from the city, ROKA chief of staff General Chae Pyong Dok made a costly mistake. There were four bridges spanning the Han River: three for rail traffic and the fourth a three-lane highway crossing. The original plan in the event of an invasion by North Korea was to destroy these bridges only when KPA tanks had entered the city, an event unlikely to occur until June 28. Despite these plans, during the night of the 27th, as South Korean high officials evacuated Seoul, Chae ordered his deputy, General Kim Paek Il, to destroy the bridges at 1:30 a.m. All four bridges were duly blown, despite the fact that some 4,000 people were on one bridge when it was destroyed, killing in the blast or drowning in the Han River some 500–800 people.

The bridges were destroyed several hours before it was necessary, and this action cut off thousands of ROKA solders from their evacuation routes. It also forced them to abandon their heavy

equipment and, in many cases, even their weapons to get across the river. Blame was assigned not to Chae but to the ROKA's chief engineer, who was executed shortly thereafter. Despite ROKA opposition, the KPA, spearheaded by tanks, continued its relentless drive on Seoul. During the night of June 27, its 3rd Division entered the city.

U.S. Army major general John Church, who headed a survey team ordered to Korea by U.S. Far East commander General Douglas MacArthur, arrived in Seoul on the night of June 27. Church, amazed at the chaos, took charge, corralling stragglers in an attempt to form a defensive line south of the Han. The capital itself fell the next day, June 28.

In a radio message to MacArthur, Church advised that only U.S. troops could contain the invasion. After a personal trip to Korea the next day, MacArthur concurred in this assessment. Meanwhile, the North Koreans in Seoul set about rounding up government officials, police officers, and remaining solders for execution.

The 3rd and 4th KPA divisions suffered 1,500 casualties in the taking of Seoul; the ROKA was shattered. By June 28, the South Korean government had fled to Taejon and the ROKA command could account for only 22,000 men of the 98,000 men on its rolls only three days earlier.

MICHAEL D. MULÉ

See also

Church Survey Mission to Korea; Korea, Democratic People's Republic of, Invasion of the Republic of Korea; Korea, Republic of, Occupation of by Democratic People's Republic of Korea; MacArthur, Douglas; Seoul; Truman, Harry S.

References

Blair, Clay. *The Forgotten War: America in Korea, 1950–1953.* New York: Times Books, 1987.

Leckie, Robert. *Conflict: The History of the Korean War, 1950–1953.* New York: Putnam, 1962.

Marshall, S. L. A. *Military History of the Korean War.* New York: F. Watts, 1963.

Millett, Allan R. *Their War in Korea: American, Asian, and European Combatants and Civilians, 1945–1953.* Princeton, NJ: Princeton University Press, 2002.

Seoul, Recapture of
Start Date: September 18, 1950
End Date: September 28, 1950

After their landing at Inchon on September 15, 1950, X Corps of the United Nations Command (UNC) forces pressed eastward with the goal of liberating the capital of the Republic of Korea (ROK, South Korea), Seoul. Hard fighting took place before the city was recaptured.

Capturing Seoul was important for several reasons. First, the city was a major industrial center and communications hub with north-south rail lines and roads running through it. Securing

Thousands of refugees stream south of Seoul, the South Korean capital, evacuating ahead of advancing communist forces, January 5, 1951. (National Archives)

INCHON–SEOUL CAMPAIGN, SEPTEMBER 1950

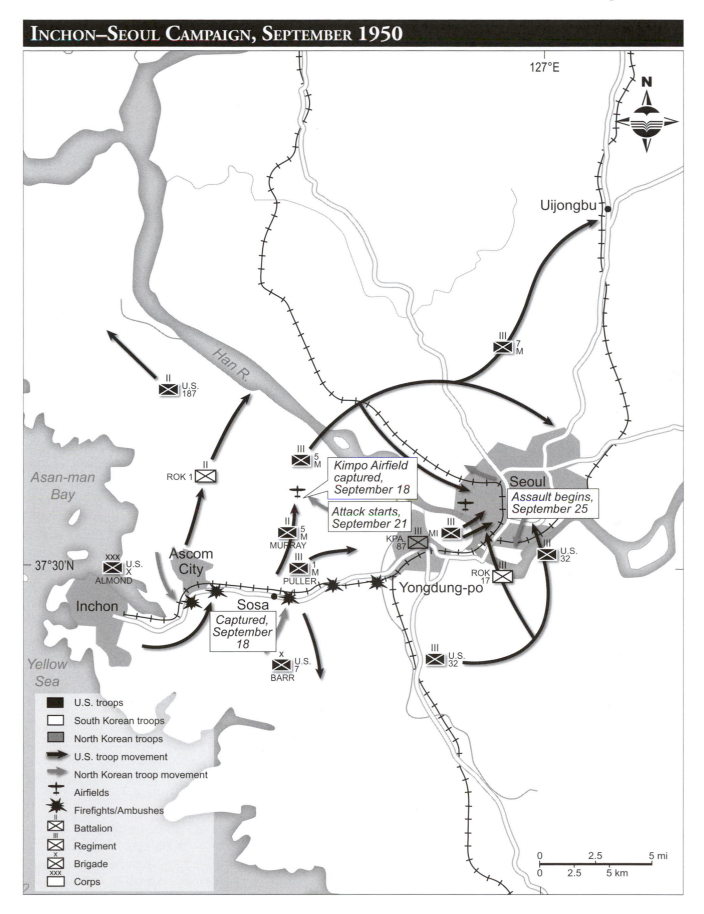

127°E

N

Uijongbu

Han R.

III 7 M

II U.S. 187

III 5 M

ROK 1 II

Kimpo Airfield captured, September 18

Attack starts, September 21

Seoul
Assault begins, September 25

Asan-man Bay

II 5 M MURRAY

III 1 M PULLER

III KPA 87

III MI

III U.S. 32

ROK 17 III

III U.S. 32

Ascom City

— 37°30'N

XXX U.S. X ALMOND

Inchon

Sosa
Captured, September 18

Yongdung-po

x U.S. 7 BARR

III U.S. 32

Yellow Sea

Legend:
- ■ U.S. troops
- □ South Korean troops
- ▨ North Korean troops
- ➤ U.S. troop movement
- ➤ North Korean troop movement
- ✈ Airfields
- ✸ Firefights/Ambushes
- ⊠ II Battalion
- ⊠ III Regiment
- ⊠ x Brigade
- ⊠ xxx Corps

0   2.5   5 mi
0   2.5   5 km

Seoul would cut off most forces of the Korean People's Army (KPA, North Korean Army) to the south along the Pusan Perimeter. Retaking the capital would also be a tremendous morale boost for the UNC, especially the Republic of Korea Army (ROKA, South Korean Army).

U.S. forces began their move toward Seoul on September 17, 1950. UNC commander General Douglas MacArthur was determined that the capital be retaken by September 25, three months to the day after the outbreak of the war. The first objective was to capture Kimpo Airfield. This would enable U.S. aircraft to resupply and provide close ground support to the attackers.

Early on September 17, the 5th Marines ambushed a column of 6 KPA T-34 tanks and 200 infantry. By the night of September 17, much of Kimpo Airfield had been taken; it was completely in Marine Corps hands the next day. That same day, the 7th Infantry Division began landing at Inchon; and on September 21, the remaining Marine regiment, the 7th, disembarked.

By the end of September 19, the 5th Marines had cleared the entire south bank of the Han River on their front; they crossed the river a day later but were then slowed by determined KPA resistance. The 1st Regiment also ran into stiff resistance from a regiment of the KPA 18th Division on September 22 before it too reached the Han.

X Corps commander Major General Edward M. Almond had made it clear to 1st Marine Division commander Major General Oliver P. Smith that Seoul must fall by September 25. Fighting was stiff, as the KPA defenders set up barricades and fought street by street and house by house. U.S. air strikes and artillery took their toll on the defenders, leveling sections of the city. The U.S. flag, soon to be replaced by that of the United Nations (UN), was not raised at the capitol building by the 5th Marines until the afternoon of September 27, although to meet MacArthur's deadline, Almond announced just before midnight on September 25 that the city had fallen. On September 29, MacArthur presided over an emotional ceremony in the capitol marking the liberation of Seoul and the restoration of the Syngman Rhee government.

On January 3, 1951, in the course of the offensive of the Third Chinese People's Volunteer Army (CPVA, Chinese Army), the South Korean government again abandoned Seoul. The Eighth Army retook the South Korean capital for a fourth and final time in the war on March 14, 1951.

Michael D. Mulé

See also

Almond, Edward Mallory; Chinese Offensive, Third; Inchon Landing; Kimpo Airfield; MacArthur, Douglas; Seoul; Seoul, Fall of; Smith, Oliver Prince; X Corps

References

Blair, Clay. *The Forgotten War: America in Korea, 1950–1953.* New York: Times Books, 1987.

Hastings, Max. *The Korean War.* New York: Simon and Schuster, 1987.

Higgins, Marguerite. *War in Korea: Report of a Woman Combat Correspondent.* Garden City, NY: Doubleday, 1951.

Marshall, S. L. A. *Military History of the Korean War.* New York: F. Watts, 1963.

Millett, Allan R. *Their War in Korea: American, Asian, and European Combatants and Civilians, 1945–1953.* Princeton, NJ: Princeton University Press, 2002.

Seoul City Sue
Birth Date: 1898
Death Date: Unknown

American-born communist radio announcer for Radio Seoul and anti-American propagandist during the Korean War. Born in Arkansas in 1898, Anna Wallace, also known as Seoul City Sue, was divorced by the age of 22 and living in Johnston County, Oklahoma, with her family. Few details of her life are known with any certainty. She later moved to Asia, where she worked as a Methodist missionary and school teacher, eventually settling in Shanghai, China, where she taught at the Shanghai American School (SAS) from 1930 to 1938. While employed at SAS she met and married a Korean journalist and took his name, Suhr. In 1943, Anna Wallace Suhr entered the Chapei Civilian Assembly Center, an internment camp operated by the Japanese just outside of Shanghai. She did continue to teach while at the center.

By 1946, Suhr was in Korea tutoring children at the U.S. Diplomatic Mission School in Seoul, where she remained until the invasion by the Democratic People's Republic of Korea (DPRK, North Korea) of the Republic of Korea (ROK, South Korea) in June 1950. On June 28, 1950, North Korean forces occupied Seoul and, by July, Suhr and her husband had pledged their loyalty to North Korea.

Most sources agree that Anna Wallace Suhr first broadcast around August 10, 1950, which is when members of the 588th U.S. Military Police Company reported first hearing her, although at least one source claims that she broadcast as early as July 18, 1950. GIs hearing her broadcasts called her by various names, including Rice Ball Maggie, Rice Bowl Maggie, and Rice Ball Kate. Seoul City Sue, however, is the nickname that stuck. The name is perhaps drawn from "Sioux City Sue," a popular 1946 song by Zeke Manners.

Much like Japan's Tokyo Rose, Nazi Germany's Axis Sally, and Vietnam's Hanoi Hannah, Seoul City Sue played the role of female propagandist radio broadcaster. Seoul City Sue's programs on Radio Seoul were North Korean propaganda designed to demoralize American troops. She routinely read the names of captured or dead American soldiers from their dog tags while tranquil music played in the background. She also welcomed ships by name as a way of illustrating a North Korean intelligence advantage in the war.

On August 13, 1950, Seoul City Sue was off the air, the result of a U.S. air strike on communications facilities in Seoul. Although the station was back in operation within two weeks, Seoul City Sue was no longer broadcasting. Seoul City Sue was first identified as Anna Wallace Suhr by the Methodist Missionary Organization on

August 27, 1950. Representatives of that organization claimed that her lack of enthusiasm during the broadcasts indicated she was being forced to participate.

Whether Anna Wallace Suhr was forced to broadcast or not remains a mystery, as her life after the August 1950 broadcasts is quite sketchy. Some American prisoners of war (POWs) at Camp 12, near Pyongyang, claim to have undergone efforts at indoctrination by Anna and her husband in February 1951. A U.S. Army defector claims to have seen her on two occasions in 1965 in North Korea. Others have reported that she was executed as a spy for South Korea. No records have been found to indicate what happened to Anna Wallace Suhr, and her fate therefore remains unknown.

TAMMY PRATER

See also
Psychological Warfare

References
Edwards, Paul M. *To Acknowledge a War: The Korean War in American Memory.* Westport, CT: Greenwood, 2000.
Lech, Raymond B. *Broken Soldiers.* Champaign: University of Illinois Press, 2000.

Service, John Stewart
Birth Date: August 8, 1909
Death Date: February 3, 1999

U.S. Foreign Service officer and one of the China Hands. In the view of many, the China Hands were the best-trained and most articulate diplomats in the history of the U.S. Foreign Service. Their reward for accurately reporting events in China during the Second World War and the years immediately afterward was to

John Stewart Service, a U.S. Foreign Service officer and expert on China who was wrongly fired because he had accurately reported that the Nationalist government lacked popular support and that, without U.S. pressure on Nationalist leader Jiang Jieshi for reform, the Communists would likely take power in China. (AP/Wide World Photos)

be systematically hounded from their posts and—for a number of them, including Service—subjected to public disgrace.

Born in China of missionary parents on August 8, 1909, John Stewart Service grew up in Sichuan Province, attended high school in Shanghai, and then studied art history at Oberlin College in Ohio. He returned to China in 1922 and, after a brief time in banking, joined the Foreign Service. When the Japanese entered Beijing (Peking), he helped escort American refugees to safety. Assigned to the new Nationalist capital at Chongqing (Chungking) as a political officer in 1941, his task was to gather information on all Chinese political parties and factions, including the communists. Service knew China extraordinarily well and had almost an uncanny instinct for gauging events there.

In the communist witch-hunt hysteria of the early Cold War period, Republican senator Joseph R. McCarthy attacked Service and other China Hands, including John Carter Vincent, John Paton Davies, and Oliver Edmund Clubb. Service was accused of being soft on communism because he had reported the truth of corruption in the government of Guomindang (GMD, Nationalist) leader Jiang Jieshi (Chiang Kai-shek). As the war progressed, Service predicted a civil war that would lead to a communist victory if things were unchanged. On March 20, 1944, Service informed his superiors: "China is a mess . . . for the sorry situation as a whole Chiang, and only Chiang, is responsible . . . Chiang will cooperate if the U.S., upon which he is dependent, makes up its mind exactly what it wants from him and then gets hard-boiled about it. . . . This may mean taking an active part in Chinese affairs. But unless we do it, China will not be of much use as an ally. And, in doing it, we may save China."

The China Hands did not—contrary to the charges of their critics—welcome communism. They simply urged that U.S. pressure be brought to bear on Jiang and—failing that—they advocated a policy of U.S. neutrality in what was an inevitable civil war. Had their advice been followed, the United States would probably have been able to maintain diplomatic relations with China and perhaps the Korean War might have been prevented. Certainly the charge that Service and other Foreign Service officials lost China to communism was patently ridiculous.

In February 1950, Senator McCarthy specifically charged Service with being "a known associate and collaborator with Communists." Although Service was subsequently cleared by a U.S. Senate committee, a Loyalty Review Board named by President Harry S. Truman said there was "reasonable doubt as to his loyalty." Secretary of State Dean G. Acheson dismissed him the same day. Service fought this, and in 1956 the Supreme Court ruled 8–0 that the board had no right to review the State Department's findings and that Acheson had no right to dismiss him. Service then rejoined the State Department, retiring from an obscure post in the Liverpool, England, consulate in 1962.

Service then earned a master's degree at the University of California, Berkeley, and became library curator of its Center for Chinese Studies. With the 1970s thaw in relations between the United States and the People's Republic of China (PRC), Service visited China, even meeting with Prime Minister Zhou Enlai in 1971. He also published several books on China. Service died in Oakland, California, on February 3, 1999.

SPENCER C. TUCKER

See also

Acheson, Dean Gooderham; China Hands; Clubb, Oliver Edmund; Davies, John Paton; Jiang Jieshi; McCarthy, Joseph Raymond; McCarthyism; Truman, Harry S.; Zhou Enlai

References

Kahn, E. J., Jr. *The China Hands: America's Foreign Service Officers and What Befell Them.* New York: Viking, 1975.
Service, John S. *Lost Chance in China: The World War II Dispatches of John S. Service.* Edited by Joseph W. Esherick. New York: Random House, 1974.

Shaw, William Hamilton
Birth Date: June 5, 1922
Death Date: September 22, 1950

U.S. Navy officer and Korean missionary. Born on June 5, 1922, in Pyongyang, Korea, William "Bill" Hamilton Shaw was the son of William Earl Shaw and Adeline Hamilton Shaw, both of whom were Methodist missionaries to Korea. Growing up in Pyongyang, Shaw graduated from Pyongyang Foreign High School in 1939 before he left for college at Ohio Wesleyan University in Delaware, Ohio, from which he graduated in 1943.

Shaw married Juanita Robinson after his graduation and completed his naval officer training in late 1943. Serving as an executive officer on *PT-518* in the European theater in the last two years of World War II, Shaw participated in the D-Day invasion of France on June 6, 1944. Eighteen days later, Shaw conducted General Dwight D. Eisenhower, supreme commander of Allied forces, and his staff to a landing craft as they set out to tour Normandy Beach.

In 1948, the Shaws returned to Korea with the U.S. Navy to assist in establishing the Korean Naval Academy at Chinhae. In October 1949, the Shaw family returned to the United States and Shaw entered a doctoral program in East Asian and Korean Studies at Harvard University with the intention of returning to Korea as a missionary professor. His studies were cut short by the outbreak of the Korean War in June 1950. Soon thereafter, Shaw rejoined the navy voluntarily.

Because of his fluency in Korean and his vast knowledge of Korean geography, Lieutenant Shaw was ordered to Tokyo and assigned to the intelligence section under Vice Admiral C. Turner Joy. Shaw then participated in the planning of the September 1950 Inchon Landing. Having led training cruises along the west coast of Korea during his service at the Korean Naval Academy, Shaw was assigned to guide the landing craft and to assist the entrance of ships to the harbor. When Inchon was secured, Shaw received permission to join the drive on Seoul with the 5th U.S. Army Regiment of the 1st U.S. Marine Division.

On September 22, 1950, the 5th Regiment split into two groups after crossing the Han River. Shaw went with the group heading toward Hongje-dong. About five miles outside of Seoul, Shaw's company was ambushed on three sides. He was killed while trying to assist a group of Korean civilians who were caught up in the fighting. He was buried in Yanghwajin (Foreigner Cemetery) in Seoul.

A monument commemorating Shaw's affection for the Korean people was subsequently erected at Nokpon-ni, the exact site of his death in action. The monument was later relocated to Ungahm Children's Park. In 2008, 58 years after his death, the South Korean government unveiled a plan to build a new, grander memorial park, at a cost of 42 billion won, to honor Shaw. He was also praised by his fellow naval officers as "an example of patriotism and moral courage."

KAI YIN ALLISON HAGA

See also

Inchon Landing; Joy, Charles Turner; Relief Efforts, Missionary

References

Clark, Donald N. *Living Dangerously in Korea: The Western Experience, 1900–1950.* Norwalk, CT: East Bridge, 2003.

Haga, Kai Yin Allison. "An Overlooked Dimension of the Korean War: The Role of Christianity and American Missionaries in the Rise of Korean Nationalism, Anti-Colonialism, and Eventual Civil War, 1884–1953." Unpublished PhD dissertation, College of William and Mary, 2007.

Shepherd, Lemuel Cornick, Jr.
Birth Date: February 10, 1896
Death Date: August 6, 1990

U.S. Marine Corps general. Born in Norfolk, Virginia, on February 10, 1896, Lemuel Cornick Shepherd Jr. graduated from the Virginia Military Institute in 1917 and then accepted a commission in the U.S. Marine Corps. Ordered to France in June 1917 as a second lieutenant, Shepherd was promoted to first lieutenant in August of the same year. He fought with the 5th Marine Regiment (part of the 2nd U.S. Army Division) in the Battle of Belleau Wood and in the Aisne-Marne, Saint-Mihiel, and Meuse Argonne campaigns, during which he was wounded three times.

In 1919, Shepherd was promoted to captain and became an aide to Marine Corps commandant General John Archer Lejeune. Following this posting he held a variety of assignments, including service on the battleships *Nevada* and *Idaho,* Norfolk Marine Corps Base, and the 4th Marines in China. After graduating from the Field Officers Course at Quantico, Virginia, in 1930, he was deployed to Haiti, where he served for four years. Promoted to

major in 1932 and to lieutenant colonel in 1935, he served on the Marine Corps Institute Staff between 1934 and 1936. After graduating from the Naval War College in 1937, Shepherd commanded a battalion of the 5th Marines. In 1940 he was promoted to colonel after completing a tour on the staff of the Marine Corps Schools.

In March 1942, Shepherd assumed command of the 9th Marine Regiment. After service under General Alexander Vandegrift in the 1st Marine Division on Guadalcanal, Shepherd was promoted to brigadier general in July 1943. Later he commanded units that fought on Cape Gloucester (December 1943) and on Guam (July–August 1944). Promoted to major general, Shepherd commanded the 6th Marine Division in the Okinawa campaign (April–June 1945).

In 1946, Shepherd became assistant commandant of the Marine Corps. From 1948 to 1950, he was commandant of the Marine Corps Schools. In June 1950, he was promoted to lieutenant general and took command of Fleet Marine Forces in the Pacific, headquartered in Honolulu.

During the Korean War, Shepherd served on General Douglas MacArthur's staff. In the course of a meeting with MacArthur on July 10, 1950, when MacArthur recalled his success with the 1st Marine Division in the Pacific during World War II, Shepherd suggested that he ask the Joint Chiefs of Staff (JCS) for that division, a request that was granted. Shepherd said the division could be in Korea in six weeks and ready for service by September 15, 1950.

Shepherd participated in planning for the Inchon Landing. He thought the operation an excellent idea but opposed Inchon as the site, particularly as another location to the south was equally well placed as a base from which to take Seoul. At MacArthur's request, Shepherd accompanied him aboard the flagship *Mount McKinley* to act as his personal adviser on amphibious matters. Shepherd was one of the first Americans to fly into Kimpo Airfield after its recapture. In January 1952, he was promoted to full general (four-star) rank and became commandant of the Marine Corps. He retired four years later, in January 1956. Recalled later that year to serve as chairman of the Inter-American Defense Board, he again retired in September 1956. Shepherd died in La Jolla, California, on August 6, 1990.

JASON B. BERG

See also

Inchon Landing; MacArthur, Douglas

References

Dupuy, Trevor N., Curt Johnson, and David L. Bongard. *The Harper Encyclopedia of Military Biography.* New York: HarperCollins, 1992.

Heinl, Robert Debs. *Soldiers of the Sea: The United States Marine Corps, 1775–1962.* Baltimore, MD: Nautical and Aviation Publishing Company of America, 1991.

Langley, Michael. *Inchon Landing: MacArthur's Last Triumph.* New York: Times Books, 1979.

Millett, Allan R. *Semper Fidelis: The History of the United States Marine Corps.* New York: Free Press, 1991.

Sherman, Forrest Percival
Birth Date: October 30, 1896
Death Date: July 22, 1951

U.S. Navy admiral and chief of naval operations between 1949 and 1951. Born on October 30, 1896, at Merrimack, New Hampshire, Forrest Percival Sherman attended the Massachusetts Institute of Technology (MIT) during 1913–1914 and then the U.S. Naval Academy at Annapolis, from which he graduated in 1917 because of the wartime accelerations. Sherman served on the gunboat *Nashville* in European waters during World War I. In 1922, he completed flight training in Pensacola, Florida. After subsequent assignments in naval aviation, he graduated from the Naval War College in 1927. He then served on the aircraft carriers *Lexington* and *Saratoga.*

Shepherd was promoted to lieutenant commander in 1930 and to commander in 1937. In the 1930s, he was an instructor at the Naval Academy, commanded a fighter squadron, had charge of the Aviation Ordnance Section of the Bureau of Ordnance, served in the aircraft carrier *Ranger,* and served on naval staffs. During 1941–1942, Captain Sherman served in the War Plans Division of the Office of the Chief of Naval Operations and was a member of the Canada–United States Permanent Joint Board on Defense. In the War Plans Division, Sherman worked closely with then U.S. Army major Albert C. Wedemeyer to produce the plan for the mobilization of the army in World War II.

Captain Sherman then took command of the carrier *Wasp.* After its loss in September 1942, he became chief of staff to Vice Admiral John W. Towers, commander of the Pacific Fleet Air Forces. He was promoted to rear admiral in April 1943. In November 1943, Sherman was appointed deputy chief of staff to commander of the Pacific Fleet Admiral Chester Nimitz, in which capacity he played a significant role in planning Pacific Theater naval operations.

After World War II, in October 1945, Sherman took command of Carrier Division I. Promoted to vice admiral, he became deputy chief of naval operations that December. In January 1948, he became chief of U.S. naval forces in the Mediterranean. In November 1949, Sherman became chief of naval operations with the rank of admiral. As chief of naval operations, Sherman forcefully defended the navy in a time of shrinking defense budgets. He secured funding for the navy's first nuclear submarine and the modernization of ships, and he was a strong advocate of naval aviation.

Once the Korean War began in June 1950, Sherman participated in the series of high-level meetings involving President Harry S. Truman, the service secretaries, presidential advisers, and congressional leaders. He also attended the first and second Blair House meetings. Truman endorsed his recommendation for a naval blockade of the Democratic People's Republic of Korea (DPRK, North Korea). Sherman supported MacArthur's call for the use of ground forces, and he oversaw the mobilization of U.S. Navy assets, including expansion of the navy. Later he won congressional approval for construction of a supercarrier.

U.S. admiral Forrest P. Sherman, shown here in November 1949, was chief of naval operations during 1949–1953. (Naval Historical Center)

Sherman and the other service chiefs expressed reservations about Operation CHROMITE, General MacArthur's proposed landing behind lines of the Korean People's Army (KPA, North Korean Army) at Inchon. Sherman opposed depriving the Atlantic Fleet Marine Force of the 1st Marine Division, since it might be needed elsewhere, and he disagreed with the site, suggesting a landing farther south at Kunsan. Yet Sherman did assure Truman that MacArthur would wisely employ units given him.

The Joint Chiefs of Staff (JCS) dispatched Sherman and General J. Lawton Collins to East Asia for more information before granting approval for Operation CHROMITE. MacArthur received them in Tokyo on August 21. The next day, the two visited Korea for talks with the Eighth Army commander Lieutenant General Walton H. Walker before flying back to Japan for MacArthur's Inchon briefing on August 23. At that time, Sherman and Collins again pressed for the Kunsan site and, subsequent to conversations with U.S. Navy and Marine officers, wanted MacArthur to consider Posung-myon, nearly 50 miles below Inchon, as a second alternative. But even before the briefing, Sherman had decided to back MacArthur's proposal. When the dangers of moving through Flying Fish Channel, the passageway heading into Inchon, which could be protected by mines and coastal batteries, were raised, Sherman broke in saying, "I wouldn't hesitate to take a ship up there." MacArthur cried out, "Spoken like a Farragut!" All expected the general's forces to advance beyond the 38th Parallel and occupy North Korea once KPA resistance was eliminated. After his last meeting with MacArthur, Sherman declared, "I wish I could share that man's confidence." On August 28, the JCS gave their qualified endorsement to Operation CHROMITE, which was carried out on September 15 with stunning success.

As United Nations Command (UNC) troops drove northward, Sherman met Defense and State Department officials on November 21 to consider changing MacArthur's mission (effecting the complete defeat of North Korea) out of concern for intervention by the People's Republic of China (PRC). Although no alteration of MacArthur's orders ensued, Sherman thought that the general was too scornful of JCS anxiety about offending China's interests.

Later, Sherman urged retaliation if Chinese air forces attacked from Manchuria. He disapproved of a cease-fire. Apparently ready to wage war to defeat communist China, Sherman emerged as a cautious supporter of MacArthur's proposals to pressure China through a naval blockade, Taiwanese military operations, guerrilla activities, and naval as well as air strikes if Chinese assaults against UNC forces carried beyond Korea.

Sherman and the other service chiefs conferred on April 5, 1951, after being informed of President Truman's displeasure at MacArthur's public defiance of administration policy. After considering the matter, they recommended that MacArthur be relieved from command. Sherman believed that dismissal was justified, since MacArthur had violated a presidential prohibition on public statements, opposed the idea of limited war, and endangered civilian control of the military. Later Sherman defended the decision at the MacArthur congressional hearings.

Sherman believed in the primacy of Europe in U.S. defense planning. In July 1951, he left for Europe on an inspection trip and negotiations regarding U.S. bases in Spain. Sherman died of a heart attack on July 22, 1951, while attending a conference on European defense in Naples, Italy.

RODNEY J. ROSS

See also
Blair House Meetings; Collins, Joseph Lawton; Collins-Sherman Visit to Tokyo; Inchon Landing; Joint Chiefs of Staff; MacArthur, Douglas; MacArthur Hearings; Walker, Walton Harris

References
Alexander, Bevin. *Korea: The First War We Lost.* New York: Hippocrene Books, 1986.

Garraty, John S., ed. *Dictionary of American Biography, Supplement Five, 1951–1955.* New York: Scribner, 1977.

Goulden, Joseph C. *Korea: The Untold Story of the War.* New York: Times Books, 1982.

James, D. Clayton. *The Years of MacArthur,* Vol. 3, *Triumph and Disaster, 1945–1964.* Boston: Houghton Mifflin, 1985.

Short, Joseph H., Jr.
Birth Date: February 11, 1904
Death Date: September 18, 1952

Journalist and press secretary to President Harry S. Truman for much of the Korean War, from December 1950 until his death in September 1952. Born in Vicksburg, Mississippi, on February 11, 1904, Joseph H. Short Jr. initially contemplated a military career. He earned a Bachelor of Arts degree from the Virginia Military Institute in 1925. Experience working on the staff of the cadet newspaper led him to switch to journalism, and in the later 1920s, he held various positions on the *Jackson* (Mississippi) *Daily News,* the *Vicksburg Post and Herald,* and the *New Orleans Times-Picayune.*

Short joined the Richmond bureau of the Associated Press (AP) in 1929. Two years later he transferred to the AP's Washington, DC, office, where he remained until 1941. A respected newsman, during the Second World War Short moved first to the *Chicago Sun* and then in 1943 to the Washington staff of the *Baltimore Sun,* where he remained until 1950. In the course of covering Harry S. Truman's vice presidential campaign of 1944, several presidential overseas and domestic trips in 1947, and the long and demanding presidential "whistle-stop" campaign of 1948, Short developed a warm relationship with the president.

When Truman's first press secretary, Charles Ross, died suddenly in December 1950, the president named Short to succeed him, an appointment that gave rise to some comment because it was the first time a professional reporter had held the position. Newspapermen widely acclaimed the selection of a hardworking and well-liked colleague and former National Press Club chairman, who prided himself on returning every telephone call made to him.

Short attempted to broaden the channels of communication between the White House and reporters and to coordinate the various cabinet departments' information activities and those of the presidency. Short advised Truman on the public relations aspects of the Korean War, attempting to provide diplomatic and tactful public explanations of some of the more controversial issues to which it gave rise, preeminent among which was his announcement of the recall in April 1951 of General Douglas MacArthur.

One of Short's early tasks was to issue a formal presidential statement denouncing the 1950 railroad strike as irresponsible and unpatriotic during a national emergency; in April 1952, he likewise depicted the president's ultimately unsuccessful seizure of the nation's steel plants as an essential wartime measure. Short also functioned as a speechwriter and general adviser to the president on both domestic and international issues, although, as might be expected, his major impact was on the presentation of policy rather than its making. Short's unexpected death from a heart attack on September 18, 1952, was widely blamed on the grueling pressures to which his job had subjected him.

PRISCILLA ROBERTS

See also
Steel Plants, Truman's Seizure of; Truman, Harry S.; Truman's Recall of MacArthur

References
Evensen, Bruce J. "Short, Joseph Hudson, Jr." In *American National Biography,* Vol. 19, edited by John A. Garraty and Mark C. Carnes, 877–878. New York: Oxford University Press, 1999.

Hamby, Alonzo L. *Man of the People: A Life of Harry S. Truman.* New York: Oxford University Press, 1995.

McCullough, David. *Truman.* New York: Simon and Schuster, 1992.

Nelson, W. Dale. *Who Speaks for the President? The White House Press Secretary from Cleveland to Clinton.* Syracuse, NY: Syracuse University Press, 1998.

"Short, Joseph (Hudson Jr.)." In *Current Biography, 1951,* edited by Anna Rothe and Evelyn Lohr, 582–583. New York: H. W. Wilson, 1952.

Stein, Meyer L. *When Presidents Meet the Press.* New York: Messner, 1969.

Swain, Martha H. "Joseph Hudson Short, Jr." In *Dictionary of American Biography, Supplement Five, 1951–1955,* edited by John A. Garraty, 626. New York: Scribner, 1977.

SHOWDOWN, **Operation**
Start Date: October 13, 1952
End Date: November 8, 1952

Limited offensive operation by United Nations Command (UNC) forces to take hills in the Iron Triangle. The communists launched their largest offensive of 1952 beginning on October 6. With substantial artillery fire and massive infantry attacks, the communist forces drove back the Eighth Army west of the Iron Triangle to split I and IX Corps. Hoping to influence U.S. public opinion in the few weeks before the U.S. presidential election, the Chinese People's Volunteer Army (CPVA, Chinese Army) pressed the attack for 10 days until resistance from the Republic of Korea Army (ROKA, South Korean Army) 9th Division artillery and close air support forced them to withdraw.

To counter the communist offensive and strengthen the battered IX Corps position on the extreme southeast apex of the Iron Triangle near Kimhwa, Eighth Army commander General James A. Van Fleet planned an immediate limited offensive to seize communist positions in the Iron Triangle complex. This offensive, Operation SHOWDOWN, was intended to convince the communists that failure to reach an agreement would prove costly to them militarily.

The attack was launched on October 13 by four battalions: two from the U.S. 7th Infantry Division and two from the ROKA 2nd Infantry Division, with one battalion from each executing a diversionary attack. The four other battalions assaulted the northeast

Men of the 17th Regiment, U.S. 7th Infantry Division, take a break along a muddy road during Operation SHOWDOWN (October 13–November 8, 1952). (National Archives)

corner of the hill at Kimhwa, where Chinese observation teams overlooked a UNC supply route through the valley.

In spite of heavy artillery and air support, the operation did not go according to the UNC plan. The Chinese put up fierce resistance, stalling the UNC attacks. Both sides then brought up more manpower. The UNC did not accurately assess Chinese resistance in its prebattle estimations; it had planned on an assault of no more than 5 days' duration with an estimated total cost of only 200 casualties to seize the entire ridge line. What was expected to be a speedy operation dragged on for 3 weeks and was the heaviest fighting since late 1951. The Chinese infantry were in fact too well dug in to be dislodged by the piecemeal UNC attacks.

By November 8, 1952, the UNC broke off its assaults. The Chinese still held most of the hills in the Triangle, with the exception of one corner of Triangle Hill, half of Sniper's Ridge, and most of Jane Russell Hill. The minor gains in territory achieved were insufficient compensation for the enormous loss of life. What was originally planned to be a limited offensive operation had resulted in a bloody stalemate in which U.S. and ROKA forces sustained an appalling 6,229 casualties in 25 days of heavy fighting, 31 times the original UNC estimate.

The Chinese forces lost twice as many men—16,000 to 19,000—but they were willing to trade men for real estate. This "limited battle in a limited war" had its effects politically in the United States. President Harry S. Truman's public approval rating plummeted below 25 percent at the conclusion of this operation. UNC commander Lieutenant General Mark Clark characterized the offensive as "unsuccessful," and it caused him to resume emphasis on air pressure tactics to break the armistice deadlock.

BRADFORD A. WINEMAN

See also

Clark, Mark Wayne; Iron Triangle; Truman, Harry S.; Van Fleet, James Alward

References

Blair, Clay. *The Forgotten War: America in Korea, 1950–1953*. New York: Times Books, 1987.

Fehrenbach, T. R. *This Kind of War: A Study in Unpreparedness*. New York: Macmillan, 1962.

Hastings, Max. *The Korean War*. New York: Simon and Schuster, 1987.

Hermes, Walter G. *U.S. Army in the Korean War: Truce Tent and Fighting Front*. Washington, DC: Office of the Chief of Military History, 1966.

Rees, David. *Korea: The Limited War*. New York: St. Martin's, 1990.

Varhola, Michael J. *Fire and Ice: The Korean War, 1950–1953*. New York: Da Capo, 2000.

Shtykov, Terentii Fomich

Birth Date: 1907
Death Date: October 25, 1964

Soviet ambassador to the Democratic People's Republic of Korea (DPRK, North Korea) between 1948 and 1951, who supported Kim Il Sung's policy of invading the Republic of Korea (ROK, South Korea). Born in the Russian province of Vitebsk in 1907, Terentii Fomich Shtykov joined the Bolshevik Party in 1920. He served as secretary for the regional party organization in Vyborg in 1937 before advancing to second secretary of the Leningrad Oblast just before the Second World War. A client of Leningrad party boss Andrei Zhdanov, Shtykov served on several fronts around Leningrad during the Second World War before being transferred to the Far Eastern front in 1945. He rose to the rank of colonel-general. Highly decorated, Shtykov received three Orders of Lenin, three Orders of Kutuzov (first class), and the Order of Suvarov, yet he was essentially a political officer.

As a member of the Military Council and deputy commander of the Maritime Military District of the Soviet Union, Shtykov played a pivotal role in the construction of the DPRK. Along with commander of the Soviet First Far Eastern Front (Army Group) marshal Kiril A. Meretskov, he led the delegation that accepted the Japanese surrender in northern Korea on August 19, 1945. Shtykov then supervised the selection of personnel for the Soviet Civil Administration in Korea, headed the Soviet delegation to the Joint Soviet-American Commission on Korea (March 20, 1946–October 18, 1947), and guided the drafting of the new constitution for North Korea, as well as the law on land reform and the Communist Party statutes in 1946.

As a negotiator, Shtykov was stubborn and followed the Stalinist line to the letter. His American counterparts noted Shtykov as a hot-tempered authoritarian who was neither politically profound nor intellectual.

Shtykov's influence on Korean politics was nonetheless immense. Through his position on the Military Council and his links to Zhdanov, Shtykov became the most authoritative voice on Soviet policy in Korea until the war turned against North Korea in late 1950. His support for Kim Il Sung over Pak Hon Yong may have been the decisive factor in Joseph Stalin's choice of the former to be chairman of the new North Korean administration in February 1946. Shtykov supported Kim and his policies unflinchingly while serving as ambassador to Pyongyang. It is likely that it was Shtykov who first convinced Stalin to approve an attack on South Korea. And it is almost certain that he used the wide latitude afforded him as ambassador to support the invasion plans in early 1950.

Shtykov was deprived of rank and reassigned to the Russian provinces in 1951. After several years as First Secretary of the Novgorod Oblast and Maritime Krai Party organization, he surfaced in 1959 as ambassador to Hungary. Recalled in 1960, he served as chairman of the State Control Commission for the Council of Ministers of the Russian Soviet Federal Republic in Moscow until his death there on October 25, 1964.

TIMOTHY C. DOWLING

See also

Kim Il Sung; Korea, Democratic People's Republic of, 1945–1953; Korea, History of, 1945–1947

References

Goncharov, Sergei N., John W. Lewis, and Xue Litai. *Uncertain Partners: Stalin, Mao, and the Korean War.* Stanford, CA: Stanford University Press, 1993.

Simmons, Robert R. *The Strained Alliance: Peking, Pyongyang, Moscow, and the Politics of the Korean Civil War.* New York: Free Press, 1975.

Van Ree, Eric. *Socialism in One Zone: Stalin's Policy in Korea, 1945–1947.* New York: St. Martin's, 1989.

Sin Ik Hui

Birth Date: July 11, 1894
Death Date: May 5, 1956

Korean nationalist, politician, and Speaker of the Republic of Korea (ROK, South Korea) National Assembly during the Korean War. Born at Kwangju, near Seoul, on July 11, 1894, Sin Ik Hui was an enthusiastic independence activist. In 1908, he went to study at Waseda University in Japan, and during this time he organized a Korean student union. Returning to Korea in 1913, he took up teaching and became deeply involved in the independence movement.

In 1918, Sin began working with overseas agitators for the independence movement in Manchuria, Beijing (Peking), and Shanghai, and he played an important role domestically in the March First Movement by discussing with other nationalists the means by which independence might be achieved. In March 1919, because of his role in the March First Movement, Sin went into enforced exile in Shanghai for 26 years, until the liberation of Korea in 1945. During his period of exile, he drafted much of the constitution for the Korean Provisional Government (KPG) and held various key posts in its government-in-exile, including minister of home affairs, minister of justice, and minister of foreign affairs.

At the conclusion of World War II, Sin returned to Korea in December 1945 as a key figure in the KPG, but his political ideas differed from those of Kim Ku. When Syngman Rhee argued in 1946 that South Korea should form a separate government from North Korea, most of the KPG groups objected. They refused to change their policy, insisting on a unified Korean government. Nonetheless, a separate South Korea was established in 1948. Sin was the most prominent KPG political leader who accepted Rhee's policy and became active in the establishment of South Korea.

Sin's strong anticommunist stance should have led him closer to Rhee. In fact, as soon as Sin returned to Korea, he had created the Chungang activist group, which operated under the KPG banner. This group made an attempt on Kim Il Sung's life, but it was soon dissolved as a result of dissension within the KPG. In 1946, Sin seceded from Kim Ku's KPG group by becoming vice president of a right-wing organization that enthusiastically followed Rhee's leadership. Furthermore, Sin took the lead in forming the Taehan Anti-communism Association, and he made a speaking tour of the country to spread his anticommunist message. At the same time, Sin founded a college and also published a newspaper.

Anticommunism, opposition to a trusteeship, and independence from the U.S. military government were Sin's political guideposts during the first few years after independence. Shortly after the establishment of South Korea, Sin suggested that Rhee's first cabinet should include the KPG group that had opposed establishment of a separate South Korean government, but Rhee rejected the idea. Because of this, Sin gradually distanced himself from Rhee. Finally, in 1947, Sin merged his group and another right-wing nationalist organization to form a new political party, and he became its leader. In February 1949, this party joined with the Korean Democratic Party to form the Democratic National Party in opposition to Rhee.

Chosen as Speaker of the National Assembly following Rhee's inauguration as president in August 1948, Sin was in that post when the Korean War began in June 1950 and was still serving during the 1952 political crisis when Rhee pressured the National Assembly to revise the constitution for his second seizure of power. Sin not only kept the position of Speaker for three terms, but he was able to increase his political power during that time.

In 1955, the Democratic National Party was expanded to form the Democratic Party, and Sin led this new opposition party. He ran against Rhee in the 1956 presidential election on the Democratic Party ticket, and a campaign speech delivered alongside the Han River brought him enormous popularity. However, Sin died suddenly on May 5, 1956, while traveling by train to campaign in the Honam (Cholla) region. His running mate for vice president, John Myon Chang, was victorious in the election. Many in Korea still remember Sin as a capable political leader who resisted Rhee's dictatorship. Although Sin opposed Rhee politically, he still supported Rhee's anticommunist and anti-Japanese platforms.

INSOOK PARK

See also

Korea, Republic of, Political Crisis; Korean Provisional Government; Rhee, Syngman

References

Kim, Hakjoon. *Haebang Konggan ui Chuyokdul* [The Principal Actors of the Liberation Period]. Seoul: Tonga Ilbo Sa, 1996.

Matray, James I., ed. *Historical Dictionary of the Korean War.* Westport, CT: Greenwood, 1991.

Park, Myong Lim. *Hanguk Chonjaeng ui Palbal kwa Kiwon* [The Outbreak and Origins of the Korean War]. Vols. 1 and 2. Seoul: Nanam, 1996.

Sin Song Mo

Birth Date: May 26, 1891
Death Date: May 29, 1960

Defense minister and concurrently acting prime minister of the Republic of Korea (ROK, South Korea) at the outbreak of the

Korean War. Born at Uiryong, South Kyongsang Province, on May 26, 1891, Sin Song Mo graduated from Posong Law School in Seoul in 1910. That same year after the Japanese annexation of Korea he fled to Vladivostok and started his life in exile under the tutelage of Sin Chae Ho, one of the best-known leaders of the Korean independence movement. Graduating from a maritime school in Shanghai in 1913, Sin Song Mo served as an ensign at Chinese navy headquarters.

In 1919, Sin joined the Korean Provisional Government, and in 1923 he was arrested in China by the Japanese police and returned to Korea and imprisoned. Upon his release in 1925, he went to Britain, where he graduated from the London School of Navigation and secured a master's license. Between 1930 and 1945, Sin worked as a captain for British and Indian commercial ship companies.

On his return to South Korea in November 1948, Sin received a cordial welcome from President Syngman Rhee. The next month, he was appointed minister of the interior. In March 1949, he left that post to become minister of defense, a post he held until May 1951. Between April and October 1950, Sin also served concurrently as the acting prime minister.

Immediately preceding the outbreak of the war in June 1950, Sin on several occasions publicly warned about the possibility of an attack by the Democratic People's Republic of Korea (DPRK, North Korea). On May 10, he held a press conference in which he stated that troops of the Korean People's Army (KPA, North Korean Army) were moving toward the 38th Parallel and there was an imminent danger of invasion. On June 8, he stated that the South Korean government was considering issuing a national mobilization order, and he actually ordered South Korean armed forces onto emergency alert. At the same time, in his public pronouncements, Sin was confident that the Republic of Korea Army (ROKA, South Korean Army) would be able to deal with the situation. In the course of the May 10 press conference, he said that following a KPA invasion, the ROKA would counterattack across the 38th Parallel. Such boasting was largely public posturing about the ability of the government to handle any possible crisis. Sin had previously said in the National Assembly that the ROKA would take breakfast at Kaesong, lunch in Pyongyang, and supper at Sinuiji. The North Korean government used Sin's boastful words after the war as evidence for their claim that the war began with an ROKA invasion of North Korea.

Sin lacked a sense of reality when the war broke out. Without undertaking any military measures, he simply urged that Rhee remove the government from Seoul. Even the emergency cabinet meeting on June 27 was not initiated by him, but rather by former Prime Minister Yi Pom Sok. Rhee, Sin, and chief of staff of the South Korean armed forces Chae Pyong Dok lacked military knowledge and experience. Blame for the poor military situation in which South Korea found itself at the beginning of the war rests in large part with those three men. Sin was remarkable in carrying out what Rhee ordered but not in counseling what the president needed. Largely because of this, of course, he had a long tenure in the cabinet.

Sin's departure from the cabinet was brought about by two incidents early in 1951. One was the scandal related to the South Korean National Defense Forces, whose leaders misappropriated public funds for themselves and as a result more than 1,000 enlisted guardsmen died of starvation and illness. The other was when ROKA troops, while searching for communists, massacred innocent civilians at Kochang in South Kyongsang Province. As defense minister, Sin was blamed for both scandals. The assembly then voted to remove him from the cabinet. Subsequently, Rhee appointed Sin chief of the South Korean mission to Japan with the equivalent rank of ambassador. Sin died in Seoul on May 29, 1960.

To Woong Chung

See also

Chae Pyong Dok; Kochang Incident; Korea, Republic of, National Defense Forces Scandal; Rhee, Syngman; Yi Pom Sok

References

Noble, H. J. *Embassy at War.* Seattle: University of Washington Press, 1975.

Park, Myong Lim. *Hanguk Chonjaeng ui Palbal kwa Kiwon* [The Outbreak and Origins of the Korean War]. Vols. 1 and 2. Seoul: Nanam, 1996.

Republic of Korea, War History Compilation Committee, Ministry of National Defense. *Hanguk Chonjaengsa* [History of the Korean War]. 9 vols. Seoul: Ministry of National Defense, 1967–1970.

Sin Tae Yong
Birth Date: 1891
Death Date: 1959

General of the Republic of Korea Army (ROKA, South Korean Army) and minister of defense for the Republic of Korea (ROK, South Korea) toward the end of the Korean War. Born in Seoul in 1891, Sin Tae Yong was educated in the same city at the Royal Boy's Military School and Royal Military School in the late Choson dynasty (1392–1910). In 1914, he graduated from the Japanese Military Academy and began his military career for Japan, attaining the rank of lieutenant colonel at the time of the Japanese surrender in 1945.

Sin spent three years in self-imposed exile, rejecting an offer to supervise the formation of the ROKA. He resumed his military career with the rank of colonel in the fall of 1948 when antigovernment and leftist elements in the military in South Korea staged the Yosu-Sunchon Rebellion. Promoted in May 1949 to brigadier general and five months later to major general, he then became the chief of staff of the ROKA. In April 1950, he resigned from the post because of differences with the U.S. Korea Military Advisory Group (KMAG). It was said that he predicted the imminent invasion by the Democratic People's Republic of Korea (DPRK, North Korea) and stressed the importance of South Korean military preparedness. Two months later, the Korean War began, and he was appointed commander of the defense of North Cholla Province but was removed in July 1950 because of conflicts with Defense Minister Sin Song Mo. In January 1952, he was reinstated, and two months later he was promoted to lieutenant general. Soon Sin Tae Yong was appointed minister of defense, a post he retained until June 1952, when Son Won Il replaced him. From 1954 to 1956, he was commander of the national militia.

Sin died in Seoul in 1959. His son, Ung Kyun, was an ROKA lieutenant general and ambassador to the Federal Republic of Germany.

Hakjoon Kim

See also

Korea, Republic of, 1947–1953; Korea, Republic of, 1953–Present; Korea Military Advisory Group; Sin Song Mo; Yosu-Sunchon Rebellion

References

Park, Myong Lim. *Hanguk Chonjaeng ui Palbal kwa Kiwon* [The Outbreak and Origins of the Korean War]. Vols. 1 and 2. Seoul: Nanam, 1996.

Republic of Korea, War History Compilation Committee, Ministry of National Defense. *Hanguk Chonjaengsa* [History of the Korean War]. 9 vols. Seoul: Ministry of National Defense, 1967–1970.

Sino-Soviet Treaty of Friendship and Alliance
Event Date: February 14, 1950

Comprehensive military and economic alliance between the Union of Soviet Socialist Republics (USSR, Soviet Union) and the newly formed People's Republic of China (PRC). Despite its name, the negotiations leading up to the Sino-Soviet Treaty of Friendship and Alliance actually exacerbated the growing tensions between the two largest communist powers and consequently may have emboldened U.S. war hawks in responding to the outbreak of hostilities in Korea.

Chinese leader Mao Zedong himself headed the Chinese delegation to Moscow in December 1949, where he also paid homage to Joseph Stalin on the occasion of his 70th birthday (December 21). Stalin expected obedience from the Chinese leader, while Mao sought respect and generosity from his senior communist comrade. Both were to be disappointed. After two months of difficult negotiations over border disputes, economic assistance, and a military alliance, a treaty was finally signed on February 14, 1950.

While the relationship between the two leaders was no warmer than before, the treaty did provide some benefits for both sides. Its centerpiece was a 30-year military alliance in which each signatory agreed to "render military and other assistance with all the means at its disposal" in the event of attack "by Japan or States allied with it" (an oblique reference to the United States). The use of Japan as the focal point meant that the Soviet Union would not be obligated to provide assistance if the United States attacked China with another ally (such as Taiwan or South Korea).

The Soviet Union also agreed to give up the strategic naval base of Port Arthur, but Soviet military forces would remain there until the end of 1952 as a deterrent to possible Japanese or U.S. imperialistic plans. Finally, the Soviet air force was to provide temporary assistance against air raids on coastal targets by the Nationalist forces in Taiwan. Reportedly, an offer by Stalin to provide military advisers (spies) was politely declined. The tepid nature of the Soviet military commitment to China may have led U.S. policy makers to assume incorrectly that China would hesitate to intervene militarily in Korea without a stronger guarantee of Soviet support.

The territorial and economic sections of the treaty were mostly decided in favor of China, but Stalin extracted numerous significant concessions. Most of the disputed territory occupied by Soviet forces during the war was returned to China, including Port Dalny, Port Arthur, the Manchurian railroads, and parts of Sinjiang. In this last area, however, the Soviets were given the right to exploit the raw materials. Mao's biggest capitulation to Soviet wishes was in agreeing that Outer Mongolia, claimed by China, would retain

Leaders of the Soviet Union and the People's Republic of China (PRC) sign the Sino-Soviet Treaty of Friendship and Alliance on February 14, 1950. Soviet foreign prosecutor Andrei Vishinsky is seated at the table. Standing directly behind are Soviet premier Joseph Stalin (left) and PRC leader Mao Zedong (right). (Bettmann/Corbis)

its nominal independence and its very real subservience to Moscow. In terms of economic assistance, Mao asked for and received a relatively paltry $300 million loan, paid out over five years, with a 1 percent annual interest rate. The 10-year repayment plan for the loan stipulated that payments would come in the form of "raw materials, tea, gold, [and] American dollars." The fact that more substantial economic aid was not offered by the more industrialized Soviet state to its almost entirely agrarian communist neighbor is an unmistakable indication that Stalin did not relish the idea of an industrialized China on his border. And yet, if China was to follow the Soviet Union's lead in building communism, it would mean first and foremost constructing a strong industrial base. This economic abandonment of a communist brother was typical, insofar as Stalin invariably placed Soviet national interests ahead of ideological considerations. In fact, his treatment of other allies (or satellites) was usually far more exploitative.

Stalin's arrogant and miserly treatment of Mao in the negotiations leading up to the Sino-Soviet Treaty of Friendship and Alliance had unintended consequences. Mao and the other leaders of the Chinese Communist Party (CCP) had to realize that they could expect only parsimonious assistance from the Soviets and that their foreign policy objectives would not always coincide. Stalin tried to isolate China and make it more dependent on the Soviet Union, but instead he pushed the CCP toward greater independence.

When word reached Washington of the growing divisions within the communist world, U.S. policy makers apparently accepted the false assumption that cracks in communist solidarity would make both China and the Soviet Union less likely to intervene in Korea. This strategic miscalculation certainly contributed to the catastrophic decision to send General Douglas MacArthur's forces across the 38th Parallel, which triggered Chinese intervention in the fall of 1950.

EDWARD SHARP

See also

China, People's Republic of; Japan; Korea, Democratic People's Republic of, Invasion of the Republic of Korea; Mao Zedong; Soviet Security Council Boycott; Soviet Union; Stalin, Joseph; Vyshinskii, Andrei Ianuarovich; Zhou Enlai

References

Beloff, Max. *Soviet Policy in the Far East, 1944–1951*. London: Oxford University Press, 1953.

Chen Jian. *Mao's China and the Cold War*. Chapel Hill: University of North Carolina Press, 2000.

Cowley, Robert, ed. *The Cold War: A Military History*. New York: Random House, 2005.

Lüthi, Lorenz M. *The Sino-Soviet Split: Cold War in the Communist World*. Princeton, NJ: Princeton University Press, 2008.

Simmons, Robert R. *The Strained Alliance: Peking, Pyongyang, Moscow, and the Politics of the Korean Civil War*. New York: Free Press, 1975.

Stueck, William W., Jr. *The Korean War: An International History*. Princeton, NJ: Princeton University Press, 1995.

———. *Rethinking the Korean War: A New Diplomatic and Strategic History*. Princeton, NJ: Princeton University Press, 2004.

SMACK, Operation
Event Date: January 25, 1953

Bungled military offensive by the U.S. 7th Infantry Division. Designed as a showpiece of air-tank-artillery coordination, its purpose was partly to impress recently sworn-in president Dwight D. Eisenhower with the military's resolve and capacity to win. Operation SMACK's failure had decidedly unfavorable repercussions for the United Nations Command (UNC) and in particular for Lieutenant General Mark W. Clark, its bellicose commander in chief, who was eager to fight until a complete victory was won and Korea's reunification accomplished.

Operation SMACK's objective was to capture the communist-held redoubt of Spud Hill in the west-central portion of the UNC lines. The UNC also hoped to take communist prisoners who might provide useful intelligence information. Numerous high-ranking U.S. Army and Air Force officers and a dozen press representatives were invited to observe the offensive. So stage-managed was the occasion that the division had produced a six-page, three-color brochure for the guests' information and convenience; the title page set out the day's "scenario."

Such blatant hubris received what might be considered its just reward. Despite careful advance preparations, including a week's prior air and artillery bombardment, SMACK quickly went astray. Far East Air Force and Marine Corps aircraft mostly missed their preselected targets, flamethrowers and automatic weapons jammed or misfired, smoke screens were incorrectly located, and the initial infantry troop assault was blocked and the men caught in a defile. All three infantry platoon leaders were wounded, and within a few hours, U.S. troops were withdrawn from Spud Hill.

Seventy-seven U.S. casualties, several hundred thousand pounds of bombs, tens of thousands of rounds of heavy- and light-caliber ammunition, 2,000 tank rounds, and 650 grenades brought a return of 65 communist casualties and none of the anticipated prisoners. Moreover, communist forces had been far less enthusiastic in their use of artillery and had employed no air power whatever. Even making all allowances for the traditional U.S. strategy of making lavish use of technology to minimize casualties, the balance sheet was disproportionately unfavorable to the Americans, who had failed to gain their objective.

Operation SMACK mushroomed into a well-publicized embarrassment when an enterprising newspaper correspondent, recently arrived in Korea and present at neither the detailed prebriefing nor the actual event, wrote a piece in which he charged that American soldiers had died needlessly in a poorly planned "demonstration" show mounted as a publicity event for the military's top brass. His story featured prominently the use of the ill-chosen word "scenario," the egregious brochure, and the presence of high-ranking spectators. Friendly reporters hastened to defend the military, and Eighth Army commander General James Van Fleet issued a public statement, but the damage had been done.

U.S. Army chief of staff General J. Lawton Collins was obliged to testify before the congressional armed services committees, where he characterized the operation as a test of coordinated assault methods rather than a needless publicity exhibition. Congress accepted his explanation, and the incident was considered closed. Even so, the failure to achieve such a small, limited, and long-prepared objective cast serious doubt on the military's competence and severely weakened Clark's credibility in dissenting from Eisenhower's policy of seeking a negotiated peace.

PRISCILLA ROBERTS

See also

Clark, Mark Wayne; Collins, Joseph Lawton; Eisenhower, Dwight David; Van Fleet, James Alward

References

Clark, Mark W. *From the Danube to the Yalu.* New York: Harper and Row, 1954.

Fehrenbach, T. R. *This Kind of War: A Study in Unpreparedness.* New York: Macmillan, 1962.

Hermes, Walter G. *U.S. Army in the Korean War: Truce Tent and Fighting Front.* Washington, DC: Office of the Chief of Military History, 1966.

Major General Oliver P. Smith was the best known U.S. Marine Corps general of the Korean War. The withdrawal of his 1st Marine Division from the Changjin (Chosin) Reservoir is considered one of the greatest accomplishments in U.S. military history. (Department of Defense)

Smith, Oliver Prince

Birth Date: October 26, 1893
Death Date: December 25, 1977

U.S. Marine Corps general and commander of the 1st Marine Division during the Korean War. Born in Menard, Texas, on October 26, 1893, Oliver Prince Smith worked his way through the University of California, Berkeley, where he was a member of the Reserve Officers Training Corps, and graduated in 1916. Smith was a Christian Scientist all his life and remained a deeply religious person who neither drank nor swore.

After graduating from the University of California, Smith worked for Standard Oil Company. When the United States entered World War I, Smith applied for a Marine Corps reserve commission, which was granted in May 1917. He was then sent to Guam, where he was awarded a regular commission.

In 1919, Smith was assigned to Mare Island Marine Barracks, San Francisco. He commanded the marine detachment on board the battleship *Texas* from 1921 to 1924. Between 1924 and 1928, he was in the personnel section of Marine Corps headquarters in Washington, DC After spending three years working with the Haitian gendarmerie, Smith attended the Army Infantry school in Fort Benning, Georgia, graduating in 1932; he was then an instructor in the Marine Corps Schools at Quantico, Virginia.

Smith served on the staff of the naval attaché at the Paris embassy from 1934 to 1936 and then returned to Quantico, where he was again an instructor from 1936 to 1939. After a year with the Fleet Marine Force, Pacific, in 1940 he commanded a battalion of the 6th Marine Regiment, and from May 1941 until March 1942,

he was with that battalion in Iceland. After two years with headquarters staff, he received command of the 5th Marine Regiment of the 1st Marine Division in January 1944 and led it through the New Britain campaign.

Promoted to brigadier general in April 1944, Smith became assistant commander of the 1st Division. He saw action on Peleliu in September and October, and in November he was made deputy chief of staff to General Simon B. Buckner's Tenth Army. After combat on Okinawa during April and June 1945, Smith was named commandant of the Marine Corps Schools at Quantico.

In April 1948, Smith became assistant commandant and chief of staff of the Marine Corps under General Clifton B. Cates. Promoted to major general in June 1950, Smith took command of the 1st Marine Division at Camp Pendleton, California. He had only 20 days to prepare the division for Korea; and on September 15, 1950, Smith led the 1st Marine Division—which made up about half of Major General Edward M. Almond's X Corps—in the Inchon Landing. Smith and Almond did not get along, primarily because Almond insisted on depreciating him and failed to understand Marine requirements.

Smith was present in Seoul for the ceremony staged by United Nations Command (UNC) commander General Douglas MacArthur turning the city back over to the South Koreans. The 1st Marine Division then relocated to Inchon and was shifted by sea to the port of Wonsan on the east coast of Korea. At the end of October, the division began an advance to the Yalu River.

Smith had serious misgivings about MacArthur's troop dispositions for the final push to the Yalu, enough so that he communicated to Marine commandant General Clifton B. Cates in Washington his doubts about the wisdom of a campaign in the bitter cold of a Korean winter with his division scattered along one road from Hungnam to the Yalu. Smith also expressed concern about the gap between his division and the Eighth Army on his left. For a Marine general in the field to counsel caution in carrying out the orders of a commander took some courage. But Smith slowed his advance to about a mile a day, took care not to string out his units any more than was absolutely necessary, and hurried the establishment of a base at Hagaru-ri. In all probability this saved his division from annihilation in the next few weeks.

When the Chinese People's Volunteer Army (CPVA, Chinese Army) resumed its offensive at the end of November, Smith's division was trapped with its main elements 78 miles north of the port of Hungnam at the Changjin (Chosin) Reservoir. On the night of November 27–28, the Chinese attacked the marines in zero-degree weather. Ultimately, the Chinese fed 12 divisions (3 armies) into the battle. The marines then began an epic 13-day retreat, in which they brought out their wounded and their equipment with them. The first stage was from Yudam-ni to the base at Hagaru-ri, which they reached on December 3 in one of the most masterful withdrawal operations in the history of war, fought against heavy odds. When Smith met U.S. correspondents at Hagaru-ri, they questioned him about the retreat, and he replied, "Gentlemen, we are not retreating. We are just attacking in another direction."

The next stage of the withdrawal, to Koto-ri, began on December 6. It took 38 hours to cover 11 miles through snow under incessant Chinese attack. Smith again regrouped his forces for a retreat 10 more miles to Chinhung-ni. On December 8, the first troops in the force began to fight their way toward the sea and safety. By December 11, what remained of the command reached the Hamhung-Hungnam area. Marines remembered the withdrawal with pride; Chinese survivors recalled the devastating effects of air strikes and artillery.

After the evacuation from Hungnam at the end of December, the divided command was ended, and Smith's 1st Marine Division was incorporated into the Eighth Army as part of IX Corps. During the February 1951 counteroffensive, when army major general Bryant E. Moore suddenly died, Eighth Army commander Lieutenant General Matthew B. Ridgway named Smith to command IX Corps, one of the rare instances in which a Marine general has commanded army troops at the division or corps level. He continued in that capacity until March.

In April 1951, Smith returned to the United States as commander of Camp Pendleton, California. Promoted to lieutenant general in 1953, he commanded the Fleet Marine Force, Atlantic, from July 1953 until September 1955. Smith retired on September 1, 1955, when he was promoted to general. Smith died in Los Altos, California, on December 25, 1977.

SPENCER C. TUCKER

See also

Almond, Edward Mallory; Cates, Clifton Bledsoe; Changjin Reservoir Campaign; Hungnam Evacuation; Inchon Landing; MacArthur, Douglas; Ridgway, Matthew Bunker; Wonsan Landing and Evacuation

References

Blair, Clay. *The Forgotten War: America in Korea, 1950–1953.* New York: Times Books, 1987.

Heinl, Robert D. *Victory at High Tide: The Inchon-Seoul Campaign.* Philadelphia: Lippincott, 1968.

Montross, Lynn, et al. *U.S. Marine Operations in Korea, 1950–1953.* 5 vols. Washington, DC: U.S. Marine Corps Historical Branch, 1954–1972.

Spiller, Roger J., ed. *Dictionary of American Military Biography*, Vol. 3. Westport, CT: Greenwood, 1984.

Smith, Walter Bedell
Birth Date: October 5, 1895
Death Date: August 9, 1961

U.S. Army officer, director of the Central Intelligence Agency (CIA) (September 1950–February 1953), then undersecretary of state until 1954. Born in Indianapolis, Indiana, on October 5, 1895, Walter Bedell Smith briefly attended Butler University. Early on, he decided to pursue a military career, and in 1910, he enlisted as a private in the Indiana National Guard. After the United States entered World War I, he was called up for active duty. He attended officer training school, and in 1918, as a second lieutenant in the 39th Infantry, he saw active service in France at Château-Thierry and the Second Battle of the Marne.

In the years following the war, Smith—who had risen to the rank of major in 1939—acquired the organizational, administrative, and planning skills essential to managing modern warfare. He served with the Bureau of Military Intelligence, the Bureau of the Budget, and the Federal Liquidation Board, and he had several assignments either studying or instructing at the Infantry School at Fort Benning, Georgia, the Command and General Staff School at Fort Leavenworth, Kansas, and the Army War College.

General George C. Marshall, chief of staff of the U.S. Army from 1939, noted Smith's abilities, and that October summoned him to Washington, DC, to assist in the rapid buildup of the U.S. military. He was promoted to lieutenant colonel in April 1941 and to colonel that July.

Named first the assistant secretary and then the secretary to the general staff, in February 1942, Smith was promoted to brigadier general and became secretary to both the newly created Joint Chiefs of Staff (JCS) and the Anglo-American Combined Chiefs of Staff. In September 1942, Smith was assigned as chief of staff to General Dwight D. Eisenhower, a position he held until the end of 1945. During the North African campaign, he was advanced to major general, and in January 1944, he became a lieutenant general. Smith won a stellar reputation as one of the finest chiefs of staff in any army. He also assisted Eisenhower in his complicated wartime dealings with the French and diplomatic negotiations leading up to the surrender of Italy.

Smith returned to Washington in January 1946 as chief of the Operations and Planning Division of the JCS, but two months later, President Harry S. Truman appointed him ambassador to the Soviet Union, where he remained until 1949. Smith's experiences in this post, as the Cold War steadily and rapidly intensified, convinced him that the United States must take a firm line to contain Soviet expansion, but he also believed that the Soviets did not deliberately seek war and would back down when confronted by U.S. strength. Smith frequently offered suggestions, all ultimately fruitless, as to possible means of breaking the Soviet-American deadlock over the future of Korea.

In September 1950, Truman named Smith, then commanding the First Army, as director of the CIA; Smith was promoted to full general in July 1951. The president hoped he would improve leadership and organization within the agency, then attracting heavy criticism for its failure to predict the invasion by the Democratic People's Republic of Korea (DPRK, North Korea) into the Republic of Korea (ROK, South Korea). Smith's reputation as both an outstanding bureaucrat and a staunch anticommunist helped to deflect further criticism from the CIA, which he centralized and coordinated, persuading General Douglas MacArthur not only to allow the agency to operate in Korea but also to utilize its intelligence. Under Smith the CIA nonetheless wrongly predicted that the People's Republic of China (PRC) would not intervene in the Korean conflict, and it also failed to anticipate assorted coups in Latin America.

Smith tightened the flow of intelligence, restricting the overall picture to a few high-ranking officers, and instituted a training program to develop a group of career intelligence officers. On occasion, notably during the 1952 presidential campaign, his uncompromising anticommunism led him to allege that communist agents had long since infiltrated both the State Department and the CIA, suggestions that provided ammunition for attacks by Joseph McCarthy on the Truman administration.

Smith took a hawkish line toward the Korean War, viewing North Korea and China as mere Soviet pawns who were being used to implement a global Soviet strategy. He believed that the Soviets, although unwilling to go to war directly with Western countries in Europe, were prepared to sanction a Sino-American war in Asia, with the objective of weakening America's commitment to Europe and impeding European rearmament. He therefore strongly supported the enhancement of U.S. budgetary and personnel commitments to the North Atlantic Treaty Organization (NATO). A hard-liner, Smith advocated that the United States should put as much pressure on China as was necessary to bring about a satisfactory settlement of the conflict. He was even ready to sanction the use of Guomindang (GMD, Nationalist) Republic of China (ROC, Taiwan) troops in the war. On the whole, the Truman administration and its United Nations (UN) allies followed a course somewhat milder than that recommended by Smith.

As one of the few Truman appointees to survive the transition to the Eisenhower administration, Smith provided a degree of continuity. As undersecretary of state in the Eisenhower administration, he helped new Secretary of State John Foster Dulles to devise policy toward Korea. Smith was particularly active in formulating a complicated compromise proposal designed to resolve the vexing question of repatriation of prisoners of war (POWs), the major sticking point in the peace negotiations, which cleared the way to the eventual 1953 Panmunjom Armistice Agreement. Smith's last major assignment in the State Department before he retired in 1954 was to represent the United States at the Geneva Conference that year, a meeting whose decidedly overoptimistic objectives included facilitating Korea's potential reunification and resolving the growing difficulties in Indochina.

After his retirement, an embittered Smith, who never received either the fifth star or the promotion to chief of staff of the army that he believed his services merited, turned to business, amassing a considerable estate. Smith took advantage of his Pentagon, CIA, and State Department connections when he actively sought assorted high positions with various corporations, including United Fruit, AMF Atomics Incorporated, the Associated Missile Products Company, the American Machine and Foundry Company, RCA, and the Corning Glass Company, at least some of which—notably United Fruit—had benefited by actions Smith took as undersecretary of state. In 1958, Dulles appointed Smith, a staunch and vocal supporter of nuclear expansion, his special advisor on disarmament. Smith died on August 9, 1961, in Washington, DC

PRISCILLA ROBERTS

See also
Central Intelligence Agency; Eisenhower, Dwight David; Joint Chiefs of Staff; MacArthur, Douglas; Truman, Harry S.

References
Ambrose, Stephen E. *Ike's Spies: Eisenhower and the Espionage Establishment.* Garden City, NY: Doubleday, 1981.

Brands, H. W., Jr. *Cold Warriors: Eisenhower's Generation and American Foreign Policy.* New York: Columbia University Press, 1988.

Breuer, William B. *Shadow Warriors: The Covert War in Korea.* New York: Wiley, 1996.

Crosswell, D. K. R. *The Chief of Staff: The Military Career of General Walter Bedell Smith.* New York: Greenwood, 1991.

Garraty, John A., ed. *Dictionary of American Biography, Supplement Seven, 1961–1965.* New York: Scribner, 1981.

Mayers, David. *The Ambassadors and America's Soviet Policy.* New York: Oxford University Press, 1995.

Montague, Ludwell Lee. *General Walter Bedell Smith as Director of Central Intelligence, October 1950–February 1953.* University Park: Pennsylvania State University Press, 1992.

Ranelagh, John. *The Agency: The Rise and Decline of the CIA.* New York: Simon and Schuster, 1986.

Smith, Walter Bedell. *My Three Years in Moscow.* Philadelphia: Lippincott, 1949.

Snyder, William P. "Walter Bedell Smith: Eisenhower's Chief of Staff." *Military Affairs* 48(1) (January 1984): 6–14.

Son Won Il
Birth Date: May 5, 1909
Death Date: February 15, 1980

Republic of Korea (ROK, South Korea) navy admiral and chief of staff at the outbreak of the Korean War in 1950, later defense minister (1953–1956). Born in Kangso, South Pyongan Province, Korea, on May 5, 1909, Son Won Il went to China and Germany during the period of the Japanese colonial administration to study navigation. He secured a master's license in Germany in 1933 and then gained maritime experience at sea in European waters. Immediately after the end of Japanese rule in 1945 and anticipating imminent Korean independence, he moved to organize the nucleus of a future navy. Son was a dominant figure in South Korean naval circles during the period from 1945 to 1950.

In November 1945, officials in the U.S. military government in Korea suggested to Son that he help establish a coast guard to maintain coastal security and stop smuggling. Believing that this would evolve into a navy, Son agreed, and the next year he became the commandant of the coast guard. In August 1948, with the establishment of the ROK, the coast guard was indeed transformed into a regular navy. Son became its chief of staff with the rank of commodore. When the Korean War began in June 1950, Son was at sea in the Pacific overseeing the passage to Korea of three patrol ships secured from the United States. He did not return to Korea until July 14.

In June 1950, the Republic of Korea Navy (ROKN, South Korean Navy) consisted of 6,900 men and 71 ships, largely ex-U.S. and ex-Japanese minesweepers and picket boats. It had bases at seven major ports—Inchon, Kunsan, Mokpo, Yosu, Pusan, Pohang, and Mukkho—and its service installations were at Chinhae. The surprise naval invasion by the Democratic People's Republic of Korea (DPRK, North Korea) of June 25 consisted of a number of small landings along the east coast of South Korea. Although no ROKN ships were immediately available in the area to oppose these landings, units did quickly put to sea from the south. In the first critical hours of the invasion, the ROKN fought well, sinking a North Korean armed steamer northeast of Pusan with 600 men aboard. Soon U.S. Navy units began to arrive, and any North Korean naval threat was largely eliminated.

In September 1950, Son participated in the Inchon Landing (Operation CHROMITE) as commander of South Korean units, including the ROK Marine Corps of 2,800 men and the 17th Infantry Regiment. Son personally led marines in street fighting in Inchon, Pupyong, Kimpo, and Seoul, and he pushed them to be first to take over the capitol in Seoul early in the morning of September 27.

In June 1953, Son retired from the navy to become defense minister, a post he retained until 1956. The next year he became the first South Korean ambassador to the Federal Republic of Germany (FRG, West Germany). He died in Seoul on February 15, 1980.

To Woong Chung

See also

Inchon Landing; Korea, Republic of, Navy

References

Hong, Un Hye, ed. *Uridul un Ibada Wihae* [We Are for This Sea: Memoirs]. Seoul: Kain Kihoek, 1990.

Republic of Korea, War History Compilation Committee, Ministry of National Defense. *Hanguk Chonjaengsa* [History of the Korean War]. 9 vols. Seoul: Ministry of National Defense, 1967–1970.

Son Yang Won
Birth Date: June 3, 1902
Death Date: September 28, 1950

Presbyterian minister killed by the Korean People's Army (KPA, North Korean Army) during the Korean War. Son Yang Won was born at Hamyang, in the present-day province of South Kyongsang in the Republic of Korea (ROK, South Korea), on June 3, 1902. He converted to Christianity in 1910 and graduated from Kyongnam Bible School in 1929. After serving as a preacher at Miryang, Ulsan, and Pusan, he entered Pyongyang Theological Seminary to study theology in April 1935. After graduating from the school in March 1938, he entered into missionary work in Pusan. In August 1939, he became a preacher who attended leprous patients at Aeyangwon, a leper colony located at Yosu, South Cholla Province, and subsequently entered the ministry there.

In the late 1930s, the Japanese began forcing Koreans to attend and worship at the Japanese Shinto shrines. In September 1939, bowing to Japanese pressure, all of the Presbyterian churches in Korea recognized the worship at the Shinto shrines as a national ceremony. They argued that attending Japanese Shinto ceremonies was not a religious service but rather a national ceremony and therefore did not violate Christian doctrines. Son was opposed to attending Shinto ceremonies, however, and was arrested by the Japanese police. He was jailed at Yosu, Kwangju, and Seoul and sentenced to life in prison in January 1944. Son was finally released from prison on August 17, 1945, two days after Korea's liberation from Japanese occupation. He returned to Aeyangwon without delay. There, he attended to some 1,200 patients.

On October 19, 1948, some 2,000 troops of the 14th Regiment of the Republic of Korea Army (ROKA, South Korean Army) rebelled at Yosu as they were about to embark for Cheju-do to suppress an uprising there. For a time, the rebellion of South Korea's own security forces seemed to threaten the foundations of the fledgling republic. Joined by local supporters of the South Korean Workers'

Party (SKWP), the rebels had seized control of the city and the nearby city of Sunchon by October 20. They established peoples' committees in the cities, which were transformed into "liberated areas." They also hunted down the police and rightists, including Christians. In the Yosu-Sunchon Rebellion, Son's two sons were captured by the local leftists and summarily executed at Sunchon on October 21, 1948. By October 27, the South Korean government forces had managed to regain control of the two cities, and the resistance finally collapsed. The leader who ordered the execution of Son's two sons was arrested by the police and sentenced to death.

Following the outbreak of the Korean War, the Korean People's Army (KPA, North Korean Army) quickly swept over most of South Korea. Yosu was taken by the North Korean forces on July 27. Son and Aeyangwon now came under strict KPA surveillance. Although he had several opportunities to escape, Son refused to leave.

On September 15, 1950, the Korean War took a dramatic new turn as U.S. forces stormed ashore at Inchon. The demoralized KPA now summarily executed several thousand people. Their targets were mainly soldiers, landowners, priests, ministers, teachers, government officials, and anyone else who might later form the core of a resistance movement. Son was arrested on September 13 and, together with many other people in Yosu, detained at the Yosu police station for 15 days. Most of the detainees were landowners, Christians, and rightist students. Son was ordered to "confess" his crimes and reflect on what he had done, but he firmly refused to do so.

On September 28, 1950, the same day that Seoul was retaken by the advancing forces of the United Nations (UN), the KPA hastily retreated to the north. Son was taken to the outskirts of Yosu with a number of other detainees and there executed. He tried to preach Christian precepts to the condemned Koreans even as execution was imminent. *Sarang ui Wonjatan* (1956), his biography authored by An Yong Jun, was later made into a movie.

JINWUNG KIM

See also

Churches and the War, Korean; Korea, Republic of, 1947–1953; Yosu-Sunchon Rebellion

References

An, Yong Jun. *Sarang ui Wonjatan* [An Atomic Bomb of Love]. Pusan: Calvin Munhwa Chulpansa, 1956.

Son, Tong Hui. *Na ui Aboji Son Yang Won Moksa* [Reverend Son Yang Won: My Father]. Seoul: Agape, 1994.

Song Chin U
Birth Date: May 8, 1889
Death Date: December 30, 1945

Conservative Korean leader during Japanese colonial rule and the post-1945 liberation period and leader of the Korean Democratic

Party (KDP). Song Chin U was born on May 8, 1889, at Tamyang, in present-day South Cholla Province of the Republic of Korea (ROK, South Korea). He studied law at Maiji University in Tokyo, graduating in 1915. During the 1919 independence demonstrations, Song was arrested and imprisoned, serving an 18-month sentence.

Following his release from prison in 1921, Song became chief of the prestigious Korean-language newspaper *Tonga Ilbo* (*East Asia Daily*), which had been founded in 1920 by Kim Song Su, a close associate. During the Pacific War, the Japanese put great pressure on Song to collaborate with them. His Korean biographers claim that he resisted by staying at home and feigning illness. Other sources, however, allege that he was a collaborator.

The Japanese had good reason to fear Korean reprisals after the end of colonial rule. Thus, on August 10, 1945, with their surrender only days away, Japanese governor-general Abe Nobuyuki took immediate steps to form a transitional government in Korea. He hoped thereby to obtain assurances for the safety of Japanese lives and property in Korea until Allied forces could arrive. Not surprisingly, there were few people he could approach to run the government who were moderate, commanded respect, and wielded informal power. Endo Ryusaku, Abe's secretary-general for political affairs, suggested contacting Song, but he refused even to meet with Endo, fearing that to do so would label him a collaborator. The Japanese then approached left-leaning nationalist Yo Un Hyong on August 14, and he accepted the responsibility for governing an interim administration. He organized the Committee for the Preparation of Korean Independence (CPKI) on August 15, 1945.

At first, conservatives such as Song and Kim tried to use the CPKI to advance their own agendas. But in the last week of August, news arrived that U.S. troops would occupy southern Korea below the 38th Parallel. This served as a critical force in enabling the establishment of rightist organizations in the south. On September 16, the KDP was officially formed in Seoul. A mainstay of the KDP was the union of landlord, manufacturing, and publishing interests, led by Song, Kim, and others. Kim proved to be an able behind-the-scenes leader, but he had neither the temperament nor the desire to be a public figure. This resulted in Song's rise as leader of the party.

Following the establishment of the American military government (AMG) on September 12, 1945, the KDP functioned essentially as its ruling party. Accordingly, on September 21, the Americans allowed Song to employ the official government radio station, JODK, to assail the Korean People's Republic, a leftwing interim government established by Yo Un Hyong on September 6. When the AMG announced the appointment of an advisory council on October 5, consisting of 11 prominent Koreans, Song and Kim were among the 4 KDP representatives. Five others were pro-KDP conservatives. Cho Man Sik could not participate because at the time he was in northern Korea. Yo Un Hyong, the one representative from the Left, refused to participate.

The AMG worked closely with Song in reaching such important decisions as the appointment of KDP member Cho Pyong Ok to head the newly created Korean National Police. The Americans also used Song as a conduit for explaining U.S. actions and policy in Korea. Song and the KDP ably used their propaganda apparatus to transmit and embellish several important decisions made by the AMG.

During the trusteeship crisis, on the night of December 29–30, 1945, Song met with Kim Ku, a rival, in Seoul. There he tried to convince Kim to avoid a head-on clash with the AMG over trusteeship. Kim failed to convince Song to support an antitrusteeship movement. Immediately after the meeting broke up at 4:00 a.m., Song was shot dead, presumably by one of Kim Ku's supporters.

JINWUNG KIM

See also

Kim Ku; Kim Song Su; Korean Democratic Party; Yo Un Hyong

References

Cumings, Bruce. *The Origins of the Korean War.* 2 vols. Princeton, NJ: Princeton University Press, 1981, 1990.

Henderson, Gregory. *Korea: The Politics of the Vortex.* Cambridge, MA: Harvard University Press, 1968.

Sim, Chi Yon. *Hanguk Hyondae Chongdang Ron: Hanguk Minjudang Yon'gu* [On Korea's Modern Political Parties: A Study of the Korean Democratic Party], Vols. 1 and 2. Seoul: Changjak kwa Pipyong-sa, 1984.

Song Shilun

Birth Date: September 10, 1907
Death Date: September 17, 1991

Chinese general; deputy commander of the Chinese People's Volunteer Army (CPVA, Chinese Army); and commander of the Ninth Army Group during the Korean War. Born in Liling, Hunan Province, on September 10, 1907, Song Shilun began his long military career when he entered the well-known Whampoa Military School in 1926. He joined the Chinese Communist Party (CCP) in 1927 and the Red Army in 1928. He was chief of staff and then commander of the Red Army's Thirty-fifth Army in 1930, and then commander of the Twenty-eighth Army. In 1938 Song was appointed commander of the Fourth Army in the Eighth Route Army during the war against Japan (1937–1945). He and Deng Hua (later the deputy commander of the CPVA) directed numerous operations in eastern Hebei Province during the Second Sino-Japanese War.

With the end of World War II and the beginning of the Chinese Civil War (1945–1949) with the Guomindang (GMD, Nationalist) forces, Song was the CCP's director of military liaison affairs stationed in Beijing. He became commander of the Tenth Army, East China Field Army, in 1946. He was promoted to commander of the Ninth Army Group in 1948, directing the cross–Yangtze River campaign and the Shanghai campaign in 1949.

When China entered the Korean War, Song led three armies of the People's Liberation Army (PLA, Chinese Communist Army) Ninth Army Group over the border in late 1950. During the Chinese Second Offensive (November 25–December 1950), he commanded the Eastern Front, including the Battle for the Changjin (Chosin) Reservoir. His army group later participated in the Chinese Fifth (Spring) Offensive campaign (April 22–30, 1951) and the Sanggamnyong campaign. He returned from Korea in 1952 and was appointed director of the PLA Advanced Infantry School in Shijiazhuang. He was promoted to general in 1955. In 1957 Song was named vice president of the PLA Academy of Military Sciences, and in 1972 he became its president. He died in Shanghai on September 17, 1991.

RICHARD WEIXING HU

See also

China, People's Republic of, Army; Chinese Offensive, Second; Chinese Offensive, Fifth; Chinese People's Volunteer Army

References

Guo Huaruo et al., eds. *Jiefangjun Junshi Dacidian* [Dictionary of PLA Military History]. Changchun: Jilin Renmin Chubanshe, 1993.

Peters, Richard, and Xiaobing Li. *Voices from the Korean War: Personal Stories of American, Korean, and Chinese Soldiers.* Lexington: University Press of Kentucky, 2004.

Wu Rugao et al., eds. *Zhongguo Junshi Renwu Dacidian* [Dictionary of Chinese Military Figures]. Beijing: Xinhua Chubanshe, 1989.

Zhongguo Junshi Dabaike Quanshu [Chinese Military Encyclopedia]. Military History, Vols. 1–3. Beijing: Junshi Kexue Chubanshe, 1997.

Zhongguo Renmin Jiefangjun Jiangshui Minglu [Brief Biographies of PLA Marshals and Generals], Vols. 1–3. Beijing: Jiefangjun Chubanshe, 1986–1987.

South Africa, Union of

Nation located on the southern tip of Africa, known since 1961 as the Republic of Africa. With a 1950 population of 13.596 million, South Africa covers 471,008 square miles, about three times the size of the U.S. state of California. It is bordered by the Indian Ocean to the south and east, the Atlantic Ocean to the west, Namibia to the northwest, Zimbabwe and Botswana to the north, and Swaziland and Mozambique to the northeast.

At the time of the Korean War, the Union of South Africa was a self-governing dominion of the British Empire, under the British Crown. The prime minister was head of government and was considered the British monarch's official representative. He was chosen from a coalition that represented the white Afrikaner (Dutch) community and other white, English-speaking populations. The organization of apartheid in South Africa at the time of the Korean War kept South Africa's majority black population in a state of perpetual subservience based upon a strict system of segregation, disenfranchisement, and discrimination.

During the war, Daniel François Malan (known as D. F. Malan), of the National Party of South Africa, served as prime minister;

Four North American F-51 Mustangs of the famed Flying Cheetah Squadron of the South African Air Force warm up before takeoff on their first combat mission in Korea on November 16, 1950. (Department of Defense)

he ruled from 1948 to 1954. Under Malan's leadership, apartheid laws were significantly strengthened, further institutionalizing the nation's legalized discrimination against black South Africans.

The South African government announced on August 4, 1950, that a fighter squadron had been offered for service with United Nations Command (UNC) forces in Korea. This offer was accepted two weeks later, and the South African Air Force (SAAF) designated 2nd Squadron as the unit. In response to a request for approximately 200 officers and men, some 332 officers and 1,094 other ranks volunteered. Of this group, 50 officers and 157 men were selected to serve in the squadron, the origins of which lay in 1940 in East Africa, the Middle East, and Italy as the "Flying Cheetahs." The 2nd Squadron's first commander in Korea was Commandant S. van Breda Theron.

After a long sea voyage to the Far East, the 2nd Squadron disembarked in Japan on November 4, 1950. There it began familiarization with U.S. Air Force (USAF) procedures, as it would fly in conjunction with U.S. forces. It also received its first aircraft, veteran USAF North American F-51 Mustang fighter-bombers.

These aircraft were subsequently painted with SAAF markings: dark blue rounders with white centers emblazoned with a red, leaping springbok; tricolor vertical tail-fin flashes; and, on occasion, red propeller spinners. The unit's first flights staged to Airfield K-9 (Pusan East) on November 16, 1950, but immediately it began preparations for moving forward to a frontline base at K-24 (Pyongyang East), where it was in place by November 22.

During the period January–November 1951, the 2nd Squadron (attached to the USAF's 18th Fighter-Bomber Wing) flew some of its most intense and frequent missions of the entire war. Missions primarily included close air support (CAS) of ground forces and interdiction of communist supply lines. Fifty-nine percent of all aircraft lost by the squadron to enemy action or accidents were destroyed between January and November 1951.

By October 1951 the nature of the ground war had changed essentially to maintaining the front lines while truce talks progressed. Aerial attacks consequently became a principal means by which the UNC exerted pressure on communist forces. South African pilots flew numerous close support and rail interdiction missions during this period, with special emphasis on flak suppression for bomber sorties.

At the end of 1952 the 2nd Squadron converted from the venerable but war-weary Mustangs to Republic F-86F Sabre fighter-bombers. Production schedules and demands by USAF units delayed delivery of the jets, but on February 25, 1953, the South Africans flew their first operational sorties. In addition to their traditional close support and interdiction roles, the Cheetahs also flew air-to-air combat missions in light of the Sabre's superior performance. Patrols ranged along the Yalu and Chongchon rivers, as well as along UNC front lines and communist supply corridors.

After the armistice, the 2nd Squadron remained operational for training and supervision of communist adherence to the ceasefire. The squadron was based at Airfield K-55 at Osan-ni, south of Seoul. On October 28, 1953, the 18th Fighter-Bomber Wing staged a formal Retreat for the Flying Cheetahs preceding the departure for South Africa of the squadron's remaining personnel.

During the squadron's three years of service, 34 SAAF members were killed in action or declared missing and presumed dead; 8 served time as prisoners of war (POWs). The squadron received presidential unit citations from both the United States and the Republic of Korea (ROK, South Korea).

DAVID R. DORONDO

See also
Aircraft; United States Air Force

References
Bruning, John R. *Crimson Sky: The Air Battle for Korea.* Dulles, VA: Brassey's, 1999.
Futrell, Robert F. *The United States Air Force in Korea, 1950–1953.* Rev. ed. Washington, DC: Office of the Chief of Air Force History, 1983.
Moore, Dermot, and Peter Bagshawe. *South Africa's Flying Cheetahs in Korea.* Johannesburg: Ashanti, 1991.

South Korea

See Korea, Republic of, 1947–1953; Korea, Republic of, 1953–Present

South Korea, Invasion of

See Korea, Democratic People's Republic of, Invasion of the Republic of Korea

Southeast Asia Treaty Organization

Multilateral, regional, political, and mutual security alliance among eight nations: the United States, Great Britain, France, Australia, New Zealand, Thailand, the Philippines, and Pakistan. The Southeast Asia Treaty Organization (SEATO) was established by the Southeast Asia Collective Defense Treaty signed in Manila on September 8, 1954. A supplementary Pacific Charter declaring the self-determination of Asian peoples accompanied SEATO's formation. While the charter established principles of economic, social, and cultural cooperation among signatory nations, SEATO's main goal was collective security. Member states agreed to defend one another and other designated nations against aggression from external or internal threats.

Established only weeks after the end of the 1954 Geneva Conference, SEATO was created in the immediate wake of the French withdrawal from Indochina. The organization was the brainchild of U.S. secretary of state John Foster Dulles, who hoped that the alliance would fill the void left by France's retreat and prevent the spread of communism in Southeast Asia. The Korean War, which had ended only 14 months before SEATO was established, also played a major role in the formation of SEATO. The United States had already made a major economic and military commitment to South Korea, and so it wished to increase its influence in Southeast Asia as well, but not unilaterally. SEATO represented the first binding commitment by the United States to the defense of the region. Moreover, it came alongside expanded efforts by President Dwight Eisenhower's administration to build a viable regime in the southern half of Vietnam.

SEATO's structure and focus were problematic from the start. Unlike the North Atlantic Treaty Organization (NATO), SEATO had no standing military force, and its membership included only two Southeast Asian nations. Thus, the organization was not truly representative of the region as a whole. The exclusion of Indonesia, Burma, and Malaya—all facing significant communist insurgencies—was a glaring weakness. In addition, the inclusion of Pakistan stirred the anger of India, driving it farther away from the Western bloc. British and French participation was viewed as anachronistic by Asian members, an unwelcome remnant of European imperialism.

London and Paris viewed SEATO and its role quite differently than did Washington, DC The British did not fully share U.S. convictions about the threat posed by the People's Republic of China (PRC) in Southeast Asia. Nor did the British see the French defeat in Indochina as an absolute failure, as did U.S. officials. The British also hoped that SEATO would serve as the basis for a broader, regional nonaggression pact, perhaps including Korea and eventually initiating détente with China. For their part, the French were never very interested in SEATO, especially given their humiliation in Indochina.

Equally troubling was Thailand's viewpoint. The Thais initially hoped that SEATO signaled a genuine commitment to fight communism on their doorstep, but they soon lost faith in it. Bangkok was chosen as SEATO headquarters, and in many ways Thailand, on the front lines of the communist advance, was the centerpiece of the organization. But against the backdrop of the worsening

The working groups of eight national delegations forming the Southeast Asia Treaty Organization (SEATO) meet at the Social Hall of Malacanang Park in Manila, capital city of the Philippines, September 8, 1954. (Bettmann/Corbis)

crisis in Laos, by the early 1960s, Thai leaders saw SEATO as little more than a paper tiger.

The crux of the problem for Thailand, and often the United States, was the rule of unanimity incorporated into the SEATO voting structure. The Thais frequently proposed forceful SEATO action against communism in the region, including resolutions approving the deployment of military forces to Laos and Vietnam by member states. The French and British refused to endorse such actions, however. Despite their anticommunist rhetoric, Pakistan and the Philippines also eschewed such commitments. SEATO planning sessions, training exercises, and joint military maneuvers were held annually, but behind this facade of unity the organization was paralyzed by dissension.

For their part, few American officials saw SEATO as anything more than a military alliance. Dulles and others hoped that SEATO provisions in the Geneva Agreements would circumvent the barring of aid to Indochina. With this in mind, the Americans insisted that SEATO declare the intention to maintain a protective area

over the Republic of Vietnam (RVN, South Vietnam), Laos, and Cambodia. Problems soon arose with other members over how this should be fulfilled. For the United States, SEATO was the principal mechanism through which military support for South Vietnam could be justified.

By the early 1960s, U.S. policy makers had less ambitious plans for SEATO. Presidents Eisenhower and John F. Kennedy both hoped that SEATO would resolve its difficulties and represent a viable alternative to unilateral commitments in the region, but as its ineffectiveness became ever more apparent, the emphasis in Washington shifted to maintaining the alliance for symbolic purposes. It was believed that the organization would at least help combat defeatism among governments in the region.

SEATO was not, however, entirely ineffective. Under the auspices of SEATO's military planning and training exercises, the Americans developed a considerable array of covert and overt operations in Thailand for use in Indochina. Washington also later used the organization to solicit commitments from Australia and

Thailand to send troops to Vietnam. Moreover, although member states knew SEATO to be generally ineffective, the specter of unified military intervention by SEATO signatories may have in fact prevented more significant support from China and the Democratic Republic of Vietnam (DRV, North Vietnam) for communist insurgencies in the region.

In Indochina, however, by the mid-1960s, SEATO was obviously toothless. As U.S. troops began pouring into Vietnam after 1965, France and Pakistan refused to sanction American policy, openly signaling SEATO's grave limitations. As the war intensified and expanded, even the pretensions of SEATO cohesion evaporated. American commitments to Asian member states, and those in the so-called protective area, were governed almost exclusively by bilateral agreements rather than by SEATO itself.

As U.S. forces began their withdrawal from Southeast Asia in the early 1970s, SEATO fell apart. Embroiled in its continuing conflict with India, Pakistan formally withdrew in November 1973. France followed in June 1974. After the communist victory in Indochina in early 1975, the remaining members decided to disband the organization in September 1975. SEATO was finally dissolved in February 1977.

ARNE KISLENKO

See also

Dulles, John Foster; Geneva Conference; Indochina War, Impact on Korea; Pacific Pact

References

Anderson, David L. *Trapped by Success: The Eisenhower Administration and Vietnam, 1953–61*. New York: Columbia University Press, 1991.

Busczynski, Leszek. *SEATO: The Failure of an Alliance Strategy*. Singapore: Singapore University Press, 1983.

Schoenl, William, ed. *New Perspectives on the Vietnam War: Our Allies' Views*. Lanham, MD: University Press of America, 2002.

Soviet Air War in Korea

Start Date: 1950
End Date: 1953

Early on the afternoon of November 1, 1950, the first Soviet Mikoyan-Gurevich MiG-15s flew into action against U.S. Air Force (USAF) units bombing targets near the Yalu River. This action marked the beginning of the air war in what came to be known as "MiG Alley" and a dramatic change in the prosecution of the war in general. The fact that the MiG-15 pilots were Soviet personnel and that at least two Fighter Air Divisions (FADs) from the Soviet Air Force or Soviet Air Defense Force fought in MiG Alley remained a Soviet state secret until the end of the Cold War. Many United Nations Command (UNC) pilots reported sighting Soviet pilots or hearing Russian spoken over the radio, but the Soviet Union and the United States never officially acknowledged the active involvement of Soviet pilots and antiaircraft troops in the Korean air war.

Top Soviet Aces during the Korean War

Name	Claimed Kills	Medal Awarded
Nikolai V. Sutyagin	21	Hero of the Soviet Union
Yevgeni G. Pepelyayev	19	Hero of the Soviet Union
Lev Kirilovich Shchukin	17	Hero of the Soviet Union
Sergei M. Kramarenko	13	Hero of the Soviet Union
Ivan V. Suchkov	12	Hero of the Soviet Union
Stepan A. Bahayev	11	Hero of the Soviet Union
Konstantin N. Sheberstov	11	Hero of the Soviet Union
Grigorii U. Ohay	11	Hero of the Soviet Union
Mikhail S. Ponomaryev	11	Hero of the Soviet Union
Dmitri A. Samoylov	10	Hero of the Soviet Union
Pavel S. Milaushkin	10	Hero of the Soviet Union
Dmitri P. Oskin	9	Hero of the Soviet Union
Mikhail I. Mihin	9	N/A
Aleksandr P. Smorchkov	8	Hero of the Soviet Union
Grigorii I. Pulov	8	Hero of the Soviet Union
Serafim P. Subbotin	8	Hero of the Soviet Union
Semen A. Fedorets	8	Lenin's Order
V. N. Alfeyev	7	Red Banner
Fiodor A. Shebanov	6	Hero of the Soviet Union
Grigorii I. Ges	6	Hero of the Soviet Union
Anatoly M. Karelin	6	Hero of the Soviet Union
Arkadii S. Boitsov	6	N/A
Nikolai I. Ivanov	6	Lenin's Order
Nikolai M. Zameskin	6	Hero of the Soviet Union
Boris S. Abakumov	5	Hero of the Soviet Union
Grigorii N. Berelidze	5	Red Banner

For the United States and UNC, the clashes between North American F-86 Sabres and MiG-15s for aerial superiority over the northwest corner of Korea quickly became the most highly publicized element of the war, often eclipsing the bloody war of attrition on the ground. Soviet pilots were not engaged in trying to gain aerial superiority or provide close air support (CAS) to communist forces. Rather, they were trying instead to ensure that the field armies of Mao Zedong, the leader of the People's Republic of China (PRC), were able to reach the battlefront and, once in action, stay supplied. The Soviet-piloted MiG-15s were ordered to Dandong (Antung) Airfield to defend the railroad bridge across the Yalu River between Dandong and Sinuiju and the hydroelectric facilities at the Supung Reservoir.

Soviet premier Joseph Stalin and Mao had cemented their official relationship by signing the Sino-Soviet Treaty of Friendship, Alliance, and Mutual Assistance on February 14, 1950. Soviet pilots began flying air defense missions over Chinese cities in the early spring of 1950, with the first MiG-15 aerial victories coming against bombers of the Guomindang (GMD, Nationalist) in southern China. When Stalin, finally convinced that the United States would not or could not intervene before victory was achieved, allowed Kim Il Sung, leader of the Democratic People's Republic of Korea (DPRK, North Korea) to invade South Korea, he became committed to a situation that would require major Soviet assistance to counteract.

Stalin ruled out the use of Soviet ground troops to shore up the defeated Korean People's Army (KPA, North Korean Army)

after the UNC's Inchon Landing on September 15 and the subsequent breakout of the U.S. Eighth Army in Korea (EUSAK) from the Pusan Perimeter. Mao, at the same time, did not want to send his forces into action without air support. The game of brinkmanship played by the two communist leaders during the first two weeks of October 1950 accelerated the feelings of mutual distrust that helped lead to the Sino-Soviet split later in the decade. Mao wanted the active participation of Soviet air units over the battlefield, while Stalin limited his involvement to defending Chinese airspace in accordance with the February treaty. On October 14, 1950, Chinese troops began crossing the Yalu River. When reports reached Stalin that U.S. aircraft were bombing targets along the North Korean–Manchurian border, he ordered into action Ivan Belov's 151st FAD (along with regiments from the 28th and 50th FADs), which had been training Chinese pilots to fly the MiG-15.

Belov's units became the initial core of the Soviet Sixty-fourth Fighter Air Corps (FAC), headquartered in Shenyang and responsible for the defense of Manchuria. The Sixty-fourth FAC included the antiaircraft divisions, ground-control radars, and radar-controlled searchlight units deployed in North Korea. These units, along with their Chinese and North Korean comrades, were responsible for shooting down more U.S. pilots than were the more glamorous MiG-15s. As many as 70,000 Soviet officers and men manned the Sixty-fourth, but even so, it was smaller than the Sixty-seventh FAC, headquartered in Beijing, which controlled Soviet air units deployed in the rest of eastern and southeastern China. These other Soviet units included bomber and Shturmovik (assault) divisions equipped with Tuploev Tu-2 and Ilyushin Il-10 aircraft. Together, the Sixty-fourth and Sixty-seventh FACs were responsible for creating a modern Chinese air force that soon became the world's third largest.

In addition to Belov's original FADs, other Soviet MiG-15 units that fought in Korea included the 303rd, 324th (commanded by the leading Allied World War II ace, Ivan Kozhedub), 97th, 216th, 32nd, and 190th FADs. Georgii Lobov commanded the 303rd; he succeeded Belov as the second commander of the Sixty-fourth FAC and was paired with the 324th from April 1951 until early 1952. These two units inflicted some of the heaviest losses suffered by the Bomber Command of the U.S. Far East Air Force (FEAF) during its campaign against the Yalu River bridges. The air battles in early April and on October 23, 1951, known to the USAF as "Black Tuesday," resulted in such heavy losses for U.S. Boeing B-29 Superfortresses that they were banned from daylight combat in MiG Alley.

While the railroad bridge between Dandong and Sinuiju was never dropped, the hydroelectric facilities at Supung did not escape the war unscathed. The USAF and U.S. Navy combined their forces in the summer of 1952 to inflict serious damage on the Yalu dams. The success of U.S. Republic F-84 Thunderjets and Douglas AD-1 Skyraiders revealed the weakness of the Soviet air defense system. The Lockheed P-3a Orion radar could not detect low-flying aircraft, and the MiG-15 was designed to fly high and blow up large bombers; it could not dogfight well at low altitudes, particularly without its accustomed ground-control direction.

As the war progressed, more Chinese and North Korean pilots flew in MiG Alley and fell victim to the increasing numbers of improved F-86s. Soviet pilots continued to bear the brunt of the aerial combat. F-86 pilots also began patrolling across the Yalu into Manchuria looking to gain an advantage over the speedy MiG-15. While the F-86 (particularly the E and F models) was a superior dogfight aircraft, particularly in the hands of highly trained U.S. pilots, and gained an impressive kill ratio, the Soviet-piloted MiG-15s kept the major supply artery open to the Chinese and North Korean field armies. The result was a stalemate in the air that paralleled the one on the ground, leaving both sides in a perpetual state of armed confrontation.

MARK A. O'NEILL

See also

Aircraft; Airpower in the Korean War; Kim Il Sung; Mao Zedong; Soviet Airfield Incident; Stalin, Joseph

References

Gagin, V. V. "Vozdushnaia voina v koree (1950–1953 g.g.)" [Air war in Korea, 1950–1953]. Voronezh: Izdatelstvo "Poligraf," 1997.

Gordon, Yefim, and Vladimir Rigmant. *MiG-15: Design, Development, and Korean War Combat History.* Osceola, WI: Motorbooks International, 1993.

No, Kum Sok, with J. Roger Osterholm. *A MiG-15 to Freedom: Memoir of the Wartime North Korean Defector Who First Delivered the Secret Fighter Jet to the Americans in 1953.* Jefferson, NC: McFarland, 1996.

O'Neill, Mark A. "The Other Side of the Yalu: Soviet Pilots in the Korean War—Phase One, 1 November 1950–12 April 1951." PhD dissertation, Florida State University, 1996.

Soviet Airfield Incident
Event Date: October 8, 1950

Incident that severely strained relations between the United States and the Soviet Union and between President Harry S. Truman and General Douglas MacArthur. Following the Inchon Landing on September 15, 1950, United Nations Command (UNC) forces under MacArthur's command drove Korean People's Army (KPA, North Korean Army) forces back into the Democratic People's Republic of Korea (DPRK, North Korea) to an area in proximity to the Yalu River, the border between North Korea and the People's Republic of China (PRC).

On September 27 the Truman administration instructed MacArthur to employ only Republic of Korea Army (ROKA, South Korean Army) units in provinces contiguous to China and under no circumstances to attack targets in Manchuria. Washington feared any incident outside of Korea might be interpreted as a direct attack rather than a military mistake. Any such attack would herald the possibility of a widened war with China or the Soviet Union and even the possibility of world war, and was therefore to be avoided at all costs.

The administration's fears were realized on October 8, 1950. Despite the order to MacArthur, two Lockheed F-80 Shooting Star fighters of the 49th Air Group repeatedly strafed a Soviet airfield 62 miles north of the Korean border and 18 miles southwest of Vladivostok. The two pilots, both young and inexperienced, made a navigational error while flying in marginal weather and mistook the airfield for a North Korean installation.

The following day, the Soviet government strongly protested what it saw as a gross violation of its territory. Initially, the State Department refused to accept responsibility for the attack and claimed that the fighter planes were under the United Nations Command (UNC) rather than U.S. command. The incident, however, may have been one of the reasons behind a conference that took place between President Truman and General MacArthur on October 15, 1950, at Wake Island in the Pacific. Four days later, on October 19, the State Department issued an apology to the Soviet government. The U.S. government promised to pay for all damages incurred in the attack.

At the same time, a report from MacArthur declared that the attack had resulted from navigational error and poor judgment, as the target was not properly identified before the strike. The report also stated that the commander of the 49th Air Group had been relieved and the two pilots punished. In actuality, the punishments were not severe nor considered career damaging. The air group commander received a new command as director of combat operations for the U.S. Fifth Air Force, and the two pilots escaped punishment when a court-martial refused to convict them.

ERIC W. OSBORNE

See also

MacArthur, Douglas; Truman, Harry S.; United States Air Force; Wake Island Conference

References

Futrell, Robert F. *The United States Air Force in Korea, 1950–1953.* Rev. ed. Washington, DC: Office of the Chief of Air Force History, 1983.

Hoyt, Edwin P. *On to the Yalu.* New York: Stein and Day, 1984.

Spanier, John W. *The Truman-MacArthur Controversy and the Korean War.* Cambridge, MA: Harvard University Press, 1959.

Soviet Security Council Boycott

Start Date: January 13, 1950
End Date: August 1, 1950

The Soviet boycott of the United Nations (UN) Security Council in 1950 was ostensibly a protest against the refusal by the United States and its allies to seat the UN ambassador from the newly established People's Republic of China (PRC). An unintended consequence of this boycott was that the United States was able to dominate the Security Council at the beginning of the Korean War, without the Soviet ambassador exercising his veto power. A single veto would have prevented the Security Council from taking action. Specifically, Soviet ambassador Jacob Malik was not able to veto the U.S. proposal of June 27, 1950, to authorize the use of military force in defense of the Republic of Korea (ROK, South Korea). Malik returned to his seat on August 1, 1950, in time to assume the rotating chairmanship of the Security Council. The end of the boycott was a tacit admission that the tactic had backfired. Malik could not undo the June resolutions on Korea, although he vigorously attacked them for propaganda purposes, but he could end U.S. domination of the Security Council, argue for a negotiated settlement of the war, and build support for UN recognition of the PRC.

The UN Security Council was made up of five permanent members (the United States, the Soviet Union, France, the United Kingdom, and the Republic of China), each of whom had veto power over the council's resolutions, and six temporary members. Dr. Tsiang Ting Fu, the delegate from the Republic of China (ROC, Taiwan), or Taiwan (then known as Formosa), held the Chinese seat, even after Mao Zedong's forces had emerged victorious in the Chinese Civil War in late 1949. Presumably, Soviet leader Joseph Stalin was distressed that his communist ally was not given a seat in the UN, although it is possible that he provoked the controversy to keep China isolated and dependent on the Soviet Union (a theory originally attributed to French UN delegate Jean Chauvel). Stalin withdrew his UN ambassador in January, causing a predictable polarization among members, most of whom had been ready to seat the PRC delegate before the boycott.

Several months later, when the Korean People's Army (KPA, North Korean Army) invaded the Republic of Korea (ROK, South Korea), the Soviets found themselves without their Security Council veto. On the first day of the invasion, June 25, 1950, the United States convened a session of the UN Security Council and pushed through a resolution condemning the attack and demanding an "immediate cessation of hostilities." Two days later, another resolution was passed allowing member nations to provide "such assistance to the Republic of Korea as may be necessary to repel the armed attack." These resolutions gave the United States a mandate to intervene militarily in the name of the UN.

The coincidence of the Security Council boycott with the commencement of hostilities in Korea provided some observers for years with sufficient circumstantial evidence that the Soviets did not plan the latter event. Soviet documents have removed any basis for accepting this conclusion as valid, since they reveal that Stalin simply made a costly blunder in allowing Kim Il Sung to proceed with his invasion of South Korea during that time. In any case, the Soviet boycott of the UN Security Council gave Harry S. Truman's administration the unexpected advantage of being able to intervene in Korea under the guise of the UN.

EDWARD SHARP

Members of the United Nations (UN) Security Council meet to discuss the crisis in Korea, June 30, 1950. The Soviet Union, whose empty seat can be seen in the photograph, was boycotting the Security Council to protest the refusal of the United States and its allies to seat the People's Republic of China. (Hulton Archive/Getty Images)

See also

China, People's Republic of; China, People's Republic of, United Nations Representation Question; China, Republic of; Cold War, Origins to 1950; Kim Il Sung; Korea, Democratic People's Republic of, Invasion of the Republic of Korea; Lie, Trygve Halvden; Malik, Jacob; Mao Zedong; Sino-Soviet Treaty of Friendship and Alliance; Soviet Union; Stalin, Joseph; Vyshinskii, Andrei Ianuarovich

References

Brook, David. *The United Nations and the China Dilemma.* New York: Vintage Press, 1956.

Chen Jian. *China's Road to the Korean War: The Making of the Sino-American Confrontation.* New York: Columbia University Press, 1994.

———. *Mao's China and the Cold War.* Chapel Hill: University of North Carolina Press, 2000.

Simmons, Robert R. *The Strained Alliance: Peking, Pyongyang, Moscow, and the Politics of the Korean Civil War.* New York: Free Press, 1975.

Stueck, William W., Jr. *Rethinking the Korean War: A New Diplomatic and Strategic History.* Princeton, NJ: Princeton University Press, 2004.

Soviet Union

In 1950 the Union of Soviet Socialist Republics (USSR, Soviet Union) was the acknowledged leader of the communist world. The Soviet Foreign Ministry played an integral role in all aspects of the diplomacy behind the Korean War, even though that role was often indirect. As the sole designer of Soviet foreign policy, Soviet Union leader Joseph Stalin attempted to be something of a puppet master in his relations with other communist states, with varying degrees of success. The Soviet Union, born out of the 1917 Bolshevik Revolution and the ensuing civil war, was the world's first communist regime. As a result of its longevity, substantial economic power, and formidable military strength, the many new socialist and communist governments created since 1945 were obliged to submit to a certain level of guidance from the Soviet Union.

The Soviet Union, by far the largest country in the world, covered more than 8.6 million square miles, 11 time zones, and 2 continents. Straddling the Ural Mountains (the traditional dividing

North Korean leader Kim Il Sung (right front) with Soviet military advisers, November 1950. (Time & Life Pictures/Getty Images)

line between Europe and Asia) gave the Soviet Union a decidedly split personality, with crucial national interests in both areas. Fifteen supposedly sovereign republics constituted the union, but most political authority was concentrated in Moscow, the Soviet capital and the country's largest city. Russia (the Russian Soviet Federated Socialist Republic) accounted for about three-quarters of the territory of the Soviet Union and contained more than half of the population, which was close to 200 million in 1950. The other 14 republics, named for their respective ethnic majorities, were on the outside edge of the country in the west and south. Of the roughly 180 distinct nationalities, whose members spoke 125 languages and dialects, the most numerous were Russians (55 percent), Ukrainians (18 percent), Uzbeks (5 percent), and Belorussians (4 percent). The many Soviet peoples, divided by language, culture, religion, and historical animosities, were united by the use of Russian as the country's lingua franca and by the experience of Soviet rule.

The ruling house of the Russian Empire for more than 300 years, the Romanov dynasty came to an abrupt end during the spontaneous February (March by the Gregorian calendar) 1917 revolution in St. Petersburg, the czarist capital. Brutal and inept, Czar Nicholas II was unable to keep his exhausted subjects united in the vast war effort during World War I. Another eight months of misery, hunger, and defeat left Russia ripe for another upheaval. Vladimir Ilyich Lenin—who incessantly promised "peace, bread, and land" for the soldiers, workers, and peasants—had gained great popularity among those groups by the autumn of 1917. Pushing his fellow Bolshevik leaders relentlessly toward armed uprising, Lenin eventually succeeded in provoking the famous October Revolution (November by the Gregorian calendar), which began 74 years of Communist Party rule in Russia. Lenin pulled Russia out of the war, despite protests from Great Britain and France, and endorsed peasant seizures of noble lands. The Bolsheviks emerged victorious from a bloody civil war that left them in control of most of the former Russian Empire. After the hostilities of the civil war had ended and British, French, Japanese, and U.S. interventions had been repulsed, Lenin abandoned the crude economic despotism of war communism in favor of the New Economic Policy

(NEP). The extreme excitement of revolution and civil war gave way to the more mundane tasks of state building and revival of the economy through a limited return to market forces, especially in the agricultural and light manufacturing sectors. The NEP was initially successful, but it gave life to the regime's class enemies (bourgeois capitalists) and eventually stalled. This was the situation that confronted Lenin's successors after his death in 1924.

Stalin's response to the NEP's temporary stagnation, once he had eliminated his main rivals, was to instigate a new revolution. By 1928 he was secure enough at the top to embark on dual policies of forced collectivization of agricultural lands and a breakneck five-year plan for rapid industrialization. Organizing peasants into collective farms gave the state control over agricultural production, but the peasants resisted, and consequently several million of them died and millions more were forced to leave their villages. The First Five-Year Plan, although chaotic and based on unachievable goals, created revolutionary excitement among communists that had been missing since 1921. More important, it produced astonishing economic growth, particularly in heavy industry (coal, oil, iron, steel, and machinery). The impressive industrial achievements of the First and Second Five-Year Plans made Stalin a legend in communist circles around the world and allowed the Soviet Union to defeat the German invaders during World War II.

The brutality of Stalin's reign extended far beyond his drastic economic policies. His infamous "purges" of the Communist Party, government, and Red Army led to the arrest, conviction, and sentencing of millions of innocent people. Some were executed, others were sent to gulag prison camps in Siberia to perform hard labor under unimaginably harsh conditions, and a lucky few were merely expelled from the Communist Party. The purges were a testament to Stalin's extreme paranoia and ruthlessness, traits that would become more pronounced as he aged. Stalin's credibility outside the Soviet Union and the fighting effectiveness of the Red Army were severely compromised by the show trials of prominent old Bolsheviks and by the decimation of the officer corps.

Although the Soviet experience in World War II began with a long series of catastrophic defeats at the hands of Germany and its allies, it ended in triumph. At a cost of well over 20 million dead, the Soviet Union emerged as the master of Eastern Europe and as one of the world's two great military superpowers. Unfortunately, the Soviet Union's wartime alliance with the other superpower, the United States, rapidly deteriorated into a relationship characterized by mutual suspicion, open hostility, and venomous rhetoric. By 1947 this conflict had become the infamous Cold War, which would last for more than 40 years. After the end of World War II, Korea became an early and bloody battlefield of the Cold War.

World War II discussions between China, Great Britain, and the United States on the future of Japanese imperial possessions lead to the Cairo Declaration of December 1, 1943. The agreement, informally accepted by Stalin in May 1945, stipulated that Korea should become an independent country "in due course." At the Yalta Conference in January 1945 Stalin agreed that Korea would be put under an international trusteeship, jointly administered by the United States, Soviet Union, China, and Great Britain. He wanted to finalize the terms at the Potsdam Conference, but by then President Harry S. Truman believed U.S. forces would occupy Korea unilaterally following Japan's surrender in response to an atomic attack. On August 12, 1945, three days before the formal Japanese surrender, the Red Army occupied the Korean Peninsula north of the 38th Parallel, ostensibly liberating it from 35 years of Japanese rule. A month later U.S. troops occupied the southern half of the peninsula. The dividing line of the 38th Parallel was intended merely as a directive for Japanese forces in Korea. Those north of the line would surrender to Soviet officers, and the rest would surrender to U.S. officers. Foreign ministers of the two occupying powers agreed on December 27, 1945, in Moscow that a united Korea would become free and independent after a 5-year trusteeship, but Cold War politics doomed this plan to failure.

Within the Democratic People's Republic of Korea (DPRK, North Korea) the Soviet Union supported veteran communist Kim Il Sung, who had received training and military experience in the Soviet Union. The communists won a series of local and regional elections in November 1946 and formed a provisional government. On May 1, 1948, a new Soviet-inspired constitution was announced and a permanent government set up soon thereafter. Kim, who ended up ruling North Korea for its first 46 years, maintained cordial relations with the Soviet Union until it dissolved in 1991, but he showed greater independence each year that he remained in power.

In contrast to North Korea, Soviet relations with the People's Republic of China (PRC) were defined partly by the fact that Mao Zedong's 1949 victory in the decades-long civil war was his own. He owed very little to Moscow, whose intermittent assistance occasionally proved to be more harmful than helpful. Nonetheless, Mao was willing to play the role of respectful junior partner to Stalin in the affairs of international communism. In February 1950 Mao and Stalin signed the Sino-Soviet Treaty of Friendship and Alliance, which solidified their relationship on the surface but also showed some underlying tensions. The two communist giants resolved their border disputes, worked out a modest economic aid package for China, and agreed to a limited military alliance. Stalin was hoping for more obedience from China, while Mao wanted greater assistance from the Soviet Union with the PRC's industrial development and national security. The result was that China followed a more independent path after the death of Stalin, who commanded great respect in Beijing despite his high-handed tactics.

The Soviet role in the start of the Korean War is not as murky as it once was, because Soviet documents record Stalin's role in approving plans for North Korea's invasion of the Republic of Korea (ROK, South Korea). Kim's attempt to unify North and South Korea by military force in June 1950 was his own idea, but the general plan was approved by both Stalin and Mao. There can be no doubt that Stalin or Mao could have prevented the initial invasion by declaring strong opposition to Kim's plan. But the

North Koreans persuaded Stalin that the risks were small and the potential gains were substantial. If his client state in North Korea swallowed the U.S. protectorate in the south, then Stalin would share the glory without expending any resources. On the other hand, if the United States intervened, the crisis would make the PRC, North Korea, and Stalin's satellites in Eastern Europe more dependent on Soviet diplomatic leadership.

Anticipating quick North Korean conquest of the peninsula, Stalin at the outset of the war made a major diplomatic blunder. Because the Soviet Union was then boycotting the United Nations (UN), the Soviet delegate was not present in the Security Council to veto the U.S.-sponsored resolutions authorizing UN members to use force against North Korea. Later, when U.S. forces were driving toward the 38th Parallel, the Soviets led the diplomatic effort to prevent them from crossing that line. Stalin was determined not to commit Soviet forces but instead applied intense pressure on the Chinese to intervene, promising to supply arms to both of his allies in the conflict. While the Soviets were not an official party to the armistice negotiations, they played a crucial behind-the-scenes role. Their initial intransigence on the issue of prisoner of war (POW) repatriation may have helped stall the negotiations, but after Stalin's death in March 1953, their position softened slightly and Soviet leaders pushed to move the talks forward again.

As the leader of the communist world, Stalin sought to manipulate the course of international affairs to consolidate his standing. By supporting Kim's invasion of South Korea, Stalin had the opportunity to expand his influence in Asia, enhance his reputation, and maintain a diplomatic wedge between the United States and China. The war did not work out as planned, and the costs for Stalin were not minimal. Most important, the United States commenced massive rearmament, leading its allies in remilitarization. Stalin also miscalculated the war's impact on Sino-Soviet relations. Mao learned two valuable lessons: Soviet aid for its communist brethren would be miserly, and China was strong enough on its own to fight the United States to a standstill. The resulting boost to Mao's confidence allowed him to chart an increasingly independent course after 1953. Although North Korea remained on good terms with the Soviet Union, Kim placed great value on self-reliance for North Korea after the war.

EDWARD SHARP

See also

China, People's Republic of; Cold War, Origins to 1950; Japan; Kim Il Sung; Korea, Democratic People's Republic of, Invasion of the Republic of Korea; Korea, History of, 1945–1947; Mao Zedong; Sino-Soviet Treaty of Friendship and Alliance; Soviet Security Council Boycott; Stalin, Joseph; Truce Talks; Vyshinskii, Andrei Ianuarovich

References

Beloff, Max. *Soviet Policy in the Far East, 1944–1951*. London: Oxford University Press, 1953.

MacKenzie, David, and Michael W. Curran. *A History of Russia, the Soviet Union, and Beyond*. 5th ed. Belmont, CA: Wadsworth, 1998.

Medish, Vadim. *The Soviet Union*. 4th ed. Englewood Cliffs, NJ: Prentice Hall, 1991.

Ulam, Adam. *Expansion and Coexistence*. 2nd ed. New York: Holt, Rinehart and Winston, 1974.

Special Operations

Unconventional warfare is a topic little discussed in connection with the Korean War, but both sides practiced it. Special operations include behind-the-lines reconnaissance, demoralization, propaganda, sabotage, and guerrilla warfare. The United Nations Command (UNC) supported guerrilla bands in the Democratic People's Republic of Korea (DPRK, North Korea), providing both training and supplies. Conversely, North Korea had units operating in the Republic of Korea (ROK, South Korea), as well as special units attached to regular infantry line units.

The UNC, and primarily the U.S. Army, supported partisan activities in North Korea. Along with equipment, the army provided the partisans with military advisers to train unconventional units in guerrilla warfare, cutting communication lines, and other sabotage. The G-3 (training) section of the U.S. Eighth Army in Korea (EUSAK) first organized these units under the command of Colonel John McGee, the former U.S. Army guerrilla leader in the Philippines during World War II. This special operations unit was later designated Army Unit 8086. Along with training, food, and ammunition, the U.S. Army also sent personnel along with the partisans to act as advisers, who actually fought alongside them. The program was very successful, and by July 1951 this force of some 7,000 partisans claimed to have killed 2,112 Chinese People's Volunteer Army (CPVA, Chinese Army) and Korean People's Army (KPA, North Korean Army) soldiers and to have captured another 169.

In the summer of 1951 Lieutenant Colonel Jay Vanderpool, who also had seen action as a guerrilla in the Philippines during World War II, replaced Colonel McGee. Vanderpool modernized a fleet of junks used by the partisans for hit-and-run operations. He also enhanced their armament to include 106-mm recoilless rifles. In March and June 1951 Vanderpool, assisted by a British officer who had served with the Special Air Service, expanded his partisan operations to include parachute infiltration. Partisan activities continued to grow. One estimate is that altogether during the war UNC partisans killed 9,095 communist soldiers and captured another 385.

In December 1952 these special operations units were reassigned from EUSAK to the Army Forces Far East, which was given sole charge of covert operations. At peak strength, special operations units consisted of seven regiments and a total of more than 22,227 personnel. After the armistice was signed in July 1953, the unit, then commanded by Colonel Glenn Muggleburg, pulled out of North Korea and was assimilated into the Republic of Korea Army (ROKA, South Korean Army).

The North Koreans also conducted special operations. At the beginning of the war, because the North Korean government

Members of a South Korean guerrilla unit pose with Lieutenant Pete Smith of the U.S. Army Rangers (kneeling) on Kye Dong Island in 1955. Both sides carried out guerrilla operations during the Korean War. (Hulton Archive/Getty Images)

expected to win the war quickly through conventional operations, there were only a few guerrilla activities conducted by the KPA. Guerrilla warfare in South Korea eventually intensified, with a force of some 5,000 partisans operating below the 38th Parallel, led by 1,700 communist advisers. At the time there were two main groups of guerrilla units opposed to the ROK. The first of these was actually a part of the KPA and was sanctioned by the government; the other was comprised mainly of bandits with only slight or no affiliation to one government or the other.

In October 1950 the CPVA brought in its own guerrilla units. At Dandong during January 7–22, 1951, UNC forces encountered the heaviest guerrilla fighting in their rear areas of the entire war. Partisans cut lines of communication and created considerable confusion.

KPA chief of staff Nam Il issued a document outlining specific missions for the Korean Workers' Party (KWP) guerrilla forces. These included forward reconnaissance of UNC positions, spreading propaganda, harassing UNC forces, reinstituting the communist way of life in southern villages, leading the people against UNC forces, cooperating with other guerrilla groups in

sabotage operations, and acting as home guards. Among actual KPA units, the most important were the 766th Independent Unit, the 560th Army Unit, and the 945th and 956th Independent Naval Infantry units. These served effectively throughout the war, conducting various covert raids on a multitude of UNC targets. These raids were conducted by rapid naval insertion at targets along the eastern coast of South Korea, such as at Chumunjin, Kangnung, Nakpung-ni, Samchok, and Imwonjin. These special operation units were often attached to regular KPA units and would change into civilian clothes or ROKA uniforms and carry out reconnaissance on UNC positions. Another technique was to blend in with the refugees prior to a large-scale communist attack, then draw out hidden weapons and strike UNC forces from behind.

Eventually the UNC recognized these guerrilla operations as a major threat to security in South Korea and to the war effort. The UNC sought to counter these widespread partisan attacks by building up the National Police force. The UNC also conducted whole operations devoted to destroying the guerrillas, such as Operation RATKILLER between December 1951 and June 1952. The sole purpose of this large operation was to end communist guerrilla activity in South Korea. The results were satisfactory. Reportedly, some 8,000 guerrillas were killed, and many sympathizers were arrested. By the July 1953 armistice, communist guerrilla activity had diminished drastically, to the point where communist guerrillas were merely fighting for survival.

ALEC MCMORRIS

See also

Nam Il; RATKILLER, Operation; United States Army Rangers

References

Bermudez, Joseph S., Jr. *North Korean Special Forces.* 2nd ed. Annapolis, MD: Naval Institute Press, 1998.

Breuer, William B. *Shadow Warriors: The Covert War in Korea.* New York: Wiley, 1996.

Evanhoe, Ed. *Dark Moon: Eighth Army Special Operations in the Korean War.* Annapolis, MD: Naval Institute Press, 1995.

Malcom, Ben S. *White Tigers: My Secret War in North Korea.* Washington, DC: Brassey's, 1996.

Matray, James I., ed. *Historical Dictionary of the Korean War.* Westport, CT: Greenwood, 1991.

Spellman, Francis Joseph
Birth Date: May 4, 1889
Death Date: December 2, 1967

Roman Catholic priest, archbishop of New York, cardinal, apostolic vicar for the U.S. armed forces (1939–1967), and ardent anti-communist. Francis Joseph Spellman was born on May 4, 1889, to a middle-class Irish-American family in Whitman, Massachusetts. Destined early for the priesthood, he was educated at Fordham College in New York, graduating in 1911, and the North American College in Rome. The anti-Americanism of the Vatican during his student years troubled him, and he forcefully challenged the assumption that the United States was godless and materialistic.

After his 1916 ordination, Spellman rose quickly in the church hierarchy. From 1925 to 1932 he served as secretariat of state in the Roman Curia, where he became a close friend of Eugenio Pacelli, who would become Pope Pius XII. With the affluent, generous American Catholic Church behind him, Spellman further consolidated his influence in Rome, and titles and appointments followed quickly. Designated archbishop of New York in 1939, he became the ranking Catholic prelate in the United States. Spellman remained in that post until his death in 1967. In February 1946 he became a cardinal.

Although small of stature, Spellman had enormous energy and ambition. When he was not establishing schools and operating orphanages, he published numerous essays and sermons. In his spare time he wrote a sentimental novel, *The Foundling,* which celebrated Catholic novelist Flannery O'Connor recommended to readers because its proceeds went to charity and it otherwise made "a good doorstop."

Spellman also soon emerged as a political power. His control of the Catholic Legion of Decency meant that he could shut down a Broadway play or launch a boycott against a motion picture that either challenged the Catholic faith or was deemed too sensual. Still, he was friendly with Jewish moguls in Hollywood, who liked to be photographed with him, and he made common cause with former Ambassador Joseph Kennedy in the struggle against communism in the 1950s, even though he refused to endorse Kennedy's son John for the U.S. presidency. His heated conflicts with former First Lady Eleanor Roosevelt and with Bishop Fulton Sheen, the most popular preacher in his church, were much publicized. Spellman's critics could be vituperative, and some accused him of deviousness and even moral turpitude.

Following World War II, Spellman became convinced that international communism posed a mortal threat to his cherished Roman Catholic Church and the United States. He thus supported Senator Joseph R. McCarthy's ill-conceived witch-hunt against communism and approved the regimes of such rightist dictators as Spain's Francisco Franco.

After the Republic of Korea (ROK, South Korea) was invaded by the Democratic People's Republic of Korea (DPRK, North Korea) on June 25, 1950, the cardinal mobilized his archdiocese into action by urging his flock to support U.S. troops in any way possible and to pray for a quick American victory. He was already impressed with South Korean president Syngman Rhee's willingness to appoint Korean Catholics to prominent offices. Accepting the domino theory of communist expansion in Asia, Spellman gave his total support to South Korea.

In 1951, responding to an invitation by General James A. Van Fleet, Spellman agreed to visit the soldiers of the U.S. Eighth Army in Korea (EUSAK), as the drama and spectacle of the military had always attracted him. Dressed in combat fatigues, he was happiest in his role as military vicar, ministering to troops in foreign lands, as close to the front lines as possible. On Christmas day 1951, he said mass in the chapel of the I Corps in Korea, with a second mass at the 1st U.S. Marine Division Headquarters, where 3,000 marines attended and more than 450 received communion.

Returning home, Spellman continued to lobby for the South Korean cause. The following year he repeated his holiday journey to the troops, offering Christmas midnight mass while artillery fire boomed out in the distance. During his visits he said mass in open-air venues, visited hospitals, and conferred with chaplains of all branches of the service. He rode jeeps into rough terrain and even assisted in pushing stranded vehicles out of the mud. Servicemen of all religions welcomed his arrival. The South Korean government eventually honored him with a stone monument bearing a complimentary inscription, which was placed in front of a rehabilitation center for blind Korean veterans that he was instrumental in establishing.

These Christmas visits to foreign-based troops became a tradition, even into the Vietnam era. Nearing the end of his life, when he had to be assisted up the steps of his airplane, the enfeebled cardinal still insisted on making the trips.

With the death of Pope Pius XII in 1958, Spellman's influence in the Vatican waned, and he did not support the reforms of Vatican II. His continued support for American involvement in Vietnam brought him into conflict with Vatican officials, and some historians have accused him of helping to perpetuate the Cold War. By the time of his death at age 78 on December 2, 1967, in New York City, the predominant influence of Irish-Americans in the American Catholic Church appeared to be on the wane.

ALLENE PHY-OLSEN

See also

McCarthy, Joseph Raymond; McCarthyism; Rhee, Syngman; Van Fleet, James Alward

References

Cannon, Robert I. *The Cardinal Spellman Story.* Garden City, NY: Doubleday, 1962.

Cooney, John. *The American Pope: The Life and Times of Francis Cardinal Spellman.* New York: Dell, 1984.

Spender, Sir Percy Claude
Birth Date: October 5, 1897
Death Date: May 3, 1985

Australian lawyer, politician, minister for external affairs from 1949 to 1951, and ambassador to the United States from 1951 to 1958. Born in Sydney on October 5, 1897, Percy Claude Spender was educated at the University of Sydney. Admitted to the New South Wales bar in 1923, Spender enjoyed a successful career as a barrister before running successfully for the House of Representatives as a Conservative member of parliament in 1937.

When the Conservatives regained power in 1949, Prime Minister Robert G. Menzies appointed Spender as minister of external affairs. Unlike the premier, who thought an alliance with the United States both unlikely and unnecessary, Spender firmly believed that Australia's security depended on entering into a regional defense pact with the United States similar to the North Atlantic Treaty Organization (NATO) alliance established by the West European countries in 1949. As did many Australians, he had bitter memories of World War II, when in his opinion Britain virtually abandoned Australia to face Japan alone, and such help as his country received came primarily from the United States.

The Korean War provided Spender with the opportunity to make his hopes reality. By early July 1950, Australia had provided naval support and a fighter squadron to the United Nations Command (UNC) in Korea, but under the anglophile Menzies it followed the British lead and was initially reluctant to commit ground forces. On July 26, when Menzies was incommunicado on the Atlantic, making a sea crossing from Britain to the United States, Spender learned that the British government had finally decided to send troops to Korea. He quickly persuaded Acting Prime Minister A. W. Fadden to follow suit; this trumped the British, as the announcement that Australia would commit one battalion (later increased to two) was made one hour before that of the British.

Despite Menzies's benevolent skepticism, the energetic Spender exploited the prestige that Australia had gained by sending ground forces to Korea to win the backing of U.S. president Harry S. Truman's administration and the U.S. Congress for the ANZUS treaty, the regional mutual security pact between Australia, New Zealand, and the United States, which was his most cherished objective. This pact was negotiated and concluded in 1951, and it was fitting that Spender, its foremost architect (who resigned as minister of external affairs in May 1951 to become Australia's ambassador to the United States), should sign his greatest triumph on his country's behalf in September 1951. The ANZUS treaty, with its implications of Australia's close alliance and cooperation with the United States and opposition to the spread of communism in Asia, formed the fundamental principles of Australian foreign policy for at least the next two or three decades.

Within this framework of his loyal support of the United States, Spender, as with other Australian diplomats, believed himself free to express some reservations on U.S. policies toward Korea. As minister of external affairs and ambassador, he was one of the more forceful and energetic participants in the Korean War briefing meetings. These somewhat sporadically scheduled Washington gatherings of representatives from the principal countries contributing to the United Nations (UN) forces in Korea were intended to promote allied unity and to ensure that all the nations involved were receiving accurate information about the course of the fighting and negotiations.

Spender also used his frequent meetings with U.S. officials to express his views. In late 1950 he made known Australia's concern that the United States might launch direct attacks on the mainland People's Republic of China (PRC) to retaliate for Chinese intervention in Korea, thereby possibly expanding the war. In December 1950 he indicated that Australia shared British prime minister Clement Attlee's alarm over the possibility that the United States might employ atomic weapons in the war.

Although Australia followed the U.S. line on nonrecognition of the PRC, early in 1951 Spender suggested that the United States consider withdrawing its support and recognition from the Guomindang (GMD, Nationalist) regime of Jiang Jieshi (Chiang Kai-shek) on Taiwan (then known as Formosa) as part of the price of a peace settlement with China, a proposal that U.S. officials refused to consider. On several other occasions he urged that the United States adopt a relatively moderate and conciliatory stance toward its communist antagonists, be circumspect in its condemnation of the Chinese, refrain from escalating the war, and make every effort to reach an acceptable negotiated peace settlement. As befitted the increasingly special Australian-American relationship, Spender's advocacy of restraint was generally undertaken in private, and when U.S. officials felt sufficiently strongly on an issue, they could normally count on public Australian support, however reluctantly given.

Spender remained ambassador to the United States until 1958, when he became a member of the International Court of Justice at The Hague, of which he served as president from 1964 to 1967. He died in Sydney on May 3, 1985.

PRISCILLA ROBERTS

See also
ANZUS Treaty; Attlee, Clement Richard; Australia; Jiang Jieshi; Menzies, Robert Gordon

References
Barclay, John St. J. *Friends in High Places: Australian-American Diplomatic Relations.* Melbourne: Oxford University Press, 1985.

Bridge, Carl, ed. *Munich to Vietnam: Australia's Relations with Britain and the United States since the 1930s.* Melbourne: Melbourne University Press, 1991.

Harper, Norman. *A Great and Powerful Friend: A Study of Australian American Relations between 1900 and 1975.* St. Lucia: Queensland University Press, 1987.

McIntyre, W. David. *Background to the Anzus Pact: Policy-Making, Strategy, and Diplomacy, 1945–55.* New York: St. Martin's, 1995.

O'Neill, Robert J. *Australia in the Korea War, 1950–1953.* 2 vols. Canberra: Australian War Memorial/Australian Government Publishing Service, 1981, 1985.

Spender, Sir Percy. *Exercises in Diplomacy: The ANZUS Treaty and the Colombo Plan.* New York: New York University Press, 1969.

———. *Politics and a Man.* Sydney: Collins, 1972.

Spring Offensive, Chinese

See Chinese Offensive, Fifth

St. Laurent, Louis Stephen
Birth Date: February 1, 1882
Death Date: July 25, 1973

Attorney, politician, and prime minister of Canada from 1948 to 1957. Born in Compton, Quebec, on February 1, 1882, Louis Stephen St. Laurent began his career as a lawyer. He moved into political life when he was chosen to be in the cabinet of Prime Minister William Lyon Mackenzie King, first as justice minister, then as secretary of state for external affairs from 1946 to 1948. After King's retirement, St. Laurent became prime minister in 1948. He thus came into the prime ministership with a knowledge of international diplomacy and with some background in the problems of post–World War II Korea.

St. Laurent was initially unconcerned about the news of the invasion by the Democratic People's Republic of Korea (DPRK, North Korea) into the Republic of Korea (ROK, South Korea). He and his cabinet believed that Canada had little or no interests in Asia and that the United States would not respond to the invasion

militarily. Thus, at first, there was no crisis atmosphere in Ottawa over the Korean problem. However, once the United Nations (UN) and the government of the United States decided to react forcefully, it then fell on Canada to follow suit.

St. Laurent's government decided to send three Royal Canadian Navy destroyers to Korean waters and to provide transport planes to ferry supplies from North America to U.S. bases in Japan. Public opinion in Canada, however, found this contribution too timid, and the U.S. government claimed that it was simply a "token" commitment.

Despite this response, St. Laurent was not yet prepared to send ground troops because Canada's already overstretched military could not easily be extended to include a significant role in Asia. It is important to note in this regard that St. Laurent was a bilingual French Canadian from Quebec, a province that traditionally distrusted Canadian involvement in foreign wars and that had opposed the use of conscription for overseas service during both world wars. Consequently, any possible force that might in the future be sent to Korea would have to be made up of volunteers, not draftees.

During much of the war, St. Laurent seemed to be overshadowed by his energetic secretary of state for external affairs, Lester Pearson. But St. Laurent and Pearson were in agreement about the difficulties that Canada faced over Korea. Both saw the "police action" as an extension of the duties of being a member of the UN and not as being part of a U.S. anticommunist crusade. Because of this, they wanted the UN to control the strategy and goals of the intervention and to limit as much as possible the enormous U.S. influence over both. The Canadian government was particularly uneasy about the possibility of the conflict spreading to other parts of Asia, or of doing anything that might provoke the People's Republic of China (PRC) or the Soviet Union. As a result, St. Laurent was determined that any Canadian contribution would be made solely in response to UN decisions, and while United Nations Command (UNC) forces would, and should, be led by the United States, they had to remain a model of collective security.

Finally, after growing domestic and foreign pressure, the Canadian government decided on July 17, 1950, to send ground troops to Korea. This decision was not announced until August 7, when St. Laurent went on national radio to explain his government's action. He claimed that while Canada's primary interest was in the defense of Western Europe through the North Atlantic Treaty Organization (NATO) alliance, there was a need for cooperation with the UN in Korea.

Because of the difficulty faced by the Canadian military in dealing with both regions, a special infantry brigade was recruited for Korea. St. Laurent called for volunteers, especially World War II veterans, to join the unit. The resulting response at recruiting stations across Canada, including Quebec, was overwhelmingly positive. Because of this, a troop commitment to Korea was made without lessening Canada's role in NATO or resorting to conscription.

The determination to send troops to Korea and the public announcement of that decision proved to be St. Laurent's most important achievements in the war. He was also involved, with Pearson, in negotiating resolutions and brokering compromises in the UN. In 1951, in particular, he worked behind the scenes in attempting to arrive at a cease-fire agreement with Indian prime minister Jawaharlal Nehru, an action that U.S. officials saw as objectionable both in method and outcome.

St. Laurent and his Liberal government were reelected in 1953 but defeated in 1957. He left public life at that point and returned to practicing law. He died in Quebec City on July 25, 1973.

ERIC JARVIS

See also

Canada; Cease-fire Negotiations; Nehru, Jawaharlal; Pearson, Lester Bowles; Wrong, Humphrey Hume

References

Granatstein, J. L., and Norman Hiller. *For Better or for Worse, Canada and the United States to the 1990s.* Toronto: Copp Clark Pitman, 1991.

Melady, John. *Korea: Canada's Forgotten War.* Toronto: Macmillan, 1983.

Stairs, Denis. *The Diplomacy of Constraint: Canada, the Korean War, and the United States.* Toronto: University of Toronto Press, 1974.

Stueck, William W., Jr., ed. *Korean War in World History.* Lexington: University Press of Kentucky, 2004.

———. *Rethinking the Korean War: A New Diplomatic and Strategic History.* Princeton, NJ: Princeton University Press, 2004.

Joseph Stalin held absolute power in the Soviet Union from the late 1920s until his death in 1953. One of history's more brutal dictators, tens of millions of Soviet citizens died as a consequence of his policies. (Library of Congress)

Stalin, Joseph
Birth Date: December 21, 1879
Death Date: March 5, 1953

Leader of the Soviet Union from the late 1920s until 1953. Joseph Stalin was born Iosif Vissarionovich Dzhugashvili in Gori, Georgia, on December 21, 1879. On his mother's insistence he entered a seminary in Tiflis in 1894. Already on the road to becoming a revolutionary, he was expelled in 1899. In 1901 he joined the Social Democratic Party in Tiflis. Arrested by the czarist police the next year, Stalin was exiled to eastern Siberia. He escaped and returned to Tiflis in 1904, where he became a Bolshevik and took the alias "Koba." Stalin helped to raise money for the Bolshevik Party by organizing bank robberies in Georgia. He spent a few years with the Baku Bolshevik Committee and then went to St. Petersburg, where he adopted the name "Stalin" ("Man of Steel"). In 1913 Stalin was arrested for a fourth time and exiled to western Siberia. There he remained until the Russian Revolution of March 1917, when he returned to St. Petersburg and became a leading figure in the Bolshevik coup d'état of November 1917.

As a key figure in the new government and holding the post of commissar for nationalities, Stalin took an active role in the civil war of 1917–1923, clashing on occasion with political rival and Commissar for War Leon Trotsky. Stalin served as secretary-general of the Communist Party between 1922 and 1953 and as Soviet premier from 1941 to 1953.

After the 1924 death of Vladimir Lenin, who was considered the father of the 1917 revolution, Trotsky and Stalin vied for power. Victorious over Trotsky by the end of the 1920s, Stalin carried out massive industrialization efforts, the forced collectivization of agriculture, and extensive purges of the party and military. His harsh policies directly resulted in the deaths of millions of Soviet citizens. Stalin anticipated a war with Nazi Germany at some point, but he sought to buy time by signing the German Soviet Non-Aggression Pact of August 23, 1939, which, in its secret provisions, divided up Eastern Europe between the Soviet Union and Germany and provided substantial economic advantages to Germany.

Stunned by the June 1941 German invasion of the Soviet Union, Stalin literally had to be forced back to leadership, but he learned to be a competent war leader and directed his country to victory in World War II, which ended in 1945. His wartime policies included an uneasy alliance with Great Britain and the United States.

At the 1943 Teheran Conference, Stalin agreed with the principle adopted at the earlier Cairo Conference, which he had not attended, that an appropriate course for Korea would be independence following a period of apprenticeship. According to U.S. president Harry S. Truman, in private talks at the 1945 Yalta Conference Stalin not only agreed with President Franklin

D. Roosevelt's plan that the Soviet Union, the United States, and China form a three-power trusteeship over Korea, but he even suggested adding Great Britain. The plan was never carried out, however.

Despite a nonaggression pact between the Soviet Union and Japan, the Soviet Union entered the war in the Far East on August 9, 1945. Stalin thus honored his pledge made at the Yalta Conference in February 1945 to go to war against Japan "two or three months" after the defeat of Germany. With Japan's military collapse imminent, the United States suggested the 38th Parallel as a practical demarcation line for the surrender of Japanese forces in Korea, and Stalin readily agreed. President Harry S. Truman and other U.S. leaders never intended this as a permanent line of division, however.

By 1948 the Soviets ensured the creation of a communist state in northern Korea under the leadership of Kim Il Sung, who had fought with the Red Army as a junior officer in World War II. The Soviet Union then provided military advisers and arms to the resultant Democratic People's Republic of Korea (DPRK, North Korea), even after the Soviet military withdrawal in December 1948. The United States also armed the Republic of Korea (ROK, South Korea) but, unlike the Soviets, never provided offensive or heavy weapons to South Korea. Less than a year later, thanks in part to Soviet assistance, Mao Zedong's Communists won control of China and established there the People's Republic of China (PRC).

Stalin approved Kim's plan to reunite Korea by force. Final approval came in March–April 1950, when Kim traveled to Moscow with a detailed plan of attack. Stalin was doubtless reassured by Washington's apparent exclusion of Korea from its defensive perimeter and by Kim's claim that the conquest would be quick and carried out before the United States could bring significant military resources to bear, should it indeed decide to intervene. Stalin ordered that North Korean weapons and equipment needs be met, and Soviet military advisers assisted in the drafting of war plans. At Stalin's insistence, Kim also visited with Mao and secured his approval and support as well. Talks between Beijing and Pyongyang led to the release of thousands of Korean troops then serving in the army of the PRC. They were sent to the DPRK and became the backbone of new divisions in the Korean People's Army (KPA, North Korean Army), which was formed for the invasion of South Korea.

Despite's Kim's optimism about a war of short duration before the United States would be able to rescue South Korea, Stalin ordered all Soviet military advisers serving with the KPA to withdraw. After the September 15, 1950, Inchon Landing completely reversed the early KPA successes, on October 1 Stalin, in response to a plea from Kim Il Sung, urged Mao to enter the war and rescue North Korea. In an October 5 telegram to Mao, Stalin stated that the United States should not be feared because together the Soviet Union and China were stronger than the United States and Great Britain. He wrote, "If war is inevitable, let it be waged now, and not in a few years when Japanese imperialism will be restored as a U.S.

ally and when the U.S. and Japan will have a ready-made bridgehead on the continent in the form of all Korea run by Syngman Rhee." Chinese foreign minister Zhou Enlai had already flown to meet with Stalin on October 11 at Sochi on the Black Sea, where he secured Soviet support in the form of sufficient tanks and artillery to equip 10 Chinese divisions. But a few hours after the initial decision, Stalin must have had second thoughts, because Zhou was then informed that the Soviet Union would loan the promised munitions and supplies and that it would be two and a half months before the Soviet Air Force could assist the Chinese.

The Kremlin also opposed a large-scale Chinese intervention because Soviet leaders feared that it might provoke a general war, which Stalin sought to avoid. This caused Mao to put Chinese entry into the war on hold until he could secure unanimous support from the Chinese politburo. This decision, made without assurances of Soviet air cover, impressed Stalin, who then promised a loan of 5.6 billion rubles to cover equipping 100 Chinese divisions. Stalin also approved turning over aircraft from two Soviet air divisions stationed in Shenyang and Shanghai to the Chinese and sent 13 air divisions to protect China, including 9 fighter divisions, 3 attack aircraft divisions, and a bomber division. This was with the proviso that the divisions would assist in China's air defense and not be used over Korea.

The Korean War gave Stalin a confidence in Mao that he had not previously held, thus placing Sino-Soviet relations on a more solid footing. This did not mean that the communist allies were always in agreement. Mao was upset at the lack of Soviet air support for Chinese ground units in combat in Korea. Also, after the Chinese military offensive in Korea had been halted and a United Nations (UN) counteroffensive had retaken Seoul, Stalin offered a proposal for a cease-fire and mutual withdrawal from the 38th Parallel.

Although Mao urged Soviet involvement in the cease-fire negotiations, Stalin insisted that the Chinese handle the particulars. Soviet documents indicate that, despite the start of negotiations, Stalin saw advantages in prolonging the war and urged Mao to take a hard line. Soviet propaganda continued to charge the United States as an aggressor looking for a future war. U.S. ambassador to Moscow Admiral Alan G. Kirk failed over a two-year period to secure a meeting with Stalin, although he did manage to meet with Deputy Foreign Minister Andrei Gromyko, who claimed ignorance of Chinese attitudes toward cease-fire talks. Before his departure from the Soviet Union, Kirk met with Foreign Minister Viacheslav Molotov, who indicated that the Soviets would not pressure communist negotiators to change their stance at the talks. Stalin was by then in poor health, and no compromise was found until after his death.

Stalin, easily one of the most horrific and fascinating individuals in world history, died in Moscow on March 5, 1953. His death clearly helped break the stalemate in the Korean armistice talks, and less than five months later a cease-fire was signed.

CLAUDE R. SASSO

See also

Gromyko, Andrei; Kim Il Sung; Kirk, Alan Goodrich; Malik, Jacob; Mao Zedong; Molotov, Viacheslav Mikhailovich; Rhee, Syngman; Soviet Air War in Korea; Truman, Harry S.; Zhou Enlai

References

Chen Jian. *Mao's China and the Cold War.* Chapel Hill: University of North Carolina Press, 2000.

Goncharov, Sergei N., John W. Lewis, and Xue Litai. *Uncertain Partners: Stalin, Mao, and the Korean War.* Stanford, CA: Stanford University Press, 1993.

Khrushchev, Nikita. *Khrushchev Remembers: With an Introduction, Commentary and Notes by Edward Crankshaw.* Boston: Little, Brown, 1970.

Stueck, William W., Jr., ed. *Korean War in World History.* Lexington: University Press of Kentucky, 2004.

———. *Rethinking the Korean War: A New Diplomatic and Strategic History.* Princeton, NJ: Princeton University Press, 2004.

Volkogonov, Dmitri. *Stalin: Triumph and Tragedy.* New York: Grove Weidenfeld, 1988.

Steel Plants, Truman's Seizure of
Event Date: April 8, 1952

Controversial action taken by President Harry S. Truman during the Korean War whereby major U.S. steel mills were seized to avert a work stoppage that might have undermined the U.S. war effort. In November 1951 a labor union representing steelworkers called for a pay increase for its members. The workers had received no increase since 1950, despite rising inflation and record steel production caused by the war, which greatly increased the profits of the companies. The union declared that, barring a wage agreement, its members would strike on December 31, 1951. Truman realized the impact that a strike would have on war production, and he tried to avert a production stoppage. He thus referred the question to the Wage Stabilization Board (WSB), and union workers decided to stay on the job until April 8, 1952, pending an agreement.

Negotiations failed when the steel companies refused the WSB's proposed pay increase unless they were allowed to raise the price of steel. On March 20, 1952, the WSB suggested an increase in wages, more fringe benefits, and a guaranteed union shop for steelworkers. The WSB's proposal would have meant an increase of about 26 cents per hour for the average steel employee. The steel companies immediately balked, alleging that they would have to raise the price of steel by $12 per ton.

The steel industry's position confronted Truman with a difficult problem. He viewed the demands of the companies as simple profiteering and refused to allow an increase in the cost of steel, fearing that a price hike would stoke inflationary pressures and add to the already immense cost of rearmament. An unintended consequence of the steel standoff was a rift between Truman and his chief mobilizer, Charles E. Wilson, director of the Office of Defense Mobilization (ODM). Wilson refused to support the WSB recommendations, and when Truman appeared to contradict earlier pledges he had made to Wilson to resolve the donnybrook, Wilson promptly resigned. Truman replaced him with John R. Steelman.

Steelman, however, was unable to broker an agreement, and the steel companies refused a compromise offer made in the first week of April. Truman believed that this decision left only one course of action to safeguard the flow of supplies to Korea and sustain the rearmament of the United States and Western Europe. On April 8, 1952, the president issued Executive Order 10340, which authorized the U.S. secretary of commerce to take control of 87 major steel factories to avert a strike.

This action did not go unchallenged by members of Congress or the public. The Justice Department was the first to act, arguing in court that Truman had no statutory support for his action. This stance baffled Truman, because he believed that he had acted well within his authority, following his declaration of a national emergency in December 1950 and the commitment of U.S. troops to Korea. Steel was absolutely indispensable to the war effort. Truman also based his order on his authority as president and commander in chief of the U.S. armed forces, the enabling war powers enumerated in the Defense Production Act of 1950, and the laws and authority of the U.S. Constitution. He saw the seizure of the mills as a last resort, forced on him by the refusal of the companies to negotiate in good faith.

The steel companies then decided to sue the federal government for the return of their property. Their suit was filed in the federal district court of Judge David A. Pine. There, Truman administration officials sought in vain to defend their position. Assistant Attorney General Homer Baldridge asserted to Judge Pine that courts could not restrict presidential power in the event of a national emergency. Not only was the administration's case weak, but the public also reacted negatively to the seizure of the steel mills. In a news conference on April 17, reporters challenged Truman's authority on the basis that a president's power cannot be absolute even in time of crisis.

Truman certainly recognized the unpopularity of his decision, and after the news conference he did his best to defuse the situation. A few days later, the president sent a letter to the Senate in which he allowed Congress to reverse his action. This letter and repeated public attempts to defend the seizures could not stop the suit in district court, however. On April 29 Judge Pine wrote a scathing opinion of the president's actions. He rejected the administration's assertion of presidential power on grounds that a strike, although it might harm the United States, was less damaging than unrestricted executive power. Pine in essence ruled Truman's seizure as unconstitutional.

The final blow to Truman's action came in a now-famous Supreme Court decision of June 2, 1952 (*Youngstown Sheet and Tube Company v. Sawyer*), when in a vote of 6–3 the high court found Truman's action unconstitutional. This was a major defeat for Truman, but more important was the effect of the vote on the country's war effort. After the Supreme Court verdict, the steel strike began, affecting some 600,000 workers and lasting for seven weeks.

On July 24 Truman intervened to end the strike, ordering a 21.5 cent-per-hour wage increase and enhanced benefits for steel workers while authorizing a $5.20 per ton increase in steel prices. The strike was over. Ironically, the price increase Truman was compelled to permit was more than what he had agreed to some months before.

The steel seizure crisis badly weakened the regime of economic controls, resulted in a loss of face for the WSB, and compelled the nation's chief mobilization official to resign. It also saw the loss of 20 million tons of steel production and cut projected civilian as well as military output substantially. The production of 520,000 automobiles (about 12 percent of annual production) was curtailed, and steel shortages resulted in the loss of $600 million–$700 million in wages.

Eric W. Osborne

See also

Defense Production Act; Mobilization; Office of Defense Mobilization; Truman, Harry S.; Truman's Domestic Agenda and the Korean War; Wage Stabilization Board; Wilson, Charles Edward

References

Fisher, Louis. *Presidential War Power.* Lawrence: University Press of Kansas, 1995.

Marcus, Maeva. *Truman and the Steel Seizure Case: The Limits of Presidential Power.* New York: Columbia University Press, 1977.

McCullough, David. *Truman.* New York: Simon and Schuster, 1992.

Pierpaoli, Paul G., Jr. *Truman and Korea: The Political Culture of the Early Cold War.* Columbia: University of Missouri Press, 1999.

Stevenson, Adlai Ewing
Birth Date: February 5, 1900
Death Date: July 14, 1965

Attorney, diplomat, governor of Illinois, and U.S. Democratic presidential candidate in 1952 and 1956. Born in Los Angeles, California, on February 5, 1900, Adlai Ewing Stevenson came from a prominent Illinois political family. After attending local Illinois schools and the elite Choate School, he spent four years at Princeton University, after which he earned a law degree, first attending Harvard Law School and then graduating from Northwestern University Law School. Entering the leading Chicago law firm of Cutting, Moore and Sidley, Stevenson rapidly won social prominence and a wide circle of intellectual friends, and he served in many public service organizations. The most notable of these organizations was the Chicago Council on Foreign Relations, of which he was elected president in 1935 and to which he devoted much of his energy, winning a reputation as a stellar public speaker.

Governor Adlai Stevenson of Illinois was the Democratic Party's nominee in the presidential elections of 1952 and 1956. Stevenson served as ambassador to the United Nations (UN) during the John F. Kennedy administration. (Library of Congress)

A firm supporter of U.S. intervention in World War II, Stevenson headed the Chicago chapter of the Committee to Defend America by Aiding the Allies in 1940. In 1941 Stevenson joined Frank Knox, a Chicago newspaper publisher and the new secretary of the navy, as his administrative assistant and speechwriter. Stevenson remained in the Navy Department until Knox's death in 1944. Shortly afterward, he joined the State Department as a special assistant to the secretary of state. He remained there until 1947, serving on the U.S. team at the 1945 San Francisco Conference that created the United Nations (UN) and on several U.S. delegations at successive UN General Assemblies.

Returning to Illinois, Stevenson was elected governor in 1948 on the Democratic ticket. As governor, he launched an activist and progressive social reform program and attempted to eradicate corruption in state government. An outspoken opponent of the rising force of McCarthyism in the early 1950s, Stevenson quickly won national recognition as a rising political star of remarkable eloquence. The Democratic National Convention in 1952 saw an open contest, as incumbent president Harry S. Truman, damaged by McCarthyism and the Korean War, had chosen not to run again. Drafted on the third ballot, Stevenson faced an uphill battle against Dwight D. Eisenhower, the popular Republican candidate and war hero.

Little divided the two presidential candidates on foreign policy; both were staunch Cold War warriors who implicitly endorsed the Truman administration's containment policy. Even so, Eisenhower acquiesced in the bitter attacks of his running mate, Senator Richard M. Nixon, and Senator Joseph R. McCarthy on Stevenson and the Democrats, accusations that followed the K1C2 strategy of focusing on the issues of Korea, communism, and corruption in government.

Stevenson, who had supported the U.S. commitment to the Republic of Korea (ROK, South Korea), attempted to distance himself from the Truman administration and especially from its successive petty corruption scandals. He established his campaign headquarters in Springfield, Illinois, and rarely asked the president to appear on his behalf. Stevenson delicately suggested that, although he supported the war, had he been president he would have avoided some of Truman's mistakes, trying to tread the fine line between disloyalty on the one hand and implication of the administration's problems on the other. He suggested that the United States should have given stronger guarantees of support to South Korea and should have been more cautious in crossing the 38th Parallel.

In practice, Stevenson's position on Korea differed little from that of Eisenhower, and he offered no new initiatives, but rather an indefinite continuation of the existing stalemate. He reversed Eisenhower's tactic of blaming the war's outbreak on Democratic incompetence, suggesting instead that responsibility lay with the Republicans for their failure to give sufficient support to the Truman administration's foreign policies. In October 1952, however, Eisenhower seized the initiative from Stevenson by promising to visit Korea in person if elected. Stevenson mocked this pledge but failed to offer any better alternative; ironically enough, he had already privately decided to make such a visit were he elected. While Eisenhower was purposely vague and did not reveal what might come of his trip to Korea, many Americans believed that he would end the war honorably and quickly.

Defeated in the November 1952 election, Stevenson embarked in 1953 on a world tour lasting several months. During the tour he visited Korea and heard the U.S. military's view that full victory would be impossible without major additional U.S. troop and budgetary commitments. In articles for *Life* magazine, he expressed admiration for many of the Taiwan Guomindang (GMD, Nationalist) government's social policies but admitted its police-state methods were unpopular and its army far weaker than the GMD portrayed; in Indochina he enunciated one of the earliest versions of the domino theory. Until his death, Stevenson never doubted that the U.S. commitment to Korea, however expensive and frustrating, was justified as part of his country's overall Cold War policy.

In 1956 Stevenson again ran unsuccessfully as the Democratic Party candidate for the presidency, this time against the incumbent Eisenhower. In 1961 Stevenson hoped that the new Democratic president, John F. Kennedy, would name him secretary of state, but both John and Robert Kennedy regarded Stevenson as overly liberal, weak, and indecisive, so they treated him rather contemptuously. For fear of provoking congressional conservatives and the China lobby, Stevenson was forbidden to express his personal preference for U.S. recognition of the communist People's Republic of China (PRC). Left ignorant of the planning for the Bay of Pigs invasion of Cuba in April 1961, Stevenson at first erroneously informed the UN that his country had played no part in it.

Stevenson's finest hour came during the Cuban Missile Crisis, when he aggressively demanded that the Soviet UN representative confirm whether or not his country had deployed nuclear missiles in Cuba. Stevenson advised the president to take a relatively moderate line during the crisis. Stevenson died in London on July 14, 1965, of a sudden heart attack.

PRISCILLA ROBERTS

See also

Containment; Eisenhower, Dwight David; K1C2; McCarthy, Joseph Raymond; McCarthyism; Nixon, Richard Milhous; Truman, Harry S.

References

Broadwater, Jeff. *Adlai Stevenson and American Politics: The Odyssey of a Cold War Liberal.* New York: Twayne, 1994.
Johnson, Walter, ed. *The Papers of Adlai E. Stevenson.* 8 vols. Boston: Little, Brown, 1972–1979.
Martin, John Bartlow. *Adlai Stevenson and the World: The Life of Adlai E. Stevenson.* Garden City, NY: Doubleday, 1977.
McKeever, Porter. *Adlai Stevenson: His Life and Legacy.* New York: William Morrow, 1989.
Reichard, Gary W. *Politics as Usual: The Age of Truman and Eisenhower.* Arlington Heights, IL: Harlan Davidson, 1988.

Stockholm Peace Appeal
Event Date: March 1950

Peace initiative and propaganda ploy, established initially as a world peace petition in March 1950 by the Soviet-sponsored World Council for Peace (WCP), that called for universal and unconditional abolition of all nuclear weapons. The Stockholm Peace Appeal also advocated the withdrawal of U.S. and United Nations Command (UNC) troops from Korea after the outbreak of war there in June 1950.

In 1947 Moscow organized the Communist Information Agency (Cominform) to consolidate its control over the international communist movement. Its predecessor agency, the Communist International (Comintern), had been disbanded to appease the Soviets' Western allies during World War II. In 1949 the Cominform created the WCP, a classic communist front-organization. Its main purpose was to blur the lines of command leading to the Kremlin, as some international left-wing forces were rightfully skeptical of Moscow's motives.

The WCP's first international conference was held in Paris in the spring of 1949, and the following year it was reported to have more than 600 million individual members in 140 countries. This figure should be taken with a grain of salt, not the least because most members were citizens of dictatorships who did not enjoy freedom of organization. It should also be noted that the Democratic People's Republic of Korea (DPRK, North Korea) accounted for 31 million members—a figure far above that country's total population. The Soviet Union sought to undermine the American effort to rearm Western Europe by employing the WCP and peace activists within the European labor movement to collect signatures in support of a total ban on nuclear weapons.

The next WCP congress was held in Stockholm, Sweden, at the Hotel Continental on March 16–19, 1950. Chairing the convention was the Swedish branch of the WCP (Svenska Fredskommitén), its leaders being Per-Olov Zennström, John Takman, and Eva Palmaer-Johansson, who also happened to be leaders in the Swedish Communist Party. They maintained strict censorship over the content of speeches made at the congress. Police surveillance later revealed the true extent of communist control over the WCP.

During the 1950 meeting, the congress created a petition, which became known as the Stockholm Peace Appeal/Petition. It called for a ban on all atomic weapons and other weapons of mass destruction. Allegedly more than 500 million people around the world signed the appeal, including 2 million in the United States through a campaign directed by W. E. B. DuBois. As with the WCP membership, figures revealing the total number of signatures on the appeal remain questionable. In Hungary, many of those who signed were minors, and in Bulgaria the name count exceeded the total population number of that country.

On June 25, 1950, North Korea, a Soviet client state, invaded the Republic of Korea (ROK, South Korea), an American client state. A Security Council Resolution was quickly passed requesting that United Nations (UN) member states provide the ROK with assistance in repulsing the attack. The Soviet Union was boycotting the Security Council at the time of the resolution over the council's failure to seat the People's Republic of China (PRC) and would presumably have otherwise used its right to veto the resolution and prevent the formation of a UN military command. A U.S.-led force, operating under the UN flag and known as the UNC, was soon fighting to stop North Korea's aggression.

By the end of July 1950, the Soviets had geared up the WCP to campaign against the U.S.-led military effort, and the March 1950 petition was amended to include anti–Korean War appeals. The appeal was bolstered by Soviet radio propaganda in Europe, which sought to undermine public confidence in the war effort in Korea by questioning the Americans' ability to combine the campaign in Korea with rearmament and a credible defense of Western Europe.

To counter the WCP and its propaganda, which labeled liberal democracy as an enemy of the arts, the U.S. Central Intelligence Agency (CIA) had sponsored the founding of the Congress for Cultural Freedom in 1949. Among its members were writer Tennessee Williams, British historian Hugh Trevor-Roper, and British philosopher Bertrand Russell. Congress waged its own propaganda battle during the Korean War.

FRODE LINDGJERDET

See also

Central Intelligence Agency; Soviet Union; United Nations Command

References

Lieberman, Robbie. *Strangest Dream: Communism, Anti-Communism, and the U.S. Peace Movement, 1945–1963.* Syracuse, NY: Syracuse University Press, 2000.

Wittner, Lawrence S. *One World or None: A History of the World Nuclear Disarmament Movement through 1953.* Stanford, CA: Stanford University Press, 1993.

STRANGLE, **Operation**
Start Date: May 1951
End Date: December 1951

United Nations Command (UNC) bombing campaign. In late May 1951, as UNC forces pushed communist troops toward the 38th Parallel, the U.S. Fifth Air Force was given responsibility for the aerial interdiction of the communists' seven main transport and communication highways leading to the front. Named for a 1944 Allied aerial interdiction campaign conducted in Italy during World War II, Operation STRANGLE unfolded as a joint campaign in which the northern region of the Republic of Korea (ROK, South Korea) was divided into three target areas to be attacked by air force fighter-bombers, Task Force 77 navy fighters, and 1st Marine Wing aircraft. Targets were mostly vehicular roads along with bridges, tunnels, and some rail lines.

Operations began on May 31, when North American F-51 Mustangs "post-holed" main roads with 500-pound bombs where repairs and bypasses were most difficult to effect. Martin B-26 Maurauders then dropped inert M-83 cluster bombs, which were detonated by communist traffic. Boeing B-29 Superfortresses attacked bridges.

As June unfolded and communist forces retreated, allied air raids turned toward airfields, rail-marshaling yards, and logistics supply centers. At first, Operation STRANGLE was very successful, but as UNC forces slowed their offensive in mid-June, communist forces were able to resupply and regroup their frontline troops more easily, and Operation STRANGLE bore diminishing results.

Much as was the case 20 years later during COMMANDO HUNT operations in Vietnam, a key to the communists' ability to thwart STRANGLE was the enormous number of labor troops deployed to quickly repair or bypass bomb damage. Repair materials such as rocks, timber, and churned-up soil were always in ready supply.

Also, as would be repeated in Vietnam, the difficulty in destroying trucks, the ease of repairing vehicles, and the vast number of new trucks supplied to the Korean People's Army (KPA, North Korean Army) by the Soviet Union made interdiction almost

Despite heavy snow, two U.S. Air Force 3rd Bomb Wing ground crew members work on a Douglas B-26 Night Intruder. These light bombers struck communist supply lines every night in all kinds of weather during Operation STRANGLE in January 1952. (National Archives)

impossible. UNC air forces, with limited resources because of Cold War commitments in Europe and elsewhere, could not long afford to maintain the initial pace of the campaign.

By July Far East Air Force (FEAF) officials reported that Operation STRANGLE was not achieving the desired results. Despite this negative report, the campaign continued, turning to such new targets as North Korean small-arms factories and Soviet and Chinese arms supplies moving by rail.

Rail traffic and tracks seemed an inviting target, but both proved to be difficult to destroy. Even when stretches of track or rail bridges were destroyed, communist forces would simply transfer supplies from one train on one side to another on the other side. Here again, large labor crews usually repaired damage very quickly. Worst of all, the communists placed very effective antiaircraft artillery (AAA) batteries or MiG interceptor fields around regularly attacked targets, dramatically elevating the price for destroying the target.

By the end of July U.S. Air Force (USAF) planners estimated that it would take six to eight months of a concentrated air campaign to interdict enemy rail or road supply efforts. Air force leaders believed that their resources allowed for no more than 90 days.

Plans for a new operation culminated on August 18, when a six-month operation, also named STRANGLE, began. To this day, there is controversy over whether this operation was STRANGLE II or STRANGLE I, Phase II. According to FEAF officials, STRANGLE II, which lasted until December 23, was designed to "cripple the communist logistics system to the extent that rapid redeployment of their forces and supplies in support of a sustained offensive is impossible."

The original operation focused on truck traffic, while the second concentrated on destroying 15- to 30-mile sections of rail track and/or rail bridges. STRANGLE II employed "group gaggles" of up to 64 fighter-bombers carrying 500-pound and 1,000-pound bombs to drop on the 56-inch-wide tracks. These raids were supported by B-29 missions against rail bridges and airfields. Only a direct hit did any real damage, and only 25 percent of bombs hit their targets. Considering that similar attacks in World War II had only a 12.9 percent success rate, the FEAF did well.

By November rail lines were being destroyed faster than the communists could repair them. As one official declared, "the United Nations' victory in the air battle against North Korea's railroads seemed imminent." An increase in MiG attacks and the effectiveness of new AAA batteries raised the price of the campaign to alarming levels. Most missions had to be reduced and replanned, and they did not reach initial levels again until late November 1951. By that time massive communist repair efforts had reversed the tide of battle. In December Fifth Air Force reports concluded that "Red railway repairmen and bridge builders 'have broken our railroad blockade . . . and won the use of all key rail arteries.'"

As with most Korean air campaigns, STRANGLE I and II had both positive and negative results. On a positive note, senior KPA prisoners captured later confirmed that their leaders had called off a major August 1951 offensive because of the destruction of 40,000 trucks. However, never in six months did the FEAF effectively stop communist resupply of their combat forces nor "isolate the battlefield."

As was the case later with aerial interdiction efforts in Vietnam, air power in Korea, requiring the efforts of both air and ground forces, hobbled the communists but did not destroy their capacity to wage war.

WILLIAM HEAD

See also
Airborne Operations; Airpower in the Korean War; Artillery, Antiaircraft; Logistics in the Korean War

References
Crane, Conrad C. *American Air Power Strategy in Korea, 1950–1953.* Lawrence: University Press of Kansas, 1999.
Futrell, Robert F. *The United States Air Force in Korea, 1950–1953.* Rev. ed. Washington, DC: Office of the Chief of Air Force History, 1983.
Mark, Eduard. *Aerial Interdiction: Air Power and the Land Battle in Three Wars.* Washington, DC: Center for Air Force History, 1994.
Thompson, Wayne. "The Air War over Korea." In *Winged Shield, Wing Sword: A History of the United States Air Force,* edited by Bernard C. Nalty, 3–52. Washington, DC: U.S. Air Force History and Museum Program, 1997.

Strategic and Tactical Airlift in the Korean War

Air transport, including the use of helicopters for the movement of personnel and supplies, came into its own during the Korean

War. The use of modern transport aircraft gave United Nations Command (UNC) forces in Korea an important advantage over their Korean People's Army (KPA, North Korean Army) and Chinese People's Volunteer Army (CPVA, Chinese Army) opponents, who did not enjoy the speed and flexibility in logistical movements that air transport afforded. The distance from the United States to the Far East and the rugged terrain of Korea itself made the use of transport aircraft and helicopters for troop movements and the delivery of high-priority cargo extremely important, although ocean transport continued to be the principal means of trans-oceanic troop and cargo movements. About 1 percent of all cargo moved from the United States to Korea during the Korean War was moved by air, as was about 5 percent of all cargo moved from Japan to Korea. Most air shipments were restricted to such critical items as whole blood, blood plasma, rockets, radio batteries, and replacement parts.

Strategic Airlift

Strategic (intercontinental) airlift was the responsibility of the Military Air Transport Service (MATS) of the U.S. Air Force (USAF). Established in 1947, MATS was organized into three main divisions: Continental, Atlantic, and Pacific. In June 1950 the MATS Pacific Division was assigned fewer than 60 transport aircraft. On the outbreak of the Korean War, the Pacific Division was immediately reinforced with 40 aircraft from the Atlantic and Continental divisions and two troop carrier groups with 75 Douglas C-54 Skymasters, the workhorse transport of the Korean War era. Canada also contributed Royal Canadian Air Force No. 426 Transport Squadron with 6 North Star aircraft, and Belgium added 2 C-54s.

By mid-August 1950 the MATS Pacific Division had more than 250 aircraft flying on three regular trans-Pacific routes, and deliveries to the Far East Command (FEC) averaged 106 tons per day. The Great Circle route from McChord Air Force Base (AFB), Washington, to Tokyo via Alaska was 5,688 miles long and took 30 hours. The mid-Pacific route from Fairfield-Suisun (Travis) AFB, California, to Tokyo via Hawaii was 6,718 miles long and took 34 hours. The other Pacific route from Travis AFB to Japan via Hawaii, Johnson Island, Kwajalein, and Guam was more than 8,000 miles long and took 40 hours.

On the long Pacific flights, the C-54 could carry about five tons. At peak utilization there were 200 such aircraft available, each of which could make three round trips per month from the West Coast to Japan. One trans-Pacific round trip by a C-54 cost about $25,000, or $5,000 per ton (or a mere $2,500 per ton if the aircraft were loaded both ways). For every ton moved by MATS over the trans-Pacific routes, the U.S. Navy moved 270 tons by sea at a cost of only about $38 per ton. Commercial charter flights were also used.

In May 1950 Japan received only 70 tons of cargo by air per month; by the end of August 1950 it was receiving more than 100 tons per day. In 1951 some 23,000 tons of cargo and 68,000 passengers were flown to the Far East. In 1952 trans-Pacific airlift

cargo tonnage increased to 30,000 tons and 175,000 passengers, plus about 54,000 medical evacuation patients. Aeromedical evacuation was an important innovation that significantly improved the survival rate of casualties and decreased the time they had to wait before reaching definitive treatment. In all, 443,196 casualties were evacuated by air from Korea to the United States during the Korean War.

Tactical Airlift

Tactical (intratheater) airlifts were the responsibility of the air force component of the U.S. FEC, Far East Air Force (FEAF), and included flights from Japan to Korea as well as within Korea itself. When the war began, FEAF lacked sufficient intratheater airlift to meet the quickly expanding requirements. On September 10, 1950, all FEAF transport assets were consolidated under the provisional Combat Cargo Command. Commanded by Major General William H. Tunner, who had directed the airlift over "the Hump" in the China-Burma-India theater during World War II, as well as the Berlin Airlift in 1948–1949, the Combat Cargo Command quickly expanded, and by mid-December 1950 it had some 260 aircraft available. On January 25, 1951, the provisional Combat Cargo Command was disestablished and replaced by the 315th Air Division (Combat Cargo). Brigadier General John P. Henebry replaced General Tunner as commander of the 315th Air Division on February 8, 1951.

Units assigned to the Combat Cargo Command/315th Air Division included the 374th Troop Carrier Wing (two squadrons of C-54s, later Douglas C-124 Globemaster IIs); the 21st Troop Carrier Squadron with Douglas C-47 Skytrains (also known as the Dakota or, more popularly, as the "Gooneybird"), augmented by the six C-47s of the Royal Hellenic Air Force's Flight 13 in November 1950 and by troop carriers of the Royal Thai Air Force; the 61st Troop Carrier Group with three C-54 squadrons; and the 314th Troop Carrier Group with four Fairchild C-119 Flying Boxcar ("Packet") squadrons. The 483rd Troop Carrier Wing, an Air Force Reserve unit from Portland, Oregon, equipped with C-119s, joined in the spring of 1952. The 315th Air Division (Combat Cargo) was also augmented by a U.S. Marine Corps squadron of R5Ds (C-54s). Because the runways and ground facilities of Korean airfields were generally limited, all of the 315th Air Division's transports were based in Japan, principally at Tachikawa Air Base outside Tokyo. In Korea the principal cargo fields were K-9 at Pusan (East), K-2 at Taegu (No. 1), K-14 at Kimpo near Seoul, K-46 at Hoengsong, and K-47 at Chunchon.

Air shipments from Japan to Korea began on June 28, 1950, when an aerial port of embarkation was established at Tachikawa. Air cargo movements from Tachikawa to Korea averaged 50 tons per day, but in October 1950 more than 12,500 tons were delivered. Air shipments from Japan to Korea between January 1 and June 30, 1951, totaled some 85,799 short tons. During the course of the Korean War, the 315th Air Division, averaging 140 combat-ready aircraft, flew 15,836,400 ton miles and 128,336,700 passenger miles in 210,343 sorties. A total of 391,773 tons of freight, 2,605,591 passengers, and 307,804 medical evacuation patients were handled. In general, the amount of cargo moved by air within the FEC exceeded that moved over the trans-Pacific routes. Between September 1, 1950, and March 1, 1951, a total of 2,123,925 measurement tons of cargo were delivered by air to Korea, 1,612,148 measurement tons (75.9 percent) from Japan, and 511,777 measurement tons (24.1 percent) directly from the United States. During the same six-month period, aircraft delivered an average of 28.49 pounds per person per day to Korea.

The FEAF air transport units participated in a number of special air operations during the Korean War. In October–November 1950 the bulk of the U.S. I and IX Corps, situated north of Pyongyang, were supported by air at a rate of 1,000 tons per day. During the December 1950 evacuation of Hungnam, the Combat Cargo Command transported 1,300 tons of cargo, 196 vehicles, 3,600 troops, and several hundred refugees. The 21st Troop Carrier Squadron and the 61st Troop Carrier Group received the Presidential Unit Citation for gallantry in support of operations around the Changjin (Chosin) Reservoir in December 1950, and in one of its more unusual operations, FEAF C-119s dropped eight treadway bridge sections to army engineers at Koto-ri, permitting Marine Corps and army units withdrawing from the Chosin Reservoir to bridge a gap in the roadway in the Funchilin Pass. FEAF troop carrier aircraft also supported parachute assaults by the 187th Airborne Regimental Combat Team (RCT) at Sukchon-Sunchon north of Pyongyang on October 20, 1950, and at Munsan-ni on March 23, 1951.

Helicopters

Helicopters had seen limited use for medical evacuation and liaison purposes during World War II, but in Korea the use of helicopters became a standard practice on the modern battlefield. The familiar Bell H-13, with two external litters, was used extensively for aeromedical evacuation from the front lines to field hospitals, and in Korea helicopters were used for the first time to move combat troops and deliver supplies to forward units. USAF and Marine Corps helicopter units led the way. The first helicopter medical evacuations in Korea were accomplished in late July 1950 by a detachment of the air force's 3rd Air Rescue Squadron under the command of Captain Oscar N. Tibbetts. Marine Corps helicopter squadron VMO-6 accomplished its first medical evacuation by helicopter on August 4, 1950. On November 11, 1951, Marine Helicopter Transport Squadron 161 lifted 950 troops to the front and returned an equal number to the rear. Another Marine battalion was relieved by helicopter the following month, and the success of the Marine Corps in utilizing helicopters for troop movements prompted U.S. Eighth Army in Korea (EUSAK) commander Lieutenant General Matthew B. Ridgway to request that four army helicopter battalions be made available. By the end of the war, aeromedical evacuation, troop movements, and supply deliveries by helicopter were almost routine procedures. U.S. Army aviators flew Mobile Army Surgical Hospital (MASH) H-13s, which were attached to each infantry division.

CHARLES R. SHRADER

See also

Aircraft; Helicopters, Employment of; Helicopters, Types and Nomenclature; Logistics in the Korean War; Military Air Transport Service; Military Sea Transport Service; United States Air Force; United States Navy

References

Boose, Donald. *U.S. Army Forces in the Korean War, 1950–1953.* Oxford, UK: Osprey, 2005.
Bruning, John R. *Crimson Sky: The Air Battle for Korea.* Dulles, VA: Brassey's, 1999.
Cowdrey, Albert E. *United States Army in the Korean War: The Medic's War.* Washington, DC: U.S. Army Center of Military History, 1987.
Futrell, Robert F. *The United States Air Force in Korea, 1950–1953.* Rev. ed. Washington, DC: Office of the Chief of Air Force History, 1983.
Hermes, Walter G. *U.S. Army in the Korean War: Truce Tent and Fighting Front.* Washington, DC: Office of the Chief of Military History, 1966.
Huston, James A. *Guns and Butter, Powder and Rice: U.S. Army Logistics in the Korean War.* Selinsgrove, PA: Susquehanna University Press, 1989.

Stratemeyer, George Edward
Birth Date: November 24, 1890
Death Date: August 9, 1969

U.S. Air Force (USAF) general and commander of the Far East Air Force (FEAF) during the Korean War. Born on November 24, 1890, in Cincinnati, Ohio, George Edward Stratemeyer grew up in Peru, Indiana. He attended the U.S. Military Academy at West Point with Dwight D. Eisenhower and Omar N. Bradley, graduating in 1915. He then served in the infantry on the Texas border.

Stratemeyer completed flight training in 1917 at Rockwell Field in San Diego, California, and was commander at the School of Military Aeronautics at Ohio State University during World War I. After assignments as chief test pilot at Kelly Air Force Base, Texas, and Chanute Field, Illinois, Stratemeyer spent three years in Hawaii. He taught tactics at West Point between 1924 and 1929. He graduated from the Air Corps Tactical School at Langley Field, Virginia, in 1930, and the Command and General Staff School at Fort Leavenworth, Kansas, in 1932. After teaching at Fort Leavenworth for several years, Stratemeyer was promoted to lieutenant colonel and commanded the 7th Bombardment Group at Hamilton Field, California, from 1936 to 1938. In the following years, he graduated from the Army War College; was appointed commander of the Southeast Air Corps Training Center at Maxwell Field, Alabama; and served as chief of the Air Corps in Washington, DC He became a major general in June 1942.

During World War II, Stratemeyer directed air operations in the China-Burma-India theater, where his men performed major air supply work. In September 1943 Stratemeyer proposed a plan whereby Boeing B-29 Superfortresses would bomb Japan from a base in India and small bases in China, and President Franklin D. Roosevelt approved the plan, code-named MATTERHORN. By April 1944 Stratemeyer was commander of the U.S. Army Air Forces (USAAF) in the China theater, with his headquarters at Chongqing (Chungking) through March 1946. Stratemeyer was widely praised for his efforts in the Chongqing airlift, in which 200,000 Chinese troops and 5,000 horses were relocated from western to eastern China. He was promoted to lieutenant general in 1945.

In February 1946 Stratemeyer returned to the United States to supervise the new Air Defense Command. He promoted air force autonomy and a large Air National Guard in the 1948 reorganization in which the Air Defense Command was renamed the Continental Air Command. Known for convincing subordinates to do what he wanted, Stratemeyer was considered a skilled military air tactician. He was certainly a forceful champion of a strengthened air force.

In April 1949 Stratemeyer was assigned to Tokyo as commanding general of the Far East Air Force (FEAF). The FEAF consisted of the Fifth Air Force in Japan, Thirteenth Air Force in the Philippines, Twentieth Air Force in Okinawa, 18 groups of fighters and fighter-bombers, and one wing of Martin B-26 Marauder and B-29 bombers. He was flying between San Francisco and Hawaii en route to Tokyo when the Korean War began on June 25, 1950. When he landed in Seoul, Republic of Korea Army (ROKA, South Korean Army) troops were already in retreat, and Americans were evacuating.

President Harry S. Truman ordered U.S. forces into action south of the 38th Parallel but believed that air power was the best way to stop the invasion. Stratemeyer agreed and helped organize direct air support during the crucial early days of the war. He ordered air attacks on advancing Korean People's Army (KPA, North Korean Army) forces and air cover for the evacuation of U.S. civilians from Seoul, and he flew reconnaissance missions and planned how to use available combat aircraft to defend South Korea. Stratemeyer proudly noted that three-fourths of the men under his command during the Korean War were from the air force reserve training program that he had established in peacetime.

When General Douglas MacArthur visited Korea on June 29, Stratemeyer asked that he approve air operations to gain control of the air and to identify targets for future air attacks in the Democratic People's Republic of Korea (DPRK, North Korea). President Truman supported MacArthur's order for bombing North Korea, and Stratemeyer cabled Fifth Air Force commander Major General Earle E. Partridge: "Take out North Korean airfields. No publicity. MacArthur approves." The goal was to "isolate the battlefield" and to attack communication lines, factories, and industries vital to the North Koreans.

The United States quickly gained air superiority over the small Korean People's Air Force (KPAF, North Korean Air Force) and proceeded to bomb supply lines and provide tactical support to ground forces. Some 100 heavy bombers in Stratemeyer's command struck a 27-mile area along the upper Naktong River in August 1950. One thousand tons of bombs were dropped within 26 minutes to rout KPA troops. This was one of the most massive U.S. bombings since the 1944 Normandy invasion. It was, however, unsuccessful. Stratemeyer instructed that no similar bombings would be ordered unless conditions were desperate.

Following the massive intervention by the Chinese People's Volunteer Army (CPVA, Chinese Army) at the end of November, Chinese and Soviet jet aircraft posed a threat to United Nations (UN) operations in far North Korea along and south of the Yalu River, an area known as MiG Alley. With United Nations Command (UNC) aircraft too far away to escort bombing missions to North Korea, Stratemeyer devised new tactics to meet this situation. Allied air power, however, was unable to prevent Chinese resupply overland. It never could "isolate the battlefield."

Stratemeyer opposed MacArthur's flouting of directives, such as ordering the bombing of bridges across the Yalu in early November 1950. He told Air Force chief of staff General Hoyt S. Vandenberg and President Truman that such raids should be limited to south of the river, restrictions that MacArthur later blamed for the failure of his Home-by-Christmas offensive. Stratemeyer did upset Secretary of Defense George C. Marshall when he suggested that the air force should be allowed to pursue unlimited military operations against the People's Republic of China (PRC). When UNC troops halted the Chinese offensive, Stratemeyer encouraged strategic bombing of industries and supply centers in North Korea instead of supporting Allied ground forces. This heightened the army–air force close support controversy.

Although loyal to MacArthur, Stratemeyer did not question Truman's presidential authority to remove MacArthur from command in April 1951. Indeed, in a March 1951 press release, Stratemeyer stressed, "A decision to extend [our operations] beyond the confines of Korea is not one that should be made by the field commander." Stratemeyer suffered a heart attack in May 1951, and General Otto P. Weyland took over his command.

Retiring from active duty on January 31, 1952, Stratemeyer focused his attention on anticommunist activities. He attempted to convince the U.S. Senate not to censure Senator Joseph R. McCarthy, and in 1954 he chaired Ten Million Americans Mobilizing for Justice, collecting signatures to oppose such censure. Angry about restrictions placed on the U.S. military during the Korean War, Stratemeyer testified to the Senate Subcommittee on Internal Security in 1954: "We were required to lose the war. We weren't allowed to win it. . . . I wasn't permitted to do a job, and certainly General MacArthur was handcuffed." Stratemeyer died in Orlando, Florida, on August 9, 1969.

ELIZABETH D. SCHAFER

See also

Aerial Combat; Airborne Operations; Aircraft; Airpower in the Korean War; Bradley, Omar Nelson; China, People's Republic of, People's Liberation Army Air Force; Close Air Support; Eisenhower, Dwight David; Far East Air Force; Home-by-Christmas Offensive; MacArthur, Douglas; Marshall, George Catlett; McCarthy, Joseph Raymond;

MiG Alley; Partridge, Earle Everard; Truman, Harry S.; United Nations Command Air Assets; United States Air Force; Vandenberg, Hoyt Sanford; Weyland, Otto Paul

References

Appleman, Roy E. *United States Army in Korea: South to the Naktong, North to the Yalu.* Washington, DC: Office of the Chief of Military History, 1961.

Blair, Clay. *The Forgotten War: America in Korea, 1950–1953.* New York: Times Books, 1987.

Bruning, John R. *Crimson Sky: The Air Battle for Korea.* Dulles, VA: Brassey's, 1999.

Current Biography, 1951. New York: H. W. Wilson, 1952.

Futrell, Robert F. *The United States Air Force in Korea, 1950–1953.* Rev. ed. Washington, DC: Office of the Chief of Air Force History, 1983.

Stratemeyer, George. *The Three Wars of Lt. Gen. George E. Stratemeyer: His Korean War Diary.* Edited by William T. Y'Blood. Washington, DC: United States Air Force/U.S. Government Printing Office, 1999.

Struble, Arthur Dewey

Birth Date: June 28, 1894
Death Date: May 1, 1983

U.S. Navy officer and commander of the Seventh Fleet at the outset of the Korean War. Born in Portland, Oregon, on June 28, 1894, Arthur Dewey Struble graduated from the U.S. Naval Academy at Annapolis in 1915 and was commissioned an ensign. Struble spent World War I on board the battleship *South Dakota*, the cruiser *St. Louis*, the store ship *Glacier*, and the destroyer *Stevens*. In 1919 and 1920 Struble served as executive officer and then commanding officer of the destroyer *Shubrick*, which was involved in the Haiti crisis of that period. For the next two decades his assignments alternated between service at sea, on battle staffs and warships, and ashore, at the U.S. Naval Academy, navy headquarters in Washington, and the naval district headquarters in San Francisco, California. The Japanese attack on Pearl Harbor on December 7, 1941, found him in command of the light cruiser *Trenton*, then operating near the Panama Canal.

After a tour in the office of the chief of naval operations during 1942–1943, during which time he was promoted to rear admiral (October 1942), Struble served as chief of staff of the Western Naval Task Force, the U.S. Navy's major command for the June 1944 Normandy invasion. Convinced of his special talents in amphibious warfare, the navy gave him command in August 1944 of Amphibious Group 2, which led the assaults on Leyte, Mindoro, and Luzon in the Philippines. His outstanding performance in these operations earned him the Distinguished Service Medal.

From September 1945 to April 1948, Struble directed the Pacific Fleet's mine clearance and amphibious forces, which gained valuable insight on coastal and inshore operations in the Far East. Rear Admiral Struble complemented this experience with service in Washington as deputy chief of naval operations and as naval deputy on the Joint Chiefs of Staff.

In May 1950 Struble was promoted to vice admiral and selected as commander of the Seventh Fleet. In Washington that June, when the Korean People's Army (KPA, North Korean Army) invaded the Republic of Korea (ROK, South Korea), Struble flew to the Far East in time to direct the first carrier strikes on Pyongyang. At the same time, he oversaw the execution of President Harry S. Truman's order on June 26 that the Seventh Fleet "neutralize" the Strait of Taiwan by placing naval forces between the mainland People's Republic of China (PRC) and Taiwan (then known as Formosa). Surface ships, carrier-based and shore-based aircraft, and submarines of his command promptly established patrols in the disputed waters off China. Units of the navy's Taiwan Patrol Force would carry out this mission for the next two decades.

The right man in the right place, Struble developed the operational plan and led the forces that executed the September 15, 1950, masterful amphibious assault at Inchon (Operation CHROMITE). Under his control as commander of Task Force Seven for Operation CHROMITE were 230 ships, including U.S. and allied aircraft carriers, the battleship *Missouri*, cruisers, destroyers, minesweepers, and amphibious vessels, as well as the U.S. X Corps, composed of the 1st Marine Division and the army's 7th Infantry Division. Careful staff planning, accurate intelligence, successful deception operations, and effective logistic support measures helped to ensure the success of Operation CHROMITE. The Inchon assault was a classic demonstration of amphibious warfare. General Douglas MacArthur's bold plan, executed by Struble and the sailors, marines, soldiers, and airmen of the United Nations (UN) coalition under his command, soon freed South Korea from the invading KPA.

In addition to the landings at Inchon and Wonsan, the latter in northeast Korea, and the successful evacuation of the X Corps from Hungnam in December 1950, Struble directed the fleet's air interdiction and close air support (CAS) strikes, naval gunfire support, and other combat operations during the critical first phase of the Korean War. Naval forces under his command helped stop KPA ground offensives and protect the allied reinforcements pouring into the port of Pusan, and brought naval power to bear on KPA forces ashore.

Detached as commander of the Seventh Fleet on March 28, 1951, Vice Admiral Struble returned to the United States to lead the First Fleet on the West Coast and then to serve with the Joint Chiefs of Staff in Washington. From May 1952 to May 1955 he worked on the Military Staff Committee of the UN. Before his retirement from the navy on July 1, 1956, Struble commanded the Eastern Sea Frontier and the Atlantic Reserve Fleet. Struble was advanced to full admiral on retirement. He died in Chevy Chase, Maryland, on May 1, 1983.

EDWARD J. MAROLDA

See also

Inchon Landing; MacArthur, Douglas; Truman, Harry S.; United States Navy

U.S. vice admiral Arthur D. Struble, shown here aboard the battleship *Missouri*, was commander of the U.S. Seventh Fleet during March 1950–May 1952. As such, he played a key role in the deployment of U.S. naval assets in the Korean War. (Naval Historical Center)

References

Cagle, Malcolm W., and Frank A. Manson. *Sea War in Korea.* Annapolis, MD: Naval Institute Press, 1957.

Field, James A., Jr. *History of United States Naval Operations, Korea.* Washington, DC: U.S. Government Printing Office, 1962.

Marolda, Edward J., ed. *The U.S. Navy in the Korean War.* Annapolis, MD: Naval Institute Press, 2007.

U.S. Navy Biographical Files, Operational Archives, Naval Historical Center, Washington, DC.

Utz, Curtis A. *Assault from the Sea: The Amphibious Landing at Inchon.* Washington, DC: Naval Historical Center, 2000.

Student Volunteer Troops, Republic of Korea

In July 1950, in a gesture that had little concrete impact on the war, student volunteer troops were sent to augment the armed forces of the Republic of Korea (ROK, South Korea). In March 1949 the South Korean government established the Student National Defense Corps, an organization whose objectives included not merely strengthening the country's security through compulsory military training but also inculcating civic values in the nation's youth. All university students were expected to devote a certain number of hours to military training.

The Republic of Korea Army (ROKA, South Korean Army) was established only in 1948, and at the outbreak of war it was still small, consisting of 67,559 officers and men, who were poorly trained and underequipped. At the start of the war, the ROKA was virtually overwhelmed by the Korean People's Army (KPA, North Korean Army), and for the most part it retreated in disarray. Calling on every available reservoir of personnel, the South Korean government quickly organized student volunteer units, which were sent to the battlefront from July 1950 onward to fight with the regular army. By no means were all these volunteers particularly eager to experience active service, and few if any had adequate military training. Those unable to learn quickly soon died in combat, and casualties among the student volunteers were high. In the war's early stages the ROKA—disorganized, ill equipped, and ill paid—was badly led and fought poorly, leading to high desertion rates. These characteristics were even more pronounced among the untried student volunteers.

In the spring of 1951 the U.S. military, determined to improve the disappointing performance of its South Korean allies, instituted a concentrated training program for all armed forces of the ROK. This included student volunteers, who were treated as regular troops for the conflict's duration. Early in the war, almost all ROKA divisions at the front were attached to U.S. Army units. This modernized training program cut casualties and losses of equipment by 50 percent and made the ROKA into an effective fighting force. It also professionalized the surviving student volunteer troops and, at least for the period of the war, virtually eliminated the difference between them and other conscripts.

After the war, military training was still a compulsory part of the program of study for South Korean college students. The Student National Defense Corps remained in existence until 1988, when it was abolished.

PRISCILLA ROBERTS

See also
Korea, Republic of, Army; Korean Augmentation to the United States Army

References
Paik Sun Yup. *From Pusan to Panmunjom.* Washington, DC: Brassey's, 1992.
Sawyer, Robert K. *Military Advisors in Korea: KMAG in Peace and War.* Washington, DC: Office of the Chief of Military History, U.S. Army, 1962.

Submachine Guns and Light Machine Guns

Pistol and rifle-caliber automatic weapons used to reinforce the firepower of ground forces. The U.S. .45-caliber Thompson Model 1928A1 submachine gun as issued to troops in Korea was an open-bolt, blowback, selective-fire weapon. Chambering the same cartridge as the Colt Model 1911 pistol, the Thompson accepted a 20-round, detachable box magazine. Although reliable, the Thompson weighed a hefty 10.45 pounds and was expensive to manufacture. During World War II, these shortcomings led the government to explore alternative submachine gun designs, which later saw service in Korea. These included the Harrington and Richardson .45-caliber Reising models 50 and 55 submachine guns, and the .45-caliber M3 and M3A1 submachine guns. In contrast to the Thompson's wooden stocks and milled steel construction, the M3 and M3A1 were equipped with retractable wire stocks and were manufactured using simplified stamped steel techniques. Although relatively reliable, their rather crude appearance earned them the nickname "grease gun."

The John Browning–designed M1918A2 Browning Automatic Rifle (BAR) provided squad-level automatic firepower for U.S. troops in World War I, World War II, and the Korean War. The gas-operated BAR fired the standard .30-06 U.S. rifle cartridge and was fed by a 20-round detachable magazine. It was a full automatic–only weapon with two settings: slow, with a cyclic rate of 300 to 450 rounds per minute; and fast, with a rate of 500 to 650 rounds per minute.

Belgian troops utilized the Vigneron M2 Submachine Gun. It chambered the 9-millimeter (mm) parabellum cartridge, fed by a 32-round magazine. The Vigneron was a selective-fire weapon, similar in operation to the British Sten, and was primarily constructed of steel stampings.

As produced by Fabrique Nationale (FN), the Belgian BAR, although chambered for the standard U.S. .30-06 caliber, boasted a number of improvements over its American cousin. The Belgian BAR Type D featured a quick-change barrel and an adjustable cyclic rate. It was also fitted with a pistol grip and a carrying handle, and it accepted either a tripod or a bipod with a butt rest.

The French 9-mm submachine gun M1949 (MAT49) was predominantly of stamped steel construction and was an excellent weapon in all respects. It was blowback operated, capable of automatic fire only, and accepted a 32-round box magazine. The M1949 was equipped with a grip safety and was very popular among French troops for its compactness afforded by a retracting wire stock and folding magazine.

The standard French squad automatic weapon was the 7.5-mm Model 1924 M29 light machine gun. It was a gas-operated selective-fire weapon very similar in function to the BAR. The M29 differed from the BAR in that it was fed by a top-mounted box magazine and was equipped with a front trigger for semiautomatic fire and a rear trigger for its fully automatic mode.

The British 9-mm selective-fire Sten Mark V submachine gun saw extensive use in Korea. Australia also issued two native-designed submachine guns—the 9-mm Austen Mark I and Mark II and the 9-mm Owen Mark I. These weapons were somewhat similar to the Sten.

The British Bren Light Machine Gun was a gas-operated, selective-fire squad weapon fitted with a top-mounted 30-round magazine. The Bren, in Marks 1 through 4, was manufactured in the standard British .303 rifle caliber in England, Canada, and Australia. It had a 30-round detachable box magazine or a 100-round detachable pan magazine.

The Soviet Union supplied the People's Republic of China (PRC) and the Democratic People's Republic of Korea (DPRK, North Korea) with tens of thousands of submachine guns. The various models were essentially similar in appearance and operation. The most common models were the PPD Model 1934/38, PPD Model 1940, PPSH Model 1941, and the PPS Model 1943. All were chambered for the 7.62-mm pistol cartridge. Later marks differed from earlier models in their more simplified construction and feed systems. All models except the full automatic-only PPS M1943 were selective-fire weapons.

The most common communist-produced squad-level automatic weapons were the 7.62-mm DP and DPM. They were conventional gas-operated, air-cooled light machine guns. Both weapons were fed by 47-round drum magazines.

JEFF KINARD

See also
Machine Guns; Pistols; Rifles

References
Hobart, F. W. A. *Pictorial History of the Machine Gun.* London: Allan, 1971.
Hogg, Ian, and John Weeks. *Military Small Arms of the Twentieth Century.* Chicago: Follett, 1973.

Smith, W. H. B. *Small Arms of the World,* 9th ed. Harrisburg, PA: Stackpole, 1969.

Willbanks, James H. *Machine Guns: An Illustrated History of Their Impact.* Santa Barbara, CA: ABC-CLIO, 2004.

Suhr, Anna Wallace

See Seoul City Sue

Sukchon and Sunchon Airborne Operation
Start Date: October 20, 1950
End Date: October 22, 1950

One of two United Nations Command (UNC) airborne operations during the Korean War. It involved dropping the 187th Airborne Regimental Combat Team (RCT) at Sukchon and Sunchon, both located north of Pyongyang, the capital of the Democratic People's Republic of Korea (DPRK, North Korea).

UNC commander General Douglas MacArthur had hoped to use airborne forces in conjunction with his amphibious landing at Inchon, but none were then available in the theater of operations. The 4,000-man 187th, commanded by Colonel Frank S. Bowen Jr., arrived in Japan only on September 20, 1950. Its operational readiness date was October 21; pending this date, MacArthur held the 187th under his control in general headquarters (GHQ) reserve at Kimpo Airfield near Seoul.

With the UNC advance north of the 38th Parallel, MacArthur planned to employ the 187th in airdrops some 25 miles north of Pyongyang to cut off the escape to the north of Korean People's Army (KPA, North Korean Army) units and North Korean officials, and to rescue UNC prisoners of war (POWs). This would be a formidable task for an RCT, especially one that had never made a combat jump and was light on equipment and firepower support.

The operation was planned to coincide with the projected 187th combat readiness date, but when he learned that the North

Paratroopers of the U.S. Army 187th Regimental Combat Team in the assault at Sukchon and Sunchon, North Korea, in October 1950, one of two United Nations Command (UNC) airborne operations of the war. (National Archives)

Korean government had fled Pyongyang along with much of the KPA, MacArthur moved it up to October 20. The plan called for the paratroopers to cut two highways and a rail line running north from Pyongyang.

On October 20 the troopers loaded aboard 113 Fairchild C-119 Flying Boxcars and Douglas C-47 Skytrains (Dakotas) of the 324th and 21st Troop Carrier squadrons. The congestion of so many aircraft at Kimpo Airfield for this operation put a crimp in other activities there, including an emergency supply lift to the U.S. Eighth Army in Korea (EUSAK). At noon the weather cleared over the drop zones and the planes took off, escorted by fighters of the Far East Air Force (FEAF). This was the first time C-119s were employed in a combat jump.

Before the drop, FEAF fighters and fighter-bombers strafed and bombed the drop zones. The air armada included MacArthur's own airplane from Tokyo, with the general and reporters aboard. MacArthur wanted to see the jump and have his presence noted.

The drops, led by Bowen himself, began about 2:00 p.m. The troopers encountered no antiaircraft fire and only sporadic ground fire. Only 1 trooper of some 2,800 was killed in the drop, and 47 were injured. For the first time in a combat operation, heavy equipment was also parachuted. This included vehicles, 12 105-mm howitzers of the 674th Field Artillery Battalion on wooden pallets (nine of which were recovered in serviceable condition), and tons of ammunition and other equipment. The drop was highly successful.

Once on the ground, the 1st Battalion secured hills east and north of Sukchon and blocked the road. The 3rd Battalion also quickly secured its objective of several low hills south of Sukchon. There was little KPA opposition.

At Sunchon, the 2nd Battalion also encountered little KPA resistance. Two of its companies set up positions south and west of Sunchon, while the third advanced on Sunchon. It was soon involved in a firefight with what turned out to be elements of the Republic of Korea Army (ROKA, South Korean Army), 6th Infantry Division, advancing toward the North Korean border with the People's Republic of China (PRC). No one had informed the paratroopers that the 6th Division would be there that day, but fortunately there were few casualties before fire was halted.

That afternoon MacArthur landed in Pyongyang and described the paratroop operation as a brilliant stroke that would bring about the final destruction of the KPA. He estimated some 30,000 KPA were trapped between the 187th and the UNC forces now moving north of Pyongyang. He did not mention the ROKA 6th Division.

On October 21 the 3rd Battalion moved south from Sukchon to meet the advancing 27th British Commonwealth Brigade of the U.S. I Corps. North of Yongyu, the 3rd Battalion ran into the rearguard KPA 239th Regiment. During the night of October 21–22, the 239th attempted to break through the paratroopers but was unsuccessful. The KPA regiment of some 2,500 men was all but destroyed. The 3rd Battalion reported that it killed about 800 troops and captured another 680.

On October 23, the 187th returned to Pyongyang. In the entire operation it had suffered 111 casualties, but more than a third of these were jump-related. While the 187th had captured 3,818 KPA prisoners, the operation was too late; none of these were high-ranking officers or North Korean officials, and the operation had failed to cut off the bulk of the KPA forces, which had already withdrawn north of Sukchon and Sunchon when the operation began. Most UNC POWs had also been removed to the north or massacred.

Spencer C. Tucker

See also

Airborne Operations; Inchon Landing; MacArthur, Douglas

References

Appleman, Roy E. *United States Army in Korea: South to the Naktong, North to the Yalu*. Washington, DC: Office of the Chief of Military History, 1961.

Blair, Clay. *The Forgotten War: America in Korea, 1950–1953*. New York: Times Books, 1987.

James, D. Clayton. *The Years of MacArthur*, Vol. 3, *Triumph and Disaster, 1945–1964*. Boston: Houghton Mifflin, 1985.

Supung and the Korean Electric Power Plant Campaign
Start Date: June 23, 1952
End Date: June 26, 1952

In the summer of 1952, with armistice negotiations at an impasse since May, U.S. Far East Air Force (FEAF) officials proposed a new campaign against hydroelectric plants in the Democratic People's Republic of Korea (DPRK, North Korea). This, they believed, would force the communists to accept United Nations Command (UNC) truce terms. On June 17, 1952, Lieutenant General Mark W. Clark, who had replaced Lieutenant General Matthew B. Ridgway as UNC commander on April 28, approved the strikes. Two days later, the Joint Chiefs of Staff and President Harry S. Truman confirmed the action, which lasted from June 23 to 27.

The targets were the Supung (Suiho), Changjin, Pujon, and Hochon power plants. The Japanese had built this large hydroelectric power complex along the Yalu River. At the time, it was the fourth-largest hydroelectric complex in the world. Centered around Supung, the complex employed impounding dams with adjacent powerhouses to exploit the large volume of water. By 1948 it was producing 300,000 kilowatts of power, with half of this going to Manchuria as surplus.

Plans called for Fifth Air Force fighter-bombers, FEAF bombers, and navy fighters/fighter-bombers to strike Supung first on June 23. Once the attack was under way, the other dams would be hit. In conjunction, Boeing B-29 Superfortresses were to make night raids against Changjin. The attacks, scheduled to begin at 9:30 a.m., were delayed by bad weather until 4:00 p.m. While 84 North American F-86 Sabres patrolled overhead, 35 Douglas AD

Skyraiders from the carriers *Boxer, Princeton,* and *Philippine Sea* dive-bombed Supung. Simultaneously, 35 Grumman F9F Panther jets flew flak suppression. This was followed by attacks from 79 Republic F-84 Thunderjets and 45 Lockheed F-80 Shooting Stars, which dropped 145 tons of bombs.

The attack was a success, and ground fire was completely neutralized. Even though 250 Mikoyan-Gurevich MiG-15s were stationed 38 miles away at Dandong (Antung), none confronted the F-86s. In fact, 160 fled to Manchuria. Only two U.S. aircraft suffered minor damage. The raid was so successful that planned night-bomber raids were diverted elsewhere.

Reconnaissance reported that 90 percent of North Korean power had been knocked out: 11 of the 13 power plants were classified as "unserviceable," and the other 2 were listed as "doubtful." In addition, 30 of 51 major factories in Manchuria, in the People's Republic of China (PRC), were without power. Supung alone was 120,000 kilowatts short for the last half of 1952, and the Chinese could never compensate for this loss.

Smaller attacks continued through the night of June 27. Altogether, the four-day effort had seen 730 Fifth Air Force fighter-bomber sorties and 238 air-superiority sorties without a single loss. Seventh Fleet had flown 546 sorties, losing two planes to ground fire, and both pilots were rescued. FEAF commander General Otto P. Weyland later declared that the hydroelectric attacks were one of two strikes that were "spectacular on their own merit."

Throughout the remainder of the year, as communist engineers and repair personnel attempted to repair the dam complex, FEAF Bomber Command sent Boeing B-26 Marauders and B-29s on night raids against the dams. On September 12–13, six B-29s, carrying 2,000-pound armor-piercing bombs, attacked Supung. They were supported by six B-26s, which knocked out 8 of 30 large searchlights and suppressed flak, and by six other radar-jamming B-29s. While one B-29 was lost and three severely damaged, they scored five direct hits, again completely neutralizing Supung.

By February 1953 Fifth Air Force intelligence discovered that two generators at Supung were again operating. Expecting more B-29 raids, the communists had positioned 141 heavy guns near the complex. Instead, on February 15, 22 F-84s of the 474th Fighter Bomber Wing, supported by 82 F-86s, made a low-level raid. It was a total success, and the Sabre jets downed three MiGs, without loss themselves.

In May 1953 General Clark gave FEAF approval to strike Supung as needed. To this end, the Fifth Air Force kept Supung shut down with raids on May 10–11 and May 30. Another raid in the works was never carried out because the Armistice Agreement was signed in July.

There has been disagreement over the influence of the Supung raids. Some have argued that they had little if any effect on communist negotiators. They argue that massive protests in Great Britain over the raids actually hardened the communist position. They have also questioned whether the raids had any major impact on the North Korean economy or its ability to wage war. It is clear

that many people in Korea and Manchuria suffered, since almost all electrical power from these plants was shut off for most of the last 13 months of the war. Moreover, the simultaneous destruction of irrigation dams and dikes flooded fields, destroyed crops, and interrupted food production and supply. This situation combined with the threat of further attacks had to have had some influence on communist leaders.

WILLIAM HEAD

See also
Clark, Mark Wayne; Far East Air Force; Joint Chiefs of Staff; Ridgway, Matthew Bunker; Truman, Harry S.; Weyland, Otto Paul

References
Clodfelter, Mark. *The Limits of Air Power: The American Bombing of North Vietnam.* New York: Free Press, 1989.

Futrell, Robert F. *The United States Air Force in Korea, 1950–1953.* Rev. ed. Washington, DC: Office of the Chief of Air Force History, 1983.

Momyer, William W. *Air Power in Three Wars: WWII, Korea, Vietnam.* Washington, DC: Department of the Air Force, 1978.

Nalty, Bernard C., and Wayne Thompson. *Within Limits: The U.S. Air Force and the Korean War.* Honolulu: University Press of the Pacific, 2005.

Thompson, Wayne. "The Air War over Korea." In *Winged Shield, Wing Sword: A History of the United States Air Force,* edited by Bernard C. Nalty, 3–52. Washington, DC: U.S. Air Force History and Museum Program, 1997.

Symington, William Stuart, III
Birth Date: June 26, 1901
Death Date: December 14, 1988

U.S. senator, secretary of the U.S. Air Force (USAF), and chairman of the National Security Resources Board (NSRB). Born in Amherst, Massachusetts, on June 26, 1901, Stuart William Symington III enlisted in the U.S. Army artillery in 1918 during World War I, eventually earning a commission. Following demobilization after the war, he attended Yale University, from which he graduated in 1923. Symington cultivated a highly successful business career as a corporate troubleshooter and eventually ran several companies, most notably St. Louis–based Emerson Electric Manufacturing from 1938 to 1945.

In 1946 Symington became assistant secretary of war for air, and in 1947 President Harry S. Truman named him the first secretary of the USAF. As such, Symington lobbied hard for the Convair B-36 Peacemaker bomber and exclusive air force control of strategic nuclear weapons. He resigned in April 1950, just prior to the Korean War, to protest cuts in the air force budget.

Within weeks Truman had appointed Symington chairman of the NSRB, an arm of the National Security Council, and Symington held the post until April 1951. In that position he was tasked with the initial mobilization effort for the Korean War, an effort that was not particularly well planned or executed. Nevertheless, Symington was among the first of Truman's advisers to lobby for a major—and rapid—mobilization effort and the imposition of economic controls soon after the Korean War began on June 25, 1950. After the massive intervention by the People's Republic of China (PRC), Symington and the NSRB were pushed aside in favor of the newly created Office of Defense Mobilization (ODM), headed by Charles E. Wilson. By January 1951 the NSRB had reverted to its former advisory role, and Symington left the agency in April to run the Reconstruction Finance Corporation.

In 1952 Symington ran successfully for the first of four terms as U.S. senator from Missouri. He served on the McCarthy Permanent Investigations Subcommittee and often engaged in public battles with its chair, particularly during the 1954 hearings on communist influence in the U.S. Army. As a prominent member of the Senate Armed Services Committee, Symington remained a leading advocate of the air force and a strong national defense.

When John F. Kennedy became president in 1961, Symington supported a larger American presence in Vietnam, and he voted for the Gulf of Tonkin Resolution in August 1964. Subsequently reevaluating his position based on the escalating costs of the Vietnam War, he argued that Washington should either lift restrictions on the use of air power in Vietnam or withdraw entirely from the conflict. By 1968, seeing no chance of victory, he turned against the war. In his last term, he was a leading critic of President Richard M. Nixon's secret war in Cambodia, and he helped secure the passage of legislation limiting military involvement there. He also argued for greater congressional oversight of the Central Intelligence Agency (CIA).

Symington retired from the Senate in December 1976. He died in New Canaan, Connecticut, on December 14, 1988.

THOMAS D. VEVE

See also

National Security Resources Board; Nixon, Richard Milhous; Office of Defense Mobilization; Truman, Harry S.; Wilson, Charles Edward

References

Barlow, Jeffrey G. *Revolt of the Admirals: The Fight for Naval Aviation, 1945–1950.* Washington, DC: Naval Historical Center, 1994.

Hogan, Michael J. *A Cross of Iron: Harry S. Truman and the Origins of the National Security State, 1945–1954.* New York: Cambridge University Press, 1998.

McFarland, Linda. *Cold War Strategist: Stuart Symington and the Search for National Security.* Westport, CT: Praeger, 2001.

Pierpaoli, Paul G., Jr. *Truman and Korea: The Political Culture of the Early Cold War.* Columbia: University of Missouri Press, 1999.

T

Taegu, Defense of
Start Date: August 1950
End Date: September 1950

During the periods August 4–24 and September 2–15, 1950, Korean People's Army (KPA, North Korean Army) forces made two significant efforts to capture Taegu, a major road and railway hub in the Republic of Korea (ROK, South Korea), as well as the site of the U.S. Eighth Army in Korea (EUSAK) headquarters. Taegu is located in southeastern South Korea, within the Pusan Perimeter. Its capture would have severed the only east–west highway and rail line serving the northern flank of the Pusan Perimeter.

Defending Taegu in August were the U.S. 1st Cavalry Division, on a 35-mile front along the Naktong River; the Republic of Korea Army (ROKA, South Korean Army), 1st Infantry Division, to the north of the 1st Cavalry, positioned along the river for 25 miles to near Naktong-ni, then facing north for 6 more miles; and the ROKA 6th Infantry Division, to the right of the 1st, on a front of 8 miles. The KPA 10th Division and part of the KPA 3rd Division faced the U.S. 1st Cavalry.

Between August 5 and 8, 1950, the KPA 13th Division crossed the Naktong River into the ROKA 1st Division's northern sector. Some of the KPA troops utilized "underwater bridges," constructed of sandbags and oil drums that made a ford a few feet below the river's surface. Air strikes, artillery, and mortar fire failed to stop the crossing. On August 7 elements of the KPA 15th Division attacked the ROKA 1st Division's southern sector, broke through, and headed east toward Tabu-dong, six miles away.

The ROKA 1st Division's 12th Regiment withdrew from its positions to occupy the high ridges north of Tabu-dong, including the towering Yuhak-san, but found them occupied by elements of the KPA 13th Division. A bloody fight ensued.

By August 15 the ROKA 1st Division, heavily engaged with the KPA 13th and 15th divisions, had requested assistance from EUSAK. Two regiments were sent: the U.S. 27th Infantry of the 24th Division and ROKA 10th Infantry of the 8th Division. While the ROKA 1st Division was thus engaged, the KPA 1st Division attacked the ROKA 6th Division, which executed a fighting withdrawal. Finally, the ROKA 6th Division dug in along the high ground northeast of Tabu-dong, on the ROKA 1st Division's right flank.

On August 9 the KPA 3rd Division's 7th Infantry Regiment crossed the Naktong River against the 5th Cavalry Regiment, seizing Hill 268 (Triangulation Hill). A counterattack by the 1st Battalion of the 7th Cavalry Regiment forced the KPA from the hill and back across the river.

On the night of August 11–12, elements of the KPA 10th Division crossed the Naktong into positions of the 2nd Battalion, 7th Cavalry Regiment, and continued attacking for the next two days. About 6:00 p.m. on August 12, the 1st Battalion of the 7th Cavalry Regiment arrived on the 2nd Battalion's left but was forced back by the KPA, refusing the 1st Cavalry Division's left flank. The 7th counterattacked on August 14 and drove the KPA back across the river with heavy losses.

That same day, elements of the KPA 3rd Division, supported by tanks of the KPA 105th Division, crossed the river into the sector of the 13th Regiment, ROKA 1st Division, just north of the town of Waegwan, then turned south and into the flank and rear of the U.S. 5th Cavalry Regiment of the 1st Cavalry Division. On August 15 a KPA force, mistaken by a U.S. officer for an expected reinforcing ROKA contingent, captured him and some 40–45 other Americans. On August 17, as counterattacking Americans began forcing

Refugees fleeing the combat area near Taegu, South Korea, on August 20, 1950. (National Archives)

the North Koreans from the hill, KPA soldiers herded their U.S. captives into a gully and massacred them. Six of the prisoners survived, but one died the following day. Some of those responsible were later captured by U.S. troops, but it is unclear what happened to them.

On August 18 the ROKA 1st Division, reinforced by the U.S. 27th Infantry, began counterattacking the KPA 13th Division. The 27th advanced up a deep valley north of Tabu-dong, while the ROKA forces attacked along high, steep mountains on each flank. The attack was halted about 8:00 p.m. Shortly thereafter, a KPA tank-infantry force attacked the 27th, but infantry rocket launchers and U.S. tank fire halted the KPA attackers, destroying at least two tanks, a self-propelled (SP) gun, and a few trucks. After the KPA force was repelled, the 27th organized a two-battalion defensive position across the valley. From August 18 through 25, the KPA attacked the 27th almost every night in what became known as the Bowling Alley (because the artillery and tank fire in the valley sounded like the noise of a bowling alley), with the KPA losing 13 tanks and five SP guns. The ROKA 1st Division flanking the 27th also held fast.

Some KPA troops infiltrated the high, steep ridges on the right of the ROKA 1st Division and attacked artillery positions and vehicles in rear areas. On August 21 the 2nd Battalion, 23rd Infantry, was deployed to protect the artillery. The KPA attacked the battalion on August 22, but it was repulsed. Counterattacking between August 23 and 25, the 2nd Battalion of the 23rd, joined by the 3rd Battalion, killed at least 523 members of the KPA 1st Regiment, ending the threat to the rear area and artillery. Elements of the ROKA 1st Division, meantime, drove KPA troops from Kasan, a high mountain overlooking the valley to Taegu.

The KPA tried again to seize Taegu in early September. This time the U.S. 1st Cavalry Division was deployed west and north of the city, with the newly arrived British 27th Brigade on the left, the 1st Cavalry Division's 5th Cavalry Regiment to the north in the Waegwan area, the 7th Cavalry Regiment in the center, and the 8th Cavalry Regiment in the old Bowling Alley area, facing north. The division front was 35 miles long. The ROKA 1st Division was on the cavalry's right. From east to west opposing the cavalry were the KPA 1st, 13th, and 3rd divisions.

On September 2 the 1st Cavalry Division launched attacks ordered by EUSAK commander Lieutenant General Walton H. Walker to try to relieve KPA pressure on the U.S. 2nd and 25th divisions to the south. Most failed, but a 5th Cavalry attack on September 4 drove the KPA from Hill 303, where the massacre had occurred the previous month.

KPA increased its pressure and retook towering Kasan. Two companies were sent to take the ridge back, but superior KPA forces drove them off on September 4–5. Also on September 2, elements of the KPA 13th Division attacked the 8th Cavalry and slowly drove it back. By September 5 the situation was worsening; KPA forces had heavily infiltrated rear areas, established blocks on the main supply route, captured Tabu-dong, and infiltrated the center south of Hill 518, which the 7th Cavalry had been fighting to take. Waegwan, on the 1st Cavalry Division's left, was in no-man's-land. It was thus imperative that the 8th Cavalry shorten its lines and reorganize and consolidate. On September 6 it carried out withdrawals of approximately two to five miles. On September 7, elements of the division began attacking their advancing enemy. Bloody fights for a number of hills ensued, including Hills 174, 203, and 314 in the 5th and 7th cavalries' area, and Hill 570 in the area of the 8th Cavalry. These battles continued until September 15. One of the bloodiest of these was over Hill 174. Won and lost several times, it was taken for the last time by Company I, 5th Cavalry, on September 16, only to find that the KPA had withdrawn.

On its new positions, the 1st Cavalry Division stopped the KPA advance but at a heavy price. The companies of the 3rd Battalion, 8th Cavalry Regiment, were at or below 50 percent strength; the 5th Cavalry's strength was so low that it was virtually not combat effective; and one company of the 1st Battalion of the 7th Cavalry Regiment was down to only 50 men.

UZAL W. ENT

See also

Haman Breakthrough; Inchon Landing; Naktong Bulge, Second Battle of; Pohang, Battle of; Pusan Perimeter and Breakout; Walker, Walton Harris

References

Appleman, Roy E. *United States Army in Korea: South to the Naktong, North to the Yalu.* Washington, DC: Office of the Chief of Military History, 1961.

Blair, Clay. *The Forgotten War: America in Korea, 1950–1953.* New York: Times Books, 1987.

Ent, Uzal W. *Fighting on the Brink: Defense of the Pusan Perimeter.* Paducah, KY: Turner, 1996.

Taejon, Defense of

Start Date: July 19, 1950
End Date: July 20, 1950

Battle in which U.S. and Republic of Korea Army (ROKA, South Korean Army) forces tried to stave off a Korean People's Army (KPA, North Korean Army) advance. By July 19, 1950, Major

General William F. Dean's 24th Division was forced into the environs of Taejon city. Dean placed Colonel Charles E. Beauchamp, commander of the 34th Infantry Regiment, in charge of its defense. Beauchamp also had the remnants of the 19th and 34th regiments, the 24th Reconnaissance Company, and what remained of the divisional artillery. A number of headquarters and service support units were in the city itself. Dean and one or two members of his staff were also in Taejon.

Beauchamp placed the 1st Battalion, 34th Infantry, with the 2nd Battalion, 19th Infantry, to its left along the Kapchon River defending the Kongju and Nonsan roads, respectively. Surviving artillery was moved from near the Taejon airstrip to the southern outskirts of the city. The 3rd Battalion, 34th Infantry, was placed west and north of the city. Elements of the 21st Infantry, not under Beauchamp's command, with an attached tank company were deployed across four miles of hills some three to four miles east of Taejon and a mile beyond where a railroad and a highway tunnel were located. Their mission was to patrol the road and keep it open east of town.

During a trip to Taejon on the morning of July 18, Eighth Army commander Lieutenant General Walton H. Walker told Dean that he needed two days to bring the newly arrived 1st Cavalry Division into position behind Taejon.

Beauchamp later wrote that Walker visited him and ordered him to hold the Taejon road network for three days. This turned out to be one day too long. Beauchamp recalled that General Dean was not present during this visit and that no one told him about the 1st Cavalry, although on July 20 Dean told him that a battalion of the 21st Infantry was coming to support the withdrawal.

The KPA's 5th Regiment attacked the 1st Battalion of the 34th Infantry Regiment before dawn on July 20, forcing it out of position and uncovering the right flank of the 2nd Battalion of the 19th Regiment. This forced the 2nd Battalion to withdraw as well. By 1:00 a.m. the road to Taejon was open. A feeble counterattack by the 3rd Battalion of the 34th Infantry failed. Just before this attack, the acting 3rd Battalion commander mysteriously disappeared, thrusting command onto a staff captain.

In the battle for Taejon, eight KPA tanks were destroyed by newly issued 3.5-inch rocket launchers. One tank was destroyed by a team led by General Dean himself. Beauchamp, his executive officer, and Dean were all absent from the command post at critical times during the battle. This produced additional confusion and delays in decision making and the execution of orders.

In fighting its way out of Taejon and running a gauntlet of ambushing fire on the road toward 21st Infantry lines, Beauchamp's command suffered terrible casualties. Beauchamp himself escaped late in the day with a small force. A belated and feeble U.S. counterattack at the tunnel area, which was the ambush's choke point, failed. Small groups of GIs made their way out cross-country, although many were killed or captured. Dean became separated and was later captured.

Of the 3,933 men engaged in and around Taejon, 1,150 were casualties. But the battles on the Kum River and at Taejon delayed

A Korean in civilian clothes lies dead in an alley shortly after he was killed by a U.S. soldier (background at left). Another American soldier (at right) looks on. This occurred during intense fighting at Taejon, South Korea, on July 20, 1950. (AP/Wide World Photos)

the KPA for six days, enabling the 25th Infantry and 1st Cavalry divisions to position themselves to slow the KPA advance.

UZAL W. ENT

See also

Dean, William Frishe; Walker, Walton Harris

References

Appleman, Roy E. *United States Army in Korea: South to the Naktong, North to the Yalu.* Washington, DC: Office of the Chief of Military History, 1961.

Blair, Clay. *The Forgotten War: America in Korea, 1950–1953.* New York: Times Books, 1987.

Ent, Uzal W. *Fighting on the Brink: Defense of the Pusan Perimeter.* Paducah, KY: Turner, 1996.

Toland, John. *In Mortal Combat: Korea, 1950–1953.* New York: William Morrow, 1991.

Taejon Agreement
Event Date: July 12, 1950

Bilateral pact between the Republic of Korea (ROK, South Korea) and the United States that established the status and rights of U.S. armed forces stationed in South Korea. The agreement was concluded with an exchange of notes between the South Korean Ministry of Foreign Affairs and the U.S. embassy at Taejon, then the interim capital of South Korea, on July 12, 1950, during the early period of the Korean War.

The formal title of the agreement is "The Agreement Relating to Jurisdiction over Criminal Offenses Committed by the United States Forces in Korea between the Republic of Korea and The United States of America." It was thus not an agreement that transferred authority over South Korean military forces to the United Nations Command (UNC), as is often mentioned in South Korea.

The origin of the agreement dates to the summer of 1948. On August 24, 1948, immediately after the creation of the South Korean government under U.S. auspices, South Korean president Syngman Rhee and commanding general of U.S. forces in Korea Lieutenant General John R. Hodge signed a pact titled "The Executive Agreement between the President of the Republic of Korea and the Commanding General, United States Army Forces in Korea, concerning Interim Military and Security Matters during the Transitional Period." Under this agreement, the South Korean government granted U.S. military authorities the right to use necessary facilities and areas as well as exclusive control over members of the U.S. armed forces, the civilian component, and their dependents until the complete withdrawal of U.S. troops. With the outbreak of the Korean War in June 1950, U.S. forces returned to Korea, and the Taejon Agreement was completed on July 12, 1950. It went into effect the same day that it was signed.

The Taejon Agreement regarded U.S. armed forces as a rescue force that had come to the assistance of South Korea in a life-or-death situation. As such, it allowed U.S. military authorities full criminal jurisdiction over U.S. forces. Regardless of the kinds and locations of crimes committed by American personnel, U.S. courts-martial could exercise exclusive jurisdiction over all U.S. troops stationed in Korea.

Also under this pact, the South Korean government and Ministry of Foreign Affairs conceded that because they were faced with stemming the North Korean military invasion, U.S. armed forces in Korea would not be subject to the authority of any institutions other than the U.S. military authorities.

Similar to this very unequal and so-called backward nation status-of-forces agreement was the "Agreement on Economic Coordination between the Republic of Korea and the United States" signed in Pusan on May 24, 1952, whereby South Korea promised to offer privileges and concessions to on-duty U.S. servicemen and military organizations. Because the American signatory was Clarence E. Meyer, a U.S. diplomat and economic mediator, this was referred to as the Meyer Agreement.

South Korean president Syngman Rhee transferred authority over South Korea's armed forces to the UNC by an arrangement separate from the Taejon Agreement. On July 14, 1950, he sent a letter to UNC commanding general Douglas MacArthur stating that for "the joint military effort of the United Nations on behalf of the Republic of Korea, I am happy to assign to you command authority over all land, sea, and air forces of the Republic of Korea during the period of the continuation of the present state of hostilities" and that "the Korean Army will be proud to serve under your command." Three days later MacArthur welcomed the transfer of the operational authority by replying, "I am proud indeed to have the gallant Republic of Korea forces under my command."

Because the Taejon Agreement was so patently unequal, the South Korean and U.S. governments agreed on negotiations to complete a status of forces agreement for U.S. troops stationed in Korea. These began immediately after the signing of the U.S–South Korean Mutual Security Treaty. It went into effect soon after the conclusion of the Korean Armistice Agreement that brought the shooting war to an end. The Mutual Security Treaty took the form of a communiqué between Rhee and U.S. secretary of state John Foster Dulles on August 7, 1953. But for a long time, negotiations fell short of the Koreans' expectations. Finally, on July 9, 1966, South Korea and the United States concluded the "Agreement under Article IV of the Mutual Defense Treaty between the United States of America and the Republic of Korea, regarding Facilities and Areas and the Status of United States

Armed Forces in the Republic of Korea," also known as the Status of Forces Agreement (SOFA).

Under Article 22 of this pact, the Taejon Agreement became null and void, with South Korea having "exclusive jurisdiction" over U.S. forces with respect to criminal offenses "except during hostilities and martial law."

JINWUNG KIM

See also

Coulter, John Breitling; Dulles, John Foster; MacArthur, Douglas; Meyer, Clarence Earle; Rhee, Syngman; United States–Republic of Korea Mutual Defense Treaty

References

Headquarters, United States Forces, Korea. *The United States of America and the Republic of Korea Status of Forces Agreement with Related Documents.* Seoul: Headquarters, U.S. FIK, 1967.

Matray, James I., ed. *Historical Dictionary of the Korean War.* Westport, CT: Greenwood, 1991.

Yi, Sok U. *Hanmi Haengjong Hyopjong Yongu* [A Study of the ROK-U.S. Status of Forces Agreement]. Seoul: Min, 1995.

Taft, Robert Alphonso
Birth Date: September 8, 1889
Death Date: July 31, 1953

Conservative quasi-isolationist U.S. senator from Ohio, Republican leader of the U.S. Senate during the Korean War, and fierce critic of President Harry S. Truman's policies toward Korea. Born in Cincinnati, Ohio, on September 8, 1889, Robert Alphonso Taft was the eldest son of Republican president William Howard Taft. The scion of a family that had been politically prominent for several previous generations, Taft was subjected to strong expectations and ambitions that he should continue this tradition, resulting in a personality both driven and self-contained. He was educated at the Taft School for Boys in Watertown, Connecticut; Yale University (graduating in 1910); and Harvard Law School (graduating in 1913), where he was at the top of his class.

In 1914 Taft joined the law firm of Maxwell and Ramsey in Cincinnati. In 1917 after U.S. intervention in World War I, Taft became assistant counsel to the newly formed U.S. Food Administration, headed by future U.S. president Herbert Hoover, and at the end of the war Taft followed his boss to Europe as a legal adviser to the American Relief Administration. For the rest of his life, Taft's views on both domestic and international affairs would reveal the influence of Hoover, who firmly believed that big government was inevitably counterproductive, inefficient, costly, and injurious to individual rights; that statist planning distorted the workings of the market; and that while the United States should play a humanitarian international role, it should give the protection of its own interests a far higher priority than defending those of other countries.

Ohio senator Robert Taft, son of former president William Howard Taft, was called "Mr. Republican," a title that not only reflected his national prominence as a political leader but also characterized the values he held dear. His isolationist position prevented him from gaining the Republican nomination for president in either 1948 or 1952, but he remained influential. (Library of Congress)

In 1920 Taft supported Hoover's unsuccessful bid for the presidency. Setting up his own law practice, Taft, Stettinius, and Hollister, which quickly became one of Cincinnati's top legal firms, Taft also became deeply involved in local and state politics, winning election to a variety of offices despite his dry, humorless, didactic, and professorial style. Hostile to most New Deal measures of the 1930s, including welfare and relief payments, progressive taxes, deficit spending, and government economic intervention, by the time Taft won election to the Senate for Ohio in 1938 he was firmly identified with his party's conservative wing.

Taft was equally critical of President Franklin D. Roosevelt's foreign policies. When World War II began, Taft opposed U.S. aid to the Allies, supporting the America First policies enunciated by Hoover and others, insisting that war would destroy American civil liberties and that Germany posed no danger to the Western Hemisphere. After U.S. intervention, Taft constantly assailed what he viewed as the excesses of domestic controls and propaganda while opposing the creation of the World Bank or any other international organization apart from the United Nations (UN). Although Taft became somewhat more liberal domestically, favoring federal aid to education, public housing, and a minimum income for all, he still believed firmly in limited government, fiscal conservatism, and checks on the power of organized labor.

In 1946 Taft became the floor leader of the Republican Party, a ratification of his existing standing as a major figure within the bipartisan conservative coalition that effectively dominated Congress. Immune to appeals for bipartisanship, as the Cold War developed he opposed heavy defense expenditures, voted in 1946 against the large American loan to Britain, complained that U.S. military and economic support for Greece and Turkey and the Marshall Plan were all too expensive, and opposed the creation of the North Atlantic Treaty Organization (NATO) as being likely to provoke the Soviet Union into escalating the Cold War. Taft believed that U.S. nuclear airpower could safeguard the United States from any foreign attack and that his country should not commit troops outside the Western Hemisphere.

By the time the Korean War began, Taft, although one of the most prominent Republican senators and who had earned the nickname "Mr. Republican," had lost two potential presidential nominations in 1940 and 1948 to more attractive candidates. Truman's unexpected presidential victory in 1948 had also shocked Taft and the Republican Party. As Republican majority leader, Taft therefore moved to take advantage of the Korean War to shore up both his party's and his own political fortunes in the forthcoming 1952 presidential campaign. Three days after the invasion of the Republic of Korea (ROK, South Korea) by the Democratic People's Republic of Korea (DPRK, North Korea), Taft decried the administration's failure to seek either a formal declaration of war or a congressional resolution authorizing the use of force in Korea. He also laid much of the responsibility for the war on the administration's "bungling and inconsistent foreign policy," by which he referred among other matters to Secretary of State Dean Acheson's National Press Club speech of January 1950. Taft even suggested that the United States might do well to pull out of Korea and base its defenses on a line running through the island positions of Taiwan and Japan. Although he reluctantly supported Truman's initial decision to commit forces to Korea, after communist China's intervention in late 1950, Taft began to accuse the president of mishandling the war.

After Truman's recall of Far East Command commander Douglas MacArthur in April 1951, Taft publicly defended the general. Abandoning his own customary restraint, he advocated MacArthur's preferred and highly provocative measures of bombing Chinese supply lines in Manchuria and including Guomindang (GMD, Nationalist) troops from the Republic of China in United Nations Command (UNC) forces. Taft tolerated the extremist tactics of Republican senator Joseph R. McCarthy, even though he found them personally distasteful, in the belief that they were likely to enhance the Republican Party's chances of victory in 1952.

Campaigning for the 1952 Republican nomination (which he lost to the internationalist war hero Dwight D. Eisenhower), Taft harped constantly on the refrain that the Democratic administration had blundered unnecessarily into an expensive war that it could neither win nor end with honor. Eisenhower and other Republican candidates continued to stress this theme in the successful autumn election campaign. Selected as Republican majority leader after the election, a more reserved Taft then unsuccessfully attempted to rein in the excesses of McCarthyism. Taft died of cancer in New York City on July 31, 1953.

PRISCILLA ROBERTS

See also

Acheson, Dean Gooderham; MacArthur, Douglas; McCarthy, Joseph Raymond; McCarthyism; Truman, Harry S.; Truman's Recall of MacArthur

References

Caridi, Ronald J. *The Korean War and American Politics: The Republican Party as a Case Study.* Philadelphia: University of Pennsylvania Press, 1968.

DeJohn, Samuel, Jr. "Robert A. Taft, Economic Conservatism, and Opposition to United States Foreign Policy, 1944–1951." Unpublished PhD dissertation, University of Southern California, Los Angeles, 1976.

Kepley, David R. *The Collapse of the Middle Way: Senate Republicans and the Bipartisan Foreign Policy, 1948–1952.* New York: Greenwood, 1982.

Matthews, Geoffrey. "Robert A. Taft, the Constitution and American Foreign Policy, 1939–53." *Journal of Contemporary History* 17(3) (July 1982): 507–522.

Paterson, James T. *Mr. Republican: A Biography of Robert A. Taft.* Boston: Houghton Mifflin, 1972.

Ricks, John Addison. "'Mr. Integrity' and McCarthyism: Senator Robert A. Taft and Senator Joseph R. McCarthy." Unpublished PhD dissertation, University of North Carolina, 1974.

Sylvester, John A. "Taft, Dulles and Ike: New Faces for 1952." *Mid-America* 76(2) (April 1994): 157–179.

Taft, Robert A. *A Foreign Policy for Americans.* Garden City, NY: Doubleday, 1951.

Taft-Hartley Act
Event Date: June 23, 1947

Congressional act cosponsored by Republican senator Robert A. Taft and Republican U.S. representative Fred A. Hartley Jr. that became law on June 23, 1947, over President Harry S. Truman's veto. The Taft-Hartley Act (also known as the Labor-Management Relations Act) was essentially designed to rein in the power of labor unions, purge them of alleged communists, and give employers more latitude in dealing with labor demands. Taft-Hartley effectively amended the 1935 National Labor Relations Act (Wagner Act), which was passed in the midst of the Great Depression and had granted significant concessions to organized labor. Many Republicans and a cabal of conservative Democrats sought to trim the power of labor unions in the post–World War II

period, and Taft-Hartley was the most far-reaching effort to do so. Detractors of the bill derided it as a "slave labor bill." Organized labor saw it as a significant step backward in employer-employee relations, and President Truman publicly lambasted the bill and angrily vetoed it. His veto was overridden, however.

Taft-Hartley enumerated numerous "unfair labor practices" that had been heretofore allowed. Specifically, it forbade jurisdictional and wildcat strikes; strikes waged solely out of political expediency or sympathy for other workers; secondary boycotts; picketing considered to be abusive, disruptive, or intimidating; closed shops; and monetary contributions to candidates for elective federal offices by an organized labor union. All union members were now required to sign sworn affidavits that they were not members of any communist organization, and individual states were given the right to pass right-to-work laws that could further impinge on labor's prerogatives and could severely limit the concept of a union shop. Finally, the federal government, mainly through the National Labor Relations Board (NLRB), was empowered to issue legally binding injunctions against unions that threatened a strike that might adversely affect "national safety or health." Each injunction could last as long as 80 days and was intended as a cooling-off period while both sides negotiated to avert a strike. During the injunction period, workers were expected to continue to work.

The Taft-Hartley Act became a thorn in the side of the Truman administration during the Korean War, as the White House sought to avert strikes that might have imperiled the war or the rearmament effort then under way. On numerous occasions, when labor unions threatened to strike, the Wage Stabilization Board (WSB), created in 1950, was asked to adjudicate labor-management disputes. This proved controversial because supporters of Taft-Hartley believed that the WSB was circumventing the law. In 1951 both the U.S. Chamber of Commerce and the National Association of Manufacturers publicly denounced the WSB's adjudication powers and asked that all labor-management disagreements be handled via the Taft-Hartley Act. They were unsuccessful in their attempt to stymie the wage board.

Taft-Hartley also figured prominently in the 1952 Steel Seizure Crisis. When organized steel workers and steel manufacturers were unable to agree on a new labor contract in late 1951, Truman was faced with a difficult decision. If he allowed a strike to take place, American national security and the safety of U.S. troops in Korea could be compromised. If he invoked Taft-Hartley and the NLRB issued an 80-day injunction, he would engender the wrath of organized labor and in an election year no less. If he allowed the WSB to handle the dispute, there would be cries of political opportunism, and U.S. industry would be put off. Truman chose the third option, as the least incendiary of the three, and handed the case to the WSB for adjudication in December 1951.

When steel makers refused to accede to the recommendations of the WSB in March 1952, Truman decided to seize most U.S. steel mills to keep workers from striking and to keep steel rolling out of plants. He was immediately challenged, and his move was ultimately ruled unconstitutional by the U.S. Supreme Court in July 1952. Truman steadfastly refused to invoke Taft-Hartley, which he had so vociferously rejected, and some 600,000 steel workers walked off the job. Not until July 24, 1952, was the strike settled, by the president himself. Some have argued that Truman should have invoked Taft-Hartley from the very beginning, which would have made the issue seem less political and may have averted a strike.

PAUL G. PIERPAOLI JR.

See also

Organized Labor; Steel Plants, Truman's Seizure of; Taft, Robert Alphonso; Truman, Harry S.; Wage Stabilization Board

References

Donovan, Robert J. *Tumultuous Years: The Presidency of Harry S. Truman.* New York: Norton, 1982.

Marcus, Maeva. *Truman and the Steel Seizure Case: The Limits of Presidential Power.* New York: Columbia University Press, 1977.

Pierpaoli, Paul G., Jr. *Truman and Korea: The Political Culture of the Early Cold War.* Columbia: University of Missouri Press, 1999.

TAILBOARD, **Operation**
Start Date: October 25, 1950
End Date: November 4, 1950

An amphibious operation by the United Nations Command (UNC). In it the U.S. X Corps headquarters, the 1st U.S. Marine Division, and supporting elements were landed at the port of Wonsan in the Democratic People's Republic of Korea (DPRK, North Korea) during October 25–31, 1950, and the 7th Infantry Division (U.S. Army) and supporting elements were landed over the shore near the town of Iwon from October 26 to November 4, 1950.

On September 15, 1950, Major General Edward M. Almond's U.S. X Corps landed on the west coast of Korea at Inchon. Soon thereafter, U.S. and South Korean forces of Lieutenant General Walton H. Walker's U.S. Eighth Army broke out of the Pusan Perimeter and attacked to the north, making contact with X Corps forces south of Seoul, the capital of the Republic of Korea (ROK, South Korea) on September 27. On that same day, U.S. president Harry S. Truman ordered implementation of the planned invasion of North Korea.

The plan was for the U.S. Eighth Army to continue its advance in the west while South Korean forces pushed north along the east coast. Meanwhile, Vice Admiral Arthur D. Struble's Joint Task Force 7 and Rear Admiral James H. Doyle's Amphibious Force Far East (Task Force 90) would land X Corps, consisting of Major General Oliver P. Smith's 1st Marine Division and Major General David G. Barr's 7th Infantry Division, at Wonsan on the northeast coast. The 187th Airborne Regimental Combat Team (RCT) would stand by to carry out an airdrop or air landing as required. Major General Robert H. Soule's 3rd Infantry Division (minus the 65th

RCT, which was operating in Korea with the U.S. Eighth Army) prepared to deploy from the port of Sasebo, Japan, to reinforce X Corps. The 65th RCT would sail to Wonsan from the southeastern Korean port of Pusan to link up with its parent 3rd Division when directed.

Brigadier General Kim Paik Il's South Korean I Corps began the offensive, with Brigadier General Choe Sok's South Korean 3rd Division crossing the 38th Parallel into North Korea to the east on October 1, 1950. On October 4 X Corps elements, the 1st Marine Division, and the 2nd Engineer Special Brigade—the U.S. Army's amphibious experts who had supported the September 15 landing—loaded on transports at Inchon while the 7th U.S. Division moved by road and rail to Pusan, from which point they were to sail. In the west, the U.S. Eighth Army began its attack north across the 38th Parallel on October 9.

General Kim's corps advanced rapidly up the east coast, capturing Wonsan on October 11. By this time, UNC naval forces had discovered that the North Koreans had heavily mined the approaches to Wonsan Harbor. The U.S. Marine Corps landing was delayed while minesweeping operations proceeded, although an advance party of X Corps Headquarters and aircraft of Major General Field Harris's 1st U.S. Marine Air Wing moved into the port area by air between October 13 and 16. Offshore, minesweeping operations continued while the ships carrying the 1st U.S. Marine Division steamed north and south off the coast in what the marines called Operation YO-YO. It was not until October 25 that the channel was declared clear and the ships were allowed to enter the port. The next day, the main ship-to-shore landing began. Unloading was completed on October 31.

With the 1st U.S. Marine Division at Wonsan, Almond no longer saw any benefit to landing the U.S. 7th Infantry Division in its wake. Instead, he decided to land it across the beach at Iwon, about 105 miles north of Wonsan, to be better able to carry out UNC commander General Douglas MacArthur's orders for a rapid advance. On October 26 Almond directed General Kim's I Corps to advance north rapidly. The 1st U.S. Marine Division was ordered to relieve South Korean forces at Wonsan and at the coastal town of Kojo to the south, concentrate one RCT in the Hamhung-Hungnam area, and advance rapidly to the north, being prepared to use one battalion landing team (BLT) for an amphibious movement to outflank pockets of Korean People's Army (KPA, North Korean Army) forces. The U.S. 7th Infantry Division was ordered to land at Iwon and advance rapidly to the northern border.

Colonel Herbert B. Powell's 17th Regimental Combat Team was selected to make the initial landing at Iwon to secure the beach. To accomplish this, his troops unloaded from the transports on which they were already embarked at Pusan harbor and reloaded aboard tank landing ships (LSTs). The 2nd Engineer Special Brigade was at sea when it received word that instead of debarking at Wonsan port, they would land over the shore at Iwon and assist the 7th Division. They arrived on October 29 to find eight LSTs already on the beach unloading the 17th RCT. The empty LSTs and other smaller landing craft then ferried ashore troops and equipment from the other units. On October 30 a storm struck, temporarily suspending unloading operations, but by November 4 more than 26,000 men of the U.S. 7th Infantry Division and supporting elements had landed, concluding Operation TAILBOARD, although some late-arriving LSTs continued to bring in supplies until November 17.

Between November 5 and 15, X Corps was bolstered by the arrival of the U.S. 3rd Infantry Division at Wonsan. With the South Korean 26th Regiment attached, the U.S. 3rd Infantry Division relieved the U.S. 1st Marine Division of responsibility for securing the port areas and took up blocking positions to deal with North Korean forces moving up from the south while the 1st Marine and 7th Infantry divisions continued north in an advance that would soon be halted by the Chinese intervention.

DONALD W. BOOSE JR.

See also

Almond, Edward Mallory; Amphibious Force Far East; Barr, David Goodwin; Doyle, James Henry; Kim Paek Il; MacArthur, Douglas; Naval Forces Far East; Smith, Oliver Prince; Struble, Arthur Dewey; X Corps; 38th Parallel, Decision to Cross; Wonsan Landing and Evacuation

References

Alexander, Joseph H. *Fleet Operation in a Mobile War, September 1950–June 1951.* Washington, DC: Naval Historical Center, 2001.

Appleman, Roy E. *Escaping the Trap: The U.S. Army X Corps in Northeast Korea, 1950.* College Station: Texas A&M University Press, 1990.

Boose, Donald W., Jr. *Over the Beach: U.S. Army Amphibious Operations in the Korean War.* Fort Leavenworth, KS: Combat Studies Institute Press, 2008.

Chisholm, Donald. "Negotiated Command Relationships: Korean War Amphibious Operations, 1950." *Naval War College Review* 53(2) (Spring 2000): 65–124.

Field, James A., Jr. *History of United States Naval Operations, Korea.* Washington, DC: U.S. Government Printing Office, 1962.

Montross, Lynn, et al. *U.S. Marine Operations in Korea, 1950–1953.* 5 vols. Washington, DC: U.S. Marine Corps Historical Branch, 1954–1972.

Taiwan, Neutralization of

U.S. plan to halt possible hostilities between the People's Republic of China (PRC) and the Republic of China (Taiwan, then known as Formosa). In 1945 at the end of World War II, the Chinese Civil War resumed between the Nationalists led by Jiang Jieshi (Chiang Kai-shek) and the Communists led by Mao Zedong. Although Mao had asked the United States to remain neutral, Washington actively supported Jiang and the Nationalists. In 1949 the communists won the war and pushed the Nationalist forces off the mainland onto the island of Taiwan. Thereafter Taiwan was known by its Nationalist government as the Republic of China (ROC, Taiwan). Both the PRC and the ROC claimed to represent all China.

By 1950 both the communists and Nationalists were posturing for diplomatic advantage. Jiang vowed to retake the mainland and restore his regime to power, while Mao pledged to reunite Taiwan with the mainland. In the United Nations (UN), despite opposition from some of its allies, the United States backed Jiang and the Nationalists as the legitimate government of China. The United States also refused to allow the PRC to be seated on the UN Security Council.

President Harry S. Truman's administration realized that Korea could easily have ramifications on the China front, and Washington sought to forestall any renewal of conflict between the two rival Chinese governments. Concurrent with the opening of hostilities in Korea, the Truman administration worked hard to prevent the two Chinas from capitalizing on the situation to attack one another. Shortly after the start of the Korean War, on June 27, 1950, President Harry S. Truman ordered the U.S. Seventh Fleet to the Taiwan Strait.

U.S. leaders at the time saw communism as monolithic, and Truman in any case believed that the PRC might seek to take advantage of fighting in Korea to seize Taiwan. Such a move would have materially strengthened the communist bloc and thus compromised U.S. national security interests in Asia. In addition, Truman sought to quiet domestic political opponents who would demand to know why U.S. forces were not being used to protect Taiwan when they were being employed in Korea.

Truman's action was meant to achieve three results: to forestall PRC leaders from using the fighting in Korea to launch an invasion of Taiwan, to prevent Jiang from initiating his promised assault to retake the mainland, and to keep UN attention focused on Korea. Either of the first two could have precipitated a wider war.

The PRC immediately denounced the U.S. action. The PRC claimed that Taiwan was a part of China and not an independent nation and asserted that the U.S. action interfered with its sovereign rights and constituted armed aggression against it. The PRC did not, however, initiate military action involving the Seventh Fleet.

The U.S. naval presence between Taiwan and the mainland indeed prevented conflict there. Overall, this neutralization of Taiwan worked to the advantage of the United States, which did not have to worry about a renewal of the Chinese Civil War as it helped the Republic of Korea (ROK, South Korea) in its war against the Democratic People's Republic of Korea (DPRK, North Korea).

When the fighting ended in Korea, the United States could no longer justify its involvement in the dispute between Taiwan and the PRC as the result of wanting to avoid a wider regional conflict. The next year, 1954, the United States signed a defensive treaty with Taiwan that considered any armed attack on Taiwan as a breach of U.S. national security interests and committed the United States to act "to meet the common danger in accordance with its constitutional processes."

Washington pursued a One China policy until 1978, when the United States officially recognized the PRC. Since then, however, the ROC has remained an ally of the United States and has maintained its independence.

DAVID R. BUCK

See also

China, People's Republic of; China, Republic of; Jiang Jieshi; Mao Zedong; Truman, Harry S.

References

Accinelli, Robert. *Crisis and Commitment: United States Policy toward Taiwan, 1950–1955.* Chapel Hill: University of North Carolina Press, 1998.

Cheng, Tun-jen, Chi Huang, and Samual S. G. Wu, eds. *Inherited Rivalry; Conflict across the Taiwan Straits.* Boulder, CO: Lynne Rienner, 1995.

Finkelstein, David M. *Washington's Taiwan Dilemma, 1949–1950: From Abandonment to Salvation.* Fairfax, VA: George Mason University Press, 1993.

Stueck, William W., Jr., ed. *Korean War in World History.* Lexington: University Press of Kentucky, 2004.

———. *The Road to Confrontation: American Policy toward China and Korea, 1947–1950.* Chapel Hill: University of North Carolina Press, 1981.

Tucker, Nancy Bernkopf. *Taiwan, Hong Kong, and the U.S., 1945–1992: Uncertain Friendships.* New York: Twayne, 1994.

Tasca, Henry Joseph
Birth Date: August 23, 1912
Death Date: August 22, 1979

Economist and U.S. diplomat. Born in Providence, Rhode Island, on August 23, 1912, Henry Joseph Tasca graduated with a bachelor's degree from Temple University in 1933. He completed his master's of business degree at the University of Pennsylvania in 1934, and three years later he earned his PhD there. He also attended the London School of Economics for one year as a Penfield scholar.

Tasca then joined the U.S. Foreign Service as an economic analyst, working in the Department of Trade Agreements. He became assistant director of the Trade Regulation and Commercial Policy Project in 1938 and was an economic adviser specializing in trade for the National Defense Commission.

During World War II, Tasca served in the U.S. Navy and rose to the rank of lieutenant commander. Immediately after the war he went to work at the Rome embassy as a representative of the Treasury Department. Additionally, he was a special assistant to the secretary of the treasury and an alternate executive director with the International Monetary Fund (IMF) during 1948 and 1949.

In 1950 Tasca was with the Department of Economic Affairs for the Marshall Plan as staff director of plans and policy. Soon afterward he served as an economic adviser to W. Averell Harriman, President Harry S. Truman's special assistant for national security affairs. After that, Tasca served overseas as a U.S. deputy special representative.

In 1953 President Dwight D. Eisenhower wanted a firsthand report on the economic situation in the Republic of Korea (ROK, South Korea), and on April 9 he named Tasca as his special representative to conduct a thorough investigation of the situation to make recommendations to the president and the National Security Council (NSC) concerning U.S. assistance to the South Korean economy.

The Tasca Mission actually followed the Meyer Mission, headed by Clarence E. Meyer and conducted in the spring of 1952. Meyer's mission had been geared more toward the financial relationship during the war between South Korea and the United Nations (UN), while Tasca surveyed the South Korean economy and the effects of the war on it.

Tasca arrived at Pusan on April 17, 1953, and for the next seven weeks he examined the situation in South Korea, meeting with various members of the UN Reconstruction Agency, the South Korean National Assembly, the Korean Chamber of Commerce, and officials in the South Korean government. Tasca returned to the United States on June 15 and submitted an extensive and comprehensive report.

Tasca's report revealed the devastating effects of the war on South Korea, including 2.5 million refugees and some 60,000 demolished homes. U.S. charities provided half of the subsistence for the population. Inflation had skyrocketed and per capita income had plummeted, leaving the population unable to achieve even its former standard of living without extensive economic assistance. Tasca's initial recommendations called for a $1 billion payout over a three-year period, although he wanted a thorough reorganization of agencies that would disperse these funds. Tasca also urged the rebuilding and expansion of the South Korean armed forces as an important step of reconstruction.

Tasca's report was reviewed by the NSC and approved by President Eisenhower on June 23, 1953. It provided concrete evidence that the Eisenhower administration was committed to a long-term involvement in restoring South Korea's economy and morale. Congress ultimately provided more than $600 million to rebuild South Korea.

Tasca next became director of the Foreign Operations Administration in Rome. In 1956 he moved to Bonn, where he served four years. Between 1960 and 1965 he was deputy assistant secretary for African affairs, and from 1965 to 1974 he served as ambassador to Morocco and then to Greece.

Tasca retired in Rome and wrote two books concerning U.S. trade policy. He died in an automobile accident in Lausanne, Switzerland, on August 22, 1979.

MONICA SPICER

See also

Eisenhower, Dwight David; Harriman, William Averell; Meyer, Clarence Earle; Refugees; Truman, Harry S.

References

Hermes, Walter G. *U.S. Army in the Korean War: Truce Tent and Fighting Front.* Washington, DC: Office of the Chief of Military History, 1966.

Matray, James I., ed. *Historical Dictionary of the Korean War*. Westport, CT: Greenwood, 1991.

Task Force Kean
Start Date: August 9, 1950
End Date: August 12, 1950

In early August 1950 Eighth Army commander Lieutenant General Walton H. Walker decided to begin the first major United Nations Command (UNC) offensive of the war to build up the confidence of his soldiers. Named Task Force Kean after 25th Division commander Major General William B. Kean, the force consisted of the 25th Division plus the just-arrived 5th Regimental Combat Team (RCT) and the 1st Marine Brigade.

Walker assigned the mission to four regiments. The 35th Infantry Regiment of the 25th Division would attack west along the northern Masan Road to Muchon-ni. The 5th RCT would attack from the southern road at Chindong-ni and link up with the 25th at Muchon-ni. The 5th Marine Regiment was to attack along the coastal road from Chindong-ni to Kosong and Sachon, and the 24th Regiment was to secure the area behind the attacking forces. In the last phase of the attack, the 5th Marines from Sachon were to link up in Chinju with the 5th RCT and the 35th Infantry, attacking west from Muchon-ni.

Eighth Army headquarters, however, was unaware of the movement of the Korean People's Army (KPA, North Korean Army) 6th Division that was attacking rapidly from the west toward Pusan and would run head-on into Task Force Kean. As early as August 2, several thousand North Koreans had infiltrated the great hill mass of Sobuk-san between the northern and southern routes to Pusan. This hill mass was very steep and was honeycombed with old mines. Most roads leading into these hills approached from the west, with few from the east.

The U.S. operation, which began on August 7, initially moved slowly because KPA forces at Sobuk-san were able to impede U.S. units massing along the coastal road at Chindong-ni. For four days, constant fighting occurred between these forces. Not until August 9 did Kean believe that lines of communication had been sufficiently cleared for the 5th RCT and the 5th Marines to begin their attack.

On August 9 the 5th Marines moved rapidly into the attack. By August 11 they reached the town of Kosong. This attack was supported by U.S. Marine Corps Chance Vought F4U Corsairs and U.S. Air Force (North American) F-51 Mustang aircraft. KPA resistance was so weakened by this air support that fresh marine units continued to push on unopposed until they were a few miles from Sachon. Here on August 12 the KPA tried to ambush the marines and counterattack. This achieved only partial success because marine ground units, supported by Corsairs, were able to control the surrounding hills and retain their positions. Subsequently, the marines received orders to return to Chindong-ni to help extricate the 5th RCT, which had been cut off by KPA units and needed assistance.

The central force of Task Force Kean encountered the heaviest fighting and experienced the most casualties. On August 10 the 1st and 2nd battalions of the 5th RCT had jumped off in the attack to link up with the 35th Infantry at Muchon-ni. In spite of light KPA resistance in the Sobuk-san hill mass, the regiment pushed on to the narrow pass beyond Pongam-ni. The 3rd Battalion of the 5th RCT passed through the other two battalions and proceeded over the pass to Songdong to link up with the 35th Infantry. Here the battalion followed the railroad tracks up Chinju pass to high ground overlooking Chinju. The battalion then dug in defense positions for the night while the rest of the regiment remained near Pongam-ni. On the morning of August 12 a company of North Koreans, their helmets camouflaged with tree branches, attacked Company I but were driven off.

While the 3rd Battalion of the 5th RCT was locked in fighting close to the Chinju objective, more activity was taking place in the regiment's rear. On the night of August 10, KPA units attacked the 1st Battalion and artillery units in Pongam-ni. KPA mortar and artillery fire landed all around, and many injuries resulted from rock fragments thrown up by the blasts. At the height of the conflict, the commanders of both the 1st Battalion and the 555th Field Artillery Battalion (FAB) were wounded. With daylight, U.S. air strikes drove the KPA units back into the hills.

Eighth Army headquarters now pressured General Kean to speed up his attack. The marines were enjoying considerable success on their route, while the 5th RCT was moving too slowly. In response, the 2nd Battalion and the 555th FAB of the 5th RCT were sent through the pass northwest of Pongam-ni to join the 3rd Battalion outside Chinju. The rest of the regiment at Pongam-ni lined up in column and prepared to traverse the pass at daybreak. Before dawn the KPA attacked the unprotected artillery and regimental supply train from all sides in what came to be known as Bloody Gulch. The attack was almost a massacre. KPA tanks approached unopposed and fired point-blank directly into the emplacements of the 555th FAB and of the newly arrived 19th FAB. These units together lost about 190 men killed and 140 wounded in the engagement.

On August 12 Task Force Kean received orders to return to its original lines. With the help of close air support from U.S. Air Force F-51s and F4U Corsairs flown by the marines, the task force withdrew. Most of the 5th RCT withdrew through the 35th Infantry. In spite of high losses, Task Force Kean was the first major offensive of the Eighth Army that stopped the KPA thrust from the southwest toward its goal of the port of Pusan.

DANIEL R. BEIRNE

See also
Eighth Army, U.S.; Kean, William Benjamin; Walker, Walton Harris

References
Appleman, Roy E. *United States Army in Korea: South to the Naktong, North to the Yalu*. Washington, DC: Office of the Chief of Military History, 1961.

Blair, Clay. *The Forgotten War: America in Korea, 1950–1953.* New York: Times Books, 1987.

Ent, Uzal W. *Fighting on the Brink: Defense of the Pusan Perimeter.* Paducah, KY: Turner, 1996.

Hoyt, Edwin P. *The Pusan Perimeter.* New York: Stein and Day, 1984.

Toland, John. *In Mortal Combat: Korea, 1950–1953.* New York: William Morrow, 1991.

Task Force 90

See Amphibious Force Far East

Task Force Smith

First U.S. Army unit to enter combat in Korea. On June 30, 1950, President Harry S. Truman authorized General Douglas MacArthur to commit ground forces under his command to Korea, and MacArthur in turn instructed General Walton H. Walker, commander of the Eighth Army, to order the 24th Division there. Early on July 1 the Eighth Army provided that a makeshift infantry battalion of the 24th Division be flown to Korea in the six Douglas C-54 Skymaster transport aircrafts that were available. The remainder of the division would follow by ship. The initial force was to make contact with the Korean People's Army (KPA, North Korean Army) and fight a delaying action. MacArthur called Task Force Smith an "arrogant display of strength" and hoped that it would fool the North Koreans into believing that a larger force was at hand. Some officers assumed that even this small U.S. force would give the North Koreans pause once they realized who they were fighting.

Task Force Smith was named for Lieutenant Colonel Charles B. ("Brad") Smith, commanding officer, 1st Battalion, 21st Regiment, 24th Infantry Division. Task Force Smith consisted of half of the battalion headquarters company, half of the communications platoon, the understrength rifle Companies B and C, two 75-millimeter (mm) recoilless rifles each and crews from Companies D and M (the heavy weapons companies of the 1st and 3rd battalions, respectively), a medical platoon from the 21st Regimental Medical Company, and two 4.2-inch mortars from the 21st Infantry's heavy mortar company, each manned by a private from that company as well as a noncommissioned officer and 4 or 5 men from Company B. In addition to their rifles, the infantrymen had six 2.36-inch bazooka rocket launchers and four 60-mm mortars. Each man was issued 120 rounds of ammunition and two days' of C rations. Most of the men were 20 years old or less; only a sixth had seen combat. As finally dug in, Task Force Smith consisted of 17 officers and 389 enlisted men in its infantry element.

The artillery element of 134 officers and enlisted men, which joined the task force on July 4, came from the 52nd Field Artillery Battalion. It consisted of a small contingent from the headquarters

Soldiers of Task Force Smith, named for its commander Lieutenant Colonel Charles B. Smith, arrive at Taejon Railroad Station in South Korea on July 2, 1950. Task Force Smith was the first U.S. Army unit to enter combat in Korea. (Department of Defense)

and service batteries and all of Battery A, with five 105-mm howitzers (one howitzer was left behind at Pyongtaek) and 73 vehicles. Lieutenant Colonel Miller O. Perry commanded the artillery element, which had 9 officers and 125 enlisted men.

From Smith on down the men of the task force were enthusiastic about the assignment and believed that the operation in Korea would be a piece of cake, with the North Koreans running away when they saw the American uniforms. The task force left Japan by air on the morning of July 1 and received an enthusiastic welcome by South Koreans on their arrival, which provided a deceiving boost to morale. General William Dean, commander of the 24th Division, then ordered Smith to block the main road to Pusan as far north as possible. This decision resulted in the July 5, 1950, Battle of Osan.

SPENCER C. TUCKER

See also

Dean, William Frishe; MacArthur, Douglas; Osan, Battle of; Truman, Harry S.; Walker, Walton Harris

References

Appleman, Roy E. *United States Army in Korea: South to the Naktong, North to the Yalu.* Washington, DC: Office of the Chief of Military History, 1961.

Collins, J. Lawton. *War in Peacetime. The History and Lessons of Korea.* Boston: Houghton Mifflin, 1969.

Gugeler, Russell A. *Combat Actions in Korea.* Rev. ed. Washington, DC: U.S. Army, Center of Military History, 1987.

Rees, David. *Korea: The Limited War.* New York: St. Martin's, 1990.

Taylor, Maxwell Davenport
Birth Date: August 26, 1901
Death Date: April 19, 1987

U.S. Army general and diplomat, commander of the Eighth Army during the Korean War, and later chairman of the Joint Chiefs of Staff (JCS). Born in Keytesville, Missouri, on August 26, 1901, Maxwell Davenport Taylor graduated in 1922 from the U.S. Military Academy at West Point as first captain and fourth in his class. Commissioned in the engineers, he transferred to the field artillery in 1926. Sent to Paris to study French, he returned to teach French and Spanish at West Point (1928–1932). After graduation from the Command and General Staff College in 1935, Taylor studied Japanese in Tokyo. He was briefly assistant military attaché in Beijing (Peking), China, and in 1940 he graduated from the Army War College and was then assigned to Latin America to study defense needs. He next commanded the 12th Artillery Battalion at San Antonio, Texas. In July 1941 he was assigned as secretary to the army chief of staff.

In the spring of 1942 Taylor became the chief of staff of Major General Matthew B. Ridgway's 82nd Infantry Division and remained with it when it became the 82nd Airborne Division. Promoted to brigadier general that December, Taylor participated in combat in Sicily and Italy in 1943, and in September he made a dramatic trip behind German lines to Rome to investigate the feasibility of a paratroop drop to secure the city. In March 1944 he took command of the 101st Airborne Division. Promoted to major general that May, he parachuted with his division into Normandy on the night of June 5–6, 1944. He commanded the 82nd Division in its September drop around Eindhoven in The Netherlands during Operation MARKET-GARDEN, when he was wounded.

After the war, Taylor served as superintendent of the U.S. Military Academy (1945–1949), where he helped to modernize its curriculum. In 1949 he commanded U.S. forces in Berlin, and in August 1951 he became deputy chief of staff of the army for operations (G-3), a position in which he favored desegregation of the army.

On February 11, 1953, Lieutenant General Taylor succeeded General James A. Van Fleet as commander of the Eighth Army in Korea. Van Fleet had grown increasingly frustrated with Washington's conduct of the last two years of the war. Taylor inherited this situation. He was acutely aware of president-elect Dwight D. Eisenhower's desire to minimize United Nations Command (UNC) casualties and bring about an early and honorable end to the war. Taylor also had to deal with South Korean president Syngman Rhee's opposition to an armistice arrangement that would leave Korea divided. Taylor chose to regard recent Chinese attacks as mere face-saving measures and refused to allow the UNC to retake Old Baldy and Pork Chop Hill. He directed military operations in Korea until the armistice in July 1953.

In November 1954 Taylor was promoted to general and was made commander in chief of the Far East Command. In June 1955 he succeeded General Matthew B. Ridgway as army chief of staff, a post that Taylor held until July 1959. He took issue with the doctrine of massive nuclear retaliation and the New Look defense policy advocated by the Eisenhower administration and chairman of the JCS Admiral Arthur W. Radford; Taylor favored a larger military capable of flexible response. When Radford's view prevailed, in July 1959 Taylor resigned.

Taylor then wrote *The Uncertain Trumpet* (1960) in which he urged a reappraisal of U.S. military policy and a buildup of conventional forces and the doctrine of flexible response. Taylor believed that brushfire wars, not nuclear conflicts, presented the greatest military challenge to the United States.

In 1961 President John F. Kennedy, a firm proponent of flexible response, made Taylor his military adviser. After a trip to the Republic of Vietnam (RVN, South Vietnam) in October 1961, Taylor urged that Kennedy send additional military aid and advisers there as well as 8,000 ground combat troops. In October 1962 in an unprecedented move, Kennedy recalled Taylor from retirement to serve as chairman of the JCS, a post he held until 1964. In this position, Taylor urged a forceful commitment to South Vietnam and the bombing of the Democratic Republic of Vietnam (DRVN, North Vietnam).

Taylor undertook his most controversial role in July 1964 when he became U.S. ambassador to South Vietnam. Disillusioned by

Eighth Army commander Lieutenant General Maxwell D. Taylor and Brigadier General Ralph M. Osborne in conference as they arrive for an inspection tour of "Freedom Village" in Panmunjom erected for the exchange of prisoners of war. (National Archives)

early 1965, Taylor urged that U.S. ground troops be used only in an enclave approach to protect major population centers. He believed that the South Vietnamese lacked motivation rather than personnel and that U.S. troops would encourage them to do less of the fighting. He lost this battle to General William Westmoreland's search-and-destroy approach of seeking out and doing battle with major communist units.

Returning to Washington in July 1965, Taylor joined the group of President Lyndon B. Johnson's senior policy consultants known as the Wise Men. In retirement Taylor wrote his memoirs, published as *Swords and Plowshares* (1972). A daring and resourceful combat leader and an important military thinker, Taylor died in Washington, DC, on April 19, 1987.

SPENCER C. TUCKER

See also

Eisenhower, Dwight David; Joint Chiefs of Staff; Massive Retaliation; New Look Defense Policy; Radford, Arthur William; Rhee, Syngman; Ridgway, Matthew Bunker; Van Fleet, James Alward

References

Blair, Clay. *The Forgotten War: America in Korea, 1950–1953.* New York: Times Books, 1987.

Taylor, John M. *General Maxwell Taylor: The Sword and the Pen.* New York: Doubleday, 1989.

Taylor, Maxwell D. *Swords and Plowshares.* New York: Norton, 1972.

Zaffiri, Samuel. *Westmoreland: A Biography of General William C. Westmoreland.* New York: William Morrow, 1994.

X Corps

Separate United Nations Command (UNC) force activated on August 26, 1950, specifically for the Inchon invasion. General Douglas MacArthur authorized Major General Edward M. Almond to establish a planning group for Operation CHROMITE, code name for the Inchon Landing. This group, known as Force X, initially experienced difficulties in requisitioning supplies because it was not listed as an official organization. Almond then requested that MacArthur upgrade it to a corps. MacArthur agreed, and Almond kept the numerical designation of X, with MacArthur noting that the World War II X Corps had been associated with the U.S. Eighth Army since 1944 and had provided occupation troops in Japan until it had been deactivated in January 1946.

X Corps came directly under MacArthur's Far East Command (FEC) as a self-sustaining miniature army of two reinforced divisions, a tactical air command, a complete artillery group, and engineer and signal units. It also had additional support units for ordnance, maintenance, medical services, transportation services, and the like. X Corps was not dependent on the U.S. Eighth Army in Korea (EUSAK) for supplies. MacArthur designated Almond, his loyal chief of staff, to command X Corps, a decision made in consultation with the Joint Chiefs of Staff (JCS).

Already concerned with the end of command unity brought by the separation of X Corps from EUSAK, the JCS believed that MacArthur was trying to avoid having to place Almond under EUSAK commander Lieutenant General Walton H. Walker, with whom he had quarreled. The JCS also pointed out that Almond was only a major general, not a lieutenant general as was usual for a corps commander, and that he had no experience with amphibious warfare. They suspected with some justification that MacArthur had selected Almond for the command because of his unquestioning loyalty and that MacArthur had planned to reward him by securing his promotion to lieutenant general later. At the same time, Almond retained his position as MacArthur's chief of staff because MacArthur professed to believe that after the Inchon Landing the war would soon be over.

On August 31, 1950, FEC General Order 24 officially gathered X Corps units to prepare for the Inchon Landing. U.S. and South Korean troops collected at embarkation camps in Japan. The 1st Marine Division was the foundation of X Corps; it was supplemented with the U.S. 7th Infantry Division and other U.S. Army and South Korean marine units.

X Corps soon grew to 70,457 men. Preinvasion difficulties to be surmounted included communication problems between U.S. and South Korean soldiers and insufficient supplies. Only the highest-ranking X Corps officers knew what was in the offing, and often requisitions were not expeditiously filled because supply sources did not recognize the urgency for the delivery of goods. Some, including General Walker, also expressed concern about an army officer commanding marines in an amphibious operation.

Despite these problems, the September 15 landing at Inchon went well. As soon as the 7th Marine Regiment was ashore and had secured the beachhead, Almond took over operational command from amphibious commander Rear Admiral James H. Doyle.

Aggressive, tactless, and egotistical, Almond soon sparred with other commanders once ashore. Anxious to recapture Seoul quickly on MacArthur's urging, Almond accused his subordinates of moving too slowly. Tensions soon developed between him and Major General Oliver P. Smith, commander of the 1st Marine Division. Almond also resisted efforts by EUSAK to join forces in pursuit of North Korean troops retreating north to Pyongyang. Almond's chief of staff, Major General Clark L. Ruffner, remarked that Almond "could precipitate a crisis on a desert island with nobody else around." Friction between Almond and his subordinates clearly affected the effectiveness of X Corps.

Members of the 1st Marine Division of X Corps come ashore at Inchon in an amphibious tractor, prepared to plant their flag in the South Korean capital of Seoul, September 1950. (Department of Defense)

Despite pleas from EUSAK after the recapture of Seoul that MacArthur restore unity of command, he refused and decided to reembark X Corps from Inchon and send it by sea around the tip of the peninsula for an amphibious landing at Wonsan. The mission of X Corps was to move west from Wonsan to assist EUSAK in capturing Pyongyang, the capital of the Democratic People's Republic of Korea (DPRK, North Korea).

South Korean troops had already secured the harbor at Wonsan while X Corps was en route. The marines spent almost two weeks at sea (which they dubbed Operation YO-YO) waiting for Wonsan Harbor to be cleared of mines. Finally landing on October 25, the 1st Marine Division began moving north to Hungnam and the Changjin Reservoir because Pyongyang had fallen to South Korean forces on October 19. MacArthur and Almond planned for X Corps to be the first troops to reach the Yalu River. By November 1950, X Corps consisted of 84,785 troops.

On November 11 Almond issued Operation Order 6 for X Corps to advance immediately to the Yalu River. Because of limited North Korean resistance, he and MacArthur hoped to end the war by Christmas. Determined to reach the China border, Almond did not consider EUSAK requests for assistance. X Corps and EUSAK were now separated by the Taebaek Mountain range. Isolated from UNC forces to the west, X Corps received its supplies from Japan.

Because Almond simply followed MacArthur's directives, his command decisions were not always the best. MacArthur discounted the threat of Chinese intervention, and Almond blindly

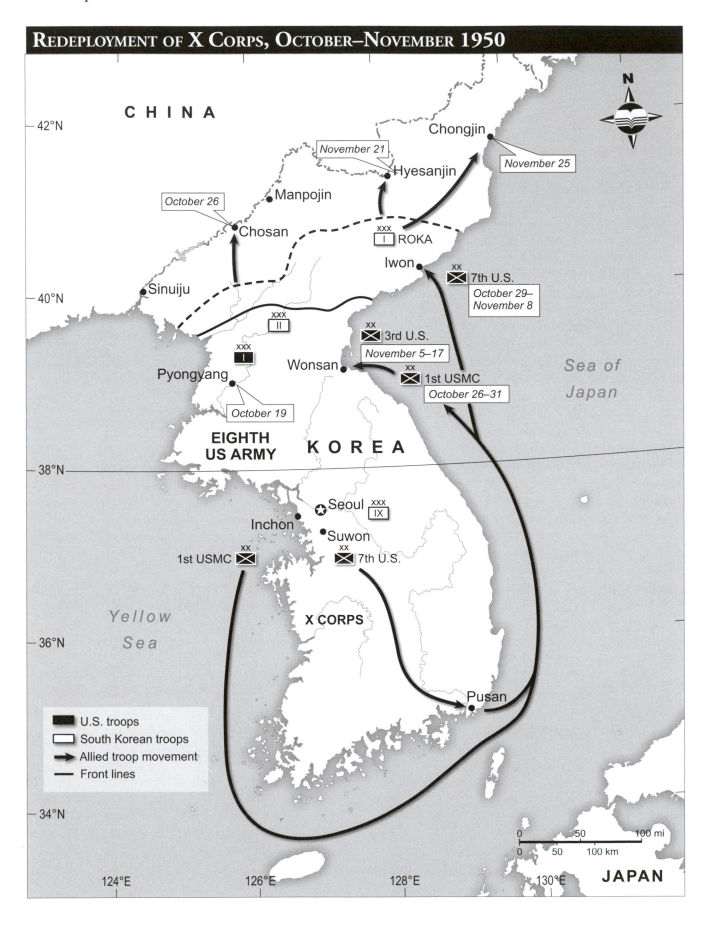

REDEPLOYMENT OF X CORPS, OCTOBER–NOVEMBER 1950

CHINA

42°N

November 21

Chongjin

Hyesanjin

November 25

Manpojin

October 26

Chosan

XXX
I ROKA

Iwon

40°N

Sinuiju

XX
7th U.S.

*October 29–
November 8*

XXX
II

XX
3rd U.S.

November 5–17

XXX
I

Wonsan

Pyongyang

XX
1st USMC

October 26–31

October 19

Sea of
Japan

EIGHTH
US ARMY

K O R E A

38°N

Seoul   XXX
IX

Inchon

Suwon

1st USMC XX   XX 7th U.S.

X CORPS

Yellow
Sea

36°N

Pusan

U.S. troops
South Korean troops
Allied troop movement
Front lines

34°N

0   50   100 mi
0   50   100 km

JAPAN

124°E   126°E   128°E   130°E

followed his orders, rushing troops forward without considering the risk posed by communist soldiers. Determined to win the race to the Yalu, Almond scattered X Corps forces across the front in an uncoordinated fashion. He also sharply criticized more conservative commanders, such as General Smith, who were much more careful in their troop dispositions. Almond diverted units, and conflicting orders created confusion that only intensified when the Chinese struck in force on November 25.

Overwhelming Chinese strength forced X Corps back on Hungnam, resulting in one of the largest amphibious evacuations in history. In February 1951 Almond received his third star for the Hungnam evacuation during early December 1950. This was in recognition of the very few casualties and equipment losses suffered by X Corps as it withdrew to Pusan.

The debacle in North Korea at the hands of the Chinese stemmed in part from the divided command. The JCS directed MacArthur to end this and to place X Corps under EUSAK control. On December 9 MacArthur directed Almond to report to new EUSAK commander Lieutenant General Matthew B. Ridgway.

For the remainder of the war, X Corps served as the third corps of EUSAK, participating in combat actions through the July 1953 armistice. In July 1951 Almond was reassigned as commander of the Army War College, Carlisle Barracks, Pennsylvania. Major General Clovis E. Byers replaced Almond as commander of X Corps. Lieutenant General Isaac D. White was commander of X Corps when the armistice was signed.

X Corps received two South Korean Presidential Unit Citations for its actions at Inchon and Hungnam and its overall combat performance. Although MacArthur had envisioned X Corps serving as the postwar U.S. military headquarters for the Republic of Korea (ROK, South Korea), it was deactivated on April 27, 1955, and its flag was retired to Fort Riley, Kansas.

ELIZABETH D. SCHAFER

See also

Almond, Edward Mallory; Amphibious Force Far East; Changjin Reservoir Campaign; Collins, Joseph Lawton; Doyle, James Henry; Eighth Army, U.S.; Far East Command; Hungnam Evacuation; Inchon Landing; Joint Chiefs of Staff; MacArthur, Douglas; Ridgway, Matthew Bunker; Smith, Oliver Prince; Walker, Walton Harris; Wonsan Landing and Evacuation

References

Appleman, Roy E. *East of Chosin: Entrapment and Breakout in Korea.* College Station: Texas A&M University Press, 1987.
———. *Escaping the Trap: The U.S. Army X Corps in Northeast Korea, 1950.* College Station: Texas A&M University Press, 1990.
———. *United States Army in Korea: South to the Naktong, North to the Yalu.* Washington, DC: Office of the Chief of Military History, 1961.
Blair, Clay. *The Forgotten War: America in Korea, 1950–1953.* New York: Times Books, 1987.
Cowart, Glenn C. *Miracle in Korea: The Evacuation of X Corps from the Hungnam Beachhead.* Columbia: University of South Carolina Press, 1992.
Heinl, Robert D. *Victory at High Tide: The Inchon-Seoul Campaign.* Philadelphia: Lippincott, 1968.
Mossman, Billy C. *United States Army in the Korean War: Ebb and Flow, November 1950–July 1951.* Washington, DC: U.S. Army Center of Military History, 1990.
Schnabel, James F. *United States Army in the Korean War: Policy and Direction, the First Year.* Washington, DC: Office of the Chief of Military History, Department of the Army, 1972.
Stanton, Shelby. *America's Tenth Legion: X Corps in Korea.* Novato, CA: Presidio, 1989.
Stewart, Richard W. *Staff Operations: The X Corps in Korea, December 1950.* Fort Leavenworth, KS: U.S. Army Command and General Staff College, 1991.

Thailand

Southeast Asian nation covering 198,455 square miles. Thailand is bordered by Burma (Myanmar) to the north and west, Laos to the southeast, Cambodia due east, and Malaysia and the Gulf of Thailand to the south. In 1950 Thailand's population was 20.42 million. Thailand is a constitutional monarchy and at the time of the Korean War was ruled by King Rama IX. Rama continues to rule today and is the longest-serving Thai monarch in history. In 1948 the staunchly anticommunist Phibun (Phibun Songkhram), who had governed as prime minister from 1938 to 1944 and was also a military officer, came back to power and ruled Thailand as a virtual military dictator until 1957. Based on Phibun's anticommunism, Washington doled out considerable military and economic aid to Thailand beginning in the late 1940s. In 1950 Thailand became part of the U.S. Military Assistance Program, and during the Korean War the Pentagon sent a Military Advisory Assistant Group to Bangkok.

The first Asian country to offer military personnel to the United Nations Command (UNC) in Korea, Thailand provided air, naval, and ground troops. Traditionally, Thailand had practiced a neutral foreign policy, remaining friendly with major Asian powers without sacrificing its independence. After World War II, however, Thailand sought an alliance with the United States to secure weapons and financial assistance. U.S. diplomats realized the importance of a stable Thailand in the midst of the Indochinese War, and Thailand would later become a critical player during the Vietnam War of the 1960s and 1970s, as the Pentagon established military bases in the country.

After the June 25, 1950, invasion of the Republic of Korea (ROK, South Korea) by the Democratic People's Republic of Korea (DPRK, North Korea), Phibun offered rice for refugee relief and said that he would send troops if asked. He hoped that by sending only a small number of troops, Thailand would secure sophisticated military aircraft and equipment for use in Korea that could be kept after the war.

Although much of the Thai press and many civilian members of the government were opposed to sending troops to Korea, Phibun addressed Parliament, emphasizing the possible economic benefits of Thai participation in the war on the U.S. side. The Thai

National Defense Council and cabinet unanimously agreed to send troops, and this united military support convinced reluctant civilian legislators to cooperate. Thailand sent 4,000 ground troops as well as 40,000 metric tons of rice valued at $4.368 million. The United States welcomed Thailand's contribution as proof of regional support for South Korea and as a counter to communist propaganda that claimed that the military action was supported solely by Western imperialists.

Attached to the U.S. 2nd Infantry Division, the Thai Infantry Battalion was perhaps best known for its defense of Pork Chop Hill in November 1952 against vicious Chinese attacks. Thailand also provided two frigates, HMRTN *Bangpakon* and *Prasae*. A detachment of Royal Thai Air Force was attached to the U.S. Air Force 21st Troop Carrier Squadron, flying Douglas C-47 Skytrain (Dakota) transport aircraft. During the war, Thai forces suffered 136 dead from all causes and 469 wounded.

Thailand also supported U.S.-sponsored resolutions in the United Nations (UN) against the People's Republic of China (PRC) and North Korea, including the February 1951 UN censure vote of the PRC for entering the war and the May 1951 embargo decision. In return for its assistance, Thailand received millions of dollars in U.S. aid for a variety of public improvement projects, and the World Bank approved a $25.4 million loan to rehabilitate Thailand's transportation and irrigation systems, the first such loan to a Southeast Asian nation.

The Mutual Defense Assistance Agreement of October 17, 1950, between the United States and Thailand confirmed that each nation would provide military equipment and services if requested and that Thailand could keep military equipment given by the United States. During the Korean War the United States sent sufficient arms to Thailand to equip 10 army battalions as well as fighter planes and naval vessels. U.S. military assistance to Thailand totaled $4.5 million in 1951, $12 million in 1952, and $56 million in 1953. Thailand participated in the 1954 Geneva Conference and was a founding member of the Southeast Asia Treaty Organization (SEATO), with Bangkok being selected as SEATO's headquarters.

ELIZABETH D. SCHAFER

See also

China, Republic of; Geneva Conference; Pork Chop Hill, Battle of; Southeast Asia Treaty Organization; United Nations Command Air Assets; United Nations Command Ground Forces, Contributions to

References

Darling, Frank C. *Thailand and the United States.* Washington, DC: Public Affairs Press, 1965.

Fineman, Daniel. *A Special Relationship: The United States and Military Government in Thailand, 1947–1958.* Honolulu: University of Hawaii Press, 1997.

Hayes, Samuel P., ed. *The Beginning of American Aid to Southeast Asia: The Griffin Mission of 1950.* Lexington, MA: Heath Lexington Books, 1971.

Kislenko, Arne. "Bending with the Wind: The Continuity and Flexibility of Thai Foreign Policy." *International Journal* 57(4) (Autumn 2002): 537–561.

Randolph, R. Sean. *The United States and Thailand: Alliance Dynamics, 1950–1985.* Berkeley: Institute of East Asian Studies, University of California, 1986.

Stueck, William W., Jr. *The Korean War: An International History.* Princeton, NJ: Princeton University Press, 1995.

Thimayya, Kadenera Subayya
Birth Date: March 31, 1906
Death Date: December 12, 1965

Indian Army general and chairman of the Neutral Nations Repatriation Commission (NNRC) in the Korean War. Born in Coorg, southern India, on March 31, 1906, Kadenera Subayya Thimayya was an Indian nationalist opposed to British rule. His socially prominent family owned a coffee plantation, and at age 16 Thimayya was selected to attend the new Prince of Wales Royal Indian Military College at Dehra Dun. An excellent student and a superb athlete, Thimayya in 1924 was one of the six Indian cadets selected for further training at the Royal Military Academy at Sandhurst. In Britain for the first time, he became aware of social and racial discrimination, and this helped fuel his own sense of Indian nationalism.

Commissioned in 1926, Thimayya returned to India and served in the Highland Light Infantry Regiment, one of the most exclusive units in the British Army. During World War II he fought against the Japanese in Burma. As an officer in the British Indian Army, he had little opportunity to take part in the Indian struggle for independence. He did, however, actively protest against the army's policy of denying promotion to qualified Indian officers. He simply refused to accept the tradition that relegated Indian officers to an inferior position.

In 1947 when India received its independence, Brigadier General Thimayya caught the attention of Prime Minister Jawaharlal Nehru. Thimayya's 4th Division helped restore order in the East Punjab, along the new Indian-Pakistan border. Thimayya emerged from this fighting as something of a national hero. He served with distinction in the 1947 war with Pakistan over Kashmir.

In 1953 during the Korean War, India was asked to provide the chairman for the NNRC and some 6,000 troops to maintain order in the prisoner of war (POW) camps. They would oversee the screening of communist and United Nations Command (UNC) POWs at Panmunjom who had refused repatriation. Nehru appointed Thimayya to the post.

Thimayya proved ideally suited for this very difficult assignment. Diplomatic yet firm, he won the respect of the POWs and of both communist and UNC representatives. Although he allowed the communists to broadcast daily 10-minute loudspeaker appeals to their countrymen to return home, he correctly predicted to UNC officials that this would have the opposite effect. Thimayya also proved adept in dealing with South Korean president Syngman Rhee. When Rhee threatened to liberate the POWs unilaterally,

Thimayya arranged to replace the South Korean marines with U.S. marines. He also made sure that the proceedings were concluded within the agreed-upon eight-week schedule.

On his return from Korea, Thimayya immediately took over the Western Command, one of India's three major military commands. However, the Korean experiences were a troubling memory, and with the help of Humphrey Evans, in late 1954 Thimayya wrote his memoirs. But because the Indian government did not believe that the time was appropriate for its publication, the manuscript was stored away for nearly 20 years. Only well after Thimayya's death, in 1981, did his widow Nina Thimayya publish his memoirs, *Experiment in Neutrality*. The book treats his activities as head of the NNRC and was translated into Korean in 1993.

Between 1957 and 1961 General Thimayya served as Indian Army chief of staff. He retired from the army on April 10, 1961. He then commanded UN peacekeeping troops on the troubled island of Cyprus. He died in Nicosia on December 12, 1965.

SUNGHUN CHO

See also

India; Nehru, Jawaharlal; Neutral Nations Repatriation Commission; Rhee, Syngman

References

Evans, Humphrey. *Thimayya of India.* New York: Harcourt Brace, 1960.

Gopal, Sarvepalli. *Jawaharlal Nehru: A Biography.* 3 vols. Cambridge, MA: Harvard University Press, 1976.

Thimayya, Kadenera Subayya. *Experiment in Neutrality.* New Delhi, India: Vision Books, 1981.

3rd Logistical Command

The U.S. Army's 3rd Logistical Command was established on September 19, 1950, to provide support for the newly formed U.S. X Corps scheduled for Operation CHROMITE, the amphibious assault at Inchon on Korea's west coast. On October 6, 1950, the 3rd Logistical Command, commanded by Brigadier General George C. Stewart, assumed responsibility for the operation of the port of Inchon. The 3rd Logistical Command subsequently supported United Nations Command (UNC) forces during the drive to Pyongyang, capital of the Democratic People's Republic of Korea (DPRK, North Korea), and on toward the Yalu River and the subsequent withdrawal southward following the Chinese intervention in November and December 1950.

In December 1950 Colonel John G. Hill replaced Brigadier General Stewart as commander of the 3rd Logistical Command and supervised the forced evacuation of the port of Inchon and other UNC logistical facilities in the Inchon-Seoul area. The evacuation was conducted successfully, but some 1.6 million gallons of petroleum products, 9,300 tons of engineer supplies, and 12 railcars of ammunition had to be abandoned or destroyed. The port of Inchon was also demolished, a senseless move because UNC

forces controlled the seaward approaches, and the communists would have been unable to utilize the port in any event.

On January 1, 1951, after the withdrawal from Inchon, the Eighth Army in Korea attached the 3rd Logistical Command to the 2nd Logistical Command. Subsequently, the 3rd Logistical Command operated the port of Pusan and logistical facilities in the Pusan area.

CHARLES R. SHRADER

See also

Inchon Landing; Logistics in the Korean War; 2nd Logistical Command; X Corps

References

Appleman, Roy E. *United States Army in Korea: South to the Naktong, North to the Yalu.* Washington, DC: Office of the Chief of Military History, 1961.

Mossman, Billy C. *United States Army in the Korean War: Ebb and Flow, November 1950–July 1951.* Washington, DC: U.S. Army Center of Military History, 1990.

38th Parallel, Decision to Cross

Two weeks after the successful Inchon Landing of September 15, 1950, United Nations Command (UNC) forces launched an offensive north across the 38th Parallel. The decision to do so had been under consideration from the opening days of the war. Initial UNC objectives established by the United Nations (UN) Security Council resolution of June 27, 1950, were to "repel the armed attack and to restore international peace and security in the area." This clearly required driving the attacking forces back to the 38th Parallel, but both U.S. policy and earlier UN General Assembly resolutions identified the long-range goal of a free, united, and independent Korea. South Korean president Syngman Rhee and some of U.S. president Harry S. Truman's advisers saw the war as an opportunity to achieve that goal.

On July 13, 1950, Rhee publicly declared that the attack by the Democratic People's Republic of Korea (DPRK, North Korea) had "obliterated" the 38th Parallel as a boundary. On the same day UNC commander General Douglas MacArthur, meeting in Tokyo with members of the U.S. Joint Chiefs of Staff (JCS), advised that he intended to destroy the North Korean forces, not just drive them back, and that he might have to occupy all of Korea to do so. Chinese intervention, he argued, could be dealt with by atomic bombs. On July 17 President Truman ordered a formal study to determine if the UNC should conduct operations north of the 38th Parallel. The issue was secretly debated over the next few weeks in a series of policy papers and meetings.

Those who favored the move argued that peace and security could not be restored while the North Korean threat existed. They saw a moral obligation to take advantage of the opportunity to reunify Korea and believed that the aggressor should be punished by more than a mere return to the status quo. Some argued that

United Nations Command (UNC) forces, driven south by the massive Chinese People's Volunteer Army intervention in the war, recross the 38th Parallel in December 1950. (National Archives)

unification of Korea under a noncommunist government would provide important strategic advantages. The arguments against moving north were based on fears of provoking Soviet or Chinese intervention, with the consequent risk of general war. Absent evidence of Moscow or Beijing joining the fight, the JCS endorsed an offensive into North Korea on July 31.

U.S. officials also sounded out the UN allies. Members of the UN Commission on Korea agreed on August 5 that the goal of the UN effort should be a unified, independent, democratic Korea. U.S. ambassador to the UN Warren R. Austin endorsed that goal in UN speeches on August 10 and 17, 1950. U.S., British, and French officials agreed on September 1 that while UN forces should not proceed north without prior UN direction, a resolution should be put before the UN General Assembly reiterating the goal of Korean independence and unification.

Clearly, the Truman administration saw the decision to cross the 38th Parallel as a weapon with which to fight its domestic critics. Under enormous pressure and vituperative attacks from conservatives (mostly Republicans), the Truman administration attempted to wrest the initiative by rolling back, not simply containing, communism. Crossing the 38th Parallel would do just that and, it was hoped, would neutralize McCarthyite attacks, which had been fully unleashed by the sudden outbreak of war in June 1950. Furthermore, reuniting Korea would inflict an embarrassing defeat on the Soviet Union in the Cold War.

On September 11 President Truman approved the final version of the formal study, NSC-81 dated September 1, that recommended postponing a final decision pending events on the battlefield but anticipated that the UN commander would receive approval to conduct operations north of the parallel unless the Soviets or Chinese intervened first. NSC-81 recommended that MacArthur be ordered to prepare plans to occupy North Korea but not to execute those plans without explicit presidential approval. The JCS informed General MacArthur of the gist of NSC-81 on September 15, the same day of the Inchon Landing.

UNC military success made it possible for President Truman and his advisers to implement the planned offensive northward. Secretary of Defense Louis Johnson's resignation and his replacement by George C. Marshall on September 21 delayed that final authorization until September 27. On that date the JCS, with Truman's approval, informed MacArthur that his objective was now the destruction of the Korean People's Army (KPA, North Korean Army); authorized him to conduct operations north of the 38th Parallel provided the Soviets had not intervened or threatened to intervene; authorized him to to continue the UNC advance if China intervened, so long as it held promise of success; and directed him to submit plans for invading and occupying North Korea.

On September 28 MacArthur submitted his plan, advising the JCS that he would issue a surrender proclamation on October 1 and, if he received no response, would then enter North Korea to accomplish his objectives. The president approved, and on September 29 the JCS ordered MacArthur to carry out his plan on schedule. Later the same day Marshall sent a personal message to MacArthur telling him not to announce in advance his intention to cross the parallel (to avoid adversely impacting the ongoing UN deliberations on the General Assembly resolution). Marshall told MacArthur to "feel unhampered tactically and strategically to proceed north of the 38th parallel."

On October 1 MacArthur broadcast his surrender message, and lead elements of the Republic of Korea Army (ROKA, South Korean Army) 3rd Division crossed the parallel on the east coast of Korea. UNC Operations Order No. 2, issued on October 2, directed the U.S. Eighth Army to attack north toward Pyongyang. X Corps was to conduct an amphibious landing at Wonsan, with a subsequent attack to link up with the Eighth Army. Resupply and the redeployment of X Corps caused a delay in executing the order.

On October 3 Chinese premier Zhou Enlai warned Indian ambassador Sardar H. M. Panikkar that if U.S. troops crossed the parallel, China would intervene. The U.S. leadership dismissed Zhou's threat as a bluff as well as a ploy in support of Soviet negotiations in the UN. Although the Chinese had begun mobilizing in Manchuria since the summer of 1950, U.S. intelligence could provide no clear-cut military indication of Chinese preparations for intervention. Both the United States and the UN were inclined to accept MacArthur's assessment that Chinese intervention was unlikely and that his forces could deal decisively with the Chinese if they did intervene.

On October 7, after a week of debate, the UN General Assembly passed a resolution recommending steps to ensure "conditions of stability throughout Korea" and actions "for the establishment of a unified, independent and democratic Government in the sovereign state of Korea." Of course, the Truman administration had decided weeks earlier to pursue Korea's forcible reunification and had already issued orders to achieve this objective. On the same day, U.S. 1st Cavalry Division patrols began to cross the parallel.

On October 9 MacArthur transmitted a second surrender message, and Lieutenant General Walton H. Walker gave orders to the U.S. Eighth Army "to strike out for Pyongyang without delay." Later on, the U.S. 1st Cavalry Division, the British 27th Brigade,

the ROKA 1st Division, and elements of the U.S. 24th Division crossed the 38th Parallel in the west in force. The offensive north to achieve the long-held U.S. goal of creating a united and sovereign Korea was now under way.

DONALD W. BOOSE JR.

See also

Austin, Warren; Collins-Vandenberg Visit to Tokyo; Johnson, Louis Arthur; Joint Chiefs of Staff; Korea, Democratic People's Republic of, United Nations Command Occupation of; MacArthur, Douglas; Marshall, George Catlett; Panikkar, Sardar K. M.; Truman, Harry S.; Zhou Enlai

References

Chen Jian. *China's Road to the Korean War: The Making of the Sino-American Confrontation.* New York: Columbia University Press, 1994.

Condit, Doris M. *History of the Office of the Secretary of Defense,* Vol. 2, *The Test of War, 1950–1953.* Washington, DC: Office of the Secretary of Defense, 1988.

Kaufman, Burton I. *The Korean War: Challenges in Crisis, Credibility and Command.* 2nd ed. New York: McGraw-Hill, 1997.

Matray, James I. "Truman's Plan for Victory: National Self-determination and the 38th Parallel Decision in Korea." *Journal of American History* 66 (September 1979): 313–314.

Schnabel, James F. *United States Army in the Korean War: Policy and Direction, the First Year.* Washington, DC: Office of the Chief of Military History, Department of the Army, 1972.

Schnabel, James F., and Robert J. Watson. *The History of the Joint Chiefs of Staff: The Joint Chiefs of Staff and National Policy,* Vol. 3, *The Korean War.* Wilmington, DE: Michael Glazier, 1979.

Stueck, William W., Jr. *The Korean War: An International History.* Princeton, NJ: Princeton University Press, 1995.

———. *Rethinking the Korean War: A New Diplomatic and Strategic History.* Princeton, NJ: Princeton University Press, 2004.

38th Parallel, Division of Korea at

Despite Korea's strategic location in Northeast Asia, the United States exhibited little interest in the peninsula until World War II in the Pacific dramatically changed the strategic balance and altered American perceptions of U.S. interests in the region. During that conflict, U.S. president Franklin D. Roosevelt viewed Soviet cooperation as essential to the war effort and to postwar peace and stability. Until the end of the war in East Asia, U.S. military and political leaders desired Soviet intervention against Japanese forces on the Asian continent, although they realized that Soviet occupation of Korea, Manchuria, and perhaps even part of Japan might jeopardize U.S. interests in the region. It was a price that Washington was willing to pay to lessen American casualties and end the war sooner than might otherwise have been possible. Moreover, the United States had no ground forces anywhere near Northeast Asia to counterbalance potential Soviet influence.

Wishing to limit the Soviet Union's postwar influence in East Asia but to avoid provoking a Soviet preemptive action, Roosevelt and his advisers formulated and proposed a vaguely defined postwar international trusteeship for Korea under the United States, Great Britain, China, and the Soviet Union. Although the Allied leaders discussed the concept from time to time during the war, they failed to agree on the details of the planned trusteeship for Korea.

In Cairo on December 1, 1943, U.S., British, and Chinese leaders declared that Korea should become free and independent "in due course," implying some temporary period of external supervision. Later, in the Teheran Conference (November 28–December 1, 1943), Soviet leader Joseph Stalin endorsed the declaration. At the Yalta Conference (February 4–11, 1945) the Soviet leader confirmed an earlier promise to enter the Pacific war two or three months after the defeat of Germany, and the U.S. and British leaders consented to Soviet concessions in Sakhalin, the Kurile Islands, and northern China. The Allies also agreed to a four-power Korean trusteeship, but again details were left ill-defined.

Although tensions were rising between the United States and the Soviet Union beforehand, after Roosevelt's death in April 1945 U.S.-Soviet relations sharply deteriorated. President Harry S. Truman's advisers favored a tougher line toward the Soviets, and conflicting U.S. and Soviet views on the termination of Lend-Lease assistance, combined operations, and the postwar treatment of Germany and Eastern Europe soured relations. As for Korea, Truman decided to postpone action to secure an agreement on trusteeship, fearing that Soviet participation in such an arrangement would provide Moscow with the opportunity to sovietize the peninsula, as in Eastern Europe.

In May, acting secretary of state Joseph C. Grew argued that the United States should seek a firm Soviet commitment to the Korean trusteeship before implementing the Yalta Agreement. The service secretaries agreed that such a commitment was desirable but noted that the United States had little political leverage. The Soviets would enter the Pacific war at a time of their choosing and could occupy mainland Northeast Asia before U.S. forces could reach these areas. Truman, however, continued to delay.

At the Potsdam Conference (July 17–August 2, 1945), the Allied chiefs of staff discussed U.S.-Soviet military operations when the Soviet Union entered the war, including the coordination of air and naval boundaries near Korea. But except for a brief and inconsequential exchange on July 22, the political leaders never discussed Korea.

While the Potsdam talks were under way, U.S. officials decided to prepare to occupy Korea as well as Japan if the Japanese surrendered unexpectedly. This decision appears to have been driven by concerns about Soviet actions and intentions and by a new confidence based on the successful U.S. atomic bomb test during the Potsdam Conference. They considered that use of the bomb might cause Japan to surrender without an invasion and before the Soviets entered the war, allowing the United States to unilaterally occupy Korea without expending American lives in the process.

On July 23, 1945, Secretary of War Henry L. Stimson advised President Truman that "now with our new weapon we would not need the assistance of the Russians to conquer Japan." But U.S. Army chief of staff George C. Marshall cautioned that with troops massed on the Manchurian border, the Soviets could attack anyway, getting "virtually what they wanted in the surrender terms."

Just before the meeting at Potsdam, the U.S. Joint Chiefs of Staff (JCS) directed the Pacific commanders to include Korea in their plans for the occupation of Japan. On July 25 after discussions at Potsdam with his Soviet counterpart, Marshall ordered the U.S. Army to prepare to move troops into Korea (Operation BLACKLIST) and alerted General Douglas MacArthur that decisions on the occupation of Japan were imminent.

MacArthur's plans for the occupation were still under development when the first atomic bomb was dropped on Hiroshima on August 6, 1945. Two days later, acting three months to the day under its pledge to enter the Pacific fighting "two to three months" after the defeat of Germany, the Soviet Union declared war on Japan. On August 9 the United States dropped a second atomic bomb at Nagasaki, and Soviet troops crossed the Manchurian border. On August 10 the Japanese asked for an armistice, sparking intense activity by U.S. planners to develop the necessary instruments of surrender. Two staff officers, colonels Charles H. Bonesteel III and Dean Rusk, were assigned the task of drafting General Order 1, designating in detail the particular Allied authority to whom the Japanese forces in each area of East Asia were to surrender. Their guidance was to place the line in Korea as far north as possible, considering that Soviet troops were advancing rapidly while the closest U.S. forces were on Okinawa, 600 miles away. Bonesteel and Rusk recommended the 38th Parallel, dividing the country roughly in half with the capital of Seoul in the American zone. On August 15 President Truman approved General Order 1, sending copies to Moscow and London. Stalin raised no objection, asking instead for a Soviet occupation zone in Japan that Truman refused to grant. This decision, though wise, nevertheless made cooperation for uniting Korea more difficult.

On August 15 the Japanese accepted the terms of surrender, and the U.S. occupation force, Lieutenant General John R. Hodge's XXIV Corps, began preparations for the imminent move to Korea. Few of the preliminary actions necessary to implement the occupation plan had been carried out, and although the corps headquarters and one division were on Okinawa, the other units and the shipping to transport them were scattered throughout the western Pacific. Shipping was at a premium, and movement of troops to Japan had first priority.

At the time of the Japanese surrender, no civil affairs units had been designated or trained for Korea. The XXIV Corps military government expertise consisted of 20 civil affairs officers (none with any knowledge of Korea) and 6 paroled Japanese-speaking Korean prisoners of war attached to the corps as translators. Even more serious was a lack of policy guidance. General MacArthur, still under the impression that the occupation was to be on a quadripartite basis, requested clarification from Washington. He was told that no other countries had "declared intentions," so the initial occupation of Korea would be by U.S. and Soviet forces only. International arrangements for Korea were under "urgent consideration" by the State Department. Neither MacArthur nor Hodge had received any instructions on such key questions as Korean independence, the severing of Korea from Japanese influence, and domestic Korean politics. The initial directive on civil affairs administration did not arrive until October 17, 1945, more than a month after Hodge's occupation force had arrived in Korea.

An advance party from Hodge's headquarters flew to Korea on September 4. There they made contact with the Soviet consulate, which had continued to operate in Seoul after the Soviet Union's declaration of war against Japan, and learned that Soviet occupation forces had stopped at the 38th Parallel. On September 5 after a week-long delay due to devastating typhoons, the lead elements of the occupation force finally embarked for Korea, landing at Inchon on the afternoon of September 8.

The occupation force entered a peninsula seething with repressed nationalism, fervor for independence, and hostility among factions of Left and Right. Returning exile groups, each with its own claim, added to the political ferment. Overlaying the domestic tensions was a growing U.S.-Soviet animosity. In December 1945 the foreign ministers of the victorious powers agreed to implement the four-power trusteeship and established a U.S.-Soviet joint commission to work out the details and begin the process toward Korean independence.

U.S.-Soviet antagonism and domestic Korean pressures soon crippled the joint commission, however, and in September 1947 the United States put the Korean question before the United Nations (UN). In November the General Assembly established the UN Temporary Commission on Korea (UNTCOK) to supervise elections with the goal of a free and independent Korea. The Soviets denied the legitimacy of the UN action and refused UNTCOK entry into northern Korea. UNTCOK duly observed elections in southern Korea, leading to the formation of the Republic of Korea (ROK, South Korea) under Syngman Rhee. Soon thereafter, the Democratic People's Republic of Korea (DPRK, North Korea) was established under Soviet auspices. By 1949 two rival regimes, each with a great power sponsor, faced each other across the 38th Parallel, and the division of Korea was complete.

DONALD W. BOOSE JR.

See also

Cairo Declaration; Hodge, John Reed; Korea, History of, 1945–1947; MacArthur, Douglas; Marshall, George Catlett; Potsdam Conference; Rhee, Syngman; Rusk, David Dean; Stalin, Joseph; Truman, Harry S.; U.S. Policy toward Korea, Pre-1950

References

Boose, Donald W., Jr. "Portentous Sideshow: The Korean Occupation Decision." *Parameters* 25 (Winter 1995): 112–29.

Cumings, Bruce. *The Origins of the Korean War.* 2 vols. Princeton, NJ: Princeton University Press, 1981, 1990.

Matray, James I. *Korea Divided: The 38th Parallel and the Demilitarized Zone.* New York: Chelsea House, 2006.

———. *The Reluctant Crusade: American Foreign Policy in Korea, 1941–1950.* Honolulu: University of Hawaii Press, 1985.

Millett, Allan R. *The War for Korea, 1945–1950: A House Burning.* Lawrence: University Press of Kansas, 2005.

Sandusky, Michael. *America's Parallel.* Alexandria, VA: Old Dominion Press, 1983.

Stueck, William W., Jr. *Rethinking the Korean War: A New Diplomatic and Strategic History.* Princeton, NJ: Princeton University Press, 2004.

Thomas, Norman Mattoon
Birth Date: November 20, 1884
Death Date: December 19, 1968

Noted socialist, ordained minister, and pacifist who helped shape much of American isolationist and pacifistic sentiments in the 20th century. Norman Mattoon Thomas was born on November 20, 1884, in Marion, Ohio, where he lived until enrolling at Princeton University, from which he graduated in 1905. He then studied at the Union Theological Seminary in New York City and was ordained a Presbyterian minister in 1911. Thomas served as an assistant pastor and then pastor of several Presbyterian churches in New York City. While in New York, he was greatly influenced by the Social Gospel movement. Demoralized by what he saw as an intolerably high rate of poverty and discouraged by American militarism, he joined the Socialist Party of America.

Thomas spoke out against American involvement in World War I and in 1918 founded and edited the *World Tomorrow*, a publication dedicated to pacifism and socialist ideals. In 1920 he cofounded the American Civil Liberties Union (ACLU) with such leftist luminaries as Upton Sinclair and Jane Addams. Thomas then turned toward politics and ran unsuccessfully as the Socialist Party candidate for the governorship of New York in 1924. He sought the office again in 1938 and also ran for mayor of New York City in 1925 and again in 1929. In 1926, when longtime Socialist Party leader Eugene Debs died, Thomas took up the leadership role of the party in the United States. He also ran in six presidential elections (1928, 1932, 1936, 1940, 1944, and 1948) as the Socialist Party candidate, but he was unsuccessful in each.

Although Thomas was a sharp and consistent critic of American-style capitalism and lambasted both the Democratic Party and the Republican Party with equal vigor, he also denounced fascism in all its forms and railed against Soviet-style communism. Thus, despite his socialist beliefs, he was firmly anti-Soviet even though he did not agree with the militaristic implementation of containment that followed World War II. Thomas also believed that U.S. involvement in World War II was a mistake, at least prior to the 1941 attack on Pearl Harbor. Indeed, in 1940 he cofounded the America First Committee, which was dedicated to maintaining American isolationism and keeping the United States out of World War II. The committee became the largest and most vocal

The leader of the Socialist Party from the 1920s to the 1960s, Norman M. Thomas was an important critic of American society and politics. (Corbis)

pacifist organization in the nation but was dissolved within days of the Pearl Harbor attack. Thomas backed the war effort after that, although he derided some of President Franklin D. Roosevelt's policies, including the decision to permit big business to control much of the war's military production.

After World War II, Thomas maintained his high profile in the peace movement and spoke out against postwar rearmament and the American involvement in the Korean War. He also spoke out loudly—and often—against the U.S. involvement in the Vietnam War and spearheaded some of the earliest organized antiwar protests of the conflict. He worked tirelessly for world disarmament throughout the 1950s and 1960s and was particularly vocal in his denunciation of the nuclear arms race. Although he resigned as head of the Socialist Party in 1955, he nevertheless remained its chief spokesman until his health began to fail in the late 1960s. He wrote numerous books during his life dealing with socialism, pacifism, disarmament, and civil liberties. Thomas died in New York City on December 19, 1968.

PAUL G. PIERPAOLI JR.

See also

Antiwar Sentiment in the United States; Isolationist Sentiment in the United States

References

Johnpoll, Bernard K. *Pacifist's Progress: Norman Thomas and the Decline of American Socialism.* San Antonio, TX: Quadrangle, 1970.

Swanberg, W. A. *Norman Thomas, the Last Idealist.* New York: Scribner, 1976.

THUNDERBOLT, **Operation**
Start Date: January 25, 1951
End Date: February 10, 1951

A reconnaissance in force launched by the U.S. I and IX Corps in late January 1951 intended to provide the commander of the U.S. Eighth Army in Korea, Lieutenant General Matthew B. Ridgway, with accurate intelligence before the drive back to the 38th Parallel by the United Nations Command (UNC).

Based on the success of Operation WOLFHOUND and Task Force Johnson, which demonstrated that few communist forces stood between the UNC and the 38th Parallel and showed the feasibility of limited offensive operations, Ridgway sought to determine the capabilities of his forces and the disposition of communist forces in the Republic of Korea (ROK, South Korea). Operation THUNDERBOLT called for a controlled advance by elements of the U.S. I and IX Corps with the intent of pressing to the Han River near Seoul while determining the communist military situation and inflicting the maximum possible punishment. The corps would advance by phase lines under the I Corps commander's direction, and the U.S. X Corps would protect the UNC's right flank. The navy planned two diversionary operations to give the appearance of amphibious invasion and draw attention away from the main effort.

The operation commenced on January 25, with the U.S. 25th Infantry Division leading I Corps and the U.S. 1st Cavalry Division leading IX Corps. Employing Ridgway's "meat grinder" technique for the first time, the offensive advanced slowly from phase line to phase line, more a result of Ridgway's requirements for close coordination and thorough ground searches than of communist opposition. Ridgway expanded the operation by adding the U.S. 3rd Infantry Division to I Corps' advance on January 27 and the U.S. 24th Infantry Division to IX Corps' advance on January 28. As the situation became clearer and communist resistance significantly increased, units measured progress in yards instead of miles.

Owing to the dramatic increase in UNC participation and communist resistance, on January 30 Ridgway converted the reconnaissance in force to a deliberate attack, and he increased the use of air assets to aid the advance. He also began planning Operation ROUNDUP, which would send his remaining forces forward in a manner similar to that of THUNDERBOLT. Operation ROUNDUP began on February 5, 1951, thus beginning an army-wide advance to the north. Continuing its methodical advance, UNC forces reached the south bank of the Han River by February 10, 1951, stopping just short of Seoul.

Conceived as a reconnaissance in force, Operation THUNDERBOLT showed that few communist forces opposed the UNC in South Korea and demonstrated the success of the "meat grinder" technique. Operation THUNDERBOLT and the follow-on offensives placed the UNC forces in a favorable position to begin subsequent operations that would allow the UNC to recapture Seoul, recross the 38th Parallel, and begin peace negotiations by mid-1951.

TIMOTHY A. SIKES

See also

"Meat Grinder" Strategy; ROUNDUP, Operation; WOLFHOUND, Operation

References

Blair, Clay. *The Forgotten War: America in Korea, 1950–1953.* New York: Times Books, 1987.

James, D. Clayton, with Anne Sharp Wells. *Refighting the Last War: Command and Crisis in Korea, 1950–1953.* New York: Free Press, 1993.

Stokesberry, James I. *A Short History of the Korean War.* New York: William Morrow, 1989.

U.S. Army, 1st Cavalry Division. *The First Cavalry Division in Korea.* Atlanta: Albert Love Enterprises, n.d.

Tomlinson, Frank Stanley
Birth Date: March 21, 1912
Death Date: September 10, 1994

British career diplomat and counselor in the British embassy in Washington, DC, between 1951 and 1953. Born in Sydney, Australia, on March 21, 1912, and educated at University College, Nottingham, Frank Stanley Tomlinson entered the British Consular Service in 1935. He held various junior positions in Japan, South Vietnam, the United States, and the Philippines before returning to Britain in 1947 to serve in the Foreign Office.

In 1951 Tomlinson was posted to the British embassy in Washington, where he attended and was one of the more active contributors to the Korean War briefing meetings. These somewhat sporadically scheduled Washington gatherings of representatives from the principal countries contributing to the United Nations Command (UNC) forces in Korea were intended to promote allied unity and ensure that all the nations involved were receiving accurate information on the course of the fighting and of negotiations. Tomlinson served as a highly dependable conduit for the passage of information between U.S. and British officials. He accurately presented and explained to U.S. government representatives London's views on issues relating to the Korean War.

Tomlinson received instructions from London, which he followed faithfully, to work for an early cease-fire and avoid any broadening of the war, concerns that were constant preoccupations of British diplomacy during the Korean War. He was particularly active on policies and issues related to the People's Republic of China (PRC), ably setting forth the relatively conciliatory attitude that the British advocated on such matters as Taiwan (then known as Formosa) and United Nations (UN) seating as an alternative to the far more uncompromising U.S. position. After leaving Washington, Tomlinson held several more second-rank Foreign Office appointments, including head of its Southeast Asia Department, British consul general in New York, and British high commissioner in Colombo, ending his career as deputy undersecretary of state at the Foreign and Commonwealth Office. On his retirement in 1972 he moved to Wiltshire. Tomlinson died on September 10, 1994.

PRISCILLA ROBERTS

See also

Churchill, Sir Winston; Eden, Robert Anthony; Franks, Oliver; United Kingdom

References

Butler, Rohan, and M. E. Pelly, eds. *Documents on British Foreign Policy Overseas,* Series 2, Vol. 4, *Korea, 1950–1951.* London: HMSO, 1995.

Danchev, Alex. *Oliver Franks: Founding Father.* New York: Oxford University Press, 1993.

Lowe, Peter. *Containing the Cold War in East Asia: British Policies toward Japan, China and Korea, 1948–1953.* Manchester, UK: Manchester University Press, 1997.

MacDonald, Callum A. *Britain and the Korean War.* Oxford, UK: Blackwell, 1990.

Stueck, William W., Jr. *The Korean War: An International History.* Princeton, NJ: Princeton University Press, 1995.

Tonghak Movement
See Chondogyo Movement

Triangle Hill, Battle of
Start Date: October 14, 1952
End Date: November 5, 1952

Battle involving United Nations Command (UNC) and Chinese People's Volunteer Army (CPVA, Chinese Army) forces following the Battle of White Horse Hill. At the time of the Battle of Triangle Hill, UNC forces were in a holding pattern defending key hilltops along the front.

Eighth Army commander General James A. Van Fleet sought to seize the initiative, and he targeted an area about three miles north of Kimhwa where only 200 yards separated the two sides. This area comprised Hill 598 (Triangle Hill) and Sniper Ridge, where UNC casualties had been high. If the Chinese could be pushed off Triangle Hill, they would have to retreat some 1,250 yards to the next defensive position.

Operation SHOWDOWN, launched on October 13, encompassed what became known as the Triangle Hill Complex: Triangle Hill, Sandy Ridge, Pike's Peak, Jane Russell Hill, and Sniper Ridge. The assault on Triangle Hill was Van Fleet's response to the ongoing Chinese attack on White Horse Hill. Triangle Hill was not expected

U.S. Army corpsmen work desperately over 7th Division wounded from the bitter struggle for Triangle Hill, October 15, 1952. (Bettmann/Corbis)

to be a difficult assault and was projected to last five days with approximately 200 UNC casualties. The attackers planned to support their infantry assault with 16 artillery battalions, consisting of 288 artillery pieces, and more than 200 fighter-bomber sorties.

From the beginning the operation was plagued with problems, however. The number of days of preparatory air strikes was cut from five to only two to support operations at White Horse Hill.

One battalion of the CPVA 135th Regiment, 45th Division, Fifteenth Army, defended Triangle Hill. It was an elite formation, well dug in and with adequate ammunition. U.S. 7th Division commander Major General Wayne Smith assigned the task of taking Triangle Hill to Colonel Lloyd Moses's 31st Infantry Regiment. Although the original plan called for only one assaulting battalion, Moses determined that he would need two.

The contest for Triangle Hill opened on October 14 and was fierce. The Chinese proved tenacious in defense. At one point U.S. troops believed that the Chinese had to have been on drugs when one Chinese battalion moved through its own artillery and mortar fire. At the end of the first day's fighting, despite taking heavy

casualties, the Chinese had repelled the two attacking U.S. battalions. On October 15 the attackers did capture Hill 598 but then encountered stiff resistance at the base of Pike's Peak.

Casualties multiplied as both sides fed additional forces into what had become a matter of face for each. Eventually, 7th Division battalions were expended at the rate of one a day. General Smith frequently rotated his troops to keep them fresh.

By October 16 the UNC had three battalions on Triangle Hill. The Chinese then committed the 134th Regiment of the 45th Division and managed to hold Pike's Peak. On October 25 when the Republic of Korea Army (ROKA, South Korean Army) 2nd Division relieved the 7th Division, the Chinese again controlled Pike's Peak.

In 12 days of battle, the 7th Division sustained more than 2,000 casualties. Eight of its nine infantry battalions fought in the battle. The ROKA 2nd Division was forced from Triangle Hill on October 30.

Because of the high number of casualties, on November 5 General Jenkins ended further attacks on Triangle Hill, conceding its possession to the Chinese. In this battle UNC forces had suffered some 9,000 casualties, while the communist side had lost more than 19,000. This UNC failure and the resulting high number of casualties was a test of the formidable strength and depth of the communist lines and led UNC commander General Lieutenant Mark W. Clark thereafter to keep his forces on the defensive.

Lessons from other hill battles were again illustrated here. These included the need for attacking troops to close quickly with defenders, to keep the attack moving, not to allow troops to become pinned down, and to dig in quickly and provide defensive cover.

During this battle, Van Fleet tested a new strategy of concentrating heavy firepower against communist artillery by reorganizing the ratio of 8-inch howitzers and 155-millimeter (mm) guns to allow maximum effect from the firepower. On November 3 Van Fleet implemented his counterbattery program, concentrating heavy firepower against communist artillery on Triangle Hill with three 8-inch howitzers and three 155-mm gun battalions. But because of caves, tunnels, and heavy overhead protection, it took more than 50 rounds of accurate fire to destroy each communist artillery piece. Thus, the counterbattery program was of limited use and could only be used within the normal ammunition allotment, at least until the overall supply of heavy artillery shells increased.

The Chinese defense of Triangle Hill and subsequent repulse of UNC forces counterbalanced the Chinese loss at White Horse Hill. The Chinese showed their willingness to absorb large losses to defend their positions. The combat on Triangle Hill is the subject of a 1956 Chinese movie, *The Battle on Shangganling Mountain,* directed by Sha Meng and Lin Shan.

CAROL J. YEE

See also

SHOWDOWN, Operation; Van Fleet, James Alward; White Horse Hill, Battle of

References

Hermes, Walter G. *U.S. Army in the Korean War: Truce Tent and Fighting Front.* Washington, DC: Office of the Chief of Military History, 1966.

MacDonald, Callum. *Korea: The War before Vietnam.* New York: Free Press, 1987.

Tripartite Meetings
Event Date: November 1951

Diplomatic discussions that dealt in part with the Korean War. The Tripartite Meetings of British, French, and U.S. foreign ministers were held during the entire month of November 1951 in conjunction with two other contemporaneous broader international gatherings: the Sixth Session of the United Nations (UN) General Assembly that met in Paris and the Eighth Session of the North Atlantic Treaty Organization (NATO) Council held in Rome. In bilateral and tripartite discussions, U.S. secretary of state Dean Acheson, British foreign secretary Anthony Eden, and French minister of foreign affairs Robert Schuman covered a wide range of issues. These included Iran, NATO, Australia, Egypt, the European Defense Community (EDC), Germany, and Korea.

The major issue involving Korea was the possibility of cease-fire arrangements, discussions concerning which were then in progress at Panmunjom between the combatants. On November 28, 1951, Acheson and Eden discussed Item 3 on the agenda, namely the establishment of an inspection organization that could supervise and enforce a cease-fire and take action on any breaches. They considered five different forms of inspection, which were, in decreasing order of severity, complete inspections anywhere behind the lines on both sides, inspections only at specified key points, air inspections, inspections limited to a zone stretching 25 miles behind the lines, and inspections limited to the demilitarized zone. Acheson faced the dilemma that although he and top U.S. military officers believed that only a strong system of inspections would enable the United States to anticipate a future North Korean offensive, he feared that demands for this would compromise and perhaps deadlock the ongoing truce talks. He wished to obtain British endorsement of a strong joint policy (greater sanctions) statement designed to emphasize that any future violation of the cease-fire would bring immediate and heavy consequences to the violators, thereby compensating for any potential shortcomings in the inspection provisions per se.

Acheson and Eden held lengthy discussions on the subject in which, as so often was the case during the war, the British were caught between their desire to please the United States and their fear of provoking the People's Republic of China (PRC) and thereby compromising their position in Hong Kong and other Asian locales. Eden promised to consult with Prime Minister Winston Churchill as to whether Britain would join in a declaration by all the powers that had contributed to the UN forces, warning of the potentially serious consequences of any future cease-fire violation and specifically suggesting that these might include bombing Chinese airfields in Manchuria or the imposition of an Anglo-American naval blockade of the Chinese coast. It was agreed, however, that this public statement would not be issued unless and until the cease-fire had been signed without reaching agreement on a system of inspections satisfactory to the Western powers. After Eden's return to London, the matter was discussed by Churchill, other government ministers, and the British chiefs of staff and within the Foreign Office.

By late December 1951 the British had watered down the proposed statement so that it bore less of the character of an ultimatum and refrained from mentioning concrete retaliatory measures, stating instead that a "breach of the armistice would be so grave that, in all probability, it would not be possible to confine hostilities within the frontiers of Korea." The British agreed that the commander of the United Nations Command (UNC), Lieutenant General Matthew Ridgway, should be authorized to conclude an armistice agreement even if supervision and inspection arrangements were considered less than satisfactory and that they would accept limited bombing raids as suitable retaliation for any breach of its terms.

Discussions continued, and in late February 1952 all 16 nations with troops in Korea agreed to endorse the much-revised and modified joint statement.

PRISCILLA ROBERTS

See also

Acheson, Dean Gooderham; Eden, Robert Anthony; European Defense Community; France; Ridgway, Matthew Bunker; United Kingdom

References

Acheson, Dean. *Present at the Creation: My Years at the State Department.* New York: Norton, 1969.

Butler, Rohan, and M. E. Pelly, eds. *Documents on British Foreign Policy Overseas,* Series 2, Vol. 4, *Korea, 1950–1951.* London: HMSO, 1995.

Dockrill, Michael. "The Foreign Office, Anglo-American Relations and the Korean Truce Negotiations, July 1951–July 1953." In *The Korean War in History,* edited by James Cotton and Ian Neary, 100–119. Manchester, UK: Manchester University Press, 1989.

Eden, Anthony. *Full Circle.* Boston: Houghton Mifflin, 1960.

Foot, Rosemary J. *A Substitute for Victory: The Politics of Peacemaking at the Korean Armistice Talks.* Ithaca, NY: Cornell University Press, 1990.

Lowe, Peter. *Containing the Cold War in East Asia: British Policies toward Japan, China and Korea, 1948–1953.* Manchester, UK: Manchester University Press, 1997.

MacDonald, Callum A. *Britain and the Korean War.* Oxford, UK: Blackwell, 1990.

Poidevin, Raymond. *Robert Schuman: Homme d'État, 1886–1963.* Paris: Imprimérie Nationale, 1986.

Stueck, William W., Jr. *The Korean War: An International History.* Princeton, NJ: Princeton University Press, 1995.

———. *Rethinking the Korean War: A New Diplomatic and Strategic History.* Princeton, NJ: Princeton University Press, 2004.

Troopships

A vital component of the U.S. war effort in Korea. The invasion of the Republic of Korea (ROK, South Korea) on June 25, 1950, presented the United States with a difficult situation. The Republic of Korea Army (ROKA, South Korean Army) was unable to stop the attack by the Democratic People's Republic of Korea (DPRK, North Korea), and President Harry S. Truman then committed U.S. forces to Korea. But the United States had few troops in Asia at the outbreak of the conflict. Large numbers of men, equipment, and supplies would have to be transported to Korea.

The distance between the United States and Korea made this task quite daunting. Almost 5,000 nautical miles separated San Francisco, one of the major embarkation points for troops on the west coast, and Korea. The distance between Korea and embarkation points on the east coast via the Panama Canal was almost 8,100 nautical miles. As large-scale transcontinental air transport was not a feasible option in 1950, troopships carried the bulk of U.S. forces to Korea.

The task of coordinating and overseeing the use of troopships lay with the U.S. Navy's Military Sea Transport Service (MSTS). MSTS used commercially chartered vessels and U.S. Navy transport ships operated by navy personnel and members of the navy's civil service branch. Because of a decline in shipbuilding after World War II, many of these ships were World War II–era transports of the Liberty and Victory types. These ships had been mass-produced during the war, and although originally designed as freighters, many were rebuilt as troop transports. MSTS's logistical efforts also benefited organizationally from the World War II experience of deploying ships with men and supplies from U.S. embarkation points across the Pacific.

Sea transport was vital in the early going. The number of transport ships rose from 25 in July 1950 to 263 by that November. The steady increase in their numbers during these months allowed the United States to transport nearly 100,000 men to Korea during the first three months of the war. Six of every 7 people who went to Korea traveled by sea. During the war, MSTS transports carried more than 4.918 million passengers to and from the United States as well as within the Asian theater of operations.

Troopships also contributed greatly to combat operations. Captain Virginius Roane commanded the U.S. Navy's Transport Force in the Asian theater and used his ships there to good effect, particularly during the September 15, 1950, Inchon Landing, when his force landed 60,000 U.S. and 6,000 ROKA troops. Roane's force also proved its worth in the December 1950 evacuation of United Nations Command (UNC) forces from Hungnam in North Korea.

It is difficult to overemphasize the logistic importance of troopships. The United States could not have projected its military might across the Pacific without them.

ERIC W. OSBORNE

See also

Logistics in the Korean War; Military Sea Transport Service; United States Navy

References

Field, James A., Jr. *History of United States Naval Operations, Korea.* Washington, DC: U.S. Government Printing Office, 1962.

Huston, James A. *The Sinews of War: Army Logistics, 1775–1953.* Washington, DC: Office of the Chief of Military History, 1966.

Love, Robert W., Jr. *History of the U.S. Navy,* Vol. 2, *1942–1991.* Harrisburg, PA: Stackpole, 1992.

Truce Talks
Start Date: July 1951
End Date: July 1953

Korean War truce talks began at Kaesong on July 10, 1951, and continued with two long recesses and one relocation of the conference site until the Korean Armistice Agreement was signed on July 27, 1953. The talks took place after the 1951 Chinese Fifth (Spring) Offensive stalled and a subsequent counteroffensive by the U.S.-led

Soldiers stand guard outside tents where military armistice negotiations are being held in Panmunjom, November 1, 1951. The truce talks were moved from Kaesong to Panmunjom by the Panmunjom Security Agreement, October 22, 1951. (National Archives)

United Nations Command (UNC) met increasing Chinese and North Korean resistance north of the 38th Parallel. The People's Republic of China (PRC) and the United States, having concluded that military victory was unobtainable at an acceptable cost, then sought a negotiated settlement. Being unable to fight on alone, the Democratic People's Republic of Korea (DPRK, North Korea) and the Republic of Korea (ROK, South Korea) could only acquiesce.

On June 23, 1951, after preliminary U.S.-Soviet contacts, Soviet deputy foreign minister Jacob Malik suggested in a radio speech that the two sides should seek a cease-fire. On June 30 Lieutenant General Matthew B. Ridgway, commander in chief of the UNC, proposed that the talks begin aboard a Danish hospital ship moored in Wonsan Harbor. In their response, Kim Il Sung, supreme commander of the Korean People's Army (KPA, North Korean Army), and Peng Dehuai, commander of the Chinese People's Volunteer Army (CPVA, Chinese Army), proposed Kaesong, a town in western Korea near the 38th Parallel. The UNC accepted. Kaesong, the old Korean capital, lay between the lines and was then unoccupied by either side. By the time liaison officers met there on July 8 to make preliminary arrangements for the talks, however, KPA and CPVA forces had moved into Kaesong, giving them control of the conference site.

Each side was represented at the truce talks by a negotiating team of five generals or admirals. These principals were assisted by liaison or staff officers who worked out the details of agreements and maintained contact during the long recesses. Much of the most productive negotiating was done by subdelegations consisting of two principals from each side aided by staff assistants. KPA and CPVA negotiators operated from a location near Kaesong. UNC negotiators maintained a base camp at Munsan, some 15 miles southeast of Kaesong.

Key KPA-CPVA policy decisions were coordinated among the Chinese, North Korean, and Soviet leaders, with China providing direction and guidance to the KPA-CPVA delegation. Instructions were transmitted through a team headed by Chinese vice foreign minister and deputy chief of staff of the CPVA Li Kenong, who directed negotiations from behind the scenes. The chief KPA-CPVA delegate at the table was Lieutenant General Nam Il, KPA chief of staff and North Korean vice foreign minister. He was assisted by two North Korean and two Chinese generals or admirals.

On the UNC side, South Korea and the major UN allies could occasionally influence policy, but the U.S. government took sole responsibility for directing the UNC negotiators, transmitting instructions through the U.S. Joint Chiefs of Staff (JCS) to Ridgway. Vice Admiral C. Turner Joy, commander of U.S. Naval Forces Far East, served as UNC chief negotiator until May 1952, when he was replaced by Lieutenant General William K. Harrison, who served as UNC chief delegate until the armistice was signed. The UNC principals also included three other U.S. generals or admirals and one Republic of Korea Army (ROKA, South Korean Army) general.

While both sides sought an armistice, each had its own objectives. Neither side trusted the intentions of the other, both believed that any concession would be taken as a sign of weakness, and each side was convinced that military pressure was essential to force the other side to compromise. Ideological differences and the bitter nature of the war intensified the mutual suspicion and hostility that marked the talks. During the first meeting both sides acted in a businesslike manner, but the underlying antagonisms were evident. UNC delegates refused food and other amenities offered by the KPA-CPVA, while the Chinese and North Koreans took advantage of their control of the setting to portray themselves as victorious hosts. They also restricted access to the conference site, denying entry to journalists accompanying the UNC negotiators. After several days of sparring on this issue, the KPA-CPVA agreed, on July 15, 1951, to establish a Kaesong Neutral Zone to which both sides would have equal access.

During the next two weeks the negotiators worked out a five-point agenda, Item 1 of which was adoption of the agenda, while Items 2 through 5 provided the format for the eventual Korean Armistice Agreement. Item 2, fixing a military demarcation line (MDL) and establishing a demilitarized zone (DMZ), became armistice Article I. Item 3, concrete arrangements for a cease-fire, an armistice, and a supervising organization, became Article II. Item 4, arrangements relating to prisoners of war, became Article III. And Item 5, recommendations to the governments of the countries concerned, became Article IV.

The first substantive issue was the location and nature of the MDL and DMZ. The KPA-CPVA side insisted on an MDL along the 38th Parallel. The UNC, whose forces had pushed north of the parallel except for an area near Kaesong, sought a line well north of the existing line of ground contact. By August 22 the two sides had narrowed their differences and were close to agreement on an MDL based on the ground contact line. The KPA-CPVA then declared a unilateral recess, ostensibly in protest of UNC air attacks against the conference site but probably to pause negotiations while they reassessed their strategy and prepared for a possible new military offensive.

During the long recess the UNC, which had been dissatisfied with the Kaesong site from the beginning, sought to relocate the talks to a more neutral location. The KPA-CPVA eventually concurred, and under the terms of the October 22 Panmunjom Security Agreement, the talks were relocated to a new site several miles to the east.

When negotiations resumed at Panmunjom on October 25, 1951, the remaining Item 2 issues were the precise location of the MDL and when it would come into effect. Ridgway believed that recent UNC ground offensives had brought the communists back to the table and feared that immediate agreement on the truce line would make further offensives impossible. He thus insisted that the truce line be the line of ground contact when the armistice was signed. The UNC also proposed adjusting the current line of contact, giving up ground near the east coast of Korea in return for placing Kaesong in the UNC zone. The KPA-CPVA insisted on immediate agreement on the location of the MDL and refused to give up Kaesong. Ridgway's efforts to regain Kaesong were prompted by recognition of the military importance of the area as the main avenue of approach into South Korea and by strong pressure from Syngman Rhee, to whom the old Korean capital had important symbolic significance. Neither of these arguments was persuasive to U.S. leaders in Washington, who believed that the armistice would soon go into effect and did not want to delay agreement over what they saw as trivial issues. They thus ordered the UNC to concede these points with the proviso that if the armistice was not concluded within 30 days, the MDL would be the line of contact at the time the armistice was signed. On this basis, Item 2 was resolved on November 27, 1951. Although the truce talks went on long after the 30-day time limit and subsequent fighting required some adjustments, the line changed little by the time of the armistice.

The two sides then addressed Item 3. They quickly agreed on the establishment of a military armistice commission (MAC) with equal representation from both sides, but they differed as to the nature and scope of its activities. The UNC wanted a supervisory mechanism with the power of inspection throughout Korea and, fearing a challenge to UNC air superiority, also called for a ban on the repair or construction of airfields. The KPA-CPVA side accepted MAC supervision inside the DMZ but rejected the airfield repair ban and inspections outside the DMZ.

On December 3, 1951, the KPA-CPVA suggested supervision of the armistice outside the DMZ by nations "neutral in the Korean War," and the UNC eventually accepted this concept. By March 1952 the two sides had agreed to Czechoslovakia, Poland, Sweden, and Switzerland as members of the Neutral Nations Supervisory Commission (NNSC) and also agreed on procedures for the rotation of military personnel through five ports of entry for each side. Thus, Item 3 had been resolved except for airfield repair and a new KPA-CPVA demand that the Soviet Union be included in the NNSC. Resolution of these matters soon became embroiled in the far more difficult issue of repatriation of prisoners of war (POWs).

Both sides had initially assumed that all POWs would be exchanged at the conclusion of an armistice. By the time negotiations began on Item 4, however, the UNC had determined that former residents of South Korea impressed into the KPA should be permitted to stay in South Korea. U.S. president Harry S. Truman had also concluded that Chinese and North Korean prisoners should not be repatriated against their will. He was heavily influenced in this by memories of the tragic post–World War II fate of millions of Soviet POWs who had been forcibly repatriated, many suffering long imprisonment or death. Truman's rationale for voluntary repatriation was humanitarian, but other U.S. officials foresaw a moral and propaganda victory if large numbers of Chinese and North Korean soldiers rejected communism. They also believed that fear of such military defectors would deter future communist aggression. General Ridgway and others argued against this policy, concerned that it would delay an armistice and jeopardize UNC prisoners held by the KPA-CPVA. There were also well-justified concerns that pro–Nationalist Chinese prisoners, South Koreans, and Nationalist Chinese with access to the camps would pressure POWs into rejecting repatriation. But President Truman remained adamant.

When discussion of Item 4 began on December 11, 1951, the KPA-CPVA proposed that all POWs simply be exchanged. The UNC, with voluntary repatriation still under debate in Washington, proposed an initial exchange of information on POWs and called for Red Cross inspections of POW camps. The KPA-CPVA rejected Red Cross visits, an issue that the UNC subsequently dropped, but the communist side agreed to exchange POW data.

When POW lists were exchanged on December 22, the UNC was shocked to discover that the KPA-CPVA lists contained only 11,559 names out of 99,500 South Korean and UNC soldiers listed as missing in action. The KPA-CPVA claimed that the discrepancy arose because they had released many prisoners at the front and because U.S. bombing had killed some UNC POWs. They in turn complained that the UNC list was more than 44,000 POWs fewer than an earlier list that the UNC had passed to the Red Cross. The UNC side acknowledged some faulty initial counting and advised that it had reclassified some 37,000 former South Korean residents as civilian internees and removed them from the POW rolls.

On January 2, 1952, the UNC proposed a method for dealing with POWs that involved voluntary repatriation. The KPA-CPVA rejected the principle, and although all the other POW-related issues were resolved by early February, voluntary repatriation was an insurmountable obstacle.

While negotiations on Items 3 and 4 stalled, Item 5, recommendations to the governments concerned, proved easy to resolve. On February 6, 1952, General Nam Il proposed a postwar political conference within three months of the signing of the armistice to discuss withdrawal of foreign forces from Korea, specific recommendations for peaceful settlement of the Korean question, and other problems relating to peace in Korea. The UNC accepted the proposal, with the replacement of the phrase "other problems relating to peace in Korea" with the nonspecific term "etc." and a few other changes. Item 5 was resolved on February 19, 1952.

In March 1952 the KPA-CPVA side began to show some flexibility on Item 4, at least regarding prisoners who had been residents of South Korea. On April 1 a UNC staff officer suggested that as many as 116,000 communist POWs might choose repatriation, but that estimate proved to be woefully optimistic. On April 19 after screening the prisoners to determine their repatriation desires, the UNC informed the KPA-CPVA that only 70,000 out of more than 170,000 prisoners held by the UNC desired repatriation. The KPA-CPVA negotiators stated flatly that such a low figure could not possibly be the "basis for further discussion." On April 28 the UNC presented what it referred to as a package proposal. It dropped the ban on airfield repair and, in return, asked the KPA-CPVA to concede on Soviet participation in the NNSC and voluntary repatriation. The KPA-CPVA accepted the first two

proposals, effectively resolving Item 3, but it firmly rejected voluntary repatriation except for former residents of South Korea.

With the talks now deadlocked, the tone at Panmunjom became increasingly hostile. The Chinese and North Koreans began an intense propaganda offensive, accusing the United States of conducting germ warfare. Bloody uprisings in the UNC-controlled POW camps provided fuel for the campaign, embarrassed the UNC, and cast doubt on its administration of the camps and the legitimacy of the screening. On October 8, with no progress in sight, the UNC declared a unilateral recess.

Neither side was prepared to initiate a major offensive, but both now increased their military activity to put pressure on their opponents. Lieutenant General Mark W. Clark, who had replaced Ridgway as UNC commander in chief in May, gained approval to conduct the largest air attacks of the war against the North Korean capital of Pyongyang and to destroy hydroelectric dams on the Yalu River. Both sides carried out ground attacks. The Chinese stepped up their propaganda campaign and conducted a major reinforcement of their forces in Korea.

With no progress at Panmunjom, the truce talks became an issue at the UN, with several countries putting forth proposals. The one that garnered the most support was that of the Indian delegation, strongly supported by the British and other Commonwealth countries. It called for a neutral nations repatriation commission (NNRC) to deal with the prisoner issue. The United States preferred a resolution that would simply endorse the UNC position but, under pressure from its allies, agreed to support the Indian resolution with some amendments. The General Assembly passed the resolution on December 3.

The Indian resolution would eventually provide the basis for resolution of the POW repatriation issue, and as 1953 began, other events that would eventually lead to an armistice were under way. The new Dwight D. Eisenhower administration took office in the United States and was committed to ending the war. North Korea, with its economy devastated, and China, strained by its war effort and eager to begin economic reconstruction, were apparently prepared to return to the truce talks, although they preferred that the United States make the first move. That came on February 22 when Clark, following up a Red Cross proposal, called for an exchange of sick and wounded POWs.

On March 5, 1953, Soviet leader Joseph Stalin died. His successors were clearly predisposed to a settlement in Korea and encouraged the Chinese and North Koreans to conclude an armistice. On March 28 the KPA-CPVA accepted Clark's proposal. Two days later Chinese premier Zhou Enlai made a speech in which he proposed that POWs not desiring repatriation be transferred to a neutral state. Kim Il Sung publicly endorsed this policy the next day, as did the Soviet foreign minister on April 1. The communists had now accepted the principle of voluntary repatriation, and events began to move quickly. The exchange of sick and wounded POWs, Operation LITTLE SWITCH, began on April 20, and the truce talks resumed on April 26. The KPA-CPVA put the NNRC concept on the table, suggesting that the NNRC be composed of the same members as the NNSC plus India.

The two sides were now close to agreement, but UNC negotiators still found some aspects of the KPA-CPVA proposal unacceptable. They also introduced two new demands: that the NNRC work on the basis of consensus rather than majority vote and that South Korean nonrepatriates not be turned over to the NNRC. Both positions were contrary to the Indian UN resolution, which the U.S. government had previously supported, and the Eisenhower administration ultimately decided not to jeopardize the armistice over these issues. On May 25 the UNC presented what it called its final position. Dropping both of the new conditions, it called for the repatriation of all POWs within 60 days after the signing of the armistice. Those refusing repatriation were to be transferred to the NNRC for a 90-day period, during which representatives of their home country would have access to them under NNRC supervision. After 90 days the postwar political conference would deal with any remaining nonrepatriates, with the proviso that after an additional 30 days the nonrepatriates would either be released or their fate decided by the UN General Assembly.

The Chinese and North Koreans were under some pressure to accept. Earlier in May the UNC had attacked irrigation dams near Pyongyang to disrupt rail and road lines. Although the North Koreans were eventually able to neutralize the effects by draining the reservoirs, these attacks further strained the North Korean infrastructure and demonstrated a UNC willingness to step up its military action. On May 20 President Eisenhower and his advisers had concluded that if the KPA-CPVA rejected the final offer, the UNC would initiate a military offensive that might include attacks on China and use of nuclear weapons. To signal this resolve, the UNC commander in chief publicly warned that if the KPA-CPVA did not accept the May 25 proposal, the UNC would widen its war effort. U.S. officials attempted to transmit veiled nuclear threats to the Chinese through India and other countries. On June 4 General Nam Il responded to the UNC by declaring, "We basically agree to the new proposal which your side put forward on May 25." On June 8 the two sides concluded an agreement on voluntary repatriation, and staff officers began a final review of the armistice language.

Feeling betrayed by the May 25 UNC concessions, South Korean president Syngman Rhee now made a final effort to derail the armistice. He made strong overtures to President Eisenhower, ordered public demonstrations, threatened to remove the ROKA from the UNC, said that he would attack any Indian troops who set foot on South Korean soil, and on June 17 unilaterally released some 27,000 Korean POWs from the UNC POW camps. Eisenhower sent a mission headed by Walter S. Robertson to negotiate with Rhee. With the promise of future U.S. support, a South Korean–U.S. mutual security treaty, and a major aid package— and after the Chinese initiated a series of heavy attacks aimed at South Korean units, nearly destroying two ROKA divisions—Rhee agreed to abide by the armistice. On July 27, 1953, General Clark, Marshal Kim Il Sung, and General Peng Dehuai signed the Korean

Armistice Agreement in separate ceremonies, Kim and Peng near Panmunjom and Clark at Munsan. At 11:00 a.m. the next morning, the Military Armistice Commission began its first meeting at Panmunjom.

DONALD W. BOOSE JR.

See also

Agenda Controversy; Armistice Agreement; Cease-fire Negotiations; Chinese Offensive, First; Chinese Offensive, Second; Chinese Offensive, Third; Chinese Offensive, Fourth; Chinese Offensive, Fifth; Chinese Offensive, Sixth; Chinese Offensives, Summer; Civilian Internee Issue; Clark, Mark Wayne; Dam Raids of 1953; Demilitarized Zone; Eisenhower, Dwight David; Harrison, William Kelly, Jr.; Joy, Charles Turner; Kaesong Bombing Proposal; Kaesong Truce Talks; Li Kenong; LITTLE SWITCH and BIG SWITCH, Operations; Malik, Jacob; Menon, Vengalil Krishnan Krishna; Military Armistice Commission; Nam Il; Neutral Nations Repatriation Commission; Neutral Nations Supervisory Commission; Panmunjom Security Agreement; Prisoners of War, Rescreening of; Repatriation, Voluntary; Rhee, Syngman; Ridgway, Matthew Bunker; Robertson Mission; SCATTER, Operation; Stalin, Joseph; Supung and the Korean Electric Power Plant Campaign; Truman, Harry S.; Zhou Enlai

References

Boose, Donald W., Jr. "The Korean War Truce Talks: A Study in Conflict Termination." *Parameters* 30(1) (Spring 2000): 102–116.

Dingman, Roger. "Atomic Diplomacy during the Korean War." *International Security* 13(3) (Winter 1988–1989): 50–91.

Foot, Rosemary J. *A Substitute for Victory: The Politics of Peacemaking at the Korean Armistice Talks.* Ithaca, NY: Cornell University Press, 1990.

Goodman, Allan E., ed. *Negotiating While Fighting: The Diary of Admiral C. Turner Joy at the Korean Armistice Conference.* Stanford, CA: Hoover Institute Press, 1978.

Hermes, Walter G. *U.S. Army in the Korean War: Truce Tent and Fighting Front.* Washington, DC: Office of the Chief of Military History, 1966.

Matray, James I. "Progress and Paralysis: The Korean Truce Talks, July 1951–May 1952." In *The Korean War at Fifty: International Perspectives,* edited by Mark F. Wilkinson, 150–175. Lexington, VA: John A. Adams Center for Military History and Strategic Analysis, 2004.

Stueck, William W., Jr. *The Korean War: An International History.* Princeton, NJ: Princeton University Press, 1995.

U.S. Department of State, Bureau of Public Affairs. *Foreign Relations of the United States, 1950,* Vol. 7, *Korea.* Washington, DC: U.S. Government Printing Office, 1976.

———. *Foreign Relations of the United States, 1951,* Vol. 7, *China and Korea.* Washington, DC: U.S. Government Printing Office, 1983.

———. *Foreign Relations of the United States, 1952–1954,* Vol. 15, *Korea.* Washington, DC: U.S. Government Printing Office, 1984.

Truman, Harry S.
Birth Date: May 8, 1884
Death Date: December 26, 1972

U.S. senator (1935–1945) and president of the United States from 1945 to 1953. Born in Lamar, Missouri, on May 8, 1884, to a family of modest means, Harry S. Truman moved several times as a youth. He spent most of his formative years in Jackson County,

Missouri, on his grandparents' 600-acre farm near Grandview. He hoped for a college education and tried to secure appointments to the U.S. Military Academy at West Point and to the U.S. Naval Academy at Annapolis, but was turned down to both because of his poor eyesight. In World War I he served as an officer with Battery D of the 129th Field Artillery and rose to the rank of captain.

After World War I Truman studied law at night at the Kansas City School of Law, although he never earned a degree. He then won election, with the aid of Thomas J. "Boss Tom" Pendergast, to a judgeship on the Jackson County court, and served from 1926 to 1934. He was elected to the U.S. Senate in 1934 and reelected in 1940, achieving prominence as the chair of the Senate committee to investigate national defense spending during World War II. By 1944 Truman had earned a reputation as a hard-working, plain-spoken, and trustworthy politician.

President Franklin D. Roosevelt chose Truman for the 1944 Democratic Party ticket as a compromise vice presidential candidate to replace Henry Wallace, who was regarded as too liberal. When Roosevelt died of a cerebral hemorrhage on April 12, 1945, Truman became the 33rd president of the United States. Although he had little experience in foreign policy and had not been included in many major policy decisions, Truman successfully guided the United States through the conclusion of World War II. He did not shrink from difficult decisions, including that of employing the atomic bomb against Japan in August 1945.

Less willing than Roosevelt to work with Soviet leader Joseph Stalin, Truman provided firm leadership in the Cold War. He implemented the policy of containing communist expansion, known as the Truman Doctrine, by coming to the aid of Greece and Turkey in 1947. His administration also undertook to strengthen Europe against communist subversion with the Marshall Plan that same year. Domestically, Truman was seen as less successful, however, and the approval ratings for his handling of the postwar economic reconversion to peace time suffered accordingly.

Truman confounded the pollsters and pundits and was reelected president in 1948 in the midst of the first major confrontation of the Cold War—the Berlin Crisis and airlift. However, the 1949 Communist victory in the Chinese Civil War and the successful testing by the Union of Soviet Socialist Republics (USSR, Soviet Union) of its first atomic bomb intensified both the Cold War and the criticism of Truman in the United States.

By 1950 Truman was coming under increasing pressure from Republicans and other detractors who saw his responses to the deepening Cold War as too tepid. Indeed, his administration was subjected to repeated—and false—allegations that it was harboring communists or communist sympathizers, especially after Republican senator Joseph R. McCarthy began his anticommunist witch-hunt, known as McCarthyism. In early 1950 Truman somewhat reluctantly gave the green light for the construction of a thermonuclear weapon (the hydrogen bomb), but when the U.S. National Security Council (NSC) presented him with a report (NSC-68) in April 1950 that called for a massive increase in defense

U.S. president Harry S. Truman signs the National Emergency Proclamation at the White House, December 16, 1950. (National Archives)

spending, the president demurred. At heart a fiscal conservative, Truman refused to embark on deficit spending or major defense increases in the absence of a major war. Only after the Korean War began in June 1950 did he accede to the recommendations of NSC-68.

In his memoirs Truman pointed out the uncompromising nature of the Soviet position after World War II regarding Korea and his appeal to the United Nations (UN) to resolve the issue there. Although the U.S. military government ended with elections and the proclamation of the Republic of Korea (ROK, South Korea) on August 15, 1948, the NSC recommended extensive military and economic aid for South Korea, and a defense agreement was signed with that country on January 26, 1950. Unfortunately, in a speech given two weeks earlier, Secretary of State Dean G. Acheson had excluded South Korea from a description of the U.S. defense perimeter. Fearful that South Korean president Syngman Rhee might start a war with the intent to reunite Korea, the Truman administration opposed providing South Korea with weapons, including tanks and aircraft, that might be used offensively.

Despite the failure of his administration to anticipate an invasion of South Korea by the Democratic People's Republic of Korea (DPRK, North Korea), Truman reacted decisively to the June 25,

1950, invasion. Truman later compared the attack to Nazi Germany's aggression in the late 1930s when he wrote, "If the Communists were permitted to force their way into the Republic of Korea without opposition from the free world, no small nation would have the courage to resist threats and aggression by stronger Communist neighbors." Truman saw Moscow's hand in the invasion and believed that the Soviet Union was trying to secure South Korea "by default" on the assumption that the United States would be too fearful of another world war to intervene. Still, he described the decision to intervene militarily as the most difficult of his presidency.

Truman adroitly handled the Korean issue in the UN. In this he benefited from the Soviet boycott of the UN Security Council—conducted in protest over the exclusion from the UN of the People's Republic of China (PRC)—and the failure of North Korea to pull back across the 38th Parallel. Truman also sent the Seventh Fleet to protect Taiwan (then known as Formosa), strengthened U.S. forces in the Philippines, and substantially increased aid to French forces fighting in Indochina.

Truman sought to limit the Korean War. He therefore rejected an offer from the Chinese Nationalists to fight in Korea, believing that this might provoke the PRC to enter the conflict. Fear of Soviet designs against Western Europe was also a major preoccupation. Truman wanted to avoid a third world war and would not approve reconnaissance flights over Darien and Port Arthur in Manchuria, or over Vladivostok in the Soviet Union, which might have provoked a Soviet response.

Truman promptly appointed General Douglas MacArthur as commander of United Nations Command (UNC) forces in Korea and supported his requests for more troops. The conflict led to the calling up of four National Guard divisions to active duty, a major increase in the size of the regular army, and an emergency appropriation of $10 billion for defense purposes. The United States was unprepared militarily for the war, however, and by summer's end Truman announced plans to significantly strengthen U.S. military forces and to double the armed forces to 3 million men, warning that the nation's defense burden would become greater still. Truman also authorized the speed-up of production of military items, including aircraft and ships.

Four days before MacArthur's September 15, 1950, landing at Inchon (Operation CHROMITE), which would dramatically change the war, Truman asked for Secretary of Defense Louis A. Johnson's resignation. General of the Army George C. Marshall replaced Johnson, whose abrasive personality and ego had offended many. Indeed, it was Johnson who had borne the brunt of criticism that the United States was unprepared for the war, although he was merely carrying out mandates established by the White House and Congress. Truman was not fond of MacArthur but approved his Inchon plan, despite reasonable concerns raised by chairman of the Joint Chiefs of Staff (JCS) General Omar N. Bradley and others. Weeks before success at Inchon, he also decided, with JCS concurrence, to authorize UNC troops to pursue the North Koreans

across the 38th Parallel with the strict proviso that his field commander not carry the war into Chinese or Soviet territory.

Truman sought a personal meeting with MacArthur, which took place on Wake Island on October 15, 1950. There they discussed the possibility of Chinese or Soviet intervention almost as an afterthought. MacArthur dismissed the possibility of Chinese intervention and maintained that, should the Chinese intervene, they would be able to get no more than 60,000 men across the Yalu River into North Korea in the face of U.S. bombing. MacArthur was proved wrong in both assessments when the PRC soon made good on its threat to enter the conflict. Truman reluctantly approved MacArthur's plea to bomb bridges over the Yalu, with the proviso that it was vital "to avoid violation of Manchurian territory and airspace."

As UNC forces reeled from the massive Chinese military intervention on November 30, 1950, Truman was asked about the possibility of using the atomic bomb in the war. He responded, "There has always been active consideration of its use." The U.S. Western European allies reacted with alarm to this statement, but at the time the Truman administration was more concerned by the fact that the Soviet Union had just completed military maneuvers involving half a million men and had consolidated their Siberian commands under one commander. While Truman declared a national emergency in December 1950, he and his principal military advisers believed that Korea was "not the place to fight a major war." Be that as it may, Truman accelerated the rearmament program, appointed a mobilization czar with sweeping powers (Charles E. Wilson), and acceded to the imposition of blanket economic controls—including price and wage controls—that began in earnest in January 1951.

Concerned with the direction of U.S. policy, British prime minister Clement R. Attlee visited Washington, DC, in December 1950. In a victory for Truman, the joint statement issued at the end of five days of talks indicated that while the two governments would seek a negotiated settlement to end the war, there would be no "thought of appeasement or rewarding aggression." Attlee received assurances, however, that Chinese industrial targets would not be bombed, that tentative plans for an economic blockade and efforts to foment internal unrest in China would be abandoned, and that the atomic bomb would not be employed there without prior consultation with London.

Although relieving General MacArthur from his command had already been suggested, Truman preferred standing by his commander in the field. Nonetheless, Truman was angered by an interview with MacArthur published in U.S. News and World Report wherein MacArthur sought to lay the blame for the UNC retreat before the Chinese forces on the administration's limited war restrictions. To curb MacArthur, the administration issued a series of extraordinary directives that required prior State Department or White House clearance before the release of any statements of a political nature. This did not keep MacArthur from announcing his own ultimatum to the Chinese, demanding their surrender and scuttling any possibility of an early cease-fire. Frustrated by MacArthur's repeated challenges to his administration's policy in Korea, Truman now began to consult his advisers about the possibility of removing the general from command. He also wanted the UNC commander to have the power to use atomic weapons in response to a massive enemy assault on U.S. forces and feared MacArthur would exploit this power to expand the war to mainland China. At the same time, Truman was concerned over the political impact of removing his field commander on Republicans in Congress and wanted the unanimous concurrence of the JCS before taking such a momentous step.

Then, on April 5, 1951, Republican house minority leader Joseph W. Martin released a letter written by MacArthur, which revealed the general's disagreements with the administration on war policy and argued that there was "no substitute for victory." After midnight on April 11, the president called a hasty news conference to announce that he was relieving MacArthur from his commands. The timing was dictated by fears that press reports of the planned action might get to MacArthur first and allow him to resign before Truman's relief order arrived. MacArthur had forced this decision, which did, however, serve to preserve the vital principle of civilian control of the military and to preserve the president's policy of fighting a limited war in Korea.

Lieutenant General Matthew B. Ridgway, MacArthur's successor, carried out the Truman administration's policy of doing nothing to broaden the conflict. Truman approved an NSC policy statement of May 17, 1951, that sought stabilization of the fighting and an armistice, but on June 10 the JCS secured approval for Ridgway to operate north of the 38th Parallel to enhance the chances for armistice talks by maximizing Chinese casualties. Although talks did get under way in July and substantial progress was made, the two sides deadlocked on the issue of repatriation of prisoners of war (POWs) by May 1952.

Although the political firestorm surrounding MacArthur's removal burned itself out rather quickly, Truman remained highly unpopular throughout the remainder of 1951 and during 1952. Still under attack from the McCarthyites, the Truman White House was besieged by the political ramifications of economic controls. The U.S. public quickly soured on the use of such measures, and the president's seizure of many of the nation's steel mills in 1952—a move taken to avert a major strike—was seen by many as too heavy-handed. When the U.S. Supreme Court ruled the action unconstitutional, whatever remained of Truman's clout had virtually evaporated. Economic controls began to unravel, and the ongoing war had worn heavily on the U.S. electorate.

Truman, now widely unpopular, chose not to stand for reelection in 1952. Following the presidential elections, Truman met on November 18 with president-elect Dwight D. Eisenhower, but he was unable to obtain Eisenhower's signature on a joint communiqué to oppose an Indian plan that required the forcible repatriation of POWs. The communist side used the Truman administration's insistence on voluntary repatriation to stall the truce talks. Despite this, Eisenhower authorized Republican senator Alexander Wiley to announce the next day that the president-elect favored "nonforcible repatriation." This, coupled with a Soviet attack on the Indian plan, helped the Truman administration reach a compromise on the issue that was closer to its position. Subsequently, when Stalin's death in March 1953 and the Eisenhower administration's threat of the use of tactical nuclear weapons helped bring about an armistice agreement, Truman made no public comment, but he did harbor some resentment that his own efforts to end the war might not be fully appreciated.

After leaving office, Truman wrote his memoirs and arranged for his papers to be placed in his presidential library in Independence, Missouri. Former Secretary of State Dean Acheson contributed his papers, as did many other administration officials. With the help of Speaker of the House of Representatives Sam Rayburn and Senate majority leader Lyndon B. Johnson, Truman urged passage of a law allowing former presidents financial support for staff and offices and free mailing privileges. Such a law was subsequently approved.

Truman was present when President Johnson came to the Truman Library on July 30, 1965, to sign the landmark Medicare bill, which was similar to legislation Truman had proposed nearly 20 years before. Truman died in Kansas City, Missouri, on December 26, 1972.

CLAUDE R. SASSO

See also

Acheson, Dean Gooderham; Attlee, Clement Richard; Bradley, Omar Nelson; Containment; Harriman, William Averell; Johnson, Louis Arthur; Joint Chiefs of Staff; MacArthur, Douglas; Marshall, George Catlett; Marshall Plan; Martin, Joseph William; McCarthyism; Munich Analogy; National Security Council Report 68; North Atlantic Treaty Organization; Rhee, Syngman; Ridgway, Matthew Bunker; Truman Doctrine; Truman-Eisenhower Transition Meeting; Truman's Cease-fire Initiative; Truman's Domestic Agenda and the Korean War; Truman's Recall of MacArthur; Wake Island Conference

References

Kaufman, Burton I. *The Korean War: Challenges in Crisis, Credibility and Command.* 2nd ed. New York: McGraw-Hill, 1997.

McCullough, David. *Truman.* New York: Simon and Schuster, 1992.

Pemberton, William E. *Harry S. Truman: Fair Dealer and Cold Warrior.* Boston: Twayne, 1989.

Pierpaoli, Paul G., Jr. *Truman and Korea: The Political Culture of the Early Cold War.* Columbia: University of Missouri Press, 1999.

Truman, Harry S. *Memoirs.* 2 vols. Garden City, NY: Doubleday, 1956.

Truman Doctrine
Event Date: March 12, 1947

U.S. foreign policy doctrine enunciated by President Harry S. Truman that formally committed the United States to fight communist expansionism abroad. On March 12, 1947, President Truman addressed a joint session of Congress and stated, "I believe that it must be the policy of the United States to support free peoples who are resisting attempted subjugation by armed minorities or by outside pressures." He was of course referring to communist pressures and thereby committed the United States to uphold the containment policy, which pledged that all necessary measures would be taken to check the spread of communism and Soviet influence.

The catalyst for the Truman Doctrine had been Britain's February 1947 announcement that it could no longer afford to provide military or financial support to Greece and Turkey. This meant that these nations might fall to communism, and this was especially true for Greece, whose pro-Western government was fighting a communist guerrilla insurgency in the northern part of the country.

The eastern basin of the Mediterranean, including the Middle East, had historically been under British influence since the 19th century. The area was still important to Britain after World War II, but it took on great importance in light of the developing Cold War. Soviet presence in the region would jeopardize the ability of the Western powers to launch strategic air strikes on the Soviet Union from bases in the area. The defense of the region had been a British preserve and rested on British military bases, the largest of which was in Egypt. British power was declining, however, while at the same time Soviet activity in the region seemed on the increase.

The Soviet Union had demanded that the Turkish government change the rules governing ship movements through the Dardanelles and allow it to participate, along with other Black Sea nations, in the defense of the straits. The U.S. interpretation of the Soviets' demand was that they intended to secure hegemony over Turkey, build bases there, and then gain control over Greece. From there the Soviet Union could dominate much of the Middle East and the eastern Mediterranean. The demand in itself was of relatively minor importance because it was made in the form of a diplomatic note, not supported by any explicit or implicit military threats.

For planners in Washington, there seemed to be a power vacuum in the region, the result of Britain's declining strength. Britain was providing military aid to Turkey, but the U.S. Joint Chiefs of Staff (JCS) thought that because of its strategic importance and in order to increase its ability to meet Soviet aggression, the United States should increase its economic and military aid to Turkey. As long as the British furnished military assistance, however, the Truman administration would provide only economic aid.

American attitudes toward the situation in Turkey were linked to the situation in Greece. Like Turkey, Greece was considered a barrier between the Soviet Union and the Mediterranean. The struggle in Greece was not one inspired by the Soviet Union but instead resulted from conflict between rightists seeking to restore the monarchy who were also failing to tackle the grave economic situation and left-wing parties seeking to install a communist regime. Washington, however, chose to view the Greek Civil War through the lens of the Cold War. A loss in Greece to the communists would not only result in a victory for the Soviets but, it was argued, would also open the entire region to communist subversion.

Thus, the Americans could not tolerate the establishment of a communist regime in Athens whether or not it was inspired by Moscow. Despite the shortcomings of the anticommunist Greek government, the Truman administration now moved to provide assistance to it. The decisive turning point came with London's announcement in February 1947 that Britain would be unable to continue its support to Greece and Turkey. It was obvious to U.S. State Department officials that the United States had to fill the breach. While preparing the draft legislation for the 1947 Greco-Turkish aid package, however, Undersecretary of State Dean Acheson found it difficult to justify the assistance request for Turkey, as it was not under a direct threat from either the Kremlin or an indigenous communist insurgency. Acheson also knew that Congress was in no mood to approve a large foreign aid request without proper justification, as it was engaged in efforts to curtail spending and pay down the national debt accrued during World War II. Also, Moscow was issuing conciliatory messages, further reducing the incentive in Congress to take strong measures against the Soviet Union.

Truman and his advisers, determined to provide military and economic assistance to both Greece and Turkey, had to find a way to sell this foreign aid package to Congress. Just prior to Truman's speech, Acheson described to the congressional leadership in stark terms the implications of Soviet domination over the eastern Mediterranean and the worldwide geopolitical consequences of such a scenario. In response, Republican senator Arthur H. Vandenberg, a formerly steadfast isolationist, informed Truman that if he were to present his request to Congress in the manner that had been used by Acheson, he and the majority of Congress would support the aid deal. As a result, Truman's request for a $400 million aid package earmarked for Turkey and Greece was presented in the Cold War terms of a struggle "between alternate ways of life," marking the emergence of the Truman Doctrine, which came to represent a concerted long-term effort to resist communist aggression around the world. Vandenberg kept his promise, and the Greco-Turkish aid package was speedily approved.

The Truman Doctrine, of course, had far wider consequences than the struggle over Greece and Turkey. It essentially put words and power behind the concept of containment and seemingly implied that the United States would come to the aid of any nation that was under siege by communist forces. The Berlin Airlift of 1948–1949 was the first test of the Truman Doctrine, which was passed with flying colors when the Truman administration orchestrated a massive airlift that eventually forced the Soviets to back down. The biggest test, however, came in June 1950 when forces of the Democratic People's Republic of Korea (DPRK, North Korea) invaded the Republic of Korea (ROK, South Korea). President Truman immediately dispatched troops to Korea and vowed to overturn the invasion and occupation. After 1950, there was no doubt that the United States had committed itself, via the Truman Doctrine, to containment on a global scale.

David Tal

See also

Acheson, Dean Gooderham; Containment; Truman, Harry S.

References

Kuniholm, Bruce R. *The Origins of the Cold War in the Near East.* Princeton, NJ: Princeton University Press, 1980.

LaFeber, Walter. *America, Russia and the Cold War, 1945–2002.* Updated 9th ed. New York: McGraw-Hill, 2004.

Leffler, Melvyn P. *A Preponderance of Power: National Security, the Truman Administration, and the Cold War.* Stanford, CA: Stanford University Press, 1992.

Truman-Eisenhower Transition Meeting
Event Date: November 18, 1952

Meeting between President Harry S. Truman and president-elect Dwight D. Eisenhower, held at the White House shortly after Eisenhower's election victory but two months before his inauguration. This was the only personal encounter between the two men during the interregnum and was largely devoted to issues arising from the Korean War, particularly the vexing question of the forced repatriation of prisoners of war (POWs). In their respective memoirs, the two presidents gave somewhat different accounts of this occasion. Truman claimed that Eisenhower was "overwhelmed" by the information he acquired, while Eisenhower recalled that the briefing "added little to my knowledge."

After a private meeting between the two in which Truman offered to provide Eisenhower with any information he required during the transition, the principals and their advisers moved to the cabinet briefing room, where Secretary of State Dean G. Acheson surveyed a variety of international issues and problems, focusing particularly on the Korean situation. At this time, Acheson and Truman were particularly concerned by the POW proposal unveiled at the United Nations (UN) the day before by Indian representative V. K. Krishna Menon, with backing from the United Kingdom and Canada. They feared its vague wording might circumvent the Truman administration's demand for exclusively voluntary repatriation. Acheson suggested that Eisenhower sign a public communiqué stating that he supported the administration's position that no POW could be "forcibly repatriated." Eisenhower, wary of committing himself at this point to any definite stance, agreed only to a vague statement that he was cooperating with Truman during the transition but that, as the U.S. Constitution decreed, Truman would be fully in control of the executive branch until the inauguration took place in January 1953.

Upon further reflection, Eisenhower essentially acceded to Truman's request. The following day, November 19, he

authorized Republican member of the Senate Foreign Relations Committee Alexander Wiley, a delegate to the UN, to state publicly that the president-elect endorsed the principle of "non-forcible repatriation." Eisenhower's open support for the Truman administration's position, together with a Soviet attack on the Menon plan, enabled Acheson to obtain modifications in the original proposal that made it acceptable to him and Truman, alterations that were enshrined in the UN resolution of December 3, 1952.

Priscilla Roberts

See also

Acheson, Dean Gooderham; Eisenhower, Dwight David; Menon, Vengalil Krishnan Krishna; Truman, Harry S.

References

Ambrose, Stephen E. *Eisenhower.* 2 vols. New York: Simon and Schuster, 1983–1984.

Brauer, Carl M. *Presidential Transitions: Eisenhower through Reagan.* New York: Oxford University Press, 1986.

Hamby, Alonzo L. *Man of the People: A Life of Harry S. Truman.* New York: Oxford University Press, 1995.

Mosher, Frederick C., W. David Clinton, and Daniel G. Lang. *Presidential Transitions and Foreign Affairs.* Baton Rouge: Louisiana State University Press, 1987.

Truman Loyalty Program

Program launched by U.S. president Harry S. Truman requiring federal employees to take an oath of loyalty to the government, which enabled federal agencies to investigate employees and, if warranted, dismiss them for activities considered suspect. In the first years after World War II, as fears of malevolent Soviet power abroad and communist subversion at home mounted, the politics of anticommunism became a potent weapon in the United States. Charges that Soviet spies or disloyal Americans were serving in important government posts began to circulate, and the Truman administration was powerless to stop the largely untruthful allegations. Soon a Red Scare erupted, and Truman felt obliged to take action to quell the resultant paranoia. Unfortunately, the Loyalty Program had unintended consequences; it further heightened anticommunist paranoia and provided fertile ground for McCarthyism, which bedeviled the Truman administration during the Korean War.

The Democrats lost control of Congress to the Republicans in 1946, placing great pressure on President Truman, himself a Democrat. At the same time, the House Un-American Activities Committee (HUAC) was uncovering alleged communist subversion in nearly all American institutions, including the federal government. Under political pressure from the Republicans and the right wing of his own party, Truman ordered the Department of Justice to develop a list of possibly subversive government employees, who were then required to sign a loyalty oath.

The Loyalty Program, established by Executive Order 9835 on March 21, 1947, mandated that all federal employees be subjected to background checks and sign a pledge of loyalty to the U.S. government. To aid in this endeavor, loyalty boards in each of the federal agencies were created. These boards performed security checks and background investigations. The loyalty review boards investigated more than 3 million federal workers, of whom roughly 3,000 were forced to resign or lost their jobs without indictment. Truman personally fired 212 executive-level employees. Soon, the loyalty oath program spread to other government agencies, especially in education.

At the time, the program seemed to some, at least, to be a violation of civil liberties and an infringement on the constitutionally guaranteed rights of targeted Americans. In the federal government, employees lost their right to openly criticize U.S. foreign policy, own books on socialism, or attend certain foreign films. In 1951 under Executive Order 10241, if the government had "reasonable" grounds for believing that a person was disloyal, it could summarily fire that person.

When Truman left office in January 1953, McCarthyism was in full swing. Truman's Executive Orders 9835 and 10241 and Public Law 733 were precedents for Executive Order 10450 signed on April 17, 1953, which President Dwight D. Eisenhower used to purge additional alleged subversives or security risks from the government. As a result, 600 federal workers resigned, and 1,500 more were fired.

In 1947 Julia Steiner of the Los Angeles County Library System, along with two unions, tried to obtain an injunction prohibiting supervisors from asking employees about reading interests, political views, or past associations. This challenge became the first of 33 cases to eventually challenge the entire Loyalty Program. From the 1950s into the late 1960s, a series of court cases gradually dismantled the various elements of the Truman-Eisenhower loyalty oath programs, largely on procedural grounds. But the concept of a loyalty oath was not overturned.

In 1972 the U.S. Supreme Court reaffirmed the legitimacy of loyalty oaths, which remain in use, most commonly by licensing boards and in public education. While the issue of such oaths has become muted, it is clear that Truman's original 1947 action helped set the stage for the corrosive politics and excesses of the McCarthy era (1950–1954) and the attendant civil liberty violations that ensued. McCarthyism, in turn, politicized the conduct and policies of the Korean War and made the conflict far more difficult to wage.

JOHN H. BARNHILL

See also

Civil Liberties in the United States; Eisenhower, Dwight David; House Un-American Activities Committee; McCarthy, Joseph Raymond; McCarthyism; Truman, Harry S.

References

Fariello, Griffin. *Red Scare: Memories of the American Inquisition: An Oral History*. New York: Norton, 1995.

Freeland, Richard M. *The Truman Doctrine and the Origins of McCarthyism: Foreign Policy, Domestic Politics, and Internal Security, 1946–1948*. New York: New York University Press, 1985.

McCullough, David. *Truman*. New York: Simon and Schuster, 1992.

Morgan, Ted. *Reds: McCarthyism in Twentieth-Century America*. Westminster, MD: Random House, 2003.

Reichard, Gary W. *Politics as Usual: The Age of Truman and Eisenhower*. Arlington Heights, IL: Harlan Davidson, 1988.

Truman's Cease-fire Initiative
Event Date: March 20, 1951

Early in 1951 President Harry S. Truman contemplated making a public appeal for a truce in the Korean War, a decision sabotaged by commander of United Nations Command (UNC) General Douglas MacArthur, who publicly demanded that his opponents surrender. MacArthur's unilateral pronouncement in this instance and on other occasions precipitated Truman's decision in April 1951 to relieve him of his command.

By late March 1951 the military situation of UNC forces in Korea was clearly improving, as they recovered from the initial shock of the massive November 1950 Chinese intervention and began to retake lost ground. Lieutenant General Matthew B. Ridgway's Eighth Army was close to regaining the 38th Parallel, the prewar boundary between the two Korean states. Encouraged by these successes, Truman's advisers began to suggest that he issue a public statement, cleared in advance with the other governments represented in the United Nations (UN) forces, requesting the communist side reach first a cease-fire and then a negotiated settlement of the war. The president also intended his message to state that, should their opponents ignore these overtures, UNC forces would have no alternative but to continue the war.

On March 20, 1951, the U.S. Joint Chiefs of Staff (JCS) informed MacArthur that this statement was in the final stages of preparation. MacArthur promptly issued his own cease-fire appeal, which demanded that the communist side surrender, denigrated Chinese Communist military capabilities, and restated the general's well-known opinion that "the fundamental questions continue to be political in nature and must find their answer in the diplomatic sphere." Truman interpreted MacArthur's statement as an example of gross insubordination, an implicit attempt to ignore his presidential prerogatives, and one that undercut his own planned declaration and tacitly criticized national policy.

In his memoirs Truman wrote that MacArthur's statement effectively presented the communist side with an ultimatum and implied that if the Chinese did not surrender, the United States and its allies might launch a full-scale attack on Chinese territory. According to Secretary of Defense George C. Marshall, MacArthur's statement was the final episode persuading Truman that he could no longer tolerate the challenges and defiance the general continually presented to his presidential authority and should therefore recall him. On April 11, 1951, Truman did just that, but the war would rage on for another 27 months.

PRISCILLA ROBERTS

See also

MacArthur, Douglas; Marshall, George Catlett; Ridgway, Matthew Bunker; Truman, Harry S.; Truman's Recall of MacArthur

References

Foot, Rosemary J. *A Substitute for Victory: The Politics of Peacemaking at the Korean Armistice Talks.* Ithaca, NY: Cornell University Press, 1990.

Hamby, Alonzo L. *Man of the People: A Life of Harry S. Truman.* New York: Oxford University Press, 1995.

James, D. Clayton, with Anne Sharp Wells. *Refighting the Last War: Command and Crisis in Korea, 1950–1953.* New York: Free Press, 1993.

Schaller, Michael. *Douglas MacArthur: The Far Eastern General.* New York: Oxford University Press, 1989.

Schnabel, James F. *United States Army in the Korean War: Policy and Direction, the First Year.* Washington, DC: Office of the Chief of Military History, Department of the Army, 1972.

Truman's Domestic Agenda and the Korean War

In his January 1949 State of the Union Address, President Harry S. Truman formally enunciated his Fair Deal program, an ambitious domestic reform agenda that traced its origins to 1945. Over the interceding years, Truman had slowly added to his vision so that by the start of 1949 the Fair Deal encompassed issues ranging from more public housing to universal health care to civil rights. By the end of 1949, however, the Fair Deal was already beginning to founder amid a barrage of foreign policy and national security crises. The final blows came in 1950, and it is no exaggeration to say that the Korean War dealt the coup de grâce to the Fair Deal, and indeed to most of Truman's domestic agenda.

The Truman administration's hopes of fulfilling the Fair Deal began to wither in early 1949. Ominous signs of a deteriorating international situation, combined with mounting tensions between the United States and the Union of Soviet Socialist Republics (USSR, Soviet Union) began to divert attention away from the Fair Deal. The Soviets' detonation of their first atomic weapon in September 1949 shocked Washington, DC, and the rest of the world. It also marked a new and dangerous turn in the Cold War, as the United States could no longer rely on its atomic monopoly. One month later, Communist forces triumphed in the Chinese Civil War. The world's most populous nation had now joined the communist bloc. At the same time, the Soviet Union formally established the German Democratic Republic (GDR, East Germany), ensuring the division of Germany for the indefinite future.

The year 1950 brought more crises. The Soviets boycotted the United Nations (UN) Security Council and signed a mutual assistance and defense pact with China. Former U.S. State Department official Alger Hiss, originally accused of espionage, was convicted of perjury, but only because the espionage charge had exceeded the statute of limitations. The British government uncovered a spy ring that seemed to prove that the Soviets had received secret atomic information through their infiltration of the Manhattan Project and other U.S. atomic weapons programs. Then came the relentless attacks of Republican senator Joseph R. McCarthy, who began a four-year-long anticommunist witch-hunt, much of which was aimed at the Truman administration and the Democratic Party. Amid this atmosphere of crisis and anti-communist hysteria, it is little wonder that the Truman administration felt obliged to further deemphasize domestic policies in the name of defense and national security.

In January 1950 Truman administration officials decided to counter the Soviets' newly acquired atomic capability by launching an all-out effort to develop, test detonate, and deploy a hydrogen, or thermonuclear, bomb. The United States accomplished this feat by 1952. Also in January 1950, Truman gave the State Department and Defense Department authority to systematically appraise the nation's military and industrial capabilities and to draw plans to augment those capabilities in light of the deepening Cold War. This planning resulted in the drafting of the seminal Cold War document prepared by the National Security Council (NSC), NSC-68. After the outbreak of war in Korea in June 1950, NSC-68 quickly became the national blueprint for waging the Cold War on a global scale. NSC-68 would serve as a U.S. defense and military guidepost for nearly a generation.

Selling NSC-68 to Truman was no small task. He was a fiscal conservative who had staked his second administration on continued domestic reform, small defense outlays, and balanced budgets. The massive defense spending envisioned in NSC-68 was therefore anathema to Truman. The president also greatly feared ceding too much authority to the military and national security establishments. Thus, the fate of NSC-68 hung in the balance until war erupted in Korea. Only after that did Truman agree, albeit reluctantly, to implement NSC-68.

The economic philosophy that underwrote the prescriptions in NSC-68 was based on the ideas of Leon Keyserling, chairman of the Council of Economic Advisors. His economic philosophy would later become the administration's de facto wartime domestic economic policy. Keyserling, a proponent of Keynesian economics, believed that sustained economic growth powered by close public-private cooperation and government supervision would enable the United States to spend considerably more for defense without harming the economy in the long term. In the short term, however, budget deficits and debt, the bane of Congress and the White House, were the most likely results. For this and other reasons enumerated above, Truman delayed taking action on NSC-68 until June, when war erupted in Korea.

After Truman decided to intervene in the war, he asked Congress to grant him specific wartime powers to place the nation

A political cartoon, entitled "Too Rough for Charley," shows President Harry S. Truman as a grinning captain at the helm of a sailing ship while Charles E. Wilson is sick over the side. The cartoon comments on Wilson's resignation as director of defense mobilization on March 30, 1952, when he disagreed with the president over how to handle a dispute between labor and management in the steel industry. (Library of Congress)

on heightened alert. Congress complied and the result was the Defense Production Act, which Truman signed into law in September 1950. He also requested an emergency $6 billion appropriation with which to augment U.S. military capacity in Korea and Western Europe. Once more, Congress complied. Thus, by July the United States had begun to mobilize, but the effort was half-hearted and disorganized.

Mobilization proceeded slowly for several reasons. First, Truman sought to keep the Korean War limited and to establish the status quo ante bellum on the Korean Peninsula, making an expansive mobilization program unnecessary. Second, Truman administration officials still clung to the hope of fulfilling the Fair Deal, which made them reluctant to spend large amounts of money on defense. The nation's attention and resources continued to be focused on the war, however, which was going badly, and on Senator McCarthy, who grew more vitriolic by the day. Truman's hopes notwithstanding, the Fair Deal seemed all but dead.

After the successful United Nations Command (UNC) landing at Inchon in September 1950, Truman changed course and decided to go for broke. Essentially circumventing the original UN resolutions, he ordered General Douglas MacArthur to move his forces north toward the Yalu River, thereby reuniting Korea. With these orders also came the decision by Truman to begin implementing fully—albeit gradually—the dictates of NSC-68. This decision marked a radical shift in U.S. defense and

mobilization policy. Once NSC-68 was approved, the Korean-era mobilization program became a dual effort: the United States continued to mobilize for the short-term Korean period and for the long haul of the Cold War. Implicit in this process was the decision to construct a permanent military and industrial mobilization base so that the nation would not again have to mobilize from scratch. Never before had the United States committed itself to such readiness in the absence of a major or total war. Until the disastrous Chinese intervention in late November 1950, the Truman administration continued to move rather slowly in its mobilization effort. No new mobilization agencies were created, and mandatory economic and material controls were eschewed in favor of voluntary efforts.

After the Chinese intervention, the Korean War and the attendant mobilization program entered a completely new phase. Fearing a wider Asian war and perhaps even a third world war, Truman decided to revert to the original goal of merely preserving the prewar integrity of the Republic of Korea (ROK, South Korea). Total victory and Korean unification were abandoned. At the same time, Truman decided to substantially accelerate the U.S. mobilization program.

On December 16, 1950, Truman declared a national emergency and began to establish a panoply of powerful civilian mobilization agencies. In doing so, Truman ensured the rapid and complete military, industrial, and economic buildup proposed in NSC-68. By 1951 the defense budget had nearly tripled from the pre–Korean War level of $13.9 billion to $42.9 billion. Such mobilization agencies as the Office of Defense Mobilization, Defense Production Administration, Office of Price Stabilization, Economic Stabilization Agency, and the Wage Stabilization Board began to exert control over vast portions of the U.S. economy. From December 1950 through the remainder of his term, Truman's domestic policy revolved around the massive mobilization program and his efforts to defend against McCarthyite attacks.

From January 1951 through April 1953 the U.S. government controlled nearly all prices and wages. In July 1951 the Truman administration implemented the Controlled Materials Plan (CMP) in response to critical shortages of industrial raw materials and bottlenecks in military production. The CMP controlled both the allocation of materials and the prioritization of industrial production. Although Korean War controls were not as sweeping as those of World War II and did not include product rationing, they were still an unprecedented foray into government planning during a period in which no war had been officially declared.

It is not surprising that the vast array of wartime controls became quickly unpopular, as did the war effort itself. Conservative Democrats and Republicans in particular came to be the most vocal opponents of Truman's wartime domestic policies. They objected to the president's military and foreign policies and they abhorred his domestic policies, which to them seemed to smack of government regimentation, if not socialism. To make matters worse, Truman's firing of the vainglorious MacArthur in April

1951 further fanned the flames of resentment and partisanship among his adversaries.

As Truman's popularity continued to plummet, so too did his relations with Congress. In the summer of 1951 and again in the summer of 1952, Congress registered its disapproval by trimming wartime controls legislation found in the Defense Production Act. By 1952 Truman had all but lost the support of Congress, which now included a significant loss of support from within the Democratic Party itself. As a result, Truman chose not to seek another term in office.

Congressional efforts to undermine wartime controls legislation had only a negligible effect on the U.S. economy. Spectacular growth combined with Truman's decision to slow down and stretch out the long-term military buildup ensured that inflation and shortages remained largely at bay. However, congressional reluctance to raise taxes high enough to keep the mobilization on a pay-as-you-go basis did result in budget deficits and a mounting national debt. For this Truman took most of the blame, even though he continued to preach about the evils of deficits and had repeatedly asked Congress to keep taxes apace with spending. Congress demurred, and Truman was forced to take the heat for perceived military failures as well as for mounting budget deficits. By early 1952 the Korean War, in the minds of many Americans, had become "Truman's War."

As the battlefield operations stabilized while the peace talks stalled, the mobilization program continued to grind on. By 1952 the United States was quantifiably stronger and safer than it had been just 18 months before. This did not mean, however, that Truman would enjoy an unremarkable last year in office. One of the last challenges that Truman and his mobilization program faced was the steel crisis of 1952. Confronted with a potentially paralyzing strike in the steel industry, and arguing that the U.S. soldiers and national defense would be imperiled by steel shortages, Truman ordered a government seizure of the nation's steel mills. The constitutionality of the order was challenged, and in June 1952 the U.S. Supreme Court handed the president a stinging defeat by overturning his order. The crisis was ended, and with it went the last vestiges of Truman's clout and popularity.

Despite the vexing economic, political, and military problems that faced the Truman administration, when viewed in its entirety Truman's wartime domestic policy can only be considered a success. His administration kept inflation in check, shortages to a minimum, and economic growth astoundingly high. What is more, U.S. industrial output soared and unemployment fell to record-low levels. There were no major or enduring dislocations to the nation's economy. To the contrary, the Dow Jones industrial average enjoyed double-digit gains from 1950 to 1952 and the nation's gross national product surged by nearly 5 percent between 1951 and 1952. As successful as his Korean War policies may have been, however, Truman remained profoundly disappointed that partisan politics and wartime exigencies had completely derailed his Fair Deal.

The singular achievement of Truman's Korean War policies may be found in the stunning successes of the military mobilization effort. In less than three years, the size of the U.S. armed forces more than doubled and production of military hard goods increased sevenfold. The number of naval ships also doubled and the strength of the air force increased from 48 to 100 wings during the same period. The Truman administration accomplished these feats by fostering and relying on administrative decentralization, increased volunteerism, equity of sacrifice, and close public-private cooperation.

Paul G. Pierpaoli Jr.

See also

Cold War, Origins to 1950; Controlled Materials Plan; Defense Production Act; Economic Stabilization Agency; Industrial Base, U.S.; MacArthur, Douglas; McCarthy, Joseph Raymond; McCarthyism; Mobilization; National Security Council Report 68; Nitze, Paul Henry; Office of Defense Mobilization; Office of Price Stabilization; Steel Plants, Truman's Seizure of; Truman, Harry S.; Truman's Recall of MacArthur; United States, Home Front; Wage Stabilization Board; Wilson, Charles Edward

References

Hamby, Alonzo L. *Beyond the New Deal: Harry S. Truman and American Liberalism.* New York: Columbia University Press, 1973.

Hogan, Michael J. *A Cross of Iron: Harry S. Truman and the Origins of the National Security State, 1945–1954.* New York: Cambridge University Press, 1998.

Kaufman, Burton I. *The Korean War: Challenges in Crisis, Credibility and Command.* 2nd ed. New York: McGraw-Hill, 1997.

Pemberton, William E. *Harry S. Truman: Fair Dealer and Cold Warrior.* Boston: Twayne, 1989.

Pierpaoli, Paul G., Jr. *Truman and Korea: The Political Culture of the Early Cold War.* Columbia: University of Missouri Press, 1999.

Truman's Recall of MacArthur
Event Date: April 11, 1951

President Harry S. Truman's recall of United Nations (UN) commander in Korea General Douglas MacArthur occurred against a backdrop of events that shocked Western policy makers. The entry of the People's Republic of China (PRC) into the war in late 1950 had increased fears about possible intervention by the Union of Soviet Socialist Republics (USSR, Soviet Union), a prospect that increased once U.S. forces advanced north of the 38th Parallel. With Washington, DC, and its allies unprepared for a global conflict, the Truman administration soon embraced the UN's measures to stop the fighting.

General MacArthur, reluctant to restrict the conflict to Korea, favored a policy to offset the military capability and perceived aggressive tendencies of the PRC. Apprehensive about a deadlock along the 38th Parallel, he urged the U.S. Joint Chiefs of Staff (JCS) in February 1951 to authorize attacks on Najin, a harbor close to Soviet territory, and electric installations on the Yalu River. The general opposed a strategy of static warfare, lamenting to

A GI, remembering the clever Burma Shave roadside signs in the United States, put these on poles along a road in central Korea. The signs echoed sentiment at the time over President Harry S. Truman's dismissal of General Douglas MacArthur as U.S. commander in the Far East in April 1951. (AP/Wide World Photos)

newspapermen on March 7, 1951, about the "savage slaughter" of U.S. forces that was sure to result from attritional combat. Openly censuring those supporting a pause at the parallel, MacArthur asked the JCS for atomic bombs to defend Japan. Despite knowledge of Truman's readiness to negotiate, he advised against military restraints, and on March 24 he made known his own scheme to end hostilities.

The UNC commander's challenge not only undercut a presidential peace bid but also defied the constitutional supremacy of civilian policy making and alarmed allied governments. After a conference with Secretary of State Dean G. Acheson, Deputy Secretary of Defense Robert A. Lovett, and Assistant Secretary of State Dean Rusk, Truman sent MacArthur a subtle rebuke, reminding him of a directive dated December 6, 1950, obligating commanders to refrain from public statements respecting delicate military and diplomatic subjects. Meanwhile, U.S. military leaders worried about a Chinese and Soviet military buildup in Asia and thought the UN commander should have standing authority to retaliate against any communist escalation. Having recommended deployment of atomic weapons to forward Pacific bases for this purpose, they were fearful that MacArthur might provoke an incident to widen the war. Moreover, U.S. allies never would consent

to providing discretion to the UN commander to order an atomic retaliation so long as MacArthur held this position.

Matters came to a head on April 5. U.S. representative Joseph W. Martin, the Republican Party minority leader, made public a letter in which the general applauded the congressman's support of MacArthur's disapproval of the U.S. European allies and strategic limitations. The general endorsed Martin's proposed aid for Jiang Jieshi's (Chiang Kai-shek) attack on the Chinese mainland, labeling the Far East the principal Cold War theater, where "no substitute for victory" should be tolerated. London's *Daily Telegraph* reported an interview with MacArthur in which he grumbled about restrictions on his military options; and *The Freeman,* a conservative U.S. journal, printed a remark credited to MacArthur saying political judgments prevented enlargement of the Republic of Korea Army (ROKA, South Korean Army).

Truman met with Acheson, Secretary of Defense George C. Marshall, JCS chairman General of the Army Omar N. Bradley, and Ambassador W. Averell Harriman—"the Big Four"—on April 6 to determine what action to take. Conferring again in Marshall's office that day, the Big Four still failed to reach a decision.

Later, Marshall, at the insistence of Truman, examined the recent communication between the JCS and MacArthur. When the Big Four gathered with the president the next day, they found him incensed over the *Freeman* article. They then recommended the general's dismissal, a determination that Truman waited to disclose until April 9, once he learned that the JCS all concurred from "a military point of view only."

Truman signed the recall orders on April 10. He hoped to have Secretary of the Army Frank Pace, who was in Korea, go to Tokyo and convey the dismissal to MacArthur in person, with the White House announcement coming thereafter. But the message failed to reach Pace, and when Truman learned that the *Chicago Tribune* planned to break the news of the general's removal, his press secretary reported the decision on April 11. Before the order could be delivered to him, MacArthur learned of his relief while at his residence, where he was entertaining guests at lunch. The orders informed the general of his dismissal as UN commander, U.S. commander in chief, supreme commander for the Allied Powers in Japan, and commanding general of U.S. Army, Far East.

The U.S. public's reaction to MacArthur's firing was extraordinarily emotional. Most letters pouring into the White House supported the general. City governments prepared cordial receptions, and Congress invited him to speak to a joint session on April 19. A California community hanged Truman in effigy, while state lawmakers debated the controversy and asked MacArthur to address them. MacArthur's legislative backers inserted in the *Congressional Record* many angry messages from constituents critical of the president. While the Hearst, McCormick, and Scripps-Howard news chains portrayed the general as a victim and Truman as a scoundrel, a number of newspapers—such as the *New York Times, Washington Post,* and *Atlanta Journal*—defended the president and his decision. A Gallup poll of mid-April found most respondents opposed to MacArthur's relief, yet the bulk of U.S. reporters assigned to Washington, DC, East Asia, and the UN sided with Truman. While Eighth Army enlisted men in Korea took their commander's dismissal in stride, Republican conservatives damned the president, and Republican senator William E. Jenner of Indiana called for his impeachment.

RODNEY J. ROSS

See also

Acheson, Dean Gooderham; Bradley, Omar Nelson; Harriman, William Averell; Jiang Jieshi; Joint Chiefs of Staff; MacArthur, Douglas; Marshall, George Catlett; Martin, Joseph William; Pace, Frank, Jr.; Truman, Harry S.

References

Donovan, Robert J. *Tumultuous Years: The Presidency of Harry S. Truman.* New York: Norton, 1982.

James, D. Clayton. *The Years of MacArthur,* Vol. 3, *Triumph and Disaster, 1945–1964.* Boston: Houghton Mifflin, 1985.

MacArthur, Douglas. *Reminiscences.* New York: McGraw-Hill, 1964.

Pearlman, Michael D. *Truman and MacArthur: Policy, Politics, and the Hunger for Honor and Renown.* Bloomington: Indiana University Press, 2008.

Spanier, John W. *The Truman-MacArthur Controversy and the Korean War.* Cambridge, MA: Harvard University Press, 1959.

Truman, Harry S. *Memoirs.* 2 vols. Garden City, NY: Doubleday, 1956.

Tsarapkin, Semion Konstantinovich
Birth Date: 1906
Death Date: September 1984

Soviet minister to Korea from 1946 to 1948, and delegate to the United Nations (UN) from 1949 to 1954. Born in a small village in the Ukraine in 1906, Semion Konstantinovich Tsarapkin went to work in a smelting plant before pursuing advanced political training. He graduated from the Institute of Oriental Studies in Moscow and entered the Soviet Foreign Service in 1937. After assisting in the negotiations for the 1941 nonaggression pact with Japan, Tsarapkin became chief of the Second Far East Department of the People's Commissariat of Foreign Affairs. In 1944 he transferred to the American Department and attended the conferences at Dumbarton Oaks (Washington, DC), San Francisco, and Potsdam (Germany). Tsarapkin was also present at the Conference of Foreign Ministers, held December 16–26, 1945, in Moscow at which the postwar fate of the Korean Peninsula was discussed. Two weeks later Tsarapkin, as minister extraordinaire and plenipotentiary, accompanied the Soviet delegation to Seoul headed by Terentii F. Shtykov. Tsarapkin continued as the principal representative of the People's Commissariat of Foreign Affairs in Korea from 1946 to 1948.

Known for his intelligence and aloofness, Tsarapkin allowed Shtykov to play the lead in negotiations and was only an occasional contributor to Soviet policy in Korea. At times, however, it appeared that Tsarapkin was the true authority within the Soviet

Agitated Soviet delegate Semion K. Tsarapkin, shown here during a United Nations Security Council meeting, June 1954. (Time & Life Pictures/Getty Images)

delegation. Like Shtykov, he was a tough negotiator who adhered faithfully to the Stalinist line, but Tsarapkin was more sophisticated and controlled than his nominal chief.

His most visible role was as one of the five commissioners in the Soviet delegation to the Joint Soviet-American Commission of 1946. Tsarapkin headed the Soviet representation to the first subcommission, charged with determining the conditions for and order of consultation with Korean parties and organizations in the process of creating an all-Korean government. He staunchly defended the Soviet position that any groups or individuals who had, at any time, opposed the Moscow Decision of December 1945 were to be prevented from participation, until Moscow ordered him to compromise. Even then Tsarapkin gave only minimal ground and on at least one occasion overruled Shtykov when it appeared the latter was ready to accede to U.S. proposals.

Upon leaving Korea, Tsarapkin joined the Soviet delegation to the UN in 1949 as a deputy to the Security Council. He often served as the Soviet spokesman when Jacob Malik was ill, and he participated in the Soviet boycott of the UN in 1950. He became the Soviets' deputy permanent representative to the UN in March 1951 and served in that capacity until he was recalled to the Union of Soviet Socialist Republics (USSR, Soviet Union) in 1954 to become head of the foreign ministry's division of internal organizations.

Tsarapkin is credited with opening the discussions that led to the armistice talks at Kaesong in 1951. In late May, as the newly arrived deputy permanent representative of the Soviet delegation to the UN, Tsarapkin casually mentioned at the end of a conversation with Thomas J. Cory, an adviser to the U.S. delegation, that the Soviet Union would support armistice talks. After tentative conversations with George F. Kennan of the U.S. State Department regarding the Soviet position and a trip to Moscow, Malik officially proposed talks in a radio broadcast on June 23, 1951. Tsarapkin participated in the Kennan-Malik talks, but the full extent of his role became clear only later. The incident is typical of Tsarapkin's style and career.

Later Tsarapkin also advised the foreign ministry on technical standards for nuclear testing control systems and served as the Soviet Union's chief delegate at the Geneva Conference of 1958 to discuss a nuclear test ban. He was posted to the Federal Republic of Germany (FRG, West Germany) from 1966 to 1971 and subsequently served as a roving ambassador until his death in September 1984.

TIMOTHY C. DOWLING

See also

Cory, Thomas J.; Kaesong Truce Talks; Kennan, George Frost; Kennan-Malik Conversations; Korea, Democratic People's Republic of, 1945–1953; Malik, Jacob; Potsdam Conference; Shtykov, Terentii Fomich; Soviet Security Council Boycott; Soviet Union

References

Goodman, Allan E., ed. *Negotiating While Fighting: The Diary of Admiral C. Turner Joy at the Korean Armistice Conference.* Stanford, CA: Hoover Institute Press, 1978.

Van Ree, Eric. *Socialism in One Zone: Stalin's Policy in Korea, 1945–1947.* New York: St. Martin's, 1989.

Tsiang Ting Fu Fuller
Birth Date: December 7, 1895
Death Date: October 9, 1965

Republic of China (ROC, Nationalist China) diplomat and scholar. Born in Shaoyang, Hunan Province, China, on December 7, 1895, Tsiang Ting Fu (Jiang Tingfu or Chiang Ting Fu) began a classical education; in 1906 he continued studies under American Presbyterian missionaries in Xiangtan. Tsiang went to the United States and attended Park University and Oberlin College, graduating in 1914 and 1918, respectively. Tsiang then moved to France as a Young Men's Christian Association (YMCA) secretary attached to the Chinese laborers assigned to assist the French Army during World War I. After the war Tsiang returned to the United States and earned his doctorate in modern history at Columbia University in 1923.

That same year Tsiang returned to China to teach at Nankai University in Tianjin. There, he pioneered the study of China's diplomatic history from a Chinese perspective. In 1929 he moved

Tsiang Ting Fu Fuller (Jiang Tigfu or Chiang Ting Fu) was a Republic of China (Nationalist China) diplomat and scholar. (Hulton Archive/Getty Images)

to Qinghua University in Beijing, where, as chairman of the history department, he assembled a comprehensive library collection and a renowned faculty, advancing modern China studies.

After Japan's invasion of China, Tsiang argued that China should avoid war until it had fully prepared for conflict and had gained allies. This caught the attention of Generalissimo Jiang Jieshi (Chiang Kai-shek), who in 1934 summoned Tsiang to discuss his views. Subsequently, Tsiang visited Moscow to garner support against the Japanese. About this time he altered his family name from Chiang to Tsiang to avoid confusion with the generalissimo's family name. Tsiang began official government service in 1935 as political director of the National Executive Committee.

In 1936 Tsiang became China's ambassador to the Union of Soviet Socialist Republics (USSR, Soviet Union). In 1937 he secured a Sino-Soviet nonaggression pact. Despite this apparent diplomatic success, he correctly predicted that the Soviets would be unenthusiastic in their support of Nationalist China. This view was contrary to that of other Chinese leaders, and Tsiang was recalled in 1938.

From 1938 to 1940 Tsiang supervised the removal of government offices and hospitals to Chongqing to escape advancing Japanese forces. He also coordinated the national budget. From 1942 through 1946 Tsiang worked in postwar relief planning. He resigned in 1946 because of a policy disagreement with T. V. Soong, Jiang's brother-in-law and financial adviser. Accepting a professorship at the University of California, he prepared to resume academic life. Pressed by friends, however, he accepted a temporary assignment as China's representative to the United Nations (UN) Economic Commission for Asia and the Far East. Shortly afterward, Tsiang became China's representative on the UN Security Council. In the UN Tsiang attempted to use Chinese influence to encourage peaceful resolutions of postwar boundary settlements.

With the establishment of the People's Republic of China (PRC) in 1949, the position of Nationalist China in the UN came under increasing challenge. In protest of Tsiang's presence, the Soviet Union boycotted the Security Council for much of 1950, a move that proved critical in allowing UN support for actions in Korea. Subsequently, as the debate on the Nationalist Chinese presence in the UN intensified, Tsiang reminded members that his state was the legitimate government, based on a constitution approved by duly elected representatives of the Chinese people. Although Tsiang failed to convert many to his cause, he did gain wide respect.

In 1961 Tsiang concurrently served as ambassador to the United States and the UN, although the next year he was replaced in the UN. Tsiang remained ambassador to the United States until April 1965, when he retired to again pursue the study of Chinese diplomatic history. Diagnosed with cancer, Tsiang returned for treatment to New York City, where he died on October 9, 1965.

K. W. T. MADDEN

See also

China, People's Republic of; China, People's Republic of, United Nations Representation Question; China, Republic of; Jiang Jieshi

References

Boorman, Howard L., ed. *Biographical Dictionary of Republican China.* New York: Columbia University Press, 1967.

Cheng, Tun-jen, Chi Huang, and Samual S. G. Wu, eds. *Inherited Rivalry: Conflict across the Taiwan Straits.* Boulder, CO: Lynne Rienner, 1995.

Current Biography, 1948. New York: H. W. Wilson, 1949.

Finkelstein, David M. *Washington's Taiwan Dilemma, 1949–1950: From Abandonment to Salvation.* Fairfax, VA: George Mason University Press, 1993.

Tucker, Nancy Bernkopf. *Taiwan, Hong Kong, and the U.S., 1945–1992: Uncertain Friendships.* New York: Twayne, 1994.

Turkey

Eurasian nation covering 300,948 square miles. Strategically located both in Europe and Asia Minor, European Turkey borders Greece and Bulgaria to the east and north; in Asia Minor it shares common borders with Georgia to the northwest, Armenia and Iran to the east, and Syria and Iraq to the south. Turkey's 1950 population was 21.1 million people. Based in Ankara, the capital, the Turkish government is a representative parliamentary democracy with a largely ceremonial president, elected by popular vote, as head of state. Real power is invested in the prime minister, who is elected by parliament. At the time of the Korean War, the Right-leaning Democratic Party held power, represented by Adnan Menderes, who served as prime minister from 1950 to 1960. Menderes was anticommunist in outlook and generally pro-Western in sympathy.

As had often happened in Turkey's modern history, the nation emerged from World War II caught between rival military and political blocks. The Union of Soviet Socialist Republics (USSR, Soviet Union) applied heavy pressure on Turkey after the war to secure control of the straits between the Black Sea and the Mediterranean. Soviet pressure on both Turkey and Greece in fact led to the Truman Doctrine of 1947 and was a major factor in galvanizing opinion in the United States regarding the Cold War. Ankara also feared outright Soviet aggression. With the invasion of the Republic of Korea (ROK, South Korea) by the Democratic People's Republic of Korea (DPRK, North Korea) in June 1950, this fear became acute, and Ankara agreed to contribute troops to a United Nations (UN) force on the Korean Peninsula.

Turkey's motives for joining the fight were not wholly altruistic. It hoped in return to gain reciprocal U.S. commitments to its defense in the eastern Mediterranean region. More specifically, the Turkish government hoped to fulfill its insistent desire for admission to the North Atlantic Treaty Organization (NATO), which had celebrated its first anniversary just two months before the outbreak of the war in the Far East. In fact, Turkey would eventually be invited to join NATO on October 22, 1951, in partial recognition for its service in Korea.

With these diplomatic considerations in mind, Turkey agreed on July 25, 1950, to raise and deploy a brigade to the UN effort in Korea. The Turkish troops arrived at Pusan in the second week of October 1950 with a nominal strength of 5,190 men. They were commanded by General Tashin Yazici, who had fought against British Empire forces at Gallipoli in World War I.

While the employment of the Turkish Brigade partially reflected both the U.S. and the UN desires to show the world a broad anticommunist coalition in Korea, the Turks' actual effectiveness in combat became a subject of allied dispute. The brigade's first major action came in the intense fighting in and around the North Korean road junction of Kunu-ri in the last week of November 1950. At that time, the brigade was positioned on the right flank of the U.S. Eighth Army's 2nd Infantry Division.

Chinese People's Volunteer Army (CPVA, Chinese Army) and Korean People's Army (KPA, North Korean Army) forces had broken the front of the Republic of Korea Army (ROKA, South Korean Army) II Corps. That unit's defeat and retreat threatened to expose the Eighth Army's right flank. The Turkish Brigade was ordered to help stem the communist advance.

Turkish participation began inauspiciously. Overwhelmed by the initial confusion of the United Nations Command (UNC) retreat, the Turks fought their first major battle and in the process mistook retreating ROKA troops for those from the KPA. In ensuing after-action reports, and more particularly in press accounts of the fighting, the Turks won praise for having won a significant victory. It would be some time before the public learned of the error. Accusations by the Turks of poor liaison on the part of the Eighth Army's contact officers heralded the beginning of a series of such charges and countercharges, all made worse by enduring linguistic difficulties.

The press also noted that individual Turkish and Greek soldiers of the UNC had to be kept separated, for they were known to fight each other as fiercely as either fought the Chinese or North Koreans. Indeed, the Turks banned wearing of the UNC colors of blue and white by their troops, as they were also the colors of Greece and therefore anathema to the Turks.

Despite initial—and, in retrospect, probably inevitable—setbacks, the Turks recovered. By all accounts they thereafter fought fiercely against communist troops, even while suffering heavy losses in an ambush of two of the brigade's supply columns south of Kunu-ri on November 29, 1950. After a northerly advance of about seven miles from the village of Sunchon toward the brigade's rear area, Turkish motorized supply columns ran into advancing communist forces and were ground down in the heavy fighting that followed.

In these first battles the Turks demonstrated behavior that subsequently came to characterize other UNC soldiers' descriptions of the brigade. Stories of Turk bravura assumed the stuff of legend: officers throwing down their hats, refusing orders to retreat further, and "dying on their fur"; repeated bayonet charges by Turkish infantry in both offensive and defensive situations; small units being wiped out rather than surrendering when isolated by Chinese forces; Chinese infantry being silently beheaded in their sleep by stealthy Turkish patrols. While such stories could not always be confirmed, many allied soldiers reported them. True or not, reports of Turks' fury with the bayonet raised morale among the UNC forces in the face of Chinese successes in the dark days of fall, winter, and early spring of 1950–1951.

U.S. Lieutenant General Matthew B. Ridgway took note of this and decided to have all infantry units fix bayonets to their rifles. Such apparent bravery on the part of the Turks and attendant casualties also flew in the face of General Douglas MacArthur's statement before the U.S. Senate that the non-U.S. and non-Korean units "had no impact on the tactical situation." This sentiment particularly galled some observers, given the fact that the Turks had deployed to Korea at a time of significant tensions in their own part of the world; and when the U.S. government quietly excused itself for the heavy losses suffered by the brigade at Kunu-ri, Ankara reportedly could not understand what the fuss was about. It was, after all, the duty of Turkish soldiers to die if necessary.

As UNC forces attempted to regain the initiative after the turn of the year, the Turks once again found themselves in action. Refitted and reorganized to replace the losses at Kunu-ri, the Turks subsequently fought in the recapture of Seoul in January 1951 and were later assigned to protect Kimpo Airfield. In the spring the brigade was assigned to the U.S. 25th Infantry Division's sector.

The front had begun to stabilize in anticipation of a successful outcome to truce talks. As both sides entered the long period of strategic stalemate and attempted to adjust the front to their respective advantage, communist forces planned a major assault. The main effort of the Chinese offensive during April 22–30, 1951, drove the brigade and other UNC forces back to the Han River, on the southern bank of which the Turks took up positions on April 30. After recovering this lost ground by June 1951, the brigade fought small actions as the main line of resistance wavered back and forth across the middle of the peninsula. In the spring of 1953, during the last of the Chinese offensives along the putative truce line, Turkish forces commanded by Brigadier General Sirri Acar fought a series of intense, sometimes hand-to-hand, battles with Chinese troops. At the time the Turks were assigned positions in the complex of outposts and bunkers called NEVADA, the retention of which the UNC deemed critical. The Turks were ordered to hold at all costs. In the course of this fighting northeast of Panmunjom, the Turks suffered approximately 395 killed and wounded but inflicted some 3,000 casualties upon communist forces. Having delayed and frustrated Chinese efforts to modify the lines, on May 29 the Turkish troops were eventually withdrawn from the line.

Although the Turkish Brigade was sometimes faulted for being badly led, the Turks replied that insufficient liaison was provided by the UNC, particularly regarding language barriers. The Turkish troops' Islamic faith also occasionally created frictions and/or misunderstandings. For example, the Turks would not allow pork in their rations. This, however, was hardly a Turkish monopoly, as other units such as Indian Hindus would eat no beef. Fortunately, more serious frictions, such as the feared hostility between Turks and British Commonwealth soldiers as a result of the memories of World War I, never materialized. In any event, the Turks' resolution in combat and ability to endure the harsh conditions of Korea were noted by other units. No Turkish troops, for example, died in captivity or went over to the communist side. Turkish casualties in the war were 721 killed, 168 missing and presumed dead, and 2,111 wounded. There is a monument in Seoul to the memory of the Turkish soldiers who fought in Korea.

DAVID R. DORONDO

See also

Kunu-ri, Battle of; MacArthur, Douglas; Ridgway, Matthew Bunker; Truman Doctrine

References

Appleman, Roy E. *United States Army in Korea: South to the Naktong, North to the Yalu.* Washington, DC: Office of the Chief of Military History, 1961.

Fehrenbach, T. R. *This Kind of War: A Study in Unpreparedness.* New York: Macmillan, 1962.

Hermes, Walter G. *U.S. Army in the Korean War: Truce Tent and Fighting Front.* Washington, DC: Office of the Chief of Military History, 1966.

Mossman, Billy C. *United States Army in the Korean War: Ebb and Flow, November 1950–July 1951.* Washington, DC: U.S. Army Center of Military History, 1990.

Twining, Nathan Farragut

Birth Date: October 11, 1897
Death Date: March 29, 1982

U.S. Air Force general, director of personnel, and deputy chief of staff during the Korean War. Born on October 11, 1897, in Monroe, Wisconsin, Nathan Farragut Twining enlisted in and served with the Oregon National Guard during June–September 1916 and March–June 1917, seeing service along the Mexican border. Twining graduated from a wartime-shortened course at the U.S. Military Academy at West Point in November 1918.

After service as an infantry lieutenant that included occupation duty in Germany and graduation from the Army Infantry School at Fort Benning, Georgia, Twining completed flight training at Brooks Field in San Antonio, Texas, in 1924 and formally transferred to the air service in 1926. He was then stationed with pursuit/fighter squadrons at bases in California, the Hawaiian Islands, and Texas. Promoted to captain in 1935, he graduated from the Air Corps Tactical School in 1936 and the Army Command and General Staff School at Fort Leavenworth, Kansas, in 1937. He was promoted to major in 1940.

During 1940–1942 Twining was on the staff of the chief of the air corps in Washington, DC, and was promoted to brigadier general in June 1942. He was chief of staff of the Allied Forces South Pacific during 1942–1943, commanded the Thirteenth Air Force on New Caledonia in January 1943, and was promoted to major general the following month. He commanded the Fifteenth Air Force in southern Italy, 1943–1944. Twining commanded the Mediterranean Allied Strategic Air Forces during 1944–1945 and was advanced to lieutenant general in June 1945. He commanded the Twentieth Air Force in the Pacific during August–October 1945. It was Twining's Boeing B-29 Superfortresses that dropped the two atomic bombs on Japan.

After commanding the Air Material Command at Wright Field, near Dayton, Ohio, between 1945 and 1947, he commanded the unified Alaska Command until he was ordered to Washington in 1950 to be director of air force personnel. In this position Twining was responsible for securing the manpower needed to enlarge the air force early in the Korean War. His major contribution in this position was weeding out incompetent National Guard and reserve officers who reported for active duty.

In October 1950 Air Force Chief of Staff Hoyt S. Vandenberg appointed Twining his deputy to supervise day-to-day air force operations. Because Vandenberg was frequently ill, Twining sometimes fulfilled his duties as well. A major problem in late 1950 was an army staff complaint that tactical aviation in Korea was inadequate. Twining sent investigators to Korea to recommend improvements and help him prepare for congressional testimony. The investigators interviewed Eighth Army commander Lieutenant General Walton H. Walker, who testified that the army could not have survived in 1950 without tactical air support. Such statements and evidence that tactical air support had enabled the

General Nathan F. Twining served with distinction in both the European and Pacific theaters in World War II. Twining was deputy chief of staff of the U.S. Air Force during the Korean War and then was chief of staff (1953–1957) and the first airman to be appointed chairman of the Joint Chiefs of Staff (1957–1960). (Library of Congress)

army to make an orderly withdrawal under massive Chinese pressure in late 1950 and early 1951 prevented a congressional inquiry. In 1952 Twining modernized aviation units in Korea to ensure air superiority and bring increased pressure on the communist side during armistice talks.

Much of Twining's time in 1951 and 1952 was spent on air force reorganization. Research and development and aircraft procurement and maintenance were under one command. Twining supervised their separation into two commands for greater efficiency in the expected expansion of the air force. He also instituted a postgraduate course at Air University so that thousands of new officers could learn air force doctrine.

Twining also devoted much time to the politics of air force expansion. When Robert A. Lovett became secretary of defense in 1951, he asked the Joint Chiefs of Staff (JCS) to recommend a force structure adequate to halt possible communist aggression, as called for in the National Security Council (NSC) report known as

NSC-68. The JCS recommended 143 wings for the air force, a victory for the politicking of Vandenberg and Twining and an increase over the 95 wings previously authorized. President Harry S. Truman accepted the plan and asked for its implementation by 1955. Still, the air force staff had to decide on the allocation of resources among the tactical and strategic bombing wings. Vandenberg and Twining favored an increase in tactical wings, but Secretary of the Air Force Thomas K. Finletter wanted more strategic bombing wings. From May to September 1952 Twining became acting chief of staff during Vandenberg's illness. Twining came to agree with Finletter's position and testified before Congress that Boeing B-52 Stratofortresses and hydrogen bombs could hold the communist powers in check.

When newly elected President Dwight D. Eisenhower began budget discussions in 1953, he proposed a severe cut in the air force budget and a decrease in the number of wings from 143 to 120. Vandenberg and General Curtis E. LeMay attacked the budget as endangering security, but Twining was willing to accept it. Vandenberg thereupon resigned in May 1953, and Twining was appointed chief of staff. Given Eisenhower's dependence on massive retaliation by strategic nuclear bombing, Twining was forced to let the budget ax fall on tactical units. By this time, however, an armistice had been concluded in Korea and the fighting there was over.

Twining was chief of staff from 1953 to 1957. During this time he instituted Eisenhower's Massive Retaliation strategy. Eisenhower appointed Twining chairman of the JCS, a position he held from August 1957 until his retirement from the air force in September 1960.

In 1966 Twining published a critique of U.S. defense policy entitled *Neither Liberty nor Safety*. This book revealed his disagreement with the Truman administration's decision to fight a limited war in Korea. Twining wrote that he was appalled that the Truman administration publicly announced that it would not use the atomic bomb and would not attack bases in China. Twining believed that such announcements had sapped the power of the air force and made the United States a "paper tiger."

After retirement from the air force, Twining served as vice chairman of textbook publisher Holt, Rinehart and Winston and as a director of United Technologies. Still interested in defense issues, Twining lobbied for an antiballistic missile program and was critical of U.S. policy during the Vietnam War. He died at Lackland Air Force Base, Texas, on March 29, 1982.

JOHN L. BELL AND SPENCER C. TUCKER

See also

Dean, William Frishe; Eisenhower, Dwight David; Finletter, Thomas Knight; Joint Chiefs of Staff; Lovett, Robert Abercrombie; Massive Retaliation; Truman, Harry S.; Vandenberg, Hoyt Sanford; Walker, Walton Harris

References

Frisbee, John L. *Makers of the United States Air Force*. Washington, DC: Air Force History and Museums Program, 1996.

McCarley, J. Britt. "General Nathan Farragut Twining: The Making of a Disciple of American Strategic Air Power, 1897–1953." Unpublished PhD dissertation, Temple University, 1989.

Twining, Nathan F. *Neither Liberty nor Safety: A Hard Look at U.S. Military Policy and Strategy*. New York: Holt, Rinehart and Winston, 1966.

Tydings Committee
Start Date: March 1950
End Date: July 1950

U.S. Senate subcommittee investigation during March–July 1950 of Republican senator Joseph R. McCarthy's allegations of communist subversion in the U.S. Department of State. The U.S. Senate Subcommittee on the Investigation of Loyalty of State Department Employees, or the Tydings Committee, was created in February 1950 and formally convened on March 8. Under the chairmanship of Democratic senator Millard E. Tydings of Maryland, the subcommittee held 31 days of hearings and heard from 34 witnesses.

On February 9, 1950, McCarthy had stated in a public address in Wheeling, West Virginia, that there were 205 State Department employees who were communists. In subsequent presentations that number fluctuated from 57 to the original 205. McCarthy proceeded to take his claims to the floor of the Senate, forcing the Democratic Party (then in the majority) to take action. McCarthy's February allegations—virtually baseless as it turned out—precipitated the anticommunist witch-hunt known as McCarthyism, which became hopelessly intertwined with the Korean War.

The committee's first witness was McCarthy. Before the Wisconsin senator was able to complete his opening statement, Tydings demanded that he provide the name of one of the alleged communists. McCarthy refused, and after Tydings proceeded to badger the witness, Republican senator Henry Cabot Lodge Jr. requested that McCarthy be allowed to present his charges as he saw fit.

During the second week of hearings, McCarthy provided the subcommittee with a list of eight names, seven of which were individuals with connections to the State Department who, he alleged, had "pro-communist proclivities" or had given "pro-Soviet" advice. One of those on the list was Owen J. Lattimore, a Johns Hopkins University professor who had been a White House adviser to Nationalist Chinese leader Jiang Jieshi (Chiang Kaishek) during World War II. In response to this charge Tydings obtained Lattimore's file from the State Department and reported to the panel on March 23 that Lattimore had no present connection to the department.

McCarthy supported his claims against Lattimore with a witness named Louis F. Budenz, a former editor of the *Communist Daily Worker*. Budenz testified that he had been told that Lattimore was a communist but that Lattimore probably was not a spy. Lattimore appeared before the committee on April 6 and dismissed Budenz's accusations as "gossip and hearsay." Although Budenz's testimony did not prove that Lattimore was disloyal, it did suggest to many media observers that McCarthy's charges might have had at least some merit.

The Tydings Committee's investigation was hindered by the inability to obtain loyalty files held by President Harry S. Truman's administration, which claimed executive privilege in refusing to release them. On May 4 Truman finally agreed to allow the committee access to the files. The committee Democrats found no evidence in them to support McCarthy's charges. Republican senators, however, claimed that the files were not tamper-proof and that the lack of findings proved nothing.

The final phase of the Tydings investigation involved a review of the *Amerasia* spy case. Several employees of *Amerasia,* a journal of East Asian affairs, were found to be in possession of classified documents concerning U.S. policy in China. In 1945 six people were arrested on conspiracy and espionage charges related to some 1,000 stolen classified government documents. Three of those arrested—Andrew Roth, Emmanuel Larsen, and John Stewart Service—were U.S. government officials. The committee reviewed the entire history of the affair and heard testimony from Larsen. The committee reached the conclusion that the federal government had handled the *Amerasia* case properly and that no agency was derelict in investigating the charges.

After four months of hearings, the committee released its report on July 17, 1950. The report was critical of McCarthy and concluded that the available evidence supported none of the senator's charges. Only the Democrats signed the report. The Senate debate on the report was bitter and partisan, with Republicans accusing Tydings of leading a "scandalous and brazen whitewash of treasonable conspiracy." In the end the committee's report only provided McCarthy and McCarthyism more fodder. And with the Korean War underway, McCarthyism became all the more hysterical and vituperative.

JOHN DAVID RAUSCH JR.

See also

McCarthy, Joseph Raymond; McCarthyism; Service, John Stewart; Truman Loyalty Program

References

Fried, Richard M. *Men against McCarthy.* New York: Columbia University Press, 1976.

Griffith, Robert. *The Politics of Fear: Joseph R. McCarthy and the Senate.* 2nd ed. Amherst: University of Massachusetts Press, 1987.

Keith, Caroline. *"For Hell and a Brown Mule": The Biography of Senator Millard E. Tydings.* Lanham, MD: Madison Books, 1991.

Klehr, Harvey, and Ronald Radosh. *The Amerasia Spy Case: Prelude to McCarthyism.* Chapel Hill: University of North Carolina Press, 1996.

U

Underwood, Horace Grant
Birth Date: July 19, 1859
Death Date: October 12, 1916

Noted Presbyterian missionary who served in Korea. Horace Grant Underwood was born in London, England, on July 19, 1859. His family immigrated to the United States in 1872. Underwood graduated from New York University in 1881 and the Dutch Reformed Theological Seminary at New Brunswick, New Jersey, in 1884. After entering the ministry that same year, he decided to engage in mission work in Korea (then under the Choson dynasty). In late 1884 he arrived in Japan and learned the Korean language from a Korean Christian named Yi Su Jong, who had translated the New Testament Gospel of Mark into Korean.

Underwood arrived in Korea on April 5, 1885, and there he adopted a Korean name, Won Tu U. He and other U.S. missionaries, including Methodist Henry G. Appenzeller, gained permission to enter Korea thanks to the efforts of the doctor-missionary Horace N. Allen, who while serving as the physician to the U.S. legation in Seoul had saved the life of Min Yong Ik, the nephew of Queen Min. Three days after he arrived in Seoul, on April 10, 1885, the Korean government established the first Western-style hospital, Royal Widespread Relief House, at the suggestion of Allen. This modern hospital was soon renamed House for People's Relief. Underwood worked in the hospital, giving lectures on physics and chemistry. In February 1886 he established an orphanage in Seoul, which later evolved into a Jesuit Academy and then Kyongsin School. The former produced such men of distinguished talent as An Chang Ho and Kim Kyu Sik.

At first, U.S. missionaries' activity was confined to the establishment of hospitals and schools, as the Korean government prohibited its people from converting to Christianity. But government officials finally capitulated. Thus, on September 27, 1887, Underwood founded the Chongdong Church, the first of Korea's Presbyterian churches, in Seoul. Three years later, in 1890, the church was renamed Saemunan Church. In November of that year, Underwood visited northern parts of Korea, including Pyongyang, preaching Christianity. He also organized a committee for the translation of the Bible into Korean in late 1887 and founded a newspaper, the *Christ Newspaper,* in April 1897.

In 1900 Underwood consulted with Appenzeller about organizing the Young Men's Christian Association (YMCA) in Korea. Finally, on October 28, 1903, the Korean YMCA was formally created. Underwood served as one of its directors until his death in 1916, contributing to the development of the YMCA movement in Korea. Meanwhile, he spent his sabbatical years in the United States between April 1891 and February 1893 and went to Europe and the United States for recuperation between September 1905 and May 1910.

Before 1910, when Japan annexed Korea as a colony, some U.S. missionaries thought a Japanese takeover would be good for Korea. After annexation, however, they realized that their thinking had been wrong. The more the U.S. missionaries sympathized with the oppressed Korean people, the more the Japanese tried to impose restrictions on their work. The Japanese colonial government persisted in its suspicion of the missionary community. Despite Japanese restrictions, Underwood enthusiastically continued his mission work in Korea. In April 1915 he established the college division of Kyongsin School at the YMCA hall in Seoul and became its dean. On April 7, 1917, this "college" was approved as Yonhui Junior College by the Japanese colonial government, which would eventually evolve into the present-day Yonsei University in

Seoul. He also led the establishment of Severance Medical School, Pearson Bible Academy, and Pyongyang Presbyterian Theological Seminary. In addition, he contributed to the translation of the Bible into Korean, publishing a Korean version of a hymnbook for the first time in Korea.

As a consequence of his hard work, Underwood's health had deteriorated, forcing him to leave for the United States for medical care in April 1916. He died in Atlantic City, New Jersey, while undergoing treatment, on October 12, 1916. Koreans erected a monument in his honor at Saemunan Church in 1927. They also erected a bronze statue on the Yonhui campus in April 1928. During the Pacific war, however, the Japanese melted down the statue to make ammunition. Immediately after the establishment of the Republic of Korea (ROK, South Korea), another statue was erected in his honor, on October 16, 1948, but it was destroyed by the Korean People's Army (KPA, North Korean Army) during the Korean War.

JINWUNG KIM

See also

Churches and the War, Korean; Kim Kyu Sik

References

Min, Kyoung Bae. *A History of Christian Churches in Korea.* Seoul: Yonsei University Press, 2005.

Pak Yong Kyu. *Hanguk Kidok Kyohoe Sa* [History of the Christian Church in Korea]. Seoul: Saengmyong ui Malssumsa, 2004.

So, Chong Min. *Underwood Ka Iyagi* [The Story of the Underwood Family]. Seoul: Sallim Chulpansa, 2005.

Underwood, Horace Grant, II
Birth Date: September 6, 1917
Death Date: January 15, 2004

U.S. Navy officer, missionary, educator, and Korean War veteran. Horace Grant Underwood II was born in Seoul on September 6, 1917. As with his grandfather, Horace Grant Underwood, and father, Horace Horton Underwood, he adopted a Korean name, Won Il Han. He left Korea with his family in May 1942, when his father was expelled by the Japanese after the outbreak of the Pacific War (part of the greater World War II conflict). Upon returning to the United States, he and his family settled in Brooklyn, New York.

In December 1942 Underwood joined the U.S. Navy. After receiving training in Boulder, Colorado, for 14 months, he was commissioned an ensign in February 1944 and first deployed to New York, serving as an intelligence officer. After he was transferred to the Joint Intelligence Center Pacific Ocean Area (JICPOA), in Honolulu, Hawaii, because of his fluency in Korean, he engaged in the interrogation of prisoners of war (POWs), in particular Korean prisoners forcibly conscripted into the Japanese army. He also worked as an interpreter officer in the Philippines and Guam.

Following Japan's surrender in August 1945, Underwood served in the headquarters of the Supreme Commander for the Allied Powers in Tokyo, Japan. He hoped to return to Korea, and in February 1946 was notified that he was to be transferred to southern Korea, which was then administered by U.S. military authorities. Underwood arrived in Seoul that May and there met with his father, who had arrived before him.

Underwood now took charge of school affairs for the U.S. Military Government in Korea (USAMGIK). Because of his experience in education, he played an important role in the establishment of present-day Seoul National University. The plan was to transform the former Kyongsong Imperial University, founded by the Japanese in 1924, into a Korean national university, which gave rise to intense conflict between the political Left and Right. Underwood served as a bridge between the USAMGIK, the newly appointed president of the university, and the Korean professors and students of the university.

Although Underwood wanted to extend his term of service, he was discharged from the navy in 1947. Thereafter, he taught English composition and English conversation at Yonhui University, which was established by his grandfather, Horace G. Underwood, in 1915.

On June 25, 1950, when the Korean War began, Underwood was at Taechon, South Chungchong Province, facing the Yellow Sea, attending the annual conference of U.S. Presbyterian missionaries. Informed of events, he hurriedly moved to Taejon, then to Taegu, and finally to Pusan. Although he was a civilian missionary at the time, he decided to become an active duty officer again. In early August 1950 he returned to the U.S. Navy and served as an intelligence officer in the Far East Naval Forces under Vice Admiral C. Turner Joy. After participating in the Inchon Landing on September 15, 1950, Underwood was transferred to the 1st Marine Division. After Seoul was recovered by United Nations Command (UNC) forces on September 28, 1950, Underwood visited Yonhui University, which had been largely destroyed.

When truce talks were held between the UNC and the communists beginning in July 1951, Underwood served as the chief interpreter for the UNC. The armistice talks dragged on as the UNC negotiators faced communist intransigence. Finally, following prolonged discussion, the Armistice Agreement was signed on July 27, 1953.

Underwood again left the navy and returned to Yonhui University, where he contributed to its reconstruction and growth, serving as a professor and member of the Board of Trustees for many years. In 1957 Yonhui University and Severance Medical School merged to form Yonsei University. Underwood died in Seoul on January 15, 2004.

JINWUNG KIM

See also

Churches and the War, Korean; Underwood, Horace Grant; Underwood, Horace Horton

References
Min, Kyoung Bae. *A History of Christian Churches in Korea.* Seoul: Yonsei University Press, 2005.
Pak Yong Kyu. *Hanguk Kidok Kyohoe Sa* [History of the Christian Church in Korea]. Seoul: Saengmyong ui Malssumsa, 2004.
So, Chong Min. *Underwood Ka Iyagi* [The Story of the Underwood Family]. Seoul: Sallim Chulpansa, 2005.

Underwood, Horace Horton

Birth Date: September 6, 1890
Death Date: February 20, 1951

U.S. missionary and educator. Horace Horton Underwood was born in Seoul on September 6, 1890, and later adopted the Korean name Won Han Gyong. In 1906 he studied in France and Switzerland for a year before attending New York University, majoring in pedagogy and psychology. After graduation, he returned to Korea as a missionary in 1912 and taught English and history at Kyongsin School, first established as an orphanage by his father, Horace Grant Underwood, in Seoul in 1886 and renamed Kyongsin in 1901. After his father died in 1916, Underwood went to the United States to perform the funeral service.

Upon returning to Korea in 1917, Underwood became a professor at Yonhui Junior College, which would eventually become Yonsei University. He taught English, pedagogy, psychology, and philosophy, and created a chair of sociology for the first time in Korea in 1917.

On March 1, 1919, Korean nationalists formed a nationwide independence movement known as the March First Movement that attracted the active participation of Korean Christians. Of all the repressive measures by the Japanese during the independence movement, the most tragic was the massacre of Christians in the village of Cheam-ni, located just south of Seoul. On April 16, 1919, Underwood and some friends visited Cheam-ni and learned that Japanese soldiers had arrived in the village the day before and ordered all male Christians into the church. When some 30 had gathered, the soldiers fired on them with rifles, then killed the survivors with swords and bayonets, and set fire to the church. Underwood and other U.S. missionaries took pictures of the atrocities, including the Cheam-ni massacre, and disseminated these with written accounts in the United States and Europe, in spite of efforts by the Japanese authorities to conceal them through their control of the post offices, railroads, and press agencies.

In September 1923 Underwood went back to study at New York University and received a doctoral degree in pedagogy in 1925. He returned to Korea the following year, and then traveled to the United States again in 1933 to launch a fund-raising campaign for Yonhui Junior College. He became dean of that school in 1934.

Just prior to the beginning of the Pacific War (part of the greater World War II conflict) in December 1941, the U.S. missionary community in Korea became completely subject to Japanese control. Missionaries could not hold meetings without police permission, and police representatives were required at all such gatherings. U.S. missionaries were not allowed to hold administrative positions in the church. Under such oppression, missionaries were compelled to withdraw from Korea, and on November 16, 1941, practically all U.S. missionaries were evacuated from the country. In December of the same year, Underwood was arrested by the Japanese police and placed in a concentration camp for foreigners. In May 1942 he was released and then expelled to the United States.

Following the liberation of Korea in August 1945, Underwood returned to the country as an interpreter for the U.S. Military Government in Korea (USAMGIK) in October 1945. Soon, he came to act as adviser to Major General Archibald V. Arnold, military governor of the USAMGIK in November 1945, and then Major General Archer L. Lerch, Arnold's successor, in July 1946. In October 1947 Underwood resigned his posts with the USAMGIK and returned to Yonhui University. He helped Paek Nak Chun, president of the university, expand and improve the school.

On March 17, 1949, Underwood's wife, Ethel Van Wagner Underwood, was killed by leftist youths who had stormed his residence on Yonhui University's campus. Frustrated and deeply saddened, Underwood traveled to the United States in May 1950. After the outbreak of the Korean War, however, he returned to Korea in October 1950 and, while serving as a civilian adviser to G-2 (military/ground intelligence) for the U.S. Army, died in Pusan, then the temporary capital of the Republic of Korea (ROK, South Korea), on February 20, 1951.

JINWUNG KIM

See also
Churches and the War, Korean; Underwood, Horace Grant; Underwood, Horace Grant, II

References
Min, Kyoung Bae. *A History of Christian Churches in Korea.* Seoul: Yonsei University Press, 2005.
Pak Yong Kyu. *Hanguk Kidok Kyohoe Sa* [History of the Christian Church in Korea]. Seoul: Saengmyong ui Malssumsa, 2004.
So, Chong Min. *Underwood Ka Iyagi* [The Story of the Underwood Family]. Seoul: Sallim Chulpansa, 2005.

Union of Soviet Socialist Republics

See Soviet Union

United Kingdom

An island nation located off the northwestern coast of the European continent. Although the United Kingdom is a solitary state, it is composed of four nations: England, Wales, Scotland, and Northern Ireland. It also has a number of overseas possessions.

Troops of the 29th British Brigade taking a break during a withdrawal to new defensive positions, April 1951. (National Archives)

The United Kingdom, a constitutional parliamentary democracy, had a 1950 population of 50 million people. The monarch is the head of state, while the prime minister is head of government. King George VI reigned until his death in February 1952, at which time his daughter, Queen Elizabeth II, ascended the throne. She remains the British monarch to this day. During the Korean War, British politics were dominated by two principal parties, the Labour Party and the Conservative Party.

The United Kingdom was the chief Western ally of the United States during the Korean War. At the outbreak of the conflict, the attention of the British people was focused on rising Cold War tensions and domestic conditions. In 1950 Prime Minister Clement R. Attlee's Labour government faced an uncertain future. The Labour Party's attempts to improve Britain's war-damaged economy after World War II resulted in continuing public hardships. The British people had grown increasingly tired of the austerity ushered in by the Labour government in the name of societal improvement through socialism. They held much less faith in the Labour government in 1950 than they had in 1945, when it assumed power.

The June 25, 1950, invasion of the Republic of Korea (ROK, South Korea) by the Democratic People's Republic of Korea (DPRK, North Korea) dashed hopes for a British economic recovery. Attlee and his senior officials were aware of the U.S. stance that a failure of the West to react in Korea would encourage communist expansion in other areas. The British concurred with this view and were particularly concerned about the threat of communist aggression in Western Europe. Attlee recognized that the United Kingdom had to support the United States, not only to meet communist expansion in Asia but also to strengthen those in the United States who advocated an American commitment to the defense of Europe. Many British officials feared a lack of support for the United States would strengthen those who believed in a Fortress America foreign policy and possibly threaten the rearmament of Europe embodied in the North Atlantic Treaty Organization (NATO).

On June 28, 1950, three days after the United Nations (UN) resolution condemning North Korea's invasion of South Korea and after the second UN resolution calling on member states to defend South Korea, Attlee spoke in the House of Commons. He told the

Commandos of the 41st Royal British Marines plant demolition charges along railroad tracks, some eight miles south of Songjin, April 10, 1951. (National Archives)

members of Parliament that Britain would fulfill its pledge to the UN and provide military assistance to South Korea.

By the end of June the British and Australian governments had offered air and naval units stationed at Japan to the United Nations Command (UNC). The issue of providing troops, however, presented two problems for Attlee's government. Any contribution of ground forces required steps toward rearmament that the Labour government had previously tried to avoid in favor of focusing resources on the domestic front. Also, British armed forces were already committed to Malaya, where communist insurgents threatened colonial rule, and to Hong Kong, after the Communist victory in the Chinese Civil War in 1949. Britain's low defense budget and overseas requirements resulted in the initial commitment to Korea of only one infantry brigade in June and an additional two infantry battalions in August. The need for a greater role necessitated greater defense spending. In January 1951 the British government projected a military spending program of £4.7 billion over the next three years. This doubled the defense estimates put forward at the beginning of 1950 and placed a considerable strain on the struggling economy.

Increasing U.S. pressure and the need for influence in U.S. foreign policy decisions in Korea required the new defense estimate, but so too did the rearmament of Europe. The drain on U.S. resources resulting from the Korean War required increased defense spending in Europe to continue Western rearmament. The inadequacy of the new defense estimate presented Attlee's government with the explosive issue of the rearmament of the Federal Republic of Germany (FRG, West Germany). Unlike the problem of defense spending, this issue proved difficult but not impossible to solve. Although the issue dogged Attlee's administration until its fall from power, the proposed European Defense Community in May 1952 defused the issue, and West German forces were eventually absorbed into NATO.

Attlee's foreign policy was similar to that of President Harry S. Truman's administration, but it had to address British interests in Asia as well. Attlee's government supported the war effort, but after the rout of the North Koreans, it maintained that all military operations in North Korea should be conducted well south of the Chinese and Soviet borders. From the outset the British demanded that the conflict not extend outside Korea without prior

British Aircraft Specifications

Aircraft	Span	Length	Height	Gross Weight (pounds)	Top Speed (mph)	Range (miles)	Ceiling (feet)
Auster A.O.P.6	36' 0"	23' 9"	8' 4 1/2"	2,160	124	315	14,000
Fairey Firefly	41' 2"	37' 11"	14' 4"	16,096	386	1,300	28,400
H.P. Hastings	113' 0"	82' 8"	22' 6"	80,000	348	1,690	26,540
Hawker Sea Fury	38' 4 3/4"	34' 8"	15' 10 1/2"	12,500	460	700	41,000
Short Sunderland	112' 9 1/2"	85' 4"	32' 10 1/2"	60,000	213	2,880	17,900
Supermarine Seafire	36' 0"	33' 7"	12' 9"	11,615	452	400	43,100

consultation. Although the Truman administration agreed that a widened war would be disastrous, many top U.S. officials, such as Secretary of State Dean G. Acheson, believed British self-interest clouded their judgment on foreign policy matters.

The mid-October 1950 intervention in the fighting by the People's Republic of China (PRC) brought about the situation that Britain had sought to avoid and strained relations with the United States. Attlee's government was profoundly opposed to direct confrontation with China because of the potential damage to Britain's Asian trade interests and the threat the PRC posed to their Far East colonies of Malaya, Hong Kong, and Singapore. The Chinese intervention clearly showed the differing attitudes between the United Kingdom and the United States over China. Attlee believed that negotiations must immediately take place over Korea. The United States, however, held that negotiations were impossible until the military situation had been stabilized. London also disagreed with Washington, DC's position that the Chinese invasion had occurred with the approval of the Union of Soviet Socialist Republics (USSR, Soviet Union). Truman administration officials believed that communism was monolithic and had to be contained. The British tried to argue that the Chinese were not pawns of the Soviets and that U.S. foreign policy must detach the two. Although this did not fall on completely deaf ears in Washington, the Truman administration refused to concede defeat in Korea, something that Attlee was willing to do in hopes of a cease-fire.

London's fear of a wider war seemed to have been realized when Truman hinted of the possibility of a nuclear attack against the Chinese. This prompted Attlee to fly to Washington in December 1950 to seek U.S. assurance that it would not exercise that option.

The British position at this point was precarious. Attlee did not want to betray the United States in Korea. This would cause a political and strategic crisis by adversely impacting the "special relationship" between the two powers and would threaten future U.S. commitment to the defense of Europe. The British consequently pursued a path of supporting the United States but also trying to influence U.S. foreign policy.

Attlee's government saw the opportunity to influence U.S. policy when the war ground to a stalemate in mid-1951. The Labour government, however, had little time to act, as it lost the general election of October 1951. The Korean War had contributed directly to the Labour Party's defeat, as the issue of rearmament burdened the economy and split the party. It was so contentious that many,

including Minister of Health Aneurin Bevan, resigned in the belief that rearmament was a threat to socialism and the welfare state in Britain.

Sir Winston Churchill, leader of the Conservative Party, became prime minister on October 26, 1951, and named R. Anthony Eden as his foreign secretary. Churchill took office the day after the Panmunjom truce talks began. He fully recognized Britain's subordinate role, because the country's military contribution was relatively small next to that of the United States. The 1st Commonwealth Division consisted of two British brigades, one Canadian brigade, two Australian battalions, and a New Zealand artillery regiment by the time he became prime minister. Britain had a large naval presence but did not have a fighter aircraft to match the Soviet Mikoyan-Gurevich MiG-15 fighter flown by the communists, which consequently handicapped naval effectiveness. Britain could barely claim the right of consultation on major issues, much less a place at the negotiating table.

Churchill's foreign policy resembled that of Attlee's, with some exceptions. The prime minister wanted a speedy end to the war but not at the price of major concessions to the communists. He believed that long-lasting peace required negotiation from a position of strength both in Asia with the Chinese and North Koreans and in Europe with the Soviets. Churchill believed such a peace would pave the way for his goal of a wide-ranging summit with the communists over global affairs.

Attaining these goals met frequent obstacles posed by the war and particularly negotiations for peace. The two stumbling blocks were safeguards for communist compliance of an armistice and the prisoner of war (POW) repatriation issue. Differing opinions in Washington and London over these problems severely strained the special relationship. The United States considered issuing a warning of the possibility of sanctions, such as an economic blockade of the Chinese coast and further military action against the PRC should the communists violate the armistice. Churchill and Eden both opposed this because of the possibility of provoking a world war. The British believed that the communists would abide by the armistice, and they wanted any warning to be in the most general terms. Truman and Acheson clearly expressed their irritation with London's stance on the issue.

A more divisive issue was that of voluntary repatriation of POWs. Truman insisted on voluntary repatriation with no concessions, which China vehemently opposed. The British supported the U.S. position but objected to another U.S. suggestion that military pressure be applied to force China to agree to voluntary repatriation. The British objected on the same grounds as in the past and began searching for an alternate solution.

The answer was to employ the help of neutral India, which had strong diplomatic channels to Beijing. Churchill saw Indian support as vital to resolving the POW issue. The Truman administration rejected this view out of distrust for the Indians because of their ties to the communist bloc. The United States also believed that the Indian proposal to the UN on POWs did not properly address the issue of defectors. The British again found themselves trying to avoid a serious clash with the United States while pursuing the course that they believed could most quickly end the war. A solution presented itself in late 1952, when the Chinese endorsed a Soviet suggestion that a cease-fire take place first before resolution of the POW issue.

The election of Dwight D. Eisenhower as president of the United States relieved the tension between Britain and the United States over foreign policy. Eisenhower was also against forcible repatriation of POWs, but he wanted a solution as soon as possible and was sympathetic to India's efforts.

Eisenhower's election, however, did not resolve basic differences of opinion between Washington and London over foreign policy in Asia. New U.S. secretary of state John Foster Dulles again considered methods of applying pressure on the PRC to break the truce talks deadlock. And Eisenhower hinted at the possibility of using nuclear weapons. Although the British did not believe that the U.S. president would authorize a nuclear strike, they did object again to increased pressure on the Chinese. In the spring of 1953 Churchill looked to Soviet assistance to solve the crisis, especially after Stalin's death in March 1953, after which the Soviets seemed more receptive to the West. Churchill tried to improve relations with Moscow and talked with Foreign Minister Viacheslav M. Molotov on the POW issue. Washington hotly contested the British action, and relations again suffered.

British policy ultimately succeeded despite the past disagreements with Washington. The Indian resolution finally gained acceptance with the communists, who agreed to a revised form of the plan on June 4, 1953. After some objection to the peace, particularly from South Korean president Syngman Rhee, the armistice was signed on July 27, 1953.

Britain made a significant military commitment to UNC forces. The Royal Navy provided the aircraft carriers HMS *Triumph, Glory, Ocean,* and *Theseus;* cruisers *Belfast, Jamaica, Birmingham, Kenya,* and *New Castle;* destroyers *Cossack, Consort, Cockade, Comus,* and *Charity;* frigates *Black Swan, Alacrity, Heart, Morecome Bay, Mounts Bay,* and *Whitesand Bay;* hospital ship *Maine;* and other ships. On August 29, 1950, the 27th Infantry Brigade, the first of the British land contingents, arrived from Hong Kong. It was followed by tank units and the 29th Infantry Brigade. Later, the 27th and 29th Brigades were joined with other Commonwealth units into the 1st Commonwealth Division. With this division were spotter aircraft from the Royal Air Force and three squadrons

of Sunderland flying boats; the Royal Navy flew Sea Fury, Firefly, and Seafire aircraft from its carriers to provide ground support and interdiction missions. Britain also provided artillery, antiaircraft artillery, and engineer units. At peak strength, British ground forces totaled 14,198 soldiers.

The British contribution to the Korean War was significant in other ways as well. Churchill's government greatly contributed to the end of the conflict through its support of the Indian initiative on POWs and conciliation with all parties concerned in the war, including the Soviets. At war's end the United Kingdom had lost 1,078 men, including those missing in action. The price was a high one for the strained resources of the United Kingdom, but participation in the war protected and furthered its interests throughout the world.

ERIC W. OSBORNE

See also

Acheson, Dean Gooderham; Alexander-Lloyd Mission; Australia; Bevan, Aneurin; Bevin, Ernest; Canada; Cassels, Sir James; Churchill, Sir Winston; Defectors; Dulles, John Foster; Eden, Robert Anthony; Eisenhower, Dwight David; European Defense Community; India; Lloyd, John Selwyn; Menon, Vengalil Krishnan Krishna; Molotov, Viacheslav Mikhailovich; Nehru, Jawaharlal; New Zealand; Panikkar, Sardar K. M.; Repatriation, Voluntary; Soviet Union; Truce Talks; Truman, Harry S.; U.S. Policy toward Korea, Pre-1950; U.S. Policy toward Korea, 1950–1953; West, Sir Michael M. A. R.

References

Bartlett, Christopher J. *A History of Postwar Britain, 1945–1974.* London: Longman, 1977.

Dimblebey, David, and David Reynolds. *An Ocean Apart: Britain and the United States in the Twentieth Century.* New York: Random House, 1998.

Greenwood, Sean. *Britain and the Cold War, 1945–1991.* New York: St. Martin's, 2000.

Grey, Jeffrey. *The Commonwealth Armies and the Korean War: An Alliance Study.* Manchester, UK: Manchester University Press, 1988.

Lowe, Peter. *Containing the Cold War in East Asia: British Policies toward Japan, China and Korea, 1948–1953.* Manchester, UK: Manchester University Press, 1997.

Renwick, Sir Robin. *Fighting with Allies: America and Britain in Peace and War.* New York: Random House, 1996.

Young, John W., ed. *The Foreign Policy of Churchill's Peacetime Administration, 1951–1955.* Worcester, UK: Leicester University Press, 1988.

United Nations and the Korean War

The United Nations (UN) was involved in Korea long before the beginning of the Korean War in June 1950. Beginning in August 1945, in accordance with wartime agreements regarding the surrender of Japanese forces at the end of World War II, Soviet forces occupied northern Korea down to the 38th Parallel, while U.S. troops occupied southern Korea the following month. After protracted negotiations and unable to resolve differences with the Union of Soviet Socialist Republics (USSR, Soviet Union) over

Soviet delegate Andrei Vyshinskii, right, shakes his fist as he accuses the United States and its allies of acting like a "master race," during a UN political committee session in New York, August 26, 1953. Listening to Vishinski's charges are, left, U.S. delegate Henry Cabot Lodge Jr. and Britain's Sir Gladwyn Jebb, center, with his head buried in his hands. (AP/Wide World Photos)

steps to reunify the peninsula, on September 17, 1947, the U.S. government laid the issue before the UN General Assembly.

On November 14, 1947, the General Assembly adopted a U.S.-sponsored resolution calling for general elections to establish a national government of Korea. In January 1948, however, Soviet authorities refused to admit into northern Korea the United Nations Temporary Commission on Korea (UNTCOK), charged with supervising the Korean elections, whereupon on February 26 the Interim Committee of the General Assembly adopted a U.S.-sponsored resolution proposing that the UNTCOK observe elections for representatives to a national assembly in those areas of Korea "accessible" to it. In May general elections were held in southern Korea, leading to the adoption of a constitution in July and the establishment of the Republic of Korea (ROK, South Korea) on August 15. Communist northern Korea then followed suit with the establishment of the Democratic People's Republic of Korea (DPRK, North Korea). On December 12, 1948, the UN

General Assembly recognized the Republic of Korea as the only lawfully constituted government on the Korean Peninsula. The same UN resolution also created the UN Commission on Korea. In April 1949, however, the Soviet Union vetoed the application by South Korea for admission to the UN.

Although there had been border fighting during the previous several years between the two Koreas along the 38th Parallel de facto border, South Korea, the United States, and the UN were all surprised by the full-scale invasion of South Korea by North Korean forces on June 25, 1950. The invasion presented the UN with the greatest challenge since its creation in 1945. The war would also be the first conflict waged under UN auspices. With the Korean People's Army (KPA, North Korean Army) rapidly overrunning the south, U.S. president Harry S. Truman authorized the insertion of U.S. air and naval forces to assist the Republic of Korea Army (ROKA, South Korean Army) in halting the invasion.

The United States brought the North Korean aggression before the UN and proposed on June 25, 1950, Resolution 82. The Security Council passed the resolution, which assigned responsibility to North Korean authorities for the attack on South Korea. It determined that this action constituted a breach of the peace and called for an immediate cessation of hostilities and a withdrawal of North Korean forces north of the 38th Parallel. When North Korea ignored the UN requests, the United States gained Security Council passage on June 27 of Resolution 83, which called upon all members to help South Korea repel the invaders and restore peace.

At the time, the Soviet Union, a permanent member of the Security Council with a right of veto, was deliberately absent in protest over the UN's refusal to seat the newly established People's Republic of China (PRC). As a consequence, for the first time, an act of aggression was directly countered with military force under the aegis of international authority. The defense of South Korea was undertaken by the United Nations Command (UNC), armed forces of 16 countries acting in the name of the UN in accordance with Security Council Resolution 84, passed on July 7, 1950, and pursuant to resolutions approved by a majority of the members. Responsibility for the enforcement action was at least nominally collective, although the United States shouldered the bulk of the responsibility and appointed the UNC commander.

There were five distinct phases to UN involvement: (1) determination of responsibility for the breach of peace, (2) establishment of a unified command (UNC) under U.S. direction and its deployment against North Korea in the successful defense of South Korea, (3) extension of UN operations north of the 38th Parallel, (4) Chinese intervention and the subsequent military stalemate, (5) negotiation and the conclusion of an armistice.

The UN decisions were largely engineered by the United States. The policy leadership of the United States, focusing on a commitment to counter communist aggression, was crucial. Moreover, the Security Council was inclined to act decisively, above all, because of the keen sense that the UN was confronted with a momentous decision on which hinged both international security and the body's prestige. To forgo collective action would have been reminiscent of the weaknesses of the ill-fated League of Nations, which had failed to avert war in the 1930s.

Security Council Resolution 84 recommended that member governments make available "to a unified command under the United States" military forces and other assistance to help repel the North Korean attack. Truman assigned command to U.S. Far Eastern commander General Douglas MacArthur, who insisted that military and political decisions in Korea were exclusively his. The UN had no supervisory authority over the command, and even few channels of communication with it except through the U.S. government. The latter was not accountable for actions on the Korean Peninsula to any UN organ. The Security Council in essence issued a blank check in authorizing the United States to establish a unified command, prompted by the accurate anticipation that it would be powerless in Korea upon the return of the Soviet Union to the Security Council.

From an initial military standpoint, U.S. predominance facilitated operations. With a solid U.S. core, UN forces for the most part enjoyed operational unity. The UNC was able to mount a successful defense of the Pusan Perimeter and subsequently dealt the North Koreans a devastating counterstroke behind enemy lines in the amphibious assault at Inchon on September 15, 1950. The shattered North Korean forces were sent scurrying back up the peninsula, above the 38th Parallel.

Had the war ended at that point, the collective UN enforcement action would have been deemed an unqualified success. Following the apparent victory, however, critical policy errors altered the situation dramatically. The UN provided no policy direction, and collective security in Korea ultimately failed because of the absence of collective responsibility at the crucial tipping point in the conflict. Truman's decision to authorize MacArthur to seek the total destruction of the North Korean forces, the unconditional surrender of the North Korean government, and the occupation of North Korea with UNC forces, pending a permanent settlement in accordance with earlier UN directives that had called for the unification of Korea, proved a grievous error in judgment.

The Truman administration, flush with MacArthur's military success at Inchon, believed that the UN resolutions of June and July provided the UNC with ample authority to send its troops into North Korea and to topple the communist regime there. Its determination to strike north required the widest possible interpretation of the legitimate role and powers of the UN as conceived in its charter. In connection with the enforcement of peace and security, the charter-prescribed provision was to restore peace, not necessarily to impose a settlement. The charter certainly did not allow, even under collective security authorization, member countries to run grave risks of triggering a chain reaction of an ever-widening conflict. Ominously, the Truman administration, as well as MacArthur, chose to ignore Beijing's explicit public warnings and those passed along by the Indian government that, if UNC forces crossed the parallel, the People's Republic of China (PRC) would enter the war. U.S. leaders chose to regard these PRC warnings as a bluff.

Most UN members were willing to follow the leadership of the United States when the General Assembly met in late September. In a major speech before the General Assembly on September 30, U.S. ambassador Warren Austin, repeating his public appeals for reunification in August, advocated that the UN forces cross the parallel to eliminate the artificial division of Korea. The United States then initiated an eight-power resolution calling for appropriate steps "to ensure conditions of stability throughout Korea" and the "establishment of a unified, independent and democratic Government in the sovereign State of Korea." The final vote on General Assembly Resolution 376 on October 7 encountered opposition only from the Soviet bloc, passing with 47 in favor, 5 opposed, with 7 abstentions. The majority accepted that North Korea had forfeited its legitimacy through its act of blatant aggression. The

UN General Assembly subsequently sanctioned the dual goals of the United States: to defeat North Korean forces and to unify the country under UN auspices. The UN, it seemed, was on the threshold of victory. The United States, however, agreed to caution in the exercise of authority. The Soviet Union, for its part, urged an immediate termination of hostilities, followed by the withdrawal of foreign troops, and all-Korean elections under UN supervision.

On October 8, 1950, MacArthur, speaking as UN commander in chief, called upon the KPA to surrender and "cooperate fully with the United Nations in establishing a unified, independent, and democratic government of Korea." He admonished the North Korean authorities that, short of immediate compliance, he would "at once proceed to take such military action as may be necessary to enforce the decrees of the United Nations." MacArthur personally drafted this ultimatum, which somewhat overstretched the mandates he had received from the UN and his superiors in Washington, DC

On October 19 UNC forces entered Pyongyang, the North Korean capital, and proceeded to advance northward. By then, the Chinese Fourth Field Army had already crossed the Yalu River and penetrated the mountainous terrain of North Korea. The first Chinese military intervention, in late October, was followed late the next month with a massive intervention that not only blunted the renewed UNC drive north but also sent UNC forces into a rapid withdrawal south. Meanwhile, Beijing had accepted a UN invitation to participate in the debate about its intervention, but after unproductive discussions its representative departed as China's forces continued their advance. When the Chinese outran the supply lines in late January 1951, UNC forces checked the advance and staged a counteroffensive, pushing communist troops back into North Korea. With both sides building defenses in depth, the front stabilized and stalemate ensued. Fighting continued, however. In these circumstances, both sides were ready to discuss peace. Prolonged talks finally led to an armistice, but not a peace settlement, on July 27, 1953.

By the end of 1950 the UN faced the dilemma of having to negotiate its objectives after having failed to impose them by force. To the original aims of restoring peace and stability were added the interests and responsibilities the UN had acquired as a belligerent in a war. It was so closely linked to the political situation in Korea that it had assumed many of the attributes of guardianship. For example, the UN created two commissions, one to supervise reunification and another to administer programs for economic reconstruction of Korea with funds raised from member nations. But pursuit of multiple and at times contradictory objectives occurred against the backdrop of bitter antagonisms. Neither the Chinese nor the North Korean governments had representation in the UN, and negotiations for a settlement were conducted in the field. MacArthur's removal from command in April 1951 enabled the U.S. government to ensure that policy decisions would be made by the governments concerned, and not by a commander in the field.

Neither the United States nor the UN worked out the modalities for ensuring that policies would reflect collective decisions. A peace agreement would necessitate the concurrence of the direct participants and presumably the majority of UN members. Acceptance of the political-military status quo entailed UN renunciation of the extended objectives that it had embraced when it endorsed approval of MacArthur's forces to cross the 38th Parallel in the autumn of 1950, although it did not have to relinquish the original limited goals of the enforcement action. The status quo preserved essentially intact the political independence and territorial integrity of South Korea as it existed prior to the invasion. Yet, the government of South Korean president Syngman Rhee sometimes asserted its own political interests so forcefully that it nearly undermined UN efforts to reach a settlement. For example, Rhee stubbornly insisted that the UNC not forgo collective enforcement until it had secured the "unified, free and democratic Korea" to which it was previously committed. Hence, UN members were negotiating on multiple levels: among themselves, with the communists, and with the South Korean regime.

The communist side proved itself able practitioners of the "fight-talk-fight-talk" Maoist strategy. When they could not win the Korean War and they were confronted with renewed heavy warfare, they assented to a shift of peace talks from Kaesong and Panmunjom, where they conducted "warfare by other means." Open warfare was complemented by the tactical uses of diplomacy. Beijing's aims were to limit U.S. influence in Asia, to establish itself as a great power in global negotiations where it would be highly visible, to maintain what it considered its sphere of influence, and to enhance its standing among other Asian countries by underscoring the peaceful coexistence theme. The half-a-loaf settlement Beijing opted for advanced all of these aims effectively.

The truce talks dragged on for nearly two years, until July 1953. The main disagreement arose over the refusal of the United States to forcibly repatriate a great many communist prisoners who did not wish to return to their respective homelands. The United States and South Korea insisted that there be no forced repatriation, while the UN was compelled to equivocate on the subject. The communists finally yielded on this issue, and an armistice was then signed. Korea remained a divided nation. An international commission was created to supervise a demilitarized zone (DMZ) near the 38th Parallel and to prevent a military buildup by either side. Negotiations for a final peace ended in deadlock, however, and more than 50 years later the two Koreas remain technically at war. By allowing itself to become embroiled in intermember politics and then to serve as an organ of U.S. military policy, the UN greatly magnified the size and scope of the Korean War, although it did exert its influence after Chinese intervention to ensure that the United States did not take unduly provocative actions that would risk extension of the fighting beyond the peninsula.

DAVID M. KEITHLY

See also

United Nations Command; United Nations General Assembly Resolution 376 (V); United Nations General Assembly Resolution 377 (V); United Nations General Assembly Resolution 498 (V); United

Nations Security Council Resolution 82; United Nations Security Council Resolution 83; United Nations Security Council Resolution 84; United Nations Security Council Resolution 85

References

Acheson, Dean. *Present at the Creation.* New York: Norton, 1969.

Bennett, A. Leroy. *International Organizations.* 2nd ed. Englewood Cliffs, NJ: Prentice Hall, 1980.

Boyd, Andrew. *Fifteen Men on a Powder Keg: A History of the U.N. Security Council.* New York: Stein and Day, 1971.

Goodrich, Leland M. *Korea: A Study in U.S. Policy in the United Nations.* New York: Council on Foreign Relations, 1956.

Riggs, Robert E., and Jack C. Plano. *The United Nations: International Organization and World Politics.* 2nd ed. Belmont, CA: Wadsworth, 1994.

Russell, Ruth B. *The United Nations and United States Security Policy.* Washington, DC: Brookings Institution, 1968.

Spanier, John. *American Foreign Policy since World War II.* 12th ed. Washington, DC: CQ Press, 1992.

United Nations Additional Measures Committee

United Nations (UN) committee established to explore sanctions against the People's Republic of China (PRC) and the Democratic People's Republic of Korea (DPRK, North Korea). The Additional Measures Committee was established by UN General Assembly Resolution 498 (V) of February 1, 1951. The United States had sought political, economic, and military countermeasures since the PRC military forces had entered the Korean War in mid-October 1950. Among the measures considered were a trade embargo and the freezing of Chinese assets in the United States.

The U.S. State Department, concerned about any action that might jeopardize support for the war by a majority of UN states, recommended against a unilateral embargo and sought UN support for collective action. U.S. efforts in the UN were complicated by an Indian-led group of Asian and Middle Eastern nations who sought to broker a cease-fire and by British reluctance to take measures against China so long as there was hope that cease-fire overtures might bear fruit. Chinese rejection of overtures by the UN Cease-Fire Group in January 1951 gave the United States added leverage and led to the passage of the February 1 resolution.

This resolution, the first passed under the Uniting for Peace procedure, condemned PRC intervention as aggression and established the Additional Measures Committee to consider and report on measures "to meet this aggression." The resolution also established a Good Offices Committee to seek a cessation of hostilities. The Additional Measures Committee was authorized to delay its report if the Good Offices Committee made satisfactory progress.

The Additional Measures Committee was to be composed of the same members as the Collective Measures Committee established by the November 7, 1950, Uniting for Peace Resolution. At the first meeting on February 16, 1950, however, the Collective Measures Committee representatives from Burma and Yugoslavia declined to participate. The membership thus consisted of representatives from Australia, Belgium, Brazil, Canada, Egypt, France, Mexico, the Philippines, Turkey, the United Kingdom, the United States, and Venezuela.

The United States sought the imposition of both political measures (nonrecognition and exclusion from the UN) and economic sanctions as soon as possible. The British, fearing a widening of the war and PRC action against Hong Kong, opposed political sanctions. Other members of the committee were inclined to wait and see if the Good Offices Committee made progress before imposing any sanctions. On March 8, 1951, the members of the Additional Measures Committee established a subcommittee consisting of Australia, France, the United Kingdom, and the United States. After a month of deliberations, the subcommittee agreed to focus on economic sanctions.

The PRC's refusal to recognize the legitimacy of the Good Offices Committee, and the initiation of the Chinese Fifth Offensive in April 1951 strengthened U.S. arguments for the imposition of sanctions. On May 3, 1951, the subcommittee recommended, and the committee accepted, a U.S. proposal for economic but not political sanctions. On May 14 the full committee delivered its report, noting that a number of countries had already imposed economic measures, and recommending an embargo on the export of weapons, munitions, and strategic materials to North Korea and the PRC. This recommendation was incorporated into UN General Assembly Resolution 500 (V) of May 18, which also called upon the Additional Measures Committee to report on the effectiveness of the embargo and the desirability of relaxing or continuing it. This report could be deferred if the Good Offices Committee reported satisfactory progress. The initiation of truce talks in July 1951 brought the efforts of the Additional Measures Committee to an end.

DONALD W. BOOSE JR.

See also

Chinese Offensive, Fifth; United Nations Cease-Fire Group; United Nations Collective Measures Committee; United Nations Good Offices Committee

References

Goodrich, Leland Matthew. *Korea: A Study of U.S. Policy in the United Nations.* New York: Council on Foreign Relations, 1956.

Seyersted, Finn. *United Nations Forces in the Law of Peace and War.* Leyden: A. W. Sijthoff, 1966.

Stueck, William W., Jr. *Rethinking the Korean War: A New Diplomatic and Strategic History.* Princeton, NJ: Princeton University Press, 2004.

United Nations. *Yearbook of the United Nations, 1950, 1951, 1952, 1953.* New York: Columbia University Press, 1951, 1952, 1953, 1954.

United Nations Cease-Fire Group

Also known as the Group of Three, the United Nations (UN) Cease-Fire Group was formed in response to UN General

Assembly Resolution 384 (V) of December 14, 1950. This resolution requested that the president of the General Assembly establish a group of three individuals, including himself, to determine the basis upon which a satisfactory cease-fire in Korea could be arranged and to make recommendations to the General Assembly as soon as possible.

Resolution 384 (V) had its genesis in lengthy UN negotiations that began after the entrance of the People's Republic of China (PRC) into the war. On November 10, 1950, following the initial clashes between United Nations Command (UNC) and Chinese People's Volunteer Army (CPVA, Chinese Army) forces, the United States proposed a Security Council resolution calling on China to withdraw its troops from Korea. When the Union of Soviet Socialist Republics (USSR, Soviet Union) vetoed this resolution, the U.S. delegation, making use of the Uniting for Peace procedure, introduced a similar resolution in the General Assembly on December 7. The earlier resolution had almost unanimous support, but by the time the General Assembly took up the proposal the situation had changed.

UN members, concerned about Chinese military success and shaken by U.S. president Harry S. Truman's November 30, 1950, public statement that he would consider using atomic bombs in Korea, were inclined to seek a negotiated settlement. Behind the scenes, the British urged the United States to exercise restraint, privately suggesting that U.S. recognition of China and withdrawal of U.S. forces from the vicinity of Taiwan (then known as Formosa) might bring an end to the Korean fighting and drive a wedge between the Chinese and the Soviets. U.S. leaders rejected these proposals but recognized that they would have to compromise to maintain allied support. Thus, the United States voted in favor of an Indian proposal put forth on December 12 by 13 Asian and Middle Eastern states for the formation of a group consisting of the General Assembly president and two other persons to investigate the possibility of a cease-fire. This proposal was incorporated in the December 14, 1950, resolution that established the Cease-Fire Group.

General Assembly president Nasrollah Entezam of Iran selected Lester B. Pearson of Canada and Sir Benegal N. Rau of India to join him in the group, which immediately set about its work by asking the United States, representing the UNC, what conditions it would accept for a cease-fire. The U.S. government had already deliberated on its cease-fire conditions and was able to respond immediately. The United States wanted a 20-mile demilitarized zone (DMZ) with its southern boundary generally along the 38th Parallel, UN supervision of the cease-fire, cessation of reinforcement or replacement of armed forces and military equipment in Korea, a one-for-one exchange of prisoners of war (POWs), and General Assembly confirmation of the cease-fire.

On December 16 the Cease-Fire Group sent messages to the Chinese ministry of foreign affairs and to a Chinese delegation that was in New York attending UN discussions on the Taiwan issue. Receiving no replies, it sent a second message to the Chinese

foreign ministry in Beijing on December 19. With CPVA forces already advancing south of the 38th Parallel, Beijing was unlikely to accept a cease-fire zone north of that line and indeed denied the legitimacy of the Cease-Fire Group. On December 21 the Chinese notified the UN that it considered the December 14 resolution null and void, because it had been passed without Chinese participation. Two days later, the Chinese government transmitted a message from Foreign Minister Zhou Enlai to Entezam as General Assembly president, ignoring his membership in the Cease-Fire Group. Zhou identified Chinese conditions for a cease-fire as withdrawal of all foreign troops, settlement of the Korean question by the Korean people themselves, U.S. withdrawal from Taiwan, and Chinese representation in the UN.

On January 2, 1951, the Cease-Fire Group reported to the First Committee that it had not been able to meet with a Chinese representative and were unable to make a recommendation. The Cease-Fire Group then privately circulated a list of "five principles" offering a step-by-step approach to a Korean settlement. On January 11 the group made a supplementary report setting forth these principles: (1) a cease-fire, including safeguards to prevent secret offensive preparations, (2) follow-up discussions on restoring peace, (3) withdrawal of all foreign forces followed by elections throughout Korea, (4) a temporary UN administration of Korea pending election arrangements, and (5) establishment of a four-party body composed of the United States, China, the Soviet Union, and the United Kingdom to settle all "Far Eastern problems." The fifth principle opened the door to discussion of Taiwan and China's UN seat and was domestically unpopular in the United States, but refusal to support the principles would have left the United States open to charges of obstructing the search for peace.

Hoping that China and the Soviet Union would reject the five principles, Truman reluctantly directed U.S. ambassador to the UN Warren Austin to endorse them. The First Committee transmitted a statement of the principles to the Chinese on January 13. The Chinese replied on January 17, rejecting the principles and counterproposing the withdrawal of all foreign troops followed by a four-party conference to be held in China to discuss Korea, the U.S. withdrawal from Taiwan, and other Far Eastern problems.

The United States saw the Chinese reply as an outright rejection of the five principles and pushed for immediate condemnation of China as an aggressor and imposition of sanctions. Others saw the reply as the potential basis for negotiations. The result of the subsequent debate was a UN resolution on February 1, 1951, accusing China of aggression, establishing an Additional Measures Committee to identify potential sanctions, and establishing a Good Offices Committee to carry on the search for a peaceful settlement. With the establishment of the Good Offices Committee, the role of the Cease-Fire Group ended.

Donald W. Boose Jr.

See also

Austin, Warren; Entezam, Nasrollah; Pearson, Lester Bowles; Rau, Sir Benegal Narsing; Truman, Harry S.; United Nations General

Assembly Resolution 377 (V); United Nations Good Offices Committee; Zhou Enlai

References

Finley, Blanche. *The Structure of the United Nations General Assembly: Its Committees, Commissions and Other Organisms, 1946–1973,* Vol. 1. Dobbs Ferry, NY: Oceana, 1977.

Goodrich, Leland Matthew. *Korea: A Study of U.S. Policy in the United Nations.* New York: Council on Foreign Relations, 1956.

Luard, Evan. *A History of the United Nations,* Vol. 1, *The Years of Western Domination, 1945–1955.* London: Macmillan, 1982.

Stueck, William W., Jr. *The Korean War: An International History.* Princeton, NJ: Princeton University Press, 1995.

United Nations. *Yearbook of the United Nations, 1950, 1951, 1952, 1953.* New York: Columbia University Press, 1951, 1952, 1953, 1954.

U.S. Army lieutenant William Millward, a Civil Assistance officer, distributes candy to Korean children at a refugee collection point in western Korea. The command was charged with assisting civilians displaced by the war. (U.S. Army Military History Institute)

United Nations Civil Assistance Command in Korea

Organization responsible for short-term assistance to Korean civilians using U.S. Army funds appropriated by the U.S. Congress under the Civilian Relief in Korea program. Before the war, U.S. aid to Korea had been funneled through the Economic Cooperation Administration (ECA), which continued to operate until April 1951. When hostilities began, the U.S.-led United Nations Command (UNC) began to provide assistance to Korean civilians caught in the combat zone. United Nations (UN) Security Council Resolution S/1657 of July 31, 1950, requested that the Unified Command (the U.S. government acting as UN executive agent in Korea) take responsibility for determining requirements and establishing procedures for the relief and support of Korean civilians. A U.S. presidential directive of September 29, 1950, gave the ECA responsibility for planning the postwar rehabilitation of Korea, while the commander in chief of the UNC (CINCUNC) was responsible for short-term civil assistance. The CINCUNC gave this task to the U.S. Eighth Army Civil Assistance Headquarters, renamed UN Civil Assistance Command in Korea (UNCACK), on January 11, 1951.

UNCACK's initial task was to safeguard the rear areas by preventing disease and unrest through provision of food, medicine, clothing, and other goods to meet immediate civilian requirements. But it eventually took on a range of responsibilities, including providing food to prisoners of war (POWs), resettling civilian internees, assisting veterans, conducting financial and economic coordination, and carrying out short-term rehabilitation and reconstruction projects.

On December 1, 1950, the General Assembly established the UN Korea Reconstruction Agency (UNKRA) to take over the task of long-term relief and rehabilitation. However, the United States was reluctant to allow an independent agency to operate in Korea while military operations were still taking place. Thus, under a December 21, 1951, memorandum of understanding, CINCUNC retained control over economic assistance and relief efforts, with

UNCACK as his oversight agency. All persons from the UN or its specialized agencies serving in Korea (except for members of the UN Commission for the Unification and Rehabilitation of Korea) came under contract to UNKRA and, with the exception of a small UNKRA planning staff, all were seconded to UNCACK.

On July 10, 1952, UNCACK was transferred to a newly organized Korean Communications Zone, which assumed responsibility for all logistic support, civil affairs, and POW control south of the combat zone in Korea. On July 1, 1953, UNCACK was redesignated Korean Civil Assistance Command (KCAC) and was placed directly under the authority of CINCUNC. KCAC retained all UNCACK responsibilities and also supervised a new Armed Forces Assistance to Korea program under which U.S. military supplies and equipment could be diverted to civilian reconstruction projects.

On August 7, 1953, the United States put in place a new postwar civil assistance structure. CINCUNC retained overall responsibility for civil assistance but was assigned an economic advisor with the title of economic coordinator. The Office of the Economic Coordinator administered U.S. bilateral assistance and coordinated the military (KCAC) and international (UNKRA) civil assistance programs. KCAC finally ceased operations in November 1955, when all its duties were assumed by the Office of the Economic Coordinator.

DONALD W. BOOSE JR.

See also

Civilian Internee Issue; Korean Communications Zone; Tasca, Henry Joseph; United Nations Command; United Nations Commission for

886   United Nations Collective Measures Committee

the Unification and Rehabilitation of Korea; United Nations Korean Reconstruction Agency

References

Hermes, Walter G. *U.S. Army in the Korean War: Truce Tent and Fighting Front.* Washington, DC: Office of the Chief of Military History, 1966.

Lyons, Gene M. *Military Policy and Economic Aid: The Korean Case, 1950–1953.* Columbus: Ohio State University Press, 1961.

United Nations. *Report of the United Nations Commission for the Unification and Rehabilitation of Korea.* General Assembly Official Records, Seventh Session, Supplement 14 (A/2181). New York: United Nations, 1952.

United Nations Command. *Civil Assistance and Economic Affairs: Korea, 1 October 1951–30 June 1952, 1 July 1952–30 June 1953, 1 July 1953–30 June 1954, and 1 July 1954–30 June 1955.* Tokyo: United Nations Command, 1952, 1953, 1954, 1955.

———. *Civilian Relief and Economic Aid: Korea, 7 July 1950–30 September 1951.* Tokyo: United Nations Command, 1951.

United Nations Collective Measures Committee

The Collective Measures Committee was established on November 3, 1950, by United Nations (UN) General Assembly Resolution 377D (V), the Uniting for Peace Resolution. This resolution also created a Peace Observation Commission, recommended that each member state maintain forces for service as UN units, and requested that the secretary-general appoint a panel of military experts to advise member states on organizing, training, and equipping those forces. The Collective Measures Committee was to consult with the secretary-general and other member states to identify ways, including the use of armed force, to "maintain and strengthen international peace and security." The committee was also to approve the panel of military experts and receive reports from member states on the forces that they had earmarked for UN service.

João Carlos Muniz of Brazil served as chairman for most of the active life of the committee, which was originally composed of representatives from Australia, Belgium, Brazil, Burma, Canada, Egypt, France, Mexico, the Philippines, Turkey, the United Kingdom, the United States, Venezuela, and Yugoslavia. On February 1, 1951, the General Assembly passed Resolution 498(V) forming the Additional Measures Committee to identify nonmilitary punitive measures against the People's Republic of China (PRC) and the Democratic People's Republic of Korea (DPRK, North Korea). By the terms of the resolution, the Additional Measures Committee was to have the same membership as the Collective Measures Committee, but representatives of Burma and Yugoslavia refused to serve in the new organization.

The Collective Measures Committee met 20 times from March 5, 1951, to August 27, 1954, and made 3 reports to the General Assembly. In its first report of October 1951, it discussed a number of political, economic, financial, and military measures that could be instituted to coordinate the efforts of states responding to aggression. Setting forth a set of "guiding principles," the committee recommended military collective action, an approach similar to that used for the United Nations Command (UNC) in Korea: one nation to provide the leadership as "executive military authority." Other states would provide national contingents under the operational control of the lead nation. The committee's report on national contributions to a UN force revealed that few of the member states that had supported the Uniting for Peace Resolution were actually willing to earmark forces, and none requested advice from the panel of experts, which never became more than a nominal list.

In its second report a year later, the committee made some preliminary observations on the concept of a UN Volunteer Reserve. The General Assembly noted but did not act on the committee's proposals. On August 30, 1954, the committee made its third report, recommending that it should remain available for further study of the issue of actions in support of collective security.

General Assembly Resolution 809(IX) of November 4, 1954, directed the Collective Measures Committee to "remain in a position to pursue further studies . . . to strengthen the capability of the United Nations to maintain peace" and to report as appropriate. In fact, the committee made no more reports after 1954 and ceased to exist in 1992.

DONALD W. BOOSE JR.

See also

United Nations Additional Measures Committee; United Nations Command; United Nations General Assembly Resolution 377 (V)

References

Finley, Blanche. *The Structure of the United Nations General Assembly: Its Committees, Commissions and Other Organisms, 1946–1973,* Vol. 1. Dobbs Ferry, NY: Oceana, 1977.

Russell, Ruth B. *The United Nations and United States Security Policy.* Washington, DC: Brookings Institution, 1968.

Seyersted, Finn. *United Nations Forces in the Law of Peace and War.* Leyden: A. W. Sijthoff, 1966.

Stueck, William W., Jr. *The Korean War: An International History.* Princeton, NJ: Princeton University Press, 1995.

United Nations. *Yearbook of the United Nations, 1950, 1951, 1952, 1953.* New York: Columbia University Press, 1951, 1952, 1953, 1954.

United Nations Command

The United Nations Command (UNC), a U.S.-led multinational force, was established in response to United Nations (UN) Security Council resolutions of June 25 and 27 and July 7, 1950. The first two resolutions condemned the Korean People's Army (KPA, North Korean Army) invasion of the Republic of Korea (ROK, South Korea) as a "breach of the peace" and recommended UN member states assist South Korea in repelling the armed attack and in restoring "international peace and security in the area." While not citing specific provisions of the UN charter, the

United Nations Command (UNC) ground combat personnel look for movement as white phosphorous shells explode in the communist-held area in the background, February 1, 1951. (Naval Historical Center)

resolution reflected the language of Chapter VII, which deals with breaches of the peace and, in Article 39, gives the Security Council the power to make recommendations. By June 30, U.S. president Harry S. Truman had authorized General Douglas MacArthur, commander in chief of the U.S. Far East Command (FEC), to use U.S. forces to assist South Korea, including air and naval strikes in the Democratic People's Republic of Korea (DPRK, North Korea), and had ordered a naval blockade of the Korean coast. The United Kingdom, Australia, Canada, New Zealand, and the Netherlands had also dispatched forces.

The United States, already engaged in Korea and providing substantial forces, was the logical choice to lead the military effort. Accordingly, the July 7 resolution recommended that UN states place their forces under a "unified command under the United States," requested the United States designate the commander, authorized the command to fly the UN flag, and asked the United States to provide reports "as appropriate."

On July 8, President Truman designated General MacArthur commander in chief of UN forces in Korea. On July 14, U.S. Army chief of staff General J. Lawton Collins presented General MacArthur a flag provided by the Security Council that had flown over the UN mission in Palestine. That same day South Korean president Syngman Rhee assigned "command authority" over all South Korean

forces to General MacArthur. On July 24, MacArthur formally established the UNC, issuing UNC General Order No. 1 and raising the UN flag over his Tokyo headquarters. In the course of the war, 15 nations, in addition to the United States and South Korea, contributed military forces to the UNC. These additional nations constituted about 10 percent of the ground, 7 percent of the naval, and 1 percent of the air forces in the UNC. Five other nations contributed medical units. During the war, the position of UNC commander in chief (CINCUNC) was held successively by General MacArthur (from July 8, 1950, to April 11, 1951), Lieutenant General Matthew B. Ridgway (from April 11, 1951, to May 12, 1952), and Lieutenant General Mark W. Clark (from May 12, 1952, to October 7, 1953).

The UNC was, for all practical purposes, a U.S. military command. The U.S. government sought UN approval for major political decisions, such as the determination of war aims, response to the Chinese intervention, civilian relief measures, and the armistice, but it maintained a free hand on operational matters. The chain of command ran from the U.S. president through the U.S. Joint Chiefs of Staff (JCS) to CINCUNC. All communications were transmitted through the army chief of staff, the designated executive agent for FEC and UNC matters. CINCUNC sent his reports through the JCS to the Defense Department. After interagency coordination, the State Department drafted the final version and

UNC Pursuit, September 23–30, 1950

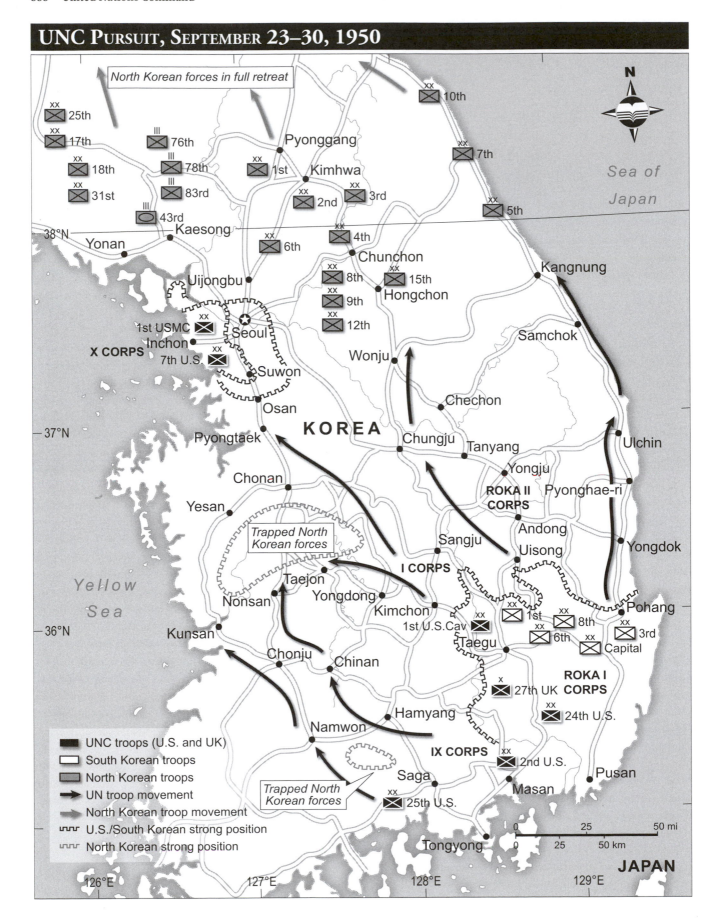

North Korean forces in full retreat

xx 25th
xx 17th
xx 18th
xx 31st
III 76th
III 78th
III 83rd
III 43rd

Pyonggang
xx 1st
Kimhwa
xx 2nd
xx 3rd

10th
xx 7th
xx 5th

Sea of Japan

38°N   Yonan
Kaesong
xx 6th
Uijongbu

xx 4th
Chunchon
xx 8th
xx 15th
Hongchon
xx 9th
xx 12th

Kangnung
Samchok

1st USMC   xx
X CORPS
Inchon
7th U.S.   xx
Seoul
Suwon
Osan

Wonju
Chechon

37°N   Pyongtaek
KOREA
Chungju   Tanyang
Yongju
Ulchin

Chonan
Yesan

Trapped North Korean forces

Sangju
ROKA II CORPS
Andong
Uisong
Pyonghae-ri
Yongdok

Taejon
Yongdong
Nonsan
Kimchon
I CORPS
1st U.S. Cav   xx
Taegu
xx 1st
xx 6th
xx 8th
xx Capital
Pohang
ROKA I CORPS

Yellow Sea

36°N   Kunsan
Chonju
Chinan
x 27th UK
xx 24th U.S.

Hamyang
Namwon
IX CORPS
xx 2nd U.S.
Pusan
Masan

Trapped North Korean forces
Saga
xx 25th U.S.
Tongyong

Legend:
- ■ UNC troops (U.S. and UK)
- □ South Korean troops
- ▨ North Korean troops
- → UN troop movement
- → North Korean troop movement
- ⊔⊔⊔ U.S./South Korean strong position
- ⊔⊔⊔ North Korean strong position

0   25   50 mi
0   25   50 km

JAPAN

126°E   127°E   128°E   129°E

presented it to the UN. The FEC headquarters, with the addition of a British deputy chief of staff in July 1952, served as the UNC headquarters. The United States rejected a proposal for a UN committee to assist CINCUNC but accepted the attachment of a representative of the secretary-general to the UNC headquarters.

Senior military representatives of the participating states had direct access to CINCUNC on major policy matters affecting their forces. Otherwise, they were to carry out CINCUNC's orders, with the right to subsequently protest in case of disagreement. The Committee of Sixteen, consisting of UN diplomatic representatives of the states providing military forces, met weekly in New York to keep the participating states informed of military operations, but it was not a mechanism for advance coordination of those operations.

UNC military operations were not charged to the UN budget. Participating states either paid for their own forces or entered into bilateral agreements with the United States for logistical support. Offers of assistance were communicated to the United States or the UN secretary-general. The United States then negotiated bilateral agreements with each government concerned.

While all operationally effective ships and air units were welcome, the minimum size for ground units was set at battalions of approximately 1,000 soldiers each (Luxembourg's small contingent served as part of the Belgian Battalion). With the exception of British Commonwealth forces, which eventually formed an entire division, incoming UN units were trained and equipped at a reception center in Taegu. These national contingents were fully integrated into the FEC component commands: U.S. Eighth Army, Far East Air Force (FEAF), and Naval Forces Far East, which were designated as UNC component commands while retaining their identity as FEC subordinates.

In the course of the war, the UNC assumed extensive powers and responsibilities for civil relief and control of resources to, in the words of one agreement, "facilitate the conduct of military operations, relieve hardship and contribute to the stabilization of the Korean economy." The UNC never entered into a status-of-forces agreement (SOFA) with South Korea, but it concluded separate agreements on such matters as economic coordination, currency control, and claims settlement as well as various ad hoc arrangements.

When Japan regained sovereignty in 1952, the United States and Japan exchanged notes governing Japanese support of UN actions. This was formalized on February 19, 1954, when Japan, the United States "acting as the Unified Command," and eight of the participating states signed a UNC-Japan SOFA providing for access, transit, and basing rights. Eventually, seven U.S. bases in Japan were designated as UNC bases.

CINCUNC signed the July 1953 Armistice Agreement on behalf of all UNC military forces. The 16 participating nations signed a joint policy statement supporting the armistice and pledging united resistance should there be a renewal of the conflict in Korea. In 1957, the UNC headquarters moved from Tokyo to Korea, leaving a small UNC (Rear) headquarters to coordinate with the Japanese government.

Security Council resolutions pertaining to the UNC contained no termination date. Pending a permanent political settlement restoring "international peace and security," the UNC remains in Korea. The UNC staff is colocated with that of the South Korean/U.S. Combined Forces Command (CFC) in Seoul and is commanded by the same U.S. four-star general who serves concurrently as commander of the CFC and commander of U.S. forces in Korea. The UNC remains responsible for the southern half of the Korean demilitarized zone. Special units assigned to the command include a UNC security force in Panmunjom, a UNC honor guard company in Seoul, the UNC component of the Military Armistice Commission, and liaison detachments from the majority of the original UN participating nations.

DONALD W. BOOSE JR.

See also

Clark, Mark Wayne; Collins, Joseph Lawton; Far East Command; MacArthur, Douglas; Rhee, Syngman; Ridgway, Matthew Bunker; Taejon Agreement; Truman, Harry S.; United Nations Command Ground Forces, Contributions to

References

Bowett, D. W. *United Nations Forces: A Legal Study*. New York: Praeger, 1964.

Chung, Kyung Young. "Status and Future Role of the United Nations Command." *Korean Journal of Security Affairs* 13(1) (June 2008): 129–154.

Hermes, Walter G. *U.S. Army in the Korean War: Truce Tent and Fighting Front*. Washington, DC: Office of the Chief of Military History, 1966.

Higgins, Rosalyn, ed. *United Nations Peacekeeping, 1945–1967: Documents and Commentary*. 4 vols. London: Oxford University Press, 1970.

Schnabel, James F., and Robert J. Watson. *The History of the Joint Chiefs of Staff: The Joint Chiefs of Staff and National Policy*, Vol. 3, *The Korean War*. Wilmington, DE: Michael Glazier, 1979.

Seyersted, Finn. *United Nations Forces in the Law of Peace and War*. Leyden: A. W. Sijthoff, 1966.

United Nations Command, Withdrawal from Seoul

See Chinese Offensive, Third

United Nations Command Air Assets

The United States provided the vast majority of the air arsenal deployed by the United Nations Command (UNC). Other nations made fairly significant contributions, however. At the start of the Korean War, the Republic of Korea Air Force (ROKAF, South Korean Air Force) deployed only 22 liaison and trainer aircraft: Piper Cub L-4 Grasshoppers, Stinson L-5Es (Sentinels), and North American T-6 Texans. Most of these were destroyed in the early

UNC and South Korean Aircraft Specifications

Aircraft	Span	Length	Height	Gross Weight (pounds)	Top Speed (mph)	Range (miles)	Ceiling (feet)
Gloster F.8	37' 2"	44' 7"	13' 0"	15,700	598	600	43,000
Piper L-18	35' 3"	22' 4 1/2"	6' 7"	1,500	110	450	13,500
Tachikawa Ki 55	38' 8 3/4"	26' 3"	11' 11 3/4"	3,660	216	750	26,740

fighting. On July 2, 1950, the United States provided 10 North American F-51s (Mustangs), and in short order ROKAF pilots were flying them in combat and carrying out interdiction and ground support roles.

British Commonwealth nations provided the remainder of other UNC air units. When the war began on June 25, 1950, the 77th Mustang Fighter Squadron of the Royal Australian Air Force was stationed in Japan. By June 29, the squadron and its North American F-51s (Mustangs) were fully operational; they were among the first UNC armed forces to fight in Korea. Australian pilots flew interdiction and ground support missions for the duration of the war, occasionally escorting bombers; and later, in Gloster F.8 (Meteor) jets, they challenged Chinese Mikoyan-Gurevich MiG-15s. In October 1951, Australia sent to Korea its only aircraft carrier, the HMAS *Sydney,* along with the 20th Carrier Air Group: two squadrons of Hawker Sea Furies and one of Fairey Fireflies. The *Sydney* remained in Korean waters until February 1952.

Great Britain sent the carriers HMS *Triumph, Ocean, Glory,* and *Theseus.* From these British pilots flew Sea Fury, Firefly, and Supermarine Seafire aircraft. British pilots also flew spotter aircraft in support of their ground units, and there were three squadrons of Sunderland flying boats for reconnaissance. South Africa sent its South African Air Force Second Squadron, the "Flying Cheetahs." It flew North American F-51s (Mustangs) and later North American F-86 (Sabre) jets.

In addition, other nations provided assistance to the UNC in the form of transport aircraft. Belgium provided several Douglas DC-4 transport aircraft; Greece supplied Flight 13 of the Royal Hellenic Air Force with eight Douglas C-47 Skytrain (also known as the Dakota and the "Gooneybird") aircraft; Canada and Thailand also provided transport aircraft during the war.

UNC land-based aircraft other than those of the United States flew a total of 44,874 sorties, including 15,359 interdiction and 6,063 close air support missions. They also flew 3,025 counterair sorties, during which they shot down three communist aircraft. UNC air forces also flew 6,578 cargo missions and 13,848 other flights. A total of 152 aircraft were lost.

FRANK D. SKIDMORE AND SPENCER C. TUCKER

See also

Aircraft; Australia; Korea, Republic of, Air Force; South Africa, Union of; United Kingdom; United States Air Force; United States Army; United States Marine Corps; United States Navy

References

Bruning, John R. *Crimson Sky: The Air Battle for Korea.* Dulles, VA: Brassey's, 1999.

Field, James A., Jr. *History of United States Naval Operations, Korea.* Washington, DC: U.S. Government Printing Office, 1962.

Futrell, Robert F. *The United States Air Force in Korea, 1950–1953.* Rev. ed. Washington, DC: Office of the Chief of Air Force History, 1983.

Hallion, Richard P. *The Naval Air War in Korea.* Baltimore: Nautical and Aviation Publishing Company of America, 1986.

United Nations Command Ground Forces, Contributions to

Twenty-one nations sent personnel to United Nations Command (UNC) forces in Korea; 16 sent military detachments and 5 sent medical detachments. During the course of the war, the United States provided some 50 percent of the total ground forces; the Republic of Korea (ROK, South Korea), 40 percent; and the remaining United Nations (UN) states, 10 percent.

On July 31, 1953, UNC ground forces' strength was 932,539 personnel: 590,911 from South Korea in both army and marines; 302,483 in the U.S. Army and Marine Corps; and 39,145 from other UN countries.

U.S. strength was in seven army divisions, one marine division, army and corps headquarters, and logistical and support forces. The United Kingdom was the second largest contributor with two brigades of five infantry battalions, two field artillery regiments, and one armored regiment; the United Kingdom also sent a Royal Marine detachment. In July 1953, the United Kingdom had a total of 14,198 personnel in UNC ground forces in Korea. Canada supplied one brigade of three infantry battalions, one artillery regiment, and supporting armored, antitank, and service forces, for a total of 6,146 personnel in July 1953.

Turkey sent a brigade (5,455 men). Australia contributed two infantry battalions (2,282 men), and New Zealand sent an artillery regiment and other supporting troops (1,389). France, then fighting its own war in Indochina, nonetheless supplied an infantry battalion, as did Belgium, Colombia, Ethiopia, Greece, the Netherlands, the Philippines, and Thailand (each with about 1,000 men). Tiny Luxembourg sent a small force that served with the Belgian battalion (a platoon of 44 men in July 1953). India provided a medical detachment (in July 1953, 70 men, down from a high of 333), as did Denmark, Italy (77), Norway (105), and Sweden (154).

SPENCER C. TUCKER

See also

Australia; Belgium; Canada; Casualties; Colombia; Ethiopia; France; Greece; India; Korea, Republic of, Army; Korea, Republic of, Marine Corps; Luxembourg, Grand Duchy of; Netherlands; New Zealand;

Philippines; Thailand; United Kingdom; United States Army; United States Marine Corps

References

Stueck, William W., Jr. *The Korean War: An International History.* Princeton, NJ: Princeton University Press, 1995.

———. *Rethinking the Korean War: A New Diplomatic and Strategic History.* Princeton, NJ: Princeton University Press, 2004.

"United Nations Allies in the Korean War." *Army Information Digest* 8(9) (1953): 57.

United Nations Commission for the Unification and Rehabilitation of Korea

Organization created in accordance with United Nations (UN) General Assembly Resolution 376 (V) of October 7, 1950, the same resolution that authorized the U.S.-led United Nations Command (UNC) to conduct operations north of the 38th Parallel. At the time, the UNC was on the counteroffensive and the United States and its allies in the UN believed that military victory and the reunification of Korea were in sight. The U.S. government, believing that the existing UN Commission on Korea (UNCOK) was inadequate to the task, had pressed the UN to create a new organization to supervise the unification, long-term reconstruction, and security of Korea.

The UN Commission for the Unification and Rehabilitation of Korea (UNCURK) was composed of representatives from Australia, Chile, the Netherlands, Pakistan, the Philippines, Thailand, and Turkey, with the chairmanship rotating monthly. UNCURK assumed UNCOK's functions of encouraging reunification and being available for observation and consultation. It was also charged with representing the UN in bringing about a "unified, independent and democratic government of all Korea" and was to exercise responsibilities regarding relief and rehabilitation as the General Assembly might direct.

Pending the commission's arrival in Korea, an interim committee composed of the same members as UNCURK met at UN headquarters "to consult with and advise the Unified Command" (the U.S. government acting for the UN in Korea). At the committee's first meeting on October 10, 1950, the Australian representative, James Plimsoll, who had been given broad powers by his government, immediately began to exercise a strong influence on the proceedings. UNC forces were already moving into the Democratic People's Republic of Korea (DPRK, North Korea), and Plimsoll was concerned that commander in chief of the UNC (CINCUNC) General Douglas MacArthur might turn the occupied territory over to the government of Syngman Rhee, president of the Republic of Korea (ROK, South Korea), ending any possibility of UNCURK-supervised elections. To forestall such an act, Plimsoll recommended, and the Interim Committee adopted on October 12, a resolution advising CINCUNC to administer the occupied territory pending future UNCURK action.

Rhee reacted strongly, calling the committee's resolution unacceptable and announcing that he was dispatching previously appointed governors to take control of the northern provinces. The United States ultimately sided with the committee, and on October 30, Rhee was persuaded to issue a statement pledging full cooperation with UNCURK. Nonetheless, the relationship had started badly, and UNCURK's view of the Rhee government was further jaundiced by press reports of torture and summary executions by South Korean officials accompanying the UNC into North Korea.

The commission then found itself divided on the key issue of elections in a reunified Korea. Rhee insisted that his appointed governors take over. Some members of the commission favored a British proposal for nationwide elections, while others accepted U.S. arguments that elections should be held only in North Korea. Plimsoll sought a compromise whereby elections would be held initially in North Korea to select an interim legislature. That body would then negotiate with the existing South Korean National Assembly to write a constitution under which nationwide elections would take place.

This issue was still unresolved on November 20, 1950, when the commission held its first meeting in Tokyo. The next day, General Douglas MacArthur welcomed the UNCURK members, encouraged them to establish a good working relationship with the Rhee government, and argued in favor of elections in North Korea only. He was optimistic that military operations would be concluded within a month, but immediately after UNCURK initiated its Korea-based operation, on November 26, the intervention of the People's Republic of China (PRC) ended all hope of early reunification and the election issue became moot.

Although most members of UNCURK believed that the Chinese attack ended their mission, their home governments directed them to stay in Korea. UNCURK left Seoul on January 3, 1951, one day ahead of advancing communist forces, and relocated its operation to Pusan, where it would remain until June 18, 1954.

With its primary mandate of supervising reunification foreclosed, UNCURK turned to its other functions. It formed a committee to study relief and economic issues, a second committee to study the situation in North Korea, and an observation group.

The observation group's first report, issued on December 7, 1950, made use of prisoner of war interrogations, information supplied by the UNC, and field visits to describe the Chinese intervention. Later that month, UNCURK established an ad hoc group to study the refugee issue. Over the years UNCURK observed and reported on the development of representative government in South Korea, UNC administration of areas north of the 38th Parallel, the South Korean government's attitude and actions toward the armistice, and economic and social matters.

While UNCURK continued to observe and report, its influence and impact were limited by declining interest on the part of many of the participating nations, an increasingly strained relationship with the Rhee government, and lack of support from the UN secretary-general and the United States. After the Chinese entered the war, UNCURK attempted to play a role in bringing about an end to hostilities, but its efforts were generally ignored. Instead, the General Assembly established a three-person cease-fire group and, later, a good offices committee to attempt cease-fire negotiations. The existence of these groups undermined UNCURK's authority, as did establishment of the UN Korea Reconstruction Agency (UNKRA) to conduct long-term relief and rehabilitation in Korea. While UNCURK remained the principal UN representative in Korea, its authority over UNKRA was limited.

When the truce talks began in July 1951 with no role for UNCURK, members of the commission began to question its value. UN secretary-general Trygve Lie argued for the abolition of UNCURK and its replacement by a single mediator. U.S. officials considered the commission ineffective and found it inconvenient to have an independent body with no U.S. representation operating in Korea. Preparing for the autumn 1951 session of the UN General Assembly, the State Department planned to recommend that UNCURK be replaced with either a single UN political representative (preferably an American) or a smaller body on which the United States would be represented. In either case, the new UN organization would be based in New York rather than Korea and would have a much narrower mandate than UNCURK. In the end, however, the U.S. delegation simply recommended, and the General Assembly agreed, that discussion of Korean political issues, including the future of UNCURK, be postponed pending the outcome of the truce talks.

UNCURK played its most prominent, and perhaps most useful, role during the South Korean political crisis of 1952. On May 24, 1952, President Rhee declared martial law in Pusan (seat of the South Korean government) and jailed numerous opposition legislators, claiming the existence of a communist conspiracy. His real motivation was to ensure victory in the upcoming election by forcing the National Assembly to pass a constitutional amendment providing for direct presidential election.

UNCURK, led by James Plimsoll and acting in close consultation with the U.S. Embassy and the UNC, called on Rhee to end martial law and release the jailed politicians. When Rhee refused, the commission made its overtures public. The crisis eventually ended in early July when Rhee released most of the prisoners and the South Korean legislators, having been rounded up by Rhee's police and confined in the National Assembly building. The assembly ultimately passed a compromise constitutional amendment, and Rhee was reelected in August.

During the crisis, the U.S. State Department found UNCURK to be a valuable asset. When, at one point, the United States contemplated using UNC forces to take Rhee into custody, they sought UNCURK's views. If carried out, the action would have been triggered by an UNCURK request. Although the U.S. military was never reconciled to UNCURK's presence as the only UN agency in Korea not under CINCUNC control, the U.S. government saw UNCURK as a useful link between the UN and the UNC and a symbol of international interest in Korea.

After the signing of the armistice and after the 1954 Geneva Conference, the issue of UNCURK's future rose once again. With no access to North Korea and little influence on the South Korean government, UNCURK's ability to carry out its mandate was essentially gone. UN secretary-general Dag Hammarskjöld argued for its dissolution, but the United States continued to view the commission as a valuable manifestation of UN involvement in Korea. UNCURK survived, making periodic reports to the General Assembly, until 1973. In that year, following the initiation of dialogue between North and South Korea, UNCURK members concluded that their presence was no longer required and recommended that the commission be dissolved. On November 28, 1973, the General Assembly, expressing the hope that the inter-Korean dialogue would continue "so as to expedite the independent peaceful reunification of the country," dissolved the commission.

DONALD W. BOOSE JR.

See also

Cease-fire Negotiations; Hammarskjöld, Dag; Korea, Democratic People's Republic of, United Nations Command Occupation of; Korea, Republic of, Political Crisis; Lie, Trygve Halvden; MacArthur, Douglas; Plimsoll, James; Rhee, Syngman; United Nations Cease-Fire Group; United Nations Good Offices Committee; United Nations Korean Reconstruction Agency

References

O'Neill, Robert J. *Australia in the Korea War, 1950–1953*. 2 vols. Canberra: Australian War Memorial/Australian Government Publishing Service, 1981, 1985.

Stueck, William W., Jr. *Rethinking the Korean War: A New Diplomatic and Strategic History*. Princeton, NJ: Princeton University Press, 2004.

United Nations. *Report of the United Nations Commission for the Unification and Rehabilitation of Korea*. General Assembly Official Records, Seventh Session, Supplement 14 (A/2181). New York: United Nations, 1952.

———. *Yearbook of the United Nations, 1950, 1951, 1952, 1953*. New York: Columbia University Press, 1951, 1952, 1953, 1954.

U.S. Department of State, Bureau of Public Affairs. *Foreign Relations of the United States, 1950*, Vol. 7, *Korea*. Washington, DC: U.S. Government Printing Office, 1976.

———. *Foreign Relations of the United States, 1951*, Vol. 7, *Korea and China*. Washington, DC: U.S. Government Printing Office, 1983.

———. *Foreign Relations of the United States, 1952–1954*, Vol. 15, *Korea*. Washington, DC: U.S. Government Printing Office, 1984.

United Nations General Assembly Resolution 376 (V)

Event Date: October 7, 1950

United Nations (UN) General Assembly resolution passed on October 7, 1950, that reiterated the UN's chief goal in Korea: the peaceful reunification of the peninsula based upon free and fair elections for the entirety of the Korean Peninsula. In 1947 the UN General Assembly had asserted that the Korean question could not be resolved by outside influence; rather, it called upon Koreans to determine their own political future through elections to be held the following year (General Assembly Resolution [II] 112). However, the General Assembly concluded in 1948 that these elections had been conducted only in the southern part of Korea, meaning that half of the Korean Peninsula had been disenfranchised. The General Assembly's Resolution 376 largely amplified its Resolution [II] 112.

The UN Security Council's approval during June 1950 of forceful action to stop the North Korean invasion of the Republic of Korea (ROK, South Korea) revealed to Moscow that its boycott of the UN over its refusal to seat a representative from the People's Republic of China (PRC) had backfired. On July 27, 1950, the Union of Soviet Socialist Republics (USSR, Soviet Union) notified Secretary-General Trygve Lie that its representative would return to his seat, although the Soviet representative was still absent when Security Council Resolution 85 was passed on July 31. Nevertheless, the Soviets' imminent return to the UN meant that the United States would not be able to further its policy toward Korea using the Security Council.

In June and July 1950 the pressing concern for the United States was to save South Korea from military collapse. As the military tide of the war shifted dramatically following the successful Inchon Landing on September 15 and the breakout of the Eighth Army from the Pusan Perimeter, the question of Korea's future became more important. Nevertheless, the United States, although it had decided to launch a military offensive into the Democratic People's Republic of Korea (DPRK, North Korea) to achieve reunification, deliberately delayed presenting a resolution on Korea's future until United Nations Command (UNC) troops had reached the 38th Parallel. Once that had been achieved, the West could deal with its adversaries from a position of strength.

Prior to the introduction of Resolution 376 in the General Assembly, a British draft suggested that new elections throughout Korea should become the basis for unification and a new government. A U.S. draft, however, which prevailed in the General Assembly vote on its 294th plenary meeting of October 7, 1950, merely called for supplementary elections to be held in North Korea only. This apparent dissent had much to do with British desires to ensure that the U.S. commitments to Europe would not be interrupted or abrogated by events in Korea. Supporting their position, the Americans noted that the government in Seoul already constituted a lawful government, based on free and fair elections held in 1948 in the most populous part of the country. Further, the resolution recommended that "appropriate steps" be taken to ensure stability throughout Korea; that a UN commission overseeing unification should be created; and that UNC troops should evacuate the Korean Peninsula as soon as these goals had been achieved. Finally, the resolution urged that plans be drawn up for humanitarian relief in both North and South Korea and for the economic rehabilitation of Korea.

General Assembly Resolution 376 was followed by Resolution 377, on November 3, 1950, affirming the fact that when the Security Council became paralyzed by dissent among its permanent members, the General Assembly could act in its place. While not mentioning Korea specifically, it clearly addressed the renewed stalemate over the conflict following the return of the Soviet representative to the Security Council.

FRODE LINDGJERDET

See also

Inchon Landing; 38th Parallel, Decision to Cross; United Nations Command; United Nations General Assembly Resolution 377 (V); United Nations Security Council Resolution 85

References

Dvorchak, Robert J. *Battle for Korea: A History of the Korean Conflict*. Cambridge, MA: Da Capo, 2003.

Stueck, William W., Jr. *The Korean War: An International History*. Princeton, NJ: Princeton University Press, 1995.

United Nations General Assembly Resolution 377 (V)
Event Date: November 3, 1950

United Nations (UN) General Assembly Resolution 377 (V) of November 3, 1950, the Uniting for Peace Resolution, was a means whereby the United States and its UN allies, then in a majority, could bypass the UN Security Council. The UN Charter confers on the Security Council primary responsibility for the maintenance of international peace and security. Because each of the five permanent members has veto power, the council can take no action without consensus among those nations. The post–World War II U.S.-Soviet confrontation frequently resulted in Security Council deadlock. Security Council resolutions that established the UN effort to assist the Republic of Korea (ROK, South Korea) were possible only because the Union of Soviet Socialist Republics (USSR, Soviet Union) was boycotting the council at the time. When the Soviet delegate resumed his UN seat in August 1950, further Security Council action on Korea became impossible. This gave impetus to long-standing efforts by the United States and its supporters to use their General Assembly majority to sidestep the Soviet veto.

These efforts came to fruition with the Uniting for Peace Resolution of November 3, 1950. The essence of the resolution was the assertion that the General Assembly could *recommend* that member states take action to maintain international peace and security when deadlock among the five permanent members prevented the Security Council from *directing* action. The resolution also provided for emergency sessions of the Assembly within 24 hours of a request from seven (later nine) Security Council members or a majority of UN members. In addition, Resolution 377 (V) established the Peace Observation Commission and the Collective Measures Committee and called on the member states to earmark and prepare military forces and other resources for use in UN-sponsored collective actions.

U.S. allies in the UN were somewhat reluctant to support the Uniting for Peace Resolution, seeing a potential danger to their own policies in General Assembly majority action and the bypassing of the great-power veto. This was not a problem for the duration of the Korean War, as the Western bloc continued to hold a commanding majority in the General Assembly. Eventually, however, the increasing number of nonaligned nations in the UN shifted the balance.

The first use of the Uniting for Peace procedure came with passage on February 1, 1951, of a General Assembly resolution identifying the People's Republic of China (PRC) as an aggressor in Korea and initiating the consideration of sanctions against China and the Democratic People's Republic of Korea (DPRK, North Korea). In November 1956 the General Assembly met in accordance with the Uniting for Peace procedures to address both the Suez Crisis and the Soviet invasion of Hungary after Franco-British and Soviet Security Council vetoes.

The Peace Observation Commission and Collective Measures Committee did no substantive work after 1954 and have since been abolished. Nothing came of the plan to have member states earmark forces for UN collective action. But the Uniting for Peace process has become a permanent part of UN procedure. Nine of the 10 emergency General Assembly sessions to date have been called in accordance with that policy, and the procedure provided a foundation for subsequent UN peacekeeping operations.

Donald W. Boose Jr.

See also

Cease-fire Negotiations; Soviet Security Council Boycott; 38th Parallel, Decision to Cross; United Nations Collective Measures Committee; United Nations Peace Observation Commission

References

Acheson, Dean. *Present at the Creation: My Years in the State Department.* New York: Norton, 1969.

Bowett, D. W. *United Nations Forces: A Legal Study.* New York: Praeger, 1964.

Luard, Evan. *A History of the United Nations,* Vol. 1, *The Years of Western Domination, 1945–1955.* London: Macmillan, 1982.

Russell, Ruth B. *The United Nations and United States Security Policy.* Washington, DC: Brookings Institution, 1968.

Stueck, William W., Jr. *The Korean War: An International History.* Princeton, NJ: Princeton University Press, 1995.

United Nations. *Yearbook of the United Nations, 1950, 1951, 1952, 1953.* New York: Columbia University Press, 1951, 1952, 1953, 1954.

United Nations General Assembly Resolution 498 (V)

Event Date: February 1, 1951

Entitled "Intervention of the Central People's Government of the People's Republic of China in Korea," United Nations (UN) General Assembly Resolution 498 (V) was passed on February 1, 1951. It demanded that the People's Republic of China (PRC) cease hostilities on the Korean Peninsula and withdraw its forces north of the Yalu River.

By late September 1950 United Nations Command (UNC) troops had reversed the Democratic People's Republic of Korea's (DPRK, North Korea) assault against the Republic of Korea (ROK, South Korea). Despite repeated warnings from the PRC threatening intervention to assist North Korea, UNC commander General Douglas MacArthur was authorized to cross the 38th Parallel—the prewar boundary between North and South Korea—into North Korean territory to achieve forcible reunification of the peninsula. On October 14 Chinese forces began to enter North Korea, and on November 25 they attacked in full force, forcing UNC troops to retreat across the 38th Parallel and indeed beyond it.

On November 16 the U.S. Department of State drafted a Security Council resolution addressing the situation, only to have it blocked by a Soviet veto on November 30. Disagreements now arose over U.S. leadership in Korea, and many noncommunist UN members were wary of the risk of escalation of the fighting beyond the Korean Peninsula. The process of adopting an official UN stance toward the Chinese intervention was delayed by several peace probes and proposals in which India was especially active. To the relief of the United States, Beijing rejected a cease-fire proposal backed by several UN member states.

Finally, on December 14, 1950, the UN General Assembly passed a resolution requesting its president to head a group seeking possible conditions for a cease-fire (General Assembly Resolution 384 [V]). When this failed, initial U.S. proposals for a new resolution condemning the PRC for aggression in Korea met with resistance from its allies Great Britain and Canada. The United States countered by reminding them how the League of Nations had failed to stem Italian and Japanese aggression in the 1930s and how lack of support in Korea would only encourage isolationist sentiments in the United States.

The U.S. State Department now amended its original resolution text, delegating to a UN committee the task of determining whether additional measures would be necessary. Resolution 498 was passed at the General Assembly's 327th plenary meeting on February 1, 1951, with India, Burma, and the communist countries voting against the measure. The resolution expressed regret that the UN Security Council had failed to exercise its responsibility to maintain peace and stability, a reminder of the stalemate following the return of the Soviet representative to the UN after its boycott over the organization's failure to seat the PRC. This led to General Assembly Resolution 376, which affirmed the assembly's power to act on behalf of the Security Council when it was paralyzed by a split among the permanent members.

The resolution's text branded the PRC as an aggressor and called for an immediate Chinese withdrawal. Further, it demanded that all other member states and authorities refrain from supporting the aggressors in the war. The resolution also repeated the request for member states to assist South Korea and the peaceful pursuit of UN goals, previously stated as the unification and reha-bilitation of Korea.

FRODE LINDGJERDET

See also
United Nations Command; United Nations General Assembly Resolution 376 (V)

References
Dvorchak, Robert J. *Battle for Korea: A History of the Korean Conflict.* Cambridge, MA: Da Capo, 2003.

Stueck, William W., Jr. *The Korean War: An International History.* Princeton, NJ: Princeton University Press, 1995.

United Nations Good Offices Committee

The Good Offices Committee was established in response to United Nations (UN) General Assembly resolution 498 (V) of February 1, 1951, which also established the Additional Measures Committee. Both committees represented attempts to deal with intervention in the Korean War by the People's Republic of China (PRC). While the United States pressed for a UN resolution that would brand China an aggressor and impose sanctions, the British Commonwealth nations and a group of Asian and Middle Eastern states opposed actions that might widen the war, and they sought ways to bring hostilities to an end. The February 1, 1951, resolu-tion reflected something of a compromise: it identified China as an aggressor and established the Additional Measures Commit-tee to explore sanctions. But it also called on General Assembly president Nasrollah Entezam of Iran to designate two persons to meet with him to use their "good offices" to "bring about a cessa-tion of hostilities in Korea and the achievement of United Nations objectives in Korea by peaceful means." The Additional Measures Committee was authorized to delay its report on recommended sanctions so long as the Good Offices Committee reported satis-factory progress.

Many UN delegates anticipated that the new committee would have the same membership as the UN Cease-Fire Group estab-lished on December 14, 1950, consisting of Entezam, Lester B. Pearson of Canada, and Sir Benegal N. Rau of India. But Rau's government had voted against the February 1 resolution and Pear-son believed that his ability to communicate with the Chinese had been undermined by his support for the resolution calling China an aggressor. Both declined to serve, and Sven Grafstrom of Swe-den and Luis Padilla Nervo of Mexico agreed to take their places. Since Mexico was already represented on the Additional Measures Committee, Padilla Nervo provided a connection between the two groups.

Although the Chinese immediately condemned the February 1 resolution as null and void, the members of the Good Offices Committee attempted to carry out their mandate. On February 14, Grafstrom tried to persuade the Chinese to establish contact with General Assembly president Entezam, but the Chinese refused to

reply to his overture. The Chinese indicated through various chan-nels that they might be interested in some other approaches, such as a multinational conference, but they would not deal with the Good Offices Committee. The Chinese Fifth (Spring) Offensive of 1951 led to increased U.S. pressure for the imposition of sanc-tions. On May 14, 1951, in the absence of progress by the Good Offices Committee, the Additional Measures Committee proposed economic sanctions against China and the Democratic People's Republic of Korea (DPRK, North Korea).

In June 1951, the members of the Good Offices Committee made a final effort to contact the communist powers but were rebuffed by both the Soviet Union and China. With the beginning of truce talks in July 1951, the committee ended its efforts.

DONALD W. BOOSE JR.

See also
Cease-fire Negotiations; Chinese Offensive, Fifth; Entezam, Nasrollah; Padilla Nervo, Luis; Pearson, Lester Bowles; Rau, Sir Benegal Nars-ing; United Nations Additional Measures Committee; United Nations Cease-Fire Group

References
Finley, Blanche. *The Structure of the United Nations General Assembly: Its Committees, Commissions and Other Organisms, 1946–1973,* Vol. 1. Dobbs Ferry, NY: Oceana, 1977.

Goodrich, Leland Matthew. *Korea: A Study of U.S. Policy in the United Nations.* New York: Council on Foreign Relations, 1956.

Stueck, William W., Jr. *The Korean War: An International History.* Princeton, NJ: Princeton University Press, 1995.

———. *Rethinking the Korean War: A New Diplomatic and Strategic History.* Princeton, NJ: Princeton University Press, 2004.

United Nations. *Yearbook of the United Nations, 1950, 1951, 1952, 1953.* New York: Columbia University Press, 1951, 1952, 1953, 1954.

United Nations Korean Reconstruction Agency

Agency established by United Nations (UN) General Assembly Resolution 410 (V) of December 1, 1950, which also provided for a negotiating committee to arrange for financial and matériel contributions. The General Assembly had already established the UN Commission for the Reunification and Rehabilitation of Korea (UNCURK), the rehabilitation functions of which were to be based on recommendations from the Economic and Social Coun-cil (ECOSOC). ECOSOC recommended a $250 million program administered by an agency separate from UNCURK and headed by an agent-general with broad operational responsibilities who would report to an advisory committee. UNCURK's role was lim-ited to advice on matters relating to Korean political unification, the designation of authorities with which the UN Korea Recon-struction Agency (UNKRA) would deal, and on the timing and location of UNKRA programs. The United States agreed to pro-vide 65 percent of UNKRA funding, while the other UN members contributed 35 percent.

On February 7, 1951, UN secretary-general Trygve Lie appointed an American, J. Donald Kingsley, as UNKRA's first agent-general. Later that month, Kingsley met with commander in chief of the United Nations Command (CINCUNC) General Douglas MacArthur in Tokyo then flew to Pusan to meet with the members of UNCURK. It soon became clear that issues of control and funding would affect UNKRA's activities. The U.S. military was adamant that UNKRA projects not interfere with military operations and that CINCUNC have final authority. UNCURK, however, pushed for an independent program under UN direction. Kingsley accepted UNC primacy, but he believed UNKRA could provide technical assistance and begin planning without affecting military operations and that such activities did not require military supervision.

Issues of control also affected UNKRA funding. The U.S. Congress insisted that CINCUNC have the final say in the use of UNKRA funds, most of which came from U.S. taxpayers. But other UN members were reluctant to contribute to a program controlled by the U.S. military.

Funding never reached adequate levels, but the control issue was finally resolved in CINCUNC's favor by a UNC-UNKRA memorandum of understanding on December 21, 1951. UNKRA was allowed to begin work, with CINCUNC retaining actual control over economic assistance and relief efforts as long as the war continued. A small number of long-range planners operated directly under the agent-general, but all other UNKRA personnel came under the UNC military relief organization: the UN Civil Assistance Command in Korea. In October 1952, rehabilitation efforts of the UNC, UNKRA, and the Republic of Korea (ROK, South Korea) were brought together under a single coordinating committee. Just before the signing of the Armistice Agreement, UNKRA, now under John B. Coulter, former Eighth Army deputy commander for civil affairs, was absorbed into the U.S.-controlled Korea foreign aid program.

When UNKRA was dissolved on August 31, 1960, its projects had been financed by international donations of just over $142 million, of which $92.9 million were provided by the United States. While the agency never developed the kind of program envisioned by its sponsors, UNKRA nonetheless made valuable contributions to the rebuilding of Korean industry, agriculture, fisheries, and community infrastructure as well as the rehabilitation of education, public health, and financial administration.

DONALD W. BOOSE JR.

See also

Coulter, John Breitling; Kingsley, John Donald; Lie, Trygve Halvden; MacArthur, Douglas; United Nations Civil Assistance Command in Korea; United Nations Commission for the Unification and Rehabilitation of Korea

References

Lyons, Gene M. *Military Policy and Economic Aid: The Korean Case, 1950–1953.* Columbus: Ohio State University Press, 1961.
United Nations. *Yearbook of the United Nations, 1950, 1951, 1952, 1953.* New York: Columbia University Press, 1951, 1952, 1953, 1954.
U.S. House of Representatives Committee on Government Operations, Subcommittee on International Operations. *Hearings on Relief and Rehabilitation in Korea.* 83rd Cong., 2nd sess., October 13, 14, and 16, 1953. Washington, DC: U.S. Government Printing Office, 1953.
———. *Relief and Rehabilitation in Korea.* 83rd Cong., 2nd. Sess., July 29, 1954. H. Rept. 2574. Washington, DC: U.S. Government Printing Office, 1954.

United Nations Peace Observation Commission

The Peace Observation Commission was established under the provisions of the Uniting for Peace Resolution: United Nations (UN) General Assembly Resolution 337A (V) of November 3, 1950. The framers of the resolution believed that both the UN Commission on Korea and the UN Special Committee on the Balkans had performed useful work in determining the facts surrounding aggression and threats to peace in Korea and Greece. Accordingly, they included a provision for the establishment of the 14-member Peace Observation Commission to "observe and report on the situation in any area where there exists international tension the continuance of which is likely to endanger the maintenance of international peace and security." The commission could be dispatched by the Security Council, the General Assembly if the Security Council was not exercising its function, or the Interim Committee when the General Assembly was not in session, but it could be sent only into the territory of states that invited or consented to the intrusion. Membership of the commission included representatives of the five permanent members of the Security Council (the People's Republic of China [PRC, Communist China], France, the Soviet Union, the United Kingdom, and the United States) plus nine others. From 1951 to 1955, these were Colombia, Czechoslovakia, India, Iraq, Israel, New Zealand, Pakistan, and Sweden.

The Peace Observation Commission played no role in the Korean War. On December 7, 1951, the General Assembly passed Resolution 508 B (VI) that requested the Peace Observation Commission establish a Balkan subcommission to replace the UN Special Committee on the Balkans. The subcommission was to consist of three to five persons and would have authority to dispatch observers into any area of international tension in the Balkans, so long as the affected states consented. In January 1952, Greece requested an observer mission be sent to its frontier areas. On January 23, 1952, the Peace Observation Commission accordingly formed a subcommission, which subsequently agreed to send observers. Colombia, France, Pakistan, Sweden, and the United States contributed observers, while the United Kingdom provided the principal observer. The observers submitted reports until 1954, when the mission was withdrawn at the request of the Greek government. That same year the Thai government requested the commission send observers to ensure that the fighting in Indochina did not spread to Thailand. The Soviet Union vetoed the proposal, and no action was taken.

In the early 1960s, the United States and the Soviet Union engaged in disarmament talks, including discussion of a UN peace force. The U.S. proposals included a role for the Peace Observation Commission, but the discussions never bore fruit. The Peace Observation Commission never met again after 1963, but it remained in existence with occasional minor changes in membership until it was abolished by a General Assembly decision on September 23, 1983.

DONALD W. BOOSE JR.

See also

United Nations Collective Measures Committee; United Nations General Assembly Resolution 377 (V)

References

Bowett, D. W. *United Nations Forces: A Legal Study.* New York: Praeger, 1964.

Russell, Ruth B. *The United Nations and United States Security Policy.* Washington, DC: Brookings Institution, 1968.

Stueck, William W., Jr., ed. *Korean War in World History.* Lexington: University Press of Kentucky, 2004.

United Nations. *Yearbook of the United Nations, 1950, 1951, 1952, 1953.* New York: Columbia University Press, 1951, 1952, 1953, 1954.

United Nations Sanctions on China
Event Date: May 18, 1951

Economic and trade embargo imposed on the People's Republic of China (PRC) on May 18, 1951, in response to that nation's intervention in the Korean War. United Nations (UN) sanctions against the PRC, championed by the United States, marked the beginning of protracted trade sanctions on the sale of strategic materials to China that sometimes became a source of considerable tension between the United States and its Cold War allies. When the Korean War began on June 25, 1950, officials from the Union of Soviet Socialist Republics (USSR, Soviet Union) had for some time boycotted sessions of the UN over its refusal to grant the PRC a permanent seat on the organization's Security Council. At the time, neither the United States nor most other Western nations—although Britain opened diplomatic relations with communist China in January 1950—recognized the legitimacy of the PRC's government, which had been in power only since October 1949. Instead, a representative of Jiang Jieshi's (Chiang Kai-shek) Guomindang (GMD, Nationalist) government-in-exile on Formosa occupied the permanent Security Council seat reserved for China.

When the PRC intervened in the war in October and November 1950, its absence from the UN assured that there would be no formal setting in which the opposing sides could air their grievances. In the absence of the Soviets, the UN Security Council adopted Resolution 82 on the same day as the North Korean invasion. It labeled the Democratic People's Republic of Korea (DPRK, North Korea) as an aggressor in the conflict, affirmed the legitimacy of the South Korean government under Syngman Rhee, and called for an immediate cessation of hostilities. By July 7, 1950, two additional resolutions had authorized a UN force, under U.S. command, to free the Republic of Korea (ROK, South Korea). The United States and South Korea provided the bulk of the forces, but 15 other UN members also contributed military troops to the UN's efforts.

In late September 1950 UN forces, after driving North Korean troops from the south, expanded their mission by crossing the 38th Parallel boundary dividing North Korea and South Korea, and continued to drive north toward the Yalu River, the border separating North Korea from China. In the midautumn of 1951 the PRC, believing its national interests were threatened by the ever-closer proximity of UN forces, launched a military probe into North Korea against UN troops. Chinese diplomats also sent indirect warnings to the United States that the PRC would not tolerate a U.S. presence in North Korea. When neither the United States nor the United Nations Command (UNC) took either these cautions or the brief incursion seriously and continued the northward advance, in late November the Chinese launched a massive intervention against UN troops. To avoid official hostilities, however, the PRC government labeled its forces "volunteers," thus enabling it to disclaim responsibility for their actions and prevent the further escalation of the crisis.

From late October 1950 the United States launched sustained efforts within the UN forum to condemn the PRC as an aggressor and called for the extension of the UN embargo on North Korea to include the PRC. In December 1950 the United States imposed a total embargo on all U.S. trade with the PRC. Meanwhile, in December 1950 and again in January 1951, the Chinese, whose forces were sweeping down into the south, rejected UN cease-fire proposals. Eventually, on February 1, 1951, the UN Security Council passed Resolution 1, condemning the PRC's entry into the conflict, a move that paved the way for economic sanctions.

After much maneuvering within the UN, including an attempt on several occasions to admit the PRC into the UN, on May 18, 1951, the UN General Assembly voted—without even one dissenting vote—for an embargo on sales of strategically important items to China and North Korea. These included petroleum, atomic energy materials, arms, ammunition, vehicles, airplanes, and other war matériel. It was hoped that such sanctions might persuade the PRC and North Korea to open negotiations for a cease-fire, although in fact hostilities continued for two additional years, until an armistice was concluded on July 27, 1953.

U.S. efforts to force its Cold War allies to observe these sanctions not just during the Korean War but for decades afterward proved internationally contentious. The British government in Hong Kong formally endorsed the sanctions but in practice often turned a blind eye to efforts to evade trade controls, since

Britain's continued control of Hong Kong depended upon Chinese acquiescence, and Hong Kong obtained much of its food and water from China. Other European allies of the United States also resented its continuing efforts throughout the 1950s and 1960s to prevent them from trading with China in materials defined as strategically valuable. Even though enforcement of these sanctions was patchy, they proved economically detrimental to such European-administered Asian outposts as Hong Kong and Macau, and for two decades the sanctions forced Japan to seek economic recovery largely through exports to the United States and other Western nations rather than by expanding trade with China. U.S. diplomats and politicians, meanwhile, often condemned as opportunistic the readiness of their European and Asian allies to trade with China in a wide variety of commodities, when the United States itself maintained a total embargo on all U.S. commercial and financial dealings with China until the end of the 1960s. Historians subsequently suggested that the severity of these economic sanctions impelled China to seek more aid from the Soviet Union than that country's leaders were willing to supply, contributing to the eventual Sino-Soviet split. Historians also argue that at least in part the disastrous policies of the Great Leap Forward of 1959–1962, which helped to precipitate major famine within China, represented a desperate effort to promote rapid internal economic development, because the PRC had only limited opportunities to obtain goods it required on the open international market.

JASON M. SOKIERA AND PRISCILLA ROBERTS

See also

China, People's Republic of; Korea, Democratic People's Republic of, 1945–1953; United Nations Command

References

Jackson, Ian. *The Economic Cold War: America, Britain and East-West Trade, 1948–63*. New York: Palgrave, 2001.

Stueck, William W., Jr., ed. *Korean War in World History*. Lexington: University Press of Kentucky, 2004.

———. *Rethinking the Korean War: A New Diplomatic and Strategic History*. Princeton, NJ: Princeton University Press, 2004.

Zhang Shu Guang. *Economic Cold War: America's Embargo against China and the Sino-Soviet Alliance, 1948–1963*. Washington, DC, and Stanford, CA: Woodrow Wilson Center Press and Stanford University Press, 2001.

United Nations Security Council Resolution 82

Event Date: June 25, 1950

Unanimous resolution passed by the United Nations (UN) Security Council in reaction to the massive invasion of the Republic of Korea (ROK, South Korea) by the armed forces of the Democratic People's Republic of Korea (DPRK, North Korea) on June 25, 1950. In the very early morning hours of Sunday, June 25, 1950, North Korean armed forces invaded South Korea, pushing south across the 38th Parallel and supported by artillery, tanks, and aircraft. Within hours of the unexpected attack, it had become clear that South Korea's meager and poorly armed defenses were no match for the Korean People's Army (KPA, North Korean Army).

The Korean War marked the first true international emergency with which the UN had to deal since its founding five years earlier. It was also the first full-scale conventional war to erupt since World War II. The UN Security Council wasted no time in approving a U.S.-drafted resolution, numbered 82, in reaction to the crisis.

Resolution 82 called for an immediate cessation of hostilities on the Korean Peninsula and an immediate pullback of North Korean forces north of the 38th Parallel. It also called for the formation of an ad hoc UN Commission on Korea, which would monitor the situation on the ground in Korea and report its findings to the Security Council. Finally, it asked all UN members to help in the implementation of the resolution and to refrain from aiding North Korea in its military endeavor.

Resolution 82 passed the Security Council unanimously, with Yugoslavia abstaining. At the time of the vote, the Soviet representative to the UN Security Council was absent, as the Union of Soviet Socialist Republics (USSR, Soviet Union) had decided the previous January to boycott the UN because of its refusal to seat a representative from the newly formed People's Republic of China (PRC). Had the Soviet ambassador to the UN been in attendance, he likely would have vetoed the measure. A veto would have prevented the Security Council from adopting the resolution. Later, the Soviets and Chinese denounced the UN resolution of June 25 and that of June 27, claiming that they were extralegal because one of the five permanent Security Council members was absent. The UN concluded, however, that because the Soviets were absent by their own volition, and that a resolution can be defeated only by an actual and specific veto, the vote and resolution were indeed valid.

The successful resolution of June 25, 1950, was followed quickly by Security Council Resolution 83, passed on June 27, again with an absent Soviet Union. Resolution 83 reinforced the previous resolution but went much farther by recommending that UN member states provide South Korea with whatever assistance "as may be necessary" to repel the North Korean attack. Taken together, the two resolutions formed the basis for international intervention in the Korean War, which would be spearheaded by the United States, working through the soon-to-be-established United Nations Command (UNC).

PAUL G. PIERPAOLI JR.

See also

United Nations and the Korean War; United Nations Security Council Resolution 83

References

Kaufman, Burton I. *The Korean War: Challenges in Crisis, Credibility and Command*. 2nd ed. New York: McGraw-Hill, 1997.

The United Nations Security Council's special Korean crisis session, June 25, 1950. Ernest Gross represented the United States, while John M. Chanf, South Korean ambassador to the United States, attended as a guest. (AP/Wide World Photos)

Stueck, William W., Jr. *The Korean War: An International History.* Princeton, NJ: Princeton University Press, 1995.

United Nations Security Council Resolution 83
Event Date: June 27, 1950

Resolution passed by the United Nations (UN) Security Council on June 27, 1950, recommending that UN member states furnish assistance, to include military assistance, to the Republic of Korea (ROK, South Korea) in repelling the attacking forces of the Democratic People's Republic of Korea (DPRK, North Korea). UN Security Council Resolution 82, passed on June 25, 1950, demanded an immediate cessation of hostilities and a withdrawal of North Korean forces to the 38th Parallel, the de facto border between the two states. Nevertheless, U.S. military advisers, U.S. ambassador to South Korea John J. Muccio, and observers of the UN Commission on Korea (UNCOK) confirmed that the attack continued with unabated force and that there was no sign of a North Korean

withdrawal. The initial invasion wave had included some 89,000 men supported with artillery and tanks, with 23,000 more troops in reserve.

Although South Korean forces were able to hold some places such as Munsan and the Eastern Coast Line, the lack of antitank weapons and heavy artillery forced the Republic of Korea Army (ROKA, South Korean Army) to pull back from these positions on June 27. By the next morning, June 28, North Korean forces had entered the South Korean capital of Seoul.

In New York (July 27 local time), the United States had already drafted a new resolution for the Security Council, Resolution 83. It confirmed the previous resolution, labeling North Korea as the sole aggressor, and demanding as well an immediate cessation of hostilities and an unconditional North Korean withdrawal behind the 38th Parallel. Second, and most important, it called upon UN member states to offer whatever assistance "as may be necessary" to help South Korea repel the attack and restore peace and stability to the peninsula. This essentially empowered the UN and its member states to intervene in the war, with military force, if necessary.

The resolution was passed on the 474th meeting of the Security Council and was made possible by the continuing boycott by the

Union of Soviet Socialist Republics (USSR, Soviet Union). A single negative vote by a permanent Security Council member would have killed the resolution, so the Soviet absence permitted the UN to organize a military effort to repel the North Korean invasion. Nonpermanent member Yugoslavia, hoping for a more neutrally worded resolution, voted against it, while two other nonpermanent members, Egypt and India, both abstained.

By the time the resolution passed, President Harry S. Truman had already ordered naval and air units of the U.S. armed forces to assist South Korea. The previous day, South Korean president Syngman Rhee had put forth a request to the Korea Military Advisory Group (KMAG) for the shipment of 10 F-51 aircraft, 74 howitzers, and 36 75-millimeter antitank guns.

Security Council Resolution 83 was quickly followed by other resolutions, which created the United Nations Command (UNC) and granted the UNC power to deliver civilian aid to South Koreans.

FRODE LINDGJERDET

See also

United Nations Security Council Resolution 82

References

Brune, Lester H., ed. *The Korean War: Handbook of the Literature and Research,* Westport, CT: Greenwood, 1996.
Kaufman, Burton I. *The Korean War: Challenges in Crisis, Credibility and Command.* 2nd ed. New York: McGraw-Hill, 1997.
Lowe, Peter. *The Origins of the Korean War.* New York: Longman, 1997.

United Nations Security Council Resolution 84
Event Date: July 7, 1950

Resolution that granted the United Nations (UN) the authority to establish a United Nations Command (UNC) designed to stop the aggression by the Democratic People's Republic of Korea (DPRK, North Korea) against the Republic of Korea (ROK, South Korea). The resolution also granted the United States the power to lead the UNC and appoint its commander. Resolution 84 essentially codified the UN's military reaction to the Korean War.

Following the North Korean attack on South Korea of June 25, 1950, the UN Security Council passed Resolution 83, demanding a cessation of hostilities and a withdrawal of North Korean forces above the 38th Parallel and calling on UN member states to offer the beleaguered South Korea aid. Meanwhile, President Harry S. Truman had ordered United States air and naval forces to come to the assistance of South Korea. With the loss of South Korea's capital of Seoul on June 28, and the continued rout of the poorly equipped Republic of Korea Army (ROKA, South Korean Army), it became clear that ground forces would be needed to stop and reverse the invasion. For the UN to accomplish this, resolving issues of command and control structure became absolutely imperative.

Addressing this need, the United States prepared a draft of UN Security Council Resolution 84. It repeated the call for assistance to South Korea and took notice of the positive response of numerous UN member states. Furthermore, the resolution placed member state forces under the leadership of the UNC, which would be led by the United States. The resolution also gave the U.S. government the authority to appoint the UNC commander. The final draft also instructed the United States to report on the course of action in Korea to the Security Council. Of added importance was the authorization of the use of the UN flag in the military campaign.

Not surprisingly, many member states, including some U.S. allies, believed that resolution 84 absolved the UN from much responsibility. Other critics addressed the lack of a clear geographic limit of operations in the resolution. The resolution was nevertheless adopted on July 7 at the 476th meeting of the Security Council, with India, Yugoslavia, and Egypt abstaining.

Eventually, 22 nations contributed to the war effort, 16 of them sending ground forces. The first non-Korean soldiers to arrive in Korea were Lieutenant Colonel Charles B. Smith's ad hoc force of 540 men from the 24th U.S. Infantry Division then on occupational duty in Japan. Meanwhile, more U.S. troops began arriving by sea and air at Pusan, on the southeastern tip of the Korean Peninsula, and President Truman tapped General Douglas MacArthur to head the UNC. Resolution 84 was followed by resolution 85, passed on July 31, which addressed the humanitarian needs of the Korean people and instructed the UNC to act as a channel for civilian aid.

FRODE LINDGJERDET

See also

United Nations Command; United Nations Security Council Resolution 83; United Nations Security Council Resolution 85

References

Dvorchak, Robert J. *Battle for Korea: A History of the Korean Conflict.* Cambridge, MA: Da Capo, 2003.
Stueck, William W., Jr. *The Korean War: An International History.* Princeton, NJ: Princeton University Press, 1995.

United Nations Security Council Resolution 85
Event Date: July 31, 1950

United Nations (UN) Security Council Resolution passed on July 31, 1950, that gave the United Nations Command (UNC) the responsibility for the oversight of humanitarian relief aid to the civilian population of the Republic of Korea (ROK, South Korea). The resolution pointed out the extreme hardships brought upon the South Korean people by the forces of the Democratic People's Republic of Korea (DPRK, North Korea) in their invasion of June 25, 1950. This had already inspired several UN agencies, nongovernmental organizations, and individual member states to offer the South Koreans humanitarian assistance. Given the desperate situation on the ground, however, only the resources and clout of the UNC could translate such offers into action.

The members of the Security Council therefore requested, through Resolution 85, a survey of the actual needs of the population and the organization and distribution of aid and assistance on the ground. Further, the UNC was to report back to the Security Council on the measures taken. Also, such UN special agencies as the Economic and Social Council were requested to offer the UNC any assistance that it might need in its aid work. As with its predecessor, Resolution 85 spelled out the unlawfulness of the North Korean attack, although it did not primarily address the issue.

Resolution 85 was adopted unanimously, with Yugoslavia abstaining, on July 31, 1950, at the 479th meeting of the UN Security Council. The Union of Soviet Socialist Republics (USSR, Soviet Union) was still absent because of its UN boycott over the failure to admit the People's Republic of China (PRC) to membership, although it had notified Secretary-General Trygve Lie on July 27 that its representative, Jacob Malik, would soon return to his seat.

FRODE LINDGJERDET

See also
United Nations Command

References
Dvorchak, Robert J. *Battle for Korea: A History of the Korean Conflict.* Cambridge, MA: Da Capo, 2003.
Stueck, William W., Jr. *The Korean War: An International History.* Princeton, NJ: Princeton University Press, 1995.

Private First Class Dwight Exe of the U.S. 5th Cavalry Regiment writes a letter home during a break in action against communist forces, November 15, 1951. (National Archives)

United States, Home Front

In the late 1940s and early 1950s, hysteria over communism gripped the United States. The world was plunged into the Cold War and communism seemed to be on the march across the globe. In 1948, the Soviet Union blockaded Berlin, and the West responded with the Berlin Airlift. In 1949, the United States took the lead in the formation of the North Atlantic Treaty Organization (NATO) to prevent, or at least impede, a Soviet invasion of western Europe. In February 1948, in a Soviet-supported coup, the communists took power in Czechoslovakia; the Soviet Union now completely dominated Eastern Europe. The next year, the communists came to power in China, the most populous nation on earth. Most troubling of all to Americans, in 1949, the U.S. nuclear monopoly ended when the Soviets successfully exploded an atomic bomb.

At home, Congress and politicians sought scapegoats to account for the distressing turn of events overseas. Congressman Richard M. Nixon made a name for himself as a member of the House Un-American Activities Committee (HUAC), which endeavored to root out suspected communists in government. Former State Department official Alger Hiss was found guilty of perjury in 1950, following the most sensational of HUAC investigations. But the person who came to symbolize the Red Scare

more than anyone else was Republican senator Joseph McCarthy. During four years of prominence (1950–1954), McCarthy brazenly leveled unprovable charges of treason against leading figures in government, the military, academia, and entertainment. Many Americans were receptive to such a demagogue, particularly with the advent of the Korean War in June 1950. As a result, hundreds of Americans lost their careers and had their lives sidetracked.

In June 1950, Americans overwhelmingly supported President Harry S. Truman's decision to intervene in Korea. The American people and their leaders in Washington believed that this latest communist aggression, which they saw as inspired by Moscow, had to be met with force. As the summer of 1950 drew on and United Nations (UN) forces continued to retreat and suffer heavy casualties, however, public support began to erode. It had been only five years since the end of World War II, and most Americans were not enthusiastic about the prospects of another protracted war or one that might end in less than total victory. Truman understood these sentiments and declared in his first press conference after the invasion by the Democratic People's Republic of Korea (DPRK, North Korea) of the Republic of Korea (ROK, South Korea), "We are not at war." He preferred to refer to the conflict as a UN "police action." This term repeatedly returned to haunt Truman as U.S. casualties mounted and the stalemate deepened.

American spirits revived briefly as, with General Douglas MacArthur's victory at Inchon in September 1950 and the Eighth

Army's breakout from the Pusan Perimeter, the tide turned in favor of the United Nations Command (UNC). To relieved Americans, it now seemed that the war would indeed be over by Christmas. However, massive intervention in November 1950 by the People's Republic of China (PRC) on behalf of North Korea dashed hopes for a quick, decisive victory.

Americans were now faced with the stark choices of bloody stalemate or escalation at the risk of sparking World War III. Public opinion polls conducted just prior to Christmas 1950 showed that more than 50 percent of Americans believed that World War III had already begun. In December 1950, President Truman sent shockwaves through the nation and the world when he announced that the use of atomic weapons was under "active consideration."

On December 16, 1950, the president declared a national emergency, upsetting the U.S. economy. As the White House moved to accelerate rearmament, inflation soared and shortages began to appear. The economic instability forced the imposition of blanket wage, price, and credit controls in January 1951, to which the U.S. public reacted warily. And as the war wore on, economic controls became more and more unpopular.

Americans, frustrated by the failure to secure victory in Korea, unused to the concept of limited war, and annoyed by continuing economic regimentation, vented their anger against the Truman administration. Public frustration reached a fever pitch when, in April 1951, Truman fired the very popular General Douglas MacArthur, UNC commander. Although many knowledgeable critics applauded the president's decision, Truman's public approval ratings sank dramatically. On his return to the United States, MacArthur received a tumultuous welcome in cities across the country as the public displayed its disdain for Truman and his handling of the war.

The vitriolic firestorm that followed the firing briefly rekindled the "Great Debate" over U.S. foreign policy. In hearings over the firing of the general, Congress debated the choices of escalation or limited war. However, it soon became clear to the press and public that the escalation favored by General MacArthur would probably lead to a wider, bloodier war. Americans thus found themselves stuck in a limited war for limited gains. As the war dragged on month after month in stalemate along the 38th Parallel, the public slowly lost interest and focused instead on living the American Dream at home.

The 1950s were a time of great prosperity in the United States. A growing middle class with money to spend brought to maturation today's consumer society. Suburbs, copying the Levittown pattern of identical houses one after another, sprang up across the United States as affluent whites moved out of urban areas in droves. The GI Bill of Rights, passed during the late stages of World War II, provided a college education and low-cost housing loans to millions of veterans. Television surpassed radio as the most popular medium for entertainment and news. In San Bernardino, California, a small drive-in hamburger stand named McDonald's catered to the needs of an increasingly mobile public. Car ownership grew dramatically throughout the fifties.

Life was not ideal for all, however, as Jim Crow racial segregation in the South, and more subtle bigotry elsewhere, conspired to maintain the status of American blacks as second-class citizens. In Greenwich Village and San Francisco, the Beat counterculture began. Led by such poets and authors as Allen Ginsberg and Jack Kerouac, the Beats decried the conformity and crass commercialism of U.S. society.

In 1952, Americans rejected the Truman administration and its policies by electing Republican Dwight D. Eisenhower, an army war hero, over Democratic opponent Adlai Stevenson. During the presidential campaign, "Ike" had promised: "I shall go to Korea." Even though he enunciated no clear plan of bringing the war to a close, Eisenhower struck a responsive chord in Americans with his promise to attend personally to ending the conflict.

Finally, on July 27, 1953, an armistice was signed that effectively ended the fighting. However, there was little celebrating in the United States. Lieutenant General Mark W. Clark reflected the sentiments of many Americans when he said, "I cannot find it in me to exult in this hour." Korea quickly became the "forgotten war" for an American public eager to get on with other things and forget the bitter stalemate that had cost thousands of U.S. war-related deaths. Sandwiched as it was between the more spectacular World War II and the more divisive Vietnam conflict, Korea would long remain the forgotten war on the American home front.

DUANE L. WESOLICK

See also

Antiwar Sentiment in the United States; Clark, Mark Wayne; Cold War, Origins to 1950; Eisenhower, Dwight David; Eisenhower's Trip to Korea; MacArthur, Douglas; MacArthur Hearings; McCarthy, Joseph Raymond; McCarthyism; National Emergency Declaration; Nixon, Richard Milhous; Police Action; Truman, Harry S.; Truman's Domestic Agenda and the Korean War; Truman's Recall of MacArthur

References

Blair, Clay. *The Forgotten War: America in Korea, 1950–1953*. New York: Times Books, 1987.

Halberstam, David. *The Fifties*. New York: Fawcett Columbine, 1993.

McCullough, David. *Truman*. New York: Simon and Schuster, 1992.

Pierpaoli, Paul G., Jr. *Truman and Korea: The Political Culture of the Early Cold War*. Columbia: University of Missouri Press, 1999.

Reeves, Thomas C. *The Life and Times of Joe McCarthy*. Lanham, MD: Madison Books, 1997.

Rose, Lisle. *The Cold War Comes to Main Street: America in 1950*. Lawrence: University Press of Kansas, 1999.

United States Air Force

The U.S. Air Force (USAF) that entered the Korean War in June 1950 was not the robust high-tech service we know today. Led by Secretary of the Air Force Thomas Finletter (from April 1950 until January 1953) and chief of staff of the air force General Hoyt S. Vandenberg (from April 1948 until July 1953), the newest U.S. military service was not yet three years old when the Democratic

People's Republic of Korea (DPRK, North Korea) launched its invasion of the Republic of Korea (ROK, South Korea) on June 25, 1950. The structure and policies of the mid-1950 USAF were deeply influenced by the experiences of—and the doctrine developed before and during—World War II, as well as the severe military budget cuts of the late 1940s.

The basis for U.S. air strategy in World War II was the Air War Plans Division's AWPD-1 report of August 1941, which became part of the Joint Board of the Army and Navy's war plan presented to President Franklin D. Roosevelt on September 11, 1941. It was written by Colonel Harold L. George, Lieutenant Colonel Kenneth Walker, and Majors Laurence S. Kutter and Haywood S. Hansell, all former instructors at the Air Corps Tactical School. The first real U.S. air power doctrine, AWPD-1 was offensive in nature and called for major increases in pilots and planes. Based on the principles and theories of air power prophets such as American Billy Mitchell and Italian Giulio Douhet, it became the basis for AWPD-42 and the 1942–1945 "Combined Bomber Offensive."

The authors of AWPD-1 believed that big, four-engine bombers—which were, at first, faster than fighters—would always get through to carry the war beyond the battle front and destroy an enemy's ability to make war as well as the will of its people. In late 1942 this doctrine became the basis of daylight precision bombing raids over Europe. There were, however, oversights in the theory. The introduction of high-speed fighters and radar, directed anti-aircraft artillery, and the resolve of civilian populations initially reduced predicted results.

In 1943, doctrine (Army Field Manual 100-20) and policy revisions introduced fighter escort to the equation and made air power a decisive factor in the Allied victory, or so reported the U.S. Strategic Bombing Survey conducted from 1944 to 1945. The survey team seemed to confirm what most airmen already believed when it concluded in its official report that even though some mistakes had been made, "Allied airpower was decisive in Western Europe." It was certainly a key factor in the Allied victory in the Pacific Theater where strategic bombing was considerably more effective. The success of the U.S. Army Air Forces (USAAF) also helped lead to the creation of the USAF in September 1947.

At the end of World War II, the USAAF had 79,000 aircraft and 2.3 million personnel. This quickly shrank during the economizing of the late 1940s, led by congressional pressures to balance the budget. To many civilian leaders, the lesson of World War II was that strategic air assets had delivered the nuclear knockout blow against Japan. As the Cold War evolved, they reasoned that future U.S. military defenses based on strategic nuclear bombers and missile forces would be more effective against the Soviet Union and other potential enemies and cheaper than maintaining "expensive" conventional military forces.

This was a policy with which USAF leadership disagreed. It caused the USAF's first secretary, W. Stuart Symington, to retire in April 1950 and General Vandenberg to describe his charges as a "shoestring air force."

A U.S. Far East Air Force Boeing B-29 Superfortress of the 19th Bomb Group attacks a communist target with 1,000-pound bombs in Korea, August 1951. (U.S. Air Force)

Faced with shrinking funds, one of the most contentious internal U.S. military controversies erupted over whether to build costly supercarriers or a fleet of B-36 intercontinental bombers. Even though Secretary of Defense Louis A. Johnson supported the Convair B-36 (Peacemaker) program and canceled the carrier program, the subsequent "Revolt of the Admirals" and heated congressional hearings significantly delayed B-36 development. While the USAF eventually survived the controversy, the delay meant that it would have to fight the Korean War with the Boeing B-29 (Superfortress) (by now designated a medium bomber) as its primary bomber asset. The Korean War made funds plentiful and the carrier program was restored, thus temporarily ending the controversy within the armed services.

The B-29 was not the only aged USAF aircraft in the early days of the Korean conflict. In spite of Vandenberg's earlier pleas for modern tactical jet aircraft, the USAF flew its earliest missions with World War II propeller-driven North American F-51 (Mustang) and Douglas B-26 (Invader) aircraft. In the first aerial engagements, North American F-82 (Twin Mustang) aircraft shot down the first three communist fighters of the war. Even the primary U.S. jet fighters of the time, the Lockheed F-80 (Shooting Star) and the Republic F-84 (Thunderjet), were not equal to the Mikoyan-Gurevich MiG-15, which the Soviet Union soon supplied in large quantities to its communist allies. Only the subsequent introduction of, and later upgrades to, the North American F-86 (Sabre) allowed the USAF to maintain air superiority during the war.

USAF forces fighting in Korea were designated the Far East Air Force (FEAF). Its personnel and aircraft helped secure the so-called Pusan Perimeter. So effective was the early B-29 bombing campaign that FEAF leaders halted the raids in September because North Korea's nonindustrial state simply provided no more targets.

Early on, USAF assets also obliterated North Korean air forces despite restrictions against flying outside of South Korea. Once pilots could fly over the entire peninsula, they found the long columns of communist troops and supplies to be ideal targets.

During the September Inchon Landing (Operation CHROMITE) and the push north, the USAF provided close air support. Following the massive Chinese military intervention of late November, the USAF helped protect the allied withdrawal. During the stalemate in negotiations between June 1951 and July 1953, the ground war became a holding action while the USAF focused on aerial interdiction, hydroelectric raids, nighttime bombing raids, and air-to-air combat over a sector of northern Korea near the Yalu River known as MiG Alley. Most of the famous air battles and pilots of the war came from the dogfights over this area.

During the war, U.S. air forces maintained air superiority in spite of being markedly outnumbered. Thus, United Nations (UN) ground forces seldom suffered communist air raids. Aerial interdiction was only partially successful, however. A lack of air assets prevented constant pressure on communist supply and communications lines. Limited ground attacks also allowed communist forces to preserve their resources, thus the basic principle of interdiction—forcing the enemy to use up its supplies faster than they can be replenished—was missing from the aerial interdiction equation in Korea.

As the two sides came closer to a cease-fire in 1953, the communists held things up with a demand that all their prisoners of war (POWs) be forcibly repatriated. President Dwight D. Eisenhower then ordered USAF attacks on northern irrigation dams and dikes. These, and the implied threat of air attacks—including nuclear strikes—against targets in Manchuria, may have been factors in the communist decision to accept an armistice agreement.

During the war, the USAF budget and force strength, as well as those of the other services, rose dramatically. The original fiscal year (FY) 1950 USAF authorizations called for 416,000 officers and airmen and $11 billion. In July 1950, the Army and Air Force Authorization Act and the first funding supplement raised these to nearly 550,000 men and $16 billion (24,000 aircraft). By the end of the conflict, USAF forces had grown to 977,593 and its funding to $22.3 billion in FY1952 and $20.7 billion in FY1953. These figures represented roughly half of the entire Pentagon budget in those years.

During most of the war, General Vandenberg, one of the air force's most dedicated and persuasive leaders, served as chief of staff of the air force. In addition, Robert A. Lovett, formerly assistant secretary of war for air from 1941 to 1945, was first Secretary of Defense George C. Marshall's deputy secretary (between September 21, 1950, and September 12, 1951) and then secretary of defense in his own right until January 20, 1953. A longtime proponent of airpower, he and Vandenberg both pushed for a more flexible and multifaceted USAF, one focused on its primary strategic mission of delivering a nuclear strike against the Soviet Union, but one also able to perform numerous conventional strategic, tactical, and airlift missions.

It was mainly because of the efforts of these men that more and better F-86s reached Korea. Even so, during the last two years of the war, only the 4th Fighter Wing and the 51st Fighter Wing with 100 to 125 F-86s were stationed in East Asia to confront 500 to 600 MiG-15s over northern Korea. Add to this a 45 percent mission incapable rate for F-86s, and the Korean aerial combat numbers are nothing short of remarkable. USAF pilots downed 792 MiGs and lost only 78 aircraft—a 10-to-1 ratio. The numbers were the result of superior U.S. pilots (Chinese and North Korean pilots fared much worse than did Russian pilots), many veterans of World War II, and such innovations as additional engine power and the A-1 radar-computed gunsight in the F-86.

Given its track record in Korea, the USAF should have fared well after the war. In relative terms it did. But under President Eisenhower and his secretary of defense Charles E. Wilson (from 1953 to 1957), and Secretary of the Air Force Harold L. Talbott (from 1953 to 1955), the postwar era saw a return to military budget cuts for all services and a focus on the strategic nuclear role of the USAF, which many civilian leaders believed provided the United States with "more bang for the buck." This was part of the New Look defense policy and the resultant doctrine of Massive Retaliation.

Indeed, it was the budget battle between Wilson and the normally congenial Vandenberg that caused the latter to retire in July 1953, to be replaced by General Nathan F. Twining (from 1953 to 1957), later first USAF chair of the Joint Chiefs of Staff. During the remainder of the 1950s, the air force experience was dominated not by the lessons of limited war taught in Korea but by the apparent lessons of Hiroshima and Nagasaki. General Curtis LeMay's Strategic Air Command (SAC) and efforts by all the services to control the development and deployment of intercontinental ballistic missiles dominated military policy and thinking throughout the Eisenhower years.

These policies, while successful in deterring Soviet expansion in Europe and Chinese designs in Asia, lost sight of the need for the United States to project its will into less-developed corners of the world and to fight what Ed Rice has dubbed "Wars of the Third Kind." Thus, many of the important skills developed in and lessons learned during Korea were forgotten by the time the United States entered the war in Southeast Asia. Lost during the Vietnam War were air-to-air combat skills, with the result that until late in the war, aerial combat ratios were 1 to 1. There was a lack of adaptable tactical weapons systems and conventional bombers, as well as a repeat of aerial interdiction mistakes during COMMANDO HUNT. Even so, during the Korea conflict, superior leadership and dedicated and selfless airmen, overcoming numerous hardships and restrictions, proved decisive in the U.S. effort to preserve the sovereignty of South Korea.

WILLIAM HEAD

See also

Aircraft; Eisenhower, Dwight David; Finletter, Thomas Knight; Johnson, Louis Arthur; Lovett, Robert Abercrombie; Marshall, George Catlett; Massive Retaliation; MiG Alley; New Look Defense Policy; Revolt of the Admirals; Twining, Nathan Farragut; Vandenberg, Hoyt Sanford

References

Condit, Doris M. *History of the Office of the Secretary of Defense,* Vol. 2, *The Test of War, 1950–1953.* Washington, DC: Office of the Secretary of Defense, 1988.

Crane, Conrad C. *American Air Power Strategy in Korea, 1950–1953.* Lawrence: University Press of Kansas, 1999.

Futrell, Robert F. *The United States Air Force in Korea, 1950–1953.* Rev. ed. Washington, DC: Office of the Chief of Air Force History, 1983.

Nalty, Bernard C., and Wayne Thompson. *Within Limits: The U.S. Air Force and the Korean War.* Honolulu: University Press of the Pacific, 2005.

Thompson, Wayne. "The Air War over Korea." In *Winged Shield, Wing Sword: A History of the United States Air Force,* edited by Bernard C. Nalty, 3–52. Washington, DC: U.S. Air Force History and Museum Program, 1997.

United States Army

As in all of the U.S. wars, the vast majority of the troops who fought in Korea were U.S. Army soldiers. The U.S. Army's direct involvement in Korea began immediately after the end of World War II. On September 8, 1945, U.S. Army and Army Air Force occupation units began moving into Korea to secure the surrender of Japanese forces south of the 38th Parallel and to preserve law and order in the country. At its peak, U.S. Army forces in Korea reached a pre–Korean War strength of almost 45,000 men. The last occupation troops left on June 29, 1949, but 482 military advisors remained in the form of the Korea Military Advisory Group (KMAG) to the Republic of Korea (ROK, South Korea).

Officially established on July 1, 1949, KMAG assumed the functions of the provisional military advisory teams that had been operating as part of the occupation force since January 1946. Its mission was "to advise the government of the Republic of Korea in the continued development of the Security Forces of that government." As a part of the U.S. Mission in Korea, KMAG was under the control of U.S. ambassador John J. Muccio. In purely military matters, KMAG coordinated directly with the Department of the Army. After the start of the war, KMAG became a subordinate command of the U.S. Eighth Army. KMAG's wartime strength rose to 1,308 men.

The principal U.S. military headquarters responsible for Korea was the Far East Command (FEC) in Tokyo. The FEC was established on January 1, 1947, as one of the worldwide geographical commands created by the National Security Act of 1947. The original intent was for the FEC to be a unified command, consisting of three coequal service component commands and a joint staff drawn from officers of all the services. In its early years, however, the FEC was little more than a continuation of its World War II predecessor, the Southwest Pacific Command. Still commanded by General of the Army Douglas MacArthur, the FEC at the outbreak of the Korean War was essentially managed by an army staff under an army commander.

In addition to being the FEC commander in chief, MacArthur was also supposed to be the commander of the army component, U.S. Army Forces Far East. (This "dual hatting" remains a common command arrangement in unified commands to this day.) That organization, however, existed only on paper. On July 24, 1951, the FEC also became the United Nations Command (UNC). The other service component commands under the FEC were Naval Forces Far East, commanded by Vice Admiral C. Turner Joy, and the Far East Air Force (FEAF), commanded by Lieutenant General George E. Stratemeyer. The FEC finally evolved into a true unified command under its last wartime commander, when Lieutenant General Mark W. Clark finally activated U.S. Army Forces Far East on October 1, 1952.

The U.S. Eighth Army was the primary command and control headquarters for army and all ground combat operations during the Korean War. At the start of the war its headquarters were in Yokohama, Japan. On July 13, 1950, the Eighth Army established its forward headquarters in Taegu, Korea, and Lieutenant General Walton H. Walker assumed command over all army forces on the peninsula. On July 14, 1951, South Korean president Syngman Rhee placed all the ground forces of the Republic of Korea Army (ROKA, South Korean Army) under the command of FEC/UNC. Three days later, the Eighth Army assumed operational control of those forces. The Eighth Army also exercised command over U.S. Marine Corps ground units committed on the peninsula.

When the Eighth Army transferred its headquarters to Korea and was activated as the U.S. Eighth Army in Korea (EUSAK) on July 13, 1950, the lack of an army component headquarters in Japan caused problems in the management of army logistical support. This led to the activation on August 24 of the Japan Logistics Command, headquartered in Yokohama. In October 1952, the Japan Logistics Command was inactivated and its functions absorbed by U.S. Army Forces Far East.

Meanwhile, on July 4, 1950, EUSAK established the Pusan Base Command to manage logistics and support operations in Korea. That organization later was designated the Pusan Logistical Command, and then the 2nd Logistical Command. In July 1952, the Korean Communications Zone (KCOMZ) was established for logistics and territorial operations behind the Eighth Army's rear boundary, which was set at roughly the 38th Parallel. A subordinate command of U.S. Army Forces Far East, KCOMZ absorbed the 2nd Logistical Command in October.

Below the level of the Eighth Army, ground combat operations in Korea were controlled by corps. Usually commanded by a lieutenant general, a corps is a flexible organization, to which divisions and other units can be assigned as needed for specific operations. Throughout the course of the war, divisions operating in Korea were assigned to different corps at different times. I Corps was established in Korea on September 13, 1950, just before the Eighth Army's breakout from the Pusan Perimeter. IX Corps was established on September 23, just after the breakout.

On August 26, X Corps was organized in Japan to command the forces for the Inchon Landing. Initially directly subordinate to the FEC, X Corps remained independent of the Eighth Army for several months after the landing. Many historians have been very critical of this unusual command arrangement. X Corps did not come under the Eighth Army until December 24, 1950. A XVI Corps headquarters was established in Japan in 1951, but that organization never operated in Korea.

The division, commanded by a major general, is normally the largest tactical unit in the U.S. Army. The two basic types of divisions in 1950 were infantry and armored. No armored divisions served in Korea, and the 1st Cavalry Division was an infantry division in all but name. The other army divisions serving in Korea included the regular 2nd, 3rd, 7th, 24th, and 25th Infantry divisions, and the 40th and 45th Infantry divisions mobilized from the California and Oklahoma National Guards, respectively.

The organization of the U.S. divisions was essentially the same as the "triangular" structure of World War II, with some modifications having been made in November 1946. A Korea-era infantry division was a fixed unit, normally consisting of nine infantry battalions, four artillery battalions, a heavy tank battalion, an engineer battalion, an air defense battalion, a medical battalion, a reconnaissance squadron, and various support companies. Its authorized wartime strength was 17,700 soldiers, 141 tanks, and 72 light and medium howitzers.

Between the division headquarters and the battalions, each division had three regiments, intermediate-level headquarters commanded by a colonel. A regiment controlled three infantry battalions, a tank company, a 4.2-inch mortar company, and a medical company. The U.S. Army today no longer uses regiments, which were fixed organizations with unique numerical designations. The command level between the divisions and the battalions is now the brigade, which is only identified by its own number within the division. The brigade has a more flexible structure but is roughly the same size as the Korea-era regiment and is commanded by a colonel.

The divisional artillery, in many divisions in Korea commanded by a brigadier general, was a regimental-size organization that controlled the division's four artillery battalions. The 3 105-mm howitzer battalions had the mission of providing direct support to each of the 3 infantry regiments, and the 155-mm howitzer battalion provided general support fires to the division as a whole. The divisional artillery also controlled the antiaircraft artillery

Wartime Authorization of a Typical Infantry Division

Designation	Number
Divisional Headquarters Company	1
Engineer Battalion	1
Heavy Tank Battalion	1
Medical Battalion	1
Reconnaissance Troop	1
Military Police Company	1
Signal Company	1
Maintenance Company	1
Supply Company	1
Replacement Company	1
Regimental Headquarters Companies*	3
Infantry Battalions*	9
Medium Tank Companies	3
4.2-in Mortar Companies	3
Medical Companies	3
Divisional Artillery Headquarters Battery**	1
105mm Artillery Battalions (DS)	3
155mm Artillery Battalion (GS)	1
Antiaircraft Automatic Weapons Battalion	1
Soldiers	17,700
Tanks	141
Howitzers	72

* Regiments of the 1st Cavalry Division were designated cavalry although they were standard infantry regiments. Their subordinate units were designated cavalry battalions and rifle companies.
** The Divisional Artillery HQ controlled the division's three direct support battalions, one general support battalion, one antiaircraft artillery automatic weapons battalion, and any other nondivisional battalions designated to reinforce the division for a specific operation.

automatic weapons battalion, which often was used in a ground support role.

The battalion, commanded by a lieutenant colonel, has always been the basic tactical unit in the U.S. Army. An infantry battalion of the period had a headquarters company, three rifle companies, and a weapons company. The headquarters company provided the battalion administration, maintenance, and supply functions. The weapons company consisted of an 81-mm mortar platoon, a 75-mm recoilless rifle platoon, and a machine gun platoon with both light and heavy machine guns. An artillery battalion had a headquarters and service battery and three firing batteries. A tank battalion had a headquarters company and three tank companies. The standard infantry battalion strength was 40 officers and 935 enlisted soldiers. An artillery battalion was somewhat smaller, with about 500 soldiers. In cavalry (reconnaissance) units the battalion-level organization is called a squadron. The battalions within a given regiment were numbered sequentially.

The company (battery in the artillery and troop in the cavalry) is the lowest level of command in the U.S. Army. Commanded by a captain, an infantry rifle company in Korea consisted of a company headquarters, three rifle platoons, and a weapons platoon with a 60-mm mortar section and a 57-mm recoilless rifle section. A rifle company had 6 officers and 195 enlisted soldiers. Artillery batteries and tank companies had only about half as many soldiers. A medium tank company had 17 tanks. At the start of the war, an artillery battery consisted of a headquarters section and four howitzer sections. During the course of the war, that increased to six howitzer sections per battery, effectively increasing the divisional artillery strength by 50 percent.

The U.S. Army designates companies, batteries, and troops alphabetically. Under the Korea-era regimental system, all the infantry companies in a regiment were lettered in sequence. The three rifle companies in the 1st Battalion were designated A, B, and C, with Company D being the weapons company. The rifle companies in the 2nd Battalion were E, F, and G, with company H being that weapons company. The headquarters company of each battalion was simply designated HQ Company, 1st Battalion, etc. The rifle platoon, led by a lieutenant, had three rifle squads and a weapons squad. The nine-man rifle squad was led by a sergeant first class squad leader and a sergeant assistant squad leader. The squad's basic firepower consisted of a corporal armed with a Browning Automatic Rifle and six riflemen armed with M-1 rifles. The weapons squad had a light machine gun section and a 2.36-inch rocket launcher (later 3.5-inch rocket launcher) section.

The army also had various separate units and organizations that operated either independently or attached to a division for specific operations. The regimental combat team (RCT) was essentially a reinforced regiment, organized to operate independently of a division. An RCT was formed around an infantry regiment with an attached artillery battalion and, in some cases, additional armor and engineer elements. Often commanded by a brigadier general, most RCTs were ad hoc organizations put together for a specific operation.

The 5th RCT operated at times as part of the 24th and 40th Infantry divisions, and at other times under the direct control of IX or X Corps. Only two battalions of the 29th RCT went to Korea, and both were later integrated into the 25th Infantry Division. The 187th Airborne RCT was officially part of the 11th Airborne Division. As the only airborne unit in Korea, however, it operated most often under the direct control of the Eighth Army. The 187th RCT made the only two airborne assaults of the war. One of the unit's commanders in Korea was William C. Westmoreland, then a brigadier general, who later commanded U.S. forces in Vietnam.

Seven ranger companies also served in Korea. Organized in Korea on October 14, 1950, the Eighth Army Ranger Company was later attached to the 25th Infantry Division. Six other ranger companies, meanwhile, were organized at the Army Infantry School at Fort Benning, Georgia, and trained for Korea. The 1st Ranger Company was assigned to the 2nd Infantry Division; the 2nd Ranger Company was assigned to the 7th Infantry Division; the 3rd Ranger Company was assigned to the 3rd Infantry Division; and the 4th Ranger Company was assigned to the 1st Cavalry Division. When the 5th Ranger Company arrived in Korea, it was assigned to the 25th Infantry Division, and the Eighth Army Ranger Company was inactivated. The last of these units to arrive in Korea was the 8th Ranger Company, which was assigned to the 24th Infantry Division.

Trained in both airborne and special operations, the 117-man ranger companies were the direct successors of the ranger battalions of World War II. They were used primarily as scout and long-range penetration units. All six companies were inactivated by August 1, 1951, and most of their soldiers were reassigned to the 187th Airborne RCT. One of the commanders of the original Eighth Army Ranger Company was Captain John Paul Vann, and one of his sergeants was David Hackworth. Both would become prominent figures in the Vietnam War.

An army unit's authorized strength and its actual strength in the field are always two different things. This was especially true in the first half of 1950, just before the start of the war. Following the post–World War II demobilizations, the U.S. Army's goal had been a combined air and ground strength of 1.5 million troops, backed up by a reserve force capable of mobilizing 4 million within a year. By early 1950, however, the army had shrunk to only 591,487 officers and men organized into 10 divisions, five separate regimental combat teams, and the constabulary force in Germany.

Considering the U.S. nuclear monopoly in the late 1940s, few people in the national leadership saw any requirement for maintaining strong, combat-ready conventional forces. Many believed the army to be obsolete.

With the exception of one division stationed in the Federal Republic of Germany (FRG, West Germany), all of the army's divisions in early 1950 were manned and equipped to no more than two-thirds of their authorized strength. Almost all of its weapons and equipment were of World War II vintage. All four of the divisions (1st Cavalry Division; 7th, 24th, and 25th Infantry divisions) occupying Japan had only two battalions per infantry regiment and two firing batteries per artillery battalion. The divisional antiaircraft artillery battalion had only one battery, and the heavy tank battalion had only one company. Rather than having heavy tanks, this tank company actually was armed with the M-24 Chaffee light tank, which soon proved worthless against the Soviet-made T-34s. The U.S. Army of 1950 was a "hollow force" in every sense of the term.

With the start of the Korean War, the army went through its third crash expansion within the last 40 years. At its peak strength in 1952, the army had 1,596,419 soldiers in the active force, which included mobilized reservists and National Guardsmen. The number of active divisions rose to 20. Eight of those divisions served in Korea, but never more than six at any given time. A total of 80 infantry battalions, 54 field artillery battalions, and 8 tank battalions served in Korea at various times during the war. The army's maximum strength in Korea was never more than 275,000 men.

The crash expansion program could do little to help EUSAK's understrength divisions in the desperate months of August and September 1950. Heavy fighting in those months reduced some American units to half of their authorized strength. The Korean Augmentation to the U.S. Army (KATUSA) program was a stopgap measure designed to keep the U.S. units in action. In theory, KATUSAs were members of the ROKA and were paid by the South

Korean government, but they were trained and equipped by the U.S. Army and assigned to U.S. units. In practice, however, many KATUSAs were little more than schoolboys drafted off the streets.

Many KATUSAs could not speak even a few words of English. Each KATUSA was supposed to be paired with an American soldier in a buddy system. Some divisions, however, grouped their KATUSA soldiers into all-Korean squads. Despite their uneven record of effectiveness from unit to unit, the KATUSAs constituted a significant percentage of many U.S. divisions. At the end of September 1950, the 1st Cavalry Division had 2,961 KATUSAs and 13,859 American troops, and KATUSAs accounted for one-third of the 7th Infantry Division. By late 1952, there were 27,000 Korean augmentation soldiers serving in U.S. Army units. The program was actually retained after the war, and in the mid-1990s there were still some 7,000 KATUSA troops in American units in Korea.

As in every major American war, with the conspicuous exception of Vietnam, a very large percentage—often the majority—of the soldiers who served were reservists or National Guardsmen. In the case of Korea, the United States clearly could not have been successful without them. On July 27, 1950, the U.S. Congress authorized President Harry S. Truman to extend involuntarily for one year all active force enlistments due to terminate prior to July 9, 1952. That, however, was little more than another stopgap measure.

Simultaneously, on June 30, 1950, Congress passed the Selective Service Extension Act of 1950, which authorized the Selective Service System to induct 50,000 men in September. It would be months, however, before those new soldiers could be trained adequately and transported to the war zone.

The army clearly needed an immediate influx of manpower. The Selective Service Extension Act also authorized the president to mobilize, for a period of 21 months, units of the National Guard and units and individual soldiers and officers of the Organized Reserve Corps (ORC). In 1950, the army's pool of trained reservists consisted of 324,761 soldiers in the Army National Guard (ARNG), and 184,015 in the Organized Reserve Corps (ORC). Both groups were categorized as "drilling reservists," citizen-soldiers who—either individually or in units—received pay for participating in regularly scheduled training. The army also had two additional reserve manpower pools, neither of which received training nor pay. Both the 324,602-man Volunteer Reserve and the 91,800-man Inactive Reserve consisted largely of World War II veterans who had not even worn a uniform since their demobilization in 1945 or 1946.

Starting on August 14, 1950, 138,600 National Guard troops were called into federal service with their units. The activated units included eight of the National Guard's 27 divisions. The 40th and 45th Infantry divisions ultimately served in Korea; the 28th and 43rd Infantry divisions were sent to Europe to reinforce NATO; and the 31st, 37th, 44th, and 47th Infantry divisions remained in the United States as training divisions and manpower pools of individual replacements.

The Army Reserve provided a total of 244,300 officers and soldiers during the war. More than 80 percent on the initial 1950 call-up of 197,727 were sent to active army units as individual replacements. Because the most pressing and immediate need was for fillers to flesh out the skeletonized active army units, the majority of those called up from the Army Reserve came from the Volunteer Reserve and Inactive Reserve, rather than from the better-trained units of the Active Reserve. Many of those units were left untouched against the contingency that they would have to be mobilized later to counter any Soviet threats in Europe. In the end, this was the most controversial aspect of the mobilization of the Army Reserve.

Arguably, the Korean War was the driving force that led to the desegregation of the U.S. Army. Although in 1948 President Truman had issued Executive Order 9981 to integrate the armed forces, the actual execution of that order was being carried out at a glacial pace. At the start of the war, the majority of African American soldiers were still assigned to segregated units, in which almost all the senior officers were white. The first major all-black unit in Korea was the 25th Infantry Division's 24th Infantry Regiment. That unit was followed by the 2nd Infantry Division's 3rd Battalion, 9th Infantry Regiment, the 3rd Infantry Division's 3rd Battalion, 15th Infantry Regiment, and the 64th Tank Battalion.

With combat units in Korea desperately short of men, and the pool of qualified African American soldiers growing in Japan, the army soon had no alternative but to start assigning them to previously all-white units. This started happening in early 1951 as an expediency measure. Later that year, FEC commander in chief General Matthew B. Ridgway finally ordered the immediate integration of all combat units in Korea.

The 24th Infantry Regiment was inactivated on October 1, and its soldiers were reassigned among other Eighth Army units. That started a ripple effect throughout the army, and by July 1953, about 90 percent of the army's black soldiers were in integrated units. Strength levels of black soldiers and officers in Army Forces, Far East (including Japan and other areas outside of Korea) reached 51,700 men.

While the Korean War was a watershed for the integration of African Americans, the integration of women into the army remained many years in the future. In 1950, all women in the army were assigned either to the Army Nurse Corps (ANC) or to the Women's Army Corps (WAC). For most of the war, WACs were not permitted to serve in Korea itself. They served at FEC headquarters in Japan, and in late 1952, about 10 female officers and soldiers did serve in Korea in administrative positions. By 1952, WAC strength armywide was about 10,000 women.

Army nurses did serve in Korea. A contingent of 57 army nurses landed at Pusan as early as July 5, 1950, and many served in Mobile Army Surgical Hospitals (MASHs) directly behind the front lines. By the end of the war, more than 540 Army nurses had served in Korea.

Between June 25, 1950, and July 27, 1953, 2,834,000 U.S. Army soldiers served in Korea. A total of 27,731 died as the result of hostile action; 2,125 died from other causes; and 77,596 were wounded in action. The majority of the 8,177 Americans listed as missing in action were U.S. Army soldiers.

DAVID T. ZABECKI

See also

African Americans and the Korean War; Clark, Mark Wayne; Eighth Army, U.S.; Executive Order 9981; Far East Command; Japan Logistical Command; Joy, Charles Turner; Korea Military Advisory Group; Korean Augmentation to the United States Army; MacArthur, Douglas; Mobile Army Surgical Hospital; Muccio, John Joseph; National Security Act; Rhee, Syngman; Ridgway, Matthew Bunker; 2nd Logistical Command; Stratemeyer, George Edward; X Corps; Truman, Harry S.; Walker, Walton Harris; Women in the Military during the Korean War

References

Appleman, Roy E. *United States Army in Korea: South to the Naktong, North to the Yalu.* Washington, DC: Office of the Chief of Military History, 1961.

Boose, Donald. *U.S. Army Forces in the Korean War, 1950–1953.* Oxford, UK: Osprey, 2005.

Collins, J. Lawton. *War in Peacetime: The History and Lessons of Korea.* Boston: Houghton Mifflin, 1969.

Donnelly, William M. *Under Army Orders: The Army National Guard during the Korean War.* College Station: Texas A&M University Press, 2001.

Hackworth, David, and Julie Sherman. *About Face: The Odyssey of an American Warrior.* New York: Simon and Schuster, 1989.

House, Jonathan M. *Toward Combined Arms Warfare: A Survey of 20-Century Tactics, Doctrine, and Organization.* Fort Leavenworth, KS: U.S. Army Command and General Staff College, 1984.

Schnabel, James F. *United States Army in the Korean War: Policy and Direction, the First Year.* Washington, DC: Office of the Chief of Military History, Department of the Army, 1972.

Stuckey, John D., and Joseph H. Pistorious. *Mobilization of the Army National Guard and Army Reserve: Historical Perspective and the Vietnam War.* Carlisle Barracks, PA: U.S. Army War College, 1984.

United States Army Engineers

The U.S. Army engineers carried out normal military engineering roles in the Korean War, and—as in past wars—they also fought in battles. Army engineers underwent a 14-week course at Fort Belvoir, Virginia. Engineers spent 6 weeks in basic infantry training and then 8 weeks learning specific military engineering skills, such as mine laying, bridge building, obstacle construction and demolition, and assault river crossings.

Army engineers were crucial to the United Nations Command (UNC) effort in the Korean War. They were involved in a cycle of building, fighting, destroying, and rebuilding. Engineers ensured the continuation of supply deliveries and communications. They also inhibited communist military movements and provided critical combat support.

When the Korean People's Army (KPA, North Korean Army) invaded the Republic of Korea (ROK, South Korea), U.S. officers from the Far East Command (FEC) headquarters traveled to Korea

Men of the 8th Engineer Battalion, 1st Infantry Division, attempt to strengthen a weakened bridge near Yangzi, Korea, to prevent its collapse until a tank retriever can arrive and remove an M-4 Sherman tank. (Department of Defense)

to evaluate the need for engineers. Taking note of the mountainous terrain and primitive nature of existing roads, ports, airfields, and railroads, they recognized the urgent need for army engineers to establish UNC supply routes as well as to create roadblocks and minefields to stop the KPA advance. Engineers soon were playing a key role in the UNC military effort.

Army engineers were assigned to infantry battalions and regiments or formed combat engineer battalions as part of infantry divisions. Special engineer units included topographical and petroleum engineers. The 3rd Engineer (Combat) Battalion of the 24th Infantry Division was the first group of engineers in the war zone, arriving at Pusan on July 5, 1950. It faced a staggering number of tasks, including normal engineer duties, assisting allied troop movement, and impeding communist forces. When needed, engineers halted their construction or demolition duties to fight. Conducting reconnaissance as well as fixing roads and bridges, engineers were also the last soldiers across the Kum River in July 1950.

During the summer of 1950, engineers defended strategic cities and sites to ensure the flow of UNC supplies. During the Inchon Landing beginning on September 15, 1950, engineers moved cargo, and, as allied troops moved north from the Pusan Perimeter, engineers helped them cross the Naktong River. Engineers used assault boats to transport troops and equipment, including tanks, while under KPA fire. With the help of Korean civilians, army engineers also helped bridge the Kum River.

When, at the end of November 1950, UNC forces withdrew southward in the face of Chinese intervention, engineers helped defend the allied perimeter. They kept routes open for retreating forces, demolished the bridges they had built earlier, and destroyed military supplies that might fall into communist hands. They also erected obstacles across roads to slow the communist advance.

In December 1950, engineers helped evacuate troops and refugees from the North Korean port of Hungnam. When the Chinese opened an offensive on New Year's Day 1951, engineers quickly built bridges for the UNC infantry to advance. Creating roads across mountains and rice paddies, engineers had to deal with frozen ground and had to clear snowfall to keep roads open. Then the spring thaw produced muddy roads and flooded streams that hindered supply deliveries. The army flood prediction service warned about the effects of torrential rains in the mountains, and engineers attempted to prevent flood debris from destroying bridges.

During the UNC spring 1951 offensive, engineers rebuilt bridges and roads that they had destroyed in the previous winter's retreat. They also cleared new paths through mountainous areas. This led the 3rd Engineers to embrace the slogan, "Where danger goes dynamite makes the way." Knowing the UNC advance depended on a reliable road network, engineers often worked under communist fire. Engineers improvised both materials and technology, such as using trams to move tons of supplies up steep grades.

In February 1951, the U.S. Army established the Engineer School, Korean Army. There U.S. soldiers taught combat engineering skills to the South Koreans. Some army engineers were also assigned to air force aviation engineer units because of a shortage of qualified aviation engineers. Known as Special Category Army with Air Force, they helped repair and improve airfields. During the war, three army engineers earned the Medal of Honor. Following the July 1953 Armistice Agreement, army engineers helped with Operation GLORY, building shelters and buildings for the exchange of war dead.

ELIZABETH D. SCHAFER

See also

Graves Registration; Hungnam Evacuation; Inchon Landing; Pusan Perimeter and Breakout; Scorched Earth Policy; United States Army

References

Armstrong, Frank H., ed. *The 1st Cavalry Division and Their 8 Engineers in Korea.* South Burlington, VT: Bull Run, 1997.

Boose, Donald. *U.S. Army Forces in the Korean War, 1950–1953.* Oxford, UK: Osprey, 2005.

Farquhar, William R., and Henry A. Jeffers. *Bridging the Imjin.* Fort Belvoir, VA: U.S. Army Corps of Engineers, 1989.

Huston, James A. *Guns and Butter, Powder and Rice: U.S. Army Logistics in the Korean War.* Selinsgrove, PA: Susquehanna University Press, 1989.

Hyzer, Peter C. "Third Engineers in Korea, July–October 1950." *Military Engineer* 43(292) (1951): 101–107.

———. "Third Engineers in Korea, Part II, November 1950–February 1951." *Military Engineer* 44(300) (1952): 252–259.

———. "Third Engineers in Korea, Part III, March–April 1951." *Military Engineer* 44(301) (1952): 356–361.

Mapp, Thomas H. "Engineer Training for Koreans." *Army Information Digest* 7 (1952): 9–16.

Strong, Paschal N. "Army Engineers in Korea." *Military Engineer* 44 (1952): 405–410.

Westover, John G. *Combat Support in Korea.* Washington, DC: Combat Forces Press, 1955.

United States Army Military Police

U.S. Army Military Police (MP) provide security, riot control, and law enforcement in both peace and war. In September 1941, the Corps of Military Police became a separate branch of the army, and during World War II, 209,250 officers and men served as military police, the largest police force in modern history.

Most military police units were demobilized with other army formations after World War II, although some MPs were stationed overseas with U.S. troops. In 1947, the MP Corps numbered 2,078 officers and 19,630 enlisted men. On July 2, 1950, the 24th MP Company moved to Korea from Japan and over the next weeks other MP companies followed, including the African American 512th, which was responsible for port security in Pusan and helped keep the main United Nations Command (UNC) supply route north open.

In Korea, MPs pursued four primary missions: controlling and screening refugees, monitoring traffic, guarding prisoners of war (POWs), and providing security, especially behind friendly lines. Keeping roads open for UNC supplies and troop movements was a major job. MPs apprehended and escorted stragglers to their units; they also provided railroad security, supervised the Korean Security Guard Company that patrolled a vital gasoline pipeline, and used trained military dogs for contraband searches. MPs monitored traffic through crucial mountain passes, road junctions, and security checkpoints, detaining suspicious individuals for questioning. They patrolled with motor vehicles, created road maps, and reported on current conditions. They also investigated abandoned dwellings searching for infiltrators.

MPs also participated in combat. An MP company was assigned to every army division, and these often provided headquarters security against attack. MPs also routinely fought communist guerrillas operating behind UNC lines. Because they were frequently in isolated locations, MPs found themselves targets for communist attacks. Often the last to leave areas after UNC troops withdrew, MPs occasionally fought advancing communist forces as infantry.

In October 1951, the 8137th MP Group was established on Koje-do off the coast of southern Korea, consisting of three MP battalions and four companies, to guard approximately 160,000 communist POWs and civilian internees. Despite being reinforced by another MP battalion, this MP group endured a POW riot in May 1952, during which the camp commander, Brigadier General Francis T. Dodd, was captured.

MPs provided security during the armistice talks. Since the signing of the Armistice Agreement in July 1953, MPs have helped monitor the demilitarized zone near the 38th Parallel. A total of 42,000 men served in the MP at the peak of the Korean War, and 54 military policemen were killed and 151 wounded in the conflict.

Today the U.S. Army Military Police School is located at Fort McClellan, Alabama. It instructs thousands of army, air force, navy, marine, and civilian personnel annually.

Elizabeth D. Schafer

See also

African Americans and the Korean War; Dodd-Colson Prisoner of War Incident; Koje-do Prisoner of War Uprising; Prisoner of War Administration, United Nations Command; Refugees; Special Operations; United States Army

References

Berryman, Eric J., and William C. Truckey, comps. and eds. *Soldiers of the Gauntlet: Memories of the 720th Military Police Battalion, United States Army, 1942–1992*. Largo, FL: 720th Military Police Association, 1995.

Boose, Donald. *U.S. Army Forces in the Korean War, 1950–1953*. Oxford, UK: Osprey, 2005.

History of the Military Police Corps. Fort McClellan, AL: U.S. Army Military Police School, 1987.

History of the Provost Marshal Section Far East Command, 1 Jan 1950 through 31 Oct 1950. U.S. Army Military Police Board Report. Fort McClellan, AL: n.p., 1951.

Westover, John G. *Combat Support in Korea*. Washington, DC: Combat Forces Press, 1955.

Wright, Robert K., Jr., comp. *Military Police*. Washington, DC: U.S. Army Center of Military History, 1992.

United States Army Rangers

The term "rangers" connotes small, highly trained elite units executing raids, patrols, or other operations behind enemy lines. The term also elicits images of intense esprit de corps and proficiency in unconventional warfare; it originated in the colonial period of U.S. history when special troops "ranged" between frontier posts. During the Korean War, senior commanders often misunderstood ranger capabilities and limitations, which frequently resulted in misuse of ranger units.

When the Korean People's Army (KPA, North Korean Army) crossed the 38th Parallel in June 1950, it employed several irregular units to infiltrate the Republic of Korea (ROK, South Korea) to seize specific objectives. U.S. commanders soon realized that Korea's rugged, mountainous terrain offered the perfect conditions for infiltrating small-unit raiders. U.S. Army chief of staff General J. Lawton Collins recommended forming a special company to be attached to each division for reconnaissance and limited attacks behind communist lines. He proposed that each company consist of a small headquarters section and three rifle platoons of three squads each. On September 29, 1950, Colonel John G. Van Houton activated the Ranger Training Center (Airborne) at Fort Benning, Georgia. Calls

for volunteers went to the 101st and 82nd Airborne divisions, as regulations required volunteers to be airborne qualified.

On October 2, the first six-week training cycle began, concentrating on methods of small-unit raids, forced marches, land navigation, demolitions, and directing artillery and tactical air support. The 1st through 4th Ranger Infantry companies (Airborne) graduated on November 13, with the 1st, 2nd, and 4th receiving orders for immediate movement to Korea. The 3rd remained at Fort Benning to assist with the second training cycle, which increased to eight weeks, followed by four weeks of cold-weather and mountain-warfare training at Camp Carson, Colorado. The 2nd Company, initially designated the 4th, was an all-black unit. As the first six ranger companies arrived in Korea, the U.S. Eighth Army did not assign all companies to specific divisions. For example, the 4th Ranger Company remained a floater and served with the 187th Regimental Combat Team (Airborne), the 1st Marine Division, and U.S. IX Corps.

A single U.S. ranger company from Japan engaged in several combat actions before the arrival of the Fort Benning companies. The 8213th Ranger Company, activated at Camp Drake, Japan, on August 25, 1950, consisted of airborne-qualified volunteers from several combat units stationed in Japan. The 8213th served with IX Corps, the Turkish Brigade, and the 25th Infantry Division until its deactivation in March 1951. The 8213th, as part of Task Force Dolvin (commanded by Lieutenant Colonel Welborn G. Dolvin), spearheaded the 25th Infantry Division's drive toward the Yalu River in November 1950. As the northernmost unit of the division, the rangers bore the brunt of the attacks by the Chinese People's Volunteer Army (CPVA) in bloody hand-to-hand combat. Of the 85 rangers who occupied defensive positions on the night of November 25–26, only 21 survived. After reorganizing with new personnel, the company joined in the recapture of Seoul in February 1951.

Periodically remaining in reserve to lead counterattacks, ranger companies generally fought as regular infantry. Company commanders with the rank of only captain sometimes faced insurmountable problems coordinating operational support with divisional staffs. Often misused by parent divisions and lacking adequate logistical support, some ranger units suffered casualty rates of 90 percent. Replacements were usually available, however, both from the United States and from volunteers from their parent units in Korea.

Occasionally the Eighth Army appropriately employed the distinctive combat capabilities of the rangers. On March 23, 1951, the 2nd and 4th Ranger companies were attached to the 187th Regimental Combat Team (RCT) and executed a parachute assault near Munsan-ni. As part of the 187th's mission to cut off retreating Chinese troops, the rangers struck southwest of the drop zones and, with minimal casualties, captured the town of Munsan-ni.

On April 7, the 4th Ranger Company was released from the 187th RCT; IX Corps commander Lieutenant General William M. Hoge planned to use the company to capture the Hwachon

Reservoir to prevent CPVA forces from flooding the Pukhan (North Han) River Valley to impede the 1st Cavalry Division's advance north along Route 17. Hoge believed the specially trained rangers were ideal to seize the dam in a small raid and put the floodgates out of commission. Hoge attached the 4th Ranger Company to the 1st Cavalry Division, but the division commander was not aware of the raid concept and assigned the 7th Cavalry Regiment to disable the floodgates. On April 8, he attached the rangers to the 2nd Battalion, 7th Cavalry, tasked to attack the dam.

Early in the afternoon of April 9, the 7th Cavalry launched its attack, but rugged terrain and heavy enemy resistance stalled the advance. Steep hills and ridgelines placed the objective outside the range of divisional artillery. Finally, a single 155-mm howitzer moved into range of the dam but provided very little support from its maximum range. Heavy Chinese mortar and interlocking machine gun fires completely halted the attack.

On April 10, CPVA forces repulsed a second attack; Hoge then ordered a determined assault by the entire 7th Cavalry Regiment. The next day the rangers and the 2nd Battalion, augmented by heavy weapons and supported by other regimental units, moved forward to attack the dam. Divisional artillery batteries displaced forward to support the offensive. Rain, sleet, and snow added to the misery of the advancing U.S. troops.

As the day wore on, the 7th Regiment commander made an attempt to utilize the rangers as Hoge envisioned. Combat engineers brought forward nine assault boats, and two platoons of rangers embarked to cross the reservoir to disable the floodgates. Under cover of darkness and poor weather conditions, both boats crossed undetected, but intense small arms fire halted the rangers on the banks of the reservoir.

After daylight, part of the assault force turned back to the south shore. The remaining rangers were unable to advance and expended most of their ammunition beating back Chinese counterattacks. An infantry company crossed in additional boats to reinforce the rangers, but by midafternoon only one platoon managed to reach them. The Chinese continued to move in more troops and halted the 7th Cavalry advance. All the rangers withdrew from the high ground they occupied to join the supporting company along the beach of the reservoir. After dark both companies returned to the south shore, and the Chinese made no strong attempt to stop the evacuation.

Lack of planning, poor coordination, lack of boats and motors, and insufficient fire support doomed any chance of success for the dam attacks. Ironically, flooding did not become a problem because of the low water level in the reservoir.

In July 1951, the U.S. Army directed the deactivation of all ranger companies in Korea. The companies continued to depend on erratic support from their parent divisions and were constantly misused. Additionally, the war had become static, preventing non-Asians from operating undetected behind communist lines.

Most airborne-qualified rangers joined the 187th RCT, while the others transferred to infantry companies. The Joint Advisory Commission, Korea, a cover name for the Central Intelligence Agency (CIA), recruited a few airborne-qualified rangers into the 8227th Army Unit (Special Activities Group), where the men participated in clandestine operations along the North Korean coast. By October 1951, all ranger companies in Korea had disbanded.

After the ranger companies disbanded, army planners realized the need for troops capable of mounting ranger operations. On October 2, 1951, the Ranger Department replaced the Ranger Training Command at Fort Benning, with the mission of training junior officers and noncommissioned officers who would return to their regular infantry units. These specially trained personnel were then expected to pass on their ranger skills to other soldiers, instilling élan and determination to all infantry units.

STANLEY S. McGOWEN

See also

Collins, Joseph Lawton; Hoge, William Morris; Special Operations; United States Army

References

Appleman, Roy E. *Disaster in Korea: The Chinese Confront MacArthur.* College Station: Texas A&M University Press, 1989.

Blair, Clay. *The Forgotten War: America in Korea, 1950–1953.* New York: Times Books, 1987.

Boose, Donald. *U.S. Army Forces in the Korean War, 1950–1953.* Oxford, UK: Osprey, 2005.

Mossman, Billy C. *United States Army in the Korean War: Ebb and Flow, November 1950–July 1951.* Washington, DC: U.S. Army Center of Military History, 1990.

Rottman, Gordon L. *U.S. Army Rangers & LRRP Units 1942–87.* 1987; reprint, London: Osprey, 1997.

United States Army Signal Corps

Military communications organization. Authorized by Congress in 1863, the U.S. Army Signal Corps played a vital role in the Korean War. In June 1950, the Army Reorganization Act stripped the Signal Corps of its combat status gained in 1920 and made it an army service branch. Major General Spencer B. Akin, the army's chief signal officer, had served on General Douglas MacArthur's staff during World War II. He retired in May 1951 and was succeeded by Major General George I. Back, who served through the remainder of the war.

When the Korean War began in June 1950, there were 48,500 personnel in the Signal Corps. Reserve officers and units were called to service, and the first signal personnel arrived in Korea in August and September 1950. A shortage of skilled cryptographers, however, delayed the receipt and interpretation of messages.

Because of post–World War II budget cuts, communications were limited by obsolete equipment and untrained personnel. This affected combat performance and troop movement early in the war. Signal Corps personnel attempted to maintain

A U.S. Army corporal with the 4th Signal Battalion works to restore telephone communication lines between Tanyang and Chechon during the Korean War. (U.S. Army Military History Institute)

communications during offensives and withdrawals, advancing or evacuating equipment as required.

Korean War signal soldiers benefited from such technological advances as radar and frequency-modulated (FM) radios. Signalmen soon realized, however, that World War II methods and equipment were not entirely suited to Korea. Extremes of climate and temperatures and rugged, mountainous terrain challenged signal operators and their equipment. Working in open, unprotected areas, members of the Signal Corps often fought communist forces to save their lives as well as protect their communications equipment. Shortages of polyethylene insulation and nylon to cover wires, synthetic manganese dioxide for batteries, and quartz crystals for radios led to creative solutions for unique situations.

During the Korean War, the Signal Corps employed such new equipment as the easier-to-transport tactical radioteletype AN/ GRC-26. Lighter field wire with improved audio transmission capabilities was also introduced, as was an improved ground radar to locate mortars. Transistorized equipment replaced vacuum-tube equipment. Signal Corps engineering laboratories at Fort Monmouth, New Jersey, produced a variety of more compact, efficient, faster, and powerful communications equipment.

The Mukden cable, buried more than three feet beneath the main highway that ran the length of the peninsula, was the primary system for telephone and telegraph communications in Korea. Signalmen repaired cable when it was struck by bombs; they also strung wire through rice paddies and across hills; and they repaired breaks in wire caused by vehicles or by civilians who cut the wire and used it to tie bundles. Signalmen often found it difficult to transport equipment for repeater stations, which weighed as much as two tons. These elevated and isolated sites were often targeted by the communists. Mobile repeater stations followed infantry units when roads allowed.

Weather conditions wreaked havoc on wire communications. In winter, batteries froze and soldiers experienced difficulties laying wire while wearing thick gloves. In summer, heat, dust, and humidity damaged equipment. As a result, wire communications were often unreliable.

Critical for quick tactical communications over long distances, very high frequency (VHF) radio companies were the backbone of the Korean War Signal Corps. Signalmen learned to bounce radio signals off steep hills and mountainsides, a technique not in the Signal Corps manual. Personnel could operate on slopes instead of summits, and this kept them out of chilling winds so harmful to humans and electronics.

Signal Corps responsibilities included taking motion pictures and photographs. These could reveal potential routes of advance and communist foxholes, but they were also used as publicity for newspapers and magazines.

The aviation section of the Signal Corps, the 304th Signal Operation Battalion, transported as much as 34,000 pounds of messages monthly between corps headquarters and the front. Delivering documents within hours instead of the days required by jeep, the cargo included maps and charts not easily transmitted by radio or telegraph. Carrier pigeons were also used to send messages.

During the war, the Signal Corps suffered 334 casualties. After the conflict, Army Signal Corps units remained in Korea to provide communications for the Eighth Army. The Signal Corps also benefited from increased defense spending during the war and new sophisticated satellite communication equipment.

ELIZABETH D. SCHAFER

See also

MacArthur, Douglas; United States Army

References

Boose, Donald. *U.S. Army Forces in the Korean War, 1950–1953.* Oxford, UK: Osprey, 2005.

Huston, James A. *Guns and Butter, Powder and Rice: U.S. Army Logistics in the Korean War.* Selinsgrove, PA: Susquehanna University Press, 1989.

Purkiser, Herman L. "What's New in Signals?" *Military Review* 31 (January 1952): 3–13.

Raines, Rebecca Robbins. *Getting the Message Through: A Branch History of the U.S. Army Signal Corps.* Washington, DC: U.S. Army Center of Military History, 1996.

Westover, John G. *Combat Support in Korea.* Washington, DC: Combat Forces Press, 1955.

Zahl, Harold A. "Toward Lighter Signal Equipment." *Army Information Digest* 8 (June 1953): 31–35.

United States Coast Guard

A branch of the U.S. armed services and one of seven uniformed U.S. services. The U.S. Coast Guard protects American ports and waterways, including inland waterways. Its chief function has been to operate as a maritime law enforcement and rescue organization that is empowered to operate in both domestic and international waters. As situations warrant, the U.S. Coast Guard may assume multiple missions and may work together with other armed services, particularly the U.S. Navy.

During the Korean War, the Coast Guard assumed a number of noncombat missions. These included search and rescue, Long Range Aid to Navigation (LORAN), and port security. Although the Coast Guard was not transferred to U.S. Navy control as occurred in the Second World War, the navy requested that the Coast Guard deploy additional search-and-rescue units in the Pacific because of the augmentation of flights from the United States to the Far East. These outfits each contained an aviation detachment, one or more cutters, and a command post with the requisite communication capability. Such units were indeed stationed at Sangley Point in the Philippines and at Guam, Wake, Midway, and Adak Islands.

LORAN, employing electronic navigational aid systems, also emerged as a role for the Coast Guard. With the other armed services dispatching supplemental forces to South Korea, safety demands on and above the western Pacific rose considerably. The Coast Guard swiftly established makeshift LORAN sites that provided coverage for heavy air and sea traffic areas between Korea and the Philippines.

With the heightened tensions of the Cold War, the U.S. Coast Guard also implemented stricter port security measures, mirroring action taken during the Second World War. Focusing on the conflict in Korea, the Coast Guard placed special emphasis on the prevention of sabotage of ships carrying military cargoes to the Far East. But the Soviet Union's 1949 detonation of an atomic bomb, combined with the war in Korea, forced the Coast Guard to implement additional protective measures, especially in the form of enhanced port security.

To accomplish its increased duties, especially port security, the Coast Guard required more personnel. These were obtained through extension of enlistments, securing new recruits, and expansion of the officer corps. Selected because they required minimal training for port security, petty officers serving at stations and on ships were transferred to port duty. To provide sufficient replacements, classes at petty officer schools were expanded to maximum-size enrollments, and larger numbers of Coast Guard personnel were sent to navy schools. In an effort to prevent disenchantment and to retain manpower, the Coast Guard permitted individuals whose enlistments were up to join the reserve instead of staying on active duty. New recruits also began to bolster the enlisted ranks of the Coast Guard, while enlargement of the officer corps emerged by commissioning recent graduates of universities and merchant marine academies and by temporary appointments. By June 1953, the Coast Guard numbered more than 34,000 officers and enlisted personnel. With the conclusion of hostilities in Korea, the Coast Guard once again shifted to its traditional peacetime activities.

R. BLAKE DUNNAVENT

See also
United States, Home Front; United States Navy

References

Capron, Walter C. *The U.S. Coast Guard.* New York: Franklin Watts, 1965.

Johnson, Robert Erwin. *Guardians of the Sea: History of the United States Coast Guard, 1915 to the Present.* Annapolis, MD: Naval Institute Press, 1987.

Waters, John M., Jr. *Rescue at Sea.* Princeton, NJ: Van Nostrand, 1966.

United States Marine Corps

The U.S. Marine Corps played a major role in the Korean War. In June 1950, the corps had fallen from an all-time high total of 485,833 personnel at the end of the Second World War to just 74,279 personnel worldwide. This did not keep Marine Corps commandant General Clifton B. Cates from proposing that marines be sent to fight in Korea immediately after the June 25, 1950, invasion of the Republic of Korea (ROK, South Korea) by the Democratic People's Republic of Korea (DPRK, North Korea). Chief of naval operations Admiral Forrest P. Sherman delayed volunteering the marines immediately and waited until July 1, the day after President Harry S. Truman decided to commit ground troops. Far East Command (FEC) commanding general Douglas MacArthur was delighted with the news, as he was already planning an amphibious operation behind the lines of the Korean People's Army (KPA, North Korean Army).

On July 2, MacArthur requested the dispatch of a marine regimental combat team; the Joint Chiefs of Staff (JCS) and Truman concurred on July 3. On July 10, at the urging of Fleet Marine Forces in the Pacific commander Lieutenant General Lemuel C. Shepherd, MacArthur revised his request to a full division with supporting aircraft.

Meanwhile, in less than two weeks, on July 12, the marines activated the 1st Brigade at Camp Pendleton, California. It consisted of the 5th Marine Regiment and Marine Aircraft Group 33, 6,600 men in all. The 1st Brigade sailed for the Far East on July 15 and debarked at Pusan beginning on August 2.

Having stripped the 1st Marine Division of much of its resources, marine headquarters had to rely on the 2nd Marine Division (then at one-third wartime strength) and reserves. On July 29, 1950, the Organized Marine Corps Reserve was activated; then on August 15, 1950, the Marine Corps Reserve was called up. By September, the marines had activated 33,258 officers and men. By the end of March 1951, the 90,044-man Marine Volunteer Reserve had activated 51,942 officers and men. Many marines were dispersed among active Marine Corps units as replacements.

Puppies adopted by members of the U.S. 7th Marine Regiment. (National Archives)

Many of the first marine reservists recalled to active duty were incorporated into the 1st Marine Division, which made the amphibious landing at Inchon on September 15, 1950. A total of 1,809 of the 3,836 men of the 3rd Infantry Regiment of the 1st Marine Division were reservists, as were nearly a fifth of the marines who participated in the Inchon Landing. Members of marine aviation units were also recalled to active duty. Eventually, 20 of 30 fighter squadrons and all 10 ground-control squadrons in the reserve were called up and integrated into regular marine aircraft wings. A year after the Korean War began, the Marine Corps had grown to nearly 200,000 personnel, and the military expansion following the start of the war envisioned a corps of 400,000 men.

The marines established an enviable fighting record during the Korean War, particularly as far as U.S. public opinion and Congress were concerned. This included operations in the August–September 1950 defense of the Pusan Perimeter, the September 15, 1950, Inchon Landing, and the October–December 1950 Changjin (Chosin) Reservoir campaign (and especially the 1st Marine Division's epic fighting withdrawal). From January 1951 to March 1952, the marines held the eastern portion of the Eighth Army's defensive positions in the Hwachon Reservoir–Punchbowl area. Then until the end of the war in July 1953, they manned the western sector and approaches to the South Korean capital, Seoul.

The 1st Marine Air Wing provided valuable service to the United Nations Command (UNC) during the conflict. Marine Chance Vought F4U-4/AU-1 (Corsair) aircraft and the new Grumman F9F-2 (Panther) jets provided valuable close air support to marine and army ground operations, the quality of this support being much envied by the army. The 1st Marine Division headquarters was unhappy over the diversion of its air assets to support other ground troops, especially as the marines believed that the army did not adequately direct close air support strikes. Marine aircraft also escorted bombers and provided battlefield reconnaissance, and the marines pioneered using helicopters in medical evacuation, transport of troops (a first in warfare), and resupply.

U.S. marines fight in the streets of Seoul, September 20, 1950. (National Archives)

A total of 424,000 marines served in Korea, suffering 4,267 killed in action, 339 deaths from other causes, and 23,744 wounded in action. Statistically, marines proved less susceptible to communist brainwashing than did U.S. Army prisoners of war (POWs). A higher percentage of marines also survived captivity than their army counterparts, and five were decorated for meritorious service while POWs. No marine was among the 192 convicted of misconduct, nor were there any marines among the 21 Americans who refused repatriation at the end of the war.

Despite the exemplary record in Korea, there were concerns over the drafting of 72,000 men into the corps during the war, which many veterans believed had reduced overall effectiveness. Marine officers also worried about using marines as conventional ground troops, and the corps certainly had much to learn about fighting in cold-weather conditions. But the marines had learned a great deal, including the potential of the helicopter in vertical envelopment. Overall, the Marine Corps emerged from the war three times larger in personnel strength than when the conflict had begun. Its place in the minds and hearts of the American public was secure thanks to the performance of its 1st Division.

SPENCER C. TUCKER

See also

Brainwashing; Casualties; Cates, Clifton Bledsoe; Changjin Reservoir Campaign; Inchon Landing; Joint Chiefs of Staff; MacArthur, Douglas; Punchbowl; Shepherd, Lemuel Cornick, Jr.; Sherman, Forrest Percival; Truman, Harry S.; United States Reserve Forces

References

Cameron, Craig M. *American Samurai: Myth, Imagination, and the Conduct of Battle in the First Marine Division, 1941–1951.* New York: Cambridge University Press, 1994.

Giusti, Ernest H. *The Mobilization of the Marine Corps Reserve in the Korean Conflict.* Washington, DC: Historical Branch, G-3 Division Headquarters, U.S. Marine Corps, 1967.

Meid, Pat, James M. Yingling, Nicholas Canzona, et al. *U.S. Marine Operations in Korea, 1950–1953.* 5 vols. Washington, DC: U.S. Marine Corps Historical Branch, 1962–1972.

Millett, Allan R. *Drive North: U.S. Marines at the Punchbowl.* Washington, DC: U.S. Marine Corps, History and Museums Division, 2001.

Changjin Reservoir Withdrawal, December 1–11, 1950

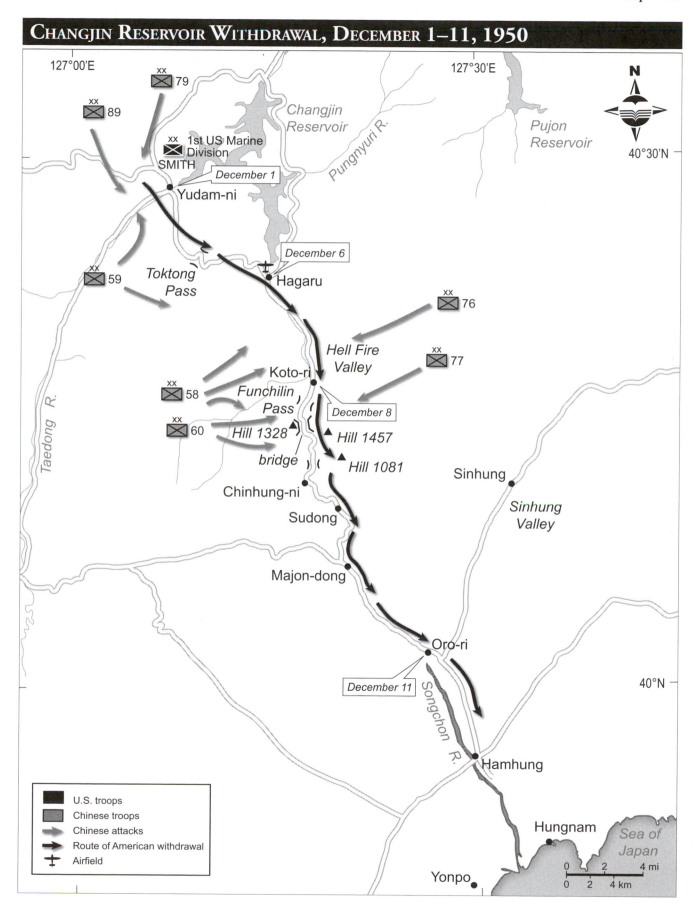

127°00'E

127°30'E

N

40°30'N

89

79

Changjin Reservoir

Pungnyuri R.

Pujon Reservoir

1st US Marine Division
SMITH

December 1

Yudam-ni

59

Toktong Pass

December 6

Hagaru

76

Hell Fire Valley

77

Koto-ri

58

Funchilin Pass

December 8

60

Hill 1328

Hill 1457

bridge

Hill 1081

Sinhung

Chinhung-ni

Sinhung Valley

Sudong

Taedong R.

Majon-dong

Oro-ri

December 11

Songchon R.

40°N

Hamhung

Hungnam

Sea of Japan

Yonpo

U.S. troops
Chinese troops
Chinese attacks
Route of American withdrawal
Airfield

0   2   4 mi

0   2   4 km

———. *Semper Fidelis: The History of the United States Marine Corps.* New York: Free Press, 1991.

Montross, Lynn. *Cavalry of the Sky: The Story of U.S. Marine Combat Helicopters.* New York: Harper and Brothers, 1954.

Montross, Lynn, et al. *U.S. Marine Operations in Korea, 1950–1953.* 5 vols. Washington, DC: U.S. Marine Corps Historical Branch, 1954–1972.

United States National Guard

At the time of the Korean War, National Guard forces were designed to augment regular forces in times of need. Certainly they played a key role in the Korean War; 84 percent of the Air National Guard (45,000 men) and 34 percent of the Army Guard (138,600 personnel) were mobilized during the conflict.

At the outset of the Korean War, the Joint Chiefs of Staff (JCS) seemed to believe that the recall of individual reservists (not National Guardsmen) and activation of logistical units from the Organized Reserve would be sufficient. On July 25, 1950, army chief of staff General J. Lawton Collins recommended against calling up full Army Guard divisions. He based this on his belief that they would have little effect on the war in Korea, since it would take months to bring the divisions to a combat-ready status. However, the rapid advance of forces of the Democratic People's Republic of Korea (DPRK, North Korea) soon changed his mind; on July 31, he recommended that four National Guard divisions and two National Guard regimental combat teams be activated.

Army National Guard

During the Korean war, a total of 8 National Guard divisions, 3 regimental combat teams (RCTs), and 714 company-sized units were called to active duty.

President Harry S. Truman did not wait for General Collins. On July 22, 1950, he alerted the first 2 of what would become a total of 19 increments of National Guard units to prepare for active duty. These included 24 battalion-sized units, 20 of which were 90- and 120-mm antiaircraft battalions, situated near major cities and military installations on both coasts of the United States. Antiaircraft commands were activated because many believed that the North Korean invasion of the Republic of Korea (ROK, South Korea) was part of a wider communist plan that might include an attack on Western Europe or the United States itself. By July 29, 3 increments of guard units had been alerted for activation in August, totaling 106 battalions and smaller commands.

As North Korean troops forced U.S. and South Korean defenders into what became known as the Pusan Perimeter, more Army Guardsmen were activated. The fourth increment, consisting of the 28th Infantry Division (Pennsylvania), 40th Infantry Division (California), 43rd Infantry Division (Rhode Island–Connecticut–Vermont), 45th Infantry Division (Oklahoma), and the 196th (South Dakota) and 278th (Tennessee) Regimental Combat Teams were alerted on July 31 and activated on September 1, 1950.

These 4 increments provided the bulk of Army Guard units that served in Korea. The final 15 increments supplied only 5 battalions and 2 smaller units for Korean service (although many other commands were called to active duty elsewhere during the war, including the 31st Infantry Division [Alabama and Mississippi], 44th Infantry Division [Illinois], 37th Infantry Division [Ohio], and 47th Infantry Division [Minnesota and North Dakota]).

The army took thousands of guardsmen from the activated divisions as individual replacements, many of them for Korea. This considerably extended the time required for these divisions to become combat ready. For example, the 28th Infantry Division was activated on September 5, 1950, with a strength of 10,416 personnel. Draftees filled the division to full strength by November, and on November 6, the 28th embarked on a 28-week training program designed to make the command combat ready. However, on February 2, 1951, and again in March, the army levied the 28th for a total of 6,000 trained fillers, destroying the division's training timetable. As a result, the 28th was not ready for deployment until mid-November 1951, when it was sent to the Federal Republic of Germany (FRG, West Germany). The 43rd Infantry Division also went to West Germany at about the same time.

General Douglas MacArthur, commander of the United Nations Command (UNC) in Korea, asked for four of the National Guard divisions for his command. Only the 40th and 45th—both partially trained—were sent to Japan in April 1951 to finish training and to provide security for Japan. Both divisions formed special commands back in the United States to train fillers who had insufficient training for deployment. When it deployed to Japan, the 45th Division was rated 43 percent combat effective. The 40th Division was in a similar situation, being 3,000 men short of operational strength.

Originally, the JCS prohibited these divisions from being employed in Korea. However, this order was later changed. The 45th deployed to Korea between December 5 and 29, 1951, replacing the 1st Cavalry Division, which went to Japan. Between early January and early February 1952, the 40th Division deployed to Korea, replacing the 24th Infantry Division, which also returned to Japan. Thus Japan was defended by two U.S. Army divisions.

The four guard divisions remaining in the U.S.—the 31st, 37th, 44th and 47th—continued to supply trained fillers for other army commands throughout their active duty during the war.

Air National Guard

Sorting out the order of battle for Air National Guard commands called to active duty in the war is difficult, as sources are at times contradictory. Some commands carried the designation of groups when mobilized but were redesignated as wings following activation. In addition to redesignated groups as wings, the Air Force also reorganized or redesignated other Air Guard units once they were mobilized.

Mission from Taegu, a painting by Gil Cohen showing operations of the 158th Fighter Bomber Squadron of the Georgia Air National Guard at Taegu Airfield, South Korea, in December 1951. (Gil Cohen/National Guard)

At the outset of the Korean War, the air force first asked for reserve volunteers to serve on active duty. In July 1950, it began to recall reservists and, the following month, began to mobilize Air Force Reserve flying units. On October 10, 1950, the air force began mobilizing Air Guard wings and their fighter squadrons and support units. The first included 1 bomber wing, 2 fighter-bomber wings, 10 fighter-bomber squadrons, and 4 fighter squadrons. Later, other units—to include reconnaissance—were sent.

Before the Korean War, Air National Guard units did not have specific wartime missions. Much of their equipment, especially aircraft, was obsolete, training was often poor, and the units were generally unprepared for combat. Guard units were almost randomly assigned to major air commands, regardless of their previous training and equipment. As with the Army Guard, Air Guard units were stripped of many key personnel for employment in other commands as fillers. As a result, most units took from three to six months to become combat ready.

Despite this, Air Guard units assigned to Japan and Korea compiled excellent combat records. They flew 39,530 combat sorties and destroyed 39 communist aircraft. Four pilots became aces, shooting down a combined 29 communist aircraft. Some units served in France, Britain, and Iceland. The 22 Air National Guard wings represented a significant increase in the air force's structure and efficiency during the Korean War.

UZAL W. ENT

See also

Collins, Joseph Lawton; Joint Chiefs of Staff; United States Air Force; United States Army Engineers; United States Army Signal Corps; United States Reserve Forces

References

Berebitsky, William. *A Very Long Weekend*. Shippensburg, PA: White Mane, 1996.

Donnelly, William M. *Under Army Orders: The Army National Guard during the Korean War*. College Station: Texas A&M University Press, 2001.

Ent, Uzal W., and Robert Grant Crist, eds. *The First Century: A History of the 28th Infantry Division*. Harrisburg, PA: Stackpole Books, 1979.

Francillon, René J. *The United States Air National Guard*. London: Aerospace Publishing, 1993.

Futrell, Robert F. *The Air National Guard and the American Military Tradition*. Washington, DC: Historical Services Division, National Guard Bureau, 1995.

———. *The United States Air Force in Korea, 1950–1953*. Rev. ed. Washington, DC: Office of the Chief of Air Force History, 1983.

Gross, Charles G. *Prelude to the Total Force: The Air National Guard 1943–1969*. Washington, DC: Office of Air Force History, United States Air Force, 1985.

Hermes, Walter G. *U.S. Army in the Korean War: Truce Tent and Fighting Front*. Washington, DC: Office of the Chief of Military History, 1966.

Hill, Jim Dan. *The Minute Man in Peace and War*. Harrisburg, PA: Stackpole, 1964.

Schnabel, James F. *United States Army in the Korean War: Policy and Direction, the First Year*. Washington, DC: Office of the Chief of Military History, Department of the Army, 1972.

United States Naval Construction Battalions

Since their creation during World War II, naval construction battalions, known as Seabees, have lived by their motto of "We build, we fight." Seabees have participated in every major conflict involving the United States since their creation. They have built entire bases, bulldozed and paved thousands of miles of roadway and airstrips, and been responsible for countless other construction projects.

During the Korean War, the Seabees were part of Task Force 90. In the course of the conflict, they grew in strength from 3,300 to 14,000 men, including reservists and active-duty personnel. Seabees first saw action during the September 1950 Inchon Landing. Contending with 30-foot tides, swift currents, and high sea walls, they put pontoon causeways into position just before the first assault, all the while under fire from the Korean People's Army (KPA, North Korean Army).

Seabees also participated in the war's other amphibious landings. At Wonsan, they not only were tasked with setting up pontoon structures but also carried out ship repair, inspected abandoned North Korean ships, and cleared mined tunnels. When the People's Republic of China (PRC) entered the war, Seabees were called on to do their work in reserve and help evacuate troops from the same harbors they were so instrumental in securing. Their pontoon causeways were now used to load troops and equipment onto ships instead of putting them ashore.

Seabees not only participated in amphibious landings but also built airfields for U.S. Marine Corps air groups. This was a difficult task, as many of the airstrips were under constant communist fire and had to remain open. On Yo-do, a small island in Wonsan harbor, in 1952, U.S. Navy aircraft often had to make forced landings without making it back to their carriers, and the Seabees were given 35 days to create an airstrip on Yo-do for emergency recovery of aircraft. Although under constant KPA fire, they constructed a 2,400-foot runway in only 16 days. In July alone, eight Chance Vought F4U-4/AU-1 (Corsair) aircraft landed safely on the island.

After the Korean War, the Seabees reorganized. From 1949 to 1953, 13 battalions of 2 distinct types were established. The first were known as amphibious construction battalions—the landing and docking units. Their mission was to place causeways and ship-to-shore fuel lines, construct pontoon docks, and perform other functions for the rapid landing of men, equipment, and supplies. The second type, naval mobile construction battalions, were land-based crews. They were responsible for various land construction tasks, including camps, roads, tank farms, airstrips, permanent waterfront structures, and many other facilities.

MATTHEW S. CARMAN

See also

Amphibious Force Far East; United States Marine Corps; United States Navy

References

Cagle, Malcolm W., and Frank A. Manson. *Sea War in Korea*. Annapolis, MD: Naval Institute Press, 1957.

Field, James A., Jr. *History of United States Naval Operations, Korea*. Washington, DC: U.S. Government Printing Office, 1962.

Marolda, Edward J., ed. *The U.S. Navy in the Korean War*. Annapolis, MD: Naval Institute Press, 2007.

United States Navy

Control of the sea was utterly necessary for the successful prosecution of the United Nations (UN) war effort during the Korean War. Reinforced by warships from allied nations, the U.S. Navy was able to maintain the logistical umbilical cord, to blockade the coast of the Democratic People's Republic of Korea (DPRK, North Korea), to back troops ashore with gunfire and close air support, and to assist in campaigns against communist communications and strategic targets. In carrying out these tasks, the U.S. Navy reaffirmed its place as a key element in the U.S. defense establishment and won the political support necessary to modernize and expand its operating forces.

These capabilities and trends ran counter to the prewar expectations of many defense analysts who saw strategic air power wielded by the air force as paramount; some planners reserved for the navy only the missions of convoy and patrol, fundamentally defensive tasks. Strapped by increasingly severe post–World War II budget cuts, the once-mighty U.S. Navy presented itself at the beginning of the Korean War as a sorry spectacle: the number of combatants had been sliced from a high of 1,200 warships and 41,000 aircraft in 1945 to 237 warships and 4,300 airplanes by June 1950. Personnel had plummeted from 3,400,000 in 1945 to 382,000 by the late spring of 1950. Ships still flying commissioning pennants were frequently manned by only two-thirds of their authorized wartime complements. The U.S. Marine Corps, meanwhile, had dropped from six large divisions and 669,000 men to two skeletal divisions and a total strength of 74,000 men.

Caught in this downward spiral, the navy's leadership had bloodied itself in a vicious fight against the air force in 1949; the so-called Revolt of the Admirals ended with both the secretary of the navy and the chief of naval operations resigning in protest. By 1950, the navy, dispirited and shorn of warships, had lost the confidence of much of the American public.

Yet when North Korea invaded the Republic of Korea (ROK, South Korea) across the 38th Parallel on June 25, 1950, U.S. command authorities immediately turned to the navy, initially to withdraw American noncombatants and then to resupply South Korean forces. The next day, the president authorized combat operations by U.S. air and naval forces in backing South Korea. On June 27, President Harry S. Truman ordered the Seventh Fleet to patrol waters off Taiwan (then know as Formosa) and Korea.

U.S. warships, with reinforcements from the British Commonwealth, quickly found themselves in action. Cruisers and destroyers conducted their first shore bombardment at Mukkho on June 29. On July 2–3, 1950, U.S. surface warships won the only sizable

A snowstorm slows Task Force 77 air operations from the U.S. aircraft carrier *Essex* (CV-9), January 18, 1952. (National Archives)

naval engagement of the war by virtually annihilating a North Korean flotilla of torpedo boats and trawlers near Chumunjin. In the Yellow Sea, carriers launched their first strikes on July 3 when aircraft from the *Valley Forge* and HMS *Triumph* struck airfields at Haeju and Pyongyang.

As warships and support vessels again proved their utility, Congress voted a $2.7 billion supplement to the navy's budget. Part of the windfall went to recommissioning 48 major combatants and 430 minor warships and auxiliaries. Other portions of the funding went to bring 1,000 aircraft back into service. This matériel buildup, which continued for the remainder of the conflict, was necessarily matched by a corresponding increase in personnel. The navy's authorized personnel strength almost doubled by June 1951 from 382,000 to 688,971. Three key sources of manpower made this expansion possible: the involuntary retention of personnel; the draft; and the recall of reservists. By the middle of the war, over 25 percent of those in navy uniform were reservists.

This investment in matériel and manpower ultimately paid great dividends. In the interim, the navy put the 1st Cavalry Division ashore on July 18, 1950, at Pohang. This force was critical to the holding of the Pusan Perimeter. Then in September, the navy

helped make possible United Nations Command (UNC) commander General Douglas MacArthur's great strategic counterstroke at Inchon. Charged with supporting the marine landing force, commander of Naval Forces Far East Vice Admiral C. Turner Joy assembled six aircraft carriers, the greatest concentration of naval air power since World War II. Directly backing the invasion force of 230 ships were 2 American and 2 British cruisers, 6 destroyers, and 3 rocket landing crafts, which beat down the North Korean coastal defenses at Flying Fish Channel and Wolmi-do.

Far less successful was the subsequent landing at Wonsan. Unnecessarily complicated, the operation saw the navy transport 30,000 troops of two divisions from Inchon and Pusan to the North Korean port. There the navy confronted a complex minefield laid with Soviet assistance. Short of minesweepers, the navy was slow to clear paths through the 2,000 mines; thus, the first waves crossed the beach 16 days after troops of the Republic of Korea Army (ROKA, South Korean Army) initially entered the city from the south.

Nonetheless, the demonstrated amphibious capability of the U.S. Navy and Marine Corps enabled the UNC later in the war to pose credible threats to North Korean rear areas on several occasions. For instance, in January 1951, navy diversionary movements in support of Operation THUNDERBOLT threatened Kansong, Kosong, and Inchon. The deception at Inchon compelled communist forces to divert at least one division to guard that key port. The next month the navy assisted Operation RIPPER by a feint at Chinnampo.

Several times the U.S. Navy also offered hard-pressed ground units a respite at the water's edge. The most noted such episode occurred in December 1950 when the navy evacuated UNC troops cut off in northeastern Korea by the entry into the war of the People's Republic of China (PRC). At Hungnam, navy vessels lifted off 105,000 troops, including almost the entire ROKA I Corps; 91,000 Korean refugees; 17,500 vehicles; and 350,000 tons of supplies. One tank landing ship (LST) left Hungnam jammed with 8,400 Korean civilians as passengers.

The navy fulfilled other combat missions. Aside from striking at strategic targets, naval aircraft played a major role in the perennial UNC attempt to deprive communist frontline forces of essential supplies. Named in 1951 Operation STRANGLE and then Operation SATURATE, the air effort was supplemented by gunfire from warships offshore and by commando raids launched from the sea.

Less heralded but more effective was the navy's blockade of North Korea. The sea barrier closed off three main avenues for the communists to reinforce and resupply their ground units: deep-water shipping along the east coast; shallow-water coastal shipping on the Yellow Sea; and deep-water shipping routes to the Asiatic seaports in China and Manchuria. Normally swarming with commercial vessels, the waters around North Korea were swept almost completely clean by UN blockaders.

For much of the struggle, the navy paid especially close attention to the three principal North Korean ports of Hungnam, Songjin, and Wonsan. The siege of the latter was especially prolonged. U.S. warships patrolled in the harbor for 861 straight days with the exception of a short period during Typhoon Karen in August 1952. So protracted did the siege become that the relieving officer, upon taking tactical command, inherited from his predecessor a golden key to the city and the honorific title of Mayor of Wonsan. Farther afield, the Seventh Fleet, beginning on June 27, 1950, patrolled in the Taiwan Strait (then known as the Formosa Strait) in response to an order from President Truman to prevent a communist attack on Taiwan, or a Guomindang (GMD, Nationalist) invasion of the mainland, thereby keeping the war limited.

Early in the conflict, navy leaders were concerned about possible Soviet submarine activity. Destroyers and naval aircraft maintained antisubmarine patrols against submarines based at Vladivostok that might interfere with UNC naval assets. Although this concern lessened as the conflict progressed, it could never be ignored. Numerous underwater contacts were reported and some were attacked, but without identifiable result. Although the U.S. Navy maintained submarines as part of the Seventh Fleet, their activities are not mentioned in official histories. However, several British commando operations were launched from U.S. Navy submarines.

Utterly essential to UNC prosecution of the war was the logistic support provided to allied forces by the navy's Military Sea Transport Service (MSTS), a unified organization set up to furnish sea transportation for Defense Department personnel and cargo. The MSTS carried the bulk of resources necessary for the conduct of the war: 4,918,919 passengers; 52,111,299 tons of cargo; and 21,828,879 tons of petroleum. For every ton of supplies airlifted to Korea, 270 tons went by sea (and every ton sent by air required 4 tons of aviation fuel to be shipped by sea). For every individual who flew to Korea, 6 traveled by sea. Overall monthly cargo requirements approximated those of World War II in the Pacific; to transport these vast quantities, approximately 360 ships were needed in the pipeline on a constant basis.

With continuous air and gunship operations, at-sea replenishment gave naval operating forces a key advantage. In July 1950, four oilers moved quickly to the theater. Improvements in technique were made, with night replenishment operations becoming standard in 1952, and by the end of that year, an entire carrier task force could be topped off with fuel, ammunition, and other necessities within a nine-hour period.

Among support vessels that once more proved invaluable was the LST, with its ability to land or evacuate forces from almost any beach without winches or stevedores. Virtually all of these amphibious ships were World War II vessels hastily returned to service, some under the auspices of the Shipping Control Administration Japan. These proved especially important early in the war, when 38 of the "Scapjap" ships brought in the supplies necessary for the maintenance of the Pusan Perimeter. Vice Admiral Joy contended that "the LST has possibly made the greatest single contribution to the success of the UN forces in Korea."

On the other hand, submarines saw little action. Early in the conflict, U.S. submarines conducted patrols off the China coast and in La Pérouse Strait. At the same time, the navy guarded against intervention by Soviet submarines. Numerous contacts were attacked early in the war, and the carriers of Task Force 77 frequently shifted station as a precautionary measure.

In one notable sphere, mine warfare, the navy revealed an important weakness. Landings at Wonsan and Chinnampo were held up by lack of minesweeping capability. Mines also caused the navy's greatest losses during the war. Five small craft (4 minecrafts—*Magpie*, *Partridge*, *Pirate*, and *Pledge*—and 1 fleet tug—*Sarsi*) were fatally damaged while conducting their dangerous work. Five destroyers (*Barton*, *Brush*, *Ernest G. Small*, *Mansfield*, and *Walke*) struck mines, although none sank. Fortunately for the U.S. Navy, the communists usually employed simple contact mines rather than more sophisticated types. Eventually, the navy extemporized effective countermeasures, in part by turning to Japan for personnel and minesweepers. By the end of the war, the navy calculated that it had destroyed 1,535 mines.

Aside from operational losses and mines, the other principal source of danger for naval personnel was gunfire from shore batteries. During the war, communist artillery fire hit 85 U.S. warships. Damage was usually minor, although the destroyer *John R. Pierce* was struck 7 times off Tanchon on August 6, 1952, and suffered 10 casualties. One hit on the heavy cruiser *Los Angeles* off Wonsan on April 2, 1953, cost the ship 13 wounded.

Given the length of the war and the navy's prominent role in it, personnel casualties were surprisingly light: 503 killed in action, died of wounds, or missing in action; 1,576 wounded; 209 prisoners; and 4,043 nonbattle deaths. Marine casualties were much higher: 4,267 fatalities to hostile action; 242 other deaths; 23,744 wounded; 616 prisoners; and 1,261 nonbattle deaths.

By the end of the war, the navy had resumed its rightful place in defense affairs. As General James Van Fleet noted, "We could not have existed in Korea without the navy." Navy funding rose from $4.1 billion in 1950 to $10 billion in 1952. Because carrier aviation had proved so useful, appropriations for naval aviation remained at a markedly higher level after the war. For virtually every year during the remainder of the 1950s, Congress authorized construction of a new supercarrier able to operate supersonic jet aircraft. Guided missile development, especially for antiaircraft work, was also accelerated. As well, the navy began construction of special minesweepers to counter magnetic mines and of improved large amphibious craft (dock landing ships and LSTs). Planning began on a helicopter assault ship capable of putting a marine battalion ashore and on large "one-stop" replenishment vessels. Oddly, surface warships fared poorly in the postwar era, as all of the navy's battleships and most of its cruisers went into mothballs. Nonetheless, the U.S. Navy was a far stronger force in 1955 than it had been in 1950.

MALCOLM MUIR JR.

See also

Inchon Landing; Joy, Charles Turner; MacArthur, Douglas; Military Sea Transport Service; Mine Warfare, Sea; Muccio, John Joseph; Naval Battles; Naval Forces Far East; Naval Gunfire Support; Revolt of the Admirals; RIPPER, Operation; SATURATE, Operation; STRANGLE, Operation; THUNDERBOLT, Operation; Troopships; Truman, Harry S.; United States Navy Air Operations; Van Fleet, James Alward; Wonsan Landing and Evacuation

References

Cagle, Malcolm W., and Frank A. Manson. *Sea War in Korea.* Annapolis, MD: Naval Institute Press, 1957.

Field, James A., Jr. *History of United States Naval Operations, Korea.* Washington, DC: U.S. Government Printing Office, 1962.

Hallion, Richard P. *The Naval Air War in Korea.* Baltimore, MD: Nautical and Aviation Publishing Company of America, 1986.

Love, Robert W., Jr., ed. *The Chiefs of Naval Operations.* Annapolis, MD: Naval Institute Press, 1980.

Marolda, Edward J., ed. *The U.S. Navy in the Korean War.* Annapolis, MD: Naval Institute Press, 2007.

Melia, Tamara Moser. *"Damn the Torpedoes": A Short History of U.S. Naval Mine Countermeasures, 1777–1991.* Washington, DC: Naval Historical Center, 1991.

Riley, John C., Jr., ed. *Operational Experiences of Fast Battleships: World War II, Korea, Vietnam.* Washington, DC: Naval Historical Center, 1989.

United States Navy Air Operations

During the Korean War, U.S. naval aircraft flying from carriers and shore bases made a major contribution to the United Nations Command (UNC) aerial campaign against communist forces. Naval aviation assisted the air force in several important missions, including attacking strategic targets well behind communist lines. The first such effort came on July 18, 1950, when the carrier Valley Forge launched strikes against the oil refineries at Wonsan in the Democratic People's Republic of Korea (DPRK, North Korea). In the spring of 1952, the navy cooperated with the air force in striking at the North Korean electrical power grid and scored substantial successes against the Supung hydroelectric facility. On September 1, 1952, 142 aircraft from 3 carriers carried out the largest navy attack of the war, wrecking the Aoji oil refinery just 8 miles from Soviet territory. So complete was the damage wrought by the strategic campaign that a shortage of targets plagued pilots toward the end of the war; at one point, jets from the Boxer were reduced to attacking a coal dump and bombing sheep.

Naval aircraft also took part in—and suffered the frustrations inherent in—the UNC interdiction effort, conducted principally in 1951 and optimistically dubbed Operation STRANGLE. Assigned the task of cutting communist supply lines in northeastern Korea, naval aviators quickly focused on a key railroad bridge near Kilchu. Damaged first on March 3 by airmen commanded by Lieutenant Commander Harold G. Carlson from the *Princeton,* the bridge was quickly repaired and again attacked. In what rapidly evolved into a campaign dubbed "the Battle of Carlson's Canyon," the contest served as a model for James Michener's *The Bridges at Toko-ri.* In a struggle that typified the entire STRANGLE campaign, after extraordinary efforts the aviators knocked out the bridge, but communist workers then built a bypass around the ruins and continued their traffic.

In October 1951, naval aviators abandoned their concentration on bridges in preference to rail cuts and again piled up impressive records, at one point slicing communist rail lines with 211 cuts in one day. Night operations from carriers began early the next year, although the lack of a specialized night carrier hurt the effort. Ultimately, naval analysts concluded that interdiction was so costly (the price of one rail cut totaled $18,000; the cost of the explosives to displace 30 cubic yards of dirt came to $100 per cubic yard) that the campaign hurt the UNC war effort more than it did the communists.

Certainly one of the most unusual attack missions flown by naval aircraft during the conflict was the May 1, 1951, attack on the Hwachon Dam. Douglas AD (Skyraider) aircraft flying from the carrier *Princeton* breached the floodgates with six torpedoes;

U.S. Navy and Marine Corps Aircraft Specifications

Aircraft	Span	Length	Height	Gross Weight (pounds)	Top Speed (mph)	Range (miles)	Ceiling (feet)
C. Vought F4U-4	41' 0"	33' 8"	14' 9"	14,670	446	1,005	41,500
Consol PB4Y-2	110' 0"	74' 7"	29' 1 1/2"	60,000	249	2,630	18,300
Douglas AD-2	50' 1/4"	38' 2"	15' 7 1/2"	18,263	321	915	32,700
Douglas F3D	50' 0"	45' 5"	16' 1"	27,681	565	1,540	38,200
Grumman AF-2	60' 8"	43' 4"	16' 2"	25,500	317	1,500	32,500
Grumman F6F-K	42' 10"	33' 10"	14' 5"	12,000	375	1,500	39,900
Grumman F7F-3N	51' 6"	45' 6 1/2"	13' 9"	21,857	447	1,750	40,600
Grumman F9F-2	38' 0"	37' 3"	11' 4"	19,494	575	1,353	44,600
Grumman TBM	54' 2"	40' 0"	16' 5"	18,250	267	1,130	23,400
Lockheed P2V	100' 0"	77' 10"	28' 1"	63,078	320	3,985	26,000
Martin PBM-5	110' 0"	79' 10"	27' 6"	56,000	215	2,700	20,200
Martin P4M	114' 0"	84' 0"	26' 1"	83,378	415	3,800	34,600
McDonnell F2H-2	44' 10"	40' 2"	14' 6"	22,312	575	1,475	44,800
N.A. AJ-2	71' 5"	63' 1"	21' 5"	50,963	449	1,723	40,800

the cascading Pukhan (North Han) River slowed the communist ground offensive. This strike was the last in warfare by planes dropping torpedoes.

Nearer the navy's taste was close air support (CAS). Early in the war, carrier aircraft proved particularly valuable in this role because they could loiter longer over the front than air force jets based in Japan. Despite initial problems in air-ground communications, soldiers and marines frequently commented on the effectiveness of naval CAS. Nowhere was this more apparent than in the withdrawal from Changjin (Chosin) and the evacuation of Hungnam in December 1950. Outside the latter port, 400 navy and marine aircraft blasted communist ground forces. When the navy found itself committed to the interdiction mission in 1951, marine aircraft and planes from two escort carriers (*Badoeng Strait* and *Sicily*) helped fill the gap in CAS until it became a top priority again in April 1952.

Much less publicized than CAS, but quite essential, was the work of the patrol squadrons. Land-based Lockheed P2V (Neptune) aircraft or Martin PBM-5 (Mariner) flying boats maintained a constant watch over the Formosa Strait, thereby freeing Seventh Fleet warships for operations off Korea. Patrol aircraft also hunted mines, enforced the naval blockade of North Korea, and made weather flights.

Several notable figures piloted naval aircraft during the conflict. Ted Williams, the famed Red Sox baseball player, flew Grumman F9F-2 (Panther) aircraft; in early 1953, his plane was set aflame by antiaircraft fire, although he managed a safe emergency landing. Two future astronauts, John Glenn and Neil Armstrong, flew combat missions in marine and navy fighters.

Fine pilots like these managed to compensate for inadequacies in their naval aircraft. The communist Mikoyan-Gurevich MiG-15 proved an unpleasant surprise, possessing distinct advantages over the frontline navy fighters (the McDonnell F2H [Banshee] and the Grumman F9F-2 [Panther]) in terms of speed and altitude capabilities. Despite these handicaps, navy pilots outscored the communists early. Other triumphs followed: in November 1952, Grumman F9F (Panther) aircraft from the *Oriskany* downed all but one or two Soviet MiGs that sortied from Vladivostok. That same

month, a navy Douglas F3D (Skyknight; "Blue Whale") won the first night combat between jet aircraft by destroying a Yakovlev-15 (Yak-15). By the end of the war, the navy had claimed 23 aerial victories and produced 1 ace in the conflict, Lieutenant Guy P. Bordelon, who shot down 5 night fliers. Nonetheless, the communist edge in matériel was sufficiently sobering that the Bureau of Aeronautics gave high priority to air superiority fighters, leading shortly after the end of the war to the Grumman F9F (Cougar) and ultimately to the supersonic Vought F8U (Crusader).

The navy was more fortunate in finding in its inventory some fine attack aircraft. Although the Chance Vought F4U-4/AU-1 (Corsair) proved vulnerable to ground fire, the Douglas AD (Skyraider) could carry large stores of ordnance and possessed a superior loiter time. The McDonnell F2H (Banshee) fighter, sturdy and easy to maintain, did double duty in the rail interdiction role.

By the end of the war, navy and marine aircraft had conducted 275,912 sorties, fully 41 percent of all combat missions flown during the conflict. These planes fired 274,189 rockets and dropped 178,399 tons of bombs—figures significantly higher than their totals for World War II. Evaluators credited the aircraft with killing 86,265 troops and destroying 44,828 buildings, 391 locomotives, 5,896 railroad cars, 7,437 vehicles, 249 tanks, and 2,005 bridges. On the debit side, the navy and marines lost 5 planes to communist fighters, 559 to antiaircraft fire, and 684 to operational causes. Some veterans argued that the Korean War, with its longer flying hours and tours, its worse weather, and its tougher antiaircraft defenses, was more demanding of aviators than World War II in the Pacific.

MALCOLM MUIR JR.

See also
Aerial Combat; Aircraft; Airpower in the Korean War; Close Air Support; Hungnam Evacuation; Muccio, John Joseph; SATURATE, Operation; STRANGLE, Operation; Supung and the Korean Electric Power Plant Campaign

References
Bruning, John R. *Crimson Sky: The Air Battle for Korea*. Dulles, VA: Brassey's, 1999.

Cagle, Malcolm W., and Frank A. Manson. *Sea War in Korea*. Annapolis, MD: Naval Institute Press, 1957.

Clark, Joseph J., with Clark G. Reynolds. *Carrier Admiral*. New York: David McKay, 1967.

Crane, Conrad C. *American Air Power Strategy in Korea, 1950–1953*. Lawrence: University Press of Kansas, 1999.

Field, James A., Jr. *History of United States Naval Operations, Korea*. Washington, DC: U.S. Government Printing Office, 1962.

Hallion, Richard P. *The Naval Air War in Korea*. Baltimore, MD: Nautical and Aviation Publishing Company of America, 1986.

United States Reserve Forces

During the Korean War, the U.S. government relied heavily on reserve-component forces to assist active-duty units in fighting the war. These components included the Army National Guard, the Air National Guard, the Army Reserve, the Air Force Reserve, the Navy Reserve, and the Marine Corps Reserve. All played important roles in the war.

In 1950, reserve units reflected the active forces in that they too were not well trained or prepared to fight a war. The United States had drastically reduced the size of its military after World War II, and in June 1950, active and reserve-component units were undermanned. They suffered from insufficient training as well as inadequate equipment to fight an all-out war.

Reserve commands trained in the United States before they were sent to Korea, Europe, or elsewhere in the world. Reserve units that remained in the United States during the war saw much of their equipment sent to Korea. For instance, the Army National Guard provided tanks and motor vehicles, and the Air National Guard sent jet aircraft as well as spare parts and other items. Stateside units found themselves stripped down to only about a third of their authorized equipment inventory.

At the start of the Korean War the army had 591,487 men and women on active duty. The Army National Guard had 324,761 personnel in 4,883 units; the Army Active Reserve had 184,015 in 934 units. In addition, there was an inactive 324,602-person Volunteer Reserve and a 91,800-person Inactive Reserve.

During the entire course of the war, 244,300 officers and soldiers of the Army Reserve were called to active duty, not including 43,000 reserve officers on active duty at the beginning of the war. Many of those called to active duty were used as fillers and for replacement.

The Air National Guard played an important role during the war. In June 1950, it had only 373 jet fighters and a total of 2,655 aircraft. Its pilots were poorly trained, the consequence of a restriction of 110 hours of flying time per year imposed for reasons of economy; there had also been little money for aviation fuel. During the war, 10 Air Force Reserve wings were activated, along with more than 100,000 individual reservists. The Air Force Reserve and the Air National Guard suffered from lack of equipment as well as insufficient training. As with the Army Reserve and the National Guard, active-duty units requisitioned much of the equipment belonging to the air units, and when they were called up, many reserve units had only about a third of their authorized equipment.

Navy Reserves made a significant contribution to the U.S. war effort. Reserve ships and crews made up a quarter of the U.S. naval presence in Korean waters during the war. On July 25, 1950, the navy activated the carrier *Princeton*. It was recommissioned on August 28, 1950, with a largely reservist crew. The carriers *Bon Homme Richard, Essex,* and *Antietam* followed in 1951. A total of 22 Naval Reserve squadrons of some 6,000 officers and 15,000 enlisted personnel were deployed with the Seventh Fleet.

The Marine Corps had to rely heavily on reserves. In June 1950, the Marine Corps had 74,279 personnel serving worldwide, down from a total of 485,833 at the end of the Second World War. Marine Corps reserves numbered twice the amount of active-duty personnel. On July 29, 1950, the Organized Marine Corps Reserve was called to active duty; on August 15, 1950, the Marine Corps Reserve was activated. By September 1950, the marines had called up 33,528 officers and soldiers. By the end of March 1951, the 90,044-man Marine Volunteer Reserve had activated 51,942 officers and soldiers. A large number of the first reservists recalled to active duty were immediately incorporated into the 1st Marine Division, which made the amphibious landing at Inchon on September 15, 1950. Nearly a fifth of the marines who participated in the landing were reservists. Many marine reservists called up were later dispersed among active units as replacements. Members of marine aviation units were also recalled to active duty. Eventually, 20 of 30 fighter squadrons and all 10 ground-control squadrons in the reserve were called up and integrated into regular marine aircraft wings.

Reserve units and personnel played an important role in the Korean War in terms of both personnel and equipment. Equipment shortages were overcome, as was, in time, their lack of training. One-quarter of the top combat decorations won in the first year of the war went to reservists.

It is noteworthy that most of the reservists called up came from the unpaid and untrained inactive and volunteer reserves, and most of them were World War II veterans. The reserve formations that were kept in the United States or sent to Europe were important in that they freed regular formations to fight in Korea.

ROBERT J. ARVIN III

See also

United States Air Force; United States Army; United States Marine Corps; United States National Guard; United States Navy

References

Collins, J. Lawton. *War in Peacetime: The History and Lessons of Korea*. Boston: Houghton Mifflin, 1969.

Donnelly, William M. *Under Army Orders: The Army National Guard during the Korean War*. College Station: Texas A&M University Press, 2001.

Field, James A., Jr. *History of United States Naval Operations, Korea*. Washington, DC: U.S. Government Printing Office, 1962.

Futrell, Robert F. *The United States Air Force in Korea, 1950–1953.* Rev. ed. Washington, DC: Office of the Chief of Air Force History, 1983.

Gugeler, Russell A. *Combat Actions in Korea.* Rev. ed. Washington, DC: U.S. Army, Center of Military History, 1987.

Montross, Lynn, et al. *U.S. Marine Operations in Korea, 1950–1953.* 5 vols. Washington, DC: U.S. Marine Corps Historical Branch, 1954–1972.

Schnabel, James F. *United States Army in the Korean War: Policy and Direction, the First Year.* Washington, DC: Office of the Chief of Military History, Department of the Army, 1972.

Stuckey, John D., and Joseph H. Pistorious. *Mobilization of the Army National Guard and Army Reserve: Historical Perspective and the Vietnam War.* Carlisle Barracks, PA: U.S. Army War College, 1984.

United States–Republic of Korea Mutual Defense Treaty
Event Date: January 26, 1954

Bilateral agreement in which the United States essentially guaranteed the security of the Republic of Korea (ROK, South Korea) against future aggression, particularly by the Democratic People's Republic of Korea (DPRK, North Korea). In the spring of 1953, recently elected U.S. president Dwight D. Eisenhower and his advisors were cautiously optimistic about the resumption of stalled armistice talks, but they recognized the need to restrain and placate South Korean president Syngman Rhee, who rejected any compromise with the communists. Rhee's continual insistence on "no armistice without unification" and his threats not to honor any truce that did not expel the Chinese People's Volunteer Army (CPVA, Chinese Army) from Korea and to continue the war alone created doubts about South Korean adherence to any negotiated settlement.

To Rhee, any agreement that left Chinese communists in Korea meant the acceptance of a "death sentence" by South Korea. Early in June 1953, President Eisenhower responded to such threats and concerns by assuring Rhee that the United States would continue to seek unification of the two Koreas by "all peaceful means" and by offering to negotiate a mutual security pact and to extend economic aid promptly after the acceptance of an armistice. But Rhee wanted an immediate defense agreement. At the same time, the Eisenhower administration realized that South Korea was in poor shape after three years of devastating war. South Korea had suffered million of casualties, and its infrastructure was almost completely destroyed.

The South Korean release of 27,000 North Korean prisoners of war (POWs) on June 18, 1953, complicated the situation and gave Washington, DC, a renewed sense of urgency to bring Rhee into line. The subsequent mission by Assistant Secretary of State Walter Robertson (June 22–July 12, 1953) resulted in the promise of a mutual security pact, among other pledges, from the United States, in exchange for a guarantee that the South Korean leader would not obstruct implementation of the terms of an armistice.

Within two weeks of the armistice signing on July 27, 1953, Secretary of State John Foster Dulles initialed the promised bilateral security pact in Seoul on August 8, 1953. Consisting of six articles, the U.S.-ROK Mutual Defense Treaty paralleled existing U.S. agreements with the Philippines and Australia/New Zealand. In the document, the United States pledged to come to the aid of South Korea in the event of an armed external attack on territory recognized by the U.S. as being lawfully brought under the administrative control of South Korea. The agreement also pledged U.S. help in expanding and improving the Republic of Korea Army (ROKA, South Korean Army), and the United States, its allies, and the United Nations (UN) agreed to give economic and humanitarian aid to South Korea so it could be rebuilt. The United States also resolved to station troops in South Korea, which remain there to this day.

Subsequent hearings before the Senate Foreign Relations Committee in January 1954 clarified that the United States held no treaty obligations in the event of any unilateral aggressive action by South Korea toward North Korea or in the event of an internal insurrection against the South Korean government; on January 26, 1954, the U.S. Senate ratified the pact by a vote of 81–6. The treaty entered into force with the exchange of ratification documents in Washington on November 17, 1954.

Despite initial efforts to limit its commitment, the United States, by agreeing to this mutual defense pact, recognized its unilateral responsibility for the security of South Korea. Between 1954 and 1960 alone, the United States provided the South Koreans with more than $1 billion in military and civilian aid.

MARK W. BEASLEY

See also

Armistice Agreement; Dulles, John Foster; Eisenhower, Dwight David; Rhee, Syngman; Rhee's Release of North Korean Prisoners of War; Robertson, Walter Spencer; Robertson Mission; Truce Talks

References

Ambrose, Stephen E. *Eisenhower.* 2 vols. New York: Simon and Schuster, 1983–1984.

Bailey, Sydney D. *The Korean Armistice.* New York: St. Martin's, 1992.

Collins, J. Lawton. *War in Peacetime: The History and Lessons of Korea.* Boston: Houghton Mifflin, 1969.

Stueck, William W., Jr. *The Korean War: An International History.* Princeton, NJ: Princeton University Press, 1995.

———. *Rethinking the Korean War: A New Diplomatic and Strategic History.* Princeton, NJ: Princeton University Press, 2004.

U.S. Department of State. *United States Treaties and Other International Agreements,* Vol. 5, Part 3, *1954.* Washington, DC: U.S. Government Printing Office, 1956.

U.S. Senate Committee on Foreign Relations. *Mutual Defense Treaty with Korea: Hearings before the Committee on Foreign Relations.* 83rd Cong., 2nd sess., January 13–14, 1954. Washington, DC: U.S. Government Printing Office.

Uniting for Peace Resolution

See United Nations General Assembly Resolution 377 (V)

Universal Military Training and Service Act
Event Date: June 19, 1951

A selective service law enacted on June 19, 1951, during the Korean War to conscript men into the armed forces of the United States. The law lowered the draft age to 18.5 years and extended the period of service from 21 to 24 months. The notion of requiring all able-bodied young men to perform military service dates back to the early years of the republic. In 1789 Secretary of War Henry Knox, with the full support of Secretary of the Treasury Alexander Hamilton and President George Washington, proposed a plan for a republican system of defense. It called for all male citizens to perform military service as a way of countering the standing armies of Europe. However, suspicions about a standing army, especially in light of the recent Revolutionary War and the British Quartering Act, prevented its enactment.

The adoption of formal conscription during peacetime was first established almost 150 years later with the passage of the 1940 Selective Service Training Act. This act expired in 1947 after the conclusion of World War II, and Congress passed a new conscription law in 1948. However, the long-standing historical opposition to universal military training remained in effect. Despite the urging of President Harry S. Truman for the establishment of a mandatory six-month training requirement for all physically fit 18-year-old males who would then become inactive reservists subject to call-up in times of war, the new law merely required registration for all men between the ages of 19 and 26. Local draft boards decided who would be selected for military service.

In June 1950, with the outbreak of the Korean War, former secretary of state and later secretary of defense (beginning in September 1950) General George C. Marshall called for a rapid expansion of the armed forces. Congress responded by extending the 1948 selective service law for one year. From July 1950 to June 1951, U.S. military personnel increased from 1.46 million to 3.25 million. A final goal of 3.6 million men was set for July 1952. Initial combat losses during the early stages of the war convinced the Truman administration and Pentagon officials of the immediate need for increased training premised upon an enduring national defense system.

Debate in Congress over a new measure for universal military training elicited many of the same antimilitarist fears dating back to the time of the Washington administration. Those fears were largely premised on the threat of a garrison state and its impact on the nation's democratic way of life. Separation of civilian and military values had a legitimate basis as defined in the U.S. Constitution with respect to the role of a civilian president as commander in chief of the nation's military. However, Cold War realities muted much of the opposition's argument against a new draft law.

On June 19, 1951, a new selective service law was enacted. Known as the Universal Military Training and Service Act, this legislation revised the 1948 law by lowering the draft age from 19 to 18.5 years of age, increasing the period of service from 21 months to 2 years, and placing a total service obligation, both active and reserve, at 8 years. All males between the ages of 18 and 26 were required to register. Lowered physical and mental standards were also part of the new law.

The Universal Military Training and Service Act remained in effect until a new law was passed in 1967 during the Vietnam War. The 1951 conscription act, as with previous ones, did not require all able-bodied 18-year-olds to perform military service immediately. It merely made them subject to a draft contingent upon manpower needs.

Almost 1.5 million men between the ages of 18 and 25 were drafted during the Korean War. Another 1.3 million volunteered, thus easing the pressure on local draft boards. One controversy over the Universal Military Training and Service Act did emerge, however. The controversy was triggered by the Truman administration's authorization of draft deferments, primarily for college students. Selective Service qualification tests were administered to those seeking deferments. Some groups, such as organized labor, criticized the measure as one of economic and class bias. Although farmers and fathers were also given deferments, public opposition was less critical of these deferments than of college waivers.

In light of the Korean conflict and the Cold War, the majority of the U.S. public backed the Universal Military Training and Service Act. Between 1950 and 1953, the defense budget nearly quadrupled, and the armed forces peaked at 3.5 million men in 1953. The new draft law did provide a measure of support to Marshall's call for a fully trained military to meet the communist threat.

CHARLES F. HOWLETT

See also
Marshall, George Catlett; Truman, Harry S.

References
Chambers, John Whiteclay. *To Raise an Army: The Draft Comes to Modern America.* New York: Basic Books, 1987.

Ekirch, Arthur A., Jr. *The Civilian and the Military.* New York: Oxford University Press, 1956.

Flynn, George Q. *The Draft, 1940–1973.* Lawrence: University Press of Kansas, 1993.

Hogan, Michael J. *A Cross of Iron: Harry S. Truman and the Origins of the National Security State, 1945–1954.* New York: Cambridge University Press, 1998.

Kaufman, Burton I. *The Korean War: Challenges in Crisis, Credibility and Command.* 2nd ed. New York: McGraw-Hill, 1997.

Unsan, Battle of
Start Date: November 1, 1950
End Date: November 2, 1950

First major battle between Chinese People's Volunteer Army (CPVA, Chinese Army) and U.S. forces in the Korean War. Reacting to the evidence of the sudden Chinese entrance into the conflict, U.S. Eighth Army in Korea (EUSAK) commander Lieutenant General Walton H. Walker ordered the 1st Cavalry Division, which had been at Pyongyang, to block the Chinese force that had overrun Republic of Korea Army (ROKA, South Korean Army) forces and was attacking toward Unsan.

On November 1 the U.S. 8th Cavalry Regiment was rushed to Unsan to replace the badly mauled ROKA units. Hardly had the 1st and 2nd battalions of the 8th taken their defensive positions north and west of Unsan when they were assaulted by the 115th and 116th divisions of the CPVA Thirty-ninth Army. Waves of Chinese infantry attacked on the evening of November 1, supported only by mortars. These attackers used bugles and signal flares as a means of control. Swarms of Chinese infantry engulfed the U.S. positions and drove a wedge between the two U.S. battalions.

The two 8th Cavalry battalions fell apart and were driven back into Unsan. The 3rd Battalion of the 8th Cavalry, three miles south of Unsan, was then ordered to help the remnants of the 1st and 2nd battalions in their withdrawal from Unsan. The Chinese attack was too rapid, however; by early morning of November 2 the attackers overran the 3rd Battalion before it could begin its mission. Hand-to-hand fighting ensued, and by midmorning of November 2 little was left of the 8th Cavalry Regiment. Small groups of survivors retreated on foot around CPVA roadblocks in the regiment's rear. A counterattack by the 5th Cavalry Regiment to break through these roadblocks was unsuccessful and resulted in more than 350 additional U.S. casualties. With more than 600 men killed or captured, the 8th Cavalry Regiment was almost destroyed.

In this first engagement with the CPVA in the Korean War, an interesting act of humanitarianism occurred. Many American walking wounded from the 5th and 8th Cavalry regiments captured by the Chinese were placed along a road for U.S. medics to pick up. By dark, numerous truckloads of these U.S. wounded had been returned to American lines.

The sudden attack by the CPVA created a period of confusion throughout EUSAK's chain of command as to Chinese intentions. Nonetheless, steps were immediately taken to withdraw the exposed I Corps below the Chongchon River.

DANIEL R. BEIRNE

See also

Chinese Military Disengagement; Chinese Offensive, First; Walker, Walton Harris

References

Blair, Clay. *The Forgotten War: America in Korea, 1950–1953.* New York: Times Books, 1987.

Hoyt, Edwin P. *The Day the Chinese Attacked, Korea, 1950: The Story of the Failure of America's China Policy.* New York: McGraw-Hill, 1990.

Spurr, Russell. *Enter the Dragon: China's Undeclared War against the U.S. in Korea, 1950–1951.* New York: Henry Holt, 1988.

U.S. Policy toward Korea, Pre-1950

The first direct contact between the United States and Korea occurred in August 1866, when W. B. Preston, an American merchant and owner of the ship *General Sherman*, attempted to persuade Korea to open trade relations with the United States. After arriving off Korea, Preston ordered the *General Sherman* up the Taedong River toward Pyongyang. Local officials warned the Americans several times not to continue, but Preston and ship captain Page ignored these warnings. The Koreans then attempted to destroy the *General Sherman* with cannon fire from the riverbanks and with fire rafts set to drift toward the American schooner. Its crew was able to maneuver the ship out of harm's way. When the Koreans tried to attack the *General Sherman* with their own ships, the schooner's superior weapons promptly repelled them. Later, Preston and Page took a local official hostage in an attempt to improve their bargaining position. This action only increased Korean outrage. When the *General Sherman* ran aground on a sandbar, the Koreans had their first opportunity to seek revenge. Again they employed fire rafts, this time with success against an immobile target. Furious at what they considered the arrogance and barbaric behavior of the Americans, the Koreans showed no mercy toward the surviving crew. When they reached the shore, all the crew members were either immediately beaten to death by angry mobs or later executed.

News of the fate of the *General Sherman* and its crew reached Washington almost a year later by way of the U.S. embassy in China. Rumors were circulating that American survivors were being held prisoner in Korea. In response to these reports, Washington dispatched Commander John C. Febiger in the screw sloop *Shenandoah,* of the Asiatic Squadron, to investigate. The *Shenandoah* sailed from Chefoo, China, in March 1868. Febiger found no evidence of survivors, but he did obtain an official Korean account of the events. The Korean government's position was that the destruction of the *General Sherman* and the execution of its crew resulted from the aggressive and irresponsible actions of the ship's crew. The Korean government also made it very clear that it had no interest in opening its doors to the West.

In April 1870 U.S. secretary of state Hamilton Fish authorized Frederick F. Low, the minister to China, to open negotiations with Korea and secure a treaty for the protection of shipwrecked seamen. After conferring with the Navy Department, the State Department directed Asiatic Squadron commander Rear Admiral John Rodgers to escort Low on his mission. The Low-Rodgers expedition, comprising an armada of five warships with more than 1,200 sailors and marines, arrived off the shores of Kanghwa Island, Korea, at the end of May 1871.

On June 1 a surveying party from the expedition came under fire from one of many Korean shore fortifications. The survey party then returned fire. The exchange lasted no longer than 10 minutes, but the Americans, while suffering no serious casualties, inflicted extensive damage to the Korean fort. Admiral Rodgers believed that it was essential to demonstrate U.S. strength and capability to the Koreans, and he developed a plan to punish the attack.

The U.S. response began on June 10, 1871, and it ended the next day. It included a massive naval bombardment of Korean shore

Japanese bringing supplies ashore at the port of Chemulpo (now Inchon) for their advance on Seoul during the Russo-Japanese War of 1904–1905. (Library of Congress)

fortifications, an amphibious assault by marines, and the capture of several Korean forts. This experiment at "gunboat diplomacy" was a failure. The Low-Rodgers mission departed Korea without the desired treaty.

In the latter part of the 19th century, Americans obtained what little they knew of Korea from accounts in the press, which were for the most part negative. An example of such reporting appeared in a *New York Times* editorial on June 21, 1880: "It does not appear that the Coreans [*sic*] are any better or any worse for their seclusion from the world . . . and they have none of the vices of barbarism, unless we should find that their uncomfortable habit of massacring all shipwrecked foreigners who fall upon the coast as barbaric." Nonetheless, the United States persisted in trying to establish relations with Korea.

During the same period, Chinese officials were increasingly concerned with growing Japanese militarism and expansionism. China supported a U.S.-Korean treaty, which it hoped could prevent Japan from securing hegemony over Korea. In May 1882 Chinese intermediary Viceroy Li Hung Chang persuaded Korea's King Kojong to sign the Treaty of Peace, Amity, Commerce, and Navigation with the United States. Central to this treaty, from King Kojong's perspective, was Article 1, which stated, "If other Powers

deal unjustly or oppressively with either Government, the other will exert their good offices, on being informed of the case, to bring about an amicable arrangement, thus showing their friendly feelings." In spite of this treaty, U.S. government officials saw little strategic or commercial value in Korea. The U.S. government saw the treaty primarily as a means to improve the treatment of U.S. sailors shipwrecked on the peninsula.

The U.S. State Department's policy toward Korea in the last decade of the 19th century demonstrates U.S. indifference toward that country. From the beginning, the State Department had no interest in Korean domestic affairs and little in Korea's foreign affairs. The State Department continuously warned its diplomats in Seoul to remain neutral and disapproved of any U.S. involvement in Korean domestic or foreign affairs. In a diplomatic dispatch, Secretary of State Frederick T. Frelinghuysen informed U.S. minister in Seoul George C. Foulk: "Seoul is the center of conflicting and almost hostile intrigues involving the interests of China, Japan, Russia, and England, and . . . it is clearly the interest of the United States to hold aloof from all this and do nothing nor be drawn into anything which would look like taking sides."

Despite Washington's policy line, U.S. diplomats in Seoul continued to give King Kojong the impression that the United States would assist in maintaining Korea's independence. One of those diplomats, Minister Horace N. Allen, informed the State Department that King Kojong was confident that the United States would ensure Korea's independence after the Russo-Japanese War.

President Theodore Roosevelt did not intend to interfere in Korea against the Japanese; however, he believed Korea to be incapable of defending itself. He also knew that there was little he could do to prevent a Japanese takeover of the peninsula and believed that Japan might play a crucial role in halting the expansion of the Russian Empire. Rather than coming to the aid of Korea, as King Kojong expected, Roosevelt supported the July 27, 1905, Taft-Katsura Memorandum, in which the United States sanctioned the Japanese takeover of Korea, and in return, the Japanese promised not to take any aggressive action against the U.S.-controlled Philippines.

In October 1905 King Kojong wrote to President Roosevelt requesting that the United States offer its "good offices" as stated in the 1882 treaty and intervene on behalf of Korea to prevent Japanese encroachment. Washington ignored the request and withdrew its legation from Seoul on November 24, 1905. Six days later, Korea became a protectorate of Japan.

In 1907 King Kojong again appealed for assistance when he sent his emissaries Yi Chun, Yi Wi Jong, and Yi Sang Sol to the Second International Peace Conference at The Hague. The envoys claimed that the protectorate convention with Japan was signed under coercion and therefore was null and void. The Japanese argued that Korea had forfeited its diplomatic rights under the protectorate convention and therefore should not be allowed a separate delegation at the conference. The Japanese prevailed and, having grown impatient with the Korean monarch's persistence, forced him to abdicate his throne. Japan formally annexed Korea in August 1910, beginning an oppressive 35-year occupation of the country.

Koreans at home and abroad continued to believe that the United States would facilitate their independence. On January 8, 1918, during World War I, President Woodrow Wilson announced his Fourteen Points for peace and espoused the principle of self-determination. Koreans became aware of what was happening in Europe, where smaller nations were about to gain their independence. Having suffered more than a decade of an oppressive Japanese government, they sought ways to capitalize on Wilson's principle of self-determination and bring about Korea's independence.

Syngman Rhee, leader of the Washington-based Korean Commission, was one of those inspired and motivated by Wilson's Fourteen Points. Rhee attempted to attend the 1919 Paris Peace Conference with the intent of drawing attention to Korea's situation and persuading President Wilson to recognize Korean independence; but the State Department refused to issue passports to Rhee and his associates, claiming that as subjects of Japan they would have to obtain their passports from Japanese officials.

During the period between the signing of the Taft-Katsura agreement and the end of World War I, the relationship between the United States and Japan changed considerably. Both had emerged as world powers with impressive naval forces, and both were equally suspicious of the other's capabilities and intentions. A naval arms race ensued, leading many to believe that war between the two nations was inevitable. In an effort to ease tensions, avoid a new arms race, and reconcile differences, the United States invited Japan to participate in the Washington Conference on the Limitation of Armaments beginning in November 1921.

The Korean Commission saw the conference as another opportunity to publicize Korea's struggle for independence. Changing its name to the Conference on Limitations of Armaments, the commission drafted an appeal, which it submitted to the U.S. delegation on October 1, 1921. The commission argued that several Western powers had negotiated a treaty with Korea before the Japanese annexation, and therefore "must still regard Korea as a separate entity and the treaties in force." U.S. secretary of state Charles E. Hughes did promise to warn the Japanese regarding their treatment of the Korean people, but the Korean Commission failed to obtain recognition of Korea's right to independence.

Not until World War II did the United States take a real interest in Korea. President Franklin D. Roosevelt favored a trusteeship in Korea, whereby the United States, Great Britain, China, and the Soviet Union would temporarily govern the country until Korea could govern itself. Roosevelt wanted to establish a lasting peace after winning the war and believed that the key to such an endeavor was strengthening U.S.-Soviet relations. He also believed that a U.S.-Soviet trusteeship in Korea would not only provide the Soviets with the incentive for entering the war in the Pacific but would also form the beginnings of U.S.-Soviet cooperation.

When President Roosevelt died in April 1945, the tone of U.S. policy toward the Soviet Union changed, as did U.S. policy toward Korea. Korea became a pawn in a power struggle between the United States and the Soviet Union. Both countries agreed to the 38th Parallel as a rough demarcation line for the surrender of Japanese forces; the Soviets would take the Japanese surrender in Korea north of that line, and the United States would do the same south of it.

Efforts to reunify the two halves of Korea foundered during the Cold War. In May 1948, when the communist northern government refused to allow a United Nations (UN) commission into its territory, the commission held elections in the southern half of Korea, and Syngman Rhee was elected president of the Republic of Korea (ROK, South Korea). Northern Korea responded by inaugurating the Democratic People's Republic of Korea (DPRK, North Korea), with Kim Il Sung as its premier.

By June 1949 the United States had withdrawn its remaining forces from South Korea and left behind the 500-man Korea Military Advisory Group (KMAG) to train South Korean forces. On January 12, 1950, Secretary of State Dean Acheson defined the U.S. strategic defense perimeter in Asia as excluding the Korean Peninsula. This situation encouraged North Korea, which had built up its military forces with substantial Soviet aid. On June 25, 1950,

North Korea launched a well-executed invasion of South Korea. This act, which caught both the United States and South Korea by surprise, initiated the Korean War and dramatically changed U.S. policy toward Korea and all of East Asia.

MARK R. FRANKLIN

See also

Acheson, Dean Gooderham; China, Republic of; Geneva Convention; Japan; Korea, Climate and Geography of; Korea, Democratic People's Republic of, 1945–1953; Korea, History of, to 1945; Korea, History of, 1945–1947; Korea, Republic of, 1947–1953; Potsdam Conference; Rhee, Syngman

References

Burnette, Scott S., ed. *Korean-American Relations: Documents Pertaining to the Far Eastern Diplomacy of the United States*, Vol. 3, *The Period of Diminishing Influence, 1896–1905*. Honolulu: University of Hawaii Press, 1989.

Cumings, Bruce. *The Origins of the Korean War*. 2 vols. Princeton, NJ: Princeton University Press, 1981, 1990.

George, Douglas Edward. "The Low-Rodgers Expedition: A Study in the Foundations of U.S. Policy in Korea." Unpublished master's thesis, Naval Post Graduate School, Monterey, CA, 1988.

Koo, Youngnok, and Dae Sook Suh, eds. *Korea and the United States: A Century of Cooperation*. Honolulu: University of Hawaii Press, 1984.

Ky, Dae Yeol. *Korea under Colonialism: The March First Movement and Anglo-Japanese Relations*. Seoul: Seoul Computer Press, 1985.

Lee, Yur Bok, and Wayne Patterson, eds. *One Hundred Years of Korea-American Relations, 1882–1982*. Tuscaloosa: University of Alabama Press, 1986.

McCune, George M., and John A. Harrison, eds. *Korean-American Relations: Documents Pertaining to the Far Eastern Diplomacy of the United States*, Vol. 1, *The Initial Period, 1883–1886*. Berkeley: University of California Press, 1951.

Millett, Allan R. *The War for Korea, 1945–1950: A House Burning*. Lawrence: University Press of Kansas, 2005.

Palmer, Spencer J., ed. *Korean-American Relations: Documents Pertaining to the Far Eastern Diplomacy of the United States*, Vol. 2, *The Period of Growing Influence, 1887–1895*. Berkeley: University of California Press, 1963.

U.S. Policy toward Korea, 1950–1953

When President Harry S. Truman began his second term of office on January 20, 1949, U.S. policy toward East Asia was in crisis. The central issue in the region, which was emerging as the Cold War's second front, was what to do about China. This decision would have profound security ramifications both for U.S.-occupied Japan and for the situation on the Korean Peninsula. In China, Mao Zedong and the Communists continued to gain in their civil war against Jiang Jieshi (Chiang Kai-shek) and the Guomindang (GMD, Nationalist) regime. Mao also appeared to be taking a more anti-American stance and was moving closer to the Soviet Union. On the Korean Peninsula, veteran communist Kim Il Sung, who had ties to both China and the Soviet Union, ruled northern Korea as president of the Democratic People's Republic of Korea (DPRK, North Korea). The Korean situation was complicated because both the DPRK and

the Republic of Korea (ROK, South Korea), led by the conservative U.S.-educated President Syngman Rhee, sought reunification of the artificially divided peninsula on their own terms.

Against the backdrop of an evolving U.S. policy of containing the Soviet Union in Europe, the situation in Asia caused Truman and Secretary of State Dean G. Acheson to seek a more realistic and pragmatic policy with both China and Korea. With the Communists controlling most of the mainland, in October 1949 Mao proclaimed in Beijing the People's Republic of China (PRC). Jiang was then forced to relocate the Nationalist government and major elements of its military to Taiwan (then known as Formosa). Despite significant political support in the U.S. Congress for maintaining military and economic assistance to the Nationalists and formulating a strategy to oppose communism in Asia, the Truman administration, which had expended considerable sums on the losing effort in China, shifted its focus to Europe, which was considered to be the most critical area for U.S. interests.

Truman's cautious policy toward Asia was in accordance with his administration's assessment that without massive U.S. military aid and assistance, and the direct involvement of U.S. military forces, the Nationalists on Taiwan would soon fall. Despite pressure from the Republican opposition, Truman announced at a press conference in January 1950 that the United States would not seek bases on Taiwan, become involved in the continuing civil war, or provide further military aid or advice to the Nationalists. U.S. domestic policy toward China was further complicated when the major U.S. European ally, Great Britain, announced in early January its recognition of the PRC. It was then obvious that the United States would have to go it alone if it adopted a pro-Jiang China policy.

The controversial and ambiguous nature of U.S. East Asia policy was further highlighted in January when Congress initially failed to pass an appropriations bill for continuing economic assistance to South Korea. This heightened the perception of an American retreat from Korea following the withdrawal of U.S. combat forces. U.S. forces had initially occupied Korea south of the 38th Parallel in September 1945 in order to receive the surrender of Japanese forces there. In early 1948 Washington began to redeploy U.S. combat units, and by early 1950 only the 500-man Korea Military Advisory Group (KMAG) remained to train and support the South Korean armed forces. Soviet military units had also been withdrawn from northern Korea, and they too had left behind administrative and training cadres.

The minimal U.S. military presence in South Korea, coupled with the failure of economic aid, signaled the reduced strategic importance of, and the diminished American commitment to, the ROK. Although the economic aid legislation was later passed, as Secretary of State Acheson later asserted, "the damage had been done. Without question, the government and the people of the United States wished to end their responsibility for the government and the future of Korea." In a speech on January 12, 1950, Acheson himself did further damage when he implied that Korea

Soldiers of the U.S. 25th Infantry Division move into Chinju, September 1950. (Department of Defense)

and Taiwan were outside the U.S. defensive perimeter in East Asia. Japan was the key regional state for U.S. Far East security.

In February 1950 the Chinese and the Soviets signed a treaty that both called on the Soviet Union to provide significant economic aid to China and established a formal alliance between the two states. The implicit withdrawal of U.S. protection from the Chinese Nationalists and from the regime in South Korea left the door wide open for Mao's planned invasion of Taiwan. With the U.S. pullback from Korea and the forging of the Sino-Soviet alliance, the way also seemed clear for Kim Il Sung's regime to reunify the Korean Peninsula by force. In addition to the apparent diplomatic withdrawal, the U.S. military order of battle in the region had been reduced significantly. General Douglas MacArthur's Far East Command (FEC) consisted of only four infantry divisions and one regimental combat team (RCT). This occupation force in Japan and Okinawa was woefully understrength and inadequately equipped and trained. The air and naval elements in the theater, while significant, also suffered from shortages and training deficiencies. Muddled diplomacy and military unpreparedness combined to expose U.S. weakness in East Asia.

The politically contentious and ambiguous U.S. policies toward both Jiang and the Nationalists on Taiwan and the regime of President Syngman Rhee in South Korea were severely tested by North Korea's attack on South Korea early on June 25, 1950. After a series of meetings with his senior foreign policy and military advisers, President Truman decided to provide military equipment to the ROK, but initially he authorized only a limited commitment of U.S. air and naval units. The president did order the Seventh Fleet into the Taiwan Strait to deter a concurrent escalation of fighting between the two Chinas. The Truman administration was concerned over possible future actions by the Soviet Union and China, along with the rapidly deteriorating situation of the South Korean forces fighting to stop the offensive by the Korean People's Army (KPA, North Korean Army).

In addition to its own unilateral actions, the United States forwarded the matter to the United Nations (UN), which condemned the North Korean invasion. The United States also requested that member states provide military support to assist the South Korean defenders. Since the Soviets were boycotting the Security Council, the UN resolution there condemning North Korea passed unanimously. (At that time the Nationalist government represented China in the UN, which was the reason for the Soviet boycott of the Security Council.) Washington then began the process of gaining UN agreement for direct military action by member states under U.S. command.

General MacArthur, who conducted a personal reconnaissance to Korea on June 29–30, 1950, passed his appraisal of the situation and of the military performance of the Republic of Korea Army (ROKA, South Korean Army) to Washington. He recommended direct U.S. military action to stem the invasion. Truman then authorized MacArthur to commit U.S. ground combat forces to the defense of South Korea. After five days of fact-finding and debate, the United States was at war with the DPRK, but on a limited scale and with no authorization to strike Soviet or Chinese targets.

Initial U.S. policy was to stop the invasion and restore the territorial integrity of South Korea. On July 7 the UN passed a resolution that called for a multinational effort under the direction of General MacArthur. Even as defenses were being organized, MacArthur began planning a bold counterstroke.

In September 1950 MacArthur's Inchon amphibious operation and a concurrent breakout by the U.S. Eighth Army in Korea (EUSAK) saw the UNC regain the offensive. After two months of tough fighting just to hang on in Korea, the Truman administration was now confronted with the policy issue of whether or not to allow MacArthur to cross the 38th Parallel with ground forces and reunite the peninsula under South Korean rule. This action had the potential to trigger direct intervention by either China or the Soviet Union or both.

The policy that emerged left MacArthur significant room for interpretation and provided wide latitude for him to react to the exigencies of the developing situation. Except for tactical actions necessary to carry out the primary military objective of the destruction of the KPA, U.S. ground forces would stay south of the 38th Parallel; ROKA forces could conduct limited operations north of that line. Under no circumstances were U.S. naval or air forces authorized to engage targets in China or the Soviet Union without prior approval by Washington. Furthermore, if Soviet forces entered the war, the UNC was to halt its offensive; but if Chinese forces intervened, the UNC was to continue advancing so long as it did not encounter serious resistance.

The KPA withdrew into North Korea but refused MacArthur's calls to surrender. On October 1 ROKA forces entered North Korea against minimal resistance. MacArthur reorganized the UN forces and prepared for further military action to destroy the KPA. In early October—avoiding the UN Security Council, as the Soviet Union had ended its boycott of that body—the United States pressed the General Assembly for a resolution to guide follow-up actions. The resultant October 7 UN General Assembly resolution called for "all appropriate steps to ensure stability throughout Korea" and for UN oversight of elections and the formation of a unified democratic Korean government. With this new "guidance," and despite specific warnings from Beijing through intermediaries and

growing intelligence evidence of a Chinese buildup in Manchuria, U.S. forces entered North Korea on October 9. Planning began in earnest for the occupation of North Korea and the implementation of a phased program under UN auspices leading to a reunified and democratic Korea.

A United Nations Command (UNC) military victory appeared to be within reach when the PRC intervened militarily. Chinese People's Volunteer Army (CPVA, Chinese Army) forces began to deploy into North Korea on October 14 and clashed with UNC troops on October 25. MacArthur, who had previously discounted Chinese intervention, now called for air strikes against Chinese targets. Washington finally agreed to air strikes against the bridges over the Yalu River, but it insisted that these strikes take place only on the Korean side of the border.

President Truman and key military leaders in Washington were now forced to reassess the situation. Truman was determined not to widen the war if at all possible, while MacArthur argued the military necessity of hitting targets in Manchuria that supported the Chinese deployment. When the Chinese then disengaged, UNC forces resumed the offensive.

The size and initial success of the massive Chinese intervention in late November changed the entire complexion of the war. In effect, the United States was now fighting China. UNC forces were driven south. After withdrawing below the 38th Parallel and losing Seoul for a second time, UNC forces rallied, stopped the Chinese, mounted a major offensive, and were able to restore a defensive line just north of the 38th Parallel.

The military stalemate on the ground and a sober appraisal of the strategic costs of all-out war with China, and possibly also the Soviet Union, precipitated a major policy change in Washington. The growing feud between Truman and MacArthur over how to deal with China culminated with the general's removal from command in April 1951. The core issues of this politically contentious action were the definition of military victory, civilian control over the military, the Truman administration's preparations to use atomic weapons if necessary in Korea but its unwillingness—and that of America's allies—to leave this decision in the hands of MacArthur, and a disagreement over the Truman administration's decision to limit the war and to seek a diplomatic settlement.

By May 1951 the war had settled into a costly stalemate with neither side willing to expend the personnel and resources for the decisive offensive operations needed to break the deadlock on the ground. The unification by force of the Korean Peninsula was no longer possible without expanding the conflict. The Truman administration now was willing to settle for a diplomatic solution and a return to the status quo ante bellum, and the communist side was also ready to negotiate.

Meetings over a negotiated settlement began on July 10, 1951. However, from the very beginning the negotiations bogged down over both major and minor issues. Off and on, the talks dragged on as disagreements over venues, meeting agendas, cease-fire agreements, the exchange of prisoners, withdrawal of foreign forces, the demarcation line, and the widening of the talks to include the Taiwan situation prolonged the complicated negotiations. In the meantime, both sides attempted to display and confirm their resolve by continuing limited military actions with significant additional casualties.

In December 1952 U.S. president-elect Dwight D. Eisenhower visited Korea to make his own personal appraisal. Despite additional pressures exerted by the new administration, there was more than six months of bitter fighting, including a major communist assault in June, before the difficult negotiations succeeded and the armistice was signed on July 27, 1953. Critical to the negotiations was South Korean president Syngman Rhee. He strongly opposed a settlement that would leave Korea divided and Chinese troops in North Korea. To secure his support, the Eisenhower administration had to promise substantial additional aid and a postconflict security pact, signed in October 1953. Rhee was placated, but the armistice that ended the fighting left Korea politically and geographically divided, and American troops were permanently garrisoned in South Korea.

J. G. D. Babb

See also

Acheson, Dean Gooderham; Acheson's National Press Club Speech; Eisenhower, Dwight David; Inchon Landing; Jiang Jieshi; Kaesong Truce Talks; Kim Il Sung; MacArthur, Douglas; Mao Zedong; Rhee, Syngman; Truce Talks; Truman, Harry S.; United States–Republic of Korea Mutual Defense Treaty; U.S. Policy toward Korea, 1953–Present

References

Acheson, Dean. *The Korean War.* New York: Norton, 1971.

Alexander, Bevin. *Korea: The First War We Lost.* New York: Hippocrene Books, 1986.

Brazinsky, Gregg. *Nation Building in South Korea: Koreans, Americans, and the Making of Democracy.* Chapel Hill: University of North Carolina Press, 2007.

Cumings, Bruce. *Child of Conflict: The Korean-American Relationship 1943–1953.* Seattle, WA: University of Washington Press, 1983.

Donovan, Robert J. *Tumultuous Years: The Presidency of Harry S. Truman.* New York: Norton, 1982.

Foot, Rosemary J. *The Wrong War: American Policy and the Dimensions of the Korean Conflict, 1950–1953.* Ithaca, NY: Cornell University Press, 1985.

Oberdorfer, Don. *The Two Koreas: A Contemporary History.* Rev. and updated ed. New York: Basic Books, 2001.

U.S. Policy toward Korea, 1953–Present

U.S. policy toward Korea since 1953 is the legacy of a conflict for which no final peace treaty has been signed. Today, nearly 60 years after the outbreak of the Korean War, the United States maintains nearly 100,000 military personnel in the Asia-Pacific theater. Some 28,500 of these are stationed in the Republic of Korea (ROK, South Korea), including the 2nd Infantry Division, which deployed to the Korean Peninsula in 1950. The United States remains committed to the defense of South Korea under the terms of a mutual security treaty promulgated in August 1953.

President Dwight D. Eisenhower took office in January 1953. Following the Truman administration's lead, he was determined to end the costly war and stalemate as soon as possible. Eisenhower saw a negotiated settlement as the only solution. However, his South Korean counterpart Syngman Rhee continued to push for the reunification of Korea by military force. This was impossible without massive U.S. assistance, and Rhee grudgingly stepped back from his position on reunification and agreed to the terms of the settlement. As a quid pro quo, he demanded assurances that the United States would not abandon the ROK and would remain fully committed to the defense of South Korea.

Within a month of the signing of the armistice, the Eisenhower administration concluded a defense treaty with the ROK. The United States also promised significant military assistance to build up the South Korean armed forces and to provide economic and humanitarian aid as well. However, the United States also began planning for a significant drawdown of its forces. A senior U.S. officer continued to command all allied forces, including South Korean units.

After further negotiations with South Korea and direct warnings to Beijing of the consequences of a renewed offensive, two of eight U.S. infantry divisions and several air force units on the peninsula were withdrawn in 1954. In addition, negotiations with the People's Republic of China (PRC) continued upon the withdrawal of its troops from the Democratic People's Republic of Korea (DPRK, North Korea). China agreed to reduce its forces, and in August 1954 Washington announced the withdrawal of four additional U.S. divisions. Despite opposition by the ROK and some U.S. members of Congress, this redeployment was completed in 1955.

A tense truce continued in Korea throughout the 1950s, as both the ROK and the DPRK continued to expand their military capabilities with equipment and training provided by their Cold War sponsors. In North Korea, the Kim Il Sung regime received massive economic support from both China and the Soviet Union, enabling it to build its economy and consolidate its power. In South Korea the increasingly autocratic, corrupt, and harsh Rhee administration was rapidly losing popular support as the economy struggled. In 1960, following a series of student demonstrations and increasing political opposition, Rhee was finally forced from office. After a brief attempt by more moderate and democratic elements to institute economic and governmental reforms failed, Major General Park Chung Hee led a successful coup and seized power in May 1961. U.S. forces and the majority of South Korean units did not interfere with the military takeover, and there was no attempt to exploit the situation by North Korea and its communist patrons.

By 1963 Park had successfully consolidated his power and gained a measure of political legitimacy when he was popularly elected as the nation's president. This period of political turbulence in South Korea coincided with a series of Cold War–related

The U.S. Navy Nimitz-class aircraft carrier *John C. Stennis* (CVN-74) and South Korean warships on March 20, 2009, at the end of the training exercise FOAL EAGLE 2009. (Department of Defense)

crises for U.S. president John F. Kennedy's administration. The 1961 Bay of Pigs fiasco, the deteriorating situation in South Vietnam, tensions with the Soviet Union in Europe, and the momentous 1962 Cuban Missile Crisis pushed the security and domestic political situation in South Korea into the background. When Lyndon B. Johnson took office in late 1963, his administration's primary focus in Asia was the expanding war in Vietnam. The United States began a gradual buildup of forces in South Vietnam that offered economic opportunities for the ROK, but also had the potential to draw off U.S. military units and equipment critical to the defense of South Korea.

To show solidarity with its ally and in an effort to ensure that U.S. forces in South Korea would not be shifted to Southeast Asia, the Park government sent two divisions of some 45,000 Republic of Korea Army (ROKA, South Korean Army) troops to Vietnam. The United States provided considerable assistance to the ROK in turn. In 1966 President Johnson and other senior members of his administration visited South Korea and pledged that no U.S. troops would be withdrawn and that American support for the defense of the ROK was a key element of U.S. Asian policy. However, two incidents in 1968 and another in 1969 tested the relationship and identified limitations in the U.S. commitment.

In January 1968 North Korean forces attacked and captured the *Pueblo*, a largely undefended U.S. Navy spy ship gathering electronic intelligence off the North Korean coast in international waters. The muted U.S. reaction to this provocation consisted of a regional show of force by aircraft carrier battle groups. This was followed by 11 months of North Korean intransigence and sporadic

negotiations before the United States issued an apology and the DPRK released the *Pueblo*'s crew (whereupon the apology was disavowed). Earlier in January 1968 North Korean commandoes attempted to assassinate President Park at the Blue House in Seoul. Again, despite a clear military provocation, Washington called for enhancing the defensive posture of South Korean and U.S. forces and responding diplomatically. At the height of American commitment to the war in Vietnam, the Johnson administration would not support a retaliatory military strike by the ROK against North Korea that could possibly escalate into wider conflict.

In April 1969, shortly after President Richard M. Nixon took office, North Korean forces shot down a U.S. intelligence collection aircraft, resulting in the loss of its 31-man crew. Again, the United States conducted a naval show of force and deployed additional aircraft to South Korea, but it carried out no punitive response. This lack of military response cast some doubts on the strength of the U.S. commitment to South Korea in any situation short of a full invasion. In June 1969 the situation was further complicated for the ROK when Nixon announced a new security doctrine.

The Nixon Doctrine represented a major policy change, and the Park regime perceived it as having a direct and negative impact on the U.S.–South Korean mutual defense relationship. Nixon attempted to assure U.S. allies that the United States would live up to its treaty commitments and continue to provide nuclear protection. What concerned the ROK was Washington's demand that allied and friendly nations now supply the troops and bear a greater share of the costs of conventional weapons for their own defense.

In early 1971 Nixon ordered the withdrawal of one of the two remaining U.S. Army divisions from Korea. More significantly, Nixon's national security adviser Henry Kissinger began secret negotiations with Beijing that led to the historic February 1972 visit by President Nixon to China. As the United States pulled out of Vietnam, the stage was set for the eventual full diplomatic recognition and normalization of relations with the PRC at the expense of the Republic of China (ROC, Taiwan). This event shook the Park regime's confidence in U.S. security commitments. Even without significant Soviet or Chinese support, the DPRK's military was superior to that of the ROK, and South Korea's ability to defend itself was problematic. The confidence of the ROK was further eroded when China reacted to North Korea's concerns over Sino-U.S. rapprochement by extending it a new military and economic aid package—this while promises of more modern U.S. equipment were being delayed and combat forces withdrawn. The Park regime began to seek direct talks with North Korea, and a short period of détente supported by the United States followed.

By the mid-1970s, as Nixon became embroiled in the Watergate scandal, the Park regime was also losing popular support, and it increasingly resorted to dictatorial methods in an attempt to retain power. Concurrently, after a period of popular and promising negotiations, relations with North Korea again began to deteriorate. Shortly after Nixon resigned in 1974, succeeding president Gerald R. Ford was confronted by a new crisis on the Korean Peninsula.

In August 1976 two U.S. Army officers were brutally murdered in the demilitarized zone (DMZ) while supervising the trimming of a tree in the Joint Security Area (JSA). Ford immediately ordered the deployment of additional air and naval forces to Korea. Under the cover of a massive show of force, which included tanks and Boeing B-52 Stratofortress bombers and other supporting aircraft, the tree was removed, but the United States took no further action. This incident did result in a change in the deployment of troops within the JSA. Once again, the United States was less than decisive or resolute in its response to North Korean aggression. President-elect Jimmy Carter campaigned for further withdrawals of U.S. forces from Korea, and Seoul again feared abandonment by its ally. The U.S. intelligence community, however, conducted an extensive reexamination of the military balance on the peninsula and concluded that North Korea was stronger militarily than was previously estimated. Caught up in a contentious domestic political debate and being pressured diplomatically by South Korea, Carter suspended the withdrawals after only one brigade of the 2nd Infantry Division had been removed. The U.S. relationship with the Park government deteriorated further when Carter called for an improvement in human rights in South Korea.

The South Korean political situation changed abruptly in October 1979, when President Park was assassinated. During the next year, key political and military factions vied for power as students, workers, and opposition parties conducted major demonstrations that often resulted in violence. General Chun Doo Hwan slowly took power and began to arrest key political opponents, censored the press, and used loyal military units to crack down on protests. In May 1980 he deployed Special Forces units and paratroopers, ostensibly under U.S. command, to quell the Kwangju riots in southern Korea, resulting in the deaths of hundreds of people.

A controversy arose over Chun's use of these troops, who had been allegedly "released" by U.S. general John A. Wickham, commander of the Combined Forces Command. The situation was further exacerbated when President Ronald Reagan lauded Chun for his decisive response to growing chaos in the country. While Washington regarded this situation in terms of the overall regional security picture, opposition groups in the ROK saw the United States as complicit in support of a brutal military dictatorship. Chun successfully stabilized the situation, and in August 1980 he was "elected" president of South Korea. He then began a major program of political and economic reforms that quieted his critics.

The deterioration in U.S.–South Korean relations during the Carter years was reversed by the close relationship that developed between Presidents Reagan and Chun. The South Korean president was the first official foreign dignitary to visit Washington during the Reagan administration. President Reagan also visited South Korea in 1983, and he increased the number of U.S. forces in Korea. Both were important gestures.

Two major incidents in 1983 also worked to bring the two countries together. On September 1 Soviet aircraft shot down Korean Airlines (KAL) Flight 007, killing both Korean and American passengers in the process. Then, on October 9, President Chun and several senior members of his government conducted a state visit to Rangoon, Burma. Two North Korean military officers had infiltrated the country, and they set off a bomb that killed several members of the Chun government, including the foreign minister. As with previous incidents, no military retaliation against the DPRK was undertaken, but the two countries worked together closely to coordinate their diplomatic responses. In a show of support, additional U.S. military forces were deployed to the region. During the next several years, the developing relationship between the Reagan administration and that of Mikhail Gorbachev in the Soviet Union, as well as Reagan's visit to China, helped to significantly lessen tensions on the Korean Peninsula.

As the international situation improved, the most significant problems in South Korea were now in the domestic political arena. Chun had promised an end to military dictatorship and wanted to oversee a peaceful transition before the 1988 Seoul Olympics. In December 1987 another ROKA officer, General Roh Tae Woo, unexpectedly won the first popular election in Korea since 1971. He defeated both Kim Young Sam and Kim Dae Jung, who would both win later elections and serve as the first two elected civilian leaders of Korea since President Syngman Rhee. In 1988 the hugely successful Seoul Olympics were held. The games were attended by virtually all of North Korea's allies and were a major embarrassment for the DPRK. The ROK, fully supported by the United States, weathered North Korea's diplomatic attempts to share the games while enduring another major terrorist incident, the bombing of KAL Flight 858. South Korea, now becoming a major economic power in Asia, had conducted a peaceful transition of government and was in a position to conduct a more independent foreign policy.

President Roh, again fully supported by the United States and taking advantage of the end of the Cold War, began to implement a policy of Nordpolitik that had its roots in the Chun era. This policy included initiatives toward normalizing relations with the DPRK and sought to improve relations with China and the Soviet Union as well.

Encouraged by Washington, Roh's policies achieved dramatic results, including a reversal of Soviet support for North Korea and closer political and economic relations with China. With the support of the major powers, the two Koreas joined the United Nations (UN) in 1991. The administration of U.S. president George H. W. Bush suggested that it was time for the United States to begin the process of moving from a leading role to a supporting role on the Korean Peninsula. The ROK was now seen as more of an equal partner and a mature, independent player in the region.

As the Cold War ended in Europe and relations with China matured, the United States began to focus on its problems in the Middle East. However, the large and well-prepared military forces of the ROK and the DPRK still confronted each other, and incidents at sea and along the DMZ occurred all too frequently. However, the booming South Korean economy, a military modernization program, and diplomatic initiatives toward China and Russia put the DPRK at a major disadvantage, and another North Korean invasion seemed a more remote possibility by the early 1990s.

Nevertheless, as William J. Clinton took office in early 1993, several issues cast doubt on this optimistic appraisal. Developments in missile technology, North Korean arms sales to the Middle East, and especially the possibility of a nuclear-armed DPRK increased tensions in the region. Clinton's first foreign visit was to South Korea, where he specifically warned North Korea of the dire consequences of using nuclear weapons against the ROK. His tour of the DMZ and his visit there with U.S. troops was a symbol of the continued U.S. commitment to the defense of South Korea. The United States led the effort to negotiate with North Korea over the issue of nuclear weapons and technology. In July 1994 "Great Leader" Kim Il Sung died after leading the DPRK for 46 years. His son Kim Jong Il, about whom little was known, took power.

In October 1994 the DPRK signed the Framework Agreement, which called for an inspection regimen conducted by the International Atomic Energy Agency (IAEA), a UN organ. North Korea was promised two light water reactors to replace its current heavy water reactors, and the United States agreed to supply oil in the interim until the new power plants came on line. After the agreement was signed, however, there were ample indications that the DPRK was not living up to the agreement. During the late 1990s, North Korea's economy was in steep decline, and there were reports of widespread famine. Millions were malnourished, and

hundreds of thousands of people may have died. Ominously, North Korea developed and launched a multistage rocket, which also increased tensions in the region. Clearly the Cold War had not ended in Korea.

Despite renewed rapprochement between the two Koreas in the late 1990s and first few years of the 21st century, relations between North and South Korea remain strained, largely because of the renewed bellicosity of the DPRK, which includes repeated tests of missiles that have the capability of striking both South Korea and Japan. Evidence of the DPRK's continuance of its nuclear weapons program has also strained relations in the region. Certainly U.S. president George W. Bush's linking of North Korea with the so-called "Axis of Evil" in January 2002 caused further angst on the Korean Peninsula. In 2003 Kim Jong Il announced that his country would withdraw from the Nuclear Non-proliferation Treaty and resume its nuclear program. After several years of multilateral talks including the United States, North Korea again agreed to freeze and dismantle its nuclear program in exchange for economic aid and other concessions. But even so Pyongyang has continued to act brazenly, conducting a crude nuclear test in 2006 and continuing with menacing missile tests as late as 2008. It is clear that U.S. policy toward North Korea after 2000 has sought to avoid backing Pyongyang into a corner, for fear that doing so could unleash a holocaust on the Korean Peninsula, where thousands of American troops remain stationed.

Meanwhile, in South Korea, President Roh Moo Hyun, who took office in February 2003, sought to continue his predecessor's rapprochement policies with North Korea. These policies included trade, aid, and reconciliation programs and a summit with Kim Jong Il in 2007, much to the consternation of Washington. Since February 2008 Lee Myung Bak, Roh's successor, has taken a tougher stand with Pyongyang, which has frozen relations between North and South Korea. He also pledged to strengthen ties to the United States, and Washington has thus far responded positively.

U.S. policy toward the Korean Peninsula remains focused on deterring the DPRK from military adventurism and defending a long-standing treaty ally. The region is the critical flash point in Asia and is specifically covered in the U.S. national security strategy as one of two areas where forces must be prepared to conduct a "Major Theater War." The United States has not relinquished its leading military role. As in 1950, the United States continues to retain vital and strategic interests in Korea.

J. G. D. BABB

See also

Eisenhower, Dwight David; Kim Il Sung; Kim Jong Il; Nixon, Richard Milhous; Rhee, Syngman; United States–Republic of Korea Mutual Defense Treaty

References

Brazinsky, Gregg. *Nation Building in South Korea: Koreans, Americans, and the Making of Democracy.* Chapel Hill: University of North Carolina Press, 2007.

Bunge, Frederica, M., ed. *North Korea: A Country Study* (DA Pam 550-81). Washington, DC: U.S. Government Printing Office, 1989.

Keon, Michael. *Korean Phoenix: A Nation from the Ashes.* Englewood, NJ: Prentice Hall International, 1977.

Kihl, Young Whan, ed. *Korea and the World: Beyond the Cold War.* Boulder, CO: Westview, 1994.

Lee, Suk Bok. *The Impact of U.S. Forces in Korea.* Washington, DC: National Defense University Press, 1987.

Oberdorfer, Don. *The Two Koreas: A Contemporary History.* Rev. and updated ed. New York: Basic Books, 2001.

Savada, Andrea M., and William Shaw, eds. *South Korea: A Country Study* (DA Pam 550-41). Washington, DC: U.S. Government Printing Office, 1990.

Stueck, William W., Jr., ed. *Korean War in World History.* Lexington: University Press of Kentucky, 2004.

V

Van Fleet, James Alward

Birth Date: March 19, 1892
Death Date: September 23, 1992

U.S. Army general and commander of the U.S. Eighth Army in Korea (EUSAK) during the Korean War. Born on March 19, 1892, in Coytesville, New Jersey, and raised in Florida, James Alward Van Fleet graduated from the U.S. Military Academy at West Point in 1915. He then served with the army along the Mexican border. After the United States entered World War I, he led a machine-gun battalion of the U.S. Army 6th Division and saw combat in the Meuse-Argonne Offensive.

In the years 1918 to 1939, Van Fleet taught military science in Reserve Officers Training Corps programs in Kansas, South Dakota, and Florida; studied and taught at the Infantry School at Fort Benning, Georgia; and eventually, as a colonel, became commander of the 8th Infantry Regiment in February 1941. Although he remained a colonel and retained command of the 8th Infantry until 1944, his rise to general officer's rank began with the June 1944 Normandy invasion, when the 8th Infantry landed at Utah Beach as a part of the U.S. 4th Division. By the time the division participated in the capture of Cherbourg, Van Fleet had earned recognition as a forceful, courageous, and competent commander. By March 1945 he was a major general and commanded III Corps.

In the postwar years, Van Fleet gained valuable experience in the exigencies of Cold War generalship. After a tour of duty in the United States, he served in occupied Germany in 1947. In 1948 he was named head of the U.S. Military Advisory and Planning Group in civil war–torn Greece. Promoted to lieutenant general and appointed to the Greek National Defense Council, Van Fleet participated in one of the first confrontations between East and West in the Cold War. He helped mold the Greek army into an effective fighting force, and by 1949 that army had defeated a communist-inspired insurgency. Van Fleet next received command of the U.S. Second Army.

In the wake of General Douglas MacArthur's removal as head of the United Nations Command (UNC) by President Truman in April 1951 and his replacement by Lieutenant General Matthew B. Ridgway, Van Fleet assumed Ridgway's former position as commander of EUSAK. He was promoted to full general on August 1. Upon his arrival in Korea, Van Fleet received orders to place EUSAK on the defensive while inflicting the heaviest possible losses on communist forces. Van Fleet repositioned the Eighth Army along and to the south of the 38th Parallel, where a rough stalemate had by then developed between UNC forces and the communists. Here his troops defeated the Fifth (Spring) Offensive by the Chinese People's Volunteer Army (CPVA, Chinese Army). Van Fleet then launched a counterattack, and by June the Eighth Army had inflicted some 270,000 casualties on the CPVA and Korean People's Army (KPA, North Korean Army).

Van Fleet chafed under the politically driven necessities of limited warfare in the age of the Cold War. Although fighting in Korea was certainly hot enough, larger considerations of international politics often determined action on the ground. Thus, through the fall and winter of 1951–1952, EUSAK fought a continuous series of defensive actions, some of them quite bloody, which Van Fleet saw as threatening to morale and discipline, and which ran counter to his predilections as a leader. On the other hand, his directives for the very defensive he was ordered to implement were perceived in the press as insufficiently aggressive. He found himself thereby caught in what would become a classic Cold War bind for U.S. battlefield commanders.

U.S. Army general James A. Van Fleet commanded the Eighth U.S. Army in Korea during April 1951–February 1953. (Hulton Archive/Getty Images)

Consequently, friction sometimes arose between Van Fleet and higher echelons over questions of tactics and ultimate goals. This atmosphere forced him to make extensive use of close air support (CAS) along Lines Kansas and Wyoming to avoid useless losses to U.S. ground troops. It also created for him the impression that the Eighth Army was intentionally being deprived of artillery ammunition in retaliation for his being politically troublesome, a charge he made after his retirement.

Despite such differences, Van Fleet kept the Eighth Army in fighting trim during the bitter and bloody stalemate of the war's last two years. At Heartbreak Ridge and Bloody Ridge in eastern Korea in the late summer of 1951, in central Korea that October, and in the Iron Triangle in the summer and autumn of 1952, Van Fleet proved to be a pugnacious, blunt spoken, and usually successful commander. Because of the nature of the Korean War, his troops sometimes suffered heavy casualties even in small-scale actions, but they almost always inflicted even greater losses on the enemy. Van Fleet inspired the political and military leadership of the Republic of Korea (ROK, South Korea) as well.

Van Fleet relinquished his command in Korea in February 1953 and retired from the army two months later as a full general. Whatever political difficulties he may have had, he went on to serve as President Dwight D. Eisenhower's special ambassador

to the Far East in 1954 and as a consultant to the secretary of the army on guerrilla warfare in 1961–1962. Van Fleet died at Polk City, Florida, on September 23, 1992.

D. R. DORONDO

See also

Cold War, Origins to 1950; Eighth Army, U.S.; MacArthur, Douglas; Ridgway, Matthew Bunker

References

Braim, Paul F. *Will to Win: The Life of General James A. Van Fleet.* Annapolis, MD: Naval Institute Press, 2001.

Hermes, Walter G. *U.S. Army in the Korean War: Truce Tent and Fighting Front.* Washington, DC: Office of the Chief of Military History, 1966.

Mossman, Billy C. *United States Army in the Korean War: Ebb and Flow, November 1950–July 1951.* Washington, DC: U.S. Army Center of Military History, 1990.

"Van Fleet Load"

In 1950 artillery ammunition requirements for the U.S. Army in the field were expressed in terms of "days of fire" (DOF), a DOF being the number of rounds allocated per gun per day. Soon after the Korean War began, the Department of the Army approved an increase in the DOF for artillery weapons in Korea to 45 rounds per day for 155-mm howitzers, and 50 rounds per day for 105-mm howitzers, 155-mm guns, and 8-inch howitzers. However, in April 1951 Lieutenant General James A. Van Fleet, commander of the U.S. Eighth Army in Korea (EUSAK), who was determined to defeat the Fifth (Spring) Offensive of the Chinese People's Volunteer Army (CPVA, Chinese Army) with massive artillery firepower, stated, "We must expend steel and fire, not men."

Accordingly, Van Fleet increased the DOF for artillery ammunition fivefold, to 300 rounds per day for 105-mm howitzers, 250 rounds per day for 155-mm howitzers, and 200 rounds per day for 155-mm guns and 8-inch howitzers. This increased allocation of artillery ammunition came to be called the Van Fleet DOF, or the "Van Fleet load." Its application significantly increased the expenditure of scarce artillery ammunition by United Nations (UN) forces in Korea. One field artillery battalion in the battle of the Soyang River in May 1951 fired 11,891 rounds of 105-mm ammunition in a single 24-hour period. The Chinese offensive was stopped cold by such massive artillery fire, but the UN logistical system was hard pressed to obtain, store, and distribute the large quantities of ammunition required.

CHARLES R. SHRADER

See also

Artillery; Chinese Offensive, Fifth; Logistics in the Korean War; Van Fleet, James Alward

References

Huston, James A. *Guns and Butter, Powder and Rice: U.S. Army Logistics in the Korean War.* Selinsgrove, PA: Susquehanna University Press, 1989.

———. *The Sinews of War: Army Logistics, 1775–1953.* Washington, DC: Office of the Chief of Military History, 1966.

Logistical Problems and Their Solutions. APO 301. Headquarters, Eighth U.S. Army Korea, Historical Section and Eighth Army Historical Service Detachment (Provisional), 1952.

Middleton, Harry J. *The Compact History of the Korean War.* New York: Hawthorn Books, 1965.

Mossman, Billy C. *United States Army in the Korean War: Ebb and Flow, November 1950–July 1951.* Washington, DC: U.S. Army Center of Military History, 1990.

Vandenberg, Hoyt Sanford

Birth Date: January 24, 1899
Death Date: April 2, 1954

U.S. Army Air Forces (USAAF) and U.S. Air Force (USAF) general; chief of staff of the air force (1948–1953). Born in Milwaukee, Wisconsin, on January 24, 1899, Hoyt Sanford Vandenberg was the nephew of future Republican senator Arthur H. Vandenberg of Michigan. He graduated from the U.S. Military Academy at West Point in 1923 and was assigned to the Air Service. In 1925 Vandenberg earned his wings, and in 1927 he was a flight instructor. In the 1930s, with a reputation as a moderate between airmen advocating big bomber development and those who believed in the need for more pursuit fighters, Vandenberg attended the Command and General Staff School at Fort Leavenworth, Kansas (1936), and the Army War College (1939). In 1939 he joined the Plans Division of the Army Air Corps and assisted with the expansion of the Air Corps. His work there ensured his promotion to colonel in 1942.

In the summer of 1942, during World War II, Vandenberg was assigned to General Dwight D. Eisenhower's staff in Britain to develop air plans for North African operations. He was promoted to brigadier general that December and was assigned as chief of staff for the Twelfth Air Force under Brigadier General James H. Doolittle.

In early 1943 Brigadier General Vandenberg became chief of strategic forces under Lieutenant General Carl Spaatz, commander of Northwest African Air Forces. In August he returned to USAAF headquarters in Washington for four months to head the air mission to the Soviet Union under Ambassador W. Averell Harriman. From there he returned to London to serve as deputy commander of Allied Expeditionary Air Forces.

In August 1944 Eisenhower advanced Vandenberg from vice commander of the tactical Ninth Air Force to its commander, replacing Lieutenant General Lewis Brereton. Along with the Royal Air Force's Second Tactical Air Force, the Ninth Air Force of some 4,000 aircraft covered the advance of Allied forces across France into Germany. Both army chief of staff George C. Marshall and Third Army commander General George Patton agreed that the Ninth Air Force performed a vital role in helping win the war

General Hoyt S. Vandenberg was chief of staff of the U.S. Air Force during 1948–1953. In that post he oversaw the growth of the air force as the linchpin of U.S. defense strategy during the early years of the Cold War. (Department of Defense)

on the western front. Vandenberg was promoted to major general in March 1945 and to lieutenant general that July, when he became assistant chief of staff for operations of the USAAF.

With the end of the war, many younger army officers like Vandenberg faced the prospect of restoration to their permanent rank, in his case brigadier general. Instead, President Harry S. Truman successfully nominated Vandenberg to remain a lieutenant general. In 1946 Vandenberg spent six months as chief of the intelligence division of the War Department's General Staff. He next served as director of the Central Intelligence Group (later Central Intelligence Agency, CIA). After 15 months he rejoined USAAF commander General Spaatz as his deputy.

Vandenberg played an important role in helping Spaatz make the air force a separate service in September 1947. Spaatz became the first chief of staff of the air force, with Vandenberg as his vice chief of staff. When Spaatz retired in April 1948, Vandenberg succeeded him.

His first task was to reorganize the USAF, which was still partially tied to the army. This was the beginning of the Cold War, and in the summer of 1948 the Soviets blockaded Berlin. It was Vandenberg who convinced Truman that the fledgling service could resupply Berlin from the air in what became known as the Berlin Airlift (Operation VITTLES). He also appointed his longtime colleagues Lieutenant General Curtis LeMay and Major General William Tunner to command the successful resupply of Berlin.

When the Korean War began in June 1950, it was a difficult time for the air force. Development of the Convair B-36 Peacemaker strategic bomber had been slowed by monetary restrictions and political controversy. This meant that the USAF would have to go to war with the Boeing B-29 Superfortress as its primary strategic bombing platform. Worst of all, the air force still faced President Truman's strict fiscal policies. As a result, weapons and resources needed by airmen were at first simply not available. A frustrated Vandenberg called it a "shoestring air force." He refused to accept the situation, and by 1953 he had resurrected the USAF into the strongest air force in the world and made it the linchpin of U.S. military policy.

Despite having available in theater only a few, mostly World War II–vintage, bombers and fighters at the start of the Korean War, the USAF played a decisive role in saving the Pusan Perimeter and in the subsequent United Nations Command (UNC) sweep north. When the Chinese People's Volunteer Army (CPVA, Chinese Army) intervened in October and November 1950, the heroic UNC rear guard and a handful of mostly World War II–veteran USAF fighter pilots flying new North American F-86 Sabres helped prevent total disaster. At Vandenberg's insistence, the deployment of more F-86s helped check communist ground forces and Mikoyan-Gurevich MiG-15s and assisted Lieutenant General Matthew B. Ridgway's forces to counterattack and restore the balance of power on the ground.

When President Truman was placed in the awkward position of recalling General Douglas MacArthur in April 1951, Vandenberg supported new secretary of defense George C. Marshall and chairman of the Joint Chiefs of Staff General Omar N. Bradley in deflecting congressional criticism of the president and U.S. military leadership. Vandenberg's levelheaded testimony and measured counsel helped convinced Congress of the ultimate folly of using nuclear weapons in Korea.

As the 1952 and 1953 stalemate and negotiations unfolded, Vandenberg urged many of his fellow air force leaders to suspend close air support (CAS) and focus on aerial interdiction. Many veterans and students of World War II Europe argued that interdiction efforts similar to those used in Europe would defeat communist forces in Korea. Vandenberg believed differently. He declared, "We used to bomb and close the Brenner Pass every day, and the Germans opened it every night." Vandenberg realized that the success of interdiction depended on ground attacks and constant and consistent bombing to force communist consumption of supplies to rise faster than they could be replenished.

Even so, Vandenberg saw no alternative to at least attempting to knock out MiG bases and utilities as best he could. Thus, despite limits against attacking enemy sanctuaries in Manchuria, these targets were attacked repeatedly. Between mid-1950 and mid-1953, USAF sorties rates grew from 100 per day to 1,000 per day. But in 1953 losses to ground fire and MiG-15s rose to alarming levels that caused even veteran pilots to question the viability of USAF tactics. To solve these problems, Vandenberg assigned B-29s to fly tactical night raids, increased the deployment of F-86s, and had new electronic gun sights installed on the Sabre jets. Vandenberg's trips to Korea and his personnel style helped convince many reluctant pilots to continue to fly.

With the arrival of Dwight D. Eisenhower's administration in 1953, military policy emphasized strategic nuclear weapons ("more bang for a buck") aimed at the Soviet threat in Europe. It was the beginning of massive retaliation and the halcyon bomber days of the Strategic Air Command (SAC). In the face of this new posture, Vandenberg fell into a policy disagreement with new Secretary of Defense Charles E. Wilson, who sought to make drastic cuts in the air force. In the ensuing public debate, Vandenberg vigorously defended the need for a flexible and technologically advanced conventional and nuclear air force capable of strategic and tactical missions.

The 1953 summer congressional hearings on the military budget were both troubling to and hard on Vandenberg, especially as he was slowly dying of cancer and in constant pain. An admirer of Eisenhower, he had been a conciliator and team player, so it hurt him deeply to air fundamental disagreements in public. But he believed he was right and that the country would be ill served by putting all its defense eggs in the basket of nuclear missiles and long-range strategic bombers. Vandenberg worried openly that a lack of conventional military preparedness would lead the nation into more Koreas, not fewer, as Wilson believed.

In the end, Vandenberg lost and was forced to retire in June 1953. Even though Eisenhower was irritated by the disagreement, he never openly criticized Vandenberg or his advisers; such was his respect for his former subordinate.

Following retirement, Vandenberg slowly wasted away from cancer. He died in Washington, DC, on April 2, 1954, firmly convinced of the correctness of his views.

WILLIAM HEAD

See also
Bradley, Omar Nelson; Eisenhower, Dwight David; Joint Chiefs of Staff; MacArthur, Douglas; Marshall, George Catlett; Massive Retaliation; Ridgway, Matthew Bunker; Truman, Harry S.; Wilson, Charles Edward

References
Meilinger, Phillip S. *Hoyt S. Vandenberg: The Life of a General.* Bloomington: Indiana University Press, 1989.

Parrish, Noel F. "Hoyt S. Vandenberg: Building the New Air Force." In *Makers of the United States Air Force,* edited by John L. Frisbee, 205–228. Washington, DC: Air Force History and Museum Programs, 1996.

Reynolds, John. "Education and Training for High Command: General Hoyt S. Vandenberg's Early Career." Unpublished PhD dissertation, Duke University, 1980.

Smith, Robert. "The Influence of USAF Chief of Staff Hoyt S. Vandenberg on United States National Security Policy." Unpublished PhD dissertation, American University, 1965.

Voorhees, Tracy Stebbins
Birth Date: June 30, 1890
Death Date: September 25, 1974

Attorney, U.S. Army officer, and undersecretary of the army, 1949–1950. Tracy Stebbins Voorhees was born in New Brunswick, New Jersey, on June 30, 1890. After earning degrees from Rutgers University and Columbia Law School, he served during World War I as assistant to the director of the War Trade Board's Bureau of Imports. From 1919 until 1942 Voorhees practiced law in New York.

In 1942, after the U.S. entry into World War II, Voorhees joined the U.S. Army with the rank of colonel. Throughout the war, Voorhees was assigned to the Surgeon General's Office, as director of its legal and control divisions. In 1947 Voorhees became administrator of food relief for occupied areas, including Germany, Japan, and Korea.

In June 1948 Voorhees was appointed assistant secretary of the army, serving on a committee that determined overall American policy toward Germany, which it was increasingly clear would remain divided indefinitely. In August 1949 he was appointed undersecretary of the army. Voorhees's staunch support for the massive increases in defense spending recommended in the April 1950 policy planning paper NSC-68 put him greatly at odds with his superior, Secretary of Defense Louis Johnson, who was determined to keep a tight lid on military expenditures. As a result of the split between the two men, Voorhees resigned his position in April 1950, the same month that NSC-68 was presented to President Harry S. Truman.

As a private citizen, Voorhees continued to campaign publicly for enhanced defense spending. In December 1950 he joined former Secretary of War Robert P. Patterson and Harvard University president James B. Conant in establishing the Committee on the Present Danger (CPD). As vice chairman of the CPD from 1951 to 1953, Voorhees was largely responsible for the organization's day-to-day operation. The committee campaigned for major long-term increases in American defense budgets and global commitments, effectively supporting the implementation of NSC-68. Its efforts were greatly facilitated by the outbreak in June 1950 of the Korean War, an event many American officials perceived as proving the existence of a major worldwide international communist threat. Once the war began, defense spending increased dramatically, and it remained quite high for the duration of the conflict.

Although formally a private organization, the CPD received strong backing and assistance from leading Truman administration officials, including Secretary of State Dean Acheson and Undersecretary of Defense Robert A. Lovett, as well as Policy Planning Staff director Paul Nitze, the principal author of NSC-68. The CPD compared the Soviet menace to the Nazi threat a decade earlier and pressed for restoring the military draft, doubling the size of the existing U.S. military, and deploying several additional divisions to Western Europe. William J. Donovan, former director of the wartime Office of Strategic Services (OSS), the precursor of the Central Intelligence Agency (CIA), soon became a prominent member.

The CPD worked closely with CIA officials and with the Psychological Strategy Board (PSB), which President Truman established in the spring of 1951 to coordinate efforts to win the loyalties of peoples in Soviet-controlled states, especially in Eastern Europe. Committee members, including Voorhees, campaigned energetically for the policies they favored, speaking and writing extensively, sponsoring films, disseminating cartoons and other publicity, briefing journalists, lobbying congressmen, and writing detailed policy recommendations and briefs for sympathetic administration officials. CPD efforts contributed significantly to the 1950–1951 Great Debate on U.S. foreign policy, the outcome of which decisively oriented the country away from isolationism and toward a militarily assertive position of high defense expenditures, large armed forces, and major overseas alliance commitments.

In 1952 Voorhees was one of several leading CPD officials who successfully urged the sympathetic General Dwight D. Eisenhower to seek the Republican Party presidential nomination, a move they hoped would check the influence of Republican isolationists and wed that party, like the Democrats, to the militarized internationalism the CPD favored. With the ending of the Korean War in 1953, the CPD largely faded away.

An unwavering anticommunist, who as a Rutgers University trustee defended the institution's decision to fire several faculty members suspected of communist affiliations, Voorhees in the mid-1950s served as the president's personal representative for Hungarian Refugee Affairs and as chairman of the president's committee for Hungarian Refugee Relief. In the late 1950s Voorhees also helped to found the Committee to Strengthen the Frontiers of Freedom, which demanded implementation of the 1958 Gaither Report's recommendations for greatly enhanced American defense budgets. Voorhees died on September 25, 1974, at Sugar Hill, New Hampshire.

PRISCILLA ROBERTS

See also
Acheson, Dean Gooderham; Central Intelligence Agency; Committee on the Present Danger; Eisenhower, Dwight David; Great Debate; Johnson, Louis Arthur; Lovett, Robert Abercrombie; National Security Council Report 68; Nitze, Paul Henry; Republican Party, United States

References
Hogan, Michael J. *A Cross of Iron: Harry S. Truman and the Origins of the National Security State, 1945–1954.* New York: Cambridge University Press, 1998.

Lucas, Scott. *Freedom War: The American Crusade Against the Soviet Union.* New York: New York University Press, 1999.

Sanders, Jerry Wayne. *Peddlers of Crisis: The Committee on the Present Danger and the Politics of Containment.* Boston: South End Press, 1983.

Vyshinskii, Andrei Ianuarovich
Birth Date: 1883
Death Date: November 22, 1954

Soviet foreign minister from March 1949 to March 1953. Born in Odessa in 1883, Andrei Ianuarovich Vyshinskii joined the Mensheviks following the split of the Russian Social Democratic Party after 1903. Trained as a lawyer at Kiev University, he met his future political patron, Joseph Stalin, when both were in prison in Baku in 1907. But Vyshinskii did not officially become a Bolshevik until 1920. He made a name for himself as the chief state prosecutor during Stalin's bloody purges in the 1930s. The high point of his legal career was his orchestration of Nikolai Bukharin's 1938 show trial.

Vyshinskii entered the foreign ministry in 1940. His rise to prominence was predicated more on opportunism than ability, but he possessed the useful knack of consistently anticipating Joseph Stalin's wishes. This was essential for Vyshinskii, because Stalin maintained tight personal control over Soviet foreign policy for the last four years of his life. Vyshinskii served as one of Viacheslav Molotov's chief deputies at the Allied conferences in Yalta and Potsdam.

In 1949 Stalin removed Molotov as foreign minister and elevated Vyshinskii in his place. Unlike his former boss, the new foreign minister did not have a significant following within the Communist Party or the general populace. The Korean War was the watershed event in Vyshinskii's four-year tenure in this post. He alternately blasted the United States and searched for negotiated settlements, depending on the exigencies of the situation.

Stalin occasionally used Vyshinskii to attack while at the same time using another official to offer a small olive branch, or vice versa. Such a contradictory foreign policy might be hard on his subordinates, but it allowed Stalin to keep several options open at once. Under Vyshinskii's direction, the Soviet foreign ministry condemned United Nations (UN) intervention in Korea with considerable ferocity. Vyshinskii himself accused United Nations Command (UNC) commanders of using disguised Japanese troops, blamed the Republic of Korea (ROK, South Korea) for starting the war, and painted the United States as an aggressor in the internal affairs of another country.

After UNC commander General Douglas MacArthur's daring September 1950 amphibious landing at Inchon, which soon put Korean People's Army (KPA, North Korean Army) forces into retreat, the Soviet position softened. Addressing the UN General Assembly, Vyshinskii focused his standard rhetorical attacks on specific hawks in President Harry S. Truman's administration and signaled a willingness to negotiate without the usual demand that U.S. forces withdraw first.

U.S. policy makers, believing that they had the diplomatic and military momentum, ignored these overtures. Vyshinskii, using unofficial intermediaries, again sought to open negotiations when UNC forces neared the 38th Parallel in October 1950 but broke off contacts once that line had been crossed. Incensed that U.S. officials, ignoring his explicit warnings, decided to invade the Democratic People's Republic of Korea (DPRK, North Korea), on November 2, 1950, Vyshinskii unleashed a vicious tirade in the UN against Truman's adviser John Foster Dulles. The next month, also in the UN, Vyshinskii justified the recent flood of Chinese "volunteers" into North Korea, continued his verbal assault against U.S. aggression in Korea, and demanded that all foreign troops be withdrawn so that "the Korean question [could] be entrusted to the Korean people themselves." Other than repetitions of such rhetoric, Soviet diplomats saw their role in the conflict diminish for a few months while events played themselves out on the battlefield after the intervention of the Chinese People's Volunteer Army (CPVA, Chinese Army).

Truce talks in Kaesong among the four combatants—South Korea, the United States, the People's Republic of China (PRC), and North Korea—began in July 1951 after the fighting had bogged down near the 38th Parallel. The Soviets had suggested a cease-fire in a June 23 radio address by Soviet UN delegate Jacob Malik, which got things going. On August 23 the talks were suspended over several disagreements, including the location of the demilitarized zone (DMZ) demarcation line.

Unexpectedly, Vyshinskii helped restart the talks two months later. After a little more than two years of service, U.S. ambassador to the Soviet Union Alan G. Kirk paid a farewell visit on October 5 to the Soviet foreign minister (Stalin was unavailable). Acting on instructions from the U.S. State Department, Kirk expressed frustration over the suspension of the truce talks and asked the Soviet government to use its influence with the Chinese and North Koreans to convince them to return to the table. Vyshinskii responded by shifting blame for the collapse of the negotiations onto commander of UNC forces Lieutenant General Matthew B. Ridgway. After this face-saving maneuver, the Soviet government agreed to intercede. Truce talks were restarted on October 25, 1951, in Panmunjom.

Although not an official participant in the Panmunjom negotiations, the Soviet Union provided considerable diplomatic support for its two allies. On several occasions during the war, Vyshinskii advocated the following formula as the basis for a truce: use of the 38th Parallel as the center of the DMZ; withdrawal of all foreign troops; and the repatriation of all prisoners of war (POWs). Once all parties agreed to accept the current battle lines as the basis for the DMZ, the main sticking point became the issue of involuntary POW repatriation. Many Chinese and North Korean prisoners did not want to return home. UN Indian delegate V. K. Krishna Menon proposed a compromise on the POW question that was reluctantly accepted by the United States. Vyshinskii preempted any possibility of a favorable Chinese response by condemning the proposal and its author in a surprisingly blunt speech in the UN on November 24, 1952. This interference maintained the deadlock in the talks for another four months, until Stalin's death in March 1953 and Vyshinskii's subsequent demotion.

The two communist combatants in the Korean War looked to Vyshinskii for diplomatic leadership. He, in turn, worked under the very close supervision of Stalin, who wished to control all aspects of Soviet foreign policy. As a result, Vyshinskii's actions were occasionally unpredictable, belligerent, and contradictory.

After being demoted in March 1953 to deputy foreign minister, Vyshinskii returned to his former position as the chief Soviet delegate to the UN, where he had served previously from 1946 to 1949. This appointment continued until his death in New York City on November 22, 1954.

EDWARD SHARP

See also

Armistice Agreement; China, People's Republic of; Cold War, Origins to 1950; Dulles, John Foster; Inchon Landing; Kaesong Truce Talks; Kim Il Sung; Kirk, Alan Goodrich; MacArthur, Douglas; Malik, Jacob; Mao Zedong; Menon, Vengalil Krishnan Krishna; Molotov, Viacheslav Mikhailovich; Ridgway, Matthew Bunker; Soviet Union; Stalin, Joseph; Truce Talks

References

Stueck, William W., Jr. *The Korean War: An International History.* Princeton, NJ: Princeton University Press, 1995.

Tucker, Robert C., ed. *Stalinism: Essays in Historical Interpretation.* New York: Norton, 1977.

Zubok, Vladislav, and Constantine Pleshakov. *Inside the Kremlin's Cold War: From Stalin to Khrushchev.* Cambridge, MA: Harvard University Press, 1996.

W

Wage Stabilization Board

U.S. government agency created by executive order on September 9, 1950, to carry out the exigencies of the Defense Production Act. Reporting directly to the Economic Stabilization Agency (ESA), as did its Office of Price Stabilization (OPS) counterpart, the Wage Stabilization Board (WSB) planned and implemented wage controls during the Korean War. In January 1951 the WSB froze wages simultaneously with the OPS general price freeze. The freeze and subsequent wage policy adjustments that followed applied to all hourly wages, salaries, and other forms of compensation. Later in 1951 the WSB created a separate Salary Stabilization Board that handled all controls pertaining to salaried employees. The work of the wage board was critical in stabilizing the economy and controlling inflationary pressures because increasing pay demands have a direct impact on prices for consumer products. If wage increases are in kept in check, manufacturers do not have to increase the prices of their products to compensate for higher employee costs.

During the war, the WSB underwent several structural and jurisdictional changes, the most important one occurring in April 1951, when President Harry S. Truman enlarged the board from 9 to 18 members. The makeup of the WSB was tripartite; that is, it comprised equal representation from industry, the ranks of organized labor, and the public at large. The president appointed members to the board first without congressional oversight. After the contentious steel strike of 1952, however, Congress insisted that WSB members be subjected to a formal approval process. In fact, the WSB played a large role in the steel strike, and its recommendations proved highly unpopular among industry executives and certain sectors of the American public.

In December 1952, as a result of a wage dispute between the United Mine Workers and the nation's coal mine operators, the WSB voluntarily disbanded, all but ceasing the activities of the board. President Dwight D. Eisenhower formally liquidated the WSB by law in the spring of 1953.

PAUL G. PIERPAOLI JR.

See also

Defense Production Act; Economic Stabilization Agency; Mobilization; Office of Price Stabilization; Steel Plants, Truman's Seizure of; United States, Home Front

References

Hogan, Michael J. *A Cross of Iron: Harry S. Truman and the Origins of the National Security State, 1945–1954.* New York: Cambridge University Press, 1998.

Pierpaoli, Paul G., Jr. *Truman and Korea: The Political Culture of the Early Cold War.* Columbia: University of Missouri Press, 1999.

Rockoff, Hugh. *Drastic Measures: History of Wage and Price Controls in the United States.* New York: Cambridge University Press, 1984.

Wake Island Conference
Event Date: October 15, 1950

On October 7, 1950, President Harry S. Truman decided he needed to confer with United Nations Command (UNC) commander General Douglas MacArthur. The meeting was to take place somewhere in the Pacific before the end of the month. Suggested by presidential administrative assistant George M. Elsey and other executive branch officials, the meeting was prompted by military and political developments in the Korean War.

As Republic of Korea Army (ROKA, South Korean Army) forces drove into the Democratic People's Republic of Korea (DPRK, North Korea), premier and foreign minister of the

U.S. president Harry S. Truman (center) and United Nations Command (UNC) commander General Douglas MacArthur (left) meet at Wake Island, October 15, 1950. (National Archives)

People's Republic of China (PRC) Zhou Enlai warned the United States about an advance beyond the 38th Parallel. After the United Nations (UN) General Assembly accepted a proposal for the unification of Korea, two U.S. aircraft strafed a Soviet air installation 60 miles above the North Korean frontier near Vladivostok. These incidents gave the White House momentary pause, and so the conference was planned to sound out MacArthur on the situation in Korea.

Once MacArthur repeated his capitulation demand to North Korea on October 9 without result, the U.S. Eighth Army in Korea (EUSAK) moved above the dividing line. With partisan Republicans urging Truman to thrust northward, administration officials sought political advantage for the Democrats in the upcoming midterm elections. At first opposed to a meeting as "too political, too much showmanship" and seeing no "real need" to confer with MacArthur, Truman eventually consented. White House press secretary Charles Ross apparently influenced Truman's decision by recalling President Franklin D. Roosevelt's conference with the general in Hawaii during World War II, before the 1944 presidential contest.

President Truman publicly announced two reasons for a meeting with General MacArthur. He wanted to discuss urgent Korean and Asian matters, and he desired face-to-face contact with the general. On October 9 Truman asked Secretary of Defense George C. Marshall to select a date and site for the meeting. Despite Truman's preference for a mid-October conference at Pearl Harbor, MacArthur chose Wake Island as the scene for an October 15 meeting. The president concurred, and on October 10 Ross reported the news to the media.

The Truman and MacArthur entourages contrasted in number and composition. Included in the president's 24-person party were Special Presidential Assistant on Foreign Affairs W. Averell Harriman, Joint Chiefs of Staff chairman General Omar N. Bradley, Secretary of the Army Frank Pace, Assistant Secretary of State for Far Eastern Affairs Dean Rusk, Ambassador-at-Large Philip C. Jessup, and Commander in Chief, Pacific and Commander in Chief, Pacific Fleet Arthur W. Radford. A group of five accompanied MacArthur from Japan, but only Ambassador to South Korea John J. Muccio and MacArthur actually took part in the Wake Island discussions.

In a private conversation with Truman before the main meeting, MacArthur downplayed the chance of China entering the war. Yet he claimed that if such a circumstance arose, his armies could manage. MacArthur reassured Truman that the battlefield victory was won and, when asked about Europe's defense, said one combat division could be transferred out of Korea in early 1951. MacArthur likewise asserted Japan's readiness for a peace treaty and apologized for any embarrassment caused by his August message to the Veterans of Foreign Wars (VFW) concerning Taiwian (then known as Formosa).

During the general session of about 90 minutes, equal attention focused on postwar Korean matters and other issues. MacArthur answered most of the inquiries addressed to his party. Some conferees and Jessup's secretary, Vernice Anderson, who was seated in an adjacent room, took notes. Moving quickly and often inconsistently from subject to subject without an agenda, the participants dealt with such questions as Korea's economic reconstruction, the military situation, Syngman Rhee's political security, and North Korean war crimes. Other Asian topics discussed included a Japanese peace treaty, a possible Pacific alliance, French Indochina, and Philippine economic difficulties. MacArthur denied the need for more UN troops and restated his conviction that there was "very little" likelihood of Chinese or Soviet intervention.

Truman ended the parley by remarking, "This has been a most satisfactory conference." While he rested, MacArthur and Muccio chatted with several of his staff. Then the president and the general endorsed the meeting's communiqué. Written by administration officials, it cited some of the issues raised and imparted the upbeat mood of the conferees. As Truman and MacArthur rode together to the air terminal, they spoke of the upcoming 1952 presidential contest. Before the general's departure, Truman gave MacArthur a box of candy for his family and presented him with a fourth Oak Leaf Cluster for his Distinguished Service Medal. In San Francisco 24 hours afterward, he praised the general and called the Wake gathering an important dialogue on Asian policies. For a short time thereafter, Truman and MacArthur traded agreeable exchanges regarding the Wake Island meeting.

Truman's satisfaction with the general soon began to erode, however, particularly over the Taiwan (Formosa) question. Once China entered the Korean War, the president and his staff complained that MacArthur had misled them.

RODNEY J. ROSS

See also

Bradley, Omar Nelson; Elsey, George McKee; Harriman, William Averell; Jessup, Philip Caryl; MacArthur, Douglas; Marshall, George Catlett; Muccio, John Joseph; Pace, Frank, Jr.; Radford, Arthur William; Rhee, Syngman; Rusk, David Dean; Soviet Airfield Incident; Truman, Harry S.; Zhou Enlai

References

Donovan, Robert J. *Tumultuous Years: The Presidency of Harry S. Truman.* New York: Norton, 1982.

James, D. Clayton. *The Years of MacArthur,* Vol. 3, *Triumph and Disaster, 1945–1964.* Boston: Houghton Mifflin, 1985.

Pearlman, Michael D. *Truman and MacArthur: Policy, Politics, and the Hunger for Honor and Renown.* Bloomington: Indiana University Press, 2008.

Schaller, Michael. *Douglas MacArthur: The Far Eastern General.* New York: Oxford University Press, 1989.

Spanier, John W. *The Truman-MacArthur Controversy and the Korean War.* Cambridge, MA: Harvard University Press, 1959.

Wilz, John E. "Truman and MacArthur: The Wake Island Conference." *Military Affairs* 42 (December 1978): 169–176.

Walker, Walton Harris
Birth Date: December 3, 1889
Death Date: December 23, 1950

U.S. Army general and commander of the U.S. Eighth Army in Korea (EUSAK) during the Korean War. Born on December 3, 1889, in Belton, Texas, Walton Harris Walker graduated from the U.S. Military Academy at West Point in 1912. During World War I he served with the 13th Machine Gun Battalion of the 5th Infantry Division in France. He saw action in the Saint-Mihiel and Meuse-Argonne offensives and earned the Silver Star for gallantry in action.

In the interwar years Walker attended the Field Artillery School at Fort Sill, the Command and General Staff College, and the Army War College. He served with the 15th Infantry Regiment in Tianjin (Tientsin), China, and he taught at the Infantry School, the Coast Artillery School, and at West Point. He also served on the General Staff's War Plans Division in Washington. Just before U.S. entry into World War II, Walker commanded the 36th Infantry Regiment. Promoted to brigadier general in July 1941, he took command of the 3rd Armored Brigade.

Promoted to major general in February 1942, Walker commanded the 3rd Armored Division. Seven months later he assumed command of the IV Armored Corps at Camp Young, California. There he established the Desert Training Center, responsible for training armored units for desert warfare in North Africa.

In February 1944 IV Armored Corps was redesignated as XX Corps and ordered to Britain. Walker's corps was committed to Normandy in July and became part of General George S. Patton's Third Army. XX Corps became known as the "Ghost Corps" for the speed of its advance. Driving east in France from the Loire River to the Moselle, Walker's corps reduced German fortifications at Metz in November 1944.

Walker's greatest challenge in World War II came during the Ardennes Offensive, when Patton swung the bulk of the Third Army north to counterattack into the southern flank of the German thrust. Walker's XX Corps was left in place to cover the front that had been held by an entire field army. In April 1945 Walker's units liberated Buchenwald concentration camp near Weimar. By May 1945 Walker's units reached Linz, Austria, the farthest

Eighth U.S. Army commander Lieutenant General Walton H. Walker believed in leading from the front and became known for his distinctive jeep. He was killed on December 23, 1950, when it was struck by a Korean civilian truck. (The Army Historical Foundation)

advance east of any of Patton's units. In that same month, he was promoted to lieutenant general.

At the end of the war Walker headed the 8th Service Command in Dallas, Texas. In June 1948 he took command of the Fifth Army, headquartered in Chicago. In September 1948 Walker went to Japan to assume command of the Eighth Army, the army ground force element of General Douglas MacArthur's Far East Command (FEC).

In 1948 the Eighth Army was what would today be called a "hollow force." Walker's four divisions in Japan had only two-thirds of their authorized wartime strength in men and equipment, and the soldiers were untrained and out of shape from several years of occupation duty. Despite the recent end of World War II, only 10 percent of Walker's troops had combat experience.

When the Korean War began in June 1950, Walker became the primary United Nations Command (UNC) ground forces commander. On July 13, 1950, he established forward headquarters of EUSAK at Taegu. Four days later, Walker also received operational control of the units of the Republic of Korea Army (ROKA, South Korean Army), and eventually of the rest of United Nations (UN) ground forces in Korea.

Despite being almost equal in numbers to the invading Korean People's Army (KPA, North Korean Army), Walker's poorly trained and equipped field army was no match for them. KPA forces steadily pushed the UNC forces southward down the Korean Peninsula until Walker finally managed to stabilize a defensive perimeter around the major port of Pusan. Bounded on the east and south by the sea and on the west by the Naktong River, the Pusan Perimeter formed a rectangle roughly 100 by 50 miles. With his back to the sea, but with the advantage of operating on interior lines, Walker on July 29 issued his famous "Stand or Die" order, in which he bluntly declared, "there will be no Dunkirk, there will be no Bataan."

During the next six weeks, Walker conducted one of the most skillful mobile defense operations in military history. Aided by the fact that his intelligence assets had broken the KPA operational codes, Walker continually shifted his mobile reserves to parry every KPA thrust. The North Koreans often broke through the UN defensive lines, but Walker always managed to find the means to close the gaps. Holding firm along the line of the Naktong River, Walker traded space for time in the north, as the communist attacks slowly collapsed the rectangular defense position from north to south. Throughout the entire campaign Walker himself spent a great deal of time at the front lines, personally appraising the situation and issuing necessary orders to commanders on the spot.

At the operational and strategic levels, Walker's primary objectives were to maintain the UNC foothold on the Korean Peninsula and buy time for the forces in Japan to prepare for and launch the landings at Inchon, deep in the KPA rear. Walker succeeded, and X Corps landed at Inchon on September 15. The result was a turning movement at operational depth, with some 100,000 KPA troops cut off from their lines of communication. Despite an initial rough start, Walker's forces counterattacked across the Naktong on September 16 and drove north. The Eighth Army linked up with X Corps on September 26. Only 25,000 to 30,000 of the KPA troops that besieged the Pusan Perimeter ever made it back to the Democratic People's Republic of Korea (DPRK, North Korea).

Walker protested MacArthur's risky decision to separate the Eighth Army and X Corps in the drive into North Korea. On October 24 Walker established his advanced command post (CP) in the North Korean capital of Pyongyang.

On October 25 Chinese People's Volunteer Army (CPVA, Chinese Army) troops first clashed with UNC troops. Walker believed that this was no minor counterattack. A U.S. regiment that went to the relief of the South Koreans was overwhelmed in fierce fighting (at Unsan) between November 1 and 3. Walker now wisely brought the bulk of his forces back behind the Chongchon River. MacArthur wanted an immediate resumption of the offensive, but Walker disagreed. One problem was that MacArthur had made X Corps dependent logistically on the Eighth Army, rather than supplying it from Japan, as should have been the case, which meant that both units were critically short of supplies. MacArthur pushed for an attack on November 15, but Walker resisted. Not until November 20 were supply elements able to deliver the 4,000 tons daily required for offensive operations. Finally, Walker agreed to resume the offensive on November 24.

On the night of November 25–26, the CPVA intervened on a massive scale, counterattacking EUSAK. This attack threatened the very survival of the Eighth Army and drove it back down the Korean Peninsula.

In the face of overwhelming odds, Walker conducted a series of delaying actions as he pulled his army back south. His withdrawal was a mixed success. Although the 24th and 25th Infantry divisions escaped largely intact, the rearguard 2nd Infantry Division was almost annihilated. On December 15 Walker established a new defensive line roughly along the 38th Parallel.

On the morning of December 23, 1950, Walker left Seoul to visit units in the vicinity of Uijongbu. Along the way his jeep was hit by a Korean civilian truck. Walker was thrown from the open vehicle and suffered multiple head injuries. He was taken to a 24th Infantry Division clearing station, where doctors pronounced him dead. Walker was promoted posthumously to (four-star) general on January 2, 1951.

Walker's performance in Korea remains a subject of debate among historians. One of his nicknames was "Bulldog," and he looked like one. His other nickname was "Johnnie Walker," because of his reputation for being able to consume large quantities of his favorite brand of Scotch. He had a flamboyant manner reminiscent of his mentor, Patton.

Although Walker's handling of the Pusan Perimeter defense had been masterful, the Eighth Army suffered a number of serious setbacks after it moved north of the 38th Parallel. Walker, however, was continually handicapped by serious command problems beyond his control. He began the war with understrength, underequipped, and untrained units. In addition to the U.S. units, Walker was also responsible for the disorganized and demoralized ROKA divisions. Never one of MacArthur's favorites, Walker had an uneasy relationship with his theater commander. MacArthur compounded Walker's problems by keeping X Corps independent of the Eighth Army, making it impossible for a single commander to synchronize all ground operations in Korea. Walker did not get along with X Corps commander Major General Edward M. Almond—but then, almost no one else did either. Walker's concern in October and November over the indicators of a large-scale Chinese intervention to the Yalu River had earned him more animosity from MacArthur's staff in Tokyo. At the time of Walker's death, MacArthur was considering relieving him.

Walker was not a good organizer, and he probably was not a great tactician, but he was a brave and tenacious warrior who believed in leading from the front. Patton once called him "a fighter in every sense of the word." Army chief of staff General J. Lawton Collins called Walker "a fine battlefield commander." Whether his success at the Pusan Perimeter was the result of effective tactics, excellent intelligence, or just sheer determination, the important thing is that he held out. Had he not done so, the Korean War could have been lost almost as soon as it started.

David T. Zabecki

See also

Collins, Joseph Lawton; Eighth Army, U.S.; Far East Command; MacArthur, Douglas; Pusan Perimeter and Breakout

References

Appleman, Roy E. *United States Army in Korea: South to the Naktong, North to the Yalu.* Washington, DC: Office of the Chief of Military History, 1961.

Blair, Clay. *The Forgotten War: America in Korea, 1950–1953.* New York: Times Books, 1987.

Mossman, Billy C. *United States Army in the Korean War: Ebb and Flow, November 1950–July 1951*. Washington, DC: U.S. Army Center of Military History, 1990.

Robertson, William G. *Counterattack on the Naktong, 1950*. Fort Leavenworth, KS: Combat Studies Institute, 1985.

Wallace, Anna

See Seoul City Sue

War Crimes Trials

U.S. State Department official and staunch anticommunist Arthur B. Emmons III initiated the debate over whether to bring war criminals of the Korean conflict to justice. A veteran Foreign Service official with impressive credentials and international service, Emmons became chief of Korean affairs at the State Department in 1950. Relegated to a secondary role in policy formation, he nonetheless formulated U.S. policy regarding war crimes trials in a series of recommendations to Assistant Secretary of State Dean D. Rusk. Despite State Department efforts, opposition from the highest ranks of the military—as well as the abandonment of United Nations (UN) aims to unify Korea after the military intervention of the Chinese People's Volunteer Army (CPVA, Chinese Army)—ultimately quashed the movement to punish war criminals.

In a memorandum of October 10, 1950, Emmons drew a distinction between war crimes of aggression and war crimes involving violation of the law, the breach of customs of war, and atrocities committed against civilians. The United Nations Command (UNC) had instructions to arrest and detain alleged North Korean war criminals until the UN charged them, but even at this early phase in the war Emmons recognized the volatility of the issue. He cautioned Rusk that the prosecution of war criminals might only intensify hatred between the Democratic People's Republic of Korea (DPRK, North Korea) and the Republic of Korea (ROK, South Korea) already engendered by intensive communist propaganda. Emmons warned that war crimes trials might counteract the greater goal of political reunification. At the very least, the United States should minimize or avoid altogether discussion of punishment in the UN, Emmons wrote.

The U.S. State Department and the UN found little support from military authorities to prosecute war criminals. Citing his own experiences with the post–World War II trials of Japanese war criminals, commander in chief of the UNC General Douglas MacArthur repeatedly expressed his opposition in principle. He told U.S. president Harry S. Truman to avoid the issue because he believed that punishing individuals in the military for war crimes was no deterrent and was of questionable propriety, since "military commanders obey the orders of their governments and have no option about waging war." In the event that the UN did adopt a policy to bring war criminals to justice, MacArthur suggested that instead of UN-sanctioned tribunals, special military commissions should try, convict, and punish those guilty of wartime atrocities.

MacArthur was well aware that civilians were often innocent victims in war. He himself supported the use of U.S. firepower with little regard for civilian casualties. This reckless expenditure of ordnance reduced U.S. casualties but took a fearsome toll on both North Korean and South Korean civilians. MacArthur was also aware of American servicemen calling in air strikes and artillery barrages on the slightest resistance. U.S. officers often destroyed entire villages to flush out single snipers. There was also the incident at Nogun-ni Railroad Bridge in July 1950. In addition, racist American attitudes toward Koreans, whom they often called "gooks," caused one army chaplain to complain to Lieutenant General Matthew B. Ridgway that the refusal to investigate serious crimes made "murder, rape, and pillage easy for the criminally inclined." He cited as evidence one U.S. soldier who had slit the throats of eight civilians near Pyongyang in 1951.

MacArthur opposed the prosecution of war criminals because he doubted the existence of a general North Korean policy toward the treatment of prisoners or civilians. There were indications that the Korean People's Army (KPA, North Korean Army) opposed the execution of UNC prisoners, and that special circumstances dictated the severity with which prisoners of war (POWs) and South Korean citizens were treated. The UNC estimated that some 20,000–22,000 South Korean soldiers, politicians, and civilians were summarily executed by the KPA during the North Korean occupation of South Korea between June and September 1950. The KPA also executed several groups of 30–40 captured U.S. soldiers each in the wake of the Inchon Landing. Some American POWs testified that these executions took place when it became impossible for the communists to transport their prisoners north.

The greatest massacres of civilians by communist forces occurred as the North Koreans withdrew from South Korea in late 1950 and when the KPA and the CPVA reoccupied North Korea during winter and spring 1950–1951. Up to 1,000 South Koreans were massacred at Mokpo and Wonsan after the September 15, 1950, UNC Inchon Landing. Later, North Korea executed tens of thousands of its own citizens in areas formerly occupied by the UNC. Many North Korean noncombatants were massacred for alleged collaboration.

Some South Korean civilian officials and military officers were also guilty of war crimes. After the KPA invasion of June 1950, the Rhee administration executed thousands of political prisoners as it retreated from Seoul, Inchon, and Taejon. The victims included two North Korean emissaries, Kim Sam Yong and Yi Chu Ha, and the "Mata Hari" of Korean communism, Kim Su Im.

Among Republic of Korea Army (ROKA, South Korean Army) unpunished war criminals was the ruthless "Tiger of Mount Paektu," Kim Chong Won. Kim earned his notoriety during the Yosu-Sunchon Rebellion of 1948, during which his soldiers beat, maimed, and executed hundreds of poor farmers and fishermen who purportedly had cooperated with communist guerrillas. After the UNC invasion of North Korea, as deputy provost marshal general of the ROKA occupational force in Pyongyang, Kim oversaw the systematic persecution and mass execution of North Korean communists during October and November 1950.

The UN continued to discuss the issue of war crimes. In late 1950 MacArthur received explicit instructions from the UN to apprehend and hold for trial "all persons who are or may be charged with atrocities or violations of the law and customs of war." But the directive quickly became a dead letter when the People's Republic of China (PRC) entered the war in late October 1950. After the Chinese intervention, the UN abandoned its goal of unifying Korea. In the armistice negotiations that followed, the matter of punishing war criminals was conveniently forgotten.

MATTHEW D. ESPOSITO

See also

Emmons, Arthur B., III; Kim Chong Won; Kochang Incident; MacArthur, Douglas; Missing in Action; Nogun-ni Railroad Bridge Incident; Ridgway, Matthew Bunker; Rusk, David Dean; Yosu-Sunchon Rebellion

References

Cumings, Bruce. *The Origins of the Korean War*. 2 vols. Princeton, NJ: Princeton University Press, 1981, 1990.
Millett, Allan R. *Their War in Korea: American, Asian, and European Combatants and Civilians, 1945–1953*. Princeton, NJ: Princeton University Press, 2002.
U.S. Department of State, Bureau of Public Affairs. *Foreign Relations of the United States, 1950*, Vol. 7, *Korea*. Washington, DC: U.S. Government Printing Office, 1976.

priority to Cold War issues for its own security and neglected to fulfill its previous commitments. Latin American leaders believed that the United States had neglected their countries and forgotten their cooperation during World War II.

Thus, when the foreign ministers met at the initiative of U.S. secretary of state Dean Acheson in Washington, the Latin American leaders did not embrace the U.S. proposal for joint participation in the Korean conflict. U.S. president Harry S. Truman's administration received only rhetorical support from its southern neighbors. The Latin American leaders approved general resolutions backing the UN, but declined to make specific commitments. The United States tied its call for increased production of strategic materials to a statement demanding economic development in Latin America. Colombia offered military assistance, but with only a battalion of volunteers.

ZSOLT VARGA

See also

Acheson, Dean Gooderham; Colombia; Latin America; Mexico; Peruvian Prisoner of War Settlement Proposal

References

Davis, Harold Eugene, and C. Wilson Larman. *Latin American Foreign Policies: An Analysis*. Baltimore, MD: John Hopkins University Press, 1975.
Matray, James I., ed. *Historical Dictionary of the Korean War*. Westport, CT: Greenwood, 1991.
Stebbins, R. P. *The United States in World Affairs, 1951*. New York: Harper and Row, 1952.

Washington Conference
Start Date: March 26, 1951
End Date: April 7, 1951

Fourth Meeting of Consultation of Foreign Ministers of American States, held in Washington, DC, to discuss Latin America's contribution to United Nations (UN) and U.S. efforts in the Korean War and to prevent the spread of communism in the western hemisphere. The general declaration concluding the conference emphasized the importance of military cooperation and readiness in case of a crisis. It also called for economic cooperation in the hemisphere and elimination of economic conditions conducive to the spread of communism.

The three previous meetings of foreign ministers occurred during World War II. The Panama (1939), Havana (1940), and Rio de Janeiro (1942) conferences were held to harmonize the war efforts of states on the American continents. The United States promised economic help in return for substantial military and economic assistance and the cooperation of Latin American countries during the war. Beginning with the 1947 Rio treaty, however, Washington pushed the defense issue and opposed Latin American initiatives regarding U.S. economic assistance. Washington gave

Webb, James Edwin
Birth Date: October 7, 1906
Death Date: March 27, 1992

Attorney, businessman, diplomat, and U.S. undersecretary of state during the Korean War. Born in Tally Ho, North Carolina, on October 7, 1906, James Edwin Webb graduated from the University of North Carolina in 1928. Two years later he joined the Marine Corps Reserve, earning his wings as a marine aviator. In 1931 Webb worked as a clerk for Congressman Edward W. Pou of North Carolina. He studied law at George Washington University between 1933 and 1936 and was admitted to the bar in the District of Columbia. Webb then became personnel director and assistant to the president of the Sperry Gyroscope Company, which manufactured and sold airplane equipment. He served as a major of the 1st Marine Air Warning Group during World War II, but did not see combat.

In 1946 Webb was named executive assistant to the undersecretary of the treasury. That same year, President Harry S. Truman appointed Webb as director of the Bureau of the Budget (BOB), and he presented the president with the first balanced budget since 1930. Fiscally conservative, Webb supported cutting the Pentagon budget, which was a top priority of both Congress and the White

House between 1946 and 1950. Frank Pace Jr., who became secretary of the army in the Korean War, worked for Webb and became budget director when Truman named Webb undersecretary of state in 1949. Secretary of State Dean G. Acheson and Webb were both experienced in economic planning and worked well together as they reorganized the department. Webb remained undersecretary of state until 1952.

Acheson directed Webb's work to secure a Korea aid bill in 1949 and 1950 to help the Republic of Korea (ROK, South Korea) recover economically and reestablish trade with Japan. Webb convinced Truman to send a supportive message to Congress about economic assistance for Korea and planned expert testimony to promote the plan, which lost by one vote. A revised aid bill passed because of changes to the bill and increased administrative lobbying.

After the June 25, 1950, invasion of South Korea by the Democratic People's Republic of Korea (DPRK, North Korea), Webb worked with other State Department officials to develop a policy position. When questioned about the U.S. decision to intervene, Webb emphasized that if North Korea had conquered South Korea, it "would have been a dagger pointed at Japan" and would have "affected the whole economy of that region."

When Truman returned to Washington on the second day of the war, Webb accompanied Acheson and Secretary of Defense Louis A. Johnson to the airport in the presidential limousine. Knowing that Acheson and Johnson did not get along, Webb suggested that Truman consider joint recommendations from his secretaries of state and defense before deciding on issues. At the first Blair House meeting, Webb spoke to the issues of military aid for South Korea, air support to evacuate American dependents, and the placement of the U.S. Seventh Fleet between Taiwan and the mainland People's Republic of China (PRC). Webb commented that he and Acheson supported the first two suggestions but thought that the United States should delay in the third. Truman agreed with this position, although he rejected Webb's recommendations that economic steps be taken to prepare the United States for war.

Webb's influence in the State Department weakened as the department focused on the Korean War, and his administrative and organizational talents were not as highly valued as the expertise of other officials in foreign policy. The relationship between Webb and Acheson also became strained. Webb, who suffered migraines and endured poor health during this time, resigned in January 1952, largely because of conflicts with Paul Nitze, who was the State Department's director of the influential Policy Planning Staff (PPS). Nitze, who had championed NSC-68 and the huge rearmament it envisioned, enjoyed Acheson's support.

Webb then became president of the Republic Supply Company and assistant to the president of Kerr-McGee Oil Industries. He also was a director of McDonnell Aircraft and president and board chairman of the Oak Ridge Institute of Nuclear Studies. Known for his excellent organizational skills, Webb in 1961 agreed to become administrator of the National Aeronautics and Space Administration (NASA). Until 1968 Webb skillfully guided NASA during its major scientific and technological successes, culminating in the 1969 Apollo XI manned moon landing shortly after his retirement. Colleagues cited Webb's excellent management techniques for NASA's success. Webb died on March 27, 1992, in Washington, DC

Elizabeth D. Schafer

See also

Acheson, Dean Gooderham; Blair House Meetings; Johnson, Louis Arthur; Korea Aid Bill of 1950; National Security Council Report 68; Nitze, Paul Henry; Pace, Frank, Jr.; Rusk, David Dean; Truman, Harry S.; Truman's Domestic Agenda and the Korean War; U.S. Policy toward Korea, Pre-1950

References

Acheson, Dean. *Present at the Creation: My Years at the State Department.* New York: Norton, 1969.

Callahan, David. *Dangerous Capabilities: Paul Nitze and the Cold War.* New York: HarperCollins, 1990.

Lambright, W. Henry. *Powering Apollo: James E. Webb of NASA.* Baltimore, MD: Johns Hopkins University Press, 1995.

McGlothlen, R. L. "Acheson, Economics, and the American Commitment in Korea." *Pacific Historical Review* 58 (February 1989): 23–54.

Webb, James E. *Space Age Management: The Large-Scale Approach.* New York: McGraw-Hill, 1969.

West, Sir Michael M. A. R.
Birth Date: October 27, 1905
Death Date: May 14, 1978

British army general who commanded the 1st Commonwealth Division from 1952 to the end of the Korean War in 1953. Born on October 27, 1905, Michael M. A. R. West was educated at Sandhurst military academy, graduating in 1925. Commissioned an army officer, he spent the remainder of the interwar years serving in Germany, Great Britain, and India. During World War II, West commanded at the regimental and brigade levels in the European theater. Because of his performance during the war, he was appointed commander of British occupation forces in Austria in 1950.

Major General West replaced Major General Archibald Cassels as commander of the Commonwealth Division in September 1952 and confronted the same problems faced by Cassels. The most serious issue was the lack of manpower in the division, particularly in British units, which were always understrength. The British had too many overseas commitments, and defense spending burdened the British economy, which had already been damaged by World War II and spending on the welfare state at home. West attempted to solve this problem by reorganizing the division in November 1952 so that all his forces were continually in service. This replaced the old method of having one brigade withdrawn while the other two remained in action.

West also implemented a new program named the Korean Augmentation Troop Commonwealth (KATCOM). Cassels first advocated this scheme, which was based on the U.S. program used to augment its divisions with Koreans (Korean Augmentation to U.S. Army, or KATUSA). It incorporated Koreans into the Commonwealth Division to relieve personnel shortages. Koreans did not see active service with the Commonwealth Division, however, until March 1953, in the last months of the war. When instituted, however, the program did ease the manpower problem.

West had a somewhat rocky relationship with his U.S. counterparts. He objected to the U.S. prosecution of the war, which was governed by political concerns as much as by military ones. The chief issue was continuing United Nations Command (UNC) offensives toward the end of the conflict, which West saw as a waste of manpower. The struggle to retain Pork Chop Hill in mid-1953 illustrated West's point of view. He saw it only as an outpost with little military significance.

General West served after the Korean War as director of the Territorial Army. After this, he was general officer commanding (GOC) of the I Corps of the British Army of the Rhine and then GOC of the Northern Command in Britain. West ended his career as chairman of the British Defense Staff in Washington and retired in 1965. He died on May 14, 1978.

ERIC W. OSBORNE

See also

Australia; Canada; Cassels, Sir James; New Zealand; United Kingdom

References

Barclay, C. N. *The First Commonwealth Division: The Story of British Commonwealth Land Forces in Korea, 1950–1953.* Aldershot, UK: Gale and Polden, 1954.

Grey, Jeffrey. *The Commonwealth Armies and the Korean War: An Alliance Study.* Manchester, UK: Manchester University Press, 1988.

Hastings, Max. *The Korean War.* New York: Simon and Schuster, 1987.

West Germany

See Germany, Federal Republic of

Weyland, Otto Paul

Birth Date: January 27, 1902
Death Date: September 2, 1979

U.S. Air Force (USAF) general and commander of the Far East Air Force (FEAF) from 1951 to 1953. Born on January 27, 1902, in Riverside, California, Otto Paul Weyland graduated from Texas A&M University in 1923 with a mechanical engineering degree and was commissioned into the U.S. Army Air Corps Reserve. He finished flight instruction at Kelly Field, Texas, then served with the 12th Observation Squadron at Fort Sam Houston, Texas.

His next assignment was as a flight instructor at Kelly Field from 1927 to 1931, when he became commander of the 4th Observation Squadron.

Weyland graduated from the Air Corps Tactical School in 1938 and from the Army Command and General Staff School in 1939. Two years later, he was the assistant commander of the aviation division of the National Guard Bureau in Washington, DC Weyland was commanding the 16th Pursuit Group in the Panama Canal Zone when the United States joined World War II.

Weyland was deputy chief of staff for the Sixth Air Force and served on the Air Corps Staff, then went to England as commander of the 84th Fighter Wing. He was promoted to brigadier general in September 1943. By February 1944 he was commander of the Nineteenth Tactical Air Command, which was part of the Ninth Air Force, providing aerial support for Patton's Third Army. Patton considered Weyland "the best damn general in the Air Corps." In 1945, now a major general, Weyland was named commander of the Ninth Air Force.

After World War II Weyland was deputy commandant of the Army Command and General Staff School at Fort Leavenworth, Kansas. When the USAF became a separate service, Weyland was first put in charge of devising plans and operations and then was named deputy commandant of the National War College in Washington, DC He became commanding general of the Tactical Air Command in July 1950.

Serving in the Far East on temporary duty when the Korean War began, Weyland was FEAF's vice commander for operations; he had been promoted to lieutenant general in April 1951. On June 10, 1951, Weyland became commanding general of FEAF, replacing General George E. Stratemeyer, who had suffered a heart attack. Weyland served in this position until the end of the Korean War.

As FEAF commander, Weyland advised military strategists about air operations. He asked for reinforcements, and the 116th Fighter-Bomber Wing joined the FEAF. Worried that the communists might gain air superiority, Weyland demanded more planes and pilots, but USAF leaders claimed that they had no additional aircraft available.

Weyland informed air force chief of staff General Hoyt S. Vandenberg that he wanted to prove that air power provided more than a supporting role for combat troops, but a year would pass before he received authority to pursue this course. At the beginning of the war, FEAF had attained air superiority, but with the entry of the People's Republic of China (PRC) into the war, it lost control of some air space over the Democratic People's Republic of Korea (DPRK, North Korea) because of Chinese sanctuaries protecting communist aircraft. When truce negotiations commenced on July 10, 1951, a new phase of the war began, with the primary goal of forcing the communists to concede. Weyland oversaw a summer campaign of interdiction against crucial targets. Known as Operation STRANGLE, these air-power assaults on North Korean railways impeded transportation of supplies but did not force the communist side to capitulate.

Portrait of U.S. Air Force general Otto P. Weyland, the commander of the Far East Air Force from June 10, 1951, to March 25, 1954. (Department of Defense)

During the fall of 1951 Weyland wanted to use air power to stop communist ground attacks and pressure settlement of the armistice on acceptable terms. USAF leaders in Washington were unsure that air power alone could achieve these goals. Weyland also came under criticism for favoring strategic bombing over close air support (CAS) of ground troops. Weyland claimed that he had "leaned over backwards to provide more than adequate close air support." Weyland struggled with trying to carry out strategic bombing at the same time as his assets provided CAS and secured air superiority over North Korea. He chafed under the constraints of limited war, which he believed had been forced on him by military tacticians unfamiliar with air power.

When Lieutenant General Mark W. Clark replaced Lieutenant General Matthew B. Ridgway as United Nations Command (UNC) commander in May 1952, he granted Weyland the authority to initiate a sustained air-pressure campaign against strategic communist targets. Ordering air attacks against targets in the communist rear areas that were necessary to launch and supply offensives, Weyland emphasized stopping communist forces before they reached the battle lines. On July 11, 1952, Weyland initiated Operation PRESSURE PUMP, in which 30 targets in Pyongyang were struck,

including the largest air attack, of 1,254 sorties, in the war. That same month Weyland was advanced to general (four-star) rank.

Lacking adequate resources to attack all communist airfields, Weyland determined which North Korean airfields were most threatening to UNC forces and ordered air attacks to neutralize them. In May 1953 he proposed bombing earthen irrigation dams north of Pyongyang to flood rice paddies. He believed that some 283,000 tons of rice might be destroyed, leading to starvation and forcing the communists to accept an armistice. Reconnaissance photographs confirmed widespread flooding from the air attacks, which Weyland called "perhaps the most spectacular of the war." The communists retaliated with offensives against UNC troops along the truce lines. During the war, Weyland personally led an unescorted bomber attack over North Korea, and he was the first USAF general to be shot at by MiG-15 jet fighters.

Returning to the United States in the summer of 1953, Weyland became commanding general of the Tactical Air Command at Langley Air Force Base, Virginia, in April 1954. He remained in that post until his retirement from active duty on July 31, 1959. Weyland then worked as a consultant for McDonnell Aircraft Corporation and was the director of a life insurance company. He died on September 2, 1979, in San Antonio, Texas.

ELIZABETH D. SCHAFER

See also

Aerial Combat; Airborne Operations; Aircraft; Airpower in the Korean War; China, People's Republic of, People's Liberation Army Air Force; Clark, Mark Wayne; Close Air Support; Far East Air Force; Korea, Democratic People's Republic of, Air Force; MiG Alley; Pyongyang; Ridgway, Matthew Bunker; STRANGLE, Operation; Stratemeyer, George Edward; Truman, Harry S.; United Nations Command Air Assets; United States Air Force; United States Navy Air Operations; Vandenberg, Hoyt Sanford

References

Futrell, Robert F. *The United States Air Force in Korea, 1950–1953.* Rev. ed. Washington, DC: Office of the Chief of Air Force History, 1983.
Weyland, Otto P. "The Air Campaign in Korea." *Air University Quarterly Review* 6 (Fall 1953): 3–28.

White Horse Hill, Battle of
Start Date: October 6, 1952
End Date: October 15, 1952

One of a series of hill battles initiated by the Chinese People's Volunteer Army (CPVA, Chinese Army) and fought largely for political reasons to improve the communist negotiating position at the armistice talks. White Horse Hill (also known as Hill 395, for its height in meters) is five miles northwest of Chorwon, just north of the 38th Parallel; it overlooks the Yokkok-chon Valley and dominates western approaches to Chorwon.

On October 3, 1952, U.S. Eighth Army in Korea (EUSAK) intelligence officers learned from a Chinese deserter that CPVA forces intended to attack the strategically situated White Horse Hill. If the defending United Nations Command (UNC) IX Corps lost this position, it would have to withdraw to higher ground south of the Yokkok-chon River in the Chorwon area, denying it the use of the Chorwon road network and leaving the Iron Triangle exposed to Chinese attack.

The Chinese attack began on October 6, 1952, and was the largest offensive of the year. The CPVA timed its attack to take advantage of the upcoming U.S. presidential elections in hopes of pressuring the United States to quit the war and also to improve their defensive positions before the onset of winter. Two battalions of the 340th Regiment, 114th Division, Thirty-eighth Army of the CPVA, targeted Major General Kim Chong O's Republic of Korea Army (ROKA, South Korean Army) 9th Division. But the ROKA soldiers were no longer the untrained troops that the Chinese had once faced. During the previous year they had greatly improved in leadership, training, and equipment. Additionally, the ROKA 9th Division was reinforced with tanks, artillery, rocket launchers, and antiaircraft weapons, and it was supported by the U.S. Fifth Air Force.

The Chinese began the attack with the diversionary tactic of opening the floodgates of the Pongnae-ho Reservoir in hopes of preventing the U.S. 2nd Division from reinforcing the ROKA 9th Division. They also attacked adjacent Arrowhead Hill (Hill 281) to fix the French Battalion and U.S. 2nd Division there. Chinese artillery and mortars fired some 4,500 rounds per day, and Chinese commanders regularly fed fresh troops into the battle. Casualties climbed as the Chinese sent wave after wave of troops in an effort to gain the objective.

ROKA defenders were aided by the fact that CPVA commanders had little latitude to change their tactics once ordered to attack. The ROKA also received excellent air, armor, and artillery support. The Fifth Air Force flew 669 daylight sorties and 76 night sorties, dropping more than 2,700 general-purpose bombs and 358 napalm bombs, and launching more than 750 5-inch rockets. On October 9 one Fifth Air Force attack hit the Chinese 335th Regiment of the 112th Division in its assembly area. Also, IX Corps artillery fired 185,000 rounds against the attacking Chinese.

Beginning on October 12, ROKA troops leapfrogged battalions within the leading regiment, which allowed them to inject fresh troops into the battle. This helped them win the battle by October 15. Although White Horse Hill changed hands a total of 24 times, 23,000 Chinese (seven of the Thirty-eighth Army's nine regiments) were unable to dislodge the ROKA 9th Division, and the CPVA lost some 15,000 men. By contrast, ROKA 9th Division casualties were only 3,500 men. Not only had the Chinese failed to seize and hold White Horse Hill, but they had also failed to pressure the United States to end the war.

CAROL J. YEE

See also
Iron Triangle

References
Blair, Clay. *The Forgotten War: America in Korea, 1950–1953.* New York: Times Books, 1987.
Fehrenbach, T. R. *This Kind of War: A Study in Unpreparedness.* New York: Macmillan, 1962.
Hermes, Walter G. *U.S. Army in the Korean War: Truce Tent and Fighting Front.* Washington, DC: Office of the Chief of Military History, 1966.
Millett, Allan R. *Their War in Korea: American, Asian, and European Combatants and Civilians, 1945–1953.* Princeton, NJ: Princeton University Press, 2002.
Toland, John. *In Mortal Combat: Korea, 1950–1953.* New York: William Morrow, 1991.

Whitney, Courtney
Birth Date: May 20, 1897
Death Date: May 21, 1969

U.S. Army officer and military secretary, and adviser to commander in chief of United Nations Command (UNC) General Douglas MacArthur during the Korean War. Courtney Whitney was born in Takoma Park, Maryland, on May 20, 1897. He enlisted as a private in the Maryland National Guard in 1917. The following year he transferred to the aviation section of the fledgling U.S. Army Signal Corps Reserve, where he was commissioned a second lieutenant in March 1918. He received a commission in the regular U.S. Army in 1920. After attending aviation school, Whitney was named assistant adjutant and then adjutant at Payne Field in Mississippi. Three years later, he earned a law degree from National University and then went to the Philippines as adjutant for the 66th Service Squadron. From 1926 to 1927 Whitney was chief of the Publications Section of the Information Division in the Office of the Chief of the U.S. Army Air Corps.

Whitney resigned his commission in 1927 and spent the next 13 years practicing corporate law in Manila, Philippine Islands. There, he forged ties with many influential Filipinos and with General Douglas MacArthur, whom he had met in Washington, DC, in the early 1920s and who from 1936 was field marshal of the Philippine armed forces. Called back into active U.S. service, MacArthur became commander of U.S. Army Forces Far East in 1941.

In 1940 Whitney was commissioned a major in the Organized Reserve Corps and became assistant chief of the legal division of the U.S. Army Air Forces (USAAF). Still assigned to that branch after the United States entered World War II, he also became a member of MacArthur's "Bataan Gang" and accompanied the general to Australia in March 1942. The following February, Whitney became assistant judge advocate of the U.S. Army Air Forces before MacArthur had him transferred to his Southwest Pacific area general headquarters to lead the Philippine Regional Section. This organization promoted guerrilla and intelligence activities in the Philippines during the Japanese occupation in preparation for U.S. landings.

After U.S. forces returned to the Philippines in the fall of 1944, Whitney became chief of the civil affairs section of MacArthur's headquarters, and into 1945 he assisted Filipino officials in restoring civil government to the liberated islands. Whitney's capacity for hard work and his loyalty impressed MacArthur, and by the end of the war he had emerged as one of the general's closest advisers and confidants. Whitney had many critics among his staff colleagues and in the media, however. They saw him as little more than an unintelligent, arrogant, and pompous sycophant.

Early in 1946 Whitney, now a brigadier general, joined MacArthur's occupation headquarters (Supreme Commander, Allied Powers) in Tokyo as chief of the government section. Putting together an able civilian and military staff, he purged militarists and ultranationalists from Japanese public life, advised the Japanese on the revision of their statutes and the writing of a new constitution, and implemented a host of administrative, civil service, electoral, fiscal, and police reforms. Although criticized by some as being unfair and heavy-handed in his methods and treatment of the Japanese, Whitney ably completed the job MacArthur wanted accomplished, and at the same time he became essential to the general.

After the beginning of the Korean War in June 1950, Whitney was appointed military secretary of the UNC. He accompanied MacArthur on trips to Korea as well as to the October 1950 Wake Island meeting with President Harry S. Truman. When Truman relieved MacArthur from command in April 1951, Whitney returned to the United States and served as the general's counsel and adviser during the Senate's inquiry into MacArthur's relief and Truman's Far Eastern policies.

At the end of May 1951, Whitney retired from the army with the permanent rank of major general to serve as MacArthur's personal secretary. Following MacArthur even into civilian life, he joined the Remington Rand Corporation as MacArthur's assistant when the general became chairman of the board. The two men remained inseparable until MacArthur's death in 1964, when Whitney was at the general's bedside. Whitney spent the remainder of his life defending his former boss, and in 1956 he published *MacArthur: His Rendezvous with History,* a book that, while panned by critics, nonetheless earned him significant royalties. Whitney died in Washington, DC, on May 21, 1969.

CLAYTON D. LAURIE

See also

MacArthur, Douglas; MacArthur Hearings; Truman, Harry S.; Truman's Recall of MacArthur

References

Blair, Clay. *The Forgotten War: America in Korea, 1950–1953.* New York: Times Books, 1987.

James, D. Clayton. *The Years of MacArthur,* Vol. 3, *Triumph and Disaster, 1945–1964.* Boston: Houghton Mifflin, 1985.

Manchester, William. *American Caesar: Douglas MacArthur, 1880–1964.* Boston: Little, Brown, 1978.

Pearlman, Michael D. *Truman and MacArthur: Policy, Politics, and the Hunger for Honor and Renown.* Bloomington: Indiana University Press, 2008.

Whitney, Courtney. *MacArthur: His Rendezvous with History.* New York: Knopf, 1956.

Williams, George Z.

Birth Date: April 7, 1907
Death Date: November 22, 1994

Physician, U.S. Navy officer, and political adviser to the U.S. Military Government in Korea (USAMGIK). Born in Inchon, Korea, on April 7, 1907, to Frank E. B. Williams, a Methodist missionary, George Z. Williams spent his childhood in Korea. At the age of 15, he left for the United States to attend high school and college. He graduated with a medical degree from the University of Colorado in 1931. After graduate study in biochemistry and a residency in anatomic and clinical pathology, he received certification from the American Board of Pathology in 1937.

Williams's work was interrupted by World War II, and he served as a medical officer in the U.S. Navy and headed the Department of Laboratories at a large hospital on the U.S. naval base in Brisbane, Australia. In 1945 he took up a new assignment as an assistant fleet surgeon; he was in charge of medical landing operations for U.S. forces. He applied for a transfer to Korea when he heard that U.S. forces would occupy southern Korea, but his request was rejected because Vice Admiral Thomas C. Kinkaid, the commander of the Seventh Fleet, wanted to keep him on his ship.

Unexpectedly, Williams met Major General John R. Hodge when the Seventh Fleet was assigned to the convoy escorting Hodge's troops to Inchon on September 8, 1945. Able to speak fluent Korean, Williams was the only available U.S. officer who could communicate with the three Korean representatives awaiting Hodge's arrival. Williams then accompanied Hodge as his personal political adviser. Hodge asked him to investigate the political conditions in Korea, to hire Koreans for the USAMGIK, and to speak on behalf of the USAMGIK to Korean leaders.

After conducting an initial political survey, Williams concluded that Yo Un Hyong's Korean People's Republic (KPR) was probably controlled by communists. Williams's religious background and church connections tended to make him more receptive to the opinions and the needs of Christian groups, educated elites, and missionary communities. He regarded the people in the Korean Democratic Party (KDP) as prominent and trustworthy Korean leaders. Despite the opposition of many Koreans, he filled the USAMGIK with a number of accused collaborators. He also recommended to Hodge that such conservatives and Christian elites as Song Chin U, Kim Ku, and Syngman Rhee be given roles of responsibility.

Soon after receiving Williams's recommendations, and against the advice of the U.S. State Department, Hodge urged General Douglas MacArthur to bring Rhee back to Korea from the United States. This decision sparked the beginning of an ongoing conflict between Hodge and the State Department throughout the occupation period.

After serving three months in Korea Williams returned to the United States in January 1946 and retired as a captain, Medical Corps, U.S. Naval Reserve. He continued his medical career and became a successful researcher and scholar in clinical pathology, receiving various awards from the leading authorities in his field. Throughout his professional life, he also helped many young Koreans to obtain medical training in the United States. Williams died on November 22, 1994, in Marin, California.

KAI YIN ALLISON HAGA

See also

Hodge, John Reed; Korea, History of, 1945–1947; Rhee, Syngman

References

Cumings, Bruce. *The Origins of the Korean War.* 2 vols. Princeton, NJ: Princeton University Press, 1981, 1990.

Haga, Kai Yin Allison. "An Overlooked Dimension of the Korean War: The Role of Christianity and American Missionaries in the Rise of Korean Nationalism, Anti-Colonialism, and Eventual Civil War, 1884–1953." Unpublished PhD dissertation, College of William and Mary, 2007.

"In Memoriam: George Williams, MD 1907–1994." *American Journal of Clinical Pathology* 103 (June 1995): 767–768.

Willoughby, Charles Andrew
Birth Date: March 8, 1892
Death Date: October 26, 1972

U.S. Army officer and assistant chief of staff for intelligence to General Douglas MacArthur and his various commands in the Far East after 1940. Willoughby's origins and ancestry are still a matter of dispute. Born on March 8, 1892, in Heidelberg, Germany, Charles Andrew Willoughby claimed he had an American mother and a German aristocratic father. He immigrated to the United States in 1910, was naturalized, and joined the 5th Infantry, U.S. Army, as Private Adolphe Charles Weidenbach. In 1914 he earned a bachelor's degree at Gettysburg College. Upon receiving a U.S. Army commission in 1916, he changed his name to Charles Andrew Willoughby.

Between 1916 and 1917 Willoughby served on the Mexican border with the 35th Infantry. Following U.S. entry into World War I, he served in France with the American Expeditionary Forces in the 16th Infantry Regiment of the 1st Division. Late in the war he joined the U.S. Army Air Corps and served as a pilot.

During the decade following World War I, Willoughby served in ground units on the Mexican border, then in Puerto Rico, and as a military attaché in Venezuela, Colombia, and Ecuador. He graduated from the Army Infantry School at Fort Benning, Georgia, in 1929 and from the Army Command and General Staff School at Fort Leavenworth, Kansas, in 1931. Later he spent some time studying at the University of Kansas, and he graduated from the Army War College at Carlisle, Pennsylvania, in 1936.

Willoughby first met General MacArthur when he was a captain at Fort Leavenworth. In 1940 MacArthur summoned him to the Philippines to be assistant chief of staff for intelligence of U.S. Army Forces in the Far East. In this capacity Willoughby helped to plan the defense of the Philippines, especially Bataan and

U.S. Army major general Charles A. Willoughby, shown here in 1951, was General Douglas MacArthur's assistant chief of staff for intelligence from 1940. In late 1950, Willoughby grossly underestimated Chinese military intentions and strength in Korea. (AP/Wide World Photos)

Corregidor, before the Japanese invasion in December 1941. Willoughby accompanied MacArthur to Australia in March 1942 and remained with the general throughout the war. That June, he was promoted to brigadier general.

MacArthur commissioned Willoughby to write the official campaign history of General Headquarters, Southwest Pacific Area. He had enormous confidence in Willoughby's ability as an intelligence chief and as a scholar. Willoughby had already written two books, *U.S. Economic Participation in the World War, 1917–1918* (1931) and *The Element of Maneuver in War* (1935), and from 1931 to 1935 he had served as the editor in chief of the *General Staff Quarterly.*

Willoughby's vague personal and family background, his origins, his pompous personality, and his extraordinarily close relationship with MacArthur produced many enemies and critics over the years, who among other things alleged that his desire to please the general often jeopardized the quality of the intelligence that Willoughby provided to MacArthur. As one historian has suggested, Willoughby's views influenced the entire intelligence community in the Far East Command, and a challenge to Willoughby was seen as being tantamount to a challenge to MacArthur. It was said that Willoughby provided MacArthur only with news he knew the general wanted to hear. In March 1945 Willoughby was promoted to major general.

Remaining with MacArthur during the occupation of Japan throughout the late 1940s, Willoughby was criticized for failing to provide warning of the June 1950 invasion of the Republic of Korea (ROK, South Korea) by the Democratic People's Republic of Korea (DPRK, North Korea). It does appear, however, that Willoughby, a vehement anticommunist, did send several reports to Washington, DC, in 1949 and 1950 indicating the possibility of a North Korean invasion in March or April 1950. However, like those in the Central Intelligence Agency (CIA) and the State Department, Willoughby thought an invasion was very unlikely anytime in the foreseeable future.

When the North Koreans did invade South Korea, Willoughby repeatedly overestimated the ability of the Republic of Korea Army (ROKA, South Korean Army) forces to stem the invasion during the early weeks of the war, and he underestimated the quality of Korean People's Army (KPA, North Korean Army) forces and the strength of their attack. But in spite of what some critics called egregiously bad intelligence collection and reporting, MacArthur continued to rely on Willoughby's interpretations of events through the fall of 1950.

Willoughby and others ignored the first hints, as early as August 1950, of a possible Chinese intervention. The same was true with later indicators that the Chinese were massing troops on the North Korean border in October and November 1950. Willoughby continued to insist that neither the Chinese nor the Soviets would seek to widen the war, because he believed that the Chinese were utterly incapable of fighting a military power such as the United States. Even as evidence continued to come in, Willoughby persisted in explaining it away as insignificant.

After the Chinese did intervene, Willoughby, who had undergone an 11th-hour conversion to realize the true nature and purpose of the Chinese presence on the border, wildly underestimated the numbers of troops involved, much to the chagrin of United Nations Command (UNC) field commanders, who were facing a much more numerous and determined enemy than had been predicted or initially realized. The charges that he steadfastly underestimated the presence, number, and danger of communist forces facing UNC forces in Korea dogged Willoughby for the remainder of his life.

After President Harry S. Truman's recall of MacArthur in April 1951, Willoughby also retired from the military. He later became editor of the *Foreign Intelligence Digest* and author of *MacArthur: 1941–1951* (1954), a book based on his personal knowledge of the general and his actions during those years. He died in Naples, Florida, on October 26, 1972.

CLAYTON D. LAURIE

See also

MacArthur, Douglas; Military Intelligence

References

Blair, Clay. *The Forgotten War: America in Korea, 1950–1953*. New York: Times Books, 1987.

"Charles Andre Willoughby." 201 File. U.S. Army Center of Military History, Washington, DC.

Goulden, Joseph C. *Korea: The Untold Story of the War*. New York: Times Books, 1982.

McGovern, James. *To the Yalu: From the Chinese Invasion to MacArthur's Dismissal*. New York: William Morrow, 1972.

Pearlman, Michael D. *Truman and MacArthur: Policy, Politics, and the Hunger for Honor and Renown*. Bloomington: Indiana University Press, 2008.

Wilson, Charles Edward

Birth Date: November 18, 1886
Death Date: January 3, 1972

President of General Electric Company and the first director of the Office of Defense Mobilization (ODM), from 1950 to 1952. Born in New York City on November 18, 1886, Charles Edward Wilson suffered tragedy at the age of 3, when his father died, reducing the family to poverty. Raised in the infamous Hell's Kitchen neighborhood of New York City, Wilson left school at age 12 to work as an office boy at General Electric. Despite his curtailed education, Wilson—often known as "Electric" Charlie to distinguish him from his namesake Charles E. "Engine" Wilson, the president of General Motors—rose from the bottom and served successively in the departments of accounting, production, engineering, manufacturing, and marketing to become president of General Electric in 1939.

In September 1942 Wilson joined the ranks of businessmen flocking to President Franklin D. Roosevelt's war mobilization effort and became a member of the War Production Board (WPB), facilitating the manufacture of an unprecedented 93,369 military airplanes in 1944. Differences with WPB chairman Donald Nelson over what Wilson considered to be unduly rapid plans for reconversion to peacetime led to his resignation in August 1944 and his return to the presidency of General Electric.

Despite, or perhaps because of, Wilson's political affiliation as a registered Republican, President Harry S. Truman regularly appointed Wilson to serve on advisory panels, including the National Security Resources Board, the National Labor-Management Panel, the University Military Training Commission, and the Taft-Hartley Advisory Board, assignments that culminated in 1946 in Wilson's chairmanship of the President's Commission on Civil Rights. In this capacity Wilson submitted a notably liberal report that demanded the legal eradication of racial violence, segregation, harassment, and discrimination in the United States.

In December 1950, after the intervention by the People's Republic of China (PRC) in the Korean War and the consequent disastrous impact on U.S. and United Nations Command (UNC) military fortunes, Truman appointed Wilson as director of the newly created ODM, an indication that the administration anticipated a lengthy and difficult conflict. Truman charged Wilson

As President Harry S. Truman (center) looks on, Chief Justice Fred Vinson administers the oath of office to Charles Wilson, formerly president of the General Electric Company, as director of the Office of Defense Mobilization, December 21, 1950. (Harry S. Truman Presidential Library)

with the task of mobilizing U.S. industry and the economy for the accelerated war effort in Korea and the broader Cold War. Wilson accepted the post on condition that he would have complete authority over all aspects of this task and be answerable only to the president. As ODM director Wilson's statutory powers exceeded those of any other civilian mobilization chief. At the time, the nation's press likened Wilson's position to a copresidency.

Wilson oversaw and facilitated a massive defense expansion, essentially that envisaged in the National Security Council's 1950 report, NSC-68, which called for rearming the nation for a potential global conflict even as it simultaneously waged a limited war in Korea. In 1951 military expenditures quadrupled from $15 billion to more than $50 billion. In this sense Wilson presided over the birth of the permanent national security state in the United States.

One of Wilson's first priorities was to stabilize the nation's overheating economy, mainly by implementing mandatory wage and price controls through the Wage Stabilization Board and the Office of Price Stabilization, which he did in late January 1951. Wilson also began to assemble industrial advisory committees from diverse sectors of the economy that aided in developing and

implementing mobilization and production priorities. Although Wilson's job was never easy, he proved to be an able administrator, negotiating the political minefields of wage and price controls, raw materials controls, and industrial expansion with much skill and success. During his tenure military and industrial output soared, inflation and economic dislocations remained largely at bay, and raw materials shortages eased considerably.

Wilson's methods were uncompromising. A staunch supporter of wage and price controls to prevent inflation and facilitate mobilization—objectives in which he largely succeeded—he was also a long-standing opponent of labor unions. In October 1946 he stated, "The problem of the United States can be captiously summed up in two words: Russia abroad, labor at home." In February 1951, when a national railroad strike jeopardized rearmament, Wilson went on the radio to appeal to the patriotism of U.S. workers to end industrial action and defeat communism abroad. In March 1952 Wilson, infuriated by Truman's decision to veto price increases in steel while accepting a Wage Stabilization Board recommendation to increase steelworkers' pay and other benefits, resigned his position and moved to W. R. Grace and Co. When management refused to acquiesce in the president's decision, a strike ensued, and in April Truman used his emergency powers to take over the steel plants, a move that the U.S. Supreme Court declared unconstitutional in the absence of an official state of war. A second strike followed, and ultimately the steel makers obtained price increases of about half of those they had originally requested.

Perhaps Wilson's greatest contribution to the Korean mobilization effort was his management technique. An early pioneer in centralized/decentralized corporate structures, Wilson sought to keep the ODM and its constituent agencies lean and compact yet powerful. He accomplished this by combining centralized management and policy making with decentralized policy implementation and operations. This management style kept administrative costs down and bureaucracies relatively small. It also resembled the multidivisional management forms that Wilson had implemented at General Electric.

During President Dwight D. Eisenhower's administration Wilson headed the People-to-People Foundation, a program intended to promote international understanding and friendship. Wilson died on January 3, 1972, in Scarsdale, New York.

PAUL G. PIERPAOLI JR. AND PRISCILLA ROBERTS

See also

Mobilization; National Emergency Declaration; National Security Council Report 68; Office of Price Stabilization; Steel Plants, Truman's Seizure of; Truman, Harry S.; Wage Stabilization Board

References

Antone, C. P. "Charles Edward Wilson." In *Dictionary of American Biography, Supplement Nine, 1971–1975,* edited by Kenneth T. Jackson, 873–874. New York: Scribner, 1994.

Hogan, Michael J. *A Cross of Iron: Harry S. Truman and the Origins of the National Security State, 1945–1954.* New York: Cambridge University Press, 1998.

Marcus, Maeva. *Truman and the Steel Seizure Case: The Limits of Presidential Power.* New York: Columbia University Press, 1977.

McCullough, David. *Truman.* New York: Simon and Schuster, 1992.

Pierpaoli, Paul G., Jr. *Truman and Korea: The Political Culture of the Early Cold War.* Columbia: University of Missouri Press, 1999.

Vander Meulen, Jacob. "Wilson, Charles Edward." In *American National Biography,* Vol. 23, edited by John A. Garraty and Mark C. Carnes, 557–559. 24 vols. New York: Oxford University Press, 1999.

"Wilson, Charles Edward." In *Current Biography, 1951,* edited by Anna Rothe and Evelyn Lohr, 663–666. New York: H. W. Wilson, 1952.

WOLFHOUND, **Operation**
Start Date: January 15, 1951
End Date: January 17, 1951

January 1951 attack on communist forces initiated by the United Nations Command (UNC). Lieutenant General Matthew B. Ridgway's assumption of command of the Eighth Army marked a dramatic change in how the war would be fought. To initiate a new aggressiveness, Ridgway ordered a reconnaissance in force to find

and destroy Chinese People's Volunteer Army (CPVA, Chinese Army) troops. The attack, known as Operation WOLFHOUND, was launched at 7:00 a.m. on January 15 by seven infantry battalions: the entire 27th Infantry (25th Division); the 1st Battalion, 15th Infantry Regiment and the 2nd Battalion, 65th Infantry Regiment (both 3rd Division); the 3rd Battalion, 2nd Infantry Regiment, Republic of Korea Army (ROKA, South Korean Army) 6th Division; and the 2nd Battalion, 12th Infantry Regiment, ROKA 1st Division. Tanks of the 89th Tank Battalion (25th Division) accompanied the 27th, while a smaller tank force went with the 3rd Division infantry. The 8th, 10th, 39th, and 90th Field Artillery Battalions supported the operation. Operation WOLFHOUND involved in all some 6,000 men.

The 1st Battalion, 27th Infantry with a tank company advanced north over a secondary road in western Korea, while the 2nd and 3rd Battalions of the regiment, with the remainder of the tank battalion, followed the main highway. The regimental objective was the Suwon-Osan area.

Neither column of the 27th Infantry met resistance, although they were slowed by roads and bridges that had been damaged by withdrawing UNC forces some days previously. The 1st Battalion stopped for the night at Pajang-ni, while the principal regimental force stopped just north of Osan, 10 miles to the east.

The 1st Battalion of the 15th with two tank companies moved rapidly over a road more or less parallel to, and some 7 to 10 miles east of, the main highway. About dusk this force entered Kumyangjang-ni, where it surprised communist forces, killing about 50 soldiers and taking the town. Turning west in darkness toward Suwon, the battalion was finally stopped by heavy communist small arms and mortar fire. The two ROKA battalions followed the 1st Battalion of the 15th, occupying Chon-ni and Kumyangjang-ni without opposition.

The 2nd Battalion of the 65th Infantry was supposed to follow a road east of but closer to the main highway than that taken by the 1st Battalion of the 15th. Finding that road impassable, the battalion doubled back and took the road previously used by 1st Battalion to the town of Songjon. There it turned west and stopped for the night in Osan, which the 27th had previously cleared.

On January 16, while the 1st Battalion approached Suwon from the west, the remainder of the 27th came in from the south. Although the 1st Battalion met no opposition, the 2nd Battalion, leading on the main road, encountered heavy machine-gun fire, while other CPVA troops attempted to cut off the battalion. The 2nd Battalion of the 65th Regiment took a path northeast out of Osan that morning and became bogged down in ice and snow.

Operation WOLFHOUND revealed that large numbers of Chinese forces were assembling in the Suwon-Kumyangjang-ni area, threatening to cut off the 27th Infantry. Accordingly, on the afternoon of January 16 the regiment was ordered to disengage and withdraw to Osan.

Total casualties among the seven battalions in the operation were only three killed and seven wounded. Communist losses

UNC ON THE DEFENSIVE, DECEMBER 31, 1950–JANUARY 24, 1951

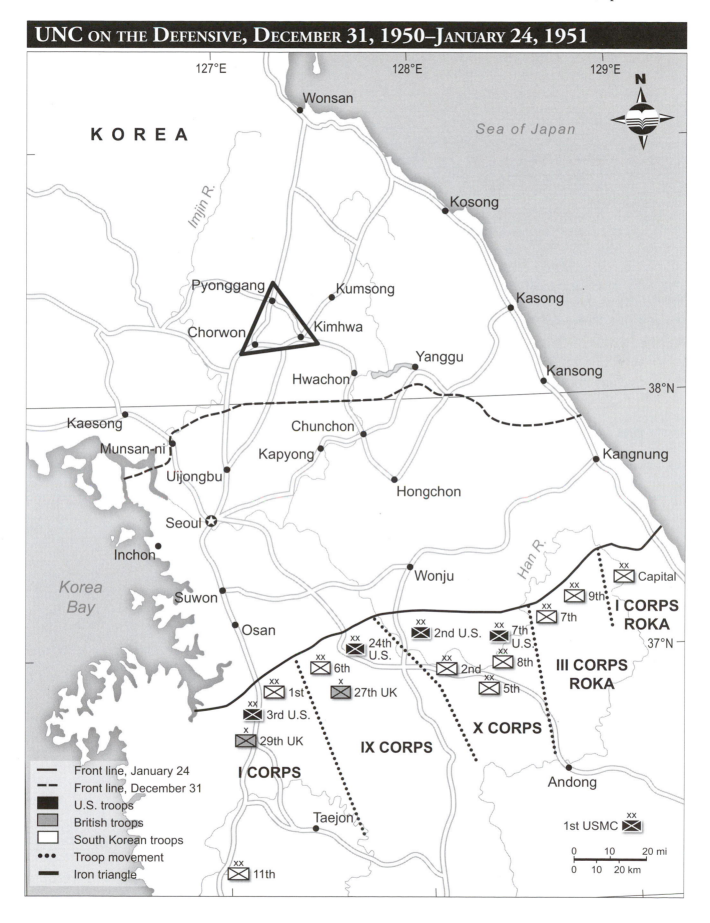

KOREA

127°E · 128°E · 129°E

N

Sea of Japan

Wonsan

Kosong

Imjin R.

Pyonggang · Kumsong

Kasong

Chorwon · Kimhwa

Yanggu

Kansong

Hwachon

38°N

Kaesong

Chunchon

Munsan-ni · Kapyong

Kangnung

Uijongbu · Hongchon

Seoul

Inchon

Wonju

Han R. · I CORPS ROKA

Capital

9th

Korea Bay

Suwon

7th

Osan

24th U.S.

2nd U.S. · 7th U.S.

III CORPS ROKA

37°N

xx 6th

xx 2nd

8th

xx 1st

xx 27th UK

5th

X CORPS

3rd U.S.

29th UK

IX CORPS

I CORPS

Andong

1st USMC

Taejon

0   10   20 mi
0 10 20 km

xx 11th

——	Front line, January 24
- - -	Front line, December 31
■	U.S. troops
▨	British troops
□	South Korean troops
••••	Troop movement
▬▬	Iron triangle

were about 1,800. On January 17 Operation WOLFHOUND forces set up a strong outpost line along the Chinwi-chon River just south of Osan.

UZAL W. ENT

See also
Ridgway, Matthew Bunker

References
Appleman, Roy E. *Ridgway Duels for Korea.* College Station: Texas A&M University Press, 1990.
Blair, Clay. *The Forgotten War: America in Korea, 1950–1953.* New York: Times Books, 1987.
Mossman, Billy C. *United States Army in the Korean War: Ebb and Flow, November 1950–July 1951.* Washington, DC: U.S. Army Center of Military History, 1990.

Women in Defense Production Administration Committees

During the Korean War women served in myriad capacities, many of which were outside the purview of the military. Indeed, women served as paid government employees in many of the mobilization and economic stabilization agencies but far more served as unpaid volunteers on mobilization advisory committees. Thousands of women served on local, regional, and national committees affiliated with the Office of Price Stabilization (OPS), while many also served on a voluntary basis in the departments of State, Defense, Labor, and the Defense Manpower Administration. Women also played an important role in the Defense Production Administration (DPA). This high level of volunteerism was in keeping with the desire of President Harry S. Truman's administration to keep the mobilization effort at a grassroots level, thereby building support for the program while eschewing large and costly bureaucracies.

The DPA was created in late December 1950 as part of the stepped-up mobilization program inaugurated by the creation of the Office of Defense Mobilization (ODM). As the ODM's first director, Charles E. Wilson moved to establish the DPA within days of his appointment on December 15, 1950. His strategy was to create policy-making agencies at the national level but to entrust day-to-day mobilization and stabilization functions to already-existing government agencies and to rely heavily upon advisory committees made up of consumers, producers, and labor representatives.

The DPA was designed to operate in a similar fashion to the War Production Board of World War II, in which Wilson had served as vice chairman and then executive vice chairman. The DPA was charged with supervising all industrial requirements and materials allocation to keep the mobilization program and the U.S. economy on an even keel. Indeed, the DPA set industrial production priorities for many U.S. manufacturers, set individual production quotas for military and military-essential products, and oversaw the pace and scope of new industrial construction in keeping with the expansion of the U.S. industrial base. The DPA also became the primary liaison with the Controlled Materials Plan (CMP), which began operation in July 1951. The CMP was designed to prevent shortages of raw materials or bottlenecks in production by closely matching and prioritizing industrial output with military requirements.

The exact extent to which women served on the various advisory committees of the DPA and its constituent agencies is difficult to determine, because many were serving in a voluntary capacity. Thus, there are no employment records to document the precise number of women involved and the extent of their activities. There were probably at least several women who served on advisory committees, with many serving on National Production Authority (NPA) industrial advisory committees, which provided the DPA with aggregate industrial production output figures and raw materials needs. By mid-June 1951, the NPA had established 397 industrial advisory committees that were operating on the local and regional level via 105 field offices located across the United States. It was mainly through the NPA, in fact, that women played a significant role in the industrial mobilization effort.

These committees drew their membership chiefly from well-organized women's groups like the Young Women's Christian Association (YWCA), the Junior League, and the League of Women Voters. Other more Korean War–specific women's groups were also involved, like Housewives United, which served the OPS in large numbers. The inclusion of women in the mobilization and stabilization effort reflected the administration's desire to keep programs decentralized and broad-based. But it also reflected the growing recognition among U.S. politicians and policy makers of women's growing stature and increased participation in the workplace and voting booth.

PAUL G. PIERPAOLI JR.

See also
Controlled Materials Plan; Housewives United; Industrial Base, U.S.; Office of Defense Mobilization; Office of Price Stabilization; Wilson, Charles Edward; Women on the Home Front, United States and Korea

References
Kaledin, Eugenia. *Mothers and More: American Women in the 1950s.* Boston: Twayne, 1984.
May, Elaine Tyler. *Homeward Bound: American Families in the Cold War Era.* New York: Basic Books, 1988.
Pierpaoli, Paul G., Jr. *Truman and Korea: The Political Culture of the Early Cold War.* Columbia: University of Missouri Press, 1999.

Women on the Home Front, United States and Korea

The trends that began to characterize U.S. society and home life when men returned from their service in World War II set the context for the Korean War years. American women throughout

A mother waves goodbye to her family as she leaves for work, 1953. The number of American women in the workforce continued to increase during the Korean War years. (Library of Congress)

the 1950s generally married at younger ages, had more children, and embraced traditional gender roles when compared to previous or subsequent generations. Thus, the marriage and birth rates soared, producing the "baby boom," men embraced their traditional roles as the primary breadwinners, and many women seemed to cherish the ideal of the contemporary homemaker. Indeed, many Americans viewed the family as a vehicle by which to attain the security and stability that had been missing during their recent experiences with economic depression and world war.

The nuclear family, in its traditional configuration, was perceived as an institution that would allow Americans to face future challenges and cope with their fears of new technology, the atomic age, economic downturns, changing residential patterns, and the threat of persistent warfare as characterized by the Cold War. While many historians have noted the high degree of optimism possessed by many World War II veterans, others have observed that by 1950 that optimism had evolved into an intense fear of communism and technology, and a destructive political disunity, especially with the advent of McCarthyism.

These fears only served to intensify the significance of the family as a safe harbor in which to weather the storms. The success of families in meeting these challenges eventually produced what historian Elaine Tyler May has characterized as "materialism, consumerism, and bureaucratic conformity." This societal context was prevalent among relatively well-educated, comfortably middle-class whites, but May also observed these trends within African American communities as well.

Throughout the 1950s women faced widespread legal, educational, medical, and employment discrimination. Although the number of women entering the workforce continued to increase during this time, their economic opportunities were generally limited to menial, subordinate, and low-paying jobs. But for those women whose husbands were unable to produce enough income to support the family—such as recent immigrants, low-income inner city residents, widows, and the elderly—these jobs were the staples of their existence. By 1950, 27 percent of all workers were female. Only 5 percent of all doctors, lawyers, architects, and those working in the natural sciences were women, however, and 70

A Korean woman sells gifts to an American soldier in a Seoul Post Exchange (PX) in 1951. (Bettmann/Corbis)

percent of "professional" women worked in the teaching, nursing, and library fields. Many women returned to the workforce as their children matured. By 1950 nearly 30 percent of all female workers were over age 45. Author Eugenia Kaledin referred to these workers as "new old ladies." Women, however, rarely received societal, institutional, or organized labor support for their professional endeavors.

The U.S. government routinely paid social security entitlements to the "primary breadwinner," even when women had significant income, and widows received a lesser amount than their husbands would have been paid. In many states women could not obtain credit, buy houses or insurance policies, and often did not have the legal standing to enter into legal contracts. Federal law barred their service on federal juries until 1957. Female students made up about 3 percent of the law school classes throughout the 1950s, and timely career advice urged them to develop stenographic skills in addition to earning their legal degree. At the time, some medical doctors still considered normal physiological events—premenstrual stress, pregnancy, childbirth, and

menopause—akin to pathological illnesses. Women were often subjected to unnecessary surgeries, forced sterilizations, and maternity room indignities.

Yet despite these inequities and prejudices, some women led the way for change during the 1950s. *Ladies Home Journal* rallied 5 million subscribers under the slogan "Never Underestimate the Power of a Woman." Hundreds wrote the magazine about their childbirth experiences, causing a reevaluation of the practice of banning husbands from the delivery room. In 1950, 43 percent of college graduates 25 years and older were female, a statistic that clearly showed that some American women were already beginning to break out of their prescribed gender roles. Scholars such as Mary R. Beard (*Woman as Force in History,* 1946) and Betty Friedan (*The Feminine Mystique,* 1963) honed the ideas that would later inform the women's movement of the 1960s. Marguerite Higgins, a journalist for the *New York Herald Tribune,* spent two years in Korea during the war and was an eyewitness to the Inchon Landing in September 1950; her reporting earned her a Pulitzer Prize, the first awarded to a woman for international reporting.

Women volunteered in schools, libraries, and hospitals, earned Olympic medals, and excelled in sports, the theater, literature, and the arts throughout the 1950s. Politically, they organized the League of Women Voters, which saw a 44 percent increase in membership between 1950 and 1958. The administration of President Dwight D. Eisenhower appointed a few women to high-level positions in government service—a cabinet member, United Nations (UN) delegate, and at least two ambassadors. Thus, although women as a group had made little progress in political or economic terms, they contributed to what Kaledin referred to as a growing consciousness that shaped the women of the next decade and compelled societal change.

Many women served as government employees and volunteers in the mobilization and economic stabilization agencies throughout the Korean War. Anna M. Rosenberg was appointed assistant secretary of defense for manpower and personnel in September 1950. She coordinated Department of Defense policies on military and civilian personnel, and recommended the formation of the Defense Advisory Committee on Women in the Services (DACOW-ITS) in 1951. At the time of her appointment, Rosenberg became the highest-ranking woman in the U.S. military establishment.

Many women also served as unpaid volunteers for such government agencies as the Departments of State, Defense, and Labor and the Defense Production Administration (DPA). The DPA was an agency similar to the War Production Board during World War II, which sought to decentralize mobilization and stabilization functions to existing local government agencies and to incorporate the expertise and support of advisory committees of consumers, producers, and labor representatives. The DPA supervised industrial requirements and materials allocation in an effort to stabilize the U.S. economy and to minimize the disruption created by wartime demands. Women participated primarily through their service on National Production Authority (NPA) industrial advisory committees that provided the DPA with industrial production output figures and raw materials needs. Women also volunteered to assist the Office of Price Stabilization (OPS) and Wage Stabilization Board (WSB), which established, monitored, and enforced price and wage controls deemed necessary to wartime mobilization, under the mandate of the Economic Stabilization Agency (ESA).

In the Republic of Korea (ROK, South Korea), many women worked as contract laborers during the war for U.S. and South Korean troops as they sought to survive the devastation visited upon their country. All told, historians report that South Korea lost two-fifths of its prewar industrial capacity, and one-third of its housing units. Women often fared poorly in terms of employment opportunities and personal and legal rights, especially under wartime conditions. Traditionally conservative Asian attitudes toward gender roles also limited women's roles. Because the war required almost full mobilization of the capable male population, the Korean National Railroad and the U.S. 3rd Transportation Military Railway Service employed women in fairly large numbers in low-level management and clerical positions.

Korean women worked in the logistical supply areas by performing all kinds of manual-labor positions that involved everything from moving cargo to construction work. The U.S. Eighth Army employed local women as waitresses in officer messes, laundresses, and janitors. Within the Republic of Korea Army (ROKA, South Korean Army), Korean women manned psychological warfare units and were primarily involved in activities designed to convince communist soldiers to surrender. Others directed traffic for the Korean National Police, and served as ROKA nurses and medical specialists aboard hospital trains and in aid stations and field hospital units. Many civilian nurses remained on the job in Seoul hospitals as that city fell to the communists in the summer of 1950. Tragically, many of these medical personnel were massacred at Uijongbu, a suburb northeast of Seoul, by North Korean secret police after the September 15, 1950, Inchon Landing. Often, educated South Korean women who fell under communist control or who were considered threatening or class enemies suffered imprisonment, torture, and execution at the hands of the secret police. Also, many Korean women experienced sexual harassment by Korean as well as foreign soldiers in both Koreas.

Korean civilian women also performed in United Service Organizations (USO) shows and served refreshments in transportation facilities. Women in North and South Korea ran family businesses, enterprises, and farms while their husbands, fathers, and brothers were away fighting the war.

Some Korean women—a few hundred per year during the war—became American military brides. Between 1950 and 1959 the U.S. Immigration and Naturalization Service reported that 1,987 Korean women had immigrated to the United States as wives of servicemen. Moreover, Americans adopted a significant number of Korean children; these connections produced longstanding migration patterns that extended into the 1980s. Women's roles in North Korea are much harder to write about with certainty, because of the closed nature of its society. Few English-language resources are available on the topic, but it is safe to say that many women in North Korea performed roles and functions similar to those in South Korea. Indeed, because of the massive dislocations to North Korea, which were bigger than those in South Korea, it is likely that they performed in an even wider array of fields. Also, communist dogma had tried to level the playing field between men and women, but the conservatism prevalent in Asian cultures at the time probably worked against that ideal to some extent. In sum, the war was a time of great trial for Korean women.

Women's activities throughout the Korean War, particularly in the United States, were conducted within the context of mobilization for not only the immediate crisis but also the long-haul of the Cold War. Be that as it may, larger societal trends tended to reinforce their traditional roles as homemakers and mothers. Although they often faced hardships and discrimination, many women excelled, setting the stage for even greater contributions and expanded roles within society beginning in the 1960s.

DEBORAH KIDWELL

See also

Economic Stabilization Agency; Mobilization; Office of Defense Mobilization; Office of Price Stabilization; United States, Home Front; Wage Stabilization Board; Women in Defense Production Administration Committees; Women in the Military during the Korean War

References

Choe, Il Song. *Hanguk Yosongsa* [History of Korean Women]. Seoul: Paeksan Charyowon, 2001.

Kaledin, Eugenia. *Mothers and More: American Women in the 1950s.* Boston: Twayne, 1984.

May, Elaine Tyler. *Homeward Bound: American Families in the Cold War Era.* New York: Basic Books, 1988.

Min, Pyong Gap. *Asian Americans.* Thousand Oaks, CA: Pine Forge, 2005.

Pierpaoli, Paul G., Jr. *Truman and Korea: The Political Culture of the Early Cold War.* Columbia: University of Missouri Press, 1999.

Rose, Lisle. *The Cold War Comes to Main Street: America in 1950.* Lawrence: University Press of Kansas, 1999.

Sibul, Eric A. "Irregular Engineers: The Use of Indigenous Labor in the Rebuilding of Critical Infrastructure During the Korean War, 1950–1953." In *Selected Papers from the 2007 Conference of Army Historians,* edited by Richard G. Davis, 125–143. Washington, DC: Center of Military History, United States Army, 2008.

Yuh, Ji-Yeon. *Beyond the Shadow of Camptown.* New York: New York University Press, 2004.

Women in the Military during the Korean War

Women served in various noncombat support roles during the Korean War, beginning soon after the invasion. In July 1950, 57 U.S. Army nurses arrived at Pusan to establish a hospital, and 12 nurses were assigned to the Mobile Army Surgical Hospital (MASH) at Taejon to treat casualties from the nearby front lines. At the start of the war the Women's Army Corps (WAC) and Women in the Air Force (WAF) groups had East Asian bases, including a WAC detachment in support of General Headquarters, Far East Command in Tokyo, Japan. None of these women, however, were permitted to serve in Korea because of the fluctuating battle lines.

The WACs, WAFs, WAVEs (Women in the Navy), and U.S. Marine Corps Women's Reserve totaled 22,000 women on active duty in June 1950. Seven thousand of these servicewomen were in health positions, while the rest served in line assignments. Women accounted for less than 1 percent of the U.S. military.

The WACs had only recently been integrated into the regular army. Having provided valuable service during World War II, they were rewarded in 1948 when Congress passed a law assuring WACs a permanent place in the army by granting them regular army and reserve status. Former WACs and officers could join the Organized Reserve Corps, which later became known as the U.S. Army Reserve. This group of reserve WACs was among the first women to serve in the Korean War effort. By July 1950 commanders in East Asia requested WAC officers and enlisted women to fill noncombat positions—such as supply clerk, corpsman, medical technician, stenographer, typist, and finance clerk—vacated by men sent to Korea.

The United States began issuing draft calls, and reservists were recalled to active duty, with entire units being assigned to Korea, overseas locations, or important support positions in the United States. A WAC training center, organized and managed by women, was established at Fort Lee, Virginia. Each week approximately 250 women enlistees and reenlistees came to Fort Lee for basic training. The women also received instruction for specific duty assignments, such as maintenance, and completed a military leadership course.

World War II WACs provided invaluable experience, acting as mentors to new enlistees. More than 1,200 WAC inactive-duty reserve officers and enlisted women voluntarily returned to active duty. Fifty WAC reservists were involuntarily recalled. In August 1950 the army suspended the discharge of WAC personnel based on marriage so that more women could serve in Korea. Both men and women had their nondisability retirements suspended by Congress, which also provided that enlisted soldiers and officers would have their obligations extended for one year.

The Defense Advisory Committee on Women in the Services (DACOWITS) was created during the Korean War and established a legacy for women in the armed services. Assistant Secretary of Defense for Manpower Anna M. Rosenberg recommended a committee to address women's military interests, and Secretary of Defense George C. Marshall approved it. The initial meeting to discuss DACOWITS was held on September 18, 1951, and Marshall formally established the committee the next month. He instructed the committee, consisting of 50 influential civilian women leaders in politics, the arts, business, and academia, to work together and recruit enlistees. Chaired by Mrs. Oswald Lord, who had led a previous army women's advisory committee, DACOWITS began a national campaign sponsored by the Department of Defense to recruit more women for the services. President Harry S. Truman officially started the campaign on November 11, 1951. It featured such patriotic slogans as "Share Service for Freedom" and "America's Finest Women Stand Beside Her Finest Men."

Marshall hoped to increase the women's services by 72,000 by July 1952. Of this number, 20,000 WACs were to be recruited. DACOWITS collectively, and as individual members, presented public programs about recruiting needs and reassured parents that their daughters would be safe in a supervised environment. DACOWITS members emphasized the career opportunities available to women in the military. They worked to improve public opinion of military women and enhance their prestige. For the most part, they promoted all of the women's service branches, permitting recruits to select which unit most interested them.

The WAC band at Fort Lee toured colleges and schools throughout the United States to welcome recruits. Actresses Helen Hayes and Irene Dunne used their fame and talents to help with the campaign. The results, however, were disappointing. By the end of 1952 the WAC had almost 500 fewer members than it had in 1951. The other

Army nurse Captain Jane Thurness uses a helmet for washing while at the front lines, February 14, 1951. (National Archives)

women's service branches did not achieve their goals either, but they did at least increase their numbers. Several thousand women joined the navy, air force, and marines. The Marine Corps, usually the smallest women's service branch, increased by 400 women over the 580 women marines on active duty when the war began.

Although there was a great need for female personnel, the Pentagon failed to attract sufficient quantities of qualified recruits to meet quotas. Many potential recruits were underage, scored poorly on aptitude tests, or were otherwise unqualified.

The disappointing WAC recruitment was the catalyst for much-needed fundamental changes for army women. Congress funded construction of a training center for WACs at Fort McClellan, Alabama, and the army approved new summer and winter uniforms for women and added more military occupational specialties to the WAC assignment list. Training courses for these specialties were developed and offered. Also, the recruiting command improved methods for training recruiters for WAC officers and enlisted women, in hopes that better communication techniques might boost enlistments.

Colonel Mary A. Hallaren was director of the WACs from 1947 to 1953. She had initiated and secured the rights of regular and reserve status for WACs and servicewomen, and during her tenure she promoted expansion of WAC services in the Korean War. On January 3, 1953, Colonel Irene O. Galloway succeeded Hallaren as the new WAC director.

Most servicewomen considered an overseas posting to be the most attractive assignment. During the Korean War most requests by eligible WACs wanting to serve in the Far East Command were approved. Two WAC units were sent to Japan in 1950, and a total of nine WAC units were there in 1953. Most of these WAC units were hospital units, although the WAC unit in Okinawa had both administrative and medical personnel. The number of women assigned to the Far East Command increased from 629 in 1950 to 2,600 in 1951, while only 300 new WACs were added to the European command in the same time period.

During the first year of the Korean War, the WAC unit formed at Fort Lee was expected to go to Pusan or Seoul to be attached to the U.S. Eighth Army, Forward. Army commanders, however, considered combat to be too unpredictable on the peninsula to assign WACs in Korea. When battle lines became stalemated in late 1951, the commander of the Eighth Army asked for a WAC unit, but recruiting had declined enough that Hallaren stated the corps strength was insufficient to keep a WAC unit in Korea. Instead, she assigned a dozen enlisted women and an officer to major headquarters in Korea during 1951. Although the number of WACs had increased from 7,259 on June 30, 1950, to 11,932 on June 30, 1951, enlistments declined when truce talks were initiated. Women who might have been inspired to enlist because of patriotism and personnel needs believed they were not needed. The other women's services also experienced decreased enlistments. In June 1951, 28,000 women served in line assignments, accounting for just over 1 percent of the military forces.

In the spring of 1952, 46,000 women were on active duty, with 13,000 WAFs, 10,000 WACs, 8,000 WAVEs, and 2,400 marines. The remaining women were in health care positions. One of the greatest needs for servicewomen was as nurses. Within the first month of the start of the Korean War, more than 100 nurses arrived in East Asia to assist with casualties. A contingent of 57 army nurses landed at Pusan early in the war, on July 5, 1950, and many served in MASHs directly behind the front lines. By the end of the war, more than 540 army nurses had served in Korea. Several thousand worked in hospitals in Japan and the Far East. Flight nurses treated casualties being evacuated, and army nurses cared for the wounded in evacuation hospitals and assisted with emergency surgery. Women physicians also served with the military.

By 1953 WACs served as administrative aides, stenographers, and translators to ease the shortage of male soldiers in some commands overseas. Women had more opportunities, having a chance to serve in supervisory positions. Increased numbers of women were employed in military occupational specialties that had been closed to them before the war. For example, in U.S. military hospitals in Japan that cared for wounded combat soldiers from Korea, WAC sergeants served as ward masters, a job previously held only by men. Women also gained jobs as senior noncommissioned officers, directing motor pools, mess halls, and post offices. In such capacities they supervised men and women. When the armistice

Distribution of American Women on Active Duty in Korea in Spring 1952

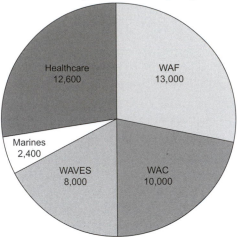

was signed in July 1953, 9,925 women were WACs and had gained military experience from the war to apply to peacetime service.

The exact number of U.S. women serving on active duty in the Korean War is unknown. In the 1980 census the Veterans Administration said that 120,300 white, black, and Hispanic women veterans of the Korean War claimed to be living in the United States. The number of women serving during the Korean War peaked at 48,700 in October 1952; this number dropped to 35,000 in June 1955.

The Korean War experience proved valuable to women serving in Vietnam and later wars. After the Korean War DACOWITS continued to address the role of women in peacetime and wartime military services.

In addition to U.S. servicewomen, women from other countries accompanied troops to Korea or provided an indigenous source of support. For example, Canadian Nurse Lieutenant J. I. MacDonald received the Associate of the Royal Red Cross citation, while another Canadian woman, Captain E. B. Pense, earned the Royal Red Cross commendation.

The Republic of Korea Women's Army Corps (ROKWAC) had been established in 1948 and served throughout the Korean War. Colonel Kim Hyon Suk was commanding officer of the ROKWAC, which she had helped organize with Korea Military Advisory Group (KMAG) advisers. Kim trained qualified women to serve as officers for ROKWAC units. She and these women developed military programs for girls in high schools and colleges to prepare more support personnel. On September 1, 1950, the ROKWAC headquarters and camps were established at Pusan as part of the Special Services Section of the Republic of Korea Army (ROKA, South Korean Army). Supervised by a U.S. adviser and a WAC officer, the ROKWAC was modeled after the U.S. WAC organization.

As the need for more servicewomen increased, the ROKWAC recruited enlistees to defend their country, but this effort was hindered by the evacuation of civilians and other limitations.

Approximately 3,000 women said they wanted to enlist in the ROKWAC, which had facilities to train only 500. Potential recruits took physical and intelligence examinations to evaluate their ability. The resulting achievement ratings were used to select the women for training. These women received such basic military training as how to use weapons and learned support skills as well. Initially, women were assigned to the regular army, where they were needed, but later, as more women received specific training, they were attached with special units to army groups.

The ROKWAC was divided into five departments. Women in the communications section operated message centers with teletypes and telephones. In the First ROKA Corps, ROKWACs were in charge of corps communications. Personnel duties involved recruiting, training, and assigning ROKWACs. Administrative work monitored supply and record keeping, consisting of secretarial duties. Some ROKWACs were heads of departments of administrative sections of rear companies. ROKWACs also conducted psychological warfare, broadcasting radio messages to the People's Republic of China (PRC) and Democratic People's Republic of Korea (DPRK, North Korea) and dropping leaflets from airplanes, as well as using airplane loudspeakers to transmit information to those on the ground. ROKWACs also worked with army intelligence officers. ROKWACs in the service unit provided recreational activities, including staffing libraries.

The Korean women did not serve as nurses or in food distribution jobs. Captain Yun Hui Yul, aide to Colonel Kim, commented about gender conflicts between military men and women: "Korean men do not like to obey women but if she is an officer they have to do it. They rationalize to themselves that they are obeying the title and not the woman." After the Korean War the ROKWACs served in a peacetime reserve program.

There is little information on North Korean and Chinese women in the Korean War in histories of the war written by both communist and noncommunist authors. The constitution of North Korea promised equal rights for women. Membership in the Worker-and-Peasant Red Guard was compulsory for men between the ages of 18 and 45 except individuals who were disabled or serving in active military duty. Many North Korean women also joined the Red Guard, where they learned guerrilla warfare, infiltration, and antiaircraft tactics and were on 24-hour alert for action. North Korean leader Kim Il Sung did not differentiate by gender when he emphasized that North Koreans "must be firmly prepared, both ideologically and militarily, for perfect self-defense."

In the PRC communist officials attempted to achieve gender equality through legal reform and administrative changes. Women remained subordinate to men in Chinese society; however, women in urban areas did benefit more from progress in gender relations than rural women.

During the 1930s and 1940s women had supported the Red Army by serving in the women's aid corps as nurses, transporting supplies to the front, and accompanying combat troops on spying or guerrilla missions. The Chinese Communist Party had established women's propaganda teams in which women urged their husbands and male relatives to enlist in the Red Army.

When the PRC entered the Korean War in October 1950, women soldiers were not expected to serve in the front lines of the Chinese People's Volunteer Army (CPVA, Chinese Army). Instead, they performed office work and logistical and medical tasks. Most women did not hold high administrative posts in the army, although some were World War II veterans. Domestically, women were employed by war industries and represented 8.9 percent of industrial employees in 1952, a 74 percent increase from 1951. Chinese leaders wanted women to try traditionally male roles, sponsoring such events as an all-woman air show held on Woman's Day in 1952. Chinese women might also have created and distributed leaflets and propaganda during the Korean War, and a smaller number might have furtively promoted peace, risking ostracism and punishment. After the 1953 armistice, China encouraged more traditional views of women and family instead of militarism.

Chinese and North Korean women also conducted sabotage against the United Nations Command (UNC) forces. North Korean women posed as refugees to infiltrate United Nations (UN) lines and inflict casualties or gather intelligence. In November 1950 the Chung Pong police detained two female agents. During interrogation, they divulged that they had been ordered by the Korean People's Army (KPA, North Korean Army) to poison wells used by UN forces. Such activities remain largely obscure. A number of women were certainly taken prisoner by UNC forces and held as prisoners of war (POWs).

ELIZABETH D. SCHAFER

See also

China, People's Republic of; Far East Command; Kim Il Sung; Korea, Democratic People's Republic of, 1945–1953; Korea, Republic of, Army; Korea Military Advisory Group; Mao Zedong; Marshall, George Catlett; Medicine, Military; Mobile Army Surgical Hospital; Truman, Harry S.; United States Air Force; United States Army; United States Marine Corps; United States Navy

References

Curtin, Ann. "Army Women on Active Duty." *Army Information Digest* 8 (1953): 22–30.

Herman, Ruby E. "Women's Army Corps Trains at Fort Lee." *Army Information Digest* 6 (1951): 26–32.

Holm, Jeanne. *Women in the Military: An Unfinished Revolution*. Novato, CA: Presidio, 1982.

Jancar, Barbara Wolfe. *Women under Communism*. Baltimore, MD: Johns Hopkins University Press, 1978.

King, Helen B. "The WACs of Korea." *Korean Survey* 4 (1955): 10–11.

Morden, Bettie J. *The Women's Army Corps, 1945–1978*. Washington, DC: U.S. Army Center of Military History, 1990.

Siu, Bobby. *Women of China: Imperialism and Women's Resistance, 1900–1949*. London: Zed, 1981.

Soderbergh, Peter A. *Women Marines in the Korean War Era*. Westport, CT: Praeger, 1994.

Stremlow, Mary V. *A History of the Women Marines, 1946–1977*. Washington, DC: History and Museums Division, Headquarters, U.S. Marine Corps, 1986.

Witt, Linda, Judith Bellafaire, and Britta Granrud. *A Defense Weapon Known to Be of Value: Servicewomen of the Korean War Era*. Hanover, NH: University Press of New England, 2005.

Won Yong Dok
Birth Date: October 19, 1907
Death Date: February 24, 1968

Republic of Korea Army (ROKA, South Korea) lieutenant general, distinguished by his unswerving loyalty to South Korean president Syngman Rhee. Born in Seoul, South Korea, on October 19, 1907, Won Yong Dok graduated from the Severance Medical School in 1931. He then became a surgeon with the rank of lieutenant colonel in the Japanese-led Manchukuo Army.

Following the end of World War II, in December 1945 Won became the assistant superintendent of the Military English Language School, established by the U.S. Army to train officers for the constabulary army in South Korea. Won himself graduated from the school in 1946 as a major. After briefly serving as the first commander of the South Korean Constabulary, in September 1946 Won became superintendent of the Korean Constabulary Academy, predecessor to the Korean Military Academy. When the Yosu-Sunchon Rebellion broke out in October 1948, Colonel Won and his 2nd Brigade, stationed at Taejon, were dispatched to the two towns to suppress the communist rebels. He next commanded the 5th Brigade between January and May 1949. After serving in the Army Staff Office immediately before the outbreak of the Korean War, he retired from active service. In January 1952 he returned to active duty as a brigadier general, becoming deputy commander of II Corps.

A political crisis in 1952 in South Korea saw Rhee in confrontation with the National Assembly. Rhee believed that only he could manage the country effectively and sought to retain his authoritarian hold. On May 25, 1952, Rhee declared martial law and appointed Won, then a major general, to implement a series of emergency measures. Won utilized strong-arm tactics that ensured Rhee's tight control over Pusan, the temporary South Korean capital, and the area around it. Ignoring the military chain of command, he issued decrees and meted out swift punishment to dissenters.

The new regulations included restrictions on holding meetings, strict censorship, and the authority to arrest any government official. One of Won's first acts was to arrest So Min Ho, a leading South Korean political figure and critic of the Rhee government. The following day 45 members of the National Assembly were arrested, although all but 12 were soon released. Many assembly members went into hiding to avoid arrest. Won helped to ensure a satisfactory vote in the National Assembly to amend the constitution, which called for the popular election of the South Korean president and the creation of an upper house. Rhee easily won the election on August 6, 1952.

As a reward for his political services, Won was advanced to lieutenant general, and in June 1953 Rhee made him commander of the Provost Marshal General's office, which placed all South Korean military police under his control rather than that of the army, whose chief of staff, Paek Son Yop, was strongly pro-American. Won continued to demonstrate his loyalty to Rhee in the sudden release on June 18, 1953, of North Korean prisoners of war (POWs). Won died in Seoul on February 24, 1968.

SPENCER C. TUCKER

See also

Korea, Republic of, Political Crisis; Paek Son Yop; Rhee, Syngman; Rhee's Release of North Korean Prisoners of War; Yosu-Sunchon Rebellion

References

Cumings, Bruce. *The Origins of the Korean War.* 2 vols. Princeton, NJ: Princeton University Press, 1981, 1990.

Matray, James I., ed. *Historical Dictionary of the Korean War.* Westport, CT: Greenwood, 1991.

Millett, Allan R. *Their War in Korea: American, Asian, and European Combatants and Civilians, 1945–1953.* Princeton, NJ: Princeton University Press, 2002.

Wonju, Battle of
Start Date: February 14, 1951
End Date: February 17, 1951

February 1951 military engagement in and around the town of Wonju in central Korea, 65 miles southeast of Seoul and 5 miles south of Hoengsong. Fighting there by the 9th and 38th Regiments of the U.S. 2nd Infantry Division, companies of the 17th Regiment of the 7th Division, elements of the 187th Airborne Regiment, and support units occurred while the division's other regiment, the 23rd, was locked in a perimeter defense in and around the village of Chipyong-ni, about 20 miles to the northwest.

In early February 1951 communist forces continued their attack on United Nations Command (UNC) forces after the latter's withdrawal from the far north of the country and struck in force in the central part of the Korean Peninsula, scattering three Republic of Korea Army (ROKA, South Korean Army) divisions and forcing other troops in that sector to withdraw southward. Communist forces aimed their attack at the key communications centers of Chipyong-ni and Wonju. Because his forces at these two locations

Vehicles of the U.S. 2nd Infantry Division stalled in an icy mountain pass south of Wonju during the Battle of Wonju, February 14–17, 1951. (National Archives)

were well forward of the main line of resistance, 2nd Division assistant division commander Brigadier General George Stewart expected that he would also be ordered to fall back. But new Eighth Army commander Lieutenant General Matthew B. Ridgway was determined to end the several-week-long practice of recoiling each time communist forces attacked, and he wanted to test the willingness and ability of his forces to withstand whatever his enemy could offer. Ridgway ordered that Chipyong-ni and Wonju be held. The ensuing fighting at Wonju became known among local commanders and troops as the "Wonju shoot" because of the effectiveness of the massive artillery fire against the attacking communist forces.

The first communist troops arriving in the area found defending UNC troops, including the Dutch Battalion, in position around Hoengsong. When they came under fire, the communists yelled, "Okay, okay, we're ROKs," whereupon the Dutch lifted their fire. The infiltrating Chinese then opened fire on the Dutch command post, killing five officers, including the commanding officer. Fourteen other men were wounded, and eight were later reported missing. On the night of February 12, orders were received to abandon Hoengsong. A perimeter defense was then established on high ground around Wonju, and all available artillery was positioned so that massed fires could be placed on any approach to the city.

At daylight on February 15 communist forces attacked from along the Som River to the west of Wonju and the defending artillery opened up in all its fury. The 2nd Division history reported:

Thunderous barrages roared across the hills as tons of shrapnel poured into the plodding troops. Thousands of shells wreaked havoc never before seen on any army as pilots reported the river running red with the blood of the massacred troops. Still they came. . . . Hour after hour the unbelievable slaughter mounted as dog-tired, exhausted artillerymen slammed an endless stream of shells into the exposed masses of Chinese. . . . The staggering losses began to tell. The once full ranks were now thin, blasted, shocked remnants without leaders, without hope. Now only unorganized bands of useless bodies, they tried to escape north out of reach of the murderous guns.

The "Wonju shoot" cost communist forces more than 5,000 casualties. Bitter fighting waged the night of February 14 and into the following day at Wonju and farther south involving troops that had bypassed Wonju. The communists then shifted their main effort to Chipyong-ni to the west and the threat to Wonju was eliminated.

SHERMAN W. PRATT

See also

Chipyong-ni, Battle of; Ridgway, Matthew Bunker

References

Blair, Clay. *The Forgotten War: America in Korea, 1950–1953*. New York: Times Books, 1987.

Munroe, Clark C. *The Second United States Infantry Division in Korea, 1950–1951*. Tokyo: Toppan Printing, n.d. [1952].

Pratt, Sherman W. *Decisive Battles of the Korean War: An Infantry Company Commander's View of the War's Most Critical Engagements.* New York: Vantage Press, 1992.

Schnabel, James F. *United States Army in the Korean War: Policy and Direction, the First Year.* Washington, DC: Office of the Chief of Military History, Department of the Army, 1972.

Wonsan, North Korea

Port city located 110 air miles north of the 38th Parallel on the east coast of the Korean Peninsula in the Democratic People's Republic of Korea (DPRK, North Korea). At present, Wonsan is the provincial capital of North Korea's Kangwon Province and has an estimated population of some 330,000 people.

During the Korean War, the 3rd and Capital divisions of the Republic of Korea Army (ROKA, South Korean Army), moving north along the east coast of the peninsula, entered Wonsan, securing both the city and its airfield on October 11, 1950. On October 19, with the city already secure, the U.S. X Corps of the United Nations Command (UNC) arrived offshore but had to await the clearing of mines laid by the North Koreans. The main body came ashore a week later, on October 26.

From the last week of October, UNC forces in the northwestern and northeastern sectors of North Korea encountered significant opposition from Chinese troops. When at the end of November Chinese forces launched massive attacks, UNC forces abandoned all of North Korea above the 38th Parallel, including Wonsan, and conducted a hurried and deep withdrawal south of that line.

JINWUNG KIM

See also

Wonsan Landing and Evacuation

References

Blair, Clay. *The Forgotten War: America in Korea, 1950–1953*. New York: Times Books, 1987.

MacDonald, Callum. *Korea: The War before Vietnam*. New York: Free Press, 1987.

Stueck, William W., Jr. *The Korean War: An International History*. Princeton, NJ: Princeton University Press, 1995.

Wonsan Landing and Evacuation
Start Date: October 25, 1950
End Date: December 7, 1950

United Nations Command (UNC) amphibious operation in October 1950. After the successful September 1950 Inchon Landing and recapture of Seoul, UNC commander General Douglas MacArthur planned an amphibious landing of X Corps on Korea's east coast as a staging site to move northwest toward the North Korean capital of Pyongyang. He selected the port town of Wonsan because of its strategic location. Some 110 miles northeast of the 38th Parallel, Wonsan had a population of some 75,000 in 1950. The site of

The entertainer Bob Hope with men of X Corps at Wonsan, North Korea, October 26, 1950. (National Archives)

a petroleum refinery that produced hundreds of tons of gasoline daily, Wonsan was also Korea's primary east coast harbor, and it had an airfield, communications facilities, and roads and railways connecting with both Seoul and Pyongyang.

Known by the code name of Operation TAILBOARD, the Wonsan landing was controversial. On September 29 MacArthur held conferences to plan the Wonsan landing, to be directed by Amphibious Force Far East commander Rear Admiral James H. Doyle, and stated that he hoped to land by October 29. Naval officers realized, however, that the landing could be delayed because of time constraints for reembarking troops at Inchon and steaming to Wonsan. They also criticized the lack of information, including current maps, on Wonsan. Proponents of the operation believed that supplying X Corps from Wonsan would relieve the supply stress on Inchon and place X Corps in an excellent strategic position to advance toward Pyongyang in conjunction with the Eighth Army. Commanders, however, differed on how X Corps should travel to Wonsan.

X Corps commander Major General Edward M. Almond stressed that "from a tactical point of view, it's cheaper to go to Wonsan by sea." He opposed moving there by land, because of the terrain, which he said would mean that "half of our heavy equipment—bulldozers, big guns, and heavy trucks—would [be] left in ditches by the side of the road." Vice Admiral C. Turner Joy, commander of U.S. Naval Forces Far East, believed X Corps "could have marched overland to Wonsan in a much shorter time and with much less effort than it would take to get the Corps around to Wonsan by sea." Other officers protested taking troops out of action when they could have been pursuing Korean People's Army (KPA, North Korean Army) forces.

MacArthur's decision to continue X Corps' status as an independent command also adversely impacted UNC logistics. To lift X Corps from Inchon, Eighth Army transportation assets had to be diverted, delaying its own movement north, and the port of Inchon was closed to other shipping until X Corps departed.

On October 7 the 1st Marine Division command post at Inchon transferred to Doyle's flagship, the *Mount McKinley*. Outloading of marines at Inchon commenced the next day. Doyle ordered the ships, carrying a total of 30,184 passengers, to begin their eastward journey of 830 sea miles on October 15.

When the ships reached Wonsan's harbor five days later, they discovered the harbor was thick with several thousand Soviet magnetic and contact mines. While minesweepers cleared a channel, Doyle ordered the ships to steam north and then return south, which the marines dubbed "Operation Yo-Yo." The crowded ships spent five days moving up and down the Korean coast, and many of those confined on them suffered from gastroenteritis and dysentery. Finally, on October 25 Doyle permitted the ships to enter the mineswept channel to Wonsan. "In retrospect, it must be said that the landing was to pay dividends for the Navy," Joy later admitted. "Had it not been undertaken we might never have become fully alerted to the menace of mine warfare nor profited from the lessons we learned about mine sweeping."

When X Corps troops landed on Wonsan's beach on October 25, they were greeted by South Korean soldiers, who had advanced overland more quickly than expected. Members of the Republic of Korea Army (ROKA, South Korean Army) Capital and 3rd divisions had secured Wonsan 15 days earlier. Air maintenance crews also beat the marines to Wonsan by a dozen days. More humiliating to the marines, the entertainers Bob Hope and Marilyn Maxwell were flown on October 24 to the objective, where they put on a show that included quips at the expense of the marines offshore.

Because Pyongyang had been captured by the ROKA 1st Division on October 19, X Corps troops headed north instead of west. The 1st Marine Division moved up the coast toward Hungnam and the Changjin Reservoir. Meanwhile, the U.S. Army's 3rd Infantry Division arrived at Wonsan in early November to join X Corps' drive against retreating KPA forces.

After the massive Chinese military intervention in late November, UNC troops withdrew to the coast, and on December 3 they were ordered to evacuate Wonsan. Some 7,009 civilian refugees, 3,834 military personnel, 1,146 vehicles, and 10,013 bulk tons of cargo were moved aboard ship; on December 7 the UNC abandoned Wonsan. Two months later, on February 16, 1951, the navy began an 861-day blockade of Wonsan in which destroyers, cruisers, battleships, and aircraft bombarded communist airfields and entrenchments. Although subject to counterbattery land fire, the UNC captured seven of Wonsan's harbor islands, one of which, Yo-do, was used for a 1,200-foot emergency airstrip. The United Nations (UN) blockade of Wonsan occupied some 80,000 KPA troops, diverting them and their artillery from military engagements in other parts of Korea. The Wonsan blockade, the longest in modern warfare, prevented the communists from using the port. It ended on July 27, 1953, when the armistice became effective.

ELIZABETH D. SCHAFER

See also

Almond, Edward Mallory; Amphibious Force Far East; Doyle, James Henry; Hope, Leslie Townes; Inchon Landing; Joy, Charles Turner; MacArthur, Douglas; Mine Warfare, Sea; Mines, Sea; X Corps; United States Marine Corps

References

Alexander, James Edwin. *Inchon to Wonsan: From the Deck of a Destroyer in the Korean War.* Annapolis, MD: Naval Institute Press, 1996.

Blair, Clay. *The Forgotten War: America in Korea, 1950–1953.* New York: Times Books, 1987.

Breuer, William B. *Shadow Warriors: The Covert War in Korea.* New York: Wiley, 1996.

Cagle, Malcolm W., and Frank A. Manson. *Sea War in Korea.* Annapolis, MD: Naval Institute Press, 1957.

Marolda, Edward J., ed. *The U.S. Navy in the Korean War.* Annapolis, MD: Naval Institute Press, 2007.

World Vision

International Christian humanitarian and relief organization founded in the United States in 1950 by Robert Pierce, an ordained minister and protestant missionary. Although Pierce had been involved in humanitarian efforts prior to World Vision's founding, chiefly in China and the Republic of Korea (ROK, South Korea), it was the outbreak of the Korean War in June 1950 that spurred him to create World Vision. Because of the nature of the war and the fact that Korea was artificially divided—communist in the Democratic People's Republic of Korea (DPRK, North Korea) and noncommunist in the Republic of Korea (ROK, South Korea)—the conflict especially affected Korean families and children. Indeed, it tore millions of families apart and left thousands of orphans behind.

Since 1947 Pierce, as a young missionary for the Youth for Christ evangelical organization founded by Reverend Billy Graham, had spent much time in China and South Korea, witnessing firsthand the ravages that poverty wrought on families and children in these developing nations. When the Korean War began, Pierce realized that there was a special need to care for South Korea's orphans and children. World Vision began as an organization dedicated solely to that endeavor. As the organization grew in size and scope, so too did its mission. Pierce led World Vision until 1967, and under his tutelage the humanitarian group began to involve itself in community development, hunger, poverty mitigation, disaster and emergency relief aid, and child and family advocacy in Developing World nations.

By the 1990s World Vision had become one of the world's largest Christian development and relief organizations, operating in 90 nations around the globe. It has maintained a focus on children and families despite its broader scope, and it continues to operate along Christian ideals, although its work encompasses people of all faiths and religions. In 2007 World Vision had an operating budget of $2.6 billion. Approximately 40 percent of its budget is derived from private donations; another 30 percent comes from governments and nongovernmental agencies. The final 30 percent comes from World Vision nonprofit organizations that funnel money back into the main budget. In more recent times the organization has also been involved with efforts to eradicate deeply ingrained, systemic causes of poverty and injustice. World Vision is probably best known for its ongoing Sponsor-a-Child program, which uses television and print media to encourage people to "adopt" or "sponsor" a child overseas by pledging to donate a certain amount of money per day to cover the child's basic living costs.

PAUL G. PIERPAOLI JR.

See also

Churches and the War, U.S.; Graham, William Franklin; Pierce, Robert Willard; Relief Efforts, Missionary

References

Boli, John, and George M. Thomas, eds. *Constructing World Culture: International Nongovernmental Organizations since 1875.* Stanford, CA: Stanford University Press, 1999.

Iriye, Akira. *Global Communities: The Role of International Organizations in the Making of the Contemporary World.* Berkeley: University of California Press, 2004.

Wrong, Humphrey Hume
Birth Date: September 10, 1894
Death Date: January 24, 1954

Canadian diplomat and ambassador to the United States during the Korean War. Born in Toronto on September 10, 1894, Humphrey Hume Wrong was the son of prominent Canadian historian George Wrong. He graduated from the University of Toronto. During World War I he was denied admission to the Canadian Expeditionary because of blindness in one eye but managed to join the British Army and saw combat before being invalided home.

Following studies at Oxford University, Wrong was hired in 1921 to teach history at the University of Toronto. In 1928 Wrong accepted an invitation to join the staff of the new Canadian legation in Washington, DC, as its first secretary. He subsequently served as a Canadian diplomat at the League of Nations, in London, again in Washington, and in Ottawa, Canada, for three years during World War II. Wrong is credited with developing the principle of functionalism; that is, that Canada has all the resources of a great power and deserves to be treated like one. Functionalism became the basis of Canada's wartime diplomacy.

In 1946 Wrong was posted to Washington again, this time as Canadian ambassador. In this capacity he played a key role in the formation of the North Atlantic Treaty Organization (NATO). During the Korean War he represented Canadian views to the U.S. State Department. These were often in the form of suggestions that revealed a growing difference of opinion between the two countries over military strategy and the role of the United Nations (UN) in the conflict. Wrong emphatically expressed Ottawa's contention that the UN effort was a collective security operation and not a vehicle for an anticommunist offensive in Asia. This position was taken despite the Canadian government's own anticommunist orientation and despite the fact that the United States provided the preponderance of United Nations Command (UNC) troops in Korea.

It was Wrong who first informed the Canadian government of the invasion of the Republic of Korea (ROK, South Korea) by the Democratic People's Republic of Korea (DPRK, North Korea), while offering his belief, widely shared in Ottawa and elsewhere, that the United States would not intervene militarily. He and his government were therefore surprised by President Harry S. Truman's quick and decisive response. From then on, Wrong was faced with the problem of relaying Canada's concerns over how the "police action" would evolve. Receiving orders from Canada's high-profile Secretary of State for External Affairs Lester Pearson, Wrong found himself inundated with Ottawa's attempts to influence U.S. policy. The main issues focused on the role of the UN and the disinclination of Canadians to allow the war to escalate. Later, with the fortunes of war swinging briefly toward the UN forces, Wrong expressed the Canadians' concern over the rhetoric and tactics of UNC commander General Douglas MacArthur. He was especially concerned over the wisdom of violating Chinese airspace with U.S. planes. Later still, he quietly informed Ottawa that even with MacArthur gone, U.S. aircraft were still unofficially conducting such overflights well into 1952.

It was because of such views that the Canadian diplomatic corps in Washington, headed by Wrong, came to be seen by the U.S. State Department as a source of unsolicited and disagreeable obstruction. This animosity escalated, on occasion, to outright hostility by the Americans toward a country that they considered a close friend and ally. Wrong was the lightning rod for these disagreements and, at times, even he would protest to Ottawa about the constant hectoring and questioning of policy that flowed across his desk aimed at U.S. actions and motives. Although he was in general agreement with the desirability of limiting U.S. "excesses," he also believed that the U.S. State Department was often harassed enough by swiftly moving events.

Overly questioning U.S. ideas could be seen in Washington as questioning U.S. sincerity. Wrong believed, in the long run, that this would prove to be self-defeating. This was particularly a problem in the early stages of the war, when Canada was perceived as not contributing sufficiently to the UNC military effort. Later, Wrong also wisely counseled his government not to push Washington too hard on Asian matters following the firing of MacArthur because of the intense political pressure the Truman administration was encountering at home.

Beyond these more controversial issues, however, Wrong was still able to negotiate with U.S. authorities for permission to allow Canadian forces bound for Korea to train first at Fort Lewis, Washington. More important, Wrong also signed an agreement in October 1950 that revived the concepts of the Hyde Park Declaration between Canada and the United States during World War II. This encouraged economic cooperation between the two countries in defense production that contributed, for better or worse, in tying the two national economies closer together during the Cold War era.

In late 1953, after the Korean War, Wrong returned to Ottawa to serve as undersecretary for external affairs, but he died in Ottawa on January 24, 1954, before he could assume that position.

ERIC JARVIS AND SPENCER C. TUCKER

See also

Canada; MacArthur, Douglas; North Atlantic Treaty Organization; Pearson, Lester Bowles; St. Laurent, Louis Stephen; Truman, Harry S.

References

Granatstein, J. L., and Norman Hillmer. *For Better or for Worse, Canada and the United States to the 1990s*. Toronto: Copp Clark Pitman, 1991.

Stairs, Denis. *The Diplomacy of Constraint: Canada, the Korean War, and the United States*. Toronto: University of Toronto Press, 1974.

Stueck, William W., Jr. *The Korean War: An International History*. Princeton, NJ: Princeton University Press, 1995.

Wu Xiuquan

Birth Date: March 6, 1908
Death Date: November 9, 1997

People's Republic of China (PRC) diplomat and chief representative to the United Nations (UN) special meeting on the Korean War and the Taiwan Strait situation in New York in November 1950. Born in the city of Wuchang, Hubei Province, China, on March 6, 1908, Wu Xiuquan (Wu Hsiu Chuan) entered Sun Yat Sen University in Moscow when he was 17. Later he worked as an interpreter for the Communist International (Comintern) at the university and joined the Russian Communist Party in 1930. Returning to China, he served as an interpreter for Comintern's adviser to China between 1930 and 1935. In that capacity, Wu attended the Chinese Communist Party (CCP) Zunyi Conference, a historic meeting in January 1935 that established Mao Zedong as leader of the entire CCP. Wu became a regimental, divisional, and then an army political commissar in the Red Army before the Long March of 1934–1935.

In 1945, just before the end of the Second Sino-Japanese War (1937–1945), Wu was transferred to northeast China as chief of staff of the Northeast China Anti-Japanese Army. Although he had excellent potential for advancement in the military, Wu was

transferred to a diplomatic career, one of a group of senior military officers selected by Mao and Zhou Enlai to hold key positions in the new Ministry of Foreign Affairs following the 1949 founding of the PRC. In the Ministry of Foreign Affairs, Wu was responsible for assisting Premier and Foreign Minister Zhou and Vice Minister of Foreign Affairs Wang Jiaxiang in dealing with Moscow and the Eastern European Communist bloc countries.

When the Korean War began in June 1950, Wu was director of the Department of Soviet and Eastern European Affairs of the Ministry of Foreign Affairs. He was involved in negotiations with Moscow concerning military assistance from the Union of Soviet Socialist Republics (USSR, Soviet Union) to China for the Korean War. Because of Wu's language skills and foreign experience, Zhou selected him to head the high-profile PRC delegation to the UN special meeting in November 1950.

Wu was the first PRC official to appear at the UN after the 1949 revolution. His job at the UN special meeting was to deliver a tough-worded condemnation of U.S. "aggression" in the Taiwan Strait and U.S. intervention in the Korean War. He later recalled this speech as one of the most important events of his life.

In 1952, when General Li Kenong fell ill, Zhou sent Wu to assist him in the Korean War armistice negotiations with the idea that Wu would replace him. But Li insisted on completing the talks before returning to Beijing. After returning from Korea in 1953, Wu became vice minister of foreign affairs and later PRC ambassador to Yugoslavia. During the Cultural Revolution, Wu was purged and jailed for eight years. Rehabilitated, he returned to the military, and in 1975 he became deputy chief of staff in charge of intelligence affairs. Wu retired in 1988 and died on November 9, 1997.

RICHARD WEIXING HU

See also

China, People's Republic of; Li Kenong; Mao Zedong; Zhou Enlai

References

Chen Jian. *Mao's China and the Cold War*. Chapel Hill: University of North Carolina Press, 2000.

Guo Huaruo et al., eds. *Jiefangjun Junshi Dacidian* [Dictionary of PLA Military History]. Changchun: Jilin Renmin Chubanshe, 1993.

Lüthi, Lorenz M. *The Sino-Soviet Split: Cold War in the Communist World*. Princeton, NJ: Princeton University Press, 2008.

Wu, Xiuquan. *Wo de Licheng* [My Journey]. Beijing: Jiefangjun Chubanshe, 1984.

Zhongguo Renmin Jiefangjun Jiangshuai Minglu [Brief Biographies of the PLA's Marshals and Generals], Vols. 1–3. Beijing: Jiefangjun Chubanshe, 1986–1987.

Xie Fang

Birth Date: 1908
Death Date: 1984

People's Liberation Army (PLA, Chinese Communist Army) general and chief of staff of the Chinese People's Volunteer Army (CPVA, Chinese Army) during the Korean War. Born in Dongfeng, Jilin Province, China, in 1908, Xie Fang (Hsieh Fang) attended the Japanese Infantry School in 1922. He first became known to the Chinese Communist Party (CCP) for his role in the Xi'an Incident in December 1936, when Jiang Jieshi (Chiang Kai-shek) was kidnapped by former warlord and Nationalist supporter General Zhang Xueliang, who forced Jiang to cooperate with the CCP forces in the fight against the Japanese. Xie was a protégé of General Zhang.

Xie joined the CCP in 1936 and was the deputy commander of the North China Field Army during 1936–1937. In the early 1940s Xie studied at Sun Yat Sen University in Moscow. He began working at the Central Party School in Yenan (Yan'an) in 1943. Beginning in the mid-1940s, Xie was associated with Lin Biao in northeast China. When the Korean War began, Xie was an experienced combat veteran and political commissar, serving as the chief of propaganda of the Northeast Military District. He was fluent in Russian, Japanese, and English and was a skilled educator and propagandist.

Xie was appointed chief of staff of the newly designated 13th Army Group in the Central Military Commission, with orders "to defend the Northeast Border Security," signed by Mao Zedong on July 13, 1950. The following month Xie drafted a report, sent to Beijing on August 31, 1950, that analyzed likely U.S. strategies and China's ability to intervene. Xie believed that the United States would launch an amphibious operation somewhere on the North Korean coast, or (with a larger force) at Seoul or Pyongyang. Although he thought the Korean People's Army (KPA, North Korean Army) would not be able to withstand a U.S. counterattack, Xie recommended that the Chinese forces not intervene until after U.S.-led forces crossed the 38th Parallel, because it would help Chinese forces both politically and militarily. Xie argued that strong air support and more equipment from the Union of Soviet Socialist Republics (USSR, Soviet Union) were essential to assisting the North Koreans. He recommended adding two additional armies with artillery and tank support to the 13th Army Group. Xie also recommended strengthening logistics and sending reconnaissance groups in advance to assess the terrain and the overall situation in the Democratic People's Republic of Korea (DPRK, North Korea).

Xie played a major role in preparing the intervention forces to advance into North Korea. He was officially named chief of staff of the CPVA on October 23, 1950, but he was recognized as chief of staff of the intervention forces from at least early October 1950. During November 1950, after the Chinese First Offensive of the month before, Peng Dehuai is said to have observed that U.S. forces were "inexperienced." Xie's opinion was more derisive; he said, "American soldiers panic easily. Their riflemen prefer to ride in trucks. They are afraid to die." Still he was concerned about logistical shortcomings that could seriously affect follow-on operations. He highlighted the shortage of sufficient transportation, which required reliance on about 500,000 laborers from northeast China. Supply lines were overextended, which would cause shortages in food and ammunition. Air support, artillery, and armor were all lacking.

Unlike Deng Hua, Xie was not a rising political figure, but he was specially selected for the Chinese negotiation team. Although

General Xie Fang, the Chinese People's Volunteer Army (CPVA, Chinese Communist Army) chief of staff. (Hulton-Deutsch Collection/Corbis)

from harsh, brow-beating, name-calling attacks, designed to harass and secure further concessions, to a quiet, reasonable, and businesslike approach. U.S. Admiral C. Turner Joy described Xie as "dangerous," with "a bitterly sharp mind." A confident negotiator, Xie would end a session if nothing could be accomplished.

Xie returned to Beijing from Korea in 1952; Chai Chengwen replaced him. Until the Cultural Revolution, Xie worked in a series of military training and education assignments as a close associate of Xiao Ke, a Long March veteran. During the Cultural Revolution, Xie was purged for his association with He Long, a leader of the Nanchang Uprising on August 1, 1927, and a Long March veteran. After the Cultural Revolution, Xie was rehabilitated and returned to work in military education as deputy director of the PLA Logistics Academy in Wuhan. Xie died in 1984.

SUSAN M. PUSKA

See also
China, People's Republic of, Army; Chinese Offensive, First; Chinese People's Volunteer Army; Deng Hua; Gao Gang; Lin Biao; Peng Dehuai

References
Joy, C. Turner. *How Communists Negotiate.* New York: Macmillan, 1955.
Spurr, Russell. *Enter the Dragon: China's Undeclared War against the U.S. in Korea, 1950–1951.* New York: Henry Holt, 1988.
Wilhelm, Alfred D., Jr. *The Chinese at the Negotiating Table.* Washington, DC: National Defense University Press, 1996.
Zhang Shu Guang. *Mao's Military Romanticism: China and the Korean War, 1950–1953.* Lawrence: University Press of Kansas, 1995.

he served as a junior member, he played a prominent role in the day-to-day negotiations, in which he participated from July 1951 to October 1952. During negotiations Xie was sometimes profane, and he often insulted the U.S. negotiators. He could shift overnight

Xinao
See Brainwashing

Y

Yalu Bridges Controversy
Event Date: November 1950

Issue that strained relations between the United States and the People's Republic of China (PRC) and also accelerated the deterioration of relations between President Harry S. Truman and United Nations Command (UNC) commander General Douglas MacArthur. MacArthur's amphibious landing at Inchon on September 15, 1950, completely reversed the progress of the war. UNC forces broke out of the Pusan Perimeter shortly thereafter, and UNC forces then crossed the 38th Parallel, invading the Democratic People's Republic of Korea (DPRK, North Korea) in pursuit of the withdrawing Korean People's Army (KPA, North Korean Army).

President Harry S. Truman became increasingly concerned as MacArthur drove north toward the Yalu River, the border with China. Truman was well aware of the PRC warning that it would not tolerate a UNC invasion of North Korea, but he dismissed it as propaganda. Beijing, however, found unacceptable the possibility of U.S. bases in North Korea, within easy range of its Manchurian industrial base.

In October 1950 UNC forces were driving on the Yalu, but Chinese forces crossed the river into North Korea beginning on October 14 and first clashed with UNC units on October 25. Although Chinese intentions at this point were unclear, MacArthur chose to believe that the units of the Chinese People's Volunteer Army (CPVA, Chinese Army) were merely covering the KPA withdrawal into Manchuria and that its clashes with UNC forces did not signal the beginning of major offensive operations by the Chinese in Korea. Nonetheless, MacArthur sought permission to bomb the bridges over the Yalu. He argued that this would serve the dual purpose of cutting off the North Koreans and Chinese from supply and hampering the potential flow of Chinese troops into Korea.

On November 6, 1950, MacArthur prepared to send 90 Boeing B-29 Superfortress bombers to destroy a bridge over the Yalu. Truman and the Joint Chiefs of Staff (JCS) quickly instructed the general to postpone the attack. They feared that any damage inflicted on the Chinese side of the Yalu would provoke a full-scale Chinese attack. World war also became a possibility because of the Sino-Soviet Treaty of Friendship and Alliance of February 14, 1950. MacArthur strongly protested the orders from Washington, DC

MacArthur did not let the issue drop and continued to insist that the bombing was necessary, especially with U.S. forces only 35 miles from the Yalu River border. After protracted discussions, the Truman administration reached a solution that it believed would placate MacArthur and serve the needs of U.S. foreign policy. It permitted MacArthur to destroy only the Korean side of the bridges.

There were 16 bridges across both the Yalu River border with China and the Tumen River border with the Union of Soviet Socialist Republics (USSR, Soviet Union). MacArthur first envisioned bombing them all, but he dropped some bridges as targets in order to concentrate on others deemed more important. Although some damage was inflicted, skirmishes with communist Mikoyan-Gurevich MiG-15 aircraft increased the prospects of war with China. Also, the diplomatic cost of the bombing outweighed its effectiveness. The bombing did not seriously interrupt the flow of supplies or troops, because half of the bridges bombed remained intact, while the frozen condition of the Yalu River permitted military transport across its surface.

Throughout the operation, the Truman administration held that the United States did not want a widened war with China or

A U.S. Navy AD-3 dive bomber drops a 2000-pound bomb on the Korean side of a bridge at Sinuiju spanning the Yalu River into Manchuria, November 15, 1950. Note the antiaircraft gun emplacements. (Department of Defense)

any other power. These statements did not mollify Beijing, because the bombing was perceived as a military threat.

The Chinese continued to build up their forces in North Korea, and on November 25, 1950, CPVA forces intervened in the war on a massive scale. As Chinese forces battered his command and drove UNC troops back south, MacArthur chafed at the restraints placed upon him by the Truman administration. This led to a deterioration in the relationship between Washington and its field commander over how to prosecute the war and, ultimately, to MacArthur's replacement.

ERIC W. OSBORNE

See also

Chinese People's Volunteer Army; Joint Chiefs of Staff; MacArthur, Douglas; Sino-Soviet Treaty of Friendship and Alliance; Truman, Harry S.; Truman's Recall of MacArthur

References

Hastings, Max. *The Korean War.* New York: Simon and Schuster, 1987.

Pearlman, Michael D. *Truman and MacArthur: Policy, Politics, and the Hunger for Honor and Renown.* Bloomington: Indiana University Press, 2008.

Spanier, John W. *The Truman-MacArthur Controversy and the Korean War.* Cambridge, MA: Harvard University Press, 1959.

Yalu River

River that forms the boundary between the Democratic People's Republic of Korea (DPRK, North Korea) and the Northeast Region (Manchuria) of the People's Republic of China (PRC). The Yalu (Amnok in Korean) River is approximately 490 miles long and drains an area covering 12,259 square miles. At its widest point, the river is about 3 miles across. The Yalu flows from the northeast to southwest, emptying into the Korea Bay (Yellow Sea) near Dandong. The river's primary source is located near Paektu-san, a

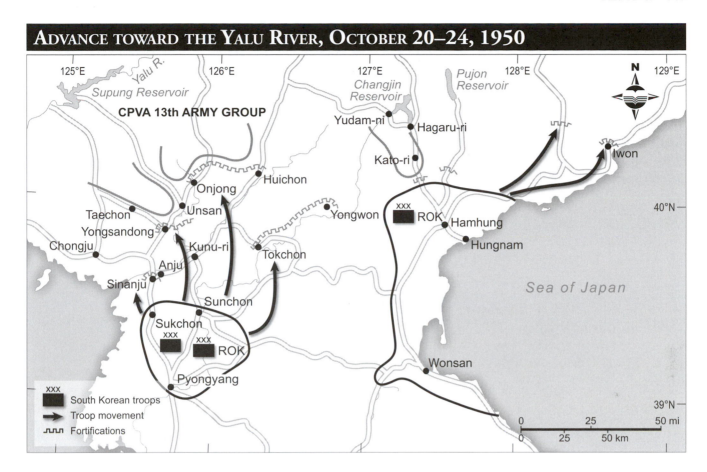

ADVANCE TOWARD THE YALU RIVER, OCTOBER 20–24, 1950

9,000-foot-high peak in northeastern North Korea. The Yalu River has three main tributaries: the Changjin, Hochon (Heochun), and Tokro rivers. Most of the Yalu is not easily navigated; it is quite shallow, in some places averaging only 10 feet in depth, and it is prone to heavy silting, which renders much of it off limits to anything but small river craft and fishing vessels.

In addition to being the location of numerous ancient Korean fortresses and archaeological sites, the Yalu River was also the site of two important modern battles: in 1894 during the Sino-Japanese War (1894–1895) and in 1904 during the Russo-Japanese War (1904–1905). The river has traditionally been the dividing line between Korea and China, but that division became even more important after the beginning of Japanese colonial rule of Korea that formally commenced in 1910. Between that date and 1945, Japan located much heavy industry in the Yalu River region. In the period after 1945 the Yalu was an important source of hydroelectric power; currently it is the site of one of the largest hydroelectric dams in Asia.

During the Korean War the Yalu River took on great significance. As United Nations Command (UNC) troops crossed the 38th Parallel into North Korea in the early fall of 1950, the PRC issued numerous warnings, all unheeded, that it would not tolerate the presence of U.S.-led UNC troops in the vicinity of the river. In mid-October PRC troops, known as the Chinese People's

Volunteer Army (CPVA, Chinese Army), began crossing the river in anticipation of a full-fledged intervention in the conflict. The CPVA crossed the Yalu at three places: Andong, Changdian, and Ji'an.

The subsequent massive Chinese intervention convinced UNC commander General Douglas MacArthur to seek permission to destroy bridges over the Yalu, which linked China with North Korea, in an effort to cripple the Chinese supply lines. Concerned about widening the war, President Harry S. Truman approved the bombing of the bridges only on the North Korean side of the river. Even when U.S. aircraft bombed some of the 16 bridges spanning the river, the Chinese were still able to cross the Yalu, particularly in the winter, when it was solidly frozen. The Yalu Bridges Controversy was a major bone of contention during the early part of the war and was cited by MacArthur as a contributing factor to the ensuing military stalemate.

PAUL G. PIERPAOLI JR.

See also
Chinese People's Volunteer Army; Yalu Bridges Controversy

References
Cumings, Bruce. *Korea's Place in the Sun: A Modern History.* New York: Norton, 1997.
Millett, Allan R. *The War for Korea, 1950–1951: They Came from the North.* Lawrence: University Press of Kansas, 2009.

Pearlman, Michael D. *Truman and MacArthur: Policy, Politics, and the Hunger for Honor and Renown.* Bloomington: Indiana University Press, 2008.

Yang Dezhi

Birth Date: January 13, 1911
Death Date: October 25, 1994

Chinese general, commander of the 19th Army Group of the Chinese People's Volunteer Army (CPVA, Chinese Army) in the Korean War, and deputy commander and commander of the CPVA. Yang Dezhi was born in Nanyangqiao in Liling County, Hunan Province, China, on January 13, 1911. As a teenager, he followed his father into the coal mines and joined the Chinese Communist Party (CCP) and the Red Army in 1928. He fought against the Guomindang (GMD, Nationalist) forces of Jiang Jieshi (Chiang Kai-shek) in the late 1920s and served under Lin Biao. After 1932 Yang commanded the 1st Regiment of the 1st Division. He took part in the Long March of 1934–1935.

Yang then commanded the 344th Brigade of the 115th Division and the Second Column of the Eighth Route Army during the Second Sino-Japanese War (1937–1945). During the Chinese Civil War (1945–1949) his forces faced strong Guomindang armies in the vicinity of Beiping (now Beijing) and were obliged to withdraw. In April 1948 Yang commanded the Second Army (later redesignated the 19th Army Group) in the Northern China Military District. In the spring of 1949 his forces besieged Taiyuan. He then proceeded to Lanzhou. He commanded the Ningxia Military District at the end of the war.

After the founding of the People's Republic of China (PRC) in October 1949, Yang commanded the Shaanxi Military District. With the beginning of the Korean War in June 1950, Yang's 19th Army Group, including the Sixty-third, Sixty-fourth, and Sixty-fifth armies, moved into the Shandong Peninsula, where it was reequipped with new Soviet weapons. Yang then led the 19th Army Group as a part of the First Field Army into Korea in February 1951 as deputy commander of the CPVA, with charge of combat operations.

Yang's army participated in the Chinese Fifth Offensive of April 1951, which aimed to take the Republic of Korea (ROK, South Korea) capital of Seoul and which inflicted heavy casualties on the Republic of Korea Army (ROKA, South Korean Army) 1st Division and the British 29th Brigade. The Chinese suffered heavy casualties themselves, however; and a subsequent United Nations Command (UNC) counterattack found them unprepared and forced into a rapid and costly withdrawal.

Yang commanded the CPVA from November 1954 to October 1955. He was promoted to full general in 1955. Following graduation from the Nanjing Advanced Military Institute in 1958, Yang assumed command of the Jinan Military Region. He held this post until the mid-1970s. He then commanded the Wuhan Military Region (1974–1979), and the Kunming Military Region (1979–1980).

Yang became chief of staff of the People's Liberation Army (PLA, Chinese Communist Army) in February 1980. Shortly thereafter he was also named to the CCP Central Military Commission, and a vice minister of National Defense. He also served on the Politburo during 1977–1987. Yang retired from his posts in 1987. In 1989 he was reported to have signed an appeal by a number of generals not to use the army against the student prodemocracy protesters at Tiananmen Square. Yang died on October 25, 1994.

SPENCER C. TUCKER

See also

China, People's Republic of; China, People's Republic of, Army; Chinese Offensive, Fifth; Chinese People's Volunteer Army; Mao Zedong; Peng Dehuai

References

Barke, Wolfgang. *Biographic Dictionary and Analysis of China's Party Leadership, 1922–1988.* New York: K. G. Saur, 1990.

Lamb, Malcolm. *Director of Officials and Organizations in China, 1968–1983.* New York: M. E. Sharpe, 1984.

Li Xiaobing, Bin Yu, and Allan R. Millett, eds. and trans. *Mao's Generals Remember Korea.* Lawrence: University Press of Kansas, 2001.

Whitson, William W., with Chen-Hsia Huang. *The Chinese High Command: A History of Communist Military Politics, 1927–71.* Westport, CT: Praeger, 1973.

Wortzel, Larry M. *Dictionary of Contemporary Chinese Military History.* Westport, CT: Greenwood, 1999.

Yang Dezhi. *Weile Heping* [For the Sake of Peace]. Beijing: Changzheng Chubanshe, 1987.

———. *Yang Dezhi Huiyilu* [Memoirs of Yang Dezhi]. Beijing: Jiefangjun Chubanshe, 1992.

Yang Yu Chan

Birth Date: February 3, 1897
Death Date: October 20, 1975

Republic of Korea (ROK, South Korea) diplomat. Born in Pusan on February 3, 1897, Yang Yu Chan spent most of his youth in the United States. He attained a bachelor's degree and then an M.D. at Boston University in 1923. Yang subsequently managed a hospital in Honolulu. Before the end of World War II, he also served as secretary-general of the Korean Young Men's Christian Association (YMCA) in Hawaii and as president of the Korean Christian Foundation in Honolulu. It was during this period that Yang became acquainted with Syngman Rhee and other leaders of the Korean independence movement who were active in the exile community in the United States. It was because of his acquaintance with Rhee that Yang became a professional diplomat.

In March 1951 Rhee, who had become the president of South Korea, appointed Yang as Korean ambassador to the United

States. Yang held that post until April 1960 and was thus the longest-serving South Korean ambassador to the United States. He played a key role in securing U.S. defense and aid commitments to South Korea, and he also mediated between the Rhee administration and Washington, DC He became the deputy head of the South Korean delegation to the 1954 Geneva Conference, held in accordance with the Korean Armistice Agreement. He also served as chief delegate to the South Korea–Japan talks held during the 1950s. In 1960 Yang became South Korean ambassador to Brazil as well as to the United States. From 1965 until his retirement in 1972 he served as South Korean ambassador-at-large. Yang died in Seoul on October 20, 1975.

JINWUNG KIM

See also
Rhee, Syngman

References
Matray, James I., ed. *Historical Dictionary of the Korean War.* Westport, CT: Greenwood, 1991.

Tonga Ilbo. *Taehan Minguk Yokdae Sambu Chongram* [General Collections of the Republic of Korea's Successive Legislative, Administrative, and Judiciary Branch Figures]. Seoul: Tonga Ilbo Sa, 1981.

Yi Chong Chan
Birth Date: March 10, 1916
Death Date: February 10, 1983

Chief of staff of the Republic of Korea Army (ROKA, South Korean Army) from June 1951 to July 1952. Born in Seoul on March 10, 1916, Yi Chong Chan graduated from the Japanese Military Academy in 1937. During World War II, he served as a major in an engineer corps of the Japanese army. In June 1946, he returned to Korea but refused an offer from the U.S. military government to lead the Korean Constabulary. In June 1949, Yi accepted the post of director of the Information and Education Bureau at the Defense Ministry with the rank of colonel.

On June 18, 1950, only a week before the invasion of the Republic of Korea (ROK, South Korea) by the Democratic People's Republic of Korea (DPRK, North Korea), Yi accepted appointment as head of the Capital Security Command at Seoul. In September, he became commander of the 3rd Division on the east coast in the defense of the Pusan Perimeter. In the pursuit phase of the breakout from that front along the Naktong River in the second half of September, Yi's troops led all units of both the ROKA and the U.S. Eighth Army in the drive northward. The 3rd Division reached the 38th Parallel on the last day of September and crossed it the next day.

On June 23, 1951, Yi was promoted to major general to take the place of Chong Il Kwon as ROKA chief of staff. He worked diligently both to augment the ROKA and to improve its fighting ability. During the time he was chief of staff, and with support from the United States, ROKA forces expanded from about 250,000 to 460,000 men.

In 1952, however, Yi found himself in conflict with President Syngman Rhee, who was then attempting to amend the constitution in his favor. On May 23, 1952, Rhee placed Pusan under martial law and ordered the arrest of some of his assembly opponents, charging them with complicity in a communist conspiracy. Rhee justified martial law as being necessary to counteract communist guerrilla operations, but his actions were much criticized both from within and outside Korea. Yi tried without success to persuade Rhee to lift the martial law decree, and he refused Rhee's order to pull two combat divisions from the front line to reinforce the weak forces in Pusan. Yi thought this might endanger military operations at the front, and he also believed that the military should not be a tool for politicians.

Although Yi enjoyed strong support from his staff, the ROKA in general, and such U.S. generals as Eighth Army commander General James A. Van Fleet and commander in chief of the United Nations Command (UNC) Lieutenant General Mark W. Clark, Rhee dismissed him in July. During the last year of the war, Yi was in the United States to attend the Command and General Staff College, from which he graduated in July 1953. The next month he was appointed president of the ROKA College. On his retirement from the military in May 1960, after Rhee's ouster following the April student uprising, Yi joined the interim government as defense minister. In 1961, he was appointed ambassador to Italy. Held in high regard by the Korean people because of his firm advocacy of a politically neutral military, Yi Chong Chan died in Seoul on February 10, 1983.

To WOONG CHUNG

See also
Chong Il Gwon; Clark, Mark Wayne; Rhee, Syngman; Van Fleet, James Alward

References
Hermes, Walter G. *U.S. Army in the Korean War: Truce Tent and Fighting Front.* Washington, DC: Office of the Chief of Military History, 1966.

Kang Song Jae. *Cham Kunin Yi Chong Chan Changgun* [The True Soldier: General Yi Chong Chan]. Seoul: Tonga Ilbo, 1986.

Tonga Ilbo. *Taehan Minguk Yokdae Sambu Chongram* [General Collections of the Republic of Korea's Successive Legislative, Administrative, and Judiciary Branch Figures]. Seoul: Tonga Ilbo Sa, 1981.

Yi Hak Ku
Birth Date: 1920
Death Date: Unknown

Senior colonel of the Korean People's Army (KPA, North Korean Army), 13th Division chief of staff, and one of the highest-ranking communist prisoners of war (POWs). Born in 1920 in

U.S. Army brigadier general George I. Back with Korean People's Army (KPA, North Korean Army) senior colonel Yi Hak Ku, former chief of staff of the KPA 13th Division, now a prisoner of war (POW) at POW Camp No. 2, Pusan, January 1951. (National Archives)

Myongchon, North Hamgyong Province, Democratic People's Republic of Korea (DPRK, North Korea), Yi Hak Ku was a primary school teacher before joining the army. Before the start of the Korean War, Yi was chief of the planning section of the Operations Planning Bureau in the KPA.

Although his wife and family remained in North Korea, Yi surrendered of his own volition with some of his men in September 1950 after the United Nations Command (UNC) landing at Inchon, when it seemed apparent that North Korea had lost the war. There were even reports that Yi had shot and wounded Choe Yongjin, the 13th Division commander. Yi also volunteered to make a broadcast urging KPA troops to stop fighting. UNC authorities segregated him from other POWs and gave him special treatment in the prison camp where he was held at Pusan.

The UNC soon determined that the KPA had ordered Yi to surrender. Sent to the POW camp on Koje-do, Yi vowed before North Korean officer POWs to devote all of his energies to resisting the "American capitalists," and he soon became popular among the POWs. Yi, along with other POW Senior Colonels Hong Chol and

Pak Sang Hyon, served as liaison with the UNC camp authorities and presented POW demands and complaints. Yi came to Compound 76 on May 7, 1952, and conducted negotiations with the UNC authorities after the POWs had captured U.S. Army brigadier general Francis T. Dodd.

On June 10, 1952, in Operation BREAKUP, Brigadier General Haydon L. Boatner summoned Yi as the spokesman of Compound 76 and instructed him to form the POWs in groups of 150 men before moving them to another compound. When the prisoners failed to move out, security troops opened fire, resulting in many casualties among the POWs. The camp authorities then segregated Yi from the other POWs and placed him in solitary confinement.

Yi returned to North Korea during Operation BIG SWITCH in 1953, but North Korea might have then purged him, and his fate remains unknown. A 1998 defector from North Korea said that the North Korean officials distrusted the returned POWs and put most of them to work in mines.

SUNGHUN CHO

See also
Dodd-Colson Prisoner of War Incident; Prisoner of War Administration, United Nations Command

References
Chu, Yong Bok. *Nae ga Kyokkun Choson Chonjaeng* [The Korean War That I Experienced]. Seoul: Koryowon, 1990.

Kim, Sun Ho. "Koje-Do in Complication: An Analysis of the Social and Political Organization of Korean Prisoners of War in UNC POW Camps, 1950–1951." Washington, DC: Human Resources Research Office, George Washington University, 1955.

Office of the Assistant Chief of Staff G 2, Intelligence, HQ, U.S. Army Forces, Far East, Advanced. "Communist Utilization of Prisoners of War." Unpublished document, 1953.

Yi Hyong Gun

Birth Date: November 2, 1920
Death Date: January 13, 2002

General and commander of the 2nd Division of the Republic of Korea Army (ROKA, South Korean Army) at the outbreak of the Korean War. Born in Kongju, South Chungchong Province, on November 2, 1920, Yi Hyong Gun graduated from the Japanese Military Academy in 1942 and rose to the rank of captain in the Japanese Army during the Second World War. Upon his return to Korea in 1945, Yi attended the Military English-Language School run by the U.S. military government in Korea. He then served as an officer in the Korean Constabulary, predecessor to the ROKA. As a result of his high marks at the Language School, Yi received serial number 1 of all commissioned officers in the ROKA.

In June 1949, Yi became the first commanding officer of the Eighth Division, stationed at Kangnung, and on June 10, 1950, just before the Korean People's Army (KPA, North Korean Army) invasion of South Korea, he became commander of the 2nd Division at Taejon, 90 miles south of Seoul. Yi immediately complained to ROKA chief of staff Chae Pyong Dok about the transfer. Yi remarked in his memoirs that shuffling divisional commanders about at such a critical time could not be justified.

On June 25, Chae ordered Yi to move his division northward and reinforce the 7th Division fighting in the area of Uijongbu about 30 miles north of Seoul. Chae's plan was for the two divisions to counterattack the next day. This was completely impossible, and Chae should have planned a delaying action, in which more ROKA units could have escaped southward. Instead, Chae ordered Yi to bring his forces into battle piecemeal as they arrived on the battlefield. Yi objected to this and told Chae that he could not launch any counterattack until he had the major part of his division in place. On the spot, Chae threatened Yi with a pistol to his head, removed Yi from his position, and ordered the commander of the 7th Division to assume command of the 2nd Division as well as his own. U.S. advisor with the ROKA chief of staff Captain James H. Hausman agreed with Yi's stance but could not prevent Chae's precipitous action at this critical time.

Chae, who was largely responsible for the disastrous defeat of the ROKA at the beginning of the war, was subsequently removed from command, and Yi returned to field command. He had charge of the ROKA III Corps in October 1950 and I Corps in January 1952. After the war, in February 1954, he was promoted to full (four-star) general and became the first chairman of the Armed Forces Joint Chiefs of Staff of the Republic of Korea (ROK, South Korea) and, in June 1956, chief of staff of the ROKA. Yi Hyong Gun retired from the army in August 1959 and died in Seoul on January 13, 2002.

To Woong Chung

See also
Chae Pyong Dok; Hausman, James Harry

References
Appleman, Roy E. *United States Army in Korea: South to the Naktong, North to the Yalu*. Washington, DC: Office of the Chief of Military History, 1961.

Hausman, James, and Il Wha H. Chung. *Hausman's Witness*. Seoul: Hankuk Moonwon, 1995.

Yi Hyong Gun. *Kunbon Ibon ui Oegil Insaeng* [Memoirs: The One Road Life of the Service's Number One Soldier]. Seoul: Chungang Ilbo Sa, 1993.

Yi Kwon Mu

Birth Date: 1915
Death Date: Unknown

Major general in the Korean People's Army (KPA, North Korean Army) and commander of the 4th Division at the beginning of the Korean War; in October 1950, he became commander of II Corps. Born in Manchuria in 1915 to a Korean refugee family, Yi Kwon Mu was a close friend of Kim Il Sung, leader of the Democratic People's Republic of Korea (DPRK, North Korea). During the Second World War, he fought with the Chinese Communist Eighth Road Army against the Japanese and after the war remained with his comrades until their victory over the Guomindang (GMD, Nationalist) was ensured. Soviet officials apparently advised Yi and other North Korean military men, who went under the name of the Korean Volunteer Army, to remain attached to Communist Chinese units even after Korea's liberation from Japanese rule in 1945, on the grounds that this would enable Korean communists to gain valuable fighting experience that they could later utilize in their own country.

In North Korea's internal politics, Yi was regarded as a member of the China-oriented Yenan (Yan'an) faction, which some believed was not entirely sympathetic to Kim Il Sung. According to some accounts, during the Second World War, Yi also spent some time as a lieutenant in the Red Army, and after the Chinese Communist victory, he apparently went to the Soviet Union for further military training.

Yi served as the KPA's first chief of staff but was temporarily relieved of his command for reasons that remain unclear. Before the Korean War began, Yi was called back to command the 4th Division, which, along with the 3rd Division, was one of the KPA's crack units. The 4th Division spearheaded North Korea's attack on the Republic of Korea (ROK, South Korea) and, on June 28, 1950, distinguished itself by occupying the capital, winning the name the Seoul Division.

Yi was one of the commanders of the ultimately unsuccessful North Korean attempt to breach the Naktong River line in August 1950, but the courage and determination he and his men displayed won the respect and admiration even of their opponents. In October 1950, Yi received command of the KPA II Corps.

Yi became commander of the KPA some time in 1958. Kim Il Sung purged Yi and numerous other adherents of both North Korea's Yenan and Soviet political factions, and Yi was removed from his posts in June 1959. No information is currently available on where and when he died.

PRISCILLA ROBERTS

See also
Kim Il Sung; Korea, Democratic People's Republic of, Army

References
Appleman, Roy E. *United States Army in Korea: South to the Naktong, North to the Yalu.* Washington, DC: Office of the Chief of Military History, 1961.

Cumings, Bruce. *The Origins of the Korean War.* 2 vols. Princeton, NJ: Princeton University Press, 1981, 1990.

Fehrenbach, T. R. *This Kind of War: A Study in Unpreparedness.* New York: Macmillan, 1962.

Kennan, George F. *Memoirs.* 2 vols. Boston: Little, Brown, 1967, 1972.

Matray, James I., ed. *Historical Dictionary of the Korean War.* New York: Greenwood, 1991.

Yi Pom Sok
Birth Date: October 20, 1900
Death Date: May 11, 1972

Prime minister and concurrently defense minister of the Republic of Korea (ROK, South Korea) from 1948 to 1950 before the start of the Korean War. Born on October 20, 1900, in Seoul, Yi Pom Sok (Lee Bum Suk) went to China and graduated from the Yunnan Military Academy Cavalry School in 1919. The following year he led an attack on Japanese forces at Chongsan-ni in northern Manchuria, gaining a reputation as one of the most famous Korean fighters against Japanese colonial rule. Serving for a time in the Guomindang (GMD, Nationalist) forces led by Jiang Jieshi (Chiang Kai-shek), Yi taught at Loyang Military Academy between 1933 and 1936.

In 1940, Yi was one of leaders of the Kwangbok Army established by the Korean Provisional Government with Jiang's support to win independence for Korea. The U.S. Office of Strategic Services (OSS) contacted Yi in the summer of 1945 and planned to use his forces in a guerrilla operation in Korea. Although Japan's surrender that August prevented the plan from being carried out, the OSS assisted Yi by providing him air transport to Korea and then back to China that same month.

Although disappointed at the decision by the U.S. Army military government in Korea not to recognize the Korean Provisional Government as the legitimate Korean government, Yi returned to Korea in the spring of 1946. He refused to participate in the constabulary, which he believed included too many individuals who were formerly pro-Japanese and too many communists. In October 1946, Yi organized the Korean National Youth Corps, which was originally intended to provide the basis for a future Korean army. This organization soon grew into a strong rightist association, which the U.S. military government later came to favor as a means of consolidating its interests in South Korea. In August 1948, Yi became both the first prime minister and first defense minister of South Korea.

Yi resigned as defense minister in February 1949 and as prime minister in April 1950, just before the start of the Korean War. After the invasion by the Democratic People's Republic of Korea (DPRK, North Korea) of South Korea on June 25, 1950, President Syngman Rhee requested that Yi provide military advice to the cabinet. Although neither an active-duty military officer nor a cabinet member, he participated in the initial meeting of senior military men on June 26. This resulted in the controversial decision insisted on by Defense Minister Sin Song Mo and army chief of staff General Chae Pyong Dok for troops of the Republic of Korea Army (ROKA, South Korean Army) to launch a counterattack against forces of the Korean People's Army (KPA, North Korean Army). Disappointed at the results of that meeting, Yi took the initiative in pushing for an emergency cabinet meeting held at 2:00 a.m. the next day. Faced with a rapidly deteriorating military situation, Yi urged evacuation of the government from Seoul. He also suggested that, after the departure of the government, bridges over the Han River be blown up to deny the KPA an easy crossing.

President Rhee and his staff left Seoul for Taejon at about 4:00 a.m., immediately after the cabinet meeting. During the day of June 27, South Korean government officials and their families also evacuated Seoul in two special trains. Learning of this evacuation, members of the assembly accused the government of deserting the people and decided that the assembly would not leave Seoul and would instead remain with the people. However, most of them had crossed the Han by that same evening.

Yi vainly sought reappointment to his former positions of prime minister or defense minister or a position as a military commander in the field. But President Rhee, who sought to capitalize on Yi's experiences in waging guerrilla warfare against the Japanese in Manchuria, offered him the task of creating a guerrilla organization in the Cholla Province, then occupied by the North Koreans. Yi sought a higher post and refused the offer.

In 1951, Yi served as ambassador to Taipei during an eight-month period. Appointed home minister in May 1952, he used police powers to coerce the assembly—then located in the temporary capital, Pusan—into accepting Rhee's demand to amend the constitution from indirect election of the president by the assembly to direct election by the people. Rhee made Yi a scapegoat for illegal methods used against the assembly, relieving him of his position as home minister.

Yi ran unsuccessfully for vice president in the elections of August 1952 and again in 1956. He died in Seoul on May 11, 1972.

To Woong Chung

See also

Jiang Jieshi; Rhee, Syngman

References

Noble, Harold J. *Embassy at War.* Seattle: University of Washington Press, 1975.

Republic of Korea, War History Compilation Committee, Ministry of National Defense. *Hanguk Chonjaengsa* [History of the Korean War]. 9 vols. Seoul: Ministry of National Defense, 1967–1970.

Yi Pom Sok. *Chulgi Yi Pom Sok Chajon* [The Autobiography of Chulgi Yi Pom Sok]. Seoul: Oekil Sa, 1991.

Yi Sang Jo
Birth Date: 1915
Death Date: 1996

Korean People's Army (KPA, North Korean Army) general Yi Sang Jo, North Korean delegate to the Panmunjom truce talks. (Hulton-Deutsch Collection/Corbis)

Deputy chief delegate and later chief delegate for the Democratic People's Republic of Korea (DPRK, North Korea) to the Panmunjom truce talks. Born in 1915 at Tongnae, South Korea, now a part of Pusan, Yi Sang Jo emigrated to China with his parents in 1932. After graduating from a Chinese military officers' training school at Nanjing, he fought with the Chinese communists against the Japanese. Later he became one of the unit commanders of the Korean Volunteer Army supported by the Chinese Communist Party (CCP). He returned to northern Korea in 1946 to become deputy chief of the organization department of the Korean Workers' Party for North Korea and to become an architect of the Korean People's Army (KPA, North Korean Army).

At the time of the North Korean invasion of the Republic of Korea (ROK, South Korea) in June 1950, Yi was vice minister of commerce of North Korea. He immediately became deputy chief of staff of the KPA. In September 1950, after the Inchon Landing, he secretly traveled to Beijing at the request of Kim Il Sung to appeal for Chinese military intervention in the war to prevent the destruction of North Korea and to ask for winter clothing for the KPA. In 1951, he was transferred to director of the Inspection Bureau of the KPA.

During the entire period of the armistice negotiations—July 10, 1951, to July 27, 1953—Major General Yi served as a member of the North Korean delegation. According to Joseph C. Goulden, "chunky and often physically filthy, Lee [Yi] had one impressive characteristic: He would permit flies to crawl over his face without brushing them away. Apparently he thought this showed iron self control."

After the cease-fire, Yi served as chief of the North Korean component of the Military Armistice Commission. In August 1955, after retiring from the army, he was appointed ambassador to Moscow. In April 1956, he was elected a candidate member of the central committee of the Korean Workers' Party. That same year, encouraged by the de-Stalinization campaign in the Soviet Union, the Chinese exile Yenan (Yan'an) faction and the Soviet exile faction challenged the personality cult of Kim Il Sung. However, Kim purged the opposition in the so-called Choe Chang Ik incident of 1957, and Yi was one of its victims. Defying a recall order, he sought political asylum in Moscow. Yi never returned to North Korea from the Soviet Union, subsequently serving as a researcher at a Soviet state-run research institute in Minsk, where he received his doctorate in political science. He resided in Minsk, living on a Soviet pension. In September 1989, Yi visited South Korea and in a press conference stated that Kim had initiated the Korean War. He died in Minsk in 1996.

Hakjoon Kim

See also

Korea, Democratic People's Republic of, 1945–1953; Korea, Democratic People's Republic of, 1953–Present; Truce Talks

Reference

Goulden, Joseph C. *Korea: The Untold Story of the War.* New York: Times Books, 1982.

Yi Sung Yop
Birth Date: February 8, 1905
Death Date: July 30, 1954

Minister of Justice of the Democratic People's Republic of Korea (DPRK, North Korea). Born in 1905 on Yonghong Island near Inchon, Yi Sung Yop was educated at Inchon Commercial School. In 1919, he participated in the March First Movement and was expelled from the school. He joined the Korean Communist Party in September 1925 and was a reporter for the *Choson Ilbo* (*Choson Daily*), a nationalist daily newspaper. His communist activities led to his imprisonment in 1931, 1937, and 1940. From 1941 to 1945, he was a board member of the Inchon District Rice Distribution Corporation, the post that would become a target for his opponents to label him pro-Japanese.

Immediately after liberation, Yi helped Pak Hon Yong in reconstructing the Korean Communist Party, and he became a member of its central committee. At the same time he became a member of the Central People's Committee at the Committee for the Preparation of Korean Independence. In November 1946, when the major leftist parties merged into a single South Korean Workers' Party (SKWP), he became a member of its central committee, chairman of its Kyonggi Province branch, and editor in chief of the party organ, *Haebang Ilbo* (*Liberation Daily*). In early 1948, Yi fled to North Korea and joined in the establishment of the DPRK, becoming its minister of justice. In June 1949, the North Korean Workers' Party absorbed the SKWP, thus becoming the Korean Workers' Party. Yi became its politburo member and a secretary of its central committee. In this capacity, he was regarded as second to Pak Hon Yong in the South Korean Workers' Party, or the domestic faction in North Korean politics.

On June 28, 1950, with the start of the North Korean occupation of the Republic of Korea (ROK, South Korea), Yi became chairman of the Seoul People's Committee. Six months later, he was engaged in the secret cease-fire negotiations of 1951 with the South Korean leftists under U.S. auspices. About this time the power struggle between Kim Il Sung's Kapsan (Manchurian) faction and Pak Hon Yong's domestic communist faction became extremely intense. Indicative of Pak's impending demise, Yi was relieved in December 1951 as minister of justice. Five months later, he was ousted from the secretariat and demoted to chairman of the People's Inspection Committee, a post he lost 10 months later. In early 1953 he, Pak, and Pak's supporters supposedly attempted a coup d'état against Kim. In April 1953, Yi was arrested with the other leaders of the SKWP faction. In August 1953, a military court sentenced him to death. A year later, on July 30, 1954, he was executed as a "state enemy who colluded with the American imperialists" to overthrow the North Korean regime.

HAKJOON KIM

See also

Korea, Republic of, 1947–1953; Korea, Republic of, 1953–Present; March First Movement; Pak Hon Yong

References

Scalapino, Robert A., and Lee Chong Sik. *Communism in Korea.* 2 vols. Berkeley: University of California Press, 1973.

Suh, Dae Sook. *Kim Il Sung: The North Korean Leader.* New York: Columbia University Press, 1988.

Yi Tong Hwi
Birth Date: August 2, 1873
Death Date: January 1, 1935

Veteran Korean independence leader in the period of the late Choson dynasty and Japanese colonial rule. Yi Tong Hwi was born at Tanchon, South Hamgyong Province in the present-day Democratic People's Republic of Korea (DPRK, North Korea) on August 2, 1873. He attended the Seoul Military Officers School between 1896 and 1897, was commissioned a second lieutenant in 1897, and then served as a court guard. He was promoted to first lieutenant in 1899, to captain in 1900, and to major in 1901. When a clandestine organization called the Reform Party was established to reinvigorate Korean society in 1902, Yi joined it. He converted to Christianity in 1903.

Organized in 1906, the Korean Self-Strengthening Society sought to establish a foundation for the recovery of Korean sovereignty through the promotion of native industry and increased educational opportunities. Yi became head of the Kanghwa-do (island) branch of the organization. Yi had spent most of his time as a career officer on the strategic island. In 1907, Yi, An Chang Ho, Yi Kap, Yang Ki Tak, and Yi Sung Hun formed a secret organization called the New People's Society to promote Korean industry and education as well as to prepare for military action against the Japanese. In 1910, Yi and other leaders of the organization were arrested and imprisoned on suspicion that they had been involved in the 1909 assassination of Ito Hirobumi, the Japanese resident-general in Korea. They were all arrested again by the Japanese in connection with the so-called Case of the One Hundred Five, in which they were accused of plotting to assassinate Japanese governor-general Terauchi Masatake in 1911. Yi was sent into exile on an island in the Yellow Sea.

After Korea became a Japanese colony in 1910, an overt independence movement became impossible. Thus, many Korean nationalist activists fled to the safety of overseas havens. While some of these exiled nationalists, including Syngman Rhee, stressed that Korea should attempt to recover its independence by diplomatic means, others advocated establishing bases for the independence movement in neighboring territories, from which operations might be expanded until Korean independence could be restored by military force. Those independence fighters who had fled just across the Yalu and Tumen rivers into Manchuria or into the Maritime Province of Russia mainly engaged in military activities of this kind. After release from exile, Yi at first took refuge in the Jiandao region in Manchuria and then in the Russian Maritime Province in 1913. At Vladivostok, he and Yi Sang Sol established the Government of the Korean Restoration Army, the first Korean provisional government, in 1914. They also organized an independence army and made plans for an armed struggle against the Japanese.

After the Korean Provisional Government (KPG) was established in Shanghai in April 1919, Yi participated in the formation of its cabinet. He served as its prime minister from November 1919 to June 1920 and again from July 1920 to January 1921. At this critical juncture, dissension developed among KPG leaders over such issues as the use of funds obtained from Russian leader Vladimir Lenin by Yi Tong Hwi. Most of the KPG leaders charged Yi with appropriating the funds to establish the Koryo Communist Party. In January 1921, Yi resigned as prime minister and left the KPG, never to return.

Following the March First Movement in 1919, the Korean struggle for independence sought to maintain its direction in a variety of alternative stratagems, and one of these was to establish ties with international socialism. The Bolshevik Revolution in Russia had just triumphed, and Lenin was urging support for independence movements among the oppressed people of the world. Encouraged by this development, Yi Tong Hwi organized the Koryo Communist Party in Shanghai in August 1920. His party secured substantial financial support from the Soviets. From then on, as part of the Korean independence movement, he devoted himself to the Korean communist movement in Russian Siberia. Yi Tong Hwi died at Vladivostok on January 1, 1935. Yi was in every way an independence fighter who dedicated his entire life to the anti-Japanese independence movement.

JINWUNG KIM

See also
An Chang Ho; Rhee, Syngman

References
Kim, Pang. *Yi Tong Hwi: Saengae wa Sasang* [Yi Tong Hwi: Life and Thought]. Seoul: Taewangsa, 1998.
———. *Yi Tong Hwi Yongu* [A Study of Yi Tong Hwi]. Seoul: Kukhak Charyowon, 1999.
Lee, Ki-baik. *A New History of Korea.* Translated by Edward W. Wagner with Edward J. Shultz. Cambridge, MA: Harvard University Press, 1984.

Yim, Louise
Birth Date: November 21, 1899
Death Date: February 17, 1977

First Korean United Nations (UN) delegate, from 1945 to 1948. The turbulent life of Louise Yim as a political activist, an educator,

and a feminist ultimately earned her the sobriquet Korea's Joan of Arc. Born Yim Yong Sin into a wealthy family at Kumsan in the central part of present-day Republic of Korea (ROK, South Korea) on November 21, 1899, she undertook a hunger strike against her parents at age 12 to gain permission to attend high school. Once at school, she refused an arranged marriage. She also formed an underground organization of students against the Japanese, who had annexed Korea in 1910. The student revolutionaries served as messengers and distributed anti-Japanese pamphlets. After the March 1, 1919, nationwide demonstration against Japan, Yim was imprisoned for seven months for her activities.

Ultimately, Yim found her way to the United States, where, on the advice of a professor, she changed her name to Louise. She earned a master's degree in political science from the University of Southern California, even as she managed a gasoline station and vegetable market. As her country's first UN delegate, from 1945 to 1948, she had helped draft the UN resolution that granted Korean independence. In June 1950, when the Democratic People's Republic of Korea (DPRK, North Korea) invaded South Korea, Yim was visiting New York as a Korean National Assembly member. Yim then embarked on a personal campaign to secure the assistance of the United States in resolving the crisis.

Yim demanded that South Korean ambassador to the United States John M. Chang (Chang Myon) place the Korean issue before the UN Security Council. She gave interviews to major media outlets, visited the White House, and lobbied an important friend from her UN days, Secretary-General Trygve Lie. Yim could take some satisfaction in that three days later, on June 27, a Security Council resolution passed calling on member states to furnish military forces to defeat the North Korean invasion.

In May 1951, South Korean president Syngman Rhee called Yim back from her efforts to enlist support for Korea in America. He directed her to organize a women's movement to supplement rear-echelon war efforts. Over the years, Yim became a close political ally of, and adviser to, Rhee. She established the United Women's Service Association and a refugee school campus in Pusan to continue higher education for youth.

After the recapture of Seoul by United Nations Command (UNC) forces, Yim returned there and created two publications, the *Women's World Magazine* and the *Commerce Daily*. She then organized the Korean Women's National Defense Association to assist veterans. Her many other accomplishments include being the first woman cabinet member in Korea (minister of commerce and industry), establishing the first YWCA in Korea, and founding Chungang (Central) University in Seoul, where she served as president. Louise Yim died in Seoul on February 17, 1977.

RICHARD A. GARVER

See also
Lie, Trygve Halvden; Rhee, Syngman

References
Millett, Allan R. *The War for Korea, 1945–1950: A House Burning.* Lawrence: University Press of Kansas, 2005.

Oliver, Robert T. *Syngman Rhee: The Man behind the Myth.* New York: Dodd, Mead, 1955.

Yim, Louise. *My Forty Year Fight for Korea.* Seoul: Chung Ang University, 1951.

Yo Un Hyong
Birth Date: May 25, 1886
Death Date: July 29, 1947

Veteran Korean nationalist during Japanese colonial rule and a prominent political leader in the immediate postliberation period. Yo Un Hyong was born at Yangpyong, Kyonggi Province, in present-day Republic of Korea (ROK, South Korea), on May 25, 1886. He studied Chinese classics for a time, but in 1908 he converted to Christianity. He traveled to China in 1913 and played an important role in the attempts to gain Korean independence in February 1919 and in the founding of the Korean Provisional Government (KPG) in Shanghai in April 1919. In 1921, Yo, Kim Kyu Sik, and some 30 other Korean nationalists attended the Congress of the Toilers of the Far East in Moscow. There Yo met the Soviet revolutionaries Vladimir Lenin and Leon Trotsky.

In 1929, the Japanese captured Yo in Shanghai and sent him back to Korea, where he served a three-year prison term. Upon his release in 1932, he assumed the editorship of the *Choson Chungang Ilbo* (*Choson Central Daily*) in Seoul. As with other prominent Koreans, Yo was pressured from 1938 on to collaborate with the Japanese in their war effort. He steadfastly resisted.

Toward the end of the Pacific War in 1945, the Japanese in Korea felt obliged to select a Korean leader to maintain order, pending the arrival of Allied forces. Spurned by Song Chin U, a conservative, who feared being labeled a collaborator, the Japanese authorities finally called on Yo. He accepted responsibility for an interim administration and organized the Committee for the Preparation of Korean Independence (CPKI) on August 15, 1945. The arrangement between Yo and the Japanese maintained order, and there was no serious violence against the Japanese.

When news arrived that the United States would occupy southern Korea, Yo's CPKI called a national convention in Seoul on September 6, 1945, to provide his regime with a stamp of legitimacy. He proclaimed the establishment of the Korean People's Republic (KPR), which had a cabinet that included distinguished nationalists of all political persuasions, right and left. Despite its efforts to represent all sides, the body was influenced the most by the Left. After the American military government was established on September 11, 1945, it refused to cooperate with the KPR. American military authorities readily accepted the premise that Yo's KPR was under Soviet domination, and most Americans dismissed Yo's claim to legitimacy.

Because the KPR was not recognized by the Americans, Yo organized the Choson People's Party (CPP) on November 12, 1945.

By doing so, he implicitly consented to the American demand that the KPR drop its claim to being a government and label itself a political party. When the KPR collapsed under American opposition, the Left in southern Korea created another leftist coalition called the Democratic National Front (DNF), a united front that included all leftists, on February 15, 1946. Yo joined the organization.

American preferential treatment toward the Right caused the Soviet Union to become more focused on creating a friendly regime in northern Korea. Thus, in mid-1946, the United States instructed its representatives in Korea to forsake their exclusive attachment to the Right in favor of a broad coalition embracing moderates. The American military government reluctantly attempted to build a moderate coalition around the leadership of Kim Kyu Sik, a leader of moderate rightists. While the chances for success seemed slim, Kim managed to join forces with Yo. At first, Yo refused to participate in the coalition movement, and he was under intense pressure from extreme leftists to quit the coalition effort. He was even kidnapped, beaten, and warned not to participate. But he finally agreed to take part in it. In August 1946, he resigned his positions in the CPP and the DNF to join the coalition movement. On October 7, 1946, the Left-Right Coalition Committee was formed, with Kim and Yo as cochairmen.

Cooperation between the United States and the Coalition Committee was short-lived. After striving to fashion a moderate alternative in Korean politics, the American military government proceeded to undermine the Coalition Committee. The failure of the U.S.-Soviet Joint Commission in the summer of 1947 had an immediate effect on politics in southern Korea. The moderate coalition that the United States had put together to support its position finally collapsed when Yo was assassinated in Seoul on July 29, 1947. The identity of his assassin and those who may have arranged his murder remain a mystery.

JINWUNG KIM

See also
Kim Kyu Sik; Pak Hon Yong; Rhee, Syngman; Song Chin U

References
Cumings, Bruce. *The Origins of the Korean War.* 2 vols. Princeton, NJ: Princeton University Press, 1981, 1990.

Yi, Ki Hyong. *Yo Un-hyong Pyongjon* [A Critical Biography of Yo Un Hyong]. Seoul: Silch'onmunhaksa, 2004.

Yongchon, Battle of
Start Date: September 2, 1950
End Date: September 12, 1950

Military engagement in early September 1950 along the Pusan Perimeter between United Nations Command (UNC) and Korean People's Army (KPA, North Korean Army) forces. Having been forced steadily back by KPA forces in the weeks following the

Battle-weary American troops withdrawing from Yongchon, September 14, 1950. (Hulton Archive/Getty Images)

June 25, 1950, invasion, UNC forces were by the end of August fighting to hold the Pusan Perimeter around the port city of Pusan. Lieutenant General Walton H. Walker's UNC forces there faced the most perilous crisis of the war. Following initial defeats around the edge of the perimeter in late August, the KPA regrouped for a final concerted push. Its ultimate military objective was to collapse the perimeter, capturing the UNC forces or driving them into the sea and thereby reunifying the entire peninsula under rule of the Democratic People's Republic of Korea (DPRK, North Korea).

Crucial to the defense of the perimeter was the east-west road running across the perimeter's northern end. This linked the eastern coastal port of Pohang with the interior city of Taegu and ran through the town of Yongchon, which lay roughly midway between them. The battle in early September for control of Yongchon, which also had roads running from there to the south, constituted one of at least five major battles around the perimeter that occurred more or less simultaneously.

On September 2, a two-division KPA offensive drove into the lines of the Republic of Korea Army (ROKA, South Korean Army) located between 20 and 35 miles north of Yongchon. The KPA's 8th Division attacked toward Yongchon from the northwest, while

the 15th Division came from the northeast. Yongchon thus became the apex of a triangle pointing southward.

In 10 days of heavy fighting, the KPA 8th Division never reached closer than about 12 miles from the road junction. Instead, the ROKA 6th Division fought the KPA to a standstill near the mountainous locality known as Hwajong. Using artillery and close air support, the South Koreans virtually destroyed the attackers.

The second prong of the KPA advance by the 15th Division made rapid initial progress, as the attackers fought their way into, and in some cases south of, Yongchon. They also severed the vital roadway linking Pohang and Taegu and established roadblocks to the southeast. While ROKA 8th Division defenders suffered initial disorder in their retreat—one regiment broke and ran—they rallied beginning about September 8. Reinforced by Korea Military Advisory Group (KMAG) cadre and two hastily deployed regiments from other ROKA divisions, the ROKA 8th Division defeated the North Koreans in fierce fighting southeast of Yongchon. Important in this was the decimation of North Korean divisional artillery that had advanced near the town without supporting infantry and then found itself caught in counterbattery fire.

By September 12, the KPA 15th Division was in full retreat. In the process it abandoned significant quantities of equipment, including large numbers of small arms, several vehicles, and at least one self-propelled gun. The KPA also left behind large numbers of killed and wounded. At about the same time that the breach in the South Korean lines was sealed, other ROKA troops from farther east reestablished contact with the 8th Division.

This ROKA victory, which came despite a relative weakness in organic artillery, helped preserve the integrity of the northern end of the perimeter at a vital point. Close air support provided by the U.S. Air Force, U.S. Navy, and U.S. Marine Corps also contributed to the South Korean success, even though the Americans' early efforts in the air frequently constituted operational improvisations. The Battle of Yongchon helped make possible the UNC breakout from the perimeter after the September 15 Inchon Landing.

D. R. DORONDO

See also

Pusan Perimeter and Breakout; Walker, Walton Harris

References

Appleman, Roy E. *United States Army in Korea: South to the Naktong, North to the Yalu.* Washington, DC: Office of the Chief of Military History, 1961.

Ent, Uzal W. *Fighting on the Brink: Defense of the Pusan Perimeter.* Paducah, KY: Turner, 1996.

Millett, Allan R. "Korea, 1950–1953." In *Case Studies in the Development of Close Air Support,* edited by Benjamin Franklin Cooling, 345–410. Washington, DC: Office of Air Force History, 1990.

Mossman, Billy C. *United States Army in the Korean War: Ebb and Flow, November 1950–July 1951.* Washington, DC: U.S. Army Center of Military History, 1990.

Yosu-Sunchon Rebellion
Event Date: October 1948

Rebellion involving the 14th Regiment of the Republic of Korea Army (ROKA, South Korean Army). The 14th came into being on May 14, 1948, based on a battalion detached from the 4th Regiment stationed in Kwangju. However, by October 19, 1948, the regiment had become embroiled in rebellion. At that time, one of the main strategies of the South Korean Workers' Party (SKWP) was to infiltrate and influence military units. The 14th Regiment was one such target. This activity was aided by the fact that the original battalion commander, Captain An Yong Gil, was a leftist sympathizer.

The regiment was split into three factions. Its overall commander, Colonel O Tong Gi, sympathized with the nationalists and belonged to the Korean Independence Party, which opposed the establishment of a separate South Korean government. The other two factions included officers and regular soldiers who were effectively controlled by the SKWP.

The SKWP in South Cholla Province placed representatives from its Military Direction Section in the 14th Regiment. They were quite successful in influencing recruitment of leftist supporters recommended by the SKWP and blocking right-wing conscripts. They even managed to eliminate many right-wing supporters who had previously been recruited. As a result, the majority of the regiment became either leftist activists or sympathizers. The seeds of rebellion had been sown.

The Cheju-do Rebellion was also underway at this time, and on October 19, 1948, army headquarters ordered the 1st Battalion of the 14th Regiment to leave for Cheju-do to help quell the riots there. Its departure was scheduled for 9:00 p.m. that evening; however, at 8:00 p.m., Sergeant-Major Chi Chang Su, a lower-ranking SKWP activist in the regiment, spontaneously ordered 40 soldiers to occupy the armory and ammunition locker. Shortly thereafter he assembled the 1st Battalion, along with soldiers from the other two battalions, and proceeded to incite them to reject their reassignment to Cheju-do, overthrow the police authorities, and establish themselves as a "people's army for national unification."

Some 3,000 soldiers decided to follow Chi. They moved into the city of Yosu, where they were joined by another 600 leftist supporters and students. They then attacked police stations, killed many police officers, and stormed the city government buildings. By dawn on October 20, the rebels had taken control of Yosu, instituted a People's Committee, and were summarily executing right-wing activists.

On the morning of October 20, between 500 and 600 rebel troops advanced on Sunchon to join forces with two other companies of the 14th Regiment already stationed there. By early afternoon, Sunchon also was controlled by the rebel forces. The next rebel step was to proceed in three directions: toward Hakgu-ri to the northwest, Kwangyang to the east, and Polgyo to the southwest. En route they again attacked police stations, killed police officers, and executed right-wing activists.

To deal with this threat, on October 21, the South Korean government established a combat command in Kwangju with seven battalions and declared a state of martial law in the region. Government forces planned to encircle the Yosu Peninsula to entrap the rebel troops and cut off any escape to the mountains in the northeast. However, the operation failed because of inefficient coordination. The commander of the 15th Regiment was apathetic in his approach to the operation and ultimately surrendered to the rebel troops without resistance, and one company of soldiers even joined the rebels. In addition, unrealistic government pressure forced troops to advance in columns rather than encircling the peninsula; consequently, many rebels were able to escape into the mountains and continue their fight by means of guerrilla warfare.

The overall cost in human lives from the rebellion was substantial. A journal record from November 9, 1948, fixed the number of deaths in south Cholla at 2,533, with a further 883 seriously wounded. However, the number of victims continued to mount from the persistent guerrilla warfare and quest for revenge.

Officially, the SKWP neither planned nor authorized the rebellion. Apparently, the uprising was rather a spontaneous event initiated from within the 14th Regiment itself. Sergeant-Major Chi decided on his own to begin the rebellion, disobeying instructions to desist from a superior SKWP officer, Lieutenant Kim Chi Hoe. However, once the rebellion was under way, the SKWP assumed the credit, and this event then paved the way for the spread of guerrilla warfare throughout most of South Korea during 1949.

The rebellion forced South Korean authorities to accelerate their efforts to eliminate SKWP influence in the army. By July 1949, more than 4,700 officers and soldiers had been dismissed. Thereafter, there were no further military revolts.

HEO MAN HO

See also

Cheju-do Rebellion

References

Cumings, Bruce. *The Origins of the Korean War.* 2 vols. Princeton, NJ: Princeton University Press, 1981, 1990.

Headquarters, U.S. Armed Forces in Korea (USAFIK). *History of the United States Armed Forces in Korea* (HUSAFIK), Vols. 1–3. Seoul: Dolbegye, 1989.

———. *G-2 Periodic Report,* Vols. 1–7. Unchon, ROK: Institute of Asian Culture Studies, Hallym University, 1988–1989.

Kim, Chom Gon. *Hanguk Chonjaeng kwa Rodongdang Chollyak* [The Korean War and the Strategy of the Korean Workers' Party]. Seoul: Pakyongsa, 1983.

Millett, Allan R. *The War for Korea, 1945–1950: A House Burning.* Lawrence: University Press of Kansas, 2005.

Younger, Kenneth

Birth Date: December 15, 1908
Death Date: May 19, 1976

Minister of state at the British Foreign Office from 1946 to 1951. Born on December 15, 1908, at Colton, Dunfermline, in Scotland, Kenneth Younger was educated at New College, Oxford, where he obtained third-class honors in philosophy, politics, and economics in 1930. As an Oxford undergraduate he also broke with his family's Conservative Party allegiance to join the Labour Party. In 1932, he was called to the bar, and he practiced law until 1939. During World War II, he served in the Intelligence Corps, eventually holding the rank of major and serving under Field Marshal Bernard Montgomery.

Younger won a parliamentary seat in 1945 and was quickly regarded as one of the most promising younger Labour members. Within a year, he was appointed minister of state in the Foreign Office, deputy to Foreign Secretary Ernest Bevin, whose deteriorating health meant that much responsibility fell on Younger's shoulders. The two men were described as resembling "an old polar bear attended by a lively cub," and Bevin quickly came to rely heavily on Younger's outstanding efficiency. Some senior Foreign Office figures, by contrast, thought him a "conceited young man" and were irritated by his readiness to accept that Britain's international world stature had changed and its foreign policies should be adapted to suit new circumstances.

During the Korean War, Younger initiated the discussion of several important issues that badly needed consideration by both the Foreign Office and the cabinet. In September 1950, he was the first to speculate as to whether United Nations Command (UNC) forces should cross the 38th Parallel if and when the Inchon Landing succeeded, a question that senior Foreign Office officials had not considered.

Younger was the leader of the British delegation at the United Nations (UN) that argued strongly in support of the resolution of October 7, 1950, authorizing offensive operations north of the parallel. Younger also raised the difficult problem of—in the event that the People's Republic of China (PRC) and the United States should go to war over Taiwan (then known as Formosa)—whether Britain should support its U.S. ally. The Foreign Office reluctantly concluded that Britain could not remain aloof from such a conflict and would be forced to assist the United States against China. Bevin, at that time ill in the hospital, agreed but declined to bring the matter up in the cabinet, partly because he feared that the issue might prove divisive and partly to preserve his freedom of action. To Younger's surprise, when he brought the subject up with Minister of Labour Aneurin Bevan, the latter concurred that, given Britain's global international alliance with the United States, the country had no choice but to join forces with its patron in the event of such a war.

In January 1951, however, Younger urged Prime Minister Clement Attlee to withstand U.S. pressure for a limited war against China involving the mainland's own territory, the imposition of economic sanctions, and the passage of a UN resolution condemning China as an aggressor. While Attlee and Bevin believed that the need to retain American goodwill was ultimately their highest priority, they followed Younger's advice insofar as was possible, attempting to restrain U.S. condemnation of China and the imposition of sanctions, successfully avoiding the war's extension to Chinese territory, and urging the opening of negotiations with the communist forces with the objective of reaching a compromise peace settlement.

Younger lost his post following the Conservative Party victory in the general election of 1951, but he retained his seat in Parliament. Suffering from poor health and finding the opposition benches somewhat unrewarding, he left Parliament in 1959 to become director of the Royal Institute of International Affairs, where he constantly urged that Britain should adjust to the loss of superpower status by placing more emphasis on its role in the UN and regional and world cooperative organizations. In addition, Younger served on numerous government and private commissions, committees, and organizations. He died in London on May 19, 1976.

PRISCILLA ROBERTS

See also

Attlee, Clement Richard; Bevan, Aneurin; Bevin, Ernest; Morrison, Herbert Stanley; United Kingdom

References

Bullock, Alan. *Ernest Bevin: Foreign Secretary, 1945–1951.* New York: Norton, 1983.

Butler, Rohan, and M. E. Pelly, eds. *Documents on British Foreign Policy Overseas,* Series 2, Vol. 4, *Korea, 1950–1951.* London: HMSO, 1995.

Grimond, J. "Younger, Sir Kenneth Gilmour (1908–1976)." In *Oxford Dictionary of National Biography: From the Earliest Times to the Year 2000,* Vol. 60, edited by H. C. G. Matthew and Brian Harrison, 961–963. Oxford: Oxford University Press, 2004.

Lowe, Peter. *Containing the Cold War in East Asia: British Policies toward Japan, China and Korea, 1948–1953.* Manchester, UK: Manchester University Press, 1997.

MacDonald, Callum A. *Britain and the Korean War.* Oxford, UK: Blackwell, 1990.

Warner, Geoffrey, ed. *In the Midst of Events: The Foreign Office Diaries and Papers of Kenneth G. Younger, February 1950–October 1951.* New York: Routledge, 2005.

Yu Chae Hung
Birth Date: August 3, 1921

General of the Republic of Korea Army (ROKA, South Korean Army) and commander of the 7th Division at the beginning of the Korean War. Born in Nagoya, Japan, on August 3, 1921, Yu Chae Hung graduated from the Japanese Military Academy in 1940. His father, Yu Sung Yol, had graduated from the same school in 1914. At the time of the liberation of Korea in 1945, both Yu and his father were officers (captain and colonel, respectively) in the Japanese Army.

Returning to Korea after the end of Japanese colonial rule in 1945, Yu entered the U.S. military government's Military English-Language School in Seoul, as did many other Koreans who had served as officers in the Japanese Army. From January 1946 until August 1948, Yu served as a high-ranking officer in the Korean Constabulary and contributed much to the creation of the ROKA. In April 1949, Colonel Yu commanded a task force charged with wiping out remaining guerrillas on Cheju-do (island) who had revolted against the American military government in southern Korea a year before. Then, promoted to brigadier general in May 1949, he became the commander of the 6th ROKA Division at Chunchon. In January 1950, he took command of the 2nd Division at Taejon, and the next May, he commanded the 7th Division at Uijongbu. Undoubtedly such frequent change of commanding officers affected the combat readiness of the ROKA at the beginning of the Korean War.

The Uijongbu corridor, only 30 miles north of Seoul, was the site of the principal Korean People's Army (KPA, North Korean Army) attack on June 25, 1950. Caught by surprise by the KPA 3rd and 4th divisions supported by tanks of the 105th Armored Brigade, Yu's 7th Division suffered heavily. Nonetheless, on the morning of June 26, Yu counterattacked and achieved a short-term success. Heavily outnumbered, his troops could not hold off the KPA advance for long, however. ROKA chief of staff Chae Pyong Dok's effort to bring up reserves and to counterattack proved both inept and futile.

Promoted to command the ROKA II Corps in July 1950, Yu showed competent and aggressive leadership in the September Battle of Yongchon and in the United Nations Command (UNC) offensive across the 38th Parallel during October and November. At Yongchon, where the KPA hoped to break through the Pusan Perimeter, Yu took a leading role in the destruction of the KPA 15th Division; and it was his 6th Division that first reached the Yalu River, on October 26. Most in the ROKA regarded Yu as their most knowledgeable general.

After the Chinese People's Volunteer Army (CPVA, Chinese Army) entered the war in October, Yu and the units under his command encountered serious problems. In the first phase of the Chinese military intervention, from late October to early November, the CPVA hit Yu's corps at Onjong and Huichon in the Chongchon River basin on the right flank of the U.S. Eighth Army. The Chinese second-phase offensive at the end of November again struck the ROKA II Corps, but this much stronger attack brought its collapse and the disastrous defeat of the U.S. Eighth Army.

In January 1951, Yu became commander of the ROKA III Corps and concurrently deputy chief of staff of the ROKA. Then, in May 1951, during the Chinese sixth offensive, Yu's III Corps at Hyon-ni suffered one of the worst defeats of the war. Facing a situation in which the corps would have been cut off, Yu ordered the 9th Division to withdraw, covered by the 3rd Division. But the Chinese succeeded in cutting off both divisions, the men of which simply fled in disorder into the hills, abandoning their equipment. This defeat was largely attributable to the fact that Yu and the two division commanders were not getting along with one another. The commander of the Eighth Army, General James A. Van Fleet, pointed out that the most pressing problem in the ROKA at the time was development of leadership qualities.

After the war, Yu attended and graduated from the U.S. Army Command and General Staff College in 1954. He then served as ROKA deputy chief of staff in 1956, chairman of the Joint Chiefs of Staff (JCS) in 1957, and commander of the First Army in 1959. He retired from the army as a lieutenant general after the student revolution in April 1960. Under the presidency of Park Chung Hee (Pak Chung-hui), he served as the minister of defense between 1971 and 1974.

To Woong Chung

See also

Chae Pyong Dok; 38th Parallel, Decision to Cross; Van Fleet, James Alward; Yongchon, Battle of

References

Appleman, Roy E. *United States Army in Korea: South to the Naktong, North to the Yalu.* Washington, DC: Office of the Chief of Military History, 1961.

Mossman, Billy C. *United States Army in the Korean War: Ebb and Flow, November 1950–July 1951.* Washington, DC: U.S. Army Center of Military History, 1990.

Yu, Jae Hung. *Kyokdong ui Sewol* [The Turbulent Years: Memoirs]. Seoul: Ulyu Munhwa Sa, 1994.

Yun Chi Yong
Birth Date: February 10, 1898
Death Date: February 9, 1996

Conservative politician in the Republic of Korea (ROK, South Korea). Born to a prominent family in Seoul on February 10, 1898, Yun Chi Yong was educated in Japan (at Waseda University) and in the United States (at the University of Hawaii; and at Princeton, Columbia, George Washington, and American universities). After 1923, he worked for Syngman Rhee in the United States, but he returned to Korea in 1937. After Korea's liberation at the end of World War II, Yun, Song Chin U, and Kim Song Su formed the Korean Democratic Party, a conservative, right-wing political party.

Yun was one of South Korean president Syngman Rhee's most trusted advisers. From August 1945 until the outbreak of the Korean War, Yun was chief secretary to Rhee. After the establishment of South Korea, Yun became Vice Speaker of the National Assembly and the first South Korean minister of home affairs. During the early years, Yun was consistent in his activities as a staunch anticommunist conservative politician.

In August 1950, Yun was appointed minister to France. He never assumed the post, as he was a member of the South Korean delegation to the United Nations (UN). He returned to Korea in January 1951. The next year he was elected to the National Assembly, defeating former minister of home affairs and chief opponent of Rhee Cho Pyong Ok.

Yun was an interesting figure, noteworthy as the only prominent conservative politician in South Korea who argued that the Korean War resulted from a U.S. attempt to test the Soviet Union's Far Eastern policy by using South Korea as bait. This position, that the Korean War was provoked by the United States, was also held by Louise Yim (Yim Yong Sin), first South Korean minister of commercial affairs and a staunch Rhee supporter.

After Park Chung Hee's May 1961 military coup d'état, Yun helped found the Democratic Republican Party, the government party, and he served as chairman of its executive committee. He was Park's chief campaign manager in the 1963 presidential election and, after Park's victory, he became mayor of Seoul. Yun remained a loyal Park supporter and a leading member of the National Assembly. He died in Seoul on February 9, 1996.

JINWUNG KIM

See also

Korean Democratic Party; Rhee, Syngman; Yim, Louise

References

Matray, James I., ed. *Historical Dictionary of the Korean War.* Westport, CT: Greenwood, 1991.

Taehan Minguk Kuksa Ochon Nyonsa Pyonchan Wiwon Hoe. *Taehan Minguk Hyondae Immulsa Taejon* [The Great Contemporary Biographical Dictionary of the Republic of Korea]. Seoul: Taehan Minguk Kuksa Ochon Nyonsa Pyonchan Wiwon Hoe, 1998.

Z

Zhang Hanfu

Birth Date: November 7, 1905
Death Date: January 1972

Vice foreign minister of the People's Republic of China (PRC) during the Korean War. Born on November 7, 1905, in Wujin, Jiangsu Province, Zhang Hanfu (Chang Han Fu) studied in the United States, where he became a communist and acquired a good command of English, which was to stand him in good stead in his years in the foreign ministry after the establishment of the PRC.

On his return to China, Zhang immediately joined the Chinese Communist Party (CCP). From 1931, he assumed positions of leadership, first in the Guangdong and then in the Jiangsu party machineries. While working in Jiangsu, in the mid-1930s, he was arrested by Guomindang (GMD, Nationalist) authorities, who imprisoned him in Suzhou.

After his release, Zhang embarked on the first of the two main facets of his career—journalism in support of the communist position. This phase lasted until the end of 1948. During this period of some 15 years, Zhang lived and wrote prolifically in Shanghai, Wuhan, Chongqing, and Hong Kong. He published numerous articles in many of the well-known journals and newspapers of the time, the more important examples of which were *Dushu Shenghuo* (*Journal of Reading Life*), *Qunzhong* (*People Magazine*), and *Xinhua Ribao* (*New China Daily*). In fact, Zhang was instrumental in starting or sustaining the last two named publications. He wrote under aliases, according to the political necessity of those days.

During the period of the Chinese Civil War (1945–1949), Zhang was in Hong Kong and Shanghai, playing a pivotal role in communist propaganda work in the former location. It was after his return to China at the end of 1948 that he began to shift to the second important aspect of his career: foreign affairs. The beginning of the change of course can be traced to the autumn of 1944, when he helped Dong Biwu prepare for the founding conference of the United Nations (UN), which took place the next year in San Francisco. Zhang had attended the conference as Dong Biwu's assistant.

After the January 1949 communist victory in Tianjin, Zhang took charge of its Foreign Affairs Department, and he assumed the same post in Shanghai after its liberation in May 1949. Zhang's performance in Tianjin and Shanghai, although brief, must have been impressive enough, as he was then transferred to Beijing, where he was appointed a vice minister in the Foreign Ministry of the newly established communist regime, working under Foreign Minister Zhou Enlai.

During the Korean War, Zhang was one of the key individuals dealing with the diplomatic aspects of the war. However, as expected, his work and contributions in the foreign ministry could hardly attract attention, the bulk of which was naturally drawn to the charismatic foreign minister. This situation persisted even after Chen Yi replaced Zhou as foreign minister early in 1958, in that Chen also was overshadowed by Zhou, who retained considerable influence in the ministry.

Until the mid-1960s, Zhang traveled widely to many parts of Asia, the Middle East, and Europe as deputy to either Zhou or Chen and participated in a number of important conferences and events. With the onslaught of the Cultural Revolution, Zhang, as with so many others who had long supported the communist cause, suddenly found himself the target of persecution. He died a painful and humiliating death in prison in January 1972.

CHAN LAU KIT CHING

See also

China, People's Republic of; Chinese Civil War; Zhou Enlai

References

Klein, Donald W., and Anne B. Clark. *Biographic Dictionary of Chinese Communism, 1921–1965.* Cambridge, MA: Harvard University Press, 1971.

Matray, James I., ed. *Historical Dictionary of the Korean War.* Westport, CT: Greenwood, 1991.

Xia, Yan. "Zhang Han Fu Wenji Daixu." In *Zhang Hanfu Wenji* [Selected Works of Zang Hanfu], edited by Xinhua Ribao and Qunzhong Zhouhan Shixuehue, 1–6. Nanjing: Jiangsu Renmin Chubanshe, 1987.

Zhang Tingfa
Birth Date: April 9, 1918

General and deputy commander of the Eleventh Army of the Chinese People's Volunteer Army (CPVA, Chinese Army) during the Korean War. Born in Sha County, Fujian Province, on April 9, 1918, Zhang Tingfa (Tsang Ting Fa) joined the Red Army in 1933 and the Chinese Communist Party (CCP) in 1936. After participating in the Long March, between 1935 and 1942 he was on the staff of the 129th Division in the Eighth Route Army. In 1942, he was promoted to director of operations in the Taihang Military District.

When the Korean War began in June 1950, Zhang's Eleventh Army of the People's Liberation Army (PLA, Chinese Communist Army) 3rd Army Group was in Sichuan Province in southwest China. In early 1951, the Eleventh Army moved to north China, and one of its divisions, the 31st, was transferred to the Twelfth Army, which entered Korea in early 1951. The remainder of the Eleventh Army, the 32nd and 33rd divisions, was combined with the 182nd Division of the Sixty-first Army to form the reorganized Eleventh Army; it entered Korea in mid-1951. Zhang's Eleventh Army was in Korea until October 1952, when it returned to China and was transferred to the new People's Liberation Army Air Force (PLAAF) Fifth Army in Zhejiang Province. Upon returning to China, Zhang was promoted to deputy chief of staff of the PLAAF and later became its chief of staff. Zhang was promoted to major general in 1955. Promoted to commander of the PLAAF in 1977, he was a member of the powerful Political Bureau (Politburo) of the CCP's Central Committee from 1978 to 1985. After seven years as commander of the PLAAF, Zhang retired in 1985.

RICHARD WEIXING HU

See also

China, People's Republic of, People's Liberation Army Air Force; Chinese People's Volunteer Army

References

Guo Huaruo et al., eds. *Jiefangjun Junshi Dacidian* [Dictionary of PLA Military History]. Changchun: Jilin Renmin Chubanshe, 1993.

Wu Rugao et al., eds. *Zhongguo Junshi Renwu Dacidian* [Dictionary of Chinese Military Figures]. Beijing: Xinhua Chubanshe, 1989.

Zhongguo Junshi Dabaike Quanshu [Chinese Military Encyclopedia]. Military History, Vols. 1–3. Beijing: Junshi Kexue Chubanshe, 1997.

Zhou Enlai
Birth Date: March 5, 1898
Death Date: January 9, 1976

Senior Communist Party leader, prime minister (1949–1976), and foreign minister (1949–1958) of the People's Republic of China (PRC). In a career spanning nearly six turbulent decades, Zhou Enlai (Chou En-lai) became known as the "indispensable man" of China's communist regime. A superhuman administrator, master diplomat, and supremely skilled political tactician, Zhou was a key party leader during the communists' long struggle for power. Named China's prime minister on the day the People's Republic was founded on October 1, 1949, he remained in that post for more than 26 years until his death. Born on March 5, 1898, in Jiangsu Province, Zhou was known as a talented actor in school plays. At 19 he went to Japan to study, but he returned two years later to join the ferment of the May Fourth Movement, named for the date of massive student demonstrations in 1919 calling for modernization and democracy (the same slogans would be revived 70 years later by student protesters in Tiananmen Square).

After being imprisoned briefly for his political activities, Zhou left China in late 1920 for France, where he helped organize a branch of the brand-new Chinese Communist Party (CCP). Returning after four years abroad, Zhou embarked on his revolutionary career, participating in the Shanghai Uprising (1927), the Long March (1934–1935), the guerrilla war against Japan (1937–1945), and the civil war against the Guomindang (GMD, Nationalists) led by Jiang Jieshi (Chiang Kai-shek) (1945–1949). In his early years in the party, Zhou outranked Mao Zedong in the leadership. But when Mao took command during the Long March, Zhou willingly assumed a subordinate role in their partnership. For more than 40 years, he would be the movement's supreme survivor—the only one of Mao's inner circle never to fall victim to the incessant purges, intrigues, power struggles, and policy shifts that characterized Mao's long and erratic reign.

When the Korean War began in June 1950, less than a year after the PRC was founded, Zhou played a key role in carrying out Mao's decisions and in orchestrating Chinese diplomacy. In early July, Zhou presided over the initial deliberations that led to the creation of the Northeast Border Defense Army (NBDA) and the Chinese military buildup in the border region. Thereafter, Zhou supervised military preparations, chairing a series of crucial meetings to decide on the structure, strategy, deployment, and logistical needs of the border force.

Meanwhile, Zhou was also responsible for managing China's relations with both its allies and adversaries. Zhou personally instructed Indian ambassador in Beijing Sardar K. M. Panikkar to

Zhou Enlai was prime minister of the People's Republic of China during 1949–1975 and concurrently foreign minister during 1949–1958. This photograph was taken in the 1950s. (Bettmann/Corbis)

warn the United States that China would enter the war if U.S. forces crossed the 38th Parallel into the Democratic People's Republic of Korea (DPRK, North Korea); it was also Zhou who led a Chinese delegation to Moscow to redeem a Soviet promise of military support, including air strikes, for Chinese troops in Korea. However, neither move achieved the desired result. U.S. leaders dismissed Zhou's warning as a bluff; in Moscow, Soviet leader Joseph Stalin reneged on providing air cover.

As the Korean peace negotiations entered their climactic phase following Stalin's death on March 5, 1953, it was Zhou, again, who signaled that China was ready to end the conflict. Shortly after returning from Stalin's funeral, Zhou offered a compromise on the prisoner of war (POW) issue that had knotted the truce talks for many months. Although the wording was oblique, Zhou in effect withdrew Beijing's demand for the forced repatriation of Chinese POWs who did not wish to return to China. The concession cleared the way for the signing of the Korean armistice four months later.

The following year, Zhou headed China's delegation to the 1954 Geneva negotiations on settling the French Indochina War. Soon after arriving, he unexpectedly encountered U.S. secretary of state John Foster Dulles in an anteroom. Zhou offered his hand, but Dulles coldly turned his back and walked out of the room. The incident symbolized the deep-frozen U.S.-Chinese hostility that

would endure for nearly two more decades. Despite Dulles's snub, Zhou became the crucial conciliator in the Geneva talks, personally persuading the Vietnamese communist leader Ho Chi Minh to make substantial concessions in return for a settlement.

During his long tenure as prime minister, working in enigmatic partnership with the mercurial Mao, Zhou used his extraordinary organizational talent to keep China's vast administrative and economic bureaucracy functioning through the constant upheavals of Mao's policies. As the party's most skilled, supple, and polished negotiator, he continued to serve as China's chief emissary to the outside world, seldom failing to charm even the most wary foreigners. He also played a crucial role as mediator and conciliator in disputes inside the party leadership.

In 1971, Zhou received President Richard Nixon's emissary, Henry Kissinger, in Beijing, paving the way for the restoration of U.S.-Chinese relations and erasing, at last, the memory of Dulles's rebuff in Geneva 17 years before.

Zhou died in Beijing on January 9, 1976, just eight months before Mao's death, leaving behind a widely accepted image of a wise, flexible, humane statesman.

ARNOLD R. ISAACS

See also

China, People's Republic of; Chinese People's Volunteer Army; Dulles, John Foster; Geneva Conference; Mao Zedong; Panikkar, Sardar K. M.

References

Chen Jian. *Mao's China and the Cold War.* Chapel Hill: University of North Carolina Press, 2000.

Gao Wenqian. *Zhou Enlai: The Last Perfect Revolutionary.* New York: Public Affairs, 2007.

Han Suyin. *Eldest Son: Zhou Enlai and the Making of Modern China, 1898–1976.* New York: Hill and Wang, 1994.

Wilson, Dick. *Zhou Enlai: A Biography.* New York: Viking, 1984.

Xia, Yafeng. *Negotiating with the Enemy; U.S.-China Talks during the Cold War, 1949–1972.* Bloomington: Indiana University Press, 2006.

Zinchenko, Konstantin E.
Birth Date: 1909
Death Date: Unknown

Assistant secretary-general at the United Nations (UN) Department of Political and Security Affairs during the Korean War. Born in Ukraine in 1909, Konstantin E. Zinchenko graduated from the Mining Academy in Moscow in 1931. He joined the Soviet Foreign Ministry in 1940 and in 1942 was counselor at the embassy in London. He returned to Moscow at the end of the war, and in June 1948, he became first counselor and secretary-general of the Soviet Union to the UN. In April 1949, he joined the UN Secretariat.

At the UN, Zinchenko was an enigmatic presence in discussions concerning the Korean War. He often attempted to influence negotiations between communist and noncommunist delegations, usually through unofficial gatherings and informal receptions. At first, U.S. diplomats took seriously his usefulness as a possible conduit for Soviet intentions; over time, as his suggestions proved to be seemingly unconnected to any communist authority, he became less and less credible.

In June 1950, as the UN voted on intervening in the Korean conflict, Zinchenko arranged a luncheon at a New York restaurant for Secretary-General Trygve Lie and 9 of the 11 Security Council members, including Soviet ambassador Jakob Malik. The Soviet Union was then boycotting the Security Council because of its refusal to seat a representative from the People's Republic of China (PRC), and discussion revolved around Lie's attempts to convince Malik to return and U.S. diplomat Ernest Gross's maneuvering to prevent it. As it worked out, Malik did not return for the crucial vote on intervention.

On August 20, 1950, Zinchenko received a copy of the secretary-general's memorandum concerning the legal basis for UN resolutions passed earlier in the summer that had authorized intervention. Sensing the potential difficulties of Zinchenko's position, Lie created a special committee within his office to deal with Korean matters, thereby avoiding Zinchenko's post of assistant secretary-general.

In April 1951, at a UN reception at Lake Success, New York, Zinchenko assembled an informal group of diplomats, including Gross, to discuss a message recently received from the Democratic People's Republic of Korea (DPRK, North Korea) suggesting withdrawal of all foreign forces from Korea. Zinchenko insisted that the North Korean request be taken seriously and, because of his involvement, many Western diplomats believed that the Soviet Union had orchestrated a proposal that could lead to substantive negotiations. This proved illusory, however, as the communists soon launched a spring offensive.

Early in 1952, Zinchenko again became a player, this time in the matter of repatriation of prisoners of war (POWs). His idea that a cease-fire could be initiated without dealing with this very divisive issue was proposed to an Israeli diplomat in New York, who then passed it on to the Americans and British. It was hinted that an armistice could be secured on the basis of items already settled and that it would be activated when the POW problem was finally resolved. Nothing came of this, however.

Finally, in June 1952, Zinchenko once again sought out Gross. The issue revolved around repatriation of POWs and possible Chinese compromise on the topic. Zinchenko indicated to Gross that the Soviet Union might be willing to agree to de facto voluntary repatriation as long as the UN agreed to the principle of general repatriation. Before Gross could meet with him again, however, Zinchenko had left New York on July 9, 1952, for "vacation" in the Soviet Union. He never returned to New York. In September, after failing to reappear as scheduled, Soviet authorities informed UN officials that he was ill.

On May 26, 1953, UN Secretary-General Dag Hammarskjold accepted Zinchenko's resignation from a term that was not to have expired until February 1, 1954. Three years after he left New York, Zinchenko surfaced as a staff member on the English-language journal *Moscow News*. There were rumors that he had spent the intervening time in prison and that his Western lifestyle and ability to mix in New York society may have contributed to his downfall. It is not clear even now that he ever represented official Soviet views on the Korean War. It seems likely that he generally exceeded his instructions and simply offered his own opinions on the war, a practice that ultimately undercut his bureaucratic position.

ERIC JARVIS

See also

Cease-fire Negotiations; Gross, Ernest Arnold; Lie, Trygve Halvden; Malik, Jacob; Repatriation, Voluntary; Soviet Security Council Boycott; Soviet Union

References

Bailey, Sydney D. *The Korean Armistice.* New York: St. Martin's, 1992.

Detzer, David. *Thunder of the Captains: The Short Summer of 1950.* New York: Cromwell, 1977.

Kaufman, Burton I. *The Korean War: Challenges in Crisis, Credibility and Command.* 2nd ed. New York: McGraw-Hill, 1997.

Stueck, William W., Jr. *The Korean War: An International History.* Princeton, NJ: Princeton University Press, 1995.

United Nations. *Yearbook of the United Nations, 1950, 1951, 1952, 1953.* New York: Columbia University Press, 1951, 1952, 1953, 1954.

Zorin, Valerian
Birth Date: January 13, 1902
Death Date: January 14, 1986

Soviet diplomat and permanent Soviet representative to the United Nations (UN) in the last year of the Korean War, 1952–1953. Born on January 13, 1902, in Novocherkassk, Rostov, Valerian Alexandrovitch Zorin was educated at the High Communist Institute of Education. From 1922 to 1932, he held an important post in the Central Committee of Komsomol; from 1933 to 1935, he pursued postgraduate education at the High Communist Institute of Education. In 1941, he transferred to the Ministry of Foreign Affairs, where, until 1942, he was assistant secretary-general. He then headed its European Department. In 1945, he became the first post–World War II Soviet ambassador to the Republic of Czechoslovakia.

In 1947, Zorin became deputy minister of foreign affairs, a post he held until 1955, and again during 1956 and 1957. He was the Soviet delegate to the UN Economic Commission on Europe and used that position to denounce U.S. aid to Greece and Turkey. In July 1947, Zorin announced that the Soviet Union would not participate in the Marshall Plan.

As deputy foreign minister, Zorin informed U.S. representatives that the Soviet Union would not intervene in the Korean War. Concurrent with his foreign ministry post, Zorin was ambassador to the UN in 1952 and 1953; he replaced Jacob Malik at the UN in October 1952 and served there until April 1953, a month after Soviet premier Joseph Stalin's death, when Andrei Y. Vyshinskii took over at the UN.

From 1955 to 1960, Zorin was ambassador to the Federal Republic of Germany (FRG, West Germany). He returned to the UN as Soviet permanent representative from 1960 to 1962. In 1956, he was made a candidate member of the Communist Party Central Committee, and in 1961, he became a full member. From 1965 to 1971, he was ambassador to France. He also served as the Soviet Union's representative to disarmament talks in Geneva. He retired from government service in 1971. Zorin died in Moscow on January 14, 1986.

Spencer C. Tucker

See also

Malik, Jacob; Soviet Union; Stalin, Joseph; Vyshinskii, Andrei Ianuarovich

References

International Who's Who, 1972–73. 36th ed. London: Europa, 1972.

Moritz, Charles, ed. *Current Biography Yearbook, 1986.* New York: H. W. Wilson, 1986.

Appendix A

Order of Battle: United Nations, Democratic People's Republic of Korea, and People's Republic of China

An order of battle (OB) is a listing of military units or organizations by nation, geographic area, campaign, or battle. This is an OB of some of the principal United Nations Command (UNC), Korean People's Army (KPA, North Korean Army), and Chinese People's Volunteer Army (CPVA, Chinese Army) Korean War commands. Unless otherwise specified, dates in parentheses are dates of arrival in Korea.

United Nations Command

Upon the outbreak of the Korean War, the United Nations (UN) Security Council passed three resolutions that condemned the attack, called upon UN member states to assist the Republic of Korea to "repel the armed attack and to restore international peace and security in the area," asked UN states to make forces available "to a unified command under the United States," and requested that the United States designate a force commander. Eventually, 15 UN nations, in addition to the United States, sent combat forces, while 5 other nations sent medical units. President Harry S. Truman designated General Douglas MacArthur, then supreme commander Allied Powers (SCAP) and commander in chief of the U.S. Far East Command (CINCFE), to be commander in chief of the United Nations Command (CINCUNC). In mid-July 1950 the president of the Republic of Korea (ROK, South Korea) placed the South Korean military forces under the CINCUNC. Thus, all military forces in the coalition opposing the communist forces of the DPRK (Democratic People's Republic of Korea, North Korea) and the People's Republic of China (PRC) came under the United Nations Command (UNC).

United States

Far East Command

In 1947 the U.S. Joint Chiefs of Staff (JCS) established two unified commands in the Pacific: the Pacific Command, headquartered in Hawaii with responsibilities in the Central Pacific, and the Far East Command (abbreviated FECOM by the JCS and FEC by the command itself), headquartered in Tokyo, Japan, with responsibility for Japan, the Ryukyu Islands (Okinawa), the Philippines, and the Mariana, Bonin, and Volcano Islands. At the start of the Korean War, Korea was added to the responsibilities of the commander in chief, Far East (CINCFE). In 1952 the responsibility for the Mariana Islands was transferred to the Pacific Command.

U.S. Army
Eighth Army

The overall U.S. Army headquarters in Korea was the U.S. Eighth Army in Korea (EUSAK, redesignated U.S. Eighth Army, EUSA, in 1952). Except for the period August to December 1950, when X Corps operated independently, all U.S. Army, U.S. Marine Corps, and United Nations (UN) ground forces as well as most of the Republic of Korea Army (ROKA, South Korea Army) came under the Eighth Army. The Eighth Army was responsible not only for planning and conducting combat operations but also for logistic support within Korea, development of the ROKA, control of prisoners of war (POWs), the administration of civil relief to the Korean civilian population in the war zone, and political and economic relations with the South Korean government. These additional tasks became an increasing burden, so in 1952 CINCFE established a separate command, the Korean Communications Zone (KCOMZ), to assume these responsibilities outside the combat zone.

The United States eventually deployed eight infantry divisions, a marine division, and numerous combat support and combat service support units to Korea during the war. Early in the war, the U.S. Army I, IX and X Corps were formed to provide command and control over these divisions. A U.S. Army corps had no fixed organization and may have consisted of from two to five divisions with varying numbers of combat support such as artillery, engineer, and antiaircraft battalions and combat service support such as medical, signal, transportation, and quartermaster battalions or companies attached to it, depending on the terrain and mission.

When the 1st Cavalry Division and the 24th and 25th Infantry divisions deployed to Korea from Japan, each of their regiments, except the 24th Infantry Regiment in the 25th Division, had but two of their three authorized battalions. The field artillery battalions (FAB) had only two of the three authorized firing batteries except the 159th FAB, which had its three batteries. Each battery was authorized six howitzers. None of the regiments had their tank company, composed of 22 tanks. Nor did these divisions have a full heavy tank battalion of 71 tanks. Instead, each division had roughly the equivalent of a tank company (about 15 or so tanks). These were M-24 light tanks and no match for the Russian T-34s they would oppose. The 21st and 34th Infantry regiments each had a 1st and 3rd Battalion. All other regiments in Japan, except the 24th, had a 1st and 2nd Battalion. When the 34th Infantry was reduced to paper status, its 1st Battalion became the 3rd Battalion, 19th Infantry, and its 3rd Battalion became the 3rd Battalion, 21st Infantry. The 24th Regiment had all three authorized battalions.

DIVISIONS

1st Cavalry Division (arrived in Korea from Japan between July 18 and 22, 1950):

- 5th, 7th, and 8th Cavalry regiments
- 61st, 77th, and 99th 105-millimeter (mm) FABs; 82nd 155-mm FAB
- Company A, 71st Heavy Tank Battalion (until October 16, 1950); 6th Medium Tank Battalion; 70th Heavy Tank Battalion (assigned, but attached to the 24th Infantry Division)
- 8th Engineer Combat Battalion (ECB); 92nd AAA/AW (antiaircraft artillery/automatic weapons) Battalion

2nd Infantry Division (arrived in Korea from the United States between July 31 and August 20, 1950):

- 9th, 23rd, and 38th Infantry regiments
- 15th, 37th, and 38th 105-mm FABs; 502nd 155-mm FAB
- 72nd Medium Tank Battalion; 2nd ECB; 82nd AAA/AW Battalion

3rd Infantry Division (arrived from the United States in September 1950):

- 7th, 15th, and 30th Infantry regiments (30th replaced by the 65th, from Puerto Rico)
- 10th, 39th, and 58th 105-mm FABs; 999th FAB. (The 9th FAB 155-mm FA, ordinarily part of the 3rd Division, was sent to Korea prior to the rest of the division in order to support ROK troops. The 999th was detailed to replace it;

when the 9th was returned to the division, the 999th became part of corps artillery.)
- 64th Medium Tank Battalion; 10th ECB; 3rd AAA/AW Battalion

7th Infantry Division (Inchon Landing from Japan, September 16, 1950):

- 17th, 31st, and 32nd Infantry regiments
- 48th, 49th, and 57th 105-mm FABs; 31st 155-mm FAB
- Company A, 77th Heavy Tank Battalion (until October 16, 1950); 73rd Medium Tank Battalion; 13th ECB; 15th AAA/AW Battalion

24th Infantry Division (from Japan, first week of July 1950):

- 19th, 21st, and 34th regiments. (The 34th RCT was replaced by 5th Regimental Combat Team [RCT] on August 27, 1950. The 5th RCT had arrived from Hawaii on August 5. The 34th was reduced to zero strength and returned to Japan.)
- 13th, 52nd, and 63rd 105-mm FABs; 11th 155-mm FAB
- Company A, 78th Heavy Tank Battalion (until October 16, 1950); 70th Medium Tank Battalion (assigned but attached to the 1st Cavalry Division); 6th Tank Battalion (attached, assigned on November 10, 1951); 3rd ECB; 26th AAA/AW Battalion

25th Infantry Division (from Japan, between July 10 and 15, 1950):

- 24th (until October 1, 1951), 27th, 35th, and 14th (after October 1, 1951) Infantry regiments. (On October 1, 1951, the 24th Infantry Regiment and the 159th FAB, composed of black enlisted men and a mix of mostly white and some black officers, were disbanded, and their personnel were transferred to other commands in Korea. The 14th Infantry Regiment replaced the 24th, and the 69th FAB replaced the 159th in the 25th Division.)
- 8th, 64th, and 159th (until October 1, 1951) and 69th (after October 1, 1951) 105-mm FABs; 90th 155-mm FAB
- Company A, 79th Heavy Tank Battalion (until October 16, 1950), 89th Medium Tank Battalion; 65th ECB; 21st AAA/AW Battalion

40th Infantry Division (California National Guard division. This division was called to active duty on September 1, 1950, and deployed to Japan in April 1951. In February 1952 the 40th deployed to Korea and replaced the 24th Infantry Division, which relocated to Japan.):

- 160th, 223rd, and 224th Infantry regiments
- 143rd, 625th, and 980th 105-mm FABs; 981st 155-mm FAB
- 140th Medium Tank Battalion; 578th ECB; 140th AAA/AW Battalion

45th Infantry Division (Oklahoma National Guard division. This division was called to active duty on September 1, 1950, and deployed to Japan in April 1951. In December 1951 the 45th replaced the 1st Cavalry Division in Korea, and the latter went to Japan.):

- 179th, 180th, and 279th Infantry regiments
- 158th, 160th, and 171st 105-mm FABs; 189th 155-mm FAB
- 245th Medium Tank Battalion; 120th ECB; 145th AAA/AW Battalion

SEPARATE REGIMENTS

5th RCT (from Hawaii, July 31, 1950; initially attached to the 25th Infantry Division and then assigned to the 24th Infantry Division to replace the 34th Infantry Regiment):

- 5th Infantry Regiment
- 555th FAB (105-mm; each of the three firing batteries had 4 howitzers)
- 72nd Engineer Combat Company (ECC)

187th Airborne Infantry RCT (arrived from the United States in October 1950):

- 187th Infantry Regiment
- 674th FAB (105-mm)

INFANTRY BATTALIONS
(EMPLOYED INITIALLY AS SEPARATE BATTALIONS)

1st and 3rd battalions, 29th Infantry Regiment (arrived from Okinawa on July 24, 1950). Badly mauled in their first battles, they were redesignated on August 6, 1950: the 1st Battalion became the 3/35th Infantry, the 3rd Battalion became the 3/27th Infantry. On August 26, 1st Cavalry Division regiments gained their third battalions from the United States: the 3/7th Infantry, 3rd Division, became the 3/8th Cavalry; the 2/30th Infantry, 3rd Division, became the 3/7th Cavalry; and the 3/5th Cavalry was formed at Fort Carson, Colorado.

SOME NONDIVISIONAL TROOPS

Armor: 71st Heavy Tank Battalion; 78th Heavy Tank Battalion (individual companies assigned to the infantry divisions in Japan; inactivated October 16, 1950).

Artillery: NOTE: In addition to battalions, both antiaircraft and field artillery were often organized into larger formations of groups or brigades. The group or brigade had no fixed number or type of battalion. Artillery groups or brigades normally are organized to control two or more artillery battalions attached to a corps or army but may also be constituted for a particular campaign or period of time or for a special mission, such as the 10th AAA Group in Korea (see below). Furthermore, the number and type of battalions attached to the group are changeable with the desires of the commander organizing the group/brigade. A group may have a certain mix of battalions at one time and another later on.

ANTIAIRCRAFT ARTILLERY

- *Groups:* 10th, 29th, 41st, 227th. The 10th, which initially served as a field artillery group supporting ground forces in Korea, consisted of the 78th FAB (90-mm gun), the 2nd Heavy Mortar Battalion (4.2-inch mortars), and the 9th FAB (155-mm howitzer). Note that only the 78th was an antiaircraft battalion. This is an unusual organization for an antiaircraft group. The composition of the other groups, which controlled air defense units, varied throughout the war.
- *Brigade:* 44th. Arrived in Korea June 15, 1953, and assumed the responsibilities of the 10th Antiaircraft Artillery (AAA) Group for overall control of Korea air defense. Assigned to the Eighth Army but detached to Far East Air Forces (FAEF) on June 15, 1953, through the end of the war. Units assigned included the 24th, 68th, 76th, 78th, 739th, and 773rd AAA battalions; the 30th, 50th, 398th, 865th, and 933rd AAA/AW battalions; and the 525th AAA Operations Detachment.
- *Antiaircraft Automatic Weapons (AAA/AW) Battalions:* 15th, 29th, 30th, 50th, 52nd, 398th, 865th, 933rd. A small contingent from the 507th, named "Detachment X," was also in Korea for the first two campaigns of the war.
- *AAA Gun Battalions* (90-mm gun): 24th, 68th, 76th, 213th, 739th, 773rd.

FIELD ARTILLERY

- *Groups:* 5th. Attached to X Corps until December 12, 1950, when its assets were used to form the Headquarters and Headquarters Battery, X Corps Artillery. Reactivated January 5, 1952, to support and train South Korean artillery units.
- *Field Artillery (FA) Observation Battalions:* 1st, 235th.
- *Rocket Field Artillery:* 2nd Rocket FA Battery.
- *Searchlight Field Artillery Battalions:* 82nd, 92nd.
- *Field Artillery Battalions* (105-mm howitzer unless otherwise specified): 10th (attached to ROKA Capital Division); 11th (attached to ROKA 3rd Division), 16th (attached to ROKA 6th Division), 17th (8-inch howitzer); 18th (attached to ROKA 7th Division), 50th (attached to ROKA 8th Division), 58th, 75th, 96th, 145th, 159th (105-mm howitzer converted to 155-mm howitzer November 20, 1951, and converted to 240-mm howitzer May 12, 1953), 196th, 204th (155-mm howitzer), 424th, 555th (part of 5th RCT), 623rd, 674th (Airborne, part of 187th RCT), 780th (8-inch towed), 936th (155-mm howitzer), 937th, 955th.
- *Armored Field Artillery Battalions* (Later redesignated as Self-Propelled Artillery): 92nd (155-mm howitzer), 176th (105-mm howitzer), 213th (converted to 240-mm howitzer March 20, 1953), 300th, 987th (105-mm howitzer), 999th (155-mm howitzer; initially attached to 3rd Infantry Division to replace the 9th 155-mm FAB, which had been sent to Korea earlier to support South Korean troops; the

9th eventually returned to the 3rd Division, and the 999th became part of the corps artillery).

- *Mortar Battalion:* 2nd Chemical Mortar Battalion, redesignated 461st Heavy Mortar Battalion on June 22, 1953.

CHEMICAL

- *Smoke Generator Battalions:* 4th, 453rd
- *Smoke Generator Companies:* 68th, 69th, 71st, 376th, 388th

ENGINEER

- *Brigades:* 2nd Engineer Special Brigade (redesignated 2nd Engineer Amphibious Support Brigade in August 1952), 409th Engineer Brigade, 417th Engineer Aviation Brigade
- *Groups:*
  - *Engineer Aviation Groups:* 930th, 931st, 934th
  - *Engineer Combat Groups:* 19th, 36th, 1169th
  - *Engineer Construction Groups:* 2nd, 24th, 32nd, 44th, 8224th
  - *Engineer Maintenance and Supply Group:* 5000th
- *Battalions:*
  - *Engineer Aviation Battalions:* 366th, 802nd, 808th, 809th, 811th, 822nd, 839th, 840th, 841st, 1903rd
  - *Engineer Combat Battalions* (ECB): 8th (minus C Company), 11th, 14th, 73rd, 74th, 116th, 151st, 185th, 194th, 378th, 1092nd, 1343rd
  - *Engineer Construction Battalions:* 44th, 62nd, 76th, 79th, 84th, 93rd, 376th, 430th, 434th, 439th, 453rd
  - *Engineer Service Battalion:* 548th
- *Companies:*
  - *Engineer Aviation Maintenance Companies:* 622nd, 919th
  - *Engineer Float Bridge Companies:* 2998th
  - *Engineer Panel Bridge Companies:* 341st, 402nd, 526th
  - *Engineer Pontoon Bridge Companies:* 138th, 573rd
  - *Engineer Treadway Bridge Companies:* 55th, 58th, 1437th, 2998th

HELICOPTER UNITS

- 1st Transportation Army Aviation Battalion (Provisional)
- 1st Helicopter Ambulance Company (Provisional)
- 6th Transportation Army Helicopter Co.
- 13th Transportation Army Helicopter Co.

Logistical Commands: 1st; Pusan Base Command (July 4–13, 1950), redesignated Pusan Logistics Command, then redesignated 2nd Logistics Command; 3rd; Japan Logistics Command (often referred to as "JLC." Since this command was in Japan, and some men, jokingly, likened General MacArthur to a deity, the troops called it "Jesus' Little Children," meaning that the JLC were MacArthur's [Jesus] little children.)

MEDICAL

- Group: 30th
- Evacuation Hospitals: 11th, 21st, 22nd, 25th, 121st, 171st, 8054th
- Field Hospitals: 1st POW (Provisional), 3rd, 4th, 14th, 64th
- Mobile Army Surgical Hospitals (MASH): 1st, 2nd, 43rd, 44th, 45th, 46th, 47th, 48th, 8055th, 8063rd, 8076th, 8225th, 8228th
- Station Hospitals: 3rd, 10th, 21st, 24th, 171st
- Surgical Hospital: 8209th
- Hospital Trains: 20th, 22nd, 8138th
- Medical Battalions: 34th (Separate), 52nd, 163rd
- Medical Service Battalion: 232nd

MILITARY POLICE

- Military Police (MP) Commands: POW Command (Provisional), redesignated 8203rd POW Command February 1, 1953
- Group: 8137th
- MP Battalions: 91st, 92nd, 93rd, 94th, 95th 96th, 97th, 519th, 525th MP Service Battalion, 772nd, 728th
- MP Companies: 1st MP Company (Provisional), 55th, 57th, 58th, 212th, 512th, 622nd, 772nd
- MP Escort Guard Companies: 165th, 551st, 552nd 555th, 556th, 595th

ORDNANCE

- Groups: 59th, 60th, 314th Ordnance Ammunition Group, 8046th Ordnance Field Group
- Ordnance Battalions: 4th, 30th, 66th, 67th, 74th, 79th, 83rd, 192rd, 328th, 335th, 801st
- Ordnance Ammunition Battalion: 32nd
- Ordnance Ammunition Companies: 55th, 58th, 65th, 69th, 363rd, 445th, 461st, 619th, 630th, 636th, 696th, 859th, 930th, 8097th
- Ordnance Heavy Automotive Maintenance Companies: 512th, 570th, 937th
- Ordnance Medium Automotive Maintenance Companies: 41st, 91st, 515th, 516th, 538th, 70th
- Ordnance Companies, Direct Automotive Support: 91st, 107th, 515th, 516th, 538th
- Ordnance Maintenance Battalions: 4th, 66th, 67th, 74th, 79th
- Ordnance Maintenance Company: 443rd
- Ordnance Field Maintenance Companies: 89th, 958th
- Ordnance Medium Maintenance Companies: 1st, 2nd, 5th, 7th, 17th, 19th, 21st, 24th, 31st, 38th, 107th, 518th
- Ordnance Heavy Maintenance Companies: 30th, 82nd, 106th, 568th
- Ordnance Companies (Direct Support): 1st, 2nd, 5th, 7th, 19th, 21st, 24th, 31st, 38th, 518th

QUARTERMASTER

- Groups: 6th, 23rd, 32nd
- Battalions: 13th, 54th, 96th, 98th, 142nd, 325th, 402nd, 501st, 8056th
- Quartermaster Service Battalion: 96th

RANGER

- 1st, 2nd, 3rd, 4th, 5th, 8th Ranger Infantry companies (Airborne)
- 8213th Army Unit, Eighth Army Ranger Company
- FEC General Headquarters (GHQ) 1st Raider Company; redesignated X Corps Special Operations Company; redesignated 8245th Army Unit, Raider Company

SIGNAL

- Groups: 1st, 22nd, 8226th Long Lines Signal Group
- Signal Battalions: 4th, 51st
- Signal Battalion, Corps: 101st
- Signal Aviation Heavy Construction Battalion: 440th
- Signal Communications Reconnaissance Battalions: 301st, 303rd, 304th
- Signal Construction Battalions: 23rd, 26th
- Signal Operations Battalion: 304th
- Signal Construction Companies: 403rd, 522nd, 532nd, 590th
- Signal Support Companies: 57th, 58th

TRANSPORTATION

- Group: 351st Transportation Highway Transport Group, 425th Transportation Traffic Regulating Group
- Railway Service: 3rd Transportation Military Railway Service (This and the following railway organizations helped to keep the South Korean railway system operating efficiently.)
- Transportation Railway Operation Battalions: 712th, 714th, 724th (These and the following railway organizations were part of the 3rd Transportation Military Railway Service.)
- Transportation Railway Shop Battalions: 764th, 765th
- Transportation Military Railway Unit: 8059th
- Transportation Truck Battalions: 1st Provisional, 52nd, 55th, 69th, 70th, 167th, 231st, 296th
- Truck Companies: 20th, 21st, 28th, 42nd, 43rd, 46th, 49th, 52nd 60th, 73rd, 74th, 107th, 121st, 131st, 167th, 231st, 252nd, 296th, 377th, 396th, 504th, 505th, 510th, 513th, 514th, 515th, 534th, 536th, 539th, 540th, 541st, 551st, 584th, 665th, 715th, 726th
- Heavy Truck Companies: 48th, 54th, 553rd, 556th
- Transportation Car Company: 95th
- Port Units: 7th Major Port, 21st Medium Port, 14th Transportation Port Battalion

AMPHIBIOUS COMMANDS

- Brigade: 2nd Engineer Special Brigade, redesignated 2nd Engineer Amphibious Support Brigade August 1952
- Regiment: 532nd Engineer Boat and Shore Regiment, redesignated 532nd Engineer Amphibious Support Regiment August 1952
- Battalion: 56th Amphibious Tank and Tractor Battalion
- Amphibious Truck Companies: 3rd, 558th, 8062nd
- Transportation Company (Heavy Boat): 18th

KOREA MILITARY ADVISORY GROUP

The Korea Military Advisory Group (KMAG) consisted of U.S. Army officer and enlisted advisers to the Republic of Korea Army (ROKA, South Korean Army).

U.S. Marine Corps

1st Marine Provisional Brigade: Arrived in Korea from the United States on August 2, 1950. In September 1950 the 5th Marine Regiment was incorporated into the 1st Marine Division, and Marine Aircraft Group 33 came under the 1st Marine Air Wing.

- 5th Marine Regiment
- 1st Battalion, 11th Marine Regiment (a 105-mm batalion of 12 howitzers)
- Co. A, 1st Medium Tank Battalion
- Co. A 1st ECB
- Co. A, 1st Amphibian Tractor Battalion
- Marine Aircraft Group 33: (MAG-33: Forward echelon of 1st Marine Aircraft Wing and part of the 1st Provisional Marine Brigade, July–September 1950)
  - Headquarters Squadron 33 (HQSQ-33); Service Squadron 33 (SMS-33)
- Marine Observation Squadron 6 (VMO-6; 6 Sikorsky HO3S helicopters, 8 Consolidated OY Sentinel observation aircraft)
- Marine Fighter Squadron 214 (VMF-214; Vought F4U Corsairs)
- Marine Fighter Squadron (VMF-323; Vought F4U Corsairs)
- Marine Night Fighter Squadron 513 (VMF[N]-513 Grumman F7F Tigercats)
- Marine Air Tactical Control Squadron 2 (MATCS-2: Controlled Marine flights and air strikes)

1st Marine Division (Inchon Landing, September 15, 1950):

- 1st Marine Regiment
- 5th Marine Regiment (part of 1st Marine Provisional Brigade August 2–September 1950)
- 7th Marine Regiment
- 11th Marine Regiment (field artillery regiment of three 105-mm howitzer battalions and one 155-mm howitzer battalion; the 1st Battalion was originally part of the 1st Marine Provisional Brigade)

- 1st Tank Battalion*; 1st Engineer Battalion*; 1st Amphibian Tractor Battalion*; 1st Armored Amphibian Battalion; 1st Shore Party Battalion*; 1st Signal Battalion**; 1st Combat Service Group**; 1st Motor Transport Battalion*; 7th Motor Transport Battalion (Fleet Marine Force unit); 1st Ordnance Battalion**; 1st Service Battalion**; 1st Medical Battalion.* (* One company from each of these battalions was part of the 1st Marine Provisional Brigade. ** A detachment from each of these units was part of the 1st Marine Provisional Brigade.)

1st Marine Aircraft Wing (MAW) (September 1950–July 1953):

- Headquarters Squadron 1 (HQSQ-1); Marine Wing Service Squadron 1 (MWSS-1)
- Marine Wing Service Group 17 (MWSG-17)
- Marine Aircraft Group 12 (MAG-12)
- Marine Aircraft Group 33 (MAG-33)
- Marine Fighter Squadron 115 (VMF-115; Grumman F9F Panthers)
- Marine Attack Squadron 121 (VMA-121; Douglas AD Skyraiders)
- Marine Fighter Squadron 212 (VMF-212; redesignated Marine Attack Squadron 212 [VMA-212] on June 10, 1952; Vought F4U Corsairs, Vought AU-1 Corsairs)
- Marine Fighter Squadron 214 (VMF-214; Vought F4U Corsairs)
- Marine Fighter Squadron 311 (VMF-311; Grumman F9F Panthers)
- Marine Fighter Squadron 312 (VMF-312; redesignated Marine Attack Squadron 312 [VMA-312] on March 1, 1952; Vought F4U Corsairs)
- Marine Fighter Squadron 323 (VMF-323; redesignated Marine Attack Squadron 323 [VMA-323] on June 30, 1952; Vought F4U Corsairs, Vought AU-1 Corsairs)
- Marine Attack Squadron 332 (VMA-332; Vought F4U Corsairs)
- Marine Attack Squadron 251 (VMA-251; Douglas AD Skyraiders)
- Marine Night-Fighter Squadron 513 (VMF[N]-513; Vought F4U Corsairs, Grumman F7F Tigercats, Douglas F3D Skyknights)
- Marine Night-Fighter Squadron 542 (VMF[N]-542; Grumman F7F Tigercats, Douglas F3D Skyknights)
- Marine Transport Squadron 152 (VMR-152; Douglas R4D Skytrains)
- Marine Ground Control Squadron 1 (MGCS-1)
- Marine Air Control Group 2 (MACG-2)
- Marine Tactical Air Control Squadron 2 (MTACS-2)
- Marine Ground Control Intercept Squadron 1 (MGCIS-1)
- Marine Ground Control Intercept Squadron 3 (MGCIS-2)
- Marine Photographic Squadron 1 (VMJ-1; McDonnell F2H-P Banshees)
- Marine Composite Squadron 1 (VMC-1; Douglas AD Skyraiders)
- Marine Helicopter Transport Squadron 161 (HMR-161; Sikorsky HRS-1 helicopters)
- Marine Observation Squadron 6 (VMO-6; Consolidated OY Sentinels, Sikorsky HO3S helicopters, Bell HTL helicopters)

U.S. Air Force

NOTE: The descending order of U.S. Air Force (USAF) commands is numbered air force, command, wing, group, squadron, and flight. During the Korean War, the USAF organizational structure was in a period of transition. The wing was a new organization established in 1948 and different from the World War II wing, which was a large administrative organization. The post-1948 combat wing consisted of a headquarters, a combat group having the same number as the wing, and other elements. On occasion, a group would be deployed forward to operate independently.

FEAF, the USAF component of the FEC:

- Fifth Air Force (Korea: exercised operational control of all USAF forces in Korea and coordination control of U.S. Navy and U.S. Marine Corps air operations in Korea); Thirteenth Air Force (Philippines); Twentieth Air Force (Guam)
- FEAF Bomber Command
- 314th Air Division (redesignated Japan Air Defense Force January 3, 1952; responsible for air defense of Japan and logistical support for USAF forces in Korea and Japan)
- 1st Troop Carrier Task Force (Provisional) (redesignated FEAF Combat Cargo Command [Provisional], September 10, 1950; redesignated 315th Air Division [Combat Cargo], January 25, 1951)
- Far East Air Matériel Command (redesignated Far East Air Logistics Force, July 2, 1952)

Tactical Air Wings and Groups
- 3rd Bombardment Wing and Group (Light)
- 4th Fighter-Interceptor Wing and Group
- 8th Fighter-Bomber Wing and Group
- 17th Bombardment Wing and Group (Light)
- 18th Fighter-Bomber Wing and Group
- 27th Fighter-Escort Wing and Group
- 35th Fighter-Interceptor Wing and Group
- 49th Fighter-Bomber Wing and Group
- 51st Fighter-Interceptor Wing and Group
- 58th Fighter-Bomber Wing and Group
- 67th Tactical Reconnaissance Wing and Group
- 116th Fighter-Bomber Wing and Group (from Air National Guard)
- 136th Fighter-Bomber Wing and Group (from Air National Guard)
- 452nd Bombardment Wing and Group (Light)
- 474th Fighter-Bomber Wing and Group

Tactical Support Wings. Formed to support the combat groups sent to Korea from fighter-bomber and bombardment wings stationed in Japan at the beginning of the war.

- 6002nd Tactical Support Wing (supported 18th Fighter-Bomber Group of 18th Fighter-Bomber Wing)
- 6131st Tactical Support Wing (supported 8th Fighter-Bomber Group of 8th Fighter-Bomber Wing)
- 6133rd Tactical Support Wing (supported 3rd Bombardment Group of 3rd Bombardment Wing)
- 6149th Tactical Support Wing (supported 49th Fighter-Bomber Group of 49th Fighter-Bomber Wing)
- 6150th Tactical Support Wing (supported 35th Fighter-Bomber Group of 35th Fighter-Bomber Wing)

Air Depot Wings
- 75th (arrived from the United States on December 12, 1952), 6148th, 6208th (Philippines), 6400th

Medium Bombardment Wings and Groups (B-29 Bombers)
- 19th Bombardment Wing and Group (Medium)
- 22nd Bombardment Group (Medium)
- 92nd Bombardment Group (Medium)
- 98th Bombardment Wing and Group (Medium)
- 307th Bombardment Wing and Group (Medium)

Troop Carrier Wings and Groups
- 1st Troop Carrier Group (Medium Provisional)
- 61st Troop Carrier Group (Heavy)
- 314th Troop Carrier Group (Medium)
- 315th Troop Carrier Wing and Group (Medium)
- 374th Troop Carrier Wing and Group (Heavy)
- 403rd Troop Carrier Wing and Group (Medium)
- 437th Troop Carrier Wing and Group (Medium)
- 483rd Troop Carrier Wing and Group (Medium)

Air Base Groups
- 3rd, 18th, 6122nd, 6167th

Air Base Wings
- 6160th, 6262nd

Air Rescue Groups
- 2nd and 3rd (evolved from 2nd and 3rd Squadrons; redesignated as groups, November 14, 1952)

Tactical Control Groups
- 502nd, 6147th, 6132nd (disbanded October 7, 1950, and absorbed into 502nd)

U.S. Navy

Prior to the Korean War, all U.S. Navy forces in the Western Pacific came under the command of U.S. Naval Forces, Far East (NAVFE, the U.S. Navy component of the FEC), except for the ships of the U.S. Seventh Fleet, which came under the Pacific Command, headquartered in Hawaii. On June 29, 1950, the Seventh Fleet was placed under the operational control of the commander of the NAVFE.

The Military Sea Transportation Service (MSTS), a unified organization within the Navy Department established in October 1949, had primary responsibility for water transportation for the military. The deputy commander for MSTS in the Western Pacific (DepComMSTS WestPac) reported directly to MSTS but coordinated closely with the NAVFE and supported operations in Far East waters.

While U.S. Navy forces were administratively assigned to type divisions (aircraft carrier, cruiser, destroyer, and so on), they were operationally assigned to task forces (TFs), task groups (TGs), and task units under the NAVFE. The NAVFE was reorganized several times throughout the war. These were the major NAVFE organizations:

Naval Forces Far East (June–July 1950):

- Amphibious Force, Far East (TF 90)
- Naval Forces, Philippines (TF 93)
- Naval Forces, Marianas (TF 94)
- Naval Forces, Japan (TF 96)

Naval Forces Far East/Naval Forces, Japan (TF 96) (July 1950–September 1950):

- Seventh Fleet (TF 70)
- Amphibious Force, Far East (TF 90)
- TGs 96.1 to 96.9 organized by function (Escort; Search and Reconnaissance; Shipping Control Administration, Japan; Towing and Salvage, Support, Minesweeping; Republic of Korea Navy [ROKN, South Korean Navy]; Royal Navy and Royal Australian Navy forces; and Submarines)

Naval Forces Far East/Naval Forces, Japan (TF 96) (September 1950–April 1951):

- Seventh Fleet (TF 70)
- Amphibious Force, Far East (TF 90)
- UN Blockading and Escort Force (TF 95)
- Minesweeping Group (TG 96.6)
- ROKN (TG 96.7)
- Fleet Activities, Japan-Korea (TG 96.1)
- Fleet Air, Japan (TG 96.2)
- Shipping Control Administration, Japan (TG 96.3)
- Service Group (TG 96.4)
- Escort Carrier Group (TG 96.8)
- Submarine Group (TG 96.9)

Naval Forces Far East/Naval Forces, Japan (TF 96) (April 1951–July 1953):

- Seventh Fleet (TF 70)
  - Striking Force (TF 77)
- Formosa Patrol (TF 72)
- Service Squadron 3 (TF 79)
- Fleet Air Wing (TG 70.6)
- Amphibious Force, Far East Task Force (TF 90)
- 1st Marine Aircraft Wing (TF 91)
- Logistic Support Force (TF 92; under operational control of the Seventh Fleet)
- Fleet Activities, Japan-Korea (TG 96.1)
- Naval Air, Japan (TG 96.2)
- Shipping Control Administration, Japan (TG 96.3; dissolved on April 1, 1952 and ships transferred to the U.S. Military Sea Transportation Service)
- Escort Carrier Group (TG 96.8)
- Submarine Group (TG 96.9)
- UN Blockading and Escort Force (TF 95)
  - West Coast Blockade Group (TG 95.1)
- East Coast Blockade Group (TG 95.2)
- Escort Group (TG 95.5)
- Minesweeping Group (TG 95.6)
- ROKN (TG 95.7)

U.S. Navy Combat Ships

Aircraft Carriers (CV); Aircraft Carriers, Attack (CVA); and Aircraft Carriers, Antisubmarine (CVS): *Antietam* (CVA 36), *Bon Homme Richard* (CVA 31), *Boxer* (CV 21), *Essex* (CVA 9), *Kearsarge* (CVA 33), *Lake Champlain* (CVA 39), *Leyte* (CVA 32), *Oriskany* (CVA 34), *Philippine Sea* (CVA 47), *Princeton* (CVS 37), *Valley Forge* (CVA 45).

Aircraft Carriers, Light (CVL): *Bataan* (CVL 29).

Aircraft Carriers, Escort (CVE): *Badoeng Strait* (CVE 116), *Bairoko* (CVE 115), *Cape Esperance* (CVE 88), *Corregidor* (CVE 58, assigned to MSTS), *Gilbert Islands* (CVE 107, served as an aircraft transport), *Point Cruz* (CVE 119), *Rendova* (CVE 114), *Sicily* (CVE 118), *Sitkoh Bay* (CVE 86), *Tripoli* (CVE 64, assigned to MSTS as an aircraft transport).

Battleships (BB): *Iowa* (BB 61), *Missouri* (BB 63), *New Jersey* (BB 62), *Wisconsin* (BB 64).

Cruisers, Heavy (CA), Cruisers, Light (CL), and Cruiser, Antiaircraft (CLAA): *Bremerton* (CA 130), *Helena* (CA 75), *Juneau* (CLAA 119), *Los Angeles* (CA 135), *Manchester* (CL 83), *Rochester* (CA 124), *St. Paul* (CA 73), *Toledo* (CA 133), *Worcester* (CL 144).

Destroyers (DD): *Agerholm* (DD 826), *Ammen* (DD 527), *Barton* (DD 722), *Brinkley Bass* (DD 887), *Beatty* (DD 756), *Fred T. Berry* (DD 858), *Black* (DD 666), *Blue* (DD 744), *John A. Bole* (DD 755), *Borie* (DD 704), *Boyd* (DD 544), *Bradford* (DD 545), *Bristol* (DD 857), *Clarence K. Bronson* (DD 668), *Brown* (DD 546), *Brush* (DD 745), *Buck* (DD 761), *Caperton* (DD 650), *Theodore E.*

Chandler (DD 717), *Chauncey* (DD 667), *Colahan* (DD 658), *Collett* (DD 730), *Cotten* (DD 669), *Cowell* (DD 547), *John R. Craig* (DD 885), *Alfred A. Cunningham* (DD 752), *Cushing* (DD 797), *Daly* (DD 519), *Dashiell* (DD 659), *De Haven* (DD 727), *Dortch* (DD 670), *English* (DD 696), *Erben* (DD 631), *Frank E. Evans* (DD 754), *Eversole* (DD 789), *Fechteler* (DD 870), *Douglas H. Fox* (DD 779), *Gatling* (DD 671), *Gregory* (DD 802), *Gurke* (DD 783), *Hailey* (DD 556), *Hale* (DD 642), *Hamner* (DD 718), *Lewis Hancock* (DD 675), *Hank* (DD 702), *Henderson* (DD 785), *Hickox* (DD 673), *Hollister* (DD 788), *John Hood* (DD 655), *Hopewell* (DD 681), *Harry E. Hubbard* (DD 748), *Hyman* (DD 732), *Ingraham* (DD 694), *Irwin* (DD 794), *Arnold J. Isbell* (DD 869), *Jarvis* (DD 799), *Jenkins* (DD 447), *Joseph P. Kennedy Jr.* (DD 850), *Kidd* (DD 661), *Kimberly* (DD 521), *James E. Kyes* (DD 787), *Laffey* (DD 724), *Laws* (DD 558), *Wallace L. Lind* (DD 703), *Lofberg* (DD 759), *Lowry* (DD 770), *George K. MacKenzie* (DD 836), *Maddox* (DD 731), *Mansfield* (DD 728), *Marshall* (DD 676), *Leonard F. Mason* (DD 852), *Massey* (DD 778), *McCord* (DD 534), *McDermut* (DD 677), *McGowan* (DD 678), *McNair* (DD 679), *Miller* (DD 535), *Moale* (DD 693), *Samuel N. Moore* (DD 747), *O'Brien* (DD 725), *Orleck* (DD 886), *Owen* (DD 536), *James C. Owens* (DD776), *Ozbourn* (DD 846), *Floyd B. Parks* (DD 884), *Picking* (DD 685), *John R. Pierce* (DD 753), *Porter* (DD 800), *Porterfield* (DD 682), *Halsey Powell* (DD 686), *Stephen Potter* (DD 538), *Preston* (DD 795), *Rooks* (DD 804), *Ross* (DD 563), *Rowan* (DD 782), *Rowe* (DD 564), *Forrest Royal* (DD 872), *Rupertus* (DD 851), *Shelton* (DD 790), *Shields* (DD 596), *Charles S. Sperry* (DD 697), *Stembel* (DD 644), *Stickell* (DD 888), *Stormes* (DD 780), *Strong* (DD 758), *Allen M. Sumner* (DD 692), *The Sullivans* (DD 537), *Lyman K. Swensen* (DD 729), *Taussig* (DD 746), *John W. Thomason* (DD 760), *Tingey* (DD 539), *Trathen* (DD 530), *Twining* (DD 540), *Uhlmann* (DD 687), *Walke* (DD 723), *Wedderburn* (DD 684), *Wiltsie* (DD 716), *Yarnall* (DD 541), *Zellars* (DD 777).

Destroyer Minesweepers (DMS): *Carmick* (DMS 33), *Doyle* (DMS 34), *Endicott* (DMS 35), *Thompson* (DMS 38).

Escort Destroyers (DDE): *Carpenter* (DDE 825), *Conway* (DDE 507), *Cony* (DDE 508), *Epperson* (DDE 719), *Fletcher* (DDE 445), *Jenkins* (DDE 447), *Keppler* (DDE 765), *McCaffery* (DDE 860), *Nicholas* (DDE 449), *Norris* (DDE 859), *O'Bannon* (DDE 450), *Philip* (DDE 498), *Radford* (DDE 446), *Renshaw* (DDE 449), *Sproston* (DDE 557), *Taylor* (DDE 468), *Walker* (DDE 517), *Waller* (DDE 466).

Radar Picket Destroyers (DDR): *Chevalier* (DDR 805), *Duncan* (DDR 874), *Fiske* (DDR 842), *Hanson* (DDR 832), *Hawkins* (DDR 873), *Higbee* (DDR 806), *Frank Knox* (DDR 742), *McKean* (DDR 784), *Perkins* (DDR 877), *Rogers* (DDR 876), *William R. Rush* (DDR 714), *Ernest G. Small* (DDR 838), *Southerland* (DDR 743), *Herbert J. Thomas* (DDR 833), *Henry W. Tucker* (DDR 875).

Destroyer Escorts (DE): *Currier* (DE 700), *Edmonds* (DE 406), *Foss* (DE 59), *Frybarger* (Amphibious Control Destroyer Escort: DEC 705), *Hanna* (DE 449), *Lewis* (DE 535), *Marsh* (DE 699), *McGinty* (DE 365), *McMorris* (DE 1036), *Ulvert M. Moore* (DE 442), *Douglas A. Munro* (DE 422), *Naifeh* (DE), *McCoy Reynolds*

(DE 440), *William Seiverling* (DE 441), *Silverstein* (DE 534), *Vammen* (DE 644), *Walton* (DE 361), *Whitehurst* (DE 634), *Wiseman* (DE 667).

Submarines: *Besugo* (SS 321), *Cabezon* (SS 334), *Diodon* (SS 349), *Greenfish* (SS 351), *Perch* (submarine transport, ASSP 313), *Pickerel* (SS 524), *Pomfret* (SS 391), *Pomodon* (SS 486), *Queenfish* (SS 393), *Redfish* (SS 305), *Remora* (SS 487), *Ronquil* (SS 396), *Sabalo* (SS 302), *Scabbardfish* (SS 397), *Sea Devil* (SS 400), *Sea Fox* (SS 402), *Segundo* (SS 398), *Sterlet* (SS 392), *Tilefish* (SS 307), *Tiru* (SS 416), *Volador* (SS 490).

Frigates (PF): *Albuquerque* (PF 7), *Bayonne* (PF 21), *Bisbee* (PF 46), *Burlington* (PF 51), *Everett* (PF 8), *Gallup* (PF 47), *Glendale* (PF 36), *Gloucester* (PF 22), *Hoquiam* (PF 5), *Sausalito* (PF 4), *Tacoma* (PF 3).

Minesweepers (except destroyer minesweepers) (AM, AMS, MHC): *Chatterer* (AMS 40), *Chief* (AM 315), *Competent* (AM 316), *Condor* (AMS 5), *Curlew* (AMS 8), *Defense* (AM 317), *Devastator* (AM 318), *Dextrous* (AM 341), *Firecrest* (AMS 10), *Gladiator* (AM 319), *Gull* (AMS 16), *Heron* (AMS 18), *Impeccable* (AM 320), *Incredible* (AM 249), *Kite* (AMS 22), *Magpie* (AM 25) (sunk), *Mainstay* (AM 261), *Merganser* (AMS 26), *Mockingbird* (AMS 27), *Murrelet* (AM 372), *Osprey* (AMS 28), *Partridge* (AM 31) (sunk), *Pelican* (AMS 32), *Pirate* (AM 275) (sunk), *Pledge* (AM 277) (sunk), *Ptarmigan* (AM 376), *Redhead* (AMS 34), *Redstart* (AMS 378), *Ruddy* (AM 380), *Shoveler* (AM 382), *Surfbird* (AM 383), *Swallow* (AMS 36), *Swift* (AM 122), *Symbol* (AM 123), *Toucan* (AM 387), *Waxbill* (MHC 50), *Waxwing* (AM 389), *Zeal* (AM 131).

Landing Ships, Dock (LSD): *Cabildo* (LSD 16), *Catamount* (LSD 17), *Colonial* (LSD 18), *Comstock* (LSD 19), *Epping Forest* (LSD 4), *Fort Marion* (LSD 22), *Gunston Hall* (LSD 5), *Tortuga* (LSD 26), *Whetstone* (LSD 27).

Fast Transports (APD, converted from destroyer escorts): *Horace A. Bass* (APD 124), *Begor* (APD), *Walter B. Cobb* (APD 106), *Diachenko* (APD 123), *Wantuck* (APD 125), *Weiss* (APD 719).

Landing Ships, Medium (Rocket) (LSM[R]): 401, 402, 403, 404, 409, 412, 525, 527, 536.

Seaplane Tenders (AV, AVP, AVS): *Corson* (AVP 37), *Curtiss* (AV 4), *Floyd's Bay* (AVP 40), *Gardiners Bay* (AVP 39), *Jupiter* (AVS 8), *Onslow* (AVP 48), *Pine Island* (AV 12), *Suisun* (AVP 53), *Kenneth Whiting* (AV 14).

Hospital Ships (AH): *Consolation* (AH 15), *Haven* (AH 12), *Repose* (AH 16).

Amphibious Force Flagships (AGC): *Eldorado* (AGC 11), *Estes* (AGC 12), *Mount McKinley* (AGC 7).

U.S. Coast Guard

U.S. Coast Guard Cutters (USCGC): USCGC *Bering Strait* (WAVP 382), USCGC *Chautauqua* (WPG 41), USCGC *Durant* (WDE 489), USCGC *Escanaba* (WPG 64), USCGC *Falgout* (WDE 424), USCGC *Finch* (WDE 428), USCGC *Forster* (WDE 434), USCGC *Gresham* (WAVP 387), USCGC *Ironwood* (WAGL 297), USCGC *Iroquois* (WPG 43), USCGC *Klamath* (WPG 66), USCGC *Koiner* (WDE 431),

USCGC *Kukui* (WAK 186), USCGC *Lowe* (WDE 425), USCGC *Minnetonka* (WPG 67), USCGC *Newell* (WDE 442), USCGC *Planetree* (WAGL 307), USCGC *Pontchartrain* (WPG 70), USCGC *Ramsden* (WDE 482), USCGC *Richey* (WDE 485), USCGC *Taney* (WPG 37), USCGC *Wachusett* (WPG 44), USCGC *Winnebago* (WPG 40), USCGC *Winona* (WPG 65).

Republic of Korea

Republic of Korea Army

Corps (Composition varied throughout the war. Each corps controlled two or more divisions):

- I: Activated July 5, 1950
- II: Activated July 15, 1950, inactivated January 1951, reactivated April 1952
- III: Activated October 16, 1950, inactivated May 1951

Divisions (Those marked with * were in existence at the beginning of the war):

1st Division*: 11th, 12th, 13th regiments (later 11, 12, 15th regiments)

2nd Division*: 5th, 16th, 25th regiments (later 17th, 31st, 32nd regiments)

3rd Division*: 22nd, 23rd regiments (26th added) (later 18th, 22nd, 23rd regiments)

5th Division*: 15th, 20th regiments; 1st Separate Battalion (later 27th, 35th, 36th regiments)

6th Division*: 7th, 8th, 19th regiments (later 2nd, 7th, 19th regiments)

7th Division*: 1st, 3rd, 9th regiments (later 3rd, 5th, 8th regiments)

8th Division*: 10th, 12th regiments (later 10th, 16th, 21st regiments)

9th Division: 28th, 29th, 30th regiments

Capital Division*: 2nd, 18th regiments (later 1st, 17th, 18th regiments then 1st Cavalry 26th regiments).

11th Division: 9th, 13th, 20th regiments
12th Division: 37th, 51st, 52nd regiments
15th Division: 38th, 39th, 50th regiments
20th Division: 60th, 61st, 62nd regiments
21st Division: 63rd, 65th, 66th regiments
22nd Division: 67th 68th, 69th regiments
25th Division: 70th, 71st, 72nd regiments
26th Division: 73rd, 75th, 76th regiments
27th Division: 77th, 78th, 79th regiments

1st Antiguerrilla Group: Organized October 8, 1950. The group included the 1st, 2nd, 3rd, 5th, 6th, 7th, 8th, 9th, 10th, 11th, 12th, 13th, and 15th Antiguerrilla battalions.

Civil Transport Corps (CTC): Although not a military organization, its activities were often vital to resupplying and sustaining UN troops deployed in rugged mountainous terrain. Parties of this force, and groups of carriers recruited earlier in the war by UN troops, brought up critical stocks of ammunition, food, water, and medical supplies and evacuated the wounded when no other means were available. GIs called them "chige bearers" (a *chige* or *jigye* was a wooden a-frame used by the Korean bearers to carry ammunition, supplies, or wounded soldiers). The CTC, organized about March–April 1951, eventually contained 65 companies, each with 240 porters. The success of UN troops in Korea often resulted from the timely arrival of these porters on some beleaguered battle position with critical provisions and ammunition. Untold numbers of them died, unheralded and forgotten.

Republic of Korea Air Force

10th Fighter Group (101st, 102nd Fighter Squadrons)
10th Maintenance and Supply Group
10th Air Base Group
10th Medical Group

Republic of Korea Navy

Frigates: *Apnok* (PF 62), *Tae Dong* (PF 63), *Dumon* (PF 64), *Nae Tong* (PF 65), *Imchin* (PF 66).

Patrol Craft: *Pak Tu San* (PC 701), *Kum Kang San* (PC 702), *Sam Kak San* (PC 703), *Chiri San* (PC 704), *Han La San* (PC 705), *Myo yang San* (PC 706).

United Kingdom and Commonwealth Forces

Some Commonwealth units remained in Korea after the Korean War cease-fire of July 27, 1953. No departure date is indicated for those units.

The 27th and 28th Commonwealth, 29th British, and 25th Canadian Infantry brigades served as independent units until July 1951, when the 1st Commonwealth Division was established, consisting of the 28th Commonwealth, 29th British, and 25th Canadian Infantry brigades and divisional troops. For simplicity, armor, artillery, engineer, and medical units are listed separately below, although some of those units were assigned to the brigades.

27th British Infantry Brigade (in Korea August 1950–April 1951; redesignated 27th Commonwealth Infantry Brigade, September 30, 1950):

- Headquarters, 27th Commonwealth Infantry Brigade (in Korea August 1950–April 1951)
- 1st Battalion, the Middlesex Regiment (in Korea August 1950–May 1951)
- 1st Battalion, the Argyll and Sutherland Highlanders (in Korea August 1950–April 1951)
- 3rd Battalion, the Royal Australian Regiment (arrived in Korea September 1950; joined 27th Brigade September 30, 1950; joined 28th Commonwealth Infantry Brigade April 1951)

- 2nd Battalion, Princess Patricia's Canadian Light Infantry (in Korea December 1950–November 1951; joined 27th Brigade February 18, 1951)

28th Commonwealth Infantry Brigade (replaced the 27th Commonwealth Infantry Brigade April 23, 1951):

- Headquarters, 28th Commonwealth Infantry Brigade (in Korea April 1951 thru armistice)
- 3rd Battalion, the Royal Australian Regiment (in Korea September 1950 thru armistice)
- 2nd Battalion, Princess Patricia's Canadian Light Infantry (in Korea April 1951–May 1951)
- 1st Battalion, the King's Own Scottish Borderers (in Korea April 1951–August 1952)
- 1st Battalion, the King's Shropshire Light Infantry (in Korea May 1951–September 1952)
- 1st Battalion, Royal Australian Regiment (in Korea March 1952–March 1953)
- 1st Battalion, the Royal Fusiliers (in Korea August 1952 thru armistice)
- 1st Battalion, the Durham Light Infantry (in Korea September 1952 thru armistice)
- 2nd Battalion, Royal Australian Regiment (relieved 1st Battalion, Royal Australian Regiment in Korea on March 21, 1953)
- 1st Battalion, the Essex Regiment (relieved 1st Battalion, the Royal Fusiliers, in Korea in August 1953)
- 1st Battalion, the Royal Warwickshire Regiment (relieved 1st Battalion, the Durham Light Infantry, in Korea in September 1953)

29th British Infantry Brigade (arrived in Korea during November 3–18, 1950, with the following battalions):

- Headquarters, 29th British Infantry Brigade (in Korea November 1950 thru armistice)
- 1st Battalion, Royal Northumberland Fusiliers (in Korea November 1950–October 1951)
- 1st Battalion, the Gloucestershire Regiment (in Korea November 1950–November 1951)
- 1st Battalion, the Royal Ulster Rifles (in Korea November 1950–October 1951)
- 1st Battalion, the Royal Norfolk Regiment (in Korea October 1951–September 1952; relieved 1st Battalion, Royal Ulsters, October 8, 1951)
- 1st Battalion, the Leicestershire Regiment (in Korea October 1951–June 1952; relieved the 1st Battalion, Royal Northumberlands, October 19, 1951)
- 1st Battalion, the Welch Regiment (in Korea November 1951–November 1952; relieved the 1st Battalion, the Gloucesters, on November 11, 1951)
- 1st Battalion, the Black Watch (in Korea November 1952–July 1953)

- 1st Battalion, the King's Regiment (in Korea September 1952–October 1953; relieved the 1st Battalion, the Royal Norfolks, on September 21, 1952)
- 1st Battalion, the Duke of Wellington's Regiment (in Korea October 1952–November 1953; relieved the 1st Battalion, the Welch Regiment, on October 31, 1952)
- 1st Battalion, the Royal Scots (relieved the 1st Battalion, the Black Watch, in Korea on July 9, 1953)
- 1st Battalion, the King's Own Royal Regiment (arrived in Korea in October 1953)
- 1st Battalion, the North Staffordshire Regiment (arrived in Korea in November 1953)

25th Canadian Infantry Brigade (in Korea May 1951 thru armistice):

- Headquarters, 25th Canadian Infantry Brigade (in Korea May 1951 thru armistice)
- 2nd Battalion, Princess Patricia's Canadian Light Infantry (in Korea May 1951–November 1952)
- 2nd Battalion, Royal Canadian Regiment (in Korea May 1951–April 1952)
- 2nd Battalion, Royal 22e Regiment (in Korea May 1951–April 1952)
- 1st Battalion, Princess Patricia's Canadian Light Infantry (in Korea October 1951–November 1952; relieved the regiment's 2nd Battalion on November 4, 1951)
- 1st Battalion, Royal Canadian Regiment (April 1952–March 1953; relieved the regiment's 2nd Battalion in Korea in mid-April 1952)
- 1st Battalion, Royal 22e Regiment (in Korea during April 1952–April 1953; relieved the regiment's 2nd Battalion in mid-April 1952)
- 3rd Battalion, Princess Patricia's Canadian Light Infantry (in Korea during October 1952–October 1953; relieved the regiment's 1st Battalion on November 3, 1952)
- 3rd Battalion, Royal Canadian Regiment (relieved the regiment's 1st Battalion on March 25, 1953)
- 3rd Battalion, Royal 22e Regiment (relieved the regiment's 1st Battalion on April 15, 1953)

Headquarters, 1st Commonwealth Division (in Korea July 1951 thru armistice):

ARMOR UNITS
- "C" Squadron, 7th Royal Tank Regiment (in Korea during November 1950–October 1951)
- 8th King's Royal Irish Hussars (in Korea during November 1950–December 1951)
- 5th Royal Inniskilling Dragoon Guards (in Korea during December 1951–December 1952; replaced the 8th Irish Hussars)
- 1st Royal Tank Regiment (replaced 5th Inniskillings, in Korea during December 1952–December 1953)
- 5th Royal Tank Regiment (replaced the 1st Royal Tank Regiment, arrived in Korea in December 1953)
- "C" Squadron, Lord Strathcona's Horse (Royal Canadians) (2nd Armour Regiment) (in Korea during May 1951–June 1952)
- "B" Squadron, Lord Strathcona's Horse (Royal Canadians) (2nd Armour Regiment) (in Korea during June 1952–May 1953; relieved "C" Squadron)
- "A" Squadrons, Lord Strathcona's Horse (Royal Canadians) (2nd Armour Regiment) (relieved "B" Squadron in May 1953)

ARTILLERY UNITS
- 45th Field Regiment, Royal Artillery (in Korea during November 1950–November 1951)
- 16th Field Regiment Royal New Zealand Artillery (in Korea during December 1950–1953)
- 14th Field Regiment, Royal Artillery (in Korea during November 1951–December 1952; relieved the 45th Field Regiment)
- 20th Field Regiment, Royal Artillery (in Korea during December 1952–December 1953; relieved the 14th Field Regiment)
- 11th (Sphinx) Independent Light AAA Battery, Royal Artillery (in Korea during November 1951–October 1951; converted to 4.2-inch mortars in June 1951)
- 170th Independent Mortar Battery (4.2-inch mortars) (in Korea during November 1950–October 1951)
- 120th Light AAA Battery, Royal Artillery (4.2-inch mortars; in Korea during October 1951–December 1952; relieved the 170th Independent Mortar Battery; joined the 61st Light Field Regiment in June 1952)
- 42nd Light AAA Battery, Royal Artillery (4.2-inch mortars; in Korea during November 1951–February 1952; replaced the 11th Light AAA Battery; joined the 61st Light Regiment in January 1952)
- 61st Light Field Regiment Royal Artillery (in Korea in January 1952 thru armistice)
- 2nd Regiment, Royal Canadian Horse Artillery (in Korea during May 1951–May 1952)
- 1st Regiment, Royal Canadian Horse Artillery (in Korea during May 1952–April 1953; relieved the 2nd Regiment)
- 81st Field Regiment Royal Canadian Artillery (in Korea in April 1953 thru armistice; relieved the 1st Regiment, Royal Canadian Horse Artillery; redesignated the 4th Regiment Royal Canadian Horse Artillery in October 1953)

ENGINEER UNITS

- 55th Field Squadron, Royal Engineers (in Korea during November 1950–July 1951; joined the 28th Field Engineer Regiment in July 1951)
- 57th Canadian Independent Field Squadron, Royal Canadian Engineers (in Korea during November 1950–July 1951; joined the 28th Field Engineer Regiment in July 1951)
- 28th Field Engineer Regiment (in Korea in July 1951 thru armistice)
- 64th Field Park Squadron, Royal Engineers (in Korea in July 1951 thru armistice; relieved the 55th Field Squadron)

MEDICAL UNITS

- 60th (Parachute) Indian Field Ambulance (in Korea in November 1950 thru armistice)
- 26th Field Ambulance, Royal Army Medical Corps (in Korea in December 1950 thru armistice)
- No. 25 Field Ambulance, Royal Canadian Army Medical Corps (in Korea during May 1951–April 1952)
- No. 25 Canadian Field Dressing Station (in Korea in July 1951 thru armistice)
- No. 37 Field Ambulance, Royal Canadian Army Medical Corps (in Korea during April 1952–May 1953; relieved No. 25 Field Ambulance)
- No. 38 Field Ambulance, Royal Canadian Army Medical Corps (in Korea in May 1953 thru armistice; relieved No. 37 Field Ambulance)

Royal Marines: 41st Independent Commando, Royal Marines (in Korea during September 1950–1953).

Royal Air Force Units: No. 88 and No. 209 Squadrons (Sunderland flying boats).

Royal Navy ships:

Aircraft carriers: HMS *Triumph, Glory, Ocean, Theseus, Unicorn* (aircraft maintenance ship).

Cruisers: HMS *Belfast, Ceylon, Jamaica, Birmingham, Kenya, Newcastle.*

Destroyers: HMS *Consort, Cockade, Comus, Concord, Consort, Constance, Charity, Cossack.*

Frigates and Sloops: HMS *Amethyst, Alacrity, Black Swan, Cardigan Bay, Crane, Hart, Modeste, Morecambe Bay, Mounts Bay, Opossum, St. Brides Bay, Sparrow, Whitesand Bay.*

Submarine: HMS *Telemachus.*

Other vessels: HMS *Tyne* (destroyer deport ship/headquarters ship); *Ladybird* (headquarters ship).

Royal Fleet Auxiliaries (RFAs) and Merchant Fleet Auxiliaries (MFAs): MFA *Choysang* (MFA armament store issuing ship), *Brown Ranger* (oiler), RFA *Echodale* (oiler), *Green Ranger* (oiler), *Maine* (hospital ship), *Wave Baron* (oiler), *Wave Chief* (oiler), *Wave Knight* (oiler), *Wave Laird* (oiler), *Wave Premier* (oiler), *Wave Prince* (oiler), *Wave Sovereign* (oiler).

Other United Nations Command Forces

Australia

1st, 2nd, and 3rd battalions, Royal Australian Regiment (see United Kingdom and Commonwealth Forces, above).

Royal Australian Air Force: No. 30 Communication Unit, No. 36 Transport Squadron, No. 77 Fighter Squadron.

Royal Australian Navy: aircraft carrier HMAS *Sydney;* destroyers HMAS *Bataan, Warramunga;* frigates HMAS *Condamine, Culgoa, Shoalhaven, Murchison.*

Belgium and Luxembourg

1st Belgian Battalion (1er Bataillon Belge) (included one Luxembourg platoon; in Korea during January 1951–August 1951).

2nd Belgian Battalion (2e Bataillon Belge) (included one Luxembourg platoon; in Korea during August 1951–June 1955).

Canada

25th Canadian Infantry Brigade (three infantry battalions, one armor squadron [equivalent to one U.S. tank company], one artillery regiment [equivalent to one U.S. artillery battalion], one engineer field squadron [equivalent to one U.S. combat engineer company], and one medical unit); joined the 1st Commonwealth Division in July 1951 (see United Kingdom and Commonwealth Forces, above).

Royal Canadian Air Force: No. 426 Transport Squadron; also 22 pilots who flew combat missions attached to U.S. Fifth Air Force.

Royal Canadian Navy: destroyers HMCS *Athabaskan, Cayuga, Crusader, Haida, Huron, Iroquois, Nootka,* and *Sioux.*

Colombia

1st Colombian Battalion (1e Batallón Colombia) (in Korea during June 1951–July 1952).

2nd Colombian Battalion (2e Batallón Colombia) (in Korea during July 1952–November 1952).

3rd Colombian Battalion (3e Batallón Colombia) (in Korea during November 1952–June 1953).

Colombian Navy: Frigates *Almirante Padilla, Captain Tono, Almirante Brion.*

Ethiopia

1st Kagnew Battalion (in Korea during May 1951–April 1952).

2nd Kagnew Battalion (in Korea during April 1952–April 1953).

3rd Kagnew Battalion (in Korea during April 1953–April 1954).

France

1er Bataillon de Corée (reinforced infantry battalion).

French Navy: frigate *La Grandière.*

Greece

Hellenic Battalion (infantry battalion).

Netherlands

Nederlands Detachement Verenigde Naties (infantry battalion).

Royal Netherlands Navy: destroyers HNLMS *Evertsen, Van Galen, Piet Hein;* frigate *Johan Maurits van Nassau.*

New Zealand

16th Field Regiment, Royal New Zealand Artillery (equivalent to one U.S. artillery battalion), joined the 1st Commonwealth Division in July 1951 (see United Kingdom and Commonwealth Forces, above).

Royal New Zealand Navy: frigates *Hawea, Kaniere, Pukaki, Rotoiti, Taupo, Tutira;* transport *Wahine.*

Philippines

10th Battalion Combat Team (Motorized) (in Korea during September 1950–September 1951).

20th Battalion Combat Team (in Korea during September 1950–June 1951).

19th Battalion Combat Team (in Korea during June 1952–April 1953).

14th Battalion Combat Team (in Korea during April 1953–April 1954).

South Africa

No. 2 Fighter Squadron, South African Air Force.

Thailand

1st Battalion, 21st Infantry Regiment, and three separate medical service elements of the Royal Thai Army.

Royal Thai Navy: frigates *Bangprakong, Prasae, Prasae II, Sichang, Tachin.*

Royal Thai Air Force: detachment flying C-47 Skytrains (also known as Dakotas and "Gooneybirds") with USAF 21st Troop Carrier Squadron.

Turkey

1st Turkish Brigade (in Korea during October 1950–September 1951).

2nd Turkish Brigade (in Korea during September 1951–July 1952).

3rd Turkish Brigade (in Korea during July 1952–September 1954).

Denmark

Medical aid only: hospital ship *Jutlandia.*

India

Medical aid only: 60th (Parachute) Field Ambulance (see United Kingdom and Commonwealth Forces, above).

Italy

Medical aid only: Italian Red Cross Hospital 68.

Sweden

Medical aid only: Swedish Red Cross Field Hospital.

Norway

Medical aid only: Mobile Army Surgical Hospital, known as NORMASH.

Communist Forces

Korean People's Army (Ground Forces Only)

Corps: NOTE: In the Korean People's Army (KPA, North Korean Army) a corps is a control headquarters, to which divisions and other commands can be attached and detached by the army or theater commander to which the corps belongs.

I: Activated June 10, 1950. In early August 1950 it included the 2nd, 4th, 6th, 7th, 9th, and 10th divisions of the 16th Armored Brigade and elements of the 105th Armored Division.

II: Activated about June 12, 1950. In early August 1950 it included the 1st, 3rd, 5th, 8th, 12th, 13th, and 15th divisions of the 17th Armored Brigade and the 766th Independent Infantry Unit (a regimental-sized command).

III: Activated October 1950. Originally included the 1st and 3rd divisions.

IV: Activated September 1950. Originally included the 9th, 18th, and 19th divisions.

V: Activated September or October 1950. Originally included the 6th, 7th, 12th, 38th, and 43rd divisions.

VI: Activated October 1950. Included the 18th, 19th, and 36th divisions.

VII: Activated September or October 1950. Included the 13th, 32nd, and 37th divisions.

VIII: Activated October 1950. Included the 42nd, 45th, and 46th divisions.

Major KPA commands at the beginning of the war:

North Korean infantry divisions consisted of three rifle regiments, an artillery regiment, an antitank battalion, an engineer battalion, a signal battalion, a recon company, and a signal company. Principal divisional weapons were 12 122-mm howitzer, 24 76-mm guns, 12 SU-76 SP guns, 12 45-mm AT guns, and 36 14.5-mm AT rifles (known as Buffalo or Elephant guns to U.S. GIs.). Division authorized strength was 12,092 men.

The KPA tank regiment was authorized 40 tanks: 13 tanks in each of three tank battalions. Tank companies each had 4 tanks. At the outbreak of the war, 120 of the 150 T-34 tanks in the KPA were in the 105th Armored Brigade. By contrast, U.S. tank platoons were authorized 5 tanks; tank companies contained 17 to 22 tanks; U.S. divisional tank battalions were authorized over 54 tanks.

1st Division (originally formed September 1946, with the 1st, 2nd, and 3rd regiments; in March 1950 the 1st Regiment was replaced by the 14th Regiment): 2nd, 3rd, and 14th regiments.

2nd Division (originally formed in 1946; regimental structure is as of December 1949): 4th, 6th, and 17th regiments.

3rd Division (activated October 1948; awarded the name "Guards-Seoul" for the capture of Seoul and Kumchon): 7th, 8th, and 9th regiments.

4th Division (activated October 1948; also awarded the name of "Guards-Seoul" for the capture of Seoul and Taejon; the name "Kim Chaek" was added in November 1950 for those remaining behind UN lines as a guerrilla command in November 1950): 5th, 16th (redesignated the 29th in 1951), and 18th regiments.

5th Division (activated August 1949 from the all-Korean 164th Division in the Fifty-fifth Army, communist China's People's Liberation Army [PLA]): 10th, 11th, and 12th regiments.

6th Division (activated July 1949 from the all-Korean 166th Division in Fifty-Sixth Army, PLA, and 1st regiment, 1st KPA Division; awarded the name "Guards" for the capture of Kimpo and Inchon on June 29–30, 1950): 13th, 14th, and 15th regiments.

7th Division (prewar 7th Division redesignated the 12th Division and the new 7th Division activated on July 2, 1950, from Border Constabulary Brigade and conscripts): 51st, 53rd, and 54th regiments.

8th Division (activated in July 1950 from the 1st Border Constabulary Brigades): 81st, 82nd, and 83rd regiments.

9th Division (activated in July 1950 from the 2nd Border Constabulary Brigade): 85th, 86th, and 87th regiments.

10th Division (activated in March 1950): 25th, 27th, and 29th regiments.

Converted to the 10th Mechanized Division in 1951: 25th and 27th Infantry and 107th Tank Regiment.

12th Division (formed as the 7th Division on April 6, 1950, from Korean troops in the PLA, with the 1st, 2nd, and 3rd regiments; redesignated the 12th Division by June 18, 1950): 30th, 31st, and 32nd regiments.

13th Division (activated in June 1950): 19th, 21st, and 23rd regiments.

15th Division (activated during May–June 1950): 45th, 48th, and 50th regiments.

105th Armored Brigade (to end of June 1950, then the 105th Seoul Armored Division). Awarded the name "Seoul" for spearheading seizure of that city in June 1950. Reportedly the division included the 206th Mechanized Regiment; the 83rd Motorized Regiment; the 107th, 109th, and 203rd Tank regiments; and the 208th Tank Training Regiment.

1st Border Constabulary Brigade (redesignated the 8th Division in July 1950).

2nd Border Constabulary Brigade (redesignated the 9th Division in July 1950).

3rd Border Constabulary Brigade.

5th Border Constabulary Brigade.

7th Border Constabulary Brigade.

766th Independent Infantry Unit (a regimental-sized command; deactivated August 1950 and personnel transferred to the 12th Division).

12th Motorcycle Regiment.

17th Motorcycle Regiment.

Other KPA Commands

17th Division (identified in defense of Seoul-Inchon in September 1950).

18th (Seoul) Division (Seoul-Inchon area in September 1950).

31st Division (Seoul-Inchon area in September 1950).

19th Antiaircraft Regiment (Seoul-Inchon area in September 1950).

2nd Artillery Regiment.

22nd Regiment, 70th Regiment, and 87th Regiment (all in the Seoul-Inchon area in September 1950).

25th Infantry Brigade (Seoul-Inchon area in September 1950).

23rd Mechanized Artillery Brigade (in June 1952 became the 21st Brigade).

24th Mechanized Artillery Brigade (organized in October 1951 from the 24th Infantry Division).

25th Coastal Defense Brigade (in October 1951 redesignated the 25th Mechanized Artillery Brigade).

26th Mechanized Artillery Brigade.

42nd Mechanized Regiment (Seoul-Inchon area in September 1950).

918th Coast Artillery Regiment (Seoul-Inchon area in September 1950).

16th Armored Brigade.

17th Armored Brigade.

849th Independent Antitank Regiment.

23rd Marine Brigade.

226th Marine Regiment.

102nd Security Regiment.

104th Security Brigade.

105th Security Regiment.

107th Security Regiment (Seoul-Inchon area in September 1950).

111th Security Regiment (Seoul-Inchon area in September 1950).

1st Air Force Division (identified at Kimpo Airfield in September 1950).

827th Air Force Unit (Seoul-Inchon area in September 1950).

10th Railroad Regiment (Seoul-Inchon area in September 1950).

Major KPA units and location, November 23, 1950:

KOREA

I, II, III, IV and V Corps, containing the 1st, 2nd, 3rd, 4th, 5th, 6th, 7th, 8th, 9th, 10th, 12th, 15th, 17th, 24th, 27th, 31st, 38th, 41st, 43rd, 47th Infantry and 105 Tank divisions.

MANCHURIA

VI, VII, and VIII Corps, with 13th, 18th, 19th, 32nd, 36th, 37th, 42nd, 45th, and 46th divisions.

Major Commands KPA, July 1, 1951:

I Corps: 8th, 19th, 47th divisions

II Corps: 2nd, 13th, 27th divisions

III Corps: 1st, 15th, 45th divisions

IV Corps: 4th, 5th, 105th Armored divisions and 26th Brigade

V Corps: 6th, 12th, 32nd divisions

VI Corps: 9th, 17th Mechanized 18th, 23rd divisions

VII Corps: 3rd, 24th, 37th, 46th divisions and 63rd Brigade

Major Commands, KPA, 1952:

I Corps: 8th Division (81st, 82nd, 83rd regiments), 9th Division (85th, 86th 87th regiments), 47th Division (2nd, 3rd, 4th regiments)

II Corps: 2nd Division (4th, 6th, 17th regiments), 13th Division (19th, 21st, 23rd regiments), 27th Division (7th, 14th, 32nd regiments)

III Corps: 1st Division (2nd, 3rd, 14th regiments; 2nd and 3rd regiments also listed for 46th Division; no doubt one is in error, but which is unknown), 15th Division (45th, 48th, 50th regiments), 45th Division (89th, 90th, 91st regiments)

IV Corps: 4th Division (5th, 18th, 29th regiments), 5th Division (10th, 11th, 12th regiments)

10th Mechanized Infantry Division: (25th Infantry, 27th Infantry, 107th Tank regiments) 105th Tank Division (1st, 2nd, 3rd Tank regiments), 21st and 23rd Brigades, 26th Mechanized Artillery Brigade

V Corps: 6th Division (1st, 13th, 15th regiments), 12th Division (30th, 31st, 32nd regiments), 46th Division (93rd, 94th, 95th regiments), 25th Mechanized Brigade

VII Corps: 3rd Division (7th, 8th, 9th regiments), 7th Division (51st, 53rd, 54th regiments), 37th Division (74th, 75th, 76th regiments)

People's Republic of China

Chinese troop formations of the CPVA are listed below in the order in which they entered Korea. China identified groups of three divisions as armies, while the United States and other countries referred to these as corps. Thus a Chinese army equated roughly to a U.S. corps. A Chinese army numbered between 21,000 and 30,000 men, a division numbered 8,000–10,000 men, and a regiment numbered 3,000 men. Chinese divisions were organized in a manner similar to those of the North Koreans. Both employed Russian-manufactured mortars and artillery pieces.

At some point during the war the Chinese developed a number code for their units. For example, 54 Unit meant Thirty-eighth Army; 55 Unit = Thirty-ninth Army; 56 Unit = Fortieth Army; 1/55 Unit = 115th Division, Thirty-ninth Army.

Thirteenth Army Group

This group came from the Fourth Field Army. The Thirty-eighth, Thirty-ninth, Fortieth, and Forty-second armies and the 1st and 2nd Motorized Artillery divisions and a cavalry regiment arrived in Korea during October 14–20, 1950. The Fiftieth and Sixty-sixth armies, Eighth Artillery, Fifth and Forty-second Truck regiments arrived near the end of October 1950. The Fiftieth and Sixty-sixth armies returned to China near the end of March 1951, but the Fiftieth Army returned to Korea in July of that year.

ARMIES

Thirty-eighth: 112th Division (334th, 335th, 336th regiments), 113th Division (337th, 338th, 339th regiments), 114th Division (340th, 341st, 342nd regiments)

Thirty-ninth: 115th Division (343rd, 344th, 345th regiments), 116th Division (346th, 347th, 348th regiments), 117th Division (349th, 350th, 351st regiments)

Fortieth: 118th Division (352nd, 353rd, 354th regiments), 119th Division (355th, 356th, 357th regiments), 120th Division (358th, 359th, 360th regiments)

Forty-second: 124th Division (370th, 371st, 372nd regiments), 125th Division (373rd, 374th, 375th regiments), 126th Division (376th, 377th, 378th regiments)

Fiftieth: 148th Division (442nd, 443rd, 444th regiments), 149th Division (445th, 446th, 447th regiments), 150th Division (448th, 449th, 450th regiments)

Sixty-sixth: 196th Division (586th, 587th, 588th regiments), 197th Division (589th, 590th, 591st regiments), 198th Division (592nd, 593rd, 594th regiments)

Ninth Army Group

This army group entered Korea the first half of November 1950.

ARMIES

Twentieth: 58th Division (172nd, 173rd, 174th regiments), 59th Division (175th, 176th, 177th regiments), 60th Division (178th, 179th, 180th regiments), 89th Division (from the 30th Army; deactivated about February 1951 with men used as replacements for other divisions) (265th, 266th, 267th regiments)

Twenty-sixth: 76th Division (226th, 227th, 228th regiments), 77th Division (229th, 230th, 231st regiments), 78th Division (232nd, 233rd, 234th regiments), 88th Division (from 30th Army; deactivated about February 1951, with men used as replacements for other divisions) (262nd, 263rd, 164th regiments)

Twenty-seventh: 79th Division (235th, 236th, 237th regiments), 80th Division (238th, 239th, 240th regiments), 81st Division (241st, 242nd, 243rd regiments), 90th Division (from the 30th Army; deactivated about February 1951, with men used as replacements for other divisions) (268th, 269th, 270th regiments)

Fourteenth Army Group

This army group entered Korea the last two weeks of February 1951.

ARMIES

Sixty-third: 187th Division (559th, 560th, 561st regiments), 188th Division (562nd, 563rd, 564th regiments), 189th Division (565th, 566th, 567th regiments)

Sixty-fourth: 190th Division (568th, 569th, 570th regiments), 191st Division (571st, 572nd, 573rd regiments), 192nd Division (574th, 575th, 576th regiments)

Sixty-fifth: 193rd Division (577th, 578th, 579th regiments), 194th Division (580th, 581st, 582nd regiments), 195th Division (583rd, 584th, 585th regiments)

Thirteenth Army Group

This army group entered Korea in March 1951.

ARMIES

Forty-seventh (replaced by First Army in June 1953): 139th Division (415th, 416th, 417th regiments), 140th Division (418th, 419th, 420th regiments), 141st Division (421st, 422nd, 423rd regiments)

Twentieth Army Group

This army group entered Korea during May–June 1951.

ARMIES

Sixty-seventh (divisions unknown)

Sixty-eighth: 203rd Division (607th, 608th, 609th regiments), 204th Division (610th, 611th, 612th regiments)

III Army Group

This army group entered Korea during the last half of March 1951.

ARMIES

Twelfth: 31st Division (92nd, 93rd, 94th regiments), 34th Division (101st, 102nd, 103rd regiments), 35th Division (104th, 105th, 106th regiments)

Fifteenth: 29th Division (86th, 87th, 88th regiments), 44th Division (131st, 132nd, 133rd regiments), 55th Division (134th, 135th, 136th regiments)

Sixtieth: 179th Division (545th, 546th, 547th regiments), 180th Division (548th, 549th 550th regiments), 181st Division (551st, 552nd, 553rd regiments)

OTHER COMMANDS

Twenty-third Army (probably included 67th, 68th, and 69th divisions)

Twenty-forth Army (probably included 70th, 71st, and 72nd divisions)

Thirty-seventh Army (probably included 109th and 111th divisions)

Forty-third Army (no details known)

1st Motorized Artillery Division

2nd Motorized Artillery Division

7th Motorized Artillery Division: Included the 9th Independent Artillery Regiment and the 11th Artillery Regiment

5th Artillery Division (entered Korea May 1951)

5th and 42nd Truck regiments

UZAL W. ENT AND DONALD W. BOOSE JR.

References

Appleman, Roy E. *United States Army in Korea: South to the Naktong, North to the Yalu.* Washington, DC: Office of the Chief of Military History, 1961.

Barclay, C. N. *The First Commonwealth Division: The Story of British Commonwealth Land Forces in Korea, 1950–1953.* Aldershot, UK: Gale and Polden, 1954.

Boose, Donald. *U.S. Army Forces in the Korean War, 1950–1953.* Oxford, UK: Osprey, 2005.

Cagle, Malcolm W., and Frank A. Manson. *Sea War in Korea.* Annapolis, MD: Naval Institute Press, 1957.

Condon, John P. *Corsairs to Panthers: U.S. Marine Aviation in Korea.* Washington, DC: History and Museums Division, HQMC, 2002.

Edwards, Paul M. *Small United States and United Nations Warships in the Korean War.* Jefferson, NC: McFarland, 2008.

Ent, Uzal W. *Fighting on the Brink: Defense of the Pusan Perimeter.* Paducah, KY: Turner Publishing, 1996.

Futrell, Robert F. *The United States Air Force in Korea, 1950–1953.* Rev. ed. Washington, DC: Office of the Chief of Air Force History, 1983.

General Orders No. 80. *Battle Credits and Assault Landings for Korea.* Washington, DC: Department of the Army, 1954.

Grey, Jeffrey. *The Commonwealth Armies and the Korean War: An Alliance Study.* Manchester, UK: Manchester University Press, 1988.

Hallion, Richard P. *The Naval Air War in Korea.* Baltimore: Nautical and Aviation Publishing Company of America, 1986.

Hermes, Walter G. *U.S. Army in the Korean War: Truce Tent and Fighting Front.* Washington, DC: Office of the Chief of Military History, 1966.

History of the North Korean Army. Military Intelligence Section, HQ. U.S. Far East Command, Tokyo, Japan, July 31, 1952.

History of the United Nations Forces in the Korean War, Vols. 1–6. Seoul: Ministry of Defense, Republic of Korea, 1972–1977.

Montross, Lynn, et al. *U.S. Marine Operations in Korea, 1950–1953.* 5 vols. Washington, DC: U.S. Marine Corps Historical Branch, 1954–1972.

Mossman, Billy C. *United States Army in the Korean War: Ebb and Flow, November 1950–July 1951.* Washington, DC: U.S. Army Center of Military History, 1990.

Rottman, Gordon L. *Korean War Order of Battle: United States, United Nations, and Communist Ground, Naval, and Air Forces, 1950–1953.* Westport, CT: Praeger, 2002.

Thomas, Nigel, Peter Abbot, and Mike Chappell. *The Korean War, 1950–1953.* Botley, Oxfordshire, UK: Osprey, 1986.

Appendix B

Military Awards and Decorations

United Nations

The United Nations Service Medal was the first military award established by the United Nations (UN). It was authorized on December 12, 1950, in accordance with Resolution 483 (V). It was originally intended to be a general service medal with bars indicating the operation or the area of service. The reverse of the medal bears the inscription "For service in defence of the principles of the charter of the United Nations." The ribbon consists of 17 alternating blue and white stripes, representing the UN colors. The ribbon is surmounted with a "Korea" bar.

The criterion for the award was 30 days in the Korea area of operations (including support bases in Japan and Okinawa) between June 27, 1950, and July 27, 1954. Military personnel of all nations that provided troops were eligible, subject to the approval of their own national forces. Civilians of international relief agencies, such as the Red Cross, the Salvation Army, the St. John's Ambulance Brigade, and the Young Men's Christian Association (YMCA), also qualified for the award.

This particular medal was never awarded for any action other than Korea, and in 1961 its name was officially changed to the United Nations Korean Medal. The award was also unique among modern medals because it was awarded in 10 different official language versions. These included English (2.760 million awarded), Korean (1.225 million), Amharic (5,650), Dutch (5,800), French (16,900), Greek (9,000), Italian (135), Spanish (1,300), Thai (10,650), and Turkish (33,700). An unofficial Tagalog version was also issued to troops from the Philippines.

United States

The first U.S. military decorations for combat in Korea were awarded for actions that took place during June 9–11, 1871. Nine U.S. sailors and six marines received the Medal of Honor when the Asiatic Squadron under Rear Admiral John Rodgers landed a shore party and captured several forts around the Korean capital in retaliation for being fired upon by the forts 10 days earlier.

The current system of U.S. military decorations came into being during World War I. Until that time, the only U.S. decoration was the Medal of Honor, first established during the American Civil War. With the establishment of additional decorations in 1918, Congress created the concept of the Pyramid of Honor. For the first time in U.S. history it was recognized that there were degrees of military service to the nation, each worthy of its own level of recognition.

At the apex of the Pyramid of Honor is the Medal of Honor (often erroneously called the Congressional Medal of Honor). The highest U.S. military award for battlefield heroism, it is awarded by the president in the name of Congress to members of the U.S. armed forces who distinguish themselves by gallantry and intrepidity at the risk of their lives above and beyond the call of duty while engaged in combat against an armed enemy of the United States. U.S. troops sometimes irreverently referred to it as the "Big Sticker" or the "Blue Max," a reference to the old imperial German Pour le Mérite and the Medal of Honor's blue ribbon. During the Korean War 131 Americans received the Medal of Honor (93 posthumously): 78 soldiers, 42 marines, 7 sailors, and 4 airmen. The Unknown Soldier of the Korean War also received the Medal of Honor.

Some levels of the Pyramid of Honor have more than one decoration because each branch of the service has its own unique award. In 1950 there were different army and navy designs for the Medal of Honor. At the next level down, the decorations even had slightly different names, but the Distinguished Service Cross (DSC) and the Navy Cross were equivalent. Many decorations, including the Silver Star, the Distinguished Flying Cross, the Legion of Merit, the Bronze Star Medal, the Air Medal, and the Purple Heart, were and are awarded by all branches of the military. In 1960 the U.S. Air Force introduced the Air Force Cross and its own design for the Medal of Honor and the Distinguished Service Medal. During the Korean War, airmen received army decorations.

The second-highest U.S. awards for combat heroism are the DSC and the Navy Cross. During the Korean War 805 Americans received the DSC, and 220 (mostly marines) received the Navy Cross. Fourteen allied soldiers also received the DSC.

Unlike many European systems of decoration, both officers and enlisted soldiers are eligible for all U.S. military awards. Some, such as the Medal of Honor, the DSC, and the Silver Star, are only for combat heroism. Others, such as the Distinguished Service Medal, are only for exceptional service. Some U.S. decorations, such as the Bronze Star Medal or the Army Commendation Medal and Navy Commendation Medal, can be awarded for either service or valor. Awards made for valor are indicated by a bronze "V" device attached to the medal's ribbon.

Most U.S. heroism decorations are for combat actions only. One exception is the Soldier's Medal, which is the highest award for noncombat heroism. The Distinguished Flying Cross is awarded for heroism in flight during either combat or noncombat situations. The Bronze Star Medal is awarded for either heroic or meritorious action. Technically it can be awarded for noncombat service, but in practice it is almost always awarded for wartime service only.

The Legion of Merit is unique in the U.S. system because it exists in four classes. Originally established in 1942 as a decoration for high-ranking foreigners, the lowest class (Legionnaire) is also awarded to Americans. The Purple Heart, established by George Washington in 1782, was America's first standing military decoration. It lapsed after the Revolutionary War, but it was reestablished in 1932 as a decoration for wounds (including mortal wounds) received in combat. Purple Hearts awarded for Korea numbered 117,315.

In some countries, such as the former Soviet Union, soldiers wear multiple medals or ribbons for subsequent awards of the same decoration. The U.S. Army and the U.S. Air Force designate subsequent awards by affixing a bronze oak leaf cluster to the medal's ribbon. The U.S. Navy and the U.S. Marine Corps use a small bronze star device. Fifth subsequent awards are indicated by a silver oak leaf cluster or a silver star device, respectively.

Although not a military decoration in the strictest sense, one of the most highly prized U.S. military awards is the Combat Infantryman Badge (CIB). A silver rifle on a blue bar backed by a silver oak wreath, the CIB was first authorized in World War II to distinguish infantrymen actively engaged in ground combat. A second award of the CIB is indicated by a star at the open top of the oak wreath. An individual can earn only one CIB per war; thus, a soldier with a star on his CIB had served as an infantryman in both World War II and the Korean War. An equally prestigious award is the Combat Field Medic Badge (CFMB) that distinguishes medics

who directly supported infantry units. Both the CIB and the CFMB are unique to the army and are worn on the left breast, above the decorations, service medals, and all other qualification badges.

Among the U.S. military services, the army has a unique way of recognizing overseas service in a combat zone. Every U.S. Army soldier wears the patch of his current unit of assignment on his left shoulder. (The U.S. Air Force, Navy, and Marine Corps do not use unit shoulder patches.) A soldier who serves overseas in a combat zone with a unit is entitled to wear that unit's patch permanently on his right shoulder. Often erroneously called a combat patch, its proper designation is "overseas service patch." Well into the late 1970s, U.S. Army soldiers could still be seen wearing patches on their right shoulder from Korean War service.

Immediately following World War II, U.S. military personnel performed occupation duty in Korea between September 3, 1945, and June 29, 1949. That service was recognized with the Army of Occupation Medal or the Navy Occupation Service Medal. All personnel who served in the U.S. armed forces anywhere in the world during the Korean War period, from June 27, 1950, to July 27, 1954, received the National Defense Service Medal (NDSM), established by Presidential Executive Order 10448. The NDSM was authorized again in subsequent wars and foreign peacekeeping missions.

Those who actually served in Korea or its contiguous airspace or waters between June 27, 1950, and July 27, 1954, received the Korean Service Medal, established by Presidential Executive Order 110179. As in previous wars, participation in each specific campaign entitled the soldier to wear a small bronze star device on the medal's ribbon. Every fifth campaign was indicated with a small silver star device. Ten campaigns were conducted during the Korean War. A bronze arrowhead device on the Korean Service Medal indicated participation in an assault operation. In addition, paratroopers who participated in a combat jump were also authorized to wear a small gold star affixed to their airborne wings.

Between October 1, 1966, and June 30, 1974, U.S. troops serving in Korea were authorized the Armed Forces Expeditionary Medal. A state of war technically still existed between the Democratic People's Republic of Korea (DPRK, North Korea) and the Republic of Korea (ROK, South Korea), and this was a period of high tension, numerous infiltration attempts by the North Koreans, and frequent armed clashes along the demilitarized zone. Some soldiers were awarded the CIB during this period, and U.S. troops did suffer casualties.

In 1956 the U.S. Congress authorized the Merchant Marine Korean Service Ribbon Bar for crew members who served aboard ships flying the American flag in Korean waters. In May 1988 the Congress also authorized the Merchant Marine Korea Service Medal to correspond to the existing campaign ribbon bar. In 1986 Congress authorized the creation of the Prisoner of War Medal for all U.S. servicemen held captive by an enemy force after April 5, 1917, thus making award of the medal retroactive to World War I.

The United States also recognizes entire units with military decorations. Individuals who are members of the unit at the time the award is won are entitled to wear the unit award permanently on their uniforms. An individual joining a decorated unit at a later time can only wear the unit award while assigned to the unit.

The Distinguished Unit Citation for army and air force units and the Presidential Unit Citation for navy units were established in 1942. In 1957 the Distinguished Unit Citation was redesignated the Presidential Unit Citation (PUC). The PUC is the equivalent of a DSC for a unit. At the next level down, the Naval Unit Citation is the unit equivalent of an individual Bronze Star Medal. The army Meritorious Unit Citation (MUC), which has stricter criteria, is considered the equivalent of a unit Legion of Merit.

The U.S. Army unit awards are easily identifiable by the gilt frame around the ribbon. The PUC is a solid blue ribbon in a gilt frame. The MUC was originally an embroidered gold wreath on an olive patch, worn on the lower left sleeve of the uniform. After the Korean War, the MUC was converted to a solid red ribbon in a gilt frame. Members of the U.S. Army wear unit awards over their right pockets. Members of the U.S. Navy, Air Force, and Marine Corps wear unit awards over their left pockets, integrated with their individual awards.

Great Britain and the Commonwealth

The British use a composite system of military awards. Some awards are only for officers, some are only for enlisted men, and some are for both. The highest British award for combat valor is the Victoria Cross (VC), established in 1856. The highest British award for noncombat valor is the George Cross (GC), established in 1940. The VC can only be awarded for gallantry in the face of enemy fire, whereas the GC is awarded for acts of noncombat heroism in either peacetime or war.

The criteria for the VC are actually more restrictive than for the U.S. Medal of Honor, which requires courage in the face of the enemy and the threat of loss of one's own life but not necessarily under direct enemy fire. Thus, U.S. soldiers have been awarded the Medal of Honor for acts of extreme heroism while prisoners of war. British soldiers under the same conditions receive the GC. Both officers and enlisted men are eligible for both the VC and the GC, and British civilians in noncombat situations are eligible for the GC. During the Korean War four British soldiers received the VC (two posthumously), and two Britons and one Australian received the GC (all as prisoners of war).

After the VC and GC, the next highest British military awards are the first three classes of the Order of the British Empire, the Distinguished Service Order (DSO), and then the last two classes of the Order of the British Empire. Only officers are generally eligible for these awards. Both orders can be given for either exceptional service or for heroism, but the DSO is given only for wartime service. Officers receiving the DSO are considered to have just missed the award of the VC. During the Korean War the DSO was awarded to 62 British, 11 Australian, 10 Canadian, and 4 New Zealand officers.

The Distinguished Conduct Medal (army and air force) and the Conspicuous Gallantry Medal (navy) are the awards for enlisted men who just missed the VC. The DSC (navy), Military Cross (army), and Distinguished Flying Cross (air force) are combat heroism decorations for officers, although in some cases warrant officers qualify. The enlisted equivalents are the Distinguished Service Medal (navy), the Military Medal (army), and the Distinguished Flying Medal (air force).

Subsequent awards of British medals and decorations are indicated by a bar affixed to the medal ribbon or by a heraldic rose device affixed to the ribbon bar. British soldiers who are Mentioned in Dispatches (MID) are authorized to wear an oak leaf device on the appropriate campaign medal. During the Korean War, more than 1,300 Commonwealth and 77 allied soldiers were MID.

During the war, two British soldiers were awarded the U.S. DSC, and 19 were awarded the Silver Star. The 1st Battalion, Gloucestershire Regiment, and the Royal Artillery's C Troop, 170th Independent Mortar Battery, both received the American Presidential Unit Citation for action at the Imjin River (April 22–25, 1951). The American PUC remains a permanent part of the Gloucestershire uniform to this day.

Commonwealth soldiers, including those of Great Britain, New Zealand, Australia, and the Union of South Africa, all received the Korea Medal for service in the Korean War. Canadians received the Korea Volunteer Service Medal, which had a different ribbon and the name "Canada" on the medal beneath the queen's profile.

France

France's highest decoration is the Légion d'Honneur, instituted by Napoleon Bonaparte in 1802 and awarded to French citizens and foreigners for outstanding services to France, civil or military. In practice, it is rarely awarded to enlisted men. For Korean War service, it was awarded in the three lower of its five classes: commander once, officer seven times, and chevalier twice.

The Médaille Militare, instituted by Louis Napoleon in 1852, is France's highest strictly military decoration. It is a most unusual decoration in that it can be awarded only to enlisted men and noncommissioned officers and to generals and admirals. Officers from the ranks of lieutenant through colonel cannot receive the award. The Médaille Militare was awarded 193 times for Korean War service.

The Croix de Guerre des Théâtres d'Operations Extérieures was awarded 2,898 times for the Korean War. Created in 1921 to recognize valor in expeditionary operations, it was similar to the Croix de Guerre of the two world wars. Because all members of the French Battalion in Korea were volunteers, they essentially all received the Croix du Combattant Volontaire. In 1980 a bar for "Corée" was authorized for that decoration.

Finally, all French servicemen in Korea received the French Korean Campaign Medal, the Médaille Commémorative Française des Opérations de l'Organisation des Nations Unies en Corée. The medal was authorized by the French Ministry of Defense on January 8, 1952.

South Korea

The highest military decoration of South Korea is the Order of Military Merit. The order has four classes: Taeguk, Ulchi, Chungmu, and Hwarang. Each class has three grades, designated by a gold star, a silver star, or no device on the ribbon and ribbon bar. Foreigners are eligible for the Order of Military Merit. After his repatriation as a prisoner of war, the Taeguk Class with Gold Star was awarded to Major General William F. Dean, former commander of the U.S. 24th Infantry Division. Dean also received the U.S. Medal of Honor.

The Defense Medal was the only other South Korean decoration for military service outside of the Order of Military Merit group. South Korea also had a Wound Medal in two classes: First Class for the loss of a limb, loss of sight, or other disabling wound, and Second Class for all other wounds. Families of soldiers killed in action received the Family of Killed in Action Award.

The South Korean War Service Medal is officially called the June 25 Incident Participation Medal. This medal was awarded to many allied soldiers, but the U.S. government declined the blanket awarding of the War Service Medal to U.S. troops. The United States did, however, allow its units to accept award of the Korean Presidential Unit Citation. As with the American PUC, the Korean PUC is a ribbon in a gilt frame. U.S. personnel wore it on their uniforms in the same manner as the American unit citations.

Other Allied Nations

Most other allied nations that sent troops to Korea recognized their service with the creation of Korean service medals or the awarding of existing general service medals with Korea bars. Those nations include Belgium, Colombia, Ethiopia, India, Luxembourg, the Netherlands, Norway, the Philippines, and Thailand. Danish personnel who served on the hospital ship *Jutlandia* received the special Jutlandia Medal.

Greece and Turkey did not institute special medals for Korean service. Their soldiers received only the United Nations Korea Medal. Ironically, most Turkish soldiers either refused to wear the medal or wore it with a plain dark red ribbon because the ribbon's original colors are also those of Turkey's bitter historical rival, Greece.

North Korea

As with most communist countries of the Cold War era, the North Korean military awards system was strongly influenced by the system of the former Soviet Union. The highest North Korean decoration is the Gold Star Medal, which carries with it the title of Hero of the Democratic People's Republic of Korea (DPRK). Its purpose is to honor heroic exploits in war. It is the equivalent of the Hero of the Soviet Union, which it resembles. As in the former Soviet system, the title of Labor Hero of the Korean DPR is a noncombat decoration considered to be of equal status.

The Order of the National Flag exists in three classes. It can be awarded for military valor or for outstanding political, cultural, or economic achievement. The Freedom and Independence Order is a combat award for commanders. The order's First Class is for division and brigade commanders, and the Second Class is for all other commanders. The Soldier's Honor Medal is a combat decoration for enlisted men and second lieutenants. It too is awarded in two classes.

The Military Merit Medal was the closest thing that the North Koreans had to a campaign medal at the time of the war. On July 25, 1985, the Fatherland Liberation Commemoration Medal was established in recognition of the 40th anniversary of the founding of the Korean Workers' Party and to commend those who served in the "Fatherland Liberation War that opposed the American invaders and their tools." Chinese People's Volunteer Army (CPVA, Chinese Army) troops who served during the war were awarded the Military Merit Medal.

China

The Commemorative Medal for Opposing America in Assisting Korea was the Chinese campaign medal for the Korean War. Because the People's Republic of China (PRC) was not officially in Korea, CPVA members were awarded this medal by the People's Political Consultative Conference National Committee. The Chinese characters on the medal read "Oppose America, Aid Korea, Commemorative." Similar commemorative medals were awarded to Chinese troops by some of the Chinese provinces close to the Korean border, Sungjiang and Liaoshi provinces among them.

The Chinese also issued two very similar-sounding medals in conjunction with the visits to Korea of high-ranking Chinese delegations. The Commemorative Medal for War to Resist U.S. Aggression and Aid Korea was awarded in March 1951 to senior CPVA officers. On September 18, 1952, the Commemorative Badge for the Victory and Peace of the Korean War was issued to all Chinese troops and to North Korean officials.

Ironically, China was the only nation to issue a victory or peace medal in connection with the Korean War. Authorized on October 25, 1953, the Peace Medal reads "Glorious Peace" on its obverse and "War to Resist U.S. Aggression and Aid Korea" on its reverse.

Relative Precedence of U.S. Military Decorations during the Korean War

Navy Medal of Honor (1861)
Army Medal of Honor (1862)
Distinguished Service Cross (1918)
Navy Cross (1919)
Army Distinguished Service Medal (1918)
Navy Distinguished Service Medal (1918)
Coast Guard Distinguished Service Medal (1949)
Silver Star (1918)
Legion of Merit (1942)
Distinguished Flying Cross (1926)
Soldier's Medal (1926)
Navy and Marine Corps Medal (1942)

Bronze Star Medal (1942)
Air Medal (1942)
Navy Commendation Medal (1944)
Army Commendation Medal (1945)
Coast Guard Commendation Medal (1951)
Purple Heart (1932)*

* Note: After the Vietnam War, the precedence of the Purple Heart was elevated to just beneath the Bronze Star Medal.

Campaigns Authorized for Wearing of the Star Device and Assaults Authorized for Wearing of the Arrowhead Device on the U.S. Korean Service Medal

UN Defensive	June 27–September 15, 1950
UN Offensive	September 16, 1950–November 2, 1950
Chinese Intervention	November 3, 1950–January 24, 1951
First UN Counteroffensive	January 25, 1951–April 21, 1951
Chinese Spring Offensive	April 22, 1951–July 8, 1951
UN Summer-Fall Offensive	July 9, 1951–November 27, 1951
Second Korean Winter	November 28, 1951–April 30, 1952
Korea Summer-Fall	May 1, 1952–November 30, 1952
Third Korean Winter	December 1, 1952–April 30, 1953
Korea Summer-Fall	May 1, 1953–July 27, 1953
Amphibious Assault, Inchon	September 15, 1950
Airborne Assault, Sunchon-Sukchon	October 20, 1950
Airborne Assault, Munsan-ni	March 23, 1951

Relative Precedence of British Orders and Decorations

Victoria Cross (VC) (1856)
George Cross (GC) (1940)
Order of the British Empire, Knight Grand Cross (GBE) (1917)
Order of the British Empire, Knight Commander (KBE) (1917)
Order of the British Empire, Commander (CBE) (1917)
Distinguished Service Order (DSO) (1886)
Order of the British Empire, Officer (OBE) (1917)
Order of the British Empire, Member (MBE) (1917)
Distinguished Service Cross (DSC) (1914)
Military Cross (MC) (1914)
Distinguished Flying Cross (DFC) (1918)
Air Force Cross (AFC) (1918)
Distinguished Conduct Medal (DCM) (1854)
Conspicuous Gallantry Medal (CGM) (1855)
George Medal (GM) (1940)
Distinguished Service Medal (DSM) (1914)
Military Medal (MM) (1916)
Distinguished Flying Medal (DFM) (1918)

Air Force Medal (AFM) (1918)
British Empire Medal (BEM) (1917)
Mentions in Dispatches (MID)

Relative Precedence of Military Decorations of South Korea

Distinguished Military Service Medal Taeguk Class (1948)
Distinguished Military Service Medal Ulchi Class (1948)
Distinguished Military Service Medal Chungmu Class (1948)
Distinguished Military Service Medal Hwarang Class (1948)
Defense Medal (1950)
First Class Special Wound Medal (1950)
Second Class Wound Medal (1950)

Relative Precedence of Military Decorations of North Korea

Title of Hero of the Korean DPR/Gold Star Medal (1950)
Title of Labor Hero of the Korean DPR (1951)
Order of the National Flag (1951)
Freedom and Independence Order (1950)
Soldier's Honor Medal (1950)
Order of Labor (1950)
Military Merit Medal (1949)

Soviet Union

The opening of records and archives since the end of the Cold War has revealed a significant presence of Soviet troops in North Korea during the war. These included advisers and liaison officers, air defense crews in the vicinity of the Manchurian airfields, and rotating units of Soviet pilots flying Mikoyan-Gurevich MiG-15s. Although the picture is still incomplete, it appears that more than 14 Soviet pilots achieved ace status in the skies over Korea. At least 21 of these pilots received the Soviet Union's highest decoration, the Gold Star Medal and the title of Hero of the Soviet Union.

DAVID T. ZABECKI

References

Borts, Lawrence H. *United Nations Medals and Missions.* Fountain Inn, SC: MOA Press, 1998.

Cunningham-Boothe, Ashley. *Marks of Courage.* Royal Leamington Spa, UK: Korvet, 1991.

Hall, Donald. *British Orders, Decorations and Medals.* St. Ives, Huntingdon, UK: Balfour, 1973.

Ingraham, Kevin R. *Honors, Medals and Awards of the Korean War, 1950–1953.* Binghamton, NY: Johnson City, 1993.

Kerrigan, Evans. *American Medals and Decorations.* London: Apple, 1990.

U.S. Senate Committee on Veterans' Affairs, 96th Cong. *Medal of Honor Recipients, 1863–1978.* Washington, DC: U.S. Government Printing Office, 1979.

Appendix C

Medal of Honor Winners

Data about Korean War Medal of Honor winners reveals patterns of places and dates of actions where high casualties occurred and also shows how quickly men of various ranks received their honor and the development of official recognition of heroism throughout the war. The ambiguity of place, sometimes listed simply as Korea or near geographic sites, shows the chaotic nature of the war. Many of the men were promoted after their award, and the rank listed in this appendix is the rank they held at the time of the action meriting their medal. When the date of presentation was not available, the date of the general order is substituted.

Two books focus on Korean War Medal of Honor winners: Edward F. Murphy's *Korean War Heroes* and Bruce Jacobs's *Korea's Heroes: The Medal of Honor Story*. For further details about an individual's biographical information such as birth date, hometown, unit, and service entry location as well as full text of award citations, see George Lang, Raymond L. Collins, and Gerard White, *Medal of Honor Recipients, 1863–1994*.

The following lists Medal of Honor winners in the Korean War chronologically by date of action. The asterisk (*) indicates that the medal was awarded posthumously.

Name	Branch/Rank	Location	Date of Action	Date Presented
*George D. Libby	USA/Sgt	near Taejon	July 20, 1950	June 20, 1951
William F. Dean Sr.	USA/MajGen	Taejon	July 20–21, 1950	January 9, 1951
*Louis J. Sebille	USAF/Maj	near Hanchang-ni	August 5, 1950	August 24, 1951
*William Thompson	USA/PFC	near Haman	August 6, 1950	June 21, 1951
*Melvin O. Handrich	USA/MSgt	near Sobuk-san Mt	August 25–26, 1950	June 21, 1951
Ernest R. Kouma	USA/SFC	near Agok-ni	August 31–September 1, 1950	May 19, 1951
*Joseph R. Ouellette	USA/PFC	near Yongsan	August 31–September 3, 1950	April 3, 1951
*Travis E. Watkins	USA/MSgt	near Yongsan	August 31–September 3, 1950	January 9, 1951
*Frederick F. Henry	USA/1Lt	near Amdong-ni	September 1, 1950	January 9, 1951
*David M. Smith	USA/PFC	near Yongsan	September 1, 1950	August 14, 1952
*Luther H. Story	USA/PFC	near Agok-ni	September 1, 1950	June 21, 1951
*Charles W. Turner	USA/SFC	near Yongsan	September 1, 1950	January 9, 1951
*Melvin L. Brown	USA/PFC	near Kasan	September 4, 1950	January 9, 1951
*Loren R. Kaufman	USA/SFC	near Yongsan	September 4–5, 1950	June 21, 1951
*Gordon M. Craig	USA/Cpl	near Kasan	September 10, 1950	April 3, 1951
*Baldomero Lopez	USMC/1Lt	Inchon invasion	September 15, 1950	August 30, 1951
*Walter C. Monegan Jr.	USMC/PFC	near Sosa-ri	September 17–20, 1950	February 8, 1952
*John W. Collier	USA/Cpl	near Chindong-ni	September 19, 1950	June 21, 1951

continued

Name	Branch/Rank	Location	Date of Action	Date Presented
*William R. Jecelin	USA/Sgt	near Saga	September 19, 1950	April 3, 1951
Henry A. Commiskey Sr.	USMC/2Lt	near Yongdungpo	September 20, 1950	August 1, 1951
*Eugene A. Obregon	USMC/PFC	Seoul	September 26, 1950	August 30, 1951
*Stanley R. Christianson	USMC/PFC	Seoul	September 29, 1950	August 30, 1951
*Robert H. Young	USA/PFC	north of Kaesong	October 9, 1950	June 21, 1951
*Samuel S. Coursen	USA/1Lt	near Kaesong	October 12, 1950	June 21, 1951
*Richard G. Wilson	USA/PFC	near Opa-ri	October 21, 1950	June 21, 1951
Archie Van Winkle	USMCR/SSgt	near Sudong	November 2, 1950	February 6, 1951
*Lee H. Phillips	USMC/Cpl	Korea	November 4, 1950	none given
*James I. Poynter	USMCR/Sgt	near Sudong	November 4, 1950	September 4, 1952
*Mitchell Red Cloud Jr.	USA/Cpl	near Chonghyon	November 5, 1950	April 3, 1951
*Robert Dale Reem	USMC/2Lt	near Chinhung-ni	November 6, 1950	February 8, 1952
*Frank N. Mitchell	USMC/1Lt	near Hansan-ni	November 26, 1950	none given
John A. Pittman	USA/Sgt	near Kujang-dong	November 26, 1950	May 19, 1951
*Reginald B. Desiderio	USA/Capt	near Ipsok	November 27, 1950	June 21, 1951
Robert S. Kennemore	USMC/SSgt	north of Yudam-ni	November 27–28, 1950	none given
*Don C. Faith Jr.	USA/LtCol	vicinity of Hagaru-ri	November 27–December 1, 1950	June 21, 1951
Hector A. Cafferata Jr.	USMCR/Pvt	Oktong Pass	November 28, 1950	November 24, 1952
*William B. Baugh	USMC/PFC	mid Koto-ri/Hagaru-ri	November 29, 1950	August 27, 1952
Reginald R. Myers	USMC/Maj	near Hagaru-ri	November 29, 1950	October 29, 1951
Carl L. Sitter	USMC/Capt	Hagaru-ri	November 29–30, 1950	October 29, 1951
*John U. D. Page	USA/LtCol	near Changjin (Chosin) Reservoir	November 29–December 10, 1950	December 19, 1956
*William G. Windrich	USMC/SSgt	near Yudam-ni	December 1, 1950	February 8, 1952
Raymond G. Davis	USMC/LtCol	near Hagaru-ri	December 1–4, 1950	November 24, 1952
William E. Barber	USMC/Capt	Changjin (Chosin) Reservoir area	December 2, 1950	August 20, 1952
*James E. Johnson	USMC/Sgt	Yudam-ni	December 2, 1950	March 29, 1954
Thomas J. Hudner Jr.	USN/LtJG	Changjin (Chosin) Reservoir area	December 4, 1950	April 13, 1951
*Junior D. Edwards	USA/SFC	near Changbong-ni	January 2, 1951	January 16, 1952
*Robert M. McGovern	USA/1Lt	near Kumyangjan-ni	January 30, 1951	January 8, 1952
Carl H. Dodd	USA/2Lt	near Sobuk	January 30–31, 1951	May 19, 1951
Hubert L. Lee	USA/MSgt	near Ipo-ri	February 1, 1951	January 29, 1952
Stanley T. Adams	USA/SFC	near Sesim-ni	February 4, 1951	July 5, 1951
Lewis L. Millett	USA/Capt	near Soam-ni	February 7, 1951	July 5, 1951
*Charles R. Long	USA/Sgt	near Hoengsong	February 12, 1951	January 16, 1952
*William S. Sitman	USA/SFC	near Chipyong-ni	February 14, 1951	January 16, 1952
*Darwin K. Kyle	USA/2Lt	near Kamil-ri	February 16, 1951	January 16, 1952
Einar H. Ingman Jr.	USA/Cpl	near Malta-ri	February 26, 1951	July 5, 1951
*Nelson V. Brittin	USA/SFC	near Yonggong-ni	March 7, 1951	January 16, 1952
Raymond Harvey	USA/Capt	near Taemi-dong	March 9, 1951	July 5, 1951
*Richard David Dewert	USN/Hn	Korea	April 5, 1951	May 27, 1952
*Herbert A. Littleton	USMCR/PFC	Chunchon	April 22, 1951	July 1, 1950
Harold E. Wilson	USMCR/TSgt	Korea	April 23–24, 1951	April 12, 1952
*Clair Goodblood	USA/Cpl	near Popsu-dong	April 24–25, 1951	January 16, 1952
Hiroshi H. Miyamura	USA/Cpl	near Taejon-ni	April 24–25, 1951	October 27, 1953
*John Essebagger Jr.	USA/Cpl	near Popsu-dong	April 25, 1951	March 26, 1952
*Charles L. Gilliland	USA/PFC	near Tongmang-ni	April 25, 1951	January 11, 1955
*Ray E. Duke	USA/SFC	near Mugok	April 26, 1951	March 19, 1954

Name	Branch/Rank	Location	Date of Action	Date Presented
*Donald R. Moyer	USA/SFC	near Seoul	May 20, 1951	January 16, 1952
Joseph C. Rodriguez	USA/PFC	near Munye-ri	May 21, 1951	January 29, 1952
*Whitt L. Moreland	USMC/PFC	Kwahchi-dong	May 29, 1951	July 19, 1951
Rodolfo P. Hernandez	USA/Cpl	near Wontong-ni	May 31, 1951	April 12, 1952
*Cornelius H. Charlton	USA/Sgt	near Chipo-ri	June 2, 1951	March 12, 1952
Benjamin F. Wilson	USA/MSgt	near Hwachon-myon	June 5, 1951	September 7, 1954
*Jack G. Hanson	USA/PFC	near Pacji-dong	June 7, 1951	January 16, 1952
*Charles G. Abrell	USMC/Cpl	Hang-nyong	June 10, 1951	September 4, 1952
*Emory L. Bennett	USA/PFC	near Sobang-san	June 24, 1951	January 16, 1952
*John Kelvin Koelsch	USN/LtJG	near Wonsan	July 3, 1951	August 1955
*Leroy A. Mendonca	USA/Sgt	near Chichon	July 4, 1951	August 14, 1952
*Lee R. Hartell	USA/1Lt	near Kobangsan-ni	August 27, 1951	January 16, 1952
*William F. Lyell	USA/Cpl	near Chupa-ri	August 31, 1951	January 7, 1953
*Edward C. Krzyzowski	USA/Capt	near Tondul	August 31–September 3, 1951	March 26, 1952
Jerry K. Crump	USA/Cpl	near Chorwon	September 6–7, 1951	June 27, 1952
*Billie G. Kanell	USA/Pvt	near Pyongyang	September 7, 1951	March 26, 1952
*Frederick Mausert III	USMC/Sgt	Songnaepyong	September 12, 1951	September 4, 1952
*George H. Ramer	USMCR/2Lt	Korea	September 12, 1951	January 7, 1953
*Jerome A. Sudut	USA/2Lt	near Kimhwa	September 12, 1951	March 13, 1952
*Edward Gomez	USMC/PFC	Hill 749	September 14, 1951	none given
*John S. Walmsley Jr.	USAF/Capt	near Yangdok	September 14, 1951	June 12, 1954
*Joseph Vittori	USMCR/Cpl	Hill 749	September 15–16, 1951	none given
*Herbert K. Pililaau	USA/PFC	near Pia-ri	September 17, 1951	March 26, 1952
*Jack A. Davenport	USMC/Cpl	near Songnae-dong	September 21, 1951	January 7, 1953
*Tony K. Burris	USA/SFC	near Mundung-ni	October 8–9, 1951	August 14, 1952
Lloyd L. Burke	USA/1Lt	near Chong-dong	October 28, 1951	April 12, 1952
*Mack A. Jordan	USA/PFC	near Kumsong	November 15, 1951	January 7, 1953
James L. Stone	USA/1Lt	near Sogogae Pass	November 21–22, 1951	October 27, 1953
*Noah O. Knight	USA/PFC	Near Kowang-san	November 23–24, 1951	January 7, 1953
Ronald E. Rosser	USA/Cpl	Near Ponggil-ri	January 12, 1952	June 27, 1952
*George Andrew Davis Jr.	USAF/Maj	Near Sinuiju-Yalu River	February 10, 1952	May 14, 1954
*Bryant E. Womack	USA/Pvt	near Sokso-ri	March 12, 1952	January 7, 1953
Duane E. Dewey	USMC/Cpl	near Panmunjom	April 16, 1952	March 12, 1953
*David B. Champagne	USMC/Cpl	Korea	May 28, 1952	none given
*John D. Kelly	USMC/PFC	Korea	May 28, 1952	September 9, 1953
David B. Bleak	USA/Sgt	near Minari-kol ravine	June 14, 1952	October 27, 1953
*Clifton T. Speicher	USA/Cpl	near Minari-kol ravine	June 14, 1952	August 5, 1953
*William E. Shuck Jr.	USMC/SSgt	Korea	July 3, 1952	September 9, 1953
*John E. Kilmer	USB/Hn	Korea	August 13, 1952	none given
*Lester Hammond Jr.	USA/Cpl	near Kimhwa	August 14, 1952	August 5, 1953
Robert E. Simanek	USMC/PFC	Outpost Irene	August 17, 1952	October 27, 1953
Alford L. McLaughlin	USMC/PFC	Outpost Bruce	September 4–5, 1952	October 27, 1953
*Edward C. Benford	USN/Hn3	Korea	September 5, 1952	July 16, 1953
*Fernando Luis Garcia	USMC/PFC	Korea	September 5, 1952	October 25, 1953
*Benito Martinez	USA/Cpl	near Satae-ri	September 6, 1952	December 16, 1953
*Donn F. Porter	USA/Sgt	near Mundung-ni	September 7, 1952	August 5, 1953
*Jack William Kelso	USMC/PFC	Korea	October 2, 1952	September 9, 1953
*Lewis G. Watkins	USMC/SSgt	Korea	October 7, 1952	September 9, 1953
Ernest E. West	USA/PFC	near Satae-ri	October 12, 1952	January 12, 1954
Edward R. Schowalter Jr.	USA/1Lt	near Kimhwa	October 14, 1952	October 12, 1953

Name	Branch/Rank	Location	Date of Action	Date Presented
*Ralph E. Pomeroy	USA/PFC	near Kimhwa	October 15, 1952	December 30, 1953
*Sherrod E. Skinner Jr.	USMCR/2Lt	Korea	October 26, 1952	September 9, 1953
George H. O'Brien Jr.	USMCR/2Lt	The Hook	October 27, 1952	October 27, 1953
*Charles J. Loring Jr.	USAF/Maj	near Sniper Ridge	November 22, 1952	May 5, 1954
*Charles George	USA/PFC	near Songnae-dong	November 30, 1952	March 18, 1954
Raymond G. Murphy	USMCR/2Lt	Ungok Hill	February 3, 1953	October 27, 1953
*Francis C. Hammond	USN/Hn	near Sanak-dong	March 26–27, 1953	December 29, 1953
William R. Charette	USN/Hn3	Panmunjom Corridor	March 27, 1953	January 12, 1954
*Daniel P. Matthews	USMC/Sgt	Vegas Hill	March 28, 1953	March 29, 1954
*Charles H. Barker	USA/PFC	near Sogogae Pass	June 4, 1953	June 7, 1955
Ola L. Mize	USA/Sgt	Near Surang-ni	June 10–11, 1953	September 7, 1954
*Richard T. Shea Jr.	USA/1Lt	Pork Chop Hill	July 6–8, 1953	May 16, 1955
*Dan D. Schoonover	USA/Cpl	Pork Chop Hill	July 8–10, 1953	July 1954
*Charles F. Pendleton	USA/Cpl	near Chungu-dong	July 16–17, 1953	none given
*Gilbert G. Collier	USA/Cpl	near Tutayon	July 19–20, 1953	January 12, 1955
*Ambrosio Guillen	USMC/SSgt	near Songuchon	July 25, 1953	none given

ELIZABETH D. SCHAFER

References

Jacobs, Bruce. *Korea's Heroes: The Medal of Honor Story.* New York: Berkley Publishing, 1961.

Lang, George, Raymond L. Collins, and Gerard White. *Medal of Honor Recipients, 1863–1994.* 2 vols. New York: Facts on File, 1995.

Murphy, Edward F. *Korean War Heroes.* Novato, CA: Presidio, 1997.

Proft, R. J., ed. *United States of America's Congressional Medal of Honor Recipients and Their Official Citations.* Columbia Heights, MN: Highland House II, 1997.

Chronology

Until January 1, 1896, Korea used the lunar calendar; all dates here have been converted to the modern calendar.

February 1866

Systematic persecution of Christians, in which nine French priests and a large number of Korean converts to Christianity are executed.

August 1886

In the *General Sherman* incident, the U.S. schooner *General Sherman,* the crew of which is attempting to trade with Korea, is burned, and its 23 crew members are killed.

October 1886

A French naval squadron of seven warships transporting 1,000 troops and commanded by Admiral Pierre Roze attacks Ganghwa (Kanghwa) Island at the mouth of the Han River. The French landing force meets Korean opposition and is unable to proceed to Seoul. The French pillage and carry off treasure and valuable cultural objects before departure.

May–June 1871

The United States dispatches a naval squadron of five warships under Rear Admiral John Rodgers in support of a diplomatic effort to investigate the imprisonment and murder of American seamen aboard the merchantman *General Sherman*. The U.S. government seeks a treaty that will guarantee proper treatment for shipwrecked sailors but also diplomatic ties and trade relations with Korea. A diplomatic impasse, however, quickly turns into armed conflict.

When his ships are fired on in the Han River on the west coast of South Korea beginning on June 10, 1871, Rodgers lands marines and sailors on Ganghwa (Kanghwa) Island in the Han River estuary. Supported by naval gunfire, the landing party seizes the forts on the island, but this American victory is devoid of significance. The Korean government refuses to negotiate (and indeed strengthens its policies against dealing with foreigners). The Americans withdraw, having failed to secure their diplomatic objectives.

February 1876

26   Japan imposes the Treaty of Ganghwa (Kanghwa) (Friendship Treaty) on Korea, forcing it to open its trade to Japan and to proclaim its independence from China in foreign relations. Japan also secures permission to maintain a legation in Seoul. Korea had traditionally been a tributary state of the Qing dynasty China.

May 1882

22   Korea concludes the Treaty of Peace, Amity, Commerce, and Navigation with the United States. The treaty enters into force on May 19, 1883. Similar treaties are concluded with Great Britain and Germany (November 26, 1883), Russia (July 7, 1884), and other European powers.

July 1882

19   Soldiers of the Muwiyong, Palace Guards Garrison, and the Changoyong, Capital Guards Garrison, believing that they have been discriminated against by the elite

Pyolgigun, Special Skills Force, established the year before, mutiny and kill Japanese training officers and burn the Japanese legation, the members of which manage to escape.

August 1882

2   To suppress the military mutiny, the Korean government asks China, the power exercising suzerainty over Korea, to send in troops.

10   Some 4,500 Chinese troops arrive in three warships at the port of Chemulpo (now Inchon).

12   The Japanese government also sends four warships to Chemulpo (Inchon) along with a battalion of troops, who proceed to Seoul. Pressed by Japan, the Korean government on August 30, 1882, concludes the Treaty of Chemulpo, which stipulates that the leaders of the military mutiny will be punished, families of Japanese victims will be indemnified to the amount of 50,000 yen, the Japanese government will receive 500,000 yen, and Japan will be permitted to station a company of guards at the Japanese legation in Seoul.

September 1882

20   Korea sends a delegation headed by Pak Yong Hyo to Tokyo to make formal apology to Japan. The Choson delegation takes the present-day South Korean national flag, Taegukki (Great Absolute Flag). The Taegukki is formally adopted as the national flag on March 6, 1883.

July 1883

8   A Korean diplomatic mission led by Min Yong Ik is dispatched to the United States.

December 1884

4   Members of the Kaehwadang (Reform Party) led by Kim Ok Kyun and allied with Japan, stage a coup d'état, killing and wounding a number of senior officials of the Sadaedang (Party of Serving the Majority) and capturing the king. The Kaehwadang then forms a new government and announces a reform program.

11   Chinese forces defeat Japanese forces that had helped the Kaehwadang members stage the coup, and they secure the king. Kim Ok Kyun and other Kaehwadang members escape to Japan.

January 1885

9   Korea and Japan conclude the Treaty of Hansong (Seoul) for indemnities to the Japanese victims of the Kaehwadang coup and compensation for rebuilding the Japanese legation.

April 1885

15   In the course of an Anglo-Russian crisis, Great Britain illegally occupies Komun-do island off the southern coast of Cholla Province. The British call the island Fort Hamilton. Despite protests from China and Korea, the British occupy the island until February 27, 1887.

May 1885

31   The Convention of Tientsin (Tianjin) is concluded between China and Japan. Troops of both countries are to be withdrawn from Korea within four months, and there is to be prior notification to the other party when troops are to be dispatched to Korea.

February 1894

15   In reaction to economic exploitation by Cho Pyong Gap, magistrate of Kobu County of Cholla Province, local peasants under the leadership of Chon Pong Jun occupy the county headquarters, initiating the Tonghak peasant war.

May 1894

10–11   Tonghak peasant forces defeat Korean government troops in the Battle of Hwangtohyon Hill, south of Kobu.

31   Tonghak peasant forces capture Chonju, the provincial capital of Cholla Province. They then advance toward Seoul.

June 1894

1   Unable to suppress the Tonghak peasant rebellion by itself, the Korean government formally requests Chinese military assistance.

6   The Chinese government formally notifies Japan in accordance with the Convention of Tianjin (Tientsin) that it is sending troops to Korea. Within days, some 2,500 Chinese troops land at Asan Bay.

8   The first of some 4,500 Japanese troops land at the Korean port of Inchon (Chemulpo).

10   The Korean government and Tonghak forces conclude the Peace of Chonju, which ends the Tonghak Rebellion and leads to the withdrawal of the latter from Chonju. Japanese forces, however, enter Seoul.

16   Mutusu Munemitsu, the Japanese foreign minister, meets with Want Fengzao, the Chinese ambassador to Japan. Wang informs the Japanese that China intends to withdraw its troops from Korea and expects Japan to do the same. He also asserts the right of China to exert suzerainty over Korea.

July 1894

11–15   Seeking to secure a protectorate, the Japanese demand that the Korean government carry out internal reforms. The Korean government, however, refuses to yield to

Japanese pressure and demands the withdrawal of Japanese troops.

23 Japanese troops enter the city of Seoul, drive the pro-Chinese faction from the Korean government, and establish a new pro-Japanese government that terminates all treaties between Korea and China and demands that Chinese troops leave Korea.

25 In a preemptive attack, three Japanese Navy cruisers attack and destroy two Chinese warships at Asan Bay, the supply route for Chinese forces in Korea.

27 The new pro-Japanese Korean government undertakes the Kabo Kyongjang (Reform of 1894).

28–29 In a land engagement near Asan Bay, Japanese forces defeat the Chinese. The Chinese suffer some 500 casualties, the Japanese only 82.

August 1894

1 War is officially declared between Japan and China.

September 1894

15 Japanese forces rout Chinese forces in the Battle of Pyongyang. The Chinese sustain some 2,000 killed and 4,000 wounded; the Japanese lose only 102 killed, 433 wounded, and 33 missing. This battle virtually assures the Japanese of victory in the Sino-Japanese War.

17 Japanese warships engage and sink 8 of 10 Chinese warships in the decisive Battle of the Yalu River, assuring Japan command of the sea.

November 1894

6 Angered at Japan taking control of Korea, Tonghak forces again take to arms.

19 Tonghak forces are defeated in the Battle of Kongju in Chungchong Province by Korean government troops reinforced by a Japanese Army contingent.

January 1895

22 The Tonghak peasant rebellion comes to an end.

April 1895

17 Japan and China conclude the Treaty of Simonoseki, which ends the Sino-Japanese War. One of the terms of the treaty is the total independence of Korea (meaning in practice that Japan replaces China in control of Korea).

October 1895

8 Queen Min, a staunch opponent of the Japanese, is assassinated with Japanese connivance at Kyongbok-kung palace. King Kojong is forced to follow Japanese orders.

February 1896

11 In the course of another insurrection, King Kojong and the crown prince flee to the Russian legation in Seoul, where they remain for a year, until February 1897. The Russians supplant the Japanese as the dominant power in Korea, and a new pro-Russian cabinet is formed.

June 1896

9 The Lobanov-Yamagata Agreement. With the Russians now ascendant in Korea, former Japanese prime minister Yamagata Aritomo and Russian foreign minister Prince Alexei Lobanov-Rostovsky sign in St. Petersburg an agreement establishing a condominium in Korea, with the aim of preserving Korea as a buffer state. The two powers agree to cooperate in reforming Korea's finances and army. Russia largely ignores the agreement and continues its penetration of Korea.

July 1896

2 So Jae Pil establishes the Tongnip Hyophoe, or Independence Club.

October 1897

11 King Kojong proclaims the establishment of the Taehan Cheguk (Great Han Empire).

25 An Anglo-Russian crisis occurs when the Russians attempt to replace the financial adviser M'Leary Brown. British warships arrive at Chemulpo (Inchon), and the Russians draw back.

April 1898

25 Japan and Russia sign an agreement pledging that neither country will interfere in Korea's internal affairs and that they will not send military instructors or financial advisers without prior mutual agreement.

October 1898

29 The Independence Club convenes a mass meeting of officials and citizenry.

November 1898

4 King Kojong orders the dissolution of the Independence Club. Rioting occurs, with the conservative (pro-Russian) and reform (pro-Japanese) groups in the country at odds with one another.

March 1900

3 The Russians attempt to secure an agreement to establish a naval base at Mesanpo, but strong Japanese opposition prevents this. The Russians and Japanese inexorably move toward war over Korea.

January 1902

30   To prevent a possible agreement between the Japanese and Russians that would render the British position in the Far East almost helpless, the British end their Splendid Isolation by signing a treaty of alliance with Japan. It affirms the independence of Korea. Both powers recognize the independence of China and Korea, but both also recognize that the other has special interests: Britain in China and Japan in Korea. If either party in defense of its interests should become involved in a war with a third power, the other is to remain neutral, but if the enemy is actively supported by another power, Britain and Japan are to fight as allies. The alliance is to last for five years or longer unless denounced one year in advance by either party.

The Japanese then enter into negotiations with the Russians, who are endeavoring to exploit a timber concession along the Yalu River secured in 1896. With negotiations proving fruitless and convinced that a war between their two states is inevitable, the Japanese decide to strike first, while the Russians are as yet unprepared.

December 1903

The Russian government proposes to Japan that Korean territory north of the 39th Parallel be declared a neutral zone into which neither country will be permitted to introduce troops. Japan rejects the Russian proposal.

February 1904

8   Japan launches a surprise attack on Russian ships at Chemulpo (Inchon), Korea, and the naval base at Port Arthur in Manchuria, initiating the Russo-Japanese War.

22   Japan forcibly incorporates the Korean island of Tok-do into its territory as Takeshima.

23   Japan forces Korea to sign a protocol permitting Japan to intervene in Korean internal affairs and occupy strategic points throughout the country.

May 1904

18   Japan forces Korea to declare all its agreements with Russia null and void.

August 1904

21   Korea is forced to accept Japanese advisers in all important government ministries.

July 1905

29   Taft-Kasura Memorandum or Agreement signed between the United States and Japan. Based on conversations on July 27 in Tokyo between U.S. secretary of war William Howard Taft and Japanese prime minister Katsura Taro, the United States recognizes Japan's sphere of influence in Korea, while Japan in turn recognizes the U.S. sphere of influence in the Philippine Islands. Only meant as an understanding to smooth Japanese-U.S. relations and not as a binding treaty, it is kept secret until 1924.

August 1905

12   Great Britain recognizes Japan's special interests in Korea.

September 1905

5   The Treaty of Portsmouth officially ends the Russo-Japanese War. At Portsmouth Navy Yard, New Hampshire, in the United States, President Theodore Roosevelt's mediation results in Japan and Russia signing this agreement. Among its provisions, Russia acknowledges Japanese control of Korea.

November 1905

17   Japan forces Korea to sign the Protectorate Treaty, and Japan takes charge of Korea's foreign affairs.

March 1906

2   Ito Hirobumi, the principal figure in his country's takeover of Korea, becomes the first Japanese resident-general in Korea.

April 1907

22   King Kojong dispatches secret envoys to the Second World Peace Conference, scheduled to be held in June in The Hague, Kingdom of the Netherlands.

July 1907

20   King Kojong is forced to abdicate the throne in favor of his son, Sunjong, who is a mere figurehead.

24   Korea is forced to cede to the Japanese resident-general full authority over all matters of internal administration.

31   Japan disbands the entire Korean Army. This leads to widespread rioting and fighting in Korea against Japanese rule.

November 1908

30   The Root-Takahira Agreement is concluded between U.S. secretary of state Elihu Root and Japanese minister to the United States Takahira Kogoro recognizing the status quo in the Pacific and each other's interests: Japan in Korea and southern Manchuria, the United States in the Philippines. Both powers also agree to support the open door policy in China and to maintain its territorial integrity.

October 1909

28   Korean nationalist An Chung Gun assassinates Japanese resident-general in Korea Ito Hirobumi at the Harbin railroad station in Manchuria.

August 1910

22   Japan formally annexes Korea in a treaty signed by the two nations.

29   Korea formally becomes a colony of Japan.

February 1919

8   Some 600 Korean students gather at the Young Men's Christian Association (YMCA) Hall in Tokyo and issue a declaration demanding Korean independence.

March 1919

1   A declaration of independence is proclaimed in Korea. This leads to some 1,500 anti-Japanese demonstrations involving more than 2 million Koreans throughout the country. Before the Japanese restore order in mid-April, more than 7,500 Koreans have been killed, more than 16,000 are wounded, and more than 46,000 have been arrested.

April 1919

13   Korean nationalists establish the Korean Provisional Government in Shanghai.

September 1919

10   New Japanese governor-general Saito Makoto announces the Cultural Policy, a new, more enlightened colonial strategy that substitutes civilian for military government and promises greater self-government for the Koreans.

June 1920

4–7   In the battle at Fengwu-dong in southeastern Manchuria, the Taehan Tongnipkun (Korean Independence Army), led by Hong Pom Do, surrounds and defeats a Japanese army contingent, inflicting casualties of more than 160 killed and 300 wounded.

October 1920

21–26   In the battle at Qingshan-li in southeastern Manchuria, Koreans of the Pungno Kunjongso (Northern Route Military Command), led by Kim Chwa Jin, crush a Japanese force, killing more than 1,200 and wounding more than 2,000.

April 1925

17   The Choson Kongsandang (Korean Communist Party) is established.

June 1926

10   On the day of Korean king Sunjong's state funeral, Korean students stage massive anti-Japanese demonstrations, known as the 10 June Independence Movement.

February 1927

15   Right-wing and left-wing Korean nationalists join to form the Singanhoe (New Main Society), a united nationalist organization.

December 1928

27   Beset by internal strife, the Korean Communist Party dissolves itself.

November 1929

3   The Kwangju Student Movement flares up. Opposing Japanese rule, it spreads over all Korea by March 1930, involving 194 schools and some 54,000 Korean students.

May 1931

15   The New Main Society, divided by internal discord, dissolves when the communists decide to leave the organization.

April 1932

29   Korean independence advocate Yun Pong Gil hurls a hand grenade into a group of high-ranking Japanese military officials at Hungkou Park in Shanghai. The blast kills and wounds more than 10 Japanese military leaders. Among the dead is Sirakawa Yoshinori, commander of Japanese armed forces in China.

April 1938

1   Japan promulgates the National General Mobilization Law, imposing mandatory war conditions on Koreans.

February 1940

11   The Name Order, which requires Koreans to use Japanese names, goes into effect.

December 1943

1   The leaders of the United States, Great Britain, and China issue the Cairo Declaration proclaiming that Korea should become free and independent "in due course." Korean nationalists condemn this announcement, which implies some temporary period of external supervision.

February 1945

8   During the Yalta Conference between Allied leaders, U.S. president Franklin D. Roosevelt tells Soviet leader Joseph Stalin that Korea should have a trusteeship of 20–30 years. Stalin replies that the shorter the period of the

trusteeship the better. He also suggests that Britain join the United States, the Soviet Union, and China as the four trustees.

July 1945

25   Following discussions at Potsdam with his Soviet counterpart, U.S. Army chief of staff George C. Marshall orders plans drawn to move U.S. troops into Korea and alerts General Douglas MacArthur that decisions on the occupation of Japan are imminent.

26   During the Potsdam Conference, the United States and Great Britain issue the Potsdam Declaration, threatening Japan with "prompt and utter destruction" if it does not surrender immediately.

August 1945

6   The United States drops an atomic bomb on Hiroshima, Japan.

8   The Soviet Union declares war on Japan, complying with its promise at the Yalta Conference, and Soviet armies invade Manchuria.

9   The United States drops an atomic bomb on Nagasaki, Japan.

14   Japan surrenders unconditionally to the Allied powers. U.S. Army staff officers colonels Charles H. Bonesteel III and Dean Rusk are assigned the drafting of General Order 1, designating the particular Allied authority to whom the Japanese forces in each area of the Far East are to surrender. Their guidance was to place the line in Korea as far north as possible, considering that Soviet troops were advancing rapidly while the closest U.S. forces are on Okinawa, 600 miles away. Bonesteel and Rusk recommend the 38th Parallel, dividing the country roughly in half, with the capital of Seoul in the American zone. On August 15 President Harry S. Truman approves General Order 1, sending copies to Moscow and London. Soviet leader Joseph Stalin raises no objection but then asks for a zone of occupation in Japan. Truman rejects his request.

16   Yo Un Hyong organizes the Committee for the Preparation of Korean Independence (CPKI) in Seoul. Encouraged by this, 145 similar committees are formed throughout the country by the end of August.

17   Cho Man Sik establishes the South Pyongan Province branch of the Committee for the Preparation of Korean Independence (CPKI).

22   Soviet forces, units of the Twenty-fifth Army, march into Pyongyang. They arrange a merger of the South Pyongan and Pyongyang branches of the Committee for the Preparation of Korean Independence (CPKI) to form the People's Political Committee, with Cho Man Sik as its chairman.

25   The Soviet command in Pyongyang, headed by Colonel General Ivan Chistiakov, authorizes the local branches of the Committee for the Preparation of Korean Independence (CPKI) to take over the administrative powers of the Japanese Government-General.

September 1945

2   The formal Japanese surrender is signed aboard the U.S. battleship Missouri in Tokyo Bay. Under the surrender terms, Japan is stripped of its overseas possessions, including Korea.

6   Yo Un Hyong proclaims the establishment of the Korean People's Republic in Seoul.

7   General Douglas MacArthur, head of the Allied Supreme Command in Japan, formally establishes American control in Korea south of the 38th Parallel.

8   Units of the U.S. Army XXIV Corps, commanded by Lieutenant General John R. Hodge, begin arriving at the port of Inchon.

9   Lieutenant General John R. Hodge, commander of U.S. forces in Korea, accepts the formal surrender of Japanese forces in Seoul.

11   The United States announces the creation of the U.S. Army Military Government in Korea (USAMGIK). Pak Hon Yong announces the reestablishment of the Korean Communist Party.

16   Formation of the rightist Korean Democratic Party in Seoul.

25   Korean nationalist and communist Kim Il Sung, who had been serving as an officer with the Soviet forces, lands at Wonsan.

October 1945

10   Governor-General Archibald Arnold declares that the American military government is the only lawful government in the zone south of the 38th Parallel, denying the legitimacy of the Korean People's Republic.

16   Korean nationalist and rightist leader Syngman Rhee returns to Korea.

25   Syngman Rhee founds the Central Council for the Rapid Realization of Korean Independence.

December 1945

16–26   The foreign ministers of the United States, Great Britain, and the Soviet Union meet in Moscow. They agree to implement a five-year trusteeship in Korea by their three states plus China. The United States and the Soviet Union are to establish a joint commission for the establishment of an interim Korean administration, in consultation with the Korean people.

17   Kim Il Sung is named chairman of the northern branch of the Korean Communist Party.

31   News of the Moscow agreement having reached Korea on December 29, two days later antitrusteeship strikes and demonstrations occur throughout the country.

January 1946

2   The Korean Communist Party alters its stand and supports trusteeship.

15   The South Korean Constabulary is established.

February 1946

8   The North Korean Interim People's Committee is established as the governing body for the Soviet zone of occupation. Kim Il Sung is named chairman.

14   The American military government creates the South Korean Representative Democratic Council as its advisory body. It soon becomes a unified rightist political coalition.

15   The Democratic People's Front, a leftist political coalition, is formed in the U.S. zone.

March 1946

5   The North Korean Interim People's Committee initiates sweeping social and economic reforms, including land reform.

20   The U.S.-Soviet Joint Commission begins meeting in Seoul.

May 1946

8   The U.S.-Soviet Joint Commission indefinitely adjourns after deadlocking over U.S. insistence on including in an interim Korean government opponents of the Moscow agreement's trusteeship plan.

August 1946

28   The North Korean Workers' Party is established.

September 1946

25   South Korean railroad workers, demanding an increase in their rice ration and pay, are rejected by the American military government and go out on strike, initiating the October People's Resistance.

October 1946

1   Serious rioting breaks out in Taegu due to general Korean dissatisfaction with the American military government.

7   The Left-Right Coalition Committee, a moderate coalition, is established by Kim Kyu Sik and Yo Un Hyong.

November 1946

23   The South Korean Workers' Party is established.

December 1946

12   The South Korean Interim Legislative Assembly convenes.

February 1947

20   The North Korean People's Committee is created as the highest executive governing body, under Kim Il Sung.

March 1947

22   The leftist labor union calls for a general strike of workers throughout South Korea.

May 1947

21   The U.S.-Soviet Joint Commission reconvenes in Seoul and meets until October.

June 1947

3   In accordance with the U.S. Koreanization policy, the South Korean Interim Government is created.

July 1947

10   Sharp confrontation in the U.S.-Soviet Joint Commission over which Korean political parties and social organizations should be consulted in pursuance of the Moscow agreement to form a provisional Korean government.

29   Ten days after the assassination of Yo Un Hyong on July 19, 1947, the Left-Right Coalition Committee collapses.

August 1947

4   The U.S. State-War-Navy Coordinating Committee approves document 176/30, outlining steps to break the Soviet-American deadlock over Korean reunification.

September 1947

U.S. Joint Chiefs of Staff (JCS) determine that Korea has no strategic significance for the United States.

17   Unable to resolve differences with the Soviet Union, the United States lays the Korean issue before the second session of the United Nations (UN) General Assembly.

November 1947

14   The UN General Assembly adopts the U.S.-sponsored resolution calling for general elections to establish a national government of Korea.

January 1948

23   The Soviet Union refuses to admit into northern Korea the United Nations Temporary Commission on Korea (UNTCOK), charged with supervising the Korean elections.

February 1948

The U.S. JCS recommends pulling U.S. forces out of South Korea even though such a move will probably result in "eventual domination of Korea by the USSR."

6   UNTCOK decides to consult with the Interim Committee of the General Assembly.

7   Opposing the anticipated establishment of a separate southern government, South Korean leftists carry out sabotage and strikes.

8   The Korean People's Army (KPA, North Korean Army) is established in North Korea.

16   The North Korean People's Committee proclaims its intention to form a government representing all Korea within the next few months.

26   The Interim Committee of the UN General Assembly adopts the U.S.-sponsored resolution proposing that the Temporary Commission observe elections for representatives to a national assembly in those areas of Korea "accessible" to it.

March 1948

22   The American Military Government in South Korea announces a program to sell formerly Japanese-owned farmland.

April 1948

2   U.S. National Security Council (NSC) paper NSC-8 calls for the United States to build up the South Korean economy and armed forces but also states that defense of South Korea should be left to the Koreans themselves; NSC-8 is accepted by President Harry S. Truman as the basis for U.S. Korea policy.

3   South Korean communists begin the Cheju-do Uprising. Guerrilla units and their supporters occupy most towns on Cheju Island and disrupt the May elections there.

19   The North-South political leaders' conference convenes in Pyongyang.

30   The North-South political leaders' conference adopts a statement calling for the withdrawal of all foreign troops, the establishment of a provisional all-Korean government, and the peaceful unification of Korea by nationwide elections.

May 1948

10   General elections are held in South Korea.

14   Protesting the general elections, North Korean leaders cut off electric power to South Korea.

31   The National Assembly convenes in Seoul.

July 1948

10   Adoption of a constitution by the People's Congress in North Korea.

12   Adoption of the first South Korean constitution.

24   Syngman Rhee is sworn in as South Korean president after being elected to the position by the National Assembly.

August 1948

15   The Republic of Korea (ROK, South Korea) is formally established.

25   Elections to choose representatives of a Supreme People's Assembly occur in North and South Korea.

September 1948

9   The Supreme People's Congress in North Korea proclaims the establishment of the Democratic People's Republic of Korea (DPRK, North Korea), with Kim Il Sung as premier.

October 1948

19–27   The Yosu-Sunchon Rebellion occurs. Some 2,000 troops of the Republic of Korea Army (ROKA, South Korean Army) 14th Regiment under communist leadership revolt against the government in the Yosu-Sunchon area. The rebellion is put down by troops loyal to the government.

27   South Korean forces completely crush the Yosu-Sunchon Rebellion.

November 1948

20   South Korean National Assembly passes the National Security Law, outlawing communism.

December 1948

12   The UN General Assembly recognizes the South Korean government as the only lawfully constituted government on the Korean Peninsula. The UN resolution also creates the UN Commission on Korea.

31   The Soviet Union announces that in compliance with a UN request in its resolution of December 12, all of its troops have left North Korea.

January 1949

General Douglas MacArthur informs the U.S. JCS that South Korean forces could not defeat a North Korean invasion of South Korea and that the United States should not commit combat troops in the event of such an invasion and should in fact remove its armed forces from South Korea as soon as possible.

February 1949

10   The Korean Democratic Party is renamed the Democratic National Party.

March 1949

17   The North Korean government and the Soviet Union conclude cultural and economic treaties as well as a secret military assistance agreement.

23   President Harry S. Truman approves NSC-8/2 as the new U.S. Korean policy, calling for action to provide economic aid to South Korea and military assistance to build the capacity for self-defense.

April 1949

8   The Soviet Union vetoes the South Korean application for admission to the UN.

May 1949

2   Establishment of the Korea Military Advisory Group (KMAG) to provide advice and training for the Republic of Korea Army (ROKA, South Korean Army).

4   Fighting breaks out along the 38th Parallel separating the two Korean states. Sporadic combat occurs thereafter, with South Korean forces initiating most of these military engagements.

June 1949

21   The South Korean government promulgates a land reform bill.

25   To forge a united front with opponents of South Korean leader Syngman Rhee, the North Korean government forms the Democratic Front for the Unification of the Fatherland (DFUF).

29   The United States withdraws the last of its combat forces from South Korea.

30   The North Korean Workers' Party and the South Korean Workers' Party are merged into the Korean Workers' Party, with Kim Il Sung as chairman.

July 1949

1   KMAG is activated in South Korea.

October 1949

1   In Bejing, China, communist leader Mao Zedong proclaims the establishment of the People's Republic of China (PRC).

January 1950

12   In the course of a National Press Club speech in Washington, U.S. secretary of state Dean Acheson excludes South Korea from the U.S. defense perimeter in East Asia, casting doubt about the U.S. security commitment.

19   The U.S. House of Representatives narrowly defeats the Truman administration's Korea Aid Bill for 1950.

January–March 1950

The U.S. Far East Command (FEC) Intelligence Section evaluates reports of an impending North Korean invasion of South Korea but concludes that it is not imminent.

February 1950

9   With additional funding added for the Republic of China (ROC, Taiwan), Congress passes a revised Korea Aid Bill, now titled the Far Eastern Assistance Act.

14   The Soviet Union and the PRC sign the Sino-Soviet Treaty of Friendship, Alliance, and Mutual Assistance.

March 30–April 25, 1950

North Korean leader Kim Il Sung visits the Soviet Union and secures approval from Soviet leader Joseph Stalin for his planned invasion of South Korea, contingent on Kim also securing the consent of Chinese leader Mao Zedong.

April 1950

3   Land reform begins in South Korea.

14   General Douglas MacArthur submits a memorandum emphasizing the strategic importance of Taiwan to U.S. security.
NSC-68 recommends substantial increases in the U.S. defense budget to counter the growing Soviet military threat.

May 1950

2   Democratic senator Tom Connally predicts the fall of South Korea to the communists.

13–16   North Korean leader Kim Il Sung visits China and secures the approval of PRC leader Mao Zedong for his planned invasion of South Korea.

30   Elections for the South Korean National Assembly produce a majority of legislators hostile to the Syngman Rhee government.

June 1950

7   The Central Committee of the DFUF proposes all-Korean elections in August to elect a unified assembly.

15   U.S. presidential representative John Foster Dulles arrives in South Korea on a fact-finding mission and pledges U.S. support for South Korea in a speech to its National Assembly two days later.

19   The North Korean Supreme People's Assembly proposes to the South Korean National Assembly the merger of the two bodies.

24   The UN Commission on Korea surveys the 38th Parallel and finds South Korean troops in defensive positions.

25   At 4:00 a.m. local time (13 hours later than in Washington, D.C.), North Korean troops, supported by tanks,

heavy artillery, and aircraft, cross the 38th Parallel and invade South Korea.

The UN Security Council passes a resolution that proclaims the North Korean attack of South Korea a breach of world peace and demands an immediate halt in the fighting.

First Blair House meeting of U.S. president Harry S. Truman with his top advisers to discuss the crisis in Korea.

26   Second Blair House meeting convenes.

27   Arrival of the General John H. Church survey mission in South Korea and the creation of the Advance Command and Liaison Group in Korea (ADCOM).

U.S. president Harry S. Truman authorizes U.S. air and naval operations against North Korean forces south of the 38th Parallel. He also announces the deployment of the U.S. Seventh Fleet in the Taiwan Strait. That same day, the UN Security Council passes a resolution calling upon members to provide assistance to South Korea in resisting aggression.

28   ROKA engineers prematurely blow bridges over the Han River, trapping many ROKA soldiers and their equipment north of the Han. Seoul falls to advancing Korean People's Army (KPA, North Korean Army) troops.

29   U.S. president Harry S. Truman authorizes a naval blockade of the North Korean coasts.

U.S. FEC commander General Douglas MacArthur visits South Korea and observes fighting at the Han River.

The Soviet Union informs the United States of its intention to remain uninvolved in Korea's civil war and declares the UN resolutions regarding Korea illegal.

The U.S. Congress approves the Deficiency Appropriations Act providing additional aid to South Korea.

30   U.S. president Harry S. Truman commits U.S. ground troops to the fighting in Korea in defense of South Korea. Congress authorizes activation of reserve components for up to 21 months. Truman agrees with a reporter's description of Korea as a "police action."

July 1950

2   U.S. president Harry S. Truman rejects ROC president Jiang Jieshi's offer of Chinese Nationalist troops for service in the Korean War.

5   First U.S. ground troops, Task Force Smith, go into action against North Korean forces just north of Osan.

7   The United Nations Command (UNC) is established. The next day President Harry S. Truman selects FEC head General Douglas MacArthur as its commander.

12   Lieutenant General Walton H. Walker takes command of U.S. troops in Korea, designated the U.S. Eighth Army, Korea (EUSAK).

13   Indian prime minister Jawaharlal Nehru urges the United States and the Soviet Union to take steps to localize and terminate the Korean War.

13–14   U.S. Army chief of staff General J. Lawton Collins and U.S. Air Force chief of staff General Hoyt S. Vandenberg visit Tokyo for discussions with UNC commander General Douglas MacArthur.

14   South Korean president Syngman Rhee places his nation's armed forces under UNC commander General Douglas MacArthur.

14–20   Battle of the Kum River.

19   U.S. president Harry S. Truman addresses the nation about the Korean crisis.

20   KPA troops seize the South Korean city of Taejon.

26   The Nogun-ni railroad bridge incident occurs in which several hundred South Korean civilians are killed by American soldiers.

29   U.S. Eighth Army commander General Walton H. Walker issues his "Stand or Die" order.

July 31–August 1, 1950

UNC commander General Douglas MacArthur visits Taiwan to discuss measures for defense of the island.

August 1950

1   The Soviet Union ends its boycott of the UN Security Council as its representative, Jacob Malik, assumes position as president of the body.

4   Having withdrawn south as far as is feasible, the UNC establishes Naktong River defenses, what becomes known as the Pusan Perimeter.

5–19   Battle of the Naktong Bulge.

6   U.S. presidential representative W. Averell Harriman visits Tokyo with Lieutenant General Matthew B. Ridgway for discussions with MacArthur until August 8.

9   Beginning of the defense of the city of Taegu.

10   First U.S. bombing raid on Rashin (Najin) in North Korea.

15   Establishment of the Korean Augmentation of the U.S. Army (KATUSA).

17   U.S. representative at the UN Warren R. Austin calls publicly for the reunification of Korea.

19   U.S. Army chief of staff General J. Lawton Collins and U.S. Navy chief of staff Admiral Forrest P. Sherman visit Tokyo to discuss plans for the Inchon Landing with UNC commander General Douglas MacArthur.

25   UNC commander General Douglas MacArthur's letter to the Veterans of Foreign Wars (VFW) is published.

U.S. secretary of the navy Francis P. Matthews refers to the possibility of waging a preventive war against the Soviet Union.

26   UNC commander General Douglas MacArthur creates the X Corps in preparation for the Inchon Landing.

September 1950

1   President Harry S. Truman addresses the U.S. Congress to explain the administration's Korean War policy.
U.S. president Harry S. Truman orders the mobilization of four U.S. National Guard divisions.

4   U.S. Navy fighters shoot down a Soviet aircraft over the Yellow Sea.

5–13 Battle of Yongchon.

8   The U.S. Congress approves the Defense Production Act.

11   U.S. president Harry S. Truman orders implementation of NSC-81, the plan for a military offensive across the 38th Parallel.

12   U.S. secretary of defense Louis A. Johnson resigns; General George C. Marshall is his replacement.

15   In Operation CHROMITE, the UNC X Corps lands at the port of Inchon.

25   The U.S. JCS authorizes ground military operations north of the 38th Parallel.
Acting chief of staff of the Chinese People's Liberation Army (PLA, Chinese Communist Army) warns that China will not "sit back with folded hands and let the Americans come up to the border."

27   EUSAK and X Corps link forces south of Seoul.
A U.S. JCS directive forbids U.S. air operations beyond the Yalu River.

28   UNC forces recapture the city of Seoul.

October 1950

1   Bent on reunifying Korea, ROKA troops cross the 38th Parallel.

2   PRC premier Zhou Enlai warns Indian ambassador K. M. Panikkar that the PRC will intervene in the Korean War if U.S. forces cross the 38th Parallel.

4   PRC leader Mao Zedong makes final decision to intervene militarily in the Korean War.

7   The UN General Assembly sanctions the advance of UNC forces into North Korea and establishes the UN Committee for the Unification and Rehabilitation of Korea (UNCURK).

8   PRC leader Mao Zedong issues an official directive turning the Northeast Border Defense Army into the Chinese People's Volunteer Army (CPVA, Chinese Army), a fig leaf enabling China to go to war with the United States without formally avowing it; Mao orders the CPVA to move immediately into North Korea "to assist the Korean comrades in their struggle."
U.S. warplanes strafe a Soviet air base in Siberia.

9   EUSAK, led by the 1st Cavalry Division, crosses the 38th Parallel into North Korea.

UNC commander General MacArthur issues an ultimatum to North Korea demanding immediate surrender. North Korean leader Kim Il Sung rejects the demand the next day.

10   ROKA troops take Wonsan.

12   The UN Interim Committee resolves that the UN recognizes no government as having "legal and effective control" over North Korea and asks the UNC to assume administrative responsibility in North Korea pending the arrival of UNCURK.

14   Troops of the CPVA begin crossing the Yalu River from China into North Korea.

15   U.S. president Harry S. Truman meets with UNC commander General Douglas MacArthur at Wake Island. The next day, troops of the CPVA begin crossing the Yalu River into North Korea.
First clashes between CPVA and UNC forces in North Korea.

19   UNC forces capture the North Korean capital of Pyongyang.

24   UNC commander General Douglas MacArthur removes restrictions on movement of non-Korean forces to provinces bordering the Yalu River.

25   X Corps lands at Wonsan Harbor.

28   The U.S. JCS sends UNC commander General Douglas MacArthur an occupation directive for North Korea.

November 1950

1   First Chinese Mikoyan-Gurevich MiG-15 jet aircraft appear along the Yalu River.

1–6 Battle of Unsan.

3   The UN approves the Uniting for Peace resolution to permit the General Assembly to act against an aggressor and to create a UN Collective Measures Committee.

6   Chinese forces attack EUSAK north of the Chongchon River and then disengage, starting a three-week lull in the fighting

7   UNC commander General Douglas MacArthur requests approval for "hot pursuit" of Chinese planes into Manchuria and destruction of the Yalu bridges.

8   Seventy-nine Boeing B-29 Superfortresses implement orders to bomb the Korean side of the bridges over the Yalu River. The first battle between manned jet aircraft in history occurs when a Lockheed F-80 Shooting Star shoots down a Mikoyan-Gurevich MiG-15.
The UN Security Council passes a resolution inviting the PRC to participate in a debate on the issues of Korea and Taiwan.

10   The Soviet Union vetoes a UN Security Council resolution calling upon the PRC to withdraw its forces from Korea.

British foreign minister Ernest Bevin submits a buffer zone proposal to the United States.

24   After a pause to resupply, UNC forces renew their offensive toward the Yalu River.

The PRC representative arrives at the UN to participate in discussions.

25   The CPVA launches a second—this time massive—offensive against UNC forces in North Korea.

28   The PRC representative at the UN denounces the United States for aggression in Korea.

30   U.S. president Harry S. Truman states at a press conference that the United States has use of atomic weapons in the Korean War under consideration.

First briefing meeting of member nations of the UNC at the Canadian embassy.

December 1950

1   UNC commander General Douglas MacArthur points to the prohibition on air strikes in Manchuria to explain the U.S. retreat in a *U.S. News and World Report* interview.

The UN passes a resolution establishing the UN Korean Reconstruction Agency (UNKRA).

4–8   British prime minister Clement Attlee meets with President Harry S. Truman and other U.S. officials about the Korean War.

5   UNC forces evacuate Pyongyang.

6   A U.S. JCS directive bans unauthorized public statements by government officials regarding the Korean War.

11–24   Evacuation of X Corps forces from the port of Hungnam.

14   The UN passes a resolution establishing the UN Cease-Fire Group.

15   UNC forces withdraw south of the 38th Parallel.

16   U.S. president Harry S. Truman declares a state of national emergency in the United States.

19   The PRC delegation leaves the UN.

20   Former U.S. president Herbert Hoover delivers his "Gibraltar America" speech.

23   EUSAK commander Lieutenant General Walton H. Walker is killed in a jeep accident; Lieutenant General Matthew B. Ridgway is his successor.

PRC premier Zhou Enlai rejects the UN Cease-Fire Group's proposal, demanding U.S. withdrawal from Korea and Taiwan and the admission of the PRC to the UN.

24   UNC forces complete their evacuation of the port of Hungnam.

26   U.S. general Matthew B. Ridgway arrives in Korea and assumes command of EUSAK.

31   Chinese forces launch their third offensive south of the 38th Parallel.

January 1951

1   U.S. president Harry S. Truman orders the mobilization of two more National Guard divisions.

3   The UN Cease-Fire Group reports the failure of negotiations with the PRC.

4   Chinese and North Korean troops recapture Seoul.

12   The U.S. JCS rejects UNC commander General Douglas MacArthur's plan for winning the Korean War through extending military operations to mainland China.

13   The United States votes in the UN in favor of a UN cease-fire resolution that promises discussion of other Far Eastern issues.

15   U.S. Army chief of staff General J. Lawton Collins and U.S. Air Force chief of staff General Hoyt Vandenberg visit Tokyo for discussions with UNC commander General Douglas MacArthur.

15–25   UNC Operation WOLFHOUND forces Chinese troops to withdraw to Osan.

17   The Chinese reject the UN Cease-Fire Group's five principles because "the purpose of arranging a cease-fire first [before negotiating] is merely to give the United States troops a breathing space."

January 25–February 1, 1951

UNC Operation THUNDERBOLT forces the Chinese to withdraw to the Han River.

February 1951

1   Passage of a UN resolution condemning the PRC for aggression in Korea and establishing the UN Additional Measures Committee and UN Good Office Committee.

5   Operation PUNCH forces the Chinese to retreat north of Seoul.

Operation ROUNDUP meets with a Chinese counterattack, forcing the X Corps on February 11 to withdraw south of Wonju.

10   South Korean National Guard units slaughter innocent civilians at the town of Kochang.

11   The Chinese open their fourth offensive to force the UNC retreat from central Korea.

13–15   Battle of Chipyong-ni.

15   UNC commander General Douglas MacArthur requests permission to bomb Rashin (Najin).

February 21–March 1, 1951

UNC Operation KILLER pushes communist forces in central Korea north of the Han River.

March 1951

7–21   UNC Operation RIPPER obliges Chinese forces to retreat north of the 38th Parallel.

UNC commander General Douglas MacArthur makes his "Die for Tie" statement at a press conference in Korea.

14   UNC forces retake Seoul.

15   UNC commander General Douglas MacArthur advocates in a press interview crossing the 38th Parallel to fulfill the UNC mission of reuniting Korea.

20   The U.S. JCS informs UNC commander General Douglas MacArthur of President Harry S. Truman's planned cease-fire initiative.

22   UNC Operation COURAGEOUS begins and by March 29 moves the UNC to a position just south of the 38th Parallel.

24   UNC commander General Douglas MacArthur issues a pronunciamento demanding immediate communist surrender.

March 26–April 7, 1951
The Washington Conference of foreign ministers of nations in the Western Hemisphere occurs.

March 1951
29   A PRC radio broadcast rejects UNC commander General Douglas MacArthur's ultimatum and calls for renewed military efforts.

April 1951
3–6   In Operation RUGGED, UNC forces cross the 38th Parallel and establish the Kansas Line.

5   U.S. Republican Party House minority leader Joseph W. Martin Jr. of Massachusetts reads in the House a letter of March 20 from UNC commander General Douglas MacArthur calling for victory in the Korean War.

6–11   UNC Operation DAUNTLESS results in UNC forces establishing the Kansas-Wyoming Line.

11   U.S. president Harry S. Truman relieves UNC commander General Douglas MacArthur of his command. His successor is Lieutenant General Matthew B. Ridgway.

14   Lieutenant General James A. Van Fleet arrives in Korea to take command of EUSAK.

19   U.S. general Douglas MacArthur delivers his "No Substitute for Victory" speech before a joint session of Congress.

22   Chinese forces open the first stage of their fifth offensive, lasting until April 28.

22–25   Battle of the Imjin River.

23–25   Battle of Kapyong.

28   The U.S. JCS authorizes UNC attacks on air bases in Manchuria if Chinese communist planes threaten the security of UNC forces on the ground.

May 3–June 25, 1951
Senate MacArthur Hearings before the Joint Committee of Armed Services and Foreign Relations.

May 1951
16   Chinese forces open the second stage of their fifth offensive, lasting until May 23.

17   U.S. president Harry S. Truman approves NSC-48/5.

18   A UN resolution is approved calling for a selective embargo against the PRC.
U.S. assistant secretary of state Dean Rusk delivers a speech referring to the PRC as "a Slavic Manchukuo on a large scale" and "not the Government of China."

30   UNC forces restore defensive positions at the Kansas Line.

31   First meeting between U.S. diplomat George F. Kennan and Soviet representative to the UN Jacob A. Malik regarding possible cease-fire negotiations in the Korean War.
The U.S. JCS sends a new directive to UNC commander General Matthew B. Ridgway on the future conduct of the Korean War.

June 1951
1   UNC Operation PILEDRIVER moves UNC forces northward to the Wyoming Line.

2   The UNC implements Operation STRANGLE.

5   A second meeting occurs between U.S. diplomat George F. Kennan and Soviet representative to the UN Jacob Malik.

15   The UNC consolidates defensive positions along the Kansas-Wyoming Line.

23   Soviet representative to the UN Jabob Malik recommends talks to bring about a cease-fire in Korea.

29   UNC commander General Matthew B. Ridgway offers to meet communist commanders in the field to discuss a cease-fire and terms for an armistice.

July 1951
10   Armistice talks open at Kaesong.

14   Communist delegation agrees to permit equal press coverage at the Kaesong armistice talks.

26   Negotiators approve an agenda for the Kaesong armistice talks.

28   The British Commonwealth Division is established.

August 18–September 5, 1951
Battle of Bloody Ridge.

August 1951

23　The communist side suspends truce talks because of alleged UNC aerial strafing in the Kaesong neutral zone.

25　A U.S. bombing raid occurs against Rashin (Najin).

September 1951

1　The ANZUS Treaty between the United States, Australia, and New Zealand is signed.

8　The Japanese Peace Treaty is signed at San Francisco.

11　U.S. secretary of state Dean Acheson meets with British foreign minister Herbert S. Morrison.

September 13–October 15, 1951

　　Battle of Heartbreak Ridge.

September 28–October 3, 1951

　　U.S. JCS chairman General Omar N. Bradley and State Department Soviet expert Charles E. Bohlen visit Tokyo and Korea.

October 1951

3–8　UNC Operation COMMANDO takes place.

5　U.S. ambassador Alan G. Kirk meets Soviet foreign minister Andrei Y. Vyshinskii and urges him to persuade the Chinese and North Koreans to resume armistice negotiations.

22　Signing of the Panmunjom Security Agreement.

24　Battle of Namsi. This is the largest air clash of the Korean War.

25　Armistice talks resume at Panmunjom.
　　Winston Churchill replaces Clement Attlee as British prime minister following the Labour Party's electoral defeat.

November 1951

12　UNC commander General Matthew B. Ridgway orders EUSAK to implement an active defense strategy.
　　Operation RATKILLER begins to kill or capture guerrillas in South Korea. It lasts until March 15, 1952.

13　At Panmunjom, the UNC proposes the line of battle as the demarcation line for a demilitarized zone (DMZ) if all other issues are settled in 30 days.

27　Agreement is reached at the Panmunjom truce talks on agenda item 2, the demarcation line and the DMZ.

28　First Anglo-American discussions occur about a Joint Policy (Greater Sanctions) statement.

December 1951

3　Negotiators at Panmunjom refer the communist proposal for settling agenda item 3, covering cease-fire inspections, to subdelegates to work out the details.

20　U.S. president Harry S. Truman approves NSC 118/2.

27　Agreement on a demarcation line at Panmunjom is invalidated, although both sides continue to accept it as the likely basis for the eventual DMZ.

January 1952

2　The UNC proposes voluntary repatriation of prisoners of war (POWs) at Panmunjom.

8　The communist delegation at Panmunjom rejects the principle of voluntary repatriation, insisting on complete respect for the provisions of the Geneva Convention on returning POWs.

18　The South Korean National Assembly rejects constitutional amendments proposed by President Syngman Rhee providing for direct popular election of the president.

27　The negotiators at Panmunjom agree to defer discussion of airfield rehabilitation.

31　Negotiators shift to subdelegation discussions of agenda item 5, political consultations between governments.

February 1952

10–15　The UNC carries out Operation CLAM-UP.

16　Communist negotiators at Panmunjom suggest that the Soviet Union should be a member of the neutral commission in charge of supervising a cease-fire.

18　The Soviet Union charges the United States with waging biological warfare in North Korea.

19　Agreement is reached at the Panmunjom truce talks on agenda item 5, providing for a political conference 90 days after the armistice to discuss withdrawal of foreign troops and Korean reunification.

March 1952

26　At the UN the United States denies communist charges of using biological warfare and criticizes them for refusing an impartial investigation.

April 1952

2　The communist delegation at Panmunjom recommends checking POW lists.

5–15　Operation SCATTER screens POWs in UNC camps.

8　U.S. president Harry S. Truman seizes the American steel mills.

10–24　Clarence E. Meyer carries out a U.S. economic mission to South Korea.

20　The UNC announces at Panmunjom that only 70,000 communist POWs desire repatriation.

28　The UNC submits a package proposal at the Panmunjom truce talks, but the communist delegation refuses to accept voluntary repatriation.

May 1952

2   At Panmunjom the communist negotiators partially accept a package proposal, dropping the Soviet Union as a Neutral National Supervisory Committee member in exchange for no limits on airfield rehabilitation.

7   A major clash occurs between UNC guards and communist prisoners at the Koje-do POW camp after the prisoners capture camp commander Brigadier General Francis T. Dodd.

11   The communist POWs release Brigadier General Francis T. Dodd.

12   General Mark W. Clark replaces General Matthew B. Ridgway as commander of U.S. forces in the Far East and of the UNC.

19   Publication of John Foster Dulles's "A Policy of Boldness" in *Life* magazine criticizing the policy of containment.

22   British foreign minister Anthony Eden sends to Washington the draft of an Anglo-Indian Five Point Plan for settling the POW controversy.

24   The United States and South Korea sign the Agreement on Economic Coordination.

25   South Korean president Syngman Rhee declares martial law in Pusan and its surrounding regions, and the next day more than 50 opposition legislators are arrested.

June 1952

2   The U.S. Supreme Court declares President Harry S. Truman's seizure of the steels plants unconstitutional in Youngstown Sheet and Tube v. Sawyer.

10   UNC forces rout militant communist POWs, ending the Koje-do Uprising.

22   British foreign minister John Selwyn Lloyd and Defense Minister Lord Alexander meet in Tokyo with UNC commander General Mark Clark.

23–26   UNC bombers raid the Suiho power plant in North Korea.

25   An assassination attempt occurs against South Korean president Syngman Rhee.

The U.S. JCS authorizes UNC commander General Mark Clark to develop Operation EVERREADY for the removal of President Syngman Rhee from power in South Korea, should this prove necessary.

June 26, 1952–March 23, 1953

Battle of Old Baldy.

July 1952

1   Operation HOMECOMING releases 27,000 civilian internees, lasting until the end of August 1952.

4   The South Korean National Assembly passes compromise legislation allowing constitutional amendments for direct presidential election as well as a limited degree of cabinet responsibility to the National Assembly.

7   The communist delegation at Panmunjom repeats demands for the repatriation of all Chinese POWs.

11   A massive UNC air raid occurs against Pyongyang.

August 1952

5   Syngman Rhee easily wins the South Korean presidential election.

27   A second major UNC air raid, the largest of the Korean War, occurs against Pyongyang.

September 1952

2   A POW settlement proposal by the government of Mexico is submitted at the UN.

28   At the Panmunjom talks, the UNC delegation presents its final proposal to settle the POW repatriation issue.

October 1952

1   The Cheju-do POW uprising begins.

6–15   The Battle of White Horse Hill occurs, signaling communist acceleration of the ground war.

8   The UNC delegation declares an indefinite recess of the Panmunjom truce talks.

13   Operation SHOWDOWN reveals the futility of ground assaults against entrenched communist defensive positions.

October 14–November 5, 1952

Battle of Triangle Hill.

October 1952

24   Republican presidential nominee Dwight D. Eisenhower pledges to "go to Korea" if elected.

The United States introduces the Twenty-one Power resolution at the UN, calling for a reaffirmation of support for the voluntary repatriation concept.

October 26, 1952–July 25, 1953

Battle of the Hook.

November 1952

3   A POW settlement proposal by the government of Peru is submitted at the UN.

4   Dwight D. Eisenhower is elected president of the United States.

10   EUSAK commander General James Van Fleet announces the mobilization of two new South Korean divisions and six regiments.

17   An Indian government POW settlement proposal is submitted at the UN.

December 1952

2–5   Fulfilling a campaign pledge, U.S. president-elect Dwight D. Eisenhower visits Korea.

3   A UN resolution endorses the Indian government POW settlement proposal.

9   A U.S. bombing raid is carried out against Rashin (Najin).

14   A POW uprising occurs at Pongam-do.

17   President-elect Dwight D. Eisenhower meets with General Douglas MacArthur, who submits his plan for victory in Korea.

January 1953

20   Dwight D. Eisenhower is inaugurated president of the United States.

25   UNC Operation SMACK tests close air support strategy.

February 1953

2   U.S. president Dwight D. Eisenhower announces in his State of the Union address the "unleashing" of Jiang Jieshi, president of Nationalist China.

7   UNC commander General Mark Clark requests permission to bomb Kaesong.

10   Lieutenant General Maxwell Taylor replaces General James Van Fleet as commander of EUSAK.

22   The UNC delegation at Panmunjom proposes the exchange of sick and wounded POWs.

March 1953

5   Soviet premier Joseph Stalin dies.

15   Soviet leader Georgi Malenkov publicly voices support for a cease-fire in Korea.

20   The U.S. JCS approves Operation MOOLAH to encourage MiG pilots to defect.

March 23–July 11, 1953

Battle of Pork Chop Hill.

March 1953

28   The communist delegation at Panmunjom accepts the UNC proposal for the exchange of sick and wounded POWs.

30   PRC foreign minister Zhou Enlai outlines in a radio broadcast a proposal for the exchange of sick and wounded POWs.

April 1953

2   U.S. president Dwight D. Eisenhower approves NSC-147, a contingency plan to escalate military operations against North Korea and the PRC.

April 17–June 15, 1953

Henry J. Tasca Mission to South Korea to study its economy.

April 1953

18   The UN passes a resolution calling for convening the General Assembly after the signing of a Korean Armistice Agreement.

April 20–May 3, 1953

Operation LITTLE SWITCH—the exchange of wounded and sick prisoners of war—occurs.

April 1953

22   U.S. president Dwight D. Eisenhower approves arms and equipment for two new ROKA divisions.

26   The Panmunjom peace talks resume.

May 1953

7   KPA lieutenant general Nam Il advances an eight-point POW settlement proposal.

13   U.S. president Dwight D. Eisenhower approves arming four additional South Korean divisions, to a total army strength of 20 divisions.

13–16   The UNC mounts raids against dams in North Korea.

22   UNC commander General Mark Clark sends the Operation EVERREADY plan to Washington for final approval. U.S. secretary of state John Foster Dulles warns the PRC through India that the United States might use atomic weapons against mainland China if the UNC POW settlement proposal is rejected.

25   The final UNC POW settlement proposal is submitted at Panmunjom with the intention to terminate truce talks if the communist delegation rejects the plan.

June 1953

4   At Panmunjom, the communist delegation accepts the UNC's final POW settlement proposal.

8   The communist delegation at Panmunjom formally accepts the principle of voluntary repatriation.

10   Communist forces open an offensive against ROKA troops.

15   U.S. president Dwight D. Eisenhower receives the Tasca Report with recommendations regarding the South Korean economy.

17   Negotiators at the Panmunjom truce talks accept a revised demarcation line.

18   Frustrated over the course of armistice negotiations that indicate U.S. acceptance of a cease-fire rather than continued pursuit of reunification, South Korean president Syngman Rhee orders the release of 27,000 North Korean POWs.

20   The UNC delegation at the Panmunjom truce talks gains
      approval for a recess.

June 22–July 12, 1953
      U.S. assistant secretary of state Walter S. Robertson car-
      ries out a mission to South Korea.

July 1953
6   Communist forces mount a new military thrust into the
      Iron Triangle.
7   U.S. president Dwight D. Eisenhower's administration
      approves NSC-154/1 and NSC-157/1.
10   South Korean president Syngman Rhee agrees not to
      disrupt the Armistice Agreement.
11   Issuance of the U.S. assistant secretary of state Walter
      S. Robertson-South Korean president Syngman Rhee
      communiqué.
13   The final Chinese offensive of the war inflicts heavy casu-
      alties on South Korean forces in the Kumsong region.
17   U.S. president Dwight D. Eisenhower's administration
      approves NSC-156/1.
19   Agreement is reached at Panmunjom on all substantive
      points of an armistice.
27   The Korean War Armistice Agreement is signed at
      Panmunjom.
      Signing of the Joint Policy (Greater Sanctions) statement,
      issued publicly on August 7.
28   The Military Armistice Commission meets for the first
      time.

August 5–September 6, 1953
      Operation BIG SWITCH, the final repatriation of Korean War
      POWS, occurs.

August 1953
8   U.S. secretary of state John Foster Dulles meets with
      South Korean president Syngman Rhee in Seoul, result-
      ing in approval of the terms of the U.S.–South Korean
      Mutual Defense Treaty.

October 1953
1   The U.S.–South Korean Mutual Defense Treaty is signed.

January 1954
26   The U.S. Senate ratifies the U.S.–South Korean Mutual
      Defense Treaty.

February 1954
1   The Neutral Nations Repatriation Commission formally
      disbands.

April 26–July 15, 1954
      A conference of the major powers takes place in Geneva,
      Switzerland, in an effort to resolve the matter of Korean
      unification and other pressing Asian matters, including
      ending the Indochina War.

May 1954
20   South Korean president Syngman Rhee's Liberal Party
      secures a majority of seats in the National Assembly
      elections.

November 1954
29   The South Korean National Assembly passes President
      Syngman Rhee's proposal to abolish the two-term limita-
      tions on the presidency.

December 1955
28   North Korean leader Kim Il Sung first enunciates his
      juche ideology.

May 1956
15   South Korean president Syngman Rhee wins reelection.

December 1958
24   The South Korean National Assembly passes a new
      National Security Law, the provisions of which amount
      to a virtual suspension of democracy.

March 1960
15   South Korean president Syngman Rhee, running unop-
      posed, wins reelection. His Liberal Party heavily rigs the
      vice presidential election to ensure the defeat of Chang
      Myon. This leads to widespread violent protests.

April 1960
19   Beginning of the South Korean April Student Revolution.
26   South Korean president Syngman Rhee is forced to
      resign. Three days later, he leaves Korea for exile in
      Hawaii. The First Republic ends.

June 1960
15   The South Korean constitution is amended to provide for
      a cabinet responsible to the legislature.

August 1960
23   Chang Myon is elected prime minister of South Korea,
      inaugurating the Second Republic.

May 1961
16   In South Korea, Major General Park Chung Hee stages a
      coup, ending the Second Republic.

December 1962

17   A public referendum in South Korea approves by a wide margin a new constitution, the outlines of which resemble those of the First Republic.

October 1963

15   Park Chung Hee is elected president of South Korea by a narrow margin. He is sworn in on December 17, inaugurating the Third Republic.

June 1965

22   South Korea and Japan establish formal diplomatic relations.

May 1967

3   Park Chung Hee wins another term as president of South Korea.

January 1968

21   A squad of 31 North Korean commandos reaches the northern edge of Seoul.

23   North Korean naval forces seize the U.S. Navy intelligence-gathering ship *Pueblo* in international waters off Wonsan Bay.

April 1969

15   North Korea shoots down an unarmed U.S. electronic intelligence-gathering EC-121 aircraft over the East Sea. All of its crew perish.

October 1969

17   South Korean president Park Chung Hee's proposal to abolish the two-term limitations on the presidency is ratified by national referendum.

April 1971

27   In heavily rigged presidential elections, South Korean president Park Chung Hee wins a third term.

December 1971

27   The South Korean National Assembly grants President Park Chung Hee emergency powers.

July 1972

4   The governments of South Korea and North Korea announce the "Joint Statement of 4 July" embodying basic principles for the reunification of Korea.

October 1972

17   In the Yushin coup d'état, South Korean president Park Chung Hee ends the Third Republic.

November 1972

21   A national referendum in South Korea ratifies the Yushin Constitution.

December 1972

23   Park Chung Hee is elected president of South Korea by the National Conference for Unification.

25   North Korea promulgates a new constitution, creating a presidential regime.

August 1973

8   Prominent South Korean opposition leader Kim Dae Jung is kidnapped by the Korean Central Intelligence Agency in Tokyo, Japan.

August 1974

15   A Korean resident of Japan attempts to assassinate Park Chung Hee, instead killing Park's wife.

August 1975

18   North Korean guards murder two U.S. Army officers in the Joint Security Area of Panmunjom.

July 1978

6   Park Chung Hee wins another term as South Korean president.

October 1979

16   In South Korea, students and other citizens demonstrate in Pusan and Masan for an end to the Yushin system. These soon turn into riots.

26   South Korean president Park Chung Hee is assassinated by Korean Central Intelligence Agency chief Kim Chae Gyu.

December 1979

12   South Korean major general Chun Doo Hwan seizes control of the armed forces in a bloody nighttime coup.

May 1980

17   Chun Doo Hwan extends martial law to all of South Korea.

18   In South Korea, students and citizens in Kawngju protest martial law in street demonstrations that soon escalate into armed revolt.

27   In a bloody confrontation, South Korean armed forces put an end to the Kwangju uprising.

August 1980

27   Chun Doo Hwan is elected president of South Korea by the National Conference for Unification.

October 1980

10   In the course of the Sixth Korean Workers' Party Congress, Kim Jong Il is publicly identified as Kim Il Sung's designated successor as leader of North Korea.

22   A national referendum approves the new constitution for the Fifth Republic in South Korea.

September 1981

1   A Soviet interceptor aircraft shoots down Korean Air Lines Flight 007, killing all 269 people aboard. The airliner had inadvertently strayed over Soviet airspace.

October 1982

9   North Korean agents detonate a bomb in the superstructure of the Aung San shrine in Rangoon, Burma, killing 17 South Korean senior government officials.

June 1987

10   In South Korea, the June Resistance begins.

29   In his eight-point democratization program, presidential candidate Roh Tae Woo agrees to the direct election of the next South Korean president.

October 1987

27   A national referendum in South Korea approves the new constitution of the Sixth Republic.

November 1987

29   North Korean agents place a bomb in a South Korean airliner. The ensuing blast over the Andaman Sea kills all 115 persons abroad.

December 1987

16   Roh Tae Woo defeats opposition leaders Kim Young Sam and Kim Dae Jung for the presidency of South Korea.

September 17–October 2, 1988

In an important recognition of its international stature, South Korea hosts the XXIV Summer Olympiad in Seoul.

October 1990

1   South Korea and the Soviet Union establish normal diplomatic relations.

August 1991

8   The UN admits both South Korea and North Korea as members.

December 1991

31   The two Korean governments adopt the "Basic Agreement on North-South Reconciliation, Nonaggression, Exchanges, and Cooperation" and the "Joint Declaration of the Denuclearization of the Korean Peninsula."

August 1992

24   South Korea and the PRC establish normal diplomatic relations.

December 1992

18   Kim Young Sam is elected president of South Korea.

March 1993

12   The government of North Korea announces its intention to withdraw from the Nuclear Non-Proliferation Treaty, initiating an acute international crisis.

July 1994

8   North Korean leader Kim Il Sung dies.

October 1994

21   The United States and North Korea sign the Agreed Framework to freeze North Korea's nuclear activity in return for economic and diplomatic benefits.

August 1996

26   The Seoul District Court sentences former South Korean presidents Chun Doo Hwan and Roh Tae Woo to death and to 22.5 years in prison, respectively, for their 1979 military mutiny, treason in 1980, the Kwangju massacre, and corruption in office.

October 1997

8   Kim Jong Il becomes secretary-general of the Korean Workers' Party in North Korea.

December 1997

18   Kim Dae Jung is elected president of South Korea.

22   In South Korea, convicted former presidents Chun Doo Hwan and Roh Tae Woo are pardoned under a special amnesty.

August 1998

31   North Korea test launches a three-stage rocket.

September 1998

5   The Supreme People's Assembly of North Korea elects Kim Jong Il chairman of the National Defense Commission.

June 1999

13   North Korean patrol boats cross the Northern Limitation Line, resulting in naval confrontation between the navies of North Korea and South Korea.

June 2000

13–15   A summit occurs between South Korean president Kim Dae Jung and North Korean leader Kim Jong Il in Pyongyang.

January 2002

29   U.S. president George W. Bush declares in his State of the Union speech that North Korea, along with Iraq and Iran, are members of an "Axis of Evil."

June 2002

13   In South Korea, a U.S. armored vehicle accidentally hits and kills two South Korean middle school girls, igniting weeks of demonstrations calling for the withdrawal of U.S. troops.

29   A North Korean patrol boat crosses the Northern Limitation Line and opens fire on a South Korean patrol boat, killing 6 South Korean sailors and wounding 19 others.

December 2002

19   Roh Moo Hyun is elected president of South Korea.

July 2006

4   North Korea conducts multiple missile tests.

October 2006

9   North Korea announces that it has successfully conducted the test of a nuclear weapon.

February 2007

13   North Korea agrees to shut down its main nuclear reactor and disable its nuclear program in exchange for energy assistance and security guarantees.

The United States and South Korea agree to complete the transition of full operational military control to South Korea on April 17, 2012.

October 2007

2–4   South Korean president Roh Moo Hyun and North Korean leader Kim Jong Il meet in Pyongyang.

December 2007

19   In the South Korean presidential election, Lee Myung Bak of the Grand National Party wins a sweeping victory.

February 2008

11   In South Korea, the opposition United Democratic Party is formed.

May 2008

2   In South Korea, a candlelight vigil begun by hundreds of teenagers, a demonstration against the importation of American beef, quickly escalates.

October 2008

10   The U.S. government removes North Korea from the list of states sponsoring terrorism.

December 2008

1   North Korea closes all overland passage through the military demarcation line and the Red Cross liaison office and all direct telephone lines between North Korea and South Korea. North Korea also rejects nuclear inspections, leading to a sharp deterioration in inter-Korean relations and jeopardizing the six-party nuclear talks.

JINWUNG KIM, JAMES MATRAY, AND SPENCER C. TUCKER

Glossary

AE — Army emergency airstrip (with number designation following).

AFB — Air force base.

A-frame — Back carrier used by porters during the war. GIs dubbed this an "A-frame" because it resembled a capital "A." The outer legs of the carrier were widespread at the bottom and came close together at the top.

AMG — American Military Government. Military government established by the United States after World War II for its zone of occupation in Korea.

Ballistics — The science of projectiles, divided into interior and exterior ballistics. Its aim is to improve the design of shells/projectiles so that increased accuracy and predictability are the result. It also deals with rockets and ballistic missiles.

Barrage — Term for a barrier formed by artillery fire (land) or an antisubmarine net or mine barrier (sea).

Battalion — Army unit, composed of a headquarters and two or more companies or batteries, from 300 to 1,000 soldiers usually commanded by a lieutenant colonel; may be part of a regiment, brigade, or division artillery.

Battery — Army tactical and administrative artillery unit corresponding to an infantry company. Usually composed of about 100 officers and men; normally commanded by a captain.

BNR — Body not returned.

Bombing raid — Military tactic in which airplanes and seaplanes drop a successive number of bombs on specified targets within a short period of time.

Boonies or boondocks — Remote woods, ridges, rice paddies, or rural areas far away from villages and settlements.

Brigade — Army unit, usually smaller than a division, to which are attached groups and/or battalions and smaller units tailored to meet anticipated requirements. During the Korean War, this was an organizational structure used by the British, Canadians, and Turks and in those cases was similar to a U.S. Army regimental combat team.

Bug-out or bugging — To retreat rapidly and in panic without orders or authority when confronted with an advancing enemy and usually leaving all weapons and equipment behind; the opposite of an orderly, organized, and authorized withdrawal or relocation.

CAS — Close air support.

CCF — Chinese communist forces. UNC term for Chinese People's Volunteer Army (CPVA, Chinese Army).

CG — Commanding general.

China Lobby — Politicians and others who believed that the United States had allowed China to fall to the communists in 1949 and who lobbied for increased military and economic support for Nationalist forces on Taiwan. Closely tied to the right wing of the Republican Party, they were generally critical of the Truman administration for making Europe rather than Asia the primary focus of its foreign policy.

CINCFE   Commander in chief, Far East. Commander of U.S. forces in the Far East.

CINCUNC   Commander in chief, United Nations Command. Commander of United Nations military forces in Korea.

CO   Commanding officer.

Containment   Strategy of the United States during most of the Cold War period aimed at preventing the spread of communist regimes around the world.

Corps   Army tactical unit larger than a division and smaller than a field army. Usually consists of two or more divisions together with auxiliary arms and services. Normally commanded by a lieutenant general.

Counterbattery   Artillery fire directed against enemy heavy weapons and artillery.

Coup   Also known as a coup d'état, a coup is a sudden, decisive use of force in politics, especially in terms of a violent overthrow of an existing government by a small group, often assisted by the military.

Court-martial   To subject to a military trial with a court consisting of a board of commissioned officers.

CP   Command post.

CPVA   Chinese People's Volunteer Army. Chinese name for their People's Liberation Army (PLA, Chinese Communist Army) forces in the Korean War, indicating Beijing's desire to avoid a full-scale conflict with the United States.

Defense perimeter   A defense without an exposed flank, consisting of forces deployed along the perimeter of a defended area.

Division   Army tactical unit, larger than a regiment or brigade and smaller than a corps. A combined arms unit for waging war, generally commanded by a major general with an authorized strength (U.S. Army) of some 20,000 men.

DOF   Days of fire. Artillery term used to express the number of rounds allocated per gun per day.

DOW   Died of wounds.

DPRK   Democratic People's Republic of Korea (North Korea).

DZ   Drop zone. Area where airborne forces are to be parachuted.

ECB   Engineer (combat) battalion.

Enfilade   To fire upon the length rather than the face of an enemy position; enfilading an enemy allows a varying range of fire to find targets while minimizing the amount of fire the enemy can return.

Envelopment   To pour fire along the enemy's line. A double envelopment means to attack both flanks of an enemy, a risky venture. A strategic envelopment was not directed against the flanks but instead was a turning movement designed to a point in the rear whereupon the enemy had to vacate his position to defend it.

EUSAK   U.S. Eighth Army in Korea.

FAA   Fleet Air Arm. British naval aviation term.

FAB   Field artillery battalion.

FAC   Forward air controller.

FEAF   Far East Air Force. Primary U.S. Air Force component serving in Korea during the Korean War.

FEC   Far East Command, today FECOM.

FO   Forward observer, artillery and mortars.

GHQ   General headquarters.

Group   A flexible administrative and tactical unit, composed of either two or more squadrons (U.S. Air Force) or two or more battalions (U.S. Army).

I&R   Intelligence and reconnaissance (platoons).

Iron Triangle   A heavily defended area in Korea encompassed by a triangle with Pyongyang at the northern angle, Chorwon at the western angle, and Kumhwa at the eastern angle. Much of the military fighting in Korea after the failure of the communist offensive in April 1951 took place within the Iron Triangle.

JATO   Jet-assisted takeoff. A pack of rockets was attached to an aircraft fuselage centerline and then ignited to add speed for liftoff. The pack was jettisoned as soon as the thrust was exhausted.

JLC Japan Logistical Command.

JOC Joint operations center.

KCOMZ Korean communications zone. In U.S. Army doctrine, a communications zone is the specified area behind the front lines where supply and administrative facilities could be established and operated to relieve the frontline commander of responsibility for functions not directly related to combat operations.

KIA Killed in action.

KPA Korean People's Army (North Korean Army).

LD Line of departure. Prominent terrain feature used to coordinate an attack.

LLC Loudspeaker and leaflet company. U.S. Army unit involved in psychological warfare operations.

Massive retaliation Foreign policy of the Eisenhower administration based on the threat of full-scale nuclear retaliation against communist aggression in any form.

MATS Military Air Transport Service (U.S. Air Force).

MIA Missing in action.

MiG Alley A 6,500-square-mile airspace in northwestern Korea, site of the most intense jet aircraft combat throughout the war.

MLR Main line of resistance.

MSR Main supply route.

MSTS Military Sea Transport Service.

Napalm An acronym for naphthenic and palmitic acids. Napalm is a jellied gasoline used in flamethrowers and aerial bombs.

NATO North Atlantic Treaty Organization.

NAVFE Naval Forces, Far East.

OPLR Outpost line of resistance.

PLA People's Liberation Army. The military forces of the People's Republic of China. The Chinese referred to their units in the Korean War as the Chinese People's Volunteer Army (CPVA, Chinese Army).

Platoon Army unit, usually four squads, of a tactical unit such as a company; usually commanded by a lieutenant.

POW Prisoner of war.

PVA People's Volunteer Army. Another term for the CPVA.

PWO Psychological warfare officers. U.S. Army officers attached to Eighth Army headquarters who decided on suitable psychological warfare targets.

R&R Rest and recuperation.

RAF Royal Air Force; United Kingdom's air force.

RCT Regimental combat team.

Red Scare Name given to the widespread fear in the United States in the 1940s and early 1950s of an internal communist conspiracy against the United States.

Regiment Army administrative and tactical unit larger than a battalion and smaller than a brigade, usually consisting of three infantry battalions plus heavy mortar, intelligence and reconnaissance, heavy tank, medical, signal, and limited transportation elements; commanded by a colonel.

ROK Republic of Korea (South Korea).

ROKA Republic of Korea Army (South Korean Army).

ROKAF Republic of Korea Air Force (South Korean Air Force).

ROKN Republic of Korea Navy (South Korean Navy).

SCAP Supreme commander, Allied powers.

Scapjap Shipping Control Administration, Japan.

Seabees Nickname for the U.S. Navy's amphibious construction battalions.

SOP Standard operating procedure.

Sortie One flight by one aircraft.

SP gun Self-propelled gun.

Squad Smallest basic tactical infantry unit, below platoon, usually 8 to 12 men; normally commanded by a sergeant.

Squadron Basic U.S. Air Force, Navy, and Marine Corps administrative aviation unit, consisting of several flights of approximately five aircraft each.

TACP Tactical air-control party.

TD Table of distribution.

TF Task force. A group of units assembled temporarily for a particular mission.

TO&E	Tables of organization and equipment. Official authorized strength, organization, and equipment of particular units.
UDT	Underwater demolition team.
UNC	United Nations Command.
UNTCOK	United Nations Temporary Commission on Korea.
USAFIK	U.S. Army Forces in Korea (designation for U.S. command in Korea at the end of World War II).
WIA	Wounded in action.
Wing	U.S. Air Force unit, normally composed of one primary mission group (designated for combat, training, airlift, or service) commanded by a colonel. A typical U.S. Air Force fighter wing consists of three fighter squadrons of 25 aircraft each. U.S. Navy wings are similar. A U.S. Marine Corps air wing contains the elements required for the air support of a Marine Corps division; commanded by a major general, it may include hundreds of aircraft.
XO	Executive officer.
ZI	Zone of the interior. During the Korean War, designation for the continental United States.

Selected Bibliography

Abner, Alan K. *Psywarriors: Psychological Warfare during the Korean War.* Shippensburg, PA: Burd Street Press, 2001.

Acheson, Dean. *The Korean War.* New York: Norton, 1971.

———. *Present at the Creation.* New York: Norton, 1969.

Aerospace Studies Institute, Air University. *Guerrilla Warfare and Airpower in Korea, 1950–1953.* Maxwell AFB, AL: Air University Press, 1964.

Aguirre, Emilio. *We'll Be Home for Christmas: A True Story of the United States Marine Corps in the Korean War.* New York: Greenwich, 1959.

Alexander, Bevin. *Korea: The First War We Lost.* New York: Hippocrene Books, 1986.

Alexander, James Edwin. *Inchon to Wonsan: From the Deck of a Destroyer in the Korean War.* Annapolis, MD: Naval Institute Press 1996.

Alexander, Joseph H. *Battle of the Barricades: U.S. Marines in the Recapture of Seoul.* Washington, DC: U.S. Marine Corps, History and Museums Division, 2000.

———. *Fleet Operation in a Mobile War, September 1950–June 1951.* Washington, DC: Naval Historical Center, 2001.

Allen, Richard C. *Korea's Syngman Rhee: An Unauthorized Portrait.* Rutland, VT: Tuttle, 1960.

Allison, John M. *Ambassador from the Prairie, or Allison Wonderland.* Boston: Houghton Mifflin, 1973.

Anderson, Christopher J. *The War in Korea: The U.S. Army in Korea, 1950–1953.* St. Paul, MN: Greenhill Books, 2001.

Anderson, Ellery. *Banner Over Pusan.* London: Evans Brothers, 1980.

Apel, Otto F., Jr., and Pat Apel. *MASH: An Army Surgeon in Korea.* Lexington: University Press of Kentucky, 1998.

Appleman, Roy E. *Disaster in Korea: The Chinese Confront MacArthur.* College Station: Texas A&M University Press, 1989.

———. *East of Chosin: Entrapment and Breakout in Korea.* College Station: Texas A&M University Press, 1987.

———. *Escaping the Trap: The U.S. Army X Corps in Northeast Korea, 1950.* College Station: Texas A&M University Press, 1990.

———. *Ridgway Duels for Korea.* College Station: Texas A&M University Press, 1990.

———. *United States Army in Korea: South to the Naktong, North to the Yalu.* Washington, DC: Office of the Chief of Military History, 1961.

Armstrong, Charles K. *The North Korean Revolution, 1945–1950.* Ithaca, NY: Cornell University Press, 2003.

Bailey, Sydney D. *The Korean Armistice.* New York: St. Martin's, 1992.

Baker, Roger G. *A USMC Tanker's War.* Oakland, OR: Elderberry Press, 2001.

Baldovi, Louis, ed. *A Foxhole View: Personal Accounts of Hawaii's Korean War Veterans.* Honolulu: University of Hawaii Press, 2002.

Baldwin, Frank, ed. *Without Parallel: The American-Korean Relationship since 1945.* New York: Random House, 1974.

Ballenger, Lee. *The Final Crucible: U.S. Marines in Korea, 1953.* Washington, DC: Brassey's 2001.

———. *The Final Outpost: U.S. Marines in Korea, 1952.* Washington, DC: Brassey's, 2000.

Barclay, C. N. *The First Commonwealth Division: The Story of British Commonwealth Land Forces in Korea, 1950–1953.* Aldershot, UK: Gale and Polden, 1954.

Barker, A. J. *Fortune Favors the Brave: The Battle of the Hook, Korea, 1953.* London: Leo Cooper, 1973.

Barth, G. Bittman. "Tropic Lightning and the Taro Leaf in Korea." Unpublished memoir, 1952–1953. Library, U.S. Army Military History Institute.

Bartlett, Norman. *With the Australians in Korea.* Canberra: Australian War Memorial, 1954.

Bateman, Robert L. *No Gun Ri: A Military History of the Korean War Incident.* Mechanicsburg, PA: Stackpole Books, 2002.

Batson, Denzil. *We Called It War: The Untold Story of the Combat Infantry in Korea.* Leawood, KS: Leathers Publishing, 1999.

Beisner, Robert L. *Dean Acheson: A Life in the Cold War.* New York: Oxford University Press, 2006.

Bercuson, David J. *Blood on the Hills: The Canadian Army in the Korean War.* Toronto: University of Toronto Press, 1999.

Berebitsky, William. *A Very Long Weekend: The Army National Guard in Korea.* Shippensburg, PA: White Mane, 1996.

Berger, Carl. *The Korea Knot: A Military and Political History.* Philadelphia: University of Pennsylvania Press, 1957.

Berry, Henry. *Hey Mac, Where Ya Been? Living Memories of the U.S. Marines in the Korean War.* New York: St. Martin's, 1988.

Biderman, Albert D. *Communist Techniques of Coercive Interrogation.* Lackland Air Force Base, TX: U.S. Air Force, 1956.

———. *March to Calumny: The Story of American POWs in the Korean War.* New York: Macmillan, 1963.

Biderman, Albert D., and Herbert Zimmer, eds. *The Manipulation of Human Behavior.* New York: Wiley, 1961.

Birtle, Andrew J. *The U.S. Army Counterinsurgency and Contingency Operations Doctrine, 1941–1975.* Washington, DC: Center of Military History, 2006.

Black, Robert. *A Ranger Born: A Memoir of Combat and Valor from Korea to Vietnam.* New York: Ballantine Books, 2002.

Black, Robert W. *Rangers in Korea.* New York: Ivy Books, 1989.

Blair, Clay. *Beyond Courage.* New York: David McKay, 1955.

———. *The Forgotten War: America in Korea, 1950–1953.* New York: Times Books, 1987.

Blanchard, Carroll H., Jr. *Korean War Bibliography and Maps of Korea.* Albany, NY: Korean Conflict Research Foundation, 1964.

Blunk, Chester L. *"Every Man a Tiger": The 731st USAF Night Intruders over Korea.* Manhattan, KS: Sunflower University Press, 1988.

Bohlen, Charles E. *Witness to History, 1929–69.* New York: Norton, 1973.

Boose, Donald. *U.S. Army Forces in the Korean War, 1950–1953.* Oxford, UK: Osprey, 2005.

Bowers, William T., William M. Hammond, and George L. MacGarrigle. *Black Soldier White Army.* Washington, DC: Center of Military History, United States Army, 1996.

Bowie, Robert R., and Richard H. Immerman. *Waging Peace.* New York: Oxford University Press, 1998.

Boyd, Arthur L. *Operation Broken Reed: Truman's Secret North Korean Spy Mission That Averted World War III.* New York: Da Capo, 2007.

Bradley, Omar N. *A Soldier's Story.* New York: Holt, 1951.

Bradley, Omar N., and Clay Blair. *A General's Life.* New York: Simon and Schuster, 1983.

Brady, James. *The Coldest War: A Memoir of Korea.* New York: St. Martin's, 2000.

Braim, Paul F. *The Will to Win: The Life of General James A. Van Fleet.* Annapolis, MD: Naval Institute Press, 2001.

Brazinsky, Gregg. *Nation Building in South Korea: Koreans, Americans, and the Making of Democracy.* Chapel Hill: University of North Carolina Press, 2007.

Breen, Bob. *The Battle of Kapyong.* Syndey: Australian Army Training Command, 1992.

———. *The Battle of Maryang San.* Sydney: Australian Army Training Command, 1991.

Breuer, William B. *Shadow Warriors: The Covert War in Korea.* New York: John Wiley, 1996.

Briggs, Ellis. *Farewell to Foggy Bottom.* New York: McKay, 1964.

Brown, Ronald J. *Counteroffensive: U.S. Marines from Pohang to No Name Line.* Washington, DC: U.S. Marine Corps, History and Museums Division, 2001.

Brune, Lester H., ed. *The Korean War: Handbook of the Literature and Research.* Westport, CT: Greenwood, 1996.

Bruning, John R. *Crimson Sky: The Air Battle for Korea.* Dulles, VA: Brassey's, 1999.

Burchett, Wilfred, and Alan Winnington. *Koje Unscreened.* London: Britain-China Friendship Association, 1953.

Bussey, Charles M. *Firefight at Yechon: Courage and Racism in the Korean War.* Washington, DC: Brassey's, 1991.

Cagle, Malcolm W., and Frank A. Manson. *Sea War in Korea.* Annapolis, MD: Naval Institute Press, 1957.

Caldwell, John C. *The Korean Story.* Chicago: Henry Regnery, 1952.

Camilleri, Joseph. *Chinese Foreign Policy: The Maoist Era and Its Aftermath.* Oxford, UK: Martin Robertson, 1980.

Canada, Historical Section, General Staff, Canadian Army. *Canada's Army in Korea.* Ottawa: Queen's Printer, 1956.

Cardwell, Thomas A., III. *Command Structure for Theater Warfare: The Quest for Unity of Command.* Maxwell Air Force Base, AL: Air University Press, 1984.

Carew, Tim. *Korea: The Commonwealth at War.* London: Cassell, 1967.

Carey, Charles W., ed. *Living through the Korean War.* Chicago: Greenhaven, 2006.

Caridi, Ronald J. *The Korean War and American Politics: The Republican Party as a Case Study.* Philadelphia: University of Pennsylvania Press, 1968.

Carlson, Lewis. *Remembered Prisoners of a Forgotten War: An Oral History of Korean War POWs.* New York: St. Martin's, 2002.

Carter, Gregory A. *Some Historical Notes on Air Interdiction in Korea.* Santa Monica, CA: Rand Corporation, 1966.

Carter, Paul A. *Another Part of the Fifties.* New York: Columbia University Press, 1983.

Casey, Steven. *Selling the Korean War: Propaganda, Politics, and Public Opinion.* New York: Oxford University Press, 2008.

Catchpole, Brian. *The Korean War.* New York: Basic Books, 2001.

Chancey, Jennie Ethell, and William R. Forstchen, eds. *Hot Shots: An Oral History of Combat Pilots of the Korean War.* New York: Morrow, 2000.

Chang, Anson, and Charles J. Hilton. *Chosin: The Untold Story.* New York: Honeoye International Association, 1993.

Chang, Gordon. *Friends and Enemies: The United States, China, and the Soviet Union.* Stanford, CA: Stanford University Press, 1990.

Chapin, John C. *Fire Brigade: U.S. Marines in the Pusan Perimeter.* Washington, DC: U.S. Marine Corps, History and Museums Division, 2000.

Chappell, Richard G., and Gerald E. Chappell. *Corpsmen: Letters from Korea.* Kent, OH: Kent State University Press, 2000.

Chen Jian. *China's Road to the Korean War: The Making of the Sino-American Confrontation.* New York: Columbia University Press, 1994.

———. *Mao's China and the Cold War.* Chapel Hill: University of North Carolina Press, 2000.

Ching, Cyrus Stewart. *Review and Reflection: A Half-Century of Labor Relations.* New York: B. C. Forbes, 1953.

Chinnery, Philip D. *Korean Atrocity!: Forgotten War Crimes, 1950–1953.* Annapolis, MD: Naval Institute Press, 2001.

Cho, Soon-Sung. *Korea in World Politics, 1940–1950.* Berkeley: University of California Press, 1967.

Choi Bong-Youn. *Korea: A History.* Rutland, VT: C. E. Tuttle, 1971.

Choi Duk-shin. *Panmunjom and After.* New York: Vantage Press, 1972.

Christensen, Thomas. *Useful Adversaries: Grand Strategy, Domestic Mobilization and Sino-American Conflict, 1947–1958.* Princeton, NJ: Princeton University Press, 1996.

Chung, Donald. *The Three-Day Promise.* Tallahassee, FL: Loiry Publishing, 1988.

Chung, Henry. *Korea and the United States through War and Peace, 1943–1960.* Seoul: Yonsei University Press, 2000.

Clark, Donald N. *Living Dangerously in Korea: The Western Experience, 1900–1950.* Norwalk, CT: Eastbridge, 2003.

Clark, Eugene F. *The Secrets of Inchon.* New York: Putnam, 2002.

Clark, Mark W. *From the Danube to the Yalu.* New York: Harper and Row, 1954.

Cleaver, Frederick W., et al. *UN Partisan Warfare in Korea, 1951–1954.* Chevy Chase, MD: Operations Research Office, Johns Hopkins University, 1956.

Cleveland, William M. *Mosquitoes in Korea.* Portsmouth, NH: Peter E. Randall, 1991.

Cochran, Bert. *Harry Truman and the Crisis Presidency.* New York: Funk and Wagnalls, 1973.

Cohen, Warren I., and Akira Iriye, eds. *The Great Powers in East Asia, 1953–1960.* New York: Columbia University Press, 1990.

Cole, Charles F. *Korea Remembered: Enough of a War; The USS Ozbourn's First Korean Tour, 1950–1951.* Las Cruces, NM: Yucca Tree, 1995.

Coleman, J. D. *Wonju: The Gettysburg of the Korean War.* Herndon, VA: Potomac Books, 2001.

Collier, Rebecca L., comp. *The Korean War.* Washington, DC: RIP 103, National Archives and Records Administration, 2003.

Collins, J. Lawton. *War in Peacetime: The History and Lessons of Korea.* Boston: Houghton Mifflin, 1969.

Condit, Doris M. *History of the Office of the Secretary of Defense,* Vol. 2, *The Test of War, 1950–1953.* Washington, DC: Office of the Secretary of Defense, 1988.

Condon, John P. *Corsairs to Panthers: U.S. Marine Aviation in Korea.* Washington, DC: History and Museums Division, HQMC, 2002.

Cooling, Benjamin Franklin III, ed. *Close Air Support.* Washington, DC: Office of Air Force History, 1999.

Cooper, Paul L. *Weekend Warriors (VF-871).* Manhattan, KS: Sunflower, 1996.

Cotton, James, and Ian Neary, eds. *The Korean War as History.* Atlantic Highlands, NJ: Humanities Press, 1989.

Courtney, Vincent R. *Hold the Hook: With the Princess Patricia's Canadian Light Infantry in Korea.* Leamington, Ontario: North American Heritage, 1996.

Cowart, Glenn C. *Miracle in Korea: The Evacuation of X Corps from the Hungnam Beachhead.* Columbia: University of South Carolina Press, 1992.

Cowdrey, Albert A. *The Medic's War.* Washington, DC: Center of Military History, Department of the Army, 1987.

Crane, Conrad C. *A Rather Bizarre War: American Airpower Strategy in Korea, 1950–1953.* Lawrence: University Press of Kansas, 2000.

Crawford, C. S. *The Four Deuces: A Korean War Story.* Novato, CA: Presidio, 1998.

Crews, Thomas. *Thunderbolt through Ripper: Joint Operations in Korea, 25 January–31 March 1951.* Carlisle Barracks, PA: Army War College, 1991.

Cumings, Bruce. *Child of Conflict: The Korean-American Relationship, 1943–1953.* Seattle: University of Washington Press, 1983.

———. *Korea's Place in the Sun: A Modern History.* New York: Norton, 1997.

———. *The Origins of the Korean War.* 2 vols. Princeton, NJ: Princeton University Press, 1981, 1990.

Cumings, Bruce, and John Halliday. *Korea: The Unknown War.* New York: Pantheon, 1988.

Cunningham, Cyril. *No Mercy, No Leniency: Communist Mistreatment of British Prisoners of War in Korea.* London: Leo Cooper, 2000.

Cunningham-Boothe, Ashley, and Peter N. Farrar. *British Forces in the Korean War.* Leamington Spa, UK: British Korean Veterans Association, 1989.

Cutforth, Rene. *Korean Reporter.* London: Allan Wingate, 1952.

Dannenmaier, William D. *We Were Innocents: An Infantryman in Korea.* Urbana: University of Illinois Press, 1999.

Davis, Larry. *The 4th Fighter Wing in the Korean War.* Atglen, PA: Schiffer Military History, 2001.

Dawson, Joseph G. III, ed. *Commander in Chief: Presidential Leadership in Modern Wars.* Lawrence: Regents Press of Kansas, 1993.

Day, William W. II. *The Running Wounded: A Personal Memory of the Korean War.* Riverton, WY: Big Bend, 1990.

Dean, William F. *General Dean's Story.* 1954; reprint, Westport, CT: Greenwood, 1973.

Deane, Phillip [pseudonym for Gerassimos Svoronos-Gigant]. *I Was a Captive in Korea.* New York: Norton, 1953.

Degovanni, George. *Air Force Support of Army Ground Operations: Lessons Learned during World War II, Korea, and Vietnam.* Carlisle Barracks, PA: Army War College, 1989.

Democratic People's Republic of Korea. *The U.S. Imperialists Started the Korean War.* Pyongyang: Foreign Language Publishing House, 1977.

Detzer, David. *Thunder of the Captains: The Short Summer of 1950.* New York: Cromwell, 1977.

Dille, John. *Substitute for Victory.* New York: Doubleday, 1954.

Dobbs, Charles M. *The Unwanted Symbol: American Foreign Policy, the Cold War, and Korea, 1945–1950.* Kent, OH: Kent State University Press, 1981.

Dong-Sum Kim, Ki-Jung Kim, and Hahnkyu Park, eds. *Fifty Years after the Korean War: From the Cold War Confrontation to Peaceful Coexistence.* Seoul: Korean Association of International Studies, 2000.

Donnelly, William M. *Under Army Orders: The Army National Guard During the Korean War.* College Station: Texas A&M University Press, 2001.

Donovan, Robert J. *Tumultuous Years: The Presidency of Harry S. Truman.* New York: Norton, 1982.

Dorr, Robert F., Jon Lake, and Warren Thompson. *Korean War Aces.* London: Osprey, 1995.

Dorr, Robert F., and Warren E. Thompson. *The Korean Air War.* Osceola, WI: Motorbooks International, 1994.

Doughty, Robert A. *Limited War in the Nuclear Age.* Lexington, MA: D. C. Heath, 1996.

Dunstan, Simon. *Armor of the Korean War, 1950–1953.* London: Osprey, 1982.

Dvorchak, Robert J. *Battle for Korea: The Associated Press History of the Korean Conflict.* Conshohocken, PA: Combined Publishing, 2000.

Dwyer, John B. *Commandos from the Sea: The History of Amphibious Special Warfare in World War II and the Korean War.* Boulder, CO: Paladin, 1998.

Ecker, Richard E. *Korean Battle Chronology: Unit-by-Unit United States Casualty Figures and Medal of Honor Citations.* Jefferson, NC: McFarland, 2005.

Eckert, Carter Jay, Lee Ki-Baik, Young Ick Lew, Michael Robinson, and Edward W. Wagner. *Korea: Old and New.* Seoul: Iljogak, for the Korea Institute, Harvard University, 1990.

Edwards, Paul G. *The Korean War: A Historical Dictionary.* Lanham, MD: Scarecrow, 2003.

———. *The Korean War: An Annotated Bibliography.* Westport, CT: Greenwood, 1998.

———. *The Inchon Landing, Korea, 1950.* Westport, CT: Greenwood, 1994.

———. *The Pusan Perimeter, Korea, 1950.* Westport, CT: Greenwood, 1993.

———. *To Acknowledge a War: The Korean War in American Memory.* Westport, CT: Greenwood, 2000.

Eisenhower, Dwight D. *The White House Years,* Vol. 2, *Mandate for Change, 1953–1956.* Garden City, NY: Doubleday, 1963.

Endicott, Stephen, and Edward Hagerman. *The United States and Biological Warfare: Secrets from the Early Cold War and Korea.* Bloomington: Indiana University Press, 1998.

Ent, Uzal W. *Fighting on the Brink: Defense of the Pusan Perimeter.* Paducah, KY: Turner Publishing, 1996.

Epley, William W., ed. *International Cold War Military Records and History.* Washington, DC: Office of the Secretary of Defense, 1996.

Evanhoe, Ed. *Dark Moon: Eighth Army Special Operations in the Korean War.* Annapolis, MD: Naval Institute Press, 1995.

Evans, Douglas. *Sabre Jets over Korea: A Firsthand Account.* Blue Ridge Summit, PA: Tab Books, 1984.

Faculty of Futan University, trans. *Stories of the Chinese People's Volunteers.* Beijing: Foreign Language Press, 1960.

Farmer, James A., and M. J. Strumwasser. *The Evolution of the Airborne Forward Air Controller: An Analysis of Mosquito Operations in Korea.* Santa Monica, CA: Rand Corporation, 1967.

Farrar-Hockley, Sir Anthony. *The British Part in the Korean War,* Vol. 1, *A Distant Obligation.* London: HMSO, 1990.

———. *The British Part in the Korean War,* Vol. 2, *An Honourable Discharge.* London: HMSO, 1994.

Fehrenbach, T. R. *The Fight for Korea.* New York: Grosset and Dunlap, 1969.

———. *This Kind of War: A Study in Unpreparedness.* New York: Macmillan, 1962.

Ferrell, Robert H. *The Eisenhower Diaries.* New York: Norton, 1981.

———. *Harry S. Truman and the Modern American Presidency.* New York: Longman, 1997.

Field, James A., Jr. *History of United States Naval Operations, Korea.* Washington, DC: U.S. Government Printing Office, 1962.

Foot, Rosemary J. *The Practice of Power: U.S. Relations with China since 1949.* New York: Oxford University Press, 1995.

———. *A Substitute for Victory: The Politics of Peacemaking at the Korean Armistice Talks.* Ithaca, NY: Cornell University Press, 1990.

———. *The Wrong War: American Policy and the Dimensions of the Korean Conflict, 1950–1953.* Ithaca, NY: Cornell University Press, 1985.

Foster, Cecil G. *MiG Alley to Mu Ghia Pass: Memoirs of a Korean War Ace.* Jefferson, NC: McFarland, 2001.

Fried, Richard M. *Nightmare in Red: McCarthyism in Perspective.* New York: Oxford University Press, 1991.

Futrell, Robert F. *The United States Air Force in Korea, 1950–1953.* Rev. ed. Washington, DC: Office of the Chief of Air Force History, 1983.

Gaddis, John Lewis. *The Cold War: A New History.* New York: Penguin, 2005.

———. *The Long Peace: Inquiries into the History of the Cold War.* New York: Oxford University Press, 1987.

———. *Strategies of Containment: A Critical Appraisal of Postwar National Security Policy.* New York: Oxford University Press, 1982.

———. *We Now Know: Rethinking Cold War History.* New York: Oxford University Press, 1998.

Galloway, Jack. *The Last of the Bugle: The Long Road to Kapyong.* Queensland, Australia: University of Queensland Press, 1994.

Gao Wenqian. *Zhou Enlai: The Last Perfect Revolutionary.* New York: Public Affairs, 2007.

Gardner, Lloyd, ed. *The Korean War.* New York: Quadrangle Books, 1972.

Geer, Andrew. *The New Breed: The Story of the U.S. Marines in Korea.* Nashville: Battery Press, 1989.

George, Alexander L. *The Chinese Communist Army in Action: The Korean War and Its Aftermath.* New York: Columbia University Press, 1967.

Gibby, Bryan R. "Fighting in a Korean War: The American Advisory Missions from 1946–1953." PhD dissertation, Ohio State University, 2004.

Giusti, Ernest H. *The Mobilization of the Marine Corps Reserve in the Korean Conflict.* Washington, DC: Historical Branch, G-3 Division Headquarters, U.S. Marine Corps, 1967.

Goncharov, Sergei N., John W. Lewis, and Xue Litai. *Uncertain Partners: Stalin, Mao, and the Korean War.* Stanford, CA: Stanford University Press, 1993.

Goodman, Allan E., ed. *Negotiating While Fighting: The Diary of Admiral C. Turner Joy at the Korean Armistice Conference.* Stanford, CA: Hoover Institute Press, 1978.

Goodrich, Leland Matthew. *Korea: A Study of U.S. Policy in the United Nations.* New York: Council on Foreign Relations, 1956.

Gordenker, Leon. *The United Nations and the Peaceful Unification of Korea: The Politics of Field Operations, 1947–1950.* The Hague: Martinus Nijhoff, 1959.

Gordon, Yefim. *Mikoyan-Gurevich MiG-15: The Soviet Union's Long-lived Korean War Fighter.* Hinckley, UK: Midland Publishing, 2001.

Gough, Terrence J. *U.S. Army Mobilization and Logistics in the Korean War.* Washington, DC: U.S. Army Center for Military History, 1987.

Goulden, Joseph C. *Korea: The Untold Story of the War.* New York: Times Books, 1982.

Grey, Jeffrey. *The Commonwealth Armies and the Korean War: An Alliance Study.* Manchester, UK: Manchester University Press, 1988.

Gugeler, Russell A. *Combat Actions in Korea.* Rev. ed. Washington, DC: U.S. Army, Center of Military History, 1987.

Gurtov, Melvin, and Byoong-Mao Hwang. *China under Threat: The Politics of Strategy and Diplomacy.* Baltimore: Johns Hopkins University Press, 1980.

Haas, Michael E. *Apollo's Warriors: United States Air Force Special Operations during the Korean War.* Honolulu: University Press of Hawaii, 2002.

———. *In the Devil's Shadow: UN Special Operations during the Korean War.* Annapolis, MD: Naval Institute Press, 2002.

Hagiwara, Ryo. *The Korean War: The Conspiracies by Kim Il-sung and MacArthur.* Tokyo: Bungli Shanja, 1993.

Haines, Richard F. *Advanced Aerial Devices Reported during the Korean War.* London: LDA Press, 1990.

Halberstam, David. *The Coldest Winter: America and the Korean War.* New York: Hyperion, 2007.

Hallion, Richard P. *The Naval Air War in Korea.* Baltimore: Nautical and Aviation Publishing Company of America, 1986.

Halperin, Morton H. *Limited War in the Nuclear Age.* Westport, CT: Greenwood, 1978.

Hamburger, Kenneth E. *Leadership in the Crucible: The Korean War Battles of Twin Tunnels & Chipyong-ni.* College Station: Texas A&M University Press, 2003.

Hamby, Alonzo L. *Man of the People: A Life of Harry S. Truman.* New York: Oxford University Press, 1995.

Hammel, Eric. *Chosin. Heroic Ordeal of the Korean War.* 1981; reprint, Novato, CA: Presidio, 1990.

Hanley, Charles J., Sang-hun Chol, and Martha Mendoza. *The Bridge at No Gun Ri: A Hidden Nightmare from the Korean War.* New York: Henry Holt, 2001.

Hansen, Kenneth. *Heroes behind Barbed Wire.* Princeton, NJ: Van Nostrand, 1957.

Hansrath, Alfred H. *The KMAG Advisor: Roles and Problems of the Military Advisor in Developing an Indigenous Army for Combat Operations in Korea.* Chevy Chase, MD: Operations Research Office, Johns Hopkins University, 1957.

———. *Problems of the Development of a Local Army (ROKA).* Chevy Chase, MD: Johns Hopkins University, 1956.

Harding, Harry, and Yuan Ming, eds. *Sino-American Relations, 1945–1955.* Wilmington, DE: Scholarly Resources, 1989.

Hastings, Max. *The Korean War.* New York: Simon and Schuster, 1987.

Haynes, Richard F. *The Awesome Power: Harry S. Truman as Commander in Chief.* Baton Rouge: Louisiana State University Press, 1973.

Headquarters, Korean People's Army. *The Heroic KPA: The Invincible Revolutionary Armed Forces.* Pyongyang: Korean People's Army Publishing House, 1990.

Heefner, Wilson A. *Patton's Bulldog: The Life and Service of General Walton H. Walker.* Shippensburg, PA: White Mane, 2001.

Heinl, Robert D. *Victory at High Tide: The Inchon-Seoul Campaign.* Philadelphia: Lippincott, 1968.

Heller, Francis H., ed. *The Korean War: A 25-Year Perspective.* Lawrence: Regents Press of Kansas, 1977.

Henderson, Gregory. *Korea: The Politics of the Vortex.* Cambridge, MA: Harvard University Press, 1968.

Hermes, Walter G. *U.S. Army in the Korean War: Truce Tent and Fighting Front.* Washington, DC: Office of the Chief of Military History, 1966.

Hickey, Michael. *The Korean War: The West Confronts Communism, 1950–1953.* London: John Murray, 1999.

Higgins, Marguerite. *War in Korea: Report of a Woman Combat Correspondent.* Garden City, NY: Doubleday, 1951.

Higgins, Rosalyn, ed. *United Nations Peacekeeping, 1945–1967: Documents and Commentary.* 4 vols. London: Oxford University Press, 1970.

Higgins, Trumbull. *Korea and the Fall of MacArthur: A Precis in Limited War.* New York: Oxford University Press, 1960.

Higham, Robin, and Donald Mrozek. *Guide to the Sources of U.S. Military History.* Hamden, CT: Archon Books, 1993.

Hightower, Charles D. *The History of the United States Air Force Airborne Forward Air Controller in World War II, the Korean War, and the Vietnam Conflict.* Fort Leavenworth, KS: Army Command and General Staff College, 1984.

Hinshaw, Arned L. *Heartbreak Ridge: Korea, 1951.* New York: Praeger, 1989.

Historical Section, General Staff, Canadian Army. *Canada's Army in Korea.* Ottawa: Queen's Printer, 1956.

History Division, General Staff. *The Battles of Turkish Armed Forces in the Korean War, 1950–1953.* Istanbul: Turkish General Staff, 1975.

History Section, Department of the Army. *The Greek Expeditionary Forces in Korea (1950–1955).* Athens, Greece: Ministry of Defense, 1977.

Hoare, James E., and Susan Pares, eds. *Conflict in Korea: An Encyclopedia.* Santa Barbara, CA: ABC-CLIO, 1999.

Hogan, Michael J. *A Cross of Iron: Harry S. Truman and the Origins of the National Security State, 1945–1954.* New York: Cambridge University Press, 1998.

———. *The Marshall Plan: America, Britain, and the Reconstruction of Western Europe, 1947–1953.* New York: Cambridge University Press, 1987.

Holober, Frank. *Raiders of the China Coast: CIA Covert Operations during the Korean War.* Annapolis, MD: Naval Institute Press, 1999.

Hoover, Herbert. *Addresses upon the American Road, 1950–1955.* Stanford, CA: Stanford University Press, 1955.

Hopkins, William B. *One Bugle No Drums: The Marines at Chosin Reservoir.* Chapel Hill, NC: Algonquin Books, 1986.

Horwitz, Dorothy, ed. *We Will Not Be Strangers: Korean War Letters Between a M.A.S.H. Surgeon and His Wife.* Urbana: University of Illinois Press, 1997.

Hoyt, Edwin P. *The Bloody Road to Panmunjom.* New York: Stein and Day, 1985.

———. *The Day the Chinese Attacked, Korea, 1950: The Story of the Failure of America's China Policy.* New York: McGraw-Hill, 1990.

———. *On to the Yalu.* New York: Stein and Day, 1984.

Huston, James A. *Guns and Butter, Powder and Rice: U.S. Army Logistics in the Korean War.* Selinsgrove, PA: Susquehanna University Press, 1989.

———. *Outposts and Allies: U.S. Army Logistics in the Cold War, 1945–1953.* Selinsgrove, PA: Susquehanna University Press, 1988.

———. *The Pusan Perimeter.* New York: Stein and Day, 1984.

Hyatt, John. *Korean War, 1950–1953: Selected References.* Maxwell Air Force Base, AL: Air University Library, 1992.

Immerman, Richard H. *John Foster Dulles: Piety, Pragmatism and Power in U.S. Foreign Policy.* Wilmington, DE: SR Books, 1998.

Industrial College of the Armed Forces. *Emergency Management of the National Economy: Reconversion and Partial Mobilization.* Washington, DC: Industrial College of the Armed Forces, 1954.

Jackson, Robert. *Air War over Korea.* New York: Scribner, 1973.

———. *Air War Korea, 1950–1953.* Osceola, WA: Motorbooks International, 1998.

Jager, Sheila Miyoshi. *Narratives of Nation Building in Korea.* Armonk, NY: M. E. Sharpe, 2003.

James, D. Clayton. *The Years of MacArthur,* Vol. 3, *Triumph and Disaster, 1945–1964.* Boston: Houghton Mifflin, 1985.

James, D. Clayton, with Anne Sharp Wells. *Refighting the Last War: Command and Crises in Korea, 1950–1953.* New York: Free Press, 1993.

Johnson, U. Alexis, with J. Olivarius McAllister. *The Right Hand of Power.* Englewood Cliffs, NJ: Prentice Hall, 1984.

Johnston, William. *A War of Patrols: Canadian Army Operations in Korea.* Vancouver: University of British Columbia, 2003.

Jordan, Kelly C. "Three Armies in Korea: The Combat Power in the U.S. 8th Army in Korea, 1950–1952." PhD dissertation, Ohio State University, 1999.

Joy, C. Turner. *How Communists Negotiate.* New York: Macmillan, 1955.

Kahn, E. J., Jr. *The Peculiar War: Impressions of a Reporter in Korea.* New York: Random House, 1952.

Kaledin, Eugenia. *Mothers and More: American Woman in the 1950s.* Boston: Twayne, 1984.

Kaufman, Burton I. *The Korean Conflict.* Westport, CT: Greenwood, 1996.

———. *The Korean War: Challenges in Crisis, Credibility and Command.* 2nd ed. New York: McGraw-Hill, 1997.

Keefer, Edward C., ed. *Foreign Relations of the United States, 1952–1954, Korea,* Vol. 15. Washington, DC: U.S. Government Printing Office, 1984.

Kennan, George F. *Memoirs.* 2 vols. Boston: Little, Brown, 1967, 1972.

Kennedy, Edgar S. *Mission to Korea.* London: Derek Verschoyle, 1952.

Kim, Byong Sik. *Modern Korea.* New York: International Publishers, 1970.

Kim Chull-Baum and James I. Matray, eds. *Korea and the Cold War: Division, Destruction, and Disarmament.* Claremont, CA: Regina Books, 1993.

Kim Chum-kon. *The Korean War, 1950–1953.* Seoul: Kwangmyong Publishing, 1973.

Kim, Dong-Sung, Ki-Jung Kim, and Hahnkyu Park, eds. *Fifty Years after the Korean War: From the Cold War Confrontation to Peaceful Coexistence.* Seoul: Korean Association of International Studies, 2000.

Kim, Gye-Dong. *Foreign Intervention in Korea.* Aldershot, UK: Dartmouth Publishing, 1993.

Kim, Il Sung. *Kim Il Sung Selected Works.* 2 vols. Pyongyang: Foreign Languages Publishing House, 1965.

Kim Ilpyong J., comp. *Historical Dictionary of North Korea.* Lanham, MD: Scarecrow, 1993.

Kim, Myung-Ki. *The Korean War and International Law.* Claremont, CA: Paige, 1991.

Kim, Richard, and Donald K. Chung. *The Three Day Promise.* Tallahassee, FL: Father and Son Publishing, 1989.

Kim, Se-Jin. *The Politics of the Military Revolution in Korea.* Chapel Hill, NC: University of North Carolina Press, 1971.

Kim, Stephen Jin-woo. *Master of Manipulation: Syngman Rhee and the Seoul-Washington Alliance, 1953–1960.* Seoul: Yonsei University Press, 2001.

Kindsvatter, Peter S. *American Soldiers: Ground Combat in the World Wars, Korea, and Vietnam.* Lawrence: University Press of Kansas, 2003.

Kinkead, Eugene. *In Every War But One.* New York: Norton, 1959.

———. *Why They Collaborated.* New York: Longman, 1960.

Knight, Peter G. "MacArthur's Eyes: Reassessing Military Intelligence Operations in the Forgotten War, June 1950–April 1951." PhD dissertation, Ohio State University, 2006.

Knott, Richard C. *Attack from the Sky: Naval Air Operations in the Korean War.* Washington, DC: Naval Historical Center, 2004.

Knox, Donald, and Albert Coppel. *The Korean War: An Oral History.* 2 vols. San Diego: Harcourt Brace Jovanovich, 1895–1988.

Kohn, Richard H., and Joseph P. Harahan, eds. *Air Interdiction in World War II, Korea, and Vietnam: An Interview with General Earle E. Partridge, General Jacob E. Smart, General John W. Vogt, Jr.* Washington, DC: Office of Air Force History, 1986.

———, eds. *Air Superiority in World War II and Korea: An Interview with General James Ferguson, General Robert M. Lee, General William W. Momyer, and General Elwood R. Quesada.* Washington, DC: Office of Air Force History, 1983.

Koo, John H., and Andrew C. Nahm. *An Introduction to Korean Culture.* Elizabeth, NJ: Hollym, 1997.

Korean Institute of Military History. *The Korean War.* 3 vols. Introduction by Allan R. Millett. Lincoln: University of Nebraska Press, 2001.

Korean Overseas Information Service. *A Handbook of Korea.* Elizabeth, NJ: Hollym, 1990.

Korean War Research Committee, War Memorial Service-Korea. *The Historical Reillumination of the Korean War.* Seoul: War Memorial Service, 1990.

Kort, Michael. *The Columbia Guide to the Cold War.* New York: Columbia University Press, 1998.

Kwak, Tae-Hwan, John Chay, Cho Soon-Sung, and Shannon McCune, eds. *U.S.-Korean Relations, 1882–1982.* Seoul: Institute for Far Eastern Studies, Kyungnam University, 1982.

Lacey, Michael, ed. *The Truman Presidency.* Cambridge, UK: Cambridge University Press, 1989.

LaFeber, Walter. *America, Russia and the Cold War, 1945–2002.* Updated 9th ed. New York: McGraw-Hill, 2004.

Langley, Michael. *Inchon Landing: MacArthur's Last Triumph.* New York: Times Books, 1979.

Lankov, Andrei. *From Stalin to Kim Il-sung: The Formation of North Korea, 1945–1950.* New Brunswick, NJ: Rutgers University Press, 2002.

Lansdown, John R. P. *With the Carriers in Korea: The Sea and Air War in SE Asia, 1950–1953.* Winslow, Cheshire, UK: Crécy, 1997.

Lautensach, Hermann. *Korea: A Geography Based on the Author's Travels and Literature.* Reprint. Berlin: Springer-Verlag, 1988.

Leckie, Robert. *Conflict: The History of the Korean War, 1950–1953.* New York: Putnam, 1962.

———. *The March to Glory.* Cleveland: World Publishing, 1960.

Lee Chae-Jin. *The Korean War: A 40-Year Perspective.* Claremont, CA: Keck Center for International and Strategic Studies, 1991.

Lee Chi-op. *Call Me "Speedy" Lee: Memoirs of a Korean War Soldier.* Seoul: Won Min, 2001.

Lee Chong Sik. *The Politics of Korean Nationalism.* Berkeley: University of California Press, 1963.

Lee, Stephen Hugh. *The Korean War.* London: Longman, 2001.

Leffler, Melvyn P. *A Preponderance of Power: National Security, the Truman Administration, and the Cold War.* Stanford, CA: Stanford University Press, 1992.

Lentz, Robert J. *Korean War Filmography.* Jefferson, NC: McFarland, 2003.

Levine, Steven I., and Jackie Hiltz, eds. *America's Wars in Asia: A Cultural Approach to History and Memory*. London: M. E. Sharpe, 1998.

Li Xiaobing, Bin Yu, and Allan R. Millett, eds. and trans. *Mao's Generals Remember Korea*. Lawrence: University Press of Kansas, 2001.

Lie, Trygve. *In the Cause of Peace: Seven Years with the United Nations*. New York: Macmillan, 1954.

Lincoln, George A. *Economics of National Defense: Managing America's Resources for Defense*. New York: Prentice Hall, 1954.

Lott, Arnold S. *Most Dangerous Sea: A History of Mine Warfare and an Account of U.S. Navy Mine Warfare Operations in World War II and Korea*. Annapolis, MD: U.S. Naval Institute, 1959.

Love, Robert W., Jr., ed. *The Chiefs of Naval Operations*. Annapolis, MD: Naval Institute Press, 1980.

Lowe, Peter. *The Korean War*. New York: Palgrave Macmillan, 2000.

———. *The Origins of the Korean War*. New York: Longman, 1997.

Lyons, Gene M. *Military Policy and Economic Aid: The Korean Case, 1950–1953*. Columbus: Ohio State University Press, 1961.

MacArthur, Douglas. *Reminiscences*. New York: McGraw-Hill, 1964.

MacDonald, Callum. *Korea: The War before Vietnam*. New York: Free Press, 1987.

MacDonald, Donald Stone. *The Koreans*. Boulder, CO: Westview, 1988.

———. *U.S.-Korean Relations from Liberation to Self-Reliance*. Boulder, CO: Westview, 1992.

Mahoney, Kevin. *Formidable Enemies: The North Korean and Chinese Soldier in the Korean War*. San Rafael, CA: Presidio, 2001.

Maihafer, Harry J. *From the Hudson to the Yalu: West Point '49 in the Korean War*. College Station: Texas A&M University Press, 1993.

Malcolm, Ben S. *White Tigers: My Secret War in North Korea*. Washington, DC: Brassey's, 1996.

Malkasian, Carter. *The Korean War, 1950–1953*. Botley, Oxfordshire, UK: Osprey, 2001.

Manhurin, Walker M. *Honest John*. New York: Putnam, 1962.

Mao Zedong. *Military Writings of Mao Tse-tung*. Beijing: Foreign Language Press, 1967.

Marcus, Maeva. *Truman and the Steel Seizure Case: The Limits of Presidential Power*. New York: Columbia University Press, 1977.

Mark, Eduard. *Aerial Interdiction: Air Power and the Land Battle in Three Wars*. Washington, DC: Center for Air Force History, 1994.

Markusen, Ann, Peter Hall, and Sabina Dietrich. *The Rise of the Gunbelt: The Military Remapping of Industrial America*. New York: Oxford University Press, 1991.

Marolda, Edward J., ed. *The U.S. Navy in the Korean War*. Annapolis, MD: Naval Institute Press, 2007.

Marshall, S. L. A. *Infantry Operations and Weapons in Korea*. San Francisco: Presidio, 1988.

———. *Military History of the Korean War*. New York: F. Watts, 1963.

———. *Pork Chop Hill*. New York: Morrow, 1956.

———. *The River and the Gauntlet*. New York: Morrow, 1953.

Matray, James I., ed. *Historical Dictionary of the Korean War*. Westport, CT: Greenwood, 1991.

———. *Korea Divided: The 38th Parallel and the Demilitarized Zone*. New York: Chelsea House, 2006.

———. *The Reluctant Crusade: American Foreign Policy in Korea, 1941–1950*. Honolulu: University of Hawaii Press, 1985.

Maurer, Maurer. *USAF Credits for Destruction of Enemy Aircraft, Korean War*. USAF Historical Study No. 81. Washington, DC: Department of the Air Force, 1963.

May, Elaine Tyler. *Homeward Bound: American Families in the Cold War*. New York: Basic Books, 1988.

McCoy, Donald R. *The Presidency of Harry S. Truman*. Lawrence: University Press of Kansas, 1984.

McCullough, David. *Truman*. New York: Simon and Schuster, 1992.

McCune, George M., with Arthur L. Grey. *Korea Today*. Cambridge, MA: Harvard University Press, 1950.

McEnaney, Laura. *Civil Defense Begins at Home: Militarization Meets Everyday Life in the Fifties*. Princeton, NJ: Princeton University Press, 2000.

McFarland, Keith D., ed. *The Korean War: An Annotated Bibliography*. New York: Garland, 1986.

McFarland, Keith D., and David L. Roll. *Louis Johnson and the Arming of America*. Bloomington: Indiana University Press, 2005.

McGibbon, Ian C. *New Zealand and the Korean War*. 2 vols. Auckland: Oxford University Press, 1996.

McGlothlen, Ronald L. *Controlling the Waves: Dean Acheson and U.S. Foreign Policy in Asia*. New York: Norton, 1993.

McLaren, David R. *Mustangs over Korea: The North American F-51 at War, 1950–1953*. Atglen, PA: Schiffer Military History, 1999.

McWilliams, Bill. *On Hallowed Ground: The Last Battle for Pork Chop Hill*. Annapolis, MD: Naval Institute Press, 2004.

Meade, E. Grant. *American Military Government in Korea*. New York: King's Crown Press, 1952.

Meador, Daniel J., ed. *The Korean War in Retrospect: Lessons for the Future*. Lanham, MD: University Press of America, 1998.

Meid, Pat, James M. Yingling, Nicholas Canzona, et al. *U.S. Marine Operations in Korea, 1950–1953*. 5 vols. Washington, DC: U.S. Marine Corps Historical Branch, 1962–1972.

Meilinger, Philip S. *Hoyt S. Vandenberg: The Life of a General*. Bloomington: Indiana University Press, 1989.

Merrill, Frank. *A Study of the Aerial Interdiction of Railways during the Korean War*. Fort Leavenworth, KS: Army Command and General Staff College, 1965.

Merrill, John. *Korea: The Peninsular Origins of the War.* Newark: University of Delaware Press, 1989.

Meyerovitz, Joanne, ed. *Not June Cleaver: Woman and Gender in Postwar America.* Philadelphia: Temple University Press, 1994.

Meyers, Edward C. *Thunder in the Morning Calm: The Royal Canadian Navy in Korea, 1950–1953.* St. Catherines, Ontario: Vanwell, 1991.

Meyers, Samuel N., and Albert D. Biderman, eds. *Mass Behavior in Battle and Captivity.* Chicago: University of Chicago Press, 1968.

Middleton, Harry J. *The Compact History of the Korean War.* New York: Hawthorn Books, 1965.

Millar, Ward M. *Valley of the Shadow.* New York: McKay, 1955.

Millett, Allan R. *Drive North: U.S. Marines at the Punchbowl.* Washington, DC: U.S. Marine Corps, History and Museums Division, 2001.

———. *The Korean War: The Essential Bibliography.* Herndon, VA: Potomac Books, 2007.

———. *The War for Korea, 1945–1950: A House Burning.* Lawrence: University Press of Kansas, 2005.

———. *Their War in Korea: American, Asian, and European Combatants and Civilians, 1945–1953.* Princeton, NJ: Princeton University Press, 2002.

Milliken, Jennifer. *The Social Construction of the Korean War: Conflict and Its Possibilities.* Manchester, UK: Manchester University Press, 2001.

Mills, Randy K., and Roxanne Mills. *Unexpected Journey: A Marine Corps Reserve Company in the Korean War.* Annapolis, MD: Naval Institute Press, 2000.

Momyer, William. *Air Power in Three Wars: WWII, Korea, Vietnam.* Washington, DC: Department of the Air Force, 1978.

Montross, Lynn. *Cavalry of the Sky: The Story of U.S. Marine Combat Helicopters.* New York: Harper and Brothers, 1954.

Montross, Lynn, et al. *U.S. Marine Operations in Korea, 1950–1953.* 5 vols. Washington, DC: U.S. Marine Corps Historical Branch, 1954–1972.

Mossman, Billy C. *United States Army in the Korean War: Ebb and Flow, November 1950–July 1951.* Washington, DC: U.S. Army Center of Military History, 1990.

Mount, Graeme S. *The Diplomacy of War: The Case of Korea.* With André Laferriere. Montreal: Black Rose Books, 2004.

Muir, Malcolm, Jr. *Sea Power on Call: Fleet Operation, June 1951– July 1953.* Washington, DC: Naval Historical Center, 2005.

Murphy, Edward F. *Korean War Heroes.* Novato, CA: Presidio, 1997.

Murphy, Robert D. *Diplomat among Warriors.* Garden City, NY: Doubleday, 1964.

Nahm, Andrew C. *Korea, Tradition and Transformation: A History of the Korean People.* Elizabeth, NJ: Hollym International, 1988.

Nakasone, Edwin M. *The Nisei Soldier: Historical Essays on World War II and the Korean War.* White Bear Lake, MN: J-Press, 1999.

Nalty, Bernard C. *Long Passage to Korea: Black Sailors and the Integration of the U.S. Navy.* Washington, DC: Naval Historical Center, 2003.

———. *Stalemate: U.S. Marines from Bunker Hill to the Hook.* Washington, DC: U.S. Marine Corps, History and Museums Division, 2001.

Nalty, Bernard C., and Wayne Thompson. *Within Limits: The U.S. Air Force and the Korean War.* Honolulu: University Press of the Pacific, 2005.

Nam Koon-woo. *The North Korean Leadership, 1945–1965.* Tuscaloosa: University of Alabama Press, 1975.

Nichols, Jack C., and Warren E. Thompson. *Korea: The Air War 1950–1953.* London: Osprey, 1991.

Nitze, Paul H., with Ann M. Smith and Steven L. Rearden. *From Hiroshima to Glasnost at the Center of Decision: A Memoir.* New York: Grove Weidenfeld, 1989.

No, Kum Sok, with J. Roger Osterholm. *A MiG-15 to Freedom: Memoir of the Wartime North Korean Defector Who First Delivered the Secret Fighter Jet to the Americans in 1953.* Jefferson, NC: McFarland, 1996.

Noble, Harold J. *Embassy at War.* Seattle: University of Washington Press, 1975.

O'Ballance, Edgar. *Korea, 1950–1953.* London: Faber and Faber, 1969.

O'Dowd, Ben. *In Valiant Company: Diggers in Battle, Korea 1950–1951.* Queensland, Australia: University of Queensland, 2000.

Office of the Provost Marshall, Department of the Army. *Prisoners of War.* 3 vols. Washington, DC: Department of the Army, 1968.

O'Neill, Mark A. "The Other Side of the Yalu: Soviet Pilots in the Korean War—Phase One, 1 November 1950–12 April 1951." PhD dissertation, Florida State University, 1996.

O'Neill, Robert J. *Australia in the Korea War, 1950–1953.* 2 vols. Canberra: Australian War Memorial/Australian Government Publishing Service, 1981, 1985.

O'Quinlivan, Michael, and James S. Santelli. *An Annotated Bibliography of the United States Marine Corps in the Korean War.* Rev. ed. Washington, DC: Historical Division, Headquarters U.S. Marine Corps, 1970.

O'Rourke, G. G., and E. T. Wooldridge. *Night Fighters over Korea.* Annapolis, MD: Naval Institute Press, 1998.

Odgers, George. *Across the Parallel: The Australian 77th Squadron with the United States Air Force in the Korean War, 1950–1953.* London: William Heinemann, 1952.

Offner, Arnold A. *Another Such Victory: President Truman and the Cold War, 1945–1953.* Stanford, CA: Stanford University Press, 2002.

Oh, Bonnie B. C., ed. *Korea under the American Military Government, 1945-1948.* Westport, CT: Praeger, 2002.

Oliver, Robert T. *Syngman Rhee: The Man behind the Myth.* New York: Dodd, Mead, 1955.

————. *Syngman Rhee and American Involvement in Korea, 1942–1960.* Seoul: Panmun Books, 1978.

————. *Verdict in Korea.* State College, PA: Bald Eagle, 1952.

————. *Why War Came in Korea.* New York: Fordham University Press, 1950.

Owen, Joseph R. *Colder Than Hell: A Marine Rifle Company at Chosin Reservoir.* Annapolis, MD: Naval Institute Press, 1996.

Paige, Glenn D. *The Korean Decision, June 24–30, 1950.* New York: Free Press, 1968.

Paik Sun Yup. *From Pusan to Panmunjom.* Washington, DC: Brassey's, 1992.

Pak, Chi-Young. *Political Opposition in Korea, 1945–1960.* Seoul: Seoul National University Press, 1980.

Paschall, Rod, ed. *Witness to War: Korea.* New York: Berkeley Publishing Group, 1995.

Paterson, James T. *Mr. Republican: A Biography of Robert A. Taft.* Boston: Houghton Mifflin, 1972.

Pearlman, Michael D. *Truman and MacArthur: Policy, Politics, and the Hunger for Honor and Renown.* Bloomington: Indiana University Press, 2008.

Pemberton, William E. *Harry S. Truman: Fair Dealer and Cold Warrior.* Boston: Twayne, 1989.

Peters, Richard, and Xiaobing Li. *Voices from the Korean War: Personal Stories of American, Korean, and Chinese Soldiers.* Lexington: University Press of Kentucky, 2004.

Pierpaoli, Paul G., Jr. *Truman and Korea: The Political Culture of the Early Cold War.* Columbia: University of Missouri Press, 1999.

Pogue, Forrest C. *George C. Marshall,* Vol. 4, *Statesman, 1945–1959.* New York: Viking, 1987.

Politella, Dario. *Operation Grasshopper.* Wichita, KS: Robert R. Longo, 1958.

Polk, Davis, comp. *Ex-Prisoners of War.* Paducah, KY: Turner Publishing for the Association of EX-POWs from the Korean War, 1993.

Poole, Walter. *The History of the Joint Chiefs of Staff: The Joint Staff and National Policy,* Vol. 4, *1950–1952.* Washington, DC: History Division, Joint Chiefs of Staff, 1979.

Portway, Donald. *Korea, Land of the Morning Calm.* London: George G. Harrap, 1953.

Prasad, S. N. *History of the Custodian Force (India) in Korea, 1953–1954.* Delhi: Government of India Press for the Ministry of Defense, 1976.

Pratt, Keith, and Richard Rutt. *Korea: A Historical and Cultural Dictionary.* London: Curzon, 1999.

Pratt, Sherman W. *Decisive Battles of the Korean War: An Infantry Company Commander's View of the War's Most Critical Engagements.* New York: Vantage Press, 1992.

Price, Scott T. *The Forgotten Service in the Korean War: The U.S. Coast Guard's Role in the Korean Conflict.* Annapolis, MD: Naval Institute Press, 2000.

Pyon Yong Tae. *Na ui Choguk* [Korea, My Country: Memoirs]. Seoul: Chayu Chulpan-sa, 1956.

Ransom, Frank E. *Air-Sea Rescue, 1941–1952.* U.S. Air Force Historical Study #95. Washington, DC: U.S. Air Force, 1953.

Rees, David. *Korea: The Limited War.* New York: St. Martin's, 1990.

————, ed. *The Korean War: History and Tactics.* London: Crescent Books, 1984.

Reeve, W. D. *The Republic of Korea.* Oxford: Oxford University Press, 1963.

Reeves, Thomas C. *The Life and Times of Joe McCarthy.* Lanham, MD: Madison Books, 1997.

Reichard, Gary W. *Politics as Usual: The Age of Truman and Eisenhower.* Arlington Heights, IL: Harlan Davidson, 1988.

Reid, Escott. *Envoy to Nehru.* New York: Oxford University Press, 1981.

Republic of Korea, Ministry of National Defense. *The Brief History of ROK Armed Forces.* Seoul: Troop Information and Education Bureau, 1986.

Republic of Korea, War History Compilation Committee, Ministry of National Defense. *Hanguk Chonjaengsa* [History of the Korean War]. 9 vols. Seoul: Ministry of National Defense, 1967–1970.

Rhee, Syngman. *Korea Flaming High.* Seoul: Office of Public Information, Republic of Korea, 1954.

Ridgway, Matthew B. *The Korean War.* Garden City, NY: Doubleday, 1967.

————. *Soldier: The Memoirs of Matthew B. Ridgway.* New York: Harpers, 1956.

Rishell, Lyle. *With a Black Platoon in Combat: A Year in Korea.* College Station: Texas A&M University Press, 1993.

Robertson, William G. *Counterattack on the Naktong, 1950.* Fort Leavenworth, KS: Combat Studies Institute, 1985.

Roe, Patrick C. *The Dragon Strikes: China and the Korean War, June–December 1950.* Novato, CA: Presidio, 2000.

Rose, Lisle. *The Cold War Comes to Main Street: America in 1950.* Lawrence: University Press of Kansas, 1999.

————. *Roots of Tragedy: The United States and the Struggle for Asia, 1945–1953.* Westport, CT: Greenwood, 1976.

Rottman, Gordon L. *Korean War Order of Battle: United States, United Nations, and Communist Ground, Naval, and Air Forces, 1950–1953.* Westport, CT: Praeger, 2002.

Rovere, Richard H. *Senator Joe McCarthy.* New York: HarperCollins, 1986.

Rusk, Dean. *As I Saw It.* Edited by Daniel S. Papp. New York: Norton, 1990.

Russ, Martin. *Breakout: The Chosin Reservoir Campaign, Korea 1950.* New York: Fromm International, 1999.

————. *The Last Parallel: A Marine's War Journal.* New York: Rinehart, 1957.

Ryan, Halford R. *Harry S. Truman: Presidential Rhetoric.* Westport, CT: Greenwood, 1993.

Ryan, Mark A. *Chinese Attitudes toward Nuclear Weapons: China and the United States during the Korean War.* Armonk, NY: M. E. Sharpe, 1990.

Sams, Crawford. *Medic!* Armonk, NY: M. E. Sharpe, 1998.

Sandler, Stanley, ed. *The Korean War: An Encyclopedia.* New York: Garland, 1995.

———. *The Korean War: No Victors, No Vanquished.* Lexington: University of Kentucky Press, 1999.

Satyasnguan, Snit. *The Thai Battalion in Korea.* Bangkok: Toppan, 1956.

Sauter, Jack. *Sailors in the Sky: Memoir of a Navy Aircrewman in the Korean War.* Jefferson, NC: MacFarland, 1995.

Sawyer, Robert K. *Military Advisors in Korea: KMAG in Peace and War.* Washington, DC: Office of the Chief of Military History, U.S. Army, 1962.

Scalapino, Robert A., and Lee Chong Sik. *Communism in Korea.* 2 vols. Berkeley: University of California Press, 1973.

Schaafsma, M. D. *The Dutch Detachment of the United Nations in Korea, 1950–1954.* The Hague: History of War Section, Royal Netherlands Army General Staff, 1960.

Schaller, Michael. *The American Occupation of Japan: The Origins of the Cold War.* New York: Oxford University Press, 1985.

———. *Douglas MacArthur: The Far Eastern General.* New York: Oxford University Press, 1989.

Schnabel, James F. *United States Army in the Korean War: Policy and Direction, the First Year.* Washington, DC: Office of the Chief of Military History, Department of the Army, 1972.

Schnabel, James F., and Robert J. Watson. *The History of the Joint Chiefs of Staff: The Joint Chiefs of Staff and National Policy,* Vol. 3, *The Korean War.* Wilmington, DE: Michael Glazier, 1979.

Schonberger, Howard B. *Aftermath of War: Americans and the Remaking of Japan, 1945–1952.* Kent, OH: Kent State University Press, 1989.

Schrader, Charles. *Communist Logistics in the Korean War.* Westport, CT: Greenwood, 1995.

Schrecker, Ellen. *Many Are the Crimes: McCarthyism in America.* Boston: Little, Brown, 1998.

Scutts, Jerry. *Air War over Korea.* London: Arms and Armour, 1982.

Sheldon, Walt J. *Hell or High Water: MacArthur's Landing at Inchon.* New York: Macmillan, 1968.

Shen Zhihua. *Mao Zedong, Stalin, and the Korean War.* Hong Kong: Tran di, 1995.

Sherwood, John Darrell. *Officers in Flight Suits: The Story of American Air Force Fighter Pilots in the Korean War.* New York: New York University Press, 1996.

Shinn, Bill. *The Forgotten War Remembered: Korea, 1950–1953.* Elizabeth, NJ: Hollym International, 1996.

Seiler, Sydney A. *Kim Il-sung: The Creation of a Legend.* Landover, MD: University Press of America, 1994.

Simmons, Edwin H. *Frozen Chosin: U.S. Marines at the Changjin Reservoir.* Washington, DC: U.S. Marine Corps, History and Museums Division, 2002.

———. *Over the Seawall: U.S. Marines at Inchon.* Washington, DC: U.S. Marine Corps, History and Museums Division, 2000.

Simmons, Robert R. *The Strained Alliance: Peking, Pyongyang, Moscow, and the Politics of the Korean Civil War.* New York: Free Press, 1975.

Skordiles, Kimon. *Kagnew: The Story of the Ethiopian Fighters in Korea.* Tokyo: Radio Press, 1954.

Slater, Michael P. *Hills of Sacrifice: The 5th RCT in Korea.* Nashville, TN: Turner Publishing, 2000.

Smith, Charles R., ed. *U.S. Marines in the Korean War.* Washington, DC: History and Museums Division, U.S. Marine Corps, 2008.

Smith, Gaddis. *Dean Acheson.* New York: Cooper Square, 1971.

Smith, Neil C., ed. *Home by Christmas: With the Australian Army in Korea, 1950–1956.* Melbourne, Australia: Mostly Unsung, 1990.

Smurthwaite, David. *Project Korea: The British Soldier in Korea, 1950–1953.* London: National Army Museum, 1988.

Song Hyo-soon. *The Fight for Freedom.* Seoul: Korean Library Association, 1980.

Spanier, John W. *The Truman-MacArthur Controversy and the Korean War.* Cambridge, MA: Harvard University Press, 1959.

Spick, Mike. *Jet Fighter Performance: Korea to Vietnam.* London: Ian Allen, 1986.

Spiller, Harry, ed. *American POWs in Korea: Sixteen Personal Accounts.* Jefferson, NC: McFarland, 1998.

Spiroff, Boris R. *Korea: Frozen Hell on Earth; A Platoon Sergeant's Diary, Korean War, 1950–1951.* Baltimore: American Literary Press, 1998.

Spurr, Russell. *Enter the Dragon: China's Undeclared War against the U.S. in Korea, 1950–1951.* New York: Henry Holt, 1988.

Stairs, Dennis. *The Diplomacy of Constraint: Canada, the Korean War and the United States.* Toronto: University of Toronto Press, 1974.

Stanton, Shelby. *America's Tenth Legion: X Corps in Korea.* Novato, CA: Presidio, 1989.

Stephens, Rudolph W. *Old Ugly Hill: A G.I.'s Fourteen Months in the Korean Trenches, 1952–1953.* Jefferson, NC: McFarland, 1995.

Stewart, James T., ed. *Airpower: The Decisive Force in Korea.* Princeton, NJ: Van Nostrand, 1957.

Stewart, Richard W. *Staff Operations: The X Corps in Korea, December 1950.* Fort Leavenworth, KS: U.S. Army Command and General Staff College, 1991.

Stokesberry, James I. *A Short History of the Korean War.* New York: William Morrow, 1989.

Stone, I. F. *The Hidden History of the Korean War, 1950–1951.* New York: Monthly Review Press, 1952.

Strawbridge, Dennis, and Nannette Kahn. *Fighter Pilot Performance in Korea.* Chicago: University of Chicago Press, 1955.

Stueck, William W., Jr., ed. *Korean War in World History.* Lexington: University Press of Kentucky, 2004.

————. *The Korean War: An International History.* Princeton, NJ: Princeton University Press, 1995.

————. *Rethinking the Korean War: A New Diplomatic and Strategic History.* Princeton, NJ: Princeton University Press, 2004.

————. *The Road to Confrontation: American Policy towards China and Korea, 1947–1950.* Chapel Hill: University of North Carolina Press, 1981.

Suh, Dae Sook. *Kim Il Sung: The North Korean Leader.* New York: Columbia University Press, 1988.

————. *The Korean Communist Movement, 1918–1948.* Princeton, NJ: Princeton University Press, 1967.

Sullivan, John A. *Toy Soldiers: A Memoir of a Combat Platoon Leader in Korea.* Jefferson, NC: McFarland, 1991.

Tae-Hoo, Yoo. *The Korean War and the United Nations.* Louvain, Belgium: Librairie Desbarax, 1965.

Tang Tsou. *America's Failure in China, 1941–1950.* Chicago: University of Chicago Press, 1963.

Taplett, Robert. *Dark Horse Six.* Williamstown, NJ: Phillips, 2002.

Taylor, Maxwell D. *Swords and Plowshares.* New York: Norton, 1972.

Terry, Addison. *The Battle for Pusan: A Memoir.* New York: Ballantine Books, 2000.

Thomas, Nigel, Peter Abbot, and Mike Chappell. *The Korean War, 1950-1953.* Botley, Oxfordshire, UK: Osprey, 1986.

Thompson, Annis G. *The Greatest Airlift: The Story of Combat Cargo.* Tokyo: Dai-Nippon Printing, 1954.

Thompson, Warren E. *Fighters over Korea: Mustang, Starfire, Shooting Star, Sabre, Tigercat, Panther, Corsair, Banshee, Thunderjet.* Osceola, WI: Motorbooks International, 1999.

————. *F-51 Mustang Units over Korea.* Oxford, UK: Osprey, 1999.

Thorgrimsson, Thor, and E. C. Russell. *Canadian Naval Operations in Korean Waters, 1950–1953.* Ottawa: Queen's Printer, 1965.

Thornton, John W. *Believed to Be Alive.* Middlebury, VT: Ericksson, 1981.

Thornton, Richard C. *Odd Man Out: Truman, Stalin, Mao and the Origins of the Korean War.* Herndon, VA: Potomac Books, 2000.

Tillman, Barrett. *Corsair: The F4U in World War II and Korea.* Annapolis, MD: Naval Institute Press, 1979.

Toland, John. *In Mortal Combat: Korea, 1950–1953.* New York: William Morrow, 1991.

Tomedi, Rudy. *No Bugles, No Drums: An Oral History of the Korean War.* New York: John Wiley, 1993.

Torkunov, Anatoly. *The War in Korea, 1950–1953.* Tokyo: IFC Publishers, 2000.

Truman, Harry S. *Memoirs.* 2 vols. Garden City, NY: Doubleday, 1956.

Tsou, Tang. *America's Failure in China, 1941–1950.* Chicago: University of Chicago Press, 1963.

Tyrrell, John V. *Air Power in Korea.* Norfolk, VA: Armed Forces Staff College, 1985.

Underwood, Horace G., with Michael Devine. *Korea in War, Revolution, and Peace: The Recollections of Horace G. Underwood.* Seoul: Yonsei University Press, 1991.

U.S. Air Force. *Far East Air Force (FEAF) Report on the Korean War.* Washington, DC: U.S. Government Printing Office for the U.S. Air Force, 1954.

————. *Operations in Korea, 1951,* Vol. 71, *U.S. Air Force Studies.* Washington, DC: United Stated Air Force Office, 1952.

U.S. Congress, Committee on Armed Services and Committee on Foreign Relations, 82nd Cong., 1st sess. *Military Situation in the Far East, May–June 1951.* 5 vols. Washington, DC: U.S. Government Printing Office, 1951.

U.S. Department of State. *Korean Problem at the Geneva Conference, April 26–June 15, 1954.* Publication 5609. Washington, DC: U.S. Government Printing Office, 1954.

U.S. Department of State, Office of the Historian, Bureau of Public Affairs. *Foreign Relations of the United States: National Security Affairs, 1950,* Vol. 1. Washington, DC: U.S. Government Printing Office, 1977.

————. *Foreign Relations of the United States: Korea 1950,* Vol. 12. Washington, DC: U.S. Government Printing Office, 1976.

————. *Foreign Relations of the United States: National Security Affairs, 1951,* Vol. 1. Washington, DC: U.S. Government Printing Office, 1980.

————. *Foreign Relations of the United States: Korea and China, 1951,* Vol. 12. Washington, DC: U.S. Government Printing Office, 1983.

————. *Foreign Relations of the United States: National Security Affairs, 1952–1954,* Vol. 1. Washington, DC: U.S. Government Printing Office, 1984.

————. *Foreign Relations of the United States: Korea, 1952–1954,* Vol. 15. Washington, DC: U.S. Government Printing Office, 1984.

U.S. Senate. *Military Situation in the Far East: Hearings before the Armed Services and Foreign Relations Committee.* U.S. Senate, 82nd Cong., 1st Sess., 1951. Washington, DC: U.S. Government Printing Office, 1951.

Utz, Curtis A. *Assault from the Sea: The Amphibious Landing at Inchon.* Washington, DC: Naval Historical Center, 2000.

Van Ree, Eric. *Socialism in One Zone: Stalin's Policy in Korea, 1945–1947.* New York: St. Martin's, 1989.

Varhola, Michael J. *Fire and Ice: The Korean War, 1950–1953.* New York: Da Capo, 2000.

Vatcher, William H., Jr. *Panmunjom.* Westport, CT: Greenwood, 1973.

Vawter, Roderick W. *Industrial Mobilization: The Relevant History.* National Defense University Press, 1983.

Vetter, Hal. *Mutiny on Koje Island.* Rutland, VT: Charles E. Tuttle, 1965.

The Victorious Fatherland Liberation War Museum. Pyongyang: Foreign Language Publishing House, 1997.

Voelkel, Harold. *Behind Barbed Wire in Korea.* Grand Rapids, MI: Zondervan Publishing, 1953.

Wainstock, Dennis D. *Truman, MacArthur and the Korean War.* Westport, CT: Greenwood, 1999.

Walker, Adrian. *A Barren Place: National Servicemen in Korea, 1950–1954.* London: Leo Cooper, 1994.

Watson, George M., Jr. *The Office of the Secretary of the Air Force.* Washington, DC: Center for Air Force History, 1993.

Watts, John Cadman. *Surgeon at War.* London: Allen and Unwin, 1955.

Weintraub, Stanley. *MacArthur's War: Korea and the Undoing of an American Hero.* New York: Free Press, 2000.

———. *War in the Wards.* Garden City, NY: Doubleday, 1964.

Werrell, Kenneth P. *Sabres over MiG Alley: The F-86 and the Battle for Air Superiority in Korea.* Annapolis, MD: Naval Institute Press, 2005.

Westad, Odd Arne. *The Global Cold War: Third World Interventions and the Making of Our Times.* New York: Cambridge University Press, 2007.

Westad, Odd Arne, ed. *Brothers in Arms: The Rise and Fall of the Sino-Soviet Alliance, 1945–1963.* Stanford, CA: Woodrow Wilson Center and Stanford University Press, 1998.

Westover, John G. *Combat Support in Korea.* Washington, DC: Office of the Chief of Military History, 1955.

Whelan, Richard. *Drawing the Line: The Korean War, 1950–1953.* Boston: Little, Brown, 1990.

White, William L. *The Captives of Korea: An Unofficial White Paper on the Treatment of War Prisoners, Our Treatment of Theirs; Their Treatment of Ours.* New York: Scribner, 1955.

Whitfield, Stephen J. *The Culture of the Cold War.* Baltimore: Johns Hopkins University Press, 1996.

Whiting, Allen S. *China Crosses the Yalu.* Stanford, CA: Stanford University Press, 1960.

Whitney, Courtney. *MacArthur: His Rendezvous with Destiny.* New York: Knopf, 1956.

Wilhelm, Alfred D., Jr. *The Chinese at the Negotiating Table.* Washington, DC: National Defense University Press, 1996.

Wilkinson, Allen B. *Up Front Korea.* New York: Vantage Press, 1967.

Wilkinson, Mark F., ed. *The Korean War at Fifty: International Perspectives.* Lexington, VA: Virginia Military Institute, 2004.

Williams, William J., ed. *A Revolutionary War: Korea and the Transformation of the Postwar World.* Chicago: Imprint Publications, 1993.

Wilson, David. *Lion over Korea: 77 Fighter Squadron RAAF, 1950–1953.* Canberra: Banner Books, 1994.

Winnington, Alan, and Wilfred Burchett. *Plain Perfidy: The Plot to Wreck Korean Peace.* London: Britain-China Friendship Association, 1962.

Witt, Linda, Judith Bellafaire, Britta Granrud, and Mary Jo Binker. *"A Defense Weapon Known to be of Value": Servicewomen of the Korean War Era.* Lebanon, NH: University Press of New England, 2005.

Wood, Herbert Fairlie. *Strange Battleground: The Operations in Korea and Their Effects on the Defense Policy of Canada.* Ottawa: Queen's Printer, 1966.

Xia, Yafeng. *Negotiating with the Enemy: U.S.-China Talks during the Cold War, 1949–1972.* Bloomington: Indiana University Press, 2006.

Y'Blood, William T. *MiG Alley: The Fight for Air Superiority.* Washington, DC: Office of Air Force History, 2000.

———, ed. *The Three Wars of George E. Stratemeyer: His Korean War Diary.* Washington, DC: Air Force History and Museums Program, 1999.

Yim, Louise. *My Forty Year Fight for Korea.* Reprint. Seoul: Chungang University, 1967.

Yonosuke, Nagai, and Akira Iriye, eds. *The Origins of the Cold War in Asia.* New York: Columbia University Press, 1977.

Yoo, Tae-ho. *The Korean War and the United Nations: A Legal and Diplomatic History.* Louvain, Belgium: Librarie Desbarax, 1965.

Yoshpe, Harry. *The National Security Resources Board, 1947–1953: A Case Study in Peacetime Mobilization.* Washington, DC: U.S. Government Printing Office, 1953.

Zelman, Walter A. *Chinese Intervention in the Korean War.* 1967; reprint, Berkeley: University of California Press, 1995.

Zhang Shu Gang. *Mao's Military Romanticism: China and the Korean War, 1950–1953.* Lawrence: University Press of Kansas, 1995.

Zhang Xiaoming. *Red Wings over the Yalu: China, the Soviet Union and the Air War in Korea.* College Station: Texas A&M University Press, 2002.

Zhang Zhu Gang and Chen Jian, eds. *Chinese Communist Foreign Policy and the Cold War in Asia: New Documentary Evidence, 1944–1950.* Chicago: Imprint Publications, 1996.

Zubok, Vladislav, and Constantine Pleshakov. *Inside the Kremlin's Cold War: From Stalin to Khrushchev.* Cambridge, MA: Harvard University Press, 1996.

RICHARD A. GARVER, PAUL G. PIERPAOLI JR., AND SPENCER C. TUCKER

List of Editors and Contributors

Volume Editor
Dr. Spencer C. Tucker
Senior Fellow
Military History, ABC-CLIO, Inc.

Associate Editor
Editor, Documents Volume
Dr. Paul G. Pierpaoli Jr.
Fellow
Military History, ABC-CLIO, Inc.

Assistant Editors
Professor Jinwung Kim
Kyungpook National University

Dr. Xiaobing Li
University of Central Oklahoma

Dr. James I. Matray
California State University, Chico

Contributors
Brian A. Arnold II
Virginia Military Institute

Robert J. Arvin
Virginia Military Institute

Jonathan D. Atkins
Virginia Military Institute

Lieutenant Colonel Joseph G. D. (Geoff)
    Babb
U.S. Army, Retired

Dr. Mark Beasley
Department of History
Texas Christian University

Colonel Daniel Randall Beirne
U.S. Army, Retired

Dr. John L. Bell Jr.
Department of History
Western Carolina University

Walter F. Bell
Information Services Librarian
Aurora University

Major Jason B. Berg
U.S. Marine Corps

Colonel Don Boose Jr.
U.S. Army, Retired

Walter Boyne
Independent Scholar

Dean Brumley
Department of History
Texas Christian University

David R. Buck
Department of History
West Virginia University

Dr. Robert J. Bunker
National Security Studies
California States University, San
    Bernardino

Dr. Paul R. Camacho
University of Massachusetts, Boston

Phillip A. Cantrell II
West Virginia University

Dr. Jack J. Cardoso
Professor of History, Emeritus
State University of New York College at
    Buffalo

Matthew S. Carman
Virginia Military Institute

Professor Chan Lau Kit-ching
Department of History
University of Hong Kong

Dr. Sunghun Cho
Dankook University
Korea

Colonel To-Woong Chung
Department of Military History
Korea Military Academy

Richard E. Coate
Independent Scholar

Dr. Don Coerver
Department of History
Texas Christian University

Dr. Finnie D. Coleman
Department of English
Texas A&M University

Dr. Jeffery B. Cook
Associate Professor of History
North Greenville University

Dean Corey
U.S. Air Force Historian
Warner Robins Air Force Base

Dr. Conrad C. Crane
Professor of History
United States Military Academy

Dr. Arthur I. Cyr
Clausen Distinguished Professor, Director
    Clausen Center
Carthage College

Dr. David R. Dorondo
Department of History
Western Carolina University

Dr. Timothy G. Dowling
Department of History
Virginia Military Institute

Dr. Joe P. Dunn
Department of History and Politics
Converse College

Dr. Blake Dunnavent
Lubbock Christian University

W. D. (Bill) Ehrhart
Independent Scholar

Brigadier General Uzal W. Ent
Pennsylvania National Guard, Retired

Mark Esposito
Department of History
West Virginia University

Dr. Matt Esposito
Department of History
Drake University

Ronald A. Fiocca
Virginia Military Institute

Lieutenant Colonel Mark Franklin
U.S. Army

Dr. Don Frazier
Department of History
McMurry University

Dr. John C. Fredricksen
Independent Scholar

Kevin J. Fromm
Virginia Military Institute

Dr. Richard A. Garver
Independent Scholar

Richard Z. Groen
Virginia Military Institute

Kai Yin Allison Haga
National Sun Yat-Sen University

William B. Harrington
Virginia Military Institute

Dr. William Head
U.S. Air Force Historian
Maxwell Air Force Base

Professor Man-ho Heo
Department of Political Science and
    Diplomacy
Kyungpook National University

John T. Hodes
Independent Scholar

Roger Horky
Texas A&M University

Dr. Charles Francis Howlett
Assistant Professor
Molloy College

Dr. Richard Weixing Hu
Department of Politics and Public
    Administration
University of Hong Kong

William Van Husen
Independent Scholar

Arnold Isaacs
Independent Scholar

Dr. Eric Jarvis
Department of History
University of Western Ontario

Major Kelly Jordan
Department of History
United States Military Academy

David M. Keithly
Independent Scholar

Mary Kelley
Department of Histor
Texas Christian University

Dr. Deborah Kidwell
US Army Command and General Staff
    College

Dr. Hakjoon Kim
President
University of Inchon

Professor Jinwung Kim
Kyungpook National University

Dr. Youngho Kim
Department of Political Science and
    Diplomacy
College of Social Sciences
Sungshin Women's University

Dr. Jeff Kinard
Guilford Technical Community College

Nicholas Krehbiel
Kansas State University

Daniel W. Kuthy
Georgia State University

Dr. Clayton D. Laurie
Intelligence Historian
Central Intelligence Agency

Professor Hochul Lee
Department of Political Science
University of Inchon

Jucheon Lee
Professor
Wonkwang University

Keith A. Leitich
Independent Scholar

Dr. Xiaobing Li
Department of History and Geography
University of Central Oklahoma

Frode Lindgjerdet
Master of Arts
Royal Norwegian Air Force Academy

Lieutenant Colonel Kevin W. T. Madden
U.S. Army Command and General Staff
    College

James R. Mahala
Virginia Military Institute

Colin Mahle
Virginia Military Institute

Dr. Edward J. Marolda
Senior Historian
Naval Historical Center

Matthew V. Martin
Virginia Military Institute

Dr. James I. Matray
Professor and Chair of History
Department of History
California State University, Chico

Dr. Jack McCallum
Department of History
Texas Christian University

Dr. Stanley S. McGowen
Department of History
Sam Houston State University

Alec McMorris
Virginia Military Institute

Professor Allan R. Millett
Director, Eisenhower Center for American
    Studies
University of New Orleans

Dr. Akitoshi Miyashita
Political Science Department
Drake University

Dr. Malcolm Muir Jr.
Department of History
Virginia Military Institute

Michael D. Mulé
Virginia Military Institute

Clint Mundinger
Virginia Military Institute

Dr. Keith Murphy
Associate Dean
Fort Valley State University

Dr. Michael R. Nichols
Tarrant County College

William Robert O'Neal Jr.
Virginia Military Institute

Dr. Mark O'Neill
Tallahassee Community College

Eric Osborne
Department of History
Virginia Military Institute

Dr. Insook Park
Independent Scholar

Natalia Petrouchkevitch
Independent Scholar

Dr. Allene Phy-Olsen
Independent Scholar

Dr. Paul G. Pierpaoli Jr.
Fellow
Military History, ABC-CLIO, Inc.

Tammy Prater
Independent Scholar

Lieutenant Colonel Sherman W. Pratt
U.S. Army, Retired

Lieutenant Colonel Susan M. Puska
U.S. Army

Robert B. Richards
United States Military Academy

Dr. Priscilla Roberts
University of Hong Kong

Professor Rodney J. Ross
Senior Professor of History/Geography
Harrisburg Area Community College

Anna Rulska
Old Dominion University

Dr. Claude R. Sasso
William Jewell College

Dr. Elizabeth D. Schafer
Independent Scholar

Captain Carl Otis Schuster
U.S. Navy, Retired
Hawaii Pacific University

Jeffery Seymour
Curator
The National Civil War Naval Museum

Dr. Edward Sharp
History Department
University of North Carolina at Greensboro

Dr. Charles R. Shrader
Independent Scholar

Timothy A. Sikes
United States Military Academy

Frank Skidmore
Department of History
Howard Payne University

Jason M. Sokiera
University of Southern Mississippi

Monica Spicer
Andrews Air Force Base

Dr. Paul Joseph Springer
Assistant Professor
United States Military Academy

Chuck Steele
Independent Scholar

Dr. Dong-Man Suh
Institute of Foreign Affairs and National
    Security
Republic of Korea

Dr. Choo Suk Suh
Research Fellow Korea Institute for Defense
    Analyses

Larry Swindell
Independent Scholar

Dr. Richard C. Thornton
George Washington University

Dr. David Trask
Department of History
Guilford Technical Community College

Dr. Stephanie Lynn Trombley
Assistant Professor of History
Embry-Riddle Aeronautical University

Dr. Spencer C. Tucker
Senior Fellow
Military History, ABC-CLIO, Inc.

Zsolt Varga
Department of History
Texas Christian University

Dr. Patricia Wadley
Independent Scholar

Jack Walker
Independent Scholar

Duane Wesolick
Western Carolina University

Dr. James Willbanks
U.S. Army Command and General Staff
    College

Sean Williams
Virginia Military Institute

Dr. Bradford A. Wineman
Department of Military History
U.S. Army Command and General Staff
    College

Dr. Anna M. Wittmann
University of Alberta

Carol J. Yee
Department of the Army

Dr. David Zabecki
Major General
Army of the United States, Retired

Norman R. Zehr
Independent Scholar

Categorical Index

Individuals

Acheson, Dean Gooderham, 6
Adams, Edward, 10
Allison, John Moore, 37
Almond, Edward Mallory, 38
An Chang Ho, 40
An Ho Sang, 40
Attlee, Clement Richard, 64
Austin, Warren, 65
Baillie, Hugh, 69
Bajpai, Girja Shankar, 70
Baldwin, Hanson Weightman, 71
Barkley, Alben William, 71
Barr, David Goodwin, 73
Baruch, Bernard, 73
Bebler, Ales, 76
Bendetsen, Karl Robin, 79
Berendsen, Sir Carl August, 79
Bevan, Aneurin, 80
Bevin, Ernest, 81
Boatner, Haydon Lemaire, 89
Bohlen, Charles Eustis, 90
Bolté, Charles Lawrence, 91
Bond, Niles W., 92
Bonnet, Henri, 92
Bowles, Chester Bliss, 94
Bradley, Omar Nelson, 96
Bricker, John William, 99
Bridgeford, Sir William, 100
Bridges, Henry Styles, 101
Briggs, Ellis Ormsbee, 102
Briscoe, Robert Pierce, 102

Burke, Arleigh Albert, 104
Campbell, Archibald, 109
Cassels, Sir James, 112
Cates, Clifton Bledsoe, 115
Chae Pyong Dok, 119
Chai Chengwen, 120
Chang Myon, 120
Chang Taek Sang, 121
Chauvel, Jean Michel Henri, 129
Chen Yi, 133
Cho Man Sik, 169
Cho Pyong Ok, 169
Choe Tok Sin, 170
Choe Yong Gon, 171
Chong Il Gwon, 172
Church, John Huston, 178
Churchill, Sir Winston, 182
Clark, Joseph James, 190
Clark, Mark Wayne, 190
Clubb, Oliver Edmund, 195
Collins, Joseph Lawton, 203
Connally, Thomas Terry, 211
Cordier, Andrew Wellington, 214
Cory, Thomas J., 216
Coulter, John Breitling, 217
Cutler, Robert, 219
Davidson, Garrison Holt, 223
Davies, John Paton, 226
Dean, Arthur Hobson, 227
Dean, William Frishe, 228
Deng Hua, 238
Doyle, James Henry, 241

Drumright, Everett Francis, 243
Du Ping, 244
Dulles, John Foster, 245
Eden, Robert Anthony, 250
Eisenhower, Dwight David, 253
Elsey, George McKee, 260
Emmons, Arthur B., III, 261
Entezam, Nasrollah, 262
Fechteler, William Morrow, 271
Finletter, Thomas Knight, 274
Foster, William Zebulon, 276
Franks, Oliver, 278
Freeman, Paul LaMarch, Jr., 280
Gao Gang, 281
Gay, Hobart Raymond, 282
Graham, William Franklin, 288
Gromyko, Andrei, 293
Gross, Ernest Arnold, 294
Guo Moruo, 295
Hammarskjöld, Dag, 298
Han Kyong Jik, 299
Han Pyo Uk, 300
Harriman, William Averell, 302
Harrison, William Kelly, Jr., 303
Hausman, James Harry, 304
Henderson, Loy Wesley, 311
Hershey, Lewis Blaine, 312
Hess, Dean Elmer, 313
Hickerson, John Dewey, 314
Hickey, Doyle Overton, 315
Higgins, Marguerite, 315
Hiss, Alger, 316

Ho Ka I, 325
Hodes, Henry Irving, 326
Hodge, John Reed, 326
Hoge, William Morris, 329
Hong Xuezhi, 334
Hope, Leslie Townes, 336
Hull, John Edwin, 342
Jackson, Charles Douglas, 367
Jamieson, Arthur B., 368
Jebb, Sir Gladwyn, 376
Jessup, Philip Caryl, 377
Jiang Jieshi, 379
Johnson, Louis Arthur, 382
Johnson, Ural Alexis, 384
Jooste, Gerhardus Petrus, 386
Joy, Charles Turner, 387
Kang Kon, 397
Katzin, Alfred G., 401
Kean, William Benjamin, 401
Keiser, Laurence Bolton, 402
Kennan, George Frost, 404
Kim Chaek, 409
Kim Chong Won, 409
Kim Il Sung, 410
Kim Jong Il, 412
Kim Ku, 413
Kim Kyu Sik, 414
Kim Paek Il, 415
Kim Sae Sun, 415
Kim Sok Won, 416
Kim Song Su, 417
Kim Tu Bong, 418
Kim Ung, 418
Kingsley, John Donald, 420
Kinsler, Francis, 421
Kirk, Alan Goodrich, 421
Knowland, William Fife, 422
Lampe, James S., 495
Lattimore, Owen, 497
Lay, James S., 498
Lee Myung Bak, 499
Lemnitzer, Lyman Louis, 501
Leviero, Anthony Harry, 501
Li Kenong, 502
Lie, Trygve Halvden, 504
Lightner, Edwin Allan, Jr., 506
Limb, Ben C., 506
Lin Biao, 507
Lippmann, Walter, 508
Lloyd, John Selwyn, 516
Lodge, Henry Cabot, Jr., 517
Lovett, Robert Abercrombie, 523

Lowe, Frank E., 524
MacArthur, Douglas, 527
Makin, Norman, 536
Makins, Sir Roger, 536
Malenkov, Georgii, 537
Malik, Jacob, 538
Mao Zedong, 541
Marshall, George Catlett, 544
Marshall, Samuel Lyman Atwood, 547
Martin, Joseph William, 550
Matthews, Francis Patrick, 552
Matthews, Harrison Freeman, 553
McCarran, Patrick Anthony, 554
McCarthy, Joseph Raymond, 555
McClure, Robert Alexis, 558
McGarr, Lionel Charles, 559
Menon, Kumara Padmanabha Sivasankara, 568
Menon, Vengalil Krishnan Krishna, 568
Menzies, Robert Gordon, 570
Merchant, Livingston Tallmadge, 571
Meyer, Clarence Earle, 573
Michaelis, John Hersey, 575
Milburn, Frank William, 578
Moffett, Howard Fergus, 593
Molotov, Viacheslav Mikhailovich, 593
Monclar, Ralph, 594
Morrison, Herbert Stanley, 596
Mu Chong, 599
Muccio, John Joseph, 599
Murphy, Charles Springs, 602
Murphy, Robert Daniel, 603
Muste, Abraham Johannes, 606
Nam Il, 611
Needham, Joseph, 624
Nehru, Jawaharlal, 625
Nie Rongzhen, 632
Nitze, Paul Henry, 633
Nixon, Richard Milhous, 635
Noble, Harold, 637
Norstad, Lauris, 638
O'Donnell, Emmett, 647
Oliver, Robert Tarbell, 651
Oppenheimer, J. Robert, 651
Pace, Frank, Jr., 659
Padilla Nervo, Luis, 661
Paek In Yop, 663
Paek Son Yop, 663
Paek Song Uk, 664
Paek Tu Jin, 665
Pak Hon Yong, 665
Pak Sun Chon, 666

Pandit, Vijaya Lakshmi Nehru, 667
Pang Ho San, 668
Panikkar, Sardar K. M., 668
Park Chung Hee, 670
Partridge, Earle Everard, 671
Pearson, Lester Bowles, 673
Peng Dehuai, 674
Pierce, Robert Willard, 677
Plimsoll, James, 681
Puller, Lewis Burwell, 704
Pyon Yong Tae, 712
Qin Jiwei, 717
Quesada, Elwood Richard, 718
Radford, Arthur William, 719
Radhakrishnan, Sarvepalli, 720
Rau, Sir Benegal Narsing, 723
Rhee, Syngman, 738
Ridgway, Matthew Bunker, 743
Roberts, William Lynn, 748
Robertson, Sir Horace, 748
Robertson, Walter Spencer, 749
Rosenberg, Julius, 754
Ruffner, Clark Louis, 757
Rusk, David Dean, 758
Ryan, Cornelius Edward, 759
Sebald, William Joseph, 767
Seoul City Sue, 774
Service, John Stewart, 775
Shaw, William Hamilton, 776
Shepherd, Lemuel Cornick, Jr., 777
Sherman, Forrest Percival, 778
Short, Joseph H., Jr., 779
Shtykov, Terentii Fomich, 781
Sin Ik Hui, 782
Sin Song Mo, 782
Sin Tae Yong, 783
Smith, Oliver Prince, 786
Smith, Walter Bedell, 787
Son Won Il, 789
Son Yang Won, 789
Song Chin U, 790
Song Shilun, 791
Spellman, Francis Joseph, 803
Spender, Sir Percy Claude, 804
St. Laurent, Louis Stephen, 805
Stalin, Joseph, 806
Stevenson, Adlai Ewing, 809
Stratemeyer, George Edward, 814
Struble, Arthur Dewey, 816
Symington, William Stuart, III, 821
Taft, Robert Alphonso, 827
Tasca, Henry Joseph, 832

Taylor, Maxwell Davenport, 835
Thimayya, Kadenera Subayya, 840
Thomas, Norman Mattoon, 845
Tomlinson, Frank Stanley, 847
Truman, Harry S., 854
Tsarapkin, Semion Konstantinovich, 865
Tsiang Ting Fu Fuller, 866
Twining, Nathan Farragut, 869
Underwood, Horace Grant, 873
Underwood, Horace Grant, II, 874
Underwood, Horace Horton, 875
Van Fleet, James Alward, 939
Vandenberg, Hoyt Sanford, 941
Voorhees, Tracy Stebbins, 943
Vyshinskii, Andrei Ianuarovich, 944
Walker, Walton Harris, 949
Webb, James Edwin, 953
West, Sir Michael M. A. R., 954
Weyland, Otto Paul, 955
Whitney, Courtney, 957
Williams, George Z., 958
Willoughby, Charles Andrew, 959
Wilson, Charles Edward, 960
Won Yong Dok, 971
Wrong, Humphrey Hume, 976
Wu Xiuquan, 977
Xie Fang, 979
Yang Dezhi, 984
Yang Yu Chan, 984
Yi Chong Chan, 985
Yi Hak Ku, 985
Yi Hyong Gun, 987
Yi Kwon Mu, 987
Yi Pom Sok, 988
Yi Sang Jo, 989
Yi Sung Yop, 990
Yi Tong Hwi, 990
Yim, Louise, 991
Yo Un Hyong, 992
Younger, Kenneth, 995
Yu Chae Hung, 996
Yun Chi Yong, 997
Zhang Hanfu, 999
Zhang Tingfa, 1000
Zhou Enlai, 1000
Zinchenko, Konstantin E., 1001
Zorin, Valerian, 1002

Events
Acheson's National Press Club Speech, 8
Agenda Controversy, 20
Airborne Operations, 21

Alexander-Lloyd Mission, 36
Blair House Meetings, 86
Bloody Ridge, Battle of, 87
BLUEHEARTS, Operation, 88
Border Clashes, 93
Bradley-Bohlen Mission to Korea, 97
Bunker Hill, Battle of, 103
Cease-fire Negotiations, 115
Changjin Reservoir Campaign, 122
Cheju-do Prisoner of War Uprising, 130
Cheju-do Rebellion, 131
Chinese Civil War, 150
Chinese Economic and Military Aid to
    North Korea, 152
Chinese Offensive, First, 154
Chinese Military Disengagement, 155
Chinese Offensive, Second, 157
Chinese Offensive, Third, 160
Chinese Offensive, Fourth, 161
Chinese Offensive, Fifth, 162
Chinese Offensive, Sixth, 163
Chinese Offensives, Summer, 164
Chipyong-ni, Battle of, 166
Chongchon River, Battle of, 174
Chunchon, Battle of, 177
Church Survey Mission to Korea, 179
Civilian Internee Issue, 187
CLAM-UP, Operation, 189
CLEANUP I and CLEANUP II, Operations, 192
Cold War, Origins to 1950, 197
Collins Visit to Tokyo, 204
Collins-Sherman Visit to Tokyo, 205
Collins-Vandenberg Discussions in Tokyo,
    206
Collins-Vandenberg Visit to Tokyo, 207
COMMANDO, Operation, 210
COURAGEOUS, Operation, 218
Dam Raids of 1953, 221
DAUNTLESS, Operation, 223
Dodd-Colson Prisoner of War Incident, 240
Dulles's Trip to Korea, 247
Eisenhower's Trip to Korea, 255
Election, U.S. Presidential, 257
Elections, U.S. Midterm, 258
EVERREADY, Operation, 265
Geneva Conference, 283
Geneva Convention, 285
Gloucester Hill, Battle of, 287
Graves Registration, 289
Great Debate, 290
Haman Breakthrough, 297
Han River Operations, 301

Heartbreak Ridge, Battle of, 305
Hoengsong, Battle of, 328
Home-by-Christmas Offensive, 331
Hook, Battles of the, 335
Hot Pursuit, 338
HUDSON HARBOR, Exercise, 341
Hungnam Evacuation, 344
Imjin River, Battle of, 349
Inchon Landing, 351
Indochina War, Impact on Korea, 359
Industrial Base, U.S., 361
Japan, Post–World War II U.S. Occupation
    of, 372
Jet Aircraft, First Manned Clash in History,
    378
Jiang Jieshi's Offer of Nationalist Troops to
    Fight in Korea, 381
Kaesong Neutral Zone Controversy, 392
Kaesong Truce Talks, 394
Kapyong, Battle of, 399
Kelly Hill, Battle of, 403
Kennan-Malik Conversations, 406
KILLER, Operation, 407
Kochang Incident, 424
Koje-do Prisoner of War Uprising, 425
Kojo Amphibious Feint, 427
Korea, Democratic People's Republic of,
    Invasion of the Republic of Korea, 443
Korea, Democratic People's Republic of,
    United Nations Command Occupation
    of, 446
Korea, Japanese Occupation of, 455
Korea, Republic of, Demonstrations for
    Unification, 470
Korea, Republic of, National Defense
    Forces Scandal, 475
Korea, Republic of, Occupation of by
    Democratic People's Republic of Korea,
    478
Korea, Republic of, Political Crisis, 480
Kum River, Battle of, 493
Kunu-ri, Battle of, 493
LITTLE SWITCH and BIG SWITCH, Operations, 514
MacArthur Hearings, 531
Meyer Mission, 575
MIG, Operation, 576
MOOLAH, Operation, 595
Munsan-ni Airborne Operation, 601
Najin, Bombing of, 607
Naktong Bulge, First Battle of, 609
Naktong Bulge, Second Battle of, 610
Namsi, Battle of, 613

Naval Battles, 620

No Name Line, Battle of, 636

Nogun-ni Railroad Bridge Incident, 638

Old Baldy, Battle of, 649

Osan, Battle of, 654

Outpost Harry, Battle for, 656

PILEDRIVER, Operation, 678

Pohang, Battle of, 682

Pongam-do Prisoner of War Uprising, 685

Pork Chop Hill, Battle of, 686

Potsdam Conference, 687

Prisoners of War, Rescreening of, 698

Pueblo Incident, 701

PUNCH, Operation, 705

Pusan Perimeter and Breakout, 707

Pyongyang, March to and Capture of, 713

RATKILLER, Operation, 722

Red Ball Express, 727

Repatriation, Voluntary, 732

Revolt of the Admirals, 737

Rhee, Syngman, Assassination Attempt on, 742

Rhee's Release of North Korean Prisoners of War, 742

RIPPER, Operation, 746

Robertson Mission, 750

ROUNDUP, Operation, 756

RUGGED, Operation, 757

SATURATE, Operation, 763

SCATTER, Operation, 764

Seoul, Fall of, 770

Seoul, Recapture of, 772

SHOWDOWN, Operation, 780

SMACK, Operation, 785

Soviet Air War in Korea, 795

Soviet Airfield Incident, 796

Soviet Security Council Boycott, 797

Special Operations, 801

Steel Plants, Truman's Seizure of, 808

STRANGLE, Operation, 811

Sukchon and Sunchon Airborne Operation, 819

Supung and the Korean Electric Power Plant Campaign, 820

Taegu, Defense of, 823

Taejon, Defense of, 825

TAILBOARD, Operation, 830

Taiwan, Neutralization of, 831

38th Parallel, Decision to Cross, 841

THUNDERBOLT, Operation, 846

Triangle Hill, Battle of, 847

Tripartite Meetings, 849

Truce Talks, 850

Truman-Eisenhower Transition Meeting, 859

Truman's Recall of MacArthur, 863

United States Navy Air Operations, 923

Unsan, Battle of, 927

Wake Island Conference, 947

War Crimes Trials, 952

Washington Conference, 953

White Horse Hill, Battle of, 956

WOLFHOUND, Operation, 962

Wonju, Battle of, 972

Wonsan Landing and Evacuation, 973

Yalu Bridges Controversy, 981

Yongchon, Battle of, 992

Yosu-Sunchon Rebellion, 994

Groups and Organizations

Abductees, South Korean, 1

Aces, 2

ADCOM, 11

African Americans and the Korean War, 16

Amphibious Force Far East, 39

Atomic Energy Commission, U.S., 61

"Bed-Check Charlies", 77

Cambridge Five, 108

Casualties, 112

Central Intelligence Agency, 118

Chaplains, U.S. Army and Republic of Korea Army, 128

China, People's Republic of, Army, 139

China, People's Republic of, Navy, 142

China, People's Republic of, People's Liberation Army Air Force, 143

China Hands, 148

China Lobby, 149

Chinese People's Volunteer Army, 165

Choson Democratic Party, 176

Churches and the War, Korean, 179

Churches and the War, U.S., 181

Committee on the Present Danger, 210

Defectors, 229

Democratic National Party, 233

Democratic Party, United States, 234

Detachment 2, 239

Economic Stabilization Agency, 249

Eighth Army, U.S., 251

European Defense Community, 264

Far East Air Force, 268

Far East Command, 269

Forward Air Controllers, 275

Hollywood Ten, 330

House Un-American Activities Committee, 338

Housewives United, 340

Japan Logistical Command, 373

Joint Chiefs of Staff, 385

Korea, Democratic People's Republic of, Air Force, 437

Korea, Democratic People's Republic of, Army, 438

Korea, Democratic People's Republic of, Navy, 446

Korea, Republic of, Air Force, 464

Korea, Republic of, Army, 465

Korea, Republic of, Korean Service Corps, 472

Korea, Republic of, Marine Corps, 474

Korea, Republic of, National Defense Forces, 475

Korea, Republic of, Navy, 476

Korea Military Advisory Group, 484

Korean Augmentation to the United States Army, 485

Korean Democratic Party, 487

Korean Independence Party, 489

Korean Provisional Government, 490

Liberal Party, 503

Medics, Combat, 567

Military Air Transport Service, 579

Military Armistice Commission, 580

Military Sea Transport Service, 584

Missing in Action, 590

Mobile Army Surgical Hospital, 590

National Security Council, 617

National Security Resources Board, 619

Naval Forces Far East, 621

Neutral Nations Repatriation Commission, 627

Neutral Nations Supervisory Commission, 629

North Atlantic Treaty Organization, 639

Office of Defense Mobilization, 648

Office of Price Stabilization, 648

Organized Labor, 652

Prisoner of War Administration, Communist, 691

Prisoner of War Administration, United Nations Command, 694

Red Cross, 727

Refugees, 729

Republican Party, United States, 733

2nd Logistical Command, 768

Southeast Asia Treaty Organization, 793

Student Volunteer Troops, Republic of Korea, 817
Task Force Kean, 833
Task Force Smith, 834
X Corps, 836
3rd Logistical Command, 841
Tydings Committee, 870
United Nations and the Korean War, 879
United Nations Additional Measures Committee, 883
United Nations Cease-Fire Group, 883
United Nations Civil Assistance Command in Korea, 885
United Nations Collective Measures Committee, 886
United Nations Command, 886
United Nations Command Air Assets, 889
United Nations Command Ground Forces, Contributions to, 890
United Nations Commission for the Unification and Rehabilitation of Korea, 891
United Nations Good Offices Committee, 895
United Nations Korean Reconstruction Agency, 895
United Nations Peace Observation Commission, 896
United States Air Force, 902
United States Army, 905
United States Army Engineers, 909
United States Army Military Police, 910
United States Army Rangers, 911
United States Army Signal Corps, 912
United States Coast Guard, 914
United States Marine Corps, 914
United States National Guard, 918
United States Naval Construction Battalions, 920
United States Navy, 920
United States Reserve Forces, 925
Wage Stabilization Board, 947
Women in Defense Production Administration Committees, 964
Women on the Home Front, United States and Korea, 964
Women in the Military during the Korean War, 968
World Vision, 975

Places
Airfields, 32

Australia, 67
Belgium, 77
Bowling Alley, 95
Canada, 110
China, People's Republic of, 135
China, Republic of, 146
Chongchon River, 173
Colombia, 208
Davidson Line, 225
Demilitarized Zone, 231
Demographics, Korean, 236
Ethiopia, 263
France, 277
Germany, Federal Republic of, 286
Greece, 291
Hong Kong, British Crown Colony of, 333
Hungnam, North Korea, 344
Imjin River, 349
India, 357
Iron Triangle, 364
Japan, 369
Kaesong, 391
Kansas-Wyoming Line, 397
Kimpo Airfield, 419
Koje-do, 424
Korea, Climate and Geography of, 429
Korea, Democratic People's Republic of, 1945–1953, 430
Korea, Democratic People's Republic of, 1953–Present, 432
Korea, History of, to 1945, 448
Korea, History of, 1945–1947, 451
Korea, Republic of, 1947–1953, 456
Korea, Republic of, 1953–Present, 459
Korea, Topography of, 481
Korean Communications Zone, 487
Korean War Veterans Memorial, U.S., 491
Latin America, 496
Luxembourg, Grand Duchy of, 525
Manchuria, 540
Mexico, 572
MiG Alley, 576
Netherlands, 626
New Zealand, 631
Northern Limitation Line, 642
Philippines, 676
Punchbowl, 706
Pusan, 706
Pyongyang, 713
Sanctuaries, 761
Sasebo, Japan, 762
Seoul, 769

South Africa, Union of, 791
Soviet Union, 798
Thailand, 839
38th Parallel, Division of Korea at, 843
Turkey, 867
United Kingdom, 875
United States, Home Front, 901
Wonsan, North Korea, 973
Yalu River, 982

Ideas and Movements
Active Defense Strategy, 9
Aerial Combat, 12
Aeromedical Evacuation, 15
Airpower in the Korean War, 33
Antiwar Sentiment in the United States, 41
Atomic Bomb, Threat to Use, 60
Biological Warfare, 83
Brainwashing, 98
Censorship and the Korean War, 117
Chemical Warfare, 133
Chondogyo Movement, 171
Civil Defense, U.S., 184
Civil Liberties in the United States, 186
Close Air Support, 193
Containment, 212
Draft, 242
Helicopters, Employment of, 307
Human Wave Attacks, 343
Industrial Dispersion, 362
Infiltration, 363
Isolationist Sentiment in the United States, 364
Juche Ideology, 388
K1C2, 428
Logistics in the Korean War, 518
Manchurian Sanctuary, 540
March First Movement, 543
Marshall Plan, 548
Massive Retaliation, 552
McCarthyism, 557
"Meat Grinder" Strategy, 560
Military-Industrial Complex, 581
Mine Warfare, Sea, 585
Mobilization, 592
Munich Analogy, 600
Naval Gunfire Support, 622
New Look Defense Policy, 630
North Korean Offensive, Delaying of, 641
Nuclear Warfare, 643
Pleven Plan, 680
Point Four Program, 683

Police Action, 685
Price Gouging, 689
Psychological Warfare, 699
Reconnaissance, 726
Relief Efforts, Missionary, 731
Rest and Recuperation, 735
Return-to-Seoul Movement, 737
"Rolling with the Punch", 753
Rotation of Troops System, 754
Schuman Plan, 765
Scorched Earth Policy, 766
Strategic and Tactical Airlift in the Korean
    War, 812
Truman Doctrine, 857
Truman Loyalty Program, 859
Truman's Cease-fire Initiative, 860
U.S. Policy toward Korea, Pre-1950, 928
U.S. Policy toward Korea, 1950–1953, 931
U.S. Policy toward Korea, 1953–Present,
    934

Technologies, Objects, and Artifacts
Aircraft, 23
Aircraft Carriers, 31
Armor, Tanks, 47
Armored Vests, 51
Artillery, 52
Artillery, Antiaircraft, 57
Atomic Bomb, 59
Bazooka, 75
Fallout Shelters, 267
Grenades, 292
Helicopters, Types and Nomenclature, 309
Hospital Ships, 336
Hydrogen Bomb, 347
Machine Guns, 533
Mines, Land, 588
Mines, Sea, 589
Mortars, 597
Napalm, 614

Pistols, 680
Railroads, Korean National, 721
Recoilless Rifles, 724
Rifles, 745
Rocket Artillery, 751
Searchlights, 767
Submachine Guns and Light Machine
    Guns, 818
Troopships, 850
"Van Fleet Load", 940

Treaties, Acts, and Other Documents
ANZUS Treaty, 43
Armistice Agreement, 43
Blacklists, 84
Cairo Declaration, 107
Defense Production Act, 230
Executive Order 9981, 265
Internal Security Act, 363
Japanese Peace Treaty, 375
Kaesong Bombing Proposal, 391
Korea Aid Bill of 1947, 482
Korea Aid Bill of 1950, 483
National Emergency Declaration, 616
National Security Act, 616
National Security Council Report 68, 618
Pacific Pact, 660
Panmunjom Security Agreement, 669
Peruvian Prisoner of War Settlement
    Proposal, 676
Price and Wage Freeze Order, 690
Prisoner of War Code of Conduct, 697
Sino-Soviet Treaty of Friendship and
    Alliance, 784
Stockholm Peace Appeal, 810
Taejon Agreement, 826
Taft-Hartley Act, 829
United Nations General Assembly
    Resolution 376 (V), 892
United Nations General Assembly
    Resolution 377 (V), 893

United Nations General Assembly
    Resolution 498 (V), 894
United Nations Security Council Resolution
    82, 898
United Nations Security Council Resolution
    83, 899
United Nations Security Council Resolution
    84, 900
United Nations Security Council Resolution
    85, 900
United States–Republic of Korea Mutual
    Defense Treaty, 926
Universal Military Training and Service
    Act, 927

Other
Atrocities, 62
Battle Fatigue, 74
"Bug-out Fever", 103
China, People's Republic of, United Nations
    Representation Question, 145
Controlled Materials Plan, 214
Film and the Korean War, 271
Historiography of the Korean War, 317
Japan, Economic Impact of the Korean War
    on, 371
Korea, Democratic People's Republic of,
    Economy, 372
Korea, Republic of, Economy, 471
Literature of the Korean War, Korean, 509
Literature of the Korean War, U.S., 511
Media and the Korean War, 562
Medicine, Military, 564
Military Intelligence, 583
Music of the Korean War, Korean, 604
Music of the Korean War, U.S., 605
Truman's Domestic Agenda and the
    Korean War, 861
United Nations Sanctions on China, 897

Index

1st Black Watch Battalion (United Kingdom), 336

1st Cavalry Division (United States), 78, 89, 154, 157 (image), 161, 167, 174, 210, 252, 282–283, 353, 399, 407, 486, 494, 586, 609, 610, 638, 641, 642, 678, 707, 711, 714, 746, 747, 757, 843, 846, 907, 908, 927–928
  Greek Battalion of, 292

1st Commonwealth Division (United Kingdom, Australia, New Zealand, Canada), 111, 210

1st Gloucestershire Regiment (United Kingdom), 78

1st Infantry Division (KPA), 440, 445

1st Infantry Division (ROKA), 156, 160, 162, 210, 301, 302, 417, 445, 466, 468, 663, 707, 714, 717, 747, 962

1st Loudspeaker and Leaflet Company (United States), 700

1st Marine Division (United States), 38, 122, 124, 125, 156, 159, 161, 205, 308, 332, 344, 345, 350, 353, 354, 355, 399, 407, 468, 474, 580, 636, 678, 746, 757, 771 (image), 816, 830, 831, 837, 837 (image), 914, 915, 975
  manpower shortage in, 592

1st Marine Provisional Brigade (United States), 707

1st Marine Regiment (ROKMC), 476

1st Marine Regiment (United States), 124, 127, 351, 704

2nd Amphibious Support Brigade (United States), 427

2nd Engineer Battalion (United States), 174

2nd Engineer Special Brigade (United States), 354

2nd Infantry Division (KPA), 177, 300, 440, 445, 610, 611, 707, 708

2nd Infantry Division (ROKA), 177, 468, 770, 848

2nd Infantry Division (United States), 19, 88, 89, 103, 156, 157, 161, 163, 165, 174, 211, 217, 280, 300, 305, 306, 328, 329, 402–403, 407, 486, 493–494, 565 (image), 609, 610, 636, 675, 683, 707, 711, 726, 727, 746, 756, 757, 907, 936, 957, 972, 972 (image), 973

2nd Infantry Regiment (ROKA), 962

2nd Logistical Command (United States), 695, **768–769**

2nd Marine Regiment (ROKMC), 475

3rd Army Group (PLA), 166

3rd Infantry Battalion (Australia), 571, 714

3rd Infantry Division (KPA), 177, 439, 445, 707, 772

3rd Infantry Division (ROKA), 177, 345, 346, 415, 445, 468, 682, 683, 709, 770, 973, 975, 985, 996

3rd Infantry Division (United States), 19, 51 (image), 77–78, 122, 127, 156, 163, 164, 165, 205, 210, 287, 288, 350, 351, 360 (image), 399, 601, 656, 746, 747, 757, 830, 831
  1st Battalion of, 403–404
  3rd Battalion of, 19, 404
  Greek Brigade of, 657, 658

3rd Logistical Command (United States), 768, 769, **841**

4th Infantry Division (KPA), 439, 445, 609, 610, 707, 772

5th Cavalry Regiment (United States), 63, 167, 168, 283, 713–714

5th Infantry Division (KPA), 177, 439, 445, 683, 708, 709

5th Infantry Division (ROKA), 164, 177, 407, 445, 468, 636, 756, 770

5th Infantry Regiment (United States), 667

5th Marine Regiment (United States), 126, 159, 351, 650 (image), 774

5th Regimental Combat Team (United States), 154, 297, 642, 707, 708, 711, 833, 907

6th Infantry Division (KPA), 297, 300, 305, 439, 445, 610, 642, 707, 708

6th Infantry Division (ROKA), 162, 177, 301, 350, 351, 445, 466, 467, 468, 607, 747, 757, 962, 993

6th Infantry Division (United States), 160, 452, 453

7th Cavalry Division (United States), 638, 713, 912

7th Infantry Division (KPA), 297, 300, 439, 445, 610, 708

7th Infantry Division (ROKA), 445, 466, 467, 636, 714, 746

7th Infantry Division (United States), 38, 73, 124, 125, 156, 159, 165, 204, 205, 209, 252, 331, 332, 344, 345 (image), 350, 351, 354, 407, 452, 453–454, 486, 725 (image), 756, 757, 780, 780 (image), 816, 830, 848, 848 (image), 907
  Ethiopian Division of, 263

7th Infantry Regiment (ROKA), 156, 159, 164, 301, 302

7th Marine Regiment (United States), 124, 126, 156, 159, 335, 336, 351, 360 (image), 678

8th Cavalry Regimental Combat Team (United States), 154, 283, 427–428, 713–714, 928

8th Infantry Division (KPA), 708

8th Infantry Division (ROKA), 161, 164, 301, 469, 707, 723, 756, 993, 994

9th Army Group (PLA), 166

9th Infantry Division (KPA), 440, 610

9th Infantry Division (ROKA), 164, 424, 469, 679, 746, 957, 996

9th Infantry Regiment (United States), 19, 88, 305–306, 494, 609, 610, 611, 972

10th Infantry Division (KPA), 439, 440, 474, 609, 708

10th Philippine Battalion (Philippines), 679

11th Airborne Division (United States), 21

11th Infantry Division (ROKA), 165, 424, 468

11th Infantry Regiment (ROKA), 714

12th Infantry Division (KPA), 305, 439, 440, 476, 682, 683, 708

12th Infantry Division (ROKA), 469

12th Infantry Regiment (ROKA), 93, 714, 962

13th Infantry Division (KPA), 439, 708, 709, 986

14th Engineer Combat Battalion (United States), 609

14th Infantry Regiment (ROKA), 994–995

15th Field Artillery Battalion (United States), 494

15th Infantry Division (KPA), 439, 440, 707, 993–994

15th Infantry Division (ROKA), 469

15th Infantry Regiment (United States), 19, 656–658, 962

16th Field Artillery Regiment (New Zealand), 399, 631

16th Infantry Regiment (KPA), 655–656

17th Infantry Division (KPA), 440

17th Infantry Division (ROKA), 609

17th Infantry Regiment (United States), 124, 331, 972

17th Regimental Combat Team (United States), 830, 831

18th Infantry Regiment (KPA), 655–656

19th Army Group (PLA), 166

19th Engineer Combat Group (United States), 354

19th Infantry Regiment (United States), 161, 493, 609, 683, 825

20th Army Group (PLA), 166

20th Infantry Division (ROKA), 470

21st Infantry Division (ROKA), 470

21st Infantry Regiment (United States), 63–64, 493, 609, 654, 683, 825

21st Regimental Medical Company (United States), 834

23rd Army Group (PLA), 166

23rd Infantry Division (United States), 650

23rd Infantry Regiment (United States), 280, 305, 306, 328, 329, 494, 610, 611, 627, 709, 972

23rd Regimental Combat Team (United States), 88, 166–168

various components of, 167

24th Infantry Division (KPA), 440

24th Infantry Division (United States), 154, 156, 160, 164, 209, 225, 228–229, 252, 297, 332, 350, 445, 486, 493–494, 609, 610, 641, 642, 683, 707, 709, 711, 713, 746, 747, 757, 825, 835, 907, 918

24th Infantry Regiment (United States), 19, 174, 297, 407, 494, 908

24th Reconnaissance Company (United States), 493, 609, 825

25th Infantry Division (United States), 19, 156, 157, 160, 164, 174, 205, 210, 252, 298, 350, 350 (image), 399, 486, 494, 609, 610, 641, 678, 705, 705 (image), 707, 708, 711, 746, 747 (image), 757, 762, 833, 846, 868, 907, 911, 932 (image), 962

26th Infantry Regiment (ROKA), 122, 124

27th British Commonwealth Brigade (United Kingdom), 68, 351, 399 707, 714, 746, 820

1st Battalion of (Argyll and Sutherland Highlanders Regiment), 399

1st Battalion of (Middlesex Regiment), 399

3rd Battalion of (Royal Australian Regiment), 67, 68, 399

27th Infantry Division (KPA), 440

27th Infantry Regiment (United States), 9, 174, 297–298, 307 (image), 609, 642, 709, 962

3rd Battalion of, 696

28th British Commonwealth Brigade (United Kingdom), 399

1st Battalion of (King's Own Scottish Borderers Regiment), 399

2nd Battalion of (Princess Patricia Canadian Light Infantry Regiment), 399

3rd Battalion (Royal Australian Regiment), 399

28th Infantry Division (United States), 918

29th Independent British Brigade (United Kingdom), 78, 160, 162, 287, 335, 876 (image)

29th Regimental Combat Team (United States), 907

31st Infantry Division (KPA), 440

31st Infantry Division (United States), 918

31st Infantry Regiment (United States), 124, 126, 127, 585 (image), 650

31st Regimental Combat Team (United States), 126, 679 (image)

32nd Infantry Regiment (United States), 124, 126, 159, 331, 455, 609, 642, 762

34th Infantry Regiment (United States), 493, 825

34th Regimental Combat Team (United States), 164, 165

35th Infantry Regiment (United States), 297, 298, 494–495, 833, 972

36th Infantry Regiment (ROKA), 88

37th Infantry Division (United States), 918

38th Infantry Division (KPA), 440

38th Infantry Regiment (United States), 88, 103, 174, 306, 494, 565 (image), 610, 611, 627

38th Parallel. See Military Demarcation Line (MDL [the 38th Parallel])

40th Infantry Division (United States), 452, 918

41st Commando Battalion (United Kingdom), 127

41st Infantry Division (KPA), 440

41st Royal British Marines (United Kingdom), 876 (image)

42nd Infantry Division (KPA), 124, 441

43rd Infantry Division (KPA), 440

43rd Infantry Division (United States), 918

44th Infantry Division (United States), 918

45th Infantry Division (CPVA), 838

45th Infantry Division (KPA), 441

45th Infantry Division (United States), 165, 475, 918

46th Infantry Division (KPA), 441

47th Infantry Division (KPA), 440

47th Infantry Division (United States), 918

50th Antiaircraft Artillery Battalion (United States), 354

52nd Field Artillery Battery (United States), 654

55th Field Artillery Battalion (United States), 833

57th Field Artillery Battalion (United States), 126, 834–835

58th Field Artillery Battalion (United States), 404

61st Field Artillery Battalion (United States), 154

63rd Field Artillery Battalion (United States), 493, 641

64th Field Artillery Battalion (United States), 297, 298

64th Tank Battalion (United States), 404

65th Infantry Regiment (Puerto Rico), 351

65th Infantry Regiment (United States), 78, 403, 404, 962

65th Regimental Combat Team (United States), 830

70th Tank Battalion (United States), 9

72nd Tank Battalion (United States), 88, 399

82nd Airborne Division (United States), 21, 744, 835

92nd Field Artillery Battalion (United States), 354

96th Field Artillery Battalion (United States), 354

101st Airborne Division (United States), 580

105th Armored Division (KPA), 439, 440, 654

105th Infantry Division (KPA), 441

107th Tank Regiment (KPA), 654

112th Infantry Division (CPVA), 957

114th Infantry Division (CPVA), 957

116th Infantry Division (CPVA), 403

124th Infantry Division (CPVA), 124

126th Infantry Division (CPVA), 124

134th Infantry Regiment (CPVA), 848

135th Infantry Regiment (CPVA), 848

148th Quartermaster Graves Registration (QMGR) Company (United States), 289

156th Infantry Division (KPA), 439

159th Field Artillery Battalion (United States), 298

180th Infantry Division (CPVA), 162

187th Airborne Regimental Combat Team (United States), 21, 22–23, 23 (image), 161, 163, 164, 165, 218, 407, 494, 580, 601, 747, 756, 757, 819, 819 (image), 820, 830, 907, 911, 972

204th Field Artillery Battalion (United States), 54 (image)

213th Field Artillery Battalion (New Zealand), 631

278th Regimental Combat Team (United States), 918

304th Signal Operation Battalion (United States), 913

335th Infantry Regiment (CPVA), 957

340th Infantry Regiment (CPVA), 957

348th Infantry Regiment (CPVA), 403
  2nd Battalion of, 403
  3rd Battalion of, 403

512th Military Police Group (United States), 910

532nd Engineer Amphibious Support Regiment (United States), 427

674th Field Artillery Battalion (United States), 820

8054th Evacuation Hospital, 567

8055th Mobile Army Surgical Hospital (MASH [United States]), 308, 590

8063rd Mobile Army Surgical Hospital (MASH [United States]), 564, 590

8076th Mobile Army Surgical Hospital (MASH [United States]), 590–591, 592

8137th Military Police Group (United States), 694, 910

8209th Mobile Army Surgical Hospital (MASH [United States]), 564, 591 (image)

8213th Ranger Company (United States), 911

8225th Mobile Army Surgical Hospital (MASH [United States]), 591

Abductees (South Korean), **1–2**
  repatriation of, 2

Acar, Sirri, 868

Aces, **2–6**, 3 (image), 4 (table)

Acheson, Dean Gooderham, **6–8**, 6 (image), 7 (image), 12, 20, 21, 66, 70, 82, 86, 87, 116, 148, 149, 206, 251, 254, 303, 383, 384, 483–484, 505, 532, 546, 555, 558, 633, 669, 758, 776, 849, 864, 878, 930, 943, 954
  friendship with Oliver Franks, 279
  National Press Club speech of, **8–9**, 42, 1115–1121**Doc.**
  position on Germany entering NATO, 286–287
  "Situation in the Far East, The," 1125–1128**Doc.**
  view of the Korean War, 7–8

Active defense strategy, **9–10**

Adams, Donald E., 3

Adams, Edward, **10–11**

Adams, James Y., 306

ADCOM (Advanced Command and Liaison Group in Korea), **11–12**

Adenauer, Konrad, 286–287, 286 (image)

Adler, Ochs, 211

Aerial combat, **12–15**, 13 (image), 14 (image)
  lack of North Korean combat aircraft, 12
  political aspects of, 13
  superiority of the USAF in, 13–14

Aeromedical evacuation, **15–16**

AFL-CIO. *See* Organized labor

African Americans, and the Korean War, **16–20**, 17 (image), 534 (image), 908, 910
  all–African American units in the Korean War, 19
  as the catalyst of the Civil Rights Movement, 19–20, 42
  early poor performance of African American units, 19
  equality for African Americans in the United States Navy (USN), 18
  integration of the United States Army, 19
  issuing of Executive Order 9981 by Truman for equality in the armed services, 17
  poor training of African American soldiers, 19
  reluctance of the United States Army to desegregate, 18

Agenda controversy, **20–21**

Air Corps Ferrying Command (ACFC), 579

Airborne operations, **21–23**, 22 (image), 23 (image)

Aircraft, **23–31**, 24 (table), 25 (image), 26 (image), 27 (image), 29 (image), 878 (table)
  Antonov An-10 Colt, 30
  Auster A.O.P.6, 28
  Bell H-13 Sioux, 29
  Boeing B-26, 584
  Boeing B-29 Superfortress, 14, 24, 221, 222, 437, 585, 613, 639, 645, 763, 811, 820, 821, 903, 903 (image), 942
  Boeing B-52 Stratofortress, 936
  Boeing RB-17 Flying Fortress, 26, 726
  Boeing RB-50A, 26
  bombers, 24–25
  British aircraft, 28–29
  Cessna L-19A Bird Dog, 28, 726
  Chance Vought F4U-4/AU-1 Corsair, 27, 833, 915, 920, 924
  Chinese and North Korean aircraft, 30–31
  Consolidated PB4Y (PB4Y-2), 27
  Convair RB-36 Peacemaker, 26, 645, 738, 821, 903
  Curtiss C-46 Gooney Bird, 601
  Curtiss-Wright C-46 Commando, 15–16, 25, 579
  de Havilland L-20 Beaver, 28
  Douglas AD (A-1) Skyraider, 35, 796
  Douglas AD-2 Skyraider, 13 (image), 27, 820–821, 924
  Douglas B-26 Invader, 24–25, 903
  Douglas C-47 Skytrain ("Gooneybird"), 16, 25, 292, 567, 579, 601, 813, 820
  Douglas C-54 Skymaster, 16, 25, 567, 579, 813, 834
  Douglas C-124 Globemaster II, 16, 25–26, 35–36, 580
  Douglas C-133 Cargomaster, 580
  Douglas F3D Skyknight, 27, 35, 924
  Fairchild C-82 Packet, 16, 601
  Fairchild C-119 Flying Boxcar, 16, 23 (image), 26, 580, 584, 601, 813, 814, 820

Fairy Firefly, 28

fighters and fighter-bombers, 23–24, 378 (table)

first recorded clash of manned jets in history, **378–379**

Gloster F.8 Meteor, 29

Grumman AF-2 Guardian, 27

Grumman F6F-K Hellcat, 27, 35

Grumman F7F Tigercat, 27–28

Grumman F9F Panther, 27 (image), 28, 821, 924

Grumman F9F-2 Panther, 915

Grumman TBM Avenger, 27, 28, 35

Handley Page Hastings, 28

Hawker Sea Fury, 28–29

Hawker Tempest, 28

Hiller H-23A Raven, 726

Hiller H-28 Raven, 29

Ilyushin Il-2 Sturmovik, 29 (image), 30

Ilyushin Il-10 Sturmovik, 30

Ilyushin Il-28 Beagle, 30, 35

Lavochkin La-7, 30

Lavochkin La-11, 30

Lisunov Li-2, 30

Lockheed C-5 Galaxy, 580

Lockheed C-130 Hercules, 580

Lockheed C-141 Starlifter, 580

Lockheed F-80 Shooting Star, 23–24, 193, 378, 437, 465, 576, 613, 672, 726, 770, 821, 903

Lockheed F-94 Starfire, 24

Lockheed P2V, 28, 924

Martin B-26 Marauder, 193, 437, 763, 811

Martin P4M Mercator, 28

Martin PBM-5 Mariner, 28, 726, 924

Martin RB-26 Invader, 726

McDonnell F2H Banshee, 28

McDonnell Douglas F-4 Phantom, 465

Mikoyan-Gurevich MiG-15, 12–13, 14 (image), 23, 30, 35, 144, 378, 420, 576–578, 577 (map), 596 (image), 613, 672, 795, 796, 821, 903, 904

Mikoyan-Gurevich MiG-19, 465

North American AJ-1 Savage, 28, 644 (image)

North American AT-6G Mosquito, 26–27

North American F-51 Mustang, 24, 25 (image), 67, 193, 465, 592, 672, 726, 763, 811, 833, 903

North American F-82 Twin Mustang, 35 (image), 770, 903

North American F-84 Twin Mustang, 24, 613

North American F-86 Sabre, 13, 24, 26 (image), 193, 465, 534–535, 578, 613, 672, 726, 795, 796, 820, 821, 904, 942

North American L-4 Navion, 726

North American RB-45 Tornado, 25

North American T-6 Texan, 672

North American/Ryan L-17 Navion, 28

Northrop F-5 Freedom Fighter, 465

Piasecki HRP-1/2 "flying banana," 30

Piasecki HUP-1/2, 30

Aircraft (continued)
  Piper L-4A, 28
  Piper L-18, 29
  Polikarpov PO-2 biplane, 13, 30
  Republic F-84 Thunderjet, 24, 193, 221, 613,
      672, 796, 821, 903
  Short Sunderland, 29
  Sikorsky H-19, 30
  Stinson L5-B Sentinel, 15
  Stinson L5-E Sentinel, 28, 726
  Supermarine Seafire, 29
  Tachikawa Ki 55, 29
  Tupelov Tu-2, 30, 35
  United Nations Command (UNC) aircraft, 29
  United States Army aircraft, 28
  United States Navy and Marine aircraft,
      27–28
  Yakolev-9, 30, 437
  Yakolev-15, 30–31, 924
  Yakolev-18, 31
Aircraft carriers, 31–32, 31 (image), 370
      (image)
  Essex class, 31
  Independence class, 31
Airfields, 32–33
Airpower, in the Korean War, 33–36, 34
      (image), 35 (image)
  air interdiction campaign to cut off
      communist forces from their supplies,
      34–35
  legacy of, 35–36
  political decisions involved in, 35
  superiority of U.S. airpower, 33–34
  use of during the Chinese invasion of Korea,
      34
  use of in the Pusan Perimeter, 34
Akin, Spencer B., 912
Alemán, Miguel, 573
Alexander-Lloyd mission, 36–37
Allen, Horace M., 179
Allen, Leven A., 252 (image)
Allison, John Moore, 37–38, 244, 384, 634, 681
Allnut, Ronald, 736
Almond, Edward M., 9, 10, 21–22, 38–39, 38
      (image), 73, 159, 194, 204, 207, 217, 308,
      351, 352 (image), 354, 407, 774, 974
  actions at the Battle of Changjin Reservoir,
      124, 125, 126, 128
  as commander of X Corps, 38–39, 122, 836,
      837, 839
  criticism of close air support (CAS) doctrine,
      194, 195
  loyalty to MacArthur, 39
  personality of, 39
  racism of, 39
  service of in World War II, 38
Alsop, Joseph, 636
American military government (AMG), 790, 791
Amphibious Force Far East, 39–40
An Chang Ho, 40
An Ho Sang, 40–41
Anderson, Alvin, 17 (image)

Antiwar sentiment, in the United States, 41–43
  among conservatives, 42
  among liberals, 42
  effect of on Truman, 41
ANZUS Treaty (1951), 43, 68, 80, 571
Appenzeller, Henry G., 179
Applegate, Dick, 595
Arbouzis, Dionyssios, 292
Armistice Agreement (1953), 43–47, 44 (image),
      45 (map), 46 (image)
  Eisenhower's radio address concerning,
      1368–1369Doc.
  major provisions of, 44–46, 1370–1383Doc.
  press release concerning, 1369–1370Doc.
Armor. See Tanks
Armored vests, 51–52, 51 (image)
Armstrong, Neil, 924
Arnold, Archibald, 453
Arnold, Henry H., 579
Artillery, 52–57, 52 (table), 53 (image), 54
      (image), 56 (image)
  antiaircraft artillery (AAA), 57–59, 58
      (image), 812
  legacy of, 56–57
  North Korean and Chinese, 55–56, 141
      (table)
  rocket artillery, 751–753, 752 (image), 753
      (image)
  UN and U.S. artillery, 52–55
Atlee, Clement, 60, 64–65, 82, 183, 206, 252,
      261, 546, 856, 876–877
  foreign policy of, 877–878
  Truman-Atlee joint communiqué,
      1252–1254Doc.
Atomic bomb, 59–60, 61 (image), 199, 205, 206
  as cornerstone of U.S. foreign policy with the
      Soviet Union, 59–60
  development of in the Soviet Union, 60, 267
  Truman's threats to use, 60–61, 65, 644, 856,
      857, 884
  use of against Japan, 59
  See also Hydrogen bomb
Atrocities, 62–64, 63 (image), 479 (image), 480
  against American soldiers, 63
  against communist prisoners, 63
  Nogun-ni railroad bridge incident, 638
  revenge killings by Americans, 63–64
  See also Kochang incident; War crimes trials
Austin, Warren R., 381, 842, 881, 884
Australia, 67–68, 368–369, 376, 400, 570–571,
      746, 794, 804–805, 877
Avery, Warren, 64

Back, George I., 912, 986 (image)
Baillie, Hugh, 69–70
Bajpai, Girja Shankar, 70–71, 70 (image), 669
Baker, Royal N., 4
Baldwin, Hanson Weightman, 71
Baldwin, Robert P., 5
Barkley, Alben William, 71–73, 72 (image)
Barr, David Goodwin, 73, 122, 124, 126, 830
Baruch, Bernard, 73–74, 74 (image)

Battle fatigue, 74–75
Battleships, 622, 623
Bazookas, 75–76, 75 (image)
Beard, Mary R., 966
Beauchamp, Charles E., 825
Bebler, Ales, 76–77
Becker, Richard S., 2
"Bed-Check Charlies," 77
Belgium, 77–79, 78 (image), 203
Belov, Ivan, 796
Bendetsen, Karl Robin, 79
Berendsen, Carl August, 79–80
Betance-Ramiriz, Carlos, 403
Bettinger, Stephen L., 5
Bevan, Aneurin, 80–81, 81 (image)
Bevin, Ernest, 64, 81–83, 82 (image), 199–200
BIG SWITCH, Operation, 230, 514–516, 515
      (image)
Biological warfare, 83–84
BLACKLIST, Operation, 844
Blacklists, 84–86, 85 (image)
  and the Hollywood community, 84–85
  and the Waldorf Statement, 85
  See also House Un-American Activities
      Committee (HUAC)
Blair, Clay, 39
Blair House meetings, 86–87
Blesse, Frederick C., 3–4
Bloody Ridge, Battle of, 87–88, 88 (image)
  casualties of, 745
BLUEHEARTS, Operation, 88–89
Blunt, Anthony, 108, 109
Boatner, Haydon Lemaire, 89–90, 191, 426,
      696–697, 986
Bohlen, Charles Eustis, 90–91, 90 (image), 97,
      213 (image), 216, 558, 633
Bolt, John F., 5
Bolté, Charles Lawrence, 91–92, 748
Bond, Niles W., 92
Bonesteel, Charles H., 452, 844
Bonnet, Henri, 92–93, 93 (image)
Bordelon, Gary, 5
Border clashes, 93–94
Bowen, Frank S., Jr., 21, 601, 819, 820
Bowles, Chester Bliss, 94–95, 95 (image), 626
Bowling Alley, 95–96
Bradley, Omar Nelson, 61, 86, 96–97, 96
      (image), 256, 287, 355, 386, 402, 532, 546,
      748, 864, 948
Bradley, Sladen, 611
Bradley-Bohlen mission to Korea, 97–98
Brainwashing, 98–99, 99 (image)
Brereton, Lewis, 527, 941
Bricker, John William, 99–100
Bricker Amendment, 1319–1320
Bridgeford, William, 100–101
Bridges, Henry Styles, 101–102, 101 (image),
      149
Briggs, Ellis Ormsbee, 102, 737
Briscoe, Robert Pierce, 102–103, 427, 621
BROILER, Operation, 644
Brown, Russell, 23

Brownell, Herbert, 256
Broz, Josip (Marshall Tito), 76, 199
Brumbaugh, Thoburn T., 181
Brussels Pact, 201
Bryan, Blackshear M., 330 (image)
Bucher, Lloyd M., 702, 703
Budenz, Louis F., 870–871
"Bug-out fever," **103**
Bunker Hill, Battle of, **103–104**
Burchett, Wilfred, 563
Burgess, Guy, 108, 108 (image), 109
Burke, Arleigh Albert, **104–105,** 104 (image),
    116, 394, 738
Burns, John J., 194
Bush, George W., 436
Buskirk, Kryder van, 592
Buttelmann, Henry, 5
Byrnes, James, 200, 212

Cairncross, John, 108, 109
Cairo Declaration, **107–108**
Cambridge Five, **108–109,** 108 (image)
Campbell, Archibald, **109–110**
Canada, **110–112,** 111 (image), 673–674,
    805–806
    casualties of in the Korean War, 112
Capehart, Homer, 291, 365
Carlson, Harold G., 923
Carne, James P., 287, 288
Carroll, George M., 129
Carter, Jimmy, 381, 461, 936
Cassels, Archibald, 954, 955
Cassels, James, **112**
Casualties, **112–115,** 113 (image), 114 (table),
    459, 564
    among POWs, 113
    Canadian, 112
    Chinese, 114–15
    difficulty in assessing total number of, 114
    North Korean, 114
    United Nations Command (UNC), 114
    U.S., 113, 114 (table)
Cates, Clifton Bledsoe, **115,** 124, 786, 787, 914
Cease-fire negotiations, **115–117**
    members of the ceasefire delegation, 116
    propaganda conflicts during, 116–117
Censorship, and the Korean War, **117–118,** 117
    (image)
Central Intelligence Agency (CIA), **118–119,**
    211, 272, 583, 595, 613, 617, 788, 943
    covert operations of in North Korea, 584
    failures of in Korea, 118–119
    founding of the Congress for Cultural
        Freedom, 811
    report on Chinese intervention in Korea,
        1222–1224**Doc.**
    report on desirability of complete UN
        conquest of Korea, 1184–1186**Doc.**
    report on North Korean armed forces'
        capabilities, 1158–1163**Doc.**
    report on Soviet intentions concerning Korea,
        1249–1250**Doc.**

report on U.S. position concerning
    Communist China, 1264–1267**Doc.**
Chae Pyong Dok, 12, **119–120,** 417, 771, 987
Chai Chengwen, **120,** 980
Chambers, Whitaker, 261
Chandler, Dan F., 586 (image)
Chang, John, 300, 416 (image)
Chang Myon, **120–121,** 472
Chang Qiankun, 143
Chang Pyong San, 394
Chang Taek Sang, **121–122**
Changjin Reservoir Campaign, **122–128,** 123
    (map), 125 (image), 127 (image), 157, 159,
    308, 344, 530, 917 (map)
    casualties of, 127–128
    Chinese counterattack, 126
    redirection of X Corps' attack, 125
    retreat of Task Force Faith during, 126, 917
        (map)
    role of the weather in, 124
Chaplains, **128–129,** 129 (image)
Chauvel, Jean Michel Henri, **129–130,** 797
Check, Gilbert, 297
Cheju-do Chinese prisoner of war uprising,
    130–131
Cheju-do Rebellion, **131–132,** 305, 994
Chemical warfare, **133**
Chen Yi, **133–135,** 134 (image)
Chennault, Claire, 149
Chiang Kai-shek. *See* Jiang Jieshi
Chicago Defender, 18
China. *See* People's Republic of China
China Hands, **148–149,** 776
China Lobby, the, 8, **149–150, 226.** 227,
    379–378, 557
Chinese Civil War, 136, 140, 142, 143, **150–152,**
    150 (image), 154, 380
    initial clashes, 150–151
Chinese Communist Party (CCP), 150–151, 281,
    282, 418, 431, 541
    collaboration of with the Guomindang
        (GMD), 151
    membership figures for, 151
Chinese People's Volunteer Air Force (CPVAF
    [Chinese Communist Air Force]), 438
Chinese People's Volunteer Army (CPVA
    [Chinese Army]), 20–21, 34, 47, 91, 122,
    141–142, 147, 150, **165–166,** 181, 204,
    281, 287–288, 293, 308, 344, 350, 365, 381,
    391–392, 458, 494, 581, 583–584, 631, 632,
    757, 884, 951, 956–957
    capture of Kimpo Airfield , 420
    casualties suffered by, 939
    disengagement of from North Korea,
        155–157
    Fifteenth Army, 717, 848
    Fiftieth Army, 10, 160, 166
    Forty-second Army, 160, 166
    Forty-seventh Army, 78
    Fourth Field Army, 882
    and human wave attacks, **343–344**
    logistics of, 521–522, 633

Logistics Department of, 334
    Ninth Army, 128, 156, 157, 159, 632
    role of women in, 971
    Sixty-sixth Army, 160, 166
    Sixty-third Army, 162
    Third Field Army, 159
    Thirteenth Army, 156, 157, 174
    Thirty-eighth Army, 160, 166, 957
    Thirty-ninth Army, 160, 166, 403
    Twenty-seventh Army, 159
    weaknesses of, 155
    See also Kaesong truce talks; People's
        Republic of China (PRC), major offensives
        of against the United Nations Command
        (UNC); Truce talks
Ching, Cyrus, 690
Chipyong-ni, Battle of, **166–168,** 167 (image),
    280
    casualties of, 168 (table)
Chistiakov, Ivan, 176
Cho Kyu Ha, 463
Cho Man Sik, **169,** 176, 430, 790
Cho Pyong Ok, **169–170**
Choe Chang Ik, 989
Choe Kyu Ha, 461
Choe Sok, 830
Choe Tok Sin, **170–171**
Choe Yong Gon, **171,** 176, 177
Choe Yongjin, 986
Chondogyo movement, **171–172**
Chong Il Kwon, **172–173,** 173 (image), 985
Chongchon River, **173**
Chongchon River, Battle of, **174,** 175 (map), **176**
Chosin Reservoir Campaign. *See* Changjin
    Reservoir Campaign
Choson Democratic Party, **176–177**
CHROMITE, Operation. *See* Inchon Landing
    (Operation CHROMITE)
Chubb, O. Edmund, 669
Chun Doo Hwan, 461
Chunchon, Battle of, **177–178**
Church, John H., 11 (image), 12, **178–179,** 609,
    771
    survey mission of to Korea, 179
Churches, and the Korean War (Korean
    churches), **179–180**
Churches, and the Korean War (U.S. churches),
    181–182
    church interests in Korea prior to the war,
        181
Churchill, Winston, 36, 37, **182–184,** 183
    (image), 199, 200, 252, 311, 451, 878, 879
    initial support of Attlee's decision to support
        UN action in Korea, 183–184
    political career of, 182–183
    as prime minister during World War II, 183
    support of UN actions in defense of South
        Korea, 184
    See also Potsdam Conference
Cinema. *See* Film, and the Korean War
Civil defense, in the United States, **184–186,** 185
    (image)

Civil liberties, in the United States, **186–187**
Civilian internees, **187–189**
Clainos, Peter, 486
CLAM-UP, Operation, **189–190,** 189 (image)
Clark, Joseph James, **190,** 427, 621
Clark, Mark, 36–37, 43, 100, 165, **191–192,** 191
    (image), 221, 241, 246, 253, 256, 268, 392,
    427, 469, 480, 595, 696, 697, 737, 743, 820,
    821, 848, 853, 887, 905, 956
  conflicts of with Syngman Rhee, 191
  crackdown of on POW uprisings, 191, 426
  establishment of the Northern Limitation
    Line (NLL), 642
  See also SMACK, Operation
Clay, Lucius, 201
CLEANUP I and CLEANUP II, Operations, **192–193**
Clifford, Clark, 260, 261
Clooney, Rosemary, 604 (image)
Close air support (CAS), **193–195,** 194 (image),
    195 (image), 795, 816, 924, 940, 942, 956
  criticism of, 194–195
Clubb, Oliver Edmund, 149, **195–196,** 384
Cold War, 367, 423, 432, 462, 470, 483, 496, 547,
    634, 855, 861
  as impetus to the growth of the military-
    industrial complex, 582
Cold War, origins of (to 1950), **197–203,** 198
    (image), 200 (image), 202 (image), 930,
    937
  and the Berlin Crisis, 201
  containment policy of the United States
    toward the Soviet Union, 201, **213–215**
  geographical concerns, 197
  Germany as the ideological/political center of,
    199
  ideological concerns, 197
  and nuclear weapons, 198
Collins, J. Lawton, 44, 165, **203–204,** 203
    (image), 206 (image), 354, 386, 532, 546,
    607, 778, 911
  discussions with Hoyt Vandenberg in Tokyo,
    203, **206–207**
  as "Lightning Joe," 203
  policy recommendations of concerning
    Korea, 204
  support for use of the atomic bomb in Korea,
    204
  visit to Tokyo with Forrest Sherman,
    205–206, 206 (image)
  visit to Tokyo with Hoyt Vandenberg,
    207–208
Colombia, **208–210,** 209 (image)
  legacy of the Korean War in, 209–10
  as only Latin American country to participate
    in the Korean War, 209, 496
Colson, Charles F., 191
  prisoner of war incident, **240–241,** 426
COMMANDO, Operation, **210,** 329
Committee Against Jim Crow in Military Service
    and Training, 17
Committee on the Present Danger, **210–211,**
    634–635, 943

Communist Information Bureau (Cominform),
    201
Conant, James B., 211, 943
Condron, Andrew, 230
Conference on European Economic Cooperation
    (CEEC), 279, 298
Congress for Cultural Freedom, 811
Connally, Thomas Terry, **211–212**
Connolly, Richard L., 630
Connor, Ollie, 654
Containment, 201–202, **212–214,** 213 (image)
Controlled Materials Plan (CMP), **214,** 362, 862,
    964
Cordero, Juan C., 403, 404
Cordier, Andrew Wellington, **214–215,** 215
    (image)
Corrigan, Frank, 216
Cory, Thomas J., **216–217**
Coulter, John Breitling, 9, **218–219**
  reputation for poor strategic leadership,
    217
Council for Mutual Economic Assistance
    (Comecon), 201
Counter-Intelligence Program (COINTELPRO),
    187
COURAGEOUS, Operation, 22, **218–219,** 219
    (image), 601
Cox, Archibald, 654
Crahay, A., 77
Craig, Gordon M., 726
Craigie, Lawrence C., 116, 394
Creighton, Richard D., 2
Cuba, 348, 810
Cutler, Robert, **219–220**
Czechoslovakia, 201, 242

Dam raids, **221–223,** 222 (image)
Dame, Hartley F., 694
Dasher, Charles L., Jr., 404
DAUNTLESS, Operation, **223,** 329, 350
Davidson, Garrison Holt, **223, 225,** 225 (image)
Davidson Line, 223, **225–226**
Davies, Albert C., 403, 404
Davies, John Paton, 149, **226–227,** 384, 555,
    558, 634
Davis, George A., 2
De Gaulle, Charles, 198
Dean, Arthur Hobson, **227–228,** 227 (image)
Dean, William Frishe, **228–229,** 228 (image),
    493, 562, 641, 825, 835
  personal bravery of, 229
DeChow, George, 297
Defectors, **229–230,** 229 (image)
Defense Advisory Committee on Women in the
    Services (DACOWITS), 968
Defense Production Act, **230–231,**
    1197–1205**Doc.**
Defense Production Administration (DPA),
    362, 862
  women in, **964**
Demilitarized Zone (DMZ), **231–232,** 232
    (image), 395, 411, 643, 698, 944

Democratic National Party (DNP [South
    Korea]), **233–234**
Democratic Party (United States), 17, 212,
    234–236, 235 (image), 257–258, 261–262,
    291, 428, 861, 943, 948
Demographics, Korean, **236–238,** 237 (image),
    238 (image)
Denfield, Louis E., 737
Deng Hua, 116, 141, 166, **238–239,** 394, 502, 979
Deng Xiaoping, 138–139, 282
Dern, George H., 718
Detachment 2, **239–240**
Dewey, Thomas E., 382, 734
Dies, Martin, 557
Dirksen, Everett, 260
DiSalle, Michael V., 690
Dodd, Francis T., 89, 191, 426, 986
Dodd-Colson prisoner of war incident, **240–241,**
    426, 696, 698
Donahue, Alphonsus, 18
Donato, Napoleon L., 736
Donovan, William J., 211
Douglas, Helen Gahagan, 339
Douglas, Paul, 257
Doyle, James Henry, 39, **241–243,** 242 (image),
    345, 354, 356, 830, 974, 975
Draft. *See* Selective Service
Drumright, Everett Francis, **243–244**
Drysdale, Douglas S., 127
Du Ping, 166, **244–245**
Dulaney, Robert L., 404
Dulles, John Foster, 60, 61, 66, 86, 121, 148, 227,
    245–247, 245 (image), 252, 251, 255, 283,
    392, 743, 750, 794, 827
  conservation with Prime Minister Nehru,
    1349–1350**Doc.**
  correspondence with Syngman Rhee,
    1351–1357**Doc.**
  friendship of with Kim Sae Sun, 416
  and the massive retaliation doctrine, 55
  as special ambassador to Japan, 375–376
  speech to the Republican Party,
    1346–1347**Doc.**
  trip to Korea, **247**
Durbrow, Eldridge, 216

Eckersley, T. W., 681 (image)
Economic Cooperation Administration (ECA),
    549, 885
Economic Stabilization Agency (ESA), **249,** 690,
    862
Eden, Robert Anthony, **250–251,** 250 (image),
    265, 279, 283, 516, 849, 878
Edwards, Bob, 244
Eekhout, W. D. H., 627
Egypt, 145
Eighth Army in Korea, U.S. (EUSAK), 21, 22,
    103, 116, 122, 125–126, 128, 156, 161, 162,
    163, 164, 174, 188, 204, 206, 217, **251–253,**
    252 (image), 329, 332, 344, 350, 355, 363,
    397, 399, 403, 427, 448, 495, 530, 583, 642,
    672, 686, 727, 766, 768, 787, 801, 820, 830,

834, 836–837, 860, 933, 939, 948, 951,
956–957, 969, 996
crossing of the 38th Parallel by, 252–253
divisional components of, 252
employment of ranger companies by,
911–912
letter to the men of from General Ridgway,
1270–1271**Doc.**
numerical strength of, 251–252
as primary command and control
headquarters, 905
shortage of divisional strength in, 270
shortage of equipment in, 270
tactical propaganda unit of, 700–701
See also "Meat Grinder" strategy; Pusan;
Pusan perimeter and breakout;
Eisenhower, Dwight D., 42, 60, 148, 192, 204,
211, 213, 220, 221, 246, **253–255,** 258
(image), 291, 380, 392, 471, 531, 576, 595,
617, 634, 645, 684, 699, 712, 720, 733, 734,
743, 810, 835, 857, 879, 904, 934, 943
annual message to Congress (1953),
1324–1333**Doc.**
armistice radio address to the American
people, 1368–1369**Doc.**
determination of to end the Korean War, 934
development of his Korean policy after trip to
Korea, **255–257,** 256 (image)
failure to defend George Marshall from
attacks by McCarthy, 556
letter to Syngman Rhee, 1350–1351**Doc.**
and the military-industrial complex, 581–582
political career of, 254
service of in World War II, 253
threats of to use atomic weapons, 854
Truman-Eisenhower transition meeting, **859**
Elections
U.S. midterm (1950), **258–260,** 259 (image)
U.S. presidential (1952), **257–258,** 428
Elliott, Nichols, 108, 109
Elsey, George McKee, **260–261**
Emmons, Arthur B., III, **261,** 952
English, William C., 404
Entezam, Nasrollah, **262,** 262 (image), 895
Ethiopia, **263–264,** 263 (image)
European Coal and Steel Community (ECSC),
277, 766
European Defense Community (EDC), **264–265,**
277, 286, 681, 766
European Union (EU), 277
Exe, Dwight, 901 (image)
EVERREADY, Operation, **265**

Fahy, Charles, 18
Faith, Don C., 126
Fallout shelters, **267–268,** 267 (image)
Far East Air Force (FEAF), **268–269,** 301, 494,
613, 672, 763–764, 796, 812, 813, 814, 815,
820, 821, 904, 955
21st Troop Carrier Squadron, 820
315th Air Division, 736
324th Troop Carrier Squadron, 820

use of napalm by, 614, 615
Far East Command (FEC), **269–271,** 270
(image), 341, 564, 583, 592, 697, 813, 905,
932
lack of training and supplies in, 270–271
numerical strength of, 269–270
Public Information Office of, 563
Far East Economic Assistance Act,
1123–1124**Doc.**
Febiger, John C., 928
Fechteler, William Morrow, **271,** 386
Federal Bureau of Investigation (FBI), 187
Federal Civil Defense Administration (FCDA),
185
Ferguson, Homer, 291, 365
Fernandez, Manuel J., 4
Film, and the Korean War, **271–274,** 272
(image)
Chinese films concerning, 849
introduction to U.S. films concerning,
271–272
Korean films concerning, 273–274
U.S. films concerning (1950–1959), 272–273
U.S. films concerning (1960–1970), 273
U.S. films concerning (1970–present), 273
Finletter, Thomas Knight, **274–275,** 275
(image), 659, 870, 902
Fisher, Adrian F., 532
Fisher, Harold E., Jr., 4
Fisher, Henry, 297
Fitzgerald, Maurice J., 695
Flanders, Ralph E., 557
Ford, Gerald R., 936
Foreign Affairs, "X" article of, 213–214
Foreign Assistance Act (1948), 200
Formosa, 145, 148, 254, 405. *See also* Republic of
China (ROC [Taiwan])
Forrestal, James V., 18, 383, 616, 738
Forward air controllers, **275–276**
Foster, Cecil G., 4
Foster, William Zebulon, 42, **276–277**
Fox, Victor, 63
France, 145, 199, 201, 264–265, **277–278,** 277
(table), 278 (image), 359
and the Indochina War, 359–361
Korea Battalion of, 277, 306
legacy of Korean War on French military
efforts in Indochina, 277–278
public opinion concerning the Korean War,
278
See also Tripartite Meetings
Franks, Oliver, **278–280**
friendship with Acheson, 279
Freeman, Paul LaMarch, Jr., 167–168, 174, **280,**
328
Frelinghuysen, Frederick T., 929
Friedan, Betty, 966
Fry, James C., 256 (image)

Gabreski, Francis S., 3
Gao Gang, **281–282**
Garrison, Vermont L., 4

Garvin, Crump, 768
Gay, Hobart Raymond, **282–283**
Geneva Conference, **283–285,** 284 (image), 712
Geneva Convention, **285,** 732
George, David Lloyd, 182
Germany, 200–201, 680–681
Germany, Federal Republic of (FRG [West
Germany]), **286–287,** 286 (image)
Gibson, Ralph D., 2
Gillespie, Dizzy, 605 (image)
Glenn, John, 924
Gloucester Hill, Battle of, **287–288**
Gómez, Laureano, 209
Gorbachev, Mikhail, 435
Gosnell, Johnnie, 35 (image)
Gouzenko, Igor, 108
Graham, William Franklin, 180, **288–289**
Granger, Lester, 18
Graves registration, **289–290**
Gray, Gordon, 18
Great Britain. *See* United Kingdom
Great Debate, **290–291,** 365, 734
Greece, 76, 199, 212, **291–292,** 858
bravery of its troops fighting in Korea, 292
Green, William, 653
Greene, J. Woodhall, 699
Grenades, **292–293,** 293 (image)
Grew, Joseph C., 844
Gromyko, Andrei, **293–294,** 505, 807
Gromyko-Roshchin telegram, 1252**Doc.**

Gromyko-Tunkin telegram, 1110–1111**Doc.**
Gross, Ernest Arnold, **294–295,** 294 (image)
Gross, H. R., 365
Guerrero, Gilbert, 88 (image)
Guo Moruo, **295**
Guomindang (GMD), 135–136, 143, 148, 149,
150, 226, 254, 379, 388, 413, 483, 505, 579,
739, 788, 795, 804, 922, 1000
corruption within, 149, 151
social policies of, 810
See also Chinese Civil War
Gwinn, Ralph W., 365

Hagerstram, James P., 4
Hallaren, Mary A., 969
Haman Breakthrough, **297–298**
Hammarskjöld, Dag, 215, 218, **298–299,** 299
(image)
Han Kyong Jik, **299–300**
Han Pyo Uk, **300–301**
Han River operations, **301–302**
Han Tong Sok, 424
Han Xianchu, 166
Harriman, William Averell, **302–303,** 302
(image), 546, 864
Harrison, William Kelly, Jr., 46 (image),
303–304, 611, 851
Hartley, Fred A., 829
Hartnett, Richard J., 736
Harvey, Laurence, 272 (image)
Hausman, James Henry, **304–305**

HAWK, Landing Plan, 22
Haynes, Loyal, 610
Heartbreak Ridge, Battle of, 87, **305–307**, 306
       (image), 307 (image)
   casualties of, 306–307, 745
Heileman, Frank A., 653
Helicopters, employment of, **307–309**, 309
       (image), 814
   drawbacks and limitations of helicopters,
       308–309
   rescuing of downed airmen, 308, 309 (image)
   transportation of wounded soldiers, 308
Helicopters, types of, **309–311**, 310 (image), 311
       (table)
   Bell Model 47 H-13 Sioux, 308, 309–310
   Hiller H-23 Raven, 308, 310
   Sikorsky H-5/HO3S-1, 15, 16 (image), 30, 308
   Sikorsky H-19 Chickasaw, 308, 311
   Sikorsky HRS-2 Chickasaw, 310 (image), 520
       (image)
   Sikorsky R-4B, 308
   Sikorsky R-5 (H-5), 311
   Sikorsky R-6 Hoverfly, 310–311
   Sikorsky S-55, 311
   United Nations Command (UNC) helicopters,
       29–30
Henderson, Loy Wesley, **311–312**
Henebry, John P., 813
Herren, Thomas W., 487
Hershey, Lewis Blaine, **312–313**
Hess, Dean Elmer, **313–314**
Hickerson, John Dewey, **314–315**, 314 (image)
Hickey, Doyle Overton, 205, **315**, 341
Higgins, Marguerite, 117 (image), **315–316**, 966
Hill, Arthur M., 618 (image), 619
Hill, John G., 609, 841
Hillenkoetter, Roscoe H., 119, 345, 618 (image)
Hiss, Alger, 8, 86, 258, 261, **316–317**, 317
       (image), 555, 758
Hitler, Adolf, 86
Ho Ka I, **325–326**
Hodes, Henry, 105, 116, **326**, 394
Hodge, John Reed, 217, **326–327**, 414, 452, 453,
       455, 457, 528, 739, 844, 958
   statement concerning aims of the United
       States regarding Korea, 1080–1081**Doc.**
Hodges, Courtney, 402
Hoengsong, Battle of, **328–329**, 328 (image)
Hoeryong Military Academy, 1
Hoffman, Paul, 549
Hoge, William Morris, **329–330**, 330 (image),
       746, 911–912
Hollywood Ten, 85, 85 (image), **330–331**
Home-by-Christmas Offensive, **331–333**, 332
       (image)
   casualties of, 332
Hong Chol, 986
Hong Jung Shik, 462 (image)
Hong Kong, 142, **333–334**, 333 (image)
Hong Xuezhi, 166, **334–335**
Hook, Battles of the, **335–336**, 335 (image)
Hoover, Herbert, 234, 291, 365

Gibraltar America address, 1259–1262**Doc.**
Hope, Bob, 974 (image)
Hope, Clifford, 291
Hope, Leslie Townes, **336**
Hospital ships, **336–338**, 337 (image)
House Un-American Activities Committee
       (HUAC), 85, 196, 272, 330–331, **338–340**,
       339 (image), 557, 859, 901
Housewives United, **340**
Hua Guofeng, 138–139
HUDSON HARBOR, Exercise, **341–342**, 645
Hughes, Charles E., 930
Hull, John Edwin, **342–343**, 343 (image)
Human wave attacks, **343–344**
Humphrey, Hubert, 17
Hungnam, **344**
Hungnam evacuation, **344–347**, 345 (image),
       346 (image)
Hutchin, Claire, 451–452
Huynh Cong Ut, 11
Hwachon Dam, attack on, 923–924
Hydrogen bomb, **347–348**, 347 (image)
Hyzer, Peter C., 609

Imjin River, **349**
Imjin River, Battle of, **349–351**, 350 (image)
Inchon Landing (Operation CHROMITE), 38, 39,
       137, 153, 203, 206, 252, 293 (image),
       351–352, 352 (image), 353 (map),
       354–359, 354 (image), 355 (image), 356
       (image), 474, 477, 530, 711, 778, 779, 796,
       816, 836, 841, 856, 951
   initial landings and advance inland, 356–359
   marine divisions and regiments involved in,
       351
   objectives of, 351–352
   opposition from MacArthur's subordinate
       commanders and the JCS, 352, 354
   planning of, 351
   Politburo protocol report (attachment 73 of
       report 78) concerning, 1209–1210**Doc.**
   problems of tidal changes and the narrowness
       of Flying Fish Channel, 352, 354
   strategic brilliance of, 351
India, **357–359**, 358 (image)
Indochina, 277–278, 284
Indochina War, impact of on Korea, **359–361**,
       360 (image)
Industrial dispersion, **362–363**
Infiltration, **363**
Internal Security Act (McCarran Act [1950]),
       363–365
International Mission Committee (IMC),
       731–732
Iran, 201, 262
Iron Triangle, **365**
Isolationism, **364–365**
Italy, 199, 265

Jabara, James, 2, 3 (image)
Jackson, Charles Douglas, **367–368**, 368
       (image), 699

Jamieson, Arthur B., 67, **368–369**
Japan, 87, 434, 450–451, **369–371**, 370 (image),
       453, 459, 807
   contribution of the Korean War to postwar
       recovery of, 369–370, **371–372**
   controversy over its trade relations with the
       PRC, 370
   impact of the Korean War on the political
       economy of, 369
   surrender of ending World War II, 689–690
   U.S. occupation of after World War II,
       372–373, 373 (image)
   See also Korea, Japanese occupation of;
       Russo-Japanese War (1904–1905); Sino-
       Japanese War (1894–1895)
Japan Logistical Command, **373–375**, 374
       (image)
Japanese Peace Treaty (1951), **375–376**, 375
       (image)
Jebb, Gladwyn, **376–379**, 880 (image)
Jessup, Philip Caryl, 201, **379–378**, 379 (image),
       558, 948
Jiang Jieshi, 7, 36, 42, 136, 139, 140, 142, 149,
       226, 254, 379, **379–381**, 379 (image), 451,
       483, 546, 660, 661, 677, 732, 739, 776, 831,
       866, 870, 931, 1000
   consolidation of political power by, 379–380
   education of, 379
   kidnapping of, 380
   offer of to send Nationalist Chinese troops to
       Korea, 380, **381–382**
   relationship of with the United States,
       380–381
   See also Chinese Civil War
Jiang Qing, 138
Jiang Tingfu. See Tsiang Ting Fu Fuller
Jiangxi Soviet Republic, 150
Johnson, James K., 4
Johnson, Louis Arthur, 18, 86, 303, **382–384**,
       382 (image), 546, 738, 842, 856, 903, 954
   opposition to sending troops to Korea, 383
   and the "revolt of the admirals," 383
Johnson, Lyndon, 173 (image), 255, 303, 601,
       634, 702–703, 836, 857
Johnson, Ural Alexis, **384–385**, 669
Johnston, Eric, 85, 690
Joint Chiefs of Staff (JCS), 60, 61, 125, 126, 203,
       204, 206, 208, 270, 351, 383, **385–386**,
       385 (image), 446, 481, 483, 530, 532, 546,
       616–617, 698, 744, 745, 787, 788, 841, 842,
       843, 857, 860
   concern of over U.S. worldwide military
       obligations, 207–208
   consideration of using nuclear weapons
       during the Korean War, 644–645
   directive outlining guidelines for General
       Ridgway, 1295–1298**Doc.**
   directive to protect Taiwan, 1266–1267**Doc.**
   report on Korea's strategic significance,
       1086–1087**Doc.**
   See also Yalu bridges controversy
Jolley, Clifford D., 3

Jones, George L., 4
Jones, Robert E., 126
Joong Ang Ilbo, 2
Jooste, Gerhardus Petrus, **386–387**
Journal of Foreign Affairs, 201
Joy, C. Turner, 20, 116, 205, 304, 345, 354, **387–388**, 387 (image), 393, 394, 394 (image), 427, 585, 620, 621, 851, 874, 905, 974
  opinion of Xie Fang, 980
Juche ideology, **388–389**, 412

K1C2 political slogan, **428–431**
Kaesong, **391**
  neutral zone controversy concerning, **392–394**, 392 (image)
  proposed bombing of, **391–392**
Kaesong truce talks, **394–397**, 394 (image), 395 (image), 396 (image)
  agenda of, 396
  establishment of the Military Demarcation Line (MDL), 395–396
  initial positions of each side, 395
Kang Kon, **397**, 707
Kang Yang Uk, 180
Kangdong Political Academy, 1
Kansas-Wyoming Line, **397**, 398 (map), **399**
Kapyong, Battle of, **399–401**, 400 (image)
Kasler, James H., 3
KATUSA Program. *See* Korean Augmentation to the United States Army (KATUSA)
Katzin, Alfred G., **401**
Kean, William Benjamin, 19, 297, **401–402**, 650, 833
Keiser, Laurence Bolton, 174, **402–403**, 403 (image), 610
Kelly, Joe W., 613
Kelly Hill, Battle of, **403–404**
  casualties of, 404
Kem, James P., 261
Kennan, George F., 90, 91, 199, 213 (image), 216, 226, 261, **404–406**, 405 (image), 630, 633
  as architect of containment policy concerning the Soviet Union, 213–214
  conversations with Kennan, **406–407**
  "Long Telegram" of, 212, 261
  "X" article of, 201, 213, 261, 404
Kennedy, John F., 226, 227, 255, 267, 303, 348, 601, 634, 639, 822, 835, 935
Kennedy, Joseph P., 291, 365, 422
Kenney, W. John, 618 (image)
Kenworthy, E. W., 18
Khrushchev, Nikita, 433, 442
KILLER, Operation, 10, 21–22, **407**, 560–561, 744
  casualties of, 407
Kim Chae Gyu, 461
Kim Chaek, **409**, 707
Kim Chong Won, **409–410**, 424, 448
  war crimes of, 952–953
Kim Chun Bae, 109
Kim Dae Jung, 436, 461, 465, 731, 936
Kim Il Sung, 1, 86, 94, 120, 137, 140, 152, 162, 176, 177, 394, **410–412**, 410 (image), 414,

418, 430, 432, 433, 433 (image), 435, 437, 438, 443–444, 454, 456, 463, 484, 594, 781, 799 (image), 800, 807, 853, 937
  attempts to join the world community, 411
  and the Choe Chang Ik incident, 989
  development of the *juche* political philosophy, 388–389, 412, 434, 435, 437, 443
  formation and administration of North Korea, 410–411
  meeting with Stalin, 1105–1106**Doc.**
  Stalin's letter to, 1103–1104**Doc.**
  as the *suryong* (great or maximum leader), 434
  telegram to Stalin, 1211–1212**Doc.**
Kim Jong Il, 388, **412–413**, 435, 436, 464, 937
Kim Ku, **413–414**, 432, 489, 491, 958
Kim Kwang Hyop, 177
Kim Kyu Sik, **414–415**, 432, 491, 992
Kim Mu Chong. *See* Mu Chong
Kim Myong Ho, 1
Kim Paek Il, **415**, 771, 830
Kim Sae Sun, **415–416**, 18 (image)
  friendship of with John Foster Dulles, 416
Kim Sok Won, **416–417**
Kim Song Ju. *See* Kim Il Sung
Kim Song Su, **417–418**, 790
Kim Tu Bong, 176, **418**
Kim Ung, **418–419**
  as commander of I Corps (KPA), 419
Kim Yong Ju, 109
Kim Young Sam, 936
Kim Yun Gun, 476
Kimpo Airfield, 216, **419–420**, 419 (image), 774, 820, 868
Kincheloe, Ivan C., 3
King Young Sam, 435, 461, 463
Kingsley, John Donald, **420–421**, 896
Kinkaid, Thomas C., 958
Kinsler, Francis, 421
Kirk, Alan Goodrich, 293, **421–422**, 807
Knowland, William F., 149, **422–424**, 423 (image)
  criticism of the Truman administration, 423
  hawkish stance toward North Korea, 423
Kochang incident, **424**
Kohlberg, Alfred, 149, 379–378
Koje-do, **424–425**
Koje-do prisoner of war uprising, **425–427**, 425 (image), 426 (image)
Kojo amphibious feint, **427–428**
Kojong (King Kojong), 929, 930
Korea, Democratic People's Republic of (DPRK [North Korea]), 1, 8, 9, 93, 279, 281, 305, 338, 349, 263, 365, 397, **430–432**, 431 (image), 457, 463, 593–594, 682, 800, 955
  Chinese economic and military aid to, **152–153**, 152 (image)
  Communist Party political power struggles in, 432–433
  economic expansion of, 435
  formal establishment of, 433

invasion of the Republic of Korea, **443–446**, **641–642**
  lack of combat aircraft in, 12
  number of casualties in the Korean War, 411
  occupation directive concerning, 1129–1132**Doc.**
  occupation of the Republic of Korea, **478–480**, 479 (image)
  original plans to invade South Korea, 177
  prevailing ideology in (*juche* ideology), **388–389**, 412, 434–435, 436, 437, 442, 443
  Stalin's support of communist state in, 431
  United Nations Command (UNC) occupation of, **446–448**, 447 (image)
Korea, Democratic People's Republic of (DPRK [North Korea]), from 1952–to present, **434–438**, 435 (image)
  destruction of economic and industrial base due to the Korean War, 411, 434, 442
  economic aid to, 434
  economic plans of (five-year; six-year; seven-year), 434, 435, 436
  nuclear program of, 435–437
  political factions within, 434
  relations with the West, 437
  support of for the PRC in the Sino-Soviet split, 434–435
  See also *Pueblo* incident
Korea, Democratic People's Republic of (DPRK [North Korea]), Air Force of. *See* Korean People's Air Force (KPAF)
Korea, Democratic People's Republic of (DPRK [North Korea]), Army of. *See* Korean People's Army
Korea, Democratic People's Republic of (DPRK [North Korea]), economy of, **441–443**, 442 (image)
  benefit of foreign aid to, 441
  decline in foreign aid, 442
  destruction of economic and industrial base due to the Korean War, 411, 432, 441
  isolation of from the rest of the world, 443
  and the *juche* philosophy, 442, 443
Korea, Democratic People's Republic of (DPRK [North Korea]), Navy of. *See* Korean People's Navy
Korea, history of (to 1945), **448–451**
  beginnings of communism in, 451
  Mongol period of, 449
  revolt of against the Japanese, 450–451
  under Chinese rule, 449
  under Japanese rule, 450, **456–458**
Korea, history of (1945–1947), **451–455**, 453 (image)
  arrival of U.S. troops in, 453–454
  determination of the line of demarcation, 452
  governing of Korea by the U.S.-Soviet Joint Commission , 453–455
  growing influence of communism in, 454
  political activity during, 452–453
Korea, Japanese occupation of, 451, **455–456**
  phases of, 456

Korea, strategic significance of, 1014–1015**Doc.**
Korea Aid Bill (1947), **482–483**
Korea Aid Bill (1950), **483–484**
Korea Workers' Party (KWP), 432, 434, 436, 478
Korean Advisory Council, 454
Korean Augmentation Troop Commonwealth (KATCOM), 955
Korean Augmentation to the United States Army (KATUSA), 467, 469, **485–487**, 486 (image), 907–908, 955
Korean Communications Zone (KCOMZ), **487**
Korean Democratic Party (KDP), 452, 459, **487–489**, 488 (image), 491, 739
Korean Independence Party (KIP), **489–490**
Korean Military Advisory Group (KMAG), 109, 179, 301, 305, 453–454, 466, **484–485**, 485 (image), 748, 759, 783, 905, 930, 931, 993
Korean Peninsula, climate, geography, and topography of, **193–194, 481–482**
Korean People's Air Force (KPAF), 77, 420, **437–438,** 770, 815
  aircraft of, 437–438
  fighter aircraft specifications (North Korean and Chinese), 437 (table)
  personnel of, 437
Korean People's Army (KPA [North Korean Army]), 9, 12, 20–21, 47, 93, 94, 163, 166, 177, 180, 181, 203, 206, 297–298, 363, 391–392, 402, 417, 424, **438–441,** 439 (image), 444–446, 457, 478–480, 581, 584, 811, 816, 880, 950, 951, 952, 986
  divisional strength and organization of, 439–440, 468, 790
  I Corps, 22, 177, 419, 440
  II Corps, 10, 161, 177, 440, 441
  III Corps, 440, 441
  number of divisions in Manchuria, 440
  operations along the Han River, 301–302
  regimental organization of, 441
  reserve units of, 442
  strength of, 440 (table), 441, 441, 444 (table), 445
  tanks of, 441
  V Corps, 10, 161, 440
  VI Corps, 440, 441
  VII Corps, 440, 441
  VIII Corps, 440, 441
  See also Kaesong truce talks; Truce talks
Korean People's Navy (KPN), **446**
Korean People's Republic (KPR), 452, 453, 739
Korean Provisional Government (KPG), 40, **490–491,** 991
Korean Service Corps (KSC), **472,** 473 (image), **474,** 475
Korean War, historiography of, **317–326**
  and the aftermath/legacy of the war, 325
  and the Allied political and military role, 323
  causes of the war, 318–319
  history of logistics and coalition warfare, 322–323
  history of the Soviet Union's role in, 324
  history of special operations, 323–324

history of U.S./South Korean military relations, 320–321
  Korean historians' view of the war, 320
  literature concerning the performance of the armed forces, 321–322
  prominent books concerning, 317–318
  U.S. politics concerning, 319–320
Korean War, logistics of, **518–523,** 519 (image), 520 (image), 521 (image)
  of the CPVA, 521–522
  impact of climate and terrain on, 518
  ordnance rebuild program, 520
  total cost of the Korean War, 520–521
  United Nations Command (UNC) logistics, 518–521
Korean War Veterans Memorial, **491–493,** 492 (image)
Korean Workers' Party (KWP), 441, 454, 802
Korei, Phillip, 755 (image)
Kouma, Ernest R., 610
Kum River, Battle of, **493**
Kung, H. H., 149
Kunu-ri, Battle of, **493–494**

Labor organizations. *See* Organized labor
Lampe, James S., **495–496**
Larsen, Emmanuel, 871
Latin America, **496–497**
Latshaw, Robert T., Jr., 3
Lattimore, Owen, 149, **497–498,** 498 (image), 870–871
Lay, James S., **498–499**
Lee Chang Chan, 481
Lee Myung Bak, 464, **499–501,** 500 (image)
LeMay, Curtis, 341, 904, 942
Lemnitzer, Lyman Louis, **591**
Lenin, Vladimir Ilyich, 799, 991
Leviero, Anthony Harry, **503–502**
Lewis, John L., 653
Li Hung Chang, 929
Li Kenong, **502–503**
Li Lisan, 295
Liberal Party, **503–504**
Lie, Trygve Halvden, 21, 145, 215, **504–506,** 504 (image), 573, 892, 893, 896, 901
  statement to the United Nations Security Council, 1164–1165**Doc.**
Lightner, Edwin Allan, Jr., **506**
Lilienthal, David, 62 (image)
Lilley, Leonard W., 4
Limb, Ben C., **506–507**
Lin Biao, 134, 137, **507–508,** 507 (image), 979
Lippman, Walter, **508–509**
Literature, of the Korean War (Korean), **509–511,** 509 (image)
Literature, of the Korean War (United States), **511–514,** 513 (image)
  novels, 512–514
  poetry, 511
  short fiction and drama, 511–512
Little Switch, Operation, 230, 285, **514–516,** 514 (image), 515 (image), 733, 853

Litzenberg, Homer, 124
Liu Shaoqi, 138
Liu Yalou, 143
Lloyd, John Selwyn, 36, **516–517**
Lobov, Georgii, 796
Lockett, Thomas H., 677
Lodge, Henry Cabot, Jr., 219, **517,** 870, 880 (image)
Long March, 150, 418, 542
"Long Telegram," the, 212, 261
Lord, Mrs. Oswald, 968
Love, Robert J., 3
Lovett, Robert Abercrombie, 211, 213 (image), **523–524,** 523 (image), 546, 547, 869, 943
Low, Frederick F., 928
Low, John F., 3
Low-Rodgers expedition, 928–929
Lowe, Frank E., **524–525**
Lucas, Scott W., 260
Lucas, Wingate, 261, 291, 365
Luce, Henry R., 149
Luckman, Charles, 18
Luxembourg, 203, **525–526**

MacArthur, Douglas, 7–8, 11 (image), 12, 21, 38, 40, 69, 70, 71, 81, 110, 144, 153, 203–204, 206 (image), 268, 301, 338, 352 (image), 381, 405, 448, 452, 453, 467, 485, **527–531,** 528 (image), 546, 607, 669, 674, 719, 758–759, 768, 771, 778, 815, 819, 841, 842, 843, 868, 882, 887, 891, 900, 905, 914, 918, 933, 948 (image)
  actions during the Battle of Changjin Reservoir, 122, 124–125, 126, 128
  actions during the Home-by-Christmas Offensive, 331–333
  advice to Eisenhower on achieving victory in Korea, 531
  as advocate of bombing military bases in China, 165
  communiqué of, 1236–1237**Doc.**
  criticism of the Truman administration's war policies, 303
  deployment of MASH units by, 590–591
  and the "Die for Tie" statement, 531, 1277–1278**Doc.**
  establishment of helicopter ambulance companies by, 15
  estimation of Chinese troops in North Korea, 331
  friendship of with Courtney Whitney, 957–958
  "home by Christmas" remark of, 331
  imposition of media censorship by, 117, 118, 562
  letter to Joseph Martin, 1280**Doc.**
  mandate to cross the 38th Parallel, 446, 841–843
  memorandum on the strategic significance of Taiwan, 1155–1157**Doc.**
  military requirements of, 207

and Operation BLUEHEARTS, 88–89
opinion of Taiwan, 146
opposition of to prosecution of war criminals, 952
prediction that China would not enter the Korean War, 34, 208, 583
"Pronunciamento" of, 1280–1281**Doc.**
recapture of Seoul, 774
request of for increased troop levels, 269–270
removal of from command by Truman, 97, 116, 182, 386, 531, 546–547, 719, 828, 862–863, **863–865,** 864 (image), 1284–1285**Doc.,** 1285–1287**Doc.**
role of in X Corps, 836–837
service of in World War II, 527–528
special report of as commander of the United Nations Command (UNC), 1235–1236**Doc.**
speech to Congress, 1287–1291**Doc.**
speech to the Veterans of Foreign Wars (VFW), 1186–1187**Doc.**
statement concerning the North Korean invasion of South Korea, 1169–1170**Doc.**
support of chaplains and religious themes, 128–129
support of Taiwan, 529
as supreme commander of the Allied Powers (SCAP) in occupied Japan, 369, 372–373
surrender ultimatum to North Korea, 1215–1216**Doc.**
Truman-MacArthur Wake Island conference, 1225–1226**Doc.**
victory proposal of, 1315–1319**Doc.**
See also Inchon Landing (Operation CHROMITE); Soviet airfield incident; Wake Island Conference; Wonsan landing and evacuation; Yalu bridges controversy
MacArthur Hearings, **531–533**
Machine guns, **533–536,** 533 (image), 534 (image)
   British, 535
   Browning 1917A1, 534
   Browning 1919A4, 534
   Browning 1919A6, 534
   Browning .50-caliber, 534
   French, 535
   Japanese, 535
   M2 heavy machine gun, 534–535
   reliance of communist forces on captured machine guns, 535
   types used by U.S. and UNC forces, 532–533
   Vickers Machine Gun Mark I, 535
   World II models used in the Korean War, 531–532, 535
   See also Submachine guns
MacLean, Allan D., 126
Maclean, Donald, 108, 109
Majury, James, 64
Makin, Norman J. O., 67, **536**
Makins, Roger, **536–537**
Makoto, Saito, 456
Malan, Daniel François, 791–792
Malenkov, Georgii, **537–538,** 538 (image)

Malik, Jacob (Yakov) A., 21, 116, 145, 201, 216, 226, 293, 406, 422, 505, **538–540,** 539 (image), 797, 901
   conversations with Kennan, 406–407
   radio address of, 851, 1298–1301**Doc.**
Manchuria, 197, 207, 338, 439, **540,** 821, 843, 849
   number of Korean People's Army (KPA) divisions in, 440
Manchurian sanctuary, **540–541, 761–762,** 762 (image)
Mao Anying, 675
Mao Zedong, 134, 135–137, 136 (image), 138, 140–141, 146, 152, 153, 154, 156, 162, 281, 343, 375, 380, 388, 433, 443, 444, 502, **541–543,** 541 (image), 546, 632, 797, 831, 931, 932, 979, 1000
   decision of to intervene in the Korean War, 542, 807
   education of, 541
   "fight-talk-fight-talk" strategy of, 882
   fighting of against the Japanese, 542
   and the Great Leap Forward, 542–543
   legacy of, 543
   and the Long March, 150, 418, 542
   relationship with Peng Dehuai, 674, 675
   Stalin's treatment of, 785
   telegram to Stalin, 1218–1219**Doc.**
   telegrams to Zhou Enlai, 1224**Doc.,** 1224–1225**Doc.**
   See also Chinese Civil War
March First Movement, **543–544**
Marcos, Ferdinand, 462
Marshall, George Catlett, 20, 42, 90, 199, 201, 206, 219, 254, 380, 384, 454, 532, **544–547,** 545 (image), 616, 618 (image), 734, 787, 815, 843, 844, 856, 860, 864, 948, 968
   McCarthy's attacks on, 555, 556, 558
   relationship of with MacArthur, 546
   role of in the dismissal of MacArthur, 546–547
   service of in World War I, 545
   service of in World War II, 545
   as special envoy to China, 545–546
   See also Marshall Plan
Marshall, Samuel Lyman Atwood, **547–548,** 756
Marshall, Winton W., 2
Marshall Plan, 6, 64, 199, 212–213, 546, 547, **548–550,** 616
   legacy of, 550
   total amount of aid, 550
Martin, Harold, 621
Martin, Joseph William, **550–551,** 551 (image)
Martin, Robert, 641
Massive retaliation defense doctrine, 552
Matsotake, Terauchi, 456
Matthews, Francis Patrick, 18, **552–553,** 553 (image), 644
Matthews, Harrison Freeman, **553–554**
May, Elaine Tyler, 965
Maybank, Burnet, 291, 365
McCarran, Patrick Anthony, **554–555**

McCarthy, Joseph R., 8, 42, 86, 90, 148, 149, 187, 254, 258, 260, 330, 338–340, 363, 379, 547, **555–557,** 556 (image), 734, 758, 788, 828, 861, 870, 871, 901
   charges of Communists in the Truman administration, 555–556, 855
   charges of Communists in the U.S. State Department, 555
   extension of his investigations from the civilian to the military, 556–557
   speech on the spread of communism, 1124–1125**Doc.**
McCarthyism, 9, 42, 187, 220, 227, 363, 365, **557–558,** 734–735, 855, 871. *See also* Blacklists; Hollywood Ten; House Un-American Activities Committee (HUAC)
McCloy, John J., 287
McClure, Robert A., 328, 403, **558–559,** 559 (image), 699, 732
McConnell, Joseph, Jr., 4
McCormack, James, 630
McDowell, John, 339 (image)
McGarr, Lionel Charles, **559–560**
McGee, John, 801
McGrath, J. Howard, 428
McKnight, Preston, 161 (image)
McMahon, Brien, 532
"Meat Grinder" strategy, **560–562,** 561 (image)
Media coverage, and the Korean War, **562–564,** 563 (image)
   censorship issues, 117, 118, 562
   official news sources, 563
Medicine, military, **564–567,** 565 (image), 566 (image)
   average casualties per division per day, 564
   common battle injuries, 564
   evacuation and transportation issues, 566–567
   infectious diseases, 565
   neuropsychiatric medicine, 565
   neurosurgery, 564
   shortage of physicians during the Korean War, 567, 591, 592
   use of whole blood transfusions, 564
   vascular injuries, 565
   See also Mobile Army Surgical Hospital (MASH)
Medics, **567**
Meirowsky, Arnold, 564
Menderes, Adnan, 867
Menon, Kumara Padmanabha Sivasankara, **568**
Menon, Vengalil Krishnan Krishna, 95, 251, 516, **568–570,** 569 (image), 626, 627
Menzies, Robert Gordon, **570–571,** 570 (image), 804
Merchant, Livingston Tallmadge, 384, **571–572**
Meretskov, Kiril A., 781
Mexico, **572–573**
Meyer, Clarence Earle, **573–575,** 574 (image), 827
Meyer Mission, **575**

Michaelis, John Hersey, **575–576**

Michener, James, 513 (image)

MIG, Operation, **576**

MiG Alley, **576,** 577 (map), **578**

Milburn, Frank W., 9, 22, 204, 217, 252 (image),
   578–579, 578 (image)

Military Air Transport Service (MATS),
   579–580, 579 (image), 580 (table), 813

Military Armistice Commission (MAC),
   580–581, 629, 643

Military Armistice Commission Headquarters
   Area (MACHA), 232

Military Demarcation Line (MDL [the 38th
   Parallel]), 20, 231, 395–396, 453, 851, 882,
   884, 944
   decision of UNC forces to cross, **841–843,** 842
      (image)
   division of Korea at, **843–845**
   establishment of as the truce line after
      ceasefire negotiations, 116

Military-industrial complex, **581–583**
   Eisenhower's fear of, 581–582
   growth of in response to both the Cold and
      Korean Wars, 582

Military intelligence, **583–584**
   See also Central Intelligence Agency (CIA)

Military Sea Transport Service (MSTS),
   584–585, 585 (image), 922
   number of ships in, 584

Miller, Ferris, 454

Miller, Gerald, 297

Milward, William, 885 (image)

Mine warfare (sea), **585–588,** 586 (image)
   clearing of mines from Korea's eastern coast,
      585–586

Mines
   land mines, **588–589,** 588 (image)
   sea mines, **589–590**

Missing in Action (MIA), **590**

Missionaries (to Korea), 179–180. See also Relief
   efforts, missionary

Mo Yun Suk, 509 (image)

Mobile Army Surgical Hospital (MASH),
   590–592, 590 (image), 744

Mobilization, **592–593**

Moffett, Howard Fergus, **593**

Molotov, Viacheslav M., 199, 230, 454, 549,
   593–594, 594 (image), 879

Monclar, Ralph, **594–595**

Monnet, Jean, 681, 765

Moodie, J. W., 631

MOOLAH, Operation, **595–596,** 596 (image)

Moore, Bryant E., 329, 407, 787

Moore, Robert H., 3

Morgan, Albert C., 695

Morrison, Herbert Stanley, **596–597**

Mortars, **597–598,** 598 (image)

Moscow Agreement, 1079–1080**Doc.**

Moses, Lloyd, 848

Mu Chong, 176, **599**

Muccio, John J., 12, 243–244, 467, **599–600,**
   748, 948

Muggleburg, Glenn, 801

Munich analogy, **600–601**

Munsan-ni airborne operation, **601–602**

Murch, Gordon E., 297

Murphy, Charles Springs, **602–603,** 602 (image)

Murphy, Robert Daniel, **603–604**

Murray, Philip, 653

Murray, Raymond L., 124

Murrow, Edward R., 211, 557

Music, of the Korean War (Korean), **604–605,**
   604 (image), 605 (image)

Music, of the Korean War (United States),
   605–606

Muste, Abraham Johannes, 42, **606**

Najin, bombing of, **607–609,** 608 (image), 608
   (table)

Naktong Bulge, First Battle of, 402, **609–610**

Naktong Bulge, Second Battle of, **610–611,** 611
   (image)

Nam Il, 116, 394, **611–612,** 612 (image), 698,
   802, 854

Namsi, Battle of, **613–614**

Napalm, **614–616,** 614 (image), 615 (image)

National Emergency Declaration, **616**

National Guard (United States), 592

National Production Authority (NPA), 362
   women serving in, 964

National Security Act (1947), **616–617**

National Security Council, 220, 254, 338, 358,
   616, **617–618,** 618 (image), 630, 636, 645
   memo (NSC-20/4), 213
   Report 8 (NSC-8), 1096–1099**Doc.**
   Report 8/1 (NSC-8/1), 1104–1105**Doc.**
   Report 8/2 (NSC-8/2), 1105–1109**Doc.**
   Report 48/5 (NSC-48/5), 1292–1294**Doc.**
   Report 68 (NSC-68), 210, 213, 230, 361, **618–**
      619, 634, 861, 869–870, 1128–1155**Doc.**
   Report 76 (NSC-76), 1179**Doc.**
   Report 80 (NSC-80), 1187–1188**Doc.**
   Report 81/1 (NSC-81/1), 446, 842,
      1188–1192**Doc.**
   Report 81/2 (NSC-81/2), 1237–1238**Doc.**
   Report 92 (NSC-92), 1250–1251**Doc.**
   Report 95 (NSC-95), 1255–1256**Doc.**
   Report 101 (NSC-101), 1267–1268**Doc.**
   Report 118 (NSC-118), 1304–1306**Doc.**
   Report 147 (NSC-147), 645, 1335–1341**Doc.**
   Report 148 (NSC-148), 1342–1346**Doc.**
   Report 154/1 (NSC-154/1), 1357–1359**Doc.**
   Report 156/1 (NSC 156/1), 1364–1368**Doc.**
   Report 157/1 (NSC 157/1), 1359–1360**Doc.**

National Security Resources Board (NSRB), 185,
   362, 616, 617, **619–620,** 653, 821–822
   Truman's ambivalence toward, 619

Naval battles, **620–621**

Needham, Joseph, **624**

Nehru, Jawaharlal, 70, 95, 221, 254, 359,
   625–626, 625 (image), 840
   conversation with John Foster Dulles,
      1349–1350**Doc.**

Nelson, Donald, 960

Netherlands, the, 201, **626–627**

Neutral Nations Repatriation Commission
   (NNRC), 45, **627–629,** 853–854

Neutral Nations Supervisory Commission
   (NNSC), 44–45, **629–630,** 852

New Deal, 235, 236

New Jersey, 623, 623 (image)

New Look defense policy, **630–631**

New Zealand, 80, 376, 400, **631–632**
   casualties suffered in the Korean War, 631

Nguyen Ngoc Loan, 10

Nie Rongzhen, **632–633**

Nitze, Paul H., 210, 211, **633–635,** 634 (image),
   943

Nixon, Richard M., 42, 149, 261 (image), 260,
   339 (image), 381, 428, 517, **635–636,** 635
   (image), 822, 901
   attacks on Truman administration, 635
   and the opening of China, 138
   policy of toward Korea, 935–936
   as vice president, 635–636

No Gun Ri strafing incident, review of,
   1385–1393**Doc.**

No Name Line, Battle of, **636–637**

Noble, Harold, **637–638**

Nogun-ni railroad bridge incident, **638**

Norstad, Lauris, **638–639,** 639 (image)

North American Treaty Organization (NATO),
   64, 65, 67, 90, 201, 208, 210, 214, 252, 264,
   265, 291, 348, 359, 365, 382, 383, 616, 633,
   639–641, 640 (image), 788, 805, 849
   controversy concerning German entrance
      into, 286–287
   See also Pleven Plan

North Korea. See Korea, Democratic People's
   Republic of (DPRK [North Korea])

North Korean Democratic Party (NKDP),
   176–177

North Korean offensive, delay of, **641–642**

North Korean Workers' Party (NKWP),
   176–177, 410, 430, 432, 739–740

Northeast Border Defense Army (NBDA [later
   the Chinese People's Volunteer Army]),
   281

Northern Limitation Line (NLL), 463, **643–644**

Norway, 145

Nuclear warfare, **643–645,** 644 (image)

O Ik Gyong, 424

October Revolution, 799

O'Daniel, J. W., 210

O'Donnell, Emmet, **647–648**
   testimony at the MacArthur Hearings, 647

Office of Civil and Defense Mobilization
   (OCDM), 186

Office of Defense Mobilization (ODM), 185–186,
   362, 619, 620, 648, 690, 808, 822, 862, 964
   under the direction of Charles E. Wilson,
      960–962, 961 (image)

Office of Price Stabilization (OPS), **648–649,**
   690, 862, 961

Office of Strategic Services (OSS), 988

Old Baldy, Battle of, **649–651,** 649 (image), 650
 (image), 686
Oliver, Robert Tarbell, **651**
Oppenheimer, Robert, 61–62, 74, 347, **651–652,**
 652 (image)
Organization of American States (OAS), 496, 497
Organization for European Economic
 Cooperation (OEEC), 200
Organized labor, **652–654**
 American Federation of Labor (AFL), 72,
  652–653
 Congress of Industrial Organizations (CIO),
  72, 652–653
 United Steel Workers, 653–654
Osan, Battle of, **654–656,** 655 (image)
 casualties of, 656
 tank battle during, 654–655
Osborne, Ralph M., 836 (image)
Ouden, M. P. A. den, 627
Outpost Harry, Battle of, **656–658,** 657 (image)
Overton, Dolphin D., III, 4

Pace, Frank, Jr., **659–660,** 660 (image), 699
Pacific Pact, **660–661**
Padilla Nervo, Luis, **661–663,** 662 (image)
Paek In Yop, **663**
Paek Son Yop, 116, 394, 394 (image), 468,
 663–664, 722–723
Paek Song Uk, **664–665**
Paek Tu Jin, **665**
Pak Hon Yong, 414, 430, 432, 457, **665–666,** 781
 telegram to Stalin, 1211–1212**Doc.**
Pak Kyong Gu, 475
Pak Sang Hyon, 986
Pak Sun Chon, **666–667**
Palmer, Dwight R. G., 18
Palmerat, Charles, 167 (image)
Palmer-Johansson, Eva, 811
Pandit, Vijaya Lakshmi Nehru, **667–668,** 667
 (image)
Pang Ho San, 445, **668**
Panikkar, Sardar K. M., 70, 312, 358–359, 583,
 668–669, 1000–1001
Panmunjom Security Agreement, **669–670,**
 1301–1304**Doc.**
Park Chung Hee, 177, 301, 460–461, 472, 667,
 670–671, 934
 assassination of, 461
Parr, Ralph S., 5
Partridge, Earle Everard, 268, **671–673,** 672
 (image)
 as commander of the Far East Air Forces
  (FEAF), 672
 service of in World War II, 671–672
Patton, George, 941, 949–950
Peach, Francis S. B., 67
Pearson, Lester Bowles, 110, **673–674,** 884
Peckham, Charles L., 127
Peng Dehuai, 137, 138, 141, 156, 157, 166, 394,
 674–676, 675 (image), 851, 979
People's Army of Vietnam (PAVN, Viet Minh),
 359

People's Liberation Army (PLA [Chinese
 Communist Army]), **139–142,** 140
 (image), 141 (table), 147, 165, 166, 380,
 438, 583
 army groups of sent to Korea, 166
 reforms of, 675
 weaknesses of, 141
 See also Chinese People's Volunteer Army
  (CPVA [Chinese Army])
People's Liberation Army Air Force (PLAAF),
 143–145
 accelerated development of because of the
  Korean War, 143–144
 formation of, 143
 primary aircraft of, 144
 Soviet support for, 144–145
 tactics of in the Korean War, 144
People's Liberation Army Navy (PLAN),
 142–143
 formation of, 142
 salvage operations of for previously sunken
  ships, 142
People's Republic of China (PRC), 1, 66, 80, 87,
 135–139, 136 (image), 137 (image), 147,
 149, 197, 204, 345, 375, 379, 389, 406, 434,
 438, 442, 451, 458, 460, 489, 505, 724, 768,
 804, 805, 815, 849, 856, 867, 878, 879, 883,
 884, 895, 922, 934
 actions of in Korea, 138
 communist revolution in, 135–136
 conflict with the Soviet Union, 138
 decision of to end hostilities in Korea,
  254–255
 economic and military aid to North Korea,
  152–153, 152 (image), 432
 economic reforms in, 139
 historiography of its role in the Korean War,
  324–325
 intervention of during the Korean War,
  136–138, 141, 204, 644–645
 and the Great Leap Forward, 138
 post-Mao era, 138–139
 pre-Korean War military buildup in,
  136–137
 question of representation of in the United
  Nations, **145–146**
 trade relations with Japan, 370
 See also Sino-Japanese War (1894–1895);
  Sino-Soviet Treaty of Friendship and
  Alliance
People's Republic of China (PRC), major
 offensives against the United Nations
 Command (UNC)
 casualties resulting from, 159, 162, 164, 165
 Fifth Offensive, **162–163,** 287–288, 349–351,
  717, 939, 940
 First Offensive, **154–155,** 155 (image)
 Fourth Offensive, **161–162**
 Second Offensive, **157,** 157 (image), 158
  (map), **159,** 159 (image)
 Sixth Offensive, **163–164,** 163 (image),
  636–637

 Summer Offensives, **164–165**
 Third Offensive, **160–161,** 161 (image)
Pepelyaev, Evgeni, 5
Perry, Matthew C., 450
Perry, Miller O., 654, 835
Peruvian prisoner of war settlement proposal,
 676
Philby, Harold Adrian ("Kim"), 108, 109
Philippines, 376, **676–677**
Pierce, Robert Willard, **677–678**
PILEDRIVER, Operation, 329, **678–680,** 679 (image)
Pistols, **680**
Pleven Plan, **680–681**
Plimsoll, James, 63, 67, **681–682,** 682 (image),
 891
Pohang, Battle of, **682–683,** 683 (image)
Point Four Program, **683–685,** 684 (image)
POLECHARGE, Operation, 78
Police action, **685**
Pongam-do prisoner of war uprising, **685–686,**
 686 (table)
Pork Chop Hill, Battle of, 165, **686–687,** 687
 (image)
Potsdam Conference, **687–689,** 688 (image), 844
 Korea as a subject of discussion at, 688
 surrender ultimatum to Japan as a result of,
  688–689
Powell, Herbert B., 830
Power, Thomas, 341
Prauty, Roman, 679 (image)
President's Committee on Equality of Treatment
 and Opportunity in the Armed Services,
 17–18
Preston, Walter, 298, 928
Price gouging, **689–690**
Price and wage freeze order, **690–691**
Prisoner of war administration, communist,
 691–694, 692 (image), 693 (image)
 camp locations, 692
 indoctrination programs, 693
 joint administration of the KPA and CPVA,
  691
 organization of prisoners, 692
 temporary camps, 691
Prisoner of war administration, United Nations
 Command (UNC), **694–697,** 695 (image),
 696 (image)
 and civilian internees (CIs), 696, 697
 Koje-do Island camp, 694
 prisoner uprisings, 696–697
 problem of camp commander turnover, 695,
  696
 problems when using ROKA guards, 694–695
Prisoner of War Military Code of Conduct,
 697–698
Prisoners of war (POWs), 20, 62, 162, 116, 184,
 188, 229, 230, 304, 384, 385, 395, 482,
 628–629, 628 (image), 674, 700, 801, 857,
 986, 1001, 1002
 Canadian, 112
 casualties among, 113
 Cheju-do Chinese POW uprising, **130–131**

Prisoners of war *(continued)*
Communist POW resettlement proposal,
1347–1349**Doc.**
harsh treatment of by the Chinese, 64
importance of the POW issue at the truce
talks, 852–854
Koje-do Island POW problem, **424–425**
Koje-do Island POW uprising, **425–427,** 425
(image), 426 (image)
marking of POW camps under the Geneva
Convention, 285
package proposal concerning, 1308**Doc.**
Peruvian POW proposal, **676**
Pongam-do POW uprising, **685–686,** 686
(table)
POW settlement proposal of Zhou Enlai,
1335–1337**Doc.**
POW uprisings, 191, 686 (table), 696–697
release of North Korean POWs, **742–743**
repatriation of, 878–879
rescreening of, **698–699**
United Nations Command (UNC) POWs, 819,
820, 840, 853
See also BIG SWITCH, Operation; Dodd-Colson
POW incident; LITTLE SWITCH, Operation;
Prisoner of war administration,
Communist; Prisoner of war
administration, United Nations Command
(UNC); Prisoner of War Military Code of
Conduct; Repatriation, voluntary; SCATTER,
Operation
Progressive Citizens of America, 95, 234
Psychological Strategy Board (PSB), 211, 219,
943
Psychological warfare, **699–701,** 700 (image)
use and importance of leaflets in, 700–701
Pueblo Incident, 465, **701–704,** 702 (image), 703
(image), 935
Puller, Lewis Burwell, 124, **704–705**
PUNCH, Operation, **705–706,** 705 (image)
Punchbowl, **706**
Pusan, **706–707**
importance of as a port, 584, 706
Pusan Perimeter and breakout, 34, 39, 354, 402,
694, **707–712,** 708 (image), 709 (image),
710 (map)
casualties of, 711
Eighth Army breakout after the Inchon
landing, 711
KPA divisions involved in, 707–708
KPA objective during, 708
Pyon Yong Tae, **712–713**
Pyongyang, 32, 40, 237, 253, 332, 396, 411, 433
(image), 447 (image), 587, 615, **713,** 766,
816, 837, 854, 882, 921, 951, 974, 975
march to and capture of, **713–717,** 714
(image)

Qiao Guanhua, 502
Qin Jiwei, **717**
Quesada, Elwood R., 194, **718**
Quick, George, 736

Quirino, Elpidio, 661, 677

Radford, Arthur W., 207, 254, 256, 354, 620,
719–720, 720 (image), 835, 948
Radhakrishnan, Sarvepalli, **720–721**
Railroads, Korean national, **721–722,** 721
(image)
Randolph, A. Philip, 17
Rankin, Ronald J., 67
RATKILLER, Operation, 664, **722–723,** 723 (image),
745, 802–803
Rau, Benegal Narsing, **723–724,** 884
Rayburn, Sam, 857
Reagan, Ronald, 211, 214, 339, 462, 936
Recoilless rifles, **724–726,** 725 (image)
Reconnaissance, **726–727,** 726 (image), 727
(table)
types of aircraft used in, 726
Red Ball Express, **727**
Red Cross, **727–729,** 728 (image)
Refugees, **729–731,** 730 (image)
number of, 729
United Nations Command response to,
729–730
Relief efforts, missionary, **731–732**
REMOVAL, Operation, 427
Repatriation, voluntary, **732–733**
Republic of China (ROC [Taiwan]), 87,
146–148, 147 (image), 196, 279, 380–381,
459, 529, 804, 856, 922
MacArthur's memorandum on the strategic
significance of, 1083–1085**Doc.**
neutralization of, **831–832**
Republic of Korea (ROK [South Korea]), 1, 8, 9,
93, 349, 365, 376, 435, 442, 800, 810
Cheju-do Rebellion in, **131–133**
Chinese military disengagement from,
155–157
demonstrations for unification in, **470–471**
economy of, **471–472**
formal establishment of, 413
occupation of by the Democratic People's
Republic of Korea, **478–480,** 479 (image)
political crisis within, **480–481**
UN recognition of, 410–411
U.S. policy toward, 1029**Doc.**
Republic of Korea (ROK), history of (1947–
1953), **456–459,** 458 (image)
First Republic of, 459
invasion of by the Korean People's Army
(KPA), 457
sharecropping and land tenure in, 459
total number of casualties suffered in the
Korean War, 458
Republic of Korea (ROK), history of (1953–
present), **459–464,** 461 (image)
continuing state of war with North Korea,
464
declining economy of after 1997, 464–465
limitations of U.S. commitment to, 460
under Chun Doo Hwan, 461–462
under Kim Dae Jung, 463–464

under Park Chung Hee, 462
under Roh Tae Woo, 462
United Nations and Western economic aid to,
460
Republic of Korea Air Force (ROKAF), 437,
464–465, 484
Republic of Korea Army (ROKA [South Korean
Army]), 19, 87, 93, 94, 121, 167, 177, 203,
297, 301, 302, 304–305, 331, 438, 446, 448,
465–470, 467 (image), 468 (table), 469
(image), 484, 880, 933
armor of, 466
artillery of, 466, 468–469
Capital Division, 164, 165, 177, 345, 415, 445,
468, 707, 746, 973, 975
chaplaincy of, 129
divisional strength and organization of, 466,
468, 468 (table)
expansion of to 12 divisions, 469
I Corps, 122, 124, 126, 161, 164, 345, 415, 468,
663, 746
II Corps, 126, 156, 157, 164, 165, 174, 217,
996
III Corps, 10, 160, 163, 397, 407, 746, 747,
996
lack of equipment and training for, 12
lack of leadership in, 179
organization of, 770 (table)
rebellion within, 467, 789–790
strength of, 770 (table)
transformation from police force to an army,
467
Republic of Korea Coast Guard (ROKCG), 484
Republic of Korea Marine Corps (ROKMC),
474–475
Republic of Korea National Defense Forces (later
V Reserve Corps), **475**
scandal within, **475–476**
Republic of Korea Navy (ROKN), **476–478,** 477
(image)
Republican Party (United States), 212, 251, 254,
257–258, 261–260, 291, 428, 555, 558,
733–735, 828, 943
founding principles of, 733
and the Great Debate, **290–291,** 365, 734
isolationism of, 734
Rest and recuperation (R&R), **735–737,** 736
(image)
Return-to-Seoul movement, **737**
Reuther, Walter, 653
Revolt of the Admirals, **737–738,** 903
Reynolds, Grant, 17
Rhee, Syngman, 44, 121, 128, 153, 164, 191,
217, 220, 222, 233, 244, 246, 255, 300, 301,
359, 417, 446, 447, 448, 454, 456, 457, 458,
459, 470, 475, 483, 489, 491, 600, 636, 664,
738–742, 739 (image), 750, 827, 835, 852,
891, 892, 926, 930, 932, 988, 990
assassination attempt on, 741, **742**
belief in Korean unification, 740, 741
conflict of with U.S. officials, 739, 740–741
conflict of with Yi Chong Chan, 985

conversion to Christianity, 738
correspondence with John Foster Dulles, 1351–1357**Doc.**
declaration of martial law in Pusan, 706–707
education of, 738
exile of in the United States, 739, 958
inauguration of, 488 (image)
inauguration address as first president of the Republic of Korea, 1099–1100**Doc.**
letters to Walter Robertson, 1360–1363**Doc.**
opposition of to the Armistice Agreement, 627–628, 854, 879, 882, 934
position on the repatriation of POWs, 697
release of North Korean POWs, **742–743**
request of for a Pacific pact, 660–661
response of to the invasion of South Korea, 458–459
return to Korea, 739
See also Liberal Party
Rice, Ed, 904
Ridgway, Matthew B., 9, 21–22, 97, 160, 161, 167, 167 (image), 208, 218, 225, 268, 303, 315, 328, 329, 330 (image), 341, 350, 394, 407, 458, 469, 601, 607–608, 729, 737, **743–745,** 734 (image), 746, 763, 766, 787, 814, 835, 846, 849, 851, 852, 857, 860, 887, 939, 942, 956
armistice message of, 1301**Doc.**
as commander of the 82nd Airborne Division, 744
as commander of Eighth Army, 744
and the establishment of the Kansas-Wyoming Line, 397, 398 (map), 399
JCS directive outlining guidelines for, 1299–1300**Doc.**
letter to the men of the Eighth Army, 1270–1271**Doc.**
motivational talents of, 744
negotiations with by W. Robertson, **750–751,** 1362–1365**Doc.**
and POW screenings and repatriation, 426
request of for the use of atomic bombs, 645
service of in World War II, 743–744
transfer of to NATO, 426, 745
as UNC commanding general after MacArthur's dismissal, 744–745
See also ROUNDUP, Operation; RUGGED, Operation; WOLFHOUND, Operation
Rifles, **745–746**
Belgian, 746
British, 746
Chinese, 746
French, 746
U.S., 745–746
See also Recoilless rifles
RIPPER, Operation, 10, 22, 218, **746–747,** 922
Risner, Robinson, 4
Roberts, Paul F., 297
Roberts, William Lynn, **748**
Robertson, Horace Clement Hugh, 67, **748–749**
Robertson, Walter Spencer, 44, 255, 741, 743, **749–750**

mission to Korea for negotiations with Syngman Rhee, 750–751, 1360–1363**Doc.**
Robeson, Paul, 42
Rocket artillery, **751–753,** 752 (image), 753 (image)
Rodgers, John, 928
Roh Moo Hyun, 464, 499, 500, 643
Roh Tae Woo, 462, 936, 937
"Rolling with the punch" battlefield tactic, **753–754**
Roosevelt, Eleanor, 257, 626, 803
Roosevelt, Franklin D., 65, 72, 197, 198, 212, 234, 235–236, 302, 451, 453, 527, 653, 828, 855, 930
Roosevelt, Theodore, 930
Rosenberg, Anna M., 968
Rosenberg, Julius, **754,** 754 (image)
judge's statement upon sentencing of, 1283–1284**Doc.**
Roshchin, N. V., 444
telegram to Soviet government containing message from Chou Enlai, 1251**Doc.**
telegram to Stalin containing message from Mao Zedong, 1121–1122**Doc.**
Ross, Thomas B., 468
Rotation of troops system, **754–756,** 755 (image)
Roth, Andrew, 871
ROUNDUP, Operation, 9, 10, 39, 560, **756–757,** 846
Royal Australian Air Force (RAAF), 67
Royal Hellenic Air Force, 81
Royal Ulster Rifles, 160
Royall, Kenneth, 618 (image)
Ruffen, David, 650
Ruffner, Clark Louis, 103, **757,** 837
Ruffner, Nick, 167
RUGGED, Operation, 329, 397, **757–758**
Rusk, David Dean, 86, 300, 315, 384, 452, **758–759,** 844, 948
Russell, Richard B., 531
Russo-Japanese War (1904–1905), 450, 455, 983
Ryan, Cornelius Edward, **759–760**
Ryusaku, Endo, 790

Sanctuaries, **540–541, 761–762,** 762 (image)
Sasebo (Japan), **762–763**
SATURATE, Operation, **763–764**
SCATTER, Operation, 188, 733, **764–765**
Schuman, Robert, 840. *See also* Schuman Plan
Schuman Plan, **765–766**
Scorched earth policy, **766–767,** 767 (image)
Seabees. *See* United States Naval Construction Battalions
Searchlights, **767**
Sebald, William Joseph, 92, **767–768**
relationship with MacArthur, 768
Selective Service, **242–243,** 592, **927**
Seoul, **769–770,** 769 (image)
fall of, **770–772,** 771 (image), 772 (image)
recapture of, **772–774,** 773 (map)
Seoul City Sue, **774–775**

Service, John Stewart, 149, 555, 558, **775–776,** 775 (image), 871
Shaw, William E., 129
Shaw, William Hamilton, **776–777**
Shazo, Thomas E. de, 305–306
Sheen, Fulton, 803
Shepherd, Lemuel Cornick, Jr., 354, 355, 386, **777,** 914
Sherman, Forrest Percival, 203, 206 (image), 354, 386, 532, 546, **778–779**
and Operation CHROMITE, 778, 779
visit to Tokyo with Lawton Collins, **206–207**
Shigeru, Yoshida, 379
Short, Joseph H., Jr., **779–780**
Shouldice, D'arcy V., 585–586
SHOWDOWN, Operation, **780–781,** 781 (image), 847
Shtykov, Terentii Fomich, 444, **781–782,** 865
report to Matveyev Zakharov on military situation in South Korea, 1165–1167**Doc.**
Shtykov-Fyn Si (Joseph Stalin) telegram, 1170–1171**Doc.**
Shtykov-Vyshinsky telegram (9/3/1949), 1110**Doc.**
Shtykov-Vyshinsky telegram (1/19/1950), 1121–1122**Doc.**
Soviet Politburo directive to, 1112–1113**Doc.**
telegram to the Soviet Ministry of Foreign Affairs, 1205**Doc.**
telegram of Stalin to, 1123**Doc.**
Shufeldt, Robert W., 451
Sikorsky, Igor, 310–311
Simmons, Ed, 63
Sin Chung Mok, 424
Sin Ik Hui, **782**
Sin Song Mo, **782–783**
Sin Tae Yong, **783–784**
Sinatra, Frank, 272 (image)
Sino-Japanese War (1894–1895), 450, 455, 983
Sino-Japanese War, Second (1937–1945), 139, 143, 146
Sino-Soviet Treaty of Friendship and Alliance, **784–785,** 784 (image), 795
SMACK, Operation, **785–786**
casualties of, 785
embarrassment caused by, 785–786
Smith, Al, 234
Smith, Charles B., 641, **834–835,** 900
actions at the Battle of Osan, 654
Smith, Frederick C., 365
Smith, Oliver P., 39, 124, 126, 127, 241, 332, 407, 774, **786–787,** 786 (image), 830, 837
as commander of the 1st Marine Division, 786
disagreements with Edward Almond, 786
service of in World War II, 786
Smith, Pete, 802 (image)
Smith, Walter Bedell, 119, 283, **787–789**
as chief of staff to General Eisenhower in World War II, 787–788
as director of the CIA, 788
Smith, Wayne, 848

Sohle, Robert H., 252 (image)
Son Won Il, **789**
Son Yang Won, **789–790**
Song Chin U, 487, **790–791**
Song Shilun, 159, 632, **791**
Soong Meiling, 149
Souers, Sidney, 618 (image)
Soule, Robert H., 830
South Africa, Union of, **791–793,** 792 (image)
　2nd Squadron of the South African Air Force
　　sent to Korea (Flying Cheetahs), 792, 792,
　　(image), 793
South Korea. *See* Republic of Korea (ROK [South
　　Korea])
South Korean Labor Party (SKLP), 457
South Korean Workers' Party (SKWP), 432, 478,
　　994–995
Southeast Asia Treaty Organization (SEATO),
　　793–795, 794 (image)
　effectiveness of, 794–795
　lack of standing military force, 793
　problematic structure and focus of, 793
Soviet air war in Korea, **795–796**
　Soviet aces, 795
　specific MiG-15 units that fought in Korea,
　　796
　weakness of the Soviet air defense system,
　　796
Soviet airfield incident, **796–797**
Soviet Union (Union of Soviet Socialist
　　Republics [USSR]), 5, 86, 141, 143, 230,
　　246, 338, 367, 389, 431, 432, 451, 452, 489,
　　549, 616, 768, **798–801,** 799 (image), 879,
　　881, 884
　boycott of the United Nations Security
　　Council, **797–798,** 798 (image), 801
　conflict with the PRC, 138
　development of the atomic bomb, 60, 267,
　　362, 375
　effect of World War II on, 197
　geographic and ethnic diversity of, 798–799
　historiography of its role in the Korean War,
　　324
　joint governing of Korea with the United
　　States, 453–455, 457, 489, 865
　missile installations of in Cuba, 348
　national interests of in both Asia and Europe,
　　798–799
　New Economic Policy (NEP) of, 800
　October Revolution, 799
　relations with China, 800
　role of in the Korean War, 800–801
　Romanov dynasty of, 799
　sale of weapons to the PRC, 633
　support of Kim Il Sung, 411
　support of the KPA by, 643, 811
　and the World Council for Peace (WCP),
　　810–811
　and World War II, 800
　See also Sino-Japanese War (1894–1895);
　　Sino-Soviet Treaty of Friendship and
　　Alliance; Soviet air war in Korea

Spaak, Paul-Henri, 199
Spaatz, Carl, 941
Special Detention Center of Laborers, 2
Special operations, **801–803,** 802 (image)
　of the Chinese People's Volunteer Army
　　(CPVA), 802
　North Korean, 801–802
　of the United Nations Command (UNC), 801
　See also RATKILLER, Operation
Spellman, Francis Joseph, **803–804**
Spender, Percy Claude, 67, 571, **804–805**
St. Laurent, Louis Stephen, **805–806**
Stalin, Joseph, 137, 143, 152, 162, 197, 212, 254,
　　293, 312, 411, 422, 430, 444, 451, 453, 454,
　　733, 781, 797, **806–808,** 806 (image)
　arrogant treatment of Mao, 785
　brutality of, 800
　commitment of to North Korea, 795–796,
　　807
　conversations with Zhou Enlai, 1308–
　　1311**Doc.,** 1311–1313**Doc.**
　leadership of in World War II, 806
　letters to Kim Il Sung, 1101–1102**Doc.,**
　　1221–1222**Doc.**
　meeting with Kim Il Sung, 1103–1104**Doc.**
　response to the New Economic Policy (NEP),
　　800
　Shtykov telegram to Fyn Si (Joseph Stalin),
　　1097–1098**Doc.**
　telegram to Mao Zedong and Zhou Enlai,
　　1216**Doc.**
　telegram to Zhou Enlai, 1173**Doc.**
　telegrams to Terentii Shtykov, 1123**Doc.,**
　　1172**Doc.**
　See also Potsdam Conference; Yalta
　　Conference
State Army-Navy-Air Force Coordinating
　　Committee (SANACC), Report 176/35,
　　1088–1095**Doc.**
State-War-Navy Coordinating Committee
　　(SWNCC), 466, 617
　excerpts from Report 176/30 of,
　　1081–1082**Doc.**
Steelman, John R., 619
Sterling, W. H., 748
Sterling, William Alexander, 36–37
Stevenson, Adlai Ewing, 257–258, **809–810,** 809
　　(image)
　education of, 809
　as governor of Illinois, 809
　position of on Korea, 810
Stevenson, William E., 18
Stewart, George C., 841
Stilwell, Joseph W., 89
Stimson, Henry L., 219, 382
Stockholm Peace Appeal, **810–811**
STRANGLE, Operation, **811–812,** 812 (image), 923
Strategic Air Command (SAC), 33
Strategic and tactical airlift, **812–814**
　strategic airlift, 813
　tactical airlift, 813–814
　use of helicopters for, 814

Stratemeyer, George E., 194, 205, 268, 341, 354,
　　814–816, 905, 955
　service of in World War II, 814–815
Strauss, Lewis, 348
Stripling, Robert, 339 (image)
Struble, Arthur D., 241, 354, 356, 477, 620, 621,
　　816–817, 817 (image), 830
Student volunteer troops (Republic of Korea),
　　817–818
Stukes, Louis, 18
Submachine guns, **818–819**
Suhr, Anna Wallace. *See* Seoul City Sue
Sukchon and Sunchon airborne operation,
　　819–820, 819 (image)
Sullivan, John L., 737
Sun Yat-sen (Sun Yixian), 135–136, 146, 150, 379
Sunshine policy, 731
Supung and the Korean Electric Power Plant
　　campaign, **820–821**
Sutyagin, Nikolai V., 5
Symington, W. Stuart, 619–620, 653, **821–822,**
　　903

Taegu, defense of, 663, **823–825,** 824 (image)
Taejon, defense of, **825–826,** 826 (image)
Taejon Agreement, **826–827**
Taft, Robert Alphonso, 42, 257, 260, 291,
　　827–829, 828 (image)
　criticism of Roosevelt's foreign policy, 828
　defense of MacArthur, 828
　as leader of the Republican Party, 828
　See also Taft-Hartley Act (1947)
Taft-Hartley Act (1947), 260, 653, **829–830**
TAILBOARD, Operation, **830–831,** 974
Taiwan. *See* Republic of China (ROC [Taiwan])
Takman, John, 811
Talbott, Harold L., 904
"Tang Chungang" (Party Center), 412
Tanks, **47–51,** 48 (image), 49 (image), 231
　　(image), 654–655
　British, 50
　Centurion Medium Cruiser Mk-5, 50
　Churchill VII Infantry, 50
　Comet A34 Heavy Cruiser, 50
　Cromwell A27M Reconnaissance, 50
　M-8 armored car, 49–50
　M-24 Chaffee, 49
　M-26 Pershing, 48
　M-46 Patton, 48–49, 48 (image)
　M4A3 and M4A3E8 Sherman, 47–48
　North Korean and Chinese, 47, 440 (image)
　T-34, 439, 439 (image), 440
　T-44/85, 47
　U.S., 47–50
Tasca, Henry Joseph, **832–833**
Task Force Dolvin, 174
Task Force Kean, **833–834**
Task Force Smith, **834–835,** 834 (image)
Taylor, Maxwell Davenport, 164, 165, 253,
　　835–836, 836 (image)
Teller, Edward, 62, 348
Thackrey, Lyman A., 345

Thailand, 793–794, 795, **839–840**
THANKSGIVING, Operation, 188
Thayer, Charles, 216
Theseus, 28, 29
Thimayya, Kadenera Subayya, 627, **840–841**
Thomas, John Parnell, 339 (image)
Thomas, Norman Mattoon, **845–846,** 846
    (image)
Thorat, S. P. P., 627
Throckmorton, John R., 154, 297
THUNDERBOLT, Operation, 9–10, 560, **846–847**
Thurness, Jane, 969 (image)
Thyng, Harrison R., 3
Tibbetts, Oscar N., 15
TOMAHAWK, Operation, 22, 22 (image), 601–602
Tomlinson, Frank Stanley, **847**
Triangle Hill, Battle of, **847–849,** 848 (image)
Tripartite Meetings, **849–850**
Troopships, **850**
Trotsky, Leon, 806
Truce talks, **850–854,** 851 (image), 944
    five-point agenda of, 852–853
    initial meetings, 851
    objectives of, 852
    U.S. control over UNC negotiators, 851
Truman, Harry S., 6, 9, 11–12, 61 (image), 70,
    71, 72 (image), 86–87, 149, 165, 199, 204,
    208, 211, 213 (image), 220, 235 (image),
    236, 252, 257, 261, 291, 380, 383, 405, 422,
    453, 469, 483, 558, 617, 618 (image), 619,
    653, 660, 669, 732, 806, 815, 821, 830,
    831, 841, 844, 852, **854–857,** 855 (image),
    870, 871, 878, 887, 900, 927, 948 (image),
    953–954, 961 (image)
    address to Civil Defense Conference,
        1291–1292**Doc.**
    address to Congress (1950), 1172–1178**Doc.**
    approval of Operation CHROMITE, 207
    attacks on by conservatives, 42, 734, 855
    authorization of atomic bomb use on Japan,
        59
    cease-fire initiative of, **860–861**
    concern over MacArthur's drive to the Yalu
        River, 981
    containment policy of, 213–214
    decision not to run for a second term, 72
    declaration of a national emergency, 902,
        1256–1257**Doc.**
    deployment of the U.S. Seventh Fleet to
        Taiwan, 143, 149
    description of the Korean War as a "police
        action," 365, **685**
    domestic agenda of, **861–863,** 862
    establishment of the Psychological Strategy
        Board (PSB), 212, 943
    Executive Order (9981), **265–266**
    factors leading to his dismissal of MacArthur
        from command, 856–857, 860–861
    farewell address of, 1320–1324**Doc.**
    and federal control of the railroads, 79
    foreign policy toward East Asia and Korea
        (1950–1953), **931–934,** 932 (image)

issuance of the National Emergency
    Declaration, **616**
and the Japanese Peace Treaty (1951),
    375–376
leadership of during the Cold War, 855
order relieving MacArthur of command,
    1284–1285**Doc.**
Point Four Program of, **683–685**
press conference on the atomic bomb,
    1240–1243**Doc.**
reactions to his dismissal of MacArthur from
    command, 182, 828
removal of MacArthur from command
    of UNC forces, 97, 116, 365, 386, 458,
    862–863, **863–865,** 864 (image),
    1284–1285**Doc.,** 1285–1287**Doc.**
report to the U.S. public on the situation in
    Korea, 1193–1196**Doc.**
response to the invasion of South Korea,
    855–856
seizure of steel plants and the United
    Steel Workers' strike, 654, **808–809,**
    1304–1308**Doc.**
statement concerning the North Korean
    invasion of South Korea, 1168**Doc.**
statement on the use of U.S. ground troops in
    South Korea, 1168–1169**Doc.**
success in guiding the United States to victory
    in World War II, 855
support of for women in service, 968
threats of to use the atomic bomb, 60–61, 65,
    644, 856, 857, 884
Truman-Atlee joint communiqué,
    1252–1254**Doc.**
Truman-Eisenhower transition meeting, 859
Truman-MacArthur Wake Island conference,
    1225–1226**Doc.**
view of the Korean War, 7–8
See also Potsdam Conference; Revolt of the
    Admirals; Soviet airfield incident; Wake
    Island Conference
Truman Doctrine, 6, 82, 201, 364–365, **857–859**
Truman Loyalty Program, **859–860**
Tsarapkin, Semion Konstantinovich, **865–866,**
    865 (image)
Tsiang Ting Fu Fuller, 797, **866–867,** 866
    (image)
Tunkin, Grigory
    Gromyko to Tunkin telegram,
        1110–1111**Doc.**
    Tunkin to Soviet Foreign Ministry telegram,
        1111–1112**Doc.**
Tunner, William H., 579, 580, 813, 942
Turkey, 199, 212, 858, **867–868**
Turkish Brigade, 156, 164
    bravery of, 868
    casualties of, 164, 868
    reputation of as good offensively and bad
        defensively, 350
Turner, Charles W., 727
Twining, Nathan Farragut, **869–870,** 869
    (image), 904

Tydings, Millard, 555
Tydings Committee, **869–870**

Underwood, Horace G., 179–180, **873–874**
Underwood, Horace G., II, **874–875**
Underwood, Horace Horton, **875**
United Kingdom, 142, 145, 199, 201, 203, 451,
    489, **875–879,** 876 (image), 877 (image),
    878 (table)
    as chief ally of the United States, 876
    commitment of the Royal Navy to UNC
        forces, 879, 890
United Kingdom, armed forces of serving in
        Korea
    British Brigade(s), 68, 78, 160, 162, 287, 335,
        399
    British Royal Northumberland Fusiliers, 350
    Gloucester Brigade, 350
    specifications for aircraft used in the Korean
        War, 878 (image)
    See also Tripartite Meetings
United Nations (UN), 153, 180, 181, 197, 198,
    201, 208, 236, 262, 279, 294–295, 359, 378,
    381, 392, 393, 406, 414, 435, 458, 460, 504,
    529, 583, 612, 636, 669, 712, 724, 740, 811,
    845, 849, 867, 930, 932–933
    Colombia's staunch support of, 209
    Peruvian prisoner of war settlement proposal,
        676
    question of Chinese representation in,
        145–146
    recognition of South Korea, 410–411
    sanctions against China, **897–898**
    Thailand's support of U.S. resolutions in, 840
United Nations Additional Measures
    Committee, **883,** 895
United Nations Cease-Fire Group, **883–885**
United Nations Civil Assistance Command in
    Korea (UNCACK), **885–886,** 885 (image)
United Nations Charter, 505
United Nations Collective Measures Committee,
    886
United Nations Command (UNC), 9, 12–13,
    20, 21, 22, 23, 77–78, 156, 166, 181, 205,
    283–284, 285, 292, 293, 315, 363, 384, 393,
    399, 420, 426, 448, 458, 476, 481, 505, 529,
    562, 585–589, 616, 682, 698, 724, 737, 753,
    805, **886–889,** 887 (image), 888 (map),
    933, 942, 973
    air power of, 437–438, **889–890,** 890 (table)
    airborne operations of, **601–602**
    and the arrest of war criminals, 952
    casualties of non-American and non-Korean
        UNC forces, 277 (table)
    composition of its forces, 264 (table), 323
    controversy concerning civilians interned by,
        187–188
    defensive position of (1951), 224 (map), 408
        (map)
    efforts of to secure a MiG-15 aircraft, 576
    establishment of, 886–887
    extensive civil powers of, 889

United Nations Command (*continued*)
  ground forces of, **890–891**
  hot pursuit strategy of UNC aircraft, 338
  invasion of the Democratic People's Republic
    of Korea (DPRK), 141, 365
  joint policy (Greater Sanctions) statement,
    1370**Doc.**
  Latin American contributions to, 496–497
  logistics of, **518–521**
  naval capabilities of, 620–621
  offensive of in the Iron Triangle, 780–781,
    781 (image)
  pursuit of North Korean forces in retreat, 888
    (map)
  and the refugee problem, 729–730
  restrictions of on air war, 144
  support of partisan activities, 801, 802–803
  Turkish participation in, 867–868
  UN Security Council resolutions pertaining
    to, 889
  voluntary repatriation issue, 732–733
  See also People's Republic of China (PRC),
    major offensives against the United
    Nations Command (UNC); Prisoner
    of war administration, United Nations
    Command; SCATTER, Operation; United
    Nations Command (UNC), reports
    concerning operations in Korea; Wonsan
    landing and evacuation
United Nations Command (UNC), reports
    concerning operations in Korea
  First Report, 1179–1182**Doc.**
  Second Report, 1183–1184**Doc.**
  Third Report, 1196–1197**Doc.**
  Fourth Report, 1205–1208**Doc.**
  Fifth Report, 1208–1209**Doc.**
  Sixth Report, 1212–1215**Doc.**
  Seventh Report, 1217**Doc.**
  Eighth Report, 1226–1227**Doc.**
  Ninth Report, 1230–1232**Doc.**
  Tenth Report, 1238–1240**Doc.**
  Eleventh Report, 1248–1249**Doc.**
  Twelfth Report, 1258–1259**Doc.**
  Thirteenth Report, 1263–1264**Doc.**
  Fourteenth Report, 1269–1270**Doc.**
  Fifteenth Report, 1272–1273**Doc.**
  Sixteenth Report, 1273–1275**Doc.**
  Seventeenth Report, 1275–1277**Doc.**
  Eighteenth Report, 1278–1279**Doc.**
  Nineteenth Report, 1281–1283**Doc.**
United Nations Commission on Korea
    (UNCOK), 368, 369, 504, 505, 891
  report on the North Korean invasion of South
    Korea, 1165**Doc.**
United Nations Commission on the Unification
    and Rehabilitation of Korea (UNCURK),
    218, 447, 448, 481, 681–682, **891–892**
United Nations Economic Commission for Asia
    and the Far East (UNECAFE), 712
United Nations General Assembly resolutions
  Resolution 337A (V), 896

  Resolution 376 (V), 881, 891, **892–893**,
    1220–1221**Doc.**
  Resolution 377 (V), 886, **893–894**,
    1232–1235**Doc.**
  Resolution 384 (V), 884, 1256**Doc.**
  Resolution 410 (V), 895, 1243–1248**Doc.**
  Resolution 498 (V), 883, **894–895**,
    1271–1272**Doc.**
  Resolution 500 (V), 883, 1294–1295**Doc.**
  Resolution 610 (VII), 1313–1315**Doc.**
  Resolution 705 (VII), 1346**Doc.**
  Resolution 809 (IX), 886
  Twenty-One Power Resolution, 1313**Doc.**
  un-numbered resolution (11/14/1947),
    1087–1088**Doc.**
  un-numbered resolution (12/12/1948),
    1102–1103**Doc.**
  un-numbered resolution (10/21/1949),
    1113–1115**Doc.**
United Nations Good Offices Committee, **895**
United Nations Interim Committee, 446–447,
    488
United Nations Korea Reconstruction Agency
    (UNKRA), 885, **895–896**
United Nations, and the Korean War, **879–883**,
    880 (image)
  influence of the United States in the UN, 881
  phases of UN involvement in the war, 881
  votes on resolutions concerning the war,
    881–882
United Nations Peace Observation Commission,
    896–897
United Nations Security Council, 7, 145, 198,
    295, 376, 505, 811, 856, 889, 899 (image),
    933
  boycott of by the Soviet Union, **797–798**, 798
    (image), 801
  Security Council Resolution 82, **898–899**,
    1163–1164**Doc.**
  Security Council Resolution 83, **899–900**,
    1167**Doc.**
  Security Council Resolution 84, 881, **900**,
    1171–1172**Doc.**
  Security Council Resolution 88, **900–901**,
    1237**Doc.**
  statement to by Trygve Lie concerning the
    invasion of South Korea, 1166–1167**Doc.**
United Nations Temporary Commission on
    Korea (UNTCOK), 368, 457, 677, 845, 880
United States, 145, 146, 153, 283–284, 285, 434,
    451, 460, 463, 489, 505, 845, 880, 881, 884,
    895
  industrial base of, **361–362**
  industrial dispersion policy of, 363
  joint governing of Korea with the Soviet
    Union, 453–455
  Mutual Defense Treaty with the Republic of
    Korea, **926**, 1383–1385**Doc.**
  See also Tripartite Meetings; United States,
    home front; United States, policy of toward
    Korea

United States, home front, **901–902**, 901
    (image)
  discontent with Truman, 902
  initial support for Truman, 901
  morale after the victory at Inchon and the
    Pusan breakout, 901–902
  prosperity of the United States, 902
  See also McCarthyism
United States, policy of toward Korea
  and the *General Sherman* incident, 928
  policy of toward Korea (1953–to present),
    934–938, 935 (image)
  policy of toward Korea (prior to 1950),
    928–931, 929 (image)
  policy of toward the Republic of Korea
    (ROK), 1101**Doc.**
  Truman's foreign policy toward East Asia and
    Korea (1950–1953), **931–934**, 932 (image)
United States Air Force (USAF), 12, 13–14, 174,
    194, 308, 465, 592, 616, 682, 707, 718, 738,
    902–905, 903 (image)
  3rd Air Rescue Squadron, 308
  7th Bomber Command, 222
  8th Fighter Wing, 420
  19th Bomb Group, 613
  21st Troop Carrier Squadron, 813, 814
  58th Fighter Interceptor Wing, 221
  61st Troop Carrier Transport, 814
  67th Tactical Reconnaissance Wing, 726
  98th Bomb Wing, 613
  116th Fighter-Bomber Wing, 955
  136th Fighter-Bomber Wing, 764
  158th Fighter Bomber Squadron, 919 (image)
  314th Troop Carrier Group, 601, 813
  315th Air Division (Combat Cargo), 813–814
  374th Troop Carrier Wing, 813
  437th Troop Carrier Wing, 601
  452nd Bomber Group, 601
  483rd Troop Carrier Wing, 813
  air superiority of during the Korean War, 904
  bombers, 24–25
  Fifth Air Force, 193, 306, 308, 437–438, 601,
    672, 764, 811, 815, 820–821, 957
  fighter aircraft specifications, 378 (table)
  fighters and fighter-bombers, 23–24
  introduction of fighter escort policies, 903
  IX Tactical Air Command, 194
  Ninth Air Force, 941
  raids of on dams, 221–223, 222 (image)
  status of after the Korean War, 904–905
  strategy of in World War II (Air War Plan
    Division [AWPD-1]), 903
  See also Airborne operations; Aircraft; Far
    East Air Force (FEAF); Najin, bombing
    of; Revolt of the Admirals; SATURATE,
    Operation; Strategic and tactical airlift
United States Army, 14, 616, **905–909**, 906
    (table)
  aircraft of, 28
  alphabetical designations for units of, 907
  Army Nurse Corps (ANC), 908

battalion and battery commands, 906–907
casualties of during the Korean War, 908–909
configuration of a typical infantry division, 906 (table)
corps command structure of, 906
Department of the Army review of the No Gun Ri strafing incident, 1387–1395**Doc.**
desegregation of, 908
divisional structure of, 906
growth of during the Korean War period, 659, 907–908
I Corps, 9, 156, 160, 161, 162, 163, 164, 174, 205, 210, 218, 350, 397, 399, 468, 678, 711, 713, 727, 780, 814, 846
II Corps, 9
IX Corps, 9, 10, 156, 157, 160, 161, 162, 163, 165, 174, 217, 350, 397, 399, 402, 407, 468, 579, 678, 679, 747, 780, 814, 846, 907, 957
numerical strength of, 907
XVI Corps, 427
XXIV Corps, 452, 528, 844
regimental combat teams (RCTs), 907
Women's Army Corps (WAC), 908
See also Eighth Army, U.S., in Korea (EUSAK); Far East Command (FEC); Korea Military Advisory Group (KMAG); Korean Augmentation to the United States Army (KATUSA); X Corps
United States Army Engineers, **909–910,** 909 (image)
United States Army Military Police (MP), **910–911**
United States Army Signal Corps, **912–913,** 913 (image)
United States Coast Guard, **913**
United States Marine Corps (USMC), 12, 14, 194–195, 308, 592, 738, 813, **914–918,** 915 (image), 916 (image), 917 (map), 920, 925
1st Marine Air Wing, 915
1st Marine Air Wing's Marine Photographic Squadron, 726
aircraft of, 27–28, 924 (table)
casualties suffered by in the Korean War, 916
drop in numerical strength of, 920
Marine Corps Reserve, 914
Marine Volunteer Reserve, 914
number of marines that served in the Korean War, 916
United States National Guard, **918–919,** 919 (image)
Air National Guard, 918–919, 925
Army National Guard, 918, 925
United States Naval Construction Battalions, **920**
United States Navy (USN), 12, 14, 194–195, 308, 592, 616, 707, 850, **920–923,** 921 (image), 925, 935 (image)
aircraft of, 27–28, 924 (table)
casualties suffered by in the Korean War, 923
evacuation of X Corps from Hungnam by, **344–346,** 345 (image), 346 (image)

gunfire support of (naval bombardment), **622–624,** 623 (image)
Joint Task Force 7, 356, 830
number of personnel, 920, 921
number of ships, 920
Seventh Fleet, 87, 143, 149, 405, 621, 719, 821, 856, 920
Task Force 70.8, 345
Task Force 72, 143
Task Force 77, 345, 437–438, 811
Task Force 90, 346, 830
Task Force 95, 621
U.S. Naval Forces Far East (NAVFE), 620, **621–622**
See also Inchon Landing (Operation CHROMITE); Military Sea Transport Service (MSTS); Mine warfare (sea); RIPPER, Operation; United States Navy air operations
United States Navy air operations, **923–925,** 924 (table)
aircraft of, 27–28, 924 (table)
attack on Hwachon Dam, 923–924
total number of enemy combatants killed by, 924
total number of sorties flown, 924
total number of vehicles and buildings destroyed by, 924
United States–Republic of Korea Mutual Defense Treaty, **926,** 1383–1385**Doc.**
United States reserve forces, **925–926**
Universal Military Training and Service Act (1951), **927**
Unsan, Battle of, 155–156, 283, **927–928**
U.S. Atomic Energy Commission (USAEC), **61–62,** 62 (image), 347–348
U.S. Military Government in Korea (USAMGIK), 131, 132, 414, 488, 958
U.S.-Soviet Joint Commission, 454, 457, 489, 865

Vail, Richard B., 339 (image)
Van Fleet, James A., 116, 163, 210, 240, 241, 252 (image), 253, 292, 305, 330 (image), 350, 353, 399, 469, 480, 664, 678, 745, 923, **939–940,** 940 (image)
actions at the Battle of Triangle Hill, 847, 849
blunt nature of, 940
extensive use of close air support (CAS), 940
the "Van Fleet Load," **940–941**
See also RATKILLER, Operation; SHOWDOWN, Operation; SMACK, Operation
Vandenberg, Hoyt, 203, 268, 386, 532, 546, 580, 613, 869, 902, 903, 904, **941–942,** 941 (image), 955
and the air supply of Berlin, 941–942
discussions with Lawton Collins in Tokyo, **207–208**
service of in World War II, 941
visit to Tokyo with Lawton Collins, **208–209**
Vandenburg, Arthur, 201, 483

Vanderpool, Jay, 801
Vasiliev, Alexandre, 444, 445
Vickery, Grady M., 300
Viet Minh. *See* People's Army of Vietnam (PAVN, Viet Minh)
Vincent, John Carter, 149, 555, 558
Vincon, Fred, 961 (image)
VITTLES, Operation, 201, 580, 941
Voorhees, Tracy Stebbins, 211, **943**
Vyshinskii, Andrei Y., 378, 880 (image), **944–945**
condemnation of UN actions in Korea, 944
Shtykov-Vyshinsky telegram (9/3/1949), 1110**Doc.**
Shtykov-Vyshinsky telegram (1/19/1950), 1123–1124**Doc.**

Wage Stabilization Board (WSB), 653–654, 690, 691, 862, **947,** 961
Wake Island Conference, **947–949,** 948 (image)
Walker, Walton H., 9, 122, 154, 156, 160, 174, 204, 205, 207, 217, 252, 297, 329, 331, 355, 402, 417, 467, 485, 530, 641, 672, 682, 708 (image), 825, 830, 837, 843, 905, **949–952,** 950 (image), 993
actions at the Battle of Unsan, 927–928
actions at the Battles of Naktong Bulge, 609, 610
aggressiveness of, 642
death of, 766
and the defense of Taejon, 825, 950–951
role of in Task Force Kean, 833
role of in Task Force Smith, 834
service of in World War II, 949–950
"stand or die" order of, 642, 707, 950, 1182–1183**Doc.**
See also Pusan; Pusan Perimeter and breakout
Wallace, Henry, 95, 260
Wang Bi, 143
Wang Bingzhang, 143
Wang Jiaxiang, 293
Wang Yong, 437
War crimes trials, **952–953**
Warren, Austin, **65–67,** 66 (image)
Washington, George, 201
Washington Conference, **953**
Wayne, John, 339
Webb, James Edwin, 383, **953–954**
Wedemeyer, Albert C., 532
Wedemeyer Report, 1082–1086**Doc.**
Wescott, William H., 3
West, Michael M. A. R., **954–955**
Westmoreland, William, 836
Weyland, Otto Paul, 268, 613, 815, **955–956,** 956 (image)
Wherry, Kenneth S., 291
Whisner, William T., 3
White Horse Hill, Battle of, **956–957**
"White Paper" on China, 379
Whitmore, Clarence, 709 (image)

Whitney, Cornelius Vanderbilt, 618 (image)
Whitney, Courtney, 352 (image), **957–958**
Wickman, John A., 936
Wilkins, John L., 300
Williams, George Z., **958–959**
Williams, Ted, 924
Willoughby, Charles A., 119, 125, 205, 699, **959–960,** 959 (image)
Wills, Lloyd E., 404
Wilson, Charles Erwin, 254, 256, 362, 616, 653, 808, 822, 856, 862 (image), 904, 942, **960–962,** 961 (image)
    belief in wage and price controls, 961
    as director of the Office of Defense Mobilization (ODM), 960–962
    opposition of to labor unions, 961–962
Wilson, Woodrow, 197, 211, 234, 930
Winnington, Alan, 563
Wolcott, Jesse P., 291
WOLFHOUND, Operation, 9, 560, **962–964,** 963 (map)
Women, on the home fronts, **964–968,** 965 (image), 966 (image)
    discrimination against women, 965–966
    educational gains made by, 966
    in the Republic of Korea, 967
    service of in government, 967
    in the United States, 964–967
Women, in the military, **968–971,** 969 (image), 970 (table)
    administrative and military occupational specialties of, 969–970
    distribution of women among different branches of military service, 970 (table)
    in North Korea, 970
    in the People's Republic of China, 970–971
    Republic of Korea Women's Army Corps (ROKWAC), 970
    total number of women on active duty (1950), 968
    total number of women on active duty (1952), 969
    Women in the Air Force (WAF), 968, 969
    Women in the Navy (WAVE), 968, 969
    Women's Army Corps (WAC), 968–969

Won Yong Dok, **971–972**
Wonju, Battle of, **972–973,** 972 (image)
Wonsan, North Korea, **973**
Wonsan landing and evacuation, **973–975,** 976 (image)
World Council for Peace (WCP), 810–811
World Vision, **975–976**
Wright, Edwin K., 352 (image)
Wright, Erwin, 125, 126
Wrong, Humphrey, **976–977**
Wu Xiuquan, 505, **977**

"X" article, the, 213–214, 261, 404
X Corps, 9, 10, 21, 38–39, 39–40, 103, 122, 124–126, 128, 156, 161, 162, 163, 164, 194, 204, 206, 328, 344–345, 352, 354–355, 363, 397, 407, 415, 468, 474, 530, 637, 678, 711, 713, 729, 746, 747, 756, 772, 774, 830, 831, **836–839,** 837 (image), 838 (map), 843, 846, 907, 951, 973, 974 (image)
    activation of, 836
    association of with Eighth Army, 836–837
    numerical strength of, 837
    redeployment of, 838 (map)
    See also Wonsan landing and evacuation
Xiao Hua, 143
Xiao Jinguang, 143
Xiao Ke, 980
Xie Fang, 116, 166, 394, **979–980,** 980 (image)

Yalta Conference, 806–807
Yalu bridges controversy, **981–982,** 982 (image), 983
Yalu River, **982–984,** 983 (map)
Yang Dezhi, 675, **984**
Yang Yu Chan, **984–985**
Yang Yu Chang, 301
Yi Chong Chan, **985**
Yi Chong Dae, 424
Yi Chun, 930
Yi Hak Ku, **985–987,** 986 (image)
Yi Hyong Gun, **987**
Yi Ki Bung, 476
Yi Kun Sok, 465
Yi Kwon Mu, **987–988**

Yi Pom Sok, **988–989**
Yi Sang Jo, 116, 394, **989–990,** 989 (image)
Yi Sang Sol, 930
Yi Sung Hun, 179
Yi Sung Yop, **990**
Yi Tok Gu, 132
Yi Tong Hwi, **990–991**
Yi Wi Jong, 930
Yi Yun Yong, 176
Yim, Louise, **991–992,** 997
Yo Un Hyong, 457, 790, 958, **992**
Yongchon, Battle of, **992–994,** 993 (image)
Yoshimichi, Hasegawa, 456
Yosu-Sunchon rebellion, **994–995**
Young, Arthur M., 309
Young, Sam P., 5
Younger, Kenneth, **995–996**
Youngstown Sheet and Tube Company v. Sawyer (1952), 808–809
Yount, Paul F., 695, 768
Yu Chae Hung, **996**
Yuan Shikai, 146
Yun Chan, 486 (image)
Yun Chi Yong, **997**
Yun Ik Hon, 475
Yun Po Son, 667

Zennström, Per-Olov, 811
Zhadanov, Andrei, 781
Zhang Hanfu, **999–1000**
Zhang Tingfa, **1000**
Zhang Xueliang, 150–151, 502
Zhou Enlai, 70, 120, 134, 136, 137, 138, 196, 230, 283, 284, 358, 379, 502, 583, 669, 674, 807, 884, 999, **1000–1001,** 1001 (image)
    conversations with Stalin, 1308–1311**Doc.,** 1311–1313**Doc.**
    prisoner of war settlement proposal, 1333–1335**Doc.**
    Stalin's telegram to, 1099**Doc.**
Zhu De, 141
Zinchenko, Konstantin E., **1001–1002**
Zorin, Valerian, **1002–1003**